ICSE Exams 2026

AF814575

All in One MATHEMATICS

Class 9

ICSE Exams 2026

All in one®

MATHEMATICS

Class 9

Authors
Laxman Prasad
Jitendra Gupta

arihant
SUCCESS AND NOTHING LESS

ARIHANT PRAKASHAN
(School Division Series)

ADMINISTRATIVE & PRODUCTION OFFICES

Regd. Office
'Ramchhaya' 4577/15, Agarwal Road, Darya Ganj, New Delhi -110002
Tele: 011- 47630600, 43518550; Fax: 011- 23280316

Head Office
Kalindi, TP Nagar, Meerut (UP) - 250002, Tel: 0121-7156203, 7156204

SALES & SUPPORT OFFICES
Agra, Ahmedabad, Bengaluru, Bareilly, Chennai, Delhi, Guwahati, Hyderabad, Jaipur, Jhansi, Kolkata, Lucknow, Nagpur & Pune.

PO No : TXT-XX-XXXXXXX-X-XX

Published By Arihant Publications (India) Ltd.

For further information about the books published by Arihant, log on to www.arihantbooks.com or e-mail at info@arihantbooks.com

Follow us on

PRICE ₹ 380.00

PRODUCTION TEAM

Publishing Managers	*Cover Designer*	*Inner Designer*
Mahendra Singh Rawat & Keshav Mohan	Salman Shaikh	Ankit Tyagi
Project Head	*Page Layouting*	*Proof Reader*
Ashwani	Shivam Prajapati	Manish Rathore

Index *cum* Study Planner

One Book- Endless Features

to Help you Succeed

Chapter Inside

At the start of each chapter, all the Chapter topics have been listed, so that students may know what they are going to study.

1

Rational and Irrational Numbers

SYLLABUS

- Rational, irrational numbers as real numbers, their place in the number system. Surds and rationalization of surds. Simplifying an expression by rationalizing the denominator. Representation of rational and irrational number on the number line. Proof of irrationality of $\sqrt{2}, \sqrt{3}, \sqrt{5}$

Rational Numbers

The numbers, which can be expressed in the form of $\frac{p}{q}$, where p, q both are coprime integers and $q \neq 0$, are known as rational numbers and are denoted by 'Q',

$$Q = \left\{\frac{p}{q} : p, q \text{ both are co prime integers and } q \neq 0\right\}.$$

e.g. $\frac{-1}{2}, \frac{3}{2}, \frac{1}{3}, \frac{7}{5}$ etc.,

Every natural number, whole number and integer is a rational number.

e.g. $1 = 1/1$ or $5 = 5/1$.

Simplified Theory

It contains the necessary study material well supported by Definitions, Facts, Figures, Flow Charts, etc.

Note Matter

Additional but informational matter related to given concept. It helps students to bring focus on important points.

Note If the equations $a_1x + b_1y + c_1 = 0$ and $a_2x + b_2y + c_2 = 0$ are written in the form $a_1x + b_1y = -c_1$ and $a_2x + b_2y = -c_2$, then by cross-multiplication method, we have

$$\frac{x}{b_2c_1 - b_1c_2} = \frac{y}{c_2a_1 - c_1a_2} = \frac{-1}{a_1b_2 - a_2b_1}.$$

Remembering Technique for Cross-multiplication

The following diagram helps in remembering the above solution

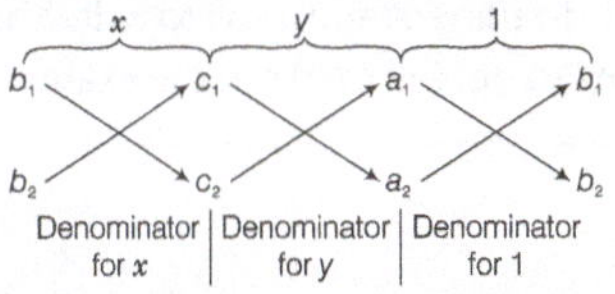

One Book- Endless Features
to Help you Succeed

Topical Exercises

To make students understand the chapter in a smooth part-by-part manner, Topical Exercises have been given in each chapter. These Exercises help students to assess the understanding of related concepts at regular interval.

Exercise 1.1

1. Express the following numbers in the form of rational numbers $\left(\frac{p}{q}\right)$
   (i) 2 (ii) −3 (iii) 2.3
2. Find two equivalent rational numbers.
   (i) $\frac{2}{3}$ (ii) $\frac{-4}{5}$
   (iii) $\frac{-21}{9}$
3. Insert a rational number lying between
   (i) −3/5 and 1/7 (ii) −7/9 and −2
   (iii) $\frac{2}{5}$ and $\frac{3}{4}$
4. Insert three rational numbers between 2.6 and 3.1.
5. Find five rational numbers between 3/5 and 4/5.
6. Find nine rational numbers between 0 and 0.1.
7. Insert three rational numbers between $\frac{4}{11}$ and $\frac{9}{16}$.
8. Find the four rational numbers between 4 and 5.
9. Insert two rational numbers between $\frac{-1}{3}$ and $\frac{-1}{2}$ and arrange them in descending order.
10. Insert eight rational numbers between $-\frac{1}{3}$ and $\frac{2}{7}$. Also, arrange them in ascending order.
11. Arrange $-\frac{5}{9}, \frac{7}{12}, -\frac{2}{3}$ and $\frac{11}{18}$ in ascending order of their magnitudes. Also, find the difference between the largest and the smallest of these fraction.
12. Represent the following rational numbers on the number line.
    (i) $-\frac{5}{4}$ (ii) $\frac{6}{5}$ (iii) $\frac{7}{2}$ (iv) $-\frac{1}{8}$

Exam Pattern Exercise

Part A - Objective Type Questions

Multiple Choice Type Questions

1. Five kingdom system of classification suggested by RH Whittaker is not based on the
   (a) presence or absence of a well-defined nucleus
   (b) mode of reproduction
   (c) mode of nutrition
   (d) complexity of body organisation
2. Which of the following statements given below is correct?
   (a) Biological classification is the scientific ordering of organisms in a hierarchical series of groups on the basis of their relationships, i.e. morphological, evolutionary and others
   (b) Whittaker classified organisms on the basis of autotrophic and heterotrophic mode of nutrition
   (c) In five kingdom system of classification, living organisms can be divided into prokaryotic and eukaryotic cells on the basis of cell structure
   (d) All of the above

Part-B Descriptive Questions

Very Short Answer Type Questions

31. Name the five kingdoms proposed by Whittaker.
32. Bacteria exchange genetic information *via* three methods out of these. Who discovered the process of transformation in bacteria?
33. Name the bacteria that causes souring of milk.
34. Expand PPLO. Also give the other name of it.

Long Answer Type Questions

70. Discuss how classification system have undergone several changes over a period of time. (NCERT)
71. Biological classification is a dynamic and ever evolving phenomenon which keeps changing with our understanding of life forms. Justify the statement by taking any two examples. (NCERT Exemplar)

Chapter Practice

To make students completely prepared for examination, this Exercise contains Exam Pattern Questions. This exercise covers all types of questions, like; 1 Mark, 2 Marks, 3 Marks, 4 Marks and 6 Marks. All the questions are fully explained helping students to understand, how to write the solutions to get full marks in the exam.

Illustrative Figures

To make the concepts completely visible, illustrative diagrams have been given at various place.

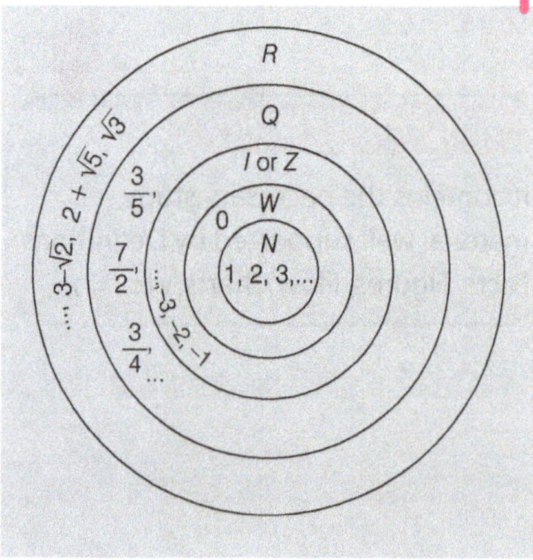

One Book- Endless Features

to Help you Succeed

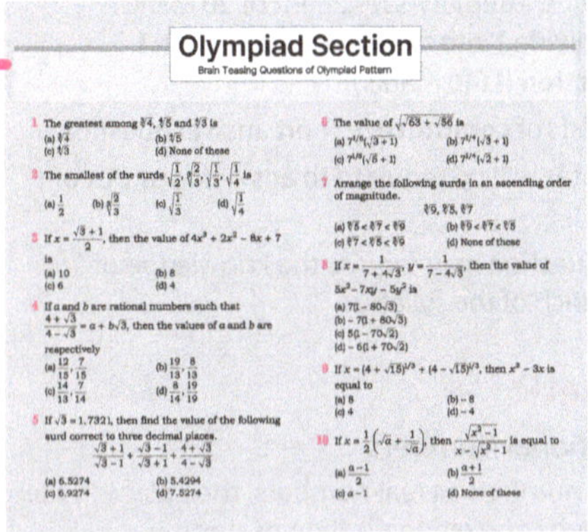
Olympiad Section
Brain Teasing Questions of Olympiad Pattern

1. The greatest among $\sqrt[4]{4}$, $\sqrt[6]{5}$ and $\sqrt[3]{3}$ is
(a) $\sqrt[4]{4}$ (b) $\sqrt[6]{5}$
(c) $\sqrt[3]{3}$ (d) None of these

2. The smallest of the surds ... is

3. If $x = \frac{\sqrt{3}+1}{2}$, then the value of $4x^3 + 2x^2 - 8x + 7$ is
(a) 10 (b) 8
(c) 6 (d) 4

4. If a and b are rational numbers such that $\frac{4+\sqrt{3}}{4-\sqrt{3}} = a + b\sqrt{3}$, then the values of a and b are respectively

5. If $\sqrt{3} = 1.732$, then find the value of the following surd correct to three decimal places.
(a) 6.5274 (b) 5.4294
(c) 6.9274 (d) 7.5274

6. The value of ... is

7. Arrange the following surds in an ascending order of magnitude.
(d) None of these

8. If $x = \frac{1}{7+4\sqrt{3}}$, $y = \frac{1}{7-4\sqrt{3}}$, then the value of $5x^2 - 7xy - 5y^2$ is

9. If $x = (4+\sqrt{15})^{1/3} + (4-\sqrt{15})^{1/3}$, then $x^3 - 3x$ is equal to
(a) 8 (b) −8
(c) 4 (d) −4

10. If $x = \frac{1}{2}\left(\sqrt{a} + \frac{1}{\sqrt{a}}\right)$, then $\frac{\sqrt{x^2-1}}{x-\sqrt{x^2-1}}$ is equal to
(d) None of these

Olympiad Section

It includes some special questions based on the pattern of Olympiad and other competitions to give the students a taste of the questions asked in competitions. These are not meant for school examinations.

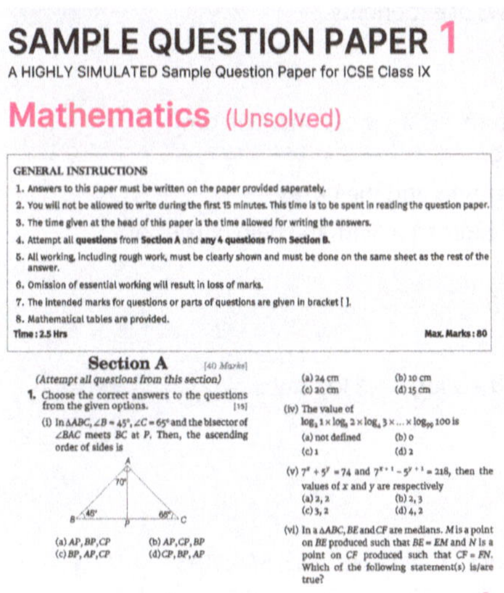
SAMPLE QUESTION PAPER 1
A HIGHLY SIMULATED Sample Question Paper for ICSE Class IX

Mathematics (Unsolved)

GENERAL INSTRUCTIONS
1. Answers to this paper must be written on the paper provided saperately.
2. You will not be allowed to write during the first 15 minutes. This time is to be spent in reading the question paper.
3. The time given at the head of this paper is the time allowed for writing the answers.
4. Attempt all questions from Section A and any 4 questions from Section B.
5. All working, including rough work, must be clearly shown and must be done on the same sheet as the rest of the answer.
6. Omission of essential working will result in loss of marks.
7. The intended marks for questions or parts of questions are given in bracket [ ].
8. Mathematical tables are provided.

Time : 2.5 Hrs Max. Marks : 80

Section A (40 Marks)
(Attempt all questions from this section)
1. Choose the correct answers to the questions from the given options. [15]
(i) In ΔABC, $\angle B = 45°$, $\angle C = 65°$ and the bisector of $\angle BAC$ meets BC at P. Then, the ascending order of sides is
(a) AP, BP, CP (b) AP, CP, BP
(c) BP, AP, CP (d) CP, BP, AP

(a) 24 cm (b) 10 cm
(c) 20 cm (d) 15 cm

(iv) The value of $\log_2 3 \times \log_3 2 \times \log_4 3 \times ... \times \log_{99} 100$ is
(a) not defined (b) 0
(c) 1 (d) 2

(v) $7^x + 5^y = 74$ and $7^{x+1} - 5^{y+1} = 218$, then the values of x and y are respectively
(a) 2, 2 (b) 2, 3
(c) 3, 2 (d) 4, 2

(vi) In a ΔABC, BE and CF are medians. M is a point on BE produced such that $BE = EM$ and N is a point on CF produced such that $CF = FN$. Which of the following statement(s) is/are true?

Internal Assessment of Practical Work

To make this book complete in all aspects, experiments based on latest syllabus have been given.

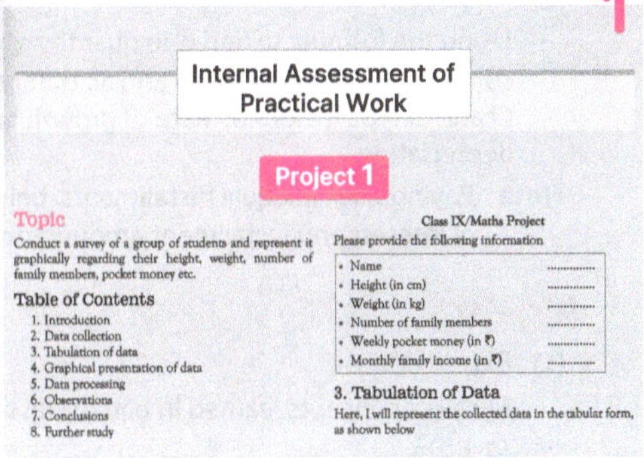
Internal Assessment of Practical Work

Project 1

Topic

Conduct a survey of a group of students and represent it graphically regarding their height, weight, number of family members, pocket money etc.

Table of Contents
1. Introduction
2. Data collection
3. Tabulation of data
4. Graphical presentation of data
5. Data processing
6. Observations
7. Conclusions
8. Further study

Class IX/Maths Project

Please provide the following information
- Name ....
- Height (in cm) ....
- Weight (in kg) ....
- Number of family members ....
- Weekly pocket money (in ₹) ....
- Monthly family income (in ₹) ....

3. Tabulation of Data

Here, I will represent the collected data in the tabular form, as shown below

Sample Question Papers

To make students practice of examination in real sense, there are 3 Sample Question Papers at the end. All these Sample Questions Papers are exactly prepared on the latest syllabus & pattern of examination.

Latest Course Structure

There will be **one** paper of **two and a half** hours duration carrying 80 Marks and Internal Assessment of 20 Marks.
The paper will be divided into two sections, **Section I** (40 Marks) and **Section II** (40 Marks).

Section I will consists of **compulsory** short answer questions.

Section II Candidates will be required to answer **four** out of **seven** questions.

The solution of a question may require the knowledge of more than one branch of the syllabus.

Pure Arithmetic

Rational and Irrational Numbers

Rational, irrational numbers as real numbers, their place in the number system. Surds and rationalization of surds.
Simplifying an expression by rationalizing the denominator.
Representation of rational and irrational numbers on the number line. Proofs of irrationality
$\sqrt{2}, \sqrt{3}, \sqrt{5}$.

Commercial Mathematics

Compound Interest

(a) Compound interest as a repeated Simple Interest computation with a growing Principal. Use of this in computing Amount over a period of 2 or 3 years.

(b) Use of formula $A = P\left(1 + \frac{r}{100}\right)^n$. Finding CI from the relation $CI = A - P$.

- Interest compounded half-yearly included.
- Using the formula to find one quantity given different combinations of *A, P, r, n, CI* and *SI*; difference between CI and SI type included. Rate of growth and depreciation.

Note Paying back in equal installments, being given rate of interest and installment amount, **not included.**

Algebra

(i) Expansions

Recall of concepts learned in earlier classes.
$(a \pm b)^2$
$(a \pm b)^3$
$(x \pm a)(x \pm b)$
$(a \pm b \pm c)^2$

(ii) Factorisation

$a^2 - b^2$
$a^3 \pm b^3$
$ax^2 + bx + c$, by splitting the middle term.

(iii) Simultaneous Linear Equations in two variables. (With numerical coefficients only)

- Solving algebraically by
  - Elimination
  - Substitution and
  - Cross-multiplication method
- Solving simple problems by framing appropriate equations.

(iv) Indices/ Exponents

Handling positive, fractional, negative and "zero" indices.
Simplification of expressions involving various exponents
$a^m \times a^n = a^{m+n}$, $a^m \div a^n = a^{m-n}$, $(a^m)^n = a^{mn}$
etc. Use of laws of exponents.

(v) Logarithms

(a) Logarithmic form vis-à-vis exponential form: interchanging.

(b) Laws of Logarithms and their uses.

Expansion of expression with the help of laws of logarithms

e.g. $y = \frac{a^4 \times b^2}{c^3}$

$\log y = 4 \log a + 2 \log b - 3 \log c$ etc.

Geometry

(i) Triangles

(a) Congruency : four cases : SSS, SAS, AAS and RHS. Illustration through cutouts. Simple applications.

(b) Problems based on

- Angles opposite equal sides are equal and converse.
- If two sides of a triangle are unequal, then the greater angle is opposite the greater side and converse.
- Sum of any two sides of a triangle is greater than the third side.
- Of all straight lines that can be drawn to a given line from a point outside it, the perpendicular is the shortest.

Proofs not required.

(c) Mid-Point Theorem and its converse, equal intercept theorem

(i) Proof and simple applications of mid-point theorem and its converse.

(ii) Equal intercept theorem: proof and simple application.

(d) Pythagoras Theorem

Area based proof and simple applications of Pythagoras Theorem and its converse.

(ii) Rectilinear Figures

(a) Proof and use of theorems on parallelogram.

- Both pairs of opposite sides equal (without proof).
- Both pairs of opposite angles equal.
- One pair of opposite sides equal and parallel (without proof).
- Diagonals bisect each other and bisect the parallelogram.
- Rhombus as a special parallelogram whose diagonals meet at right angles.
- In a rectangle, diagonals are equal, in a square they are equal and meet at right angles.

(b) Constructions of Polygons

Construction of quadrilaterals (including parallelograms and rhombus) and regular hexagon using ruler and compasses only.

(c) Proof and use of Area theorems on parallelograms:

- Parallelograms on the same base and between the same parallels are equal in area.
- The area of a triangle is half that of a parallelogram on the same base and between the same parallels.
- Triangles between the same base and between the same parallels are equal in area (without proof).
- Triangles with equal areas on the same bases have equal corresponding altitudes.

(iii) Circle

(a) Chord properties

- A straight line drawn from the centre of a circle to bisect a chord which is not a diameter is at right angles to the chord.
- The perpendicular to a chord from the centre bisects the chord (without proof).
- Equal chords are equidistant from the centre.
- Chords equidistant from the centre are equal (without proof).
- There is one and only one circle that passes through three given points not in a straight line.

(b) Arc and chord properties

- If two arcs subtend equal angles at the centre, they are equal and its converse.
- If two chords are equal, they cut off equal arcs and its converse (without proof).

Note Proofs of the theorems given above are to be taught unless specified otherwise.

Statistics

Introduction, collection of data, presentation of data, Graphical representation of data, Mean, Median of ungrouped data.

(i) Understanding and recognition of raw, arrayed and grouped data.

(ii) Tabulation of raw data using tally-marks.

(iii) Understanding and recognition of discrete and continuous variables.

(iv) Mean, median of ungrouped data.

(v) Class intervals, class boundaries and limits, frequency, frequency table, class size for grouped data.

(vi) Grouped frequency distributions: the need to and how to convert discontinuous intervals to continuous intervals.

(vii) Drawing a frequency polygon.

Mensuration

Area and perimeter of a triangle and a quadrilateral. Area and circumference of circle. Surface area and volume of Cube and Cuboids. .

(a) Area and perimeter of triangle (including Heron's formula), all types of Quadrilaterals.

(b) Circle: Area and Circumference. Direct application problems including Inner and Outer area.
Areas of sectors of circles other than quarter-circle and semi-circle are not included.

(c) Surface area and volume of 3-*D* solids : cube and cuboid including problems of type involving:

- Different internal and external dimensions of the solid.
- Cost.
- Concept of volume being equal to area of cross-section x height.
- Open/closed cubes/cuboids.

Trigonometry

(a) Trigonometric Ratios: sine, cosine, tangent of an angle and their reciprocals.

(b) Trigonometric ratios of standard angles– 0°, 30°, 45°, 60°, 90°. Evaluation of an expression involving these ratios.

(c) Simple 2-*D* problems involving one right-angled triangle.

(d) Concept of trigonometric ratios of complementary angles and their direct application

$\sin A = \cos (90° - A)$, $\cos A = \sin (90° - A)$

$\tan A = \cot (90° - A)$, $\cot A = \tan (90° - A)$

$\sec A = \operatorname{cosec} (90° - A)$, $\operatorname{cosec} A = \sec (90° - A)$

Coordinate Geometry

Cartesian System, Plotting of points in the plane for given coordinates, solving simultaneous linear equations in 2 variables graphically and finding the distance between two points using distance formula.

(a) Dependent and independent variables.

(b) Ordered pairs, coordinates of points and plotting them in the Cartesian plane.

(c) Solution of Simultaneous Linear Equations graphically.

(d) Distance formula.

INTERNAL ASSESSMENT

A minimum of two assignments are to be done during the year as prescribed by the teacher.

Suggested Assignments

- Conduct a survey of a group of students and represent it graphically - height, weight, number of family members, pocket money, etc.
- Planning delivery routes for a postman/milkman.
- Running a tuck shop/canteen.
- Study ways of raising a loan to buy a car or house, e.g. Bank loan or purchase a refrigerator or a television set through hire purchase.
- Cutting a circle into equal sections of a small central angle to find the area of a circle by using the formula $A = \pi r^2$.
- To use flat cutouts to form cube, cuboids and pyramids to obtain formulae for volume and total surface area.
- Draw a circle of radius r on a $\frac{1}{2}$ cm graph paper and then on a 2 mm graph paper. Estimate the area enclosed in each case by actually counting the squares. Now try out with circles of different radii. Establish the pattern, if any, between the two observed values and the theoretical value (area = πr^2). Any modifications?

CHAPTER

01

Rational and Irrational Numbers

SYLLABUS

- Rational, irrational numbers as real numbers, their place in the number system. Surds and rationalization of surds. Simplifying an expression by rationalizing the denominator. Representation of rational and irrational number on the number line. Proof of irrationality of $\sqrt{2}$, $\sqrt{3}$, $\sqrt{5}$

1. **Natural Numbers** Numbers, which are used for counting, i.e. 1, 2, 3, 4, ..., are called natural numbers and are denoted by 'N'.
$$N = \{1, 2, 3, 4, \dots\}$$
2. **Whole Numbers** All natural numbers including zero are known as whole numbers and are denoted by 'W'.
$$W = \{0, 1, 2, 3, 4, \dots\}$$
3. **Integers** The collection of all whole numbers and negative numbers are called integers. The collection of integers is denoted by 'Z' or 'I'.
$$Z \text{ or } I = \{\dots, -4, -3, -2, -1, 0, 1, 2, 3, 4, \dots\}$$
4. **Prime Numbers** The numbers, which are divisible by 1 and itself, are called prime numbers.
$$P = \{2, 3, 5, 7, 11, 13, 17, 19, \dots\}$$
5. **Coprime Numbers** Those numbers which have no common factors other than 1, are known as coprime numbers.
e.g. (2, 3), (8, 9) etc., 2 is the smallest prime number. It is the only even prime number.
6. **Composite Numbers** Composite numbers are those numbers, which have more than two factors.
e.g. $4 = 2 \times 2 \times 1$, $8 = 2 \times 2 \times 2 \times 1$, $9 = 3 \times 3 \times 1$, $12 = 2 \times 2 \times 3 \times 1$, etc.
The smallest composite even number is 4 and smallest composite odd number is 9.

Rational Numbers

The numbers, which can be expressed in the form of $\frac{p}{q}$, where p, q both are coprime integers and $q \neq 0$, are known as rational numbers and are denoted by 'Q',

$$Q = \left\{\frac{p}{q} : p, q \text{ both are co prime integers and } q \neq 0\right\}.$$

e.g. $\frac{-1}{2}, \frac{3}{2}, \frac{1}{3}, \frac{7}{5}$ etc.,

Every natural number, whole number and integer is a rational number.

e.g. $1 = 1/1$ or $5 = 5/1$.

Equivalent Rational Numbers

Equivalent rational numbers are those numbers which have same numerical value but different representation.

e.g. $\frac{1}{2}, \frac{2}{4}, \frac{10}{20}$ and $\frac{25}{50}$ all are equivalent rational numbers which have same numerical value, i.e. 1/2 and different representation.

Properties of Rational Numbers

(i) The sum of two or more rational numbers is always a rational number.
e.g. If $\frac{2}{3}, \frac{5}{2} \in Q$, then $\frac{2}{3} + \frac{5}{2} = \frac{19}{6} \in Q$.

(ii) The difference of two rational numbers is always a rational number.
e.g. If $\frac{1}{2}, \frac{1}{3} \in Q$, then $\frac{1}{2} - \frac{1}{3} = \frac{1}{6} \in Q$

(iii) The product of two or more rational numbers is always a rational number.
e.g. If $\frac{1}{2}, \frac{2}{3} \in Q$, then $\frac{1}{2} \times \frac{2}{3} = \frac{1}{3} \in Q$.

(iv) The division of rational number by a non-zero rational number is always a rational number.
e.g. If $\frac{2}{3}, \frac{4}{3} \in Q$, then $\frac{2}{3} \div \frac{4}{3} = \frac{1}{2} \in Q$.

(v) For every rational number $\frac{a}{b}$, there is another rational number $\frac{-a}{b}$ such that $\frac{a}{b} + \left(\frac{-a}{b}\right) = 0$. Then, $\left(\frac{-a}{b}\right)$ is called additive inverse of $\frac{a}{b}$. If $\frac{a}{b} + 0 = \frac{a}{b}$, then 0 is called **additive identity** for rational numbers.

(vi) For every rational number $\frac{a}{b}$, there is another rational number $\frac{b}{a}$ such that $\frac{a}{b} \times \frac{b}{a} = 1$. Then, $\frac{b}{a}$ is called **multiplicative inverse** of $\frac{a}{b}$. If $\frac{a}{b} \times 1 = \frac{a}{b}$, then 1 is called **multiplicative identity**.

(vii) There are infinitely many rational numbers between any two given rational numbers.

(viii) The set of rational numbers is ordered.
i.e. $a, b \in Q$ then either $a < b$ or $a > b$ or $a = b$

Example 1. Which one is the greatest rational number $\frac{4}{5}$ and $\frac{9}{7}$?

Sol. Here, $\frac{4}{5}$ and $\frac{9}{7} \Rightarrow \frac{4 \times 7}{5 \times 7} = \frac{28}{35}$ and $\frac{9 \times 5}{7 \times 5} = \frac{45}{35}$

[$\because$ LCM of 7 and 5 = 35].

Since, $28 < 45$

$\Rightarrow \frac{28}{35} < \frac{45}{35} \Rightarrow \frac{4}{5} < \frac{9}{7} \Rightarrow \frac{9}{7}$ is greater.

Methods to Determine Rational Numbers between Two Numbers

For determining one or more than one rational numbers between two given numbers, we use the following methods.

I. When one Rational Number is Determined

Let x and y be any two rational numbers, $\frac{x+y}{2}$ is a rational number lying between x and y

(a) if $x > y \Rightarrow x > \frac{x+y}{2} > y$ (b) if $x < y \Rightarrow x < \frac{x+y}{2} < y$

Example 2. Find a rational number lying between

(i) 3 and $\frac{4}{7}$ (ii) $-\frac{2}{3}$ and $-\frac{5}{7}$.

Sol. (i) Here, $3 > \frac{4}{7}$

$$\frac{4}{7} < \frac{3 + \frac{4}{7}}{2} < 3 \Rightarrow \frac{4}{7} < \frac{25}{14} < 3$$

Hence, a rational number between 3 and $\frac{4}{7}$ is $\frac{25}{14}$.

(ii) Here, $\frac{-2}{3} > \frac{-5}{7}$

$$\Rightarrow \quad \frac{-2}{3} > \frac{-\frac{2}{3} + \left(\frac{-5}{7}\right)}{2} > \frac{-5}{7} \Rightarrow \frac{-2}{3} > \frac{-29}{42} > \frac{-5}{7}$$

Hence, $\frac{-29}{42}$ lies between $\frac{-2}{3}$ and $\frac{-5}{7}$.

II. When More than One Rational Numbers are Determined

Let x and y be any two rational numbers, and we have to find indefinite rational numbers between x and $y\,(x < y)$.

i.e. Equating the denominators can be done either by finding their LCM or by multiplying the denominators of one to both the numerator and denominator of the other and make given rational numbers with same denominator then multiplying the numerator and denominator by $n + 1$.

Example 3. Find four rational numbers lying between $\frac{3}{5}$ and $\frac{2}{3}$.

Sol. We have, $\frac{3}{5}$ and $\frac{2}{3}$

LCM of 5 and 3 = 15

$\therefore$ Write the given rational numbers with the same denominator, we get

$$\frac{3 \times 3}{5 \times 3} \text{ and } \frac{2 \times 5}{3 \times 5} \text{ or } \frac{9}{15} \text{ and } \frac{10}{15}$$

or
$$\frac{9 \times 5}{15 \times 5} \text{ and } \frac{10 \times 5}{15 \times 5} \text{ or } \frac{45}{75} \text{ and } \frac{50}{75}$$

$\therefore$ Rational numbers lying between

$$\frac{45}{75} \text{ and } \frac{50}{75} \text{ are } \frac{46}{75}, \frac{47}{75}, \frac{48}{75} \text{ and } \frac{49}{75}.$$

Hence, the required rational numbers between $\frac{3}{5}$ and $\frac{2}{3}$ are $\frac{46}{75}, \frac{47}{75}, \frac{48}{75}$ and $\frac{49}{75}$.

Alternate Method

Here, $\frac{3}{5} < \frac{2}{3}$, so let $x = \frac{3}{5}$, $y = \frac{2}{3}$ and $n = 4$

Now, $d = \frac{y - x}{n + 1} \Rightarrow d = \frac{\frac{2}{3} - \frac{3}{5}}{4 + 1} = \frac{\frac{10 - 9}{15}}{5} = \frac{1}{15 \times 5} = \frac{1}{75}$

So, the four rational numbers between x and y are $(x + d)$, $(x + 2d)$, $(x + 3d)$ and $(x + 4d)$.

Here, $x + d = \frac{3}{5} + \frac{1}{75} = \frac{45 + 1}{75} = \frac{46}{75}$

$\Rightarrow \quad x + 2d = \frac{3}{5} + \frac{2}{75} = \frac{45 + 2}{75} = \frac{47}{75}$

$\Rightarrow \quad x + 3d = \frac{3}{5} + \frac{3}{75} = \frac{45 + 3}{75} = \frac{48}{75}$

and $\quad x + 4d = \frac{3}{5} + \frac{4}{75} = \frac{45 + 4}{75} = \frac{49}{75}$

Hence, the required four rational numbers lying between $\frac{3}{5}$ and $\frac{2}{3}$ are $\frac{46}{75}, \frac{47}{75}, \frac{48}{75}$ and $\frac{49}{75}$.

Example 4. Find five rational numbers between $\frac{8}{5}$ and $\frac{7}{2}$. Also, arrange in ascending order.

Sol. We have $\frac{8}{5}$ and $\frac{7}{2}$

LCM of 2 and 5 = 10

∴ Write the given rational numbes with the same denominator, we get

$$\frac{8}{5} \times \frac{2}{2} = \frac{16}{10} \text{ and } \frac{7}{2} \times \frac{5}{5} = \frac{35}{10}$$

∴ Rational numbers lying between

$$\frac{8}{5} \text{ and } \frac{7}{2} \text{ are } \frac{17}{10}, \frac{18}{10}, \frac{19}{10}, \frac{20}{10}, \frac{21}{10}$$

In ascending order

$$\frac{8}{5} < \frac{17}{10} < \frac{18}{10} < \frac{19}{10} < 2 < \frac{21}{10} < \frac{7}{2}$$

Example 5. Find four rational numbers between 0 and 0.3.

Sol. We have, $\frac{0}{1}$ and $\frac{3}{10}$

LCM of 1 and 10 = 10

∴ Write the given rational numbers with the same denominator, we get

$$\frac{0}{1} \times \frac{10}{10} = \frac{0}{10} \text{ and } \frac{3}{10} \times \frac{1}{1} = \frac{3}{10}$$

∵ Multiplying the numerator and denominator by 4 + 1 = 5

$$\Rightarrow \quad \frac{0}{10} \times \frac{5}{5} = \frac{0}{50} \text{ and } \frac{3}{10} \times \frac{5}{5} = \frac{15}{50}$$

Thus, rational numbers are

$$\frac{1}{50}, \frac{2}{50}, \frac{3}{50}, \frac{4}{50}$$

Representation of a Rational Number on a Number Line

Let us represent $\frac{1}{2}, \frac{-3}{2}, \frac{-1}{2}$ etc., on a number line XY. So, we take one half of the unit and mark all these points as follows

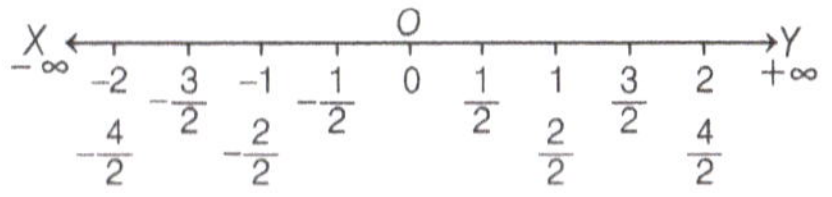

Similarly, represent $\frac{1}{3}, \frac{2}{3}, \frac{3}{3}, \frac{4}{3}$, ... and $\frac{-1}{3}, \frac{-2}{3}, \frac{-3}{3}, \frac{-4}{3}$, ... and so on, then we take one-third of the unit and mark as follows

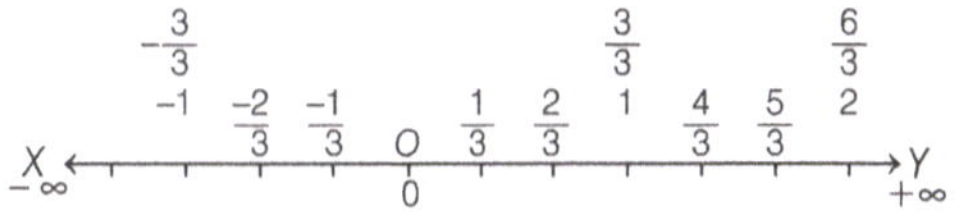

Thus, every rational number has been represented by one and only one point on the number line XY.

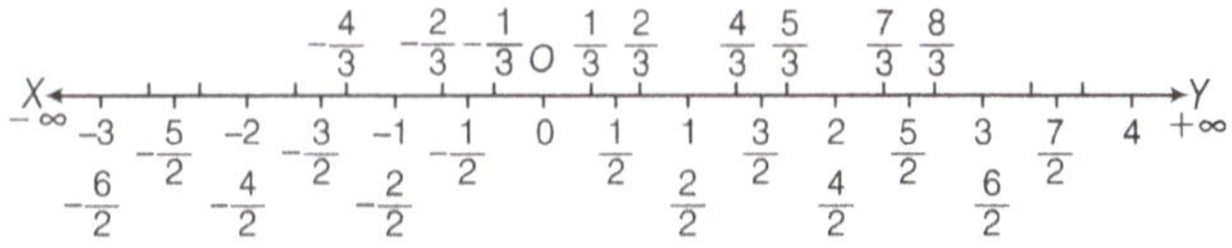

Example 6. Represent the following rational numbers on the number line.

(i) $\frac{2}{3}$ (ii) $\frac{1}{4}$ (iii) $-\frac{3}{5}$

Sol.

(i) Here, 2/3 lies between 0 and 1.

∴ We take one-third of unit length and mark points on the number line XY on both sides of 0 (zero), then we represent 2/3 as point A.

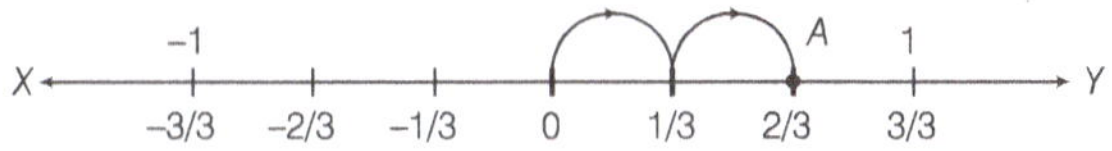

(ii) Here, 1/4 lies between 0 and 1.

∴ We take one-fourth of unit length and mark points on the number line XY on both sides of 0 (zero), then we represent 1/4 as point A.

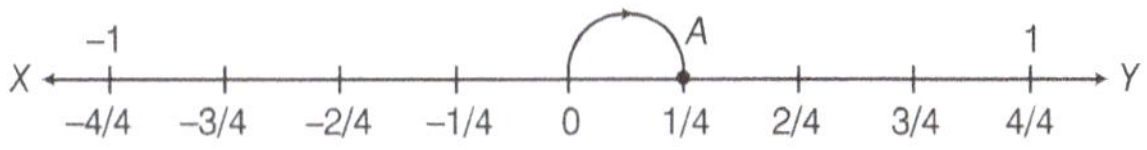

(iii) Here, – 3/5 lies between – 1 and 0.

∴ We take one-fifth of unit length and mark points on the number line XY on both sides of 0 (zero), then we represent – 3/5 as point$A$.

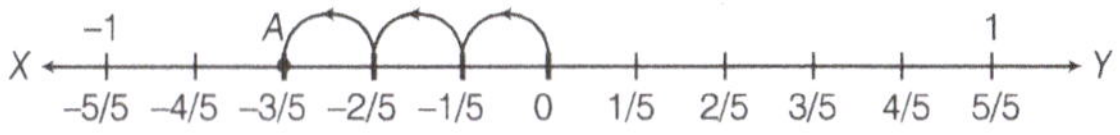

Exercise 1.1

1. Express the following numbers in the form of rational numbers $\left(\frac{p}{q}\right)$
   (i) 2 (ii) – 3 (iii) 2.3
2. Find two equivalent rational numbers.
   (i) $\frac{2}{3}$ (ii) $\frac{-4}{5}$
   (iii) $\frac{-21}{9}$
3. Insert a rational number lying between
   (i) – 3/5 and 1/7 (ii) – 7/9 and – 2
   (iii) $\frac{2}{5}$ and $\frac{3}{4}$
4. Insert three rational numbers between 2.6 and 3.1.
5. Find five rational numbers between 3/ 5 and 4/ 5.
6. Find nine rational numbers between 0 and 0.1.
7. Insert three rational numbers between $\frac{4}{11}$ and $\frac{9}{16}$.
8. Find the four rational numbers between 4 and 5.
9. Insert two rational numbers between $\frac{-1}{3}$ and $\frac{-1}{2}$ and arrange them in descending order.
10. Insert eight rational numbers between $-\frac{1}{3}$ and $\frac{2}{7}$. Also, arrange them in ascending order.
11. Arrange $-\frac{5}{9}, \frac{7}{12}, -\frac{2}{3}$ and $\frac{11}{18}$ in ascending order of their magnitudes. Also, find the difference between the largest and the smallest of these fraction.
12. Represent the following rational numbers on the number line.
    (i) $-\frac{5}{4}$ (ii) $\frac{6}{5}$ (iii) $\frac{7}{2}$ (iv) $-\frac{1}{8}$

Irrational Numbers

The numbers, which cannot be expressed in the form $\frac{p}{q}$, where p, q both are coprime integers and $q \neq 0$, are called irrational numbers.

In other words, the square roots, cube roots and nth roots etc., of natural number are irrational numbers, if their exact value cannot be obtained.

e.g. $\sqrt{2}, \sqrt{3}, \frac{1}{\sqrt{3}}, 5+\sqrt{7}, \sqrt{2}-\sqrt{5}$ etc., are irrational numbers.

Properties of Irrational Numbers

(i) There are infinitely many irrational numbers between any two given irrational numbers.

(ii) The negative of an irrational number is always an irrational number. e.g. $(-1)\times\sqrt{3} = -\sqrt{3}$

(iii) The sum of a rational and an irrational number is always an irrational number. e.g. $4+\sqrt{3}$

(iv) The sum of two irrational numbers may or may not be an irrational number.
e.g. (a) $(2+\sqrt{7})+(3-\sqrt{7}) = 5$; 5 is a rational number.
(b) $(\sqrt{5}+8)+(\sqrt{3}-8) = \sqrt{5}+\sqrt{3}$; $\sqrt{5}+\sqrt{3}$ is an irrational number.

(v) The subtraction of a rational and an irrational number is always an irrational number. e.g. $5-\sqrt{2}$

(vi) The difference of two irrational numbers may or may not be an irrational number.
e.g. (a) $(4-\sqrt{11})-(2-\sqrt{11}) = 2$; 2 is a rational number.
(b) $(\sqrt{5}+8)-(-\sqrt{5}-7) = 2\sqrt{5}+15$; $2\sqrt{5}+15$ is an irrational number.

(vii) The product of a non-zero rational and an irrational number is always an irrational number.
e.g. $4\times\sqrt{5} = 4\sqrt{5}$

(viii) The product of two irrational numbers may or may not be an irrational number.
e.g. (a) $(7-\sqrt{7})\times(7+\sqrt{7}) = 42$; 42 is a rational number.
(b) $(5+\sqrt{3})\times(7-\sqrt{5}) = 35-5\sqrt{5}+7\sqrt{3}-15$; which is an irrational number.

(ix) The division of a non-zero rational and an irrational number is always an irrational number.
e.g. $\frac{4}{\sqrt{2}}$

(x) $p+q\sqrt{x} = r+s\sqrt{x}$
$\Rightarrow \quad p = r$ and $q = s$

Example 7. Classify the following number as rational number or an irrational number.

(i) $2-\sqrt{5}$ (ii) $(3+\sqrt{23})-\sqrt{23}$
(iii) $\frac{1}{\sqrt{2}}$ (iv) $3\sqrt{5}\times\sqrt{35}$
(v) $(5-\sqrt{2})^2$ (iv) $(7-\sqrt{7})(7+\sqrt{7})$

Sol.

(i) We have, $2-\sqrt{5}$

Here, 2 is a rational number and $\sqrt{5}$ is an irrational number. The sum or difference between a rational number or an irrational number is always irrational number.

Hence, $2-\sqrt{5}$ is an irrational number.

(ii) We have, $(3+\sqrt{23})-\sqrt{23}=3+\sqrt{23}-\sqrt{23}=3$

Hence, $(3+\sqrt{23})-\sqrt{23}$ is a rational number.

(iii) We have, $\frac{1}{\sqrt{2}}$

Here, 1 is a rational number and $\sqrt{2}$ is an irrational number. We know that, division of a rational number and an irrational number is always an irrational number.

Hence, $\frac{1}{\sqrt{2}}$ is an irrational number.

(iv) Here, $3\sqrt{5}\times\sqrt{35}=3\sqrt{5\times 35}=3\sqrt{5\times 5\times 7}=15\sqrt{7}$

Since, 15 and $\sqrt{7}$ are rational and irrational numbers, respectively.

We know that product of a rational number and an irrational number is always an irrational number.

Hence, $3\sqrt{5}\times\sqrt{35}$ is an irrational number.

(v) Here, $(5-\sqrt{2})^2=25+2-10\sqrt{2}$ $[\because (a-b)^2=a^2+b^2-2ab]$

$=27-10\sqrt{2}$

Since, 27 is a rational number and $10\sqrt{2}$ is an irrational number and we know that the subtraction of a rational and an irrational number is always an irrational number.

Hence, $(5-\sqrt{2})^2$ is an irrational number.

(iv) Here, $(7-\sqrt{7})(7+\sqrt{7})$

$=(7)^2-(\sqrt{7})^2$ $[\because (a+b)(a-b)=a^2-b^2]$

$=49-7$

$=42$ is a rational number.

Hence, $(7-\sqrt{7})(7+\sqrt{7})$ is a rational number.

Note (i) Let p be a number and a be any positive integer. If p divides a^2, then p divides a.

(ii) Let p be a number and a, b be any two positive integers. If p divides ab, then p divides a or p divides b or p divides both a and b.

Example 8. Prove that $\sqrt{2}$ is an irrational number.

Sol. Let us assume $\sqrt{2}$ be a rational number.

Now, $\sqrt{2}=\frac{a}{b}$

On squaring both sides, we get

$$2=\frac{a^2}{b^2}\Rightarrow 2b^2=a^2 \quad ...(i)$$

$\Rightarrow$ 2 divides a^2 $\Rightarrow$ 2 divides a

Then, a can be written as $2m$, where m is an integer.

On putting $a=2m$ in Eq. (i), we get

$$2b^2=(2m)^2\Rightarrow 2b^2=4m^2$$

$$\Rightarrow b^2=2m^2$$

So, 2 divides b^2 $\Rightarrow$ 2 divides b

Thus, 2 is a common factor of a and b.

But this contradicts the fact that a and b have no common factor other than 1.

The contradiction arises by assuming that $\sqrt{2}$ is a rational. Our assumption is wrong.

Hence, $\sqrt{2}$ is an irrational number. **Hence proved.**

Example 9. Show that $\frac{1}{\sqrt{5}}$ is an irrational number.

Sol. Assume that $\frac{1}{\sqrt{5}}$ is a rational number.

$\Rightarrow \frac{1}{\sqrt{5}}=\frac{p}{q}$, where p and q are coprime integers, $q\neq 0$

Squaring both sides,

$$\frac{1}{5}=\frac{p^2}{q^2}$$

$$q^2=5p^2 \quad ...(i)$$

$\Rightarrow q^2$ is divisible by 5 but 5 is a prime number.

$\Rightarrow$ 5 divides q

Again, let $q=5m$ ...(ii)

From Eqs. (i) and (ii), we get

$$(5m)^2=5p^2$$

$$25m^2=5p^2$$

$$p^2=5m^2$$

$\Rightarrow$ 5 divides p^2 $\Rightarrow$ 5 divides p

[if a is prime number and if it divides p^2, then a divides p, where a is positive integer]

Thus, 5 in a common factor of p and q.

$\therefore$ This is a contradiction. [$\because$ p and q are coprime integers]

$\Rightarrow$ Our assumption is wrong.

Hence, $\frac{1}{\sqrt{5}}$ is an irrational number.

Example 10. Show that $\sqrt{7}-\sqrt{5}$ is an irrational number.

Sol. Assume that $\sqrt{7}-\sqrt{5}$ is a rational number.

$\Rightarrow \sqrt{7}-\sqrt{5}=x$, a rational number.

Squaring both sides,

$$(\sqrt{7}-\sqrt{5})^2=x^2$$

$$\Rightarrow 7+5-2\sqrt{35}=x^2 \quad [\because (a-b)^2=a^2+b^2-2ab]$$

$$\Rightarrow 12-2\sqrt{35}=x^2$$

$$\sqrt{35}=\frac{12-x^2}{2} \quad ...(i)$$

Here, x is rational $\Rightarrow x^2$ is rational

$\Rightarrow 12-x^2$ is rational

$\Rightarrow \frac{12-x^2}{2}$ is rational ...(ii)

But we know that $\sqrt{35}$ is irrational.

$\Rightarrow \frac{12-x^2}{2}$ is irrational [by Eq. (i)] ...(iii)

which is a contradiction.

$\therefore$ Our assumption is wrong.

Thus, $\sqrt{7}-\sqrt{5}$ is an irrational number.

Example 11. Show that $5-\sqrt{3}$ is an irrational number.

Sol. Assume that $5-\sqrt{3}$ is a rational number.

Now, $5-\sqrt{3}=\frac{a}{b}$

On rearranging, we get $5-\frac{a}{b}=\sqrt{3}$

Since, 5 and $\frac{a}{b}$ are rational numbers.

So, their difference will be a rational number.

$\therefore$ $\sqrt{3}$ is a rational number.

But we know that, $\sqrt{3}$ is an irrational number.

This contradicts the fact that $\sqrt{3}$ is an irrational number.

Hence, $5-\sqrt{3}$ is an irrational number.

Irrational Number between Two Rational Numbers

Let a and b be two positive irrational numbers and ab is not a perfect square, then $\sqrt{ab}$ is an irrational number lying between a and b.

Now, we insert another irrational number between a and $\sqrt{ab}$ is $\sqrt{a \times \sqrt{ab}}$.

Similarly, we can insert another irrational number.

Example 12. Find two irrational numbers between 2 and $\frac{5}{2}$.

Sol. Firstly, we insert one irrational number between 2 and $\frac{5}{2}$, which is $\sqrt{2\times\frac{5}{2}}=\sqrt{5}$.

Thus, $\sqrt{5}$ is an irrational number between 2 and $\frac{5}{2}$.

Now, we insert another irrational number between 2 and $\sqrt{5}$, which is $\sqrt{2\times\sqrt{5}}$.

Thus, $\sqrt{5}$ and $\sqrt{2\sqrt{5}}$ are irrational numbers between 2 and $\frac{5}{2}$.

Example 13. Insert three irrational numbers between 5 and 6.

Sol. We have, 5 and 6 two numbers.

It can be rewritten as

$$5=\sqrt{5^2}=\sqrt{25}$$

and $$6=\sqrt{6^2}=\sqrt{36}$$

We can write any three numbers between 25 and 36.

$$25<26<27<28<\dots<36$$

So, $\sqrt{26}$, $\sqrt{27}$ and $\sqrt{28}$ are three irrational numbers between 5 and 6.

Irrational Number between Two Irrational Numbers

Let a and b be two rational numbers, then $\sqrt{a}$ and $\sqrt{b}$ are two irrational numbers, then irrational number between two irrational numbers $\sqrt{a}$ and $\sqrt{b}$ is $(\sqrt{ab})^{1/2}$.

Example 14. Find an irrational number between $\sqrt{5}$ and $\sqrt{7}$.

Sol. We know that irrational number lying between a and b is $\sqrt{ab}$.

$\therefore$ Irrational number between $\sqrt{5}$ and $\sqrt{7}$ is

$$\sqrt{\sqrt{5}\times\sqrt{7}}=(\sqrt{35})^{1/2}=(35)^{1/4}$$

Example 15. Insert two irrational numbers between $\sqrt{2}$ and $\sqrt{7}$.

Sol. Consider the squares of $\sqrt{2}$ and $\sqrt{7}$, we get

$$(\sqrt{2})^2=2 \quad \text{and} \quad (\sqrt{7})^2=7$$

We know that $2<3<5<7$

i.e. 3 and 5 are two rational numbers between 2 and 7.

Hence, $\sqrt{2}<\sqrt{3}<\sqrt{5}<\sqrt{7}$

i.e. $\sqrt{3}$ and $\sqrt{5}$ are two irrational numbers between $\sqrt{2}$ and $\sqrt{7}$.

Example 16. Find four irrational numbers between $4\sqrt{2}$ and $3\sqrt{3}$.

Sol. Taking squares of $4\sqrt{2}$ and $3\sqrt{3}$.

$(4\sqrt{2})^2=32$ and $(3\sqrt{3})^2=27$

$\Rightarrow$ $32>31>30>29>28>27$

Taking square root, we get

$\sqrt{32}>\sqrt{31}>\sqrt{30}>\sqrt{29}>\sqrt{28}>\sqrt{27}$

Thus, $\sqrt{31}$, $\sqrt{30}$, $\sqrt{29}$ and $\sqrt{28}$ lie between $4\sqrt{2}$ and $3\sqrt{3}$.

Method to Locate an Irrational Number on the Number Line

We can locate some of the irrational numbers of the form $\sqrt{n}$, where n is a positive integer on the number line by using following steps.

Step I Write the given number (without root) as the sum of the squares of two natural numbers (say a and b, where $a>b$).

Step II Take the distance equal to these two natural numbers on the number line (a on number line and b vertically) starting from O (say OA and AB) in such a way that one is perpendicular to other (say $AB \perp OA$).

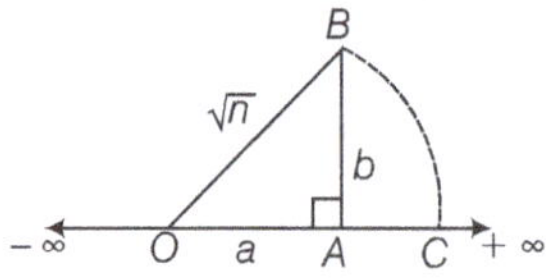

Step III Use Pythagoras theorem to find the distance OB.

Step IV Take O as centre and OB as radius, draw an arc, which cut the number line at C (say).

Thus, the point C will represent the location of $\sqrt{n}$ on the number line.

Example 17. Locate irrational number on the line.
(i) $\sqrt{5}$ (ii) $2+\sqrt{5}$

Sol.

(i) Here, $5 = 4 + 1 = 2^2 + 1^2$

Now, draw $OQ = 2$ units on number line and then draw $PQ = 1$ unit, such that $PQ \perp OQ$.

$\because \quad OP = \sqrt{OQ^2 + PQ^2}$ [by Pythagoras theorem]

$= \sqrt{5}$

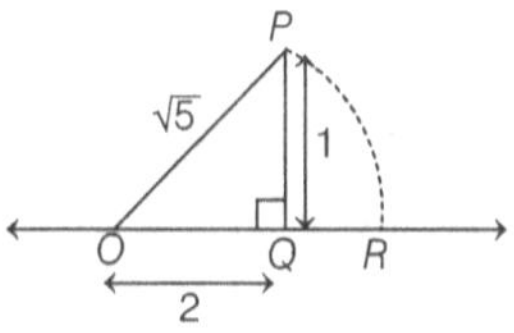

Taking O as centre and radius equal to OP draw an arc, which cuts the number line at R.

Hence, OR represents $\sqrt{5}$ on the number line.

(ii) To locate $2+\sqrt{5}$ on the number line.

Firstly, we mark a 2 units distance from the origin on the number line, say A and further apply the same procedure as in part (i).

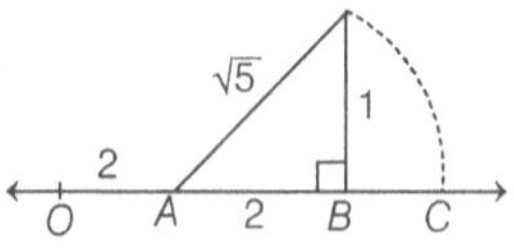

Hence, OC represents $2+\sqrt{5}$ on the number line.

Example 18. Locate $-\sqrt{2}$ on the number line.

Sol. Here, $2 = 1^2 + 1^2$

So, first draw $OA = 1$ unit on number line and then draw $AB = 1$ unit, such that $AB \perp OA$

$\Rightarrow \quad OB = \sqrt{OA^2 + OB^2}$ [by Pythagoras theorem]

$= \sqrt{2}$

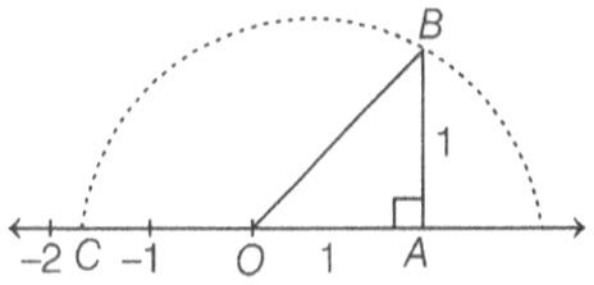

On taking O as centre and radius equal to OB, then draw an arc on the left side of the centre O.

$\therefore OC = -\sqrt{2}$ unit

Example 19. Locate $2\sqrt{2}$ on the number line.

Sol. Here, $2 = 1^2 + 1^2$

Firstly, we draw $OA = 1$ unit on number line and then draw $AB = 1$ unit such that $AB \perp AO$.

$OB = \sqrt{OA^2 + AB^2}$ [by Pythagoras theorem]

$= \sqrt{2}$

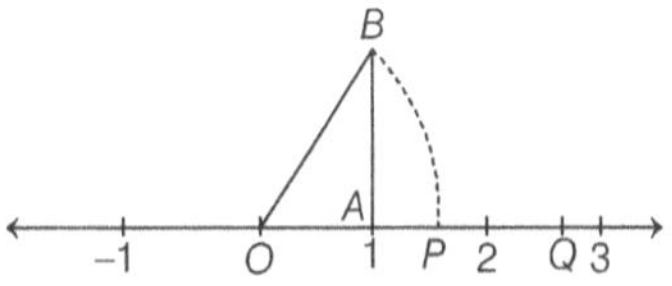

On taking O as centre and radius OB, draw an arc P on number line

$\Rightarrow \quad OP = \sqrt{2}$

Again draw an arc with centre P and radius OP, which meets the number line at Q.

$\Rightarrow OQ = 2 \times OP = 2\sqrt{2}$

Hence, OQ represents $2\sqrt{2}$ on the number line.

Example 20. Locate $\sqrt{7.5}$ on the number line.

Sol. First, we draw a line AB with length 7.5 units. Now from the point B, mark a distance of 1 unit, called as point C.

Draw a line bisector at point O on the number line and draw a semi-circle with centre O and radius OA.

Last, we draw a perpendicular line on B, which interests the semi-circle at point D.

Thus, $BD = \sqrt{7.5}$

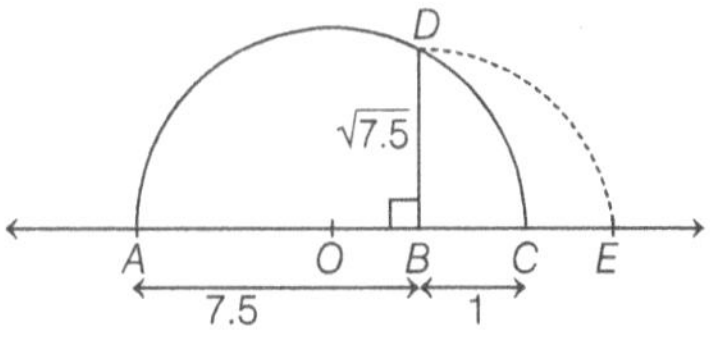

Hence, draw an arc with centre B and radius BC, which intersects the number line at point E.

$\Rightarrow BE$ represents $\sqrt{7.5}$ on the number line.

Exercise 1.2

1. Classify the following numbers as rational or irrational.
   (i) $\frac{1}{\sqrt{2}}$ (ii) $7\sqrt{5}$ (iii) -3
   (iv) $(4+\sqrt{8})-2\sqrt{2}$
   (v) $\sqrt{24}+(7\sqrt{6}-2\sqrt{6})$
2. Prove the following as an irrational numbers.
   (i) $\sqrt{6}$ (ii) $\sqrt{5}$ (iii) $\sqrt{7}$
3. Prove that $3+2\sqrt{5}$ is an irrational number.
4. Prove that $2\sqrt{3}-\sqrt{7}$ is an irrational number.
5. Insert the following number of irrational numbers between these two numbers.
   (i) Two irrational numbers between 3 and 7/3.
   (ii) Three irrational numbers between 7 and 8.
6. Insert a rational and an irrational number between 3 and 5.
7. Insert an irrational number between $\sqrt{6}$ and $\sqrt{11}$.
8. Insert two irrational numbers between $\sqrt{3}$ and $\sqrt{8}$.
9. Locate the following irrational numbers on the number line. (i) $\sqrt{2}$ (ii) $\sqrt{17}$

Real Numbers

The collection of all rational and irrational numbers together form a collection of real numbers. Every real number can be represented by a unique point on the number line and denoted by *R*.

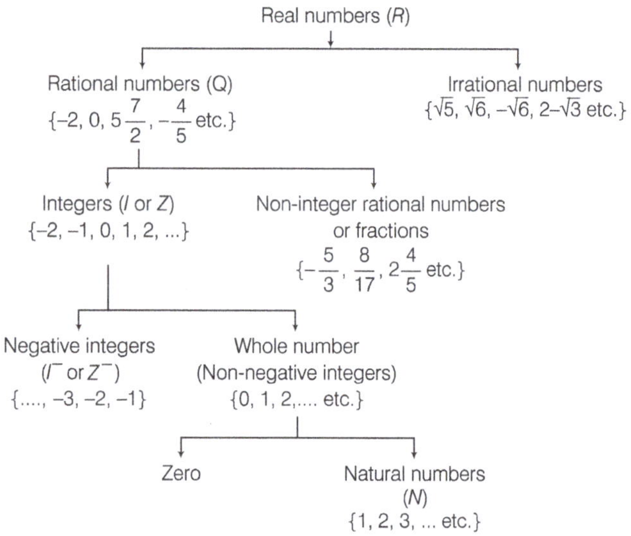

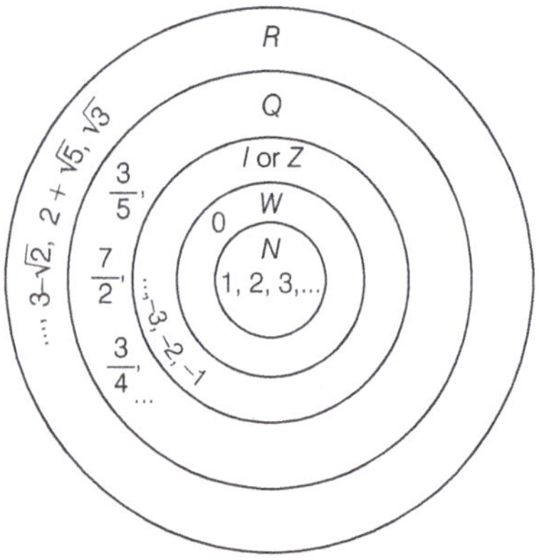

Properties of Real Numbers

If a and b are any two real numbers, then

(i) $a+b$ is a real number.
(ii) $a-b$ is a real number.
(iii) $a \times b$ is a real number.
(iv) $\frac{a}{b}$ is also a real number but $b \neq 0$.

If $a, b \in R$ and $a < b$, then $\frac{a+b}{2} \in R$ and $a < \frac{a+b}{2} < b$

The collection of real numbers is ordered i.e., if $a, b \in R$ then either $a < b$ or $a > b$ or $a = b$ is called **tricotomy law**.

Example 21. Find a real number lying between $\sqrt{3}$ and $\sqrt{5}$

Sol. $\sqrt{3}, \sqrt{5} \in R$

$\Rightarrow \quad 3 < 5 \Rightarrow \sqrt{3} < \sqrt{5}$

$\Rightarrow \frac{\sqrt{3}+\sqrt{5}}{2}$ lies between $\sqrt{3}$ and $\sqrt{5}$.

Example 22. Find a rational number between $\sqrt{2}$ and $\sqrt{3}$.

Sol. Consider the squares of $\sqrt{2}$ and $\sqrt{3}$, which are perfect squares.

$\Rightarrow 2 < 2.25 < 3 \Rightarrow \sqrt{2} < 1.5 < \sqrt{3}$

Hence, 1.5 is a rational number between $\sqrt{2}$ and $\sqrt{3}$.

Decimal Expansion of Real Numbers

A real number can be expressed as a decimal number. The decimal expansion of real numbers can be either terminating or non-terminating repeating or non-terminating non-repeating (3.45 or 2.6565 ...... or 0.325 ......).

Therefore, there are two types of decimal expansions

1. Decimal Expansion of Rational Numbers

On dividing p by q, two main cases occur either the remainder becomes zero after a certain stage or never becomes zero and we get a repeating (or non-repeating) string of remainders.

***Case* I When remainder becomes zero**

On dividing p by q, if remainder becomes zero after some steps, then decimal expansion terminates or ends after a finite number of steps. Such decimal expansion is called terminating decimal expansion.

(i) $\frac{1}{4}$

4) 1.0 (0.25
8
20
20
0

$\therefore \frac{1}{4} = 0.25$

On dividing 1 by 4, we get the exact value 0.25, i.e. remainder is zero, so 1/4 has the terminating decimal expansion.

(ii) $\frac{639}{250}$

250) 639 (2.556
500
1390
1250
1400
1250
1500
1500
0

$\therefore \frac{639}{250} = 2.556$

On dividing 639 by 250, we get the exact value 2.556, i.e. remainder is zero, so 639/250 has the terminating decimal expansion.

***Case* II When remainder never becomes zero**

On dividing p by q, if remainder never becomes zero and set of digits repeats periodically (or in same interval), then the decimal expansion is called **non-terminating repeating decimal**. It is also known as **non-terminating recurring decimal** expansion. The block of repeated digit is denoted by the bar over it.

e.g.

(i) $\frac{2}{3}$

3) 2.0 (0.66
18
20
18
2

$\therefore \frac{2}{3} = 0.666... = 0.\overline{6}$

On dividing 2 by 3, we get the block of repeated number 6 again and again, i.e. remainder never becomes zero, so 2/3 is a non-terminating repeating decimal expansion.

(ii) $\frac{1}{7}$

7) 1.0 (0.142857142857
7
30
28
20
14
60
56
40
35
50
49
10
7
30
28
20
14
60
56
40
35
50
49
1

$\frac{1}{7} = 0.1428571428571 \ \ldots = 0.\overline{142857}$

On dividing 1 by 7, we get the block of repeated number 142857 again and again, i.e. remainder never becomes zero, so 1/7 has the **non-terminating repeating decimal** expansion.

Some Important Points

(i) A rational number is said to be a pure recurring decimal, if all the digits in it after the decimal point are repeated.
e.g. $0.\overline{4}$, $0.\overline{7}$ etc.

(ii) A rational number is said to be a mixed recurring decimal, if there is atleast one non-repeated digit.
e.g. $3.6\overline{75}$, 42.78333 ... .

Example 23. Write the following in decimal form and state what kind of decimal expansion each has?

(i) $\frac{39}{100}$ (ii) $5\frac{1}{8}$

(iii) $\frac{4}{13}$ (iv) $\frac{2}{15}$

(v) $\frac{329}{500}$ (vi) $\frac{1}{13}$

Sol.

(i) $\frac{39}{100} = 0.39$, so it has terminating decimal expansion.

(ii) $5\frac{1}{8} = \frac{41}{8} = 5.125$, so it has terminating decimal expansion.

(iii) $\frac{4}{13} = 0.\overline{307692}$, so it has non-terminating repeating decimal expansion.

(iv) $\frac{2}{15} = 0.1\bar{3}$, so it has non-terminating repeating decimal expansion.

(v) $\frac{329}{500} = 0.658$, so it has terminating decimal expansion.

(vi) $\frac{1}{13} = 0.076923076923... = 0.\overline{076923}$, so it has non-terminating repeating decimal expansion.

Some Important Types of Questions Based on Decimal Expansion of Rational Numbers

Type 1 Let x be a rational number whose decimal expansion terminates. Then, x can be expressed in the form p/q, where p, q are coprimes and the prime factorisation of q is of the form $2^n 5^m$, where n and m are non-negative integers.

Example 24. Express 23.3408 in the form of rational number.

Sol. Let us consider the rational number whose decimal expansion terminates, i.e. 23.3408

Now, $23.3408 = \frac{233408}{10000} = \frac{233408}{10^4}$

Denominator of the above rational number is the power of 10 and prime factor of 10 is 2 and 5.

$$\therefore \quad 23.3408 = \frac{233408}{10^4} = \frac{233408}{2^4 \cdot 5^4} = \frac{2^6 \times 7 \times 521}{2^4 \times 5^4} = \frac{2^2 \times 7 \times 521}{5^4}$$

[cancel the factors common to both numerator and denominator]

Thus, 23.3408 can be expressed as $\frac{2^2 \times 7 \times 521}{5^4}$.

Type 2 Let $x = p/q$ be a rational number, such that the prime factorisation of q is of the form $2^n 5^m$, where n and m are non-negative integers. Then, x has a decimal expansion, which terminates.

Example 25. If $\frac{13}{125}$ is a rational number, find the decimal expansion of it, which terminate.

Sol. Given rational number is $\frac{13}{125}$.

$\therefore$ Prime factorisation of $125 = 5^3$

Now, $\frac{13}{125} = \frac{13}{5^3} = \frac{13 \times 2^3}{5^3 \times 2^3}$

[make the denominator in the power of 10]

$= \frac{104}{10^3} = 0.104$

Thus, 0.104 is decimal expansion, which terminates.

Type 3 Let $x = p/q$ be a rational number, such that the prime factorisation of q is not of the form $2^n 5^m$, where n and m are non-negative integers. Then, x has a decimal expansion, which is non-terminating repeating (recurring).

Example 26. Without actually performing the long division, state whether the following rational numbers will have a terminating decimal expansion or not. Also, write decimal expansion

(i) $\frac{3}{8}$ (ii) $\frac{14588}{625}$ (iii) $\frac{31}{343}$

Sol.

(i) We have, $\frac{3}{8}$

The factors of the denominator 8 are $2^3 \times 5^0$.

So, $\frac{3}{8}$ has a terminating decimal expansion.

Now, $\frac{3}{8} = \frac{3}{2^3} \times \frac{5^3}{5^3} = \frac{375}{10^3} = 0.375$

which is the required decimal expansion.

(ii) We have, $\frac{14588}{625}$

The factors of the denominator 625 are $5^4 \times 2^0$.

So, it has a terminating decimal expansion.

Now, $\frac{14588}{625} = \frac{14588}{5^4} \times \frac{2^4}{2^4} = \frac{233408}{10^4} = 23.3408$

which is the required decimal expansion.

(iii) We have, $\frac{31}{343}$

The factor of the denominator 343 is 7^3, which is not of the form $2^n 5^m$. So, it has non-terminating repeating decimal expansion.

Now, $\frac{31}{343} = 0.090379008 ...$

Method to Convert Non-terminating Recurring Decimal Expansion into Rational Number

Suppose, the number of the form $x = a \cdot b\bar{c}$, where a, b and c are the digits of the number (i.e. $a, b, c \in \{0, 1, 2, 3, ..., 9\}$, we have to transform the given number in the form of $\frac{p}{q}$, where p and q are coprime integers and $q \neq 0$.

The following steps are given below

Step I First, transform the non-repeated digit(s) between decimal point and recurring number to the left side of decimal by multiplying both sides by 10^r, where 'r' is the number of digits between decimal point and recurring number (i.e. $x = a \cdot b\bar{c}$, we see that one digit 'b' exist between decimal point and recurring number).

So, we multiply both sides by 10^1, we get

$$10x = ab \cdot \bar{c} \quad \text{...(i)}$$

Step II Count the number of digits in recurring number (say R) and then multiply Eq. (i) by that power of 10 (i.e. 10^R) and the equation becomes

$$10(10x) = abc \cdot \bar{c} \quad \text{...(ii)}$$

Step III Lastly, subtract Eq. (i) from Eq. (ii), we get the required result as

$$100x - 10x = abc \cdot \bar{c} - ab \cdot \bar{c}$$

$$\Rightarrow \quad x = \frac{abc \cdot \bar{c} - ab \cdot \bar{c}}{90} = \frac{abc - ab}{90}$$

Example 27. Show that the following repeating decimals are rational numbers

(i) $1.\bar{9}$

(ii) $0.3\overline{25}$

(iii) $0.0\overline{72}$

Sol.

(i) Let $x = 1.999$ ...(i)

Thus, one digit is repeating.

So, on multiplying both sides of Eq. (i) by 10, we get

$$10x = 19.999... \quad \text{...(ii)}$$

It can be written as

$$10x = 18 + 1.999...$$

$\Rightarrow$ $10x = 18 + x$ [using Eq. (i)]

$\Rightarrow$ $10x - x = 18$

$\Rightarrow$ $9x = 18$

$\Rightarrow$ $x = \frac{18}{9} = 2$

or $\frac{2}{1}$

Hence, 1.999 ... is approximately equal to 2.

(ii) Given, $x = 0.3\overline{25}$

First, to shift the decimal point just before the recurring term, we multiply by 10, we get

$$10x = 3.\overline{25} \quad \text{...(i)}$$

Thus, two digits are repeating.

So, on multiplying Eq. (i) by 100, we get

$$1000x = 325.\overline{25}$$

Rewrite it as

$$1000x = 322 + 3.\overline{25}$$

$\Rightarrow$ $1000x = 322 + 10x$ [using Eq. (i)]

$\Rightarrow$ $990x = 322$

$x = \frac{322}{990}$

$\Rightarrow$ $x = \frac{161}{495}$

Hence, $\frac{161}{495}$ is a rational representation of $0.3\overline{25}$.

(iii) Let $x = 0.0\overline{72}$

First, to shift the decimal point just before the recurring term, we multiply by 10, we get

$$10x = 0.\overline{72} \quad \text{...(i)}$$

Thus, two digits are repeating.

So, on multiplying Eq. (i) by 100, we get

$$1000x = 72.\overline{72}$$

It can be written as

$1000x = 72 + 0.\overline{72} = 72 + 10x$ [using Eq. (i)]

$990x = 72$

$x = \frac{72}{990}$

$x = \frac{36}{495}$

Hence, $\frac{36}{495}$ is a rational representation of $0.0\overline{72}$.

Example 28. Find the sum of 0.0333 ... and 0.444... .

Sol. Let $x = 0.0333$ ...(i)

Here, to shift the decimal point just before the recurring term, we multiply by 10, we get

$$10x = 0.333... \quad \text{...(ii)}$$

Thus, one digit is repeating.

So, on multiplying Eq. (ii) by 10, we get

$$100x = 3.333...$$

It can be written as $100x = 3 + 0.333...$

$\Rightarrow$ $100x = 3 + 10x$ [from Eq. (ii)]

$\Rightarrow$ $90x = 3$

$\Rightarrow$ $x = \frac{3}{90}$ ...(iii)

Again, let $y = 0.444...$ ...(iv)

Thus, one digit is replacing.

So, on multiplying Eq. (iv) by 10, we get

$$10y = 4.444...$$

It can be written as

$$10y = 4 + 0.444...$$

$\Rightarrow$ $10y = 4 + y$ [using Eq. (iv)]

$\Rightarrow$ $9y = 4$

$\Rightarrow$ $y = \frac{4}{9}$

$\therefore$ Sum of 0.333... and 0.444... $= x + y$

$$= \frac{3}{90} + \frac{4}{9} = \frac{3 + 40}{90} = \frac{43}{90}$$

2. Decimal Expansion of Irrational Numbers

The decimal expansion of an irrational number is non-terminating non-recurring. In other words, a number whose decimal expansion is non-terminating non-recurring is an irrational number.

e.g. Let $\sqrt{2}$ and π be irrational numbers, then their decimal expansions are

$\sqrt{2} = 1.41421356237309504880168872420 96...$

and $\pi = 3.14159265358979323846264338327950...$

Generally, $\frac{22}{7}$ is an approximate value of π but $\pi \neq \frac{22}{7}$.

Example 29. Find an irrational number between

(i) $\frac{1}{7}$ and $\frac{1}{3}$ (ii) $-\frac{2}{7}$ and $\frac{2}{5}$.

Sol.

(i) We have, $\frac{1}{7} = 0.\overline{142857}$ and $\frac{1}{3} = 0.\overline{3}$

It implies that they are non-terminating recurring decimals.

Hence, the required irrational number which lies between $\frac{1}{7}$ and $\frac{1}{3}$ is 0.2101001000... .

(ii) We have, $\frac{-2}{7} = -0.\overline{285714}$ and $\frac{2}{7} = \overline{285714}$

$\Rightarrow$ They are non-terminating recurring decimals.

Hence, the required irrational number which lies between $\frac{-2}{7}$ and $\frac{2}{7}$ is 0.101001000....

(i) There are infinitely many non-terminating non-recurring numbers which exists between two irrational numbers.
(ii) Students can write other number also as per their choice.
(iii) There is no specification in it.

Exercise 1.3

1. What can be the maximum number of digits in the repeating block of digits in the decimal expansion of 1/17? Perform the division to check your answer.
2. Write the following in decimal form and say what kind of decimal expansion each has?

   (i) $\frac{64}{100}$ (ii) $\frac{2}{11}$ (iii) $7\frac{1}{8}$ (iv) $\frac{5}{13}$ (v) $\frac{7}{3}$ (vi) $\frac{169}{400}$

3. Express decimal number 0.18696 in the form of rational number.
4. Without doing any actual division, find which of the following rational numbers have terminating decimal representation.

   (a) $\frac{129}{2^2 5^7 7^5}$ (b) $\frac{6}{15}$ (c) $\frac{35}{50}$

   (d) $\frac{125}{441}$ (e) $\frac{77}{210}$ (f) $\frac{13}{3125}$

   (g) $\frac{17}{8}$ (h) $\frac{64}{455}$ (i) $\frac{15}{1600}$

   (j) $\frac{29}{343}$ (k) $\frac{23}{2^3 5^2}$

5. Express the following decimals in the form of p/q.

   (i) $0.\overline{4}$ (ii) $0.\overline{54}$ (iii) $0.\overline{621}$ (iv) $0.00\overline{32}$ (v) $2.0\overline{15}$

6. Find an irrational number between 1/9 and 1/7.
7. Find two irrational numbers between

   (i) 1/7 and 2/7, when it is given that $\frac{1}{7} = 0.\overline{142857}$.

   (ii) 2/3 and 8/9.

4. Surds

Let $a > 0$ be a positive rational number and n be a positive integer, such that $a^{1/n} = \sqrt[n]{a}$ is an irrational number, then n is called **exponent**, a is called **radicand** and '$\sqrt{\ }$' is called **surd**. $\sqrt{3}, \sqrt[5]{16}, \sqrt[3]{20}$ are surds as 3, 16, 20 are positive real numbers.

But $\sqrt{16}, \sqrt[4]{81}, \sqrt[3]{27}$ etc are not surds because $\sqrt{16} = 4, \sqrt[4]{81} = 3, \sqrt[3]{27} = 3$, i.e. $\sqrt{16}, \sqrt[4]{81}, \sqrt[3]{27}$ are not irrational numbers.

In other words, $\sqrt[n]{a}$ is a surd (of order n) if

(i) a is a positive real number,
(ii) $n(> 1)$ is a positive integer, and
(iii) $\sqrt[n]{a}$ is not a rational number.

Every surd is an irrational number but every irrational number is not a surd. e.g. π is an irrational number but not a surd.

Example 30. State which of the following are surds and which are not? Give reason.

(i) $\sqrt{48}$ (ii) $\sqrt[3]{256}$
(iii) $\sqrt{20} \times \sqrt{45}$ (iv) $\sqrt[3]{8} \times \sqrt[3]{54}$
(v) $3\sqrt{12} \div 6\sqrt{27}$

Sol.

(i) We have, $\sqrt{48} = \sqrt{3 \times 4 \times 4} = 4\sqrt{3}$
$= 4\sqrt{3}$, which is not a rational number.
Hence, $\sqrt{48}$ is a surd.

(ii) $\sqrt[3]{256} = \sqrt[3]{2^3 \times 2^3 \times 2^2} = 2 \times 2 \times \sqrt[3]{2^2}$, which is not a rational number.
Hence, $\sqrt[3]{256}$ is a surd.

(iii) We have, $\sqrt{20} \times \sqrt{45} = \sqrt{900} = \sqrt{3 \times 3 \times 10 \times 10}$
$= 3 \times 10 = 30$, which is a rational number.
Hence, $\sqrt{20} \times \sqrt{45}$ is not a surd.

(iv) We have, $\sqrt[3]{8} \times \sqrt[3]{54} = \sqrt[3]{432} = \sqrt[3]{2^4 \times 3^3}$
$= (2^4)^{1/3} \ (3^3)^{1/3} = 2^{4/3} \ 3^{3 \times 1/3} = 3 \cdot \sqrt[3]{16}$
which is not a rational number.
Hence, $\sqrt[3]{8} \times \sqrt[3]{54}$ is a surd.

(v) We have, $3\sqrt{12} \div 6\sqrt{27} = \dfrac{3\sqrt{12}}{6\sqrt{27}} = \dfrac{3 \times \sqrt{4 \times 3}}{6 \times \sqrt{3 \times 3 \times 3}} = \dfrac{3 \times 2 \times \sqrt{3}}{6 \times 3\sqrt{3}} = \dfrac{1}{3}$,
which is a rational number.
Hence, $3\sqrt{12} \div 6\sqrt{27}$ is not a surd.

Types of Surds

(i) **Pure surds** A surd is a pure surd, if it does not have any other rational coefficient except unity.
e.g. $\sqrt{3}, \sqrt{2}, \sqrt[3]{7}$, etc.,

(ii) **Mixed surds** A surd is a mixed surd, if it has some rational coefficient other than unity.
e.g $3\sqrt{7}, 2\sqrt{11}, 54\sqrt[3]{8}$, etc.,

(iii) **Similar surds** Two or more surds are said to be similar or like, if they have the same surd factor and same radical sign, i.e. the surds which have same irrational factor are called similar surds.
e.g. $3\sqrt{13}, \sqrt{13}, \sqrt{52}$ etc.

Laws of Surds

Let $a, b \in R^+$

(i) $(\sqrt[n]{a})^n = a \ (n > 1)$
(ii) $\sqrt[n]{ab} = \sqrt[n]{a} \cdot \sqrt[n]{b}$
(iii) $\sqrt[n]{\dfrac{a}{b}} = \dfrac{\sqrt[n]{a}}{\sqrt[n]{b}}$
(iv) $(\sqrt{a} + \sqrt{b})(\sqrt{a} - \sqrt{b}) = a - b$
(v) $(\sqrt{a} + \sqrt{b})^2 = a + 2\sqrt{ab} + b$
(vi) $(\sqrt{a} - \sqrt{b})^2 = a - 2\sqrt{ab} + b$
(vii) $(\sqrt{a} + \sqrt{b})(\sqrt{c} + \sqrt{d}) = \sqrt{ac} + \sqrt{ad} + \sqrt{bc} + \sqrt{bd}$
(viii) If $\sqrt{a}$ and $\sqrt{b}$ are two positive irrational numbers, then
(a) $\sqrt{a} < \sqrt{b}$, if $a < b$
(b) $\sqrt{a} > \sqrt{b}$, if $a > b$
(ix) If a is a positive rational number and $\sqrt{b}$ is an irrational number, then
(a) $a < \sqrt{b}$, if $a^2 < b$
(b) $a > \sqrt{b}$, if $a^2 > b$
(x) $\sqrt{a} + \sqrt{b} \neq \sqrt{a + b}; \ a \neq b$

Example 31. Sum of $\left(\dfrac{2}{3}\sqrt{7} - \dfrac{1}{2}\sqrt{2} + 6\sqrt{11}\right)$ and $\left(\dfrac{1}{3}\sqrt{7} + \dfrac{3}{2}\sqrt{2} - \sqrt{11}\right)$

Sol. We have, $\dfrac{2}{3}\sqrt{7} - \dfrac{1}{2}\sqrt{2} + 6\sqrt{11} + \dfrac{1}{3}\sqrt{7} + \dfrac{3}{2}\sqrt{2} - \sqrt{11}$

$= \left(\dfrac{2}{3} + \dfrac{1}{3}\right)\sqrt{7} + \left(\dfrac{-1}{2} + \dfrac{3}{2}\right)\sqrt{2} + (6 - 1)\sqrt{11}$

$= \left(\dfrac{3}{3}\right)\sqrt{7} + \left(\dfrac{2}{2}\right)\sqrt{2} + 5\sqrt{11} = \sqrt{7} + \sqrt{2} + 5\sqrt{11}$

Example 32. Solve the following

(i) Find the sum of $(8 + 3\sqrt{2})$ and $(8 - 3\sqrt{2})$.
(ii) Find the square of $(8 + 5\sqrt{3})$.
(iii) Find the product of $\left(\sqrt{\dfrac{3}{5}} + \sqrt{\dfrac{5}{2}}\right)$ and $(\sqrt{5} + \sqrt{2})$.

Sol.

(i) $(8 + 3\sqrt{2}) + (8 - 3\sqrt{2}) = 8 + 3\sqrt{2} + 8 - 3\sqrt{2} = 16$

(ii) $(8 + 5\sqrt{3})^2 = (8)^2 + 2 \times 8 \times 5\sqrt{3} + (5\sqrt{3})^2$
[$\because (a + b)^2 = a^2 + b^2 + 2ab$]
$= 64 + 80\sqrt{3} + 75 = 139 + 80\sqrt{3}$

(iii) $\left(\sqrt{\frac{3}{5}}+\sqrt{\frac{5}{2}}\right)(\sqrt{5}+\sqrt{2})=\left(\frac{\sqrt{3}}{\sqrt{5}}+\frac{\sqrt{5}}{\sqrt{2}}\right)(\sqrt{5}+\sqrt{2})$

$=\frac{\sqrt{3}}{\sqrt{5}}\times\sqrt{5}+\frac{\sqrt{3}}{\sqrt{5}}\times\sqrt{2}+\frac{\sqrt{5}}{\sqrt{2}}\times\sqrt{5}+\frac{\sqrt{5}}{\sqrt{2}}\times\sqrt{2}$

$=\sqrt{3}+\frac{\sqrt{6}}{\sqrt{5}}+\frac{5}{\sqrt{2}}+\sqrt{5}$

Example 33. Simplify $\sqrt{7+2\sqrt{10}}+\sqrt{12-2\sqrt{35}}$.

Sol. Here, $\sqrt{7+2\sqrt{10}}=\sqrt{5+2+2\sqrt{10}}$

$=\sqrt{(\sqrt{5}+\sqrt{2})^2}=\sqrt{5}+\sqrt{2}$

and $\sqrt{12-2\sqrt{35}}=\sqrt{7+5-2\sqrt{35}}$

$=\sqrt{(\sqrt{7}-\sqrt{5})^2}$

$=\sqrt{7}-\sqrt{5}$

$\therefore\ \sqrt{7+2\sqrt{10}}+\sqrt{12-2\sqrt{35}}=\sqrt{5}+\sqrt{2}+(\sqrt{7}-\sqrt{5})$

$=\sqrt{5}+\sqrt{2}+\sqrt{7}-\sqrt{5}$

$=\sqrt{2}+\sqrt{7}$

Example 34. Find the greatest number.

(i) $\sqrt[3]{3}$ and $\sqrt{2}$

(ii) $2\sqrt[4]{3}$ and $2\sqrt[3]{2}$

Sol.

(i) We have, $\sqrt[3]{3}$ and $\sqrt{2}$.

As LCM of 2 and 3 is 6.

$\Rightarrow\quad \sqrt[3]{3}=(3)^{1/3}=(3^2)^{\frac{1}{6}}=(9)^{1/6}$

and $\quad \sqrt{2}=2^{1/2}=(2^3)^{1/6}=(8)^{1/6}$

Thus, $9>8\Rightarrow(9)^{1/6}>(8)^{1/6}$

Hence, $\sqrt[3]{3}>\sqrt{2}$

(ii) Here, $2\sqrt[4]{3}$ and $2\sqrt[3]{2}$

LCM of 3 and 4 is 12.

$\Rightarrow 2\sqrt[4]{3}=\sqrt[4]{2^4\times3}=\sqrt[4]{48}=(48)^{\frac{1}{4}}=(48^3)^{\frac{1}{12}}=(110592)^{\frac{1}{12}}$

and $2\sqrt[3]{2}=\sqrt[3]{2^3\times2}=\sqrt[3]{16}=(16)^{\frac{1}{3}}=(16^4)^{\frac{1}{3}}=(65536)^{\frac{1}{12}}$

Thus, $110592>65536\Rightarrow(110592)^{\frac{1}{12}}>(65536)^{\frac{1}{12}}$

Hence, $2\sqrt[4]{3}>2\sqrt[3]{2}$

Example 35. Express $4\sqrt{5}, 5\sqrt{3}, 10, 3\sqrt{7}$ and $6\sqrt{2}$ in ascending order.

Sol. Now, write all the numbers in pure surds like,

$4\sqrt{5}=\sqrt{16}\times\sqrt{5}=\sqrt{80},\ 5\sqrt{3}=\sqrt{25}\times\sqrt{3}=\sqrt{75}$

$10=\sqrt{100},\ 3\sqrt{7}=\sqrt{9}\times\sqrt{7}=\sqrt{63}$

and $\quad 6\sqrt{2}=\sqrt{36}\times\sqrt{2}=\sqrt{72}$

Since, $\quad 63<72<75<80<100$

$\Rightarrow\quad \sqrt{63}<\sqrt{72}<\sqrt{75}<\sqrt{80}<\sqrt{100}$

$\Rightarrow\quad 3\sqrt{7}<6\sqrt{2}<5\sqrt{3}<4\sqrt{5}<10$

Hence, given surds in ascending order are

$3\sqrt{7}, 6\sqrt{2}, 5\sqrt{3}, 4\sqrt{5}$ and 10.

Example 36. Express $\sqrt{5}, \sqrt[3]{2}$ and $\sqrt[4]{3}$ in descending order.

Sol. First, we take LCM of 2, 3 and 4 which is 12.

$\sqrt{5}=5^{\frac{1}{2}}=(5^6)^{\frac{1}{12}}=(15625)^{\frac{1}{12}}$

$\sqrt[3]{2}=2^{\frac{1}{3}}=(2^4)^{\frac{1}{12}}=(16)^{\frac{1}{12}}$

$\sqrt[4]{3}=(3)^{\frac{1}{4}}=(3^3)^{\frac{1}{12}}=(27)^{\frac{1}{12}}$

Thus, $15625>27>16$

$\Rightarrow\quad (15625)^{\frac{1}{12}}>(27)^{\frac{1}{12}}>(16)^{\frac{1}{12}}$

$\Rightarrow\quad \sqrt{5}>\sqrt[4]{3}>\sqrt[3]{2}$

Hence, $\sqrt{5}, \sqrt[4]{3}$ and $\sqrt[3]{2}$ are in descending order.

Rationalisation of Surds

When we multiply a surd by another surd we get a rational number. This process is known as rationalisation of surds or simple rationalisation. In this result, each surd is known as rationalising factor of the other surd.

Example 37. Find the product of following surds.

(i) $2\sqrt{5}\times4\sqrt{5}$ (ii) $\sqrt{7}\times\frac{2}{\sqrt{7}}$

(iii) $(\sqrt{2}+3)(\sqrt{2}-3)$

Sol.

(i) $2\sqrt{5}\times4\sqrt{5}=2\times4\sqrt{5\times5}=8\times5=40$

$\therefore 2\sqrt{5}$ and $4\sqrt{5}$ are rationalising factors of each other.

(ii) $\sqrt{7}\times\frac{2}{\sqrt{7}}=2$

$\therefore \sqrt{7}$ and $\frac{2}{\sqrt{7}}$ are rationalising factors of each other.

(iii) $(\sqrt{2}+3)(\sqrt{2}-3)=(\sqrt{2})^2-3^2$ $\quad[\because (a+b)(a-b)=a^2-b^2]$

$=2-9=-7$

$\therefore (\sqrt{2}+3)$ and $(\sqrt{2}-3)$ are rationalising factor of each other.

Example 38. Write the lowest rationalising factor of the following.

(i) $\sqrt{32}$

(ii) $(\sqrt{2}-2)$

(iii) $\sqrt{40}-\sqrt{360}$

(iv) $15-3\sqrt{2}$

Sol.

(i) We have, $\sqrt{32}=\sqrt{2^2\times2^2\times2}=2\times2\sqrt{2}=4\sqrt{2}$

Here, we have to multiply by $\sqrt{2}$, so that it becomes rationalise.

Hence, lowest rationalising factor of $\sqrt{32}$ is $\sqrt{2}$.

(ii) We have, $(\sqrt{2}-2)$

Here, we have to multiply by $(\sqrt{2}+2)$, so that it becomes rationalise.

Hence, lowest rationalising factor of $(\sqrt{2}-2)$ is $(\sqrt{2}+2)$.

(iii) We have, $\sqrt{40}-\sqrt{360}=2\sqrt{10}-6\sqrt{10}=-4\sqrt{10}$
Here, we have to multiply by $\sqrt{10}$, so that it becomes rationalise.
Hence, lowest rationalise factor is $\sqrt{10}$.

(iv) We have, $15-3\sqrt{2}=3(5-\sqrt{2})$
Here, we have to multiply by $5+\sqrt{2}$, so that it becomes rationalise. Hence, lowest rationalise factor is $5+\sqrt{2}$.

Rationalising the Denominator

If the denominator of an expression contains a term with a square root (or a number under a radical sign), then we multiply and divide the numerator and denominator of the given expression by the conjugate of its denominator and simplify.

Conjugate of $\sqrt{a}+\sqrt{b}$ is $\sqrt{a}-\sqrt{b}$

and $\sqrt{a}-\sqrt{b}$ is $\sqrt{a}+\sqrt{b}$

Conjugate of $a+\sqrt{b}$ is $a-\sqrt{b}$

and $a-\sqrt{b}$ is $a+\sqrt{b}$

Example 39. Rationalise the denominator of $\dfrac{5}{\sqrt{3}-\sqrt{5}}$.

Sol. Let $y=\dfrac{5}{\sqrt{3}-\sqrt{5}}$ and its denominator $=\sqrt{3}-\sqrt{5}$

Here, the conjugate of denominator $(\sqrt{3}-\sqrt{5})$ is $(\sqrt{3}+\sqrt{5})$.

$$y=\frac{5}{\sqrt{3}-\sqrt{5}}\times\frac{\sqrt{3}+\sqrt{5}}{\sqrt{3}+\sqrt{5}}=\frac{5(\sqrt{3}+\sqrt{5})}{(\sqrt{3})^2-(\sqrt{5})^2}$$

[using the formula, $(a-b)(a+b)=a^2-b^2$]

$$=\frac{5(\sqrt{3}+\sqrt{5})}{3-5}=-\frac{5}{2}(\sqrt{3}+\sqrt{5})$$

Example 40. If $\sqrt{2}=1.4142$, then find the value of $\sqrt{\dfrac{\sqrt{2}-1}{\sqrt{2}+1}}$.

Sol. Given, $\sqrt{2}=1.4142$

We have, $\sqrt{\dfrac{\sqrt{2}-1}{\sqrt{2}+1}}=\sqrt{\dfrac{(\sqrt{2}-1)}{(\sqrt{2}+1)}\times\dfrac{(\sqrt{2}-1)}{(\sqrt{2}-1)}}$

[by rationalising the denominator]

$$=\sqrt{\frac{(\sqrt{2}-1)^2}{2-1}}=\frac{\sqrt{(\sqrt{2}-1)^2}}{1}=\sqrt{2}-1$$

$=1.4142-1=0.4142$ [put $\sqrt{2}=1.4142$]

Example 41. If $\dfrac{3+\sqrt{7}}{3-\sqrt{7}}=a+b\sqrt{7}$, find the values of a and b.

Sol. Given, $a+b\sqrt{7}=\dfrac{3+\sqrt{7}}{3-\sqrt{7}}$

$\Rightarrow \quad a+b\sqrt{7}=\dfrac{3+\sqrt{7}}{3-\sqrt{7}}\times\dfrac{3+\sqrt{7}}{3+\sqrt{7}}$ [by rationalising]

$\Rightarrow \quad a+b\sqrt{7}=\dfrac{(3+\sqrt{7})^2}{(3)^2-(\sqrt{7})^2}$ [$\because (a-b)(a+b)=a^2-b^2$]

$=\dfrac{9+7+6\sqrt{7}}{9-7}$ [$\because (a+b)^2=a^2+b^2+2ab$]

$\Rightarrow \quad a+b\sqrt{7}=\dfrac{16+6\sqrt{7}}{2}=8+3\sqrt{7}$

On comparing the coefficient of a and b on both sides, we get

$$a=8 \text{ and } b=3$$

Example 42. Rationalise the following :

(i) $\dfrac{4\sqrt{3}+5\sqrt{2}}{\sqrt{48}+\sqrt{18}}$

(ii) $\dfrac{2}{\sqrt{5}+\sqrt{3}+2}$

(iii) $\dfrac{1}{3-\sqrt{8}}-\dfrac{1}{\sqrt{8}-\sqrt{7}}+\dfrac{1}{\sqrt{7}-\sqrt{6}}-\dfrac{1}{\sqrt{6}-\sqrt{5}}+\dfrac{1}{\sqrt{5}-2}$

Sol.

(i) $\dfrac{4\sqrt{3}+5\sqrt{2}}{\sqrt{48}+\sqrt{18}}=\dfrac{4\sqrt{3}+5\sqrt{2}}{4\sqrt{3}+3\sqrt{2}}\times\dfrac{4\sqrt{3}-3\sqrt{2}}{4\sqrt{3}-3\sqrt{2}}$ [by rationalising]

$$=\frac{4\sqrt{3}(4\sqrt{3}-3\sqrt{2})+5\sqrt{2}(4\sqrt{3}-3\sqrt{2})}{48-18}$$

$$=\frac{48-12\sqrt{6}+20\sqrt{6}-30}{30}$$

$$=\frac{18+8\sqrt{6}}{30}=\frac{9+4\sqrt{6}}{15}$$

(ii) $\dfrac{2}{\sqrt{5}+\sqrt{3}+2}=\dfrac{2}{(\sqrt{5}+\sqrt{3})+2}\times\dfrac{(\sqrt{5}+\sqrt{3})-2}{(\sqrt{5}+\sqrt{3})-2}$

[by rationalising]

$=\dfrac{2(\sqrt{5}+\sqrt{3}-2)}{(\sqrt{5}+\sqrt{3})^2-2^2}$ [$\because (a+b)(a-b)=a^2-b^2$]

$$=\frac{2(\sqrt{5}+\sqrt{3}-2)}{5+3+2\sqrt{5}\sqrt{3}-4}=\frac{2(\sqrt{5}+\sqrt{3}-2)}{4+2\sqrt{15}}$$

$=\dfrac{\sqrt{5}+\sqrt{3}-2}{2+\sqrt{15}}=\dfrac{\sqrt{5}+\sqrt{3}-2}{2+\sqrt{15}}\times\dfrac{2-\sqrt{15}}{2-\sqrt{15}}$ [by rationalising]

$$=\frac{2\sqrt{5}+2\sqrt{3}-4-\sqrt{5}\sqrt{15}-\sqrt{3}\sqrt{15}+2\sqrt{15}}{2^2-(\sqrt{15})^2}$$

[$\because (a+b)(a-b)=a^2-b^2$]

$$=\frac{2\sqrt{5}+2\sqrt{3}-4-5\sqrt{3}-3\sqrt{5}+2\sqrt{15}}{4-15}$$

$$=\frac{-\sqrt{5}-3\sqrt{3}-4+2\sqrt{15}}{-11}$$

$$=\frac{\sqrt{5}+3\sqrt{3}-2\sqrt{15}+4}{11}$$

(iii) $\dfrac{1}{3-\sqrt{8}}-\dfrac{1}{\sqrt{8}-\sqrt{7}}+\dfrac{1}{\sqrt{7}-\sqrt{6}}-\dfrac{1}{\sqrt{6}-\sqrt{5}}+\dfrac{1}{\sqrt{5}-2}$

$$=\frac{1}{3-\sqrt{8}}\times\frac{3+\sqrt{8}}{3+\sqrt{8}}-\frac{1}{\sqrt{8}-\sqrt{7}}\times\frac{\sqrt{8}+\sqrt{7}}{\sqrt{8}+\sqrt{7}}$$

$$+\frac{1}{\sqrt{7}-\sqrt{6}}\times\frac{\sqrt{7}+\sqrt{6}}{\sqrt{7}+\sqrt{6}}$$

$$-\frac{1}{\sqrt{6}-\sqrt{5}}\times\frac{\sqrt{6}+\sqrt{5}}{\sqrt{6}+\sqrt{5}}+\frac{1}{\sqrt{5}-2}\times\frac{\sqrt{5}+2}{\sqrt{5}+2}$$ [by rationalising]

$$=\frac{3+\sqrt{8}}{3^2-(\sqrt{8})^2}-\frac{\sqrt{8}+\sqrt{7}}{(\sqrt{8})^2-(\sqrt{7})^2}+\frac{\sqrt{7}+\sqrt{6}}{(\sqrt{7})^2-(\sqrt{6})^2}-\frac{\sqrt{6}+\sqrt{5}}{(\sqrt{6})^2-(\sqrt{5})^2}+\frac{\sqrt{5}+2}{(\sqrt{5})^2-2^2}$$

$[\because (a+b)(a-b)=a^2-b^2]$

$$=\frac{3+\sqrt{8}}{9-8}-\frac{\sqrt{8}+\sqrt{7}}{8-7}+\frac{\sqrt{7}+\sqrt{6}}{7-6}-\frac{\sqrt{6}+\sqrt{5}}{6-5}+\frac{\sqrt{5}+2}{5-4}$$

$$=(3+\sqrt{8})-(\sqrt{8}+\sqrt{7})+(\sqrt{7}+\sqrt{6})-(\sqrt{6}+\sqrt{5})+(\sqrt{5}+2)$$

$$=3+2=5$$

Example 43. If $x=2-\sqrt{3}$, then find the value of $\left(x-\frac{1}{x}\right)^3$.

Sol. Let $x=2-\sqrt{3}$

$$\Rightarrow \frac{1}{x}=\frac{1}{2-\sqrt{3}}=\frac{1}{2-\sqrt{3}}\times\frac{2+\sqrt{3}}{2+\sqrt{3}}$$ [by rationalising]

$$=\frac{2+\sqrt{3}}{2^2-(\sqrt{3})^2}$$ $[\because (a+b)(a-b)=a^2-b^2]$

$$=\frac{2+\sqrt{3}}{4-3}=\frac{2+\sqrt{3}}{1}=2+\sqrt{3}$$

$$\therefore x-\frac{1}{x}=(2-\sqrt{3})-(2+\sqrt{3})=-2\sqrt{3}.$$

Thus, $\left(x-\frac{1}{x}\right)^3=(-2\sqrt{3})^3=(-2)^3(\sqrt{3})^3$

$$=-8\times3\sqrt{3}=-24\sqrt{3}$$

Example 44. If $a=\frac{2-\sqrt{5}}{2+\sqrt{5}}$ and $b=\frac{2+\sqrt{5}}{2-\sqrt{5}}$, then find the value of $(a+b)^3$.

Sol. Here, $a+b=\frac{2-\sqrt{5}}{2+\sqrt{5}}+\frac{2+\sqrt{5}}{2-\sqrt{5}}=\frac{(2-\sqrt{5})^2+(2+\sqrt{5})^2}{(2+\sqrt{5})(2-\sqrt{5})}$

$$=\frac{(4+5-4\sqrt{5})+(4+5+4\sqrt{5})}{2^2-(\sqrt{5})^2}$$

$[\because (a+b)(a-b)=a^2-b^2]$

$$=\frac{18}{4-5}=\frac{18}{-1}=-18$$

Hence, $(a+b)^3=(-18)^3=-5832$

Exercise 1.4

1. State which of the following are surds and which are not? Give reason.
   (i) $\sqrt{169}$ (ii) $\sqrt{1331}$
   (iii) $\sqrt[3]{64}$ (iv) $\sqrt{243}$
   (v) $\sqrt[4]{16}$ (vi) $\sqrt[3]{625}$
   (vii) $\sqrt[3]{-125}$
2. Simplify the following.
   (i) $3\sqrt{3}+2\sqrt{27}+7\sqrt{3}$
   (ii) $8\sqrt{15}\div2\sqrt{3}$
3. Simplify the following.
   (i) $(\sqrt{3}-\sqrt{7})^2$
   (ii) $(\sqrt{3}+\sqrt{5})(\sqrt{2}+\sqrt{7})$
   (iii) $(7+\sqrt{7})(7-\sqrt{7})$
4. Arrange $\sqrt{3}$, $3\sqrt{5}$, $4\sqrt{8}$ in ascending order.
5. Write the lowest rationalising factor of the following
   (i) $\sqrt{75}$
   (ii) $\sqrt{3}-3$
   (iii) $\sqrt{28}-\sqrt{567}$
6. Rationalise the denominator of the following.
   (i) $\frac{4}{3\sqrt{5}}$ (ii) $\frac{3}{4-\sqrt{7}}$
   (iii) $\frac{1}{\sqrt{6}-\sqrt{5}}$ (iv) $\frac{6}{3\sqrt{2}-2\sqrt{3}}$
7. If $\sqrt{2}=1.414$, then find the value of
   $3\sqrt{32}-2\sqrt{50}+4\sqrt{128}-20\sqrt{18}$.
8. If $\sqrt{3}=1.732$, then find the value of
   (i) $\sqrt{27}+\sqrt{75}+\sqrt{108}-\sqrt{243}$.
   (ii) $5\sqrt{12}-3\sqrt{48}+6\sqrt{75}+7\sqrt{108}$.
9. If $x=2+\sqrt{3}$, then find the value of $x-1/x$.
10. Find the values of a and b
    (i) $\frac{5+3\sqrt{2}}{5-3\sqrt{2}}=a+b\sqrt{2}$
    (ii) $\frac{5+2\sqrt{3}}{7+4\sqrt{3}}=a+b\sqrt{3}$
11. If $x=9+4\sqrt{5}$, then find the value of $\sqrt{x}-\frac{1}{\sqrt{x}}$
12. If $p=\frac{\sqrt{5}-\sqrt{3}}{\sqrt{5}+\sqrt{3}}$ and $q=\frac{\sqrt{5}+\sqrt{3}}{\sqrt{5}-\sqrt{3}}$, then find the value of p^2+q^2.

Chapter Practice

a. 1 Mark Questions

1. Which of the following pair is equivalent rational numbers?

   (a) $\frac{3}{5}, \frac{15}{25}$ (b) $\frac{1}{2}, \frac{3}{4}$

   (c) $\frac{2}{7}, \frac{3}{7}$ (d) None of these

2. Which of the following is a rational number lying between 2 and $\frac{4}{7}$?

   (a) $\frac{9}{7}$ (b) $\frac{16}{7}$ (c) $\frac{18}{7}$ (d) $\frac{13}{7}$

3. The sum of two irrational numbers is

   (a) an irrational number

   (b) a rational number

   (c) an integer

   (d) may or may not be irrational

4. Determine the irrational number from the following.

   (a) $\sqrt{36}$ (b) $\sqrt{\frac{9}{25}}$ (c) $\sqrt{\frac{2}{3}}$ (d) $\sqrt{49}$

5. Determine the number from the following which has terminating decimal representation

   (a) $\frac{4}{13}$ (b) $\frac{7}{6}$ (c) $\frac{4}{5}$ (d) $\frac{8}{13}$

6. $\sqrt{7} \times \sqrt{6}$ is equal to

   (a) $3\sqrt{2}$ (b) $3\sqrt{7}$ (c) $2\sqrt{7}$ (d) $\sqrt{42}$

7. On rationalising the denominator of $\frac{1}{\sqrt{5}-3}$, we get

   (a) $\frac{\sqrt{3}+5}{4}$ (b) $-\frac{(\sqrt{3}+5)}{4}$

   (c) $-\frac{(\sqrt{5}+3)}{4}$ (d) $\frac{5+\sqrt{3}}{4}$

b. 3 Marks Questions

8. Find the five rational numbers lying between $\frac{2}{5}$ and $\frac{3}{4}$.

9. Represent the following rational numbers on the number line.

   (i) $\frac{5}{7}$ (ii) $-\frac{7}{2}$ (iii) $-\frac{3}{8}$

10. Classify the following numbers as rational or irrational with justification.

    (i) $3\sqrt{18}$ (ii) $(1+\sqrt{5})-(4+\sqrt{5})$

    (iii) 1.030030003 ...... (iv) $\sqrt{\frac{9}{27}}$

    (v) 0.3796

11. Show that $3\sqrt{2}$ is an irrational number.

12. Show that $(\sqrt{5}+\sqrt{3})$ is an irrational number.

13. Write two rational numbers between $\sqrt{2}$ and $\sqrt{3}$.

14. Write three irrational numbers between $\sqrt{3}$ and $\sqrt{5}$.

15. Represent $\sqrt{10}$ on the number line.

16. Locate a point P on the number line such that it represents $\sqrt{29}$.

17. Write the lowest rationalising factor of the following.

    (i) $\sqrt{24}$ (ii) $\sqrt{5}-3$ (iii) $\sqrt{18}-\sqrt{50}$

18. Express $1.272727... = 1.\overline{27}$ in the form $\frac{p}{q}$, where p, q are integers and $q \neq 0$.

19. Express the following real numbers in ascending order.

    $$4\sqrt{2},\ 3\sqrt{3},\ 2\sqrt{11},\ 6,\ \sqrt{17}$$

20. If $\sqrt{2} = 1.414$, then evaluate

    $$\sqrt{8}+\sqrt{50}+\sqrt{72}+\sqrt{98}.$$

21. Rationalise the denominator of $\frac{2}{\sqrt{3}-\sqrt{5}}$.

c. 4/5 Marks Questions

22. Express each of the following as a rational number in the simplest form.

    (i) $1.3\overline{7}$ (ii) $2.\overline{23}$

    (iii) $34.\overline{5678}$ (iv) $111.32\overline{35}$

23. Express $0.6 + 0.\overline{7} + 0.4\overline{7}$ in the form p/q, where p, q are integers and $q \neq 0$.

24. Simplify (i) $(\sqrt{11}-\sqrt{7})(\sqrt{11}+\sqrt{7})$

    (ii) $(5+\sqrt{7})(2+\sqrt{5})$

25. Simplify each of the following expressions.

    (i) $(3+\sqrt{3})(2+\sqrt{2})$

    (ii) $(3+\sqrt{3})(3-\sqrt{3})$

    (iii) $(\sqrt{5}+\sqrt{2})^2$

    (iv) $(\sqrt{5}-\sqrt{2})(\sqrt{5}+\sqrt{2})$

26. Rationalise the denominators of the following.

(i) $\frac{1}{\sqrt{7}}$ (ii) $\frac{1}{\sqrt{7}-\sqrt{6}}$ (iii) $\frac{1}{\sqrt{5}+\sqrt{2}}$ (iv) $\frac{1}{\sqrt{7}-2}$

27. If $\sqrt{5} = 2.236$, then find the value

$$\frac{21}{\sqrt{20}-\sqrt{40}-\sqrt{80}-\sqrt{5}+2\sqrt{10}}.$$

28. If $\sqrt{2} = 1.414$ and $\sqrt{3} = 1.732$, then find the value of

$$\frac{4}{3\sqrt{3}-2\sqrt{2}}+\frac{3}{3\sqrt{3}+2\sqrt{2}}.$$

29. If $x = 3+\sqrt{8}$, then find the value of $\left(x^2+\frac{1}{x^2}\right)$.

30. If $x = 1+\sqrt{2}$, then find the value of $\left(x-\frac{1}{x}\right)^3$.

31. Show that $\frac{15}{\sqrt{10}+\sqrt{20}+\sqrt{40}-\sqrt{5}-\sqrt{80}} = \sqrt{10}+\sqrt{5}$.

d. 6 Marks Questions

32. Locate $5+\sqrt{2}$ on the number line.

33. Prove that the following are irrational numbers

(i) $\sqrt[3]{5}$ (ii) $\frac{1}{2+\sqrt{3}}$

34. If a and b are rational numbers and $\frac{2+\sqrt{3}}{2-\sqrt{3}} = a+b\sqrt{3}$, then find the value of $a+b$.

35. Find the values of a and b, if

$$\frac{7+3\sqrt{5}}{3+\sqrt{5}}-\frac{7-3\sqrt{5}}{3-\sqrt{5}} = a+\sqrt{5}b$$

36. Rationalise $\frac{1}{\sqrt{7}+\sqrt{3}-\sqrt{2}}$.

37. Simplify $\frac{x-\sqrt{x^2-1}}{x+\sqrt{x^2-1}}-\frac{x+\sqrt{x^2-1}}{x-\sqrt{x^2-1}}$.

38. If $a = \frac{1}{7-4\sqrt{3}}$ and $b = \frac{1}{7+4\sqrt{3}}$, then find the values of the following.

(i) a^2+b^2

(ii) a^3+b^3

39. Simplify $\frac{4-\sqrt{5}}{4+\sqrt{5}}+\frac{4+\sqrt{5}}{4-\sqrt{5}}$.

40. If $x = \sqrt{3}+\frac{1}{\sqrt{3}}$, calculate the value of

$\left(x-\frac{\sqrt{126}}{\sqrt{42}}\right)\cdot\left(x-\frac{1}{x-\frac{2\sqrt{3}}{3}}\right)$ correct to two decimal places.

41. If $x = \frac{\sqrt{5}-2}{\sqrt{5}+2}$ and $y = \frac{\sqrt{5}+2}{\sqrt{5}-2}$, find the value of x^2+y^2+xy.

Hints and Answers

Exercise 1.1

1. (i) $\frac{2}{1}$ (ii) $-\frac{3}{1}$ (iii) $\frac{23}{10}$

2. (i) $\frac{4}{6}, \frac{6}{9}$ (ii) $\frac{-12}{15}, \frac{-24}{30}$ (iii) $\frac{-7}{3}, \frac{-28}{12}$

3. Hint Do same as Example 2.

Ans. (i) $-\frac{8}{35}$ (ii) $-\frac{25}{18}$ (iii) $\frac{23}{40}$

4. Hint Do same as Example 4.

Ans. $\frac{27}{10} = 2.7, \frac{28}{10} = 2.8, \frac{29}{10} = 2.9$

5. Hint Do same as Example 4.

Ans. $\frac{19}{30}, \frac{20}{30}, \frac{21}{30}, \frac{22}{30}$ and $\frac{23}{30}$

6. Hint Do same as Example 5.

Ans. $\frac{1}{100}, \frac{1}{50}, \frac{3}{100}, \frac{1}{25}, \frac{1}{20}, \frac{3}{50}, \frac{7}{100}, \frac{2}{25}$ and $\frac{9}{100}$

7. Hint Do same as Example 3. **Ans.** $\frac{17}{38}, \frac{13}{27}, \frac{22}{43}$

8. Hint Do same as Example 4.

Ans. $\frac{21}{5}, \frac{22}{5}, \frac{23}{5}$ and $\frac{24}{5}$

9. Hint Do same as Example 4.

Ans. $\frac{-4}{9}, \frac{-7}{18}$ and $-\frac{1}{2} > -\frac{4}{9} > -\frac{7}{18} > -\frac{1}{3}$

10. Hint Do same as Example 4.

$\frac{-2}{7}, \frac{-5}{21}, \frac{-4}{21}, \frac{-1}{7}, \frac{-2}{21}, \frac{-1}{21}, 0, \frac{1}{21}$

In ascending order,

$\frac{-2}{7} > \frac{-5}{21} > \frac{-4}{21} > \frac{-1}{7} > \frac{-2}{21} > \frac{-1}{21} > 0 > \frac{1}{21}$

11. Hint magnitude of $\frac{-24}{36}, \frac{-20}{36}, \frac{21}{36}$ and $\frac{22}{36}$ is $\frac{24}{36}, \frac{20}{36}, \frac{21}{36}$ and $\frac{22}{36}$, respectively.

Ans. $\frac{20}{36} < \frac{21}{36} < \frac{22}{36} < \frac{24}{36}$; difference is $\frac{1}{9}$.

12. **Hint** Do same as Example 6.

Ans. (i)

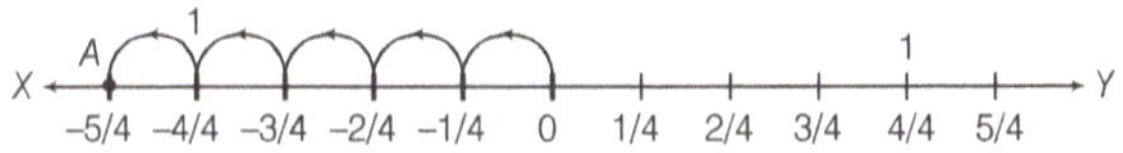

(ii)

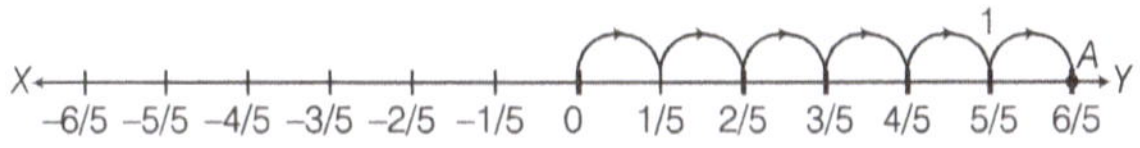

(iii)

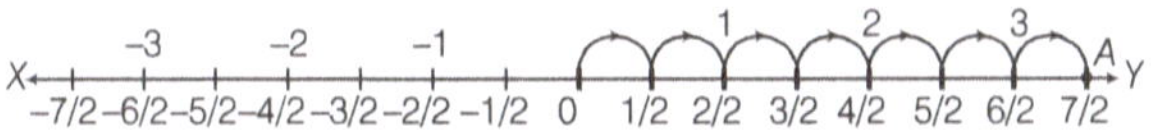

(iv)

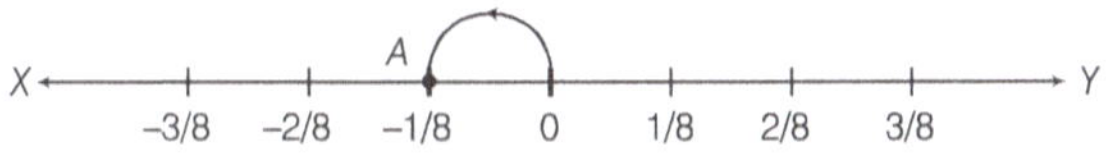

Exercise 1.2

1. **Hint** Do same as Example 7.

Ans. (i) Irrational (ii) Irrational (iii) Rational (iv) Rational (v) Irrational

2. **Hint** Do same as Example 8.
3. **Hint** Do same as Example 10.
4. **Hint** Do same as Example 10.
5. (i) Do same as Example 12. **Ans.** $\sqrt{7}, \sqrt{3\sqrt{7}}$

(ii) Do same as Example 13. **Ans.** $\sqrt{50}, \sqrt{51}, \sqrt{52}$

6. **Hint** A rational number between 3 and 5 is $\frac{3+5}{2} = \frac{8}{2} = 4$

and an irrational number between 3 and 5 is $\sqrt{3 \times 5} = \sqrt{15}$.

Ans. $4, \sqrt{15}$

7. **Hint** Do same as Example 14. **Ans.** $(66)^{1/4}$
8. **Hint** Do same as Example 15. **Ans.** $\sqrt{5}, \sqrt{6}$
9. (i) **Hint** Do same as Example 17.

Ans.

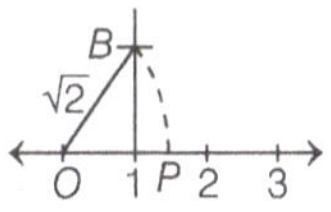

(ii) **Hint** Do same as Example 17.

Ans.

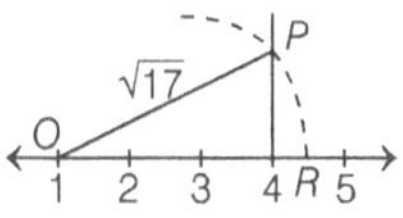

Exercise 1.3

1. **Hint** Do same as Case II part (ii). **Ans.** 16.
2. **Hint** Do same as Example 23.

Ans. (i) 0.64, terminating decimal expansion.

(ii) $0.\overline{18}$, non-terminating repeating decimal expansion.

(iii) 7.125, terminating decimal expansion.

(iv) $0.\overline{384615}$, non-terminating repeating decimal expansion.

(v) $2.\overline{3}$, non-terminating repeating decimal expansion.

(vi) 0.4225, terminating decimal expansion.

3. **Hint** Do same as Example 24. **Ans.** $\frac{19 \times 123}{2^2 \times 5^5}$
4. **Hint** Do same as Example 26.

Ans. (a) Non-terminating repeating

(b) Terminating

(c) Terminating

(d) Non-terminating repeating

(e) Non-terminating repeating

(f) Terminating

(g) Terminating

(h) Non-terminating repeating

(i) Terminating

(j) Non-terminating repeating

(k) Terminating

5. **Hint** Do same as Example 27.

Ans. (i) $\frac{4}{9}$ (ii) $\frac{6}{11}$ (iii) $\frac{23}{37}$ (iv) $\frac{8}{2475}$ (v) $\frac{133}{66}$

6. **Hint** Do same as Example 29.

Ans. 0.1303003000 ...

7. **Hint** Do same as Example 29.

Ans. (i) 0.1430143001430001 ... and 0.254025400254 ...

(ii) 0.6868868886 ... and 0.7070070007 ...

Exercise 1.4

1. **Hint** Do same as Example 30.

(i) Not surd (ii) Surd (iii) Not surd (iv) Surd (v) Not surd (vi) Surd (vii) Not surd

2. (i) **Hint** $3\sqrt{3} + 2\sqrt{3 \times 3 \times 3} + 7\sqrt{3}$

$= 3\sqrt{3} + 2 \times 3\sqrt{3} + 7\sqrt{3}$

$= 3\sqrt{3} + 6\sqrt{3} + 7\sqrt{3}$ **Ans.** $16\sqrt{3}$

(ii) **Hint** $8\sqrt{3} \times \sqrt{5} \times \frac{1}{2\sqrt{3}}$ **Ans.** $4\sqrt{5}$

3. **Hint**

(i) Use the identity, $(a-b)^2 = a^2 + b^2 - 2ab$.

(ii) Do same as Example 32(iii).

(iii) Use the identity, $(a+b)(a-b) = a^2 - b^2$.

Ans. (i) $10 - 2\sqrt{21}$ (ii) $\sqrt{6} + \sqrt{21} + \sqrt{10} + \sqrt{35}$ (iii) 42

4. **Hint** Do same as Example 35.

Ans. $\sqrt{3}, 3\sqrt{5}, 4\sqrt{8}$

5. **Hint** Do same as Example 38.
Ans. (i) $\sqrt{3}$ (ii) $\sqrt{3}+3$ (iii) $\sqrt{7}$

6. **Hint** Do same as Example 39.
Ans. (i) $\frac{4}{15}\sqrt{5}$ (ii) $\frac{4+\sqrt{7}}{3}$ (iii) $\sqrt{6}+\sqrt{5}$
(iv) $3\sqrt{2}+2\sqrt{3}$

7. **Hint** $3\sqrt{32}-2\sqrt{50}+4\sqrt{128}-20\sqrt{18}$
$=12\sqrt{2}-10\sqrt{2}+32\sqrt{2}-60\sqrt{2}=-26\sqrt{2}$
Ans. – 36.764

8. **Hint** Do same as Q. 7.
Ans. (i) 8.660 (ii) 121.24

9. **Hint** $\frac{1}{x}=\frac{1}{2+\sqrt{3}}\times\frac{2-\sqrt{3}}{2-\sqrt{3}}$ **Ans.** $2\sqrt{3}$

10. **Hint** Do same as Example 41.
Ans. (i) $a=\frac{43}{7}$ and $b=\frac{30}{7}$
(ii) $a=11$ and $b=-6$

11. **Hint** Do same as Example 43. **Ans.** ± 4

12. **Hint** Do same as Example 44. **Ans.** 62

Chapter Exercise

1. (a) 2. (a) 3. (d) 4. (c)
5. (c) 6. (d) 7. (c)

8. **Hint** Do same as Example 3.
Ans. $\frac{55}{120},\frac{62}{120},\frac{69}{120},\frac{76}{120},\frac{83}{120}$
or $\frac{11}{24},\frac{31}{60},\frac{23}{40},\frac{19}{30},\frac{83}{120}$

9. **Hint** Do same as Example 6.
(i) **Ans.**

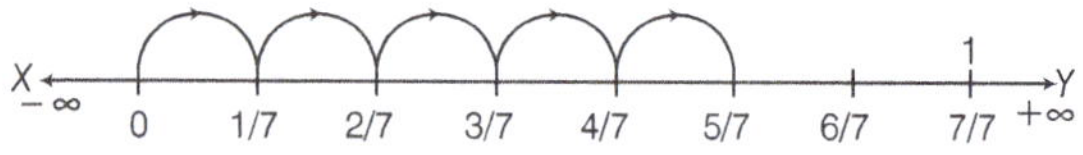

(ii) **Ans.**

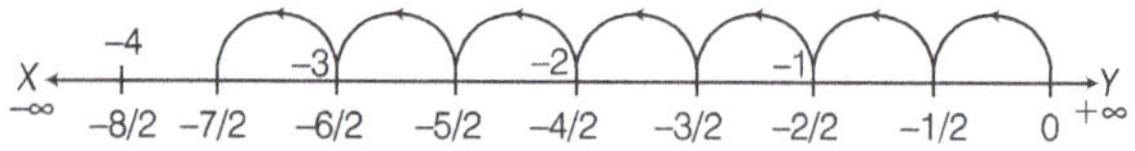

(iii) **Ans.**

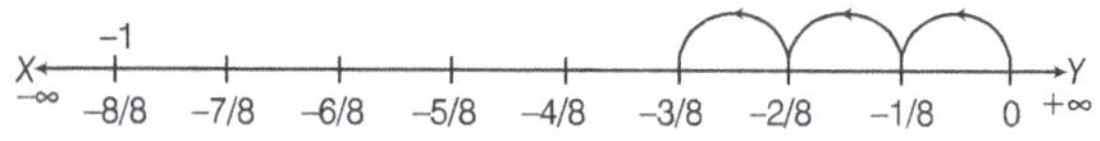

10. **Hint** Do same as Example 7.
Ans. (i) Irrational (ii) Rational (iii) Irrational
(iv) Irrational (v) Rational

11. **Hint** Do same as Example 8.

12. **Hint** Do same as Example 10.

13. **Hint** $\sqrt{2}=1.414\ldots$ and $\sqrt{3}=1.732$.
Ans. 1.5 and 1.6

14. **Hint** $\sqrt{3}=1.732\ldots$ and $\sqrt{5}=2.236\ldots$
Ans. 1.8010010001..., 1.9010010001..., 2.010010001...

15. **Hint** Do same as Example 17 (i).

16. **Hint** Here, $29=25+4=5^2+2^2$
Now, proceed same as Example 17 (i).

17. (i) **Hint** $\sqrt{24}=\sqrt{4\times 6}=4\sqrt{6}$
Ans. $\sqrt{6}$
(ii) **Hint** Here, no further simplification.
Ans. $\sqrt{5}+3$
(iii) **Hint** $\sqrt{18}-\sqrt{50}=\sqrt{2\times 9}-\sqrt{2\times 25}$
$=3\sqrt{2}-5\sqrt{2}=-2\sqrt{2}$
Ans. $\sqrt{2}$

18. **Hint** Do same as Example 27 (i). **Ans.** $\frac{14}{11}$

19. **Hint** Do same as Example 35.
Ans. $\sqrt{17}, 3\sqrt{3}, 4\sqrt{2}, 6, 2\sqrt{11}$

20. **Hint** $2\sqrt{2}+5\sqrt{2}+6\sqrt{2}+7\sqrt{2}=20\sqrt{2}$
Put $\sqrt{2}=1.414$
Ans. 28.28

21. **Hint** Do same as Example 39.
Ans. $-(\sqrt{3}+\sqrt{5})$

22. (i) **Hint** Let $n=1.3\overline{7}$
Multiplying both sides by 10, we have
$10x=13.\overline{7}$
(ii) **Hint** Do same as Example 27(i).
(iii) **Hint** Do same as Example 27(i).
(iv) **Hint** Do same as part (i).
Ans. (i) $\frac{62}{45}$ (ii) $\frac{221}{99}$
(iii) $\frac{345644}{9999}$ (iv) $\frac{1102103}{9900}$

23. **Hint** Do same as Example 28.
Ans. 167/90

24. (i) **Hint** Apply the law of surd
$(\sqrt{a}+\sqrt{b})(\sqrt{a}-\sqrt{b})=a-b$. **Ans.** 4
(ii) **Hint** Do same as Example 32 (iii).
Ans. $10+5\sqrt{5}+2\sqrt{7}+\sqrt{35}$

25. **Hint** Do same as Example 32.
Ans. (i) $6+3\sqrt{2}+2\sqrt{3}+\sqrt{6}$ (ii) 6
(iii) $7+2\sqrt{10}$ (iv) 3

26. **Hint** Do same as Example 39.
Ans. (i) $\frac{\sqrt{7}}{7}$ (ii) $\sqrt{7}+\sqrt{6}$
(iii) $\frac{\sqrt{5}-\sqrt{2}}{3}$ (iv) $\frac{\sqrt{7}+2}{3}$

27. **Hint** $\dfrac{21}{\sqrt{20}-\sqrt{40}-\sqrt{50}-\sqrt{5}+2\sqrt{10}}$

$$= \frac{21}{2\sqrt{5}-2\sqrt{2}\sqrt{5}-4\sqrt{5}-\sqrt{5}+2\sqrt{2}\sqrt{5}}$$

Ans. –3.1305

28. **Hint** $\dfrac{4}{3\sqrt{3}-2\sqrt{2}} \times \dfrac{3\sqrt{3}+2\sqrt{2}}{3\sqrt{3}+2\sqrt{2}}$

$$+ \frac{3}{3\sqrt{3}+2\sqrt{2}} \times \frac{3\sqrt{3}-2\sqrt{2}}{3\sqrt{3}-2\sqrt{2}}$$

$$= \frac{4(3\sqrt{3}+2\sqrt{2})}{27-8} + \frac{3(3\sqrt{3}-2\sqrt{2})}{27-8}$$

$$= \frac{21\sqrt{3}+2\sqrt{2}}{19}$$

Ans. 2.063

29. **Hint** Do same as Example 43. **Ans.** 34

30. **Hint** Do same as Example 43. **Ans.** 8

31. **Hint** $\dfrac{15}{\sqrt{10}+2\sqrt{5}+2\sqrt{10}-\sqrt{5}-4\sqrt{5}} = \dfrac{15}{3(\sqrt{10}-\sqrt{5})}$

32. **Hint** Do same as Example 17 (ii).

33. (i) **Hint** Do same as Example 8.

(ii) **Hint** Rationalise the denominator and then do same as Example 11.

34. **Hint** Do same as Example 41. **Ans.** 11

35. **Hint** Do same as Example 41. **Ans.** $a = 0$, $b = 1$

36. **Hint** Do same as Exampel 42(ii).

Ans. $\dfrac{3\sqrt{3}-4\sqrt{2}+\sqrt{42}-\sqrt{7}}{10}$

37. **Hint** By rationalising

Ans. $-4x\sqrt{x^2-1}$

38. **Hint** Rationalise the denominator

Ans. (i) 194 (ii) 2702

39. **Hint** Do same as Example 42 (i). **Ans.** 42/11

40. **Hint** Substitute the value of x and simplify. **Ans.** 0.83

41. **Hint** Do same as Example 44. **Ans.** 323

Olympiad Section

Brain Teasing Questions of Olympiad Pattern

1 The greatest among $\sqrt[3]{4}$, $\sqrt[4]{5}$ and $\sqrt[4]{3}$ is

(a) $\sqrt[3]{4}$ (b) $\sqrt[4]{5}$
(c) $\sqrt[4]{3}$ (d) None of these

2 The smallest of the surds $\sqrt{\frac{1}{2}}, \sqrt[3]{\frac{2}{3}}, \sqrt{\frac{1}{3}}, \sqrt{\frac{1}{4}}$ is

(a) $\frac{1}{2}$ (b) $\sqrt[3]{\frac{2}{3}}$ (c) $\sqrt{\frac{1}{3}}$ (d) $\sqrt{\frac{1}{4}}$

3 If $x = \frac{\sqrt{3}+1}{2}$, then the value of $4x^3 + 2x^2 - 8x + 7$ is

(a) 10 (b) 8
(c) 6 (d) 4

4 If a and b are rational numbers such that $\frac{4+\sqrt{3}}{4-\sqrt{3}} = a + b\sqrt{3}$, then the values of a and b are respectively

(a) $\frac{12}{15}, \frac{7}{15}$ (b) $\frac{19}{13}, \frac{8}{13}$
(c) $\frac{14}{13}, \frac{7}{14}$ (d) $\frac{8}{14}, \frac{19}{19}$

5 If $\sqrt{3} = 1.7321$, then find the value of the following surd correct to three decimal places.

$$\frac{\sqrt{3}+1}{\sqrt{3}-1} + \frac{\sqrt{3}-1}{\sqrt{3}+1} + \frac{4+\sqrt{3}}{4-\sqrt{3}}$$

(a) 6.5274 (b) 5.4294
(c) 6.9274 (d) 7.5274

6 The value of $\sqrt{\sqrt{63}+\sqrt{56}}$ is

(a) $7^{1/6}(\sqrt{3}+1)$ (b) $7^{1/4}(\sqrt{3}+1)$
(c) $7^{1/5}(\sqrt{5}+1)$ (d) $7^{1/4}(\sqrt{2}+1)$

7 Arrange the following surds in an ascending order of magnitude.

$$\sqrt[3]{9}, \sqrt[9]{5}, \sqrt[3]{7}$$

(a) $\sqrt[9]{5} < \sqrt[3]{7} < \sqrt[3]{9}$ (b) $\sqrt[3]{9} < \sqrt[3]{7} < \sqrt[9]{5}$
(c) $\sqrt[3]{7} < \sqrt[9]{5} < \sqrt[3]{9}$ (d) None of these

8 If $x = \frac{1}{7+4\sqrt{3}}$, $y = \frac{1}{7-4\sqrt{3}}$, then the value of $5x^2 - 7xy - 5y^2$ is

(a) $7(1-80\sqrt{3})$
(b) $-7(1+80\sqrt{3})$
(c) $5(1-70\sqrt{2})$
(d) $-6(1+70\sqrt{2})$

9 If $x = (4+\sqrt{15})^{1/3} + (4-\sqrt{15})^{1/3}$, then $x^3 - 3x$ is equal to

(a) 8 (b) -8
(c) 4 (d) -4

10 If $x = \frac{1}{2}\left(\sqrt{a} + \frac{1}{\sqrt{a}}\right)$, then $\frac{\sqrt{x^2-1}}{x-\sqrt{x^2-1}}$ is equal to

(a) $\frac{a-1}{2}$ (b) $\frac{a+1}{2}$
(c) $a-1$ (d) None of these

Answers

1. (a) **2.** (d) **3.** (a) **4.** (b) **5.** (a) **6.** (d) **7.** (a) **8.** (b) **9.** (a) **10.** (a)

* *These questions may or may not be asked in the examination, have been given just for additional practice required for olympiads Scholarship Exams etc. For detailed explanations refer Page No. 332.*

CHAPTER

02

Compound Interest

SYLLABUS

- (a) Compound interest as a repeated Simple Interest computation with a growing Principal. Use of this in computing Amount over a period of 2 or 3 years. (b) Use of formula $A = P(1+\frac{r}{100})^n$. Find CI from the relation CI = A – P
- Interest compounded half-yearly included. ▪ Using the formula to find one quantity given different combinations of A, P, r, n CI and SI; difference between CI and SI type included. Rate of growth and depreciation.

Note Paying back in equal installments, being given rate of interest and installment amount, not included.

Interest

When a person borrows some amount of money (principal) from another person or organisation (bank), then the person borrowing money (borrower) pays some extra money during repayment, that extra money during repayment is called interest.

Simple Interest (SI)

$$= \frac{\text{Principal } (P) \times \text{Rate } (R) \times \text{Time } (T)}{100}$$

and Amount (A) = Principal (P) + Simple Interest (SI)

Compound Interest (CI)

The difference between the original principal and the final amount is called the compound interest.

Compound interest (CI)

= Final amount (A) – Original principal (P)

Computation of Compound Interest as a Repeated Simple Interest

Simple interest for the first period, add it to the original amount and then calculate the simple interest on the accumulated amount for the next period and so on, until the amount for the last period has been found.

Example 1. ₹ 15000 is lent at 6% compound interest per year for 2 yr. Find the final amount and the compound interest.

Sol. **For the first year,**

$$P = ₹\,15000,\ R = 6\% \text{ and } T = 1\text{yr}$$

$$\therefore \text{ Interest} = \frac{P \times R \times T}{100} = \frac{15000 \times 6 \times 1}{100} = ₹\,900$$

Amount after first year = ₹(15000 + 900) = ₹15900

Now, principal for the second year = ₹ 15900

Now, for the second year,

$$P = ₹\,15900,\ R = 6\% \text{ and } T = 1 \text{ yr}$$

$$\therefore \text{ Interest} = \frac{P \times R \times T}{100} = \frac{15900 \times 6 \times 1}{100} = ₹\,954$$

Amount after second year = ₹ (15900 + 954) = ₹ 16854

∴ Compound interest = Final amount – Original amount

= ₹ (16854 – 15000)

= ₹ 1854

Example 2. Calculate the interest on ₹ 6000 in 3 yr at 5% per annum compounded annually.

Sol. **For the first year,**

Principal (P) = ₹ 6000, R = 5% and T = 1yr

$$\therefore \text{ Interest} = \frac{P \times R \times T}{100} = \frac{6000 \times 5 \times 1}{100} = ₹\,300$$

Amount after first year = ₹ (6000 + 300) = ₹ 6300

Now, for the second year,

Principal (P) = ₹ 6300, R = 5% and T = 1 yr

$\therefore$ Interest $= \dfrac{P \times R \times T}{100}$

$= \dfrac{6300 \times 5 \times 1}{100} =$ ₹ 315

Amount after second year = ₹ (6300 + 315) = ₹ 6615

Now, for the third year,

Principal (P) = ₹ 6615, R = 5% and T = 1 yr

$\therefore$ Interest $= \dfrac{P \times R \times T}{100} = \dfrac{6615 \times 5 \times 1}{100}$

= ₹ 330.75

Hence, total interest is ₹ (300 + 315 + 330.75) = ₹ 945.75

Example 3. Find the compound interest to the nearest rupee on ₹ 7500 for 2 yr 4 months at 12% per annum compounded annually.

Sol. **For the first year,**

Principal (P) = ₹ 7500, R = 12% and T = 1 yr

$\therefore$ Interest $= \dfrac{P \times R \times T}{100}$

$=$ ₹ $\left(\dfrac{7500 \times 12 \times 1}{100}\right)$

= ₹ 900

Amount after first year = ₹ (7500 + 900) = ₹ 8400

Now, for the second year,

Principal (P) = ₹ 8400, R = 12% and T = 1 yr.

$\therefore$ Interest $= \dfrac{P \times R \times T}{100} =$ ₹ $\left(\dfrac{8400 \times 12 \times 1}{100}\right)$

= ₹ 1008

Amount after second year = ₹ (8400 + 1008) = ₹ 9408

Now, for the next 4 months,

Principal (P) = ₹ 9408, R = 12% and $T = \dfrac{4}{12} = \dfrac{1}{3}$ yr

$\therefore$ Interest $= \dfrac{P \times R \times T}{100} =$ ₹ $\left(\dfrac{9408 \times 12 \times 1/3}{100}\right)$

= ₹ 376.32

Hence, the compound interest for 2 yr 4 months

= ₹ (900 + 1008 + 376.32)

= ₹ 2284 (to nearest rupee)

Example 4. Calculate the amount due and the compound interest on ₹ 16000 for 3 yr when the rate of interest on successive years are 10%, 14% and 15%, respectively.

Sol. **For the first year,**

Principal (P) = ₹ 16000, R = 10% and T = 1 yr

$\therefore$ Interest $= \dfrac{P \times R \times T}{100}$

$=$ ₹ $\left(\dfrac{16000 \times 10 \times 1}{100}\right) =$ ₹1600

Amount after first year = ₹ (16000 + 1600) = ₹ 17600

Now, for the second year,

Principal (P) = ₹ 17600, R = 14% and T = 1 yr

$\therefore$ Interest $= \dfrac{P \times R \times T}{100} =$ ₹ $\left(\dfrac{17600 \times 14 \times 1}{100}\right) =$ ₹2464

Amount after second year = ₹ (17600 + 2464) = ₹ 20064

Now, for the third year,

Principal (P) = ₹ 20064, R = 15% and T = 1 yr.

$\therefore$ Interest $= \dfrac{P \times R \times T}{100}$

$=$ ₹ $\left(\dfrac{20064 \times 15 \times 1}{100}\right) =$ ₹3009.6

Amount after third year

= ₹ (20064 + 3009.6) = ₹23073.6

Hence, compound interest is ₹(23073.6 − 16000) = ₹7073.6

Example 5. Kriti invests ₹ 50000 for 2 yr at certain rate of interest, compound annually. At the end of one year, this sum amounts to ₹ 54500. Find

(i) the rate of interest per annum.

(ii) the amount due to the end of second year.

(iii) the compound interest earned in 2 yr.

Sol. Let the rate of interest be R% per annum.

(i) **For the first year,**

Principal (P) = ₹ 50000, Rate = R%, T = 1 yr

and Amounts (A) = ₹ 54500

$\because$ Interest for the first year = Final amount − Original amount

= ₹ (54500 − 50000) = ₹ 4500

$\therefore$ Interest $= \dfrac{P \times R \times T}{100} =$ ₹ $\left(\dfrac{50000 \times R \times 1}{100}\right) =$ ₹$(500R)$

$\Rightarrow \quad 4500 = 500R$

$\Rightarrow \quad R = 9$

$\therefore$ Rate of interest is 9% per annum.

(ii) **Now, for the second year,**

Principal (P) = ₹54500, R = 9% and T = 1 yr

$\therefore$ Interest $= \dfrac{P \times R \times T}{100} =$ ₹ $\left(\dfrac{54500 \times 9 \times 1}{100}\right) =$ ₹4905

Amount after second year = ₹(54500 + 4905) = ₹59405

(iii) Compound interest earned in 2 yr

= ₹(59405 − 50000) = ₹9405

Example 6. Calculate the amount and the compound interest on ₹ 6000 at 20% per annum for $1\frac{1}{2}$ yr, when interest is compounded half-yearly.

Sol. **For the first half-year,**

P = ₹ 6000, R = 20% and T = 1/2 yr

$\therefore$ Interest $= \dfrac{P \times R \times T}{100}$

$=$ ₹ $\left(\dfrac{6000 \times 20 \times \frac{1}{2}}{100}\right) =$ ₹600

Amount after first half-year

= ₹(6000 + 600) = ₹6600

Now, for the second half-year,

P = ₹ 6600, R = 20% and T = 1/2 yr

$\therefore$ Interest $= \dfrac{P \times R \times T}{100} =$ ₹ $\left(\dfrac{6600 \times 20 \times \frac{1}{2}}{100}\right) =$ ₹660

Amount after second half-year

$= ₹(6600 + 660) = ₹7260$

For the third half-year,

$P = ₹\ 7260,\ R = 20\%$ and $T = 1/2$ yr.

$\therefore$ Interest $= \frac{P \times R \times T}{100}$

$= ₹\left(\frac{7260 \times 20 \times \frac{1}{2}}{100}\right) = ₹726$

Amount after third half-year $= ₹(7260 + 726) = ₹7986$

Hence, compound interest $= ₹(7986 - 6000) = ₹1986$

Exercise 2.1

1. Find the amount and the compound interest on ₹ 2500 for 2 yr at 11% per annum.
2. Neha invests ₹ 8000 in post office at 12% per annum compound interest for 2 yr. Find
   (i) the interest for the first year.
   (ii) the amount standing to his credit at the end of second year.
3. Rohit deposited ₹ 8000 with a finance company for 3 yr at an interest of 15% per annum. What is the compound interest that Rohit gets after 3 yr?
4. Find the compound interest on ₹ 20000 for 2 yr 3 months at 10% per annum, compounded annually.
5. Calculate the amount and the compound interest on ₹ 8000 in $2\frac{1}{2}$ yr at 15% per annum.
6. Calculate the amount and the compound interest on ₹ 4600 in 2 yr, when the rate of interest for successive years are 10% and 12%, respectively.
7. Find the amount and the compound interest on ₹ 15000 in 2 yr when the rate of interest for the successive years 8% and 9%, respectively.
8. Deposited a sum of ₹ 7400 in a bank for 1 yr, compounded half-yearly at 5% per annum, find the compound interest, he gets.
9. Roma borrowed ₹ 64000 from a bank for $1\frac{1}{2}$ yr at the rate of 10% per annum. Compute the total compound interest payable by Roma after $1\frac{1}{2}$ yr, if the interest is compounded half-yearly.
10. Find the amount and the compound interest on ₹ 25000 for $1\frac{1}{2}$ yr at 10% per annum, the interest being compounded semi-annually.

Compound Interest, When Interest is Compounded Yearly

$$A = P\left(1 + \frac{R}{100}\right)^n$$

where, P = Principal, R = Rate of interest per annum,

n = Time (number of years).

$\therefore$ Compound Interest, CI $= A - P$

$$\Rightarrow \quad \text{CI} = P\left(1 + \frac{R}{100}\right)^n - P = P\left[\left(1 + \frac{R}{100}\right)^n - 1\right]$$

If the rate of interest for the successive years are $R_1\%$, $R_2\%$ and $R_3\%$, then compound interest is given by

$$\text{CI} = P\left[\left(1 + \frac{R_1}{100}\right)\left(1 + \frac{R_2}{100}\right)\left(1 + \frac{R_3}{100}\right)\ldots - 1\right]$$

Example 7. Calculate the compound interest and amount for 2 yr at 10% per annum on ₹ 4700.

Sol. Given, rate of interest, $R = 10\%$, principal, $P = ₹\ 4700$ and number of years, $n = 2$ yr.

Now, amount $(A) = P\left(1 + \frac{R}{100}\right)^n$

$$= 4700\left(1 + \frac{10}{100}\right)^2$$

$$= 4700\left(1 + \frac{1}{10}\right)^2$$

$$= 4700\left(\frac{11}{10}\right)^2$$

$$= \frac{4700 \times 121}{100} = 47 \times 121 = ₹\ 5687$$

$\therefore$ Compound interest, $CI = A - P = ₹\ (5687 - 4700) = ₹987$

Example 8. Find the compound interest on ₹ 10000 for 3 yr, if the rate of interest is 4% for the first year, 5% for the second year and 6% for the third year.

Sol. Here, $P = 10000$, $R_1 = 4\%$, $R_2 = 5\%$ and $R_3 = 6\%$.

∴ Compound interest,

$$CI = P\left[\left(1+\frac{R_1}{100}\right)\left(1+\frac{R_2}{100}\right)\left(1+\frac{R_3}{100}\right)-1\right]$$

$$= 10000\left[\left(1+\frac{4}{100}\right)\left(1+\frac{5}{100}\right)\left(1+\frac{6}{100}\right)-1\right]$$

$$= 10000\left[\left(1+\frac{1}{25}\right)\left(1+\frac{1}{20}\right)\left(1+\frac{3}{50}\right)-1\right]$$

$$= 10000\left[\left(\frac{26}{25}\right)\left(\frac{21}{20}\right)\left(\frac{53}{50}\right)-1\right]$$

$$= 10000\,[1.15752 - 1]$$

$$= 10000\,(0.15752) = ₹\,1575.2$$

Formula for Compound Interest, When the Interest is Compounded Half-yearly or Quarterly (Not for Annually)

(i) **When compound interest is compounded half-yearly** (6 months) In this case, the rate of interest 'R' becomes $\frac{R}{2}$ and time 'n' becomes $2T$, where T is the number of years.

$$\therefore \quad A = P\left(1+\frac{R}{2\times 100}\right)^{2T}$$

and $$CI = A - P = P\left[\left(1+\frac{R}{2\times 100}\right)^{2T} - 1\right]$$

(ii) **When compound interest is compounded quarterly** (3 months) In this case, the rate of interest 'R' becomes $\frac{R}{4}$ and time 'n' becomes $4T$.

$$\therefore \quad A = P\left(1+\frac{R}{4\times 100}\right)^{4T}$$

and $$CI = A - P = P\left[\left(1+\frac{R}{4\times 100}\right)^{4T} - 1\right]$$

Important Facts Related to CI Using Formula

(i) SI (Simple Interest) and CI (Compound Interest) are equal for the first conversion period on the same sum and at the same rate.

(ii) CI of second conversion period is more than the CI of first conversion period.

(iii) CI for the kth conversion period
= Amount after k conversion periods
− Amount after $(k-1)$ conversion periods

(iv) When the total time is not a complete number of conversion periods, then we consider simple interest for the last partial period.

(v) CI of second conversion period
− CI of first conversion period
= SI on the interest of the first conversion period.

Example 9. Find the compound interest on ₹ 25000 for 2 yr at 10% per annum interest being compounded semi-annually.

Sol. Here, $P = ₹\,25000$, $R = 10\%$ and $T = 2$ yr.

Since, the interest is compounded semi-annually.

$$\therefore \quad A = P\left(1+\frac{R}{2\times 100}\right)^{2T}$$

$$= 25000\left(1+\frac{10}{2\times 100}\right)^{4}$$

$$= 25000\left(1+\frac{1}{20}\right)^{4}$$

$$= 25000\left(\frac{21}{20}\right)^{4}$$

$$= 25000\times\frac{21}{20}\times\frac{21}{20}\times\frac{21}{20}\times\frac{21}{20}$$

$$= ₹\,30387.65$$

Hence, $CI = A - P = ₹\,(30387.65 - 25000) = ₹5387.65$

Example 10. Find the compound interest on ₹ 31250 at 16% per annum for $\frac{3}{4}$ yr (or 9 months) when interest being compounded quarterly.

Sol. Here, $P = ₹\,31250$, $R = 16\%$ and $T = \frac{3}{4}$ yr or 9 months.

Since, the interest is compounded quarterly.

$$\therefore \quad A = P\left(1+\frac{R}{400}\right)^{4T}$$

$$= 31250\left(1+\frac{16}{400}\right)^{4\times\frac{3}{4}}$$

$$= 31250\left(1+\frac{1}{25}\right)^{3}$$

$$= 31250\times\frac{26}{25}\times\frac{26}{25}\times\frac{26}{25}$$

$$= ₹35152$$

$$\therefore \quad CI = A - P = ₹(35152 - 31250)$$

$$= ₹3902$$

Example 11. Find the amount when ₹ 10000 is invested for $2\frac{1}{2}$ yr at 10% interest compounded yearly.

Sol. First find the amount in 2 yr.

Amount in 2 yr $= ₹\,10000\left(1+\frac{10}{100}\right)^{2} = ₹\,12100$

After two years, ₹ 12100 is the principal for the remaining half-year and so interest for next half-year

$$= \frac{P\times R\times T}{100} = ₹\left(\frac{12100\times 10\times 1/2}{100}\right)$$

$$= ₹\,605$$

⇒ Amount in $2\frac{1}{2}$ yr $= ₹\,(12100 + 605) = ₹\,12705$

To Find the Principal, When Rate, Time and Amount (or CI) are Given

Example 12. What sum of money will amount to ₹ 15972 in 3 yr at 10% per annum compounded yearly?

Sol. Let P (principal) be the required money.

Given, amount (A) = ₹15972, rate of interest (R) = 10% and time (n) = 3 yr.

$$\because \quad A = P\left(1+\frac{R}{100}\right)^n$$

$$\therefore \quad 15972 = P\left(1+\frac{10}{100}\right)^3 \Rightarrow 15972 = P\left(\frac{11}{10}\right)^3$$

$$\Rightarrow \quad 15972 = P \times \frac{11}{10} \times \frac{11}{10} \times \frac{11}{10}$$

$$\therefore \quad P = \frac{15972 \times 10 \times 10 \times 10}{11 \times 11 \times 11}$$

$$= ₹(12 \times 1000) = ₹12000$$

To Find Rate, When Principal, Time and Amount (or CI) are Given

Example 13. At what rate per cent per annum compound interest will ₹ 5000 amount to ₹ 5832 in 2 yr?

Sol. Let the rate of interest be R% per annum.

Given, principal (P) = ₹5000, amount (A) = ₹5832 and time (n) = 2 yr.

$$\text{Now,} \quad A = P\left(1+\frac{R}{100}\right)^n$$

$$\therefore \quad 5832 = 5000\left(1+\frac{R}{100}\right)^2 \Rightarrow \frac{5832}{5000} = \left(1+\frac{R}{100}\right)^2$$

$$\Rightarrow \quad \frac{729}{625} = \left(1+\frac{R}{100}\right)^2 \Rightarrow \left(\frac{27}{25}\right)^2 = \left(1+\frac{R}{100}\right)^2$$

$$\Rightarrow \quad \frac{27}{25} = 1+\frac{R}{100} \quad \text{[taking square root]}$$

$$\Rightarrow \quad \frac{R}{100} = \frac{27}{25} - 1 \Rightarrow \frac{R}{100} = \frac{27-25}{25}$$

$$\Rightarrow \quad \frac{R}{100} = \frac{2}{25} \Rightarrow R = 8$$

Hence, the rate of interest is 8%.

To Find the Time, When Rate, Principal and Amount (or CI) are Given

Example 14. In what time will ₹ 390625 amount to ₹ 456976 at 4% compound interest?

Sol. Let n yr be the required time.

Given, principal (P) = ₹ 390625, amount (A) = ₹ 456976 and rate of interest (R) = 4%.

$$\because \quad A = P\left(1+\frac{R}{100}\right)^n$$

$$\therefore \quad 456976 = 390625\left(1+\frac{4}{100}\right)^n \Rightarrow \frac{456976}{390625} = \left(1+\frac{1}{25}\right)^n$$

$$\Rightarrow \quad \left(\frac{26}{25}\right)^4 = \left(\frac{26}{25}\right)^n \Rightarrow n = 4$$

Hence, the required time is 4 yr.

Example 15. A sum ₹ 25000 invested at 8% per annum compounded semi-annually amounts to ₹ 28121.60. Compute the time period of investment.

Sol. Let the number of conversion periods be n.

Given, principal (P) = ₹25000, Amount (A) = ₹ 28121.60 and R = 8%.

$$\because \quad A = P\left(1+\frac{R}{200}\right)^n$$

$$\therefore \quad 28121.60 = 25000\left(1+\frac{8}{200}\right)^n = 25000\left(1+\frac{1}{25}\right)^n$$

$$\Rightarrow \quad \frac{2812160}{100} = 25000\left(\frac{26}{25}\right)^n$$

$$\Rightarrow \quad \left(\frac{26}{25}\right)^n = \frac{2812160}{100 \times 25000} = \frac{17576}{15625} = \left(\frac{26}{25}\right)^3$$

$$\therefore \quad n = 3$$

Hence, the time period of investment is 3 half-years, i.e. $1\frac{1}{2}$ yr.

Example 16. In what time will ₹ 1200 yield ₹ 252 as compound interest at 10% per year compounded annually?

Sol. Let 'n' yr be the required time period.

Given, principal (P) = ₹ 1200, CI = ₹ 252 and R = 10%.

$$\because \quad \text{CI} = P\left[\left(1+\frac{R}{100}\right)^n - 1\right]$$

$$\Rightarrow \quad 252 = 1200\left[\left(1+\frac{10}{100}\right)^n - 1\right] \Rightarrow \frac{252}{1200} = \left(\frac{11}{10}\right)^n - 1$$

$$\Rightarrow \quad \left(\frac{11}{10}\right)^n = \frac{252}{1200} + 1 = \frac{1452}{1200}$$

$$\Rightarrow \quad \left(\frac{11}{10}\right)^n = \frac{121}{100} = \left(\frac{11}{10}\right)^2 \Rightarrow n = 2 \text{ yr}$$

Hence, the required time is 2 yr.

To Find the Principal, When the Difference between Compound and Simple Interests, Rate and Time are Given

Example 17. The difference between simple interest and compound interest for 2 yr at 5% per annum is ₹ 20. Find the principal amount.

Sol. Given, CI – SI = ₹ 20, n = 2 yr and R = 5%.

$$\text{Clearly,} \quad \text{CI} = \left[P\left(1+\frac{R}{100}\right)^n - 1\right] = P\left[\left(1+\frac{5}{100}\right)^2 - 1\right]$$

$$= P\left[\left(\frac{21}{20}\right)^2 - 1\right] = P\left(\frac{441}{400} - 1\right) = P \times \frac{41}{400}$$

$$\therefore \quad \text{SI} = \frac{P \times R \times T}{100} \Rightarrow = \frac{P \times 5 \times 2}{100} = \frac{P}{10}$$

$$\because \quad \text{CI} - \text{SI} = 20 \Rightarrow \frac{41P}{400} - \frac{P}{10} = 20$$

$$\Rightarrow \quad \frac{P}{400} = 20 \Rightarrow P = ₹8000$$

To Find the Rate, When the Difference between Compound and Simple Interest, Principal and Time are Given

Example 18. The difference between CI and SI on ₹ 6000 for 2 yr is ₹ 15 at the same rate of interest per year. Find the rate of interest.

Sol. Let the rate of interest be $R\%$ per annum.

Given, principal (P) = ₹ 6000, time $(n) = 2$ yr

and CI – SI = ₹15

Clearly, $\text{CI} = P\left[\left(1+\frac{R}{100}\right)^n - 1\right] = 6000\left[\left(1+\frac{R}{100}\right)^2 - 1\right]$

and $\text{SI} = \frac{P \times R \times T}{100} = \frac{6000 \times R \times 2}{100}$

$\because$ CI – SI = 15

$$\therefore \quad 6000\left(1+\frac{R}{100}\right)^2 - 6000 - \frac{6000 \times R \times 2}{100} = 15$$

$$\Rightarrow \quad 6000\left[1+\frac{R^2}{10000}+\frac{2R}{100}-1-\frac{2R}{100}\right] = 15$$

$$\Rightarrow \quad 6000\left[\frac{R^2}{10000}\right] = 15 \Rightarrow \frac{R^2}{10} = \frac{15}{6}$$

$$\Rightarrow \quad R^2 = \frac{15 \times 10}{6} = 25 \Rightarrow R = 5$$

Hence, the rate of interest is 5%.

Exercise 2.2

1. ₹ 7500 is borrowed at CI at the rate of 4% per annum. What will be the amount to be paid after 2 yr?
2. Find the compound interest on ₹ 1600 for 3 yr at $3\frac{3}{4}\%$ per annum.
3. Find the amount of ₹ 6250 at 8% per annum compound interest for 2 yr. Also, calculate the compound interest.
4. A and B borrowed ₹ 60000 and ₹ 50000 respectively for a period of 3 yr. A paid simple interest at the rate of 10% per annum, while B paid compound interest at the rate of 10% per annum compounded annually. Find who paid more interest and by how much?
5. Rohit lends ₹ 20000 at CI for 3 yr. If the rate of interest for the first two successive years is 15% per annum and for the third year it is 16%. Calculate the sum that Rohit will get at the end of the third year.
6. Find the amount of ₹ 12500 for 2 yr compounded annually, the rate of interest being 15% for the first year and 16% for the second year.
7. Calculate the compound interest on ₹ 4000 in $1\frac{1}{2}$ yr at 10% per annum compounded half-yearly.
8. Deepak borrowed ₹ 16000 from a finance company at 10% per annum compounded half-yearly. What amount of money will discharge his debt after 1 yr and 6 months.
9. On what sum of money will compound interest for 2 yr at 5% per annum amount to ₹ 205?
10. Rachna borrowed a certain sum at the rate of 15% per annum. If she paid at the end of two years ₹ 1290 as interest compounded annually, find the sum she borrowed.
11. At what rate per cent will ₹ 12000 yield ₹ 1891.50 as compound interest in 3 yr?
12. A person invests ₹ 10000 for two years at a certain rate of interest compounded annually. At the end of 1 yr this sum amounts to ₹ 11200. Calculate
    (i) the rate of interest
    (ii) the amount at the end of second year.
13. At what rate per cent compound yearly will ₹ 80000 amount to ₹ 88200 in 2 yr?
14. What rate of compound interest will a sum of money become $\frac{125}{64}$ times of itself in 3 yr?
15. In what time will ₹ 6250 amount to ₹ 6632.55 at 4% compound interest payable half-yearly?
16. In what time will ₹ 2400 amount to ₹ 2646 at 10% per annum compounded semi-annually?
17. Find the difference between the simple interest and compound interest on ₹ 4000 for 2 yr at 8% per annum compounded annually.
18. Find the difference between simple interest and compound interest on ₹ 9500 for 2 yr at 8% per annum.
19. If the difference between the simple interest and compound interest on a certain sum of money for 2 yr at 5% per annum is ₹ 1.50, then find the sum.
20. The difference between the SI and CI on a certain sum of money for 2 yr at 4% per annum is ₹ 20. Find the sum.

Rate of Growth

The relative increase in a quantity is called its growth and the growth per year (or unit of time) is the rate of growth.

Important Formulae Related to Population Growth

(i) If P is the population of a city at the beginning of a certain year and r% per annum be the constant rate of growth of population, then

Population after n yr $= P\left(1+\frac{r}{100}\right)^n$.

(ii) If P is the population at the beginning of a certain year. If the rate of growth be r_1% during first year, r_2% during second year, r_3% during third year, then

Population after 2 yr $= P\left(1+\frac{r_1}{100}\right)\left(1+\frac{r_2}{100}\right)$

and population after 3 yr

$$= P\left(1+\frac{r_1}{100}\right)\left(1+\frac{r_2}{100}\right)\left(1+\frac{r_3}{100}\right)$$

(iii) If P_0 is the population of city, n yr ago and P is the present value of population, then

$$P = P_0\left(1+\frac{r}{100}\right)^n.$$

Example 19. The population of a city in the year 2016 was 424000. What will be the population in 2018, if it increases 5% per year.

Sol. Here, $P = 424000$, $r = 5\%$ per annum and $n = 2$ yr.

$\therefore$ Population after 2 yr

$$= 424000\left(1+\frac{5}{100}\right)^2 = 424000\left(\frac{21}{20}\right)^2$$

$$= 424000 \times \frac{21}{20} \times \frac{21}{20} = 467460$$

Example 20. The population of a particular area A of a city is 5000. It increases by 10% in 1st yr. It decreases by 20% in the 2nd yr because of some reason. In the 3rd yr, the population increases by 30%. What will be the population of area A at the end of 3 yr?

Sol. Given that, $P = 5000$, $R_1 = 10\%$, $R_2 = -20\%$ (decrease) and $R_3 = 30\%$

$\therefore$ Population at the end of 3rd year

$$= P\left(1+\frac{R_1}{100}\right)\left(1+\frac{R_2}{100}\right)\left(1+\frac{R_3}{100}\right)$$

$$= 5000\left(1+\frac{10}{100}\right)\left(1-\frac{20}{100}\right)\left(1+\frac{30}{100}\right)$$

$$= 5000 \times \frac{11}{10} \times \frac{4}{5} \times \frac{13}{10} = 10 \times 11 \times 4 \times 13 = 5720$$

Example 21. The population of a place increased to 54000 in 2003 at a rate of 5% per annum.

(i) Find the population in 2001.

(ii) What would be its population in 2005?

Sol.

(i) Here, population in 2003 = 54000,

Rate of increase = 5% and time period (n) = 2 yr

Let the population in 2001 be P.

$\therefore$ Present population $= P\left(1+\frac{R}{100}\right)^n$

$$= P\left(1+\frac{5}{100}\right)^2 = P\left(1+\frac{1}{20}\right)^2$$

$$\Rightarrow \quad 54000 = P \times \left(\frac{21}{20}\right)^2$$

$$\Rightarrow \quad 54000 = P \times \frac{21}{20} \times \frac{21}{20}$$

$$\therefore \quad P = \frac{54000 \times 20 \times 20}{21 \times 21} = \frac{21600000}{21 \times 21}$$

$$= 48979.59 = 48980 \text{ (approx.)}$$

Hence, the population in 2001 is 48980.

(ii) For population in 2005, i.e. 2 yr after 2003,

Initial population = 54000, i.e. in the year 2003

Time $(n) = 2$ yr, Rate of increase $(R) = 5\%$

Let population in 2005 be A.

$$\therefore \quad A = P\left(1+\frac{R}{100}\right)^n$$

$$= 54000\left(1+\frac{5}{100}\right)^2$$

$$= 54000\left(1+\frac{1}{20}\right)^2 = 54000\left(\frac{21}{20}\right)^2$$

$$= 54000 \times \frac{21}{20} \times \frac{21}{20} = 135 \times 21 \times 21 = 59535$$

Hence, the population in 2005 is 59535.

Example 22. In a laboratory, the count of bacteria in a certain experiment was increasing at the rate of 2.5% per hour. Find the bacteria at the end of 2 h, if the count was initially 506000.

Sol. Here, initial count of bacteria $(P) = 506000$, time $(n) = 2$ h

Rate of increasing bacteria $(R) = 2.5\%$ per hour

$$= \frac{25}{10}\% \text{ per hour} = \frac{5}{2}\% \text{ per hour}$$

Bacteria count after 2 h $(A) = P\left(1+\frac{R}{100}\right)^n$

$$= 506000\left(1+\frac{5}{2 \times 100}\right)^2 = 506000\left(1+\frac{1}{40}\right)^2$$

$$= 506000\left(\frac{41}{40}\right)^2$$

$$= 506000 \times \frac{41}{40} \times \frac{41}{40}$$

$$= \frac{5060 \times 41 \times 41}{4 \times 4} = \frac{1265 \times 41 \times 41}{4}$$

$$= \frac{2126465}{4} = 531616.25 = 531616 \text{ (approx.)}$$

Hence, the number of bacteria count at the end of 2 h are 531616.

Depreciation

The relative decrease in the value of a machine or article is called its depreciation and the decrease in the value per year (or unit of time) is called rate of depreciation.

(i) If V is the value of a machine at a certain time and r% per annum is the rate of depreciation, then V_n, the depreciated value of machine after n yr is given by

$$V_n = V\left(1 - \frac{r}{100}\right)^n.$$

(ii) If V_0 is the value of a machine n yr ago and V is the present value, then

$$V = V_0\left(1 - \frac{r}{100}\right)^n.$$

Example 23. The value of a residential flat constructed at a cost of ₹ 112000 is depreciating at the rate 15% per annum. What will be its value 3 yr after construction.

Sol. Here, present value = ₹ 112000,

rate of depreciation = 15% per annum and $n = 3$ yr.

$\therefore$ Value after 3 yr $= 112000\left(1 - \frac{15}{100}\right)^3$

$$= \left[112000 \times \left(\frac{85}{100}\right)^3\right]$$

$$= \left(112000 \times \frac{17}{20} \times \frac{17}{20} \times \frac{17}{20}\right)$$

$$= (14 \times 17 \times 17 \times 17) = ₹\ 68782$$

Exercise 2.3

1. The present population of a town is 140000. What will be the population after 2 yr, if it increase 5% annually.
2. The population of a particular area X of a city is 10000. It increases by 20% in 1st yr. It increases by 40% in the 2nd yr because of some reason. In the 3rd yr, the population increases by 60%. What will be the population of area X at the end of 3 yr?
3. The population of a town increases by 20% every year. If its present population is 432000, then find its population 2 yr ago.
4. The present population of a village is 5408. If it has increased at the rate of 4% every year, what was its population two years ago?
5. The population of a village 2 yr ago was 6250. Due to migration to cities, it decreases at the rate of 8% every year. Find the decrease in its population in the last 2 yr.
6. 6000 workers were employed to construct a river bridge in four years. At the end of first year, 20% workers were retrenched. At the end of second year, 5% of the workers at that time were retrenched. However, to complete the project in time, the number of workers was increased by 15% at the end of third year. How many workers were working during the fourth year?
7. 24000 blood donors were registered with 'red cross' at Kolkata. The number of donors increased at the rate of 5% every six months. Find the time period at the end of which the total number of blood donors becomes 27783.
8. A machine depreciates every year at the rate of 20% of its value at the beginning of the year. The machine was purchased for ₹ 500000 when new. Find its price after 3 yr.
9. A machine depreciates every year at the rate of 20% of its value at the beginning of the year. The machine was purchased for ₹ 250000 when new, and the scrap value realised when sold was ₹ 128000. Find the number of years that the machine was used.
10. The cost of a machine is supposed to depreciate each year by 12% of its value at the beginning of the year. If the machine is valued ₹ 44000 at the beginning of 2008, find its value
    (i) at the end of 2009.
    (ii) at the beginning of 2007.
11. The value of a car depreciates by 12.5% every year. By what per cent will the value of the car decrease after 3 yr?

Chapter Practice

a. 1 Mark Questions

1. The compound interest on ₹ 100 at 10% per annum compounded annually for 2 yr is
   (a) ₹ 121 (b) ₹ 120
   (c) ₹ 210 (d) ₹ 190

2. The compound interest on ₹ 5000 at 20% per annum for $1\frac{1}{2}$ yr compounded half yearly is
   (a) ₹ 1655 (b) ₹ 1665
   (c) ₹ 1500 (d) ₹ 1565

3. If the number of conversion periods ≥ 2, then the compound interest is
   (a) greater than or equal to simple Interest
   (b) equal to simple interest
   (c) less than simple interest
   (d) greater than simple interest.

4. In how many years will ₹ 1000 amount to ₹ 1331 at 10% compound interest is
   (a) 3 (b) 2
   (c) 5 (d) 1

5. The compound interest on ₹ 25000 in 2 yr, if rates are successive 4% and 5% per year is
   (a) ₹ 27300 (b) ₹ 23700
   (c) ₹ 27330 (d) ₹ 23770

b. 3 Marks Questions

6. Find the amount and the compound interest on ₹ 25000 for 3 yr at 12% per annum compounded annually.

7. A farmer obtained a loan of ₹ 12800 from HDFC Bank for buying a tractor. If the bank charges compound interest $7\frac{1}{2}$% per annum, what amount he will have to pay after 3 yr.

8. Determine the amount and the compound interest on ₹ 20000 in 2 yr when the rate of interest for the successive years is 7% and 8% per annum, respectively.

9. Find the amount of ₹ 12500 for 2 yr compounded annually, the rate of interest being 15% for the first year and 16% for the second year.

10. If the interest is compounded half-yearly, calculate the amount when the principal is ₹ 7400, the rate of interest is 5% per annum and the duration is 1 yr.

11. Compound interest on a certain sum of money at 5% per annum for two years is ₹ 246. Calculate the simple interest on the same sum for 3 yr at 6% per annum.

12. At what rate percent compounded yearly will a sum of money become eight times in three years?

13. The population of a city is 20000. If the annual birth rate is 4% and annual death rate is 2%, calculate the population after two years.

14. The value of a machine, purchased two years ago, depreciates at the annual rate of 10%. If its present value is ₹ 97200, find its value when it was purchased.

c. 6 Marks Questions

15. Shivam borrowed ₹ 16000 from Sanjeev at 15% per annum simple interest. If Shivam lent it to Rohit at the same rate but compounded annually, then find the gain of Shivam after 3 yr.

16. The simple interest on a certain sum of money for 3 yr at 10% is ₹ 3600. Find the amount due and the compound interest on this sum of money at the same rate after 3 yr, interest is compounded annually.

17. On a certain sum of money, the difference between the compound interest for a year, payable half-yearly, and the simple interest for a year is ₹ 180. Find the sum lent out, if the rate of interest in both the cases is 10%.

18. At what rate per cent per annum compound interest will ₹ 2000 amount to ₹ 2315.25 in 3 yr?

19. The difference between compound interest and simple interest on ₹ 20000 for 2 yr is ₹ 128 at the same rate of interest per annum. Find the rate of the interest.

20. On a certain sum, the compound interest for 2 yr is ₹ 2172. If the rates of interest for successive years are 6% and 8% per annum, then find the sum.

21. A sum of money at compound interest amounts in two years to ₹ 2809 and in three years to ₹ 2977.54. Find the rate of interest and the original sum.

22. ₹ 39527 is divided between Seeta and Geeta, both aged 28 yr and 26 yr, respectively. Their money is invested at 5% per annum compound interest in such a way that both receive equal money at the age of 30 yr. Find the share of each.

23. A man borrowed a sum of money and agrees to pay it off by paying ₹ 43200 at the end of the first year and ₹ 34992 at the end of the second year. If the rate of compound interest is 8% per annum, then find the sum borrowed.

24. The present population of a village is 6250. If it increases at the rate of 4% every year, what will be population
 (i) at the end of 2 yr
 (ii) at the end of 3 yr.

25. The population of a town in China increases by 20% every year. If its present population is 216000, then find
 (i) its population after 2 yr
 (ii) its population 2 yr ago.

26. Calculate the compound interest on ₹ 3500. For first 2 yr at 8% per annum, interest paid half yearly, 12% per annum for the third year interest compounded annually and 5% per annum for the fourth year interest compounded annually. Find the earning at the end of 4 yr.

27. The compound interest calculated yearly at 10% on a certain sum of money amounts to ₹ 665.50 in the fifth year. Calculate
 (i) compound interest for the sixth year at the same rate and same sum.
 (ii) compound interest for the fourth year on the same sum and at the same rate.

28. Prabsimran won a lottery of ₹ 50000, 30% was paid as income tax. She deposited the balance in a bank paying 10% per annum, interest compounded bi-annually. What sum will she get after 3 yr?

29. Carbon decays at a constant rate in such a way that it reduces to 50% in 5568 yr. Find the age of an old wooden piece in which the carbon is only 12.5% of the original.

30. The cost of a washing machine depreciates by ₹ 720 during the second year and by ₹ 648 during the third year. Calculate
 (i) the rate of depreciation per annum
 (ii) the original cost of the machine
 (iii) the value of the machine at the end of third year.

31. The population of a town increases 4% annually but it decreases by emigration annually to the extent of 1%. Find the increase percent in 3 yr.

32. Rohan borrowed ₹ 40000 at 10% per annum simple interest. He immediately invested this month 10% per annum the interest compounded half-yearly. Calculate Rohan's gain in 18 month.

33. A man borrows ₹ 5000 at 12% compound interest payable every six months. He pays ₹ 1800 at the end of every six months. Calculate the third payment he has to make at the end of 18 months in order to clear the entire loan.

34. A sum of ₹ 9800 is invested for 3 yr at 10% per annum at compound interest.
 (i) What is the sum due at the end of first year?
 (ii) What is the sum due at the end of second year?
 (iii) Find the difference between the answers in (ii) and (i) and find the interest on this sum (difference) for one year.
 (iv) Write down the compound interest for the third year.

Hints and Answers

Exercise 2.1

1. **Hint** Do same as Example 1.
 Ans. ₹ 3080.25, ₹ 580.25
2. **Hint** Do same as Example 1.
 Ans. (i) ₹ 960 (ii) ₹ 10035.20
3. **Hint** Do same as Example 2. **Ans.** ₹ 4167
4. **Hint** Do same as Example 3. **Ans.** ₹ 4805
5. **Hint** For first year, $P =$ ₹ 8000, $R = 15$ and $T = 1$ yr
 For second year, $P =$ ₹ 9200, $R = 15$ and $T = 1$ yr
 For next half-year, $P =$ ₹ 10580, $R = 15$ and $T = \frac{1}{2}$ yr
 Ans. ₹ 11373.50, ₹ 3373.50
6. **Hint** Do same as Example 4.
 Ans. ₹ 5667.20, ₹ 1067.20
7. **Hint** Do same as Example 4.
 Ans. ₹ 17658, ₹ 2658
8. **Hint** Do same as Example 6. **Ans.** ₹ 374.63
9. **Hint** Do same as Example 6. **Ans.** ₹ 10088
10. **Hint** Do same as Example 6.
 Ans. ₹ 28940.65, ₹ 3940.65

Exercise 2.2

1. **Hint** Do same as Example 7. **Ans.** ₹ 8112
2. **Hint** Do same as Example 7. **Ans.** ₹ 186.83
3. **Hint** Do same as Example 7.
 Ans. ₹ 7290, ₹ 1040
4. **Hint** Do same as Example 7.
 Ans. Interest paid by $A =$ ₹ 18000

Interest paid by B = ₹16550

A paid more by ₹1450

5. **Hint** Do same as Example 8.

Ans. CI = ₹ 30682

6. **Hint** Do same as Example 8. **Ans.** ₹ 16675
7. **Hint** Do same as Example 9. **Ans.** ₹ 630.50
8. **Hint** Do same as Example 9.

Here, $n = 3$ **Ans.** ₹ 18522

9. **Hint** Use the formula, $CI = P\left[\left(1+\frac{R}{100}\right)^n - 1\right]$

Ans. ₹ 2000

10. **Hint** Do same as Example 12. **Ans.** ₹ 4000
11. **Hint** Use the formula, $CI = P\left[\left(1+\frac{R}{100}\right)^n - 1\right]$

Ans. 5%

12. **Hint** (i) Let R be the rate of interest. Then,

$$\text{CI for first year} = \frac{P \times R \times T}{100}$$

[∵ SI = CI for first conversion period]

$$\Rightarrow (11200 - 10000) = \frac{10000 \times R \times 1}{100}$$

(ii) Amount at the end of second year

$$= P\left(1+\frac{R}{100}\right)^2$$

Ans. (i) 12% (ii) ₹ 12544

13. **Hint** Do same as Example 13.

Ans. 5%

14. **Hint** Let rate of interest be R% per annum and sum of money be ₹ P.

$$\text{Then, } \frac{125P}{64} = P\left(1+\frac{R}{100}\right)^3 \quad \left[\because A = P\left(1+\frac{R}{100}\right)^n\right]$$

Now, find R.

Ans. 25% per annum.

15. **Hint** Do same as Example 15. **Ans.** $1\frac{1}{2}$ yr
16. **Hint** Do same as Example 15. **Ans.** 1yr
17. **Hint** SI for 2 yr

$$= ₹\left(\frac{4000 \times 8 \times 2}{100}\right) = ₹\ 640$$

and compound interest earn in 2 yr

$$= 4000\left[\left(1+\frac{8}{100}\right)^2 - 1\right] = ₹\ 665.6$$

Ans. ₹ 25.60

18. **Hint** Do same as Q. 17.

Ans. ₹ 60.80

19. **Hint** Do same as Example 17. **Ans.** ₹ 600
20. **Hint** Do same as Example 17. **Ans.** ₹ 12500

Exercise 2.3

1. **Hint** Do same as Example 19. **Ans.** 154350
2. **Hint** Do same as Example 20. **Ans.** 26880
3. **Hint** Let P_0 be the population 2 yr ago.

$$\text{Then, } 432000 = P_0\left(1+\frac{20}{100}\right)^2$$

Ans. 300000

4. **Ans.** 5000
5. **Hint** The decrease in the population

= Present population − Population 2 yr ago

Ans. 960

6. **Hint** The number of workers who were working during the fourth year

$$= 6000\left(1-\frac{20}{100}\right)\left(1-\frac{5}{100}\right)\left(1+\frac{15}{100}\right)$$

Ans. 5244

7. **Hint** Let the number of units of time (six months) be n.

$$\text{Using } P = P_0\left(1+\frac{r}{100}\right)^n, \text{ we get}$$

$$27783 = 24000\left(1+\frac{5}{100}\right)^n$$

$$\Rightarrow \left(\frac{21}{20}\right)^n = \frac{27783}{24000} = \frac{9261}{8000} = \left(\frac{21}{20}\right)^3$$

Ans. $1\frac{1}{2}$ yr

8. **Hint** Do same as Example 23. **Ans.** ₹ 256000
9. **Hint** $128000 = 250000\left(1-\frac{20}{100}\right)^n$

$$\Rightarrow \frac{128000}{250000} = \left(\frac{80}{100}\right)^n = \left(\frac{4}{5}\right)^n$$

$$\Rightarrow \left(\frac{4}{5}\right)^n = \left(\frac{4}{5}\right)^3$$

Ans. $n = 3$

10. (i) **Hint** ∴ Required value $= (44000)\left(1-\frac{12}{100}\right)$

Ans. ₹ 38720

(ii) **Hint** Value at 2008 = (Value at 2007) $\left(1-\frac{12}{100}\right)$

∴ Value at 2007 $= 44000 \times \frac{100}{88}$ **Ans.** ₹ 50000

11. **Hint** Let the present value of the car be ₹ P_0.

Value of the car after 3 yr

$$= (\text{Present value}) \times \left(1-\frac{12.5}{100}\right)^3$$

$$= ₹\ P_0 \times \left(1-\frac{1}{8}\right)^3$$

$$= ₹\ P_0 \times \left(\frac{7}{8}\right)^3$$

∴ Decrease in the value of car

$$= ₹ P_0 - ₹ P_0 \times \left(\frac{7}{8}\right)^3$$

∴ Percentage decrease in the value of the car after 3 yr

$$= \left(\frac{\text{Decrease in value}}{\text{Present value}} \times 100\right)\%$$

Ans. $33\frac{1}{128}\%$

Chapter Exercise

1. (a) 2. (a) 3. (d)
4. (a) 5. (a)
6. **Hint** Do same as Example 2.
Ans. ₹ 35123.20; ₹ 10123.2
7. **Hint** Required amount $= 12800\left(1 + \frac{7\frac{1}{2}}{100}\right)^3$
Ans. ₹ 15901.40
8. **Hint** Use the formula, $A = P\left(1 + \frac{R_1}{100}\right)\left(1 + \frac{R_2}{100}\right)$,
Compound interest, CI = A − P
Ans. ₹ 23112; ₹ 3112
9. **Hint** Use the formula, $A = P\left(1 + \frac{R_1}{100}\right)\left(1 + \frac{R_2}{100}\right)$.
Ans. ₹ 16675
10. **Hint** Do same as Example 9. **Ans.** ₹ 7774.63
11. **Hint** First, use the formula,
$CI = P\left[\left(1 + \frac{R}{100}\right)^n - 1\right]$, to find P.
Then, use the formula, $SI = \frac{P \times R \times T}{100}$. **Ans.** ₹ 432
12. **Hint** Do same as Example 13.
Ans. 100% per annum.
13. **Hint** Here, population after 2 yr $= 20000\left(1 + \frac{2}{100}\right)^2$
and rate of growth = (4 − 2)% = 2% **Ans.** 20808
14. **Hint** Let V_0 be the purchased value. Then,
$97200 = V_0\left(1 - \frac{10}{100}\right)^2$ **Ans.** ₹ 120000
15. **Hint** Here, $P = ₹16000$, $R = 15$ and $T = 3$ yr.
$$\therefore \quad SI = \frac{P \times R \times T}{100} = \frac{16000 \times 15 \times 3}{100} = ₹ 7200$$
and $$CI = P\left[\left(1 + \frac{R}{100}\right)^T - 1\right]$$
$$= 16000\left[\left(1 + \frac{15}{100}\right)^3 - 1\right]$$
$$= 16000\left(\frac{4167}{8000}\right) = ₹ 8334$$
∴ Gain of Shivam = ₹(8334 − 7200) **Ans.** ₹ 1134
16. **Hint** First, use the formula $SI = \frac{P \times R \times T}{100}$ to find P.
Then, do same as Example 7. **Ans.** ₹ 15972; ₹ 3972
17. **Hint** Let principal be ₹ x.
SI for 1 yr $= ₹\left(\frac{x \times 10 \times 1}{100}\right) = ₹\frac{x}{10}$
Rate of interest per conversion period (half-year)
$$= \frac{1}{2} \text{ of } 10\% = 5\%$$
and n (the number of conversion periods) = 2
$$\therefore CI = ₹\, x\left[\left(1 + \frac{R}{100}\right)^2 - 1\right] = ₹\frac{41}{400}x$$
$$CI - SI = ₹\left(\frac{x}{400}\right)$$
The sum lent out = ₹ 72000
18. **Hint** Do same as Example 13. **Ans.** 5%
19. **Hint** Do same as Example 18. **Ans.** 8%
20. **Hint.** Let P be the principal.
Clearly, $A = P\left(1 + \frac{R_1}{100}\right)\left(1 + \frac{R_2}{100}\right)$
$$A = P\left(1 + \frac{6}{100}\right)\left(1 + \frac{8}{100}\right)$$
$$= P\left(\frac{53}{50}\right)\left(\frac{27}{25}\right) = \frac{1431}{1250}P$$
$$\because \quad CI = A - P \Rightarrow 2172 = \frac{1431}{1250}P - P$$
$$\therefore \quad P = \frac{1250 \times 2172}{181}$$
Ans. ₹ 15000
21. **Hint** Let P be the original sum and R% be the rate of interest.
Then, according to the question,
$$P\left(1 + \frac{R}{100}\right)^2 = 2809 \quad \text{...(i)}$$
and $$P\left(1 + \frac{R}{100}\right)^3 = 2977.54 \quad \text{...(ii)}$$
On dividing Eq. (ii) by Eq. (i), we get the value of R and then substituting the value of R in Eq. (i), we get the value of P. **Ans.** 6%, ₹ 2500
22. **Hint** Let Seeta's share = ₹ x. Then,
Geeta's share = ₹ (39527 − x)
Amount received by Seeta at the age of 30 yr
$$= x\left(1 + \frac{5}{100}\right)^2$$
Amount received by Geeta at the age of 30 yr
$$= (39527 - x)\left(1 + \frac{5}{100}\right)^4$$
According to the question,
$$x\left(1 + \frac{5}{100}\right)^2 = (39527 - x)\left(1 + \frac{5}{100}\right)^4$$
Ans. Seeta's share = ₹ 20727
Geeta's share = ₹ 18800

23. Hint Let the money borrowed be ₹ x. Then,

Amount to be paid after first year

$$= x\left(1+\frac{8}{100}\right) = ₹\ x\left(\frac{27}{25}\right)$$

Money refunded at the end of first year

$$= ₹\ 43200$$

$$\therefore \text{Principal for the 2nd year} = ₹\left(\frac{27}{25}x - 43200\right)$$

Amount at the end of 2nd year

$$= \left(\frac{27}{25}x - 43200\right)\left(1+\frac{8}{100}\right)$$

$$= \left(\frac{27}{25}x - 43200\right)\left(\frac{27}{25}\right)$$

But the money paid at the end of the 2nd year

$$= ₹\ 34992$$

$$\therefore \left(\frac{27x}{25} - 43200\right)\left(\frac{27}{25}\right) = 34992$$

Ans. ₹ 70000

24. (i) **Hint** Population at the end of 2 yr

$$= 6250\left(1+\frac{4}{100}\right)^2$$

Ans. 6760

(ii) Population at the end of 3 yr

$$= 6250\left(1+\frac{4}{100}\right)^3$$

Ans. 7030

25. (i) **Hint** Population after 2 yr

$$= 216000\left(1+\frac{20}{100}\right)^2$$

Ans. 311040

(ii) **Hint** Let P_0 be the population of 2 yr ago.

Then, $216000 = P_0\left(1+\frac{20}{100}\right)^2$ **Ans.** 150000

26. Hint $P =$ ₹ 3500

$R_1 = 8\%$ per annum and $T_1 = 2$ yr

$= 4\%$ half yearly or $n = 4$ (half years)

$R_2 = 12\%$ per annum and $T_2 = 1$ yr

$R_3 = 15\%$ per annum and $T_3 = 1$ yr

$$\because \text{Amount} = P\left(1+\frac{R_1}{100}\right)^n\left(1+\frac{R_2}{100}\right)^n\left(1+\frac{R_3}{100}\right)^n$$

Ans. ₹ 1773.72

27. (i) **Hint** Compound interest for the 6th yr

= Compound interest of 5th yr

+ Interest on it for 1 yr

Ans. ₹ 732.05

(ii) **Hint** Let compound interest for 4th yr be ₹ x.

Now, compound interest for 5th yr

= Compound interest of 4th yr

+ Interest on it for 1 yr

$\Rightarrow$ ₹ 665.50 = ₹ x + 10% of ₹ x

Ans. ₹ 605

28. Hint Income tax paid $= ₹\left(\frac{30}{100}\times 50000\right)$

$= ₹ 15000$

$\therefore$ Principal = ₹ (50000 − 15000) = ₹ 35000

$R = 10\%$ per annum $= \frac{10}{2}\%$ (semi-annually) and

Time = 3 yr or $n = 3\times 2 = 6$ (half years)

Now, $A = 35000\left(1+\frac{5}{100}\right)^6 = 35000\left(\frac{21}{20}\right)^6$

Ans. ₹ 46903.35

29. Hint Let rate of decay $R\%$ per annum and the age of wooden piece n yr.

$$\left(1-\frac{R}{100}\right)^{5568} = 50\% = \frac{50}{100} = \frac{1}{2}$$

$$1-\frac{R}{100} = \left(\frac{1}{2}\right)^{\frac{1}{5568}} \quad \ldots\text{(i)}$$

and $$\left(1-\frac{R}{100}\right)^n = \frac{12.5}{100} = \frac{1}{8}$$

$$1-\frac{R}{100} = \left(\frac{1}{2}\right)^{\frac{3}{n}} \quad \ldots\text{(ii)}$$

On comparing Eqs. (i) and (ii), we have $\frac{1}{5568} = \frac{3}{n}$

Ans. 16704 yr

30. (i) **Hint** Given, $P\left(1-\frac{R}{100}\right) - P\left(1-\frac{R}{100}\right)^2 = 720$

and $P\left(1-\frac{R}{100}\right)^2 - P\left(1-\frac{R}{100}\right)^3 = 648$

Ans. 10% per annum

(ii) **Ans.** ₹ 8000

(iii) Value of the machine at the end of third year

$$= ₹\ P\left(1-\frac{R}{100}\right)^3$$

Ans. ₹ 5832

31. Increase in population of a town in 3 yr over 100

$$= 100\left(1+\frac{3}{100}\right)^3 - 100 \qquad [\because 4\% - 1\% = 3\%]$$

Ans. 9.27%

32. Hint Principal = ₹ 40000, Rate = 10% per annum

and Time = 18 month $= \frac{18}{12} = \frac{3}{2}$ yr

$$\text{SI} = ₹\left(\frac{40000\times 10\times 3}{100\times 2}\right) = ₹\ 6000$$

$$\therefore \quad A = P\left(1+\frac{r}{100}\right)^n$$

$\Rightarrow$ ₹ $40000\left(1+\frac{5}{100}\right)^3$ = ₹ 46305

$\therefore$ CI earned by Rohan in 18 month

= ₹(46305 − 40000) = ₹ 6305

Rohan's gain in 18 month

= ₹ (6305 − 6000) = ₹ 305

Ans. ₹ 305

33. Hint Interest for the first six months

= ₹ $\left(\frac{5000\times 6\times 1}{100}\right)$ = ₹ 300

Amount after first six months

= ₹ (5000 + 300) = ₹ 5300

Principal for the second six month

= ₹(5300 − 1800) = ₹ 3500

Interest for the second six months

= ₹$\left(\frac{3500\times 6\times 1}{100}\right)$ = ₹ 210

Principal for the third six months

= ₹ (3710 − 1800)

= ₹ 1910

Interest for the third six month

= ₹ $\left(\frac{1910\times 6\times 1}{100}\right)$

= ₹ 114.60

$\therefore$ The payment to be made at the end of 18 month to clear the entire loan

= ₹ (1910 + 114.60) = ₹ 2024.60

Ans. ₹ 2024.60

34. Hint

(i) Interest for the 1st yr = ₹ $\left(\frac{9800\times 10\times 1}{100}\right)$

= ₹ 980

The sum due at the end of the 1st yr

= ₹ (9800 + 980)

Ans. ₹ 10780

(ii) Interest fo the 2nd yr

= ₹ $\left(\frac{10780\times 10\times 1}{100}\right)$ = ₹ 1078

The sum due at the end of the 2nd yr

= ₹ (10780 + 1078)

Ans. ₹ 11858

(iii) $\therefore$ Required difference

= ₹ (11858 − 10780) = ₹ 1078

Interest for one year on this difference

= ₹ $\left(\frac{1078\times 10\times 1}{100}\right)$

Ans. ₹ 107.80

(iv) Compound Interest for the 3rd yr

= ₹ (1078 + 107.80)

Ans. ₹ 1185.80

Olympiad Section

Brain Teasing Questions of Olympiad Pattern

1 Ravi lent Ramu a certain sum of money at the rate of $2\frac{1}{2}$% per annum, interest compounded annually. After two years, Ramu paid a sum of ₹ 2560 to Ravi. What sum of money did Ramu borrow from Ravi?

(a) ₹ 2036.64
(b) ₹ 2236.54
(c) ₹ 2436.64
(d) ₹ 2636.64

2 A certain money doubles in 4 yr under compound interest. In how many more years will it become 4 times the principal under the same conditions?

(a) 8 (b) 4
(c) 12 (d) 16

3 Ajay borrowed a sum of ₹ 4000 at 10% per annum for 4 yr under simple interest. But after 2 yr he was asked to pay compound interest for the remaining 2 yr on the sum borrowed initially. How much more did Ajay have to pay if interest was compounded annually?

(a) ₹ 40 (b) ₹ 20
(c) ₹ 80 (d) ₹ 160

4 In how many years will a sum of ₹ 25600, interest compounded quarterly, at the rate of 25% per annum amount to ₹ 28900?

(a) 1 yr (b) $\frac{1}{2}$ yr
(c) 2 yr (d) 4 yr

5 At compound interest of 8%, 10% and 12% for three consecutive years, the interest earned in the third year is ₹ 891. The principal is

(a) ₹ 5000 (b) ₹ 6250
(c) ₹ 7000 (d) ₹ 7250

6 The difference between the compound interest on a sum of ₹ 4000, interest being compounded annually and the simple interest on it for two years is ₹ 250. Find the rate of interest (pa).

(a) 15% (b) 10%
(c) 25% (d) 20%

7 A sum of money invested at compound interest doubles itself in six years. In how many years will it become 64 times itself at the same rate of compound interest?

(a) 30 (b) 36
(c) 42 (d) 48

8 A sum of ₹ 4000 is split into two parts. One part is lent at simple interest and the other at compound interest, interest being compounded annually. At the end of two years, the total interest earned is ₹ 1720. Find the sum of lent at simple interest, if each part is lent at 20% pa (in ₹).

(a) 1200 (b) 1000
(c) 800 (d) 1500

9 The cost of an electronic device reduces at the rate of 5% per annum. If its present cost is ₹ 32490, what was its cost before two years?

(a) ₹ 37000 (b) ₹ 35400
(c) ₹ 36000 (d) ₹ 37200

10 Two persons P and Q lent certain amounts at the same rate of interest for 2 yr and 3 yr, respectively under compound interest. If their final amounts are in the ratio of 3 : 5, Q's amount at the end of the first year being ₹ 8500 and P earned an interest of ₹ 510 for the first year, then find the ratio of their principals.

(a) 33 : 50 (b) 27 : 47
(c) 35 : 61 (d) 22 : 51

Answers

1. (c) **2.** (b) **3.** (a) **4.** (b) **5.** (b) **6.** (c) **7.** (b) **8.** (b) **9.** (c) **10.** (a)

* *These questions may or may not be asked in the examination, have been given just for additional practice required for olympiads Scholarship Exams etc. For detailed explanations refer Page No. 333.*

CHAPTER 03

Expansions

SYLLABUS

- Expansion of the Form $(a \pm b)^2$
- Expansion of the Form $(a \pm b)^3$
- Expansion of the Form $(x \pm a)(x \pm b)$
- Expansion of the Form $(a \pm b \pm c)^2$

For algebraic expressions, expansion means the expanded form of an algebraic expression i.e. conversion of product form to addition/subtraction form. e.g. $a^2 + 2ab + b^2$ is an expanded form of $(a + b)^2$. In other words, we can say, $a^2 + 2ab + b^2$ is an expansion of $(a + b)^2$.

Expansion of the Form $(a \pm b)^2$

$(a + b)^2 = a^2 + 2ab + b^2$

$(a - b)^2 = a^2 - 2ab + b^2$

Example 1. Expand by using suitable identities.

(i) $(2a + 3b)^2$ (ii) $(4x^2y + 6z)^2$

Sol. (i) $(2a + 3b)^2 = (2a)^2 + 2(2a)(3b) + (3b)^2 = 4a^2 + 12ab + 9b^2$

(ii) On comparing $(4x^2y + 6z)^2$ with $(a + b)^2$, we get

$$a = 4x^2y \text{ and } b = 6z$$

By using the identity $(a + b)^2 = a^2 + 2ab + b^2$, we get

$$(4x^2y + 6z)^2 = (4x^2y)^2 + 2(4x^2y)(6z) + (6z)^2$$
$$= 16x^4y^2 + 48x^2yz + 36z^2$$

Example 2. Expand the following by using suitable identities.

$$\left(2x - \frac{1}{2x}\right)^2$$

Sol. On comparing $\left(2x - \frac{1}{2x}\right)^2$ with $(a - b)^2$, we get $a = 2x$ and $b = \frac{1}{2x}$

By using identity $(a - b)^2 = a^2 - 2ab + b^2$, we get

$$\left(2x - \frac{1}{2x}\right)^2 = (2x)^2 - 2 \times 2x \times \frac{1}{2x} + \left(\frac{1}{2x}\right)^2 = 4x^2 - 2 + \frac{1}{4x^2}$$

Example 3. If $x^2 + 4x + a = (x + 2)^2$, then find the value of a.

Sol. We have, $x^2 + 4x + a = (x + 2)^2$

$\Rightarrow \quad x^2 + 4x + a = x^2 + 2 \times x \times 2 + 2^2$

$[\because (a + b)^2 = a^2 + 2ab + b^2]$

$\Rightarrow \quad x^2 + 4x + a = x^2 + 4x + 4$

On comparing both sides, we get

$$a = 4$$

Example 4. Using a suitable identity, evaluate

(i) $(1008)^2$ (ii) $(9.98)^2$

Sol.

(i) Consider, $(1008)^2 = (1000 + 8)^2 = (1000)^2 + (8)^2 + 2(1000)(8)$

$[\because (a + b)^2 = a^2 + b^2 + 2ab]$

$= 1000000 + 64 + 16000 = 1016064$

(ii) Consider, $(9.98)^2 = (10 - 0.02)^2$

$= (10)^2 + (0.02)^2 - 2(10)(0.02)$

$[\because (a - b)^2 = a^2 + b^2 - 2ab]$

$= 100 + 0.0004 - 0.4 = 99.6004$

Example 5. Evaluate $(4a + 3b)^2 - (4a - 3b)^2 + 48ab$.

Sol. We have, $(4a + 3b)^2 - (4a - 3b)^2 + 48ab$

$= (4a)^2 + (3b)^2 + 2(4a)(3b) - [(4a)^2 + (3b)^2 - 2(4a)(3b)] + 48ab$

$[\because (A + B)^2 = A^2 + B^2 + 2AB \text{ and } (A - B)^2 = A^2 + B^2 - 2AB]$

$= 16a^2 + 9b^2 + 24ab - [16a^2 + 9b^2 - 24ab] + 48ab$

$= 24ab + 24ab + 48ab = 96ab$

Example 6. If $x - 2 = \frac{1}{4x}$, then find the value of

(i) $x^2 + \frac{1}{16x^2}$ (ii) $x^4 + \frac{1}{256x^4}$

Sol.

(i) We have, $x - 2 = \frac{1}{4x} \Rightarrow x - \frac{1}{4x} = 2$

On squaring both sides, we get

$$\left(x - \frac{1}{4x}\right)^2 = 2^2$$

$$\Rightarrow (x)^2 + \left(\frac{1}{4x}\right)^2 - 2 \times x \times \frac{1}{4x} = 4$$

$[\because (a-b)^2 = a^2 + b^2 - 2ab]$

$$\Rightarrow x^2 + \frac{1}{16x^2} - \frac{1}{2} = 4$$

$$\Rightarrow x^2 + \frac{1}{16x^2} = 4 + \frac{1}{2} = \frac{9}{2}$$

(ii) Now, consider $x^2 + \frac{1}{16x^2} = \frac{9}{2}$

On squaring both sides, we get

$$\left(x^2 + \frac{1}{16x^2}\right)^2 = \left(\frac{9}{2}\right)^2$$

$$\Rightarrow x^4 + \frac{1}{256x^4} + 2 \times x^2 \times \frac{1}{16x^2} = \frac{81}{4}$$

$[\because (a+b)^2 = a^2 + b^2 + 2ab]$

$$\Rightarrow x^4 + \frac{1}{256x^4} + \frac{1}{8} = \frac{81}{4} \Rightarrow x^4 + \frac{1}{256x^4} = \frac{81}{4} - \frac{1}{8}$$

$$\Rightarrow x^4 + \frac{1}{256x^4} = \frac{162-1}{8} = \frac{161}{8}$$

Example 7. In the expansion of $(5x-3)(x+2)^2$, find

(i) coefficients of x^3, x^2 and x.

(ii) constant term.

Sol. We have, $(5x-3)(x+2)^2 = (5x-3)(x^2+4+4x)$

$[\because (a+b)^2 = a^2 + b^2 + 2ab]$

$= 5x^3 + 17x^2 + 8x - 12$

(i) Coefficient of $x^3 = 5$, coefficient of $x^2 = 17$

and coefficient of $x = 8$

(ii) Constant term $= -12$

Expansion of the Form $(x \pm a)(x \pm b)$

$(x+a)(x+b) = x^2 + (a+b)x + ab$

$(x-a)(x-b) = x^2 - (a+b)x + ab$

Example 8. Expand the following products.

(i) $(x+3)(x+7)$ (ii) $(x+6)(x-5)$

(iii) $(x-4)(x+6)$ (iv) $(x-2)(x-5)$

Sol. (i) $(x+3)(x+7) = x^2 + (3+7)x + 3 \times 7$

$[\because (x+a)(x+b) = x^2 + (a+b)x + ab]$

$= x^2 + 10x + 21$

(ii) $(x+6)(x-5) = (x+6)[x+(-5)]$

$= x^2 + [6+(-5)]x + 6 \times (-5)$

$[\because (x+a)(x+b) = x^2 + (a+b)x + ab]$

$= x^2 + x - 30$

(iii) $(x-4)(x+6) = [x+(-4)](x+6)$

$= x^2 + (-4+6)x + (-4) \times 6$

$[\because (x+a)(x+b) = x^2 + (a+b)x + ab]$

$= x^2 + 2x - 24$

(iv) $(x-2)(x-5) = x^2 - (2+5)x + 2 \times 5 = x^2 - 7x + 10.$

$[\because (x-a)(x-b) = x^2 - (a+b)x + ab]$

Example 9. Evaluate 105×106 without multiplying directly.

Sol. First, write 105 as $100+5$ and 106 as $100+6$.

Then, $105 \times 106 = (100+5)(100+6)$

$= (100)^2 + (5+6)(100) + (5 \times 6)$

$[\because (x+a)(x+b) = x^2 + (a+b)x + ab]$

$= 10000 + 11 \times 100 + 30$

$= 10000 + 1100 + 30$

$= 11130$

Expansion of the Form $(a \pm b \pm c)^2$

$(a+b+c)^2 = a^2 + b^2 + c^2 + 2ab + 2bc + 2ca$

$(a-b-c)^2 = a^2 + b^2 + c^2 - 2ab + 2bc - 2ca$

Example 10. Write the following in the expanded form.

(i) $(3x+y+2)^2$ (ii) $(2x-y+4z)^2$

(iii) $(4x-2y-3z)^2$ (iv) $\left(\frac{2}{3}x - \frac{3}{4}y + \frac{4}{5}z\right)^2$

Sol.

(i) We have, $(3x+y+2)^2$

On comparing with $(a+b+c)^2$, we get

$a = 3x$, $b = y$ and $c = 2$

We know that $(a+b+c)^2 = a^2 + b^2 + c^2 + 2ab + 2bc + 2ca$

On putting the values of a, b and c in the above identity, we get

$(3x+y+2)^2 = (3x)^2 + (y)^2 + (2)^2 + 2 \times (3x) \times (y) + 2 \times y \times 2 + 2 \times 2 \times 3x$

$= 9x^2 + y^2 + 4 + 6xy + 4y + 12x$

(ii) We have, $(2x-y+4z)^2$

On comparing with $(a+b+c)^2$, we get

$a = 2x$, $b = -y$ and $c = 4z$

We know that $(a+b+c)^2 = a^2 + b^2 + c^2 + 2ab + 2bc + 2ac$

On putting the values of a, b and c in the above identity, we get

$(2x-y+4z)^2 = (2x)^2 + (-y)^2 + (4z)^2 + 2 \times 2x \times (-y) + 2 \times (-y) \times (4z) + 2 \times 4z \times 2x$

$= 4x^2 + y^2 + 16z^2 - 4xy - 8yz + 16xz$

(iii) We have, $(4x-2y-3z)^2$

On comparing $(4x-2y-3z)^2$ with $(a-b-c)^2$, we get

$$a = 4x,\ b = 2y \text{ and } c = 3z$$

By using identity $(a-b-c)^2$

$$= a^2+b^2+c^2-2ab+2bc-2ca, \text{ we get}$$

$$(4x-2y-3z)^2 = (4x)^2+(2y)^2+(3z)^2 - 2(4x)(2y)+2(2y)(3z)-2(3z)(4x)$$

$$\Rightarrow (4x-2y-3z)^2 = 16x^2+4y^2+9z^2-16xy+12yz-24xz$$

(iv) We have, $\left(\frac{2}{3}x-\frac{3}{4}y+\frac{4}{5}z\right)^2$

On comparing with $(a+b+c)^2$, we get

$$a = \frac{2}{3}x,\ b = -\frac{3}{4}y \text{ and } c = \frac{4}{5}z$$

We know that $(a+b+c)^2 = a^2+b^2+c^2+2ab+2bc+2ca$

On putting the values of a, b and c in the above identity, we get

$$\left(\frac{2}{3}x-\frac{3}{4}y+\frac{4}{5}z\right)^2 = \left(\frac{2}{3}x\right)^2+\left(-\frac{3}{4}y\right)^2+\left(\frac{4}{5}z\right)^2+2\left(\frac{2}{3}x\right)\left(-\frac{3}{4}y\right) + 2\left(-\frac{3}{4}y\right)\left(\frac{4}{5}z\right)+2\left(\frac{4}{5}z\right)\left(\frac{2}{3}x\right)$$

$$= \frac{4}{9}x^2+\frac{9}{16}y^2+\frac{16}{25}z^2+2\left[\frac{-xy}{2}+\left(\frac{-3yz}{5}\right)+\frac{8zx}{15}\right]$$

$$= \frac{4}{9}x^2+\frac{9}{16}y^2+\frac{16}{25}z^2+2\left[\frac{-xy}{2}-\frac{3yz}{5}+\frac{8zx}{15}\right]$$

$$= \frac{4}{9}x^2+\frac{9}{16}y^2+\frac{16}{25}z^2-xy-\frac{6yz}{5}+\frac{16zx}{15}$$

Example 11. Simplify $(x+y+z)^2+(x-y-z)^2$.

Sol. Consider, $(x+y+z)^2+(x-y-z)^2$

$$= x^2+y^2+z^2+2xy+2yz+2zx+x^2+y^2+z^2-2xy+2yz-2zx$$

$$\left[\because (a+b+c)^2 = a^2+b^2+c^2+2ab+2bc+2ca \text{ and } (a-b-c)^2 = a^2+b^2+c^2-2ab+2bc-2ca\right]$$

$$= 2x^2+2y^2+2z^2+4yz$$

$$= 2(x^2+y^2+z^2+2yz)$$

Expansion of the Form $(a \pm b)^3$

$(a+b)^3 = a^3+b^3+3ab(a+b)$

$(a-b)^3 = a^3-b^3-3ab(a-b)$

Example 12. Simplify the following expansions.

(i) $(2x+3y)^3$ (ii) $(5a-7b)^3$

Sol. (i) $(2x+3y)^3 = (2x)^3+(3y)^3+3\times 2x\times 3y\times(2x+3y)$

$$[\because (a+b)^3 = a^3+b^3+3ab(a+b)]$$

$$= 8x^3+27y^3+18xy(2x+3y)$$

$$= 8x^3+27y^3+36x^2y+54xy^2$$

(ii) $(5a-7b)^3 = (5a)^3-(7b)^3-3\times 5a\times 7b\times(5a-7b)$

$$[\because (A-B)^3 = A^3-B^3-3AB(A-B)]$$

$$= 125a^3-343b^3-105ab(5a-7b)$$

$$= 125a^3-343b^3-525a^2b+735ab^2$$

Example 13. Simplify $(4x+2y)^3-(4x-2y)^3$.

Sol. Consider, $(4x+2y)^3-(4x-2y)^3$

$$= \{(4x)^3+(2y)^3+3(4x)^2(2y)+3(4x)(2y)^2\} - \{(4x)^3-(2y)^3-3(4x)^2(2y)+3(4x)(2y)^2\}$$

$$\left[\because (a+b)^3 = a^3+b^3+3a^2b+3ab^2 \text{ and } (a-b)^3 = a^3-b^3-3a^2b+3ab^2\right]$$

$$= (64x^3+8y^3+96x^2y+48xy^2)-(64x^3-8y^3-96x^2y+48xy^2)$$

$$= 64x^3+8y^3+96x^2y+48xy^2-64x^3+8y^3+96x^2y-48xy^2$$

$$= 8y^3+96x^2y+8y^3+96x^2y = 16y^3+192x^2y$$

Example 14. Evaluate $(999)^3$ by using identity.

Sol. We have, $(999)^3 = (1000-1)^3$

$$= (1000)^3-(1)^3-3(1000)^2(1)+3(1000)(1)^2$$

$$[\because (a-b)^3 = a^3-b^3-3a^2b+3ab^2]$$

$$= 1000000000-1-3000000+3000$$

$$= 1000000000-1-2997000 = 997002999$$

Example 15. Find the cube of $x-\frac{1}{x}+y$, where $x \neq 0$.

Sol. Consider, $\left(x-\frac{1}{x}+y\right)^3 = \left[\left(x-\frac{1}{x}\right)+y\right]^3$

$$= \left(x-\frac{1}{x}\right)^3+y^3+3\left(x-\frac{1}{x}\right)^2y+3\left(x-\frac{1}{x}\right)y^2$$

$$[\because (a+b)^3 = a^3+b^3+3a^2b+3ab^2]$$

$$= \left[x^3-\frac{1}{x^3}-3x^2\left(\frac{1}{x}\right)+3x\left(\frac{1}{x}\right)^2\right]+y^3 + 3\left(x^2+\frac{1}{x^2}-2\times x\times\frac{1}{x}\right)y+3\left(x-\frac{1}{x}\right)y^2$$

$$\left[\because (a-b)^3 = a^3-b^3-3a^2b+3ab^2 \text{ and } (a-b)^2 = a^2+b^2-2ab\right]$$

$$= \left(x^3-\frac{1}{x^3}-3x+\frac{3}{x}\right)+y^3+3\left(x^2+\frac{1}{x^2}-2\right)y+3\left(x-\frac{1}{x}\right)y^2$$

$$= x^3-\frac{1}{x^3}-3x+\frac{3}{x}+y^3+3x^2y+\frac{3y}{x^2}-6y+3xy^2-\frac{3y^2}{x}$$

$$= x^3-3x+\frac{3}{x}-\frac{1}{x^3}+3x^2y+\frac{3y}{x^2}-6y+3xy^2-\frac{3y^2}{x}+y^3$$

Expansion of the form

(i) $(a+b+c)(a^2+b^2+c^2-ab-bc-ca) = a^3+b^3+c^3-3abc$

(ii) $(x+a)(x+b)(x+c) = x^3+(a+b+c)x^2 + (ab+bc+ca)x+abc$

(iii) If $a+b+c=0$, then $a^3+b^3+c^3 = 3abc$.

Example 16. Find the product of

$$(x+y+3z)(x^2+y^2+9z^2-xy-3yz-3xz).$$

Sol. We have, $(x+y+3z)(x^2+y^2+9z^2-xy-3yz-3xz)$

$$= (x+y+3z)[x^2+y^2+(3z)^2-x\times y-y\times 3z-3z\times x]$$

On comparing it with

$(a+b+c)(a^2+b^2+c^2-ab-bc-ca)$, we get

$a = x$, $b = y$ and $c = 3z$

Now, as

$(a+b+c)(a^2+b^2+c^2-ab-bc-ca) = a^3+b^3+c^3-3abc$

$$\therefore (x+y+3z)(x^2+y^2+9z^2-xy-3yz-3xz) = [x^3+y^3+(3z)^3-3\times x\times y\times 3z] = x^3+y^3+27z^3-9xyz$$

Example 17. Find the product of the following $(x+1)(x+2)(x+3)$.

Sol. We have, $(x+1)(x+2)(x+3)$

We know that

$$(x+a)(x+b)(x+c) = x^3+(a+b+c)x^2 + (ab+bc+ca)x+abc$$

On comparing it with

$a = 1$, $b = 2$ and $c = 3$

On putting the values of a, b and c in the above identity, we get

$$(x+1)(x+2)(x+3) = (x^3)+(1+2+3)x^2 + (1\times 2+2\times 3+3\times 1)x+1\times 2\times 3 = x^3+6x^2+11x+6$$

Example 18. If $x = y+5$, then find the value of $x^3-y^3-15xy-125$.

Sol. Given, $x = y+5 \Rightarrow x-y-5=0$

$\Rightarrow \quad x+(-y)-5=0$

$\Rightarrow (x)^3+(-y)^3+(-5)^3 = 3(x)(-y)(-5)$

[$\because (a+b+c)=0$, then $a^3+b^3+c^3=3abc$]

$\Rightarrow \quad x^3-y^3-125 = 15xy$

$\Rightarrow x^3-y^3-15xy-125=0$

Miscellaneous Solved Examples

Example 19. If $x\neq 0$, $x+\dfrac{1}{2x} = p$ and $x-\dfrac{1}{2x}=q$, then find a relation between p and q.

Sol. We have, $\quad x+\dfrac{1}{2x}=p \quad$ ...(i)

and $\quad x-\dfrac{1}{2x}=q \quad$ ...(ii)

On squaring both sides of Eq. (i), we get

$$\left(x+\frac{1}{2x}\right)^2 = p^2 \Rightarrow x^2+\frac{1}{4x^2}+2\times x\times\frac{1}{2x}=p^2$$

[$\because (a+b)^2=a^2+b^2+2ab$]

$$\Rightarrow \quad x^2+\frac{1}{4x^2}+1=p^2 \Rightarrow x^2+\frac{1}{4x^2}=p^2-1 \quad \text{...(iii)}$$

Now, squaring both sides of Eq. (ii), we get

$$\left(x-\frac{1}{2x}\right)^2=q^2$$

$$\Rightarrow \quad x^2+\frac{1}{4x^2}-2\times x\times\frac{1}{2x}=q^2 \quad [\because (a-b)^2=a^2+b^2-2ab]$$

$$\Rightarrow \quad x^2+\frac{1}{4x^2}-1=q^2 \Rightarrow x^2+\frac{1}{4x^2}=q^2+1 \quad \text{...(iv)}$$

From Eqs. (iii) and (iv), we get

$$p^2-1=q^2+1 \Rightarrow p^2-q^2=2$$

Example 20. If $a+b=6$ and $ab=8$, then find the value of $(a-b)$.

Sol. Consider, $(a-b)^2=(a+b)^2-4ab$

$= 6^2-4\times 8 \quad$ [$\because a+b=6$ and $ab=8$]

$\Rightarrow \quad (a-b)^2 = 36-32=4$

$\Rightarrow \quad (a-b)^2=4 \quad$ [taking square root on both sides]

$\Rightarrow \quad a-b=\pm 2$

Example 21. Prove that

$$\left(2x-\frac{1}{2x}\right)^2-\left(2x+\frac{1}{2x}\right)\left(2x-\frac{1}{2x}\right)=\frac{1}{2x^2}-2.$$

Sol. Consider, LHS $=\left(2x-\dfrac{1}{2x}\right)^2-\left(2x+\dfrac{1}{2x}\right)\left(2x-\dfrac{1}{2x}\right)$

$$=(2x)^2+\left(\frac{1}{2x}\right)^2-2-\left[(2x)^2-\left(\frac{1}{2x}\right)^2\right]$$

$$\left[\because \left(a-\frac{1}{a}\right)^2=a^2+\frac{1}{a^2}-2 \text{ and } (a+b)(a-b)=a^2-b^2\right]$$

$$=4x^2+\frac{1}{4x^2}-2-4x^2+\frac{1}{4x^2}$$

$$=2\times\frac{1}{4x^2}-2=\frac{1}{2x^2}-2=\text{RHS}$$ **Hence proved.**

Example 22. If $x^2+\dfrac{1}{x^2}=20$, then find the value of each of the following

(i) $x+\dfrac{1}{x}$ (ii) $x-\dfrac{1}{x}$

Sol. We have, $x^2+\dfrac{1}{x^2}=20$

(i) Consider, $\left(x+\dfrac{1}{x}\right)^2 = x^2+\dfrac{1}{x^2}+2$ [$\because (a+b)^2=a^2+b^2+2ab$]

$= 20+2=22 \quad \left[\because x^2+\dfrac{1}{x^2}=20\right]$

Hence, $x+\dfrac{1}{x}=\pm\sqrt{22}$ [taking square root on both sides]

(ii) Consider, $\left(x-\dfrac{1}{x}\right)^2 = x^2+\dfrac{1}{x^2}-2\times x\times\dfrac{1}{x}=x^2+\dfrac{1}{x^2}-2$

[$\because (a-b)^2=a^2+b^2-2ab$]

$=20-2=18 \quad \left[\because x^2+\dfrac{1}{x^2}=20\right]$

Hence, $x-\dfrac{1}{x}=\pm\sqrt{18}$ [taking square root on both sides]

Example 23. If $a^2-4a-1=0$ and $a\neq 0$, then find the values of

(i) $a-\dfrac{1}{a}$ (ii) $a+\dfrac{1}{a}$ (iii) $a^2-\dfrac{1}{a^2}$

Sol.

(i) We have, $a^2-4a-1=0 \Rightarrow a^2-1=4a$

$$\Rightarrow \quad \frac{a^2-1}{a}=4 \Rightarrow a-\frac{1}{a}=4 \quad \text{...(i)}$$

(ii) Consider, $\left(a+\frac{1}{a}\right)^2 = a^2 + \frac{1}{a^2} + 2$

$[\because (A+B)^2 = A^2 + B^2 + 2AB]$

$= a^2 + \frac{1}{a^2} - 2 + 2 + 2 = a^2 + \frac{1}{a^2} - 2 \times a \times \frac{1}{a} + 4$

$= \left(a - \frac{1}{a}\right)^2 + 4 \qquad [\because A^2 + B^2 - 2AB = (A-B)^2]$

$= 4^2 + 4 = 16 + 4 = 20 \qquad$ [from Eq. (i)]

$\Rightarrow \quad a + \frac{1}{a} = \pm\sqrt{20} = \pm 2\sqrt{5}$

[taking square root on both sides] ...(ii)

(iii) We have, $a^2 - \frac{1}{a^2} = \left(a - \frac{1}{a}\right)\left(a + \frac{1}{a}\right)$

$[\because (x-y)(x+y) = x^2 - y^2]$

$= 4 \times (\pm 2\sqrt{5}) = \pm 8\sqrt{5} \qquad$ [from Eqs. (i) and (ii)]

Example 24. If $a + b = 1 + ab$, then prove that $a^3 + b^3 = 1 + a^3b^3$.

Sol. We have, $a + b = 1 + ab$ ...(i)

On cubing both sides in Eq. (i), we get

$(a+b)^3 = (1+ab)^3$

$\Rightarrow a^3 + b^3 + 3ab(a+b) = 1^3 + (ab)^3 + 3 \times 1 \times ab(1+ab)$

$[\because (A+B)^3 = A^3 + B^3 + 3AB(A+B)]$

$\Rightarrow a^3 + b^3 + 3ab(1+ab) = 1 + a^3b^3 + 3ab(1+ab)$

[from Eq. (i)]

$\Rightarrow \quad a^3 + b^3 = 1 + a^3b^3 + 3ab(1+ab) - 3ab(1+ab)$

$\Rightarrow \quad a^3 + b^3 = 1 + a^3b^3$ **Hence proved.**

Example 25. If $2x - 5y = 10$ and $xy = 15$, then find the value of $8x^3 - 125y^3$.

Sol. We have, $2x - 5y = 10$ ...(i)

and $xy = 15$ ...(ii)

On cubing both sides of Eq. (i), we get

$(2x - 5y)^3 = 10^3$

$\Rightarrow (2x)^3 - (5y)^3 - 3(2x)(5y)(2x - 5y) = 1000$

$[\because (a-b)^3 = a^3 - b^3 - 3ab(a-b)]$

$\Rightarrow \quad 8x^3 - 125y^3 - 30xy(2x - 5y) = 1000$

$\Rightarrow \quad 8x^3 - 125y^3 - 30(15)(10) = 1000$

[from Eqs. (i) and (ii)]

$\Rightarrow \quad 8x^3 - 125y^3 - 4500 = 1000$

$\Rightarrow \quad 8x^3 - 125y^3 = 1000 + 4500 = 5500$

Example 26. Without actually calculating the cubes, evaluate $29^3 - 11^3$.

Sol. We have, $29^3 - 11^3 = (20+9)^3 - (20-9)^3$

$= 2\{9^3 + 3 \times (20)^2 \times 9\}$

$[\because (a+b)^3 - (a-b)^3 = 2(b^3 + 3a^2b)]$

$= 2(729 + 27 \times 400) = 2(729 + 10800)$

$= 1458 + 21600 = 23058$

Example 27. If $\frac{a}{b} = \frac{b}{c}$, then prove that $(a+b+c)(a-b+c) = a^2 + b^2 + c^2$.

Sol. We have, $\frac{a}{b} = \frac{b}{c} = k$ (say)

$\Rightarrow \quad a = bk$ and $b = ck$

$\Rightarrow \quad a = ck^2$

Consider, LHS $= (a+b+c)(a-b+c)$

$= (ck^2 + ck + c)(ck^2 - ck + c)$

$[\because a = ck^2$ and $b = ck]$

$= c^2(k^2 + k + 1)(k^2 - k + 1)$

$= c^2[\{(k^2+1) + k\}\{(k^2+1) - k\}]$

$= c^2\{(k^2+1)^2 - k^2\}$

$[\because (a+b)(a-b) = a^2 - b^2]$

$= c^2\{k^4 + 1 + 2k^2 - k^2\}$

$[\because (a+b)^2 = a^2 + b^2 + 2ab]$

$= c^2\{k^4 + k^2 + 1\}$ ...(i)

Now, consider RHS $= a^2 + b^2 + c^2 = (ck^2)^2 + (ck)^2 + c^2$

$[\because a = ck^2$ and $b = ck]$

$= c^2k^4 + c^2k^2 + c^2$

$= c^2(k^4 + k^2 + 1)$ ...(ii)

From Eqs. (i) and (ii), we get

LHS = RHS **Hence proved.**

Example 28. If $x + y + z = 0$, then find the value of $\frac{x^2}{yz} + \frac{y^2}{xz} + \frac{z^2}{xy}$.

Sol. Given, $x + y + z = 0$

$\therefore \quad \frac{x^2}{yz} + \frac{y^2}{xz} + \frac{z^2}{xy} = \frac{x^3 + y^3 + z^3}{xyz}$

$= \frac{3xyz}{xyz} \quad [\because$ if $x + y + z = 0$, then $x^3 + y^3 + z^3 = 3xyz]$

$= 3$

Example 29. If the difference between two positive numbers is 5 and the difference between their cubes is 650, then find

(i) their product.

(ii) the sum of their squares.

Sol. Let two positive numbers be x and y, where $x > y$.

According to the statement, we have

$x - y = 5$ and $x^3 - y^3 = 650$

(i) Consider, $x - y = 5$

On cubing both sides, we get $(x-y)^3 = 5^3$

$\Rightarrow \quad x^3 - y^3 - 3xy(x-y) = 125$

$[\because (a-b)^3 = a^3 - b^3 - 3ab(a-b)]$

$\Rightarrow \quad 650 - 3xy(5) = 125$

$[\because x - y = 5$ and $x^3 - y^3 = 650]$

$\Rightarrow \quad 650 - 125 = 15xy \Rightarrow 15xy = 525$

$\Rightarrow \quad xy = \frac{525}{15} = 35 \Rightarrow xy = 35$ ...(i)

(ii) Again, consider $x - y = 5$

On squaring both sides, we get $(x-y)^2 = (5)^2$

$[\because (a-b)^2 = a^2 + b^2 - 2ab]$

$\Rightarrow \quad x^2 + y^2 - 2xy = 25$

$\Rightarrow \quad x^2 + y^2 - 2 \times 35 = 25 \qquad$ [from Eq. (i)]

$\Rightarrow \quad x^2 + y^2 - 70 = 25$

$\Rightarrow \quad x^2 + y^2 = 95$

Chapter Practice

a. 1 Mark Questions

1. Value of x, $(x + 2)^2 = 49$
   (a) 9 (b) 7 (c) 2 (d) 5

2. Value of x, $(x + 2)^2 - 4 = (3x - 5) + x^2$
   (a) 5 (b) $-5/7$ (c) -5 (d) $5/7$

3. If $x^2 + \frac{1}{x^2} = 2$, then value of $x + \frac{1}{x}$ is
   (a) 2 (b) 1 (c) 0 (d) 1/2

4. If $x - \frac{1}{x} = 4$, then value of $x^2 + \frac{1}{x^2}$ is
   (a) 16 (b) 20
   (c) 18 (d) 14

5. Simplify $(x + y)^3 - (x - y)^3$
   (a) $3(y^3 + 3x^2y)$ (b) $2(y^3 + 3x^2y)$
   (c) $(y^3 + 2x^2y)$ (d) $2y^3 + 3x^2y$

6. Value of x, $(x - 7)(x - 9) = x^2 - 1$
   (a) 2 (b) 6
   (c) -4 (d) 4

b. 3 Marks Questions

7. Expand the following.
   (i) $(2x + 4y^2)^2$ (ii) $(3a - 5ab)^2$

8. Expand the following.
   (i) $(3x^2y + 5z)^2$ (ii) $\left(\frac{1}{2}x + \frac{2}{3}y\right)^2$

9. Find the expansions of the following.
   (i) $(3x - 4y)^2$ (ii) $\left(\frac{3a}{2} - \frac{2}{3b}\right)^2$

10. Use $(a + b)^2 = a^2 + 2ab + b^2$ to evaluate the following.
    (i) $(102)^2$ (ii) $(10.2)^2$
    (iii) $(10.3)^2$

11. Using the suitable identity to evaluate the following.
    (i) $(1003)^2$ (ii) $(998)^2$

12. Use $(a - b)^2 = a^2 - 2ab + b^2$ to evaluate the following.
    (i) $(9.2)^2$ (ii) $(6.1)^2$

13. Find the product of the following.
    (i) $(x + 7)(x + 9)$ (ii) $(x + 2y)(x + 3y)$
    (iii) $(x + 5y)(x - 8y)$

14. Find the product of the following.
    (i) $(x - 4)(x - 5)$ (ii) $(x - 3y)(x - 5y)$

15. Expand
    (i) $(9x + 2y + z)^2$ (ii) $(2x + 3y - 5z)^2$
    (iii) $(-x + 2y + z)^2$ (iv) $\left(\frac{2x}{5} + \frac{3y}{4} - \frac{4z}{7}\right)^2$

16. Find the expansions of the following.
    (i) $(2a + b)^3$
    (ii) $(3x - 4y)^3$
    (iii) $\left(x - \frac{2}{3}y\right)^3$
    (iv) $\left(x - \frac{2}{3y}\right)^3 - \left(x + \frac{2}{3y}\right)^3$

17. Using a suitable identity, find the value of $(98)^3$.

18. If $4y^2 - 12y + b = (2y - 3)^2$, then find the value of b.

19. Evaluate 95×96 without multiplying directly.

20. If $x + \frac{1}{x} = 5$, then find
    (i) $x^2 + \frac{1}{x^2}$ (ii) $x^4 + \frac{1}{x^4}$

c. 4/5 Marks Questions

21. Simplify $\left(\frac{a}{2b} + \frac{2b}{a}\right)^2 - \left(\frac{2b}{a} - \frac{a}{2b}\right)^2$.

22. If $a^2 + b^2 = 42$ and $ab = 12$, then find
    (i) $3(a + b)^2 + 5(a - b)^2$
    (ii) $7(a - b)^2 - 2(a + b)^2$

23. Simplify $(a + b + c)^2 - (a - b - c)^2$.

24. Simplify $(3x + 2y)^3 + (3x - 2y)^3$.

25. Find the expansion of $(x + y - 1)^3$.

26. If $x - y = 6$ and $xy = 24$, then find the value of $x + y$.

27. If $a + b = 7$ and $ab = 12$, then find the value of $a^2 - ab + b^2$.

28. If $(3a + 4b) = 16$ and $ab = 4$, then find the value of $(9a^2 + 16b^2)$.

29. If $4x^2 + y^2 = 40$ and $xy = 6$, then find the value of $2x + y$.

30. (i) Find the coefficients of x^2 and x in the product of $(x - 1)(x + 3)(x - 4)$.
    (ii) Find the coefficients of x^2 and x in the expansion of $(x - 5)(x + 3)(x + 7)$.

31. If $x + 2y = 5$, then prove that
$$x^3 + 8y^3 + 30xy = 125$$

32. If $(a + 2b) = 6$, then show that
$$a^3 + 8b^3 + 36ab = 216$$

33. If $x = 2y + 6$, then find the value of
$$x^3 - 8y^3 - 36xy = 216$$

34. Simplify : $\dfrac{(x^2 - y^2)^3 + (y^2 - z^2)^3 + (z^2 - x^2)^3}{(x - y)^3 + (y - z)^3 + (z - x)^3}$.

35. Without actually calculating the cubes, find the value of $(15)^3 + (-10)^3 - (-5)^3$.

36. If $a = 2$, $b = 8$ and $c = 8$, then find the value of $\dfrac{ab + bc + ca - a^2 - b^2 - c^2}{3abc - a^3 - b^3 - c^3}$, using suitable identity.

37. If $a^2 + b^2 + c^2 - ab - bc - ca = 0$, prove that $a = b = c$.

38. If $3x - 2y = 5$ and $xy = 6$, then find the value of $27x^3 - 8y^3$.

39. If $2x - 3y = 10$ and $xy = 10$, then find the value of $8x^3 - 27y^3$.

40. If $x + \dfrac{1}{x} = 4$, then find the value of $x^3 + \dfrac{1}{x^3}$.

41. If $a + \dfrac{1}{a} = b$ and $a \neq 0$, then show that
$a^3 + \dfrac{1}{a^3} = b(b^2 - 3)$.

42. If $a + b + c = 12$ and $a^2 + b^2 + c^2 = 100$, then find $ab + bc + ca$.

43. If $a^2 + b^2 + c^2 = 50$ and $ab + bc + ca = 47$, then find $a + b + c$.

44. If $a^2 + b^2 + c^2 = 250$ and $ab + bc + ca = 3$, then find $a + b + c$.

45. If $x + y - z = 4$ and $x^2 + y^2 + z^2 = 38$, then find the value of $xy - yz - zx$.

46. If $3(x^2 + 1) = 10x$, where $x > 1$, then find

(i) $x - \dfrac{1}{x}$ (ii) $x^3 - \dfrac{1}{x^3}$

47. If $a = \dfrac{1}{a - 5}$, where $a \neq 5$ and $a \neq 0$, then find the values of

(i) $a - \dfrac{1}{a}$ (ii) $a + \dfrac{1}{a}$

48. If $x \neq 0$ and $x + \dfrac{1}{x} = 2$, then show that
$$x^2 + \frac{1}{x^2} = x^3 + \frac{1}{x^3} = x^4 + \frac{1}{x^4}$$

49. If $a^2 + \dfrac{1}{a^2} = 66$, then find the values of

(i) $a - \dfrac{1}{a}$ (ii) $a^3 - \dfrac{1}{a^3}$

50. If $\left(a^2 + \dfrac{1}{a^2}\right) = 20$, then find the values of

(i) $a + \dfrac{1}{a}$ (ii) $a^3 + \dfrac{1}{a^3}$

51. If $x > 0$ and $x^2 + \dfrac{1}{9x^2} = \dfrac{25}{36}$, then find $x^3 + \dfrac{1}{27x^3}$.

52. If $x^2 + \dfrac{1}{25x^2} = 8\dfrac{3}{5}$, then find the value of $x^3 + \dfrac{1}{125x^3}$.

53. If $x^4 + \dfrac{1}{x^4} = 47$, where $x > 0$, then prove that $x^3 + \dfrac{1}{x^3} = 18$.

54. If $a + b = 10$ and $a^2 + b^2 = 58$, then find the value of $a^3 + b^3$.

55. If $x = 7 + 4\sqrt{3}$, then find the value of $\sqrt{x} + \dfrac{1}{\sqrt{x}}$.

56. If $x = 3 + 2\sqrt{2}$, then find the value of $x^3 - \dfrac{1}{x^3}$.

57. If $x = 5 - 2\sqrt{6}$, then find the value of $x^3 - \dfrac{1}{x^3}$.

58. Find the coefficient of x^4 in the expansion of $(x^2 + x + 1)^2 + (x^2 - x + 1)^2$.

59. Find the coefficient of x^2 in the expansion of $(x^2 + 2x + 3)^2 + (x^2 - 2x + 3)^2$.

60. If the number x is 2 more than the number y and the sum of the squares of x and y is 34, then find the product of x and y.

61. If the number p is 7 more than the number q and the sum of the squares of p and q is 85, then find the product of p and q.

62. The sum of two numbers is 9 and their product is 20. Find the sum of their

(i) squares
(ii) cubes

63. If the sum of two numbers is 7 and the sum of their cubes is 133, then find the sum of their squares.

64. (i) If $a^2 + b^2 + c^2 = 29$ and $a + b + c = 9$, find $ab + bc + ca$.

(ii) If $a + b - c = 4$ and $a^2 + b^2 + c^2 = 38$, find $ab - bc - ca$.

(iii) If $a - b - c = 3$ and $a^2 + b^2 + c^2 = 77$, find $ab - bc + ca$.

Hints and Answers

1. (d) **2.** (c) **3.** (a)

4. (c) **5.** (b) **6.** (d)

7. (i) **Hint** Do same as Example 1 (ii).
Ans. $4x^2 + 16y^4 + 16xy^2$

(ii) **Hint** Do same as Example 1 (i).
Ans. $9a^2 + 25a^2b^2 - 30a^2b$

8. (i) **Hint** Do same as Example 1 (ii).
Ans. $9x^4y^2 + 25z^2 + 30x^2yz$

(ii) **Hint** Do same as Example 2.
Ans. $\frac{1}{4}x^2 + \frac{4}{9}y^2 + \frac{2}{3}xy$

9. (i) **Hint** Do same as Example 1.
Ans. $9x^2 + 16y^2 - 24xy$

(ii) **Hint** Do same as Example 2.
Ans. $\frac{9}{4}a^2 - 2\frac{a}{b} + \frac{4}{9b^2}$

10. (i) **Hint** $(102)^2 = (100 + 2)^2$ **Ans.** 10404

(ii) **Hint** $(10.2)^2 = (10 + 0.2)^2$ **Ans.** 104.04

(iii) **Hint** Do same as part (ii). **Ans.** 106.09

11. (i) **Hint** Do same as Example 4 (i).
Ans. 1006009

(ii) **Hint** Do same as Example 4 (ii).
Ans. 996004

12. **Hint** (i) $(9.2)^2 = (10 - 0.8)^2$
(ii) $(6.1)^2 = (6 + 0.1)^2$

Ans.
(i) 84.64 (ii) 37.21

13. (i) **Hint** Do same as Example 8 (i).
Ans. $x^2 + 16x + 63$

(ii) **Hint** $(x + 2y)(x + 3y)$
$= (x)^2 + (2y + 3y)x + (2y)(3y)$
Ans. $x^2 + 5xy + 6y^2$

(iii) **Hint** Do same as part (ii).
Ans. $x^2 - 3xy - 40y^2$

14. (i) **Hint** Do same as Example 8 (iv).
Ans. $x^2 - 9x + 20$

(ii) **Hint** $(x - 3y)(x - 5y)$
$x(x - 5y) - 3y(x - 5y)$
Ans. $x^2 - 8xy + 15y^2$

15. **Hint** Use the identity,
(i) $(a + b + c)^2 = a^2 + b^2 + c^2 + 2ab + 2bc + 2ca$
Ans. $81x^2 + 4y^2 + z^2 + 36xy + 4yz + 18xz$

(ii) **Hint** Use the identity,
$(a + b - c)^2 = a^2 + b^2 + c^2 + 2ab - 2bc - 2ca.$
Ans. $4x^2 + 9y^2 + 25z^2 + 12xy - 30yz - 20xz$

(iii) **Hint** Write $(-x + 2y + z)^2$
$= [-(x - 2y - z)]^2 = (x - 2y - z)^2$
Use the identity,
$(a - b - c)^2 = a^2 + b^2 + c^2 - 2ab + 2bc - 2ca$
Ans. $x^2 + 4y^2 + z^2 - 4xy + 4yz - 2xz$

(iv) **Hint** Use the identity, $(a + b - c)^2$
$= a^2 + b^2 + c^2 + 2ab - 2bc - 2ca$
Ans. $\frac{4}{25}x^2 + \frac{9}{16}y^2 + \frac{16}{49}z^2 + \frac{3}{5}xy - \frac{6}{7}yz - \frac{16}{35}zx$

16. (i) **Hint** Do same as Example 12 (i).
Ans. $8a^3 + b^3 + 12a^2b + 6ab^2$

(ii) Do same as Example 12 (ii).
Ans. $27x^3 - 64y^3 - 108x^2y + 144xy^2$

(iii) **Hint** Use the identity,
$(a - b)^3 = a^3 - b^3 - 3ab(a - b)$
Ans. $x^3 - \frac{8}{27}y^3 - 2x^2y + \frac{4}{3}xy^2$

(iv) **Hint** Use the identity,
$(a - b)^3 = a^3 - b^3 - 3ab(a - b)$
and $(a + b)^3 = a^3 + b^3 + 3ab(a + b)$
Ans. $\frac{-16}{27y^3} - \frac{4x^2}{y}$

17. **Hint** Write $(98)^3 = (100 - 2)^3$.
Use the identity,
$(a - b)^3 = a^3 - b^3 - 3ab(a - b)$
Ans. 941192

18. **Hint** Do same as Example 3.
Ans. $b = 9$

19. **Hint** Write $95 \times 96 = (100 - 5)(100 - 4)$
Use the identity, $(x - a)(x - b)$
$= x^2 - (a + b)x + ab.$
Ans. 9120

20. **Hint** Do same as Example 6.
Ans. (i) 23 (ii) 527

21. **Hint** Given, expression can be rewritten as
$$\left(\frac{a}{2b} + \frac{2b}{a}\right)^2 - \left\{-\left(\frac{a}{2b} - \frac{2b}{a}\right)\right\}^2$$
$$= \left(\frac{a}{2b} + \frac{2b}{a}\right)^2 - \left(\frac{a}{2b} - \frac{2b}{a}\right)^2$$
Use the identity, $(a + b)(a - b) = a^2 - b^2$.
Ans. 4

22. **Hint** Using the identities,
$(a + b)^2 = a^2 + b^2 + 2ab$
and $(a - b)^2 = a^2 + b^2 - 2ab$
Ans. (i) 288 (ii) – 6

23. **Hint** Do same as Example 11.
Ans. $4a(b + c)$

24. **Hint** Do same as Example 13.
Ans. $54x^3 + 72xy^2$

25. **Hint** $(x + y - 1)^3 = [(x + y) - 1]^3$

$$= (x + y)^3 - (1)^3 - 3(x + y)(1)[(x + y) - 1]$$
$$= (x + y)^3 - 1 - 3(x + y)[(x + y) - 1]$$

Ans. $x^3 + y^3 + 3x^2y + 3xy^2 - 3x^2 - 6xy - 3y^2 + 3x + 3y - 1$

26. **Hint** Consider, $(x + y)^2 = (x - y)^2 + 4xy$.
Ans. 132

27. **Hint** Write $a^2 - ab + b^2 = (a + b)^2 - 3ab$.
Ans. 13

28. **Hint** $(3a + 4b)^2 = 9a^2 + 16b^2 + 24ab$ **Ans.** 160

29. **Hint** $(2x + y)^2 = 4x^2 + y^2 + 4xy$. **Ans.** ± 8

30. (i) Do same as Example 7.
Ans. $-2, -11$
(ii) Do same as Example 7. **Ans.** $5, -29$

31. **Hint** Use the identity,
$$(a + b)^3 = a^3 + b^3 + 3ab(a + b).$$

32. Do same as Q. 31.

33. Do same as Q. 31.

34. Use the identity, if $a + b + c = 0$
Then $a^3 + b^3 + c^3 = 3abc$
So, $x - y + y - z + z - x = 0$
Ans. $(x + y)(y + z)(z + x)$

35. **Hint** Use the identity, if $x + y + z = 0$, then $x^3 + y^3 + z^3 = 3xyz$
Ans. 2250

36. **Hint** Use the identity,
$a^3 + b^3 + c^3 - 3abc = (a + b + c)$
$(a^2 + b^2 + c^2 - ab - bc - ca)$
Ans. $\frac{1}{18}$

37. **Hint** $a^2 + b^2 + c^2 - ab - bc - ca = 0$
Multiply by 2 on both sides, we get
$(a - b)^2 + (b - c)^2 + (c - a)^2 = 0$
$(a - b)^2 = 0, (b - c)^2 = 0, (c - a)^2 = 0$

38. Do same as Example 25. **Ans.** 665

39. Do same as Example 25. **Ans.** 2800

40. **Hint** Cubing both sides and use the identity,
$$(a + b)^3 = a^3 + b^3 + 3ab(a + b)$$
Ans. 52

41. Do same as Q. 40.

42. **Hint** Use the identity,
$$(a + b + c)^2 = a^2 + b^2 + c^2 + 2(ab + bc + ca)$$
Ans. 22

43. **Hint** Use the identity,
$$(a + b + c)^2 = a^2 + b^2 + c^2 + 2(ab + bc + ca)$$
Ans. ± 12

44. Do same as Q. 43.
Ans. ± 16

45. **Hint** Use the identity,
$$(x + y - z)^2 = x^2 + y^2 + z^2 + 2(xy - yz - zx)$$
Ans. -11

46. (i) **Hint** $x + \frac{1}{x} = \frac{10}{3}$

Now, $x - \frac{1}{x} = \sqrt{\left(x + \frac{1}{x}\right)^2 - 4}$

Ans. $\pm \frac{8}{3}$

(ii) **Hint** $x^3 - \frac{1}{x^3} = \left(x - \frac{1}{x}\right)^3 + 3\left(x - \frac{1}{x}\right)$

Ans. $\frac{728}{27}$

47. **Hint** (i) $a = \frac{1}{a - 5} \Rightarrow \frac{1}{a} = a - 5 \Rightarrow a - \frac{1}{a} = 5$

Ans. (i) 5

(ii) **Hint** $a + \frac{1}{a} = \sqrt{\left(a - \frac{1}{a}\right)^2 + 4}$

Ans. $\pm\sqrt{29}$

48. **Hint** Squaring both sides of $x + \frac{1}{x} = 2$, we get

$$x^2 + \frac{1}{x^2} = 2$$

and cubing both sides of $x + \frac{1}{x} = 2$, we get

$$x^3 + \frac{1}{x^3} = 2$$

Again, squaring both sides of $x^2 + \frac{1}{x^2} = 2$, we get

$$x^4 + \frac{1}{x^4} = 2$$

So, $x^2 + \frac{1}{x^2} = x^3 + \frac{1}{x^3} = x^4 + \frac{1}{x^4}$

49. (i) **Hint** $\left(a - \frac{1}{a}\right)^2 = a^2 + \frac{1}{a^2} - 2$. **Ans.** ± 8

(ii) **Hint** $\left(a^3 - \frac{1}{a^3}\right) = \left(a - \frac{1}{a}\right)^3 + 3\left(a - \frac{1}{a}\right)$

Ans. ± 536

50. (i) **Hint** $\left(a + \frac{1}{a}\right)^2 = a^2 + \frac{1}{a^2} + 2$

Ans. $\pm\sqrt{22}$

(ii) **Hint** $a^3 + \frac{1}{a^3} = \left(a + \frac{1}{a}\right)^3 - 3\left(a + \frac{1}{a}\right)$

Ans. $\pm 19\sqrt{22}$

51. Hint $\because \left(x+\frac{1}{3x}\right)^2 = x^2 + \frac{1}{9x^2} + \frac{2}{3}$

Now, $x^3 + \frac{1}{27x^3} = x^3 + \left(\frac{1}{3x}\right)^3$

$= \left(x+\frac{1}{3x}\right)^3 - \left(x+\frac{1}{3x}\right)$

Ans. $\pm\frac{91}{216}$

52. Do same as Q. 51. **Ans.** $\pm 25\frac{1}{5}$

53. Hint Use the identity $\left(x^2+\frac{1}{x^2}\right)^2 = x^4 + \frac{1}{x^4} + 2$, and we get the value of $x^2 + \frac{1}{x^2} = \pm 7$

Again the identity use the identity

$\left(x+\frac{1}{x}\right)^2 = x^2 + \frac{1}{x^2} + 2$, then we get the value of $x + \frac{1}{x} = 3$.

Now, use the identity,

$$a^3 + b^3 = (a+b)^3 - 3ab\,(a+b)$$

54. Hint Use the identity $a^2 + b^2 = (a+b)^2 - 2ab$ and find value of ab.

Then, use the identity,

$$a^3 + b^3 = (a+b)^3 - 3ab(a+b).$$

Ans. 370

55. Hint $\frac{1}{x} = \frac{1}{7+4\sqrt{3}} = \frac{7-4\sqrt{3}}{(7)^2-(4\sqrt{3})^2} = 7-4\sqrt{3}$

Thus, $x + \frac{1}{x} = 14$

$\Rightarrow (\sqrt{x})^2 + \left(\frac{1}{\sqrt{x}}\right)^2 = 14$

$\Rightarrow \left(\sqrt{x}+\frac{1}{\sqrt{x}}\right)^2 = 14 + 2$

Ans. ± 4

56. Hint Do same as Q. 55 and $x - \frac{1}{x} = 4\sqrt{2}$.

Ans. $140\sqrt{2}$

57. Hint Do same as Q. 55 and $x - \frac{1}{x} = -4\sqrt{6}$.

Ans. $-396\sqrt{6}$

58. Use identity

$(a+b+c)^2 = a^2 + b^2 + c^2 + 2(ab + bc + ca)$

Ans. 2

59. Do same as Q. 58. **Ans.** 20

60. Hint Given, $x = 2 + y$ and $x^2 + y^2 = 34$

$\because \quad x = 2 + y$

$\therefore \quad (x-y)^2 = 4$

and use the identity, $(a-b)^2 = a^2 + b^2 - 2ab$

Ans. 15

61. Do same as Q. 60.

Ans. 18.

62. Hint Let $x + y = 9$ and $xy = 20$

(i) $x^2 + y^2 = (x+y)^2 - 2xy$

(ii) $x^3 + y^3 = (x+y)^3 - 3xy(x+y)$

Ans. (i) 41 (ii) 189

63. Hint Let $x + y = 7$ and $x^3 + y^3 = 133$.

Then, use $(x+y)^3 = x^3 + y^3 + 3xy\,(x+y)$

Finally, use the identity,

$$a^2 + b^2 = (a+b)^2 - 2ab.$$

Ans. 29

64. Hint Use identity

$(a+b+c)^2 = a^2 + b^2 + c^2 + 2(ab + bc + ca)$

Ans.

(i) 26

(ii) -11

(iii) 34

Olympiad Section

Brain Teasing Questions of Olympiad Pattern

1 If $x^3 + y^3 + z^3 = 3xyz$, then the relation between x, y and z is

(a) $x = y = z$ (b) $x > y > z$
(c) $x < y = z$ (d) $x < y > z$

2 If $x^{1/3} + y^{1/3} + z^{1/3} = 0$, then the value of $(x + y + z)^3$ is

(a) $22xyz$ (b) $23xyz$
(c) $27xyz$ (d) $24xyz$

3 If $a^{1/2} + b^{1/2} - c^{1/2} = 0$, then the value of $(a + b - c)^2$ is

(a) $5ab$ (b) $4ab$
(c) $6ab$ (d) $7ab$

4 If $p = 2 - a$, then the value of $a^3 + 6ap + p^3 - 8$ is

(a) 1 (b) 2
(c) 4 (d) 0

5 $(3a + 2b - c + d)^2 - 12a(2b - c + d)$ is a

(a) perfect square
(b) not perfect square
(c) cube root
(d) None of the above

6 If $a + b + c = 15$ and $a^2 + b^2 + c^2 = 83$, then find the value of $a^3 + b^3 + c^3 - 3abc$.

(a) 180 (b) 170
(c) 160 (d) 190

7 If $\frac{x^2+1}{x} = 2\frac{1}{2}$, then the value of $x^3 - \frac{1}{x^3}$ is

(a) $-7\frac{7}{8}$ (b) $\frac{1}{2}$
(c) $\frac{4}{5}$ (d) None of these

8 If $x - y + z = 4$ and $x^2 + y^2 + z^2 = 38$, then the value of $xy + yz - xz$ is

(a) 11 (b) -21
(c) -44 (d) 45

9 If $a + b + c = 2$, $ab + bc + ca = -1$ and $abc = -2$, then the value of $a^3 + b^3 + c^3$ is

(a) 7 (b) 6
(c) 8 (d) 9

10 If $a^2 + 4b^2 + 25c^2 = 2ab + 10bc + 5ca$, then

(a) $a = 2b = 5c$ (b) $a > 2b = 5c$
(c) $a < 2b = 5c$ (d) None of these

Answers

1. (a) **2.** (c) **3.** (b) **4.** (d) **5.** (a) **6.** (a) **7.** (a) **8.** (a) **9.** (c) **10.** (a)

* *These questions may or may not be asked in the examination, have been given just for additional practice required for olympiads Scholarship Exams etc. For detailed explanations refer Page No. 335.*

CHAPTER

04

Factorisation

SYLLABUS

- Factorisation $a^2 - b^2$, $a^3 \pm b^3$, $a^2 + bx + c$, by splitting the middle term.

The process of expressing an algebraic expression as the product of two or more algebraic expressions is called factorisation, these expressions are called factors of given algebraic expression.

In this chapter, we will study the methods of expressing an algebraic expression as the product of its factors.

Factorisation by Taking Out Common Factors

If various terms of an expression have common factors, then the given expression can be factorised by dividing the each term of expression by the common factor and expression is shown as the product of common term and remaining expression (enclosed in bracket).

Example 1. Factorise the following :

(i) $7x - 42$ (ii) $-16z + 20z^3$

(iii) $10a^2 - 15b^2 + 20c^2$ (iv) $20l^2m + 30alm$

(v) $x^2yz + xy^2z + xyz^2$

Sol.

(i) $7x - 42$

In the given expression, we see that each term can be divided by 7. So, 7 is the common term.

$$7x - 42 = 7\left(\frac{7x}{7} - \frac{42}{7}\right) = 7(x - 6),$$

which is the required factorisation of the given expression.

(ii) $-16z + 20z^3$

In the given expression, we can see that each term can be divided by $4z$. So, $4z$ is the common term.

$$-16z + 20z^3 = 4z\left(\frac{-16z}{4z} + \frac{20z^3}{4z}\right)$$

$$= 4z(-4 + 5z^2),$$

which is the required factorisation of the given expression.

(iii) $10a^2 - 15b^2 + 20c^2$

In the given expression, we can see that each term can be divided by 5. So, 5 is the common term.

$$10a^2 - 15b^2 + 20c^2 = 5\left(\frac{10a^2}{5} - \frac{15b^2}{5} + \frac{20c^2}{5}\right)$$

$$= 5(2a^2 - 3b^2 + 4c^2),$$

which is the required factorisation of the given expression.

(iv) $20l^2m + 30alm$

In the given expression, we can see that each term can be divided by $10lm$. So, $10lm$ is common term.

$$20l^2m + 30alm = 10lm\left(\frac{20l^2m}{10lm} + \frac{30alm}{10lm}\right)$$

$$= 10lm(2l + 3a),$$

which is the required factorisation of the given expression.

(v) $x^2yz + xy^2z + xyz^2$

In the given expression, we can see that each term can be divided by xyz. So, xyz is common term.

$$x^2yz + xy^2z + xyz^2 = xyz\left(\frac{x^2yz}{xyz} + \frac{xy^2z}{xyz} + \frac{xyz^2}{xyz}\right)$$

$$= xyz(x + y + z),$$

which is the required factorisation of the given expression.

Example 2. Factorise $27a^3b^3 - 18a^2b^3 + 75a^3b^2$.

Sol. In the given expression, we can see that each term can be divided by $3a^2b^2$. So, $3a^2b^2$ is the common term.

$$27a^3b^3 - 18a^2b^3 + 75a^3b^2 = 3a^2b^2\left(\frac{27a^3b^3}{3a^2b^2} - \frac{18a^2b^3}{3a^2b^2} + \frac{75a^3b^2}{3a^2b^2}\right)$$
$$= 3a^2b^2\,(9ab - 6b + 25a),$$

which is the required factorisation of the given expression.

Note Generally, we take that term as common term, which has least power in the given expression.

Example 3. Factorise $18x^3y - 45x^2yz + 63x^3yz^2$.

Sol. In the given expression, we see that each term can be divided by $9x^2y$. So, $9x^2y$ is the common term.

$$18x^3y - 45x^2yz + 63x^3yz^2 = 9x^2y\left(\frac{18x^3y}{9x^2y} - \frac{45x^2yz}{9x^2y} + \frac{63x^3yz^2}{9x^2y}\right)$$
$$= 9x^2y\,(2x - 5z + 7xz^2),$$

which is the required factorisation of the given expression.

Example 4. Factorise

$$10x\,(x + 2y)^3 - 15y\,(x + 2y)^2 + 35\,(x + 2y).$$

Sol. In the given expression, we see that each term can be divided by $5\,(x + 2y)$. So, $5(x + 2y)$ is the common term.

$$5(x + 2y)\left[\frac{10x\,(x + 2y)^3}{5(x + 2y)} - \frac{15y\,(x + 2y)^2}{5(x + 2y)} + \frac{35\,(x + 2y)}{5(x + 2y)}\right]$$
$$= 5\,(x + 2y)\,[2x(x + 2y)^2 - 3y\,(x + 2y) + 7],$$

which is the required factorisation of the given expression.

Factorisation by Grouping of Terms

Sometimes all the terms in the given expression do not have common factor but different terms can be grouped in such a way that each group has a common factor. In this way, we find a common factor across all the groups and factorise the given expression.

Example 5. Factorise $px - qy + qx - py$.

Sol. We have, $px - qy + qx - py$

$$= px + qx - qy - py$$
$$= (p + q)x - (q + p)y$$
$$= (p + q)x - (p + q)y$$

Now, $(p + q)$, is common factor across in both groups.

So, $(p + q)\,(x - y)$ which is the required factorisation of the given expression.

Example 6. Factorise $a^3 - 4a^2 + 3a - 12$.

Sol. Here, first two terms have a^2 as common factor and last two terms have 3 as common factor.

$\therefore \quad a^3 - 4a^2 + 3a - 12 = a^2(a - 4) + 3(a - 4).$

Now, we see that $(a - 4)$ is common factor in both groups.

So, $\quad a^3 - 4a^2 + 3a - 12 = (a - 4)(a^2 + 3).$

Example 7. Factorise $pq^2 - 4pq + 4q - 16$

Sol. Here, first two terms have pq as common factor and last two terms have 4 as common factor.

$$pq^2 - 4pq + 4q - 16 = pq(q - 4) + 4(q - 4)$$

Now, $(q - 4)$ is common factor in both groups

So, $pq^2 - 4pq + 4q - 16 = (pq + 4)\,(q - 4)$

Example 8. Factorise $l(x - y)^2 + (mx - my) + 5x - 5y$.

Sol. We have, $l(x - y)^2 + (mx - my) + (5x - 5y)$

$$= l(x - y)^2 + m(x - y) + 5(x - y)$$

Now, $(x - y)$ is common factor across all the groups.

So, $l(x - y)^2 + (mx - my) + (5x - 5y) = (x - y)[l(x - y) + m + 5]$

which is the required factorisation of the given expression.

Example 9. Factorise $xy\,(a^2 - b^2) + ab\,(x^2 - y^2)$.

Sol. We have, $xy\,(a^2 - b^2) + ab(x^2 - y^2)$

$$= xya^2 - xyb^2 + abx^2 - aby^2$$
$$= xya^2 + abx^2 - aby^2 - xyb^2$$
$$= ax(ay + bx) - by(ay + bx)$$

Now, $(ay + bx)$ is common factor for each group, so

$xy(a^2 - b^2) + ab(x^2 - y^2) = (ay + bx)(ax - by)$ which is the required factorisation of given expression.

Example 10. Factorise

$3ax - 6ay - 8by + 4bx + 9az + 12bz.$

Sol. We have, $3ax - 6ay - 8by + 4bx + 9az + 12bz$

Now, arranging the given expression into groups,

$$= (3ax + 4bx) - 6ay - 8by + 9az + 12bz$$
$$= (3ax + 4bx) - (6ay + 8by) + (9az + 12bz)$$
$$= x(3a + 4b) - 2y(3a + 4b) + 3z(3a + 4b)$$

Now, $(3a + 4b)$ is common factor for each group, so

$3ax - 6ay - 8by + 4bx + 9az + 12bz = (3a + 4b)\,(x - 2y + 3z)$

which is the required factorisation of the given expression.

Factorisation by Making the Perfect Square

Sometimes a given expression can be written as the perfect square of combination of two or more terms. In this case, the given expression can be expressed as the product of terms involved in perfect square.

(i) $(a + b)^2 = a^2 + 2ab + b^2$

(ii) $(a - b)^2 = a^2 - 2ab + b^2$

Example 11. Factorise $9x^2 + 12xy + 4y^2$.

Sol. We have, $9x^2 + 12xy + 4y^2$

Given, expression can be rewritten as

$$(3x)^2 + 2\cdot 3x\cdot 2y + (2y)^2$$

Now, take $3x = a$ and $2y = b$, then the expression becomes
$$a^2 + 2ab + b^2 = (a + b)^2$$
Hence, the expression becomes $(3x + 2y)^2$.
So, the required factors are $(3x + 2y)$ and $(3x + 2y)$.

Example 12. Factorise $49y^2 + 84yz + 36z^2$.

Sol. We have, $49y^2 + 84yz + 36z^2 = (7y)^2 + 2\cdot(7y)\cdot(6z) + (6z)^2$

Now, take $7y = a$ and $6z = b$, then the expression becomes
$$a^2 + 2ab + b^2 = (a + b)^2.$$
Hence, the expression becomes $(7y + 6z)^2$.
So, the required factors are $(7y + 6z)$ and $(7y + 6z)$.

Example 13. Find the factors of $121b^2 - 88bc + 16c^2$.

Sol. We have, $121b^2 - 88bc + 16c^2 = (11b)^2 - 2\cdot(11b)(4c) + (4c)^2$

Now, take $11b = A$ and $4c = B$, then the expression becomes $A^2 - 2AB + B^2 = (A - B)^2$.
Hence, the expression becomes $(11b - 4c)^2$.
So, the required factors are $(11b - 4c)$ and $(11b - 4c)$.

Factorisation of Difference of Two Squares

If the given expression is expressible as the difference of two squares, we use the following identity to factorise it.
$$a^2 - b^2 = (a + b)(a - b)$$

Example 14. Factorise $4x^2 - 169y^2$.

Sol. We have, $4x^2 - 169y^2 = (2x)^2 - (13y)^2$

$\therefore \quad (2x)^2 - (13y)^2 = (2x + 13y)(2x - 13y)$
$[\because a^2 - b^2 = (a + b)(a - b)]$

which is the required factorisation of the given expression.

Example 15. Factorise $x^4 - 81y^4$.

Sol. We have, $x^4 - 81y^4 = (x^2)^2 - (9y^2)^2$

$\because \quad a^2 - b^2 = (a + b)(a - b)$

$\therefore \quad (x^2)^2 - (9y^2)^2 = (x^2 + 9y^2)(x^2 - 9y^2)$

We see that $x^2 - 9y^2$ is again expressed as a difference of two squares.

$\therefore \quad (x^2 + 9y^2)(x^2 - 9y^2) = (x^2 + 9y^2)[(x)^2 - (3y)^2]$
$= (x^2 + 9y^2)(x + 3y)(x - 3y) [\because a^2 - b^2 = (a + b)(a - b)]$

which is the required factorisation of the given expression.

Example 16. Factorise $x^8 - 256$.

Sol. We have, $x^8 - 256 = (x^4)^2 - (16)^2$

$= (x^4 + 16)(x^4 - 16) \quad [\because a^2 - b^2 = (a + b)(a - b)]$
$= (x^4 + 16)[(x^2)^2 - 4^2]$
$= (x^4 + 16)(x^2 + 4)(x^2 - 4) \quad [\because a^2 - b^2 = (a + b)(a - b)]$
$= (x^4 + 16)(x^2 + 4)[(x)^2 - (2)^2]$
$= (x^4 + 16)(x^2 + 4)(x - 2)(x + 2) \quad [\because a^2 - b^2 = (a + b)(a - b)]$

which is the required factorisation of the given expression.

Example 17. Factorise $1 - (p + q)^2$

Sol. We have, $1 - (p + q)^2$

$= 1^2 - (p + q)^2$
$= [1 - (p + q)][1 + (p + q)] \quad [\because a^2 - b^2 = (a - b)(a + b)]$

$\therefore 1 - (p + q)^2 = (1 - p - q)(1 + p + q)$

which is the required factorisation of the given expression.

Example 18. Factorise $5x^3 - 125x$.

Sol. We have, $5x^3 - 125x$

$= 5x(x^2 - 25)$
$= 5x(x^2 - 5^2)$
$= 5x(x - 5)(x + 5) \quad [\because a^2 - b^2 = (a + b)(a - b)]$

So, $5x^3 - 125x = 5x(x - 5)(x + 5)$

which is the required factorisation of the given expression.

Example 19. Factorise $a^2 - 3b + ab - 9$.

Sol. We have, $a^2 - 3b + ab - 9$

$= a^2 - 9 + ab - 3b = a^2 - 3^2 + b(a - 3)$
$= (a - 3)(a + 3) + b(a - 3) \quad [\because a^2 - b^2 = (a + b)(a - b)]$

Now, $(a - 3)$ is common factor in both groups

$\therefore \quad a^2 - 3b + ab - 9 = (a - 3)(a + 3 + b)$

which is the required factorisation of the given expression.

Example 20. Factorise $2(ab + cd) - a^2 - b^2 + c^2 + d^2$.

Sol. We have, $2(ab + cd) - a^2 - b^2 + c^2 + d^2$

$= 2ab + 2cd - a^2 - b^2 + c^2 + d^2$
$= (c^2 + d^2 + 2cd) - (a^2 + b^2 - 2ab)$
$= (c + d)^2 - (a - b)^2$
$[\because A^2 + 2AB + B^2 = (A + B)^2 \text{ and } A^2 - 2AB + B^2 = (A - B)^2]$
$= (c + d + a - b)(c + d - a + b) \quad [\because A^2 - B^2 = (A + B)(A - B)]$

which is the required factorisation of the given expression.

Factorisation of Sum and Difference of Two Cubes

The sum and difference of two cubes can be factorised by using the following formulae

(i) $a^3 + b^3 = (a + b)(a^2 - ab + b^2)$.

(ii) $a^3 - b^3 = (a - b)(a^2 + ab + b^2)$.

Example 21. Factorise $a^6 + 512b^6$.

Sol. We have, $a^6 + 512b^6 = (a^2)^3 + (8b^2)^3$

$\because \quad A^3 + B^3 = (A + B)(A^2 - AB + B^2)$

$\therefore \quad a^6 + 512b^6 = (a^2 + 8b^2)[(a^2)^2 - a^2 \times 8b^2 + (8b^2)^2]$
$= (a^2 + 8b^2)(a^4 - 8a^2b^2 + 64b^4)$

which is the required factorisation of the given expression.

Example 22. Factorise $8x^3 - (3x-4y)^3$.

Sol. We have, $8x^3 - (3x-4y)^3 = (2x)^3 - (3x-4y)^3$

$\therefore \quad (2x)^3 - (3x-4y)^3 = [2x - (3x-4y)]$
$[(2x)^2 + 2x(3x-4y) + (3x-4y)^2]$
$[\because a^3 - b^3 = (a-b)(a^2+ab+b^2)]$

$= (2x - 3x + 4y)\ [4x^2 + 6x^2 - 8xy + 9x^2 + 16y^2 - 24xy]$
$[\because (a-b)^2 = a^2 - 2ab + b^2]$

$= (4y - x)(19x^2 - 32xy + 16y^2)$

which is the required factorisation of the given expression.

Example 23. Factorise $8(x+y)^3 - 27(x-y)^3$.

Sol. Let $x + y = a$ and $x - y = b$. Then, the given expression reduces to $8a^3 - 27b^3$ and it can be rewritten as $(2a)^3 - (3b)^3$.

So, factorise it by using formula

$A^3 - B^3 = (A-B)(A^2 + AB + B^2)$, we get

$(2a)^3 - (3b)^3 = (2a - 3b)(4a^2 + 6ab + 9b^2)$ ...(i)

Now, substituting the values of a and b in Eq. (i), we get

$8(x+y)^3 - 27(x-y)^3 = [2(x+y) - 3(x-y)] \times [4(x+y)^2 + 6(x+y)(x-y) + 9(x-y)^2]$

$= (2x + 2y - 3x + 3y)$
$[4(x^2 + 2xy + y^2) + 6(x^2 - y^2) + 9(x^2 - 2xy + y^2)]$
$[\because (A+B)^2 = A^2 + 2AB + B^2, (A-B)^2 = A^2 - 2AB + B^2$ and $(A^2 - B^2) = (A+B)(A-B)]$

$= (-x + 5y)(4x^2 + 8xy + 4y^2 + 6x^2 - 6y^2 + 9x^2 + 9y^2 - 18xy)$

$= (-x + 5y)(19x^2 - 10xy + 7y^2)$

which is the required factorisation of the given expression.

Example 24. Factorise $a^3 - 27b^3 + 2a^2b - 6ab^2$.

Sol. We have, $a^3 - 27b^3 + 2a^2b - 6ab^2$

$= (a)^3 - (3b)^3 + 2ab(a - 3b)$

$= (a - 3b)(a^2 + 9b^2 + 3ab) + 2ab(a - 3b)$
$[\because x^3 - y^3 = (x-y)(x^2 + xy + y^2)]$

$= (a - 3b)(a^2 + 3ab + 9b^2 + 2ab)$ [taking $(a - 3b)$ common]

$= (a - 3b)(a^2 + 5ab + 9b^2)$

which is the required factorisation of the given expression.

Example 25. Factorise $x^3 - 3x^2y + 3xy^2 - 2y^3$.

Sol. We have, $x^3 - 3x^2y + 3xy^2 - 2y^3$

$= x^3 - 3x^2y + 3xy^2 - y^3 - y^3$

$= (x-y)^3 - y^3 \quad [\because (a-b)^3 = a^3 - 3a^2b + 3ab^2 - b^3]$

On putting $x - y = p$, we get

$p^3 - y^3 = (p - y)(p^2 + py + y^2)$
$[\because (a^3 - b^3) = (a-b)(a^2 + ab + b^2)]$

On replacing p by $x - y$, we get

$(x - y - y)[(x-y)^2 + (x-y)y + y^2]$

$= (x - 2y)[x^2 + y^2 - 2xy + xy - y^2 + y^2]$

$= (x - 2y)[x^2 - xy + y^2]$

which is the required factorisation of the given expression.

Example 26. Factorise $\dfrac{x^6}{343} + \dfrac{343}{x^6}$.

Sol. We have, $\dfrac{x^6}{343} + \dfrac{343}{x^6} = \left(\dfrac{x^2}{7}\right)^3 + \left(\dfrac{7}{x^2}\right)^3$

$= \left(\dfrac{x^2}{7} + \dfrac{7}{x^2}\right)\left[\left(\dfrac{x^2}{7}\right)^2 - \dfrac{x^2}{7} \times \dfrac{7}{x^2} + \left(\dfrac{7}{x^2}\right)^2\right]$
$[\because a^3 + b^3 = (a+b)(a^2 - ab + b^2)]$

$= \left(\dfrac{x^2}{7} + \dfrac{7}{x^2}\right)\left(\dfrac{x^4}{49} - 1 + \dfrac{49}{x^4}\right)$

which is the required factorisation of the given expression.

Example 27. Factorise $a^{12} - b^{12}$.

Sol. We have, $a^{12} - b^{12} = (a^6)^2 - (b^6)^2 = (a^6 + b^6)(a^6 - b^6)$
$[\because x^2 - y^2 = (x+y)(x-y)]$

$= [(a^2)^3 + (b^2)^3][(a^3)^2 - (b^3)^2]$

$= [(a^2)^3 + (b^2)^3](a^3 - b^3)(a^3 + b^3)$
$[\because x^2 - y^2 = (x+y)(x-y)]$

$= [(a^2 + b^2)(a^4 + b^4 - a^2b^2)][(a-b)(a^2 + ab + b^2)]$
$[(a+b)(a^2 - ab + b^2)]$
$\left[\begin{array}{l}\because x^3 + y^3 = (x+y)(x^2 - xy + y^2) \\ \text{and } x^3 - y^3 = (x-y)(x^2 + xy + y^2)\end{array}\right]$

$= (a+b)(a-b)(a^2 + b^2)(a^2 - ab + b^2)$
$(a^2 + ab + b^2)(a^4 + b^4 - a^2b^2)$

which is the required factorisation of the given expression.

Factorisation of Trinomial by Splitting the Middle Term

A trinomial (expression with three terms) of the form $ax^2 + bx + c$, where $a \neq 0$ and a, b and c are constants, can be factorised splitting the middle term.

To factorise $ax^2 + bx + c$, b is written as the sum of two numbers, whose product is equal to ac and factorisation can be done by grouping the terms.

In case of expression $ax^2 + bx - c$, b is written as the difference of two numbers, whose product is equal to ac.

Example 28. Factorise $6x^2 + 17x + 12$.

Sol. We have, $6x^2 + 17x + 12$

Here, 17 is to be written as sum of two numbers, whose product is $12 \times 6 = 72$.

By hit and trial, we find that such numbers are 9 and 8, whose sum $(9 + 8)$ is 17 and product (9×8) is 72.

$= 6x^2 + (9 + 8)x + 12$ [by splitting the middle term]
$= 6x^2 + 9x + 8x + 12$
$= (6x^2 + 9x) + (8x + 12)$
$= 3x(2x + 3) + 4(2x + 3)$

On taking $(2x + 3)$ common from the above expression, we get

$$6x^2 + 17x + 12 = (2x + 3)(3x + 4)$$

which is the required factorisation of the given expression.

Example 29. Factorise $5x^2 - 32x + 12$.

Sol. We have, $5x^2 - 32x + 12$

Here, 32 is to be written as sum of two numbers, whose product is $12 \times 5 = 60$.

By hit and trial, we find that such numbers are 30 and 2, whose sum $(30 + 2)$ is 32 and product (30×2) is 60.

$= 5x^2 - (30 + 2)x + 12$
[by splitting the middle term]
$= 5x^2 - 30x - 2x + 12$
$= (5x^2 - 30x) - (2x - 12) = 5x(x - 6) - 2(x - 6)$
$= (x - 6)(5x - 2)$

which is the required factorisation of the given expression.

Example 30. Factorise $2x^2 + 5x - 12$.

Sol. We have, $2x^2 + 5x - 12$

Here, 5 is to be written as difference of two numbers, whose product is $12 \times 2 = 24$.

By hit and trial, we find that such numbers are 8 and 3, whose difference $(8 - 3)$ is 5 and product (8×3) is 24.

$= 2x^2 + (8 - 3)x - 12$
[by splitting the middle term]
$= 2x^2 + 8x - 3x - 12 = (2x^2 + 8x) - (3x + 12)$
$= 2x(x + 4) - 3(x + 4) = (x + 4)(2x - 3)$

which is the required factorisation of the given expression.

Example 31. Factorise $(x^2 - 4x)^2 - 8(x^2 - 4x) - 20$.

Sol. We have, $(x^2 - 4x)^2 - 8(x^2 - 4x) - 20$

On putting $x^2 - 4x = y$, we get

$y^2 - 8y - 20 = y^2 + (-10 + 2)y - 20$
[by splitting the middle term]
$= y^2 - 10y + 2y - 20$
$= y(y - 10) + 2(y - 10) = (y - 10)(y + 2)$

On replacing y by $(x^2 - 4x)$, we get

$$(x^2 - 4x - 10)(x^2 - 4x + 2)$$

which is the required factorisation of given expression.

Example 32. Factorise $12(3x - 2y)^2 - 3x + 2y - 1$.

Sol. We have, $12(3x - 2y)^2 - 3x + 2y - 1$

$= 12(3x - 2y)^2 - (3x - 2y) - 1$

On putting $3x - 2y = z$, we get

$12z^2 - z - 1 = 12z^2 + (-4 + 3)z - 1$
[by splitting the middle term]
$= 12z^2 - 4z + 3z - 1$
$= 4z(3z - 1) + 1(3z - 1)$
$= (3z - 1)(4z + 1)$

On replacing z by $(3x - 2y)$, we get

$12(3x - 2y)^2 - 3x + 2y - 1 = [3(3x - 2y) - 1][4(3x - 2y) + 1]$
$= (9x - 6y - 1)(12x - 8y + 1)$

which is the required factorisation of the given expression.

Example 33. Factorise $5 - (3x^2 - 2x)(6 - 3x^2 + 2x)$.

Sol. We have, $5 - (3x^2 - 2x)(6 - 3x^2 + 2x)$

On putting $3x^2 - 2x = y$

Then, the given expression reduces into

$= 5 - y(6 - y) = 5 - 6y + y^2$

Now, splitting the middle term, we get

$y^2 - 6y + 5 = y^2 - (5 + 1)y + 5$
$= y^2 - 5y - y + 5$
$= y(y - 5) - 1(y - 5) = (y - 5)(y - 1)$

On replacing y by $3x^2 - 2x$, we get

$5 - (3x^2 - 2x)(6 - 3x^2 + 2x) = (3x^2 - 2x - 5)(3x^2 - 2x - 1)$

Now, again splitting the middle term, we get

$3x^2 - 2x - 5 = 3x^2 - (5 - 3)x - 5$

and $3x^2 - 2x - 1 = 3x^2 - (3 - 1)x - 1$

$= (3x^2 - 5x + 3x - 5)(3x^2 - 3x + x - 1)$
$= \{x(3x - 5) + 1(3x - 5)\}\{3x(x - 1) + 1(x - 1)\}$
$= (3x - 5)(x + 1)(x - 1)(3x + 1)$

which is the required factorisation of the given expression.

Chapter Practice

a. 1 Mark Questions

1. Which one is the common factor of $9a^2b^4 + 12a^3b^3$
   (a) $3a^3b^3$ (b) $3ab^3$
   (c) $3a^2b^3$ (d) $3a^2b^2$

2. By using suitable formula, value of $102^2 - 98^2$ is
   (a) 800 (b) 200
   (c) 1800 (d) 400

3. Without multiplication, 48×52 is equal to
   (a) 2486 (b) 2496
   (c) 2497 (d) 2476

4. If $\frac{x}{y} + \frac{y}{x} = 1$, then $x^3 + y^3$ is
   (a) 1 (b) $2y^3$ (c) $-2y^3$ (d) 0

5. Simplify $\frac{0.87 \times 0.87 \times 0.87 + 0.13 \times 0.13 \times 0.13}{0.87 \times 0.87 - 0.87 \times 0.13 + 0.13 \times 0.13}$.
   (a) 0.87 (b) 1 (c) 0.74 (d) 0

b. 3 Marks Questions

6. By taking common factor, find factors of the following questions.
   (a) (i) $8ab^2 + 12a^2b$
   (ii) $4(x+y)^2 - 3(x+y)$
   (iii) $2(2x-5y)(3x+4y) - 6(2x-5y)(x-y)$
   (b) $a - 1 - (a-1)^2 + ax - x$
   (c) $5\sqrt{5}x^2 + 20x + 3\sqrt{5}$
   (d) $px^2 + (4p^2 - 3q)x - 12pq$
   (e) $4(2a-3)^2 - 3(2a-3)(a-1) - 7(a-1)^2$
   (f) $(3p-1)^2 - (3p-2)(3p-1)$
   (g) $\frac{a}{b}x^2 + \left(\frac{a}{b} + \frac{c}{d}\right)x + \frac{c}{d}$, $b \neq 0$ and $d \neq 0$
   (h) $25a(x-y) + 30b(y-x)$
   (i) $px - (px+qy)^2 + p^2x + pqy + qy$
   (j) $8x^3 - 6x^2 + 10x$
   (k) $18p^2q^2 - 24pq^2 + 30p^2q$
   (l) $6xy^2 + 9x^2y - 21xy$
   (m) $a(a+b-c) - bc$
   (n) $a^2x^2 + (ax^2+1)x + a$
   (o) $4(x-y)^2 - 12(x^2-y^2) + 9(x+y)^2$
   (p) $a^2b + ab^2 - abc - b^2c + axy + bxy$
   (q) $32a^2x^3 - 8b^2x^3 - 4a^2y^3 + b^2y^3$
   (r) $x^3p^2 - 8y^3p^2 - 4x^3q^2 + 32y^3q^2$
   (s) $x^2 - \left(\frac{a+b}{a} + \frac{a}{a+b}\right)x + 1$
   (t) $x^3 + xy(2-3x) - 6y^2$
   (u) $(1+x)^2(1+y^2) - (1+y)^2(1+x^2)$
   (v) $x^6 - 7x^3 - 8$
   (w) $9x^2 - 4(y+2x)^2$
   (x) $2x^2 + 13xy - 24y^2$
   (y) $pq(x^2+y^2) - xy(p^2+q^2)$
   (z) $a^3 + 2a^2 + 5a + 10$

7. By using the formula $A^2 - B^2 = (A+B)(A-B)$, factorise the following questions.
   (a) $4x^2 - 25$
   (b) $x^2 - 21$
   (c) $a^2 + \frac{1}{a^2} - 18$
   (d) $a^4 - 7a^2 + 1$
   (e) $x^2 + \frac{1}{x^2} - 11$
   (f) $2x^4 - 32$
   (g) $a^4 + b^4 - 11a^2b^2$
   (h) $x^4 + 5x^2 + 9$
   (i) $25(2a-b)^2 - 81b^2$
   (j) $(a^2-b^2)(c^2-d^2) - 4abcd$
   (k) $\left(2x - \frac{1}{2x}\right)^2 - 4x^2 + \frac{1}{4x^2}$
   (l) $x^8 - y^8$
   (m) $9x^2 - 4a^2 + 4ay - y^2$
   (n) $x^4 - 11x^2 + 49$
   (o) $x^4 + 36x^2 - 12x^3 - 49$
   (p) $36(x-y)^2 - 25(2x+y)^2$
   (q) $25x^2 - y^2 + 4yz - 4z^2$
   (r) $(x^2 + y^2 - z^2) - 2xy$

8. Factorise by splitting the middle term.
   (a) $4x^2 + 7x + 3$ (b) $5x^2 - 18x + 9$
   (c) $2x^2 + 14x - 16$ (d) $p^2 - 6p - 27$

c. 4/5 Marks Questions

9. Factorise the following questions.
   (a) $\left(x - \frac{1}{x}\right)^2 + 6\left(x - \frac{1}{x}\right) + 9$
   (b) $(a^2 - 3a)(a^2 - 3a + 7) + 10$
   (c) $5(3a+b)^2 + 6(3a+b) - 8$

(d) $3(2a-b)^2-19(2a-b)+28$

(e) $(a^2-a)(4a^2-4a-5)-6$

(f) $(p^2+4p)^2+21(p^2+4p)+98$

(g) $(x^2-4x)(x^2-4x-1)-20$

10. Factorise the following questions. By using the formulae $(A \pm B)^2 = A^2 + B^2 \pm 2AB$.

(a) $(ax+by)^2+(bx-ay)^2$

(b) $x^2+\frac{1}{x^2}-2-3x+\frac{3}{x}$

11. Simplify the following to apply $A^3 \pm B^3 = (A \pm B)(A^2 + B^2 \mp AB)$.

(a) a^3+27b^3 (b) $8a^3-27b^3$

(c) $a^3-5\sqrt{5}b^3$ (d) $216x^3+\frac{1}{27}$

(e) $a^3-0.064$ (f) $7a^3+56b^3$

(g) $64x^3-125y^3$

(h) $a^3-\frac{1}{a^3}-2a+\frac{2}{a}$

(i) $27a^3+\frac{1}{64b^3}+\frac{27a^2}{4b}+\frac{9a}{16b^2}$

12. Factorise

(a) $1-8a^3$

(b) $64-a^3b^3$

(c) $64x^6-729y^6$

(d) $(x+1)^6-(x-1)^6$

(e) $3a^7b-81a^4b^4$

(f) $9(x+y)^2-24(x^2-y^2)+16(x-y)^2$

(g) $2x^7-128x$

(h) $250(a-b)^3+2$

(i) $64-a^3b^3+8-2ab$

(j) $32x^4-500x$

(k) a^6-1

(l) $64a^6-b^6$

(m) a^7-ab^6

(n) $a^3b-a^2b+5ab-5b$

(o) $a^2x^3-8a^2y^3-4b^2x^3+32b^2y^3$

(p) $(x+y)^2+64(x-y)^2-16(x^2-y^2)$

d. 6 Marks Questions

13. Show that 35^3+27^3 is divisible by 62.

14. If $x-\frac{1}{x}=\sqrt{2}$, then find $x^2+\frac{1}{x^2}$.

15. If $a^2+6a+x=(a+3)^2$, then find the value of x.

16. If $a>1$ and $a+\frac{1}{a}=\frac{9}{2}$, find the values of

(a) $a^2+\frac{1}{a^2}$. (b) $a-\frac{1}{a}$.

(c) $a^4-\frac{1}{a^4}$. (d) $a^3-\frac{1}{a^3}$.

Hints and Answers

1. (c) 2. (a) 3. (b)

4. (d) 5. (b)

6. (a) (i) **Hint** $4ab\left[\frac{8ab^2}{4ab}+\frac{12a^2b}{4ab}\right]$

Ans. $4ab(2b+3a)$

(ii) **Hint** Taking $(x+y)$ common

Ans. $(x+y)(4x+4y-3)$

(iii) **Hint** Taking $(2x-5y)$ common

Ans. $14y(2x-5y)$

(b) **Hint** $(a-1)-(a-1)^2+x(a-1)$

Taking $(a-1)$ common

Ans. $(a-1)(x-a+2)$

(c) **Hint** $5\sqrt{5}x^2+15x+5x+3\sqrt{5}$

Ans. $(5x+\sqrt{5})(\sqrt{5}x+3)$

(d) **Ans.** $(px-3q)(x+4p)$

(e) **Ans.** $(a-5)(3a-4)$

(f) **Ans.** $(3p-1)$

(g) **Hint** $\left(\frac{a}{b}x^2+\frac{a}{b}x\right)+\left(\frac{c}{d}x+\frac{c}{d}\right)$

$=\frac{a}{b}x(x+1)+\frac{c}{d}(x+1)$

Ans. $(x+1)\left(\frac{ax}{b}+\frac{c}{d}\right)$

(h) **Hint** $(x-y)(25a-30b)$

Ans. $5(x-y)(5a-6b)$

(i) **Hint** $(px+qy)-(px+qy)^2+p(px+qy)$

Ans. $(px+qy)(1-px-qy+p)$

(j) **Hint** Taking $2x$ common

Ans. $2x(4x^2-3x+5)$

(k) **Hint** Taking $6pq$ common

Ans. $6pq(3pq-4q+5p)$

(l) **Hint** Taking $3xy$ common

Ans. $3xy(2y+3x-7)$

(m) **Hint** $a^2+ab-ac-bc=a(a+b)-c(a+b)$

Ans. $(a+b)(a-c)$

(n) **Hint** $a^2x^2+ax^3+x+a=ax^2(x+a)+1(x+a)$

Ans. $(x+a)(ax^2+1)$

(o) **Ans.** $(-x-5y)^2=(x+5y)^2$

(p) **Hint** $(a^2b+ab^2)-(abc+b^2c)+(axy+bxy)$

$=ab(a+b)-bc(a+b)+xy(a+b)$

Ans. $(a+b)(ab-bc+xy)$

(q) **Hint** $(32\,a^2x^3-8\,b^2x^3)-(4\,a^2y^3-b^2y^3)$

Ans. $(2a+b)(2a-b)(2x-y)(4x^2+2xy+y^2)$

(r) **Hint** $p^2(x^3-8y^3)-4q^2(x^3-8y^3)$

$=(x^3-8y^3)(p^2-4q^2)$

Ans. $(x-2y)(x^2+4y^2+2xy)(p+2q)(p-2q)$

(s) **Hint** $x^2-\dfrac{a+b}{a}x-\dfrac{a}{a+b}x+1$

$=x\left(x-\dfrac{a+b}{a}\right)-\dfrac{a}{a+b}\left(x-\dfrac{a+b}{a}\right)$

Ans. $\left(x-\dfrac{a+b}{a}\right)\left(x-\dfrac{a}{a+b}\right)$

(t) **Hint** $x^3+2xy-3x^2y-6y^2$

$=(x^3-3x^2y)+(2xy-6y^2)$

$=x^2(x-3y)+2y(x-3y)$

Ans. $(x-3y)(x^2+2y)$

(u) **Hint** $(1+x^2+2x)(1+y^2)-(1+y^2+2y)(1+x^2)$

$=1+y^2+x^2+x^2y^2+2x+2xy^2$
$\qquad -1-x^2-y^2-x^2y^2-2y-2x^2y$

$=2x-2y+2xy^2-2x^2y$

$=2(x-y)-2xy(x-y)$

Ans. $2(x-y)(1-xy)$

(v) **Hint** $(x^3)^2-7x^3-8=(x^3)^2-8x^3+x^3-8$

$=x^3(x^3-8)+1(x^3-8)$

$=(x^3-8)(x^3+1)$

$=(x^3-2^3)(x^3+1^3)$

Ans. $(x-2)(x^2+2x+4)(x+1)(x^2-x+1)$

(w) **Hint** $-7x^2-14xy-2xy-4y^2$

$=-7x(x+2y)-2y(x+2y)$

Ans. $-(7x+2y)(x+2y)$

(x) **Hint** $2x^2-3xy+16xy-24y^2$

$=x(2x-3y)+8y(2x-3y)$

Ans. $(x+8y)(2x-3y)$

(y) **Hint** $pqx^2+pqy^2-p^2xy-q^2xy$

$=(pqx^2-p^2xy)-(q^2xy-pqy^2)$

$=px(qx-py)-qy(qx-py)$

Ans. $(px-qy)(qx-py)$

(z) **Hint** $a^2(a+2)+5(a+2)$

Ans. $(a+2)(a^2+5)$

7. (a) $4x^2-25;\ (2x)^2-(5)^2$

Ans. $(2x+5)(2x-5)$

(b) **Hint** $x^2-(\sqrt{21})^2$

Ans. $(x-\sqrt{21})(x+\sqrt{21})$

(c) **Hint** $\left(a-\dfrac{1}{a}\right)^2-16\Rightarrow\left(a-\dfrac{1}{a}\right)^2-4^2$

Ans. $\left(a-\dfrac{1}{a}+4\right)\left(a-\dfrac{1}{a}-4\right)$

(d) **Hint** $(a^2+1)^2-(3a)^2$

Ans. $(a^2+1+3a)(a^2+1-3a)$

(e) **Hint** $x^2+\dfrac{1}{x^2}-2-9=x^2+\dfrac{1}{x^2}-2\cdot x\cdot\dfrac{1}{x}-9$

$=\left(x-\dfrac{1}{x}\right)^2-(3)^2$

Ans. $\left[\left(x-\dfrac{1}{x}+3\right)\left(x-\dfrac{1}{x}-3\right)\right]$

(f) **Hint** $2(x^4-16)=2[(x^2)^2-(4)^2]$

Ans. $2(x^2+4)(x+2)(x-2)$

(g) **Hint** $(a^2)^2+(b^2)^2-2a^2b^2-9a^2b^2=(a^2-b^2)^2-(3ab)^2$

Ans. $(a^2-b^2+3ab)(a^2-b^2-3ab)$

(h) $(x^2+3+x)(x^2+3-x)$

(i) $(10a+4b)(10a-14b)$

(j) **Hint** $(a^2c^2+b^2d^2-2abcd)-(a^2d^2+b^2c^2+2abcd)$

$=(ac-bd)^2-(ad+bc)^2$

Ans. $(ac-bd-ad-bc)(ac-bd+ad+bc)$

(k) **Hint** $\left(2x-\dfrac{1}{2x}\right)^2-\left[(2x)^2-\dfrac{1}{(2x)^2}\right]$

$=\left(2x-\dfrac{1}{2x}\right)^2-\left(2x-\dfrac{1}{2x}\right)\left(2x+\dfrac{1}{2x}\right)$

$=\left(2x-\dfrac{1}{2x}\right)\left(2x-\dfrac{1}{2x}-2x-\dfrac{1}{2x}\right)$

Ans. $-\dfrac{1}{x}\left(2x-\dfrac{1}{2x}\right)$

(l) **Hint** $(x^4+y^4)(x^4-y^4)$

Ans. $(x^4+y^4)(x-y)(x+y)(x^2+y^2)$

(m) **Hint** $(3x)^2-(y-2a)^2$

Ans. $(3x-y+2a)(3x+y-2a)$

(n) **Hint** $(x^4+49+14x^2-25x^2)$

Ans. $(x^2-5x+7)(x^2+5x+7)$

(o) **Hint** $(x^2-6x)^2-(7)^2$

Ans. $[(x^2-6x)+7][(x^2-6x)-7]$

(p) **Ans.** $-(16x-y)(4x+11y)$

(q) **Hint** $(5x)^2-[y^2-2\cdot y\cdot(2z)+(2z)^2]$

$=(5x)^2-(y-2z)^2$

Ans. $(5x+y-2z)(5x-y+2z)$

(r) $(x-y-z)(x-y+z)$

8. (a) **Hint** Do same as Example 28.

Ans. $(4x+3)(x+1)$

(b) **Hint** Do same as Example 29.

Ans. $(5x-3)(x-3)$

(c) **Hint** Do same as Example 30.
Ans. $2(x-1)(x+8)$

(d) **Hint** Do same as Example 31.
Ans. $(p+3)(p-9)$

9. (a) **Hint** Put $\left(x-\frac{1}{x}\right)=y$, we get y^2+6y+9.
Ans. $\left(x-\frac{1}{x}+3\right)^2$

(b) **Ans.** $(a^2-3a+5)(a-2)(a-1)$

(c) **Hint** Let $3a+b=x$
$\therefore$ Given expression becomes $5x^2+6x-8$.
Ans. $(3a+b+2)(15a+5b-4)$

(d) **Hint** Let $2a-b=x$.
Now, factorise $3x^2-19x+28$
Ans. $(2a-b-4)(6a-3b-7)$

(e) **Hint** Let $a^2-a=x$
$\therefore (a^2-a)[4(a^2-a)-5]-6$
$=x(4x-5)-6=4x^2-5x-6$
$=4x^2-8x+3x-6$
$=4x(x-2)+3(x-2)=(4x+3)(x-2)$
On putting $x=a^2-a$, we get
$[4(a^2-a)+3](a^2-a-2)$
$=(4a^2-4a+3)(a^2-2a+a-2)$
Ans. $(4a^2-4a+3)(a-2)(a+1)$

(f) **Hint** Let $p^2+4p=x$
Now, factorise $x^2+21x+98$
Ans. $(p^2+4p+7)(p^2+4p+14)$

(g) **Hint** Let $x^2-4x=a$.
$\therefore (x^2-4x)[(x^2-4x)-1]-20=a(a-1)-20$
$=a^2-a-20=a^2-5a+4a-20$
$=(a-5)(a+4)$
$=(x^2-4x-5)(x^2-4x+4)$
$=(x^2-4x-5)[x^2-2(2)x+2^2]$
Ans. $(x-5)(x+1)(x-2)^2$

10. (a) **Ans.** $(a^2+b^2)(x^2+y^2)$

(b) **Hint** $\left(x^2+\frac{1}{x^2}-2\cdot x\cdot\frac{1}{x}\right)-3\left(x-\frac{1}{x}\right)$
$=\left(x-\frac{1}{x}\right)^2-3\left(x-\frac{1}{x}\right)$
Ans. $\left(x-\frac{1}{x}\right)\left(x-\frac{1}{x}-3\right)$

11. (a) **Hint** $a^3+(3b)^3$
$(a+3b)[(a)^2-a\times 3b+(3b)^2]$
Ans. $(a+3b)(a^2-3ab+9b^2)$

(b) **Hint** $(2a)^3-(3b)^3$
Ans. $(2a-3b)(4a^2+6ab+9b^2)$

(c) **Hint** $a^3-(\sqrt{5}b)^3$
Ans. $(a-\sqrt{5}\,b)(a^2+5b^2+\sqrt{5}ab)$

(d) **Hint** $(6x)^3+\left(\frac{1}{3}\right)^3$
Ans. $\left(6x+\frac{1}{3}\right)\left(36x^2-2x+\frac{1}{9}\right)$

(e) **Hint** $a^3-(0.4)^3$
Ans. $(a-0.4)(a^2+0.4a+0.16)$

(f) **Hint** $7(a^3+8b^3)=7[a^3+(2b)^3]$
Ans. $7(a+2b)(a^2-2ab+4b^2)$

(g) **Hint** $(4x)^3-(5y)^3$
Ans. $(4x-5y)(16x^2+20xy+25y^2)$

(h) **Hint** $a^3-\frac{1}{a^3}-2\left(a-\frac{1}{a}\right)$
$=\left(a-\frac{1}{a}\right)\left(a^2+\frac{1}{a^2}+1\right)-2\left(a-\frac{1}{a}\right)$
Ans. $\left(a-\frac{1}{a}\right)\left(a^2+\frac{1}{a^2}-1\right)$

(i) **Hint** $(3a)^3+\frac{1}{(4b)^3}+\frac{9a}{4b}\left(3a+\frac{1}{4b}\right)$
$=\left(3a+\frac{1}{4b}\right)\left[(3a)^2+\frac{1}{(4b)^2}-3a\times\frac{1}{4b}\right]+\frac{9a}{4b}\left(3a+\frac{1}{4b}\right)$
Ans. $\left(3a+\frac{1}{4b}\right)\left(3a+\frac{1}{4b}\right)\left(3a+\frac{1}{4b}\right)$

12. (a) **Hint** $(1)^3-(2a)^3$
$(1-2a)[(1)^2+1\times 2a+(2a)^2]$
Ans. $(1-2a)[1+2a+4a^2]$

(b) **Hint** $(4)^3-(ab)^3$
$(4-ab)[(4)^2+4\times ab+(ab)^2]$
Ans. $(4-ab)(16+4ab+a^2b^2)$

(c) **Hint** Use the formulae,
$a^3\pm b^3=(a\pm b)(a^2\mp ab+b^2)$
and $a^2-b^2=(a+b)(a-b)$
Ans. $(2x+3y)(2x-3y)(16x^4+36x^2y^2+81y^4)$

(d) **Hint** $[(x+1)^3]^2-[(x-1)^3]^2$
Then, use $(a^2-b^2)=(a+b)(a-b)$
and $(a\pm b)^3=a^3\pm b^3\pm 3ab(a\pm b)$
Ans. $4x(x^2+3)(3x^2+1)$

(e) **Hint** $3a^4b(a^3-27b^3)=3a^4b[a^3-(3b)^3]$
Ans. $3a^4b(a-3b)(a^2+3ab+9b^2)$

(f) **Hint** $[3(x+y)]^2-2\cdot 3(x+y)\cdot 4(x-y)+[4(x-y)]^2$
$=[3(x+y)-4(x-y)]^2$
Ans. $(7y-x)^2$

(g) **Ans.** $2x(x+2)(x^2-2x+4)(x-2)(x^2+2x+4)$

(h) **Ans.** $2(5a-5b+1)(25a^2+25b^2-50ab-5a+5b+1)$

(i) **Hint** $(64 - a^3 b^3) + (8 - 2ab)$

$= [(4)^3 - (ab)^3] + 2(4 - ab)$

Ans. $(4 - ab)(18 + 4ab + a^2 b^2)$

(j) $4x(2x - 5)(4x^2 + 10x + 25)$

(k) **Ans.** $(a - 1)(a^2 + a + 1)(a + 1)(a^2 - a + 1)$

(l) **Hint** $(2a)^6 - b^6 = [(2a)^3]^2 - (b^3)^2$

Ans.
$(2a + b)(2a - b)(4a^2 - 2ab + b^2)(4a^2 + 2ab + b^2)$

(m) **Hint** $a(a^6 - b^6) = a[(a^3)^2 - (b^3)^2]$

Ans. $a(a + b)(a^2 - ab + b^2)(a - b)(a^2 + ab + b^2)$

(n) **Hint** $a^2b(a - 1) + 5b(a - 1)$ **Ans.** $b(a - 1)(a^2 + 5)$

(o) **Ans.** $(x - 24)(x^2 + 4y^2 + 2xy)(a - 2b)(a + 2b)$

(p) **Hint** $(x + y)^2 + [8(x - y)]^2 - 2 \cdot 8 \cdot (x + y)(x - y)$

$= [(x + y) - 8(x - y)]^2$

Ans. $(9y - 7x)^2$

13. **Hint** $(35 + 27)(35^2 + 27^2 - 35 \times 27)$ is a multiple of 62. Hence, $35^3 + 27^3$ is divisible by 62.

14. **Hint** Given, $x - \frac{1}{x} = \sqrt{2}$

Squaring on both sides, we get

$$\left(x - \frac{1}{x}\right)^2 = (\sqrt{2})^2$$

$$\Rightarrow x^2 + \frac{1}{x^2} - 2 \cdot x \cdot \frac{1}{x} = 2$$

Ans. 4

15. **Hint** We have, $a^2 + 6a + x = a^2 + (3)^2 + 6a$.

Ans. $x = 9$

16. **Ans.** (i) $\frac{73}{4}$ (ii) $\frac{\sqrt{65}}{2}$ (iii) $\frac{657\sqrt{65}}{16}$ (iv) $\frac{77\sqrt{65}}{8}$

Olympiad Section

Brain Teasing Questions of Olympiad Pattern

1 Factorise $(3-4y-7y^2)^2-(4y+1)^2$.

(a) $(4-7y^2)(2-8y-7y^2)$

(b) $(7-4y^2)(2-8y-7y^2)$

(c) $(4-7y^2)(8y-7y^2)$

(d) $(7-4y^2)(2+8y-7y^2)$

2 Factorise $px^2+(4p^2-3q)x-12pq$.

(a) $(x+3p)(px-4q)$
(b) $(x+4p)(px-3q)$
(c) $(x+3p)(px-3q)$
(d) None of the above

3 Factorise y^3-2y^2-y+2.

(a) $(y-2)(y+1)(y-1)$
(b) $(y+2)(y+1)(y-1)$
(c) $(y-2)(y-1)(y-1)$
(d) None of the above

4 Factorise $\left(3x-\frac{1}{y}\right)^2+8\left(3x-\frac{1}{y}\right)+16$
$+\left(z+\frac{1}{y}-2x\right)\left(3x-\frac{1}{y}+4\right)$.

(a) $\left(3x-\frac{1}{y}+4\right)(x+z+4)$

(b) $\left(3x+\frac{1}{y}-4\right)(x+z+4)$

(c) $\left(3x-\frac{1}{y}-4\right)(x+z+4)$

(d) $\left(3x+\frac{1}{y}+4\right)(x+z+4)$

5 If $xya^2=(x-y)^2(a+1)$, then the value of $1+\frac{4}{a}+\frac{4}{a^2}$ is

(a) $\left(\frac{x-y}{x+y}\right)^2$ (b) $\left(\frac{x+y}{x-y}\right)^2$

(c) $\left(\frac{x}{x+y}\right)^2$ (d) $\left(\frac{y-x}{y}\right)$

6 Factorise $5x^2-y^2-4xy+7x-7y$.

(a) $(x-y)(5x-y+7)$
(b) $(x-y)(5x+y-7)$
(c) $(x-y)(5x+y+7)$
(d) $(x+y)(5x+y+7)$

7 Factorise $12(3x-4y)^2-3x+4y-1$.

(a) $(9x-12y+1)(12x-16y+1)$
(b) $(9x-12y+1)(12x+16y-1)$
(c) $(9x+12y-1)(12x+16y-1)$
(d) $(9x-12y-1)(12x-16y+1)$

8 Factorise $(x^2+4y^2-9z^2)^2-16x^2y^2$.

(a) $(x-2y+3z)(x+2y-3z)(x-2y+3z)(x-2y-3z)$
(b) $(x+2y+3z)(x+2y-3z)(x-2y+3z)(x-2y-3z)$
(c) $(x-2y-3z)(x+2y-3z)(x-2y+3z)(x-2y-3z)$
(d) None of the above

9 Factorise x^4-625.

(a) $(x^2+25)(x+5)(x-5)$

(b) $(x^2-25)(x+5)(x-5)$

(c) $(x^2+25)(x+5)^2$

(d) $(x^2+5)(x+25)(x-25)$

10 Factorise $4x^2-12ax-y^2-z^2-2yz+9a^2$.

(a) $(2x+y+z-3a)(2x-y-z-3a)$
(b) $(2x+y+z-3a)(2x+y-z-3a)$
(c) $(2x-y+z+3a)(2x-z+y-3a)$
(d) $(2x+y-z+3a)(2x+y-z-3a)$

Answers

1. (a) **2.** (b) **3.** (a) **4.** (a) **5.** (b) **6.** (c) **7.** (d) **8.** (b) **9.** (a) **10.** (a)

* *These questions may or may not be asked in the examination, have been given just for additional practice required for olympiads Scholarship Exams etc. For detailed explanations refer Page No. 336.*

CHAPTER

05

Simultaneous Linear Equations in Two Variables

SYLLABUS

- Simultaneous Linear Equation is Two variables (with numerical coefficients only)
- Solving algebraically by : Substitution, Elimination and Cross Multiplication method
- Solving simple problems by framing appropriate equations.

In previous chapter, we have studied linear equations in one variable like, $x+2=0, \sqrt{2}y+\sqrt{5}=0$, etc. We also know that such equations have a unique solution and their solution can be represented on a number line. In this chapter, the knowledge of linear equation in one variable will be extended to that of two variables.

Linear Equation in Two Variables

An equation $ax + by + c = 0$, where a, b and c are real numbers (a and b together cannot be zero) and x, y are variables, (each with degree 1) is called a general linear equation in two variables.

e.g. (i) $3x + 2y = 4$

(ii) $1.2s + 3t = 5$

(iii) $\pi u + 5v = 9$

Solution of a Linear Equation in Two Variables

Any pair of values of x and y which satisfies the given equation in x and y, is called its solution. This solution is written as an ordered pair (x, y).

A linear equation in two variables has **infinitely many solutions**. e.g. Linear equation $3x+2y=14$ is satisfied by $(x=0,\ y=7)$, $(x=2,\ y=4)$, $(x=4,\ y=1)$, $(x=-2,\ y=10)$ and $(x=5,\ y=-1/2)$, etc. So, these pairs are the solutions of given linear equation. But $(x=1,\ y=5)$ does not satisfy the given linear equation, so it is not the solution of the given linear equation.

Example 1. Find four solutions of the equation $4x+3y=12$.

Sol. Given, linear equation in two variables is

$$4x+3y=12 \quad \text{...(i)}$$

On putting $x=0$ in Eq. (i), we get

$$4(0)+3y=12 \Rightarrow 3y=12 \Rightarrow y=\frac{12}{3}=4$$

So, (0, 4) is a solution of given equation.

On putting $y=0$ in Eq. (i), we get

$$4x+3(0)=12 \Rightarrow 4x=12 \Rightarrow x=\frac{12}{4}=3$$

So, (3, 0) is a solution of given equation.

On putting $x=1$ in Eq. (i), we get

$$4(1)+3y=12 \Rightarrow 3y=12-4=8 \Rightarrow y=\frac{8}{3}$$

So, $\left(1, \frac{8}{3}\right)$ is a solution of the given equation.

On putting $x = 2$ in Eq. (i), we get

$$4(2) + 3y = 12$$

$$\Rightarrow \quad 3y = 12 - 8 = 4 \Rightarrow y = \frac{4}{3}$$

So, $\left(2, \frac{4}{3}\right)$ is a solution of the given equation.

Hence, four solutions of given equation are (0, 4), (3, 0), $\left(1, \frac{8}{3}\right)$ and $\left(2, \frac{4}{3}\right)$.

System of Simultaneous Linear Equations

Two linear equations in the two variables say x and y, is said to form a system of simultaneous linear equations. The general form of system of simultaneous linear equation in two variables x and y is $a_1x + b_1y + c_1 = 0$ and $a_2x + b_2y + c_2 = 0$ where $a_1, b_1, c_1, a_2, b_2, c_2$ are all real numbers and $a_1^2 + b_1^2 \neq 0$, $a_2^2 + b_2^2 \neq 0$.

Solving a System of Simultaneous Linear Equations

Solving a system of simultaneous linear equations, we mean to find the values of variables, which simultaneously satisfy all the equations occurring in the system.

$$a_1x + b_1y + c_1 = 0$$

and $$a_2x + b_2y + c_2 = 0$$

means to find the value of x and y, which satisfy both the equations simultaneously. Generally, this solution is written as an ordered pair (x, y).

Example 2. Show that $x = 5$, $y = 4$ is the solution of system of linear equations.

$$4x - 3y = 8 \text{ and } x - 2y = -3$$

Sol. Consider the given system of linear equations

$$4x - 3y = 8 \quad \text{...(i)}$$

and $$x - 2y = -3 \quad \text{...(ii)}$$

Now, on substituting $x = 5$, $y = 4$ in LHS of Eq. (i), we get

$$\text{LHS} = 4(5) - 3(4) = 20 - 12 = 8 = \text{RHS of Eq. (i)}$$

$\therefore$ $x = 5$ and $y = 4$ satisfy Eq. (i).

Now, on substituting $x = 5$, $y = 4$ in LHS of Eq. (ii), we get

$$\text{LHS} = 5 - 2(4)$$
$$= 5 - 8 = -3 = \text{RHS of Eq. (ii)}$$

$\therefore$ $x = 5$, $y = 4$ satisfy Eq. (ii).

Thus, $x = 5$, $y = 4$ satisfy both the equations.

Hence, $x = 5$ and $y = 4$ is the solution of given system of simultaneous linear equation.

Methods of Solving System of Simultaneous Linear Equations

1. Substitution Method

In this method, value of one variable can be found out in terms of other variable from any equation and this value is substituted in other equation. In this way, we find an equation in one variable, which can be solved easily.

Thus, we get the values of x and y which gives the required solution.

Verification To verify this solution, put the values of both variables in given equations, we get LHS = RHS, then the solution is correct, otherwise not.

Sometimes when we put the value of one variable in terms of other variable in another equation, we get an equation with no variable. Then,

(i) if the equation is true (i.e. LHS = RHS), then we can conclude that the pair of linear equations has infinitely many solutions.

(ii) if the equation is false (i.e. LHS $\neq$ RHS), then we can conclude that the pair of linear equations has no solution.

Example 3. Solve the following system of equations $x + 8y = 19$ and $2x + 11y = 28$, by substitution method and verify it.

Sol. Given, equations are

$$x + 8y = 19 \quad \text{...(i)}$$

and $$2x + 11y = 28 \quad \text{...(ii)}$$

From Eq. (i), $$x = 19 - 8y \quad \text{...(iii)}$$

On substituting $x = 19 - 8y$ in Eq. (ii), we get

$$2(19 - 8y) + 11y = 28$$

$$\Rightarrow \quad 38 - 16y + 11y = 28$$

$$\Rightarrow \quad 5y = 38 - 28 = 10 \Rightarrow y = \frac{10}{5} = 2$$

On putting $y = 2$ in Eq. (iii), we get

$$x = 19 - 16 = 3$$

Hence, $x = 3$ and $y = 2$ is the required solution.

For verification

Put the values of x and y in the given equations.

From Eq. (i), we get LHS $= x + 8y = 3 + 8(2)$
$= 3 + 16 = 19 =$ RHS

From Eq. (ii), we get LHS $= 2x + 11y = 2(3) + 11(2)$
$= 6 + 22 = 28 =$ RHS

Hence, the solution is correct (or verified).

Example 4. Solve the following system of equations $3x - y = 3$ and $9x - 3y = 9$ by substitution method.

Sol. Given, system of equations are

$$3x - y = 3 \quad \text{...(i)}$$

and $$9x - 3y = 9 \quad \text{...(ii)}$$

Now, consider Eq. (i), i.e. $3x - y = 3 \Rightarrow y = 3x - 3$ ...(iii)

Now, substituting the value of y in Eq. (ii), we get

$$9x - 3(3x - 3) = 9 \Rightarrow 9x - 9x + 9 = 9 \Rightarrow 9 = 9$$

This equation has no variable but it is true for all values of x. So, this system of linear equation has infinitely many solutions, which can be given by taking y (or x) $= k$ in Eq. (iii), where k is an arbitrary real number.

Now, taking $x = k$ in Eq. (iii), we get

$$y = 3k - 3$$

Hence, infinite solutions are given by $x = k$, $y = 3k - 3$, where k is an arbitrary real number.

Example 5. Solve the simultaneous linear equations $3x - y = 5$ and $5x - 3y = -1$. Hence, find m, if $y = mx - 3$.

Sol. Given, system of equations are

$$3x - y = 5 \quad \text{...(i)}$$

and $$5x - 3y = -1 \quad \text{...(ii)}$$

From Eq. (i), we have $y = 3x - 5$ ...(iii)

On putting the value of y from Eq. (iii) in Eq. (ii), we get

$$5x - 3(3x - 5) = -1$$

$\Rightarrow$ $$5x - 9x + 15 = -1$$

$\Rightarrow$ $$-4x + 15 = -1$$

$\Rightarrow$ $-4x = -1 - 15 = -16 \Rightarrow x = 4$

On putting $x = 4$ in Eq. (iii), we get

$$y = 3(4) - 5 = 12 - 5 = 7$$

Hence, the required solution is $x = 4$ and $y = 7$.

Now, $y = mx - 3 \Rightarrow 7 = 4m - 3$

$\Rightarrow$ $$10 = 4m \Rightarrow m = \frac{5}{2}$$

2. Elimination Method

In this method, one variable out of the two variables is eliminated by making the coefficients of that variable equal in both the equations.

We can make coefficients of one variable out of the two variables equal by multiplying one or both the equations by an appropriate number or numbers in such a way that either the coefficients of x or the coefficients of y in both the equations will be equal.

After eliminating that variable, the equation left is an equation in one variable, which can be solved easily. Value of one variable obtained in this way can be substituted in any one of the two equations to find the value of other variable.

Verification To verify the solution put the values of x and y in both equations. If these values satisfy both equations, i.e. LHS = RHS, then the solution is correct, otherwise not.

Example 6. Solve the following pair of linear equations by elimination method.

$$x + y = 5 \text{ and } 2x - 3y = 4$$

Also, verify the solution.

Sol. Given, system of linear equations are

$$x + y = 5 \quad \text{...(i)}$$

and $$2x - 3y = 4 \quad \text{...(ii)}$$

For making the coefficients of y numerically equal, multiply Eq. (i) by 3 and Eq. (ii) by 1, and write the above equations as

$$3x + 3y = 15 \quad \text{...(iii)}$$

and $$2x - 3y = 4 \quad \text{...(iv)}$$

On adding Eqs. (iii) and (iv), we get

$$3x + 2x = 15 + 4 = 19 \Rightarrow x = \frac{19}{5}$$

On putting $x = \frac{19}{5}$ in Eq.(i), we get

$$\frac{19}{5} + y = 5 \Rightarrow y = 5 - \frac{19}{5}$$

$\Rightarrow$ $$y = \frac{25 - 19}{5} \Rightarrow y = \frac{6}{5}$$

Hence, $x = \frac{19}{5}$ and $y = \frac{6}{5}$ is the required solution.

For verification

Put $x = \frac{19}{5}$ and $y = \frac{6}{5}$ in Eqs. (i) and (ii), respectively.

From Eq. (i), we get LHS $= x + y = \frac{19}{5} + \frac{6}{5} = \frac{25}{5} = 5 =$ RHS

From Eq. (ii), we get LHS $= 2x - 3y = 2 \times \frac{19}{5} - 3 \times \frac{6}{5}$

$$= \frac{38}{5} - \frac{18}{5} = \frac{20}{5} = 4 = \text{RHS}$$

Hence, the solution is verified.

Example 7. The expression $ax + by$ has value 7, when $x = 2$ and $y = 1$. When $x = -1$ and $y = 1$, it has value 1. Find the values of a and b.

Sol. According to the question, we have

$$2a + b = 7 \quad \text{...(i)}$$

and $$-a + b = 1 \quad \text{...(ii)}$$

On subtracting Eq. (ii) from Eq. (i), we get

$$3a = 6 \Rightarrow a = 2$$

On putting $a = 2$ in Eq. (ii), we get

$$-2 + b = 1 \Rightarrow b = 1 + 2 = 3$$

Hence, $a = 2$ and $b = 3$.

Example 8. Use elimination method to find all possible solutions of the following pair of linear equations.

$$2x + 3y = 8 \text{ and } 4x + 6y = 7$$

Sol. Given, pair of linear equations is

$$2x + 3y = 8 \quad \text{...(i)}$$

and $$4x + 6y = 7 \quad \text{...(ii)}$$

On multiplying Eq. (i) by 2 to make the coefficients of x equal, we get the equations as

$$4x + 6y = 16 \quad \text{...(iii)}$$

and $$4x + 6y = 7 \quad \text{...(iv)}$$

On subtracting Eq. (iv) from Eq. (iii), we get

$$(4x - 4x) + (6y - 6y) = 16 - 7 \Rightarrow 0 = 9$$

which is a false equation involving no variable.

So, the given pair of linear equations has no solution.

3. Cross-multiplication Method

According to this method, the solution of system of two linear equations

$$a_1x + b_1y + c_1 = 0 \quad \ldots(i)$$

$$a_2x + b_2y + c_2 = 0 \quad \ldots(ii)$$

is given by $x = \dfrac{(b_1c_2 - b_2c_1)}{(a_1b_2 - a_2b_1)}$ and $y = \dfrac{(c_1a_2 - c_2a_1)}{(a_1b_2 - a_2b_1)}$,

provided $a_1b_2 - a_2b_1 \neq 0$.

Working Rule to Solve the Problems by Cross-multiplication Method

Step I First, write the given equations in standard form

$$a_1x + b_1y + c_1 = 0 \text{ and } a_2x + b_2y + c_2 = 0$$

Step II With the help of these equations, draw the following diagram

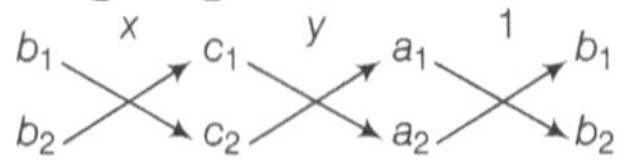

Step III With the help of diagram write the following equation

$$\frac{x}{b_1c_2 - b_2c_1} = \frac{y}{c_1a_2 - c_2a_1} = \frac{1}{a_1b_2 - a_2b_1}$$

Step IV Find the values of x and y by solving them taking two at a time, provided $a_1b_2 - a_2b_1 \neq 0$.

Verification We substitute the value of variables in both equations, if LHS = RHS, then the solution is correct, otherwise not.

Note If the equations $a_1x + b_1y + c_1 = 0$ and $a_2x + b_2y + c_2 = 0$ are written in the form $a_1x + b_1y = -c_1$ and $a_2x + b_2y = -c_2$, then by cross-multiplication method, we have

$$\frac{x}{b_2c_1 - b_1c_2} = \frac{y}{c_2a_1 - c_1a_2} = \frac{-1}{a_1b_2 - a_2b_1}.$$

Remembering Technique for Cross-multiplication

The following diagram helps in remembering the above solution

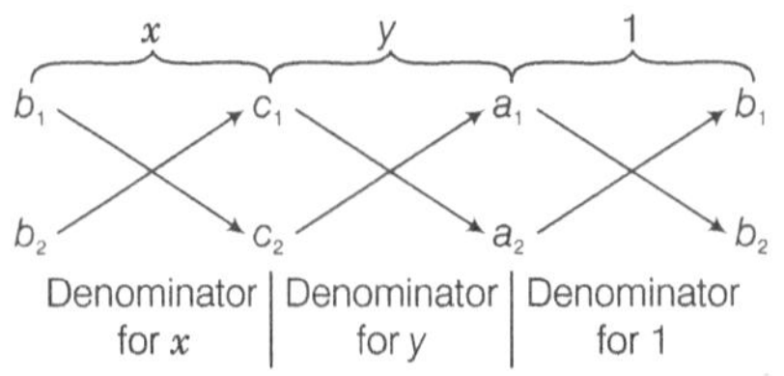

In the above pattern, the arrow (→) between the two numbers b_1 and c_2 indicates that the two numbers are to be multiplied and the arrow (→) between the two numbers b_2 and c_1 indicates that the two numbers are to be multiplied and this product is to be subtracted from first product which means, product of the numbers with upward arrow (↑) will be subtracted from the product of numbers with downward arrow (↓).

Example 9. Solve the following system of equations by cross-multiplication method.

$$2x + 3y = 46 \text{ and } 3x + 5y = 74$$

Also, verify the solution.

Sol. Standard form of above equations are

$$2x + 3y - 46 = 0 \quad \ldots(i)$$

and $$3x + 5y - 74 = 0 \quad \ldots(ii)$$

Diagram for above equations is

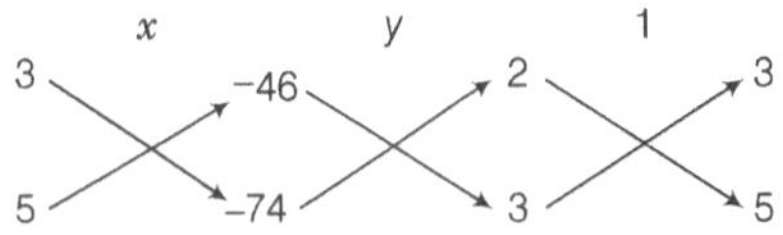

With the help of diagram, we have

$$\frac{x}{(3)(-74) - (5)(-46)} = \frac{y}{(-46)(3) - (-74)(2)} = \frac{1}{(2)(5) - (3)(3)}$$

$$\Rightarrow \frac{x}{-222 + 230} = \frac{y}{-138 + 148} = \frac{1}{10 - 9}$$

$$\Rightarrow \frac{x}{8} = \frac{y}{10} = \frac{1}{1}$$

I II III

On taking I and III terms, we get

$$\frac{x}{8} = \frac{1}{1} \Rightarrow x = 8$$

On taking II and III terms, we get

$$\frac{y}{10} = \frac{1}{1} \Rightarrow y = 10$$

Hence, $x = 8$ and $y = 10$ is the required solution.

For verification

Put $x = 8$ and $y = 10$ in Eqs. (i) and (ii), respectively.

From Eq. (i), we get

$$\text{LHS} = 2x + 3y - 46 = 2(8) + 3(10) - 46$$

$$= 16 + 30 - 46 = 0 = \text{RHS}$$

From Eq. (ii), we get LHS

$$= 3x + 5y - 74 = 3(8) + 5(10) - 74$$

$$= 24 + 50 - 74 = 0 = \text{RHS}$$

Hence, the solution is verified.

Example 10. Solve the following system of equations by cross-multiplication method.

$x + 4y - 5 = 0$ and $4x + 4y = 13$

Sol. Given, pair of linear equations can be written as

$$x + 4y - 5 = 0 \quad \ldots(i)$$

and $$4x + 4y - 13 = 0 \quad \ldots(ii)$$

Diagram for the above equation is

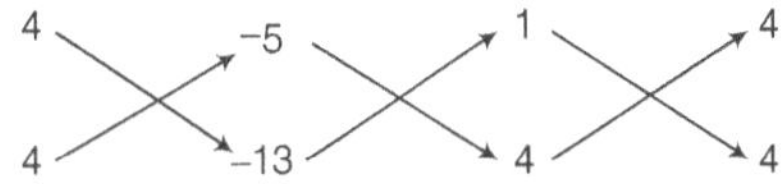

With the help of diagram, we have

$$\frac{x}{4(-13)-4(-5)} = \frac{y}{-5(4)-(-13)(1)} = \frac{1}{(1)(4)-(4)(4)}$$

$$\Rightarrow \quad \frac{x}{-52+20} = \frac{y}{-20+13} = \frac{1}{4-16}$$

$$\Rightarrow \quad \underset{\text{I}}{\frac{x}{-32}} = \underset{\text{II}}{\frac{y}{-7}} = \underset{\text{III}}{\frac{1}{-12}}$$

On taking I and III terms, we get

$$\frac{x}{-32} = \frac{1}{-12} \Rightarrow x = \frac{-32}{-12} = \frac{8}{3}$$

On taking II and III terms, we get

$$\frac{y}{-7} = \frac{1}{-12} \Rightarrow y = \frac{-7}{-12} = \frac{7}{12}$$

Hence, $x = \frac{8}{3}$ and $y = \frac{7}{12}$ is the required solution.

Example 11. Solve the following system of equations by cross-multiplication method.

$$3(px - qy) + (p + 5q) = 0$$

and $\quad 3(qx + py) + (q - 4p) = 0, \; p^2 + q^2 \neq 0$

Sol. Given, pair of linear equation is

$$3px - 3qy + (p + 5q) = 0 \quad \text{...(i)}$$

and $\quad 3qx + 3py + (q - 4p) = 0 \quad$ ...(ii)

Diagram for the above equations is

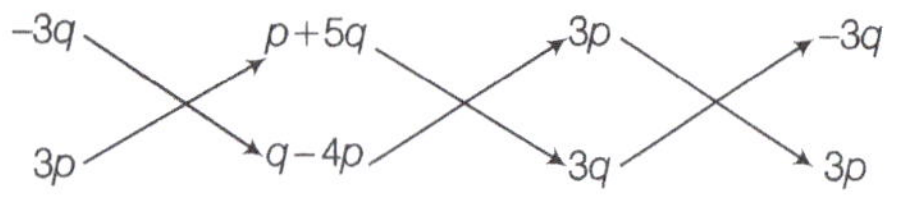

With the help of diagram, we have

$$\frac{x}{-3q(q-4p)-3p(p+5q)} = \frac{y}{(p+5q)3q-(q-4p)3p} = \frac{1}{(3p)(3p)-3q(-3q)}$$

$$\Rightarrow \quad \frac{x}{-3q^2-3p^2} = \frac{y}{15q^2+15p^2} = \frac{1}{9p^2+9q^2}$$

$$\Rightarrow \frac{x}{-3(q^2+p^2)} = \frac{y}{15(q^2+p^2)} = \frac{1}{9(p^2+q^2)}$$

$$\Rightarrow \quad \underset{\text{I}}{\frac{x}{-3}} = \underset{\text{II}}{\frac{y}{15}} = \underset{\text{III}}{\frac{1}{9}}$$

On taking I and III terms, we get

$$\frac{x}{-3} = \frac{1}{9} \Rightarrow x = -\frac{3}{9} = -\frac{1}{3}$$

On taking II and III terms, we get

$$\frac{y}{15} = \frac{1}{9} \Rightarrow y = \frac{15}{9} = \frac{5}{3}$$

Hence, $x = -\frac{1}{3}$ and $y = \frac{5}{3}$ is the required solution.

Equations Reducible to a Pair of Linear Equations

Sometimes, the equations are not linear but they can be reduced to a pair of linear equations by making some suitable substitutions. Some of the situations are given below

(i) If equations are in the form of $\frac{1}{x}, \frac{1}{y}$, then put $\frac{1}{x} = p, \frac{1}{y} = q$, to convert them into linear form.
After solving, put the values of p and q in above substitutions, to get the values of x and y.

(ii) If equations are in the form of $\frac{1}{x \pm a}, \frac{1}{y \pm b}$, then put $\frac{1}{x \pm a} = p, \frac{1}{y \pm b} = q$, to convert them into linear form. After solving, put the values of p and q in above substitutions, to get the values of x and y.

(iii) If equations are in the form of $\frac{1}{x+y}, \frac{1}{x-y}$, then put $\frac{1}{x+y} = u$ and $\frac{1}{x-y} = v$, to convert them into linear form. After solving, put the values of u and v in above substitutions and again get linear equations in x and y. Now, solve these equations to get the values of x and y.

Example 12. Solve the pair of equations and verify the solution $\frac{2}{x} + \frac{3}{y} = 13$ and $\frac{5}{x} - \frac{4}{y} = -2$.

Sol. Given, pair of linear equations is not linear.

On putting $\frac{1}{x} = p$ and $\frac{1}{y} = q$, we get

$$2p + 3q = 13 \quad \text{...(i)}$$

and $\quad 5p - 4q = -2 \quad$ ...(ii)

The pair obtained after substitution, is the pair of linear equations.

Now, let us solve these equations by elimination method.

On multiplying Eq. (i) by 4 and Eq. (ii) by 3 and then adding, we get

$$(8p + 12q) + (15p - 12q) = 52 - 6$$

$$\Rightarrow \quad 8p + 15p = 52 - 6 \Rightarrow 23p = 46 \;\Rightarrow\; p = \frac{46}{23} = 2$$

On putting $p = 2$ in Eq. (i), we get

$$2(2) + 3q = 13 \;\Rightarrow\; 3q = 13 - 4 = 9 \;\Rightarrow\; q = \frac{9}{3} = 3$$

Since, $p = \frac{1}{x}$ and $q = \frac{1}{y}$ we put the values of p and q, we get

$$2 = \frac{1}{x} \text{ and } 3 = \frac{1}{y} \;\Rightarrow\; x = \frac{1}{2} \text{ and } y = \frac{1}{3}$$

which is the required solution.

Verification Put $x = \frac{1}{2}$ and $y = \frac{1}{3}$ in given equations, both equations get satisfied.

$$\Rightarrow \quad \frac{2}{x} + \frac{3}{y} = 13$$

$$\text{LHS} = \frac{2}{\frac{1}{2}} + \frac{3}{\frac{1}{3}} = 4 + 9 \qquad \left[\because \frac{\frac{a}{b}}{\frac{c}{d}} = \frac{a \times d}{b \times c}\right]$$

$= 13 = \text{RHS}$

$\Rightarrow \frac{5}{x} - \frac{4}{y} = -2 \Rightarrow \text{LHS} = \frac{\frac{5}{1}}{2} - \frac{\frac{4}{1}}{3} = 10 - 12$ $\left[\because \frac{\frac{a}{b}}{\frac{c}{d}} = \frac{a \times d}{c \times b}\right]$

$= -2$

Hence, the solution is correct (or verified).

Example 13. Solve the following pair of equations by reducing them to a pair of linear equations.

$$\frac{10}{(x+y)} + \frac{2}{(x-y)} = 4 \text{ and } \frac{15}{(x+y)} - \frac{5}{(x-y)} = -2$$

Sol. Given, pair of linear equations is

$$\frac{10}{(x+y)} + \frac{2}{(x-y)} = 4 \text{ and } \frac{15}{(x+y)} - \frac{5}{(x-y)} = -2$$

On putting $\frac{1}{x+y} = u$ and $\frac{1}{x-y} = v$, we get

$10u + 2v = 4$ ...(i)

and $15u - 5v = -2$ ...(ii)

On multiplying Eq. (i) by 5 and Eq. (ii) by 2 and then adding, we get

$5(10u + 2v) + 2(15u - 5v) = 5 \times 4 + 2 \times (-2)$

$\Rightarrow 50u + 10v + 30u - 10v = 20 - 4$

$\Rightarrow 80u = 16$

$\Rightarrow u = \frac{1}{5}$

On substituting $u = \frac{1}{5}$ in Eq. (i), we get

$10 \times \frac{1}{5} + 2v = 4 \Rightarrow 2 + 2v = 4$

$\Rightarrow 2v = 2 \Rightarrow v = 1$

If $u = \frac{1}{5}$, then by $\frac{1}{x+y} = u$, we get

$\frac{1}{x+y} = \frac{1}{5} \Rightarrow x + y = 5$ ...(iii)

If $v = 1$, then by $\frac{1}{x-y} = v$, we get

$\frac{1}{x-y} = 1 \Rightarrow x - y = 1$ ...(iv)

On adding Eqs. (iii) and (iv), we get

$2x = 6 \Rightarrow x = 3$

On putting $x = 3$ in Eq. (iv), we get

$3 - y = 1 \Rightarrow y = 2$

Hence, $x = 3$ and $y = 2$, which is the required solution.

Exercise 5.1

1. Find the solution of the following system of equations by substitution method.
   (i) $x + y = 8$ and $2x - 3y = 1$
   (ii) $3x + 2y = 10$ and $12x + 8y = 30$
   (iii) $2x - 7y = 11$ and $6x - 21y = 33$
   (iv) $\sqrt{2}x + \sqrt{5}y = 0$ and $\sqrt{6}x + \sqrt{15}y = 0$
   (v) $x + 2y = -1$ and $2x - 3y = 12$.

2. Solve the following system of equations by substitution method.
   $$\frac{x}{7} + \frac{y}{3} = 5 \text{ and } \frac{x}{2} - \frac{y}{9} = 6$$

3. Find the solution for the pair of equations
   $0.2x + 0.3y = 1.3$ and $0.4x + 0.5y = 2.3$
   by substitution method.

4. Find the solution for the pair of equations
   $\frac{x}{10} + \frac{y}{5} - 1 = 0$ and $\frac{x}{8} + \frac{y}{6} = 15$. Hence, find λ, if $y = \lambda x + 5$.

5. Solve the following pair of equations by using elimination method.
   (i) $8x + 5y = 11$ and $x + y = 4$
   (ii) $4x - 3y = 8$ and $6x - y = \frac{29}{3}$
   (iii) $11x + 15y + 23 = 0$ and $7x - 2y - 20 = 0$
   (iv) $3x - 5y = 4$ and $9x - 2y - 7 = 0$
   (v) $0.4x + 0.3y = 1.7$ and $0.7x - 0.2y = 0.8$
   (vi) $\frac{x}{4} + \frac{y}{3} = -\frac{1}{12}$ and $\frac{x}{2} - \frac{5}{4}y = \frac{7}{4}$
   (vii) $\frac{x}{2} + \frac{2y}{3} = -1$ and $x - \frac{y}{3} = 3$

6. Solve the following pair of linear equations by cross-multiplication method.
   (i) $4x + 6y = 5$ and $2x + 9y = 3$
   (ii) $5x + 4y - 4 = 0$ and $x - 12y - 20 = 0$
   (iii) $3x - 5y + 1 = 0$ and $2x + 3y - 12 = 0$
   (iv) $\frac{x}{7} + \frac{y}{3} = 5$ and $\frac{x}{2} - \frac{y}{9} = 6$
   (v) $8x + 5y = 9$ and $3x + 2y = 4$

7. Solve the following pair of equations.
   (i) $\frac{1}{2x} - \frac{1}{y} = -1$ and $\frac{1}{x} + \frac{1}{2y} = 8$; $x, y \neq 0$
   (ii) $\frac{4}{x} + 3y = 14$ and $\frac{3}{x} - 4y = 23$
   (iii) $\frac{2xy}{x+y} = \frac{3}{2}$ and $\frac{xy}{2x-y} = -\frac{3}{10}$,
   where $x + y \neq 0$ and $2x - y \neq 0$

8. Solve the following pair of linear equations.
   $$x + y = 14xy \text{ and } 2x - y = 4xy$$

9. Solve the following pair of linear equations by reducing them to a pair of linear equations.
   $$\frac{5}{(x-1)} + \frac{1}{(y-2)} = 2 \text{ and } \frac{6}{(x-1)} - \frac{3}{(y-2)} = 1$$

Applications of Linear Equations in Two Variables

Here, we will discuss some different types of word problems that you may deal in day-to-day life situations. The following points should be kept in mind to form the pair of linear equations from the given data.

Problem solving techniques for different types of word problems are given below

Problems Based on Numbers

For these types of problems, we generally let the numbers as x, y and then formulate the equations.

Example 14. The sum of two numbers is 24 and their difference is 4. Find the numbers.

Sol. Let the numbers are x and y. Then, we have

$$x + y = 24 \quad \text{...(i)}$$

and $$x - y = 4 \quad [\text{assuming } x > y] \quad \text{...(ii)}$$

On adding Eqs. (i) and (ii), we get

$$2x = 28 \Rightarrow x = 14$$

On substituting $x = 14$ in Eq. (i), we get

$$14 + y = 24 \Rightarrow y = 24 - 14 = 10$$

Hence, the required numbers are 14 and 10.

Problems Based on Digits

For these types of problems, we generally let the digit in unit's place be x and that in ten's place be y. Then, two-digit number is given by $10y + x$.

On interchanging the positions of the digits, i.e. the digit in unit's place becomes y and in ten's place becomes x, then two-digit number becomes $10x + y$.

Formulate the equations and then solve them.

Example 15. The sum of a two-digit number and number obtained by reversing the order of digits is 99. If the digits of the number differ by 3. Then, find the numbers.

Sol. Let the unit's place digit be x and ten's place digit be y.

$\therefore$ Original number $= 10y + x$

Number obtained by reversing the order of digits

$$= 10x + y$$

$\because$ Sum of both numbers $= 99$

$\therefore \quad (10y + x) + (10x + y) = 99$

$\Rightarrow \quad 11x + 11y = 99$

$\Rightarrow \quad x + y = 9 \quad$ [dividing both sides by 11] ...(i)

Also, given that the digits of the numbers differ by 3.

$\therefore$ If $y > x$, then $y - x = 3$ ...(ii)

and if $y < x$, then $x - y = 3$ ...(iii)

On adding Eqs. (i) and (ii), we get

$$2y = 12 \Rightarrow y = \frac{12}{2} = 6$$

Then, from Eq. (i), we get

$$x = 9 - y = 9 - 6 = 3 \quad [\because y = 6]$$

$\therefore$ Number $= 10y + x = 10 \times 6 + 3 = 60 + 3 = 63$

On adding Eqs. (i) and (iii), we get

$$2x = 12 \Rightarrow x = \frac{12}{2} = 6$$

Then, from Eq. (i), we get

$$y = 9 - x = 9 - 6 = 3 \quad [\because x = 6]$$

$\therefore$ Number $= 10y + x = 10(3) + 6 = 36$

Hence, the required numbers are 63 and 36.

Example 16. The sum of digits of a two-digit number is 10. If the digits of the number are reversed, the new number increased by 2, which is equal to 3 times the original number. Then, determine the original number.

Sol. Let the unit's place digit be y and ten's place digit be n.

$\therefore$ Original number $= 10x + y$

Number obtained by reversing the order of digits

$$= 10y + x$$

According to the question,

$$x + y = 10 \quad \text{...(i)}$$

$\Rightarrow \quad 10y + x + 2 = 3(10x + y)$

$\Rightarrow \quad 10y + x + 2 = 30x + 3y$

$\Rightarrow \quad 29x - 7y = 2$ ...(ii)

Multiplying Eq. (i) by 7, we get

$$7x + 7y = 70 \quad \text{...(iii)}$$

On adding Eqs. (ii) and (iii), we get

$$36x = 72 \Rightarrow x = \frac{72}{36} = 2$$

From Eq. (i), we get

$$y = 10 - x = 10 - 2 = 8 \quad [\because x = 2]$$

$\therefore$ The required number $= 10x + y = 10(2) + 8 = 28$

Problems Based on Fractions

For these types of problems we generally, let the numerator of the fraction be x and denominator be y. Then, the fraction is x/y.

Formulate the linear equations on the basis of given conditions and solve for x and y, to get the value of the fraction.

Example 17. A fraction becomes 4/5, if 1 is added to both numerator and denominator. If however, 5 is subtracted from both numerator and denominator, the fraction becomes 1/2. What is the fraction?

Sol. Suppose the numerator is x and denominator is y of the fraction.

Condition I When 1 is added to both numerator and denominator, then

New fraction $= \dfrac{x + 1}{y + 1}$

According to the question,

$$\frac{x+1}{y+1}=\frac{4}{5} \Rightarrow 5(x+1)=4(y+1)$$

$\Rightarrow$ $5x+5=4y+4$

$\Rightarrow$ $5x-4y=-1$ ...(i)

Condition II When 5 is subtracted from both numerator and denominator.

Then, new fraction $=\frac{x-5}{y-5}$

According to the question,

$$\frac{x-5}{y-5}=\frac{1}{2} \Rightarrow 2(x-5)=1(y-5)$$

$\Rightarrow$ $2x-10=y-5 \Rightarrow 2x-y=10-5$

$\Rightarrow$ $2x-y=5$ ...(ii)

On multiplying Eq. (ii) by 4, we get

$8x-4y=20$ ...(iii)

On subtracting Eq. (i) from Eq. (iii), we get

$\Rightarrow$ $3x=21 \Rightarrow x=7$

On putting $x=7$ in Eq. (i), we get

$$5(7)-4y=-1 \Rightarrow 4y=35+1$$

$\Rightarrow$ $y=\frac{36}{4}=9$

Hence, the required fraction is $\frac{7}{9}$.

Problems Based on Time and Work

The concept to be used for these types of problems, is given below.

If a person can do a piece of work in n days, then he will do $1/n$ of the work in one day and *vice-versa*.

Formulate the equations and then solve them.

Example 18. **2 women and 5 men can together finish an embroidery work in 4 days, while 3 women and 6 men can finish it in 3 days. Find the time taken by one woman alone to finish the work and also that taken by one man alone.**

Sol. Let one woman finishes the work in x days and one man finishes the work in y days.

Then, work done by one woman in one day $=1/x$
and work done by one man in one day $=1/y$

[assuming total work = 1]

$\therefore$ Work done by 2 women and 5 men in one day

$$=\frac{2}{x}+\frac{5}{y}=\frac{5x+2y}{xy}$$

$\therefore$ The number of days required for complete the work by 2 women and 5 men $=\frac{xy}{5x+2y}$

According to the question, $\frac{xy}{5x+2y}=4$ ...(i)

Similarly, in second case, $\frac{xy}{6x+3y}=3$ ...(ii)

Eqs. (i) and (ii) can be rewritten as

$$\frac{5x+2y}{xy}=\frac{1}{4} \text{ and } \frac{6x+3y}{xy}=\frac{1}{3}$$

$\Rightarrow$ $\frac{20x+8y}{xy}=1$ and $\frac{18x+9y}{xy}=1$

$\Rightarrow$ $\frac{20}{y}+\frac{8}{x}=1$ and $\frac{18}{y}+\frac{9}{x}=1$

On putting $\frac{1}{x}=u$ and $\frac{1}{y}=v$ in given equations, we get

$20v+8u=1$ ...(iii)

and $18v+9u=1$ ...(iv)

On multiplying Eq. (iii) by 9 and Eq. (iv) by 8 and then subtracting, we get

$$(20v \times 9+8u \times 9)-(18v \times 8+9u \times 8)=9-8$$

$\Rightarrow$ $180v-144v=1 \Rightarrow 36v=1 \Rightarrow v=\frac{1}{36}$

On substituting $v=\frac{1}{36}$ in Eq. (iv), we get

$$18 \times \frac{1}{36}+9u=1 \Rightarrow \frac{1}{2}+9u=1 \Rightarrow u=\frac{1}{18}$$

Thus, we get $u=\frac{1}{18}$ and $v=\frac{1}{36}$

$\Rightarrow$ $\frac{1}{x}=\frac{1}{18}$ and $\frac{1}{y}=\frac{1}{36}$ $\left[\because \text{put } u=\frac{1}{x} \text{ and } v=\frac{1}{y}\right]$

$\therefore$ $x=18$ and $y=36$

Hence, a single woman can finish the work in 18 days and a single man can finish the work in 36 days.

Problems Based on Distance, Speed and Time

Some formulae to be used for these types of problems, are given below

$$\text{Speed}=\frac{\text{Distance}}{\text{Time}}$$

To solve problems related to speed of boat going downstream and upstream, let the speed of boat in still water be x km/h and speed of stream be y km/h.

Then, speed of the boat downstream $=(x+y)$ km/h and speed of the boat upstream $=(x-y)$ km/h.

Example 19. **Roohi travels 300 km to her home partly by train and partly by bus. She takes 4 h, if she travels 60 km by train and the remaining by bus. If she travels 100 km by train and the remaining by bus, she takes 10 min longer. Find the speed of the train and the bus separately.**

Sol. Let the speed of the train be x km/h and the speed of the bus be y km/h. In first case, Roohi travels 60 km by train and 240 km by bus in 4 h.

Thus, $\frac{60}{x}+\frac{240}{y}=4$ $\left[\because \text{time}=\frac{\text{distance}}{\text{speed}}\right]$

$\Rightarrow$ $\frac{15}{x}+\frac{60}{y}=1$ [dividing both sides by 4] ...(i)

Similarly, in second case,

$$\frac{100}{x}+\frac{200}{y}=4+\frac{1}{6} \quad \left[\because 10 \text{ min}=\frac{1}{6}\text{h}\right]$$

$\Rightarrow$ $\frac{100}{x}+\frac{200}{y}=\frac{25}{6}$

$\Rightarrow \quad \frac{24}{x}+\frac{48}{y}=1\left[\text{multiplying both sides by } \frac{6}{25}\right]$ ...(ii)

On putting $\frac{1}{x}=u$ and $\frac{1}{y}=v$ in Eqs. (i) and (ii), we get

$15u + 60v = 1$ ...(iii)

and $24u + 48v = 1$ ...(iv)

On multiplying Eq. (iii) by 4 and Eq. (iv) by 5 and then subtracting, we get

$4(15u + 60v) - 5(24u + 48v) = 4 \times 1 - 5 \times 1$

$\Rightarrow \quad 60u - 120u = -1 \Rightarrow -60u = -1$

$\Rightarrow \quad u = \frac{1}{60}$

On putting $u = \frac{1}{60}$ in Eq. (iii), we get

$15 \times \frac{1}{60} + 60v = 1$

$\Rightarrow \quad 60v = 1 - \frac{1}{4} = \frac{3}{4} \Rightarrow v = \frac{1}{80}$

Thus, we get $u = \frac{1}{60}$ and $v = \frac{1}{80}$

$\Rightarrow \quad \frac{1}{x} = \frac{1}{60}$ and $\frac{1}{y} = \frac{1}{80}$ $\left[\because \text{putting } u = \frac{1}{x} \text{ and } v = \frac{1}{y}\right]$

$\therefore \quad x = 60$ and $y = 80$

Hence, the speed of train is 60 km/h and the speed of bus is 80 km/h.

Example 20. A train leaves Agra for Punjab, 420 km away, at 6 am. One hour later, another train leaves Punjab for Agra. They met at 9 am, if the second train had started at 6 am and the first train at 7 : 30 am, they would still have met at 9 am. Find the speed of each train.

Sol. Let the speed of the first train be x km/h and that of the second train be y km/h. The two trains meet at 9 am.

Let us consider the following chart

	Time (in hours)	Speed (in km/h)	Distance (in km)
First train	3	x	$3x$
Second train	2	y	$2y$
First train	1.5	x	$1.5x$
Second train	3	y	$3y$

Since, the two trains meet, therefore the sum of distances covered by them is 420 km.

$\therefore \quad 3x + 2y = 420$ ...(i)

and $1.5x + 3y = 420$ ...(ii)

On multiplying Eq. (ii) by 2, we get

$3x + 6y = 840$ ...(iii)

On subtracting Eq. (i) from Eq. (iii), we get

$4y = 420 \Rightarrow y = 105$

On substituting $y = 105$ in Eq. (i), we get

$3x + 210 = 420$

$\Rightarrow \quad 3x = 420 - 210$

$\Rightarrow \quad 3x = 210 \Rightarrow x = 70$

Hence, the speed of the first train is 70 km/h and that of second train is 105 km/h.

Example 21. A boat goes 30 km upstream and 44 km downstream in 10 h. In 13 h, it can go 40 km upstream and 55 km downstream. Determine the speed of the stream and that of the boat in still water.

Sol. Let speed of the boat in still water be x km/h and speed of the stream be y km/h.

Then, speed of the boat downstream $= (x + y)$ km/h

and speed of the boat upstream $= (x - y)$ km/h

Condition I When boat goes 30 km upstream, then the time taken,

$t_1 = \frac{30}{x-y}$ h $\left[\because \text{time} = \frac{\text{distance}}{\text{speed}}\right]$

When boat goes 44 km downstream, then the time taken,

$t_2 = \frac{44}{x+y}$ h

But, total time taken = 10 h

$\Rightarrow \quad t_1 + t_2 = 10\text{ h} \Rightarrow \frac{30}{x-y} + \frac{44}{x+y} = 10$ ...(i)

Condition II When boat goes 40 km upstream, then the time taken,

$T_1 = \frac{40}{x-y}$ h $\left[\because \text{time} = \frac{\text{distance}}{\text{speed}}\right]$

When boat goes 55 km downstream, then the time taken,

$T_2 = \frac{55}{x+y}$ h

But, total time taken = 13 h

$\Rightarrow \quad T_1 + T_2 = 13\text{ h}$

$\Rightarrow \quad \frac{40}{x-y} + \frac{55}{x+y} = 13$ ...(ii)

Here, Eqs. (i) and (ii) are not in linear form, so we reduce them in linear form by putting $\frac{1}{x-y} = u$ and $\frac{1}{x+y} = v$.

From Eq. (i), we get

$30u + 44v = 10$

$\Rightarrow \quad 30u + 44v - 10 = 0$ ...(iii)

and from Eq. (ii), we get

$40u + 55v = 13$

$\Rightarrow \quad 40u + 55v - 13 = 0$ ...(iv)

Eqs. (iii) and (iv) are in linear form.

Now, by cross-multiplication method, we get

$$\frac{u}{(44)(-13)-(55)(-10)} = \frac{v}{40(-10)-30(-13)} = \frac{1}{30(55)-44(40)}$$

$$\left[\because \frac{u}{b_1c_2 - b_2c_1} = \frac{v}{c_1a_2 - c_2a_1} = \frac{1}{a_1b_2 - a_2b_1}\right]$$

$\Rightarrow \quad \frac{u}{-572+550} = \frac{v}{-400+390} = \frac{1}{1650-1760}$

$\Rightarrow \quad \frac{u}{-22} = \frac{v}{-10} = \frac{1}{-110}$

I II III

On taking I and III terms, we get

$\frac{u}{-22} = \frac{1}{-110}$

$\Rightarrow \quad u = \frac{22}{110} = \frac{1}{5}$

On taking II and III terms, we get

$$\frac{v}{-10} = \frac{1}{-110}$$

$\Rightarrow \quad v = \frac{10}{110} = \frac{1}{11}$

Now, putting the values of u and v in $\frac{1}{x-y} = u$ and $\frac{1}{x+y} = v$, we get

$$\frac{1}{x-y} = \frac{1}{5} \Rightarrow x - y = 5 \quad ...(v)$$

and $\quad \frac{1}{x+y} = \frac{1}{11} \Rightarrow x + y = 11 \quad ...(vi)$

On adding Eqs. (v) and (vi), we get

$$2x = 16 \Rightarrow x = \frac{16}{2} = 8$$

On putting $x = 8$ in Eq. (v), we get

$$8 - y = 5 \Rightarrow y = 8 - 5 = 3$$

Hence, speed of the boat in still water is 8 km/h and speed of the stream is 3 km/h.

Problems Based on Commercial Mathematics

(i) To solve questions based on ticket fare, we generally let the fare of 1 full ticket as ₹ x and the reservation charges as ₹ y. Thus, total fare of 1 full ticket = ₹ $(x + y)$ and 1 half ticket = ₹ $\left(\frac{x}{2} + y\right)$.

(ii) To solve questions based on profit and loss, take the cost price of 1st article as ₹ x and that of 2nd article as ₹ y.

(iii) To solve questions based on simple interest, let the amount invested as ₹ x at some rate of interest and ₹ y at some other rate of interest.

Example 22. 37 pens and 53 pencils together cost ₹ 320, while 53 pens and 37 pencils together cost ₹ 400. Find the cost of a pen and that of a pencil.

Sol. Let the cost of a pen be ₹ x and that of a pencil be ₹ y.

According to the question,

$$37x + 53y = 320 \quad ...(i)$$

and $\quad 53x + 37y = 400 \quad ...(ii)$

On adding Eqs. (i) and (ii), we get

$$90x + 90y = 720$$

$\Rightarrow \quad x + y = 8 \quad ...(iii)$

On subtracting Eq. (i) from Eq. (ii), we get

$$16x - 16y = 80 \Rightarrow x - y = 5 \quad ...(iv)$$

Now, adding Eqs. (iii) and (iv), we get

$$2x = 13 \Rightarrow x = 6.5$$

On substituting $x = 6.5$ in Eq. (iii), we get

$$6.5 + y = 8 \Rightarrow y = 8 - 6.5 = 1.5$$

Hence, cost of one pen is ₹ 6.5 and cost of one pencil is ₹ 1.5.

Problem Based on Ages

(i) If the present age is x, then n times the present age $= nx$.

(ii) If the present age is x, then age n yr later $= x + n$.

(iii) If present age is x, then age n yr ago $= x - n$

Example 23. 4 yr ago, a mother was four times as old as her daughter. 6 yr later, the mother will be two and a half times as old as her daughter at that time. Find the present ages of mother and her daughter.

Sol. Let the present age of mother = x yr

and present age of daughter = y yr

For year ago,

The age of mother = $(x - 4)$ yr

the age of daughter = $(y - 4)$ yr

$$(x - 4) = 4(y - 4)$$

$$x - 4y + 12 = 0 \quad ...(i)$$

Six year later,

the age of mother = $(x + 6)$ yr

the age of daughter = $(y + 6)$ yr

$$(x + 6) = \frac{5}{2}(y + 6)$$

$\Rightarrow \quad 2x - 5y - 18 = 0 \quad ...(ii)$

From Eq. (i), we get

$$x = 4y - 12 \quad ...(iii)$$

On substituting value of x from Eq. (iii) in Eq. (ii), we get

$$2(4y - 12) - 5y - 18 = 0$$

$$8y - 24 - 5y - 18 = 0$$

$$3y = 42$$

$$y = 14$$

On substituting $y = 14$ in Eq. (iii), we get

$$x = 4 \times 14 - 12 \Rightarrow x = 44$$

Hence, the age of mother = 44 yr and the age of daughter = 14 yr.

Problems Based on Geometry and Mensuration

For these types of problems, we generally use the following concepts

(i) In case of a triangle, angle sum property of triangle, is used.

(ii) In case of a parallelogram, opposite angles are equal and sum of adjacent angles is 180°.

(iii) In case of a cyclic quadrilateral, opposite angles are supplementary.

Example 24. The area of a rectangle gets reduced by 9 sq units, if its length is reduced by 5 units and breadth is increased by 3 units. If we increase the length by 3 units and the breadth by 2 units, the area increases by 67 sq units. Find the dimensions of the rectangle.

Sol. Let x units be the length and y units be the breadth of a rectangle, then area of rectangle $= xy$ sq units.

In the first case, area is reduced by 9 sq units, when length $= (x - 5)$ units and breadth $= (y + 3)$ units,

i.e. $xy - (x - 5) \times (y + 3) = 9$

$\Rightarrow xy - (xy + 3x - 5y - 15) = 9$

$\Rightarrow -3x + 5y + 15 = 9$

$\Rightarrow 3x - 5y = 6$ ...(i)

In the second case, area is increased by 67 sq units, when length $= (x + 3)$ units and breadth $= (y + 2)$ units

i.e. $(x + 3) \times (y + 2) - xy = 67$

$\Rightarrow xy + 2x + 3y + 6 - xy = 67$

$\Rightarrow 2x + 3y = 61$ ...(ii)

On multiplying Eq. (i) by 3 and Eq. (ii) by 5, we get

$9x - 15y = 18$ ...(iii)

and $10x + 15y = 305$ ...(iv)

On adding Eqs. (iii) and (iv), we get

$19x = 323 \Rightarrow x = 17$

On substituting $x = 17$ in Eq. (ii), we get

$34 + 3y = 61 \Rightarrow 3y = 27 \Rightarrow y = 9$

Hence, the length of rectangle is 17 units and the breadth of rectangle is 9 units.

Exercise 5.2

1. The difference between two numbers is 26 and one number is three times the other. Find the numbers.
2. Find two numbers, such that the larger number added to three times the smaller number gives 7 and twice the larger number added to the smaller number gives 9.
3. The sum of the digits of a two-digit number is 9. Also, nine times this number is twice the number obtained by reversing the order of the digits. Find the number.
4. The sum of the digits of a two-digit number is 15. The number obtained by reversing the order of digits of the given number exceeds the given number by 9. Find the given number.
5. The sum of the digits of a two-digit number is 8 and the difference between the number and the number formed by reversing the digits is 18. Find the number.
6. A fraction becomes 1/3, when 1 is subtracted from the numerator and it becomes 1/4, when 8 is added to its denominator. Find the fraction.
7. A fraction is such that, if the numerator is multiplied by 3 and the denominator is reduced by 3, we get 18/11, but if the numerator is increased by 8 and the denominator is doubled, we get 2/5. Find the fraction.
8. If we add 1 to the numerator and subtract 1 from the denominator, a fraction reduces to 1. It becomes 1/2, if we only add 1 to the denominator. What is the fraction?
9. A fraction becomes 9/11, if 2 is added to both the numerator and the denominator. If 3 is added to both the numerator and the denominator, it becomes 5/6. Find the fraction.
10. Ritu can row downstream 20 km in 2 h and upstream 4 km in 2 h. Find her speed of rowing in still water and the speed of the current.
11. The coach of a cricket team buys 7 bats and 6 balls for ₹ 3800. Later, she buys 3 bats and 5 balls for ₹ 1750. Find the cost of each bat and each ball.
12. 2 tables and 3 chairs together cost ₹ 2000, where as 3 tables and 2 chairs together cost ₹ 2500. Find the total cost of 1 table and 5 chairs.
13. The taxi charges in a city consist of a fixed charge together with the charge for the distance covered. For a distance of 10 km, the charge paid is ₹ 105 and for a journey of 15 km, the charge paid is ₹ 155. What are the fixed charges and the charge per kilometre? How much does a person have to pay for travelling a distance of 25 km?
14. Five years ago, Nuri was thrice as old as Sonu. Ten years later, Nuri will be twice as old as Sonu. How old are Nuri and Sonu?
15. The present ages of A and B are in the ratio 9 : 4. Seven years hence, the ratio of their ages will be 5 : 3. Find their present ages.
16. If twice the son's age (in years) is added to the father's age, the sum is 70. But if twice the father age is added to the son's age, the sum is 95. Find the ages of father and son.
17. The area of a rectangle gets reduced by 9 sq units, if its length is reduced by 5 unit and breadth is increased by 3 units. If we increase the length by 3 units and breadth by 2 units, then the area is increased by 67 sq units. Find the dimensions of the rectangle.

Chapter Practice

a. 1 Mark Questions

1. The sum of two numbers is 12 and their difference is 2, then the numbers are
   (a) 7 and 5 (b) 5 and 3
   (c) 6 and 4 (d) None of these

2. The sum of two natural numbers is 240 and their ratio is 3 : 5. Then, the greater number is
   (a) 180 (b) 160
   (c) 150 (d) 90

3. Sum of digits of a two digit number is 8.If the number obtained by reversing the digits is 18 more than the original number, then the original number is
   (a) 35 (b) 53
   (c) 26 (d) 62

4. Which one is satisfies the equations
   $\frac{x}{a}+\frac{y}{b}=a+b$
   and $\frac{x}{a^2}+\frac{y}{b^2}=2,\ a\neq 0,\ b\neq 0$
   (a) $x=a^2$ and $y=b^2$ (b) $x=a$ and $y=b$
   (c) $x=b^2$ and $y=a^2$ (d) $x=b$ and $y=a$

5. The sum of two natural number is 25 and their difference is 7. The numbers are
   (a) 17 and 8 (b) 16 and 9
   (c) 18 and 7 (d) 15 and 10

b. 3 Marks Questions

6. Solve the following pair of equations.
   $43x + 67y = -24$ and $67x + 43y = 24$

7. Solve $2x + 3y = 11$ and $2x - 4y = -24$ and hence find the value of m, for which $y = mx + 3$.

8. Solve $2ax - by = 2a^2 - b^2$ and $ax + 2by = a^2 + 2b^2$.

9. In a two-digit number, the ten's digit is six times the unit's digit. When the number is decreased by 45, the digits are reversed. Find the number.

10. In a two-digit number, the unit's digit is twice the ten's digit. If 27 is added to the number, the digits interchange their places. Find the number.

11. 5 pencils and 7 pens together cost ₹ 50, whereas 7 pencils and 5 pens together cost ₹ 46. Find the cost of one pencil and that of one pen.

12. Find the cost of 2 T-shirts and 3 pants, if the cost of 2 T-shirts and one pant is ₹ 625 and 3 T-shirts and 2 pants together cost ₹ 1125.

13. Find the values of x and y in the following rectangle.

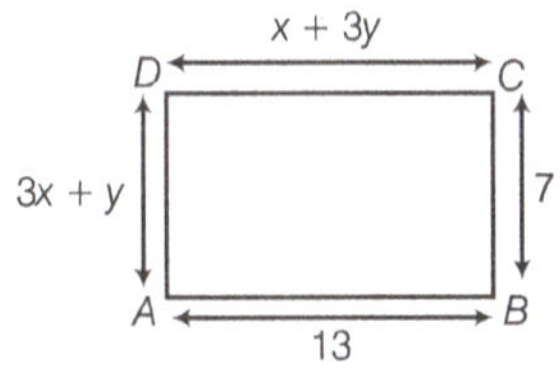

c. 4/5 Marks Questions

14. Solve, using the method of elimination by equating coefficients.
    $x + y = 3.3$ and $\frac{0.6}{3x - 2y} = -1.$
    Given, $3x - 2y \neq 0$

15. The sum of two number is 400 and the difference between their squares is 40000. Find the numbers.

16. Mala buys postage stamps of denominations 75 paise and 50 paise for ₹ 20. She buys 32 stamps in all. Find the number of 75 paise stamps bought by her.

17. If three times the larger of two numbers is divided by the smaller one, we get 4 as the quotient and 3 as the remainder. Also, if seven times the smaller number is divided by the larger one, we get 5 as the quotient and 1 as the remainder. Find the numbers.

18. Ten percent of the red balls were added to twenty percent of the blue balls and the total was 24. Yet three times the number of red balls exceeds the number of blue balls by 20. How many were red balls and how many were blue balls?

19. At a certain time in a deer park, the number of heads and the number of legs of deer and human visitors were counted and it was found that there were 41 heads and 136 legs. Find the number of deer and human visitors in the park.

20. Solve the following pairs of linear equations
    $\frac{2}{\sqrt{x}}+\frac{3}{\sqrt{y}}=2;\ \frac{4}{\sqrt{x}}-\frac{9}{\sqrt{y}}=-1$

21. Solve the following pairs of linear equations
$(a-b)x+(a+b)y=a^2-2ab-b^2$
$(a+b)(x+y)=a^2+b^2$

22. Solve the following pair of linear equations for x and y
$$\frac{b}{a}x+\frac{a}{b}y=a^2+b^2 \text{ and } x+y=2ab.$$

23. The sum of two numbers is 13 and the sum of their reciprocals is $\frac{13}{36}$. Find the numbers.

24. The ratio of incomes of two persons is 9 : 7 and the ratio of their expenditures is 4 : 3. If each of them manages to save ₹ 2000 per month, find their monthly incomes.

25. A train covered a certain distance at a uniform speed. If the train had been 6 km/h, faster, it would have taken 4 h less than the scheduled time. And, if the train were slower by 6 km/h, it would have taken 6 h more than the scheduled time. Find the length of the journey.

d. 6 Marks Questions

26. Solve the following system of linear equations by cross-multiplication method
$$3(ax-by)+(a+6b)=0$$
and $$3(bx+ay)+(b-6a)=0$$

27. Solve $\frac{2x-8}{3}-\frac{3y-7}{2}=1$ and $\frac{3-2x}{7}-\frac{5-y}{3}=-1.$

28. Can the following equations hold simultaneously?
$$\frac{7x-2y}{xy}=5;\ \frac{8x+7y}{xy}=15 \text{ and } 2x+3y=5$$

29. Solve the following pair of equations by reducing them to a pair of linear equations.
$$\frac{1}{(3x+y)}+\frac{1}{(3x-y)}=\frac{3}{4}$$
and $$\frac{1}{2(3x+y)}-\frac{1}{2(3x-y)}=\frac{-1}{8}$$

30. A and B each have a certain number of mangoes. A says to B, if you give 30 of your mangoes, I will have twice as many as left with you. B replies, if you give me 10, I will have thrice as many as left with you. How many mangoes does each have?

31. Places A and B are 100 km apart on a highway. One car starts from A and another from B at the same time. If the cars travel in the same direction at different speeds, they meet in 5 h. If they travel towards each other, they meet in 1 h. What are the speeds of the two cars?

32. X takes 3 h more than Y to walk 30 km. But if X doubles his pace, he is ahead of Y by $1\frac{1}{2}$ an hour. Find their speed of walking.

33. A train covered a certain distance at a uniform speed. If the train would have been 10 km/h faster, it would have taken 2 h less than the scheduled time and if the train were slower by 10 km/h, it would have taken 3 h more than the scheduled time. Find the distance covered by the train.

34. The total railway fare for 4 members travelling in 3-Tier coach and 3 members travelling in 2-Tier coach is ₹ 5100, whereas the total railway fare for 3 members travelling in 3-Tier coach and 4 members travelling in 2-Tier coach is ₹ 5400. Find the fare to be paid by a couple travelling through 2-Tier.

35. A railway half ticket costs half the full fare, but the reservation charges are the same on a half ticket as on a full ticket. One reserved first class ticket from the station A to B costs ₹ 2530. Also, one reserved first class ticket and one reserved first class half ticket from station A to B costs ₹ 3810. Find the full first class fare from station A to B and also the reservation charges for a ticket.

36. A lending library has a fixed charge for the first three days and an additional charge for each day thereafter. Sarita paid ₹ 27 for a book kept for seven days, while Susy paid ₹ 21 for the book she kept for five days. Find the fixed charge and the charge for each extra day.

37. Mr. A and Mr. B together can do a piece of work in 15 days. If one day's work of Mr. B is $\frac{2}{3}$ times one day's work of Mr. A, find in how many days, each alone will do the work?

38. In a ΔABC, if $\angle C=3\angle B=2(\angle A+\angle B)$, then find the three angles.

39. The length of the sides of a triangle is given as
$$2x+\frac{y}{2},\ \frac{5x}{3}+y+\frac{1}{2} \text{ and } \frac{2}{3}x+2y+\frac{5}{2}.$$
Given that the triangle is equilateral, find its area.

40. Sonia invests a certain sum at the rate of 10% per annum of interest and another sum at the rate of 8% per annum and get a yield of ₹ 1640 in one year's time. Next year, she interchanges the rates and gets a yield of ₹ 40 less than the previous year. How much did she invest in each type in the first year?

Hints and Answers

Exercise 5.1

1. (i) **Hint** Given, equations are $x + y = 8$ ...(i)

and $2x - 3y = 1$ ...(ii)

From Eq. (i), we get $y = 8 - x$

Then, from Eq. (ii), we get

$2x - 3(8 - x) = 1 \Rightarrow 5x = 25 \Rightarrow x = 5$

$\therefore$ $y = 8 - 5 = 3$ **Ans.** $x = 5, y = 3$

(ii) **Hint** Given, equations are $3x + 2y = 10$ ...(i)

and $12x + 8y = 30$ ...(ii)

From Eq. (i), we get $y = \frac{10 - 3x}{2}$

Then, from Eq. (ii), we get

$12x + 8\left(\frac{10 - 3x}{2}\right) = 30$

$\Rightarrow 12x + 40 - 12x = 30 \Rightarrow 40 = 30$

Ans. No solution exists.

(iii) **Hint** Given, equations are $2x - 7y = 11$ ...(i)

and $6x - 21y = 33$ ...(ii)

From Eq. (i), we get $y = \frac{2x - 11}{7}$

Then, from Eq. (ii), we get $6x - 21\left(\frac{2x - 11}{7}\right) = 33$

$\Rightarrow 6x - 6x + 33 = 33 \Rightarrow 33 = 33$

Ans. Infinitely many solutions.

(iv) **Hint** Do same as part (iii).

Ans. Infinitely many solutions.

(v) **Hint** Do same as part (i). **Ans.** $x = 3, y = -2$

2. **Hint** Given, equations are

$$\frac{x}{7} + \frac{y}{3} = 5 \quad ...(i)$$

and $$\frac{x}{2} - \frac{y}{9} = 6 \quad ...(ii)$$

On multiply Eq. (i) by LCM (7, 3) = 21 and Eq. (ii) by LCM (9, 2) = 18. Then, we get

$$3x + 7y = 105 \text{ and } 9x - 2y = 108$$

Now, do same as Example 3.

Ans. $x = 14, y = 9$

3. **Hint** Given, pair of linear equations is

$$0.2x + 0.3y = 1.3 \quad ...(i)$$

and $$0.4x + 0.5y = 2.3 \quad ...(ii)$$

On multiplying both equations by 10, we get

$$2x + 3y = 13 \quad ...(iii)$$

and $$4x + 5y = 23 \quad ...(iv)$$

Now, do same as Example 3.

Ans. $x = 2, y = 3$

4. **Hint** Given, pair of equations is

$$\frac{x}{10} + \frac{y}{5} - 1 = 0 \quad ...(i)$$

and $$\frac{x}{8} + \frac{y}{6} = 15 \quad ...(ii)$$

Now, multiplying both sides of Eq. (i) by LCM (10, 5) = 10, we get

$$x + 2y - 10 = 0$$

$$\Rightarrow \quad x + 2y = 10 \quad ...(iii)$$

Again, multiplying both sides of Eq. (ii) by LCM (8, 6) = 24, we get

$$3x + 4y = 360 \quad ...(iv)$$

Now, do same as Example 5.

Ans. $x = 340, y = -165$ and $\lambda = -\frac{1}{2}$

5. (i) **Hint** Given, pair of linear equations is

$$8x + 5y = 11 \quad ...(i)$$

and $$x + y = 4 \quad ...(ii)$$

On multiplying Eq. (ii) by 8 and then subtracting from Eq. (i), we get

$$-3y = -21 \Rightarrow y = 7$$

Putting $y = 7$ in Eq. (ii), we get

$$x = 4 - 7 = -3$$

Ans. $x = -3, y = 7$

(ii) **Hint** Do same as part (i). **Ans.** $x = \frac{3}{2}, y = -\frac{2}{3}$

(iii) **Hint** Do same as part (i). **Ans.** $x = 2, y = -3$

(iv) **Hint** Do same as part (i).

Ans. $x = \frac{9}{13}, y = \frac{-5}{13}$

(v) **Hint** Given, pair of linear equations is

$$0.4x + 0.3y = 1.7 \quad ...(i)$$

and $$0.7x - 0.2y = 0.8 \quad ...(ii)$$

On multiplying Eq. (i) by 20 and Eq. (ii) by 30 and then adding both equations, we get

$$29x = 58 \Rightarrow x = 2$$

On putting $x = 2$ in Eq. (ii), we get

$$0.7 \times 2 - 0.8 = 0.2y \Rightarrow y = 3$$

Ans. $x = 2$ and $y = 3$

(vi) **Hint** Given, pair of linear equations is

$$\frac{x}{4} + \frac{y}{3} = -\frac{1}{12}$$

$$\Rightarrow \quad 3x + 4y = -1 \quad ...(i)$$

and $$\frac{x}{2} - \frac{5}{4}y = \frac{7}{4} \Rightarrow 2x - 5y = 7 \quad ...(ii)$$

On multiplying Eq. (i) by 5 and Eq. (ii) by 4 and then adding both equations, we get

$$23x = 23 \Rightarrow x = 1$$

On putting $x = 1$ in Eq. (ii), we get

$$2 \times 1 - 7 = 5y \Rightarrow y = -1$$

Ans. $x = 1, y = -1$

(vii) **Hint** Do same as part (vi).

Ans. $x = 2, y = -3$

6. (i) **Hint** Given, pair of equations is

$4x + 6y - 5 = 0$ and $2x + 9y - 3 = 0$.

By cross-multiplication method, we get

$$\frac{x}{-18+45}=\frac{y}{-10+12}=\frac{1}{36-12}$$

Ans. $x=\frac{9}{8}, y=\frac{1}{12}$

(ii) **Hint** Do same as part (i).

Ans. $x=2, y=-\frac{3}{2}$

(iii) **Hint** Do same as part (i).

Ans. $x=3, y=2$

(iv) **Hint** $\frac{x}{\frac{-6}{3}-\frac{5}{9}}=\frac{y}{-\frac{5}{2}+\frac{6}{7}}=\frac{1}{-\frac{1}{63}-\frac{1}{6}}$

Ans. $x=14$ and $y=9$

(v) **Hint** Given pair of linear equations can be written as

$$8x+5y-9=0 \quad \text{...(i)}$$

and $$3x+2y-4=0 \quad \text{...(ii)}$$

Now, do same as Example 9.

Ans. $x=-2, y=5$

7. (i) Hint Do same as Example 12.

Ans. $x=\frac{1}{6}, y=\frac{1}{4}$

(ii) **Hint** Do same as Example 12.

Ans. $x=\frac{1}{5}, y=-2$

(iii) **Hint** Equation $\frac{2xy}{x+y}=\frac{3}{2}$, where $x+y\neq 0$, can be written as

$$\frac{1}{y}+\frac{1}{x}=\frac{4}{3} \quad \text{...(i)}$$

and the equation $\frac{xy}{2x-y}=\frac{-3}{10}$, where $2x-y\neq 0$, can be written as

$$\frac{2}{y}-\frac{1}{x}=\frac{-10}{3} \quad \text{...(ii)}$$

Now, do same as Example 12.

Ans. $x=\frac{1}{2}, y=-\frac{3}{2}$

8. **Hint** Here, $x=0$ and $y=0$ is a solution of the given system of equations.

Now, when $x\neq 0$ and $y\neq 0$, then divide both sides of each equation by xy,

i.e. $$\frac{1}{y}+\frac{1}{x}=14 \quad \text{...(i)}$$

and $$\frac{2}{y}-\frac{1}{x}=4 \quad \text{...(ii)}$$

Now, do same as Example 12.

Ans. $x=0, y=0$ and $x=\frac{1}{8}, y=\frac{1}{6}$

9. **Hint** Do same as Example 13.

Ans. $x=4, y=5$

Exercise 5.2

1. **Hint** Let the two numbers be x and y $(x>y)$.

According to the question,

$$x-y=26 \quad \text{...(i)}$$

and $$x=3y \quad \text{...(ii)}$$

Ans. 39 and 13

2. **Hint** Let larger number and smaller number be x and y, respectively.

Then, according to the question,

$$x+3y=7 \quad \text{...(i)}$$

and $$2x+y=9 \quad \text{...(ii)}$$

Ans. Larger number is 4 and smaller number is 1.

3. **Hint** Let x be the digit at unit's place and y be the digit at ten's place of the required two-digit number.

Then, two-digit number $=x+10y$

According to the question,

$$x+y=9 \quad \text{...(i)}$$

When we reverse the order of the digits, then

New two-digit number $=y+10x$

According to the question,

$$9\times(x+10y)=2\times(y+10x)$$

$$\Rightarrow 9x+90y=2y+20x$$

$$\Rightarrow 88y=11x \Rightarrow x=8y \quad \text{...(ii)}$$

Ans. 18

4. **Hint** Let the digit at the unit's place be x and digit at the ten's place be y. Then, number formed $=10y+x$

Number formed by reversing the digits

$$=10x+y$$

According to the question,

$$x+y=15 \quad \text{...(i)}$$

and $10x+y=(10y+x)+9$

$$\Rightarrow x-y=1 \quad \text{...(ii)}$$

Ans. 78

5. **Hint** Do same as Q. 4. **Ans.** 53

6. **Hint** Let the fraction be $\frac{x}{y}$.

For condition I, we get

$$\frac{x-1}{y}=\frac{1}{3} \Rightarrow 3x-y=3 \quad \text{...(i)}$$

For condition II, we get $\frac{x}{y+8}=\frac{1}{4}$

$$\Rightarrow 4x-y=8 \quad \text{...(ii)}$$

Now, by solving Eqs. (i) and (ii), we get the required fraction.

Ans. $\frac{5}{12}$

7. **Hint** Do same as Example 17. **Ans.** $\frac{12}{25}$

8. **Hint** Do same as Example 17. **Ans.** $\frac{3}{5}$

9. **Hint** Do same as Example 17. **Ans.** 7/9

10. **Hint** Let speed of Ritu in still water = x km/h
and speed of current = y km/h
Then, downstream speed = $(x + y)$ km/h
and upstream speed = $(x - y)$ km/h
According to the question,
$$\frac{20}{x+y} = 2 \quad \left[\because \text{time} = \frac{\text{distance}}{\text{speed}}\right]$$
$$\Rightarrow \quad x + y = 10 \quad \ldots(i)$$
and $$\frac{4}{x-y} = 2 \Rightarrow x - y = 2 \quad \ldots(ii)$$
Ans. Speed of Ritu in still water = 6 km/h;
Speed of current = 4 km/h

11. **Hint** Let cost of one bat = ₹ x and cost of one ball = ₹ y
According to the question,
Cost of 7 bats and 6 balls = ₹ 3800
i.e. $7x + 6y = 3800$ ...(i)
Cost of 3 bats and 5 balls = ₹ 1750
i.e. $3x + 5y = 1750$ ...(ii)
Now, by solving Eqs. (i) and (ii), we get the value of x and y.
Ans. Cost of one bat = ₹ 500, Cost of one ball = ₹ 50

12. **Hint** Do same as Q. 11. **Ans.** ₹1700

13. **Hint** Let fixed charge be ₹ x and the charge per kilometre be ₹ y.
According to the question,
$x + 10y = 105$ ...(i)
and $x + 15y = 155$ ...(ii)
Ans. Fixed charges = ₹ 5; Charges per kilometre = ₹10;
Charges for 25 km = ₹ $(5 + 25 \times 10)$ = ₹ 255

14. **Hint** Let the present age of Nuri be x yr and the present age of Sonu be y yr.
5 yr ago, Nuri's age = $(x - 5)$ yr
and Sonu's age = $(y - 5)$ yr
According to the question,
$x - 5 = 3(y - 5) \Rightarrow x - 3y = -10$ ...(i)
After 10 yr, Nuri's age = $(x + 10)$ yr
and Sonu's age = $(y + 10)$ yr
According to the question,
$x + 10 = 2(y + 10)$
$\Rightarrow \quad x - 2y = 10$ ...(ii)
Ans. Nuri's age = 50 yr, Sonu's age = 20 yr

15. **Hint** Let present age of A and B be x and y, respectively.
Then, according to the question,
$$\frac{x}{y} = \frac{9}{4} \quad \ldots(i)$$
and $$\frac{x+7}{y+7} = \frac{5}{3}$$
Ans. A's present age is 18 yr and B's present age is 8 yr.

16. **Hint** Let son's age and father's age be x and y, respectively.
Then, according to the question,
$2x + y = 70$ ...(i)
$x + 2y = 95$ ...(ii)
Ans. Ages of father and son are 40 yr and 15 yr, respectively.

17. **Hint** Let the length and breadth of rectangle be x units and y units.
$(x - 5)(y + 3) = xy - 9$ and $(x + 3)(y + 2) = xy + 67$
$xy + 2x + 3y + 6 = xy + 67$
$3x - 5y - 6 = 0$ ...(i)
$2x + 3y - 61 = 0$ ...(ii)
$y = 9$
Subtituting this value of y in Eq. (ii)
$x = 17$
Hence the length of rectangle = 17 units and breadth = 9 units.

Chapter Exercise

1. (a) 2. (c) 3. (a)
4. (a) 5. (b)

6. **Hint** On adding given equations, we get
$x + y = 0$...(i)
On subtracting given equations, we get
$x - y = 2$ ...(ii)
Ans. $x = 1$ and $y = -1$

7. **Hint** Do same as Example 5.
Ans. $x = -2$, $y = 5$ and $m = -1$

8. **Hint** Given equations are
$2ax - by = 2a^2 - b^2$ ...(i)
and $ax + 2by = a^2 + 2b^2$ ...(ii)
Now, on multiplying Eq. (ii) by 2 and then subtracting from Eq. (i).
After that put the value of y in Eq. (i) and get the value of x.
Ans. $x = a$, $y = b$

9. **Hint** Let the unit's digit be x and ten's digit be y.
Then, the number is $10y + x$.
Now, according to the question,
$y = 6x$ ...(i)
Also, it is given that, when the number is decreased by 45, the digits are reversed. Therefore, we have
$10y + x - 45 = 10x + y$
$\Rightarrow \quad x - y = -5$ ...(ii)
Now, solving Eqs. (i) and (ii), we get the required result.
Ans. 61

10. **Hint** Do same as Q. 9.
Ans. 36

11. **Hint** Do same as Example 22.
Ans. Cost of a pencil = ₹ 3 and cost of a pen = ₹ 5

12. **Hint** Let the cost of one T-shirt be ₹ x and that of one pant be ₹ y. Then,

According to the question,

$$2x + y = 625 \quad \dots(i)$$

and $$3x + 2y = 1125 \quad \dots(ii)$$

Cost of 2 T-shirts and 3 pants = ₹ $(2x + 3y)$.

Ans. ₹ 1375

13. Hint Use the property of rectangle that its opposite sides are equal, to form linear equations and then solve by any suitable method.

Ans. $x = 1$ and $y = 4$

14. Hint Rewrite it as ...(i)

$$\frac{0.6}{3x - 2y} = -1$$

$$\Rightarrow \quad 0.6 = -3x + 2y$$

Solve, we get the result

$$x = 1.2 \text{ and } y = 2.1$$

Ans. $x = 1.2$ and $y = 2.1$

15. Hint Let the larger number be x and the smaller number be y, then

$$x + y = 400 \quad \dots(i)$$

and $$x^2 - y^2 = 40000 \quad \dots(ii)$$

On dividing Eq. (ii) by Eq. (i), we get

$$x - y = 100 \quad \dots(iii)$$

On adding Eqs. (i) and (iii), we get

Ans. 250, 150

16. Hint Let the number of 75 paise stamps is x and number of 50 paise stamps is y.

According to the question,

$$x + y = 32 \quad \dots(i)$$

and $$75x + 50y = 2000 \quad [\because ₹\ 20 = 20 \times 100 \text{ paise}]$$

$$\Rightarrow \quad 3x + 2y = 80 \quad \dots(ii)$$

Ans. Number of 75 paise stamps is 16.

17. Hint Let the larger number be x and the smaller be y.

We know that

Dividend = (Divisor × Quotient) + Remainder

According to the question,

$$3x = 4y + 3 \quad \dots(i)$$

$$7y = 5x + 1 \quad \dots(ii)$$

Ans. The required number are 25 and 18.

18. Hint Let there be x red balls and y blue balls.

According to the question,

$$10\% \text{ of } x + 20\% \text{ of } y = 24$$

$$x + 2y = 240$$

and $$3x - y = 20$$

Ans. There were 40 red balls and 100 blue balls.

19. Hint Let there is x deer and y human.

As a deer and a human each has one head,

$$x + y = 41 \quad \dots(i)$$

As a deer has 4 legs and a human has 2 legs

$$4x + 2y = 136 \quad \dots(ii)$$

Solve and get the result

Ans. There were 27 deer and 14 human.

20. Hint Substituting $\frac{1}{\sqrt{x}} = a$ and $\frac{1}{\sqrt{y}} = b$, we get

$$2a + 3b = 2 \quad \dots(i)$$

and $$4a - 9b = -1 \quad \dots(ii)$$

Solve and get the result. **Ans.** $x = 4$, $y = 9$

21. Hint $(a - b)x + (a + b)y = a^2 - 2ab - b^2 \quad \dots(i)$

$$(a + b)(x + y) = a^2 + b^2 \quad \dots(ii)$$

Rewrite the Eq. (ii),

$$(a + b)x + (a + b)y = a^2 + b^2 \quad \dots(iii)$$

Solve and get the result

Ans. $x = a + b$ and $y = -\frac{2ab}{a + b}$

22. Hint $\frac{b}{a}x + \frac{a}{b}y = a^2 + b^2 \quad \dots(i)$

and $$x + y = 2ab \quad \dots(ii)$$

Use substitution method and get the result

Ans. $x = ab$ and $y = ab$

23. Hint Let the required numbers be x and y

According to the statements,

$$x + y = 13 \quad \dots(i)$$

And $$\frac{1}{x} + \frac{1}{y} = \frac{13}{36}$$

$$xy = 36$$

We know $(x - y) = \sqrt{(x + y)^2 - 4xy}$

Ans. The required numbers are 9 and 4.

24. Hint Let the monthly income of two persons be ₹x and ₹ y.

Savings = ₹ 2000

Expenditure are ₹ $(x - 2000)$ and ₹$(y - 2000)$

According to the question,

$$\frac{x}{y} = \frac{9}{7}$$

$$\Rightarrow \quad \frac{x - 2000}{y - 2000} = \frac{4}{3}$$

Ans. Monthly incomes are ₹ 18000 and ₹ 14000.

25. Hint Let the original speed of the train is x km/h and the time taken to complete the journey is y h.

Length of whole journey = (xy) km.

Case I Speed = $(x + 6)$ km/h

and time = $(y - 4)$ h

Length of total journey = $(x + 6)(y - 4)$ km

$$\therefore \quad xy = (x + 6)(y - 4)$$

or $$xy = xy - 4x + 6y - 24$$

or $$4x - 6y = -24$$

or $2x - 3y = -12$ ... (i)

Case II Speed $= (x - 6)$ km/h

and time $= (y + 6)$ h

Length of total journey $= (x - 6)(y + 6)$ km

$\therefore \quad xy = (x - 6)(y + 6)$

or $\quad xy = xy + 6x - 6y - 36$

or $\quad 6x - 6y = 36$

or $\quad x - y = 6$ ...(ii)

Multiplying Eq. (ii) by 3 and subtracting Eq. (i)

Ans. Length of the journey = 720 km

26. Hint On writing the coefficients in pattern of cross-multiplication, we get

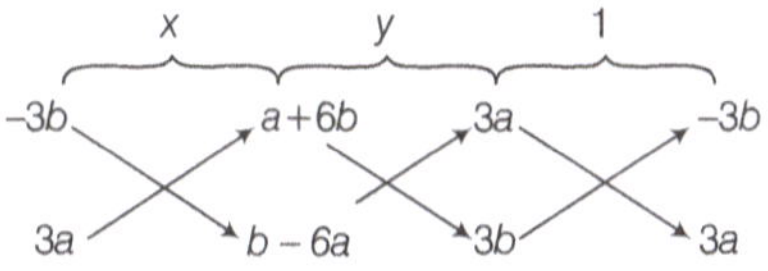

Ans. $x = -\frac{1}{3}$ and $y = 2$

27. Hint Given, system of equation is

$$\frac{2x-8}{3} - \frac{3y-7}{2} = 1 \quad \text{...(i)}$$

and $$\frac{3-2x}{7} - \frac{5-y}{3} = -1 \quad \text{...(ii)}$$

Now, to remove fraction multiply Eq. (i) by 6 and Eq. (ii) by 21.

[$\because$ LCM of 3 and 2 = 6 and LCM of 7 and 3 = 21]

Ans. $x = -2$ and $y = -1$

28. Hint Given, system of equations are

$$\frac{7}{y} - \frac{2}{x} = 5 \quad \text{...(i)}$$

$$\frac{8}{y} + \frac{7}{x} = 15 \quad \text{...(ii)}$$

and $$2x + 3y = 5 \quad \text{...(iii)}$$

Now, let us solve the first two equations simultaneously.

On putting $\frac{1}{x} = u$ and $\frac{1}{y} = v$ in given equations, we get

$$7v - 2u = 5 \quad \text{...(iv)}$$

and $$8v + 7u = 15 \quad \text{...(v)}$$

Thus, $x = 1$ and $y = 1$ is the solution of Eqs. (i) and (ii).

Now, putting $x = 1$ and $y = 1$ in Eq. (iii), we get

$$2 \times 1 + 3 \times 1 = 5$$

$\Rightarrow \quad 2 + 3 = 5$

$\Rightarrow \quad 5 = 5$, which is true.

Ans. The three given equations can hold simultaneously and the solution is $x = 1$ and $y = 1$.

29. Hint On putting $\frac{1}{(3x+y)} = u$ and $\frac{1}{(3x-y)} = v$ in given equations, we get

$$u + v = \frac{3}{4} \quad \text{...(i)}$$

and $$\frac{1}{2}u - \frac{1}{2}v = -\frac{1}{8}$$

$\Rightarrow \quad u - v = -\frac{1}{4}$ ...(ii)

Now, solving Eqs. (i) and (ii), we get the result.

Ans. $x = 1$ and $y = 1$.

30. Hint Let A has x mangoes and B has y mangoes.

According to the question,

$$x + 30 = 2(y - 30)$$

$\Rightarrow \quad x - 2y = -90$ ...(i)

and $\quad y + 10 = 3(x - 10)$

$\Rightarrow \quad 3x - y = 40$ ...(ii)

Now, solving Eqs. (i) and (ii), we get the result.

Ans. A has 34 mangoes and B has 62 mangoes.

31. Hint Let speed of car I = x km/h

and speed of car II = y km/h.

Car I starts from point A and car II starts from point B.

Case I Cars travel in the same direction

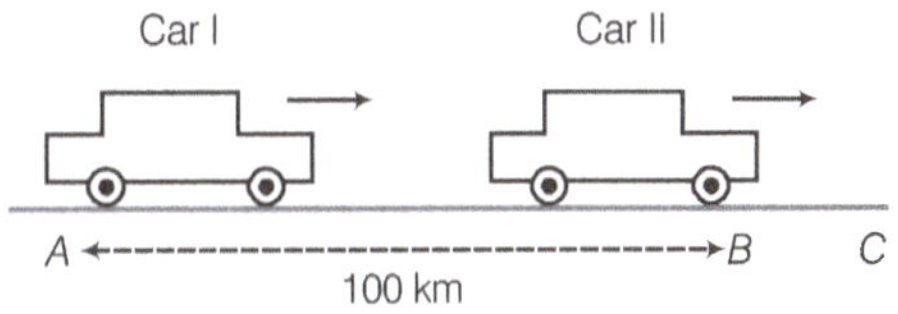

Since, two cars meet at C after 5 h, therefore

AC = Distance travelled by car I in 5 h = $5x$ km

BC = Distance travelled by car II in 5 h = $5y$ km

We know that $AC - BC = AB$

$\Rightarrow \quad 5x - 5y = 100$ [$\because AB = 100$ km]

$\Rightarrow \quad x - y = 20$ [dividing by 5] ...(i)

Case II Cars travel towards each other

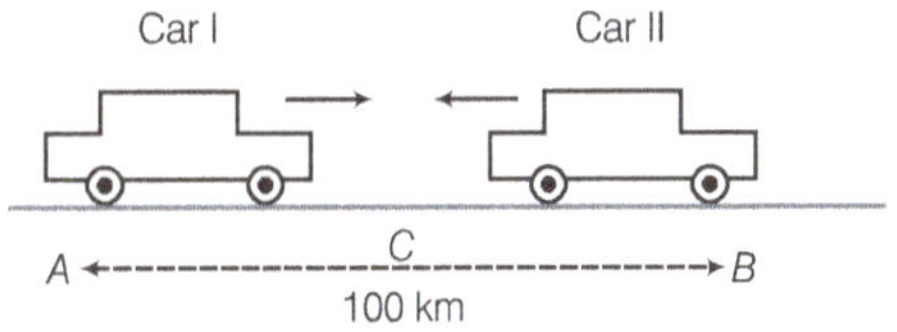

Since, two cars met at C after one hour, therefore

$$AC + CB = 100 \Rightarrow x + y = 100 \quad \text{...(ii)}$$

Ans. The speed of the two cars are 60 km/h and 40 km/h, respectively.

32. Hint Let the speed of X and Y be x km/h and y km/h, respectively.

According to the question,

$$\frac{30}{x} - \frac{30}{y} = 3 \quad \left[\because \text{time} = \frac{\text{distance}}{\text{speed}}\right]$$

$\Rightarrow \quad \frac{10}{x} - \frac{10}{y} = 1$ [dividing both sides by 3] ...(i)

If X doubles his pace, then speed of X is $2x$ km/h.

Then, according to the question,

$$\frac{30}{y} - \frac{30}{2x} = 1\frac{1}{2} \Rightarrow -\frac{10}{x} + \frac{20}{y} = 1 \quad \text{...(ii)}$$

Now, solving Eqs. (i) and (ii), we get the result.

Ans. Speed of X and Y are $\frac{10}{3}$ km/h and 5 km/h, respectively.

33. Hint Let the speed of train be x km/h and the scheduled time is y h.

Then, according to the question,

$$xy = (x + 10)(y - 2)$$

[$\because$ distance = speed × time and distance will remain same]

and $xy = (x - 10)(y + 3)$

The above equations can be written as

$$x - 5y = -10 \quad \text{...(i)}$$

and $3x - 10y = 30$ ...(ii)

Now, solving Eqs. (i) and (ii), we get the result.

Ans. 600 km

34. Hint Let fare for one member in 3-Tier be ₹ x and fare for one member in 2-Tier be ₹ y.

According to the question,

$$4x + 3y = 5100 \quad \text{...(i)}$$

and $3x + 4y = 5400$ ...(ii)

Now, solving Eqs. (i) and (ii), we get the result.

Ans. ₹ 1800

35. Hint Let the cost of full and half first class fare be ₹ x and ₹ $\frac{x}{2}$, respectively and reservation charges be ₹ y per ticket.

Case I Cost of one reserved first class ticket from the station A to B = ₹ 2530

$$\Rightarrow \quad x + y = 2530 \quad \text{...(i)}$$

Case II Cost of one reserved first class ticket and one reserved first class half ticket from station A to B = ₹ 3810

$$\Rightarrow \quad x + y + \frac{x}{2} + y = 3810$$

$$\Rightarrow \quad 3x + 4y = 7620 \quad \text{...(ii)}$$

Ans. Full first class fare from stations A to B is ₹ 2500 and the reservation charges for a ticket is ₹ 30.

36. Hint Let the fixed charge for the first three days be ₹ x

and the additional charge per day be ₹ y.

According to the question,

Sarita paid for 7 days = ₹ 27

$$\Rightarrow \quad x + 4 \times y = 27$$

$$\Rightarrow \quad x + 4y = 27 \quad \text{...(i)}$$

[$\because$ ₹ $4y$ are to be paid for extra 4 days]

Susy paid for 5 days = ₹ 21

$$\Rightarrow \quad x + 2y = 21 \quad \text{...(ii)}$$

[$\because$ ₹ $2y$ are to be paid for extra 2 days]

Ans. The fixed charge for first three days is ₹ 15 and additional charge for each extra day is ₹ 3.

37. Hint Let Mr. A alone will do the work in x days and Mr. B alone will do the work in y days.

According to the question, $\frac{1}{y} = \frac{2}{3} \times \frac{1}{x}$

$$\Rightarrow \quad \frac{2}{x} - \frac{3}{y} = 0 \quad \text{...(i)}$$

Also, we have $\frac{1}{x} + \frac{1}{y} = \frac{1}{15}$

$\left[\because \text{in 1 day, they do } \frac{1}{15} \text{ work}\right]$

Ans. Mr. A alone will do the work in 25 days and Mr. B alone will do the work in 37.5 days.

38. Hint Let $\angle A = x$ and $\angle B = y$.

Then, $\angle C = 3\angle B = 3y$.

$\because \quad 3\angle B = 2(\angle A + \angle B)$ [given]

$\therefore \quad 3y = 2(x + y) \Rightarrow y = 2x$ ...(i)

Also, we know that the sum of interior angles of a triangle is 180°.

$$\therefore \quad \angle A + \angle B + \angle C = 180^\circ$$

$$\Rightarrow \quad x + y + 3y = 180 \quad \text{...(ii)}$$

Ans. The angles are $\angle A = 20^\circ$, $\angle B = 40^\circ$ and $\angle C = 120^\circ$.

39. Hint Use the property of an equilateral triangle, i.e. all sides are equal in length, to form a pair of linear equations. Then, any pair of linear equations can be solved by any suitable method.

Now, find the length of side, by substituting the value of x and y in the given lengths.

Also, use the formula,

$\therefore$ Area of equilateral triangle $= \frac{\sqrt{3}}{4}(\text{Side})^2$

Ans. 18.295 sq units

40. Hint Let us assume that Sonia invests ₹ x at the rate of 10% and ₹ y at the rate of 8% in the first year.

We know that simple interest, $\text{SI} = \frac{PRT}{100}$

According to the question,

$$\frac{x \times 10 \times 1}{100} + \frac{y \times 8 \times 1}{100} = 1640$$

$$\Rightarrow \quad 10x + 8y = 164000 \quad \text{...(i)}$$

Now, after interchanging the rates, we get

$$\frac{y \times 10 \times 1}{100} + \frac{x \times 8 \times 1}{100} = 1640 - 40 = 1600$$

$$\Rightarrow \quad 10y + 8x = 160000$$

$$\Rightarrow \quad 8x + 10y = 160000 \quad \text{...(ii)}$$

On adding Eqs. (i) and (ii), we get

$$18x + 18y = 324000$$

$$\Rightarrow \quad x + y = 18000 \quad \text{...(iii)}$$

On subtracting Eq. (ii) from Eq. (i), we get

$$2x - 2y = 4000 \Rightarrow x - y = 2000$$

[dividing both sides by 2] ...(iv)

Ans. Sonia invests ₹ 10000 at the rate of 10% and ₹ 8000 at the rate of 8%.

Olympiad Section

Brain Teasing Questions of Olympiad Pattern

1 If $(a + b, a - b)$ is the solution of the equations $3x + 2y = 20$ and $4x - 5y = 42$, then the value of b is

(a) 8 (b) -2
(c) -4 (d) 5

2 There are two numbers. The predecessor of the larger number exceeds the successor of the smaller number by 6. The sum of the numbers is 32. Then, the difference of numbers is

(a) 0 (b) 8
(c) 10 (d) 12

3 X is a three-digit number. The number formed by reversing the digits of X is 891 less than X. Find its unit's digit.

(a) 0 (b) 1
(c) 2 (d) Cannot be determined

4 $7^x + 5^y = 74$ and $7^{x+1} - 5^{y+1} = 218$, then the values of x and y are respectively

(a) 2, 2 (b) 2, 3
(c) 3, 2 (d) 4, 2

5 Shashi has decided fixed distance to walk on a tread mill. First day, she walks at a certain speed. Next day, she increases the speed of the tread mill by 1 km/h, she takes 6 min less and if she reduces the speed by 1 km/h, then she takes 9 min more. What is the distance that she has decided to walk everyday?

(a) 4 km (b) 6 km
(c) 5 km (d) 3 km

6 A vessel contains a mixture of 24 L milk and 6 L water and second vessel contains a mixture of 15 L milk and 10 L water, then how much mixture of milk and water should be taken from the first and the second vessel separately and kept in a third vessel, so that the third vessel may contain a mixture of 25 L milk and 10 L water?

(a) 15 L and 15 L
(b) 20 L and 10 L
(c) 20 L and 15 L
(d) None of the above

7 A hybrid mango tree, whose life span is 10 yr, starts giving fruits from the first year onwards. In the nth year it produces $11n$ raw mangoes. But during the first half of the tree's life, every year, a certain number, which is constant, fail to ripen into fruits. During the second half of the tree's life, every year, the number of raw fruits that fail to ripen is half the corresponding number in the first half of the tree's life. In the fourth year of the tree's life, it produces 36 ripe mangoes. How many mangoes ripen during the 9th year of the tree's life?

(a) 100 (b) 96
(c) 95 (d) 86

Answers

1. (d) **2.** (b) **3.** (a) **4.** (a) **5.** (d) **6.** (c) **7.** (c)

* *These questions may or may not be asked in the examination, have been given just for additional practice required for olympiads Scholarship Exams etc. For detailed explanations refer Page No. 337.*

CHAPTER 06

Indices/Exponents

SYLLABUS

• Handling positive, Fractional, Negative and zero indices • Simplification of expressions involving various exponents $a^m \times a^n = a^{m+n}$, $a^m \div a^n = a^{m-n}$, $(a^m)^n = a^{mn}$ etc. Use of laws of exponents.

We have already learnt that exponent is a mathematical concept for expressing very large numbers into the shorter form, which make them easy to read and understand. e.g. if a is any real number and n is any natural number, then $a \times a \times a \times a \times \ldots$ upto n times can be expressed as a^n. Here, a is called the **base**, n is called the **exponent** or **index** and a^n is called the **exponential** form of a. e.g. $9765625 = 5 \times 5 \times 5 \times 5 \times \ldots$ upto 10 times $= 5^{10}$.

Handling Positive, Fractional, Negative and Zero Indices

1. **Indices with Positive Integer** If a is any non-zero real numbers and n is a positive integer,
   then $\sqrt[n]{a} = a^{1/n}$. e.g. $\sqrt[2]{27} = (27)^{1/2}$ etc.
2. **Indices with Fractional/Rational Number** If a is any non-zero real number and m, n are fractional/rational numbers. Then,
   $a^{m/n} = (a^m)^{1/n} = \sqrt[n]{a^m}$.
   e.g. $(2)^{5/3} = [(2)^5]^{1/3} = (32)^{1/3}$
   $= \sqrt[3]{32} = \sqrt[3]{(4)^2 \times 2} = 4\sqrt[3]{4} = 4(2)^{1/3}$
   and $(-7)^{2/5} = [(-7)^2]^{1/5} = (49)^{1/5} = \sqrt[5]{49}$ etc.
3. **Indices with Negative Integer** If a is any non-zero real number and n is any positive integer, then $a^{-n} = \frac{1}{a^n}$.
   e.g. $4^{-3} = \frac{1}{4^3} = \frac{1}{4 \times 4 \times 4} = \frac{1}{64}$
4. **Indices with Zero** For any non-zero number raised to the power zero, is always equal to 1.
   i.e. $a^0 = 1$
   e.g. $(-289)^0 = 1$
   and $(7^5)^0 = 1$ etc.

Example 1. Find the value of $3^{-a} \times 2^b \times 5^{-c} \times 7^d$, if $17640 = 2^a \,.\, 3^b \,.\, 5^c \,.\, 7^d$.

Sol. We have, $17640 = 2^a \,.\, 3^b \,.\, 5^c \,.\, 7^d$

$\Rightarrow \quad 2^3 \times 3^2 \times 5^1 \times 7^2 = 2^a \,.\, 3^b \,.\, 5^c \,.\, 7^d$

On comparing the exponents of 2, 3, 5 and 7 on both the sides, we get

$a = 3,\ b = 2,\ c = 1,$ and $d = 2$

$\therefore\ 3^{-a} \times 2^b \times 5^{-c} \times 7^d = 3^{-3} \times 2^2 \times 5^{-1} \times 7^2$

$= \frac{1}{27} \times 4 \times \frac{1}{5} \times 49 \qquad \left[\because \left(\frac{a}{b}\right)^n = \left(\frac{b}{a}\right)^{-n}\right]$

$= \frac{196}{135} = 1\frac{61}{135}$

Laws of Exponents

1. Product Law

If a is any non-zero real number and m, n are rational numbers, then $a^m \times a^n = a^{m+n}$.

Example 2. Evaluate

(i) $3^4 \times 3^5$

(ii) $5^{2/3} \times 5^{4/3}$

Sol.

(i) We have, $3^4 \times 3^5 = 3^{4+5}$ $[\because a^m \times a^n = a^{m+n}]$

$\Rightarrow \quad 3^9 = 19683$

(ii) We have, $5^{2/3} \times 5^{4/3} = 5^{2/3+4/3}$ $[\because a^m \times a^n = a^{m+n}]$

$= 5^{\frac{2+4}{3}} = 5^{\frac{6}{3}} = 5^2 = 25$

2. Division Law

If a is any non-zero real number and m, n are rational numbers, then $\dfrac{a^m}{a^n} = a^{m-n}$ or $a^m \div a^n = a^{m-n}$.

Note (i) Why $a^0 = 1$?

Reason We know that $\dfrac{a^m}{a^n} = a^{m-n}$.

If $m = n$, then $\dfrac{a^m}{a^m} = a^{m-m} \Rightarrow 1 = a^0$

(ii) $\dfrac{1}{a^n} = \dfrac{a^0}{a^n} = a^{0-n} = a^{-n}$. Thus, $a^{-n} = \dfrac{1}{a^n}$

or $\dfrac{1}{a^{-n}} = a^n$, for any rational number n.

Example 3. Solve

(i) $3^7 \div 3^5$ (ii) $\left(\dfrac{2}{3}\right)^{7/2} \div \left(\dfrac{2}{3}\right)^{3/2}$

Sol.

(i) We have, $3^7 \div 3^5 = 3^{7-5} = 3^2 = 9$ $\left[\because \dfrac{a^m}{a^n} = a^{m-n}\right]$

(ii) We have, $\left(\dfrac{2}{3}\right)^{7/2} \div \left(\dfrac{2}{3}\right)^{3/2} = \left(\dfrac{2}{3}\right)^{7/2-3/2}$ $\left[\because \dfrac{a^m}{a^n} = a^{m-n}\right]$

$= \left(\dfrac{2}{3}\right)^{\frac{7-3}{2}} = \left(\dfrac{2}{3}\right)^{4/2} = \left(\dfrac{2}{3}\right)^2 = \dfrac{4}{9}$

Example 4. Express each of the following in the simplest form.

(i) $a^{-7} \times a^0 \times a^7$ (ii) $(a^{-1} + b^{-1}) \div (a^{-2} - b^{-2})$

Sol.

(i) We have, $a^{-7} \times a^0 \times a^7 = a^{-7+0+7}$ $[\because a^m \times a^n = a^{m+n}]$

$\Rightarrow \quad a^0 = 1$ $[\because a^0 = 1]$

(ii) We have, $(a^{-1} + b^{-1}) \div (a^{-2} - b^{-2}) = \dfrac{a^{-1} + b^{-1}}{a^{-2} - b^{-2}}$

$= \dfrac{\frac{1}{a} + \frac{1}{b}}{\frac{1}{a^2} - \frac{1}{b^2}} = \dfrac{\frac{b+a}{ab}}{\frac{b^2 - a^2}{a^2b^2}}$ $\left[\because a^{-n} = \dfrac{1}{a^n}\right]$

$= \dfrac{b+a}{ab} \times \dfrac{a^2b^2}{b^2 - a^2}$ $\left[\because \dfrac{a}{b} \div \dfrac{c}{d} = \dfrac{ad}{bc}\right]$

$= \dfrac{ab(b+a)}{(b+a)(b-a)}$

$[\because A^2 - B^2 = (A+B)(A-B)]$

$= \dfrac{ab}{b-a}$

Example 5. Prove that

$$\frac{x^{-1}}{x^{-1} + y^{-1}} + \frac{x^{-1}}{x^{-1} - y^{-1}} = \frac{2y^2}{y^2 - x^2}.$$

Sol. LHS $= \dfrac{x^{-1}}{x^{-1} + y^{-1}} + \dfrac{x^{-1}}{x^{-1} - y^{-1}}$

$= \dfrac{\frac{1}{x}}{\frac{1}{x} + \frac{1}{y}} + \dfrac{\frac{1}{x}}{\frac{1}{x} - \frac{1}{y}}$ $\left[\because a^{-n} = \dfrac{1}{a^n}\right]$

$= \dfrac{\frac{1}{x}}{\frac{y+x}{xy}} + \dfrac{\frac{1}{x}}{\frac{y-x}{xy}}$

$= \dfrac{xy}{(x+y)x} + \dfrac{xy}{(y-x)x}$ $\left[\because \dfrac{a}{b} \div \dfrac{c}{d} = \dfrac{ad}{bc}\right]$

$= \dfrac{y}{x+y} + \dfrac{y}{y-x} = \dfrac{y(y-x) + y(x+y)}{(y+x)(y-x)}$

$= \dfrac{y^2 - xy + xy + y^2}{y^2 - x^2}$ $[\because (a+b)(a-b) = a^2 - b^2]$

$= \dfrac{2y^2}{y^2 - x^2} =$ RHS **Hence proved**

Example 6. If $x = -3$ and $y = 2$, then find the value of $x^x + y^y + x^y + y^x$.

Sol. We have, $x^x + y^y + x^y + y^x = (-3)^{-3} + (2)^2 + (-3)^2 + (2)^{-3}$

[given, $x = -3$ and $y = 2$]

$= \dfrac{1}{(-3)^3} + 4 + 9 + \dfrac{1}{2^3}$ $\left[\because a^{-n} = \dfrac{1}{a^n}\right]$

$= -\dfrac{1}{27} + 13 + \dfrac{1}{8}$

$= \dfrac{104+1}{8} - \dfrac{1}{27} = \dfrac{105 \times 27 - 8 \times 1}{27 \times 8}$

$= \dfrac{2835 - 8}{216} = \dfrac{2827}{216} = 13.09$

Example 7. Prove that

$$\frac{1}{1 + x^{m-n} + x^{l-n}} + \frac{1}{1 + x^{n-l} + x^{m-l}} + \frac{1}{1 + x^{l-m} + x^{n-m}} = 1.$$

Sol. Consider, LHS $= \dfrac{1}{1+x^{m-n}+x^{l-n}} + \dfrac{1}{1+x^{n-l}+x^{m-l}} + \dfrac{1}{1+x^{l-m}+x^{n-m}}$

$$= \frac{1}{1+\frac{x^m}{x^n}+\frac{x^l}{x^n}} + \frac{1}{1+\frac{x^n}{x^l}+\frac{x^m}{x^l}} + \frac{1}{1+\frac{x^l}{x^m}+\frac{x^n}{x^m}} \quad \left[\because a^{m-n} = \frac{a^m}{a^n}\right]$$

$$= \frac{1}{\frac{x^n+x^m+x^l}{x^n}} + \frac{1}{\frac{x^l+x^n+x^m}{x^l}} + \frac{1}{\frac{x^m+x^l+x^n}{x^m}}$$

$$= \frac{x^n}{x^l+x^m+x^n} + \frac{x^l}{x^l+x^m+x^n} + \frac{x^m}{x^l+x^m+x^n}$$

$$= \frac{x^l+x^m+x^n}{x^l+x^m+x^n} = 1 = \text{RHS}$$ **Hence proved**

3. Power Law

If a and b are non–zero real numbers and m is a rational number, then

(i) $(ab)^m = a^m \cdot b^m$ (ii) $\left(\dfrac{a}{b}\right)^m = \dfrac{a^m}{b^m}$

Note (i) $(-a)^m = a^m$, if m is even number.
(ii) $(-a)^m = -a^m$, if m is odd number.

Example 8. Solve : (i) 6^4 (ii) $\left(\dfrac{2}{3}\right)^4$

Sol.

(i) We have, $6^4 = (2\times 3)^4 = 2^4 \times 3^4 = 16\times 81 = 1296$ $[\because (ab)^m = a^m b^m]$

(ii) We have, $\left(\dfrac{2}{3}\right)^4 = \dfrac{2^4}{3^4} = \dfrac{16}{81}$ $\left[\because \left(\dfrac{a}{b}\right)^m = \dfrac{a^m}{b^m}\right]$

Example 9. Solve : $(-3)^3 + (4)^2 + (-8)^2 - (-2)^5$

Sol. $-27+16+64-(-32)$

[$\because$ $(-a)^m = a^m$, if m is even number $(-a)^m = -a^m$, if m is odd number]

$= -27+16+64+32 = 85$

4. Power-to-Power Law

If a is any non-zero real number and m, n are rational numbers, then $(a^m)^n = a^{mn}$.

Note $a^{m/n} = (a^m)^{1/n} = (a^{1/n})^m$ or $\sqrt[n]{a^m} = (\sqrt[n]{a})^m$, where $n > 0$.

Example 10. Evaluate :

(i) $(4^2)^3$ (ii) $\left[\left(\dfrac{2}{3}\right)^{5/2}\right]^{6/5}$

Sol.

(i) We have, $(4^2)^3 = 4^{2\times 3} = 4^6$ $[\because (a^m)^n = a^{mn}]$
Hence, $4^6 = 4096$

(ii) We have, $\left[\left(\dfrac{2}{3}\right)^{5/2}\right]^{6/5} = \left(\dfrac{2}{3}\right)^{\frac{5}{2}\times\frac{6}{5}} = \left(\dfrac{2}{3}\right)^3$ $[\because (a^m)^n = a^{mn}]$
$= \dfrac{8}{27}$

Example 11. Evaluate

(i) $(4)^{3/2}$

(ii) $(27)^{4/3}$

(iii) $(243)^{3/5}$

(iv) $\dfrac{1}{(27)^{-2/3}}$

Sol.

(i) We have, $4^{3/2} = (4^{1/2})^3$ $[\because (a^{m/n}) = (a^{1/n})^m]$
$= (2)^3 = 8$

(ii) We have, $(27)^{4/3} = (27^{1/3})^4$ $[\because a^{m/n} = (a^{1/n})^m]$
$= [(3^3)^{1/3}]^4 = (3^{3\times(1/3)})^4$ $[\because (a^m)^n = a^{mn}]$
$= 3^4 = 81$

(iii) We have, $(243)^{3/5}$
$= (3\times 3\times 3\times 3\times 3)^{3/5}$
$= (3^5)^{3/5}$
$= 3^{5\times\frac{3}{5}} = 3^3$ $[\because (a^m)^n = a^{m\times n}]$
$= 3\times 3\times 3 = 27$

(iv) We have, $\dfrac{1}{(27)^{-2/3}} = (27)^{2/3}$ $\left[\because \dfrac{1}{a^{-n}} = a^n\right]$
$= (3\times 3\times 3)^{2/3}$
$= (3^3)^{2/3}$
$= 3^{3\times(2/3)} = 3^2$
$= 3\times 3 = 9$ $[\because (a^m)^n = a^{m\times n}]$

Example 12. Find the value of $3^3 \times (243)^{-2/3} \times 9^{1/3}$.

Sol. We have, $3^3 \times (243)^{-2/3} \times 9^{1/3}$
$= 3^3 \times (3\times 3\times 3\times 3\times 3)^{-2/3} \times (3\times 3)^{1/3}$
$= 3^3 \times (3^5)^{-2/3} \times (3^2)^{1/3}$
$= 3^3 \times 3^{5\times(-2/3)} \times 3^{2\times 1/3}$ $[\because (a^m)^n = a^{m\times n}]$
$= 3^3 \times 3^{-10/3} \times 3^{2/3}$
$= 3^{3-\frac{10}{3}+\frac{2}{3}}$ $[\because a^l \times a^m \times a^n = a^{l+m+n}]$
$= 3^{\frac{9-10+2}{3}} = 3^{\frac{11-10}{3}} = 3^{1/3}$

Example 13. Evaluate $5^{-4} \times (125)^{5/3} \div (25)^{-1/2}$.

Sol. We have, $5^{-4} \times (125)^{5/3} \div (25)^{-1/2}$
$= 5^{-4} \times (5\times 5\times 5)^{5/3} \div (5\times 5)^{-1/2}$
$= 5^{-4} \times (5^3)^{5/3} \div (5^2)^{-1/2}$
$= 5^{-4} \times 5^{3\times\frac{5}{3}} \div 5^{2\times\left(-\frac{1}{2}\right)}$ $[\because (a^m)^n = a^{m\times n}]$
$= \dfrac{5^{-4}\times 5^5}{5^{-1}} = \dfrac{5^{-4+5}}{5^{-1}}$ $[\because a^m \times a^n = a^{m+n}]$

$$= \frac{5^1}{5^{-1}} = 5^{1-(-1)} \qquad \left[\because \frac{a^m}{a^n} = a^{m-n}\right]$$

$$= 5^{1+1} = 5^2 = 25$$

Example 14. Simplify $\dfrac{5\cdot(25)^{m+1} - 25\cdot(5)^{2m}}{5\cdot(5)^{2m+3} - (25)^{m+1}}$.

Sol. We have, $\dfrac{5\cdot(25)^{m+1} - 25\cdot(5)^{2m}}{5\cdot(5)^{2m+3} - (25)^{m+1}} = \dfrac{5\times(5^2)^{m+1} - 5^2\times 5^{2m}}{5\times 5^{2m+3} - (5^2)^{m+1}}$

$$= \frac{5\times 5^{2(m+1)} - 5^2\times 5^{2m}}{5\times 5^{2m+3} - 5^{2(m+1)}} \qquad [\because (a^m)^n = a^{m\times n}]$$

$$= \frac{5^1\times 5^{2m+2} - 5^2\times 5^{2m}}{5^1\times 5^{2m+3} - 5^{2m+2}}$$

$$= \frac{5^{2m+2+1} - 5^{2+2m}}{5^{2m+3+1} - 5^{2m+2}} \qquad [\because a^m\cdot a^n = a^{m+n}]$$

$$= \frac{5^{2m+3} - 5^{2m+2}}{5^{2m+4} - 5^{2m+2}} = \frac{5^{2m+2}(5-1)}{5^{2m+2}(5^2-1)}$$

[taking 5^{2m+2} common from both numerator and denominator]

$$= \frac{4}{(25-1)} = \frac{4}{24} = \frac{1}{6}$$

5. Reciprocal Law

If a and b are non-zero real numbers and n is any rational number, then $\left(\dfrac{a}{b}\right)^n = \left(\dfrac{b}{a}\right)^{-n}$.

Example 15. Find the value of x, when $\sqrt{\dfrac{2}{3}} = \left(\dfrac{3}{2}\right)^{1-2x}$.

Sol. We have, $\sqrt{\dfrac{2}{3}} = \left(\dfrac{3}{2}\right)^{1-2x}$

We know that $\dfrac{a}{b} = \left(\dfrac{b}{a}\right)^{-1}$ [reciprocal law]

$$\therefore \quad \sqrt{\frac{2}{3}} = \left[\left(\frac{2}{3}\right)^{-1}\right]^{1-2x}$$

$$\Rightarrow \quad \left(\frac{2}{3}\right)^{1/2} = \left(\frac{2}{3}\right)^{-1(1-2x)} \qquad [\because (a^m)^n = a^{m\times n}]$$

$$\Rightarrow \quad \left(\frac{2}{3}\right)^{1/2} = \left(\frac{2}{3}\right)^{2x-1}$$

On comparing the exponents of $\dfrac{2}{3}$ from both sides, we get

$$2x - 1 = \frac{1}{2}$$

$$\Rightarrow \quad 2x = 1 + \frac{1}{2} = \frac{3}{2}$$

$$\Rightarrow \quad x = \frac{3}{4}$$

Example 16. Find the value of x, when

$$\sqrt{\left(\frac{4}{5}\right)^{1-2x}} = 1\frac{9}{16}$$

Sol. We have, $\sqrt{\left(\dfrac{4}{5}\right)^{1-2x}} = 1\dfrac{9}{16}$

$$\Rightarrow \quad \left(\left(\frac{4}{5}\right)^{1-2x}\right)^{1/2} = \frac{25}{16}$$

$$\Rightarrow \quad \left(\frac{4}{5}\right)^{\frac{1-2x}{2}} = \frac{5^2}{4^2} \qquad [\because (a^m)^n = a^{m\times n}]$$

$$\Rightarrow \quad \left(\frac{4}{5}\right)^{\frac{1-2x}{2}} = \left(\frac{5}{4}\right)^2 \qquad \left[\because \left(\frac{a}{b}\right)^m = \frac{a^m}{b^m}\right]$$

We know that $\dfrac{a}{b} = \left(\dfrac{b}{a}\right)^{-1}$ [reciprocal law]

$$\therefore \quad \left(\frac{4}{5}\right)^{\frac{1-2x}{2}} = \left(\frac{4}{5}\right)^{-2}$$

On comparing the exponents of $\dfrac{4}{5}$ from both the sides, we get

$$\frac{1-2x}{2} = -2$$

$$\Rightarrow \quad 1 - 2x = -4 \Rightarrow -2x = -4 - 1$$

$$\Rightarrow \quad x = \frac{-5}{-2} \Rightarrow x = \frac{5}{2}$$

Example 17. Find the value of x, when

$$3^3(7^0 + 4^{3x}) = 27\frac{27}{64}$$

Sol. We have, $3^3(7^0 + 4^{3x}) = 27\dfrac{27}{64}$

$$\Rightarrow \quad 27(1 + 4^{3x}) = 27 + \frac{27}{64}$$

$$\Rightarrow \quad 27 + 27\times 4^{3x} = 27 + \frac{27}{64}$$

$$\Rightarrow \quad 27\times 4^{3x} = \frac{27}{64}$$

[subtracting 27 from both the sides]

$$\Rightarrow \quad 4^{3x} = \frac{1}{64} \quad \text{[dividing both the sides by 27]}$$

$$\Rightarrow \quad 4^{3x} = \frac{1}{4^3}$$

We know that $\dfrac{a}{b} = \left(\dfrac{b}{a}\right)^{-1}$ [reciprocal law]

$$\therefore \quad 4^{3x} = 4^{-3}$$

On comparing the exponents of 4 from both the sides, we get

$$3x = -3 \Rightarrow x = -1$$

Note (i) If $n \neq 0$ and $a^n = b^n$, then $a = b$

(ii) If $a \neq 1$ and $a^m = a^n$, then $m = n$

Chapter Practice

a. 1 Mark Questions

1. Value of $\sqrt[5]{\sqrt[3]{9^2}}$ is

(a) $(9)^{1/5}$ (b) $3^{6/5}$

(c) $3^{4/15}$ (d) $9^{4/5}$

2. $[\{(-1) \times (-1)\}^2]^3 - (1)^{(-2)}$

(a) 1 (b) 0 (c) 2 (d) 3

3. $\{(2^0)^3\}^{-1/5}$

(a) 32 (b) $\frac{1}{32}$ (c) 1 (d) $2^{-3/5}$

4. Which one is the value of x, if

$$\sqrt{\frac{p}{q}} = \left(\frac{q}{p}\right)^{1-3x}$$

(a) $-\frac{3}{4}$ (b) $-\frac{4}{3}$

(c) $\frac{4}{3}$ (d) $\frac{1}{2}$

5. Value of x, $(13)^{\sqrt{x}} = 4^4 - 3^4 - 6$

(a) 4 (b) 3

(c) 2 (d) 2

b. 3 Marks Questions

6. Evaluate

(i) $(64)^{-\frac{1}{3}}$ (ii) $16^{\frac{3}{2}} - 4(5)^0 - \left(\frac{1}{64}\right)^{-\frac{1}{2}}$

(iii) $\left(\frac{64}{216}\right)^{-\frac{2}{3}} \div \frac{1}{\left(\frac{343}{1000}\right)^{\frac{1}{3}}} \times \sqrt{\frac{144}{169}}$

7. Evaluate $\frac{(4 \times 10^8)(6 \times 10^{-6})}{8 \times 10^{11}}$.

8. If $x = 2$, $y = -1$, find the value of

(i) $x^x + y^y$ (ii) $x^y + y^x$

9. Simplify $[1 - \{1 - (1 - n)^{-1}\}^{-1}]$

10. If $5^{3x} = 125$ and $10^y = 0.001$, then find $5x + y$.

11. Prove that $\frac{a + b + c}{a^{-1}b^{-1} + b^{-1}c^{-1} + c^{-1}a^{-1}} = abc$

12. If $2^x = 3^y = 6^{-z}$, then show that $x^{-1} + y^{-1} + z^{-1} = 0$

13. Evaluate

(i) $27^{4/3} \times 27^{-2/3}$ (ii) $(-32)^{2/5}$

14. Simplify $(7x^5y^3z^2)(19x^7y^5z^3)$

15. Evaluate (i) $(256)^{-(4^{-3/2})}$ (ii) $\sqrt[4]{28} \div \sqrt[3]{7}$

16. Simplify, $(32)^{0.8} + \left(\frac{1}{81}\right)^{0.25} + (625)^{0.5}$

17. Evaluate $\sqrt{\frac{1}{9}} + (0.01)^{-1/2} - (64)^{2/3}$. Find your answer as a fraction.

18. Simplify $\frac{729x^7y^4z^5}{27x^{11}y^3z^7}$

19. Simplify $\left(\frac{81}{16}\right)^{-3/4} \times \left[\left(\frac{25}{9}\right)^{-3/2} \div \left(\frac{5}{2}\right)^{-3}\right]$

20. Evaluate $\frac{(32)^{2/5} \times (4)^{-1/2} \times (8)^{1/3}}{2^{-2} \div (64)^{-1/3}}$

21. Evaluate $\frac{3 \times 27^{n+1} + 9 \times 3^{3n-1}}{8 \times 3^{3n} - 5 \times 27^n}$.

22. Evaluate $\frac{3^{-3} \times 6^2 \times \sqrt{98}}{5^2 \times \sqrt[3]{125} \times (15)^{-4/3} \times 3^{1/3}}$.

23. If $3^x = 9 \times 3^y$ and $8 \times 2^y = 4^x$, then find the value of $3x + 2y$.

24. Solve for y, if $(\sqrt[3]{4})^{2y + \frac{1}{2}} = (\sqrt[3]{8})^5$.

25. Prove that $\left(\frac{a^m}{a^n}\right)^{m+n} \left(\frac{a^n}{a^l}\right)^{n+l} \left(\frac{a^l}{a^m}\right)^{l+m} = 1$

26. Simplify $\left[\left(\frac{x^a}{x^b}\right)^{a+b-c} \cdot \left(\frac{x^b}{x^c}\right)^{b+c-a} \cdot \left(\frac{x^c}{x^a}\right)^{c+a-b}\right]$

27. Show that $\left[\left\{\frac{x^{l(l-m)}}{x^{l(l+m)}}\right\} \div \left\{\frac{x^{m(m-l)}}{x^{m(m+l)}}\right\}\right]^{a+b} = 1$

28. Show that $\{(x^{a-a^{-1}})^{1/(a-1)}\}^{a/(a+1)} = x$

29. Simplify $(x^{1/3} - x^{-1/3})(x^{2/3} + 1 + x^{-2/3})$

30. If $x = 2^{1/3} + 2^{2/3}$, then find the value of $x^3 - 6x$.

c. 4/5 Marks Questions

31. Solve for x, $3(2^x + 1) - 2^{x+2} + 5 = 0$.

32. Simplify each of the following

(i) $\left(\dfrac{27^{-3}}{9^{-3}}\right)^{1/5}$ (ii) $(32)^{-2/5} \div (125)^{-2/3}$

33. Simplify $\left(\dfrac{64}{125}\right)^{-2/3} \div \dfrac{1}{\left(\dfrac{256}{625}\right)^{1/4}} + \left(\dfrac{\sqrt{25}}{3}\right)^{0}$.

34. Evaluate $\left(\dfrac{16}{81}\right)^{-3/4} \times \left(\dfrac{49}{9}\right)^{3/2} \div \left(\dfrac{343}{216}\right)^{2/3}$.

35. Prove that $\dfrac{\sqrt{2} \times \sqrt[3]{3} \times \sqrt[4]{4}}{(10)^{-1/5} \times (5)^{3/5}} \div \dfrac{(3)^{4/3} \times (5)^{-7/5}}{(4)^{-3/5} \times 6} = 10$

36. Solve for x,

$$(81)^{3/4} - \left(\frac{1}{32}\right)^{-2/5} + x\left(\frac{1}{2}\right)^{-1} \times 2^0 = 27$$

37. If $5^{2x-1} = 25^{x-1} + 100$, then find the value of 4^{3+x}

38. If $\dfrac{9^y \times 3^2 \times (3^{-y/2})^{-2} \div (27)^x}{3^{3x} \times 3^2} = \dfrac{1}{27}$, then show that $2x - y = 1$.

39. Prove that $\dfrac{x^{-1}}{x^{-1} + y^{-1}} + \dfrac{x^{-1}}{x^{-1} - y^{-1}} = \dfrac{2y^2}{y^2 - x^2}$

40. Solve for x and y such that

$$3^x \times 3^{-y} = 9 \text{ and } 2^y \times 4^{-x} = \frac{1}{8}$$

41. Solve for x and y such that $27^{x+1} = 81^{y+2}$ and $\left(\dfrac{1}{3}\right)^{3+x} = \left(\dfrac{1}{9}\right)^{3y}$

42. Find the values of m and n, if

$$4^{2m} = (\sqrt[3]{16})^{-6/n} = (\sqrt{8})^2$$

43. Solve for x and y such that

$$(\sqrt{32})^x \div 2^{y+1} = 1 \text{ and } 8^y \div 16^{4-\frac{x}{2}} = 1$$

44. Solve for x and y such that

$(\sqrt{3125})^x \div 5^{y+1} = 1$ and $(625)^{4-x/2} - 125^y = 0$.

45. If $a^x = b$, $b^y = c$ and $c^z = a$, then prove that $xyz = 1$.

46. If $p^x = q^y = r^z$ and $q^2 = pr$, then show that $y = \dfrac{2xz}{z + x}$.

47. If $2^a = 3^b = 12^c$, then show that $\dfrac{1}{c} = \dfrac{1}{b} + \dfrac{2}{a}$.

d. 6 Marks Questions

48. Simplify

$$\left(\frac{x^a}{x^b}\right)^{a^2+ab+b^2} \times \left(\frac{x^b}{x^c}\right)^{b^2+bc+c^2} \times \left(\frac{x^c}{x^a}\right)^{c^2+ac+a^2}.$$

49. Prove that

$$\left(\frac{x^{a^2+b^2}}{x^{ab}}\right)^{a+b} \times \left(\frac{x^{b^2+c^2}}{x^{bc}}\right)^{b+c} \times \left(\frac{x^{c^2+a^2}}{x^{ac}}\right)^{a+c} = x^{2(a^3+b^3+c^3)}$$

50. Prove that

$$\left(\frac{3^{a+1}}{3^{b+1}}\right)^{a+b} \times \left(\frac{3^{b+2}}{3^{c+2}}\right)^{b+c} \times \left(\frac{3^{c+3}}{3^{a+3}}\right)^{c+a} = 1$$

51. Prove that $(x^{1/(a-b)})^{1/(a-c)} \times (x^{1/(b-c)})^{1/(b-a)} \times (x^{1/(c-a)})^{1/(c-b)} = 1$

52. If $a = x^{m+n} \cdot y^l$, $b = x^{n+l} \cdot y^m$ and $c = x^{l+m} \cdot y^n$, then show that $a^{m-n} \cdot b^{n-l} \cdot c^{l-m} = 1$.

53. $\left(\dfrac{p^{-1}q^2}{p^3q^{-2}}\right)^{1/3} \div \left(\dfrac{p^6q^{-3}}{p^{-2}q^3}\right)^{1/2} = p^aq^b$, prove that $a + b + 1 = 0$, where p and q are different positive primes.

54. Show that $\sqrt[bc]{\dfrac{x^b}{x^c}} \times \sqrt[ca]{\dfrac{x^c}{x^a}} \times \sqrt[ab]{\dfrac{x^a}{x^b}} = 1$.

55. If $x = 2 + 2^{1/3} + 2^{2/3}$, then find the value of $x^3 - 6x^2 + 6x - 7$.

56. Simplify, $\left\{\dfrac{4^{m+\frac{1}{4}} \times \sqrt{2 \times 2^m}}{2\sqrt{2^{-m}}}\right\}^{\frac{1}{m}}$

57. If $a\sqrt[3]{x^2} + b\sqrt[3]{x} + c = 0$, then show that $a^3x^2 + b^3x + c^3 = 3abcx$

58. If $l^2 = m^3$, then show that

$$\left(\frac{l}{m}\right)^{3/2} + \left(\frac{m}{l}\right)^{2/3} = \sqrt{l} + \frac{1}{\sqrt[3]{m}}$$

59. If $1176 = 2^p \cdot 3^q \cdot 7^r$, then find the value of $2^p \cdot 3^q \cdot 7^{-r}$ as a fraction.

60. If $\dfrac{9^{n+1}(3^{-n/2})^{-2} - 27^n}{(2 \times 3^m)^3} = \dfrac{1}{729}$, then prove that $m - n = 2$.

61. If $\sqrt{11^0 - \dfrac{3}{7}} = (1.75)^{3-4x}$, then find the value of x.

Hints and Answers

1. (c) **2.** (b) **3.** (c)

4. (d) **5.** (a)

6. (i) **Hint** Do same as Example 11(iv). **Ans.** 4

(ii) **Hint** Do same as Example 11. **Ans.** 56

(iii) **Hint** Do same as Example 11, use the law,

$\therefore (a^m)^n = a^{mn},\ a^{-1} = \frac{1}{a}$

7. **Hint** $\frac{(4\times 10^8)(6\times 10^{-6})}{8\times 10^{11}} = \frac{4\times 6\times 10^{8-6}}{8\times 10^{11}}$ $[\because a^n \times a^t = a^{n+n}]$

$= 3\times 10^{2-11}$ $\left[\because \frac{a^m}{a^n} = a^{m-n}\right]$

Ans. 3×10^{-9}

8. **Hint** (i) $(2)^2 + (-1)^{-1}$ **Ans.** 3

(ii) $(2)^{-1} + (-1)^2$ **Ans.** $\frac{3}{2}$

9. **Hint** $\left[1-\left\{1-\frac{1}{1-n}\right\}^{-1}\right]^{-1} = [1-\{-n\}^{-1}]^{-1} = \left[1+\frac{1}{n}\right]^{-1}$

Ans. $\frac{n}{n+1}$

10. **Hint** We have, $5^{3x} = 5^3$ and $10^y = 10^{-3}$

Ans. 2

11. **Hint** $\frac{a+b+c}{\frac{1}{a}\cdot\frac{1}{b}+\frac{1}{b}\cdot\frac{1}{c}+\frac{1}{c}\cdot\frac{1}{a}} = \frac{(a+b+c)}{\frac{(c+a+b)}{abc}}$

[taking LCM]

12. **Hint** Let $2^x = k \Rightarrow 2 = k^{1/x}$ ...(i)

$3^y = k \Rightarrow 3 = k^{1/y}$ ...(ii)

and $6^{-z} = k \Rightarrow 6 = k^{-1/z}$ ...(iii)

Now, $6 = 2\times 3 \Rightarrow k^{-1/z} = k^{1/x+1/y}$

[from Eqs. (i), (ii) and (iii)]

$\Rightarrow \frac{1}{x}+\frac{1}{y} = -\frac{1}{z}$ [comparing both sides]

13. (i) **Hint** First, apply $a^m \times a^n = a^{m+n}$, then do same as Example 12. **Ans.** 9

(ii) **Hint** $(-32)^{2/5} = \{(-32)^{1/5}\}^2$ $[\because (-2)^5 = -32]$

Ans. 4

14. **Hint** $7\times 19\times x^5\times x^7\times y^3\times y^5\times z^2\times z^3$

Apply product law to get the required result

Ans. $133x^{12}y^8z^5$

15. (i) **Hint** Here, $(256)^{-(4^{-3/2})} = (256)^{-[(2^2)^{-3/2}]}$

$= (256)^{-[2^{2\times(-3/2)}]}$ $[\because (a^m)^n = a^{mn}]$

$= (256)^{-(2^{-3})} = (2^8)^{(-1/8)}$

$= 2^{8\times(-1/8)}$ $[\because (a^m)^n = a^{mn}]$

Ans. $\frac{1}{2}$

(ii) **Hint** Here, $\sqrt[4]{28} \div \sqrt[3]{7} = (28)^{1/4} \div (7)^{1/3}$

$= (4\times 7)^{1/4} \times \frac{1}{7^{1/3}}$

$= (4)^{1/4}\times 7^{1/4}\times\frac{1}{7^{1/3}}$ $[\because (ab)^m = a^m b^m]$

$= (2^2)^{\frac{1}{4}} \times 7^{\frac{1}{4}-\frac{1}{3}}$ $[\because a^m \div a^n = a^{m-n}]$

$= 2^{1/2}\times 7^{-1/12} = 2^{\frac{1\times 6}{2\times 6}} \times \frac{1}{7^{1/12}}$ $\left[\because a^{-m} = \frac{1}{a^m}\right]$

$= \frac{2^{6/12}}{7^{1/12}}$ **Ans.** $\sqrt[12]{\frac{64}{7}}$

16. **Hint** $(2)^{5\times 0.8} + \left(\frac{1}{3}\right)^{4\times 0.25} + (5)^{4\times 0.5}$ **Ans.** $41\frac{1}{3}$

17. **Hint** $\frac{1}{3} + (100)^{1/2} - (4)^2$ $\left[\because a^{-n} = \left(\frac{1}{a}\right)^n\right]$

$= \frac{1}{3} - 16 + (10)^{2\times\frac{1}{2}}$ **Ans.** $-5\frac{2}{3}$

18. **Hint** Apply Division law. **Ans.** $\frac{27y}{x^4z^2}$

19. **Hint** $\left(\frac{3^4}{2^4}\right)^{-3/4} \times \left[\left(\frac{5^2}{3^2}\right)^{-3/2} \div \left(\frac{5}{2}\right)^{-3}\right]$

$= \left[\left(\frac{3}{2}\right)^4\right]^{-3/4} \times \left\{\left[\left(\frac{5}{3}\right)^2\right]^{-3/2} \div \left(\frac{5}{2}\right)^{-3}\right\}$ $\left[\because \frac{a^m}{b^m} = \left(\frac{a}{b}\right)^m\right]$

Now, do same as Example 11. **Ans.** 1

20. **Hint** Given, expression $= \frac{(2^5)^{2/5}\times(2^2)^{-1/2}\times(2^3)^{1/3}}{\frac{1}{2^2}\times\frac{1}{(2^6)^{-1/3}}}$

Now, use $(a^m)^n = a^{mn}$. **Ans.** 4

21. **Hint** Do same as Example 14. **Ans.** -28

22. **Hint** $\frac{3^{-3}\times(2\times 3)^2\times(2\times 7^2)^{1/2}}{5^2\times(5^3)^{1/3}\times(3\times 5)^{-4/3}\times 3^{1/3}}$

$= \frac{3^{-3}\times 2^2\times 3^2\times(2)^{1/2}\times(7^2)^{1/2}}{5^2\times 5^1\times 3^{-4/3}\times 5^{-4/3}\times 3^{1/3}}$ $[\because (ab)^m = a^m b^m]$

$= \frac{3^{-3+2-\left(-\frac{4}{3}\right)-\frac{1}{3}}\times 2^{\frac{1}{2}+2}\times 7}{5^{2+1-\frac{4}{3}}}$ **Ans.** $\frac{28\sqrt{2}}{5^{5/3}}$

23. **Hint** We have, $3^x = 9\times 3^y$ and $8\times 2^y = 4^x$

$\Rightarrow 3^x = 3^2\times 3^y$ and $2^3\times 2^y = (2^2)^x$

$\Rightarrow 3^x = 3^{y+2}$ and $2^{y+3} = 2^{2x}$

$[\because a^m\cdot a^n = a^{m+n}$ and $(a^m)^n = a^{mn}]$

Now, comparing the exponents of 3 and 2, we get

$x = y+2$ ...(i)

and $y+3 = 2x$ ...(ii)

On solving Eqs. (i) and (ii), we get $x = 1$ and $y = -1$

Ans. 1

24. Hint $(\sqrt[3]{4})^{2y+\frac{1}{2}} = (\sqrt[3]{8})^5 \Rightarrow (2^{2/3})^{2y+\frac{1}{2}} = 2^5$

Comparing the power of 2.

$\Rightarrow \frac{2}{3}\left(2y+\frac{1}{2}\right) = 5$ **Ans.** $3\frac{1}{2}$

25. Hint LHS $= \left(\frac{a^m}{a^n}\right)^{m+n}\left(\frac{a^n}{a^l}\right)^{n+l}\left(\frac{a^l}{a^m}\right)^{l+m}$

$= (a^{m-n})^{m+n}(a^{n-l})^{n+l}(a^{l-m})^{l+m}$ $\left[\because \frac{A^x}{A^y} = A^{x-y}\right]$

$= a^{(m-n)(m+n)}a^{(n-l)(n+l)}a^{(l-m)(l+m)}$ $[\because (A^x)^y = A^{xy}]$

$= a^{m^2-n^2}a^{n^2-l^2}a^{l^2-m^2}$ $[\because (A-B)(A+B) = A^2 - B^2]$

$= a^{m^2-n^2+n^2-l^2+l^2-m^2}$ $[\because A^x \cdot A^y = A^{x+y}]$

26. Hint Do same as Q. 25. **Ans.** 1

27. Hint LHS $= \left[\left\{\frac{x^{l^2-lm}}{x^{l^2+lm}}\right\} \div \left\{\frac{x^{m^2-ml}}{x^{m^2+ml}}\right\}\right]^{a+b}$

$= [x^{l^2-lm-l^2-lm} \div x^{m^2-ml-m^2-ml}]^{a+b}$

$= [x^{-2lm} \div x^{-2lm}]^{a+b}$

$= [x^{-2lm-(-2lm)}]^{a+b}$

28. Hint Consider, LHS $= \{(x^{(a-1/a)})^{1/(a-1)}\}^{a/(a+1)}$ $\left[\because a^{-1} = \frac{1}{a}\right]$

$= \{(x^{(a^2-1)/a})^{1/(a-1)}\}^{a/(a+1)}$

$= \left\{x^{\frac{(a-1)(a+1)}{a}\times\frac{1}{(a-1)}}\right\}^{a/(a+1)}$ $[\because (a^m)^n = a^{mn}]$

$= x^{(a+1)/a \times a/(a+1)}$

29. Hint We have, $(x^{1/3} - x^{-1/3})(x^{2/3} + 1 + x^{-2/3})$

$= \left(x^{1/3} - \frac{1}{x^{1/3}}\right)\left(x^{2/3} + 1 + \frac{1}{x^{2/3}}\right)$ $\left[\because a^{-m} = \frac{1}{a^m}\right]$

$= (x^{1/3})^3 - \left(\frac{1}{x^{1/3}}\right)^3$ $[\because (a-b)(a^2+b^2+ab) = a^3 - b^3]$

Ans. $x - \frac{1}{x}$

30. Hint We have, $x = 2^{1/3} + 2^{2/3}$

$\Rightarrow x^3 = (2^{1/3} + 2^{2/3})^3$

$= (2^{1/3})^3 + (2^{2/3})^3 + 3 \cdot 2^{1/3} \cdot 2^{2/3}(2^{1/3} + 2^{2/3})$ $[\because (a+b)^3 = a^3 + b^3 + 3ab(a+b)]$

$= 2 + 2^2 + 3 \cdot 2^{1/3+2/3} \cdot x$ **Ans.** 6

31. Hint We have, $3 \cdot 2^x + 3 - 2^x \cdot 2^2 + 5 = 0$

$\Rightarrow 3 \cdot 2^x - 4 \cdot 2^x + 8 = 0 \Rightarrow -2^x + 8 = 0$

Ans. $x = 3$

32. (i) **Hint** Here, $\left(\frac{27^{-3}}{9^{-3}}\right)^{1/5} = \left(\frac{27}{9}\right)^{-3/5}$ **Ans.** $(3)^{-3/5}$

(ii) **Hint** $\frac{(32)^{-2/5}}{(125)^{-2/3}} = \frac{(2^5)^{-2/5}}{(5^3)^{-2/3}}$ **Ans.** $6\frac{1}{4}$

33. Hint $\left(\left(\frac{4}{5}\right)^4\right)^{-2/3} + \frac{1}{\left(\left(\frac{4}{5}\right)^4\right)^{1/4}} + \left(\sqrt{\frac{25}{3}}\right)^0$

Use the law $(a^m)^n = a^{mn}$ and $a^0 = 1$ **Ans.** $\frac{9}{4}$

34. Hint Do same as Example 12. **Ans.** 31.5

35. Hint LHS $= \frac{2^{1/2} \cdot 3^{1/3} \cdot 2^{1/2}}{2^{-1/5} \cdot 5^{-1/5} \cdot 5^{3/5}} \times \frac{2^{-6/5} \times 2 \times 3}{3^{4/3} \times 5^{-7/5}}$

$= 2^{\frac{1}{2}+\frac{1}{2}+\frac{1}{5}-\frac{6}{5}+1} \cdot 3^{\frac{1}{3}+1-\frac{4}{3}} \cdot 5^{\frac{1}{5}-\frac{3}{5}+\frac{7}{5}}$

36. Hint We have,

$(81)^{3/4} - \left(\frac{1}{32}\right)^{-2/5} + x\left(\frac{1}{2}\right)^{-1} \times 2^0 = 27$

$\Rightarrow (3^4)^{3/4} - (2^{-5})^{-2/5} + x(2^{-1})^{-1} = 27$ $\left[\because \frac{1}{a^n} = a^{-n} \text{ and } a^0 = 1\right]$

$\Rightarrow 3^{4\times\frac{3}{4}} - 2^{(-5)\times\left(-\frac{2}{5}\right)} + x \times 2^{(-1)\times(-1)} = 27$ $[\because (a^m)^n = a^{mn}]$

$\Rightarrow 3^3 - 2^2 + x \times 2 = 27$

Ans. $x = 2$

37. Hint We have, $5^{2x-1} = 25^{x-1} + 100$

$\Rightarrow 5^{2x-1} = 5^{2\times(x-1)} + 100$ $[\because (a^m)^n = a^{mn}]$

$\Rightarrow 5^{2x-1} - 5^{2x-2} = 100$

$\Rightarrow 5^{2x-2}[5-1] = 100$

$\Rightarrow 5^{2x-2} \times 4 = 100$

$\Rightarrow 5^{2x-2} = 25 = 5^2$

Now, equating exponents from 5 both sides, we get

$2x - 2 = 2$

$\Rightarrow x = 2$ **Ans.** 1024

38. Hint We have, $\frac{9^y \times 3^2 \times (3^{-y/2})^{-2} \div (27)^x}{3^{3x} \times 3^2} = \frac{1}{27}$

$\Rightarrow \frac{3^{2y} \times 3^2 \times 3^y \div 3^{3x}}{3^{3x} \times 3^2} = \frac{1}{3^3}$ $[\because (a^m)^n = a^{mn}]$

$\Rightarrow \frac{3^{2y+2+y-3x}}{3^{3x+2}} = \frac{1}{3^3}$ $[\because a^m \times a^n = a^{m+n}]$

$\Rightarrow 3^{3y-3x+2-3x-2} = 3^{-3}$ $\left[\because \frac{1}{a^n} = a^{-n}\right]$

$\Rightarrow 3^{3y-6x} = 3^{-3}$

Now, equating exponents from 3 both sides, we get

$3y - 6x = -3$

39. Hint $\frac{\frac{1}{x}}{\frac{x+y}{xy}} + \frac{\frac{1}{x}}{\frac{y-x}{xy}} = \frac{y}{x+y} + \frac{y}{y-x}$

$= y\frac{[y - x + x + y]}{(x+y)(y-x)}$

40. Hint We have, $3^{x-y} = 3^2$ and $2^{y-2x} = 2^{-3}$

$\Rightarrow x - y = 2$ and $2x - y = 3$

On solving above equations, we get the required values.

Ans. $x = 1$ and $y = -1$

41. Hint We have, $(27)^{x+1} = (81)^{y+2}$

and $\left(\frac{1}{3}\right)^{3+x} = \left(\frac{1}{9}\right)^{3y} \Rightarrow 3^{3x+3} = 3^{4y+8}$

and $\left(\frac{1}{3}\right)^{3+x} = \left(\frac{1}{3}\right)^{6y}$

On equating exponent from both sides, we get

$3x + 3 = 4y + 8$

and $3 + x = 6y$

or $3x - 4y = 5$

and $x - 6y = -3$

On solving the above equations, we get the required result. **Ans.** $x = 3$ and $y = 1$

42. Hint We have, $4^{2m} = (\sqrt[3]{16})^{-6/n} = (\sqrt{8})^2$

$\Rightarrow (2^2)^{2m} = [(2^4)^{1/3}]^{-6/n} = [(2^3)^{1/2}]^2$

$\Rightarrow 2^{4m} = 2^{4\times\frac{1}{3}\times\left(-\frac{6}{n}\right)} = 2^3 \Rightarrow 2^{4m} = 2^{-8/n} = 2^3$

$\therefore 2^{4m} = 2^3$ and $2^{-8/n} = 2^3$

On equating exponents from both sides, we get

$4m = 3$ and $-\frac{8}{n} = 3$

Ans. $m = \frac{3}{4}$ and $n = \frac{-8}{3}$

43. Hint We have, $(\sqrt{32})^x \div 2^{y+1} = 1$

$\Rightarrow [(2^5)^{1/2}]^x \div 2^{y+1} = 1$

$\Rightarrow 2^{\frac{5x}{2}-(y+1)} = 2^0$ $[\because (a^m)^n = a^{mn}$ and $a^0 = 1]$

On comparing the exponents from 2 both sides, we get

$5x - 2y - 2 = 0$ ...(i)

and $8^y \div 16^{4-x/2} = 1$

$\Rightarrow 2^{3y} \div 2^{4(4-x/2)} = 2^0$

$\Rightarrow 2^{3y-16+2x} = 2^0$

$\Rightarrow 2x + 3y - 16 = 0$ ...(ii)

On solving Eqs. (i) and (ii), we get the required result.

Ans. $x = 2$ and $y = 4$

44. Hint Do same as Q. 41. **Ans.** $x = 2$ and $y = 4$

45. Hint Given, $a^x = b, b^y = c$ and $c^z = a$

Now, $a^x = b \Rightarrow (c^z)^x = b \Rightarrow c^{xz} = b$

$\Rightarrow (b^y)^{xz} = b \Rightarrow b^{xyz} = b^1$

46. Hint Suppose $p^x = q^y = r^z = K$

$\therefore p = K^{\frac{1}{x}}, q = K^{\frac{1}{y}}$ and $r = K^{\frac{1}{z}}$

$q^2 = pr$ $[\because$ Given$]$

$\Rightarrow (K^{\frac{1}{y}})^2 = K^{\frac{1}{x}} \cdot K^{\frac{1}{z}}$

47. Hint Do same as Q. 46.

48. Hint Do same as Q. 25. **Ans.** 1

49. Hint Do same as Q. 25.

50. Hint Do same as Q. 25.

51. Hint Consider,

LHS $= (x^{1/(a-b)})^{1/(a-c)} \times (x^{1/(b-c)})^{1/(b-a)} \times (x^{1/(c-a)})^{1/(c-b)}$

$= x^{\frac{1}{(a-b)}\times\frac{1}{(a-c)}} \times x^{\frac{1}{(b-c)}\times\frac{1}{(b-a)}} \times x^{\frac{1}{(c-a)}\times\frac{1}{(c-b)}}$ $[\because (a^m)^n = a^{mn}]$

$= x^{1/(a-b)(a-c)+1/(b-c)(b-a)+1/(c-a)(c-b)}$

$= x^{-1/(a-b)(c-a)-1/(b-c)(a-b)-1/(c-a)(b-c)}$

$= x^{-\left[\frac{b-c+c-a+a-b}{(a-b)(b-c)(c-a)}\right]} = x^0$

52. Hint Consider, LHS $= a^{m-n} \cdot b^{n-l} \cdot c^{l-m}$

$= (x^{m+n} \cdot y^l)^{m-n} \cdot (x^{n+l} \cdot y^m)^{n-l} \cdot (x^{l+m} \cdot y^n)^{l-m}$

$= [x^{(m+n)(m-n)} \cdot y^{l(m-n)} \cdot x^{(n+l)(n-l)} \cdot y^{m(n-l)} \cdot x^{(l+m)(l-m)} \cdot y^{n(l-m)}]$ $[\because (a^m)^n = a^{mn}]$

$= [x^{m^2-n^2} y^{l(m-n)} \cdot x^{n^2-l^2} \cdot y^{m(n-l)} x^{l^2-m^2} \cdot y^{n(l-m)}]$ $[\because (a+b)(a-b) = a^2 - b^2]$

$= x^{m^2-n^2+n^2-l^2+l^2-m^2} \cdot y^{lm-nl+mn-lm+nl-mn}$

53. Hint $\left(\frac{p^{-1}q^2}{p^3q^{-2}}\right)^{1/3} = (p^{-1-3}q^{2-(-2)})^{1/3} = p^{-4/3}q^{4/3}$

$\left(\frac{p^6q^{-3}}{p^{-2}q^3}\right)^{1/2} = (p^{6-(-2)}q^{-3-3})^{1/2}$

$= (p^8q^{-6})^{1/2} = p^4q^{-3}$

$\therefore \left(\frac{p^{-1}q^2}{p^3q^{-2}}\right)^{1/3} \div \left(\frac{p^6q^{-3}}{p^{-2}q^3}\right)^{1/2} = p^aq^b$

$\Rightarrow p^{-\frac{16}{3}}q^{\frac{13}{3}} = p^aq^b$

$\therefore a = -\frac{16}{3}$ and $b = \frac{13}{3}$

54. Hint Let LHS $= \left(\frac{x^b}{x^c}\right)^{1/bc} \times \left(\frac{x^c}{x^a}\right)^{1/ca} \times \left(\frac{x^a}{x^b}\right)^{1/ab}$

$= (x^{b-c})^{1/bc} \times (x^{c-a})^{1/ca} \times (x^{a-b})^{1/ab}$ $\left[\because \frac{a^m}{a^n} = a^{m-n}\right]$

$= (x^{b-c})^{a/abc} \times (x^{c-a})^{b/abc} \times (x^{a-b})^{c/abc}$

$= x^{\frac{a(b-c)+b(c-a)+c(a-b)}{abc}}$ $[\because (a^m)^n = a^{mn}]$

$= x^{\frac{ab-ac+bc-ab+ac-bc}{abc}}$

55. Hint We have, $x = 2 + 2^{1/3} + 2^{2/3}$

$\Rightarrow x - 2 = 2^{1/3} + 2^{2/3}$ ...(i)

On cubing both sides, we get

$(x-2)^3 = (2^{1/3} + 2^{2/3})^3$

$\Rightarrow x^3 - (2)^3 - 3x(2)(x-2) = (2^{1/3})^3 + (2^{2/3})^3 + 3 \times 2^{1/3} \times 2^{2/3}(2^{1/3} + 2^{2/3})$

$[\because (a \pm b)^3 = a^3 \pm b^3 \pm 3ab(a \pm b)]$

$\Rightarrow x^3 - 8 - 6x(x-2) = 2^{3\times\frac{1}{3}} + 2^{3\times\frac{2}{3}} + 3 \times 2^{1/3+2/3}(x-2)$

$[\because (a^m)^n = a^{mn}, a^m \cdot a^n = a^{m+n}$ and from Eq. (i)$]$

$\Rightarrow x^3 - 8 - 6x(x-2) = 2 + 2^2 + 3 \times 2(x-2)$

$\Rightarrow x^3 - 6x^2 + 6x = 2$

On subtracting 7 from both sides, we get the required value.

Ans. -5

56. Hint $\left\{\dfrac{(2^2)^{m+\frac{1}{4}} \times (2^{m+1})^{\frac{1}{2}}}{2 \times 2^{-\frac{m}{2}}}\right\}^{\frac{1}{m}}$

$$= \left\{2^{2m} + \frac{1}{2} + \frac{m}{2} + \frac{1}{2} - 1 + \frac{m}{2}\right\}^{\frac{1}{m}}$$

Ans. 8

57. Hint We have, $ax^{2/3} + bx^{1/3} = -c$ ...(i)

$\Rightarrow (ax^{2/3} + bx^{1/3})^3 = (-c)^3$ [cubing both sides]

$\Rightarrow a^3x^2 + b^3x + 3ax^{2/3} \cdot bx^{1/3}(ax^{2/3} + bx^{1/3}) = -c^3$

$[\because (A+B)^3 = A^3 + B^3 + 3AB(A+B)]$

$\Rightarrow a^3x^2 + b^3x + 3abx(-c) = -c^3$ [from Eq. (i)]

58. Hint LHS $= \left(\dfrac{l}{m}\right)^{3/2} + \left(\dfrac{m}{l}\right)^{2/3}$

$= \left(\dfrac{l}{m}\right)^{3/2} + \left(\dfrac{l}{m}\right)^{-2/3}$ $\left[\because \left(\dfrac{a}{b}\right)^m = \left(\dfrac{b}{a}\right)^{-m}\right]$

$= \left(\dfrac{l^3}{m^3}\right)^{1/2} + \left(\dfrac{l^2}{m^2}\right)^{-1/3}$ $[\because a^{mn} = (a^m)^n]$

$= \left(\dfrac{l^3}{l^2}\right)^{1/2} + \left(\dfrac{m^3}{m^2}\right)^{-1/3}$ [given, $l^2 = m^3$]

59. Hint First, we find $p = 3$, $q = 1$ and $r = 2$.

Then, we get $2^p\, 3^q\, 7^{-r} = \dfrac{24}{49}$. **Ans.** $\dfrac{24}{49}$

60. Hint $\dfrac{9^{n+1}(3^{-n/2})^{-2} - 27^n}{(2 \times 3^m)^3} = \dfrac{1}{729}$

$\Rightarrow \dfrac{(3^2)^{n+1}\left(3^{\left(-\frac{n}{2}\right)(-2)}\right) - (3^3)^n}{2^3 \times 3^{m \times 3}} = \dfrac{1}{729}$

$\Rightarrow \dfrac{3^{2n+2} \times 3^n - 3^{3n}}{2^3 \times 3^{3m}} = \dfrac{1}{3^6}$

$\Rightarrow \dfrac{3^{3n+2} - 3^{3n}}{2^3 \times 3^{3n}} = \dfrac{1}{36}$

$\Rightarrow \left(\dfrac{9-1}{2^3}\right)\left[\dfrac{1}{3^{3m-3n}}\right] = \dfrac{1}{3^6}$

61. Hint Use reciprocal law

Ans. $x = \dfrac{7}{8}$

Olympiad Section

Brain Teasing Questions of Olympiad Pattern

1 The value of $\left(\sqrt[6]{27}-\sqrt{6\frac{3}{4}}\right)^2$ is

(a) $\frac{1}{4}$ (b) $\frac{3}{4}$

(c) $\frac{1}{3}$ (d) $\frac{5}{4}$

2 If $x=\sqrt{3}+\sqrt{2}$, then the value of $x^2+\frac{1}{x^2}$ is

(a) 10 (b) 11

(c) 9 (d) 7

3 If $x=7-4\sqrt{3}$, then the value of $\frac{x^2+1}{7x}$ is

(a) 3 (b) 4

(c) 2 (d) 1

4 If $x^3=\sqrt[3]{8}+\sqrt[3]{27}+\sqrt[3]{64}+\sqrt[3]{125}+\sqrt[3]{216}+\sqrt[3]{343}$, then x^2 equals

(a) 9 (b) 1

(c) 4 (d) 6

5 $\frac{3^{30}+3^{29}+3^{28}}{3^{31}+3^{30}-3^{29}}+\frac{2^{30}+2^{29}+2^{28}}{2^{31}+2^{30}-2^{29}}$ equals

(a) $\frac{369}{311}$ (b) $\frac{367}{332}$

(c) $\frac{361}{330}$ (d) None of these

6 The value $\sqrt{3^2\sqrt{9^2\sqrt{81^2\sqrt{16^{16}}}}}$ is

(a) 430 (b) 429

(c) 435 (d) 432

7 If $x=\frac{1}{2-\sqrt{3}}$, then the value of $x^3-2x^2-7x+10$ is

(a) 0 (b) 8

(c) 9 (d) 5

8 If $x=1+5^{1/3}+5^{2/3}$, then the value of $x^3-3x^2-12x+6$ is

(a) 22 (b) 21

(c) 20 (d) 25

Answers

1. (b) **2.** (a) **3.** (c) **4.** (a) **5.** (c) **6.** (d) **7.** (b) **8.** (a)

* *These questions may or may not be asked in the examination, have been given just for additional practice required for olympiads Scholarship Exams etc. For detailed explanations refer Page No. 338.*

CHAPTER

07

Logarithms

SYLLABUS

(a) Logarithmic form vis-a-vis exponential form : interchanging. (b) Laws of Logarithmic and their uses. Expansion of expression with the help of laws of logarithms e.g. $y = \frac{a^4 b^2}{c^3} \Rightarrow \log y = 4 \log a + 2 \log b - 3 \log c$ etc.

If a is any positive real number ($a \neq 1$) and m is any rational number and n be any real number such that $a^m = n$, then $m = \log_a n$, where m is called **logarithm** of n to the base a. Thus, $a^m = n$ is called the **exponential form** and $m = \log_a n$ is called the **logarithmic form**.

Interchanging
(Logarithmic form vis-a-vis expontential form)

Exponential form	Logarithmic form
$2^4 = 16$	$4 = \log_2 16$
$5^0 = 1$	$0 = \log_5 1$
$3^{-4} = \frac{1}{3^4} = \frac{1}{81}$	$-4 = \log_3 \frac{1}{81}$
$(10)^{-4} = \frac{1}{(10)^4} = \frac{1}{10000}$	$-4 = \log_{10} \frac{1}{10000}$

Properties of Logarithms

1. $a^0 = 1 \Rightarrow \log_a 1 = 0, a \neq 1,$
2. $a^1 = a \Rightarrow \log_a a = 1,$
3. If base of logarithm is not given, then we always take 10 as a base. Logarithms to the base 10 are called common logarithms. e.g. $\log 50 = \log_{10} 50$
4. If $x = a^m$ and $y = a^m$, then $x = y$.
   Hence, $\log_a x = \log_a y \Rightarrow x = y$.

Example 1. Write each of the following in the logarithmic form.

(i) $7^3 = 343$ (ii) $2^{-10} = \frac{1}{1024}$ (iii) $4^{3/2} = 8$

(iv) $(0.2)^3 = 0.008$

Sol.

(i) We have, $7^3 = 343$

$\Rightarrow \quad 3 = \log_7 343 \quad [\because a^m = n \Rightarrow m = \log_a n]$

(ii) We have, $2^{-10} = \frac{1}{1024}$

$\Rightarrow \quad -10 = \log_2 \frac{1}{1024} \quad [\because a^m = n \Rightarrow m = \log_a n]$

(iii) We have, $4^{3/2} = 8$

$\Rightarrow \quad \frac{3}{2} = \log_4 8 \quad [\because a^m = n \Rightarrow m = \log_a n]$

(iv) We have, $(0.2)^3 = 0.008$

$\Rightarrow \quad 3 = \log_{0.2}(0.008) \quad [\because a^m = n \Rightarrow m = \log_a n]$

Example 2. Find the values of x in each of the following.

(i) $\log_3 x = 3$ (ii) $\log_4 x = 3/2$ (iii) $\log_{10} x = -3$

(iv) $\log_x 16 = 2$ (v) $\log_9 27 = 2x + 3$

Sol.

(i) We have, $\log_3 x = 3$

$\Rightarrow \quad x = (3)^3 = 27 \quad [\because \log_a n = m \Rightarrow a^m = n]$

(ii) We have, $\log_4 x = \frac{3}{2}$

$\Rightarrow \quad x = (4)^{3/2} = 8 \quad [\because \log_a n = m \Rightarrow a^m = n]$

(iii) We have, $\log_{10} x = -3$

$\Rightarrow \quad x = (10)^{-3}$ $\quad [\because \log_a n = m \Rightarrow a^m = n]$

$\therefore \quad x = \frac{1}{10^3} = \frac{1}{1000}$ $\quad \left[\because a^{-m} = \frac{1}{a^m}\right]$

(iv) We have, $\log_x 16 = 2$

$\Rightarrow \quad x^2 = 16$ $\quad [\because \log_a n = m \Rightarrow a^m = n]$

$x = 4$

(v) We have, $\log_9 27 = 2n + 3$

$\Rightarrow \quad (9)^{2n+3} = 27$ $\quad [\because \log_a n = m \Rightarrow a^m = n]$

$\Rightarrow \quad 3^{4x+6} = 3^3$

$\therefore \quad x = -3/4$

Example 3. Find the logarithm in each of the following.

(i) 64 to the base 4

(ii) $\frac{1}{81}$ to the base 27

(iii) 0.008 to the base 5

Sol.

(i) Let $\log_4 64 = x$, then $64 = 4^x$ $\quad [\because \log_a n = m \Rightarrow a^m = n]$

$\Rightarrow \quad 4^x = 4 \times 4 \times 4 \Rightarrow 4^x = 4^3$

On comparing the exponents of 4 both sides, we get

$x = 3$

Hence, $\log_4 64 = 3$.

(ii) Let $\log_{27} \frac{1}{81} = x$, then $\frac{1}{81} = (27)^x$ $\quad [\because \log_a n = m \Rightarrow a^m = n]$

$\Rightarrow \quad \frac{1}{3 \times 3 \times 3 \times 3} = (3 \times 3 \times 3)^x \Rightarrow \left(\frac{1}{3}\right)^4 = (3^3)^x$

$\Rightarrow \quad 3^{-4} = 3^{3x}$ $\quad \left[\because \frac{1}{a^n} = a^{-n} \text{ and } (a^m)^n = a^{mn}\right]$

On comparing the exponents of 3 both sides, we get

$3x = -4 \Rightarrow x = -\frac{4}{3}$

Hence, $\log_{27} \frac{1}{81} = -\frac{4}{3}$.

(iii) Let $\log_5 0.008 = x$, then

$0.008 = 5^x$ $\quad [\because \log_a n = m \Rightarrow a^m = n]$

$\Rightarrow \quad \frac{8}{1000} = 5^x \Rightarrow \frac{1}{125} = 5^x$

$\Rightarrow \quad (5)^{-3} = (5)^x$ $\quad \left[\because \frac{1}{a^n} = a^{-n}\right]$

On comparing the exponents of 5 both sides, we get

$x = -3$

Hence, $\log_5 0.008 = -3$

Laws of Logarithms and their uses

(i) **Product Law** $\log_a m \cdot n = \log_a m + \log_a n$

e.g. $\log (10) = \log (2 \times 5) = \log 2 + \log 5$

(ii) **Quotient Law** $\log_a \left(\frac{m}{n}\right) = \log_a m - \log_a n$

e.g. $\log \frac{10}{3} = \log 10 - \log 3$

(iii) **Power Law** $\log_a (m)^n = n \log_a m$

e.g. $\log (10)^3 = 3 \log 10$

(iv) $\log_n m = \frac{\log_a m}{\log_a n}, m > 0, n, a > 0, a \neq 1, n \neq 1$

e.g. $\log_2 3 = \frac{\log_{10} 3}{\log_{10} 2}$

(v) $a^{\log_a m} = m$

e.g. $4^{\log_4 64} = 64$

(vi) $x^{\log_a y} = y^{\log_a x}$

e.g. $3^{\log_{10} 4} = 4^{\log_{10} 3}$

(vii) **Reciprocal Law** $\log_a b = \frac{1}{\log_b a}$

Example 4. Evaluate the following.

(i) $\frac{\log 8 \log 9}{\log 27}$ (ii) $\frac{\log 625}{\log 125}$

(iii) $3 + \frac{1}{2} \log_{10} 9 - 2 \log_{10} 5$

(iv) $4 + \log_{10} (0.001)$

Sol.

(i) We have, $\frac{\log 8 \log 9}{\log 27} = \frac{\log (2)^3 \times \log (3)^2}{\log (3)^3}$

$= \frac{3 \log 2 \times 2 \log 3}{3 \log 3} = 2 \log 2$

(ii) We have, $\frac{\log 625}{\log 125} = \frac{\log 5^4}{\log 5^3} = \frac{4 \log 5}{3 \log 5}$ $\quad [\because \log m^n = n \log m]$

$= \frac{4}{3}$

(iii) We have, $3 + \frac{1}{2} \log_{10} 9 - 2 \log_{10} 5$

$= 3 \times 1 + \frac{1}{2} \log_{10} (3 \times 3) - 2 \log_{10} 5$

$= 3 \log_{10} 10 + \frac{1}{2} \log_{10} 3^2 - 2 \log_{10} 5$ $\quad [\because 1 = \log_{10} 10]$

$= \log_{10} 10^3 + \log_{10} 3^{2 \times \frac{1}{2}} - \log_{10} (5)^2$ $\quad [\because n \log m = \log m^n]$

$= \log_{10} 1000 + \log_{10} 3 - \log_{10} 25$

$= \log_{10} (1000 \times 3) - \log_{10} 25$ $\quad [\because \log m + \log n = \log mn]$

$= \log_{10} \frac{3000}{25}$ $\quad \left[\because \log m - \log n = \log \frac{m}{n}\right]$

$= \log_{10} 120$

(iv) $4 + \log_{10} (0.001)$

$= 4 + \log_{10} (10)^{-3}$

$= 4 - 3 \log_{10} 10$ $\quad$ [by power law]

$= 4 - 3 \times 1$ $\quad [\because \log_{10} 10 = 1]$

$= 1$

Example 5. Express $\log 4.5 + \log \frac{25}{50}$ in terms of $\log 2$ and $\log 3$.

Sol. We have, $\log 4.5 + \log \frac{25}{50} = \log \frac{45}{10} + \log \frac{25}{50} = \log \frac{9}{2} + \log \frac{1}{2}$

$= \log 9 - \log 2 + \log 1 - \log 2$ $\left[\because \log \frac{m}{n} = \log m - \log n\right]$

$= \log 3^2 - 2\log 2$ $[\because \log 1 = 0]$

$= 2\log 3 - 2\log 2$ $[\because \log m^n = n \log m]$

$= 2(\log 3 - \log 2)$

Example 6. If $\log_{10} 2 = m$ and $\log_{10} 3 = n$, then express each of the following in terms of m and n.

(i) $\log_{10} 90$ (ii) $\log_{10} 0.54$

Sol. Given, $\log_{10} 2 = m$ and $\log_{10} 3 = n$

(i) We have, $\log_{10} 90 = \log_{10} (10 \times 9)$

$= \log_{10} 10 + \log_{10} 3^2$ $[\because \log mn = \log m + \log n]$

$= 1 + 2\log_{10} 3$ $[\because \log m^n = n \log m]$

$= 2 \log_{10} 3 + 1 = 1 + 2n$ $[\because \log_a a = 1]$

(ii) $\log_{10} 0.54 = \log_{10} \frac{54}{100} = \log_{10} \frac{27 \times 2}{100}$

$= \log_{10} 27 \times 2 - \log_{10} 100$ $\left[\because \log \frac{m}{n} = \log m - \log n\right]$

$= \log_{10} 27 + \log_{10} 2 - \log_{10} 100$ $[\because \log mn = \log m + \log n]$

$= \log_{10} 3^3 + \log_{10} 2 - \log_{10} 10^2$

$= 3\log_{10} 3 + \log_{10} 2 - 2\log_{10} 10$ $[\because \log m^n = n \log m]$

$= 3n + m - 2$ $[\because \log_{10} 10 = 1]$

$= m + 3n - 2$

Example 7. If $\log_{10} 8 = 0.90$, then find the value of $\log \sqrt{32}$.

Sol. We have, $\log_{10} 8 = 0.90$

$\Rightarrow \log_{10} 2^3 = 0.90$

$\Rightarrow 3\log_{10} 2 = 0.90$

$\Rightarrow \log_{10} 2 = \frac{0.90}{3} = 0.30$ ...(i)

Now, $\log\sqrt{32} = \log_{10} (32)^{1/2} = \frac{1}{2}\log_{10} 32$ $[\because \log m^n = n \log m]$

$= \frac{1}{2}\log_{10} 2^5 = \frac{5}{2}\log_{10} 2$

$= \frac{5}{2} \times 0.30 = 5 \times 0.15 = 0.75$ [from Eq. (i)]

Example 8. Determine the logarithmic expansion of $y = \frac{5^p 7^p}{3^r}$.

Sol. Given, $y = \frac{5^p 7^p}{3^r}$

On taking log both sides, we get

$\log y = \log \frac{5^p 7^q}{3^r}$

$\Rightarrow \log y = \log 5^p 7^q - \log 3^r$ $\left[\because \log \frac{m}{n} = \log m - \log n\right]$

$\log y = \log 5^p + \log 7^q - \log 3^r$ $[\because \log mn = \log m + \log n]$

$\log y = p \log 5 + q \log 7 - r \log 3$ $[\because n \log m = \log m^n]$

Hence, $\log y = p \log 5 + q \log 7 - r \log 3$ is the logarithmic expansion of $y = \frac{5^p 7^q}{3^r}$.

Example 9. If $\log 7 - \log 2 + \log 16 - 2\log 3 - \log \frac{7}{45} = 1 + \log x$, then find x.

Sol. We have, $\log 7 - \log 2 + \log 16 - 2\log 3 - \log \frac{7}{45} = 1 + \log x$

$\Rightarrow \log 7 - \log 2 + \log 16 - \log 3^2 - \log \frac{7}{45} = 1 + \log x$

$[\because n \log m = \log m^n]$

$\Rightarrow \log 7 - \log 2 + \log 16 - \log 9 - (\log 7 - \log 45) = 1 + \log x$

$\left[\because \log \frac{m}{n} = \log m - \log n\right]$

$\Rightarrow \log 7 - \log 2 + \log 16 - \log 9 - \log 7 + \log 45 = 1 + \log x$

$\Rightarrow (\log 16 + \log 45) - (\log 2 + \log 9) = 1 + \log x$

$\Rightarrow \log(16 \times 45) - \log(2 \times 9) = 1 + \log x$

$[\because \log m + \log n = \log mn]$

$\Rightarrow \log \frac{16 \times 45}{2 \times 9} = 1 + \log x$ $\left[\because \log m - \log n = \log \frac{m}{n}\right]$

$\Rightarrow \log 40 = 1 + \log x = \log 10 + \log x$ $[\because 1 = \log 10]$

$\Rightarrow \log 40 = \log 10x$

$\Rightarrow 10x = 40$

On comparing the coefficient of log both sides, we get

$x = 4$

Example 10. Solve for x, if $\log_{10} (x^2 - 21) = 2$.

Sol. We have, $\log_{10} (x^2 - 21) = 2$

$\Rightarrow x^2 - 21 = (10)^2$ $[\because \log_a n = m \Rightarrow a^m = n]$

$\Rightarrow x^2 - 21 = 100 \Rightarrow x^2 = 100 + 21 = 121$

$\therefore x^2 = (11)^2 \Rightarrow x = \pm 11$ [taking square root]

Example 11. Solve for x, if

$$\log(x + 3) - \log(x - 3) = 1.$$

Sol. We have, $\log(x + 3) - \log(x - 3) = 1$

$\Rightarrow \log\left(\frac{x+3}{x-3}\right) = 1$ $\left[\log m - \log n = \log \frac{m}{n}\right]$

$\Rightarrow \log\left(\frac{x+3}{x-3}\right) = \log 10$ $[\because 1 = \log 10]$

$\Rightarrow \left(\frac{x+3}{x-3}\right) = 10$

$\Rightarrow x + 3 = 10(x - 3)$

$\Rightarrow x + 3 = 10x - 30$

$\Rightarrow x - 10x = -30 - 3$

$\Rightarrow -9x = -33$

$\therefore x = \frac{33}{9} = \frac{11}{3} = 3\frac{2}{3}$

Example 12. Solve for x, if

$$(\log_{10} x)^2 - (\log_{10} x) - 2 = 0.$$

Sol. We have, $(\log_{10} x)^2 - (\log_{10} x) - 2 = 0$

Let $\log_{10} x = t$, then the given expression reduces to

$t^2 - t - 2 = 0$

Now, factorise by splitting the middle term, we get

$$t^2 - 2t + t - 2 = 0$$

$\Rightarrow$ $t(t-2) + 1(t-2) = 0$

$\Rightarrow$ $(t-2)(t+1) = 0$

$t - 2 = 0$ or $t + 1 = 0$

$\Rightarrow$ $t = 2$ or $t = -1$

On putting the value of t, we get

$\log_{10} x = -1$ or $\log_{10} x = 2$

$\Rightarrow$ $x = (10)^{-1}$ or $x = (10)^2$ $\quad [\because \log_a n = m \Rightarrow a^m = n]$

Hence, $x = \frac{1}{10}$ and 100.

Example 13. Simplify $\dfrac{\log_3 8}{\log_9 16 \log_4 10}$.

Sol. We have, $\dfrac{\log_3 8}{\log_9 16 \log_4 10}$

$$= \frac{\dfrac{\log_{10} 8}{\log_{10} 3}}{\dfrac{\log_{10} 16}{\log_{10} 9} \times \dfrac{\log_{10} 10}{\log_{10} 4}} \quad \left[\because \log_n m = \frac{\log_{10} m}{\log_{10} n}\right]$$

$$= \frac{\log_{10} 8 \times \log_{10} 9 \times \log_{10} 4}{\log_{10} 16 \times \log_{10} 3 \times \log_{10} 10} \quad \left[\because \frac{a/b}{c/d} = \frac{ad}{bc}\right]$$

$$= \frac{\log_{10} 2^3 \times \log_{10} 3^2 \times \log_{10} 2^2}{\log_{10} 2^4 \times \log_{10} 3 \times 1} \quad [\because \log_{10} 10 = 1]$$

$$= \frac{3\log_{10} 2 \times 2\log_{10} 3 \times 2\log_{10} 2}{4\log_{10} 2 \times \log_{10} 3}$$

$$= 3\log_{10} 2$$

Example 14. If $p = \log_x yz$, $q = \log_y zx$ and $r = \log_z xy$, then prove that $\dfrac{1}{1+p} + \dfrac{1}{1+q} + \dfrac{1}{1+r} = 1$.

Sol. Let $\dfrac{1}{1+p} = \dfrac{1}{1+\log_x yz} = \dfrac{1}{\log_x x + \log_x yz}$ $\quad [\because 1 = \log_x x]$

$$= \frac{1}{\log_x xyz} \quad [\because \log m + \log n = \log mn]$$

$$= \log_{xyz} x \quad \left[\because \frac{1}{\log_b a} = \log_a b\right]$$

Similarly, $\dfrac{1}{1+q} = \log_{xyz} y$ and $\dfrac{1}{1+r} = \log_{xyz} z$

$\therefore$ LHS $= \dfrac{1}{1+p} + \dfrac{1}{1+q} + \dfrac{1}{1+r}$

$= \log_{xyz} x + \log_{xyz} y + \log_{xyz} z$

$= \log_{xyz} xyz = 1$ $\quad [\because \log m + \log n = \log mn]$

= RHS **Hence proved**

Example 15. Prove that $\log_{3^4} 4^3 = \dfrac{3}{4}\log_3 4$.

Sol. Let $\log_{3^4} 4^3 = x$

$\Rightarrow$ $(3^4)^x = 4^3$ $\quad [\because a^m = n \Rightarrow \log_a n = m]$

$\Rightarrow$ $3^{4x} = 4^3$

Taking log with base 3 both sides, we get

$\Rightarrow$ $\log_3 3^{4x} = \log_3 4^3$

$\Rightarrow$ $4x = \log_3 4^3$ $\quad [\because \log_a a = 1]$

$\Rightarrow$ $4x = 3\log_3 4$

$\Rightarrow$ $x = \dfrac{3}{4}\log_3 4$

$\therefore$ LHS = RHS **Hence proved**

Example 16. Find the value of $\log_3 2 \cdot \log_4 3 \cdot \log_5 4 \ldots \log_8 7$.

Sol. We have, $\log_3 2 \cdot \log_4 3 \cdot \log_5 4 \ldots \log_8 7$

By base changing formula,

$$\log_3 2 \cdot \log_4 3 \cdot \log_5 4 \ldots \log_8 7$$

$$= \frac{\log 2}{\log 3} \cdot \frac{\log 3}{\log 4} \cdot \frac{\log 4}{\log 5} \cdots \frac{\log 7}{\log 8} = \frac{\log 2}{\log 8}$$

$$= \frac{\log 2}{3\log 2} = \frac{1}{3}$$

Example 17. Solve the equations for x

$$\log_x 2 \times \log_{x/16} 2 = \log_{x/64} 2$$

Sol. Given, $\log_x 2 \times \log_{x/16} 2 = \log_{x/64} 2$

$$\Rightarrow \frac{1}{\log_2 x} \times \frac{1}{\log_2\left(\frac{x}{16}\right)} = \frac{1}{\log_2\left(\frac{x}{64}\right)} \quad \left[\because \log_a b = \frac{1}{\log_b a}\right]$$

By cross multiplication, we get

$\Rightarrow$ $\log_2(x/64) = \log_2 x \times \log_2(x/16)$

$\Rightarrow$ $\log_2 x - \log_2 64 = \log_2 x(\log_2 x - \log_2 16)$ $\quad \left[\because \log_a \frac{m}{n} = \log_a m - \log_a n\right]$

$\Rightarrow$ $\log_2 x - \log_2 2^6 = \log_2 x(\log_2 x - \log_2 2^4)$

$\Rightarrow$ $\log_2 x - 6\log_2 2 = \log_2 x(\log_2 x - 4\log_2 2)$ $\quad [\because \log_a m^n = n\log_a m]$

$\Rightarrow$ $\log_2 x - 6 \times 1 = \log_2 x(\log_2 x - 4 \times 1)$ $\quad [\because \log_a a = 1]$

$\Rightarrow$ $(\log_2 x)^2 - 5\log_2 x + 6 = 0$

Let $y = \log_2 x$

$\Rightarrow$ $y^2 - 5y + 6 = 0$ $\quad$ ...(i)

$\Rightarrow$ $y^2 - 3y - 2y + 6 = 0$

$\Rightarrow$ $y(y-3) - 2(y-3) = 0$

$\Rightarrow$ $(y-3)(y-2) = 0 \Rightarrow y = 3$ or $y = 2$

Putting the values of y in Eq. (i),

$\log_2 x = 3$ or $\log_2 x = 2$

$\Rightarrow$ $x = 2^3$ or $x = 2^2 \Rightarrow x = 8$ or $x = 4$.

Hence, the solutions of the given equation are 8, 4.

Chapter Practice

a. 1 Mark Questions

1. If $\log_2 x = a$, then find 4^{2a-1} is

(a) $\frac{x^4}{2}$ (b) $\frac{x^4}{4}$ (c) $\frac{x^2}{4}$ (d) $\frac{x^8}{4}$

2. Simplify $\log_{10} \sqrt[5]{32}$ is

(a) $\log_{10}(2)^{1/5}$ (b) $\log_{10}^{2}$ (c) $\log_{10} 5$ (d) $-\log_{10} 2$

3. Value of $\log_{10} \frac{50}{\sqrt{25}}$ is

(a) 1 (b) $\frac{1}{5}$ (c) -1 (d) 2

4. Find the value of x, when $\log(97 + \sqrt{x^2 - 16}) = 2$

(a) 5 and -7 (b) 2 and -5
(c) -5 and 5 (d) -2 and -5

5. Express $\log_{\sqrt{2}} 8$

(a) 12 (b) -12 (c) 6 (d) -6

6. Simplify $\log_{10} \frac{a^2}{\sqrt{b}}$ in terms of $\log_{10} a$, $\log_{10} b$.

(a) $2\log_{10} a - \frac{1}{2}\log_{10} b$ (b) $2\log_{10} a - \log_{10} b$

(c) $2\log_{10} a - 2\log_{10} b$ (d) $\frac{1}{2}\log_{10} a - 2\log_{10} b$

7. If $\frac{\log a}{b-c} = \frac{\log b}{c-a} = \frac{\log c}{a-b}$, then $a^a \cdot b^b \cdot c^c$ is

(a) 1 (b) 0 (c) -1 (d) 3

8. If $\frac{1}{\log_a n} + \frac{1}{\log_c n} = \frac{2}{\log_b n}$, then the value of b^2 is

(a) nb (b) an (c) ab (d) ac

9. Solve $\log_5 2 \times \log_2 5$

(a) -1 (b) 2 (c) 0 (d) 1

b. 3 Marks Questions

10. Express each of the following in the logarithmic form.

(i) $3^6 = 729$ (ii) $(81)^{3/4} = 27$
(iii) $8^{-1} = 0.125$ (iv) $5^3 = 125$
(v) $25^{1/2} = 5$

11. Prove that

(i) $\log_{10} 0.001 = -3$ (ii) $\log_5 125 = 3$
(iii) $\log_a 1 = 0$ (iv) $\log_{10} 100 = 2$
(v) $\log_{10}(0.0001) = -4$

12. Solve for x of each of the following.

(i) $\log_{10} x = -4$ (ii) $\log_{\sqrt{5}}(x-1) = 2$
(iii) $\log_{\sqrt{3}} x = 6$

13. Find the logarithm of each of the following.

(i) 256 to the base 4 (ii) 8 to the base 2
(iii) $\frac{1}{125}$ to the base 5 (iv) 625 to the base 25
(v) $\frac{1}{256}$ to the base 16

14. Solve each of the following.

(i) $\log_{125} 625$ (ii) $\log_{1/8} \frac{1}{256}$
(iii) $\log_{12} 1728$

15. Evaluate $\log_{2\sqrt{3}} 1728$.

16. Simplify the following.

(i) $\log_2(\log_2(\log_2 16))$ (ii) $3^{-\frac{1}{2}\log_3 9}$

17. Express $\log \frac{27}{4} + \log \frac{4}{32}$ in terms of log 2 and log 3.

18. If $\log v = 2\log 2 - \log 3 + \log \pi + 3\log r$, then find v.

19. Simplify $\log_{10} 8 + \log_{10} 25 + 2\log_{10} 3 - \log_{10} 18$.

20. Prove that

$$2\log\frac{15}{18} - \log\frac{25}{162} + \log\frac{4}{9} = \log 2.$$

21. If $\log_{10} m = n$, then evaluate 10^{2n-3} in terms of m.

22. If $\log_{10} 2 = m$ and $\log_{10} 3 = n$, then express $\log_{10} 120$ in terms of m and n.

23. Solve for x, if $\log_{10}(x^2 - 24) = 3$.

24. Solve for x, if $\log(x + 4) - \log(x + 5) = 1$.

25. Solve for x, if $(\log_{10} x)^2 + 5(\log_{10} x) + 6 = 0$.

26. Prove that

$$\log\frac{70}{33} + \log\frac{22}{135} - \log\frac{7}{18} = 3\log 2 - 2\log 3.$$

27. If $(x + y)^2 = 9xy$, then prove that

$$2\log(x + y) = \log x + \log y + 2\log 3.$$

28. If $\frac{3}{2}\log m + \frac{2}{3}\log n - 1 = 0$, then evaluate $m^9 n^4$.

29. If $x = \log 0.6$, $y = \log 1.25$ and $z = \log 3 - 2\log 2$, then find $5^{(x+y-z)}$.

30. Given that $x = 1 + \log 2 - \log 5, y = 2\log 3$ and $z = \log a - \log 5$. If $x + y = 2z$, then find the value of a.

31. If $\log 27 = 1.431$, then evaluate $\log 9$.

32. If $\log_{10} x = m + n$ and $y = 10^{2m-n}$, then evaluate $\log_{10} x^3y^4$ in terms of m and n.

33. Find the value of x, if
$$5^{\log x} + 3^{\log x} = 3^{\log x + 1} - 5^{\log x - 1}.$$

34. Show that $\dfrac{\log\sqrt{27} + \log\sqrt{8} - \log\sqrt{125}}{\log 6 - \log 5} = \dfrac{3}{2}$.

c. 4/5 Marks Questions

35. If $a^{3-x} \cdot b^{5x} = a^{x+5} \cdot b^{3x}$, then show that
$$x\log\frac{b}{a} = \log a.$$

36. Solve for x, if $\log(3x + 2) + \log(3x - 2) = 5\log 2$.

37. If $a^{2x-3} \cdot b^{2x} = a^{6-x} \cdot b^{5x}$, then prove that
$$3\log a = x\log\frac{a}{b}.$$

38. If $\log 2 = 0.3010$ and $\log 3 = 0.4771$, then find the value of $\log 3 + \log 8 - \log\sqrt{6}$.

39. Simplify $\dfrac{\log\sqrt{27} + \log 64 + \log\sqrt{1000}}{\log 480}$.

40. Solve for x and y, if
$$\log xy = 2 \text{ and } \log\frac{x}{y} + 2\log 2 = 2.$$

41. Solve for x, if $\log_x 49 - \log_x 7 + \log_x \dfrac{1}{343} + 2 = 0$.

42. If $\dfrac{\log_{10}x}{\log_{10}y} = \dfrac{3}{2}$ and $\log_{10} xy = 5$, then find the values of x and y.

43. If $a = 1 + \log_x yz$, $b = 1 + \log_y zx$ and $c = 1 + \log_z xy$, then show that $ab + bc + ca = abc$.

44. If $\log_a x = \dfrac{1}{\alpha}$, $\log_b x = \dfrac{1}{\beta}$, $\log_c x = \dfrac{1}{\gamma}$, then find the value of $\log_{abc} x$.

45. Solve for x and y, if $\log_{10} x^3y^4 = 7$ and $\log_{10}\dfrac{x^2}{y} = 1$.

46. Evaluate $\log_3\sqrt{6} + \log_3\sqrt{\dfrac{2}{3}} - \log_3(\log_3 9)$.

47. Solve for x, if
$$\log(x + 2) + \log(x - 2) = \log 3 + 3\log 4.$$

48. Solve for x, if
$$\log_{10} 5 + \log_{10}(5x + 1) = \log_{10}(x + 5) + 1.$$

49. Solve for x, if $\log_3(3 + x) + \log_3(8 - x)$
$$- \log_3(9x - 8) = 2 - \log_3 9.$$

d. 6 Marks Questions

50. Solve for x and y, if
$$\frac{\log(x + y)}{\log 2} = \frac{\log(x - y)}{\log 5} = \frac{\log 4}{\log(0.5)}.$$

51. If $x^2 + y^2 = 23xy$, then prove that
$$\log\left(\frac{x + y}{5}\right) = \frac{1}{2}(\log x + \log y).$$

52. Find the value of x, if
$$(\log_{10} x)^2 - 11(\log_{10} x) + 10 = 0.$$

53. If $x = (100)^a$, $y = (10000)^b$ and $z = (10)^c$, then express $\log\left(\dfrac{10\sqrt{y}}{x^2z^3}\right)$ in terms of a, b and c.

54. If $2x - \log 48 + 3\log 2 = \dfrac{1}{3}\log 125 - \log 3$, then find $(100)^x$.

55. Solve for a and b:
$$\log_{10}(ab) = 2,\ \log_{10}\left(\frac{a}{b}\right) + 2\log_{10} 2 = 2$$

Hints and Answers

1. (b)	**2.** (b)	**3.** (a)	**4.** (c)
5. (c)	**6.** (a)	**7.** (a)	**8.** (d)

9. (d)

10. Hint Do same as Example 1.

Ans. (i) $6 = \log_3 729$ (ii) $\log_{81} 27 = 3/4$

(iii) $-1 = \log_8 0.125$ (iv) $3 = \log_5 125$

(v) $\dfrac{1}{2} = \log_{25} 5$

11. Hint Apply $\log_a n = m \Rightarrow a^m = n$

(i) $(10)^{-3} = 0.001$ (ii) $5^3 = 125$

(iii) $a^0 = 1$ (iv) $10^2 = 100$

(v) $10^{-4} = 0.0001$

12. Hint Do same as Example 2.

Ans. (i) $x = \frac{1}{10000} = 0.0001$ (ii) $x = 6$

(iii) $x = 27$

13. Do same as Example 3.

Ans. (i) 4 (ii) 3 (iii) −3

(iv) 2 (v) − 2

14. Hint Apply power law

$\log_a(m)^n = n\log_a m$ and $\log_{a^n} m = \frac{1}{n}\log_a m$

Ans. (i) $\frac{4}{3}$ (ii) $\frac{8}{3}$ (iii) 3

15. Hint $\log_{2\sqrt{3}} 1728 = \log_{(12)^{1/2}}(12)^3$ **Ans.** 6

16. Hint (i) $\log_2(\log_2(\log_2 2^4)) = \log_2(\log_2 4)$, **Ans.** 1

(ii) $3^{-\frac{1}{2}\log_2(3)^2} = 3^{-\frac{1}{2}\times 2}$ **Ans.** $\frac{1}{3}$

17. Hint Do same as Example 5. **Ans.** $3\log 3 - 5\log 2$

18. Hint $\log v = \log\frac{4\pi r^3}{3}$. **Ans.** $v = \frac{4\pi r^3}{3}$

19. Hint $3\log_{10}2 + 2\log_{10}5 + 2\log_{10}3$

$- \log_{10}9 - \log_{10}2$ **Ans.** 2

20. Hint Use the formulae, $\log m - \log n = \log\frac{m}{n}$,

$n\log m = \log m^n$ and $\log m + \log n = \log mn$.

21. Hint $\because \log_{10} m = n \Rightarrow m = 10^n$

Now, $10^{2n-3} = (10^n)^2 \cdot 10^{-3} = \frac{m^2}{10^3}$ **Ans.** $\frac{m^2}{1000}$

22. Hint Do same as Example 6. **Ans.** $2m + n + 1$

23. Hint Do same as Example 10. **Ans.** $x = \pm 32$

24. Hint Do same as Example 11. **Ans.** $\frac{-46}{9}$

25. Hint Do same as Example 12.

Ans. $x = \frac{1}{1000}, \frac{1}{100}$

26. Hint Let LHS $= \log 70 - \log 33 + \log 22 - \log 135$

$- \log 7 + \log 18$

$= (\log 2 + \log 5 + \log 7) - (\log 11 + \log 3)$

$+ (\log 11 + \log 2) - (3\log 3 + \log 5)$

$- \log 7 + (\log 2 + 2\log 3)$

27. Hint $(x + y)^2 = 9xy$

Taking log on both sides, we get

$2\log(x + y) = \log x + \log y + 2\log 3$

28. Hint $\because \log m^{\frac{3}{2}} \cdot n^{\frac{2}{3}} = \log 10$

$\Rightarrow m^{\frac{3}{2}} \cdot n^{\frac{2}{3}} = 10 \Rightarrow m^{\frac{3}{2}\times 6} \cdot n^{\frac{2}{3}\times 6} = 10^6$ **Ans.** 10^6

29. Hint $x + y - z = \log 0.6 + \log 1.25 - (\log 3 - 2\log 2)$

$= \log(0.6\times 1.25\times 4) - \log 3$

$= \log\frac{0.6\times 1.25\times 4}{3}$

$= \log\frac{6}{10}\times\frac{125}{100}\times\frac{4}{3}$

$= \log 1 = 0$

$\therefore \quad 5^{x+y-z} = 5^0$ **Ans.** 1

30. Hint Given, $x + y = 2z$

$\Rightarrow \quad 1 + \log 2 - \log 5 + 2\log 3 = 2(\log a - \log 5)$

$\Rightarrow \log 10 + \log 2 - \log 5 + 2\log 3 = 2(\log a - \log 5)$

$[\because 1 = \log 10]$

$\Rightarrow \quad \log 36 = \log\frac{a^2}{25}$ **Ans.** $a = \pm 30$

31. Hint $\log 3^3 = 1.431$

$\Rightarrow \quad 3\log 3 = 1.431$ $[\because \log m^n = n\log m]$

Now, $\log 9 = \log 3^2 = 2\log 3$

$= 2\times\frac{1.431}{3}$ [substituting the value of log 3]

Ans. 0.954

32. Hint $\log_{10} x^3y^4 = \log_{10} x^3 + \log_{10} y^4$

$= 3\log_{10} x + 4\log_{10} y$

Ans. $11m - n$

33. Hint $5^{\log x} + 5^{\log x - 1} = 3^{\log x + 1} - 3^{\log x}$

$\Rightarrow \quad 5^{\log x}\left[1 + \frac{1}{5}\right] = 3^{\log x}[3 - 1] \Rightarrow \left(\frac{5}{3}\right)^{\log x} = \left(\frac{5}{3}\right)^1$

Ans. $x = 10$

34. Hint Let LHS $= \frac{\log(3)^{3/2} + \log(2)^{3/2} - \log(5)^{3/2}}{\log 6 - \log 5}$

$= \frac{\frac{3}{2}[\log 6 - \log 5]}{\log 6 - \log 5}$

35. Hint $\frac{b^{2x}}{a^{2x+2}} = 1 \Rightarrow \left(\frac{b}{a}\right)^{2x} = a^2$

Taking log on both sides, we get

$x\log\left(\frac{b}{a}\right) = \log a$

36. Hint $\log(3x + 2)(3x - 2) = \log 2^5$

$\Rightarrow \quad 9x^2 - 4 = 32$ **Ans.** $x = 2$

37. Hint Do same as Q. 35.

38. Hint $\log 3 + 3\log 2 - \frac{1}{2}(\log 2 + \log 3)$

$= 0.4771 + 3\times 0.3010 - \frac{1}{2}[0.3010 + 0.4771]$

Ans. 0.99105

39. Hint $\frac{\frac{3}{2}\log 3 + 6\log 2 + \frac{3}{2}[\log 2 + \log 5]}{5\log 2 + \log 15}$ **Ans.** $\frac{3}{2}$

40. Hint $\log x + \log y = 2$ and $\log x - \log y = 2 - 2\log 2$

Ans. $x = \pm 50$, $y = \pm 2$

41. Hint We have, $\log_x 49 - \log_x 7 + \log_x\frac{1}{343} + 2 = 0$

$\Rightarrow \quad 2\log_x 7 - \log_x 7 - 3\log_x 7 + 2 = 0$

Ans. $x = 7$

42. Hint $\dfrac{\log_{10} x}{\log_{10} y} = \dfrac{3}{2}$

$\Rightarrow \quad \log_{10} x^2 = \log_{10} y^3 \Rightarrow x^2 = y^3$

$\Rightarrow \quad x = y^{3/2}$ ...(i)

$y \cdot y^{3/2} = 10^5$ $[\because xy = 10^5]$

$\Rightarrow \quad y^{1/2} = 10 \Rightarrow y = 100$

$100x = 10^5$ $[\because xy = 10^5]$

Ans. $x = 1000,\ y = 100$

43. Hint $a = 1 + \log_x yz = \log_x x + \log_x yz = \log_x xyz$

$\Rightarrow \dfrac{1}{a} = \log_{xyz} x$

Similarly, $\dfrac{1}{b} = \log y_{xyz}$ and $\dfrac{1}{c} = \log z_{xyz}$

$\Rightarrow \dfrac{1}{a} + \dfrac{1}{b} + \dfrac{1}{c} = \log x_{xyz} + \log y_{xyz} + \log z_{xyz}$ **Ans.** 1

44. Hint $\dfrac{1}{\alpha} = \log_a x = \dfrac{\log x}{\log a}$

$\Rightarrow \log a = \alpha \log x$

Similarly, $\log b = \beta \log x$, $\log c = \gamma \log x$

$\log x_{abc} = \dfrac{\log x}{\log abc} = \dfrac{\log x}{\log a + \log b + \log c}$

45. Hint We have, $\log_{10} x^3 \cdot y^4 = 7$

$\Rightarrow \quad 3\log_{10} x + 4\log_{10} y = 7$ ...(i)

and $\quad \log_{10} \dfrac{x^2}{y} = 1$

$\Rightarrow \quad 2\log_{10} x - \log_{10} y = 1$ ...(ii)

$\Rightarrow \quad \log_{10} x = 1$ and $\log_{10} y = 1$

$[\because \log_a n = m \Rightarrow a^m = n]$

$\Rightarrow \quad x = (10)^1$ and $y = (10)^1$

Ans. $x = 10$ and $y = 10$

46. Hint $\log_3 \sqrt{6} \times \sqrt{\dfrac{2}{3}} - \log_3 2 = \log_3 2 - \log_3 2$

Ans. 0

47. Hint Do same as Q. 36.

Ans. $x = 14$

48. Hint $\log_{10} 5(5x + 1) = \log_{10}(x + 5)10$

Ans. $x = 3$

49. Hint $\log_3\left[\dfrac{(3 + x)(8 - x)(9)}{(9x - 8)}\right] = 2$

Ans. $x = 4$

50. Hint $\dfrac{\log(x + y)}{\log 2} = \dfrac{\log 4}{\log(0.5)}$

$\Rightarrow \quad x + y = \dfrac{1}{4}$ ...(i)

and $\quad \dfrac{\log(x - y)}{\log 5} = \dfrac{\log 4}{\log(0.5)}$

$\Rightarrow \quad x - y = \dfrac{1}{25}$ ...(ii)

On solving Eqs. (i) and (ii), we get the required result.

Ans. $x = \dfrac{29}{200}$ and $y = \dfrac{21}{200}$

51. Hint We have, $x^2 + y^2 = 23xy$

$\Rightarrow \quad (x + y)^2 = 25xy$ [adding $2xy$ on both sides]

$\Rightarrow \quad \left(\dfrac{x + y}{5}\right)^2 = xy$

Taking log on both sides, we get the required result.

52. Hint $(\log_{10} x - 1)(\log_{10} x - 10) = 0$

Ans. $x = 10, 10^{10}$

53. Hint $\log \dfrac{10\sqrt{y}}{x^2 z^3} = \log 10 + \dfrac{1}{2}\log y - 2\log x - 3\log z$

$= 1 + \dfrac{1}{2}\log(10000)^b - 2\log(100)^a - 3\log(10)^c$

Ans. $-4a + 2b - 3c + 1$

54. Hint $2x + \log\dfrac{1}{6} = \log 5 - \log 3$

$\Rightarrow \quad 2x - \log 2 - \log 5 = 0$

$\Rightarrow \quad 2x = \log 10$

Ans. 10

55. Hint $ab = (10)^2 = 100$ and $\log_{10}\dfrac{a}{b} = 2 - 2\log_{10} 2$

$= 2\log_{10} 10 - 2\log_{10} 2$

$\therefore \quad \log_{10}\dfrac{a}{b} = 2\log_{10}\dfrac{10}{2} = 2\log_{10} 5 = \log_{10} 25$

$\therefore \quad \dfrac{a}{b} = 25$ so, $ab \cdot \dfrac{a}{b} = 100 \times 25$

Ans. $a = 50, b = 2, a = -50, b = -2$

Olympiad Section

Brain Teasing Questions of Olympiad Pattern

1 If $x = \log_3 27$ and $y = \log_9 27$, then the value of $\frac{x+y}{xy}$ is

(a) $\frac{1}{3}$ (b) $\frac{1}{9}$
(c) 3 (d) 1

2 The value of $\log_{(a-b)}(a^3 - b^3) - \log_{(a-b)}(a^2 + ab + b^2)$, $(a > b)$ is

(a) 0 (b) 1
(c) 3 (d) not defined

3 The value of $\log_2 1 \times \log_3 2 \times \log_4 3 \times \ldots \times \log_{99} 100$ is

(a) not defined (b) 0
(c) 1 (d) 2

4 If $\log_a \frac{13^2}{\sqrt{2^3} \times 5} = 2\log_a 13 - \log_a 5 - x$, then

(a) $a^x = 2^{3/2}$ (b) $x^a = 2^{3/2}$
(c) $a^x = 2^{2/3}$ (d) $x^a = 2^{2/3}$

5 If $\log[4 - 5\log_{32}(x + 3)] = 0$, then the value of x is

(a) 32 (b) 8
(c) 2 (d) 5

6 If $x^6 - y^6 = k^6$, then $\log_k(x^2 - y^2) + \log_k(x^2 + y^2 - xy) + \log_k(x^2 + y^2 + xy)$ equals

(a) 3 (b) 4
(c) 5 (d) 6

7 $\log_2 [\log_4 \{\log_5 (625)^4\}]$ equals

(a) 1 (b) 0
(c) 3 (d) None of these

8 If $x^4 + y^4 = 83x^2y^2$, then $\log\left(\frac{x^2 - y^2}{9}\right)$ is equal to

(a) $\log x + \log y$
(b) $\log x - \log y$
(c) $\log xy$
(d) $\frac{\log x}{\log y}$

9 If $\log x + \log 5 = 2 + \log 64$, then the value of x is

(a) 1240 (b) 1280
(c) 1310 (d) 1100

10 The value of $\log_{11} 3 \cdot \log_3 1331$ is

(a) 4 (b) 0
(c) 3 (d) 1

Answers

1. (d) **2.** (b) **3.** (b) **4.** (a) **5.** (d) **6.** (d) **7.** (a) **8.** (a) **9.** (b) **10.** (c)

* *These questions may or may not be asked in the examination, have been given just for additional practice required for olympiads Scholarship Exams etc. For detailed explanations refer Page No. 339.*

CHAPTER

08

Triangles

SYLLABUS

• (a) Congruencey : Four cases : SSS, SAS, AAS and RHS. Illustration through cutouts. Simple applications. • (b) Problems based on (i) Angles opposite equal sides are equal and converse. (ii) If two sides of a triangle are unequal, then the greater angle is opposite the greater side and converse. (iii) Sum of any two sides of a triangle is greater than the thire side. (iv) Of all straight lines that can be drawn to a given line from a point outside it, the perpendicular is the shortest. Proofs not required.

A plane figure closed by three intersecting lines is called a **triangle**. A triangle has three sides, three angles and three vertices and it is denoted by the symbol 'Δ'. A triangle ABC is shown in the given figure

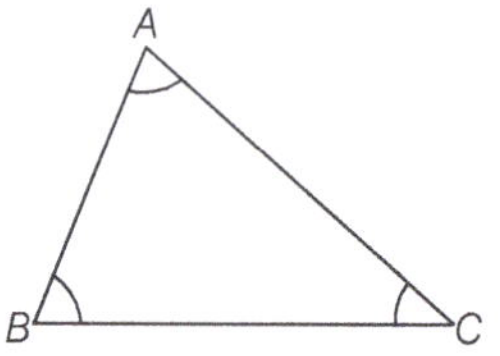

Triangle ABC can be denoted as ΔABC, in which AB, BC, CA are three sides, $\angle A$, $\angle B$, $\angle C$ are angles and A, B, C are three vertices.

Types of Triangles

Triangles are classified according to the length of their sides and the measure of their angles.

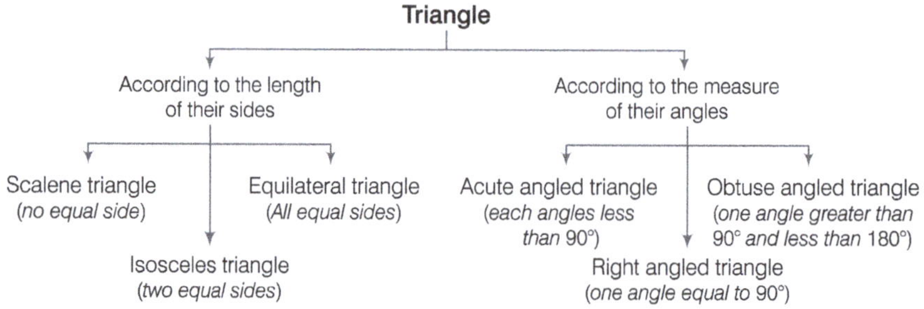

Important Properties of Triangles

(i) The sum of all angles of a triangle is 180°. It is called angle sum property of a triangle.

(ii) In an equilateral triangle, all sides and all angles are equal. So, each angle of an equilateral triangle is 60°.

(iii) A triangle cannot have more than one right angle.

(iv) A triangle cannot have more than one obtuse angle.

(v) In a right angled triangle, sum of the two acute angles is 90°.

(vi) If the side BC of a ΔABC is produced to D, then $\angle ACD$ so formed is called an exterior angle of ΔABC and it is equal to sum of its interior opposite angles, i.e. $\angle ACD = \angle BAC + \angle ABC$.

This is called exterior angle property of a triangle.

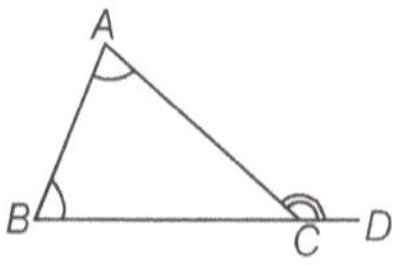

Some Important Terms Related to a Triangle

Median

The median of a triangle is a line segment joining a vertex of a triangle to the mid-point of the opposite side.

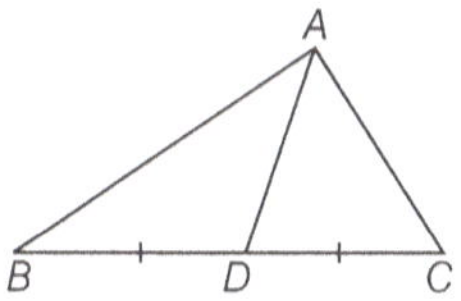

(i) A triangle has three medians and all the three medians intersect each other at one point only.

(ii) The point of intersection of the medians is called the '**centroid**' of the triangle.

(iii) The centroid of a triangle divides each median in the ratio 2 : 1.

Altitude

Perpendicular drawn from a vertex of a triangle to the opposite side is called an altitude of the triangle.

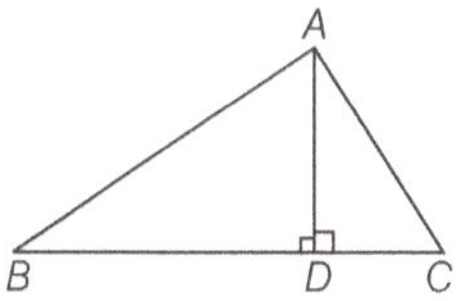

(i) A triangle has three altitudes and all the three altitudes are concurrent i.e. they intersect each other at one point only.

(ii) The point of intersection of the Altitudes is called the '**orthocentre**'.

Incentre and Incircle

When a circle touches all the sides of the triangle, called incircle and the centre of the incircle is called incentre. An incentre is the point of intersection of all three interior angle bisectors of the triangle.

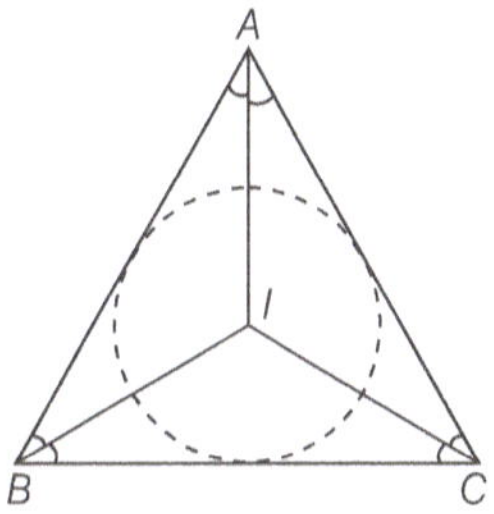

Circumcentre and Circumcircle

When a circle passes through all the vertices of a triangle, called circumcircle. And centre of circumcircle is called the circumcentre.
Circumcentre is the point of intersection of all three right bisectors of a triangle, where a right bisector is a line bisecting a side of a triangle and perpendicular to it.

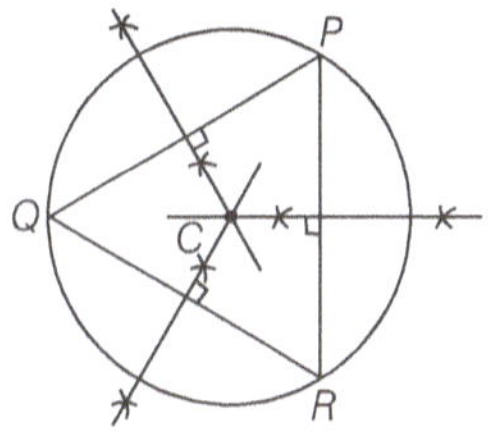

Congruence of Triangles

Two figures are said to be congruent, if they are of same shape and size ('congruent' means equal in all aspects). e.g. Two circles of the same radii and two squares of the same sides are congruent.

Two triangles are congruent, if sides and angles of a triangle are equal to the corresponding sides and angles of the other triangle.

Or

If a triangle superimposed on the other triangle and they cover each other completely, then the two triangles are congruent.

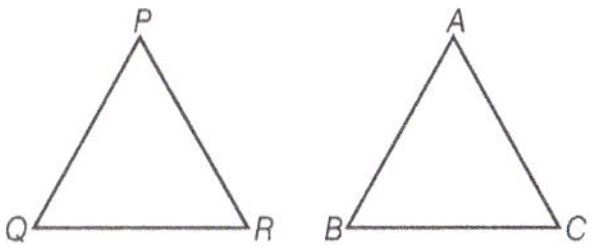

If ΔPQR is congruent to ΔABC, then we write $\Delta PQR \cong \Delta ABC$.

In congruent triangles, corresponding parts are equal and therefore we will write it in short as 'CPCT',
i.e. corresponding parts of congruent triangles.

(i) Every triangle is congruent to itself.

(ii) It is necessary to write the correspondence of vertices correctly for writing the congruence of triangles in symbolic form. The order of letters in the names of triangles shows the corresponding relationship.

i.e. $\Delta PQR \cong \Delta ABC$

Example 1. It is given that $\Delta ABC \cong \Delta RPQ$. Is it true to say that $BC = QR$? Give reason to support your answer.

Sol. No, because we know that triangles are congruent, if the sides and angles of one triangle are equal to the corresponding sides and angles of other triangle.

Here, $\Delta ABC \cong \Delta RPQ$

$\therefore$ $AB = RP$, $BC = PQ$

and $AC = RQ$

Hence, it is not true to say that $BC = QR$.

Example 2. It is given that $\Delta ABC \cong \Delta FDE$. If $AB = 5$ cm, $\angle B = 40°$ and $\angle A = 80°$, then find the length of DF and also measurement of $\angle E$.

Sol. Given, $AB = 5$ cm, $\angle B = 40°$ and $\angle A = 80°$

Since, $\Delta ABC \cong \Delta FDE$ [given]

$\therefore$ $\left.\begin{aligned} FD &= AB = 5\text{ cm} \\ \angle D &= \angle B = 40° \\ \angle F &= \angle A = 80° \end{aligned}\right\}$ [by CPCT]

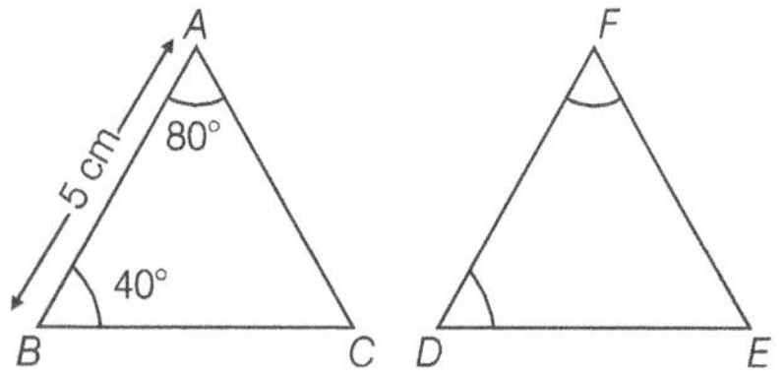

Also, in ΔFDE, $\angle F + \angle D + \angle E = 180°$

$\angle E = 180° - \angle F - \angle D$

[by angle sum property of a triangle]

$\therefore$ $\angle E = 180° - 80° - 40°$ [$\because \angle D = 40°$ and $\angle F = 80°$]

$= 60°$

Hence, $DF = 5$ cm and $\angle E = 60°$.

Criterias for Congruence of Triangles

SAS (Side-Angle-Side) Congruence Rule

Two triangles are congruent, if two sides and the included angle of a triangle are equal to the two sides and the included angle of the other triangle.

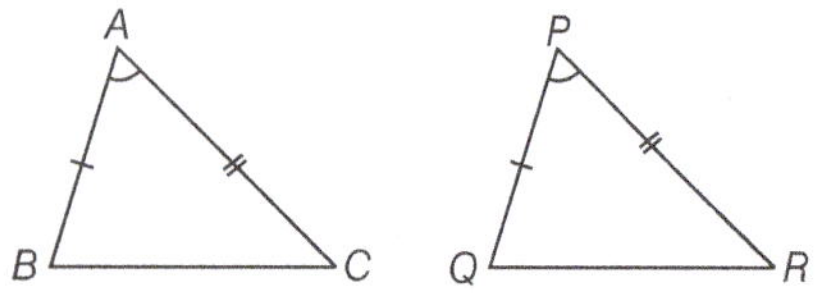

In ΔABC and ΔPQR, if $AB = PQ$, $\angle A = \angle P$, $AC = PR$

or $AC = PR$, $\angle C = \angle R$, $CB = RQ$

or $CB = RQ$, $\angle B = \angle Q$, $BA = QP$.

Then, $\Delta ABC \cong \Delta PQR$.

Here, for triangles to be congruent by SAS rule, it is very important that the equal angles are included between the pair of equal sides.

Example 3. In the given figures, find the measure of $\angle B'A'C'$.

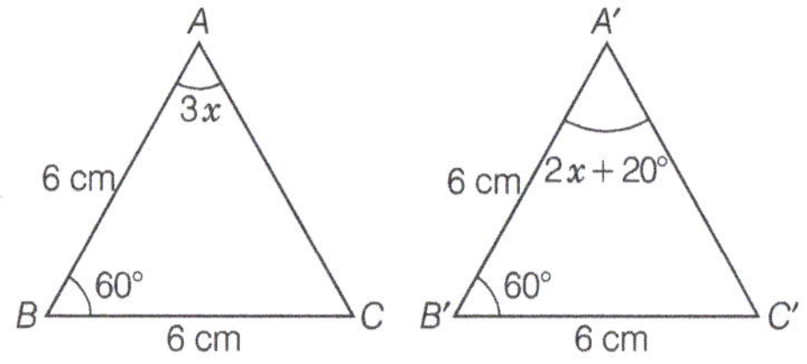

Sol. In ΔABC and $\Delta A'B'C'$,

$AB = A'B' = 6$ cm [given]

$\angle ABC = \angle A'B'C' = 60°$ [given]

and $BC = B'C' = 6$ cm [given]

$\therefore$ $\Delta ABC \cong \Delta A'B'C'$ [by SAS congruence rule]

Then, $\angle BAC = \angle B'A'C'$ [by CPCT]

$\Rightarrow$ $3x = 2x + 20°$ [from figure]

$\Rightarrow$ $3x - 2x = 20°$

$\Rightarrow$ $x = 20°$

$\therefore$ $\angle B'A'C' = 2x + 20° = 2 \times 20° + 20° = 60°$

Example 4. In the given figure,

$OB = OA$ and $OC = OD$

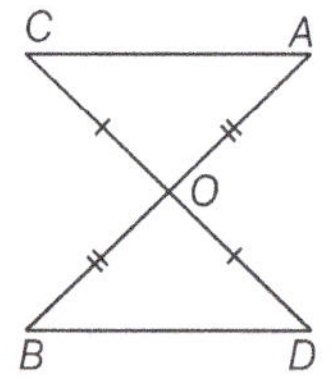

Show that

(i) $\Delta AOC \cong \Delta BOD$ (ii) $AC \parallel BD$

Sol.

(i) In ΔAOC and ΔBOD,

$OA = OB$ [given]

$OC = OD$ [given]

$\angle AOC = \angle BOD$ [vertically opposite angles]

$\therefore$ $\Delta AOC \cong \Delta BOD$ [by SAS congruence rule]

(ii) $\angle OBD = \angle OAC$ [CPCT]

These form a pair of alternate angles for line segment AC and BD.

Therefore, $AC \parallel BD$ **Hence proved**

Example 5. In a quadrilateral $ACBD$, $AC = AD$ and AB bisects $\angle A$ (see the figure). Show that $\Delta ABC \cong \Delta ABD$. What can you say about BC and BD?

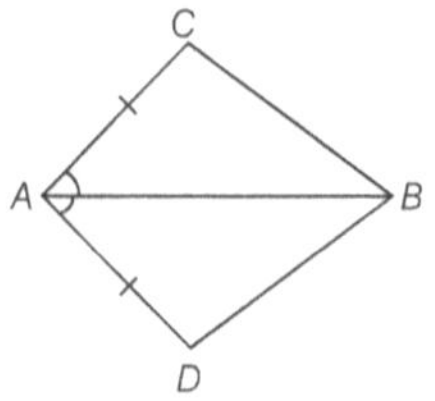

Sol. **Given** In quadrilateral $ACBD$,

$AC = AD$ and $\angle BAC = \angle BAD$

To prove $\Delta ABC \cong \Delta ABD$

Proof In ΔABC and ΔABD, $AC = AD$ [given]

$\angle BAC = \angle BAD$ [given]

and $AB = AB$ [common side]

Thus, $\Delta ABC \cong \Delta ABD$ [by SAS congruence rule]

$\Rightarrow$ $BC = BD$ [by CPCT]

Hence, BC and BD are equal.

Example 6. AB is a line segment and line l is a perpendicular bisector of AB. If a point P lies on l, then show that P is equidistant from A and B.

Sol. **Given** Line l is a perpendicular bisector of AB.

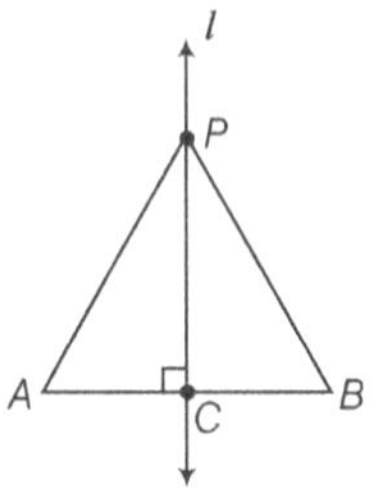

To prove P is equidistant from A and B.

i.e. to prove $PA = PB$

Proof Since, line l is perpendicular bisector of AB.

$\therefore$ $\angle ACP = \angle BCP = 90°$ ...(i)

and $AC = BC$ [$\because$ C is the mid-point of AB] ...(ii)

In ΔPCA and ΔPCB,

$AC = BC$ [from Eq. (ii)]

$\angle ACP = \angle BCP$ [each 90°, from Eq. (i)]

and $PC = PC$ [common side]

$\therefore$ $\Delta PCA \cong \Delta PCB$ [by SAS congruence rule]

$\Rightarrow$ $PA = PB$ [by CPCT]

Hence proved

Example 7. In the given figure, $AC = AE$, $AB = AD$ and $\angle BAD = \angle EAC$. Show that $BC = DE$.

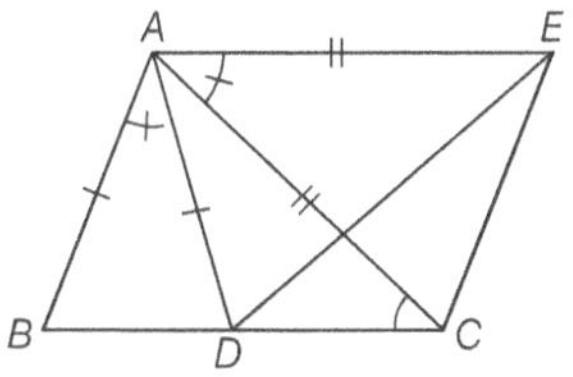

Sol. In ΔABC and ΔADE,

$AB = AD$ [given]

$\angle BAD = \angle EAC$ [given] ...(i)

On adding $\angle DAC$ both sides of Eq. (i), we get

$\angle BAD + \angle DAC = \angle EAC + \angle DAC \Rightarrow \angle BAC = \angle EAD$

$AC = AE$ [given]

$\therefore$ $\Delta ABC \cong \Delta ADE$ [by SAS congruence rule]

$\Rightarrow$ $BC = DE$ [by CPCT]

Hence proved

Example 8. In the given figure, $OP = OQ$, $OR = OS$ and $\angle POQ = \angle ROS$. Prove that $PR = QS$.

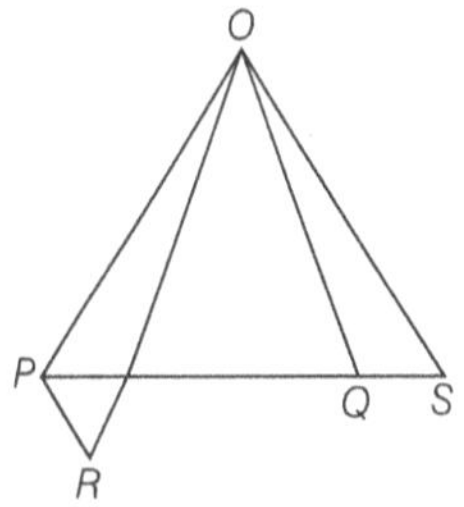

Sol. Given, $\angle POQ = \angle ROS$

$\Rightarrow$ $\angle POQ - \angle ROQ = \angle ROS - \angle ROQ$

[subtracting $\angle ROQ$ from both sides]

$\angle POR = \angle QOS$

In ΔPOR and ΔQOS,

$OP = OQ$ [given]

$OR = OS$ [given]

$\angle POR = \angle QOS$ [proved above]

$\therefore$ $\Delta POR \cong \Delta QOS$ [by SAS congruence rule]

$\Rightarrow$ $PR = QS$ [CPCT]

Hence proved

Example 9. In the given figure, ΔABC and ΔABD are such that $AD = BC$, $\angle 1 = \angle 2$ and $\angle 3 = \angle 4$. Prove that $BD = AC$.

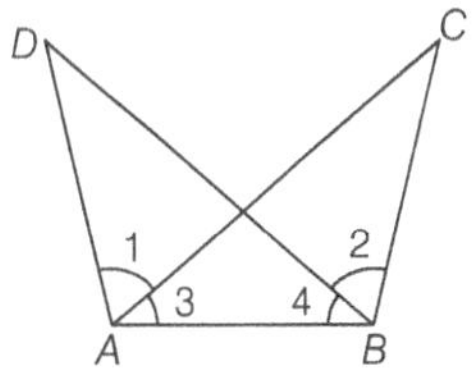

Sol. **Given** $AD = BC$, $\angle 1 = \angle 2$ and $\angle 3 = \angle 4$

To prove $BD = AC$

Proof Since, $\angle 1 = \angle 2$ and $\angle 3 = \angle 4$

$\therefore$ $\angle 1 + \angle 3 = \angle 2 + \angle 4$

$\Rightarrow$ $\angle DAB = \angle CBA$ ...(i)

Thus, in ΔABD and ΔABC, we have

$AB = AB$ [common side]

and $\angle DAB = \angle CBA$ [from Eq. (i)

$AD = BC$ [given]

$\therefore$ $\Delta ABD \cong \Delta BAC$ [by SAS congruence rule]

$\Rightarrow$ $BD = AC$ [by CPCT]

Hence proved

Example 10. In the given figure, $PQ = PR$ and PL is bisector of $\angle P$.

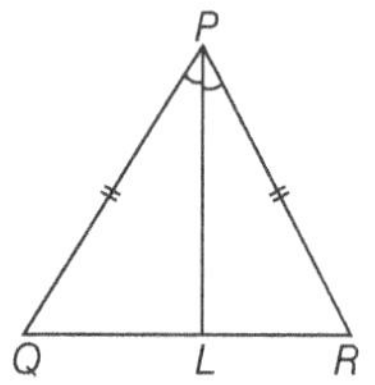

Prove that

(i) L is the mid-point of QR. (ii) $PL \perp QR$

Sol. **Given** In ΔPQR, $PQ = PR$ and $\angle QPL = \angle RPL$

To prove (i) $QL = RL$ (ii) $\angle PLQ = 90°$

Proof In ΔQPL and ΔRPL,

$PQ = PR$ [given]

$\angle QPL = \angle RPL$ [PL is bisector of $\angle P$]

$PL = PL$ [common]

$\Delta QPL \cong \Delta RPL$ [by SAS congruence rule]

(i) $QL = RL$ [CPCT] **Hence proved.**

(ii) $\angle PLQ = \angle PLR$ [CPCT]...(i)

$\angle PLQ + \angle PLR = 180°$ [QLR is a straight line]

$\Rightarrow \angle PLQ + \angle PLQ = 180°$ [from Eq. (i)]

$\Rightarrow 2\angle PLQ = 180°$

$\Rightarrow \angle PLQ = 90°$ or $PL \perp QR$ **Hence proved**

AAS (Angle-Angle-Side) Congruence Rule

Two triangles are congruent, if any two angles and a side of one triangle are equal to two angles and the corresponding side of other triangle.

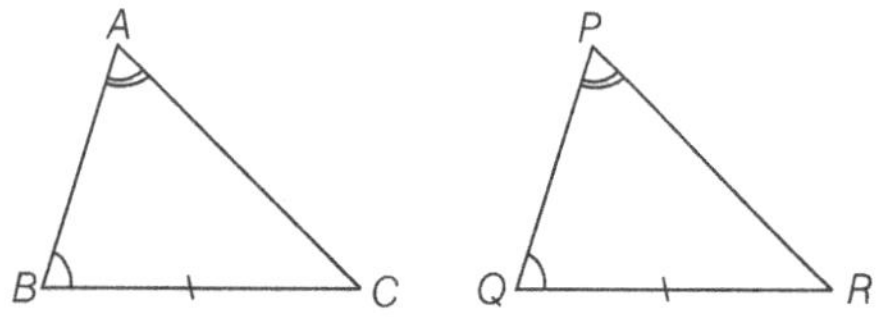

In ΔABC and ΔPQR, if

$\angle A = \angle P$, $\angle B = \angle Q$ and $BC = QR$.

or $\angle A = \angle P$, $\angle C = \angle R$ and $AB = PQ$

or $\angle B = \angle Q$, $\angle C = \angle R$ and $AC = PR$

Then, $\Delta ABC \cong \Delta PQR$.

AAS congruence rule is equivalent to ASA congruence rule. But in ASA congruence rule, the side of the triangle is included side.

Example 11. In the given figure, $AB = AC$ and $\angle B = \angle C$. Prove that

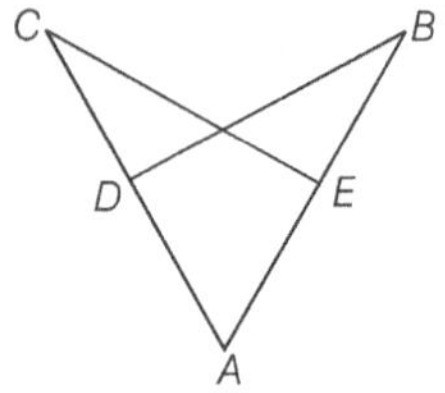

(i) $\Delta ABD \cong \Delta ACE$ (ii) $BD = CE$.

Sol.

(i) In ΔABD and ΔACE, we have

$\angle B = \angle C$ [given]

$\angle A = \angle A$ [common]

and $AB = AC$ [given]

$\therefore$ $\Delta ABD \cong \Delta ACE$ [by AAS congruence rule]

(ii) $\because \Delta ABD \cong \Delta ACE$

$\therefore$ $BD = CE$ [by CPCT]

Example 12. If the altitudes AD, BE and CF of a ΔABC are equal, then prove that ΔABC is an equilateral triangle.

Sol. **Given** In ΔABC, altitudes are equal,

i.e. $AD = BE = CF$

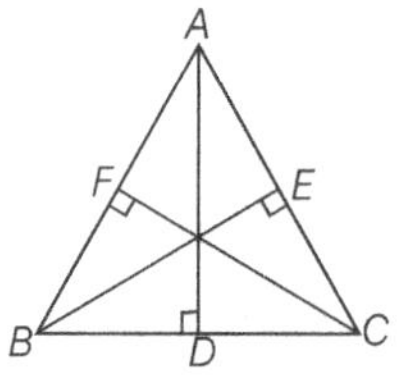

To prove ΔABC is an equilateral triangle, i.e. to prove $AB = BC = CA$.

Proof In ΔADC and ΔBEC,

$\angle ADC = \angle BEC$ [each 90°]

$\angle ACD = \angle BCE$ [common angle]

and $AD = BE$ [given]

$\therefore$ $\Delta ADC \cong \Delta BEC$ [by AAS congruence rule]

$\Rightarrow$ $AC = BC$ [by CPCT] ...(i)

Similarly, we can prove that $\Delta ADB \cong \Delta CFB$ [by AAS congruence rule]

$\Rightarrow$ $AB = CB$ ...(ii)

From Eqs. (i) and (ii), we get

$AB = BC = AC$

Thus, ΔABC is an equilateral triangle. **Hence proved**

Example 13. Line segment AB is parallel to another line segment CD. O is the mid-point of AD. Show that

(i) $\Delta AOB \cong \Delta DOC$

(ii) O is also the mid-point of BC.

Sol. **Given** $AB \| CD$ and O is the mid-point of AD.

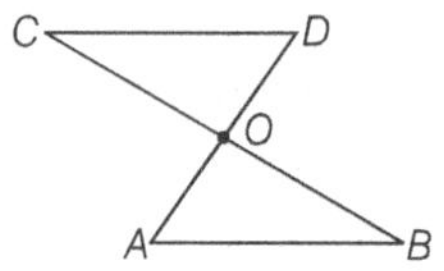

$\therefore$ $AO = OD$ ...(i)

To prove

(i) $\Delta AOB \cong \Delta DOC$

(ii) O is also the mid-point of BC, i.e. to prove $OB = OC$.

Proof

(i) In ΔAOB and ΔDOC, $\angle ABO = \angle DCO$

[alternate angles as $AB \parallel CD$ and BC is a transversal line]

$\angle AOB = \angle DOC$ [vertically opposite angles]

and $OA = OD$ [from Eq. (i)]

$\therefore$ $\Delta AOB \cong \Delta DOC$ [by AAS congruence rule]

(ii) By using corresponding part of congruent triangles, we get

$OB = OC$

Thus, O is also the mid-point of BC. **Hence proved.**

Example 14. In the given figure, line l is the bisector of an angle P and Q is any point on l. QA and QB are perpendiculars from Q to the arms of $\angle P$.

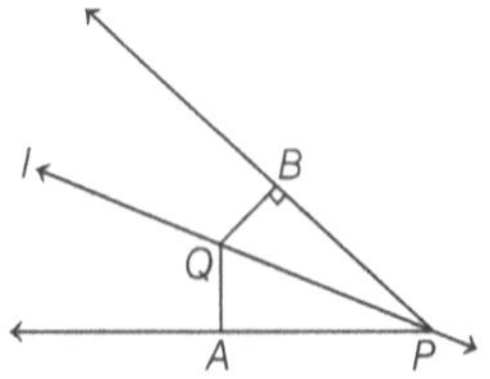

Show that

(i) $\Delta PAQ \cong \Delta PBQ$

(ii) Q is equidistant from the arms of $\angle P$.

Sol.

(i) In ΔPAQ and ΔPBQ,

$\angle QPA = \angle QPB$ [$\because$ line l is bisector of $\angle P$]

$\angle PAQ = \angle PBQ$ [each $= 90°$]

and $PQ = PQ$ [common]

$\therefore$ $\Delta PAQ \cong \Delta PBQ$ [by AAS congruence rule]

(ii) $QA = QB$ [CPCT]

$\Rightarrow$ Q is equidistant from the arms of $\angle P$.

Example 15. In a quadrilateral $ABCD$, perpendiculars BM and DN are drawn to AC, such that $BM = DN$. If $BR = 8$ cm, then find the length of BD.

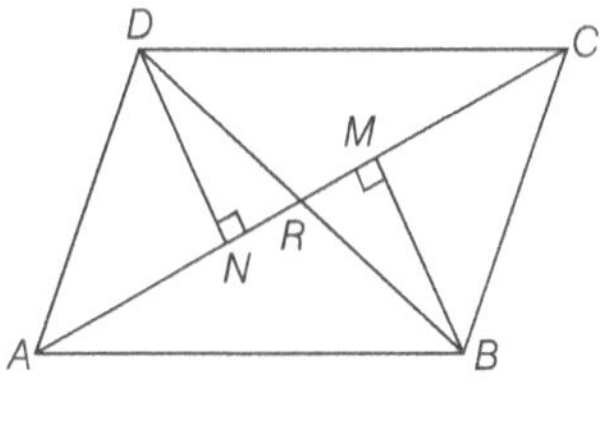

Sol. In ΔDNR and ΔBMR,

$\angle DNR = \angle BMR$

[each $90°$, because $DN \perp AC$ and $BM \perp AC$]

and $\angle DRN = \angle BRM$ [vertically opposite angles]

$DN = BM$ [given]

$\therefore$ $\Delta DNR \cong \Delta BMR$ [by AAS congruence rule]

$\Rightarrow$ $DR = BR$ [by CPCT]

$\Rightarrow$ $DR + BR = BR + BR$ [adding BR both sides]

$\therefore$ $BD = 2BR$

$= 2 \times 8 = 16\,\text{cm}$ [$\because BR = 8$ cm, given]

Example 16. AD is a median and BL, CM are perpendiculars drawn from B and C respectively on AD produced to M. Prove that $BL = CM$.

Sol. **Given** AD is a median and BL, CM are perpendiculars drawn from B and C respectively on AD produced to M.

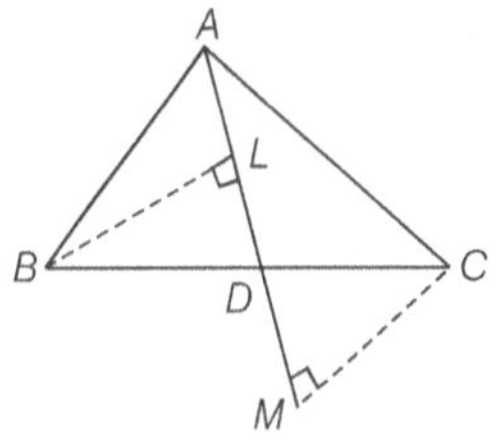

To prove $BL = CM$

Proof In ΔBDL and ΔCDM,

$\angle BLD = \angle CMD$ [each $90°$]

$\angle BDL = \angle CDM$ [vertically opposite angles]

and $BD = CD$

[$\because AD$ is a median, so D is the mid-point of BC]

$\therefore$ $\Delta BDL \cong \Delta CDM$ [by AAS congruence rule]

$\Rightarrow$ $BL = CM$ [by CPCT] **Hence proved**

Example 17. In the given figure, $AB = CB$ and $\angle x = \angle y$. Prove that $QA = PC$.

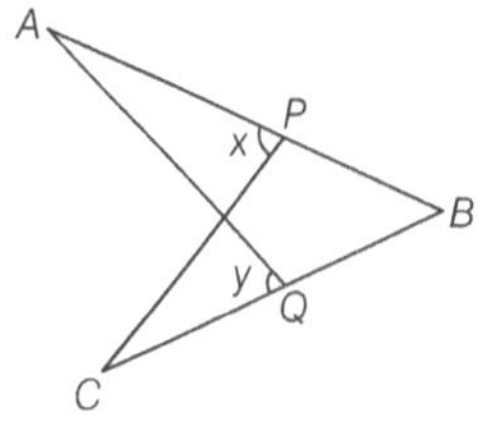

Sol. For ΔPBC,

$\angle x = \angle B + \angle PCB$

[external angle = sum of two internal opposite angles]

For ΔQAB,

$\angle y = \angle B + \angle QAB$

[external angle = sum of two internal opposite angles]

But $\angle x = \angle y$ [given]

$\Rightarrow$ $\angle B + \angle PCB = \angle B + \angle QAB$

$\Rightarrow$ $\angle PCB = \angle QAB$

In ΔQAB and ΔPCB,

$\angle QAB = \angle PCB$ [proved above]

$\angle B = \angle B$ [common]

$AB = CB$ [given]

$\therefore$ $\Delta QAB \cong \Delta PCB$ [by ASA congruence rule]

$\therefore$ $QA = PC$ [CPCT] **Hence proved**

SSS (Side-Side-Side) Congruence Rule

If three sides of one triangle are equal to the three sides of another triangle, then the triangles are congruent.

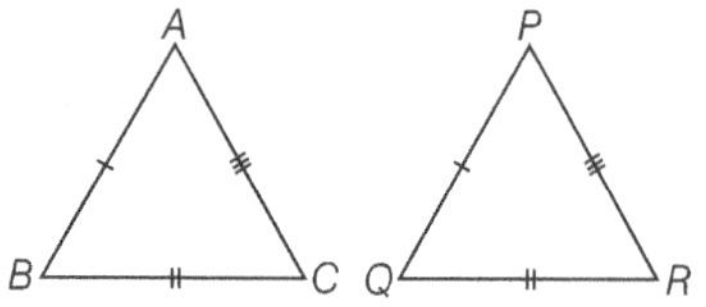

In ΔABC and ΔPQR, if $AB = PQ$, $BC = QR$ and $AC = PR$, then $\Delta ABC \cong \Delta PQR$.

Example 18. ΔABC and ΔDBC are two isosceles triangles on the same base BC and vertices A and D are on the same side of BC (see the figure). If AD is extended to intersect BC at P, then show that

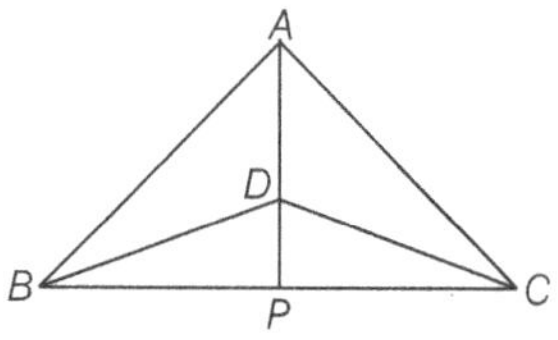

(i) $\Delta ABD \cong \Delta ACD$ (ii) $\Delta ABP \cong \Delta ACP$

(iii) AP bisects $\angle A$ as well as $\angle D$

Sol. **Given** ΔABC and ΔDBC are two isosceles triangles in which $AB = AC$ and $BD = DC$.

To prove

(i) $\Delta ABD \cong \Delta ACD$ (ii) $\Delta ABP \cong \Delta ACP$

(iii) AP bisects $\angle A$ as well as $\angle D$.

Proof

(i) In ΔABD and ΔACD,

$AB = AC$ [given]

$BD = DC$ [given]

and $AD = AD$ [common side]

$\therefore$ $\Delta ABD \cong \Delta ACD$ [by SSS congruence rule]

$\Rightarrow$ $\angle BAD = \angle CAD$ [by CPCT]

(ii) In ΔABP and ΔACP,

$AB = AC$ [given]

$AP = AP$ [common side]

and $\angle BAP = \angle CAP$ [proved earlier]

$\therefore$ $\Delta ABP \cong \Delta ACP$ [by SAS congruence rule]

$\Rightarrow$ $BP = CP$ (CPCT)

(iii) Now, as $\Delta ABD \cong \Delta ACD$ ...(i)

$\therefore$ $\angle BAD = \angle CAD \Rightarrow AP$ bisects $\angle A$

Also, as $\Delta ABP \cong \Delta ACP$ ...(ii)

Now, subtracting Eq. (i) from Eq. (ii), we get

$\Delta ABP - \Delta ABD \cong \Delta ACP - \Delta ACD$

$\Rightarrow$ $\Delta DBP \cong \Delta DCP$

$\therefore$ $\angle BDP = \angle CDP$ [by CPCT]

Hence, AP bisects $\angle A$ as well as $\angle D$.

RHS (Right Angle-Hypotenuse-Side) Congruence Rule

If in two right triangles, the hypotenuse and one side of one triangle are equal to the hypotenuse and one side of the other triangle, then the two triangles are congruent.

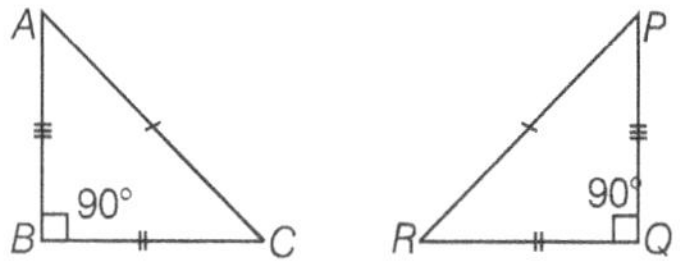

In ΔABC and ΔPQR, if

$\angle B = \angle Q$, $AC = PR$ and $AB = PQ$

or $\angle B = \angle Q$, $AC = PR$ and $BC = RQ$.

Then, $\Delta ABC \cong \Delta PQR$.

Example 19. AD is an altitude of an isosceles ΔABC in which $AB = AC$. Show that

(i) AD bisects BC (ii) AD bisects $\angle A$

Sol. Given, $AD \perp BC$ and $AB = AC$

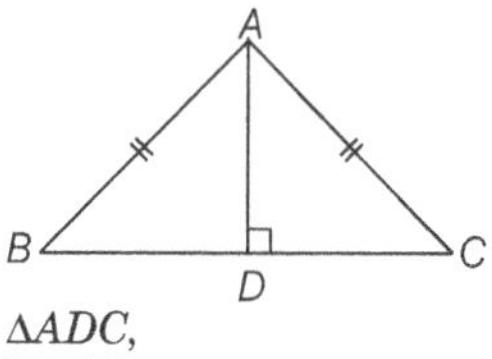

In ΔADB and ΔADC,

$AB = AC$ [given]

$\angle ADB = \angle ADC$ [each 90°]

and $AD = AD$ [common]

$\therefore$ $\Delta ADB \cong \Delta ADC$ [by RHS congruence rule]

$\Rightarrow$ $BD = DC$ [by CPCT]

and $\angle BAD = \angle CAD$ [by CPCT]

$\Rightarrow$ AD bisects BC and AD bisects $\angle A$.

Example 20. In the given figure AB and CD are perpendiculars on BD. Also, $AB = CD$ and $AF = CE$. Prove that (i) $ABF \cong CDE$ (ii) $BE = FD$.

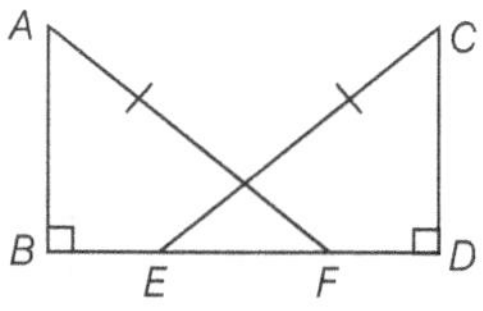

Sol. **Given** $AB \perp BD$, $CD \perp BD$, $AB = CD$ and $AF = CE$.

To prove $BE = FD$

Proof (i) In ΔABF and ΔCDE,

$AB = CD$ [given]

$AF = CE$ [given]

and $\angle ABF = \angle CDE = 90°$

$\therefore$ $\Delta ABF \cong \Delta CDE$ [by RHS congruence rule]

(ii) As we know $\Delta ABF \cong \Delta CDE$

$\Rightarrow$ $BF = ED$ [by CPCT]

$\Rightarrow \quad BF - EF = ED - EF$ [subtract EF from both sides]

$\Rightarrow \quad BE = FD$ **Hence proved**

Example 21. In the given figure, two sides PQ, PR and altitude PN of ΔPQR are respectively equal to two sides AB, AC and altitude AM of ΔABC.

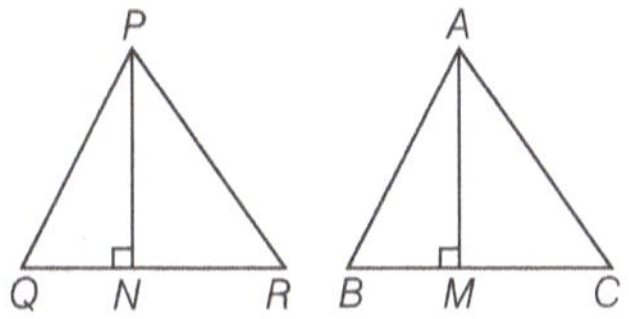

Prove that $\Delta PQR \cong \Delta ABC$.

Sol. In ΔPQN and ΔABM,

$\angle PNQ = \angle AMB$ [each 90°]

$PQ = AB$ [given]

$PN = AM$ [given]

$\therefore \quad \Delta PQN \cong \Delta ABM$ [by RHS congruence rule]

$\therefore \quad QN = BM$ [CPCT] ...(i)

In ΔPNR and ΔAMC,

$\angle PNR = \angle AMC$ [each 90°]

$PR = AC$ [given]

$PN = AM$ [given]

$\therefore \quad \Delta PNR \cong \Delta AMC$ [by RHS congruence rule]

$\therefore \quad NR = MC$ [CPCT] ...(ii)

From Eqs. (i) and (ii), we get

$QN + NR = BM + MC$

$\Rightarrow \quad QR = BC$ [from figure]

In ΔPQR and ΔABC

$PQ = AB$ [given]

$PR = AC$ [given]

$QR = BC$ [proved above]

$\therefore \quad \Delta PQR \cong \Delta ABC$ [by SSS congruence rule]

Important Theorems Based on Isosceles Triangle

Theorem 1 *Angles opposite to equal sides of a triangle are equal.*

Given An isosceles ΔPQR is given in which $PQ = PR$

To prove $\angle Q = \angle R$

Construction Draw PL bisector of $\angle P$ to meet QR at L.

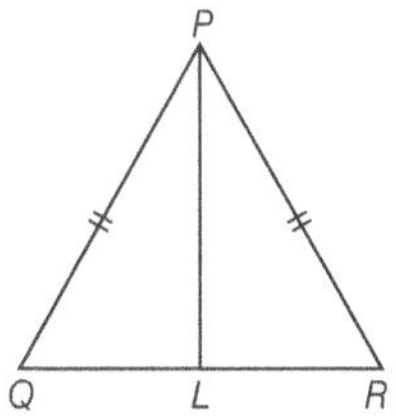

Proof In ΔPQL and ΔPRL,

$PQ = PR$ [given]

$PL = PL$ [common]

$\angle QPL = \angle RPL$

[PL is bisector of $\angle P$ by construction]

$\therefore \quad \Delta PQL \cong \Delta PRL$ [by SAS congruence rule]

$\therefore \quad \angle Q = \angle R$ [CPCT]

Theorem 2 (Converse of Theorem 1) *The sides opposite to equal angles of a triangle are equal.*

Given A ΔPQR in which $\angle Q = \angle R$

To prove $PQ = PR$

Construction Draw PL bisector of $\angle P$ to meet QR at L.

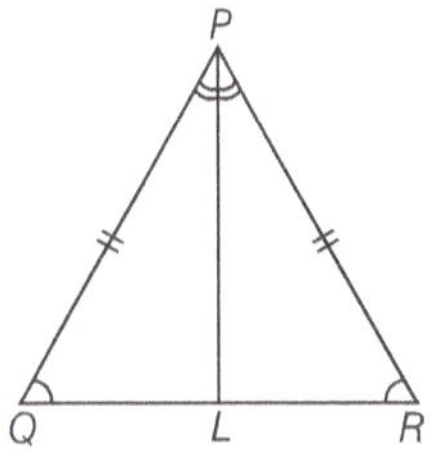

Proof In ΔPQL and ΔPRL,

$\angle Q = \angle R$ [given]

$PL = PL$ [common]

$\angle QPL = \angle RPL$

[PL is bisector of $\angle P$ by construction]

$\therefore \quad \Delta PQL \cong \Delta PRL$ [by AAS congruence rule]

$\therefore \quad PQ = PR$ [CPCT]

Example 22. In a ΔABC, if $AB = 3$ cm, $AC = 3$ cm and $\angle A = 50°$, then find $\angle B$.

Sol. In ΔABC, we have $AB = AC = 3$ cm

$\therefore \quad \angle C = \angle B$

[$\because$ angles opposite to equal sides of a triangle are equal]

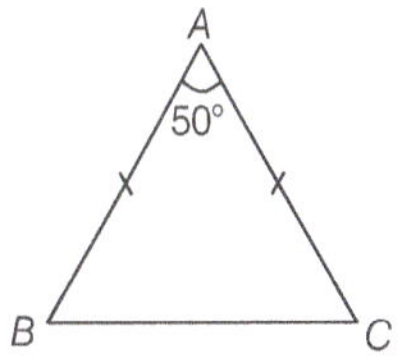

But $\angle A + \angle B + \angle C = 180°$

[by angle sum property of a triangle]

$\Rightarrow \quad 50° + \angle B + \angle B = 180°$ [$\because \angle A = 50°$ and $\angle C = \angle B$]

$\Rightarrow \quad 50° + 2\angle B = 180°$

$\Rightarrow \quad 2\angle B = 130°$

$\Rightarrow \quad \angle B = \frac{130°}{2}$

$\Rightarrow \quad \angle B = 65°$

Example 23. In the given figure, ABC and DBC are two isosceles triangles on the same base BC. Show that $\angle ABD = \angle ACD$.

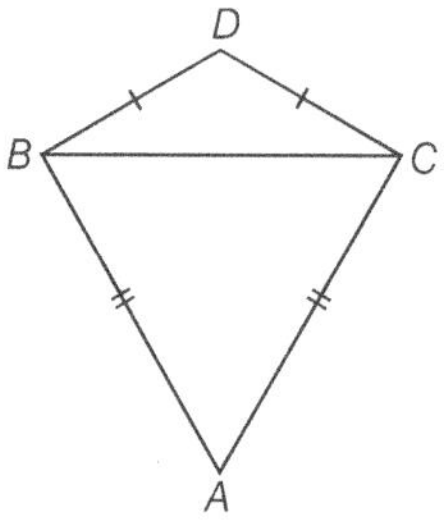

Sol. $CD = BD$ [given]

$\angle CBD = \angle BCD$ ...(i)

[$\because$ angles opposite to equal sides are equal]

$AC = AB$ [given]

$\Rightarrow$ $\angle ABC = \angle ACB$ ...(ii)

On adding Eqs. (i) and (ii), we get

$\angle CBD + \angle ABC = \angle BCD + \angle ACB$

$\Rightarrow$ $\angle ABD = \angle ACD$ **Hence proved**

Example 24. ABC is a triangle, in which $AB = AC$, D is any point of AB. Through D, a line parallel to AC intersects BC at E. If $DB = 1.5$ cm, then find the length of DE.

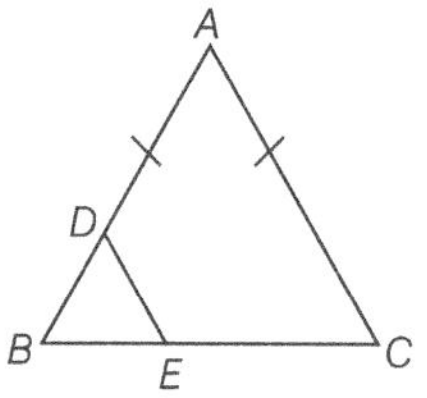

Sol. Given, $AB = AC$

$\Rightarrow$ $\angle C = \angle B$ ...(i)

[$\because$ angles opposite to equal sides of a triangle are equal]

Also, $DE \parallel AC$

$\angle DEB = \angle C$ [corresponding angles] ...(ii)

From Eqs. (i) and (ii), we get

$\angle B = \angle DEB$

Hence, $DE = DB$

[$\because$ sides opposite to equal angles of a triangle are equal]

Thus, $DE = 1.5\,\text{cm}$ [$\because DB = 1.5\,\text{cm}$, given]

Example 25. PQR is an isosceles triangle in which QM and RN are drawn to equal sides PR and PQ respectively. Show that these altitudes are equal.

Sol. Given, $PR = PQ$

$\Rightarrow$ $\angle Q = \angle R$

[$\because$ angles opposite to equal sides are equal]

In ΔQMR and ΔRNQ,

$\angle R = \angle Q$ [from above]

$QR = RQ$ [common]

$\angle QMR = \angle RNQ$ [each 90°]

$\therefore$ $\Delta QMR \cong \Delta RNQ$ [by AAS congruence rule]

$QM = RN$ [CPCT] **Hence proved**

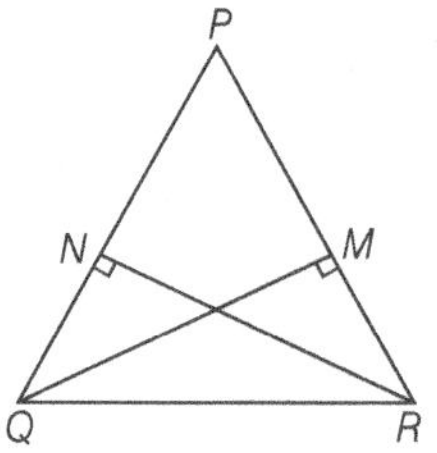

Example 26. In the given figure, ΔABC is an isosceles triangle in which $AB = AC$ and LM is parallel to BC. If $\angle A = 50°$, then find $\angle LMC$.

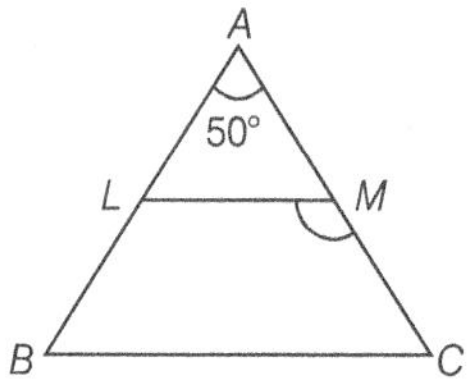

Sol. Given, ΔABC is an isosceles triangle with $AB = AC$.

$\therefore$ $\angle ACB = \angle ABC$ ...(i)

[$\because$ angles opposite to equal sides of a triangle are equal]

By using angle sum property of a triangle,

$\angle ABC + \angle ACB + \angle CAB = 180°$

$\Rightarrow$ $\angle ACB + \angle ACB + 50° = 180°$ [from Eq. (i)]

$\Rightarrow$ $2\angle ACB = 130°$

$\Rightarrow$ $\angle ACB = 65°$

Since, lines $LM \parallel BC$.

$\therefore$ $\angle LMC + \angle BCM = 180°$ [$\because$ co-interior angles]

$\Rightarrow$ $\angle LMC + 65° = 180°$ [$\because \angle BCM = \angle ACB$]

$\Rightarrow$ $\angle LMC = 115°$

Example 27. In the given figure, $AB = BC$ and $AC = CD$. Prove that $\angle BAD : \angle ADB = 3 : 1$.

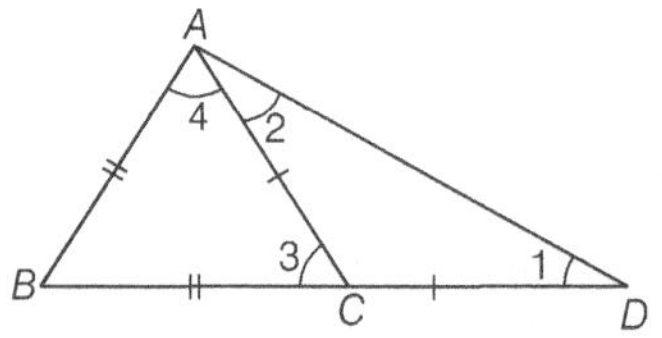

Sol. **Given** $AB = BC$ and $AC = CD$

To prove $\angle BAD : \angle ADB = 3 : 1$

Proof $CA = CD$ [given]

$\Rightarrow$ $\angle 1 = \angle 2 = x$ (say) ...(i)

[$\because$ angles opposite to equal sides of a triangle are equal]

Considering ΔADC whose side DC is extended to B, we have

$\angle 3 = \angle 1 + \angle 2$

[since, exterior angle is equal to the sum of interior opposite angles]

$\Rightarrow$ $\angle 3 = x + x = 2x$ ...(ii)

Also, $BA = BC$ [given]

$\Rightarrow$ $\angle 3 = \angle 4$ ...(iii)

[$\because$ angles opposite to equal sides of a triangle are equal]

From Eqs. (ii) and (iii), we get

$\angle 4 = 2x$ ...(iv)

Now, $\angle BAD = \angle BAC + \angle CAD = \angle 4 + \angle 2$

$= 2x + x = 3x$ [from Eqs. (i) and (iv)] ...(v)

Thus, $\angle BAD : \angle ADB = 3x : x$

$\Rightarrow$ $\angle BAD : \angle ADB = 3 : 1$ **Hence proved**

Example 28. In an isosceles ΔABC with $AB = AC$, D and E are the points on BC such that $BE = CD$. Show that $AD = AE$.

Sol. Given, ΔABC is an isosceles triangle in which

$AB = AC$ ...(i)

and D, E are points on BC such that

$BE = CD$ ...(ii)

Since, $AB = AC$

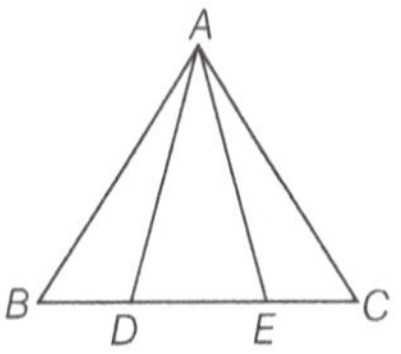

So, $\angle C = \angle B$ ...(iii)

[$\because$ angles opposite to equal sides are also equal]

From Eq. (ii), we have

$BE = CD$

$\Rightarrow$ $BE - DE = CD - DE$

[subtracting DE from both sides]

$\Rightarrow$ $BD = CE$ ...(iv)

In ΔABD and ΔACE, $AB = AC$ [from Eq. (i)]

$\angle B = \angle C$ [from Eq. (iii)]

and $BD = CE$ [from Eq. (iv)]

$\therefore$ $\Delta ABD \cong \Delta ACE$ [by SAS congruence rule]

$\Rightarrow$ $AD = AE$ [by CPCT]

Exercise 8.1

1. If ΔABC is congruent to ΔPQR, then find the length of QR.

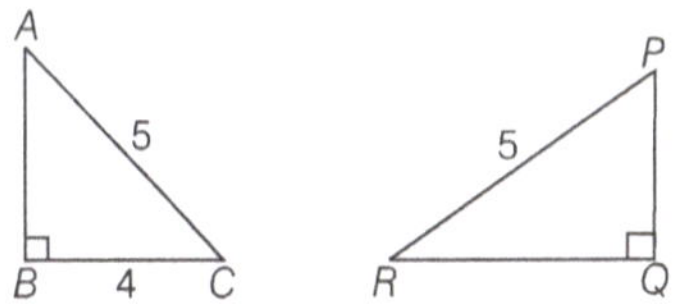

2. In the given figures, find the measure of $\angle B' A' C'$.

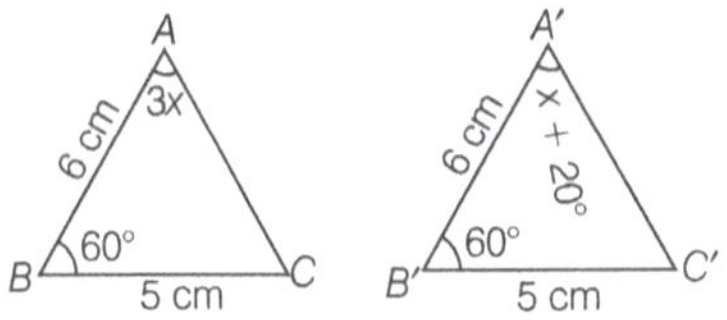

3. In the given figure, if $BC = 2.6$ cm, then find the value of $2BD + \dfrac{BC}{2}$.

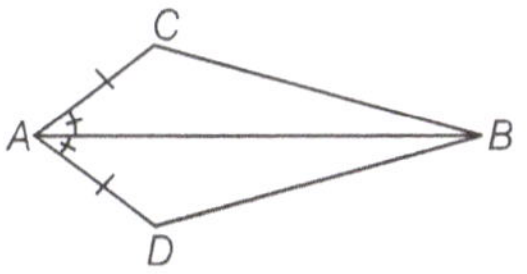

4. In the given figure, L and M are mid-points of equal sides PQ and PR respectively of ΔPQR. Prove that $QM = RL$.

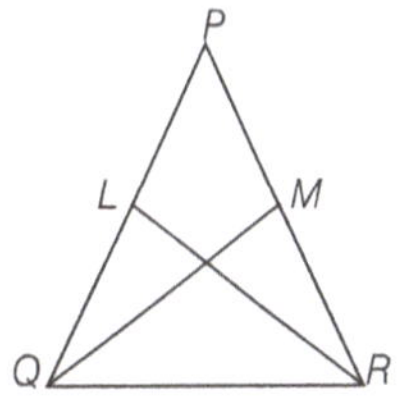

5. $ABCD$ is a quadrilateral in which $AD = BC$ and $\angle DAB = \angle CBA$ (see the figure).

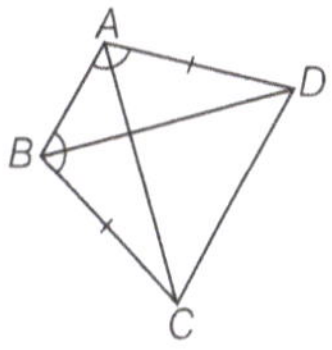

Prove that

(i) $\Delta ABD \cong \Delta BAC$ (ii) $BD = AC$

(iii) $\angle ABD = \angle BAC$.

6. In ΔABC, AD is the perpendicular bisector of BC (see the figure). Show that ΔABC is an isosceles triangle, i.e. $AB = AC$.

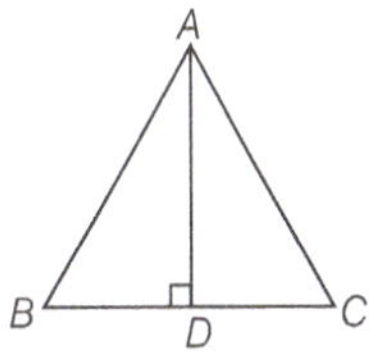

7. AB is a line segment and P is its mid-point. D and E are points on the same side of AB, such that $\angle BAD = \angle ABE$ and $\angle EPA = \angle DPB$ (see the figure).

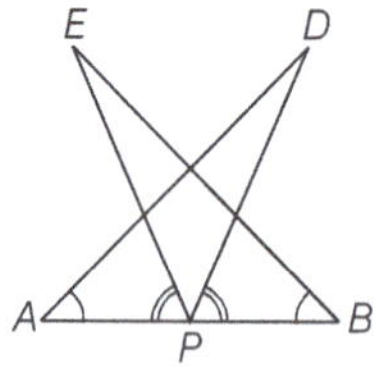

Show that

(i) $\Delta DAP \cong \Delta EBP$ (ii) $AD = BE$.

8. In the given figures, $AB = DE$, $BC = EF$ and median AP = median DQ. Prove that $\angle B = \angle E$.

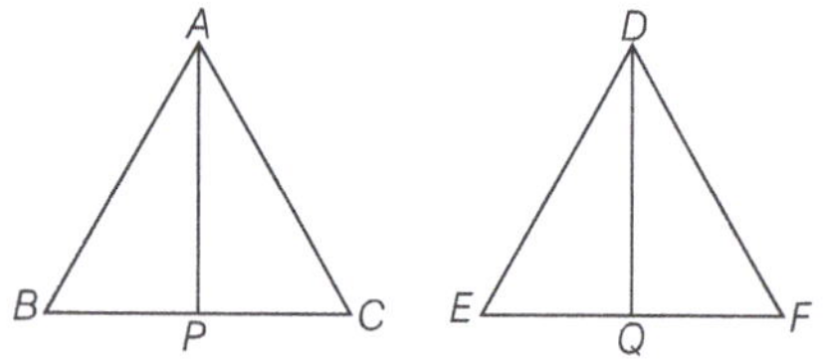

9. The given figure shows a circle with centre O. N is mid-point of AB. Show that ON is perpendicular to AB.

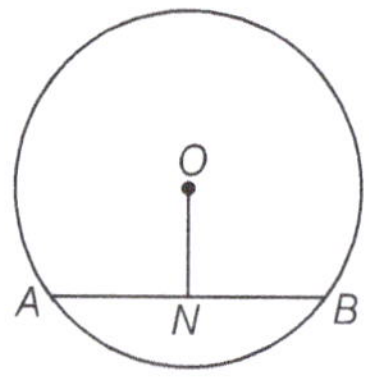

10. In the given figure, P is a point equidistant from two lines l and m intersecting at point A. Prove that ΔABP and ΔACP are congruent and length of AC is 8 cm.

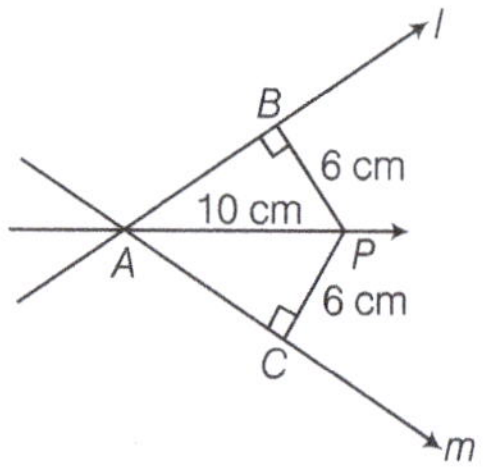

11. Use congruency of triangles to find the value of x and y.

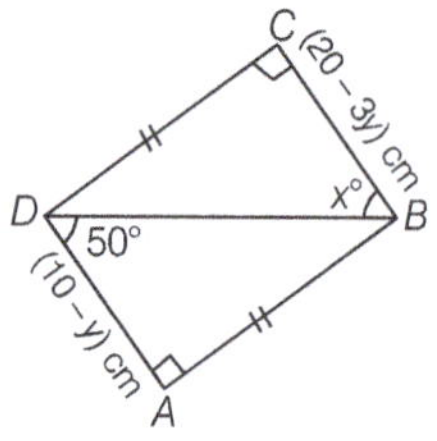

12. A is any point in the $\angle PQR$ such that the perpendiculars drawn from A on PQ and QR are equal. Prove that QA bisects $\angle PQR$.

13. $ABCD$ is a square, X and Y are points on sides AD and BC respectively such that $AY = BX$. Prove that $BY = AX$ and $\angle BAY = \angle ABX$.

14. In the following figure, ABC is a right triangle with $AB = AC$. Bisector of $\angle A$ meets BC at D. Prove that $BC = 2AD$.

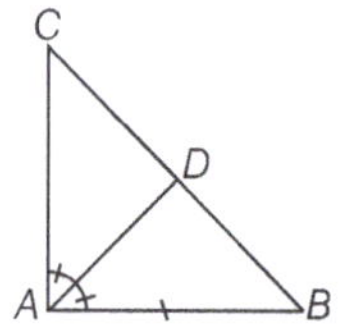

15. ΔABC is a right angled triangle in which $\angle A = 90°$ and $AB = AC$. Find $\angle B$ and $\angle C$.

16. In the given figure, $\angle BAC = 85°$, $CA = CB$ and $BD = CD$. Find the measures of $\angle x$, $\angle y$ and $\angle z$. Given reasons to support your answer.

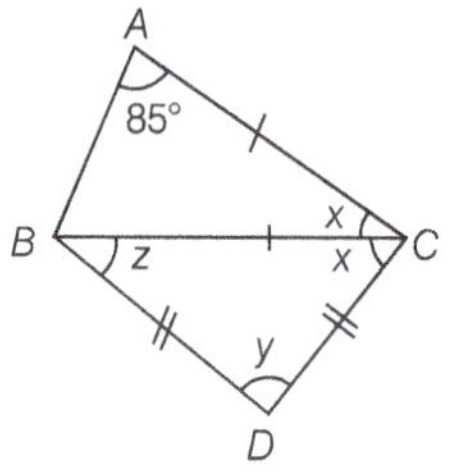

17. In ΔABC, $AB = AC$ and AD is bisector of $\angle BAC$. Then, prove that $\Delta ABD \cong \Delta ACD$.

18. In the given figure, MN is parallel to PR, $\angle LBN = 70°$ and $AB = BC$. Find the value of $\angle ABC$.

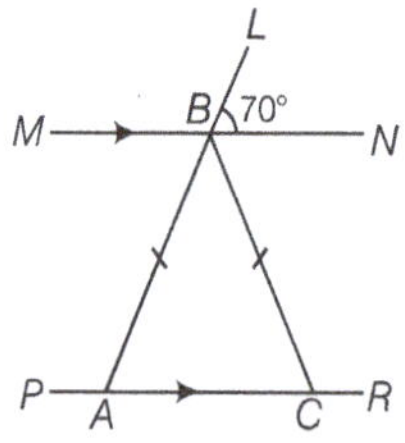

19. Points E and F are the mid-point of equal sides AB and AC of a ΔABC, respectively. Show that $BF = CE$.

20. In the given figure, $PQRS$ is a square and A is mid-point of PS. QA and RA are joined. Prove that $\angle AQR = \angle ARQ$.

21. In an isosceles ΔABC with $AB = AC$, the bisectors of $\angle B$ and $\angle C$ intersect each other at O. Join A to O. Show that
(i) $OB = OC$
(ii) AO bisects $\angle A$

22. Suppose ΔABC is an isosceles triangle in which $AB = AC$ and LM is parallel to BC. If $\angle A = 60°$, find $\angle LMC$.

23. In the given figure, $DE = EF$, $BE = EC$, $ED \perp AB$ and $EF \perp AC$. Prove that $AB = AC$.

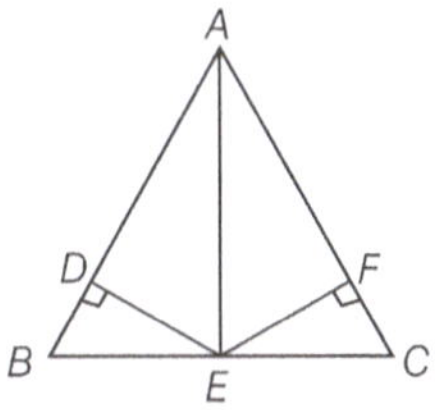

24. In the ΔPQR, PL bisects angle P and is perpendicular to QR. If the lengths of the sides of the triangle are expressed in terms of x and y as shown in the figure, find the value of x and y.

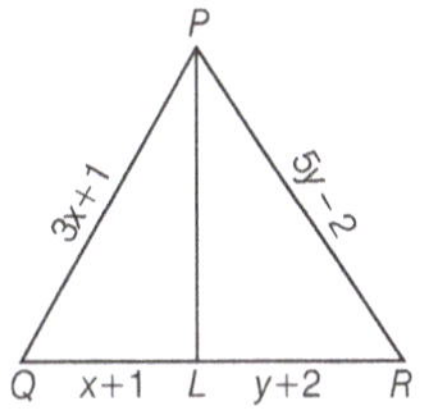

25. In ΔABC, bisectors of $\angle B$ and $\angle C$ meet at point P. Through P, a line LM is drawn parallel to BC, meeting AB at L and AC at M. Show that $LM = BL + CM$.

26. D and E are points on the base BC of ΔABC, such that $BD = CE$. If $AD = AE$, then prove that $\Delta ABE \cong \Delta ACD$.

27. In the given figure, $AD = AE$ and $BD = EC$. Prove that $AB = AC$.

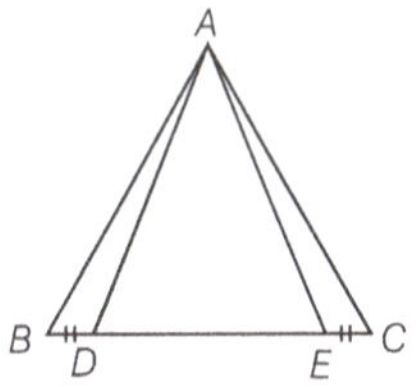

Inequalities in A Triangle

In this topic, there are some relations between unequal sides and unequal angles of a triangle. These relation are stated in the form of theorems which are given below

Theorem 1 *If two sides of a triangle are unequal, then the angle opposite to longer side is larger (or greater).*

Given A ΔPQR in which $PQ > PR$.

To prove $\angle PRQ > \angle Q$

Construction From PQ, cut $PL = PR$. Join L and R.

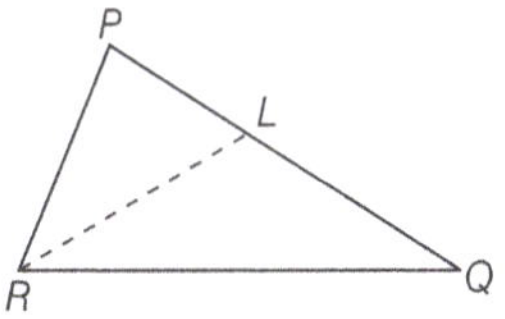

Proof In ΔPRL,

$PL = PR$ [by construction]

$\angle PRL = \angle PLR$

[angles opposite to equal sides]...(i)

In ΔLQR,

Exterior $\angle PLR > \angle Q$

[exterior angle of a triangle is always greater than each of its interior opposite angles]

$\therefore$ $\angle PRL > \angle Q$ [from Eq. (i)]

$\therefore$ $\angle PRQ > \angle Q$

Since, $\angle PRL$ is a part of $\angle PRQ$.

$\angle PRQ > \angle PRL > \angle Q$ **Hence proved.**

Theorem 2 (Converse of Theorem 1) *In any triangle, the side opposite to the larger (or greater) angle is longer.*

Given A ΔPQR in which $\angle RPQ > \angle Q$.

To prove $QR > PR$

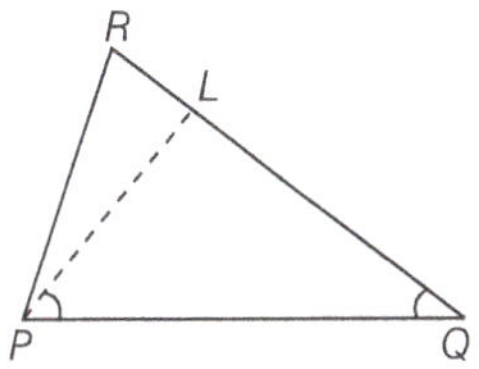

Construction Draw $\angle QPL = \angle Q$

Proof In ΔPQL, $PL = QL$ ...(i)

[sides opposite to equal angles]

In ΔPLR, $PL + LR > PR$

[sum of any two sides of a triangle is always greater than the third side]

$\therefore$ $QL + LR > PR$ [from Eq. (i)]

$\therefore$ $QR > PR$ [$\because$ $QL + LR = QR$]

Hence proved

Some More Important Theorems

Theorem 3 *The sum of any two sides of a triangle is greater than the third side.*

Given A ΔPQR.

To prove $QP + PR > QR$

Construction Produce QP to L such that $PL = PR$.

Join L and R.

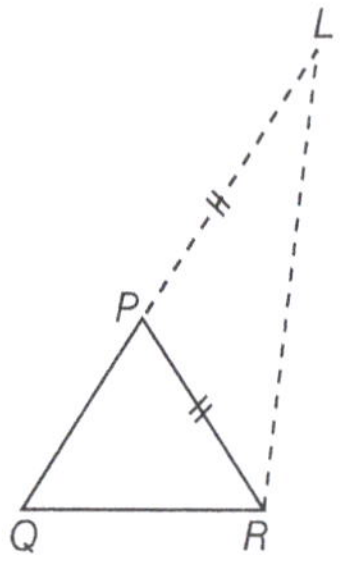

Proof $\angle PRL = \angle PLR$ ...(i)

[$\because$ $PL = PR$ by construction and angle opposite to equal sides are equal]

$\angle QRL > \angle PRL$ [whole is greater than a part]...(ii)

$\angle QRL > \angle PLR$ [from Eqs. (i) and (ii)]

$QL > QR$

[greater angle has greater side opposite to it]

$QP + PL > QR$

[QPL is a straight line, $QL = QP + PL$]

$QP + PR > QR$ [$PL = PR$, by construction]

Hence proved

Theorem 4 *Of all straight lines, that can be drawn to a given straight line from a point outside it, the perpendicular is the shortest line.*

Given A point O outside the line PQ and OA perpendicular to PQ.

To prove OA is the shortest of all the lines that can be drawn from O to PQ.

Construction Join O with any point B in PQ.

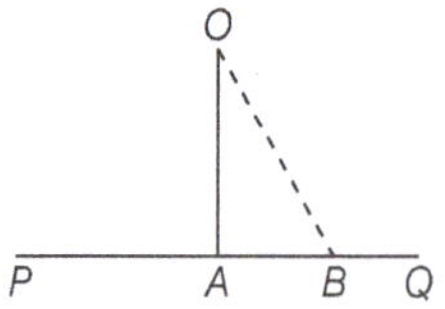

Proof In right angled ΔOAB,

$\angle OAB > \angle OBA$

[right angle is the greatest angle in right angled triangle]

$OB > OA$ [side opposite to greater angle is greater]

Similarly, it can be shown that OA is smaller than any other line that can be drawn from O to PQ.

$\therefore$ OA is the shortest line drawn from O to PQ.

Hence proved

Example 29. In ΔPQR, $\angle P = 70°$ and $\angle R = 30°$. Which side of this triangle is the longest? Give reason for your answer.

Sol. Given, in ΔPQR, $\angle P = 70°$ and $\angle R = 30°$

We know that the sum of angles of a triangle is 180°.

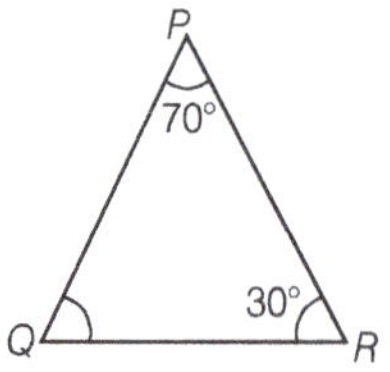

$\therefore$ $\angle P + \angle Q + \angle R = 180°$

$\Rightarrow$ $70° + \angle Q + 30° = 180°$

$\Rightarrow$ $\angle Q = 180° - (70° + 30°) = 80°$

Here, $\angle Q$ is greatest, so side PR is longest.

[$\because$ side opposite to the greatest angle of a triangle is the longest]

Example 30. Is it possible to construct a triangle with lengths of its sides as 4 cm, 3 cm and 7 cm? Give reason for your answer.

Sol. No, it is not possible to construct a triangle with lengths of its sides as 4 cm, 3 cm and 7 cm, because here we see that sum of the lengths of two sides is equal to third side, i.e. $4 + 3 = 7$. We know that the sum of any two sides of a triangle is greater than its third side, so given statement is not correct.

Example 31. In the given figure, $AB = 8.5$ cm, $BC = 6$ cm and $CA = 7.2$ cm. Write x, y and z in ascending order.

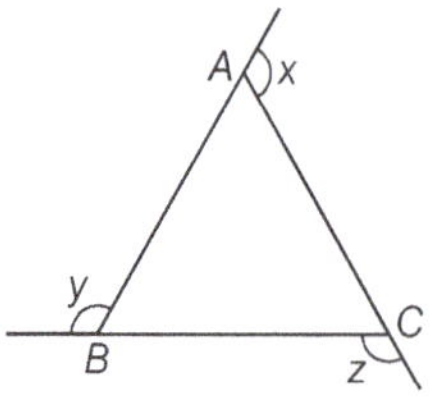

Sol. Given, $AB = 8.5$ cm, $BC = 6$ cm and $CA = 7.2$ cm

$\therefore \quad AB > CA > BC \Rightarrow \angle C > \angle B > \angle A$

[$\because$ angle opposite to longer side is greater]

On multiplying each term of an inequality by -1, we get

$-\angle C < -\angle B < -\angle A$

[when we multiply the '–' sign, the sign of inequality will be reverse]

On adding 180° in each term, we get

$(180^\circ - \angle C) < (180^\circ - \angle B) < (180^\circ - \angle A)$

[triangle inequalities]

$\Rightarrow \quad z < y < x$

Hence, angles in ascending order are x, y and z.

Example 32. If AB and CD are the smallest and largest sides of a quadrilateral $ABCD$, out of $\angle B$ and $\angle D$ decide which is greater.

Sol. **Given** In quadrilateral $ABCD$, AB is the smallest and CD is the largest side.

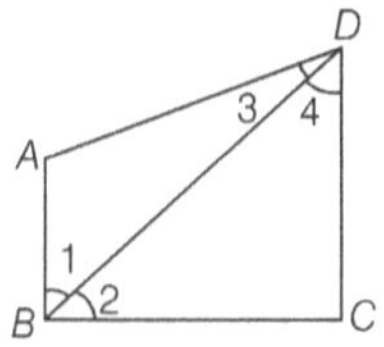

To check $\angle B < \angle D$ or $\angle D < \angle B$.

Now, join BD.

Proof Now, in ΔABD, $AD > AB$

[since, AB is the smallest side in $ABCD$]

$\Rightarrow \quad \angle 1 > \angle 3 \quad$ ...(i)

[$\because$ angle opposite to largest side of a triangle is greater]

In ΔBCD, $CD > BC$

[since, CD is the largest side in $ABCD$]

$\Rightarrow \quad \angle 2 > \angle 4 \quad$ ...(ii)

[$\because$ angle opposite to larger side is greater]

On adding Eqs. (i) and (ii), we get

$\angle 1 + \angle 2 > \angle 3 + \angle 4 \Rightarrow \angle B > \angle D$

Hence, $\angle B > \angle D$

Example 33. In the given figure, AD bisects $\angle A$. Then, find the relation between the sides AB, AC and DC.

Sol. **Given** AD is the bisector of $\angle BAC$.

In ΔABC, sum of three angles of a triangle is 180°.

$\therefore \quad \angle A = 180^\circ - (\angle B + \angle C) = 180^\circ - (70^\circ + 30^\circ) = 80^\circ$

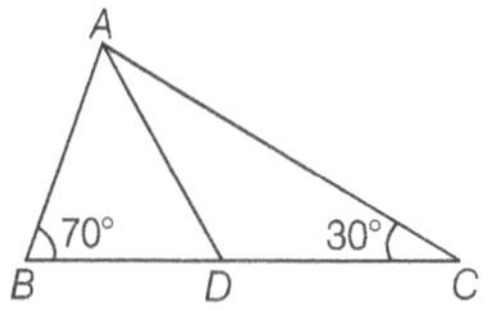

$\Rightarrow \angle BAD = \angle DAC = \dfrac{80^\circ}{2} = 40^\circ$

[since, AD is the bisector of $\angle A$]

In ΔABD, $\quad \angle ADB = 180^\circ - (\angle BAD + \angle ABD)$

[$\because$ sum of three angles of a triangle is 180°]

$= 180^\circ - (40^\circ + 70^\circ) = 70^\circ$

Thus, $\quad \angle DBA = \angle ADB \Rightarrow AD = AB$

[$\because$ sides opposite to equal angles of a triangle are equal]

In ΔADC, $\quad \angle ADC = 180^\circ - (\angle DAC + \angle ACD)$

[$\because$ sum of three angles of a triangle is 180°]

$= 180^\circ - (40^\circ + 30^\circ) = 110^\circ$

Thus, $\quad \angle DCA < \angle CAD < \angle ADC$

[$\because \angle DCA = 30^\circ$, $\angle CAD = 40^\circ$ and $\angle ADC = 110^\circ$]

$\Rightarrow \quad AD < DC < AC$

But $\quad AB = AD$

Hence, $AB < DC < AC$.

Example 34. D is a point on side BC of ΔABC, such that $AD = AC$. Show that $AB > AD$.

Sol. **Given** In ΔABC, $AD = AC$

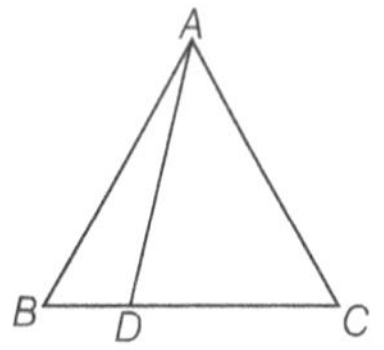

To prove $AB > AD$

Proof Since, $\quad AD = AC$

$\therefore \quad \angle ACD = \angle ADC \quad$ ...(i)

[$\because$ angles opposite to equal sides of a triangle are equal]

Now, $\angle ADC$ is an exterior angle of ΔABD.

$\therefore \quad \angle ADC > \angle ABD$

[$\because$ exterior angle is greater than interior opposite angles]

$\Rightarrow \quad \angle ACD > \angle ABD \quad$ [from Eq. (i)]

$\Rightarrow \quad \angle ACB > \angle ABC$

[$\because \angle ABD = \angle ABC$ and $\angle ACD = \angle ACB$]

$\Rightarrow \quad AB > AC$

[$\because$ side opposite to greater angle in a triangle is greater]

$\therefore \quad AB > AD \quad$ [$\because AD = AC$, given]

Hence proved

Example 35 Show that in a quadrilateral $ABCD$, $AB + BC + CD + DA < 2(BD + AC)$.

Sol. **Given** $ABCD$ is a quadrilateral.

To prove $AB + BC + CD + DA < 2(BD + AC)$

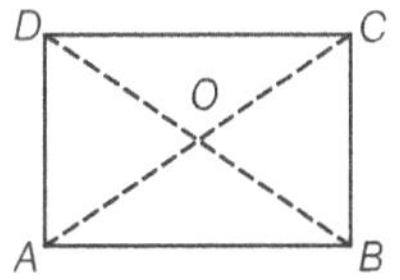

Proof In ΔOAB, $OA + OB > AB \quad$ ...(i)

[$\because$ sum of any two sides of a triangle is greater than the third side]

Similarly, in ΔOBC, $OB + OC > BC \quad$ ...(ii)

In ΔOCD, $OC + OD > CD \quad$ ...(iii)

and in ΔODA, $OD + OA > DA$ ...(iv)

On adding Eqs. (i), (ii), (iii) and (iv), we get

$$2[(OA + OB + OC + OD)] > AB + BC + CD + DA$$

$\Rightarrow$ $2[(OA + OC) + (OB + OD)] > AB + BC + CD + DA$

$\Rightarrow$ $2(AC + BD) > AB + BC + CD + DA$

[$\because$ $OA + OC = AC$ and $OB + OD = BD$]

$\Rightarrow$ $AB + BC + CD + DA < 2(BD + AC)$ **Hence proved**

Example 36. Show that the sum of three altitudes of a triangle is less than the sum of the three sides of the triangle.

Sol. Consider a ΔABC and let AL, BM and CN are the altitudes.

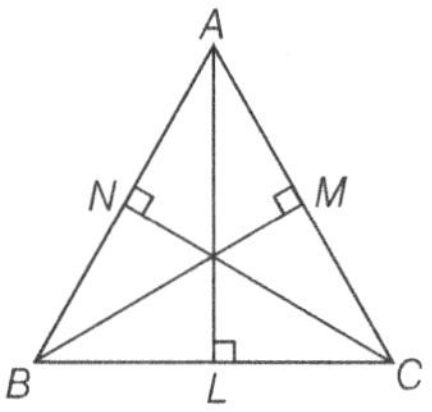

To prove $AL + BM + CN < AB + BC + AC$

Proof Clearly, the perpendicular AL drawn from the point A to the line BC is shorter than the line segment AB drawn from point A to the line BC.

$\therefore$ $AL < AB$ ...(i)

Similarly, $BM < BC$ ...(ii)

and $CN < AC$ ...(iii)

On adding Eqs. (i), (ii) and (iii), we get

$AL + BM + CN < AB + BC + AC$ **Hence proved**

Example 37. If S is any point on side QR of a ΔPQR, then show that $PQ + QR + RP > 2PS$.

Sol. **Given** In ΔPQR, S is any point on side QR.

To prove $PQ + QR + RP > 2PS$

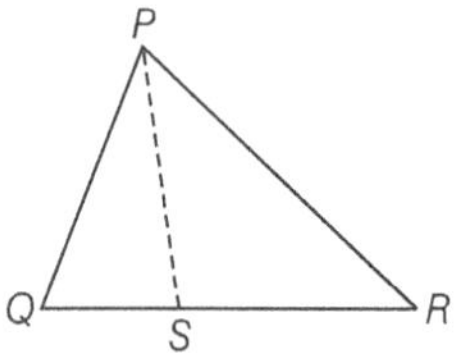

Proof In ΔPQS, $PQ + QS > PS$ ...(i)

[$\because$ sum of any two sides of a triangle is greater than the third side]

Similarly, in ΔPRS, $SR + RP > PS$ ...(ii)

[$\because$ sum of any two sides of a triangle is greater than the third side]

On adding Eqs. (i) and (ii), we get

$$PQ + QS + SR + RP > 2PS$$

$\Rightarrow$ $PQ + (QS + SR) + RP > 2PS$

$\Rightarrow$ $PQ + QR + RP > 2PS$ [$\because$ $QR = QS + SR$]

Hence proved

Example 38. In the given figure, $PQ > PR$, QS and RS are the bisectors of $\angle Q$ and $\angle R$ respectively, then find the relation between the sides SQ and SR.

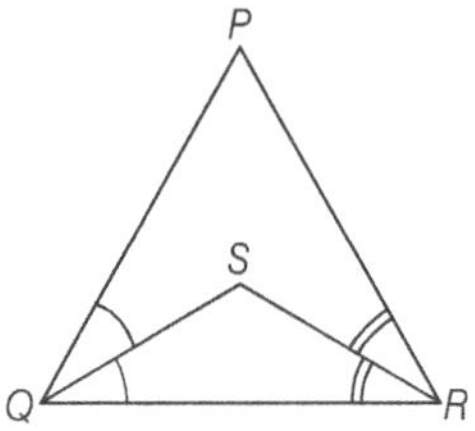

Sol. Given, $PQ > PR$

$\Rightarrow$ $\angle PRQ > \angle PQR$

[$\because$ angle opposite to longer side is greater]

$\Rightarrow$ $\frac{1}{2}\angle PRQ > \frac{1}{2}\angle PQR$ [dividing by 2]

$\Rightarrow$ $\angle SRQ > \angle SQR$

[since, QS and RS are the bisectors of $\angle Q$ and $\angle R$, respectively]

$\therefore$ $SQ > SR$

[$\because$ side opposite to greater angle of a triangle is longer]

Example 39. In the given figure, T is a mid-point of side QR of ΔPQR and S is a point such that $RT = ST$. Prove that $PQ + PR > QS$.

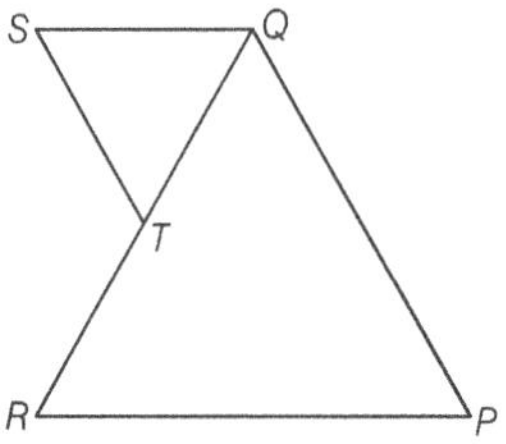

Sol. **Given** T is a mid-point of side QR of ΔPQR and S is a point such that $RT = ST$.

To prove $PQ + PR > QS$

Proof In ΔPQR, $PQ + PR > QR$

[$\because$ sum of any two sides of a triangle is greater than the third side]

$\Rightarrow$ $PQ + PR > QT + RT$ [$\because$ $QR = QT + RT$]

$\Rightarrow$ $PQ + PR > QT + ST$ [$\because$ $RT = ST$, given] ...(i)

In ΔQST, $QT + ST > QS$ ...(ii)

[$\because$ sum of any two sides of a triangle is greater than the third side]

From Eqs. (i) and (ii), we get

$PQ + PR > QS$ **Hence proved**

Example 40. Show that the difference of any two sides of a triangle is less than the third side.

Sol. Consider a ΔABC.

To prove $AC - AB < BC$, $BC - AC < AB$

and $BC - AB < AC$

Construction Take a point D on AC such that $AD = AB$ and join BD.

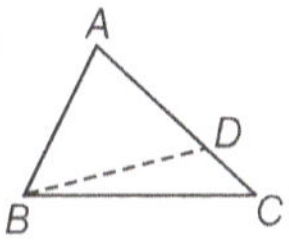

Proof In ΔABD, $\angle BDC$ is an exterior angle.

$\therefore \quad \angle BDC > \angle ABD \quad$ ...(i)

[$\because$ exterior angle is greater than opposite interior angles]

In ΔBDC, $\angle ADB$ is an exterior angle.

$\therefore \quad \angle ADB > \angle DBC \quad$ ...(ii)

[$\because$ exterior angle is greater than opposite interior angles]

In ΔABD, $\quad AB = AD \quad$ [by construction]

$\Rightarrow \quad \angle ADB = \angle ABD \quad$ ...(iii)

[$\because$ angles opposite to equal sides are equal]

From Eqs. (i) and (iii), we get

$\angle BDC > \angle ADB \quad$ ...(iv)

$\Rightarrow \quad \angle BDC > \angle DBC \quad$ [from Eq. (ii)]

$\Rightarrow \quad BC > CD$

[$\because$ side opposite to greater angle is larger]

$\Rightarrow \quad CD < BC \Rightarrow AC - AD < BC$

$\Rightarrow \quad AC - AB < BC \quad$ [$\because AD = AB$, by construction]

Similarly, $BC - AC < AB$ and $BC - AB < AC$.

Hence proved

Example 41. Prove that, the sum of any two sides of a triangle is greater than twice the median drawn to the third side.

Or

AD is a median of ΔABC. Prove that $AB + AC > 2AD$.

Sol. Consider a ΔABC and let AD be the median drawn to side BC.

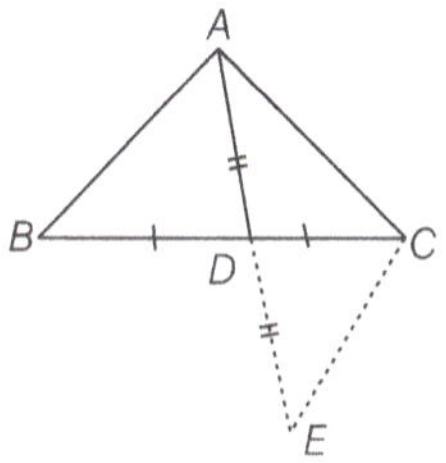

To prove $AB + AC > 2AD$

Construction Produce AD upto a point E such that $AD = DE$, i.e. $AE = 2AD$. Also, join C and E.

Proof As we know that sum of any two sides of a triangle is greater than the third side.

$\therefore$ In ΔACE, $AC + CE > AE$ i.e. $\quad AC + CE > 2AD \quad$ ...(i)

Now, we will prove that $AB = CE$.

Consider ΔADB and ΔEDC

Clearly, $\angle ADB = \angle EDC \quad$ [vertically opposite angles]

$AD = DE \quad$ [by construction]

and $\quad BD = DC \quad$ [$\because D$ is mid-point of BC]

$\Rightarrow \quad \Delta ADB \cong \Delta EDC \quad$ [by SAS congruence rule]

$\Rightarrow \quad AB = EC \quad$ [by CPCT] ...(ii)

Now, from Eqs. (i) and (ii), we get

$AB + AC > 2AD \quad$ **Hence proved**

Example 42. Prove that the perimeter of a triangle is greater than the sum of its three medians.

Sol. Consider a ΔABC and let AD, BE and CF are the medians of ΔABC.

We know that the sum of any two sides of a triangle is greater than twice the median drawn to the third side.

$\therefore \quad AB + AC > 2AD \quad$ ...(i)

$AB + BC > 2BE \quad$ ...(ii)

and $\quad BC + AC > 2CF \quad$ ...(iii)

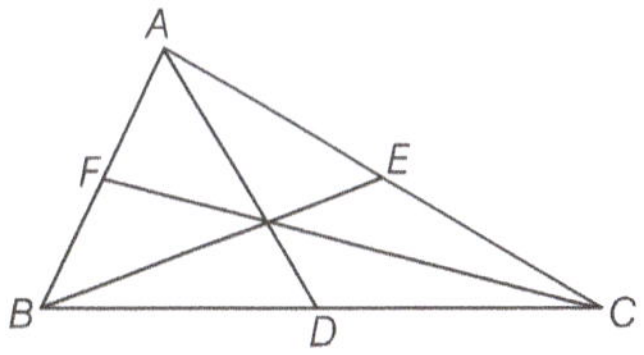

On adding Eqs. (i), (ii) and (iii), we get

$2(AB + BC + AC) > 2(AD + BE + CF)$

$\therefore \quad AB + BC + AC > AD + BE + CF$

Hence, the perimeter of a triangle is greater than the sum of its three medians. **Hence proved**

Exercise 8.2

1. Is it possible to construct a triangle with lengths of its sides as 9 cm, 7 cm and 17 cm? Give reason for your answer.
2. In the given figure, AL bisects $\angle A$. Arrange AB, BL and LC in the descending order of their lengths.

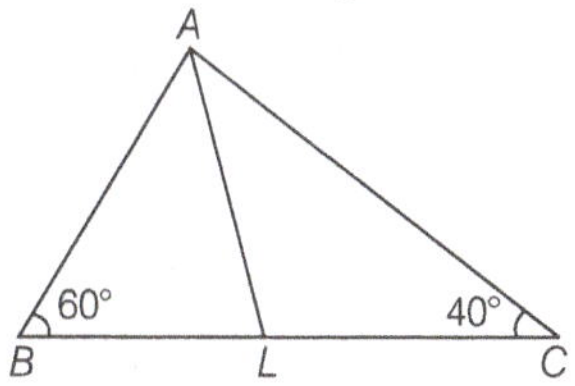

3. In ΔABC, if $\angle A = 50°$ and $\angle B = 30°$, then which side of the triangle is longest and which side is shortest?
4. In the given figure, ABC is triangle, having sides BC and CA produced to D and E, respectively. Then, $AC > BC$. Is it true?

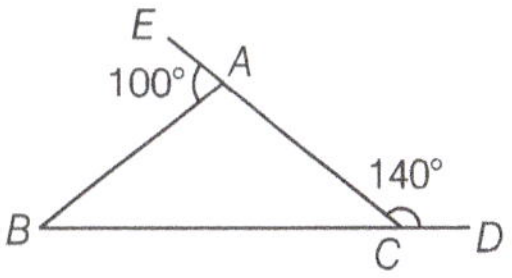

5. In the given figure, PR is perpendicular to line AB and $QR = RS$. Show that PT is greater than PQ.

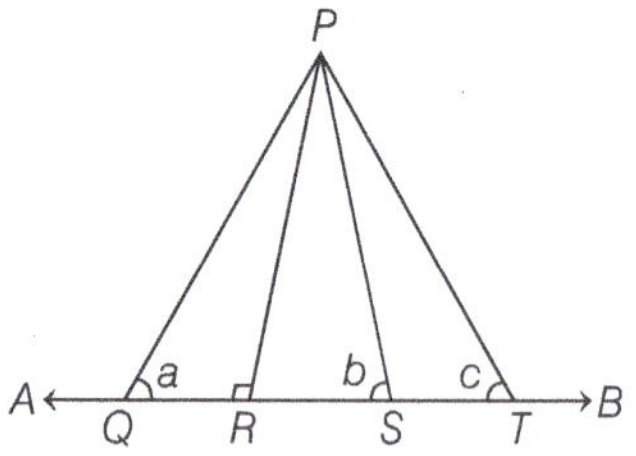

6. AB and CD are respectively the smallest and longest sides of a quadrilateral $ABCD$ (see the figure). Show that $\angle A > \angle C$.

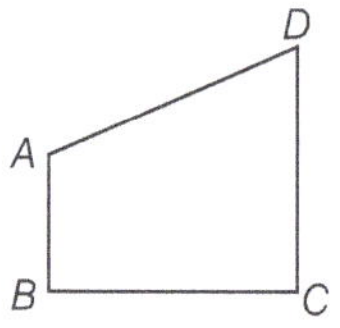

7. Show that in a right angled triangle, hypotenuse is the longest side.

8. In the given figure, $AB > AC$. Then, what is the relation between the sides AB and AD ?

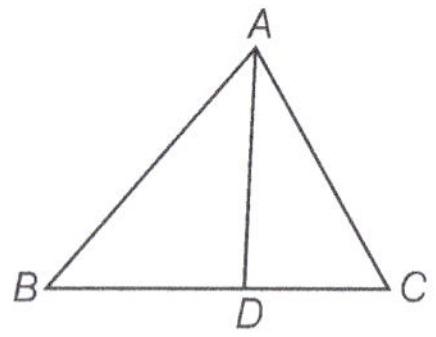

9. In the given figure, $\angle B < \angle A$ and $\angle C < \angle D$, then show that $AD < BC$.

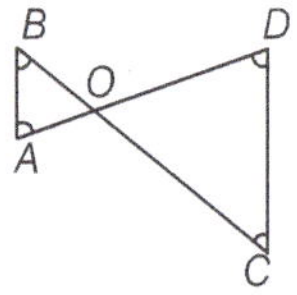

10. O is any point in the interior of ΔABC. Show that $OB + OC < AB + AC$.

11. In the figure, if AD is the bisector of $\angle A$, then show that

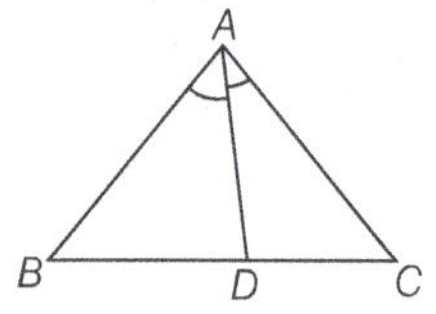

(i) $AB > BD$
(ii) $AC > CD$.

12. In the given figure, if $\angle B = \angle C = 55°$ and $\angle D = 25°$, then show that $BC > CA$ and $CA < AD$.

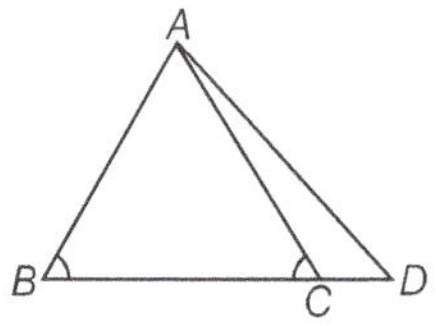

13. In the given figure, $PR > PQ$ and PS bisects $\angle QPR$. Prove that $\angle PSR > \angle PSQ$.

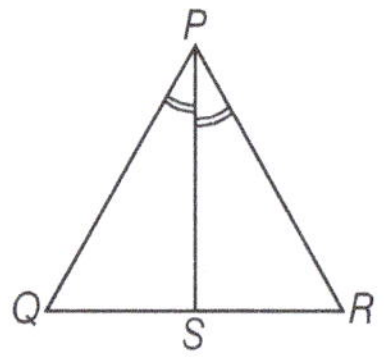

14. In the given figure, sides AB and AC of ΔABC are extended to points P and Q, respectively. Also, $\angle PBC < \angle QCB$. Show that $AC > AB$.

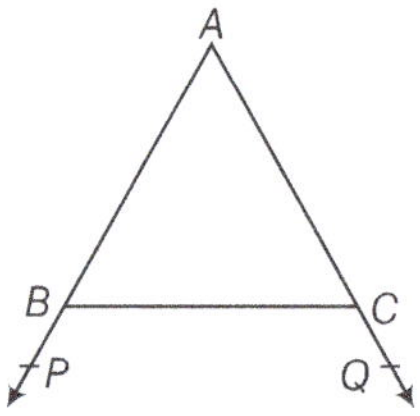

15. In the given figure, $PQ = PR$. Prove that $PF > PE$.

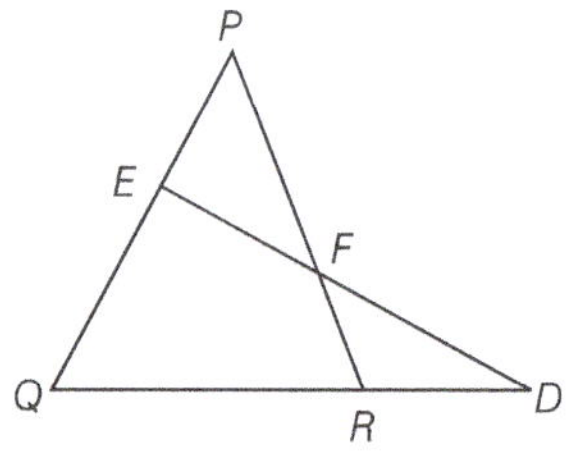

16. If ABC is an isosceles triangle and $60° < A < 90°$, then show that $c < a < \sqrt{2}c$.

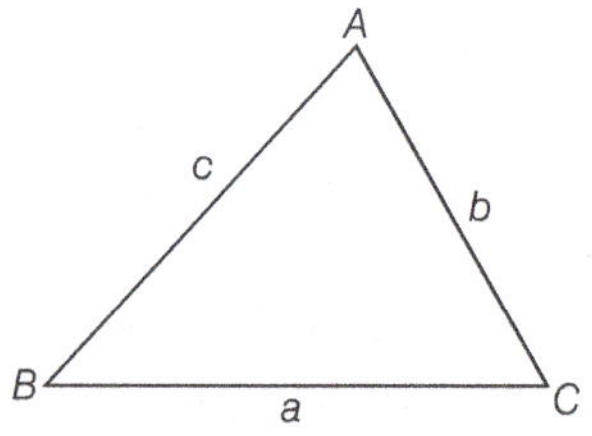

17. Prove that in a triangle other than an equilateral triangle, angle opposite to the longest side is greater than 2/3 of a right angle.

18. Show that in a quadrilateral $ABCD$, $AB + BC + CD + DA > AC + BD$.

Chapter Practice

a. 1 Mark Questions

1. The three angles of a triangle are $a+15°$, $2a-20°$ and $a-15°$. The angles are
   (a) 65°, 70° and 45° (b) 65°, 80° and 35°
   (c) 45°, 100° and 35° (d) 65°, 60° and 55°

2. If $\Delta PQR \cong \Delta ABC$ and given $PR = 6$, $AC = 6$ and $BC = 3$, then the value of QR is
   (a) 3 (b) 4 (c) 5 (d) 6

3. In the given figure, if side $AO = 3$ cm, then the length of side BO is

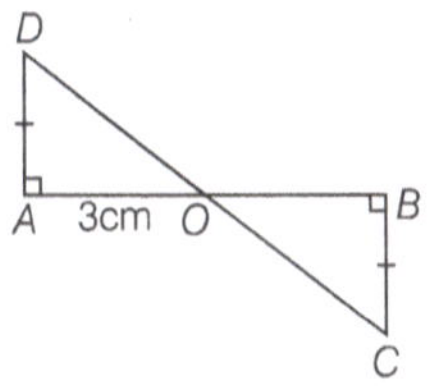

   (a) 9 cm (b) 6 cm
   (c) 3 cm (d) $\sqrt{3}$ cm

4. In the given figure, $AB = CD$, $\angle ABC = \angle BCD$ and $AC = 4$ units, then BD is equal to

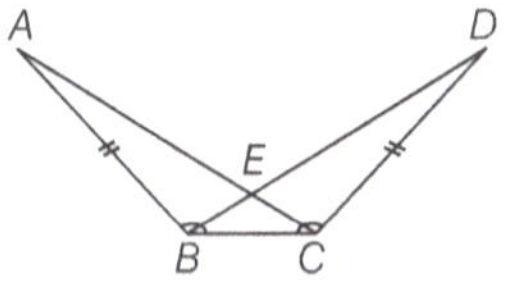

   (a) 2 units (b) 3 units
   (c) 4 units (d) 8 units

5. In the given figure BD, bisects $\angle B$ and BD is perpendicular to AC. The value of x and y are

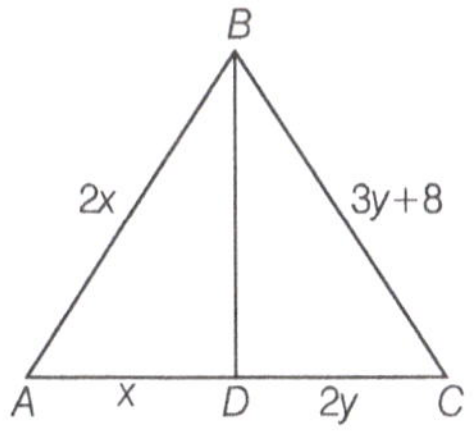

   (a) $x = 8,\ y = 8$ (b) $x = 8,\ y = 16$
   (c) $x = 16,\ y = 16$ (d) $x = 16,\ y = 8$

b. 3 Marks Questions

6. In ΔPQR, if $\angle R = \angle P$, $QR = 4$ cm and $PR = 5$ cm, then find the length of PQ.

7. In the given figures, $AB = DE$, $BC = EF$ and $\angle ABC = \angle DEF$. Then, what is the possible relation between both triangles?

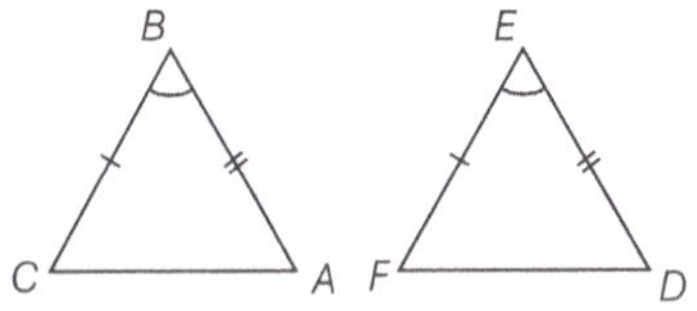

8. Line segment joining the mid-points M and N of parallel sides PQ and SR respectively of a trapezium $PQRS$ is perpendicular to both the sides PQ and SR. Prove that $PS = QR$.

9. In the given figures, by which rule $\Delta ABC \cong \Delta DEF$?

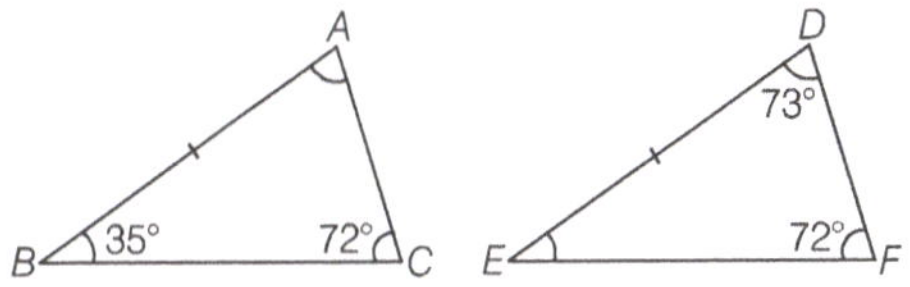

10. If $ABCD$ is a parallelogram, then prove that ΔABD is congruent to ΔCDB.

11. $ABCD$ is a parallelogram and E is the point on side BC. If DE and AB produced to meet at F, such that $DE = EF$. Prove that $AF = 2AB$.

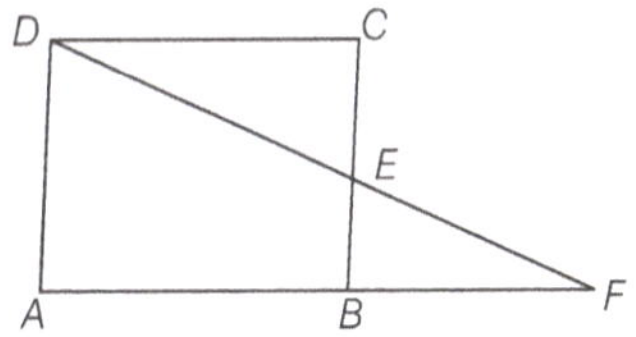

12. In the given figure, $PS \perp QR$, $PS \perp AB$ and $\angle 1 = \angle 4$. Prove that $\Delta PQS \cong \Delta PRS$.

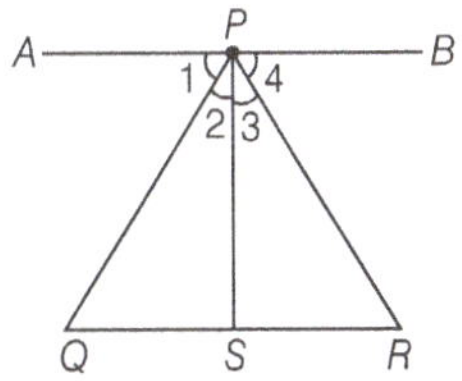

13. In the given figure, $\angle Q = \angle T$, $QS = RT$ and $\angle 1 = \angle 2$. Prove that $\Delta PQR \cong \Delta PTS$.

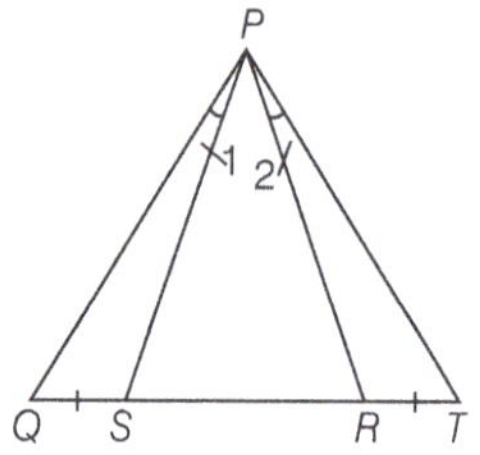

14. In the given figure, $PQ = RS$ and $\angle PQR = \angle QRS$. Prove that

(i) $PR = QS$

(ii) $QT = RT$

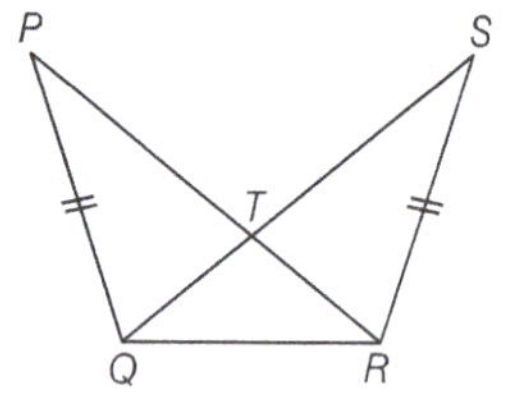

15. If the diagonals of a quadrilateral bisect each other at right angle, then prove that the quadrilateral is a rhombus.

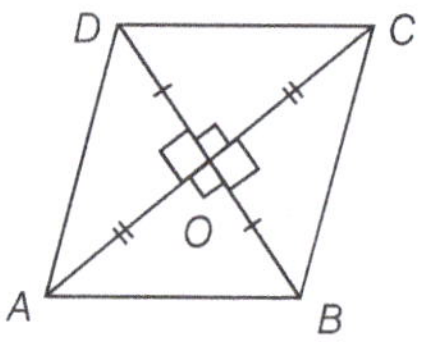

16. In the given figure, if $AB = AC$ and $\angle 1 = \angle 2$, then prove that $\angle PBC = \angle PCB$.

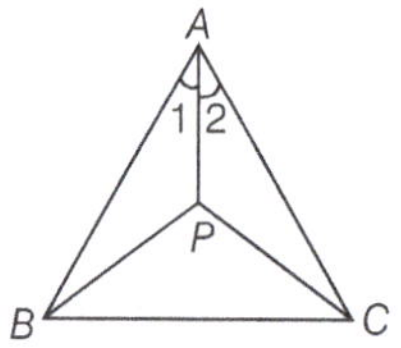

17. In a rhombus $PQRS$, O is any interior point such that $OP = OR$. Prove that points Q, O and S are collinear.

18. In the given figure, find the values of x and y.

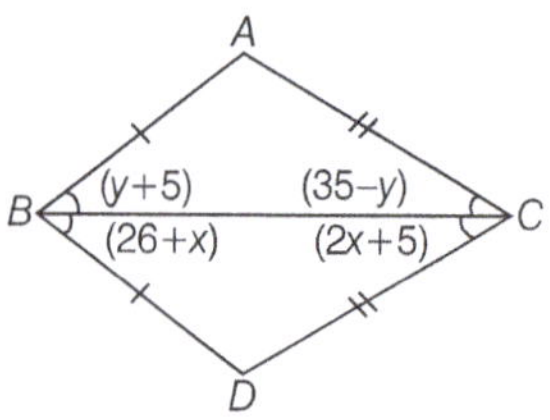

19. In the given figure, $l \parallel m$ and M is the mid-point of a line segment AB. Show that M is also the mid-point of any line segment CD having its end points on l and m, respectively.

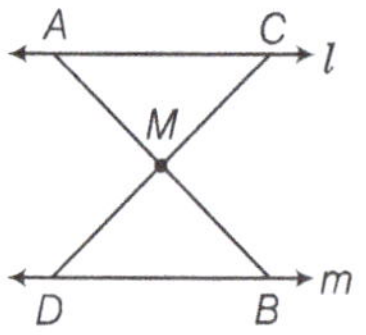

20. In the given figure, if $AB = AC$ and $DB = DC$, then find the ratio of $\angle ABD$ to $\angle ACD$.

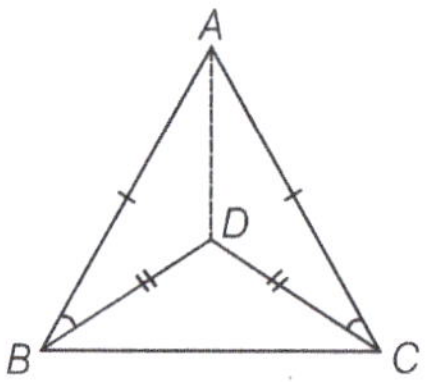

21. In the given figure, $BA \perp AC$, $DE \perp DF$ such that $BA = DE$ and $BF = EC$. Show that $\Delta ABC \cong \Delta DEF$.

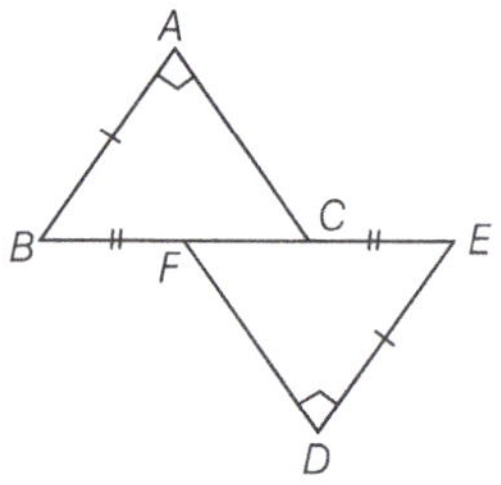

22. In the given figure, $BL \perp AC$, $MC \perp LN$, $AL = CN$ and $BL = CM$. Prove that $\Delta ABC \cong \Delta NML$.

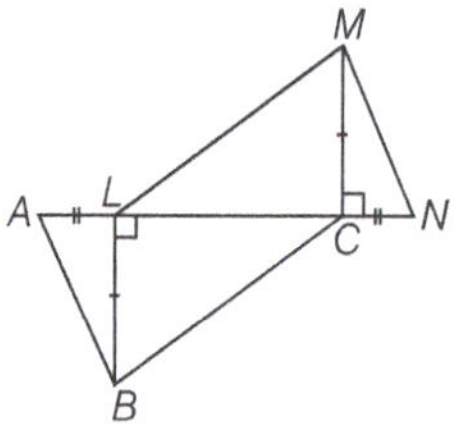

23. In ΔABC, if $\angle A = 40^\circ$ and $\angle B = 60^\circ$, then which side of the triangle is longest and which side is shortest?

24. In the given figure, $AB = AC$, $CE = CB$ and $EF \parallel BC$. If $\angle CAD = 137^\circ$, find $\angle CEF$.

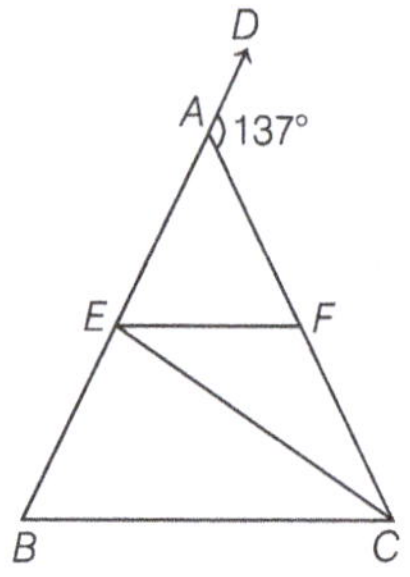

25. From the given figure, find the value of P.

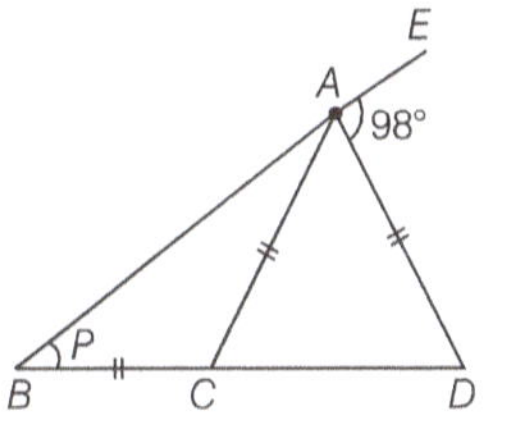

26. In ΔABC, $AB = AC$ and D is a point on AB such that $AD = DC = BC$. Show that $\angle BAC = 36°$.

27. $ABCD$ is a square and ABE is an equilateral triangle outside the square, prove that $\angle ACE = \frac{1}{2} \angle ABE$.

28. In the given figure, $\angle OAB = \angle OBA$ and $AC = BD$. Prove that $AD = BC$.

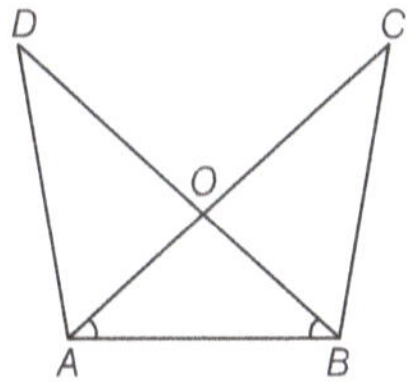

29. In the given figure, $AB = AC$ and BD, CE are bisectors of $\angle B$, $\angle C$ respectively. Prove that

(i) $\Delta DBC \cong \Delta ECB$

(ii) $BD = CE$

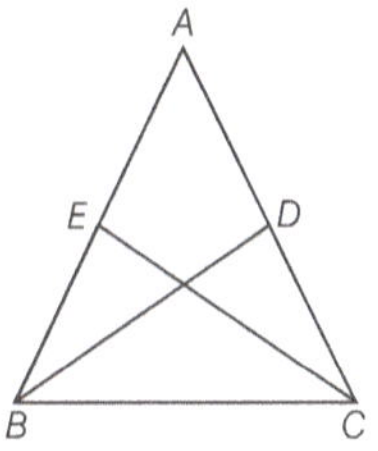

30. In the given figure, $EA = ED$ and $\angle 1 = \angle 2$. Prove that ΔEBC is an isosceles triangle.

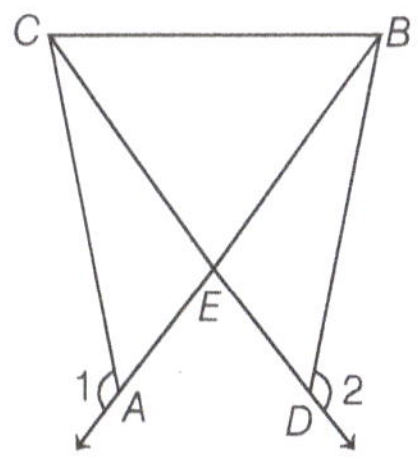

31. In an isosceles ΔABC, with $AB = AC$, the bisectors of $\angle B$ and $\angle C$ intersect each other at I. Show that

(i) $IB = IC$

(ii) IA bisects $\angle A$

32. In the given figure, $PQ = PR$ and S is any point on QR. Prove that $PQ > PS$.

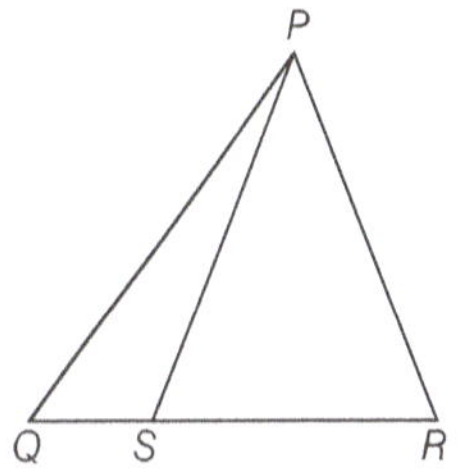

33. In the given figure, $AB = AC$. Prove that $AB > CD$.

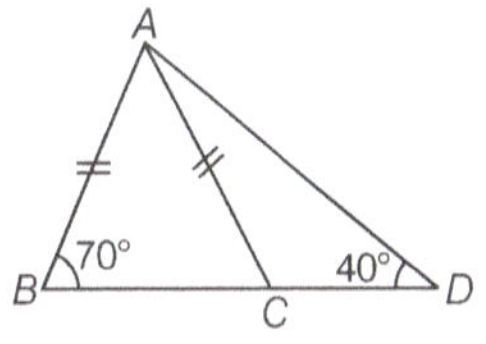

C. 4/5 Marks Questions

34. In the given figure, $\angle PQD = 130°$ and $\angle EPR = 118°$. Prove that $PQ > PR$.

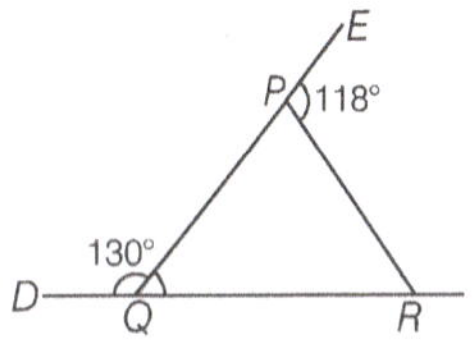

35. Using the information given in the following figure, write the sides AB, BC and AC in the descending order of their lengths.

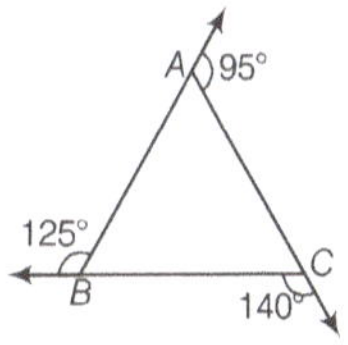

36. In the given triangle, $AC = AD$, $\angle CAD = 50°$ and $\angle BAD = 23°$. Then, $AB > BC$. Is it true?

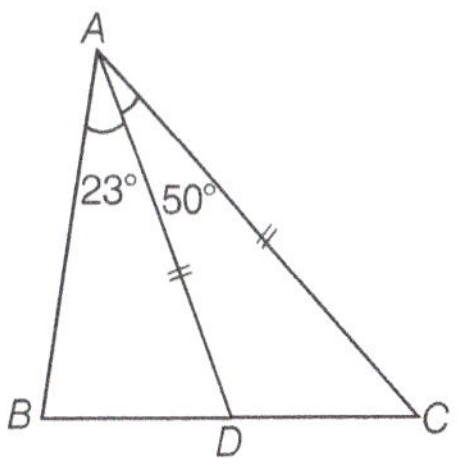

37. Prove that the medians of an equilateral triangle are equal.

38. In the given figure, $AB = AD$, $\angle BAE = \angle FAD$ and $\angle EAC = \angle CAF$. Prove that $AE = AF$.

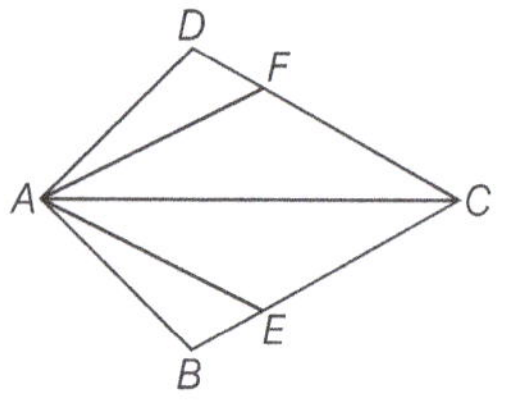

39. In a ΔABC, the internal bisector of $\angle B$ and $\angle C$ meet at O. Prove that OA is also internal bisector of $\angle A$.

40. In the given figure, PQ is a line segment. A and B are points on opposite sides of PQ such that each of them is equidistant from the points P and Q. Show that the line AB is the perpendicular bisector of PQ.

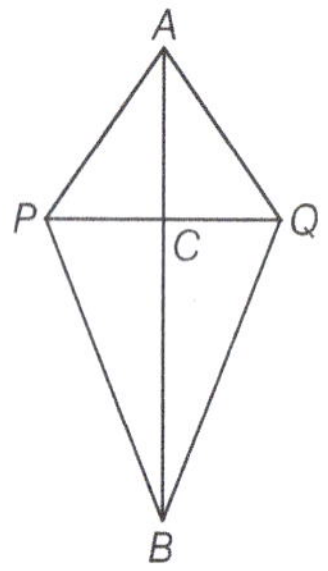

41. In the given figure, $BA \parallel PQ$, $CA \parallel RS$ and $BP = RC$. Prove that

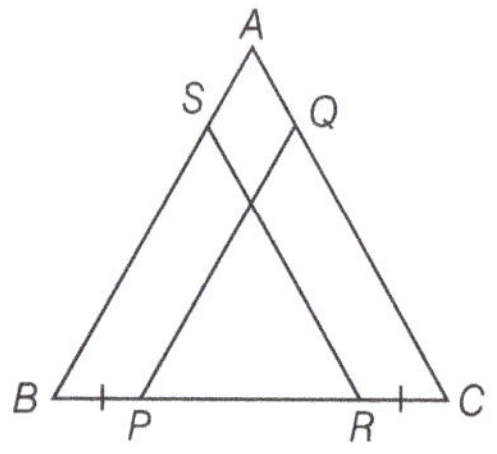

(i) $BS = PQ$ (ii) $RS = CQ$.

42. O is a point in the interior of a square $ABCD$ such that OAB is an equilateral triangle. Show that ΔCOD is an isosceles triangle.

43. Two lines l and m intersect at the point O and P is a point on a line n passing through the point O such that P is equidistant from l and m. Prove that n is the bisector of the angle formed by l and m.

44. In the given figure, two sides AB, BC and median AM of ΔABC are respectively equal to sides PQ, QR and median PN of ΔPQR.

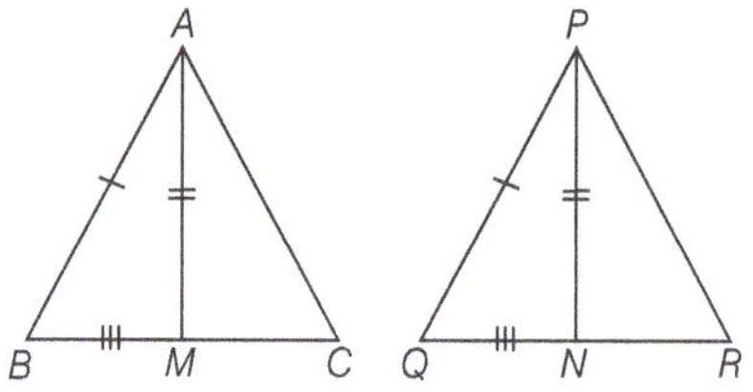

Show that

(i) $\Delta ABM \cong \Delta PQN$

(ii) $\Delta ABC \cong \Delta PQR$.

45. In ΔABC, $AB = AC$, $\angle A = (5x + 20°)$ and $\angle B = \frac{2}{5}$th of $\angle A$. Find the measure of $\angle A$.

46. Find the measure of each lettered angle in the following figure.

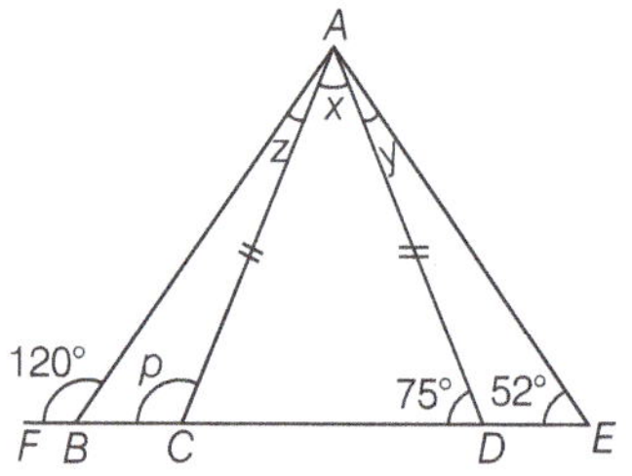

47. A point O is taken inside an equilateral four sided figure $ABCD$ such that its distance from the angular points D and B are equal. Show that AO and OC are in the same straight line.

48. In ΔABC, the sides AB, AC are equal and the base BC is produced to any point D. From D, DE is drawn perpendicular to BA produced and DF perpendicular to AC produced. Prove that BD bisects $\angle EDF$.

49. If the bisector of an angle of a triangle also bisects the opposite side, prove that the triangle is isosceles.

50. If ABC is a right angled triangle such that $AB = AC$ and bisector of angle C intersects the side AB at D, then prove that $AC + AD = BC$.

51. O is any point in the interior of ΔPQR. Show that $OQ + OR < PQ + PR$.

52. In the given figure, PS bisects $\angle P$. Arrange PQ, QS and SR in ascending order.

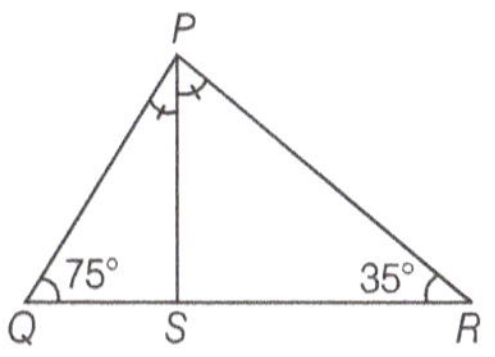

53. In the given figure, $AB = AC$. Prove that $AO > AE$.

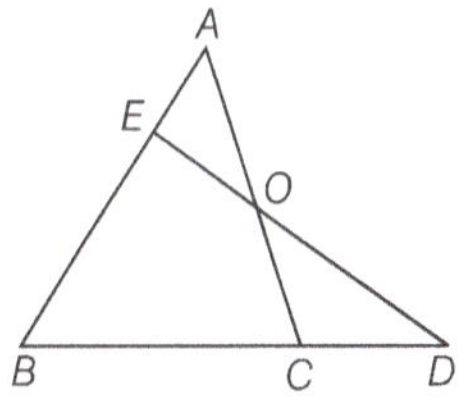

Hints and Answers

Exercise 8.1

1. Since, $\Delta ABC \cong \Delta PQR$

Thus, $BC = QR$ [by CPCT]

Ans. 4

2. **Hint** Do same as Example 3. **Ans.** 30°

3. **Hint** Do same as Example 5. **Ans.** 6.5

4. **Hint** In ΔPQM and ΔPRL,

$PQ = PR$ [given]

$\Rightarrow \frac{PQ}{2} = \frac{PR}{2}$

$\Rightarrow PL = PM$

and $\angle P = \angle P$ [common]

$\therefore \Delta PQM \cong \Delta PRL$

[by SAS congruence rule]

$QM = RL$ [CPCT]

5. (i) **Hint** Use SAS rule to show congruence of triangles

(ii) **Hint** Use CPCT

(iii) **Hint** Use CPCT in the proving result.

6. **Hint Given** $AD \perp BC$ and $BD = DC$

To prove $AB = AC$

Consider ΔADB and ΔADC and use SAS congruence rule.

To prove $AB = AC$, Use CPCT.

7. (i) **Hint** Here, we have $\angle EPA = \angle DPB$

On adding $\angle EPD$ to both sides, we get

$\angle EPA + \angle EPD = \angle DPB + \angle EPD$

$\Rightarrow \angle DPA = \angle EPB$

or $\angle EPB = \angle DPA$ ...(i)

Now, in ΔDAP and ΔEBP, we have

$AP = BP$ [given]

$\Rightarrow \angle PAD = \angle PBE$ [given]

and $\angle DPA = \angle EPB$ [from Eq. (i)]

$\Delta DAP \cong \Delta EBP$

(ii) **Hint** Use CPCT to show the result.

8. First, prove that $\Delta APB \cong \Delta DQE$ by SSS congruence rule, then show that $\angle B = \angle E$ by CPCT.

9. **Hint** First prove $\Delta OAN \cong \Delta OBN$ by SSS congruence

$\therefore \angle ONA = \angle ONB$ [by CPCT]

Now, $\angle ONA + \angle ONB = 180°$

$\Rightarrow \angle ONA + \angle ONA = 180°$

$\Rightarrow \angle ONA = 90°$

10. First, prove that $\Delta ABP \cong \Delta ACP$ by RHS and then show that $AC = 8$ cm by Pythagoras theorem.

11. **Hint** In ΔDAB and ΔBCD, we have

$BD = BD$ [common]

$\angle DAB = \angle BCD$ [each 90°]

$AB = CD$ [given]

$\therefore \Delta DAB \cong \Delta BCD$ [by RHS congruence rule]

Use CPCT, $10 - y = 20 - 3y$ and $x = 50$

Ans. $x = 50°$ and $y = 5$ cm

12. **Hint Construction** Join A and Q.

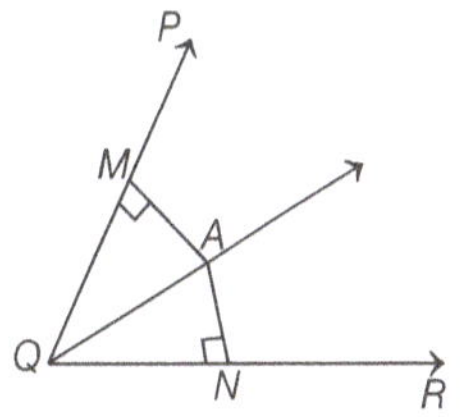

Now, In ΔAMQ and ΔANQ,

$AM = AN$ [given]

$\angle AMQ = \angle ANQ$ [each 90°]

$AQ = AQ$ [common]

$\therefore \Delta AMQ \cong \Delta ANQ$

[by RHS congruence rule]

$\Rightarrow \angle AQM = \angle AQN$ [CPCT]

QA bisects $\angle PQR$.

13. Hint First, prove that $\Delta XAB \cong \Delta YBA$ by RHS congruence rule, then show that $BY = AX$ and $\angle BAY = \angle ABX$ by CPCT.

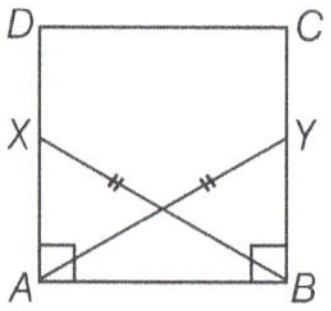

14. Hint In ΔABC, $\angle A = 90°$ and $AB = AC \Rightarrow \angle C = \angle B$

But $\angle A + \angle B + \angle C = 180° \Rightarrow \angle B = 45°$

As AD is bisector of $\angle A$, $\angle BAD = \angle CAD = 45°$

$\Delta ABD \cong \Delta ACD$ (SAS) $\Rightarrow BD = CD$ [by CPCT]

In ΔABD, $\angle BAD = \angle ABD$ (each 45°) $\Rightarrow AD = BD$

$\therefore \quad BC = BD + CD = BD + BD = 2BD = 2AD$

15. Hint Do same as Example 22.

Ans. $\angle B = 45°$ and $\angle C = 45°$

16. Hint Use the result that, the angles opposite to equal sides of a triangle are equal.

Ans. $\angle x = \angle z = 10°$ and $\angle y = 160°$

17. Hint $\because AB = AC$

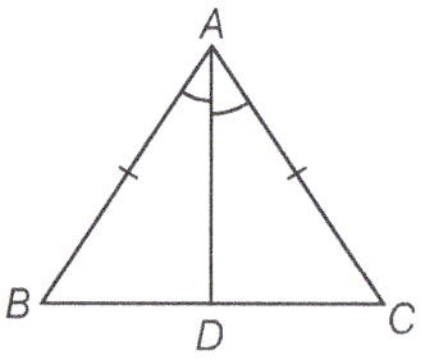

$\Rightarrow \quad \angle C = \angle B$ ...(i)

Also, we have $\quad \angle BAD = \angle CAD$ ...(ii)

Now, use AAS congruence rule to prove the result.

18. Hint $\because \angle LBN = \angle LAC$ and $\angle A = \angle C$. **Ans.** 40°

19. Hint $\because \quad AB = AC$

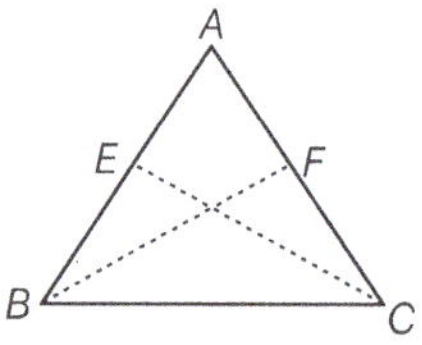

$\Rightarrow \quad \angle C = \angle B$ ...(i)

and $\quad \frac{1}{2} AB = \frac{1}{2} AC$

$\Rightarrow \quad BE = CF$ ...(ii)

Now, prove that $\Delta BEC \cong \Delta CFB$ using SAS rule.

20. Hint In ΔPQA and ΔSRA,

$PA = SA$

$PQ = SR$ [sides of a square are equal]

$\angle QPA = \angle RSA$ [each 90°]

$\therefore \quad \Delta PQA \cong \Delta SRA$ [by SAS congruence rule]

$QA = RA$ [CPCT]

$\Rightarrow \quad \angle AQR = \angle ARQ$

[angles opposite to equal sides are equal]

21. (i) **Hint** Here, we have $AB = AC$ [given]

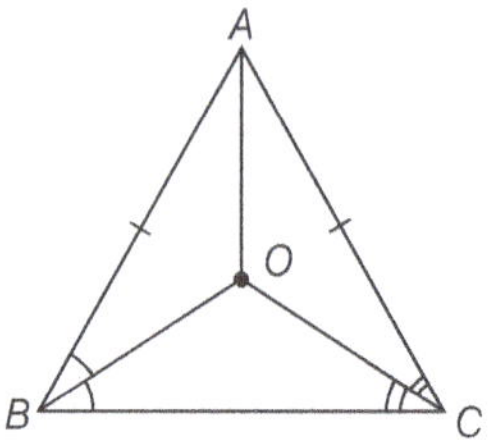

$\Rightarrow \quad \angle C = \angle B$

[$\because$ angles opposite to equal sides are equal]

$\Rightarrow \quad \frac{1}{2} \angle B = \frac{1}{2} \angle C$

$\Rightarrow \quad \angle OBC = \angle OCB$

and $\quad \angle OBA = \angle OCA$ ...(i)

$\Rightarrow \quad OC = OB$ ...(ii)

[$\because$ sides opposite to equal angles of a triangle are equal]

(ii) **Hint** Firstly, show that $\Delta ABO \cong \Delta ACO$, then use CPCT to shown the required result.

22. Hint Do same as Example 26.

Ans. 120°

23. Hint Prove that $\Delta BDE \cong \Delta CFE$ by RHS congruence rule.

Then, by CPCT, we get $\angle B = \angle C$.

Use the result that, the sides opposite to equal angles are equal.

24. Hint First prove that $\Delta PQL \cong \Delta PRL$ by ASA congruence rule.

Then, by CPCT, we get

$3x + 1 = 5y - 2$ ...(i)

and $\quad x + 1 = y + 2$ ...(ii)

Now, solve both equations.

Ans. $x = 4, \ y = 3$

25. Hint Here, we have

$\angle 1 = \angle 2$ and $\angle 3 = \angle 4$

[$\because$ BP bisects $\angle B$ and CP bisects $\angle C$] ...(i)

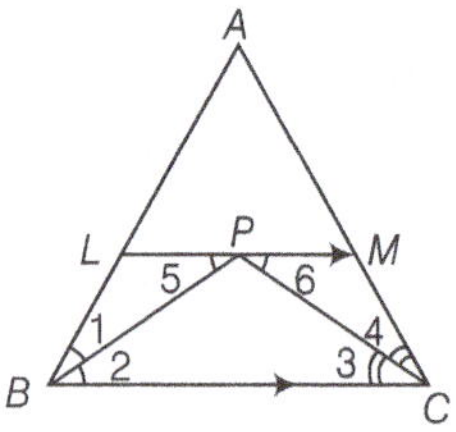

Since, $LM \parallel BC$

$\therefore \quad \angle 5 = \angle 2$ and $\angle 6 = \angle 3$ ...(ii)

From Eqs. (i) and (ii), we get

$\angle 1 = \angle 5$ and $\angle 4 = \angle 6$

$\Rightarrow \quad LP = BL$ and $PM = CM$

Now, add them and get the required result.

26. **Hint** In ΔADE, $AD = AE$ [given]

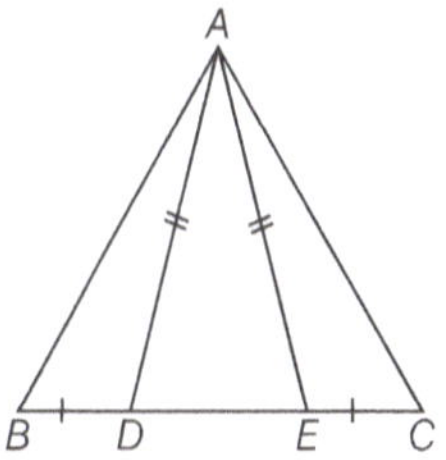

$\Rightarrow \quad \angle AED = \angle ADE$

$\Rightarrow \quad \angle ADC = \angle AEB \quad \ldots(i)$

$[\because \angle ADE = \angle ADC$ and $\angle AED = \angle AEB]$

Since, $BD = CE$ [given]

On adding DE both sides, we get

$BD + DE = CE + DE$

$\Rightarrow \quad BE = CD \quad \ldots(ii)$

$[\because BE = BD + DE$ and $CD = CE + DE]$

Hence, using SAS congruence rule.

$\Delta ABE \cong \Delta ACD$

27. $\because AD = AE \Rightarrow \angle AED = \angle ADE$

$\Rightarrow \quad 180 - \angle AED = 180 - \angle ADE$

$\Rightarrow \quad \angle AEC = \angle ADB$

Now, prove $\Delta ADB \cong \Delta AEC$ using SAS rule, then by CPCT $AB = AC$

Exercise 8.2

1. **Hint** Do same as Example 30.

Ans. No

2. **Hint** $\angle BAC = 180° - (60° + 40°) = 80°$

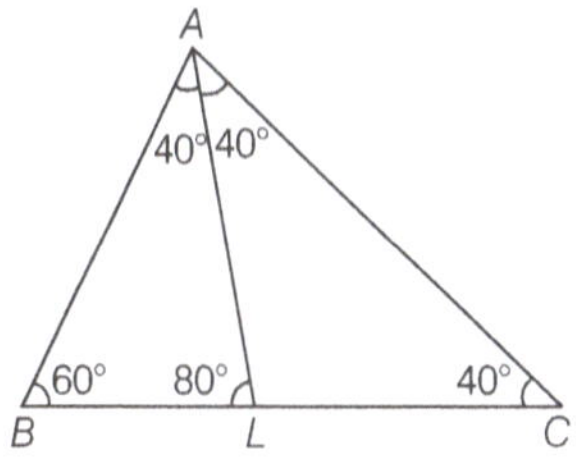

Since, AL bisects $\angle A$.

$\therefore \angle BAL = \angle CAL = \frac{80°}{2} = 40°$

$\angle ALB = 180° - (60° + 40°) = 80°$

In ΔABL, $AB > AL > BL$

[side opposite to greater angle is greater)...(i)

In ΔALC, $AL = LC$

[side opposite to equal angles are equal]...(ii)

$\therefore AB > LC > BL$ [from Eqs. (i) and (ii)]

3. **Hint** Do same as Example 29.

Side opposite to the smallest angle is smaller.

Ans. AB = Longest side and AC = Shortest side.

4. **Hint** In ΔABC, $\angle A = 80°$, $\angle C = 40°$ and $\angle B = 60°$

Ans. No

5. **Hint** First show $\Delta PQR \cong \Delta PSR$ by SAS congruence rule.

Then, by CPCT, we get

$PQ = PS$

$\therefore \quad \angle a = \angle b$

In ΔPST, exterior $\angle b = \angle c + \angle SPT$

[$\because$ exterior angle = sum of interior opposite angles]

$\Rightarrow \quad \angle b > \angle c$

$\angle a > \angle c \quad [\because \angle a = \angle b]$

In ΔPQT, $\angle a > \angle c \Rightarrow PT > PQ$

[in a triangle, side opposite to greater angle is greater]

Hence proved.

6. **Hint** Join AC then do same as Example 32.

7. **Hint** Let ΔABC be a right angled triangle in which $\angle B = 90°$.

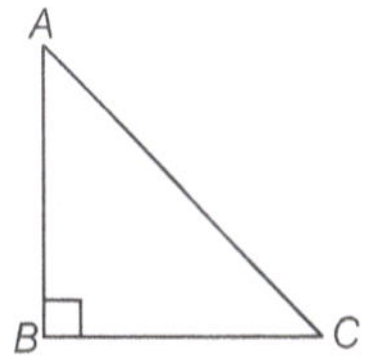

$\Rightarrow \quad \angle A < \angle B$ and $\angle C < \angle B$

$\Rightarrow \quad BC < AC$ and $AB < AC$

Thus, AC is the longest side.

8. **Hint** In ΔABC, $AB > AC$

$\Rightarrow \quad \angle C > \angle B \quad \ldots(i)$

[$\because$ angle opposite to longer side is greater]

In ΔABD, $\angle ADB > \angle C \quad \ldots(ii)$

$\therefore \quad \angle ADB > \angle B$ [from Eqs. (i) and (ii)]

$\Rightarrow \quad AB > AD$

9. **Hint** In ΔAOB, $\angle B < \angle A$

$\Rightarrow \quad OA < OB \quad \ldots(i)$

In ΔDOC, $\angle C < \angle D$

$\Rightarrow \quad OD < OC \quad \ldots(ii)$

Now, add Eqs. (i) and (ii) and get the result.

10. **Hint** Clearly $\angle OBC < \angle B$

and $\angle OCB < \angle C$

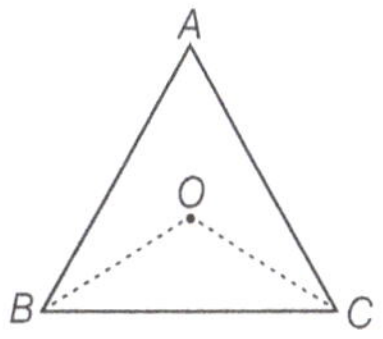

$\Rightarrow \quad OC < AC$ and $OB < AB$

11. (i) **Hint** $\angle ADB > \angle CAD$

[$\because$ exterior angle is greater than opposite interior angle]

$\Rightarrow \quad \angle ADB > \angle BAD \quad [\because \angle BAD = \angle CAD]$

$\Rightarrow \quad AB > BD$

(ii) **Hint** Similarly, by considering,

$\angle ADC > \angle BAD$, we get

$AC > CD$

12. **Hint** $\angle BAC = 70°$ and $\angle ACD = 125°$

13. **Hint** $PR > PQ \Rightarrow \angle PQR > \angle PRQ$

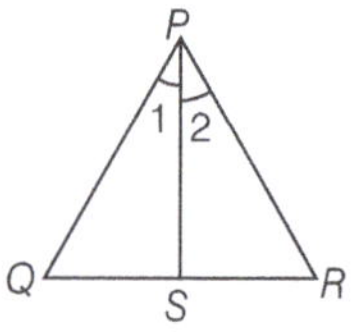

$\Rightarrow \quad \angle PQR + \angle 1 > \angle PRQ + \angle 1$

$\Rightarrow \quad \angle PQR + \angle 1 > \angle PRQ + \angle 2$

$\Rightarrow \quad \angle PSR > \angle PSQ$

14. **Hint** We have, $\angle PBC < \angle QCB$

$\Rightarrow \quad -\angle PBC > -\angle QCB$

$\Rightarrow \quad 180° - \angle PBC > 180° - \angle QCB$

$\Rightarrow \quad \angle B > \angle C$

15. **Hint** Since, $PQ = PR$

$\therefore \quad \angle Q = \angle R$ ...(i)

Clearly, $\angle PEF > \angle Q$ ...(ii)

$\angle R > \angle RFD \Rightarrow \angle Q > \angle RFD$ ...(iii)

From Eqs. (ii) and (iii), we get

$\angle PEF > \angle RFD = \angle PFE$

[$\because$ vertically opposite angles]

$\Rightarrow \quad \angle PEF > \angle PFE$

16. **Hint** Here, we have $AB = AC$

$\Rightarrow \quad \angle B = \angle C$

$\because \quad A + B + C = 180°$

$\therefore \quad A + 2C = 180°$

$\Rightarrow \quad A = 180° - 2C$

Now, as $60° < A < 90°$

$\therefore \quad 60° < 180° - 2C < 90°$

$\Rightarrow \quad -120° < -2C < -90°$

$\Rightarrow \quad 90° < 2C < 120°$

$\Rightarrow \quad 45° < C < 60°$

$\Rightarrow \quad C < A \Rightarrow c < a$ ...(i)

If $A = 90°$, then $a^2 = b^2 + c^2$

$\Rightarrow \quad a^2 = 2c^2 \Rightarrow a = \sqrt{2}c$ [$\because b = c$]

But $A < 90°$

$\therefore \quad a < \sqrt{2}c$ ...(ii)

From Eqs. (i) and (ii), we shows the result.

17. **Hint** In ΔABC, let BC be the longest side.

Then, $\quad BC > AB \Rightarrow \angle A > \angle C$ ...(i)

and $\quad BC > AC \Rightarrow \angle A > \angle B$ ...(ii)

On adding Eqs. (i) and (ii), we get

$2\angle A > \angle B + \angle C \Rightarrow 3\angle A > \angle A + \angle B + \angle C$

$\Rightarrow \quad \angle A > \frac{2}{3}$ of a right angle.

18. **Hint** In ΔABC, $AB + BC > AC$ ...(i)

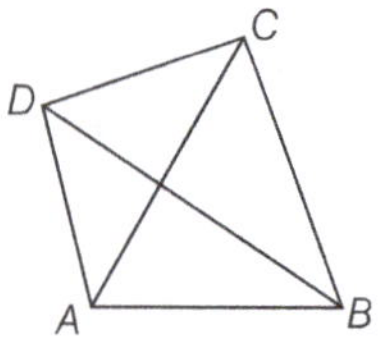

In ΔBCD, $BC + CD > BD$ ...(ii)

In ΔCDA, $CD + DA > AC$ ...(iii)

In ΔDAB, $DA + AB > BD$ ...(iv)

On adding Eqs. (i), (ii), (iii) and (iv), we show the result.

Chapter Exercise

1. (b) **Hint** Sum of angles of a triangle = 180°

2. (a) **Hint** By CPCT, if $\Delta PQR \cong \Delta ABC$.

$QR = BC = 3$

3. (c) **Hint** $\Delta OAD \cong \Delta OBC$ [by AAS congruence rule]

$\therefore \quad OA = OB \Rightarrow OB = OA = 3$ cm

4. (c) **Hint** $\Delta ABC \cong \Delta DCB$ [by SAS congruence rule]

$\therefore \quad AC = DB$

$\Rightarrow \quad 4 = DB$

$\Rightarrow \quad BD = 4$

5. (d) **Hint** $\Delta ABD \cong \Delta CBD$ [ASA congruence rule]

$\therefore \quad x = 2y$ [by CPCT]...(i)

and $\quad 2x = 3y + 8$ [by CPCT]...(ii)

Solving Eqs. (i) and (ii), we get

$x = 16, \; y = 8$

6. **Hint** In ΔPQR, $\angle P = \angle R$ [given]

$\therefore \quad PQ = QR$

[$\because$ sides opposite to equal angles are equal]

Ans. 4 cm

7. **Hint** Use SAS congruence rule.

Ans. $\Delta ABC \cong \Delta DEF$

$\therefore \; AC = FD, \; \angle BCA = \angle EFD$ [by CPCT]

$\angle BAC = \angle EDF$

8. **Hint** Join RM and SM.

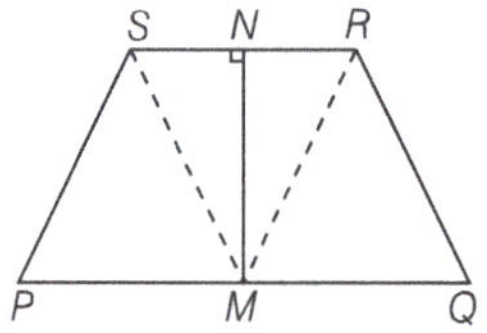

Now, show $\Delta RMN \cong \Delta SMN$ [by SAS]

$\therefore \quad RM = SM$ [CPCT]

and $\quad \angle RMN = \angle SMN$ [CPCT] ...(i)

As, $MN \perp PQ$, $\angle PMN = \angle QMN$ [each 90°]

$\Rightarrow \quad \angle PMN - \angle SMN = \angle QMN - \angle RMN$ [from Eq. (i)]

$\Rightarrow \quad \angle PMS = \angle QMR$

Now, show $\quad \Delta PMS \cong \Delta QMR$ [by SAS]

$\therefore \quad PS = QR$ [CPCT]

9. **Hint** In ΔDEF, $\angle E = 180° - 73° - 72° = 35°$

Ans. AAS congruence rule.

10. **Hint** In ΔABD and ΔCDB, $AD = CB$ and $AB = CD$

[$\because$ opposite sides of a parallelogram are equal]

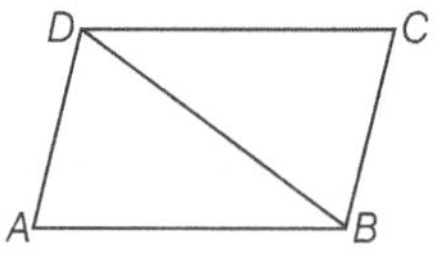

Also, $\angle DAB = \angle BCD$
[opposite angles of a parallelogram are equal]

11. Hint In ΔECD and ΔEBF; $\angle DEC = \angle FEB$
[vertically opposite angles]
$\angle DCB = \angle EBF$ [alternate angles]
and $DE = EF$ [given]
$\therefore$ $\Delta ECD \cong \Delta EBF$ [by AAS congruence rule]
$\Rightarrow$ $CD = BF$ [by CPCT]

12. Hint Since, $PS \perp AB$, $\angle APS = 90° = \angle SPB$
$\therefore$ $\angle 1 + \angle 2 = 90°$ and $\angle 3 + \angle 4 = 90°$
But $\angle 1 = \angle 4$ [given]
$\Rightarrow$ $\angle 2 = \angle 3$
In ΔPQS and ΔPRS, we have
$\angle 2 = \angle 3$
$\angle PSQ = \angle PSR$ [each 90°]
$PS = PS$ [common]
$\therefore$ $\Delta PQS \cong \Delta PRS$ [by ASA]

13. Hint $QS = RT$ [given]
$QS + SR = RT + SR$
$\Rightarrow$ $QR = TS$
Also, $\angle 1 = \angle 2$ [given]
$\Rightarrow$ $\angle 1 + \angle SPR = \angle 2 + \angle SPR$
$\Rightarrow$ $\angle QPR = \angle TPS$
By $\angle Q = \angle T$, $\angle QPR = \angle TPS$, $QR = TS$
$\Delta PQR \cong \Delta PTS$ [by AAS]

14. Hint $\Delta PQR \cong \Delta SRQ$ [by SAS]
(i) $PR = QS$ [CPCT]
(ii) In ΔPTQ and ΔSTR,
$\angle QPT = \angle TSR$ [$\because \angle QPR = \angle QSR$]
$\angle PTQ = \angle RTS$ [vertical opposite angles]
$PQ = RS$
$\therefore$ $\Delta PTQ \cong \Delta STR$ [by AAS]
$\Rightarrow$ $QT = RT$ [CPCT]

15. Hint In ΔAOB and ΔCOB,
$OA = OC$, $OB = OB$ and $\angle AOB = \angle BOC$
$\therefore$ $\Delta AOB \cong \Delta COB$ [by SAS congruence rule]
$\Rightarrow$ $AB = BC$ ...(i)
Similarly, by proving that $\Delta BOC \cong \Delta DOC$ and $\Delta COD \cong \Delta AOD$, we get
$BC = CD$ and $CD = DA$ ...(ii)
$\therefore$ From Eqs. (i) and (ii), we get
$AB = BC = CD = DA$

16. Hint Prove that $\Delta APB \cong \Delta APC$ by SAS congruence rule.

17. Hint In $PQRS$, join OQ and OS.

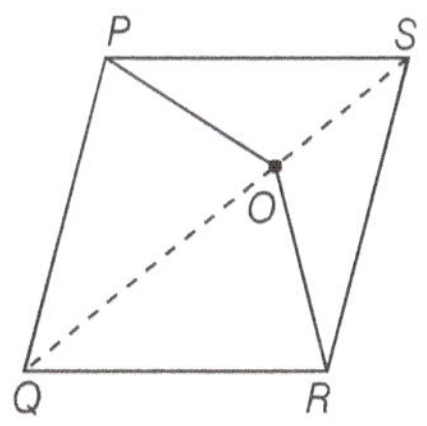

Now, show $\Delta OQP \cong \Delta OQR$ [by SSS]
$\therefore$ $\angle POQ = \angle QOR$ [CPCT] ...(i)
Similarly, $\Delta OPS \cong \Delta ORS$
$\therefore$ $\angle POS = \angle ROS$ [CPCT]...(ii)
As sum of angles at a point is 360°.
$\angle POQ + \angle QOR + \angle ROS + \angle POS = 360°$
$\Rightarrow$ $2(\angle QOR + \angle ROS) = 360°$ [using Eqs. (i) and (ii)]
$\Rightarrow$ $\angle QOR + \angle ROS = 180°$
Sum of two adjacent angles is 180°, so QOS is a straight line.

18. Hint $\Delta ABC \cong \Delta DBC$ [by SSS]

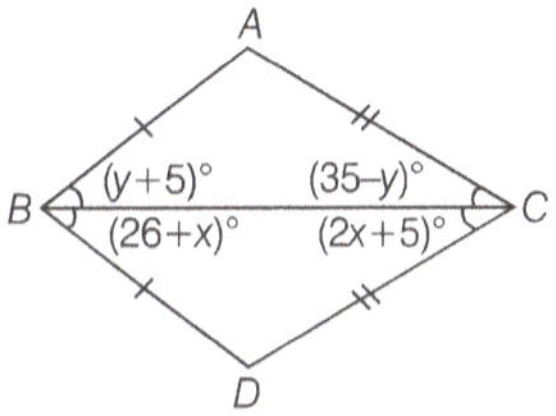

$\therefore$ $y + 5 = 26 + x$ [CPCT] ...(i)
and $2x + 5 = 35 - y$ [CPCT]...(ii)
On solving Eqs. (i) and (ii), we get
$x = 3°$ and $y = 24°$

19. Hint Do same as Example 13.

20. Hint First prove that $\Delta ADB \cong \Delta ADC$ by SSS congruence rule. Then, show that $\angle ABD = \angle ACD$ by CPCT.

Ans. 1 : 1

21. Hint Use RHS congruence rule to show the given result.

22. Hint Prove $\Delta ALB \cong \Delta NCM$
Then, we have $\angle A = \angle N$
and $AB = NM$ [by CPCT]
Since, $AL = CN$, therefore $AL + LC = CN + LC$
$\Rightarrow$ $AC = NL$
Further prove that $\Delta ABC \cong \Delta NML$.

23. Hint Do same as Example 29.

Ans. AB is the longest side and BC is the shortest side.

24. Hint In ΔABC, $AB = AC$
$\angle ACB = \angle ABC$ ...(i)
[angle opposite equal sides are equal]
$\angle CAD = \angle ACB + \angle ABC$
[external angle = sum of two internal opposite angles]
$\Rightarrow$ $137° = \angle ACB + \angle ACB$ [from Eq. (i)]
$\Rightarrow$ $\angle ACB = \left(\frac{137}{2}\right)^\circ = 68\frac{1}{2}^\circ$
$\Rightarrow$ $\angle ABC = 68\frac{1}{2}^\circ$ i.e. $\angle EBC = 68\frac{1}{2}^\circ$
In ΔEBC, $CE = CB$ [given]
$\therefore$ $\angle CEB = \angle EBC$
[angle opposite equal sides are equal]
$\Rightarrow$ $\angle CEB = 68\frac{1}{2}^\circ$ $\left[\because \angle EBC = 68\frac{1}{2}^\circ\right]$

$\Rightarrow \angle EBC + \angle CEB + \angle BCE = 180°$

[sum of angle of a triangle]

$\Rightarrow \quad 68\frac{1}{2}^{\circ} + 68\frac{1}{2}^{\circ} + \angle BCE = 180° \Rightarrow \angle BCE = 43°$

Now, $EF \parallel BC$ [given]

and CE is a transversal.

$\angle CEF = \angle BCE$ [alternate angles]

$\Rightarrow \quad \angle CEF = 43°$ [$\because \angle BCE = 43°$]

25. Hint In ΔABC, $BC = AC$ [given]

$\therefore \angle BAC = P$ [angles opposite equal sides are equal]

In ΔACD, $\angle ACD = P + P$

[external angle = sum of two internal opposite angles]

$\Rightarrow \angle ACD = 2P$

In ΔACD, $AC = AD$ [given]

$\therefore \angle ADC = 2P$ [angles opposite equal sides are equal]

In ΔABD, $\angle EAD = \angle ABD + \angle ADB$

[$\because$ external angle = sum of two internal opposite angles]

$\Rightarrow \quad 98° = P + 2P$

$\Rightarrow \quad 3P = 98°$

$\Rightarrow \quad P = \left(\frac{98}{3}\right)^{\circ} = 32°40'$

26. Hint Let $\angle BAC = a$

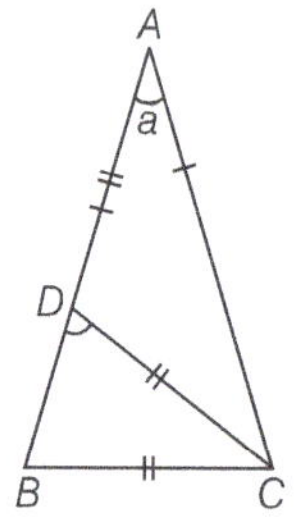

In ΔADC, $AD = DC$

$\therefore \quad \angle ACD = a$

$\therefore \quad \angle BDC = a + a$

[sum of two internal opposite angles]

$= 2a$

In ΔBDC, $DC = BC$

$\therefore \quad \angle DBC = 2a$

In ΔABC, $AB = AC$

$\therefore \quad \angle ACB = 2a$

Also, $\angle BAC + \angle ABC + \angle ACB = 180°$

[angles of a triangle]

$\Rightarrow \quad a + 2a + 2a = 180° \Rightarrow 5a = 180° \Rightarrow a = 36$

$\therefore \angle BAC = 36°$, as required.

27. Hint Draw the figure and mark the angles as shown.

We know that each angle of an equilateral triangle is 60° and each angle of a square is 90°.

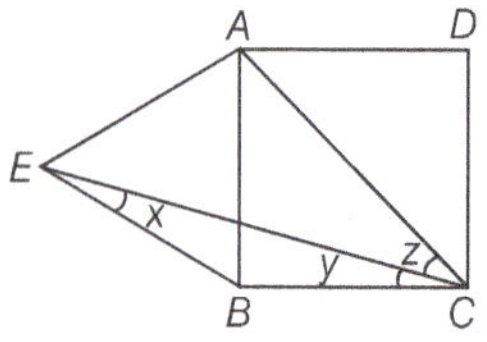

As, AC is a diagonal of the square $ABCD$,

$\angle ACB = 45°$.

In ΔEBC, $\angle EBC = \angle EBA + \angle ABC$

$= 60° + 90° = 150°$

$EB = BC$ [$\because EB = AB$ and $AB = BC$]

$\Rightarrow \quad \angle y = \angle x$

[$\because$ angle opposite equal sides are equal]

$\Rightarrow \angle x + \angle y + \angle EBC = 180°$

[sum of angles of a triangle]

$\Rightarrow \quad \angle y + \angle y + 150° = 180°$

$\Rightarrow \quad 2\angle y = 30°$

$\Rightarrow \quad \angle y = 15°$

$\Rightarrow \quad \angle ACE = \angle ACB - \angle y$

$= 45° - 15° = 30°$

$\Rightarrow \quad \angle ACE = \frac{1}{2} \times 60° = \frac{1}{2} \angle ABE$

Hence, $\angle ACE = \frac{1}{2} \angle ABE$.

28. Hint In ΔOAB,

$\angle OAB = \angle OBA$ [given]

$\therefore \quad OB = OA$

[sides opposite equal angle are equal]

Given, $BD = AC$

$\Rightarrow \quad BD - OB = AC - OA$ [$\because OB = OA$, prove above]

$\Rightarrow \quad OD = OC$

In ΔAOD and ΔBOC,

$AO = BO$ [proved above]

$OD = OC$ [proved above]

$\angle AOD = \angle BOC$ [vertical opposite angles]

$\therefore \quad \Delta AOD \cong \Delta BOC$ [SAS rule]

$\therefore \quad AD = BC$ [CPCT]

29. Hint $AB = AC$ [given]

$\Rightarrow \quad \angle C = \angle B$ [angle opposite equal sides are equal]

As BD and CE are bisectors of $\angle B$ and $\angle C$ respectively,

$\angle DBC = \frac{1}{2} \angle B$

and $\angle ECB = \frac{1}{2} \angle C$

$\Rightarrow \quad \angle DBC = \angle ECB$ [$\because \angle B = \angle C$, proved above]

(i) In ΔDBC and ΔECB,

$\angle DCB = \angle EBC$

[$\because \angle DCB = \angle C$ and $\angle EBC = \angle B$]

$\angle DBC = \angle ECB$ [proved above]

$BC = BC$ [common]

$\Delta DBC \cong \Delta ECB$

[ASA rule of congruency]

(ii) $\Delta DBC = \Delta ECB$ [proved in part (i)]

$\Rightarrow \quad BD = CE$ [CPCT]

30. Hint $\angle 1 + \Delta EAC = 180°$ [linear pair]

$\angle 2 + \angle EDB = 180°$ [linear pair]

$\Rightarrow \quad \angle 1 + \angle EAC = \angle 2 + \angle EDB$

but $\angle 1 = \angle 2$ [given]

$\Rightarrow \quad \angle EAC = \angle EDB$

In ΔEAC and ΔEDB,

$\angle EAC = \angle EDB$ [proved above]

$\Rightarrow \angle AEC = \angle DEB$ [vertical opposite angles]

$\Rightarrow EA = ED$ [given]

$\therefore \Delta EAC \cong \Delta EDB$ [by ASA rule of congruency]

$\therefore EC = EB$ [CPCT]

$\Rightarrow \Delta EBC$ is an isosceles triangle.

31. Hint

(i) Given, $AB = AC \Rightarrow \angle B = \angle C$

[$\because$ angle opposite equal sides are equal]

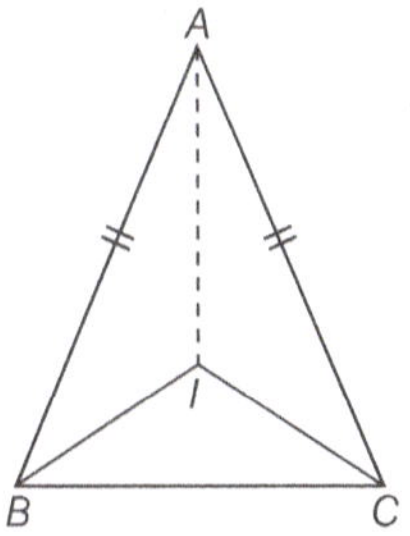

$\Rightarrow \frac{1}{2}\angle B = \frac{1}{2}\angle C$

$\Rightarrow \angle IBC = \angle ICB$

[$\because$ IB and IC are bisectors of $\angle B$ and $\angle C$]

$\Rightarrow IB = IC$ [sides opposite equal angles are equal]

(ii) Also, $\frac{1}{2}\angle B = \frac{1}{2}\angle C$

$\Rightarrow \angle ABI = \angle ACI$

[$\because$ IB and IC are bisectors of $\angle B$ and $\angle C$ respectively]

In ΔIAB and ΔIAC,

$\angle ABI = \angle ACI$ [proved above]

$IB = IC$ [proved above]

$AB = AC$ [given]

$\therefore \Delta IAB \cong \Delta IAC$ [by SAS rule of congruency]

$\therefore \angle IAB = \angle IAC$ [CPCT]

$\Rightarrow IA$ bisects $\angle A$.

32. Hint $PQ = PR \Rightarrow \angle Q = \angle R$ [given]

In ΔPSR, $\angle PSQ > \angle R$

[external angle is greater than each internal opposite angles]

$\Rightarrow \angle PSQ > \angle Q$ [$\because \angle R = \angle Q$]

$\Rightarrow PQ > PS$

[sides opposite to greater angle is longer]

33. Hint Clearly, $\angle ACB = 70°$

and this implies $\angle ACD = 110°$

and $\angle CAD = 30°$

Now, in ΔACD, $\angle ADC > \angle CAD$

$\Rightarrow AC > CD$

34. Hint $\angle RPQ = 62°$ [linear pair]

$\angle QRP = 68°$

[external angle = sum of two internal opposite angles]

$\angle PQR = 50°$ [linear pair]

35. Hint Do same as Example 31.

Ans. BC, AC, AB

36. Hint $AC = AD$

$\Rightarrow \angle ADC = \angle C$

$\because$ In ΔADC, $\angle DAC + \angle ADC + \angle C = 180°$

$\therefore \angle ADC = \angle C = 65°$

Now, in ΔABC,

$\angle A = 73°$, $\angle B = 42°$ and $\angle C = 65°$

$\Rightarrow BC > AB$

Ans. No

37. Hint By using congruency rule SAS.

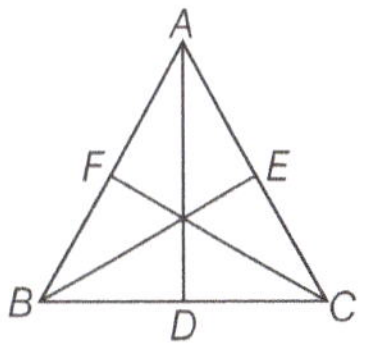

Show that $\Delta ADC \cong \Delta BEA$, then by CPCT

$\Rightarrow AD = BE$

Similarly, we can prove that $BE = CF$

$\therefore AD = BE = CF$

38. Hint $\angle BAE = \angle FAD$, $\angle EAC = \angle CAF$ [given]

$\Rightarrow \angle BAE + \angle EAC = \angle FAD + \angle CAF$

$\Rightarrow \angle BAC = \angle CAD$

Now, $\Delta ABC \cong \Delta ADC$ [bySAS]

[$\because$ $AB = AD$, $AC = AC$ and $\angle BAC = \angle CAD$]

$\therefore \angle ABC = \angle ADC$ [CPCT]

$\Rightarrow \angle ABE = \angle ADF$

Now, $\Delta ABE \cong \Delta ADF$ [by ASA]

[$\because$ $AB = AD$, $\angle BAE = \angle FAD$ and $\angle ABE = \angle ADF$]

$\Rightarrow AE = AF$

39. Hint Draw $OL \perp BC$, $OM \perp CA$ and $ON \perp AB$

$\Delta OLC \cong \Delta OMC$ [by AAS]

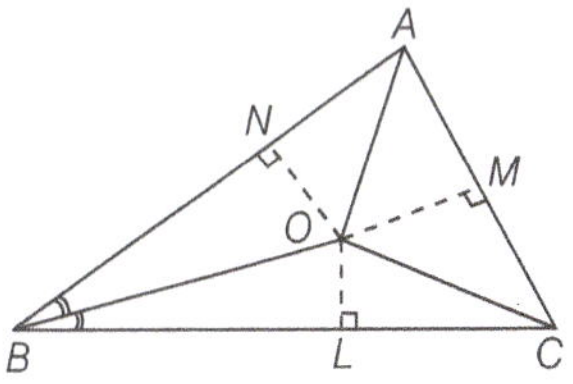

$\therefore OL = OM$ [CPCT] ...(i)

$\Rightarrow OL = ON$

[$\because$ similarly, $\Delta OBL \cong \Delta OBN$] ...(ii)

In ΔOAM and ΔOAN,

$OM = ON$ [from Eqs. (i) and (ii)]

$\angle OMA = \angle ONA$ [each 90°]

$OA = OA$ [common]

$\Delta OAM \cong OAN$ [by RHS]

$\therefore \angle OAM = \angle OAN$ [CPCT]

40. Hint Given, $PA = QA$ and $PB = QB$

To show, $AB \perp PQ$ and AB bisects PQ.

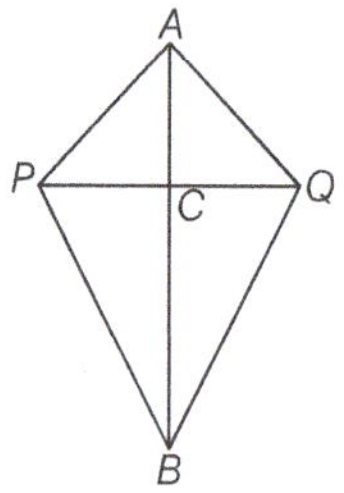

In $\Delta PAB \cong \Delta QAB$, [by SSS]

$\because$ $PA = QA$, $PB = QB$ and $AB = AB$ [common]

$\therefore$ $\angle PAB = \angle QAB$ [CPCT]

In $\Delta PAC \cong \Delta QAC$, [by SAS]

$\because$ $PA = QA$, $\angle PAC = \angle QAC$ and $CA = CA$ [common]

$\therefore$ $PC = QC \Rightarrow PC = CQ \Rightarrow C$ is mid-point of AB

$\Rightarrow$ AB bisects PQ.

Also, $\angle PCA = \angle QCA$ [CPCT]

But $\angle PCA + \angle QCA = 180°$ [linear pair]

$\Rightarrow$ $\angle PCA + \angle PCA = 180°$

$\Rightarrow$ $\angle PCA = 90° \Rightarrow AB \perp PQ$

41. Hint Show that $\Delta BSR \cong \Delta PQC$ by using AAS rule, then by CPCT we prove the required result.

42. Hint Show $\Delta AOD \cong \Delta BOC$ by SAS congruence rule.

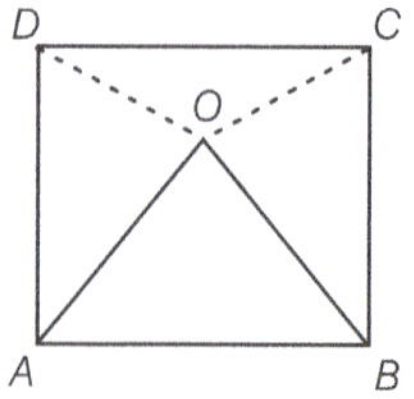

Then, $OC = OD$ [by CPCT]

43. Hint

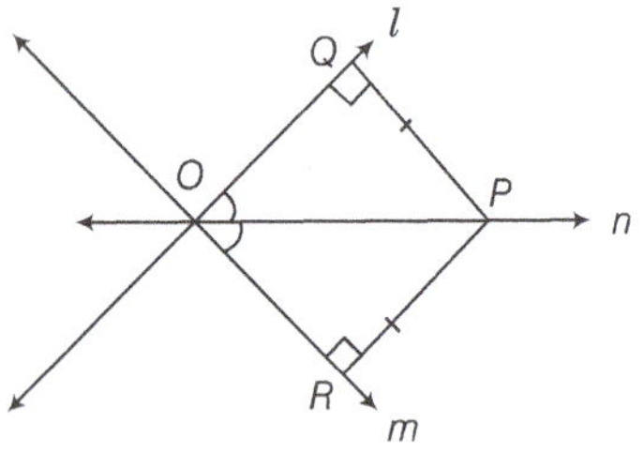

Show $\Delta OQP \cong \Delta ORP$ [by RHS congruence rule]

then $\angle POQ = \angle POR$ [by CPCT]

44. (i) **Hint** We know that median bisects the opposite side. Use this property and then show the given parts by using SSS congruence rule.

(ii) **Hint** Use SAS congruence rule.

45. Hint $\angle B = \angle C$ and use sum of three angles of a triangle is 180°.

Ans. $\angle A = 100°$

46. Hint $AC = AD$

$\Rightarrow$ $\angle ACD = 75°$

$\Rightarrow$ $x = 180° - 150° = 30°$

Also, we have

$120° = p + z$

$p = x + 75°$

$75° = y + 52°$

Ans. $x = 30°$, $y = 23°$, $p = 105°$ and $z = 15°$

47. Hint By SSS rule, show that $\Delta AOB \cong \Delta AOD$

$\Rightarrow$ $\angle 1 = \angle 2$

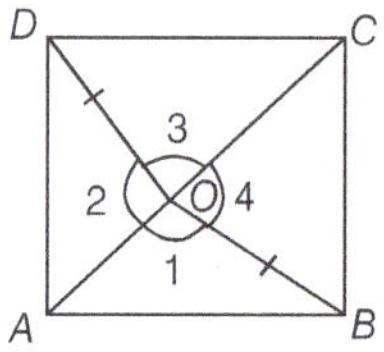

Similarly, $\Delta DOC \cong \Delta BOC \Rightarrow \angle 3 = \angle 4$

But $\angle 1 + \angle 2 + \angle 3 + \angle 4 = 360°$

$\Rightarrow$ $2(\angle 2 + \angle 3) = 360°$

$\Rightarrow$ $\angle 2 + \angle 3 = 180°$

$\Rightarrow$ AO and OC are in the same straight line.

48. Hint $AB = AC$

$\Rightarrow$ $\angle B = \angle C$

$\Rightarrow$ $\angle B = \angle DCF$

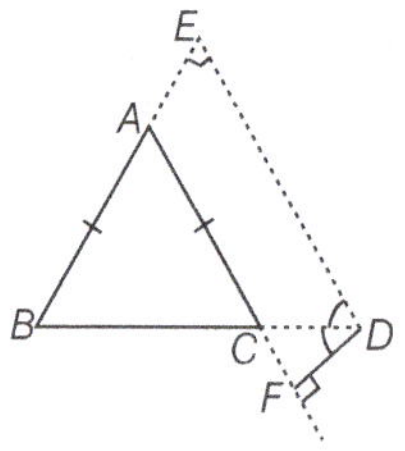

Now, in ΔBDE and ΔCDF,

$\angle B = \angle DCF$

and $\angle E = \angle F = 90°$

$\Rightarrow$ $\angle EDB = \angle FDC$

49. Hint Assume the bisector PS of $\angle P$ meet side QR of ΔPQR at point S.

As, the bisector PS bisects opposite side QR, so S is mid-point of QR.

Produce PS to a point T such that $ST = PS$.

Join R and T.

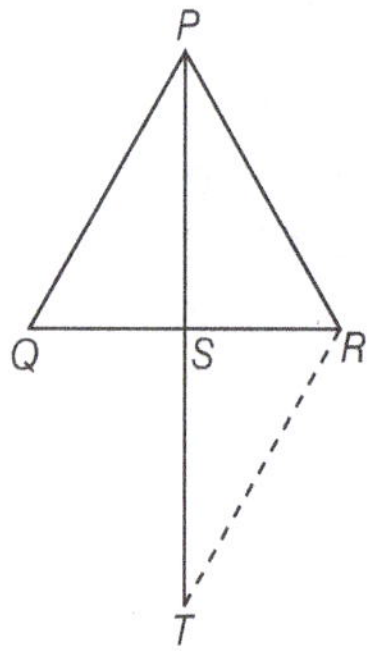

In ΔPQS and ΔTRS,

$QS = RS$ [$\because S$ is mid-point of QR]

$PS = ST$ [by construction]

$\angle PSQ = \angle TSR$ [vertical opposite angles]

$\therefore \Delta PQS \cong \Delta TRS$ [by SAS rule]

$\therefore PQ = TR$ and $\angle QPS = \angle RTS$ [CPCT]

As, PS is bisector of $\angle P$,

$\angle QPS = \angle RPS$

$\Rightarrow \angle RTS = \angle RPS$

$\Rightarrow \angle RTP = \angle RPT$

Thus, in ΔPRT,

$\angle RTP = \angle RPT$

$\Rightarrow PR = TR$

[sides opposite to equal angles are equal]

$\therefore PQ = TR = PR$

$\Rightarrow PQ = PR$

50. Hint Construction Draw $DE \perp BC$

Firstly show $\Delta DAC \cong \Delta DEC$ using AAS congruence rule

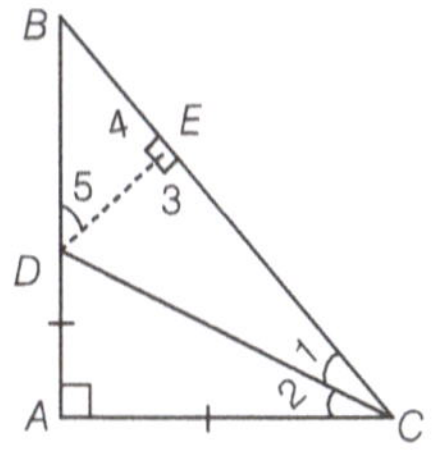

Then, by CPCT, $DA = DE$ ...(i)

and $AC = EC$ ...(ii)

In ΔABC, $AB = AC$

$\Rightarrow \angle C = \angle B$ ...(iii)

$\therefore \angle B = 45°$

In ΔBED, $\angle B = \angle 5 = 45°$ [$\because \angle 4 = 90°$ by construction]

$\Rightarrow DE = BE$ ...(iv)

From Eqs. (i) and (iv), we get

$DA = DE = BE$

51. Hint Produce QO to intersect PR at A.

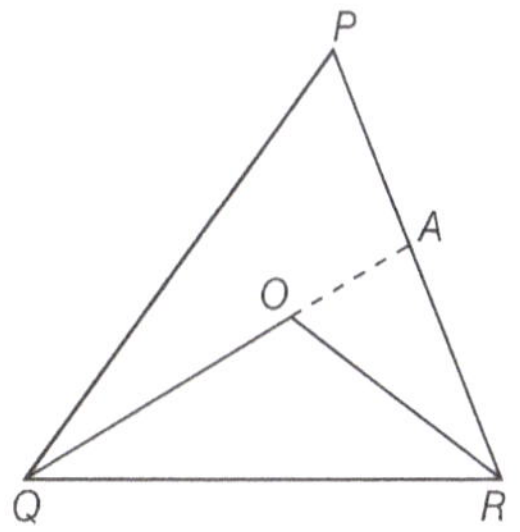

In ΔPQA, $PQ + PA > QA$

[$\because$ sum of two sides of a triangle > third side]

$\Rightarrow PQ + PA > OQ + OA$ ...(i)

In ΔOAR, $OA + AR > OR$ ...(ii)

On adding Eqs. (i) and (ii), we get

$PQ + PA + OA + AR > OQ + OA + OR$

$\Rightarrow PQ + (PA + AR) > OQ + OR$

$\Rightarrow PQ + PR > OQ + OR$ [$\because PA + AR = PR$]

$\Rightarrow OQ + OR < PQ + PR$

52. Hint $\angle P = 180° - 75° - 35° = 70°$

Since, PS bisects $\angle P$,

$\angle QPS = \angle SPR = \frac{1}{2} \times 70° = 35°$

$\therefore \angle PSQ = \angle SPR + \angle R = 35° + 35° = 70°$

[external angle = sum of opposite internal angles]

$\therefore$ In ΔPQS, $\angle QPS < \angle PSQ < \angle PQS$

$\Rightarrow QS < PQ < PS$ ...(i)

[sides opposite to smaller angle is smaller]

Also, in ΔPSR,

$\angle SPR = 35° = \angle R$

$\Rightarrow PS = SR$ ...(ii)

$\therefore QS < PQ < SR$ [from Eqs. (i) and (ii)]

53. Hint $\angle B = \angle ACB$ [$\because AB = AC$ given]

$\angle AEO > \angle B$ ...(i)

[$\because \angle AEO$ is external angle of ΔEBD and external angle is greater than each internal opposite angles]

$\angle ACB > \angle COD$

[$\because \angle ACB$ is external angle of ΔCOD and external angle is greater than each internal opposite angles]

$\angle B > \angle COD$ [$\because \angle B = \angle ACB$] ...(ii)

$\angle AEO > \angle COD$ [from Eqs. (i) and (ii)] ...(iii)

$\angle EOA = \angle COD$ [vertical opposite angle] ...(iv)

$\angle AEO > \angle EOA$ [from Eqs. (iii) and (iv)]

$AO > AE$

[$\because$ greater angle has greater opposite side]

Olympiad Section

Brain Teasing Questions of Olympiad Pattern

1 In ΔABC, if $A - B = 15°$, $B - C = 30°$, then $\angle A$, $\angle B$ and $\angle C$ are respectively

(a) 80°, 65°, 35° (b) 65°, 80°, 35°
(c) 35°, 80°, 65° (d) 80°, 35°, 65°

2 In ΔABC, $\angle B = 45°$, $\angle C = 65°$ and the bisector of $\angle BAC$ meets BC at P. Then, the ascending order of sides is

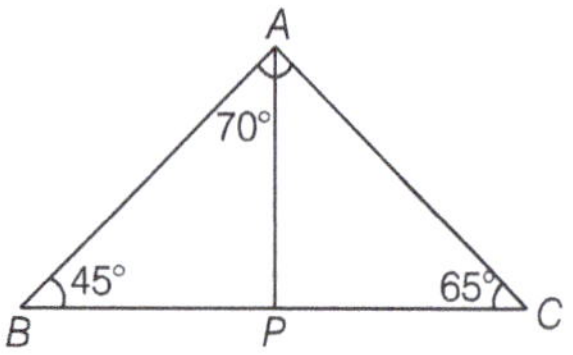

(a) AP, BP, CP (b) AP, CP, BP
(c) BP, AP, CP (d) CP, BP, AP

3 The sides of a triangle are 2006 cm, 6002 cm and m cm, where m is a positive integer. The number of such possible triangles is

(a) 1 (b) 2006 (c) 3996 (d) 4011

4 In the given figure, AC is the median as well as altitude to BD. In ΔACE, AD is the median to CE.

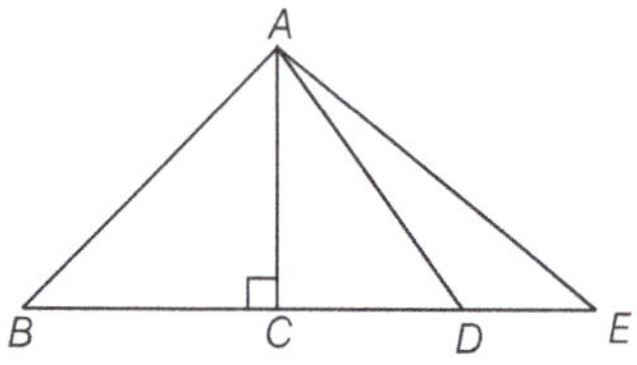

Which one of the following is true?

(a) $AB + CD > AE$ (b) $AB + BC = AE$
(c) $AB + DE < AE$ (d) None of these

5 In the given figure, $AY \perp ZY$ and $BY \perp XY$, such that $AY = ZY$ and $BY = XY$, then

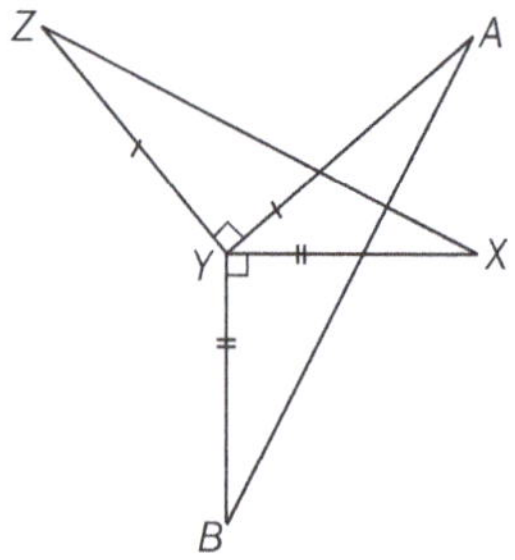

(a) $AB = ZX$ (b) $AB = AY$
(c) $ZX = AY$ (d) $ZX = BY$

6 In ΔABC, $AB = AC$ and D is a point on AB such that $AD = DC = BC$. Then, $\angle BAC$ is equal to

(a) 30° (b) 40° (c) 36° (d) 45°

7 If $\angle ACB$ is a right angle and $AC = CD$ and $CDEF$ is a parallelogram. If $\angle FEC = 10°$, then $\angle BDE$ equals

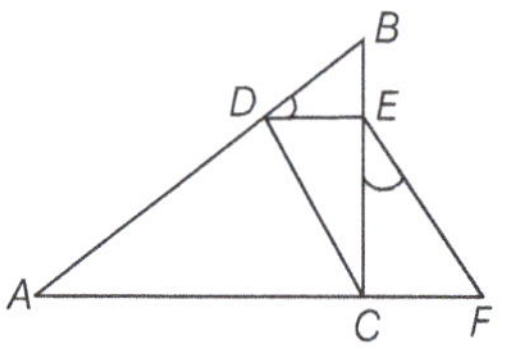

(a) 60° (b) 70° (c) 50° (d) 55°

8 In the given figure, $\angle BCD = 40°$, $\angle EDC = 35°$, $\angle CBF = 30°$ and $\angle DEG = 40°$, then $\angle BAE$ equals

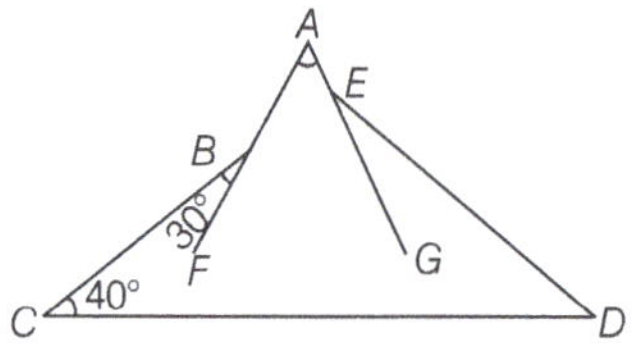

(a) 70° (b) 50° (c) 110° (d) 35°

9 If $PQRS$ is a quadrilateral, where PQ is its longest side and RS is its shortest side, then which one of the given relations is correct?

(a) $\angle R < \angle P$ and $\angle S > \angle Q$ (b) $\angle R > \angle P$ and $\angle S > \angle Q$
(c) $\angle R > \angle P$ and $\angle S < \angle Q$ (d) Cannot be determined

10 Line segment joining the mid-points M and N of parallel sides AB and DC, respectively of a trapezium $ABCD$ is perpendicular to both the sides AB and DC. Then,

(a) $AD = BC$ (b) $AD = 2BC$
(c) $AD \parallel BC$ (d) $AD < BC$

Answers

1. (a) **2.** (d) **3.** (d) **4.** (a) **5.** (a)
6. (c) **7.** (c) **8.** (d) **9.** (b) **10.** (a)

* *These questions may or may not be asked in the examination, have been given just for additional practice required for olympiads Scholarship Exams etc. For detailed explanations refer Page No. 340.*

CHAPTER

09

Mid-Point and Pythagoras Theorems

SYLLABUS

- (a) Mid-Point Theorem and its converse, equal intercept theorem. (i) Proof and simple applications of mid-point theorem and its converse. (ii) Equal intercept theorem : proof and simple application. • (b) Pythagoras Theorem (i) Area based proof and simple applications of Pythagoras Theorem and its converse.

Many properties of triangles have been studied so far, such as congruence of triangles and inequalities in a triangle. In this chapter, we will study some important theorems related to triangles, such as mid-point theorem, equal intercept theorem, Pythagoras theorem and its converse alongwith their applications.

Mid-Point and Equal Intercept Theorems

Mid-Point Theorem

The line segment joining the mid-points of any two sides of a triangle is parallel to the third side and equal to half of it.

Given A ΔABC, E and F are the mid-points of AB and AC, respectively.

To prove $EF \parallel BC$

and $EF = \frac{1}{2} BC$.

Construction Through vertex C, draw $CD \parallel AB$ and let it meet extended EF at D.

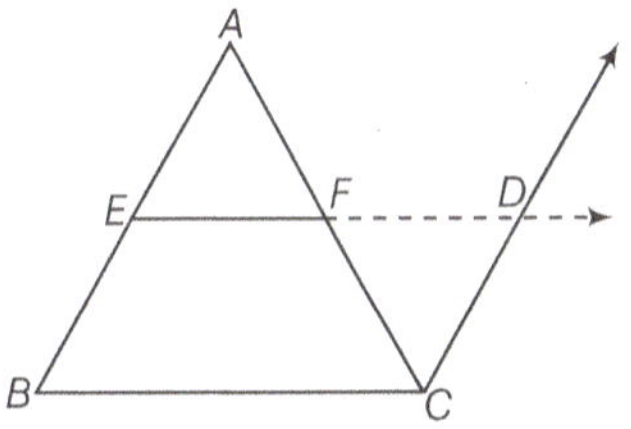

Proof Now, in ΔAEF and ΔCDF,

$\angle AFE = \angle CFD$ [vertically opposite angles]

$AF = FC$ [∵ given]

and $\angle AEF = \angle FDC$ [alternate interior angles]

∴ $\Delta AEF \cong \Delta CDF$ [by AAS congruence rule]

Then, $AE = CD$ and $EF = FD$ [by CPCT] ...(i)

Also, $AE = BE$ [∵ given] ...(ii)

From Eqs. (i) and (ii), we get

$AE = BE = CD$ ...(iii)

and $BE \parallel CD$ [by construction]

So, $BCDE$ is a parallelogram.

[∵ one pair of opposite sides is parallel and equal]

Then, $ED \parallel BC$ or $EF \parallel BC$ and $ED = BC$

[opposite sides of parallelogram]

Now, $BC = ED = EF + FD = 2EF$

[from Eq. (i), $EF = FD$]

⇒ $EF = \frac{1}{2} BC$

Hence, the line segment joining the mid-points of two sides of a triangle is parallel to the third side and equal to half of it. **Hence proved**

Converse of Mid-Point Theorem

The line drawn through the mid-point of one side of a triangle, parallel to another side bisect the third side.

Given A ΔABC, E is the mid-point of AB and $EF \parallel BC$.

Then, $BE = AE$

To prove F is the mid-point of AC.

Construction Draw $CM \parallel AB$ and extend EF such that it intersects CM at D.

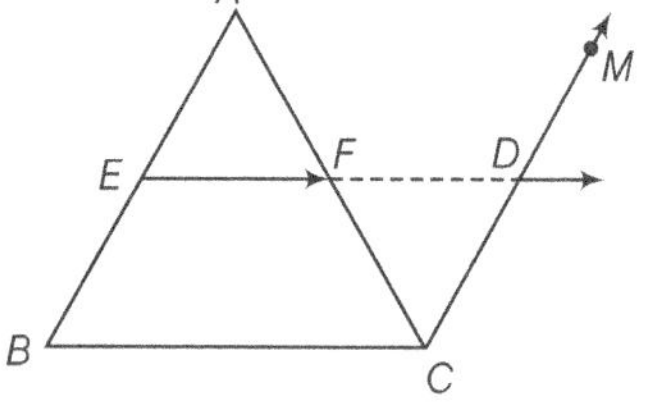

Proof In ΔAEF and ΔCDF, $\angle FAE = \angle FCD$

[$\because$ alternate angles]

$\angle AFE = \angle CFD$ [$\because$ vertically opposite angles]

$AE = CD$

[$\because$ $BCDE$ is a parallelogram, so $CD = BE = AE$]

$\therefore$ $\Delta AEF \cong \Delta CDF$ [by AAS congruence rule]

Then, $AF = CF$ [by CPCT]

Hence, F is the mid-point of AC.

Example 1. ΔABC is an isosceles triangle in which $AB = AC$. D and E are the mid-points of sides AB and AC, respectively and $DE = 3.5$ cm. Find the perimeter of ΔABC, when $AD = 4.5$ cm.

Sol. Given, A ΔABC, in which $AB = AC$ and D and E are the mid-points of AB and AC, respectively.

$\therefore$ $AD = DB = 4.5$ cm [as D is the mid-point of AB]

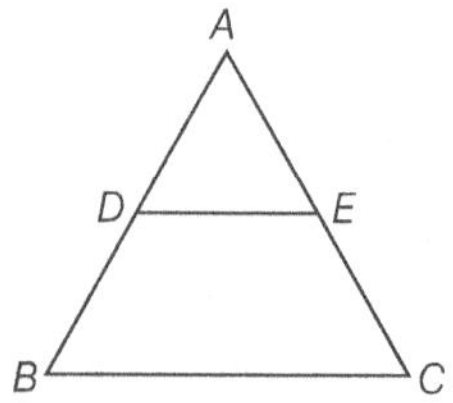

Then, $AB = 2AD = 2 \times 4.5 = 9$ cm

So, $AB = AC = 9$ cm [given]

Since, D and E are the mid-points of AB and AC.

By mid-point theorem,

$$DE \parallel BC \text{ and } DE = \frac{1}{2} BC$$

Then, $BC = 2DE = 2 \times 3.5 = 7$ cm

Now, perimeter of $\Delta ABC = AB + BC + CA$

$= 9 + 7 + 9 = 25$ cm

Example 2. In ΔABC, $AB = 5$ cm, $BC = 8$ cm and $CA = 7$ cm. If D and E are respectively the mid-points of AB and BC, determine the length of DE.

Sol. **Given** In ΔABC, we have $AB = 5$ cm, $BC = 8$ cm and $CA = 7$ cm. Since, D and E are the mid-points of AB and BC, respectively.

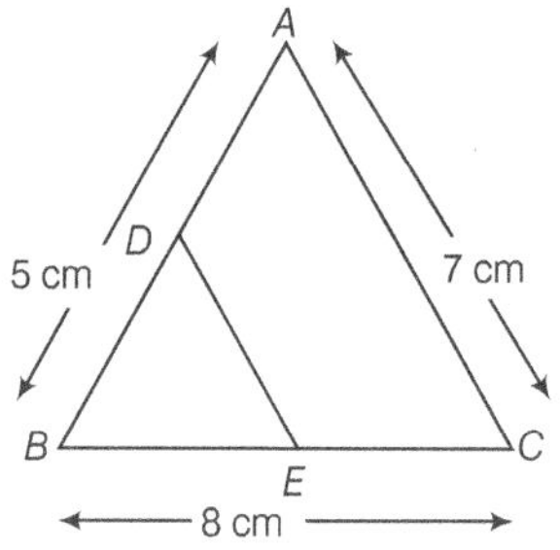

By mid-point theorem,

$$DE \parallel AC \text{ and } DE = \frac{1}{2} AC = \frac{7}{2} = 3.5$$

Thus, $DE = 3.5$ cm

Example 3. ABC is an equilateral triangle and L, M and N are the mid-points of the sides AB, BC and CA, respectively. Prove that ΔLMN is an equilateral triangle.

Sol. **Given** ΔABC is an equilateral triangle and L, M and N are the mid-points of the sides AB, BC and CA, respectively.

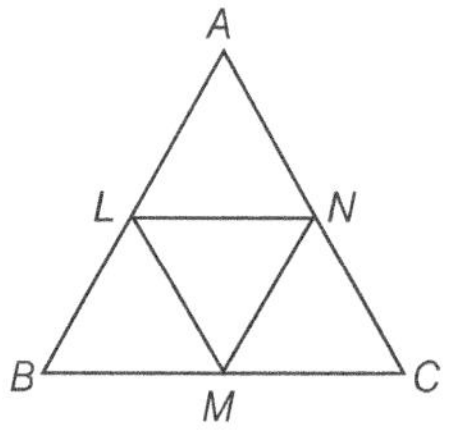

To prove ΔLMN is an equilateral triangle.

Proof Since, L and N are the mid-points of AB and AC, respectively.

By mid-point theorem,

$$LN = \frac{1}{2} BC$$

Similarly, $LM = \frac{1}{2} AC$

and $MN = \frac{1}{2} AB$

Now, ΔABC is an equilateral triangle.

$\therefore$ $AB = BC = CA$

$\Rightarrow$ $\frac{1}{2} AB = \frac{1}{2} BC = \frac{1}{2} CA$

$\Rightarrow$ $MN = LN = LM$

Hence, ΔLMN is an equilateral triangle. **Hence proved**

Example 4. *E* and *F* are respectively the mid-points of non-parallel sides *AD* and *BC* of a trapezium *ABCD*. Prove that $EF \parallel AB$ and $EF = \frac{1}{2}(AB + CD)$.

Sol. **Given** *E* and *F* are respectively the mid-points of non-parallel sides of *AD* and *BC* of trapezium *ABCD*.

To prove $EF \parallel AB$ and $EF = \frac{1}{2}(AB + CD)$

Construction Join *CE* and produce it to meet *BA* at *P*.

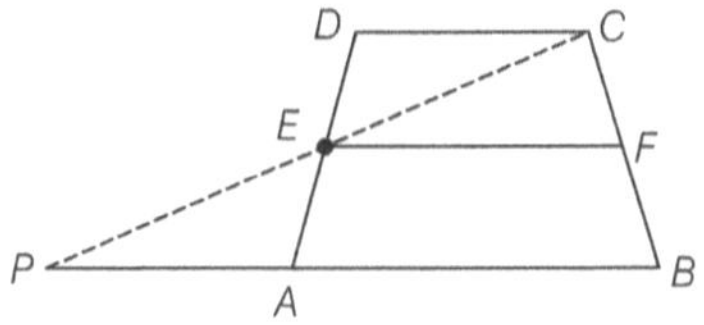

Proof In ΔDEC and ΔAEP, we have

$\angle DEC = \angle AEP$ [vertically opposite angles]

$\angle DCE = \angle APE$

[$\because DC \parallel PB$ and *PC* is transversal, so alternate angles are equal]

$DE = AE$ [$\because$ *E* is the mid-points of *AD*]

$\therefore$ $\Delta DEC \cong \Delta AEP$ [by AAS congruence rule]

Then, $CE = PE$ [by CPCT]

and $CD = PA$ [by CPCT]

Now, in ΔCPB, *E* is the mid-point of *CP*. [$\because CE = PE$]

Also, *F* is the mid-point of *BC*. [given]

So, by mid-point theorem,

$EF \parallel PB$ and $EF = \frac{1}{2} PB$

$\Rightarrow$ $EF \parallel AB$ and $EF = \frac{1}{2}(PA + AB)$

$= \frac{1}{2}(CD + AB)$ [$\because PA = CD$]

Hence, $EF \parallel AB$ and $EF = \frac{1}{2}(AB + CD)$ **Hence proved.**

Example 5. *ABCD* is a kite with $AB = AD$ and $CD = CB$. Prove that the figure formed by joining the mid-points of the consecutive sides is a rectangle.

Sol. Let *P*, *Q*, *R* and *S* be the mid-points of the sides *AB*, *BC*, *CD* and *DA*, respectively. Join *AC* and *BD* which intersects each other at *O*.

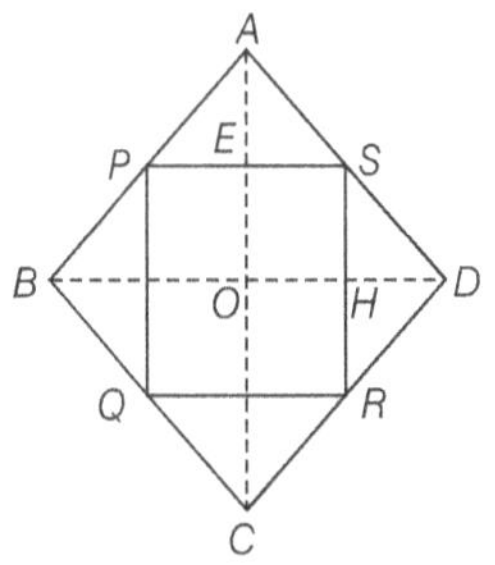

Now, in ΔABC,

$\because$ *P* and *Q* are the mid-points of *AB* and *BC*.

$\therefore$ $PQ \parallel AC$ and $PQ = \frac{1}{2} AC$ [by mid-point theorem] ...(i)

and in ΔACD,

$\because$ *R* and *S* are the mid-points of *CD* and *DA*.

$\therefore$ $RS \parallel AC$ and $RS = \frac{1}{2} AC$ [by mid-point theorem] ...(ii)

From Eqs. (i) and (ii), we get $PQ \parallel RS$ and $PQ = RS$

Since, a pair of opposite sides are equal and parallel

So, *PQRS* is a parallelogram.

Also, $AB = AD$ [given]

So, *A* lies on the perpendicular bisector of *BD*. ...(iii)

Further, $CB = CD$ [given]

So, *C* lies on the perpendicular bisector of *BD*. ...(iv)

From Eqs. (iii) and (iv), *AC* is the perpendicular bisector of *BD*.

i.e. $AC \perp BD$

$\Rightarrow$ $\angle AOD = 90°$

Clearly, $HS \parallel OE$ and $SE \parallel OH$.

So, *SEOH* is a parallelogram.

Hence, $\angle ESH = \angle EOH = 90°$

[$\because$ opposite angles of a parallelogram are equal]

So, parallelogram *PQRS* is a rectangle as each angle is 90°.

Hence proved

Example 6. *ABCD* is a trapezium in which $AB \parallel DC$ and $AD = BC$. If *P*, *Q*, *R* and *S* be respectively, the mid-points of *BA*, *BD*, *CD* and *CA*, then show that *PQRS* is a rhombus.

Sol. In ΔABC, *P* and *S* are respectively the mid-points of sides *AB* and *AC*.

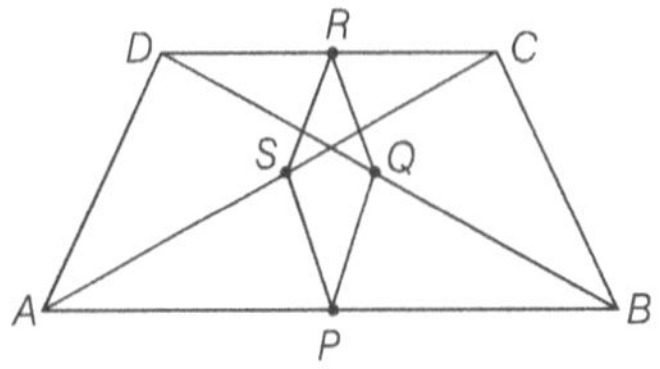

$\therefore$ $PS \parallel BC$ and $PS = \frac{1}{2} BC$

[by using mid-point theorem] ...(i)

Similarly, $QR \parallel BC$ and $QR = \frac{1}{2} BC$ ...(ii)

Now, from Eqs. (i) and (ii), we get

$PS \parallel QR$

and $PS = QR$ ...(iii)

$\Rightarrow$ *PQRS* is a parallelogram.

[$\because$ one pair of opposite side are parallel and equal]

Further, in ΔACD, *S* and *R* are respectively the mid-points of *AC* and *CD*.

$\therefore$ $SR \parallel AD$

and $SR = \frac{1}{2} AD = \frac{1}{2} BC$ [$\because AD = BC$] ...(iv)

Similarly, $PQ \parallel AD$

and $PQ = \frac{1}{2} AD = \frac{1}{2} BC$ [$\because AD = BC$] ...(v)

From Eqs. (i), (ii), (iv) and (v), we get

$PS = QR = SR = PQ$

Hence, *PQRS* is a rhombus. **Hence proved**

Example 7. ABC is a triangle. D is a point on AB such that $AD = \frac{1}{4}AB$ and E is a point on AC such that $AE = \frac{1}{4}AC$. Prove that $DE = \frac{1}{4}BC$.

Sol. **Given** In ΔABC, $AD = \frac{1}{4}AB$ and $AE = \frac{1}{4}AC$

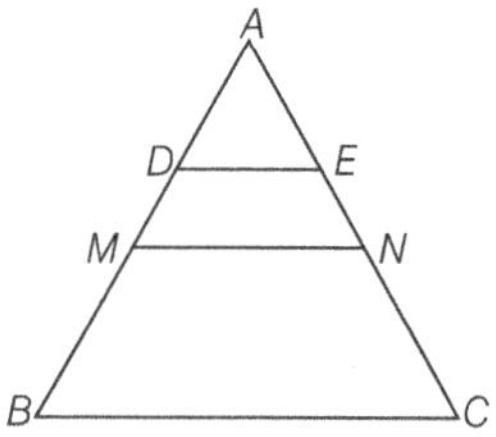

To prove $DE = \frac{1}{4}BC$

Proof Let M and N be the mid-points of sides AB and AC, respectively.

By mid-point theorem,

$$MN \parallel BC \text{ and } MN = \frac{1}{2}BC \quad \text{...(i)}$$

We have, $AM = \frac{1}{2}AB$ [$\because$ M is mid-point of AB]

$\Rightarrow$ $\frac{1}{2}AM = \frac{1}{4}AB$

$\therefore$ $\frac{1}{2}AM = AD$ [given]

So, D is mid-point of AM.

Similarly, $AN = \frac{1}{2}AC$ [$\because$ N is mid-point of AC]

$\Rightarrow$ $\frac{1}{2}AN = \frac{1}{4}AC \Rightarrow \frac{1}{2}AN = AE$ [given]

So, E is mid-point of AN.

In ΔAMN, D and E are the mid-points of AM and AN, respectively.

By mid-point theorem,

$$DE \parallel MN \text{ and } DE = \frac{1}{2}MN$$

$\Rightarrow$ $DE = \frac{1}{2}\left(\frac{1}{2}BC\right)$ [from Eq. (i)]

$\Rightarrow$ $DE = \frac{1}{4}BC$ **Hence proved**

Example 8. In the following figure, AD is a median of ΔABC and E is the mid-point of AD. Also, BE produced meets AC at F. Prove that $AF = \frac{1}{3}AC$.

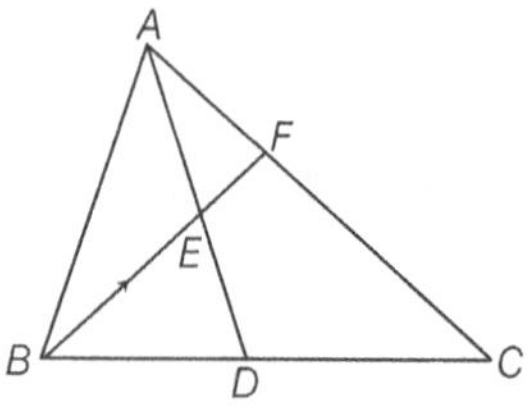

Sol. **Given** In ΔABC, AD is a median and E is mid-point of AD.

To prove $AF = \frac{1}{3}AC$

Construction Draw $DP \parallel BF$, which intersect AC at P.

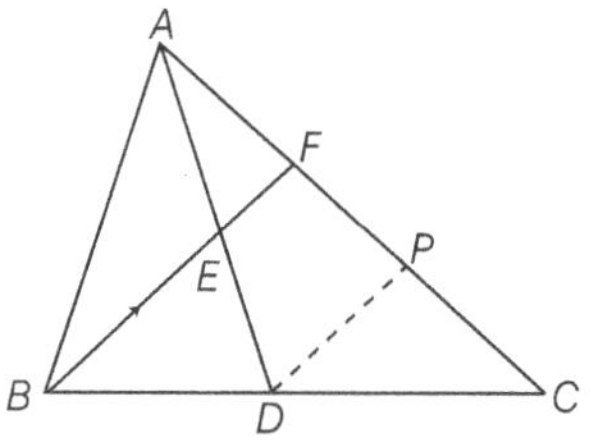

Proof In ΔADP, E is the mid-point of AD and $EF \parallel DP$. [by construction]

$\therefore$ F is the mid-point of AP

$\Rightarrow$ $AF = FP$ ...(i)

[by converse of mid-point theorem]

In ΔFBC, D is the mid-point of BC and $DP \parallel BF$. [$\because$ AD is a median of ΔABC]

$\therefore$ P is the mid-point of FC

$\Rightarrow$ $FP = PC$ ...(ii)

[by converse of mid-point theorem]

From Eqs. (i) and (ii),

$$AF = FP = PC$$

Now, $AF + FP + PC = AC$

$AF + AF + AF = AC$

$3AF = AC$

$\therefore$ $AF = \left(\frac{1}{3}\right)AC$ **Hence proved**

Example 9. In the given figure, AD is a median of ΔABC, E is the mid-point of AD and $DP \parallel AC$, prove that $BE : EQ = 3 : 1$.

Sol. **Given** AD is a median of ΔABC, E is the mid-point of AD and $DP \parallel AC$.

To prove $BE : EQ = 3 : 1$

Proof In ΔBCQ, D is the mid-point of side BC and $PD \parallel CQ$.

Therefore, by converse of mid-point theorem, P is the mid-point of BQ.

i.e. $BP = PQ$ ...(i)

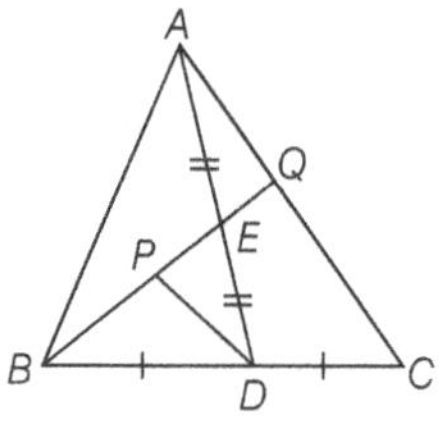

In ΔAEQ and ΔDEP,

$\angle AEQ = \angle DEP$ [vertically opposite angles]

$\Rightarrow$ $AE = ED$ [given]

$\Rightarrow$ $\angle AQE = \angle DPE$ [alternate angles as $PD \parallel AC$]

$\therefore$ $\Delta AEQ \cong \Delta DEP$ [by AAS congruency axiom]

$\Rightarrow \quad EQ = PE$ [CPCT]

i.e. E is the mid-point of PQ.

or $\quad EQ = \frac{1}{2}PQ$ ...(ii)

and $\quad PE = \frac{1}{2}PQ$ ...(iii)

On adding Eqs. (i) and (iii), we get

$$BP + PE = PQ + \frac{1}{2}PQ$$

$\Rightarrow \quad BE = \frac{3}{2}PQ = \frac{3}{2} \times 2EQ$ [$\because PQ = 2EQ$]

$\Rightarrow \quad BE = 3EQ$

$\Rightarrow \quad \frac{BE}{EQ} = \frac{3}{1} \Rightarrow BE : EQ = 3:1$

Example 10. In the given figure, $ABCD$ is a parallelogram and E, F are the mid-points of the sides AB, CD respectively. Show that the line segments AF and EC trisect the diagonal BD.

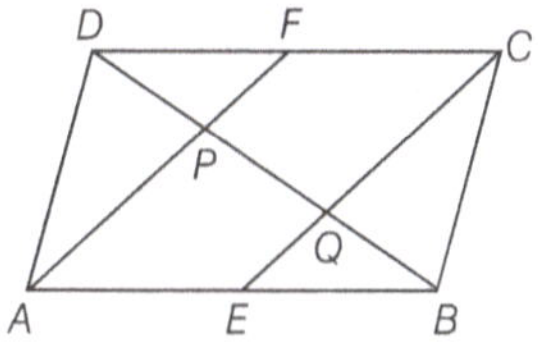

Sol. As, $ABCD$ is a parallelogram, $AB \parallel DC$

$\Rightarrow \quad AE \parallel FC$

Also, $\quad AB = DC$

[$\because$ opposite sides of a parallelogram are equal]

$\Rightarrow \quad \frac{1}{2}AB = \frac{1}{2}DC$

$\Rightarrow \quad AE = FC$ [given]

Thus, in the quadrilateral $AECF$, $AE = FC$ and $AE \parallel FC$

$\Rightarrow$ $AECF$ is a parallelogram

$\Rightarrow \quad AF \parallel EC$

In ΔDQC, $\quad PF \parallel QC$ [$\because AF \parallel EC$, proved above]

and F is mid-point of CD. [given]

$\therefore$ P is mid-point of DQ.

[by converse of mid-point theorem]

$\Rightarrow \quad DP = PQ$ ...(i)

In ΔABP, $\quad EQ \parallel AP$ [$\because EC \parallel AF$, from above]

and E is mid-point of AB [given]

$\therefore$ Q is mid-point of BP.

[by converse of mid-point theorem]

$\Rightarrow \quad BQ = PQ$ ...(ii)

From Eqs. (i) and (ii), we get

$$DP = PQ = BQ$$

Hence, the line segments AF and EC trisect the diagonal BD.

Intercept

If a line l cut two lines m and n (parallel or non-parallel) at points A and B respectively, then the line-segment AB is called intercept made on line 'l' by the lines m and n.

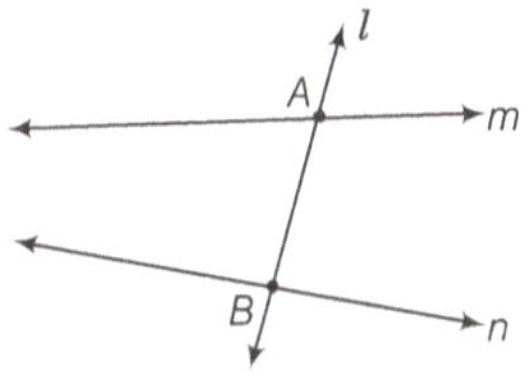

Equal Intercept Theorem

If a transversal makes equal intercepts on three (or more) parallel lines, then any other line cutting them will also makes equal intercepts.

Given $l \parallel m \parallel n$ and a transversal p cutting them at points A, B and C respectively, such that $AB = BC$. Also, any other line q cuts them at points D, E and F, respectively.

To prove $DE = EF$

Construction Join AF which cuts BE at G.

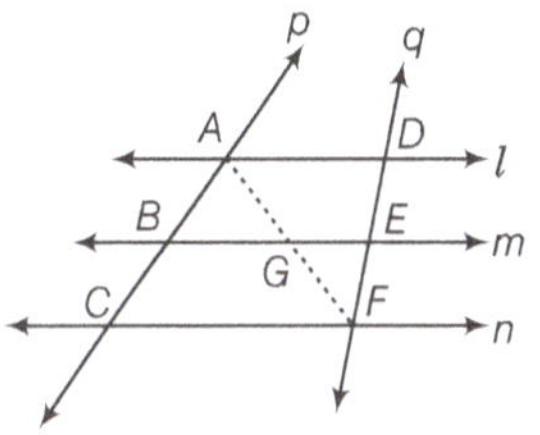

Proof In ΔACF, B is the mid-point of AC

[$\because AB = BC$, given]

and $\quad BG \parallel CF$ [$\because m \parallel n$, given]

By converse of mid-point theorem,

G is the mid-point of AF.

Now, in ΔAFD, G is the mid-point of AF.

and $\quad GE \parallel AD$ [$\because l \parallel m$, given]

By converse of mid-point theorem,

E is the mid-point of DF.

Then, $\quad DE = EF$

Hence, the line q makes equal intercept at l, m and n.

Hence proved

Example 11. In the given figure l, m and n are the three lines parallel to each other. S_1 and S_2 are transversal such that $AB = BC = 5$ cm, find PQ and QR, if $PR = 12$ cm.

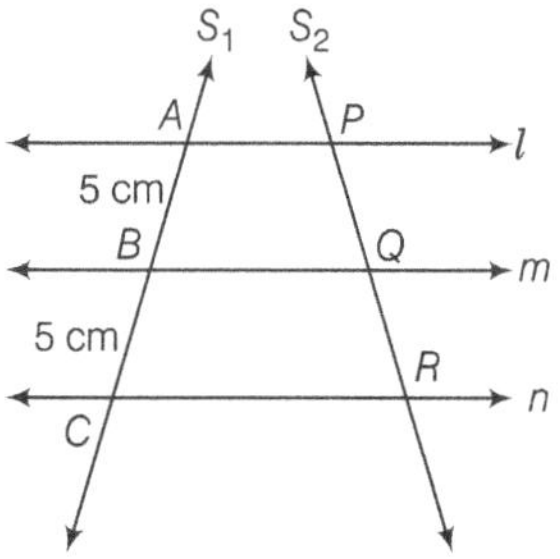

Sol. Given, $l \parallel m \parallel n$, $AB = BC = 5$ cm and $PR = 12$ cm

Since, the transversal S_1 makes equal intercepts AB and BC on parallel lines l, m and n, therefore by equal intercept theorem, we have

$$PQ = QR$$

$\because$ $PR = PQ + QR$

$\Rightarrow$ $PQ + QR = 12$

$\Rightarrow$ $2PQ = 12$ $\quad [\because PQ = QR]$

$\Rightarrow$ $PQ = 6$ cm

Hence, $PQ = QR = 6$ cm

Example 12. In the given figure, $l \parallel m \parallel n$ and $AB = BC$. If $DC = 5.6$ cm, find DG.

Sol. Given, $l \parallel m \parallel n$, $AB = BC$ and $DC = 5.6$ cm

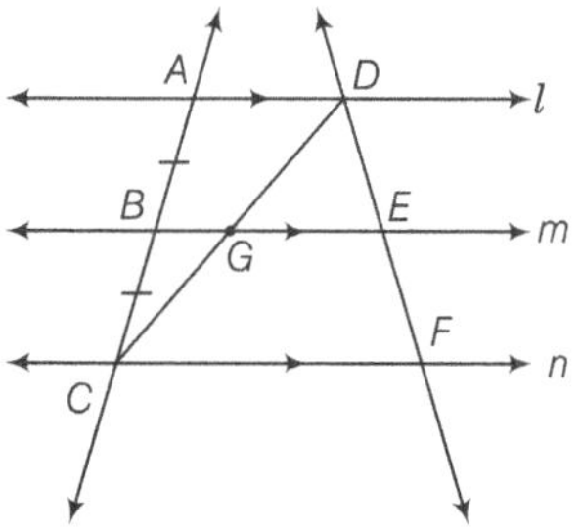

In ΔACD, B is a mid-point of AC and $BG \parallel AD$. [given]

$\therefore$ By converse of mid-point theorem, G is mid-point of CD.

$\Rightarrow$ $CG = GD$ ...(i)

Since, $CD = CG + GD$

$\Rightarrow$ $CD = GD + GD$ [from Eq. (i)]

$\Rightarrow$ $DG = \frac{1}{2}CD = \frac{1}{2} \times 5.6 = 2.8$ cm

Example 13. In the given figure, M and N divide AB into three equal parts. Line segments MP and NQ are both parallel to BC and meet AC in P and Q, respectively. Prove that P and Q divide AC into three equal parts.

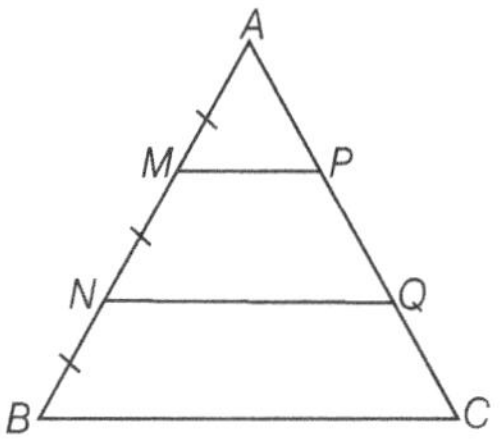

Sol. **Given** In ΔABC, $AM = MN = NB$; $MP \parallel BC$ and $NQ \parallel BC$.

To prove $AP = PQ = QC$

Construction Through A draw a line DE parallel to BC.

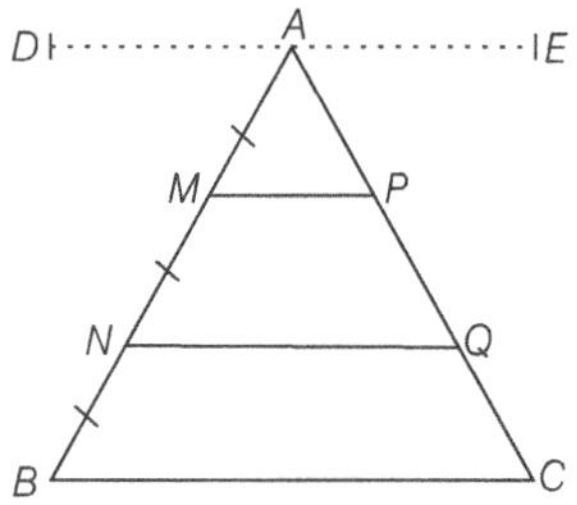

Proof Since, $DE \parallel BC$, $MP \parallel BC$ and $NQ \parallel BC$

Therefore, $DE \parallel MP \parallel NQ \parallel BC$.

Now, as the transversal AB makes equal intercepts AM, MN and NB on parallel lines DE, MP, NQ and BC into three equal parts. Therefore, by equal intercept theorem, transversal AC also makes equal intercepts on these parallel lines.

Hence, $AP = PQ = QC$.

Example 14. In the given figure, $ABCD$ is a parallelogram. E and F are the mid-points of sides AB and CD, respectively. PQ is any line that meets AD, EF and BC in points P, O and Q, respectively. Prove that $PO = OQ$.

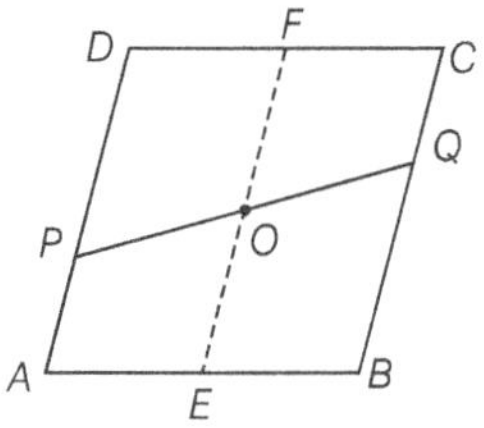

Sol. **Given** $ABCD$ is a parallelogram. E and F are the mid-points of AB and CD, respectively.

To prove $PO = OQ$

Proof Since, E and F are the mid-points of AB and CD, respectively

$\therefore$ $AE = \frac{1}{2}AB$ ...(i)

and $DF = \frac{1}{2}CD$ ...(ii)

Also, we know that opposite sides of parallelogram are equal,

$\therefore$ $AB = CD$ ...(iii)

Now, from Eqs. (i), (ii) and (iii), we get

$$AE = DF$$

Also, $AE \parallel DF$ [$\because AB \parallel CD$]

$\Rightarrow$ $AEFD$ is a parallelogram.

[$\because$ if a pair of opposite sides of a quadrilateral are parallel and equal, then the quadrilateral is a parallelogram]

$\Rightarrow$ $AD \parallel EF$

Also, $AD \parallel BC$ [$\because ABCD$ is a parallelogram]

$\therefore$ $AD \parallel BC \parallel EF$

Now, E is the mid-point of AB.

$\therefore$ $AE = EB$

By equal intercept theorem, we can say that PQ also makes equal intercepts on these parallel lines,

i.e. $PO = OQ$ **Hence proved**

Exercise 9.1

1. In ΔPQR, S and T are mid-points of the sides PQ and PR, respectively. If $QR = 6$ cm and $\angle Q = 60°$. Find (i) ST (ii) $\angle PST$.

2. In the given figure, X and Y are the mid-points of AB and AC, respectively. Given that $BC = 6$ cm, $AB = 5.4$ cm and $AC = 5.0$ cm, calculate the perimeter of trapezium $YXBC$.

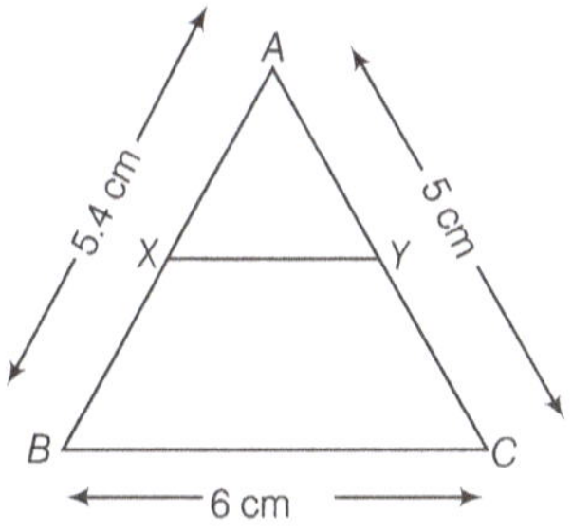

3. In ΔABC, D, E and F are the mid-points of sides AB, BC and AC, respectively. Then, prove that quadrilateral $DECF$ is a parallelogram.

4. In ΔABC, M is mid-point of AB and a straight line through M and parallel to BC cuts AC at N. Find the lengths of AN and MN, if $BC = 7$ cm and $AC = 5$ cm.

5. In the given figure, AD and CE are medians and $DF \parallel CE$. Prove that $FB = \frac{1}{4} AB$.

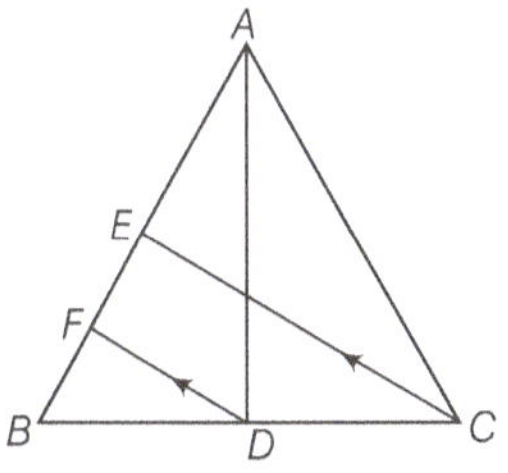

6. $ABCD$ is a trapezium in which $AB \parallel DC$, BD is a diagonal and E is the mid-point of AD. A line is drawn through E parallel to AB intersecting BC at F (see the figure). Show that F is the mid-point of BC.

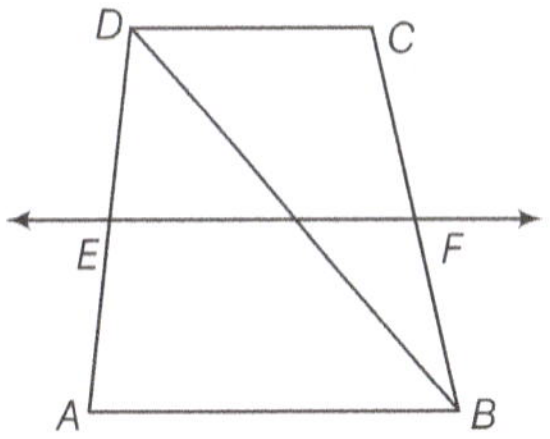

7. In the given figure D, E and F are the mid-points of BC, CA and AB, respectively. P, Q and R are the mid-points of EF, FD and DE, respectively. If $AB = 4$ cm, $BC = 7$ cm and $CA = 6$ cm. Find the sides of ΔPQR.

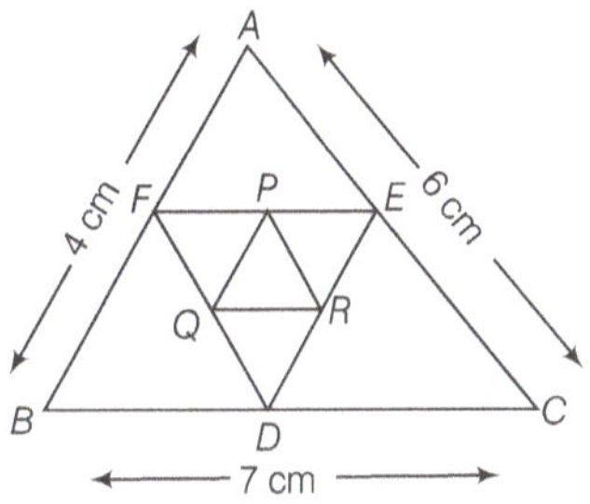

8. In an isosceles ΔABC, $AB = C$ and D, E, F are the mid-points of the edges BC, CA, AB, respectively. Prove that EF and AD bisect each other at right angles.

9. Prove that the line joining the mid-points of the diagonals of a trapezium is parallel to the parallel sides of the trapezium and is equal to half the difference of these sides.

10. Show that the line segments joining the mid-points of the opposite sides of a quadrilateral bisect each other.

11. Prove that the figure obtained by joining the mid-points of the adjacent sides of a quadrilateral is a parallelogram.

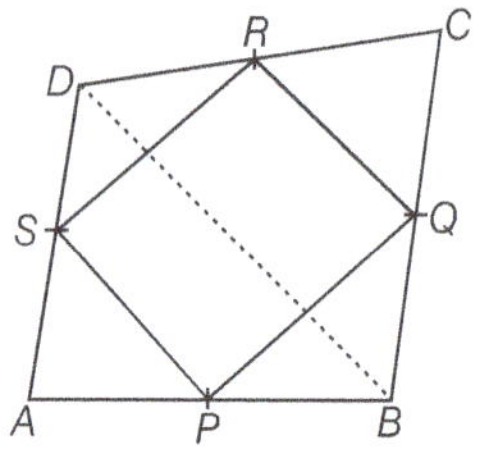

12. In ΔABC, the medians BE and CF are produced to points P and Q respectively such that $EP = BE$ and $FQ = CF$. Prove that

(i) Q, A and P are collinear

(ii) A is mid-point of QP.

13. Show that the quadrilateral formed by joining the mid-points of the adjacent sides of a square is also a square.

14. $ABCD$ is a quadrilateral in which P, Q, R and S are mid-points of the sides AB, BC, CD and DA, respectively AC is a diagonal.

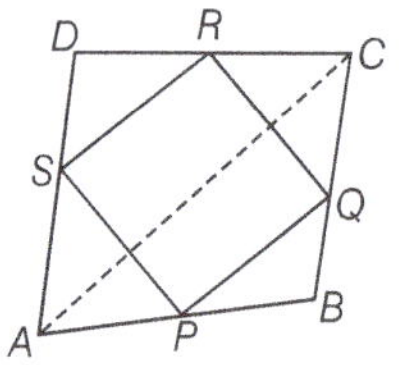

Show that

(i) $SR \parallel AC$ and $SR = \frac{1}{2} AC$.

(ii) $PQ = SR$.

(iii) $PQRS$ is a parallelogram.

15. In a right-angled ΔABC, $\angle ABC = 90°$ and D is mid-point of AC. Prove that $BD = \frac{1}{2} AC$.

16. In the given figure, $MN \parallel KL \parallel GH$ and $AB = BC$. If $DE = 3.2$ cm, find DF.

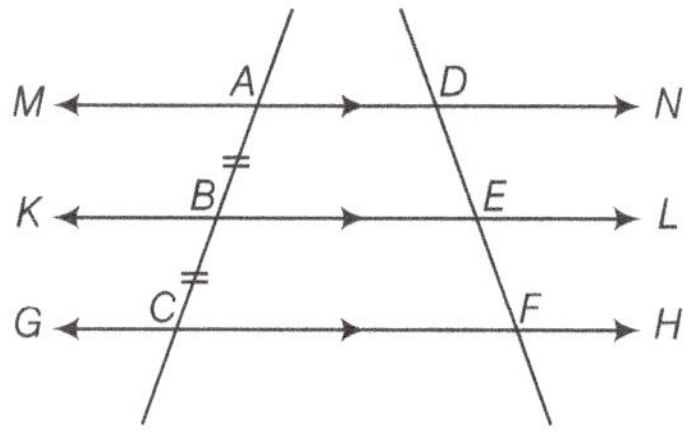

17. In ΔXYZ, D is mid-point of XY and E is mid-point of YZ.

Calculate

(i) DE, if $XZ = 6$ cm (ii) $\angle DEY$, if $\angle XZY = 60°$

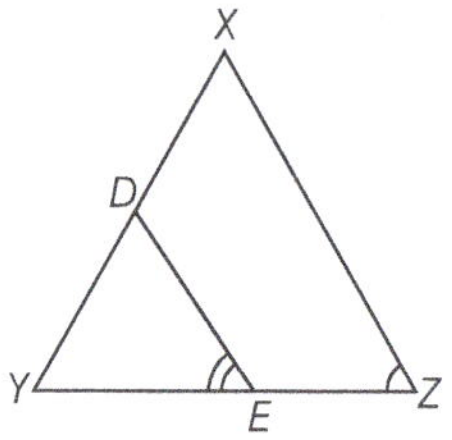

18. In the given figure, $XYZT$ is a parallelogram. Points E and F are the mid-points of sides XY and ZT, respectively. The straight lines XF and YF meet the straight lines ET and EZ in points G and H, respectively.

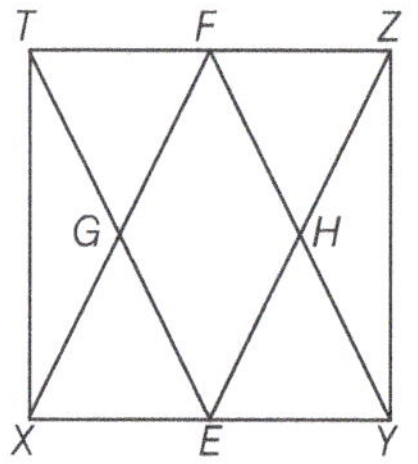

Prove that

(i) $\Delta HEY \cong \Delta FHZ$ (ii) $GEHF$ is a parallelogram

Pythagoras Theorem (Area Based Proof)

In a right angled triangle, the square on the hypotenuse is equal to the sum of the squares on the remaining two sides.

Given A ΔABC is a right angled triangle, right angled at B.

To prove $AC^2 = AB^2 + BC^2$

Construction Draw squares $ABFG$, $BCHI$ and $ACDE$ on sides AB, BC and AC, respectively. Draw line $BN \perp DE$ which intersect AC at M, DE at N. Join GC and BE.

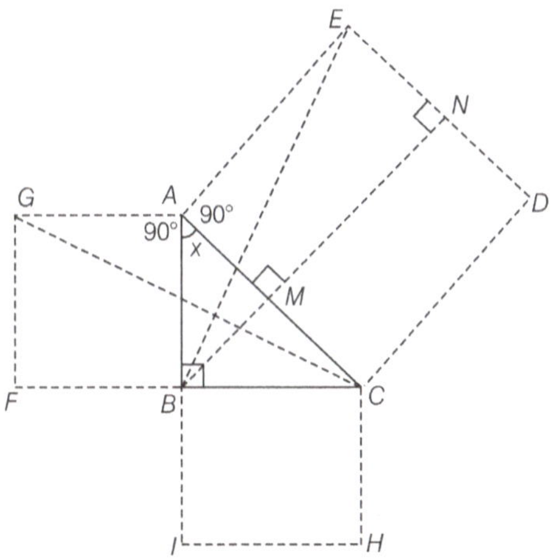

Proof $\angle FBC = \angle FBA + \angle ABC = 90° + 90° = 180°$

Hence, FBC is a straight line.

Since, GA and FB are opposite sides of a square.

$\therefore \quad GA \parallel FB \Rightarrow GA \parallel FC$

Since, $BN \perp AC$ and $AE \perp AC \Rightarrow AE \parallel BN$

As each angle of quadrilateral $AMNE$ is 90°.

$\Rightarrow$ $AMNE$ is a rectangle.

Now, let $\angle BAC = x°$

In ΔGAC and ΔBAE,

$AG = AB$ [sides of square]

$\angle GAC = \angle BAE = 90° + x°$

and $AC = AE$ [sides of square]

$\therefore \quad \Delta GAC \cong \Delta BAE$ [by SAS congruence rule]

$\therefore \quad$ ar (ΔGAC) = ar (ΔBAE) ...(i)

[congruent figures are equal in area]

Now, ar $(\Delta GAC) = \frac{1}{2} \times$ area of square $ABFG$ ...(ii)

[$\because$ ΔGAC and square $ABFG$ are on same base AG and between the same parallel lines AG and CF, so area of triangle is half of the area of square parallelogram]

Similarly, ar $(\Delta BAE) = \frac{1}{2}$ area of rectangle $AMNE$ ...(iii)

From Eqs. (i), (ii) and (iii), we get

area of square $ABFG$ = area of rectangle $AMNE$ ...(iv)

Similarly, area of square $BCHI$

= area of rectangle $CMND$ ...(v)

On adding Eqs. (iv) and (v), we get

area of square $ABFG$ + area of square $BCHI$

= area of rectangle $AMNE$ + area of rectangle $CMND$

$\Rightarrow$ area of square $ABFG$ + area of square $BCHI$

= area of square $ACDE$

$\Rightarrow$ square on AB + square on BC = square on AC

$\Rightarrow \quad AB^2 + BC^2 = AC^2 \Rightarrow AC^2 = AB^2 + BC^2$

Alternate Proof of Pythagoras Theorem

In a right-angled triangle, the square on the hypotenuse is equal to the sum of the squares on the remaining two sides.

Given A ΔABC in which $\angle ABC = 90°$

To prove $AC^2 = AB^2 + BC^2$

Construction Draw $BD \perp AC$

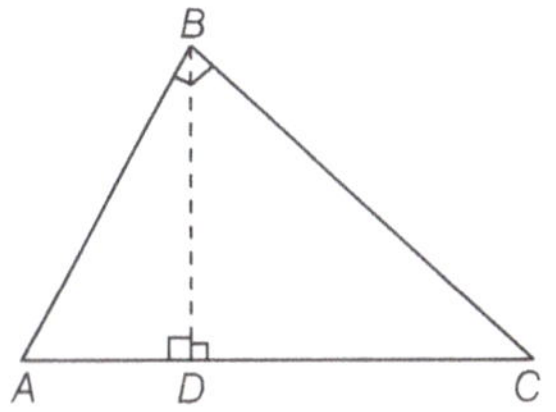

Proof In ΔABC and ΔBDC,

(i) $\angle ABC = \angle BDC = 90°$

(ii) $\angle BCA = \angle BCD$ [common]

$\therefore \Delta ABC \sim \Delta BDC$ [AA similarity]

$\Rightarrow \quad \frac{BC}{DC} = \frac{AC}{BC} \Rightarrow BC^2 = AC \times DC$ ...(i)

Now, in ΔABC and ΔADB,

(i) $\angle ABC = \angle ADB = 90°$

(ii) $\angle BAC = \angle BAD$ [common]

$\therefore \Delta ABC \sim \Delta ADB$ [AA similarity]

$\Rightarrow \quad \frac{AB}{AD} = \frac{AC}{AB}$

$\Rightarrow \quad AB^2 = AC \times AD$ ...(ii)

Adding Eqs. (i) and (ii), we get

$$AB^2 + BC^2 = AC \times AD + AC \times DC$$

$$\Rightarrow AB^2 + BC^2 = AC(AD + DC) = AC \times AC = AC^2$$

Converse of Pythagoras Theorem

In ΔABC, if BC is the largest side and $BC^2 = AB^2 + AC^2$, then $\angle A = 90°$.

Given In a ΔABC, $BC^2 = AB^2 + AC^2$

To prove $\angle A = 90°$

Construction Construct an another ΔPQR such that $\angle P = 90°$, $PQ = AB$ and $PR = AC$.

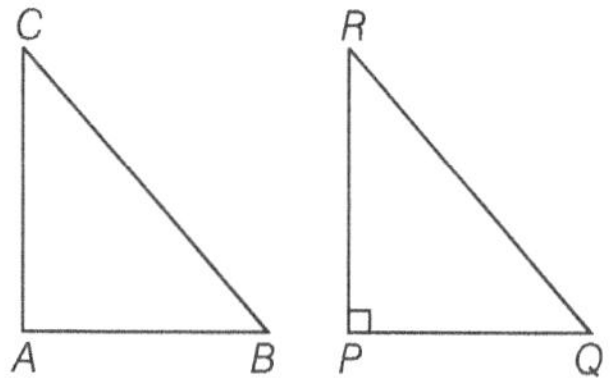

Proof In ΔPQR

By Pythagoras theorem,

$QR^2 = PQ^2 + PR^2$

$\Rightarrow QR^2 = AB^2 + AC^2$ [by construction]

But $BC^2 = AB^2 + AC^2$ [given]

$\therefore QR^2 = BC^2 \Rightarrow QR = BC$

In ΔABC and ΔPQR,

$AB = PQ$ [by construction]

$AC = PR$ [by construction]

and $BC = QR$ [proved above]

$\therefore \Delta ABC \cong \Delta PQR$ [by SSS of congruence rule]

$\Rightarrow \angle A = \angle P$ [by CPCT]

$\Rightarrow \angle A = 90°$

Example 15. A ladder 17 m long, reaches a window of a building 15 m above the ground. Find the distance of the foot of the ladder from the building.

Sol. Let AC be the ladder and AB be the building. Then, we need to find BC.

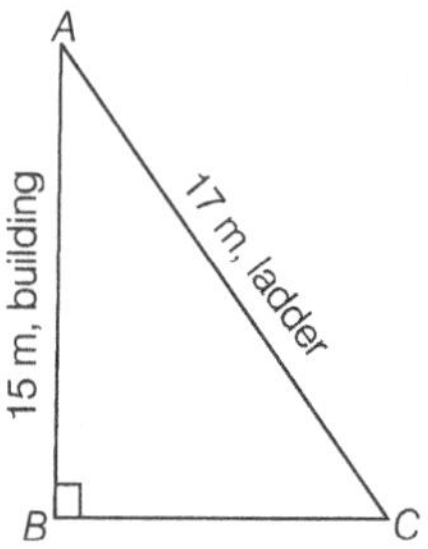

Now, in ΔABC, $AB^2 + BC^2 = AC^2$ [by Pythagoras theorem]

$\Rightarrow 15^2 + BC^2 = 17^2$ [$\because AB = 15$ m, $AC = 17$ m]

$\Rightarrow 225 + BC^2 = 289 \Rightarrow BC^2 = 289 - 225$

$\Rightarrow BC^2 = 64 \Rightarrow BC = 8$ m

Hence, distance of the foot of the ladder from building is 8 m.

Example 16. ΔABC is an isosceles triangle, right angled at C. Prove that $AB^2 = 2AC^2$.

Sol. Draw an isosceles ΔABC, which makes right angle at C and $AC = BC$.

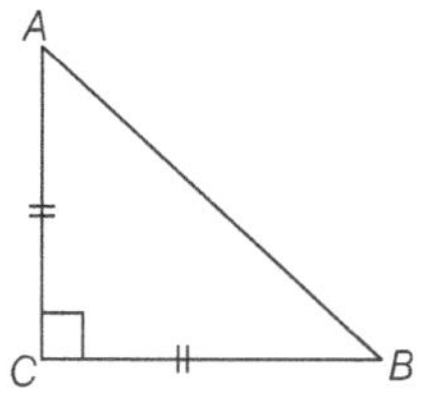

By Pythagoras theorem, we have

$AB^2 = AC^2 + BC^2 = AC^2 + AC^2$ [$\because BC = AC$, given]

$\therefore AB^2 = 2AC^2$ **Hence proved**

Example 17. ΔABC is an equilateral triangle of side $2a$. Find its altitudes.

Sol. Draw an equilateral ΔABC having each side as $2a$. Also, draw $AD \perp BC$, where AD is an altitude.

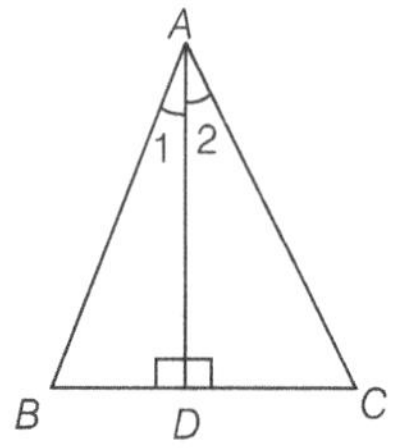

In ΔADB and ΔADC,

$AD = AD$ [common side]

$AB = AC$ [sides of an equilateral triangle]

and $\angle ADB = \angle ADC$ [each 90°]

$\therefore \Delta ADB \cong \Delta ADC$ [by RHS congruency rule]

Then, $BD = CD = \frac{1}{2} BC = a$ [by CPCT]

In ΔADB, using Pythagoras theorem, we get

$AB^2 = AD^2 + BD^2$

$\Rightarrow (2a)^2 = AD^2 + a^2$

$\Rightarrow 4a^2 = AD^2 + a^2 \Rightarrow AD^2 = 3a^2$

$\therefore AD = \sqrt{3}a$

Hence, the altitude of ΔABC is $\sqrt{3}a$ units

Example 18. Prove that the sum of the squares of the sides of a rhombus is equal to the sum of the squares of its diagonals.

Sol. Suppose $ABCD$ is a rhombus in which

$$AB = BC = CD = DA = a \text{ (say)}$$

Here, the diagonals AC and BD are right angle bisectors of each other at O.

In ΔAOB, $\angle AOB = 90°$

$$OA = \frac{1}{2}AC \quad [\because OA = OC] \quad ...(i)$$

and $$OB = \frac{1}{2}BD \quad [\because OB = OD] \quad ...(ii)$$

By using Pythagoras theorem, we get

$$OA^2 + OB^2 = AB^2$$

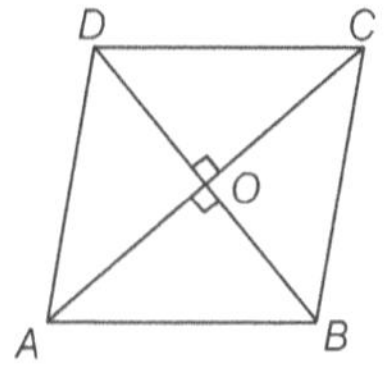

$$\Rightarrow \left(\frac{1}{2}AC\right)^2 + \left(\frac{1}{2}BD\right)^2 = AB^2 \quad \text{[from Eqs. (i) and (ii)]}$$

$$\Rightarrow AC^2 + BD^2 = 4AB^2$$

$$\Rightarrow AB^2 + BC^2 + CD^2 + DA^2 = AC^2 + BD^2$$

$[\because AB = BC = CD = DA]$

Hence proved

Example 19. In an equilateral triangle, prove that three times the square of one side is equal to four times the square of one of its altitudes.

Sol. Let ΔABC be an equilateral triangle of side a.

Draw $AD \perp BC$. Again, let $AD = x$ is an altitude.

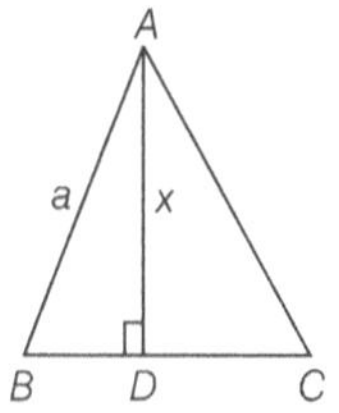

Now, $BD = CD$

[$\because$ in an equilateral triangle, altitude AD is perpendicular bisector of base BC]

$$= \frac{1}{2}BC = \frac{1}{2}a$$

[$\because$ each side of an equilateral triangle is a]

In right angled ΔADB, using Pythagoras theorem, we get

$$AB^2 = AD^2 + BD^2$$

$$\Rightarrow a^2 = x^2 + \left(\frac{1}{2}a\right)^2$$

$$\Rightarrow a^2 = x^2 + \frac{1}{4}a^2$$

$$\Rightarrow 4a^2 = 4x^2 + a^2$$

$$\therefore 3a^2 = 4x^2$$

Thus, we have three times the square of one side (a) is equal to four times the square of one of its altitudes.

Hence proved

Example 20. Two poles of heights 6 m and 11 m stand on a plane ground. If the distance between the feet of the poles is 12 m, then find the distance between their tops.

Sol. Let x be the distance between tops of the poles. i.e. $DC = x$ m

Given $BC = 11$ m, $AD = 6$ m

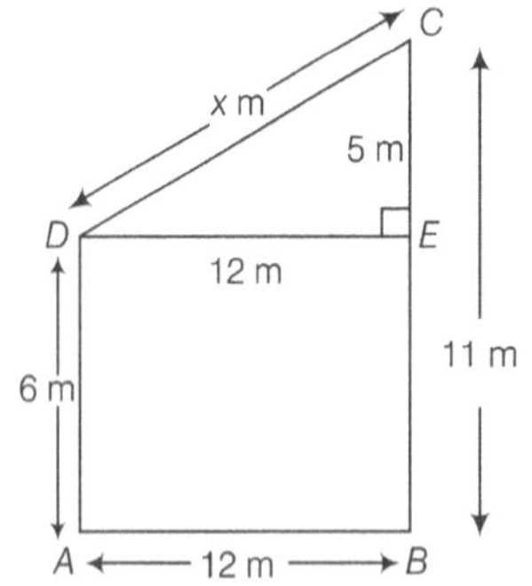

Then, $CE = BC - AD = 11 - 6 = 5$ m $\quad [\because AD = BE]$

Also, $AB = 12$ m

In ΔDEC, using Pythagoras theorem, we get

$$DC^2 = DE^2 + CE^2$$

$$\Rightarrow x^2 = 12^2 + 5^2$$

$$= 144 + 25 = 169$$

$$\therefore x = \sqrt{169} = 13 \quad \text{[taking positive square root]}$$

Hence, the distance between the tops of the poles is 13 m.

Example 21. Suppose D and E are points on the sides CA and CB, respectively of ΔABC right angled at C. Prove that $AE^2 + BD^2 = AB^2 + DE^2$.

Sol. Consider a right angled ΔABC, right angled at C. D and E are two points on sides CA and CB. Join ED, BD and EA.

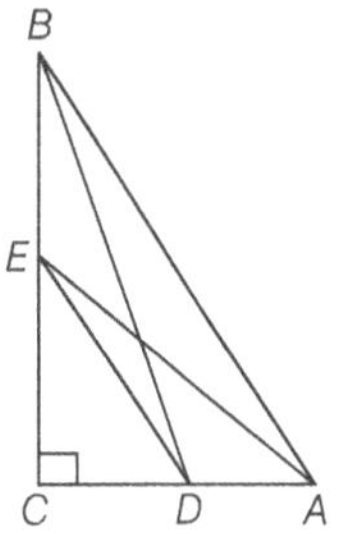

By using Pythagoras theorem

In ΔACE,

$$AE^2 = CA^2 + CE^2 \quad ...(i)$$

In ΔBCD,

$$BD^2 = BC^2 + CD^2 \quad ...(ii)$$

In ΔECD, we get

$$CD^2 + CE^2 = DE^2 \quad ...(iii)$$

and in ΔACB, we get

$$CA^2 + CB^2 = BA^2 \quad ...(iv)$$

On adding Eqs. (i) and (ii), we get

$$AE^2 + BD^2 = (CA^2 + CE^2) + (BC^2 + CD^2)$$
$$= (BC^2 + CA^2) + (CD^2 + CE^2)$$
$$\Rightarrow \quad AE^2 + BD^2 = BA^2 + DE^2 \quad \text{[from Eqs. (iii) and (iv)]}$$

Hence proved

Example 22. In the given figure, ABC is a triangle in which $\angle ABC > 90°$ and $AD \perp CB$ produced. Prove that $AC^2 = AB^2 + BC^2 + 2BC \cdot BD$.

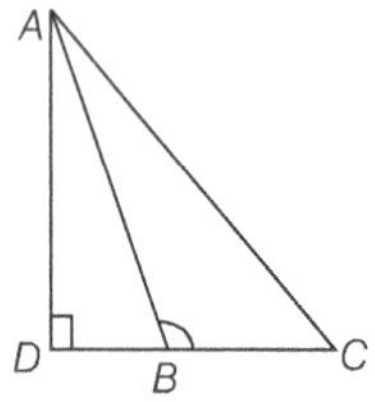

Sol. **Given** In figure, ABC is a triangle in which $\angle ABC > 90°$ and $AD \perp CB$ produced.

To prove $AC^2 = AB^2 + BC^2 + 2BC \cdot BD$

Proof In right angled ΔADC, $\angle D = 90°$

$$\therefore \quad AC^2 = AD^2 + DC^2 \quad \text{[by Pythagoras theorem]}$$
$$= AD^2 + (BD + BC)^2 \quad [\because DC = DB + BC]$$
$$= (AD^2 + BD^2) + BC^2 + 2BD \cdot BC$$
$$[\because (a+b)^2 = a^2 + b^2 + 2ab]$$
$$\Rightarrow \quad AC^2 = AB^2 + BC^2 + 2BC \cdot BD$$
$$[\because \text{in right angled } \Delta ADB,\ AB^2 = AD^2 + DB^2]$$

Hence proved

Example 23. In an equilateral ΔABC, D is a point on side BC, such that $BD : DC = 2 : 1$. Prove that $9AD^2 = 7AB^2$.

Sol. **Given** A equilateral ΔABC, where D is a point on BC such that $BD : DC = 2 : 1$.

To prove $9\,AD^2 = 7\,AB^2$

Construction Draw $AE \perp BC$

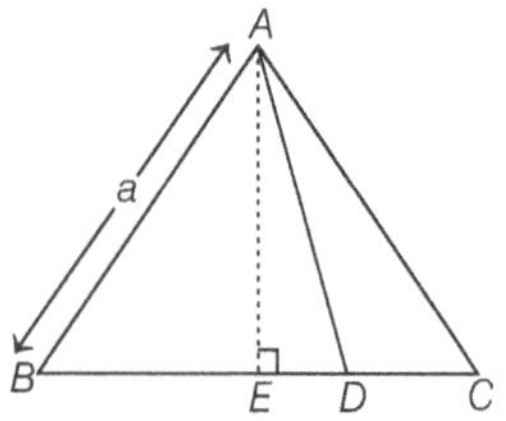

Proof Since, ABC is an equilateral triangle.

$$\therefore \quad AB = BC = CA = a \text{ (say)} \quad \text{...(i)}$$

Also, as $BD : DC = 2 : 1$, therefore

$$BD = \frac{2}{3}BC = \frac{2}{3}a \quad \text{...(ii)}$$

Now, since $AE \perp BC$

$$\therefore \quad BE = EC = \frac{1}{2}a$$

[in an equilateral triangle, altitude is a perpendicular bisector]

$$\Rightarrow \quad DE = BD - BE$$
$$= \frac{2}{3}a - \frac{1}{2}a = \left(\frac{4-3}{6}\right)a = \frac{1}{6}a \quad \text{...(iii)}$$

Now, from ΔAED, we have

$$AD^2 = AE^2 + ED^2 \quad \text{[using Pythagoras theorem]}$$
$$\Rightarrow \quad AD^2 = AB^2 - BE^2 + ED^2$$
$$[\text{in } \Delta ABE,\ AB^2 = BE^2 + AE^2]$$
$$AD^2 = a^2 - \left(\frac{1}{2}a\right)^2 + \left(\frac{1}{6}a\right)^2$$
$$\text{[using Eqs. (i), (ii) and (iii)]}$$
$$\Rightarrow \quad AD^2 = a^2 - \frac{1}{4}a^2 + \frac{1}{36}a^2$$
$$\Rightarrow \quad AD^2 = a^2\left(\frac{36-9+1}{36}\right)$$
$$= \frac{28}{36} \times a^2$$
$$\Rightarrow \quad AD^2 = \frac{7}{9} \times AB^2 \quad \text{[using Eq. (i)]}$$
$$\Rightarrow \quad 9AD^2 = 7AB^2$$

Hence proved

Example 24. Let BL and CM are medians of a ΔABC right angled at A. Prove that $4(BL^2 + CM^2) = 5BC^2$.

Sol. Since, BL and CM are medians, then lines BL and CM divides AC and AB into two equal parts.

$$\therefore \quad CL = AL = \frac{AC}{2} \quad \text{...(i)}$$

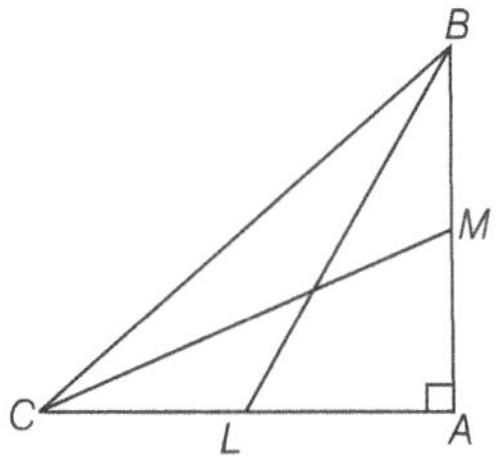

$$\text{and} \quad AM = BM = \frac{AB}{2} \quad \text{...(ii)}$$

In ΔBAC, $\angle A = 90°$

By using Pythagoras theorem, we get

$$BC^2 = AB^2 + AC^2 \quad \text{...(iii)}$$

In ΔBAL, $\angle A = 90°$

By using Pythagoras theorem, we get

$$BL^2 = AB^2 + AL^2$$
$$\Rightarrow \quad BL^2 = AB^2 + \left(\frac{AC}{2}\right)^2 \quad \text{[using Eq. (i)]}$$
$$\Rightarrow \quad BL^2 = AB^2 + \frac{AC^2}{4}$$
$$\Rightarrow \quad 4BL^2 = 4AB^2 + AC^2 \quad \text{...(iv)}$$

In ΔMAC, $\angle A = 90°$

By using Pythagoras theorem, we get

$$CM^2 = AC^2 + AM^2$$
$$\Rightarrow \quad CM^2 = AC^2 + \left(\frac{AB}{2}\right)^2 \quad \text{[using Eq. (ii)]}$$
$$\Rightarrow \quad 4CM^2 = 4AC^2 + AB^2 \quad \text{...(v)}$$

On adding Eqs. (iv) and (v), we get

$$4(BL^2 + CM^2) = 5(AC^2 + AB^2)$$

$\Rightarrow \quad 4(BL^2 + CM^2) = 5BC^2$ [using Eq. (iii)]

Hence proved

Example 25. If the sides of a triangle are 3 cm, 4 cm and 5 cm long, determine whether the triangle is a right angled triangle.

Sol. Let the sides of the triangle be $AB = 3$ cm, $BC = 4$ cm and $AC = 5$ cm.

$\therefore \quad AB^2 = 3^2 = 9, BC^2 = 4^2 = 16$

and $\quad AC^2 = 5^2 = 25$

Since, $AB^2 + BC^2 = AC^2$

Then, by converse of Pythagoras theorem, triangle is a right-angled triangle.

Example 26. In ΔPQR, $PS \perp QR$ and $PS^2 = QS \times RS$. Prove that ΔPQR is a right angled triangle.

Sol. In right angled ΔPSQ and ΔPSR, we have

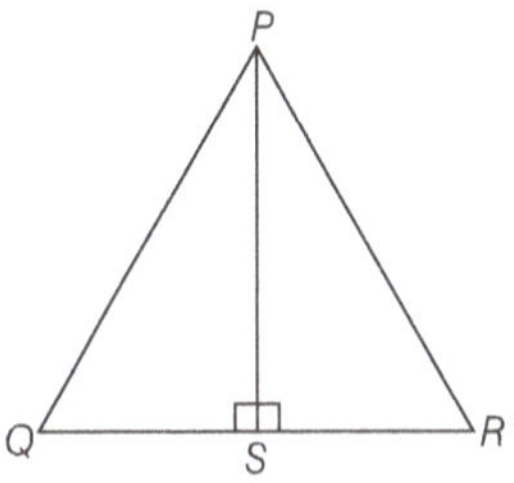

$PQ^2 = PS^2 + QS^2$ ...(i)

and $\quad PR^2 = PS^2 + SR^2$ ...(ii)

On adding Eqs. (i) and (ii), we get

$$PQ^2 + PR^2 = 2PS^2 + QS^2 + SR^2$$

$= 2(QS \times SR) + QS^2 + SR^2$ [given]

$= (QS + SR)^2$ [$\because (a + b)^2 = a^2 + b^2 + 2ab$]

$\Rightarrow \quad PQ^2 + PR^2 = QR^2$

Hence, ΔPQR is a right angled triangle, by converse of Pythagoras theorem.

Exercise 9.2

1. PQR is an equilateral triangle with each side of length $2p$ units. If $PS \perp QR$, then find the length of PS.
2. A wire attached to a vertical pole of height 18 m is 24 m long and has a stake attached to the other end. How far from the base of the pole should the stake be driven, so that the wire will be taut?
3. In the given figure, if $CD = 17$ m, $BD = 8$ m and $AD = 4$ m, then find the value of AC.

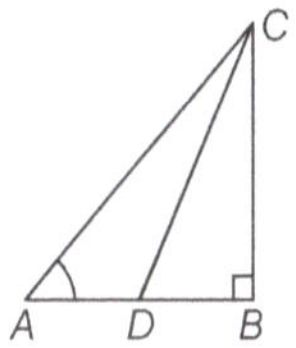

4. In the given figure, ABC is a triangle with $AB = 8$ cm, $BC = 6$ cm and $AC = 3$ cm. Find the length of OC.

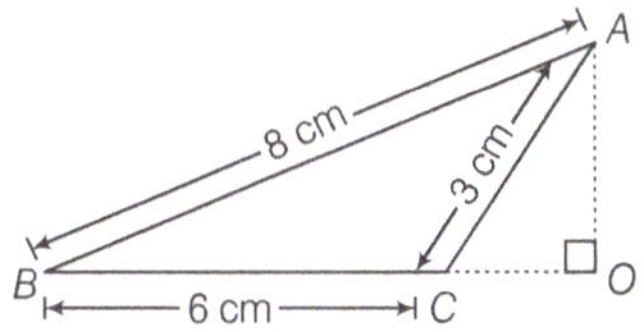

5. In ΔABC, if $AB = 6\sqrt{3}$ cm, $AC = 12$ cm and $BC = 6$ cm. Then, find $\angle B$.
6. Is the triangle with sides 13 cm, 16 cm and 18 cm a right angled triangle? Give reason.
7. A ladder 10 m long reaches a window 8 m above the ground. Find the distance of the foot of the ladder from base of the wall.
8. In the given figure, O is any point inside a rectangle $ABCD$.

   Prove that $OB^2 + OD^2 = OA^2 + OC^2$.

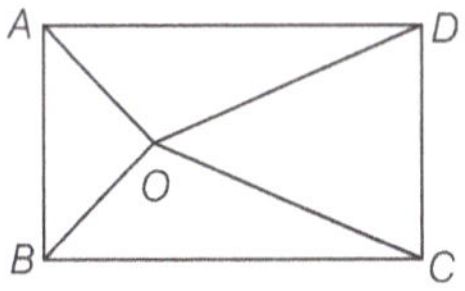

9. Two poles of height 9 cm and 14 cm stand vertically on a plane ground. If the distance between their feet is 12 cm. Find the distance between their tops.
10. In ΔABC, $\angle B = 90°$ and D is the mid-point of BC. Prove that $AC^2 = AD^2 + 3CD^2$.

11. In the given figure, ABC is a triangle in which $\angle ABC < 90°$ and $AD \perp BC$. Prove that $AC^2 = AB^2 + BC^2 - 2BC \cdot BD$.

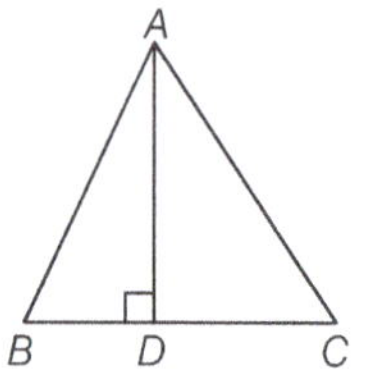

12. In the given figure,

$AE = DC = 17$ cm, $BE = 8$ cm, $\angle ABC = 90°$ and $AD = EC = x$ cm.

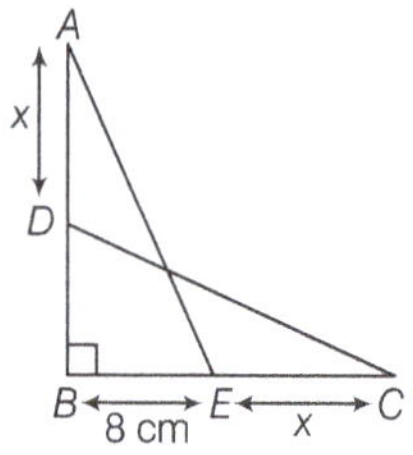

Find x.

13. In ΔABC, if $AB = AC$ and D is a point on BC.

Prove that $AB^2 - AD^2 = BD \times CD$

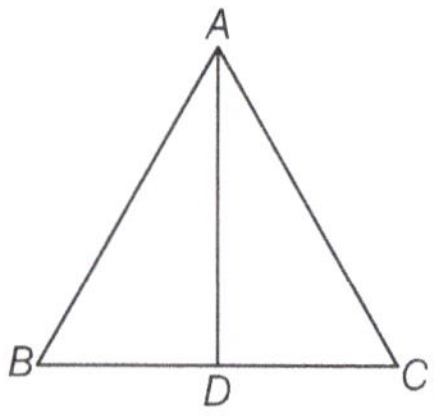

14. The perpendicular from A on side BC of a ΔABC intersects BC at D such that $DB = 3\,CD$ (see the figure).

Prove that $2AB^2 = 2AC^2 + BC^2$.

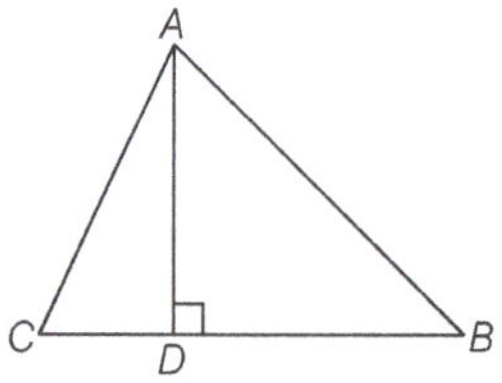

15. D and E are points on the sides CA and CB, respectively of a ΔABC right angled at C.

Prove that $AE^2 + BD^2 = AB^2 + DE^2$.

16. An aeroplane leaves an airport and flies due North at a speed of 1000 km/h. At the same time, another aeroplane leaves the same airport and flies due West at a speed of 1200 km/h.

How far apart will be the two planes after $1\frac{1}{2}$ h?

17. A ladder reaches a window which is 9 m above the ground on one side of the street. Keeping its foot at the same point, the ladder is turned to the other side of the street to reach a window 12 m high. Find the width of the street, if the ladder is of 15 m.

18. In the given figure, $3AB = 9CD = 54$ cm and $6BP = 8CP = 72$ cm. Show that the measure of $\angle APD = 90°$.

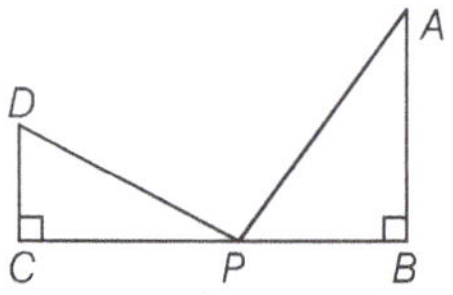

19. In a quadrilateral $XYZT$, $\angle Y = 90° = \angle T$. Prove that $2XZ^2 - YZ^2 = XY^2 + XT^2 + TZ^2$.

Chapter Practice

a. 1 Mark Questions

1. Determine which of the following is right angled triangles.
(a) 7 cm, 24 cm, 25 cm (b) 50 cm, 80 cm, 100 cm
(c) 8 cm, 40 cm, 41 cm (d) 3 cm, 5 cm, 6 cm

2. Which statement is true for the ΔABC, AD is perpendicular to BC?
(a) $AB^2 = AC^2 + BD^2$
(b) $AB^2 = CD^2 + AC^2 + BD^2$
(c) $AB^2 + AC^2 = CD^2 + BD^2$
(d) $AB^2 + CD^2 = AC^2 + BD^2$

3. Which conditions satisfy for the quadrilateral formed by joining the mid-points of the sides of a quadrilateral $PQRS$, taken in order, is a rectangle
(a) $PQRS$ is a parallelogram
(b) $PQRS$ is a rhombus
(c) the diagonals of $PQRS$ are perpendicular to each other
(d) the diagonals of $PQRS$ are equal

4. If the length of a side of rhombus is 11 cm and one of the diagonals is 18 cm, then determine the length of the other diagonal
(a) 12 cm (b) $4\sqrt{10}$ cm
(c) $6\sqrt{10}$ cm (d) 20 cm

5. Which is satisfy for a ΔABC?

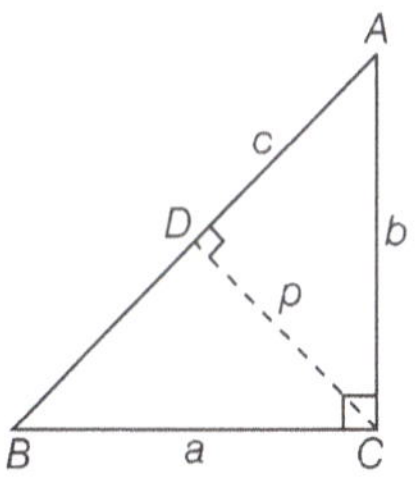

(a) $\dfrac{1}{p^2} = \dfrac{1}{a^2} + \dfrac{1}{b^2}$
(b) $\dfrac{1}{p^2} = \dfrac{1}{a^2} - \dfrac{1}{b^2}$
(c) $p^2 = a^2 + b^2$
(d) $p^2 = a^2 - b^2$

b. 3 Marks Questions

6. In ΔABC, AD is the median and E is the mid-point of AD. BE produced meets AC at F. If $AC = 9$ cm, then find the length of AF.

7. Suppose D and E are the mid-points of sides AB and AC, respectively of ΔABC. If the perimeter of $\Delta ABC = 38$ cm. Find the perimeter of ΔADE.

8. In ΔABC, $AB = 13$ cm, $BC = 16$ cm and $AC = 8$ cm. Find the perimeter of the triangle formed by joining the mid-points of the sides of the triangle.

9. Suppose D, E and F are the mid-points of sides BC, CA and AB, respectively of ΔABC. If perimeter of ΔABC is 12.8 cm, then find the perimeter of ΔDEF.

10. In the given figure, it is given that $BDEF$ and $FDCE$ are parallelograms. If $BD = 8$ cm, then determine CD.

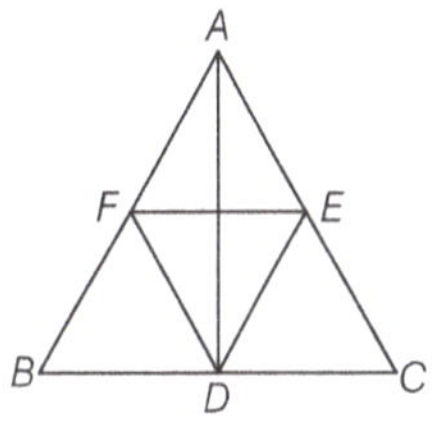

11. In the given figure, $ABCD$ is a rhombus, $AO = 4$ cm and $DO = 3$ cm. Then, find the perimeter of the rhombus.

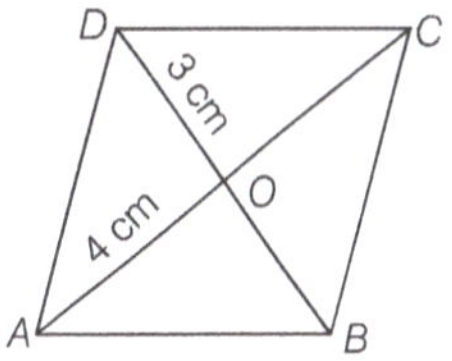

12. Use the information, given in the adjoining figure, to show that $AB = AC$.

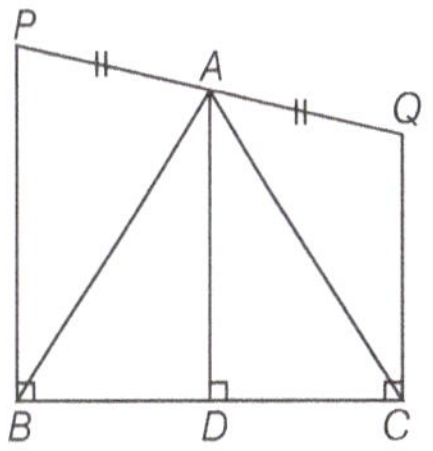

13. In ΔABC, $\angle B = 90°$. Find the sides of the triangle if $AB = (x - 3)$ cm, $BC = (x + 4)$ cm and $AC = (x + 6)$ cm.

14. A boy goes 24 m due East and 7 m due South. How far is he from the starting point?

15. Find the altitude of an equilateral ΔABC of side 8 cm.

C. 4/5 Marks Questions

16. In the given figure, O is any point inside a rectangle $ABCD$ such that $OB = 6$ cm, $OD = 8$ cm and $OA = 5$ cm. Find the length of OC.

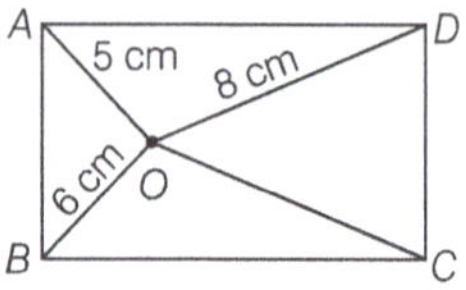

17. In a quadrilateral $ABCD$, $\angle A + \angle D = 90°$. Prove that $AC^2 + BD^2 = AD^2 + BC^2$.

18. In right angled ΔABC, right angled at C, P and Q are points of sides CA and CB respectively, which divide these sides in the ratio 2 : 1.

Prove that (i) $9AQ^2 = 9AC^2 + 4BC^2$.

(ii) $9BP^2 = 9BC^2 + 4AC^2$

19. If S is a point on side PQ of a ΔPQR such that $PS = QS = RS$, prove that $PR^2 + QR^2 = PQ^2$.

20. In the given figure, $PQRS$ is a parallelogram, L is the mid-point of sides SR and SN is drawn parallel to LQ which meets RQ produced at N and cut side PQ at M. Prove that

(i) $SN = 2LQ$. (ii) $SP = \frac{1}{2} RN$.

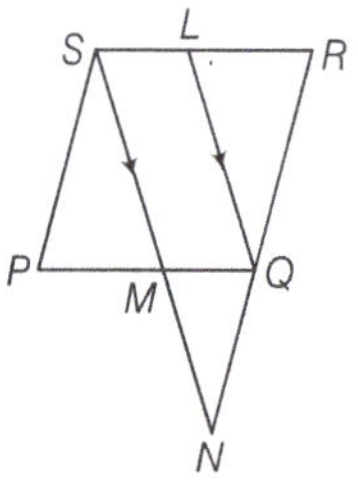

21. ΔABD is a right angled triangle, right-angled at A and $AC \perp BD$. Show that

(a) $AB^2 = BC \times BD$

(b) $AC^2 = BC \times DC$

(c) $AD^2 = BD \times CD$

22. In the given figure, ΔABC is a right angled triangle, right angled at C and D is the mid-point of BC. Prove that $AB^2 = 4AD^2 - 3AC^2$.

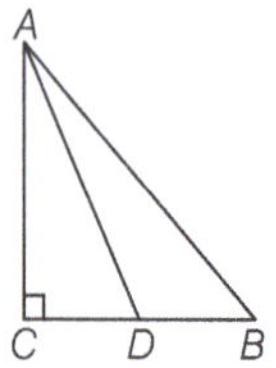

23. In ΔPQR, $PD \perp QR$ such that D lies on QR, if $PQ = a$, $PR = b$, $QD = c$ and $DR = d$, then prove that $(a + b)(a - b) = (c + d)(c - d)$.

24. ABC is an isosceles triangle in which $AB = AC = 20$ cm and $BC = 24$ cm. $PQRS$ is a rectangle drawn inside the isosceles triangle. Given, $PQ = SR = y$ cm and $PS = QR = 2x$ cm.

Prove that : $y = 16 - \frac{4x}{3}$

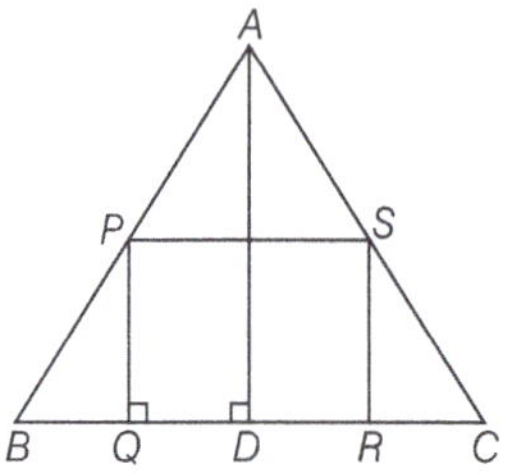

25. A 5 m long ladder is placed leaning towards a vertical wall such that it reaches the wall at a point 4 m high. If the foot of the ladder is moved 1.6 m towards the wall, then find the distance by which the top of the ladder would slide upwards on the wall.

26. From a point O in the interior of a ΔABC, perpendiculars OD, OE and OF are drawn to the sides BC, CA and AB respectively. Prove that

(i) $AF^2 + BD^2 + CE^2 = OA^2 + OB^2 + OC^2 - OD^2 - OE^2 - OF^2$

(ii) $AF^2 + BD^2 + CE^2 = AE^2 + CD^2 + BF^2$

27. Prove that the sum of the squares of the diagonals of a parallelogram is equal to the sum of squares of its sides.

28. In the given figure, OP, OQ and OR are drawn perpendiculars to the sides BC, CA and AB respectively of ΔABC. Prove that

$AR^2 + BP^2 + CQ^2 = AQ^2 + CP^2 + BR^2$

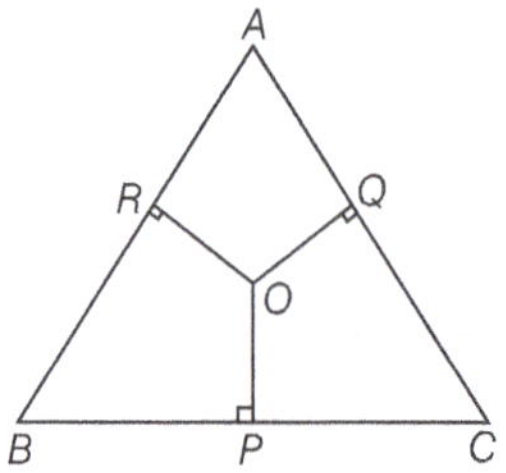

29. Use the intercept theorem to prove the converse of the mid-point theorem.

30. In the given figure, $2XD = XY$, P is mid-point of XY, Q is mid-point of DR and $PR \parallel YS$. Prove that

(i) $XQ \parallel YS$

(ii) $DS = 3RS$

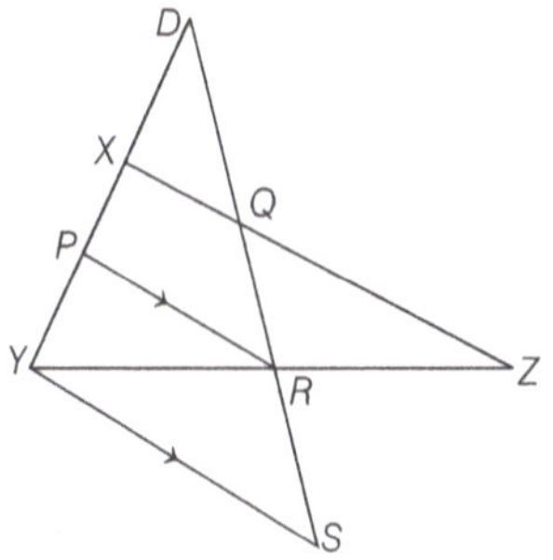

31. $ABCD$ is a rhombus, $EABF$ is a straight line such that $EA = AB = BF$. Prove that ED and FC when produced meet at right angle.

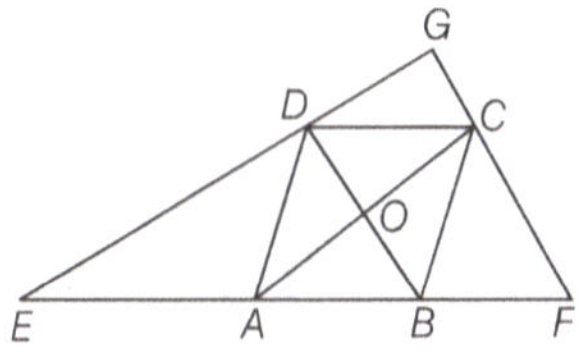

32. P, Q and R are the mid-points of the sides BC, CA and AB respectively of a ΔABC. PR and BQ meet at X, CR and PQ meet at Y.

Prove that $XY = \frac{1}{4} BC$.

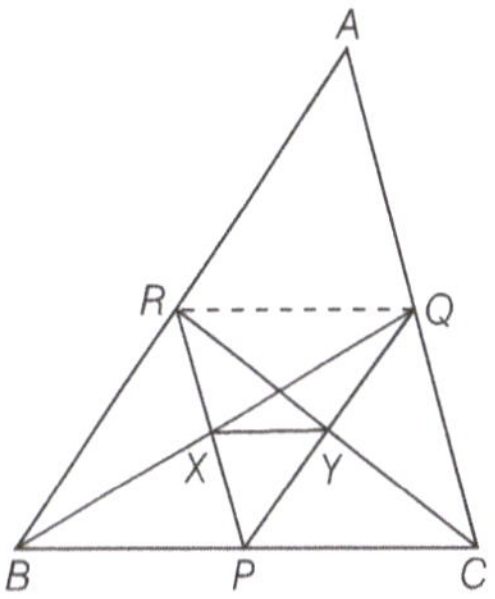

33. $ABCD$ is a rectangle and P, Q, R and S are the mid-points of the sides AB, BC, CD and DA, respectively. Show that the quadrilateral $PQRS$ is a rhombus.

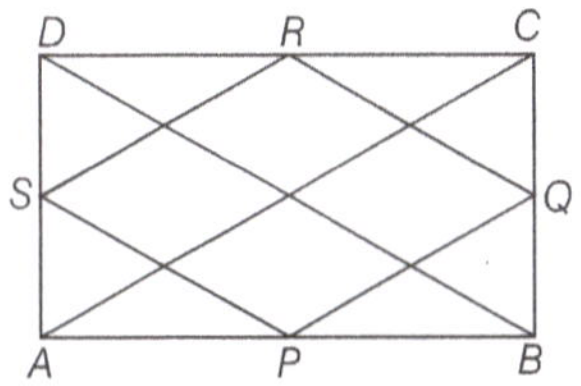

34. In the given figure D, E and F are the mid-points of the sides AB, BC and CA respectively of a ΔABC. Show that ΔABC is divided into four congruent triangles by joining the points D, E and F.

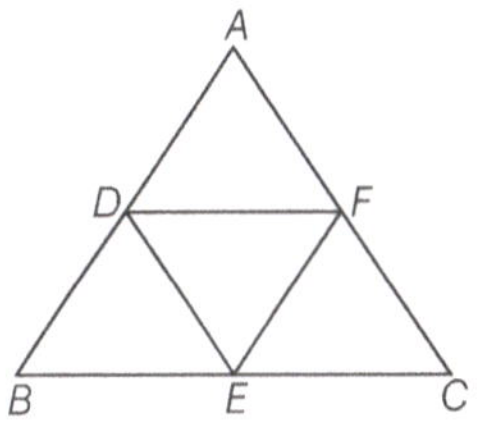

Hints and Answers

Exercise 9.1

1. (i) **Hint** S and T are the mid-points of the sides PQ and PR.

$\Rightarrow \quad ST \parallel QR$ and $ST = \frac{1}{2} QR$

[by mid-point theorem]

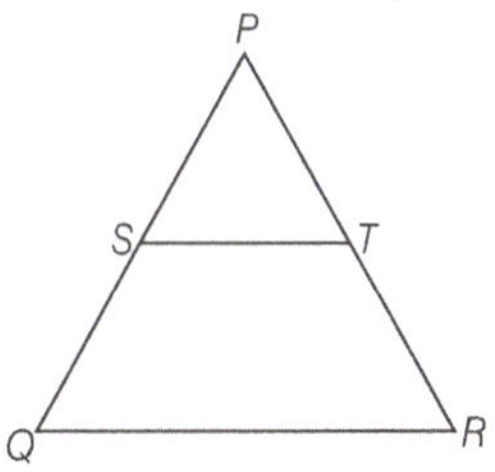

$\Rightarrow \quad ST = \frac{1}{2} \times 6$ **Ans.** 3 cm

(ii) **Hint** $ST \parallel QR$

$\Rightarrow \quad \angle PST = \angle PQR \qquad [\because \angle Q = \angle PQR = 60°]$

Ans. 60°

2. **Hint** $XB = \frac{1}{2} AB$ and $YC = \frac{1}{2} AC$

and by mid-point theorem,

$XY = \frac{1}{2} BC.$

Ans. 14.2 cm

3. **Hint** By using mid-point theorem,

$DE \parallel AC$ and $DE = \frac{1}{2} AC = FC$

[as F is the mid-point of AC]

$\Rightarrow \quad DE \parallel FC$

Similarly, $DF \parallel EC$ and $DF = EC$

4. **Hint** Use converse of mid-point theorem,

$MN \parallel BC$ and M is the mid-point of AB.

$\therefore \quad AN = \frac{1}{2} AC$

$= \frac{1}{2} \times 5 = 2.5$ cm

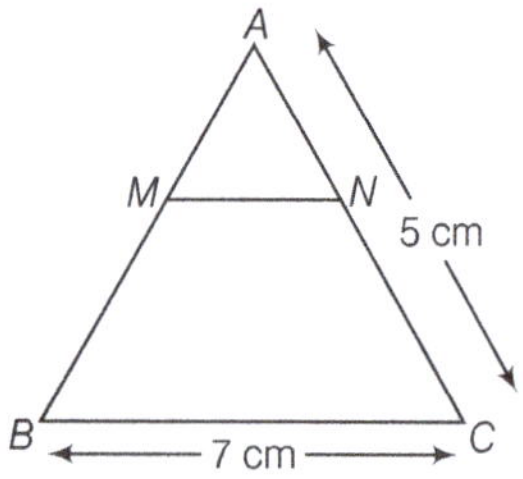

and by mid-point theorem,

$MN = \frac{1}{2} BC$

$= \frac{1}{2} \times 7 = 3.5$ cm

5. **Hint** Do same as Example 8.

6. **Hint** Use converse of mid-point theorem.

7. **Hint** Use mid-point theorem. In ΔABC, we get

$EF = \frac{1}{2} BC = \frac{1}{2} \times 7 = 3.5$ cm

$DF = \frac{1}{2} AC = \frac{1}{2} \times 6 = 3.0$ cm

and $\quad DE = \frac{1}{2} AB = \frac{1}{2} \times 4 = 2$ cm

Again, use mid-point theorem in ΔDEF.

Ans. $PQ = 1$ cm, $QR = 1.75$ cm and $PR = 1.5$ cm

8. **Hint**

Join DE and DF.

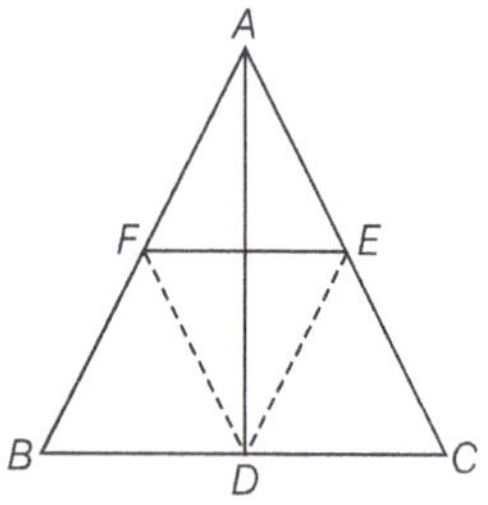

By mid-point theorem,

$DE \parallel BA$ and $DE = \frac{1}{2} BA$ ...(i)

Also, $DF \parallel CA$ and $DF = \frac{1}{2} CA$ ...(ii)

From Eqs. (i) and (ii), we get

$DE \parallel FA$ and $DF \parallel EA$; $DE = DF$

$\Rightarrow DEAF$ is a parallelogram with two adjacent sides equal.

So, $DEAF$ is a rhombus.

9. **Hint** Join DE and produce it to meet AB at G.

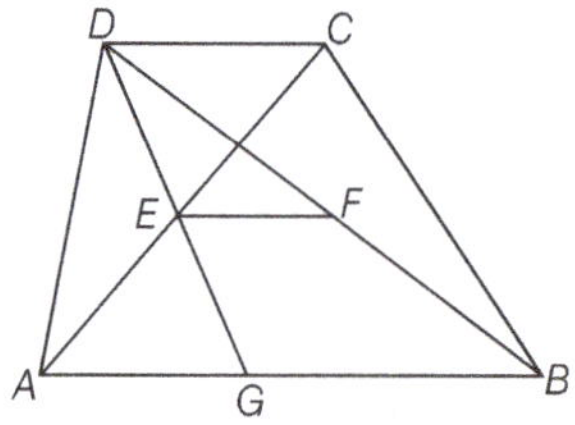

Now, prove, $\Delta ECD \cong \Delta EAG$, then $AG = DC$ and $DE = EG$.

By using mid-point theorem

$EF \parallel GB$ and $EF = \frac{1}{2} GB$

But, $GB = AB - AG = AB - DC$

10. **Hint** In ΔABC, P and Q are the mid-points of sides AB and BC respectively, therefore

$PQ \parallel AC$ and $PQ = \frac{1}{2} AC$

Similarly, $SR \parallel AC$ and $SR = \frac{1}{2} AC$

$\Rightarrow PQ \parallel SR$ and $PQ = SR \Rightarrow PQRS$ is a parallelogram.

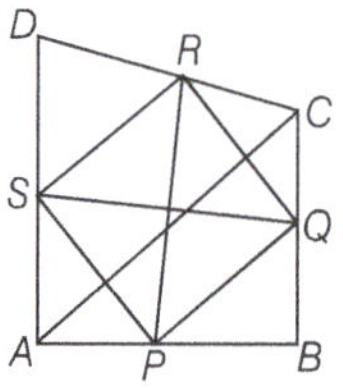

As the diagonals of a parallelogram bisect each other, therefore, the line segments PR and SQ bisect each other.

11. **Hint** In ΔABD, $PS \parallel BD$ and $PS = \frac{1}{2} BD$ ...(i)

In ΔBCD, $QR \parallel BD$ and $QR = \frac{1}{2} BD$ ...(ii)

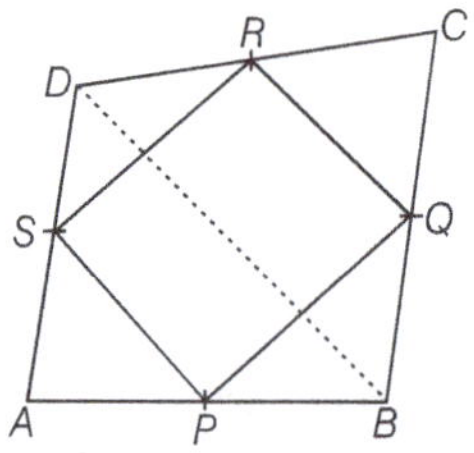

$\therefore \quad PS \parallel QR$ and $PS = QR$ [from Eqs. (i) and (ii)]

$\Rightarrow \quad PQRS$ is a parallelogram.

12. (i) **Hint** In ΔABP, by mid-point theorem,

$FE \parallel AP$ and $FE = \frac{1}{2} AP$ ...(i)

Similarly, In ΔACQ,

$FE \parallel QA$ and $FE = \frac{1}{2} QA$ ...(ii)

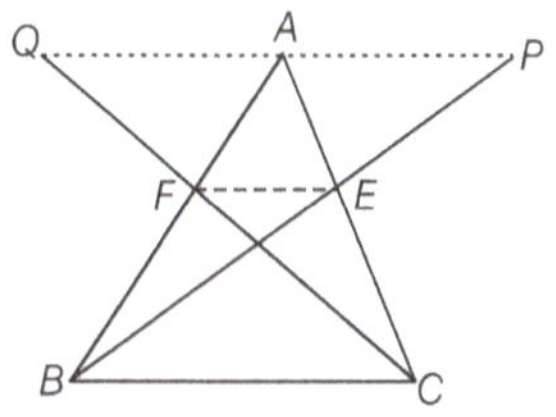

(ii) **Hint** From Eqs. (i) and (ii), we get

$$\frac{1}{2}AP = \frac{1}{2}QA$$

$\Rightarrow \quad AP = QA$

13. **Hint** In ΔACD,

$RS = \frac{1}{2}AC \quad \left[\because RS \,||\, AC \text{ and } RS = \frac{1}{2}AC\right]$

$SP = \frac{1}{2}BD \quad \left[\because SP \,||\, BD \text{ and } SP = \frac{1}{2}BD\right]$

$PQ = \frac{1}{2}AC \quad \left[\because PQ \,||\, AC \text{ and } PQ = \frac{1}{2}AC\right]$

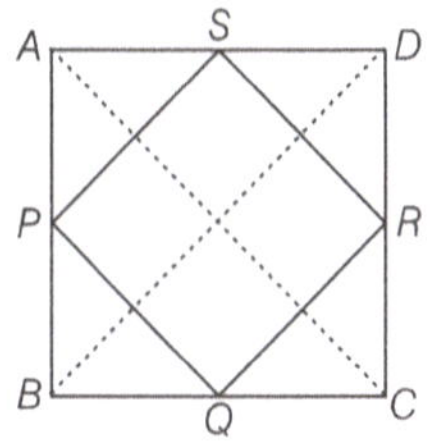

$QR = \frac{1}{2}BD \quad \left[\because QR \,||\, BD \text{ and } QR = \frac{1}{2}BD\right]$

$AC = BD$ [diagonals of a square]

Hence, $RS = SP = PQ = QR$

$\angle DOC = \angle QRS = 90°$

14. (i) **Hint** In ΔDAC, use mid-point theorem.

(ii) **Hint** Joining mid-points of a quadrilateral forms a rectangle.

$\therefore$ Opposite sides are equal.

(iii) **Hint** Use results from parts (i) and (ii).

15. **Hint** Since, $DE \,||\, CB$ and AB is transversal.

$\Rightarrow \quad \angle AED = \angle ABC$ [corresponding angles]

$= 90° = \angle DEB$

In ΔAED and ΔBED,

$\angle AED = \angle BED$, $AE = BE$

and $\quad DE = DE$

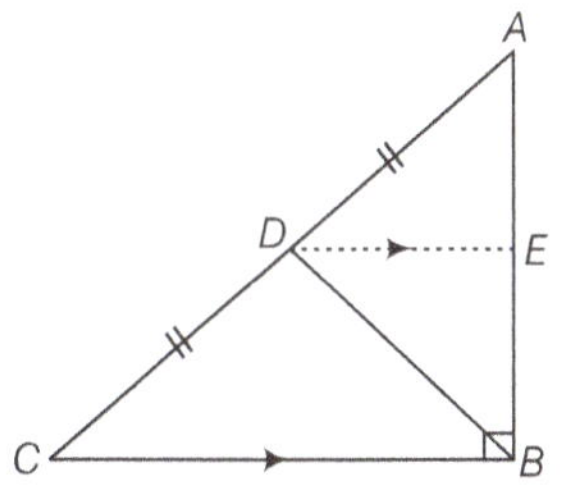

$\therefore \quad \Delta AED \cong \Delta BED$ [by SAS]

$\Rightarrow \quad BD = AD = \frac{1}{2}AC$ [by CPCT]

16. **Hint** Transversal AC makes equal intercepts, AB and BC on the parallel sides MN, KL and GH.

Using Equal intercepts theorem,

$DE = EF = 3.2$ cm

Ans. 6.4 cm

17. (i) **Hint** Since, D is the mid-point of XY and E is the mid-point of YZ.

$\therefore \quad DE \,||\, XZ$ and $DE = \frac{1}{2}XZ$

As, $XZ = 6$ cm

$\therefore \quad DE = \frac{1}{2} \times 6$

Ans. 3 cm

(ii) **Hint** Since, $DE \,||\, XZ$ and YZ is transversal, therefore $\angle DEY = \angle XZY$

Ans. 60°

18. (i) **Hint** In ΔHEY and ΔFHZ, $XYZT$ is a parallelogram.

$\therefore \quad XY = TZ$

$\Rightarrow \quad \frac{1}{2}XY = \frac{1}{2}TZ$

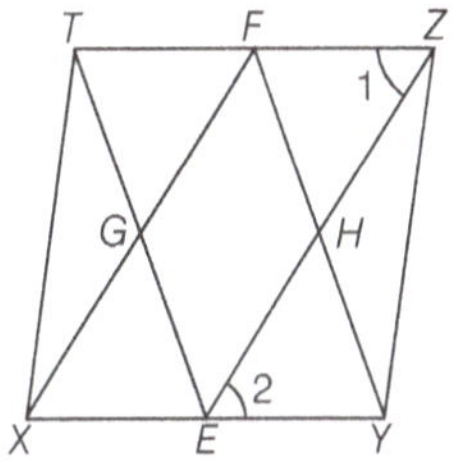

$\Rightarrow \quad EY = FZ$

Since, $TZ \,||\, XY$.

$\therefore \quad \angle 1 = \angle 2$ [alternate angles]

$\angle FHZ = \angle EHY$ [vertically opposite angles]

$\therefore \quad \Delta HEY \cong \Delta FZH$ [by AAS congruency]

(ii) **Hint** $FZ = XE$ ...(i)

[$\because FZ = EY$ (proved in part (i))]

$XY \,||\, ZT \Rightarrow XE \,||\, FZ$ ...(ii)

From Eqs. (i) and (ii), we get

$XEZF$ is a parallelogram.

It is mid-point of EZ [$\because \Delta HEY \cong \Delta FHZ$]

Similarly, G is the mid-point of XF.

$\therefore \; XG = FG = \frac{1}{2} \times XF$

and $\quad EH = ZH = \frac{1}{2}EZ$

$\Rightarrow \quad FG = HE$ ...(iii)

Also, $XE \,||\, FZ$

$\Rightarrow \quad FG \,||\, HE$ ...(iv)

Exercise 9.2

1. Hint In ΔPSQ,

$$PQ^2 = PS^2 + QS^2$$

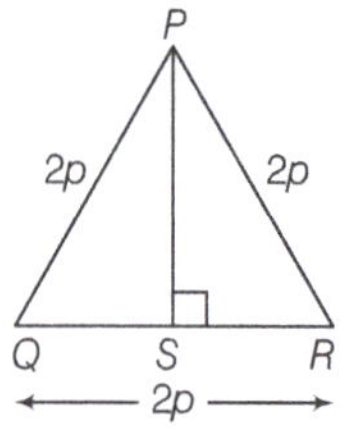

$\Rightarrow \quad (2p)^2 = PS^2 + p^2$ **Ans.** $\sqrt{3}p$

2. Hint Using Pythagoras theorem in ΔABC.

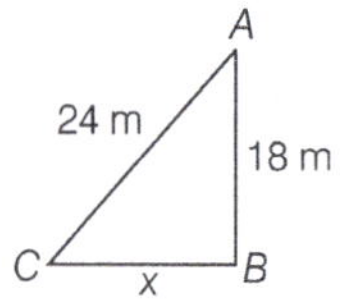

Ans. $6\sqrt{7}$ m

3. Hint In ΔDBC, using Pythagoras theorem to find $BC = 15$ m.

Now, in ΔABC, using Pythagoras theorem,

$$AC = \sqrt{AB^2 + BC^2}$$

$$= \sqrt{(12)^2 + (15)^2}$$

Ans. $\sqrt{369}$ m

4. Hint Let $OC = x$ and $OA = y$

In ΔAOC, using Pythagoras theorem, we have

$$y^2 = 9 - x^2 \quad \ldots(i)$$

Again, In ΔAOB, using Pythagoras theorem, we have

$$y^2 = 64 - (6 + x)^2 \quad \ldots(ii)$$

Solve Eqs. (i) and (ii) to get the required result.

Ans. $1\frac{7}{12}$ cm

5. Hint Using Pythagoras theorem. **Ans.** 90°

6. Hint No, because it does not satisfy the Pythagoras theorem.

7. Hint In ΔBAC, using Pythagoras theorem, we get

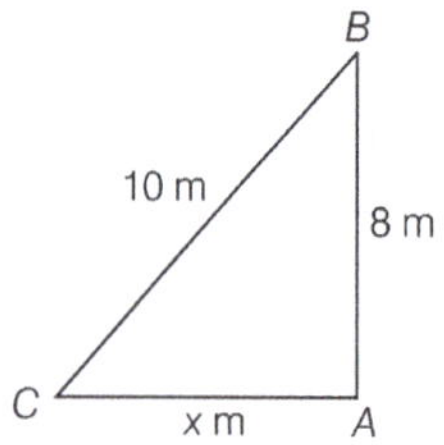

$$AC^2 + AB^2 = BC^2$$

$\Rightarrow \quad x^2 + (8)^2 = (10)^2$

Ans. $x = 6$ m

8. Hint Since, $PQ \parallel BC$

$\therefore \quad PQ \perp AB$ and $PQ \perp DC$

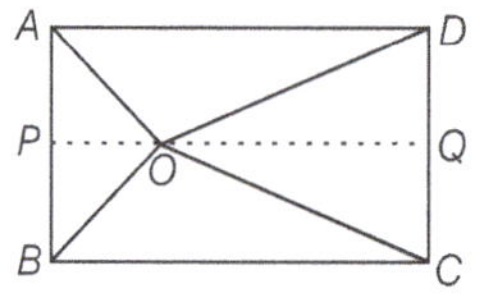

In ΔOPB, using Pythagoras theorem, we get

$$OB^2 = OP^2 + BP^2 \quad \ldots(i)$$

In ΔOAP, using Pythagoras theorem, we get

$$OA^2 = OP^2 + AP^2 \quad \ldots(ii)$$

In ΔOQC, using Pythagoras theorem, we get

$$OC^2 = OQ^2 + CQ^2 \quad \ldots(iii)$$

and in ΔOQD, using Pythagoras theorem, we get

$$OD^2 = OQ^2 + QD^2 \quad \ldots(iv)$$

On adding Eqs. (i) and (iv), we get

$$OB^2 + OD^2 = OP^2 + BP^2 + OQ^2 + QD^2$$

$$= OP^2 + CQ^2 + OQ^2 + AP^2$$

[$\because BP = CQ$ and $DQ = AP$, opposite sides of rectangles]

$$= CQ^2 + OQ^2 + OP^2 + AP^2$$

$$= OC^2 + OA^2 \quad \text{[from Eqs. (ii) and (iii)]}$$

9. Hint Do same as Example 20. **Ans.** 13 cm

10. Hint Given, as D is mid-point of BC, $BD = CD$ and $BC = 2CD$.

In ΔABD, $AB^2 = AD^2 - BD^2$

In ΔABC, $AC^2 = AB^2 + BC^2 = (AD^2 - BD^2) + BC^2$

$\Rightarrow \quad AC^2 = AD^2 - CD^2 + (2CD)^2$ [given]

11. Hint Do same as Example 22.

12. Hint Using Pythagoras theorem. In ΔABE,

$AB = 15$ cm $\Rightarrow BD = 15 - x$ [$\because AD = EC = x$]

In ΔBCD, using Pythagoras theorem,

$$DC^2 = BD^2 + BC^2$$

Ans. 7 cm

13. Hint Draw $AN \perp BC$

Then, prove $\Delta ABN \cong \Delta ANC$ [by RHS congruence rule]

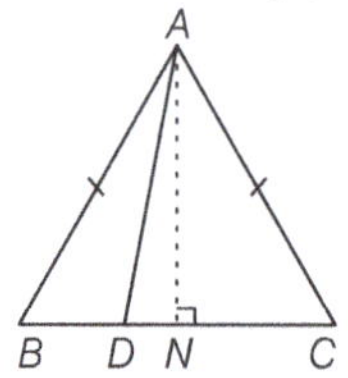

$$BN = NC \quad \text{[by CPCT]}$$

In ΔABN, $AB^2 = AN^2 + BN^2 \quad \ldots(i)$

In ΔADN, $AD^2 = AN^2 + DN^2 \quad \ldots(ii)$

Now, subtracting Eqs. (i) and (ii).

14. Hint $DB = 3CD$ [given]

and $\quad DB + CD = BC$

$\therefore \quad 3CD + CD = BC$

$$CD = \frac{1}{4}(BC) \quad \ldots(i)$$

and $$BD = \frac{3}{4}(BC) \quad \ldots(ii)$$

In ΔADC, using Pythagoras theorem, we have

$$AD^2 = AC^2 - CD^2 \quad \ldots(iii)$$

In ΔADB, using Pythagoras theorem, we have

$$AB^2 = AD^2 + DB^2$$

Using Eq. (iii), we have

$$AB^2 = AC^2 - CD^2 + DB^2$$

Now, using Eqs. (i) and (ii) we can determine the required result.

15. Hint Do same as Example 24.

16. Hint O be the position of airport.

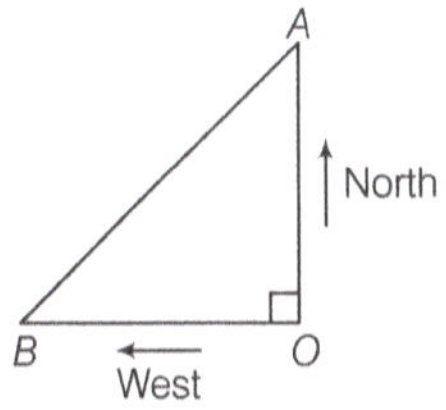

$$OA = 1000 \times \frac{3}{2} = 1500 \text{ km}$$

[$\because$ distance = speed × time]

and $$OB = 1200 \times \frac{3}{2} = 1800 \text{ km}$$

By using Pythagoras theorem, we get

$$AB^2 = OB^2 + OA^2$$

$$\Rightarrow \quad AB^2 = (1800)^2 + (1500)^2 = 5490000$$

Ans. $300\sqrt{61}$ km

17. Hint Find AC and BC, by using Pythagoras theorem.

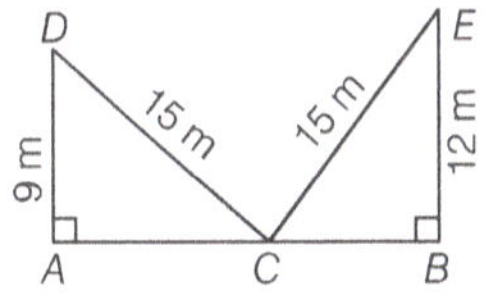

Ans. 21 m

18. Hint We have, $AB = 18$ cm, $CD = 6$ cm, $BP = 12$ cm, $CP = 9$ cm.

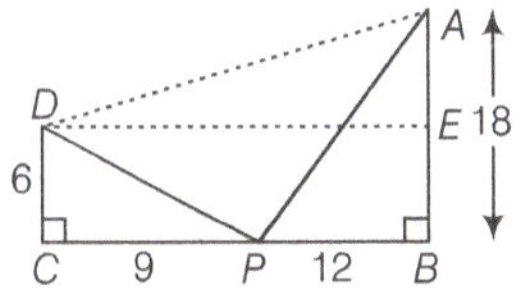

In ΔDCP, $DP^2 = DC^2 + CP^2$

$$= 6^2 + 9^2 = 36 + 81 = 117$$

In ΔABP, $AP^2 = AB^2 + BP^2 = 18^2 + 12^2 = 324 + 144$

$$\Rightarrow \quad AP^2 = 468$$

$$\Rightarrow AP^2 + DP^2 = 468 + 117 = 585 \quad \ldots(i)$$

In ΔAED, $AD^2 = AE^2 + DE^2 = 12^2 + 21^2$

$$\Rightarrow \quad AD^2 = 144 + 441 = 585 \quad \ldots(ii)$$

From Eqs. (i) and (ii), we get $\angle APD = 90°$

19. Hint In right angled ΔXYZ and ΔXTZ,

$$XZ^2 = XY^2 + YZ^2 \quad \ldots(i)$$

and $$XZ^2 = XT^2 + TZ^2 \quad \ldots(ii)$$

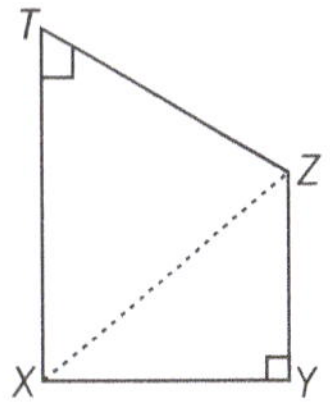

On adding Eqs. (i) and (ii), we get

$$2XZ^2 - YZ^2 = XY^2 + XT^2 + TZ^2$$

Chapter Exercise

1. (a) **2.** (d) **3.** (b)

4. (b) **5.** (a)

6. Hint Do same as Example 8.

Ans. 3 cm

7. Hint $AB + BC + CA = 38$ units

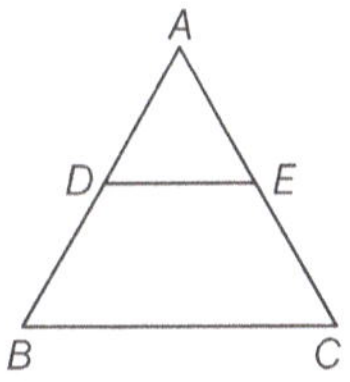

$$\Rightarrow \quad \frac{1}{2}AB + \frac{1}{2}BC + \frac{1}{2}CA = \frac{38}{2}$$

$$\Rightarrow \quad AD + DE + AE = 19$$

Ans. 19 cm

8. Hint $DF = \frac{1}{2}AC = \frac{8}{2} = 4$

$$FE = \frac{1}{2}AB = \frac{13}{2} = 6.5$$

$$ED = \frac{1}{2}BC = \frac{16}{2} = 8$$

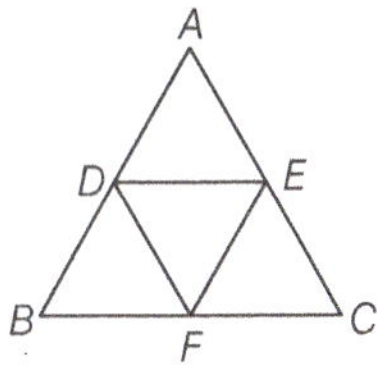

Ans. 18.5 cm

9. Hint Do same as Q. 8.

Ans. 6.4 cm

10. Hint In parallelogram $BDEF$,

$$BD \,||\, FE \text{ and } BD = FE \quad \ldots(i)$$

In parallelogram $FDCE$,

$$DC \,||\, FE \text{ and } DC = FE \quad \ldots(ii)$$

From Eqs. (i) and (ii), we get

$BD = DC = FE = 8$ cm **Ans.** 8 cm

11. Hint We know that, diagonals of a rhombus bisect each other at right angle.

$\therefore$ $OB = OD$ and $OA = OC$. **Ans.** 20 cm

12. Hint By using equal intercept and then $\Delta ABD \cong \Delta ACD$ by SAS congruence

13. Hint Use Pythagoras theorem.

Ans. $AB = 8$ cm, $BC = 15$ cm and $AC = 17$ cm

14. **Hint** Use Pythagoras theorem. **Ans.** 25 m

15. **Hint** Use Pythagoras theorem. **Ans.** $4\sqrt{3}$ cm

16. **Hint** Do same as Q. 8 of Exercise 9.2. **Ans.** $5\sqrt{3}$ cm

17. **Hint Construction** Produce AB and CD to meet at point E. Also, join AC and BD.

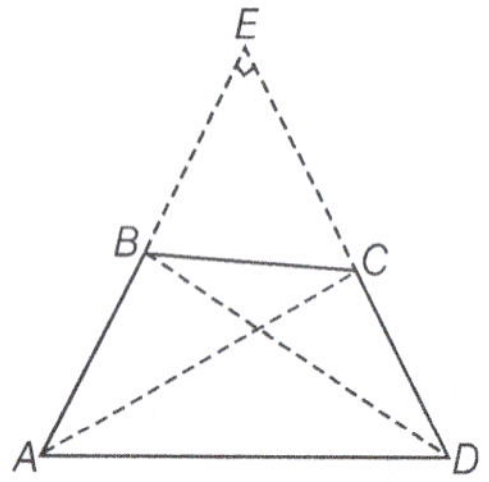

In ΔAED, $\angle E = 90°$ [$\because \angle A + \angle D = 90°$ (given)]

$$AD^2 = AE^2 + DE^2 \quad \text{...(i)}$$

[by Pythagoras theorem]

In ΔBEC,

$$BC^2 = BE^2 + EC^2 \quad \text{...(ii)}$$

[by Pythagoras theorem]

On adding Eqs. (i) and (ii), we have

$$AD^2 + BC^2 = AE^2 + DE^2 + BE^2 + CE^2 \quad \text{...(iii)}$$

In ΔAEC,

$$AC^2 = AE^2 + CE^2 \quad \text{...(iv)}$$

[by Pythagoras theorem]

In ΔBED,

$$BD^2 = BE^2 + DE^2 \quad \text{...(v)}$$

[by Pythagoras theorem]

On adding Eqs. (iv) and (v), we have

$$AC^2 + BD^2 = AE^2 + CE^2 + BE^2 + DE^2 \quad \text{...(vi)}$$

Using Eqs. (iii) and (vi) get the required result.

18. **Hint** Join AQ and BP.

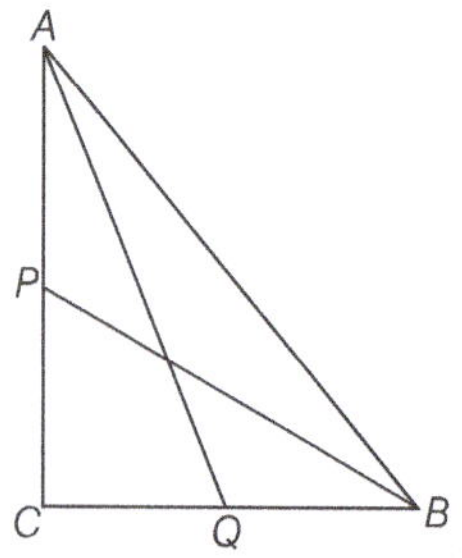

$$CP = \frac{2}{3}AC \quad \text{...(i)}$$

[$\because P$ divides CA in 2 : 1 (given)]

Also, $$QC = \frac{2}{3}BC \quad \text{...(ii)}$$

[$\because Q$ divides CB in 2 : 1 (given)]

(i) In ΔACQ, using Pythagoras theorem and Eq. (ii), we get

$$9AQ^2 = 9AC^2 + 4BC^2$$

(ii) In ΔBCP, using Pythagoras theorem and Eq. (i), we get

$$9BP^2 = 9BC^2 + 4AC^2$$

19. **Hint** In ΔPQR, $PS = QS = RS$ [given]

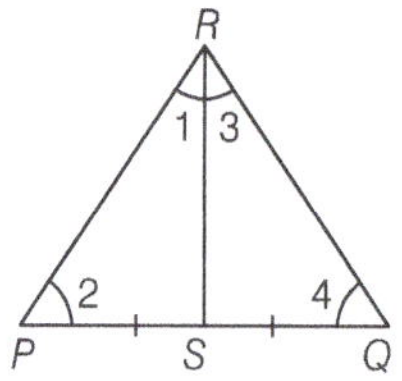

In ΔPSR, $PS = SR$

$\Rightarrow \quad \angle 1 = \angle 2$

In ΔRSQ, $SQ = SR$

$\Rightarrow \quad \angle 3 = \angle 4$

Now, in ΔPQR, $\angle P + \angle Q + \angle R = 180°$

$\Rightarrow \quad \angle 1 + \angle 3 = 90° \Rightarrow \angle R = 90°$

$\Rightarrow \quad \Delta PRQ$ is a right angled triangle at R.

20. (i) **Hint** In ΔRNS, L is the mid-point of SR and $LQ \parallel SN$

$\Rightarrow Q$ is the mid-point of RN.

[by converse of mid-point theorem]

$\Rightarrow \quad LQ = \frac{1}{2}SN \Rightarrow SN = 2LQ$

(ii) **Hint** $QR = \frac{1}{2}RN \Rightarrow SP = \frac{1}{2}RN$

[by mid-point theorem]

21. **Hint**

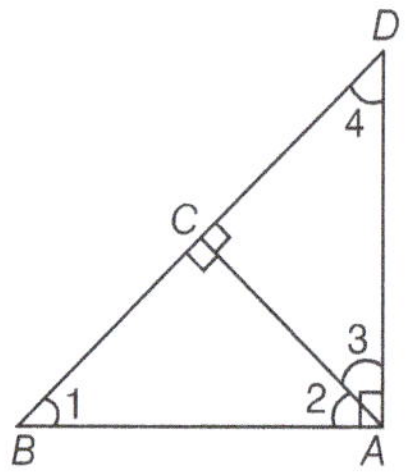

$\angle 1 = \angle 3$, $\angle 2 = \angle 4$

By AA similarity

(i) $\Delta ABC \sim \Delta DBA \Rightarrow BC \cdot BD = AB^2$

(ii) $\Delta ABC \sim \Delta DAC \Rightarrow BC \cdot DC = AC^2$

(iii) $\Delta DAC \sim \Delta DBA \Rightarrow BD \cdot CD = AD^2$

22. **Hint** $DC = \frac{1}{2}BC$ ...(i)

[$\because D$ is the mid-point of BC (given)]

By Pythagoras theorem,

In ΔABC, $AB^2 = AC^2 + BC^2$ ...(ii)

In ΔADC, $AD^2 = AC^2 + DC^2$ ...(iii)

From Eqs. (i) and (iii), we have

$$AC^2 = AD^2 - \left(\frac{1}{2}BC\right)^2$$

$\Rightarrow \quad 4AC^2 = 4AD^2 - BC^2$

$\Rightarrow \quad 3AC^2 + AC^2 = 4AD^2 - BC^2$

Using Eq. (ii), we have

$$AB^2 = 4AD^2 - 3AC^2$$

23. Hint In ΔPDQ, $PQ^2 = PD^2 + QD^2$ ...(i)

In ΔPDR, $PR^2 = PD^2 + DR^2$ ...(ii)

Simplify Eqs. (i) and (ii) for PD^2 and equate the obtained results.

24. Hint By using Pythagoras theorem $AD = 16$ cm

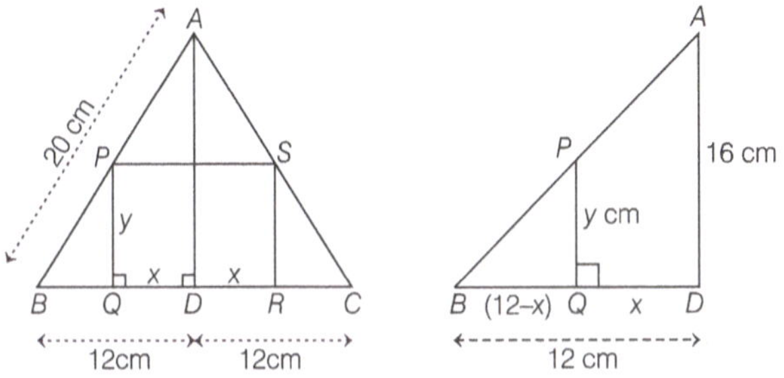

$$\frac{y}{12 - x} = \frac{4}{3}$$ [By AA similarity]

25. Hint

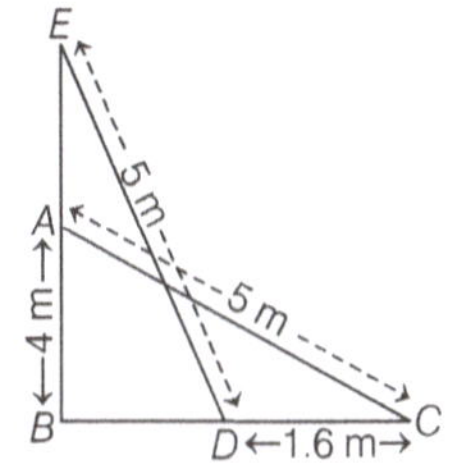

We need to find the length of AE.

Apply Pythagoras theorem in ΔABC and find the length of BD.

$$BD = 1.4 \text{ m}$$

Again, apply pythagoras theorem in ΔEBD and find the length of AE

$$BE = 4.8 \text{ m}$$

Ans. 0.8 m

26. Hint Join OB and OC.

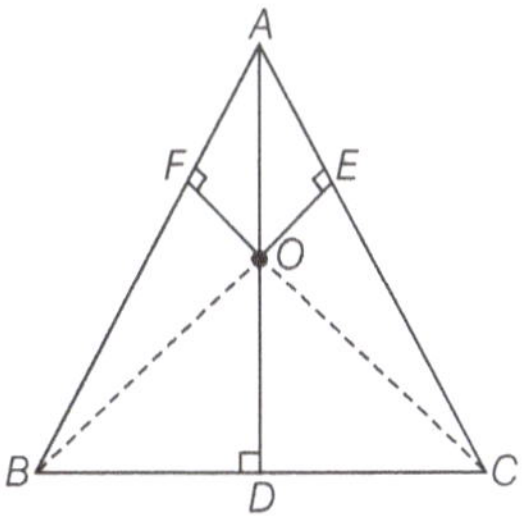

(i) By Pythagoras theorem,

In ΔOFA, $OA^2 = AF^2 + OF^2$ ...(i)

In ΔODB, $OB^2 = BD^2 + OD^2$ ...(ii)

and, In ΔOEC, $OC^2 = CE^2 + OE^2$ ...(iii)

Add Eqs. (i), (ii) and (iii) to get the required result.

(ii) By Pythagoras theorem,

In ΔODB, $OB^2 = OD^2 + BD^2$ ...(i)

and in ΔODC, $OC^2 = OD^2 + CD^2$ ...(ii)

Subtracting Eq. (ii) from Eq. (i), we get

$$OB^2 - OC^2 = BD^2 - CD^2 \quad \text{...(iii)}$$

Similarly, we have

$$OC^2 - OA^2 = CE^2 - AE^2 \quad \text{...(iv)}$$

and $$OA^2 - OB^2 = AF^2 - BF^2 \quad \text{...(v)}$$

Adding Eqs. (iii), (iv) and (v) to get the required result.

27. Hint

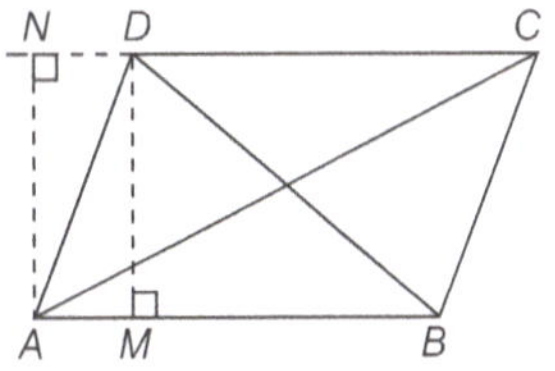

To prove $AC^2 + BD^2 = AD^2 + BC^2 + AB^2 + CD^2$

In ΔANC, $AC^2 = AN^2 + NC^2$ [by Pythagoras theorem]

$\Rightarrow$ $AC^2 = AN^2 + (ND + DC)^2$

$\Rightarrow$ $AC^2 = AD^2 + DC^2 + 2.\, ND.\, DC$

[$\because AD^2 = AN^2 + ND^2$] ...(i)

In ΔDMB, $BD^2 = DM^2 + BM^2$ [by Pythagoras theorem]

$\Rightarrow$ $BD^2 = DM^2 + (AB - AM)^2$

$\Rightarrow$ $BD^2 = AD^2 + AB^2 - 2.\, AB.\, AM$

[$\because AD^2 = DM^2 + AM^2$] ...(ii)

Add Eqs. (i) and (ii) to get the required result.

28. Hint

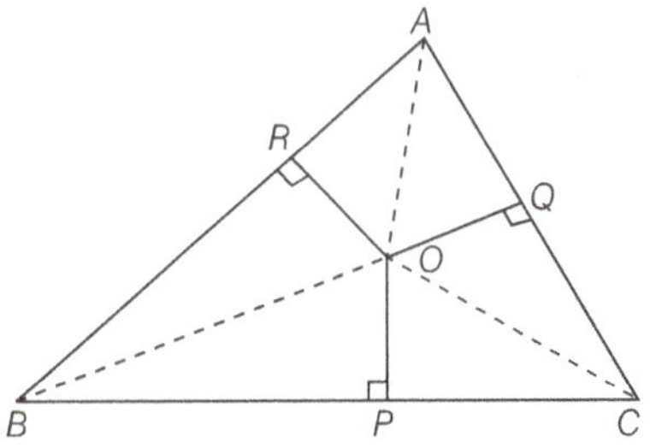

By Pythagoras theorem,

In ΔARO, $AR^2 = AO^2 - OR^2$ ...(i)

In ΔBPO, $BP^2 = BO^2 - OP^2$ ...(ii)

In ΔCQO, $CQ^2 = CO^2 - OQ^2$ ...(iii)

Adding Eqs. (i), (ii) and (iii), we get

$$AR^2 + BP^2 + CQ^2 = AQ^2 + CP^2 + BR^2$$

29. Hint Converse of mid-point theorem is

The straight line drawn through the mid-point of one side of a triangle and parallel to another side bisects the third side.

Given, In ΔABC, D is mid-point of side AB and DE is parallel to BC.

To Prove $AE = CE$

Construction Draw FG parallel to BC through vertex A.

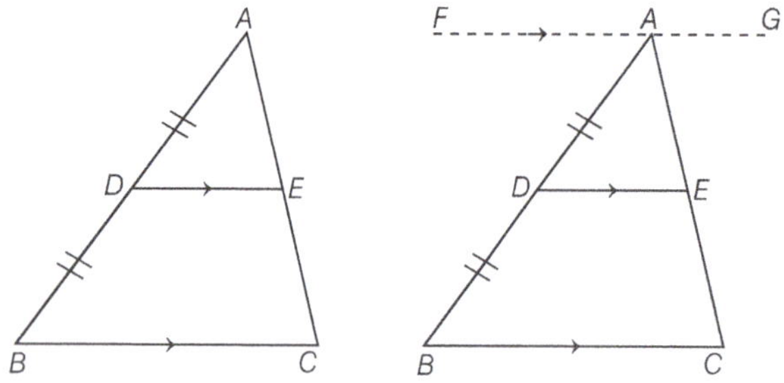

Proof Since, $FG \parallel DE \parallel BC$ and the transversal AB makes equal intercepts i.e. $AD = DB$.

Also, AC is an another transversal by intercept theorem,

$$AE = CE$$

30. Hint

(i) By using mid-point theorem.

$$XD = \frac{1}{2} XY = XP$$

$\Rightarrow \quad XQ \parallel PR \quad \ldots(i)$

$PR \parallel YS \quad$ (given) ...(ii)

From Eqs. (i) and (ii), we get

$$XQ \parallel YS$$

(ii) $DR : RS = 2 : 1$

and Q is the mid-point of DR

$\Rightarrow \quad DS = 3RS$

31. Hint $OA = OC$, $OB = OD$ and $\angle COD = 90°$

By mid-point theorem,

In ΔBDE, A and O are mid-points of BE and BD, respectively.

$\therefore \quad OA \parallel DE \Rightarrow OC \parallel DG \quad \ldots(i)$

In ΔCFA, B and O are mid-points of AF and AC, respectively.

$\therefore \quad OB \parallel CF \Rightarrow OD \parallel GC \quad \ldots(ii)$

Thus, in quadrilateral $OCGD$, $OC \parallel DG$ and $OD \parallel CG$. Therefore, $OCGD$ is a parallelogram.

$\angle CGD = \angle COD$ but $\angle COD = 90°$

$\angle CGD = 90°$

32. Hint By using mid-point theorem

$$RQ \parallel BC$$

$\Rightarrow \quad RQ = \frac{1}{2} BC = BP = PC$

$\Rightarrow \quad RQ \parallel BP$ and $RQ \parallel PC$

$\Rightarrow BPQR$ and $PCQR$ is a parallelogram.

We know, diagonals of parallelogram bisect each other. Y is mid-point of PQ.

$\Rightarrow \quad XY \parallel RQ$

and $\quad XY = \frac{1}{2} RQ$

$\Rightarrow \quad XY = \frac{1}{4} BC$

33. Hint By using mid-point theorem

$PQ \parallel AC$ and $PQ = \frac{1}{2} AC \quad \ldots(i)$

Similarly, $SR \parallel AC$ and $SR = \frac{1}{2} AC \quad \ldots(ii)$

From Eqs. (i) and (ii),

$PQRS$ is a parallelogram

$\Delta APS \cong \Delta BPQ \quad$ [by SAS congruency]

$\therefore \quad PS = PQ \quad$ [CPCT]

$\therefore \quad PQ = RS = PS = RQ$

[$\because$ opposite sides of a parallelogram is equal]

Thus, $PQRS$ is a rhombus.

34. Hint To prove

$$\Delta DEF \cong \Delta EDB \cong \Delta CFE \cong \Delta FAD$$

By mid-point theorem,

$$DF \parallel BC \Rightarrow DF \parallel BE$$

Similarly, $EF \parallel BE$

Therefore, $BEFG$ is a parallelogram.

$\therefore \quad \Delta EDB \cong \Delta DEF \quad$ [by SSS congruency]

Similarly, $\Delta DEF \cong \Delta CFE$ and $\Delta DEF \cong \Delta FAD$.

Olympiad Section

Brain Teasing Questions asked in Previous Olympiads

1 In the following figure, ΔABC is right angled at C and M is the mid-point of hypotenuse AB. If $AC = 32$ cm and $BC = 60$ cm, then the length of CM is

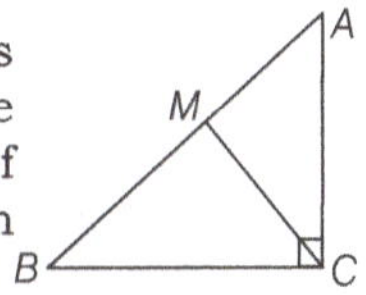

(a) 32 cm (b) 30 cm
(c) 17 cm (d) 34 cm

2 In the adjoining figure, the side AC of ΔABC is produced to E such that $CE = \frac{1}{2}AC$. If D is the mid-point of BC and ED produced to meet AB at F and CP, DQ are drawn parallel to BA, then FD is equal to

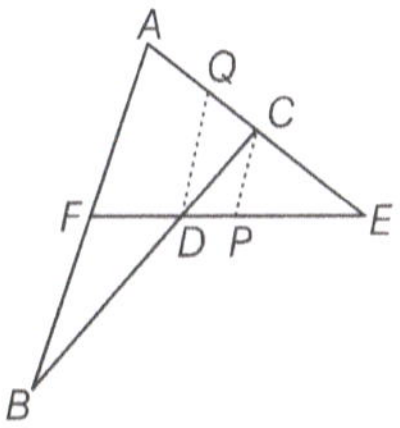

(a) $\frac{1}{2}FE$ (b) $\frac{1}{3}FE$
(c) FE (d) $\frac{1}{4}FE$

3 In the given figure, ΔABC is an isosceles triangle, in which $AB = AC$ and D, E and F are the mid-points of BC, CA and AB, respectively. Then,

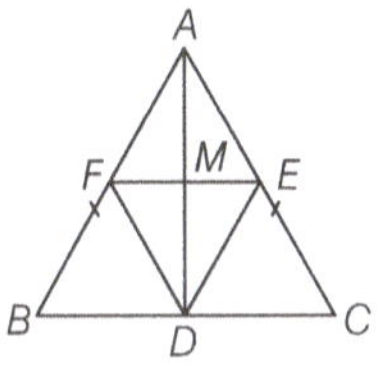

(a) $AD \perp FE$
(b) $AD \parallel FE$
(c) AD is bisected by FE
(d) Both (a) and (c)

4 Suppose D, E and F are the mid-points of the sides AB, BC and CA respectively of ΔABC, AE meets DF at O. P and Q are the mid-points of OB and OC, respectively. $DPQF$ is a

(a) square (b) parallelogram
(c) rectangle (d) rhombus

5 ABC is a triangle and through A, B and C lines are drawn parallel to BC, CA and AB respectively intersecting at P, Q and R, then perimeter of ΔPQR is equal to

(a) $2 \times$ perimeter of ΔABC
(b) $3 \times$ perimeter of ΔABC
(c) perimeter of ΔABC
(d) None of the above

6 In ΔABC, $\angle A = 70°$, $\angle B = 30°$ and $\angle C = 80°$. What are the angles of the triangle formed by joining the mid-points of the sides of this triangle?

(a) 80°, 40°, 30° (b) 40°, 80°, 30°
(c) 80°, 70°, 30° (d) 50°, 60°, 75°

7 A 5 m long ladder is placed leaning towards a vertical wall such that it reaches the wall at a point 4 m high. If the foot of the ladder is moved 1.6 m towards the wall, then find the distance by which the top of the ladder would slide upwards on the wall.

(a) 0.5 m (b) 0.8 m (c) 0.4 m (d) 0.6 m

8 ΔABC is an isosceles triangle with $AB = AC = 13$ cm and the length of altitude from A on BC is 5 cm. Then, BC is equals to

(a) 24 cm (b) 10 cm (c) 20 cm (d) 15 cm

9 In the given figure, O is a point inside a ΔABC such that $\angle AOC = 90°$, $OA = 6$ cm and $OR = 8$ cm. If $AB = 24$ cm and $\angle BAC = 90°$, then BC is equal to

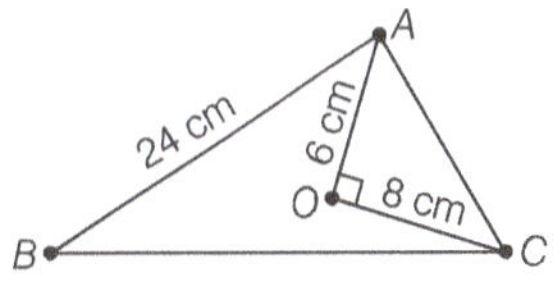

(a) 25 cm (b) 26 cm (c) 30 cm (d) 32 cm

10 In a ΔABC, BE and CF are medians. M is a point on BE produced such that $BE = EM$ and N is a point on CF produced such that $CF = FN$. Which of the following statement(s) is/are true?

I. NAM is a straight line.

II. A is the mid-point of MN.

(a) I is true (b) II is true
(c) Both I and II are true (d) None of these

Answers

1. (d)	**2.** (b)	**3.** (d)	**4.** (b)	**5.** (a)
6. (c)	**7.** (b)	**8.** (a)	**9.** (b)	**10.** (c)

** These questions may or may not be asked in the examination, have been given just for additional practice required for olympiads Scholarship Exams etc. For detailed explanations refer Page No. 342.*

CHAPTER 10

Rectilinear Figures

SYLLABUS

- **Proof and Use of Theorems on Parallelogram** (i) Both pair of opposite sides equal (without proof). (ii) Both pairs of opposite angles equal. (iii) One pair of opposite sides equal and parallel (without proof). (iv) Diagonals bisect each other and bisect the parallelogram. (v) Rhombus as a special parallelogram whose diagonals meet at right angles. (vi) In a rectangle, diagonals are equal in a square, they are equal and meet at right angels.

Rectilinear figure

Here, 'Recti' means 'Straight' and 'Linear' means 'Line'. So, a rectilinear figure is a plane figure formed only by line segments. Some rectilinear figures are shown below

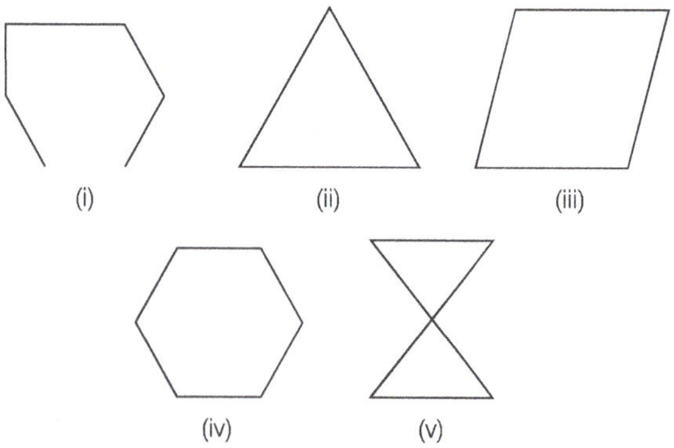

Polygon

A simple closed rectilinear figure, is called a polygon.

Convex Polygon When each interior angle of a polygon is less than 180°, then it is called a convex polygon.

Concave Polygon When atleast one angle of a polygon is greater than 180°, then it is called concave polygon.

Quadrilaterals

Here, 'Quad' means 'Four' and 'Lateral' means 'Sides', so a closed figure having four sides, is called a quadrilateral.

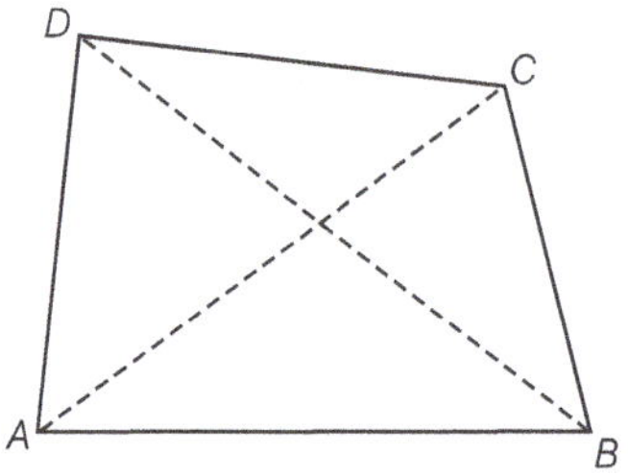

In a quadrilateral $ABCD$ AB, BC, CD and DA are the four sides, A, B, C and D are the four vertices and $\angle A$, $\angle B$, $\angle C$ and $\angle D$ are the four angles formed at the vertices.

(i) **Opposite Sides** Two sides of a quadrilateral, which have no common end point (vertex) i.e. do not intersect each other.

(ii) **Consecutive or Adjacent Sides** Two sides of a quadrilateral, which have a common end point i.e. intersect each other.

(iii) **Opposite Angles** Two angles of a quadrilateral are said to be opposite angles, if they do not have a common arm.

(iv) **Consecutive or Adjacent Angles** Two angles of a quadrilateral are said to be consecutive or adjacent angles, if they have a common arm.

(v) **Diagonals** The line segment joining the opposite vertices, is called a diagonal.

Angle Sum Property of a Quadrilateral

'The sum of the four angles of a quadrilateral is 360°.'

Verification Let *ABCD* be a quadrilateral and *AC* be a diagonal.

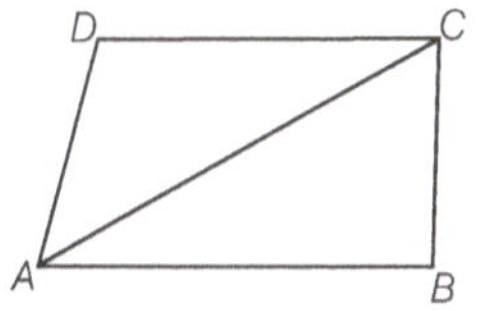

We know that in ΔADC,

$\angle DAC + \angle ACD + \angle ADC = 180°$ ...(i)

[since, sum of angles of a triangle is 180°]

Similarly, in ΔABC,

$\angle CAB + \angle ACB + \angle ABC = 180°$ ...(ii)

[since, sum of angles of a triangle is 180°]

On adding Eqs. (i) and (ii), we get

$$\angle DAC + \angle ACD + \angle ADC + \angle CAB + \angle ACB + \angle ABC = 180° + 180° = 360° \quad ...(iii)$$

Also, $\angle DAC + \angle CAB = \angle BAD$

and $\angle ACD + \angle ACB = \angle BCD$ ...(iv)

From Eqs. (iii) and (iv), we get

$$\angle ABC + \angle BAD + \angle ADC + \angle BCD = 360°$$

$$\Rightarrow \angle A + \angle B + \angle C + \angle D = 360°$$

Example 1. The angles of a quadrilateral are in the ratio 3 : 5 : 9 : 13. Find all the angles of the quadrilateral.

Sol. Given, the ratio of the angles of a quadrilateral is 3 : 5 : 9 : 13.

Let the angles of the quadrilateral be $3x$, $5x$, $9x$ and $13x$.

We know that sum of the angles of a quadrilateral is 360°.

$\therefore \quad 3x + 5x + 9x + 13x = 360°$

$\Rightarrow \quad 30x = 360°$

$\Rightarrow \quad x = \frac{360°}{30} = 12°$

Hence, angles of the quadrilateral are

$3x = 3 \times 12° = 36°$,

$5x = 5 \times 12° = 60°$,

$9x = 9 \times 12° = 108°$

and $13x = 13 \times 12° = 156°$.

Types of Quadrilaterals

1. Trapezium

A quadrilateral in which one pair of opposite sides are parallel, is called a trapezium.

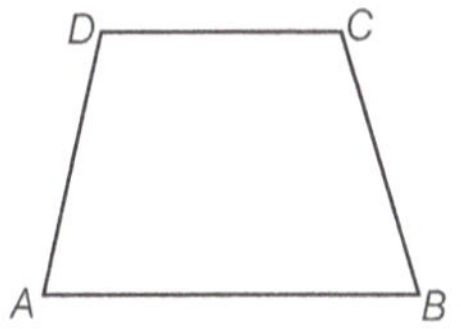

If two non-parallel sides of a trapezium are equal, then it is called an isosceles trapezium.

2. Parallelogram

A quadrilateral in which both pairs of opposite sides are parallel, is called parallelogram.

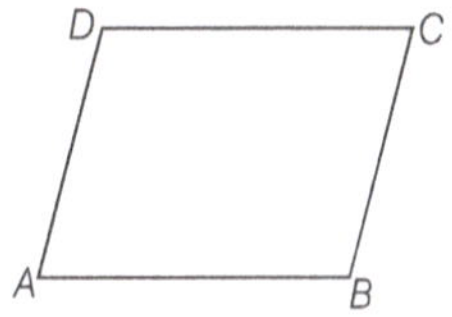

In the figure, *ABCD* is a parallelogram in which

$AB \parallel DC$ and $AB = DC$

$BC \parallel AD$ and $BC = AD$

$\angle A = \angle C$ and $\angle B = \angle D$

Also, $\angle A + \angle B = 180°$, $\angle B + \angle C = 180°$,

$\angle C + \angle D = 180°$ and $\angle D + \angle A = 180°$

Properties of Parallelogram

1. The opposite sides are parallel and equal.
2. The opposite angles are equal in measure.
3. The diagonals bisects each other.
4. The sum of adjacent angles of a parallelogram is 180°.

3. Rectangle

A parallelogram in which one of its angles is right angle, is called rectangle.

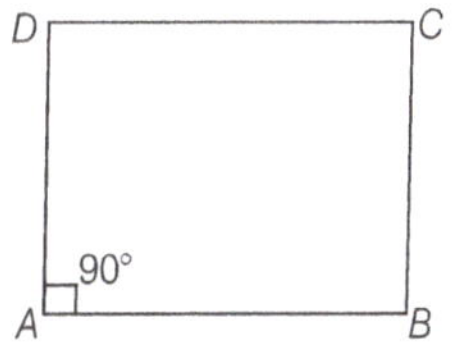

In the figure, *ABCD* is a rectangle in which

$AB \parallel DC$ and $AB = DC$

$BC \parallel AD$ and $BC = AD$

and $\angle A = 90°$.

Also, $\angle B = \angle C = \angle D = 90°$.

Properties of Rectangle

1. Every rectangle is a parallelogram, so it exist all the properties of parallelogram i.e.
   (i) opposite sides of rectangle are equal.
   (ii) diagonals of rectangle bisect each other, etc.
2. Diagonals of a rectangle are equal.

Note If one angle of a parallelogram is 90°, then all angles will be 90°. Instead to prove each interior angle of rectangle is 90°, it is sufficient to prove anyone angle equals to 90°.

4. Rhombus

A parallelogram in which all sides are equal, is called a rhombus.

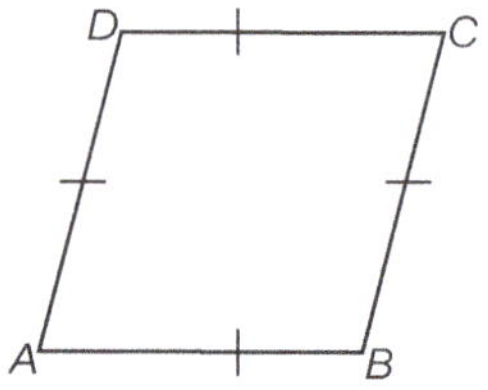

In the figure, *ABCD* is a rhombus in which

$AB = BC = CD = DA$

and $AB \parallel CD$, $BC \parallel DA$

Properties of Rhombus

1. Every rhombus is a parallelogram, so it exist all the properties of parallelogram i.e.
   (i) opposite angles of rhombus are equal.
   (ii) diagonals of rhombus bisect each other, etc.
2. Diagonals of a rhombus intersect at right angles.

5. Square

A rectangle, whose two consecutive sides are equal, is called a square.

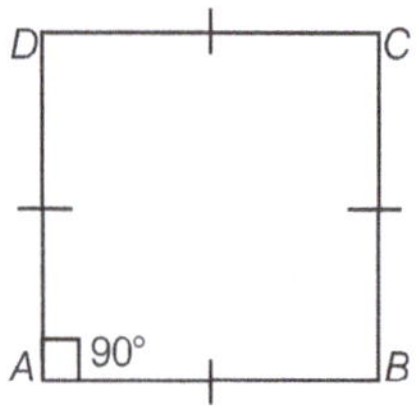

In the figure, *ABCD* is a square in which

$AB \parallel CD$, $BC \parallel AD$, $AB = BC = CD = DA$

and $\angle A = 90°$

Properties of Square

1. It satisfies all the properties of parallelogram.
2. Each interior angle is right angle and all sides are equal.
3. Diagonals of a square are equal and intersect at right angles.

6. Kite

A quadrilateral in which two pairs of adjacent sides are equal, is known as kite.

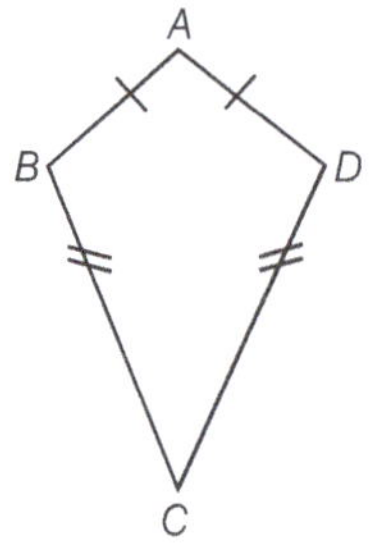

In the figure, *ABCD* is a kite in which $AB = AD$ and $BC = CD$.

Example 2. All the angles of a quadrilateral are equal. What special name is given to this quadrilateral?

Sol. We know that sum of all angles in a quadrilateral is 360°.

If *ABCD* is a quadrilateral, then

$\angle A + \angle B + \angle C + \angle D = 360°$ ...(i)

But it is given, $\angle A = \angle B = \angle C = \angle D$

From Eq. (i), we get

$\angle A + \angle A + \angle A + \angle A = 360° \Rightarrow 4\angle A = 360°$

$\therefore \angle A = 90°$

So, all angles of a quadrilateral are 90°.

Hence, given quadrilateral is a rectangle or square.

Theorems Based on Parallelogram and Their Uses

Theorem 1 *A diagonal of a parallelogram divides it into two congruent triangles.*

Or

Each diagonal of a parallelogram bisects the parallelogram.

Given *ABCD* is a parallelogram and *AC* is its diagonal.

$\therefore AB \parallel CD$ and $BC \parallel AD$

To prove $\Delta ABC \cong \Delta CDA$

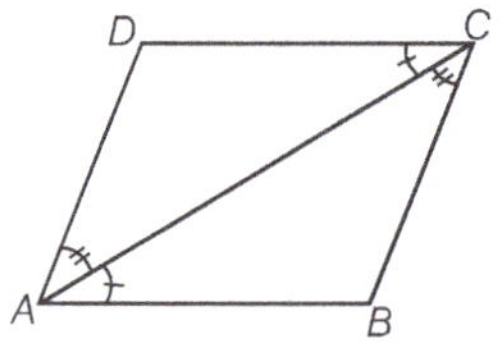

Proof In ΔABC and ΔCDA, $\angle BCA = \angle DAC$

[$\because$ alternate angles are equal]

$AC = AC$ [common sides]

$\angle BAC = \angle DCA$

[$\because$ alternate angles are equal]

$\therefore$ $\Delta ABC \cong \Delta CDA$ [by ASA congruence rule]

Similarly, we can prove that $\Delta ABD \cong \Delta CDB$

Hence, diagonal of a parallelogram divides it into two congruent triangles.

Theorem 2 *In a parallelogram, opposite sides are equal.*

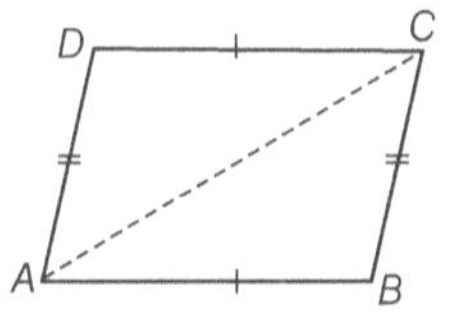

$AB = CD$

and $BC = AD$

Theorem 3 **(Converse of Theorem 2)** *If each pair of opposite sides of a quadrilateral is equal, then it is a parallelogram.*

Theorem 4 *In a parallelogram, opposite angles are equal.*

Given $ABCD$ is a parallelogram.

$\therefore$ $AB \parallel CD$ and $BC \parallel AD$

To prove $\angle A = \angle C$ and $\angle B = \angle D$

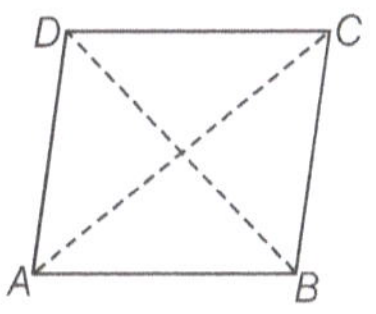

Proof Since, $AB \parallel CD$ and AD is a transversal, then

$\angle A + \angle D = 180^\circ$ [co-interior angles] ...(i)

Similarly, $AD \parallel BC$ and CD is a transversal, then

$\angle D + \angle C = 180^\circ$ [co-interior angles] ...(ii)

From Eqs. (i) and (ii), we get

$$\angle A + \angle D = \angle D + \angle C \Rightarrow \angle A = \angle C$$

Similarly, we can prove that $\angle B = \angle D$.

Theorem 5 **(Converse of Theorem 4)** *If in a quadrilateral, each pair of opposite angles is equal, then it is a parallelogram.*

Given $ABCD$ is a quadrilateral, in which

$\angle A = \angle C$ ...(i)

and $\angle B = \angle D$ ...(ii)

To prove $ABCD$ is a parallelogram.

Proof On adding Eqs. (i) and (ii), we get

$\angle A + \angle B = \angle C + \angle D$ ...(iii)

Now, by angle sum property of a quadrilateral, we have

$\angle A + \angle B + \angle C + \angle D = 360^\circ$ ...(iv)

On putting the value from Eq. (iii), we get

$$\angle A + \angle B + \angle A + \angle B = 360^\circ$$

$\Rightarrow$ $2(\angle A + \angle B) = 360^\circ$

$\Rightarrow$ $\angle A + \angle B = 180^\circ$

$\therefore$ $\angle A + \angle B = \angle C + \angle D = 180^\circ$ [from Eq. (iii)]

Since, the line AB intersect AD and BC at points A and B, respectively such that

$\angle A + \angle B = 180^\circ$ [co-interior angles]

$\therefore$ $AD \parallel BC$

Similarly, $AB \parallel DC$

Hence, $ABCD$ is a parallelogram.

Theorem 6 *A quadrilateral is a parallelogram, if a pair of opposite sides are equal and parallel.*

Theorem 7 *The diagonals of a parallelogram bisects each other.*

Given $ABCD$ is a parallelogram, whose diagonals AC and BD intersect each other at O.

To prove $OA = OC$ and $OB = OD$.

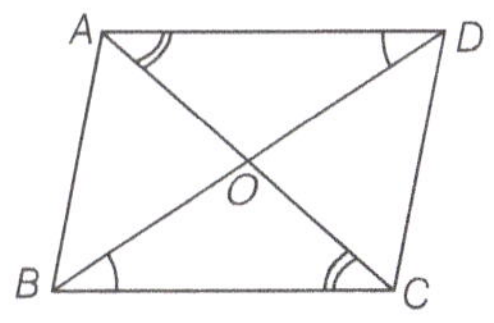

Proof In ΔAOD and ΔCOB, $\angle ODA = \angle OBC$

[$\because$ alternate angles]

$\angle OAD = \angle OCB$ [$\because$ alternate angles]

and $AD = BC$

[opposite sides of a parallelogram are equal]

$\therefore$ $\Delta AOD \cong \Delta COB$ [by ASA congruence rule]

Then, $OA = OC$ and $OB = OD$. [by CPCT]

Theorem 8 **(Converse of Theorem 7)** *If the diagonals of a quadrilateral bisects each other, then it is a parallelogram.*

Given $ABCD$ is a quadrilateral, whose diagonals AC and BD bisect each other

i.e. $OA = OC$ and $OB = OD$

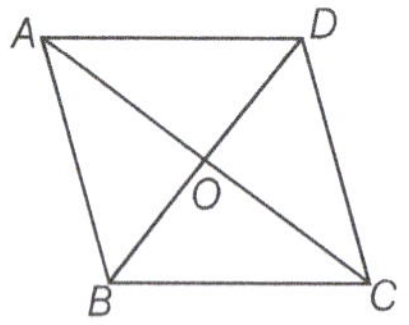

To prove $ABCD$ is a parallelogram.

Proof In ΔAOB and ΔCOD,

$OA = OC$ [given]

$\angle AOB = \angle COD$ [vertically opposite angles]

$OB = OD$ [given]

$\therefore$ $\Delta AOB \cong \Delta COD$ [by SAS congruence rule]

Then, $\angle ODC = \angle OBA$ [by CPCT]

But these are alternate angles, which are formed, when transversal BD intersects lines AB and DC.

$\therefore$ $AB \parallel CD$

Similarly, we can prove that $BC \parallel AD$.

Hence, $ABCD$ is a parallelogram.

Example 3. The perimeter of a parallelogram is 32 cm. If the longer side measures 9.5 cm, then what is the measure of the shorter side?

Sol. Let the measure of shorter side = x cm

Given, longer side measure = 9.5 cm

and perimeter = 32 cm

$\Rightarrow$ 2 (longer side + shorter side) = 32

[$\because$ In parallelogram, opposite sides are equal]

$\Rightarrow$ $9.5 + x = \frac{32}{2} = 16$

$\Rightarrow$ $x = 16 - 9.5$

$\therefore$ $x = 6.5$ cm

Example 4. In the given figure, $ABCD$ is a parallelogram, in which $\angle A = 60°$. Find $\angle B$, $\angle C$ and $\angle D$.

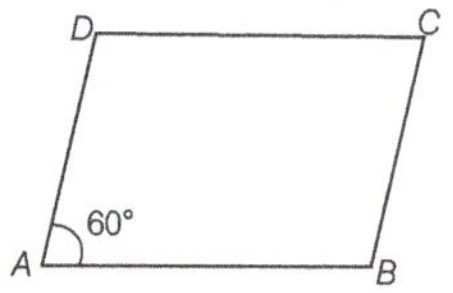

Sol. We know that opposite angles of parallelogram are equal

Therefore, $\angle C = \angle A = 60°$ and let $\angle B = \angle D = x$.

Now, using angle sum property of a quadrilateral,

we have $\angle A + \angle B + \angle C + \angle D = 360°$

$\Rightarrow$ $60° + x + 60° + x = 360°$

$\Rightarrow$ $120° + 2x = 360°$

$\Rightarrow$ $2x = 360° - 120°$

$\Rightarrow$ $2x = 240°$

$\Rightarrow$ $x = 120°$

Hence, $\angle B = 120°$, $\angle C = 60°$ and $\angle D = 120°$.

Example 5. In the following figure, $ABCD$ and $AEFG$ are two parallelograms. If $\angle C = 55°$, then determine $\angle F$.

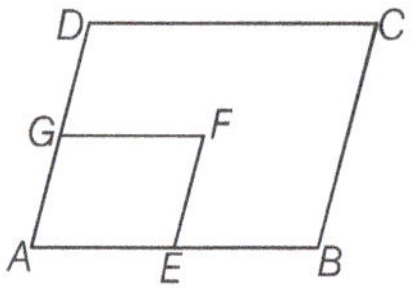

Sol. Given, $ABCD$ is a parallelogram.

$\therefore$ $\angle A = \angle C = 55°$ [$\because$ opposite angles are equal]

Also, $AEFG$ is a parallelogram.

$\therefore$ $\angle A = \angle F = 55°$

Example 6. In the given figure, $ABCD$ is a parallelogram. What is the sum of the angles x, y and z?

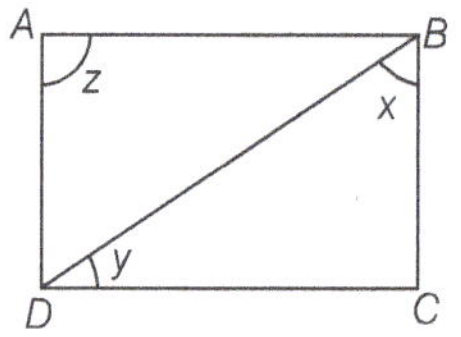

Sol. Given, $ABCD$ is a parallelogram.

$\Rightarrow$ $\angle DAB = \angle DCB = z$

In ΔBCD,

$\angle DBC + \angle BCD + \angle CDB = 180°$

[$\because$ angle sum property of a triangle]

$\Rightarrow$ $x + y + z = 180°$

Example 7. In a parallelogram $ABCD$, if $\angle A = (3x - 20)°$, $\angle B = (y + 15)°$ and $\angle C = (x + 40)°$, then find the values of x and y.

Sol. Given, $ABCD$ is a parallelogram.

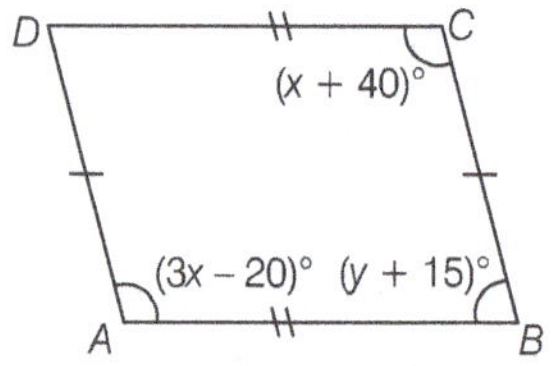

Then, $\angle A = \angle C$

[opposite angles of a parallelogram are equal]

$\Rightarrow$ $(3x - 20)° = (x + 40)°$

$\Rightarrow$ $3x - x = 40° + 20°$

$\Rightarrow$ $2x = 60°$

$\Rightarrow$ $x = 30°$

Also, $\angle A + \angle B = 180^\circ$ [$\because$ co-interior angles]

$\Rightarrow$ $3x - 20^\circ + y + 15^\circ = 180^\circ$

$\Rightarrow$ $3x + y = 185^\circ$

On putting $x = 30^\circ$, we get

$3(30^\circ) + y = 185^\circ$

$\Rightarrow$ $y = 185^\circ - 90^\circ = 95^\circ$

Example 8. *ABCD* is a parallelogram in which *P* and *Q* are the mid-points of opposite sides *AB* and *CD* (given in figure). If *AQ* intersects *DP* at *S* and *BQ* intersects *CP* at *R*, then show that

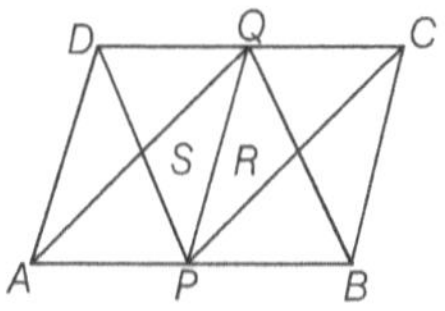

(a) *APCQ* is a parallelogram.
(b) *DPBQ* is a parallelogram.
(c) *PSQR* is a parallelogram.

Sol. Given, *ABCD* is a parallelogram.

$\therefore$ $AB \parallel CD$, $AB = CD$ and $AD \parallel BC$, $AD = BC$

Also, given *P* and *Q* are the mid-points of sides *AB* and *CD*, respectively.

(a) In quadrilateral *APCQ*,

$AP \parallel CQ$ [$\because AB \parallel CD$] ...(i)

Now, $AP = \frac{1}{2}AB$

and $CQ = \frac{1}{2}CD$ ...(ii)

Since, $AB = CD$ [given]

$\Rightarrow$ $\frac{1}{2}AB = \frac{1}{2}CD$

$\Rightarrow$ $AP = CQ$ [using Eq. (ii)]

Thus, we have $AP \parallel CQ$ and $AP = CQ$.

Hence, *APCQ* is a parallelogram.

(b) Similarly, in quadrilateral *DPBQ*,

$BP \parallel QD$ and $BP = QD$

$\therefore$ *DPBQ* is a parallelogram.

(c) Since, *DPBQ* is a parallelogram.

$\therefore$ $DP \parallel BQ$

$\Rightarrow$ $PS \parallel QR$ ...(iii)

and *APCQ* is also a parallelogram.

$\therefore$ $AQ \parallel PC \Rightarrow SQ \parallel PR$ ...(iv)

From Eqs. (iii) and (iv), we have

$PS \parallel QR$ and $SQ \parallel PR$

Hence, *PSQR* is also a parallelogram.

Example 9. In a parallelogram *ABCD*, diagonals *AC* and *BD* intersect at *O* and $AC = 6.8$ cm and $BD = 5.6$ cm. Find the measures of *OC* and *OD*.

Sol. We know that the diagonals of a parallelogram bisect each other. Therefore, *O* is the mid-point of *AC* and *BD*.

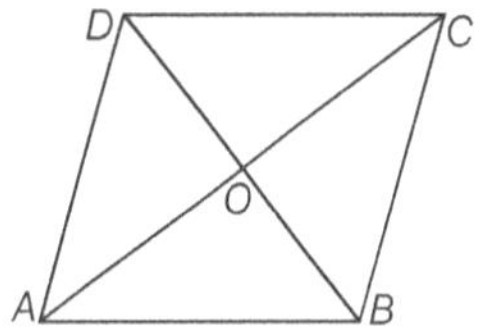

$\therefore$ $OC = \frac{1}{2} \times AC = \frac{1}{2} \times 6.8 = 3.4$ cm

and $OD = \frac{1}{2}BD = \frac{1}{2} \times 5.6 = 2.8$ cm

Example 10. In a parallelogram, show that the angle bisectors of two adjacent angles intersect at right angles.

Sol. Let *ABCD* be a parallelogram, such that angle bisectors of adjacent angle *A* and *B* intersect at point *P*.

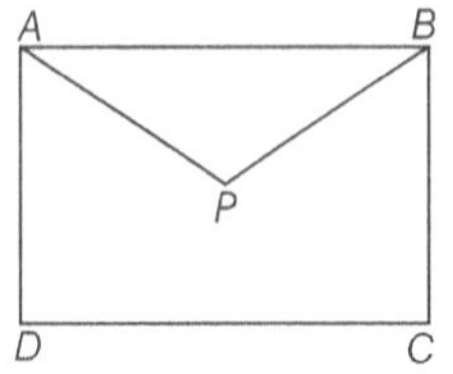

To show that $\angle APB = 90^\circ$

Here, $\angle A + \angle B = 180^\circ$

[$\because AD \parallel BC$ and $\angle A$ and $\angle B$ are consecutive interior angles]

$\Rightarrow$ $\frac{1}{2}\angle A + \frac{1}{2}\angle B = 90^\circ$ [dividing on both sides by 2] ...(i)

But in ΔAPB, we have $\frac{1}{2}\angle A + \frac{1}{2}\angle B + \angle APB = 180^\circ$

[by angle sum property of a triangle]

$\Rightarrow$ $90^\circ + \angle APB = 180^\circ$ [using Eq. (i)]

$\therefore$ $\angle APB = 90^\circ$ **Hence proved**

Example 11. Quadrilateral *ABCD* is a parallelogram and *AP* and *CQ* are perpendicular from vertices *A* and *C* on diagonal *BD* (see the figure).

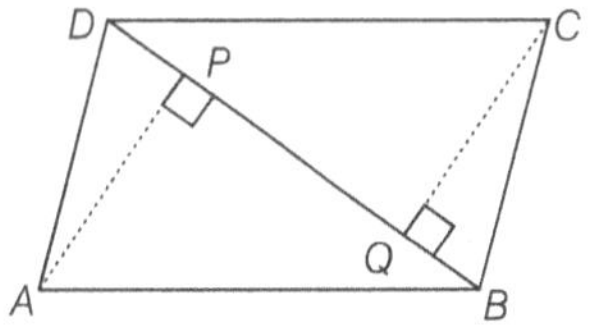

Show that

(i) $\Delta CQD \cong \Delta APB$.
(ii) $AP = CQ$.

Sol. Given, *ABCD* is a parallelogram.

$\therefore$ $\angle CDB = \angle DBA$ ...(i)

and *AP* and *CQ* are perpendicular from vertices *A* and *C* on diagonal *BD*.

(i) Now, in ΔCQD and ΔAPB, we have

$CD = AB$

[opposite sides of a parallelogram]

$\angle CQD = \angle APB = 90^\circ$ [given]

$\angle CDQ = \angle ABP$ [from Eq. (i)]

$\therefore \quad \Delta CQD \cong \Delta APB$ [by AAS congruence rule]

(ii) Since, $\Delta APB \cong \Delta CQD$

$\therefore \quad AP = CQ$ [by CPCT]

Important Results Based on Rectangle, Rhombus and Square

Here, we study special types of parallelogram in which we can find (or prove or shown) the important results of rectangle, rhombus and square.

Result 1 *If the diagonals of a parallelogram are equal, then it is a rectangle.*

Given Let parallelogram be $ABCD$, whose diagonals AC and BD are equal i.e. $AC = BD$.

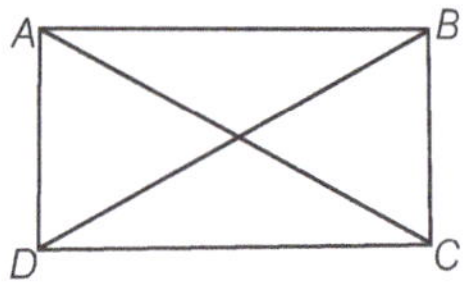

To prove $ABCD$ is a rectangle.

Proof In ΔABC and ΔDCB, we have

$AB = CD$ [opposite sides of parallelogram]

$BC = CB$ [common sides]

and $AC = BD$ [given]

$\therefore \quad \Delta ABC \cong \Delta DCB$ [by SSS congruence rule]

So, $\angle ABC = \angle DCB$ ...(i)

But $DC \parallel AB$ and transversal CB intersects them.

$\therefore \quad \angle ABC + \angle DCB = 180^\circ$ [co-interior angles]

$\Rightarrow \quad \angle ABC + \angle ABC = 180^\circ$ [from Eq. (i)]

$\Rightarrow \quad 2\angle ABC = 180^\circ$

$\Rightarrow \quad \angle ABC = 90^\circ = \angle DCB$

Thus, $ABCD$ is a parallelogram and one of its angle is 90°.

Hence, $ABCD$ is a rectangle. **Hence proved**

Result 2 *If the diagonals of a parallelogram intersect each other at right angles, then it is a rhombus.*

Given A parallelogram $ABCD$, whose diagonals AC and BD intersect each other at right angles i.e.

$$\angle AOD = \angle AOB = \angle COD = \angle BOC = 90^\circ$$

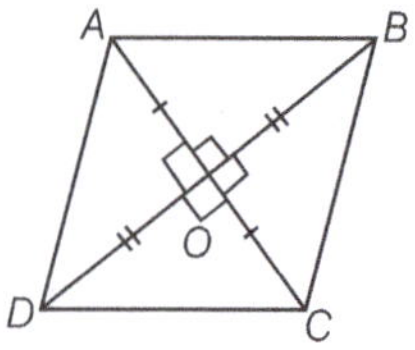

To prove $ABCD$ is a rhombus.

Proof In ΔAOB and ΔCOD, $OA = OC$ and $OB = OD$

[$\because$ diagonals of a parallelogram bisect each other]

$\angle AOB = \angle COD$ [given]

$\therefore \quad \Delta AOB \cong \Delta COD$ [by SAS congruence rule]

Then, $AB = CD$ [by CPCT] ...(i)

Again, in ΔAOD and ΔCOB, we have

$OA = OC$ and $OD = OB$

[$\because$ diagonals of a parallelogram bisect each other]

and $\angle AOD = \angle BOC$ [given]

$\therefore \quad \Delta AOD \cong \Delta COB$ [by SAS congruence rule]

Then, $AD = BC$ [by CPCT] ...(ii)

Similarly, we can prove that

$AB = AD$ and $CD = BC$ ...(iii)

From Eqs. (i), (ii) and (iii), we get

$$AB = BC = AD = CD$$

Hence, $ABCD$ is a rhombus. **Hence proved**

Result 3 *If the diagonals of a parallelogram are equal and intersect each other at right angles, then it is a square.*

Given A parallelogram $ABCD$, in which $AC = BD$ and $AC \perp BD$.

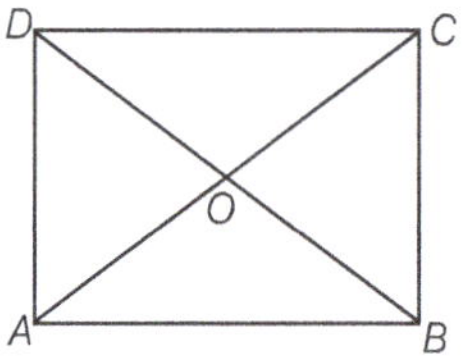

To prove $ABCD$ is a square.

Proof Let AC and BD intersect at a point O.

In ΔABO and ΔADO, we have

$BO = OD$ [given]

$AO = OA$ [common sides]

$\angle AOB = \angle AOD = 90^\circ$ [given]

$\therefore \quad \Delta ABO \cong \Delta ADO$ [by SAS congruence rule]

Then, $AB = AD$ [by CPCT]

Also, $AB = DC$ and $AD = BC$

[$\because$ opposite sides of a parallelogram are equal]

$\therefore \quad AB = BC = DC = AD$ ...(i)

Again, in ΔABC and ΔBAD, we have

$AB = BA$ [common sides]

$AC = BD$ [given]

$BC = AD$ [from Eq. (i)]

$\therefore \quad \Delta ABC \cong \Delta BAD$

[by SSS congruence rule]

Then, $\angle ABC = \angle BAD$ [by CPCT] ...(ii)

Also, $\angle ABC + \angle BAD = 180^\circ$ [co-interior angles]

$\therefore \quad \angle ABC = \angle BAD = 90^\circ$ [using Eq. (ii)]

Thus, $AB = BC = CD = DA$ and $\angle A = 90^\circ$

Hence, $ABCD$ is a square. **Hence proved**

Example 12. In the given figure, $ABCD$ is a rhombus. Then, find the value of x.

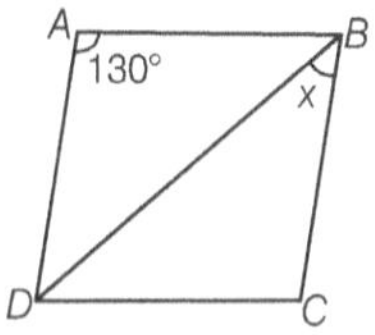

Sol. Given, $ABCD$ is a rhombus in which $\angle BAD = 130°$ and $\angle DBC = x$.

$\therefore \quad \angle B = 2\angle DBC = 2x$

[$\because$ diagonals bisect the angles in rhombus]

Now, $\angle DAB + \angle B = 180°$ [co-interior angles]

$\Rightarrow \quad 130° + 2x = 180°$ [from figure]

$\Rightarrow \quad 2x = 180° - 130° = 50°$

$\therefore \quad x = 25°$

Example 13. In the following figure, $ABCD$ is a square. A line segment DX cuts the side BC at X and the diagonal AC at O, such that $\angle COD = 105°$. Find the value of x.

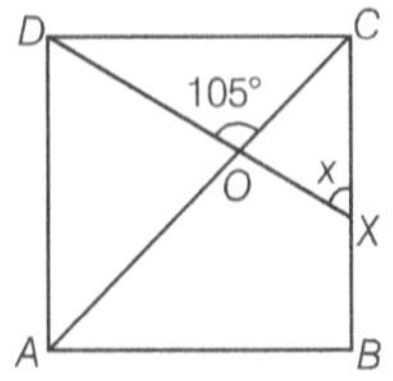

Sol. Given, $ABCD$ is a square in which $\angle COD = 105°$.

We know that the diagonal AC of square $ABCD$ will bisect the $\angle C$.

$\therefore \quad \angle OCX = \frac{1}{2}\angle C = \frac{1}{2} \times 90° = 45°$ ...(i)

Now, we have

$\angle COD + \angle COX = 180°$ [linear pair]

$\Rightarrow \quad 105° + \angle COX = 180°$

$\Rightarrow \quad \angle COX = 180° - 105°$

$\Rightarrow \quad \angle COX = 75°$ ...(ii)

Now, in ΔCOX, we have $\angle COX + \angle OXC + \angle OCX = 180°$

[angle sum property of a triangle]

$\Rightarrow \quad 75° + x + 45° = 180°$ [using Eqs. (i) and (ii)]

$\Rightarrow \quad x = 180° - 120°$

$\therefore \quad x = 60°$

Example 14. Prove that the quadrilateral formed by the bisectors of the angles of a parallelogram is a rectangle.

Sol. **Given** Let $ABCD$ be a parallelogram and AP, BR, CR and DP be the bisectors of $\angle A$, $\angle B$, $\angle C$ and $\angle D$, respectively.

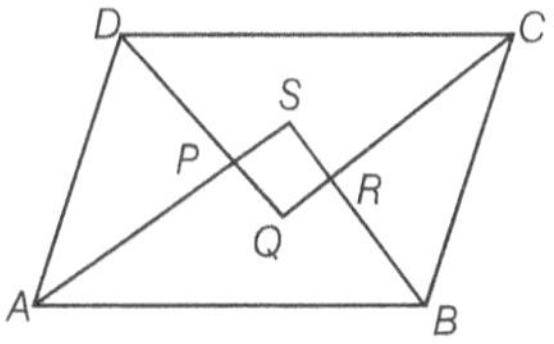

To prove Quadrilateral $PQRS$ is a rectangle.

Proof Since, $ABCD$ is a parallelogram.

$\therefore$ $DC \parallel AB$ and DA is a transversal.

We have,

$\angle A + \angle D = 180°$ [corresponding interior angles]

$\Rightarrow \quad \frac{1}{2}\angle A + \frac{1}{2}\angle D = 90°$

$\Rightarrow \quad \angle PAD + \angle PDA = 90°$

$\Rightarrow \quad \angle APD = 90°$

[$\because$ sum of the angles of a triangle is 180°]

$\therefore \quad \angle SPQ = 90°$ [vertically opposite angles]

Similarly, $\quad \angle PQR = 90°$,

$\angle QRS = 90°$

and $\quad \angle PSR = 90°$

Thus, $PQRS$ is a quadrilateral, each of whose angles is 90°. Hence, $PQRS$ is a rectangle. **Hence proved**

Example 15. In the given figure, two parallel lines l and m are intersected by a transversal X. Show that the quadrilateral formed by the bisectors of interior angles, is a rectangle.

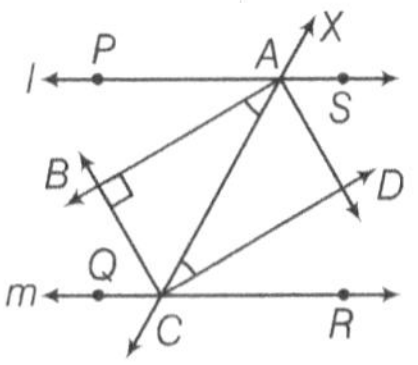

Sol. Given, lines l and m are parallel i.e. $PS \parallel QR$ and transversal X intersects PS and QR at points A and C, respectively.

The bisectors of $\angle PAC$ and $\angle ACQ$ intersect each other at B and bisectors of $\angle ACR$ and $\angle SAC$ intersect each other at D. Now, we have to show that quadrilateral $ABCD$ is a rectangle. Since, $PS \parallel CR$ and X is a transversal.

$\therefore \quad \angle PAC = \angle ACR$ [alternate angles]

$\Rightarrow \quad \frac{1}{2}\angle PAC = \frac{1}{2}\angle ACR$

[multiplying by 1/2 on both sides]

$\Rightarrow \quad \angle BAC = \angle ACD$

These form a pair of alternate angles for lines AB and CD with AC as transversal.

So, $\quad AB \parallel CD$

Similarly, $\quad BC \parallel AD$

Therefore, quadrilateral $ABCD$ is a parallelogram.

Now, PS is a straight line.

So, $\quad \angle PAC + \angle SAC = 180°$ [linear pair]

$\Rightarrow \quad \frac{1}{2}\angle PAC + \frac{1}{2}\angle SAC = \frac{1}{2} \times 180°$

[multiplying by 1/2 on both sides]

$\Rightarrow \quad \angle BAC + \angle DAC = 90°$

$\Rightarrow \quad \angle BAD = 90°$

Thus, one angle of parallelogram $ABCD$ is a right angle.

Hence, $ABCD$ is a rectangle.

Example 16. A diagonal of a parallelogram bisects one of its angles. Show that it is a rhombus.

Sol. *ABCD* is a parallelogram, in which diagonal *AC* bisects the $\angle A$.

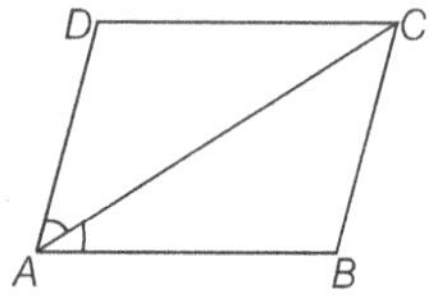

To show *ABCD* is a rhombus.

Proof Since, diagonal *AC* bisects $\angle A$.

$\therefore \quad \angle CAB = \angle CAD$ ...(i)

Since, $AB \| CD$ and *AC* is a transversal.

$\therefore \quad \angle CAB = \angle ACD$ ...(ii)

[alternate interior angles]

Again, $AD \| BC$ and *AC* is a transversal.

$\angle DAC = \angle ACB$ ...(iii)

[alternate interior angles]

From Eqs. (i), (ii) and (iii), we get

$\therefore \quad \angle ACD = \angle ACB$

$\Rightarrow$ *AC* bisects $\angle C$.

Now, $\angle A = \angle C$ [$\because$ opposite angles of a parallelogram]

$\Rightarrow \quad \frac{1}{2}\angle A = \frac{1}{2}\angle C$

$\Rightarrow \quad \angle DAC = \angle DCA \Rightarrow CD = AD$ ...(iv)

[$\because$ sides opposite to equal angles of a triangle]

But $AB = CD$ and $AD = BC$

[$\because$ opposite sides of parallelogram]

$\therefore \quad AB = BC = CD = AD$ [$\because$ from Eq. (iv)]

Hence, *ABCD* is a rhombus.

Example 17. *ABCD* is a rhombus and *AB* is produced of *E* and *F*, such that $AE = AB = BF$. Prove that *ED* and *FC*, when produced, meet at right angle.

Sol. **Given** *ABCD* is a rhombus. *AB* produced to *E* and *F*, such that $AE = AB = BF$ ...(i)

Construction Join *ED* and *CF* and produced it to meet at *G*.

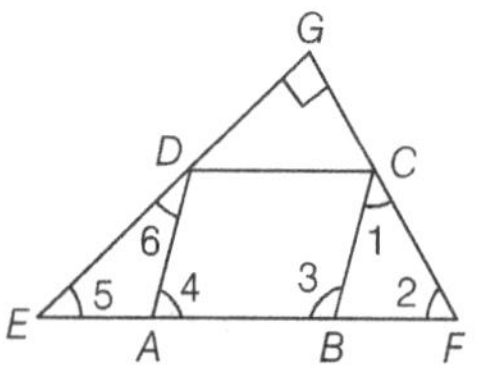

To prove $EG \perp FG$

Proof Since, *ABCD* is a rhombus.

$\therefore \quad AB = CD = BC = AD$ ...(ii)

Now, in ΔBCF, we have

$BC = BF$ [from Eqs. (i) and (ii)]

$\Rightarrow \quad \angle 2 = \angle 1$

[$\because$ angles opposite to equal sides are equal]

and $\quad \angle 3 = \angle 1 + \angle 2$ [exterior angles]

$\Rightarrow \quad \angle 3 = 2\angle 2$ ...(iii)

Similarly, in ΔADE, we have $AE = AD$

$\Rightarrow \quad \angle 6 = \angle 5$

and $\quad \angle 4 = \angle 5 + \angle 6 = 2\angle 5$ ...(iv)

On adding Eqs. (iii) and (iv), we get

$\angle 4 + \angle 3 = 2\angle 5 + 2\angle 2 \Rightarrow 180^\circ = 2(\angle 5 + \angle 2)$

[since, $\angle 4$ and $\angle 3$ are consecutive interior angles]

$\Rightarrow \quad \angle 5 + \angle 2 = 90^\circ$ ...(v)

Now, in ΔEGF, we have

$\angle 5 + \angle 2 + \angle EGF = 180^\circ \Rightarrow 90^\circ + \angle EGF = 180^\circ$

$\therefore \quad \angle EGF = 90^\circ$

Hence, $EG \perp FG$. **Hence proved**

Example 20. If the figure given below, *PQRS* is a rhombus and *SRFE* is a square.

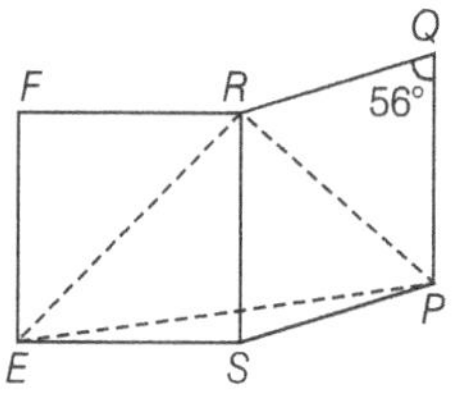

If $\angle PQR = 56^\circ$, evaluate

(a) $\angle SPE$ (b) $\angle FEP$ (c) $\angle EPR$ (d) $\angle PER$

Sol. Given, *PQRS* is a rhombus

$\therefore \quad PS = RS$ and $\angle PSR = \angle PQR = 56^\circ$

Also, *SRFE* is a square.

$\therefore \quad ES = RS$

and $\angle FES = \angle ESR = \angle SRF = \angle RFE = 90^\circ$

$\Rightarrow \quad PS = RS = ES$

(a) In ΔPES,

$PS = ES \Rightarrow \angle SPE = \angle PES$ ...(i)

[$\because$ angles opposite to equal sides of a triangle are equal]

$\therefore \angle SPE + \angle PES + \angle PSE = 180^\circ$

[angle sum property of a triangle]

$\Rightarrow 2\angle SPE + 146^\circ = 180^\circ$

[$\because \angle PSE = \angle ESR + \angle PSR = 90^\circ + 56^\circ = 146^\circ$]

$\Rightarrow \quad 2SPE = 34^\circ \Rightarrow \angle SPE = 17^\circ$

(b) $\angle SEP = 17^\circ$ ...(ii) [using Eq. (i)]

In rhombus *PQRS*,

$\angle PQR + \angle QRS + \angle RSP + \angle SPQ = 360^\circ$

[angle sum property of a quadrilateral]

$\Rightarrow 56^\circ + 56^\circ + 2SPQ = 360^\circ$

[$\because$ opposite angles of a rhombus are equal]

$\Rightarrow \quad 2\angle SPQ = 360^\circ - 112^\circ \Rightarrow \angle SPQ = 124^\circ$

$\therefore \quad \angle SPR = \frac{124^\circ}{2} = 62^\circ$

[$\because$ diagonals of a rhombus bisect its angles]

$\angle FEP = \angle FES - \angle SEP = 90^\circ - 17^\circ = 73^\circ$

[using Eq. (ii) and each angle of a square is 90°]

(c) $\angle EPR = \angle SPR - \angle SPE = 62^\circ - 17^\circ = 45^\circ$

(d) $\angle RES = \frac{90^\circ}{2} = 45^\circ$

[$\because$ the diagonals of a square bisect its angles]

$\therefore \angle PER = \angle RES - \angle SEP$

$= 45^\circ - 17^\circ = 28^\circ$

Chapter Practice

a. 1 Mark Questions

1. $PQ = QR = RS = SP$, $\angle P = 90°$, $PQ \parallel RS$ and $RQ \parallel PS$.

(a) Square (b) Rectangle
(c) Parallelogram (d) Rhombus

2. $PQ \parallel SR$, $QR \parallel PS$ and $PQ = QR = RS = SP$.

(a) Square
(b) Rectangle
(c) Parallelogram
(d) Rhombus

3. $PQ \parallel SR$ and $QR \parallel PS$.

(a) Square
(b) Rectangle
(c) Parallelogram
(d) Rhombus

4. $PQ \parallel SR$ and $QR \parallel PS$ and $\angle P = 90°$.

(a) Square
(b) Rectangle
(c) Parallelogram
(d) Rhombus

5. Diagonals of a rectangle are equal and perpendicular. Is this statement true?

(a) Yes
(b) No
(c) Diagonals equal but not perpendicular
(d) None

6. The given figure shows a rhombus $ABCD$. Find the value of y.

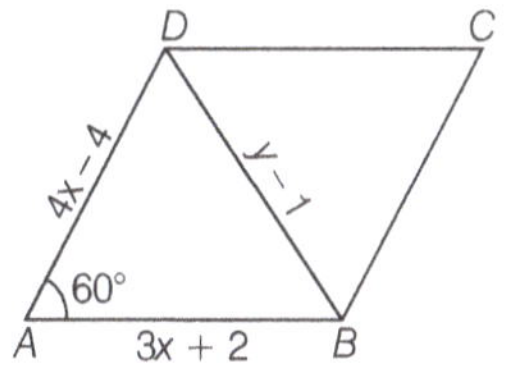

(a) 21 (b) 6 (c) 12 (d) 8

b. 3 Marks Questions

7. In the following figure, $ABCD$ is a parallelogram. Find the values of x and y.

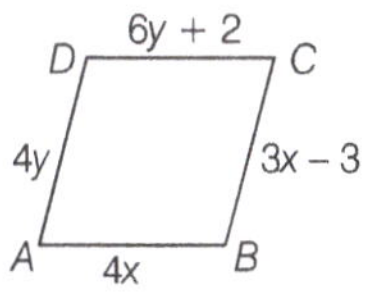

8. The perimeter of a parallelogram $ABCD$ is 40 cm. $AB = 3x$ cm, $BC = 2x$ cm and $CD = 2(y+1)$ cm. Find the values of x and y.

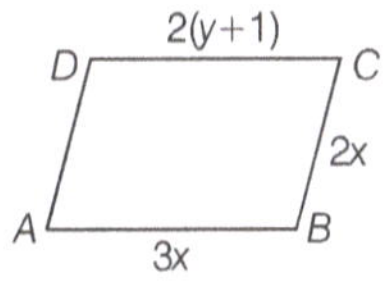

9. In the following figure, $ABCD$ is a parallelogram. Find the value of y.

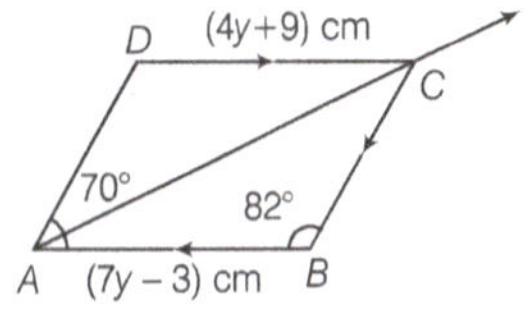

10. In the following figure, $ABCD$ is parallelogram. Find the values of x, y and z.

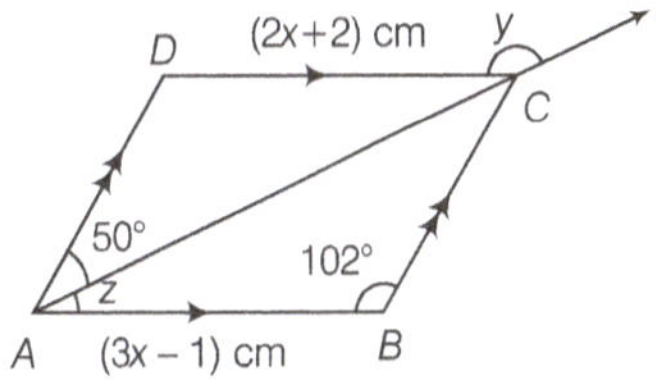

11. Two opposite angles of a parallelogram are $(3x-2)°$ and $(63-2x)°$. Find all the angles of the parallelogram.

12. In the following figure, $ABCD$ is a parallelogram. Find the measure of the angles x and y.

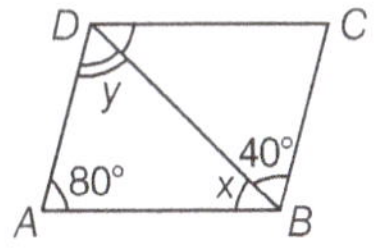

13. In the given rectangle, $\angle ABE = 30°$ and $\angle CFE = 144°$. Find the measure of $\angle BEF$.

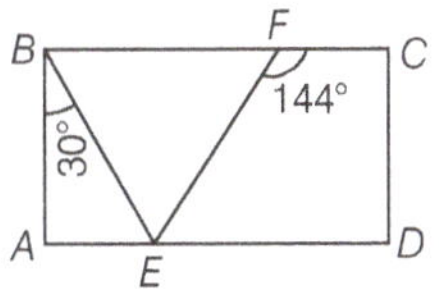

14. A diagonal of a rectangle is inclined to the one side of the rectangle at 25°. Find the acute angle between the diagonals.

15. If $ABCD$ is a rhombus, such that $\angle ACB = 40°$. Then, find $\angle ADB$.

16. In the given figure, $ABCD$ is a parallelogram. If $\angle A = 65°$, then find the value of $\angle B + \angle D$.

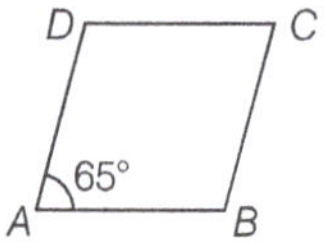

17. If an angle of a parallelogram is 2/3 of its adjacent angle, then find the smallest angle of the parallelogram.

18. Prove that sum of any two consecutive angle is 180° in parallelogram.

19. Diagonals of a quadrilateral $ABCD$ bisects each other. If $\angle A = 35°$, then find the value of $\angle B$.

20. If $ABCD$ is a square and ΔBOC is an equilateral triangle. Find the values of x and y.

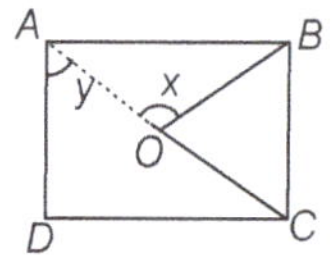

21. In a rectangle $ABCD$, diagonals intersect at O. If $\angle OAB = 30°$, find

(i) $\angle ACB$ (ii) $\angle ABO$ (iii) $\angle COD$ (iv) $\angle BOC$

22. If BEC is an equilateral triangle in the square $ABCD$. Find the value of x in the figure.

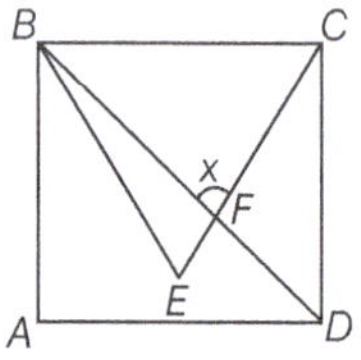

C. 4/5 Marks Questions

23. Diagonal AC of a parallelogram $ABCD$ bisects $\angle A$ (see the figure). Show that

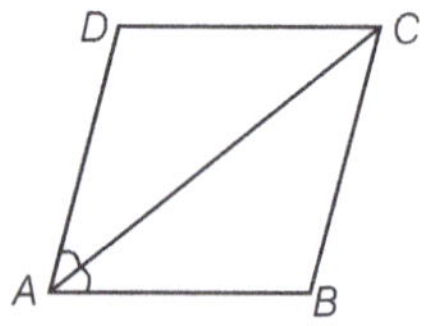

(i) it bisects $\angle C$ also.
(ii) $ABCD$ is a rhombus.

24. In a quadrilateral $ABCD$, AO and BO are the bisectors of $\angle A$ and $\angle B$, respectively. Prove that $\angle AOB = \frac{1}{2}(\angle C + \angle D)$.

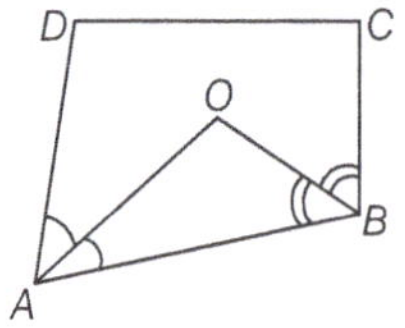

25. In a parallelogram $ABCD$, $AB = 30$ cm and $AD = 20$ cm. The bisector of $\angle A$ meets DC at E and BC produced at F. Find the length of CF.

26. The angle between two altitudes of a parallelogram through the vertex of an obtuse angle of the parallelogram is 60°. Find the angles of the parallelogram.

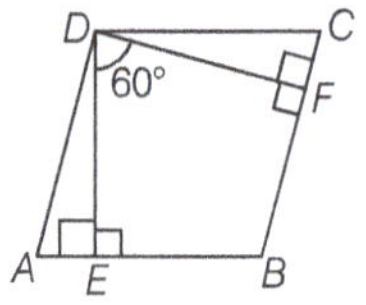

27. In the given figure, $ABCD$ and $PBCQ$ are parallelograms. Prove that

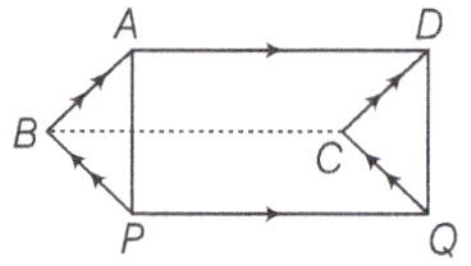

(a) $APQD$ is a parallelogram.
(b) $AP = DQ$.
(c) $\Delta ABP \cong \Delta DCQ$.

28. In the given figure, $ABCD$ is a parallelogram. E is the mid-point of side BC, DE and AB, when produced, meet at F. Prove that $AF = 2AB$.

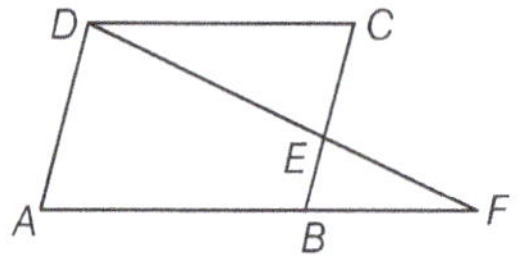

29. In parallelogram $ABCD$, two points P and Q are taken on diagonal BD such that $DP = BQ$ (see the figure). Show that $APCQ$ is a parallelogram.

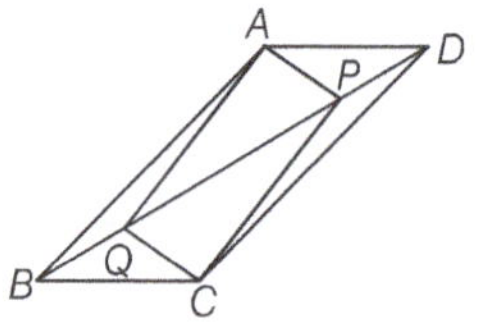

30. In the given figure, bisectors of $\angle A$ and $\angle C$ of quadrilateral $ABCD$ meet DC and BA produced at Q and P respectively. Show that

$$\angle P + \angle Q = \frac{1}{2}(\angle A + \angle C)$$

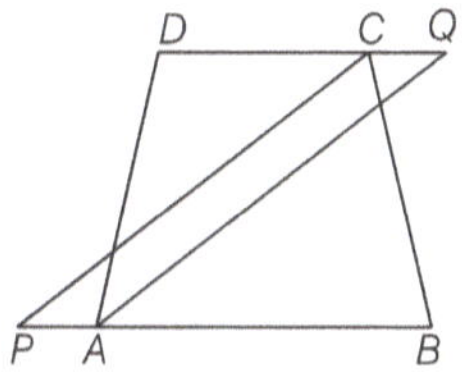

31. In the following figure, P is the mid-point of side BC of a parallelogram $ABCD$, such that $\angle BAP = \angle DAP$. Prove that

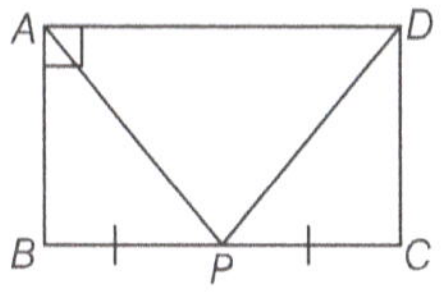

(i) $CP = CD$. (ii) $AD = 2CD$.
(iii) DP bisects $\angle D$. (iv) $\angle APD = 90°$.

32. Prove that the bisectors of the interior angles of a rectangle form a square.

33. In a ΔABC, median BM is produced to a point D such that $DM = BM$. Prove that $ABCD$ is a parallelogram.

34. In the following figure, $ABCD$ is a parallelogram and $\angle DAB = 60°$. If the bisectors AP and BP of $\angle A$ and $\angle B$, respectively, meet at P on CD. Then, prove that P is the mid-point of CD.

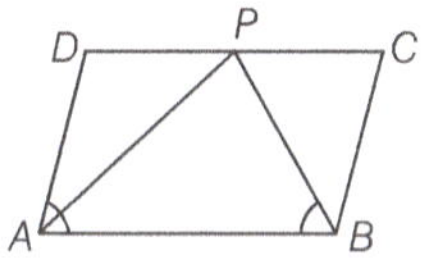

35. $ABCD$ is a rhombus, in which altitude from D to side AB bisects AB. Find the angles of the rhombus.

36. $ABCD$ is a parallelogram. If the bisectors of $\angle A$ and $\angle C$ meet the diagonal BD at P and Q, respectively. Prove that the quadrilateral $PCQA$ is a parallelogram.

37. In the parallelogram $ABCD$, M is mid-point of AC and X, Y are points on AB and DC, respectively such that $AX = CY$. Prove that

(i) ΔAXM is congruent to ΔCYM.
(ii) XMY is a straight line.

38. In the figure shown below, $WXYZ$ is a rhombus such that $\angle W = 65°$. If ZAY is an equilateral triangle, determine

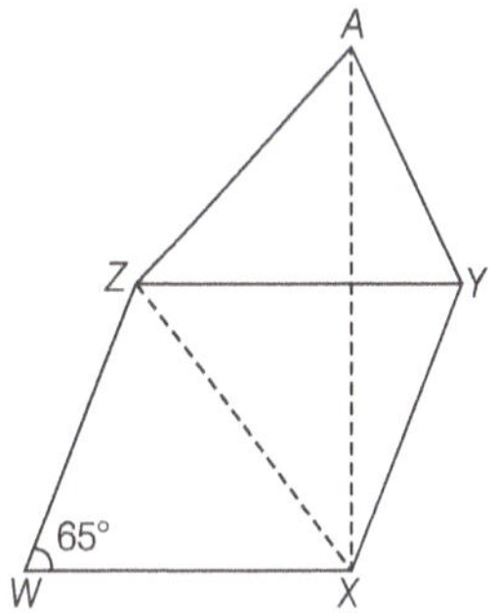

(i) $\angle YXA$
(ii) $\angle ZXA$

Hints and Answers

1. (a) **2.** (d)
3. (c) **4.** (b)
5. (c) **6.** (a)

7. Hint $6y + 2 = 4x$ ...(i)
and $4y = 3x - 3$ ...(ii)
[$\because$ in parallelogram opposite sides are equal]
Ans. $x = 5$ and $y = 3$

8. Hint Opposite sides of a parallelogram are equal.
$\therefore$ $AD = 2x$ and $2(y + 1) = 3x$
Also, $3x + 2x + 2(y + 1) + 2x = 40$
Ans. $x = 4$ and $y = 5$

9. Hint $7y - 3 = 4y + 9$
Ans. $y = 4$ cm

10. Hint $3x - 1 = 2x + 2 \Rightarrow x = 3$
Now, $\angle D = \angle B = 102°$
Also, $y = 50° + \angle D$
$\therefore$ $\angle DAB + 102° = 180° \Rightarrow \angle DAB = 78°$
Ans. $x = 3$, $y = 152°$ and $z = 28°$

11. Hint $(3x - 2)° = (63 - 2x)°$
[$\because$ opposite angles of a parallelogram are equal]
Ans. 37°, 143°, 37° and 143°

12. Hint $\because \angle DAB + \angle CBA = 180°$
[$\because$ sum of co-interior angles are supplementary]
Also, $80° + x + 40° = 180°$
$\Rightarrow$ $y + 80° + 60° = 180°$
[$\because$ angle sum propety of a trinagle]
Ans. $\angle x = 60°$ and $\angle y = 40°$

13. Hint From the figure,
$\angle ABE + \angle EBF = \angle ABF$
and $\angle BFE + \angle CFE = 180°$
Ans. 84°

14. Hint Angle less than 90° is an acute angle. Since, the diagonals of a rectangle bisects each other.

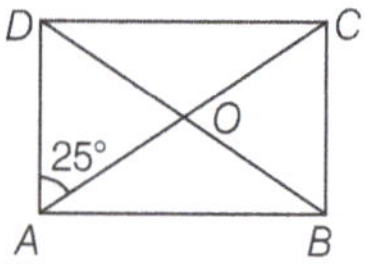

Then, $\frac{1}{2}AC = \frac{1}{2}BD$ **Ans.** 50°

15. Hint $\because AB = CD = BC = AD$

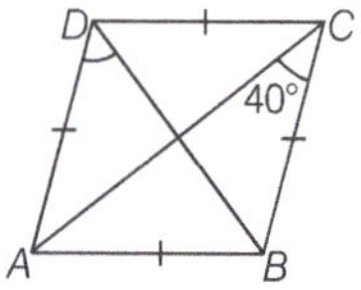

In ΔABC, $AB = BC \Rightarrow \angle BAC = 40°$

$\therefore \quad \angle ABC = \angle ADC = 100°$

Ans. $\angle ADB = 50°$

16. Hint Do same as Example 4. **Ans.** 230°

17. Hint Let the angle be x, then $x = \frac{2}{3}(180° - x)$

Ans. 72°

18.

$AD \parallel BC$

$\angle A + \angle B = 180°$

[$\because$ sum of interior angles on the same side of the transversal is 180°]

Similarly, $\angle B + \angle C = 180°$, $\angle C + \angle D = 180°$

and $\angle D + \angle A = 180°$

19. Hint The diagonals of the quadrilateral bisect each other so, $ABCD$ is a parallelogram.

$\angle B = 180° - \angle A = 180° - 35° = 145°$ **Ans.** 145°

20. Hint

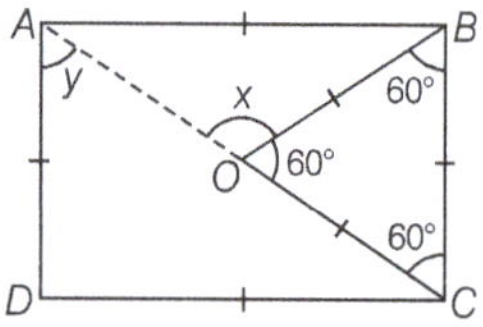

Ans. $x = 75°$ and $y = 15°$

21. (i) **Hint** $\angle ABC = 90°$

$\therefore \angle ACB + 30° + 90° = 180°$

[sum of angles in a triangle is 180°]

Ans. 60°

(ii) **Hint** $\because AC = BD$ [diagonals are equal]

$2AO = 2BO \Rightarrow AO = BO$

[diagonals bisect each other]

Ans. 30°

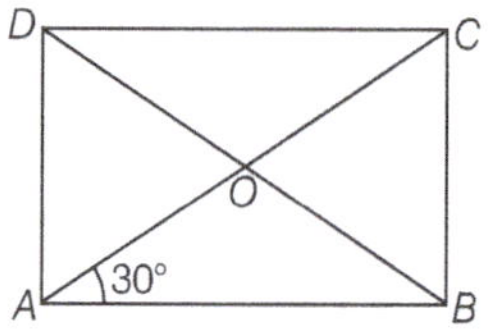

(iii) **Hint** $\angle AOB + 30° + 30° = 180°$ **Ans.** 120°

(iv) **Hint** $\angle BOC + 120° = 180°$ **Ans.** 60°

22. Hint Since, $ABCD$ is a square and BD is a diagonal.

$\therefore \quad \angle DBC = 45°$.

$\because BEC$ is an equilateral triangle.

$\therefore \angle BCE = 60°$.

In ΔBFC, $x + 45° + 60° = 180°$

Ans. $x = 75°$

23. (i) **Hint** Given, diagonal AC of a parallelogram $ABCD$ bisects $\angle A$.

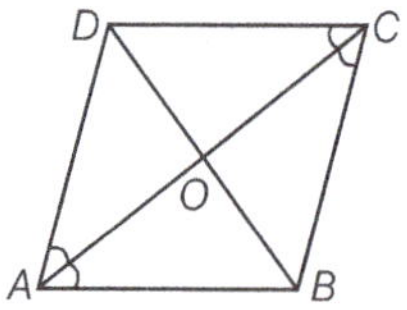

i. e. $\quad \angle DAC = \angle BAC$

$= \frac{1}{2}\angle BAD$ ...(i)

Here, $AB \parallel DC$ and AC is a transversal.

$\therefore \quad \angle DCA = \angle BAC$

[pair of alternate angles] ...(ii)

$\therefore \quad \angle BCA = \angle DAC$

[pair of alternate angles] ...(iii)

From Eqs. (i), (ii) and (iii), we get result

$\angle DAC = \angle BCA = \angle BAC = \angle DCA$ ...(iv)

Hence, diagonal AC also bisects $\angle C$.

(ii) **Hint** From Eq. (iv),

$\angle DAC = \angle DCA$

$\Rightarrow \quad CD = DA$

[$\because$ sides opposite to equal angles are equal]

But $AB = DC$ and $AD = BC$

[$\because ABCD$ is a parallelogram]

$\therefore AB = BC = CD = DA$

Hence, $ABCD$ is a rhombus.

24. Hint In ΔAOB, $\angle OAB + \angle OBA + \angle AOB = 180°$ ...(i)

[angle sum property of a triangle]

$\Rightarrow \angle A + \angle B + \angle C + \angle D = 360°$

[sum of angles of a quadrilateral is 360°]

$\Rightarrow \frac{1}{2}\angle A + \frac{1}{2}\angle B + \frac{1}{2}\angle C + \frac{1}{2}\angle D = 180°$ ...(ii)

Equating Eqs. (i) and (ii), we have

$\angle AOB = \frac{1}{2}(\angle C + \angle D)$

25. Hint $\angle ADE = \angle ECF$ [alternate angles]

$\angle 1 = \angle F$

$\Rightarrow \angle 2 = \angle F$ [$\because \angle 1 = \angle 2$, given]

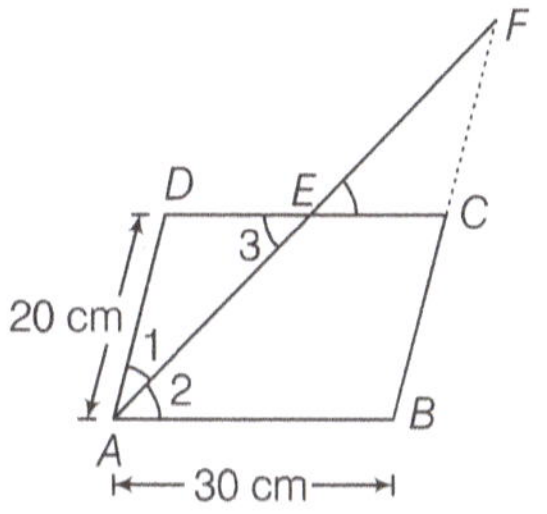

Thus, in ΔAFB, we have

$\angle 2 = \angle F$

$\Rightarrow BF = AB$

[$\because$ sides opposite to equal angles of a triangle are equal]

$\Rightarrow BC + CF = 30$

$\Rightarrow AD + CF = 30$

[$\because BC = AD$, opposite sides of a parallelogram]

$\Rightarrow 20 + CF = 30$

$\Rightarrow CF = 30 - 20$

Ans. 10 cm

26. Hint $\angle BED = \angle BFD = 90°$

$\therefore \angle FBE = 360° - (\angle FDE + \angle BED + \angle BFD)$

[angle sum property of a quadrilateral]

$= 360° - (60° + 90° + 90°)$

Since, $ABCD$ is a parallelogram.

$\therefore \angle ADC = 120°$

Now, $\angle A + \angle B = 180°$

[interior angles of a parallelogram]

$\Rightarrow \angle A = 180° - \angle B$

$= 180° - 120°$ [$\because \angle FBE = \angle B$]

Also, $\angle C = \angle A$

Ans. Angles of the parallelogram are 60°, 120°, 60° and 120°, respectively.

27. (a) **Hint** Since, $ABCD$ is a parallelogram. Therefore, we have

$AD \parallel BC$

and $AD = BC$ ...(i)

[$\because$ opposite sides of a parallelogram are equal and parallel]

(b) **Hint** $AP = QD$

[$\because$ opposite sides of a parallelogram $APQD$ are equal]

(c) **Hint** $\Delta ABP \cong \Delta DCQ$ by SSS congruence rule.

28. Hint Given, $ABCD$ is a parallelogram.

$\therefore AB = CD$ and $AD = BC$

Also, E is the mid-point of side BC

i.e. $BE = CE$

Now, in ΔDEC and ΔBEF, we have

$\angle DEC = \angle BEF$ [vertically opposite angles]

$CE = BE$ [given]

and $\angle DCE = \angle FBE$ [alternate interior angles]

$\therefore \Delta DEC \cong \Delta BEF$ [by ASA congruence rule]

So, $DC = BF$ [by CPCT] ...(i)

Also, we have $DC = AB$ [given] ...(ii)

From Eqs. (i) and (ii), we get

$AB = BF$

$\therefore AF = 2AB$

29. Hint In ΔAPD and ΔCQB

$\angle ADP = \angle CBQ$ [alternate interior angles]

$\Rightarrow AD = CB$ [opposite sides of parallelogram]

$\Rightarrow DP = BQ$ [given]

$\therefore \Delta APD \cong \Delta CQB$ [by SAS congruence rule]

$\therefore AP = CQ$ [CPCT]

Similarly, $\Delta AQB \cong \Delta CDP$ [by SAS congruence rule]

So, $AQ = CP$ and $AP = CQ$

30. Hint $\angle DAQ = \frac{1}{2}\angle A$ [$\because AQ$ is bisector of $\angle A$] ...(i)

and $\angle BCP = \frac{1}{2}\angle C$ [$\because PC$ is bisector of $\angle C$] ...(ii)

$\Rightarrow \angle DAQ + \angle D + \angle Q + \angle BCP + \angle B + \angle P = 360°$

[$\because$ sum of angles of a quadrilateral is 360°] ...(iii)

From Eqs. (i), (ii) and (iii), we get

$\angle P + \angle Q = \frac{1}{2}(\angle A + \angle C)$

31. (i) **Hint** We have, $\angle BAP = \angle DAP$ ...(i)

Clearly, $\angle DAP = \angle BPA$ ...(ii)

[alternate interior angles]

(ii) **Hint** Clearly, $BC = 2CP$

[$\because P$ is the mid-point of BC]

$\Rightarrow AD = 2CP$

[$\because BC = AD$, opposite sides of a parallelogram are equal]

$\Rightarrow AD = 2CD$

[$\because$ from part (i), we have $CP = CD$]

(iii) In ΔDPC, $CP = CD$ [from part (i)]

$\therefore \angle CDP = \angle CPD$ ...(iii)

[$\because$ angles opposite to equal sides are equal]

Also, $\angle ADP = \angle CPD$ ...(iv)

[alternate interior angles]

Now, from Eqs. (iii) and (iv), we get

$\angle ADP = \angle CDP$

$\therefore DP$ bisects $\angle D$.

(iv) **Hint** Clearly, $\angle DAP = \frac{1}{2}\angle A$ [$\because \angle BAP = \angle DAP$] ...(v)

and $\angle ADP = \frac{1}{2}\angle D$ [$\because DP$ bisects $\angle D$] ...(vi)

On adding Eqs. (v) and (vi), we get

$\angle DAP + \angle ADP = \frac{1}{2}(\angle A + \angle D)$

$= \frac{1}{2} \times 180° = 90°$

[$\because \angle A + \angle D = 180°$ as co-interior angles]

Now, in ΔAPD,

$\angle APD = 180° - 90° = 90°$

[angle sum property of a triangle]

32.

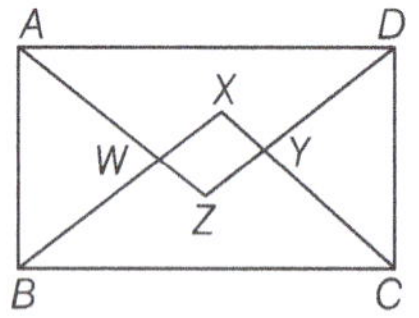

In ΔABW,

$\angle ABW + \angle BAW = \frac{1}{2}\angle B + \frac{1}{2}\angle A$

$= \frac{1}{2} \times 180° = 90°$

[adjacent angles of rectangle]

By angle sum property of triangle,

In ΔABW, $\angle AWB = 90°$

$\therefore$ $\angle XWZ = 90°$ [vertically opposite angle]

Similarly, $\angle XYZ = 90°$

Also, $\angle WXY = \angle YZW = 90°$

So, $WXYZ$ is a rectangle or square.

Here, $\angle ABW = \angle BAW = 45°$

[$\because$ BX and AZ are bisectors of $\angle B$ and $\angle A$ respectively]

$\therefore$ $AW = BW$

[$\because$ angles opposite to equal sides are equal]

Similarly, $BX = CX$ and $CY = DY$

By Pythagoras theorem,

In ΔBAW, $AB^2 = AW^2 + BW^2$

$\Rightarrow$ $AB = \sqrt{2}\ BW$

Similarly, In ΔDYC, $CD = \sqrt{2}\ CY$

Here, $AB = CD$ [opposite sides of rectangle]

$\Rightarrow$ $BW = CY$

In ΔBXC, $BX = CX$

$\Rightarrow$ $BW + WX = CY + YX$

$\Rightarrow$ $WX = YX$ [$\because BW = CY$]

So, $WX = YX = ZY = WZ$

[$\because$ opposite sides of rectangle are equal]

33. Hint

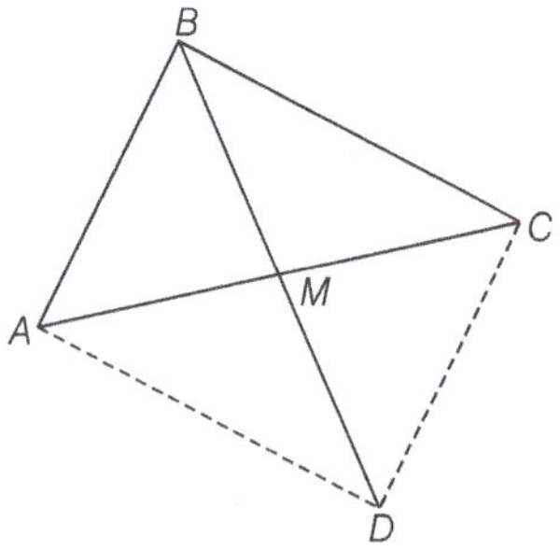

As BM is median, so M is mid-point of AC.
i.e. $AM = CM$

34. Hint $\angle PAB = \angle DAP = \frac{1}{2}\angle DAB = \frac{1}{2} \times 60° = 30°$

$\Rightarrow$ $\angle PAB = \angle APD = 30°$ [alternate interior angles]

$\therefore$ $AD = PD$ ...(i)

[sides opposite to equal angles are equal]

$\angle A + \angle B = 180°$

[co-interior angles of parallelogram $ABCD$]

$\therefore$ $\angle B = 180° - 60° = 120°$

$\Rightarrow$ $\angle ABP = \angle PBC = 60°$ [$\because$ PB is the bisector of $\angle B$]

So, $\angle ABP = \angle BPC = 60°$ [alternate interior angles]

$\therefore$ $BC = PC$ ...(ii)

[sides opposite to equal angles are equal]

Use property of parallelogram with Eqs. (i) and (ii) to get the required result.

35. Hint

Construction $DM \perp AB$ and join DB

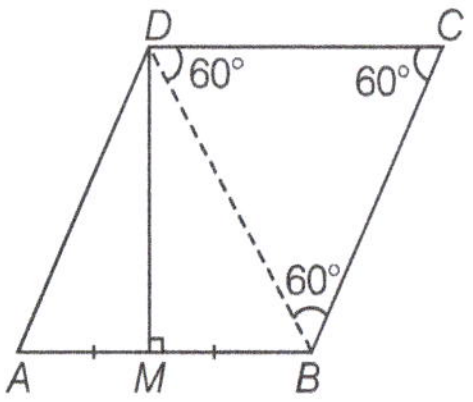

$\Delta AMD \cong BMD$ [by SAS congruence rule]

$\therefore$ $AD = DB = BC = DC = AB$

Ans. Angles of rhombus are 60°, 120°, 60° and 120°.

36. Hint

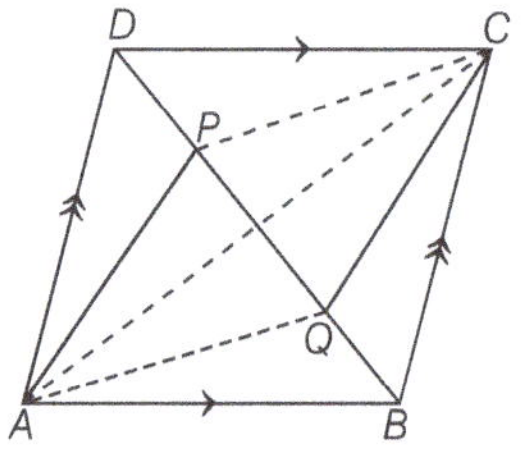

Construction. Join AC.

$\Delta ABQ \cong \Delta CDP$ [by ASA congruence rule]

$\therefore$ $AQ = CP$ [CPCT]

Similarly, $QC = AP$

37. Hint

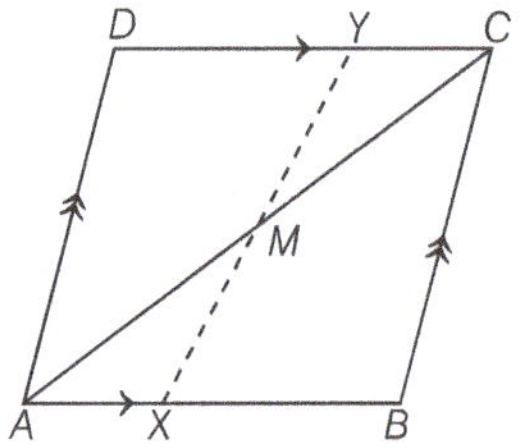

Construction. Join XM and MY.

38. Hint

(i) $\angle XYZ = \angle ZWX = 65°$ [opposite angles of a rhombus]

and $\angle AYZ = 60°$ [angle of an equilateral triangle]

$\therefore$ $\angle AYX = 125°$

Now, $AY = XY$ [$\because AY = YZ$ and $YZ = XY$]

$\therefore$ $\angle YAX = \angle YXA$ [angle opposite to equal sides]

Ans. $\angle YXA = 27.5$

(ii) $\angle YXZ = \frac{1}{2}\angle X = \frac{115°}{2}$

[sum of adjacent angles of a parallelogram is 180°]

Ans. $\angle ZXA = 30°$

Olympiad Section

Brain Teasing Questions of Olympiad Pattern

1 *ABCD* and *MNOP* are quadrilaterals as shown in the figure below. Then,

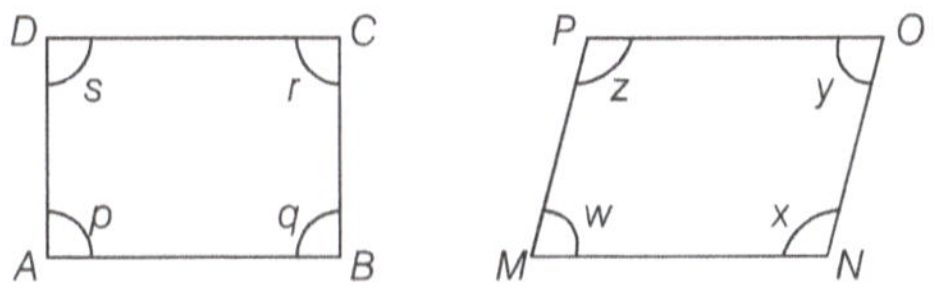

(a) $p+q+r+s<w+x+y+z$
(b) $p+q+r+s=w+x+y+z$
(c) $p+q+r+s>w+x+y+z$
(d) None of the above

2 In a parallelogram *ABCD*, $AB = 4$ cm and $BC = 7$ cm. Then, each of its diagonals is less than

(a) 3 cm (b) 4 cm
(c) 7 cm (d) 11 cm

3 In the given figure, *ABC* is an isosceles triangle, in which $AB = AC$. *AEDC* is a parallelogram. If $\angle CDF = 70°$ and $\angle BFE = 100°$, then $\angle FBA$ is equal to

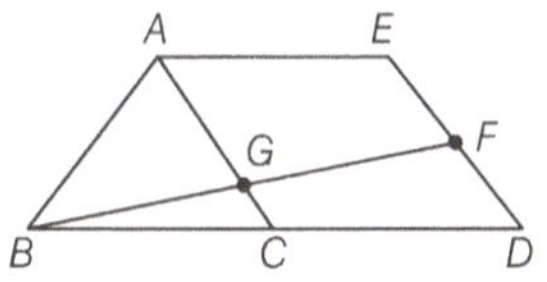

(a) 30° (b) 40°
(c) 50° (d) 80°

4 In the given figure, *ABC* is a square having $AO = AX$. Then, $\angle XOB$ equals

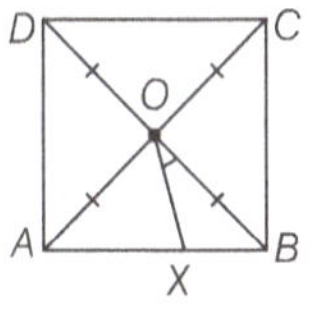

(a) 23.6° (b) 21.5°
(c) 20.2° (d) 22.5°

5 If *X* is any point within a square *ABCD* and on side *AX*, a square *AXYZ* described such that *D* is within it, then *BX* is equal to

(a) *DZ* (b) *AZ*
(c) *BZ* (d) *CZ*

6 *ABCD* is a square. If *P*, *Q*, *R* and *S* are points on the sides *AB*, *BC*, *CD* and *DA* respectively, such that $AP = BQ = CR = DS$, then the value of $\angle SPQ$ is equal to

(a) 90° (b) 70°
(c) 120° (d) 60°

7 *ABCD* is a quadrilateral such that $BC = BA$ and $CD > AD$. Which one of the following is correct?

(a) $\angle BAD = \angle BCD$ (b) $\angle BAD > \angle BCD$
(c) $\angle BAD < \angle BCD$ (d) $2\angle BAD = \angle BCD$

8 In the following figure, *ABCD* is a trapezium. If $\angle AOB = 126°$ and $\angle PDC = \angle QCD = 52°$, find the values of *x* and *y*.

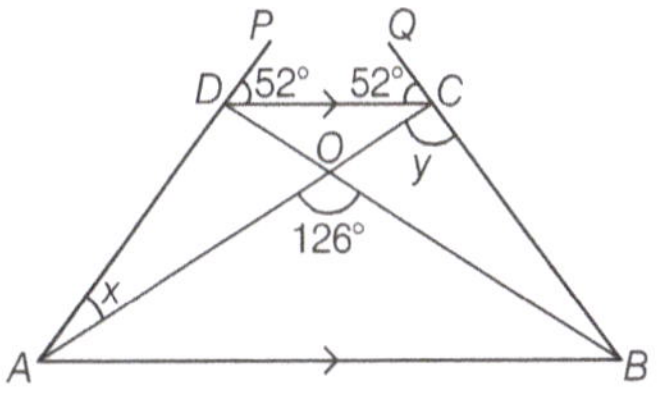

(a) $x = 20°$, $y = 100°$
(b) $x = 25°$, $y = 101°$
(c) $x = 25°$, $y = 110°$
(d) None of the abvoe

9 *ABCD* is a parallelogram. If the bisectors of $\angle A$ and $\angle C$ meet the diagonal *BD* at *P* and *Q* respectively, then quadrilateral *PCQA* is a.

(a) parallelogram (b) rectangle
(c) square (d) None of these

Answers

1. (b) **2.** (d) **3.** (b) **4.** (d) **5.** (a) **6.** (a) **7.** (b) **8.** (b) **9.** (a)

* *These questions may or may not be asked in the examination, have been given just for additional practice required for olympiads Scholarship Exams etc. For detailed explanations refer Page No. 344.*

CHAPTER 11

Construction of Polygons

SYLLABUS

- Construction of quadrilaterals (including parallelograms and rhombus) and regular hexagon using ruler and compasses only.

In the earlier classes, we studied the various constructions of line segments, angles (i.e. 30°, 45°, 60°,...), triangles and quadrilateral. In this chapter, we will study the construction of various quadrilaterals such as parallelograms, rhombus, rectangles, squares etc. and regular hexagon.

Construction

Construction means, drawing of correct and accurate figure from the given data. Always draw a rough diagram before constructing the figure (using ruler and compass).

Construction of Quadrilateral

A closed bounded plane figure by four line segments is called a Quadrilateral.

Construction 1 *To construct a quadrilateral, when its four sides and one angle are given.*

Example 1. Construct a quadrilateral *ABCD*, where *AB* = 7.0 cm, *BC* = 5.8 cm, *CD* = 6.3 cm, *DA* = 4.3 cm and $\angle A = 75°$.

Sol. Given, a quadrilateral *ABCD* in which *AB* = 7.0 cm, *BC* = 5.8 cm, *CD* = 6.3 cm, *DA* = 4.3 cm and $\angle A = 75°$.

Steps of construction

1. Draw a line segment *AB* of length 7.0 cm.
2. At point *A*, construct $\angle PAB = 75°$. [$\because 75° = 30° + 45°$]

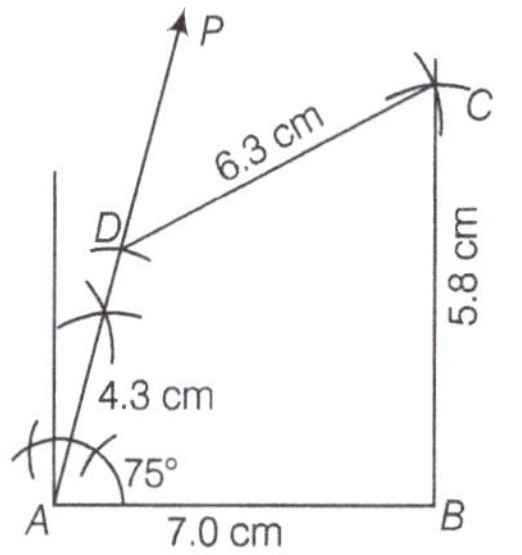

3. Taking *A* as centre, make an arc of radius 4.3 cm, which cuts *AP* at *D*.
4. Taking *B* and *D* as centres, make arcs of radii 5.8 cm and 6.3 cm respectively, which cut each other at *C*.
5. Join *BC* and *CD*.

Thus, *ABCD* is the required quadrilateral.

Construction 2 *To construct a quadrilateral, when three sides and two angles are given.*

Example 2. Construct a quadrilateral *KITE*, given that *KI* = 3.8 cm, *IT* = 2.9 cm, *KE* = 4.2 cm, $\angle K = 90°$ and $\angle I = 120°$.

Sol. Given, *KI* = 3.8 cm, *IT* = 2.9 cm, *KE* = 4.2 cm, $\angle K = 90°$ and $\angle I = 120°$ of the quadrilateral *KITE*.

Steps of construction

1. Draw a line segment *KI* of length 3.8 cm.
2. At points *K* and *I*, construct $\angle XKI$ and $\angle YIK$ of 90° and 120°, respectively.

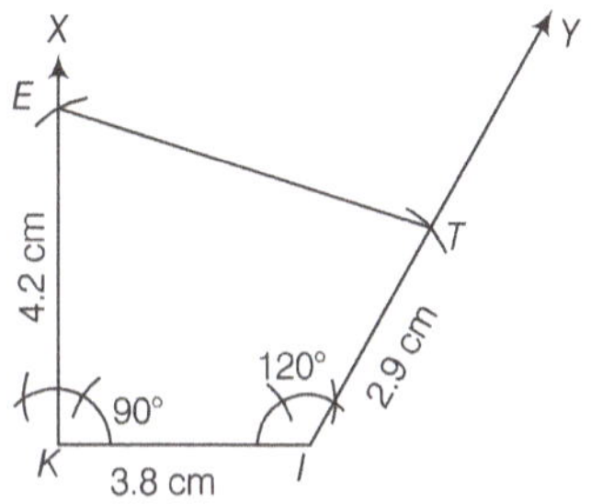

3. Taking K and I as centres, make arcs of radii 4.2 cm and 2.9 cm respectively, which cut KX and IY at E and T, respectively.
4. Join T and E. Thus, $KITE$ is the required quadrilateral.

Construction 3 *To construct a quadrilateral, when four sides and one diagonal are given.*

Example 3. Construct a quadrilateral $PQRS$ with $PQ = 3.7$ cm, $QR = 3.2$ cm, $RS = 2.5$ cm, $PS = 3.1$ cm and $QS = 3.5$ cm.

Sol. Given, $PQ = 3.7$ cm, $QR = 3.2$ cm, $RS = 2.5$ cm, $PS = 3.1$ cm and $QS = 3.5$ cm of the quadrilateral $PQRS$.

Steps of construction

1. Draw a line segment $PQ = 3.7$ cm.
2. Taking P and Q as centres, make arcs of radii 3.1 cm and 3.5 cm respectively, which cut each other at S.

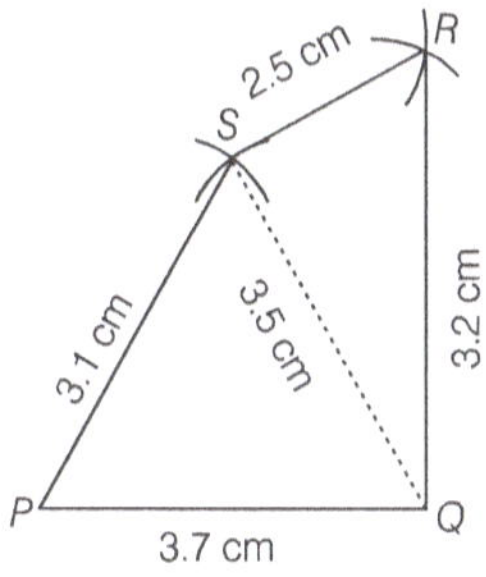

3. Taking S and Q as centres, make arcs of radii 2.5 cm and 3.2 cm respectively, which cuts each other at R.
4. Join PS, SR and RQ.

   Thus, $PQRS$ is the required quadrilateral.

Construction 4 *To construct a quadrilateral, whose three sides and two diagonals are given.*

Example 4. Construct a quadrilateral $ABCD$ whose three sides, i.e. $AB = 2.7$ cm, $BC = 1.9$ cm, $AD = 3.6$ cm and two diagonals, i.e. $AC = 3.5$ cm, $BD = 5.3$ cm are given.

Sol. Given, $AB = 2.7$ cm, $BC = 1.9$ cm, $AD = 3.6$ cm, $AC = 3.5$ cm and $BD = 5.3$ cm of the quadrilateral $ABCD$.

Steps of construction

1. Draw a line segment $AB = 2.7$ cm.
2. Taking A and B as centres, make arcs of radii 3.5 cm and 1.9 cm respectively, which cut each other at C.

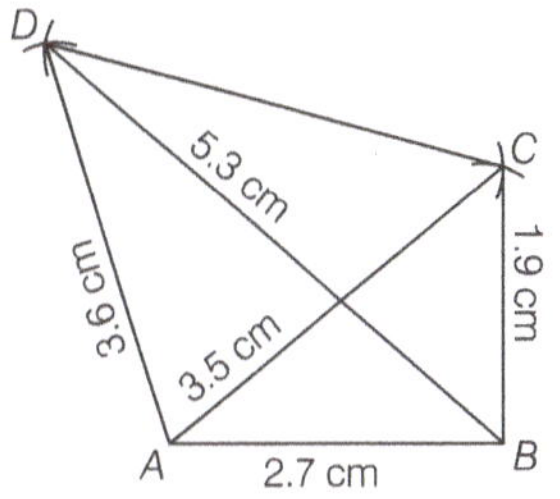

3. Again, taking A and B as centres make arcs of radii 3.6 cm and 5.3 cm respectively, which cut each other at D.
4. Join BC, CD and DA.

   Thus, $ABCD$ is the required quadrilateral.

Construction of Parallelograms

A quadrilateral in which opposite sides equal and parallel is called a Parallelogram.

Construction 5 *To construct a parallelogram, when two adjacent sides and the including angle are given.*

Example 5. Construct a parallelogram, whose adjacent sides $AB = 3.6$ cm, $BC = 5.4$ cm and including angle $\angle B = 60°$ are given.

Sol. Given, $AB = 3.6$ cm, $BC = 5.4$ cm and $\angle B = 60°$ of the parallelogram $ABCD$.

Steps of construction

1. Draw a line segment BC of length 5.4 cm.
2. At B as centre, construct $\angle MBC = 60°$.

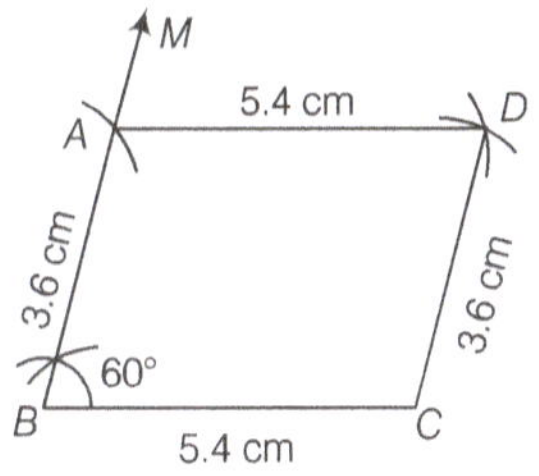

3. Taking B as centre, cut an arc of radius 3.6 cm, which cut the line BM at A.
4. Taking A as centre, make an arc of radius 5.4 cm.
5. Taking C as centre, make another arc of radius 3.6 cm, which cut previous arc at D.
6. Join AD and CD.

   Thus, $ABCD$ is the required parallelogram.

Construction 6 *To construct a parallelogram, when two adjacent sides and one diagonal are given.*

Example 6. If $AB = 5.4$ cm, $AD = 4.1$ cm and $BD = 5.1$ cm, then construct a parallelogram $ABCD$.

Sol. Given, a parallelogram $ABCD$ in which $AB = 5.4$ cm, $AD = 4.1$ cm and diagonal $BD = 5.1$ cm.

Steps of construction

1. Draw a line segment AB of length 5.4 cm.
2. Taking A as centre, make an arc of radius 4.1 cm.

3. Taking B as centre, make another arc of radius 5.1 cm, which cuts previous arc at D.
4. Taking D as centre, make an arc of radius 5.4 cm.

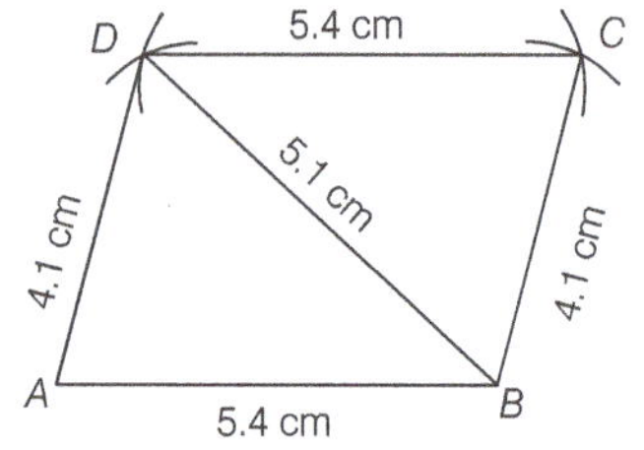

5. Taking B as centre, make another arc of radius 4.1 cm, which cuts previous arc at C.
6. Join AD, BC and CD.

Thus, $ABCD$ is the required parallelogram.

Construction 7 *To construct a parallelogram, when one side and both diagonals are given.*

Example 7. Contruct a parallelogram, whose one side is 4.5 cm and diagonals are 6.0 cm and 5.6 cm.

Sol. Let $AB = 4.5$ cm, $AC = 6.0$ cm and $BD = 5.6$ cm

Steps of construction

1. Draw a ΔAOB having base $AB = 4.5$ cm

$$OA = \frac{1}{2} \times AC = \frac{1}{2} \times 6.0 = 3\text{cm}$$

and $$OB = \frac{1}{2} \times BD = \frac{1}{2} \times 5.6 = 2.8\text{cm}$$

[using the concept that diagonals of a parallelogram bisect each other]

2. Now, produce the side AO to C such that $OC = OA$.
3. Also, produce the side BO to D such that $OD = OB$.

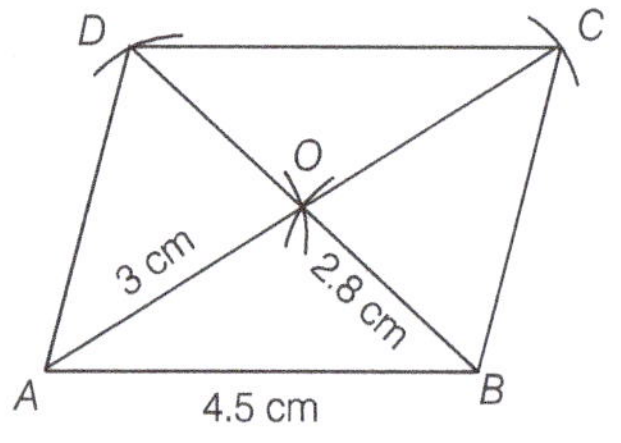

4. Join AD, DC and CB.

Hence, $ABCD$ is the required parallelogram.

Construction 8 *To construct a parallelogram, when two diagonals and an included angle are given.*

Example 8. Given that $AC = 6$ cm, $BD = 5.2$ cm and $\angle COD = 60°$, where O be the point of intersection of diagonals, then construct a parallelogram $ABCD$.

Sol. Given, a parallelogram $ABCD$ in which $AC = 6$ cm, $BD = 5.2$ cm and $\angle COD = 60°$, where O is the point of intersection of diagonals.

Steps of construction

1. Draw a line segment AO, which is the half of the line AC, i.e. 3 cm and produce AO to C such that $OC = OA$.
2. Taking O as centre, construct $\angle COP = 60°$.

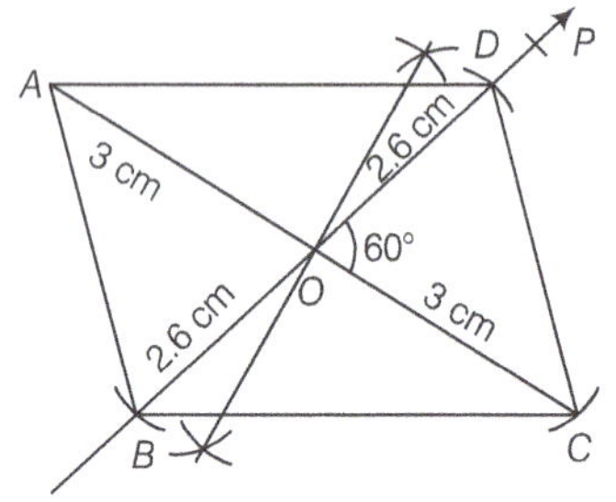

3. Taking O as centre, make an arc of radius 2.6 cm to line OP, where $OB = OD = 2.6$ cm.
4. Join AB, BC, CD and DA.

Thus, $ABCD$ is the required parallelogram.

Construction 9 *To construct a parallelogram, when two adjacent sides and height are given.*

Example 9. Construct a parallelogram, whose adjacent sides are 4.7 cm and 3.4 cm. Also, height from 4.7 cm side, is 2.6 cm.

Sol. Let $ABCD$ be a parallelogram in which $AB = 4.7$ cm and $BC = 3.4$ cm are adjacent sides and $AN = 2.6$ cm is the height from side AB.

Steps of construction

1. Draw a line segment AB of length 4.7 cm.
2. At point A, draw a line AP, which is perpendicular to AB.
3. Taking A as centre, draw an arc of radius 2.6 cm, which cuts AP at N.
4. Through N, draw a line $AP \perp QR$
5. Taking A as centre, make an arc of radius 3.4 cm, which cuts QR at D.

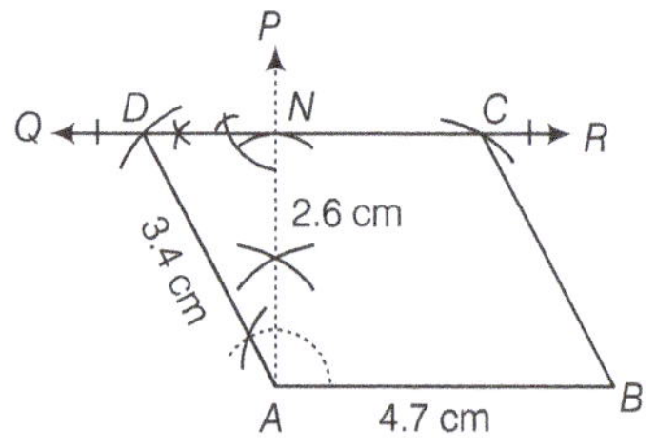

6. Taking D as centre, draw an arc of radius 4.7 cm, which meets QR at C.
7. Join BC and AD.

Thus, $ABCD$ is the required parallelogram.

Construction 10 *To construct a parallelogram, when one side, one diagonal and one height are given.*

Example 10. Construct a parallelogram, whose one side, one diagonal and height from the given sides are respectively 4 cm, 3.5 cm and 2 cm.

Sol. Let $AB = 4$ cm, $AC = 3.5$ cm and height from $AB = 2$ cm.

Steps of construction

1. Draw $AB = 4$ cm.
2. At point A, draw $AP \perp AB$. From AP, cut-off $AN = 2$ cm.

3. Through N, draw a line $AP \perp QR$
4. Taking A as centre and radius = 3.5 cm, draw an arc to meet QR at C.

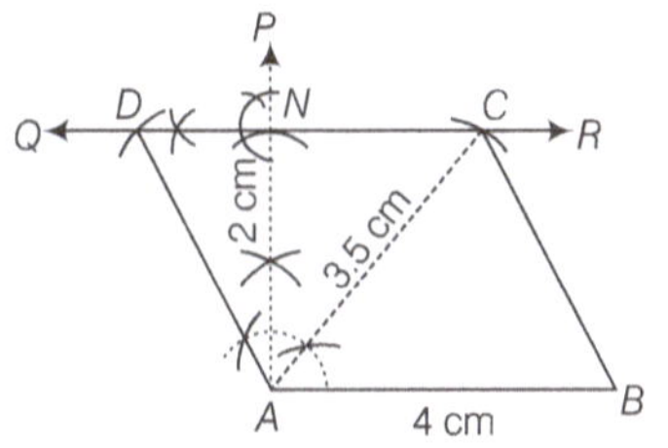

5. Taking C as centre and radius = 4 cm, draw an arc to meet QR at D.
6. Join BC and AD.

Thus, $ABCD$ is the required parallelogram.

Construction 11 *To construct a parallelogram, when both heights and the angle between two sides are given.*

Example 11. Construct a parallelogram $ABCD$, whose height from AB is 2.3 cm and height from BC = 4.2 cm. Also, $\angle BAD = 60°$.

Sol. Given, The heights from AB = 2.3 cm, BC = 4.2 cm and the $\angle BAD = 60°$.

Steps of construction

1. Draw a line PQ of any length and take a point A on it.
2. At point A, construct $\angle QAF$ of 60°.
3. At point A, draw a line AE perpendicular to PQ.

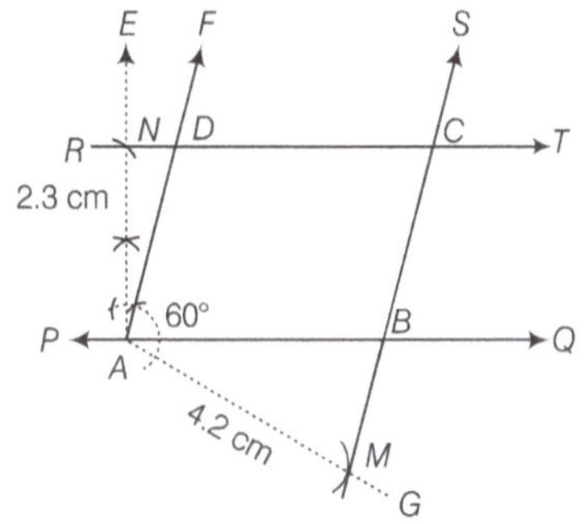

4. Taking A as centre, cut an arc of radius 2.3 cm, which cuts AE at N.
5. Through N, draw a line $RT \parallel PQ$ to meet AF at D.
6. At point A, draw a line AG perpendicular to AD.
7. Taking A as centre make an arc of radius 4.2 cm, which cuts AG at M.
8. Through M, draw a line $MS \perp AG$ to meet AQ at B and MS at C.

Thus, $ABCD$ is the required parallelogram.

Construction of Trapezium

A quadrilateral in which one pair of opposite sides is parallel is called a Trapezium.

Construction 12 *To construct a trapezium, when four sides are given.*

Example 12. Construct a trapezium $ABCD$, where AB = 5 cm, BC = 3.1 cm, CD = 3.1 cm and DA = 2.7 cm.

Sol. Given, AB = 5 cm, BC = 3.1 cm, CD = 3.1 cm and DA = 2.7 cm of the trapezium $ABCD$.

Steps of construction

1. Draw a line segment AB of length 5 cm.
2. Taking A as centre, cut-off an arc of radius 3.1 cm, which cuts AB at E.
3. Taking E and B as centres, make arcs of radii 2.7 cm and 3.1 cm respectively, which cut each other at C and complete ΔEBC.

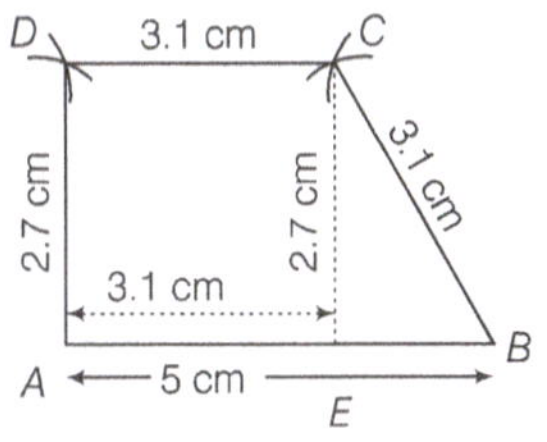

4. Taking A as centre, make an arc of radius 2.7 cm.
5. Taking C as centre, make another arc of radius 3.1 cm, which cuts previous arc at D.
6. Join AD and DC.

Thus, $ABCD$ is the required trapezium.

Construction of Rectangle

A parallelogram in which each angle is a right angle is called a Rectangle.

Construction 13 *To construct a rectangle, when one side and one diagonal are given.*

Example 13. If AB = 5.2 cm and AC = 5.7 cm, then construct a rectangle $ABCD$.

Sol. Given, AB = 5.2 cm and AC = 5.7 cm of the rectangle $ABCD$.

Steps of construction

1. Draw a line AB = 5.2 cm.
2. At point B, construct a line BP, which is perpendicular to AB.
3. Taking A as centre, make an arc of radius 5.7 cm, which cuts BP at C.

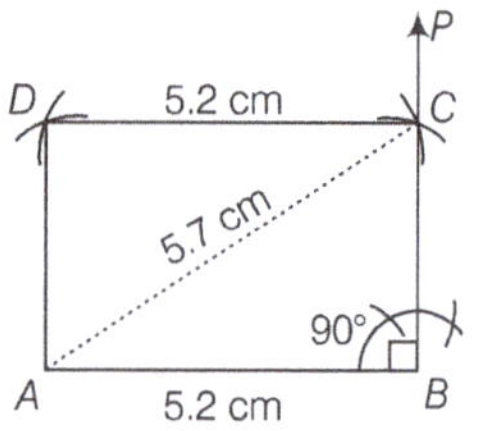

4. Taking C as centre, make an arc of radius 5.2 cm.
5. Taking B as centre, make another arc of radius 5.7 cm, which cuts previous arc at D.
6. Join AD and DC.

   Thus, $ABCD$ is the required rectangle.

Construction of Square

A rectangle in which all sides are equal is called a Square.

Construction 14 *To construct a square, when one diagonal is given.*

Example 14. Construct a square $ABCD$, whose one diagonal $AC = 5.2$ cm.

Sol. Given, a square $ABCD$, whose length of a diagonal AC is 5.2 cm.

Steps of construction

1. Make a line segment AO, which is the half of AC, i.e. 2.6 cm and produce AO to C, such that $AO = OC$.

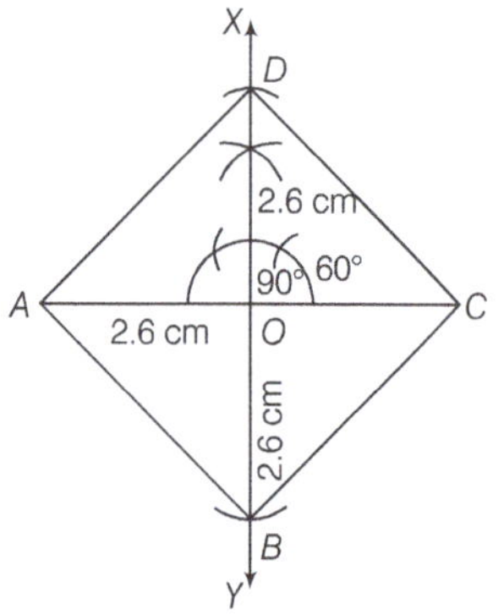

2. At point O, construct $\angle AOX = 90°$.
3. Taking O as centre, cut-off an arc of radius equal to the half of BD, i.e. $\left(\frac{1}{2} \times 5.2 = 2.6\right)$, which cuts OX at D.
4. Produce DO to B, such that $DO = OB$.
5. Join AB, BC, CD and DA.

   Thus, $ABCD$ is the required square.

Construction 15 *To construct a square whose one side is given.*

Example 15. Construct a square $ABCD$, in which its side is 6 cm.

Sol. Steps of construction

1. Draw a line segment $AB = 6$ cm.
2. Draw AP perpendicular to AB.
3. From AP, cut $AD = 6$ cm.

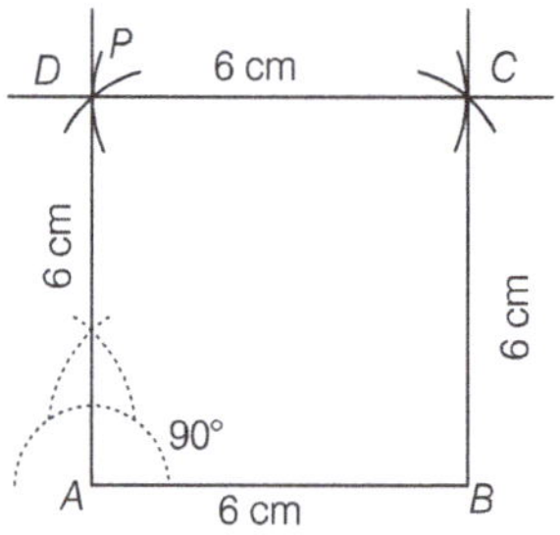

4. Taking B and D as centres, make arcs of radii 6 cm each, which cut each other at C.
5. Join BC and DC.

   Thus, $ABCD$ is the required square.

Construction of Rhombus

A parallelogram in which all sides are equal is called a Rhombus.

Construction 16 *To construct a rhombus, when diagonals are given.*

Example 16. Given that diagonal $AC = 5.2$ cm and diagonal $BD = 6.8$ cm, then construct a rhombus $ABCD$.

Sol. Given, a rhombus whose diagonals $AC = 5.2$ cm and $BD = 6.8$ cm.

Steps of construction

1. Draw a line segment AC of length 5.2 cm.

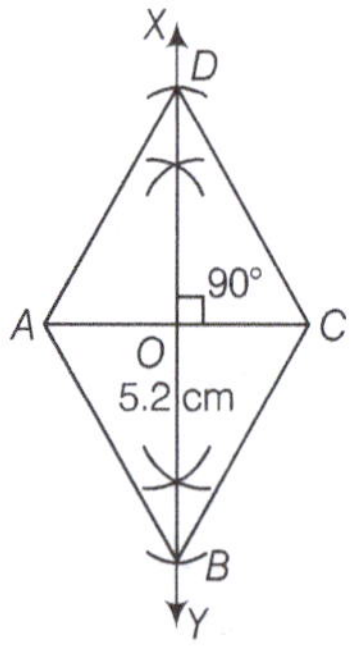

2. Draw perpendicular bisector XY of AC, which cuts each other at O.
3. Taking O as centre cut of two arcs of length half of the length of BD $\left(\text{i.e. } \frac{1}{2} \times 6.8 = 3.4\right)$, which cuts line XY at B and D, respectively.
4. Join AB, BC, CD and DA.

Thus, $ABCD$ is the required rhombus.

Construction 17 *To construct a rhombus whose one side and one angle is given.*

Example 17. Construct a rhombus *ABCD*, when its side = 6 cm and $\angle A = 60°$.

Sol. ***Steps of construction***

1. Draw a line segment $AB = 6$ cm.
2. Draw *AP* making angle 60° with *AB*.
3. Taking *A* as centre, makes an arc of radius 6 cm, which cuts *AP* at point *D*.

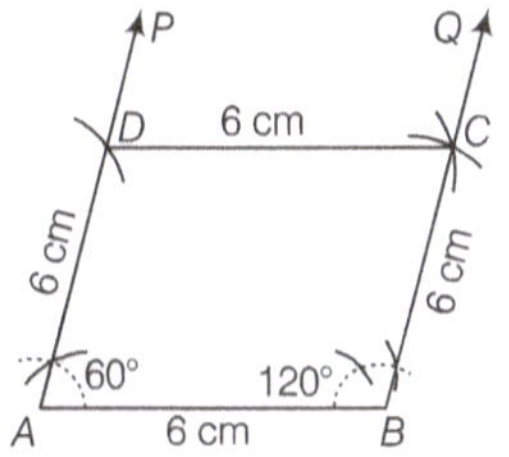

4. Since, *ABCD* is a rhombus.

$\therefore \quad \angle A + \angle B = 180°$ [co-interior]

$\Rightarrow \quad \angle B = 180° - 60° = 120°$ [$\because \angle A = 60°$]

Draw *BQ*, making an angle 120° with *AB* and from *BQ*, cut $BC = 6$ cm.

5. Join *DC*.

Thus, *ABCD* is the required rhombus.

Construction of Regular Hexagon

If in a polygon, all 6 sides and angles are equal is called a Regular Hexagon.

Construction 18 *To construct a regular hexagon, when side is given.*

Example 18. If each side of regular hexagon is 2.8 cm, then construct a regular hexagon.

Sol. Let each side of regular hexagon *ABCDEF* is 2.8 cm.

Steps of construction

1. Draw a line segment $AB = 2.8$ cm.
2. At point *B*, draw $\angle ABP = 120°$ and cut-off an arc of radius 2.8 cm, which cuts *BP* at *C*.
3. At point *C*, draw $\angle BCQ = 120°$ and cut-off an arc of radius 2.8 cm, which cuts *CQ* at *D*.

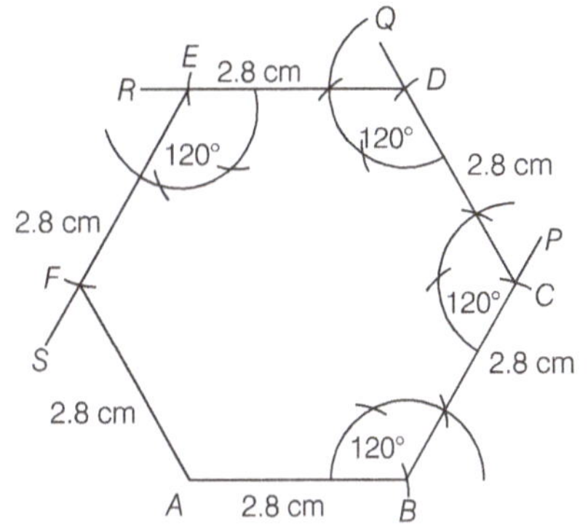

4. At point *D*, draw $\angle CDR = 120°$ and cut-off an arc of radius 2.8 cm, which cuts *DR* at *E*.
5. At point *E*, draw $\angle DES = 120°$ and cut-off an arc of radius 2.8 cm, which cuts *ES* at *F*.
6. Join *AF*.

Thus, *ABCDEF* is the required regular hexagon.

Alternate Method

Steps of construction

1. Draw a circle of radius 2.8 cm.
2. Take any point *A* on the circumference of a circle.

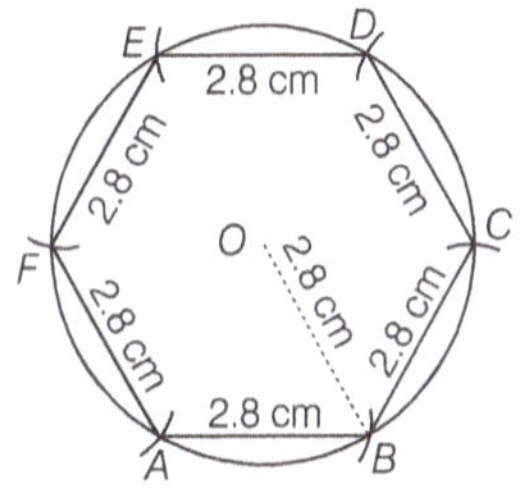

3. Taking *A* as centre having radius = 2.8 cm, draw two arcs which cuts the circle at points *B* and *F*.
4. Taking *B* as centre having radius = 2.8 cm, draw an arc which cuts the circle at point *C*.
5. Taking *C* as centre, draw an arc of radius 2.8 cm, which cuts the circle at point *D*.
6. Taking *D* as centre draw an arc of radius 2.8 cm, which cuts the circle at point *E*.
7. Join *AB*, *BC*, *CD*, *DE*, *EF* and *FA*.

Thus, *ABCDEF* is the required regular hexagon.

Chapter Practice

a. 1 Mark Questions

1. Which of the following represents the proper conditions under which we can construct a quadrilateral?
(a) Length of three sides and one diagonal is given.
(b) Length of one diagonal and four sides are given.
(c) Length of one diagonal and two sides are given.
(d) None of the above

2. If the length of two diagonals and three sides are given, then which of the following is possible?
(a) We don't have enough information
(b) We can construct a quadrilateral
(c) We can't construct a quadrilateral
(d) None of the above

3. If the length of three sides are given, then we need to know the value of ...... included angles to construct a quadrilateral.
(a) Two (b) Three (c) Four (d) One

4. What parameters we require for the geometrical construction of a square?
(a) The length of all four sides
(b) The measure of all interior angles
(c) The length of one side
(d) The measure of one interior angle

5. How many parameters are necessary to construct a unique quadrilateral?
(a) Two (b) Five (c) Three (d) Seven

6. If only the length of diagonals are given, then which of the following can be drawn?
(a) Rhombus (b) Rectangle
(c) Parallelogram (d) Kite

b. 3 Marks Questions

7. Using ruler and pair of compasses only, construct the quadrilateral $ABCD$ in which $\angle BAD = 45°$, $AD = 6$cm, $AB = 5.8$ cm, $BC = 3.6$ cm and $CD = 5$ cm.

8. Construct a quadrilateral $MADE$, when $MA = 6$ cm, $AD = 3.9$ cm, $ME = 4.6$ cm and $\angle EMA = 90°$ and $\angle MAD = 105°$.

9. Construct a quadrilateral $ABCD$ in which $AB = 3.2$ cm, $BC = 5.2$, $CD = 6.1$ cm, $DA = 4.3$ cm and $BD = 5$ cm.

10. Construct a quadrilateral $ABCD$ in which $AB = 3.2$ cm, $BC = 4.2$ cm, $CD = 5.0$ cm, $DA = 3.5$ cm and diagonal $AC = 4.5$ cm.

11. Construct a quadrilateral $PQRS$, where $PQ = 2.7$ cm, $QR = 1.9$ cm, $PS = 3.6$ cm, $PR = 3.5$ cm and $QS = 5.3$ cm.

12. Using ruler and pair of compasses only, construct a parallelogram $ABCD$ using the data $AB = 6$ cm, $AD = 3$ cm and $\angle DAB = 45°$.

13. Construct a parallelogram $ABCD$, when $AB = 4.3$ cm, $AD = 6.3$ cm and $AC = 4.8$ cm.

14. Construct a parallelogram having one side $AB = 6.0$ cm and diagonals are $AC = 7.0$ cm and $BD = 6.2$ cm.

c. 4/5 Marks Questions

15. Draw a parallelogram whose diagonals are 4 and 6 cm long and contain an angle of 75°.

16. Construct a parallelogram $ABCD$ with sides $AB = 6$ cm, $BC = 4$ cm and altitude = 3.5 cm.

17. Construct a parallelogram $PQRS$ in which $PQ = 4.5$cm, $PR = 3.8$ cm and height from $PQ = 2.5$ cm.

18. Construct a parallelogram $CUTE$, whose height from $CU = 4$ cm height from $UT = 5.5$ cm. Also, $\angle UCE = 45°$

19. Construct a trapezium $ABCD$, when $AB = 3$ cm, $BC = 2.5$ cm, $CD = 5.0$ cm and $DA = 2.8$ cm and $AD || BC$.

20. Construct a rectangle $ABCD$, whose $BC = 4.8$ cm and diagonal $AC = 6.4$ cm.

21. Construct a rectangle $ABCD$, when its sides are 7 cm and 8.2 cm.

22. Construct a square $MAKE$, whose one diagonal is 4.8 cm.

23. Construct a square $PQRS$, in which its side is 7 cm.

24. Construct a rhombus, whose diagonals are 7 cm and 8 cm.

25. Construct a rhombus $ABCD$, when its side = 5 cm and $\angle A = 60°$.

d. 6 Marks Questions

26. Construct a rhombus $ABCD$, in which, $\angle A = 60°$ and height = 3.0 cm.

27. Construct a regular hexagon $ABCDEF$, whose one side is 3.2 cm.

Hints and Answers

1. (b) 2. (b) 3. (a)
4. (c) 5. (b) 6. (a)
7. Do same as Example 1.
8. Do same as Example 2.
9. Do same as Example 3.
10. Do same as Example 3.
11. Do same as Example 4.
12. Do same as Example 5.
13. Do same as Example 6.
14. Do same as Example 7.
15. Do same as Example 8.
16. Do same as Example 9.
17. Do same as Example 9.
18. Do same as Example 11.
19. Do same as Example 12.
20. Do same as Example 13.
21. **Hint**
   1. Draw a line segment $AB = 8.2$ cm

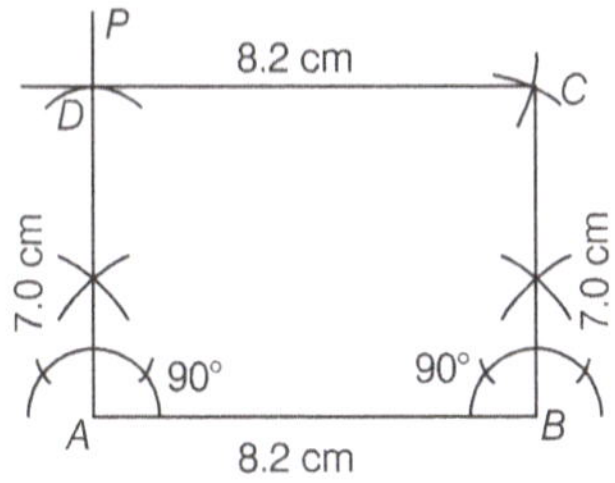

   2. Draw AP perpendicular to AB.
   3. Cut $AD = 7$ cm from AP.
   4. Taking B and D as centres, make arcs of radii 7 cm and 8.2 cm respectively, which cuts each other at C.
   5. Join BC and DC
      Thus, $ABCD$ is the required rectangle.
22. Do same as Example 14.
23. Do same as Example 15.
24. Do same as Example 16.
25. Do same as Example 17.
26. **Hint**
   1. Draw a line segment PQ of any length.
   2. Take any point L on PQ.
   3. Draw $RL \perp PQ$.
   4. From LR, cut $LB = 3.0$ cm.
   5. Through B, draw $BM \perp RL$

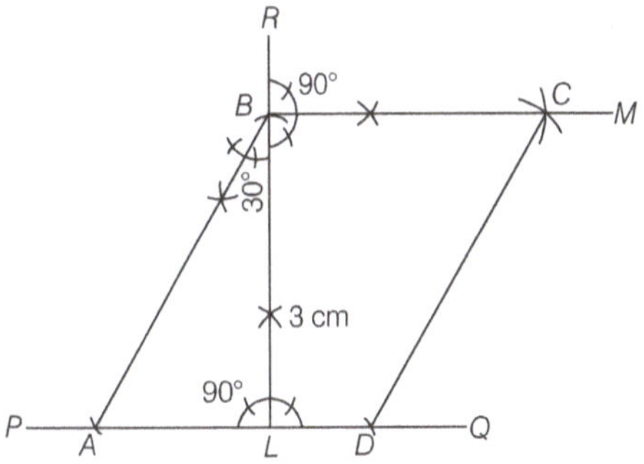

   6. Draw $\angle ABL = 30°$, so that arm BA of $\angle ABL$ meets PQ at A, since $\angle A = 60°$.
   7. With A as centre and radius = AB, draw an arc, which cuts PQ at D.
   8. With B as centre and radius $= AB$, draw an arc, which cuts BM at C.
   9. Join CD.
27. Do same as Example 18.

CHAPTER

12

Areas Theorems on Parallelograms & Triangles

SYLLABUS

- Proof and use of Area theorems on parallelograms : (i) Parallelograms on the same base and between the same parallels are equal in area. (ii) The area of a triangle is half that of a parallelogram on the same base and between the same parallels. (iii) Triangles between the same base and between the same parallels are equal in area (without proof). (iv) Triangles with equal area on the same bases have equal corresponding altitudes.

In earlier classes, we have studied some formulae for finding the areas of some plane figures such as triangle, rectangle, square, parallelogram etc.

In this chapter, we shall study some relationship between the areas of these geometric figures under the condition when they lie on the same base (or equal bases) and between the same parallel lines.

Figures on the Same Base and between the Same Parallels

Two figures are said to be on the same base and between the same parallels, if they have a common base (or side) and the vertices (or vertex) opposite to the common base of each figure lie on a parallel line to the base.

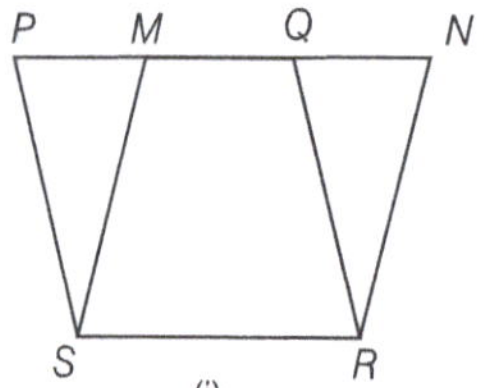

(i)

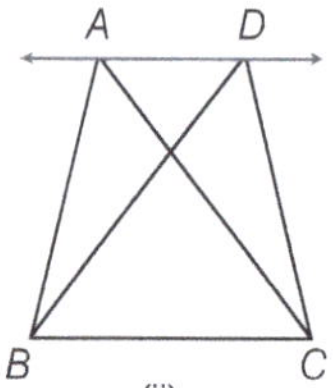

(ii)

In given figure, ΔDQR and ΔPQR lie on the same base QR but not lie between the same parallels QR and PM, because vertex D does not lie on PM.

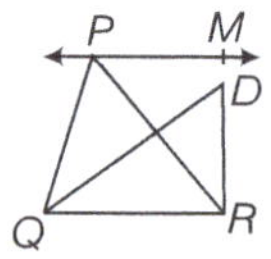

Areas of Parallelograms on the Same Base and between the Same Parallels

Theorem 1 *Parallelograms on the same base and between the same parallels are equal in area.*

Given $ABCD$ and $PQCD$ are two parallelograms on same base DC and between same parallels PB and DC.

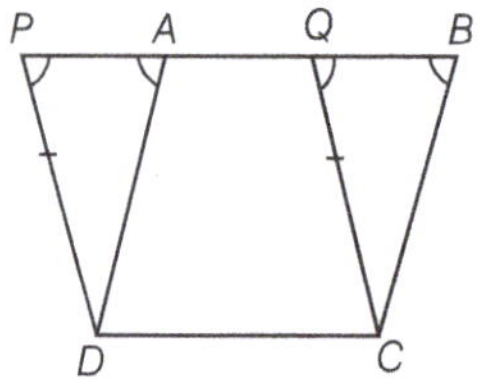

To prove Area of parallelogram $ABCD$

= Area of parallelogram $PQCD$

Proof In ΔPDA and ΔQCB,

$\angle DPA = \angle CQB$ [corresponding angles]

$\angle DAP = \angle CBQ$ [corresponding angles]

Also, $PD = QC$

[$\because$ opposite sides of the parallelogram are equal]

So, $\Delta PDA \cong \Delta QCB$ [by AAS congruence rule]

$\Rightarrow$ ar (ΔPDA) = ar (ΔQCB) ...(i)

[congruent figures have equal areas]

Now, adding both sides of Eq. (i) to common area of trapezium $AQCD$, we get

ar (ΔPDA) + ar (trapezium $AQCD$)

= ar (ΔQCB) + ar (trapezium $AQCD$)

$\Rightarrow$ ar (parallelogram $PQCD$) = ar (parallelogram $ABCD$)

Hence, parallelograms on the same base and between the same parallels are equal in area. **Hence proved.**

Converse of theorem Parallelograms on the same base and having equal areas lie between same parallel lines.

Corollary 1 *If a parallelogram and a rectangle are on the same base and between the same parallel lines, then they are equal in area.*

Given A parallelogram $ABCD$ and a rectangle $ABEF$ are on the same base AB and between the same parallel lines AB and DE.

To prove Area of parallelogram $ABCD$

= Area of rectangle $ABEF$

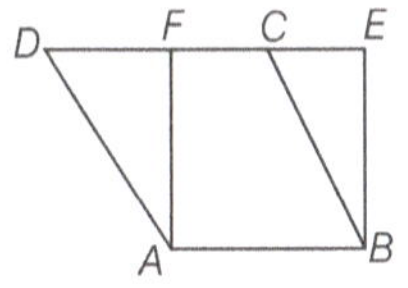

Proof Since, every rectangle is a parallelogram, therefore by above theorem, we can say that

Area of parallelogram $ABCD$ = Area of rectangle $ABEF$

Hence proved.

Corollary 2 *Area of a parallelogram = Base × Height*

Given A parallelogram $ABCD$.

To prove Area of parallelogram $ABCD$ = base × height

Construction Construct a rectangle $ABEF$ with same base AB and between the parallel lines AB and CD.

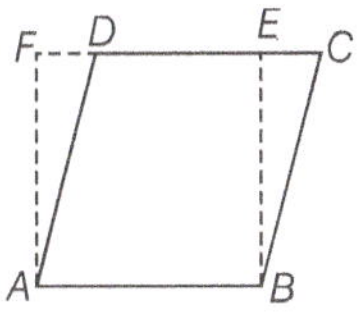

Proof Clearly, area of parallelogram $ABCD$ = area of rectangle $ABEF$ [by Corollary 1]

$\Rightarrow$ Area of parallelogram $ABCD = AB \times BE$

[$\because$ area of rectangle = length × breadth]

$\therefore$ Area of parallelogram $ABCD$ = Base × Height

Hence proved.

Corollary 3 *Parallelograms with equal bases and between the same parallels are equal in area.*

Given $ABCD$ and $EFGH$ are two parallelograms with equal bases $AB = EF$ and between the same parallel lines EB and HC.

To prove Area of parallelogram $ABCD$

= Area of parallelogram $EFGH$

Construction Draw $BM \perp DC$ and $EN \perp HG$.

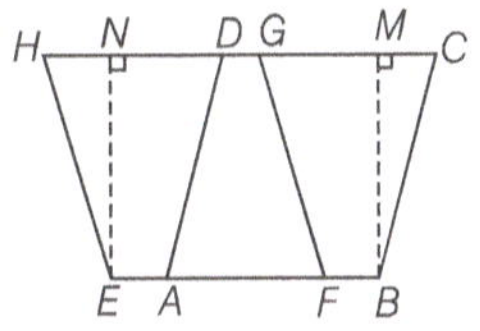

Proof Since, $EB \parallel HC$, therefore

$BM = EN$ ...(i)

[perpendicular distance between two parallel lines are always equal]

Now, area of parallelogram $ABCD = AB \times BM$ ...(ii)

[by Corollary 2]

and area of parallelogram $EFGH = EF \times EN$

$= AB \times EN$ [$\because AB = EF$, given]

$= AB \times BM$ [using Eq. (i)] ...(iii)

Now, from Eqs. (ii) and (iii), we get

ar (parallelogram $ABCD$) = ar (parallelogram $EFGH$)

Hence proved.

Example 1. In the given figure, $ABCD$ and $ABFE$ are two parallelograms and ar (quadrilateral $EABC$) = 17 cm^2 and ar (parallelogram $ABCD$) = 25 cm^2. Then, find ar (ΔBCF).

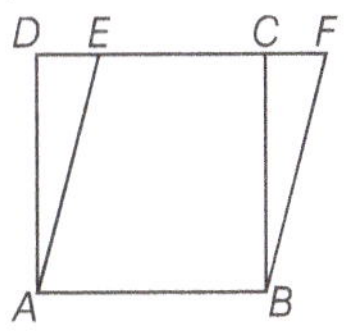

Sol. Given, $ABCD$ and $ABFE$ are two parallelograms on the same base AB and between same parallel lines AB and DF.

Also, ar (quadrilateral $EABC$) = 17 cm^2

and ar (parallelogram $ABCD$) = 25 cm^2

We have,

ar (parallelogram $ABCD$) = ar (parallelogram $ABFE$)

[$\because$ parallelograms on the same base and between same parallel are equal in area]

$\Rightarrow$ ar (parallelogram $ABFE$)

$= \text{ar (parallelogram } ABCD) = 25 \text{ cm}^2$

$\therefore \quad \text{ar } (\Delta BCF) = \text{ar (parallelogram } ABFE) - \text{ar (quadrilateral } EABC)$

$= 25 - 17 = 8 \text{ cm}^2$

Hence, the area of ΔBCF is 8 cm^2.

Example 2. In the given figure, $ABCD$ is a parallelogram, $AE \perp DC$ and $CF \perp AD$. If $CD = 18$ cm, $AE = 9$ cm and $CF = 10$ cm, then find AD.

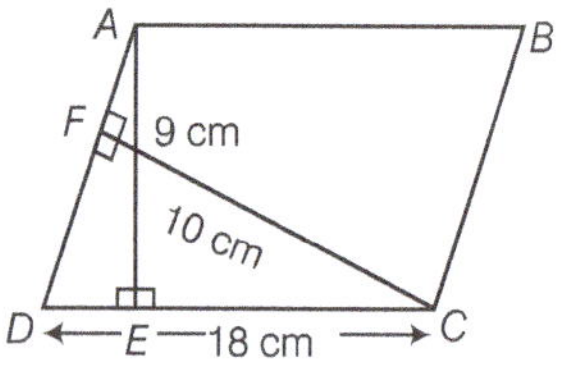

Sol. We have, $CD = 18$ cm, $AE = 9$ cm and $CF = 10$ cm.

We know that,

Area of parallelogram = Base × Height

$\therefore \quad \text{ar (parallelogram } ABCD) = CD \times AE$

$= 18 \times 9 = 162 \text{ cm}^2 \qquad \text{...(i)}$

Also, $\text{ar (parallelogram } ABCD) = AD \times CF$

$\Rightarrow \quad 162 = AD \times 10 \qquad$ [using Eq. (i)]

$\Rightarrow \quad AD = \dfrac{162}{10} = 16.2 \text{ cm}$

Theorem 2 *If a triangle and a parallelogram are on the same base and between the same parallels, then the area of the triangle is equal to half the area of the parallelogram.*

Given ΔABP and parallelogram $ABCD$ are on the same base AB and between the same parallels AB and PC.

To prove $\text{ar } (\Delta ABP) = \dfrac{1}{2} \times \text{ar (parallelogram } ABCD)$

Construction Draw $BQ \parallel AP$ to get another parallelogram $ABQP$.

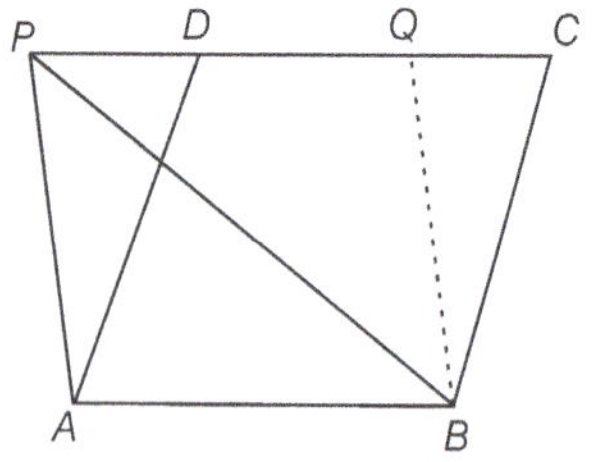

Proof Since, parallelograms $ABCD$ and $ABQP$ lie on the same base AB and between the same parallels AB and PC.

So, $\text{ar (parallelogram } ABCD) = \text{ar (parallelogram } ABQP) \qquad \text{...(i)}$

[$\because$ Parallelograms on the same base and between the same parallels are equal in area]

Now, diagonal PB of parallelogram $ABQP$ divides it into two congruent triangles, i.e. ΔABP and ΔBPQ.

$\therefore \qquad \text{ar } (\Delta ABP) = \text{ar } (\Delta BPQ) \qquad \text{...(ii)}$

Now, $\text{ar } (\Delta ABP) + \text{ar } (\Delta BPQ) = \text{ar (parallelogram } ABQP)$

$\Rightarrow \quad \text{ar } (\Delta ABP) + \text{ar } (\Delta ABP) = \text{ar (parallelogram } ABQP)$

[using Eq. (ii)]

$\Rightarrow \quad 2 \times \text{ar } (\Delta ABP) = \text{ar (parallelogram } ABQP)$

$\Rightarrow \quad \text{ar } (\Delta ABP) = \dfrac{1}{2} \times \text{ar (parallelogram } ABQP)$

$\Rightarrow \quad \text{ar } (\Delta ABP) = \dfrac{1}{2} \times \text{ar (parallelogram } ABCD)$

[using Eq. (i)]

Hence proved.

Corollary 1 *Area of triangle* $= \dfrac{1}{2} \times$ *Base* × *Height*

Given A ΔABC with base BC and $AN \perp BC$, i.e. with height AN.

To prove $\text{ar } (\Delta ABC) = \dfrac{1}{2} \times BC \times AN$

Construction Through A and C, draw lines parallel to BC and AB to meet at D.

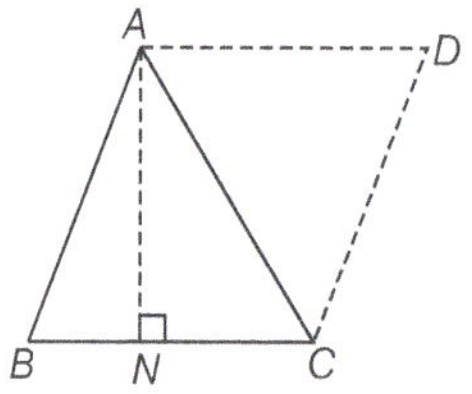

Proof Since, ΔABC and parallelogram $ABCD$ are on the same BC and between the same parallel lines BC and AD,

$\therefore$ We have,

$\text{ar } (\Delta ABC) = \dfrac{1}{2} \times \text{ar (parallelogram } ABCD) \quad$ [by theorem 2]

$= \dfrac{1}{2} \times BC \times AN$

[$\because$ area of parallelogram = base × height]

$= \dfrac{1}{2} \times \text{Base} \times \text{Height} \qquad$ **Hence proved.**

Corollary 2 *A triangle is divided into two triangles of equal area by its median.*

Given A ΔABC in which AD is one of its median.

To prove $\text{ar } (\Delta ABD) = \text{ar } (\Delta ACD)$

Construction From A, draw $AM \perp BC$

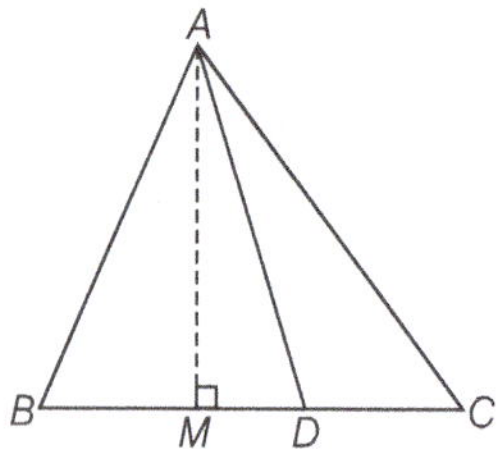

Proof ar $(\Delta ABD) = \frac{1}{2} \times$ Base $\times$ Height

$= \frac{1}{2} \times BD \times AM$ ...(i)

and ar $(\Delta ACD) = \frac{1}{2} \times DC \times AM$

$= \frac{1}{2} \times BD \times AM$ ...(ii)

[$\because$ D is the mid-point of BC, so $BD = DC$]

From Eqs. (i) and (ii), we get

ar (ΔABD) = ar (ΔACD)

Corollary 3 *Area of a trapezium*

$= \frac{1}{2} \times$ *(Sum of parallel sides)* $\times$ *Height*

Given A trapezium $ABCD$ in which $AB \parallel DC$ and $CN \perp AB$, height of trapezium = CN

To prove Area of trapezium $ABCD = \frac{1}{2}(AB + DC) \times CN$

Construction Join AC and draw $AM \perp CD$ (produced)

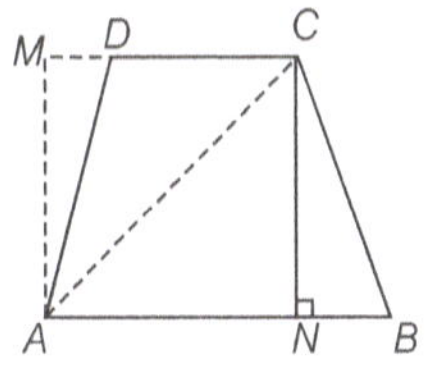

Proof Clearly, $AM = CN$ ...(i)

[$\because$ perpendicular distance between two parallel lines are equal]

Now consider, ar (trapezium $ABCD$)

= ar (ΔABC) + ar (ΔADC)

$= \frac{1}{2} \times AB \times CN + \frac{1}{2} \times DC \times AM$

[AM = height of ΔADC corresponding to the base CD]

$= \frac{1}{2} \times AB \times CN + \frac{1}{2} \times DC \times CN$ [using Eq. (i)]

$= \frac{1}{2} \times CN \times (AB + DC)$

$= \frac{1}{2} \times$ (Sum of parallel sides) $\times$ Height

Example 3. The area of the parallelogram $ABCD$ is 90 cm^2.

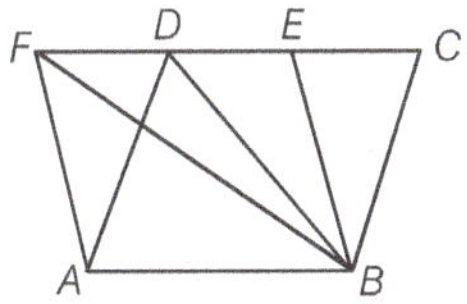

Find

(i) ar $(ABEF)$ (ii) ar (ΔABD) (iii) ar (ΔBEF)

Sol. Given, area of parallelogram $ABCD = 90\text{ cm}^2$

(i) We know that parallelogram on the same base and between the same parallel lines are equal in area.

$\therefore$ ar $(ABEF)$ = ar (parallelogram $ABCD$) = 90 cm^2

(ii) We know that if a triangle and a parallelogram are on the same base and between the same parallels, then area of triangle is equal to half of the area of the parallelogram.

$\therefore$ ar $(\Delta ABD) = \frac{1}{2} \times$ ar (parallelogram $ABEF$)

[$\because$ parallelogram lie on same base AB and between same parallels AB and EF]

$= \frac{1}{2} \times 90$

$\Rightarrow$ ar$(\Delta ABD) = 45\text{ cm}^2$

(iii) Similarly, ΔBEF and parallelogram $ABEF$ are on the same base EF and $EF \parallel AB$.

$\therefore$ ar$(\Delta BEF) = \frac{1}{2} \times$ ar$(ABEF)$

$= \frac{1}{2} \times 90 = 45\text{ cm}^2$

Example 4. In the given figure, parallelograms $ABCD$ and $PBCQ$ are given. If R is a mid-point on PB, then show that ar $(\Delta QRC) = \frac{1}{2}$ ar (parallelogram $ABCD$).

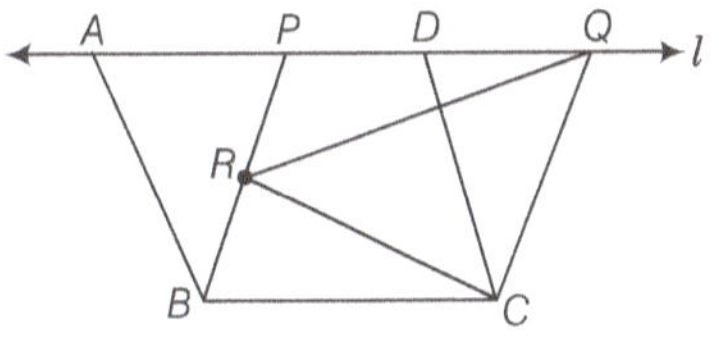

Sol. **Given** $ABCD$ and $PBCQ$ are two parallelograms and R is a mid-point on PB.

To prove ar $(\Delta QRC) = \frac{1}{2}$ ar (parallelogram $ABCD$)

Proof Here, parallelograms $PBCQ$ and $ABCD$ lie on the same base BC and between the same parallels BC and AQ.

So, ar (parallelogram $PBCQ$)

= ar (parallelogram $ABCD$) ...(i)

Now, ΔQRC and parallelogram $PBCQ$ lie on the same base CQ and between the same parallels CQ and BP.

So, ar $(\Delta QRC) = \frac{1}{2}$ ar (parallelogram $PBCQ$) ...(ii)

From Eqs. (i) and (ii), we get

ar $(\Delta QRC) = \frac{1}{2}$ ar (parallelogram $ABCD$)

Hence proved.

Example 5. If P and Q are any two points lying on the sides DC and AD respectively of a parallelogram $ABCD$. Show that ar(ΔAPB) = ar(ΔBQC).

Sol. **Given** In a parallelogram $ABCD$, P and Q are any two points lying on the sides DC and AD, respectively.

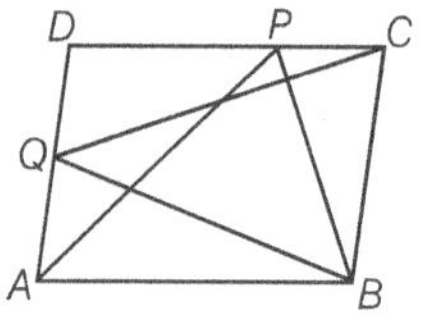

To prove ar (ΔAPB) = ar (ΔBQC)

Proof Here, parallelogram $ABCD$ and ΔBQC stand on the same base BC and lie between the same parallel lines BC and AD.

$\therefore \quad$ ar (ΔBQC) = $\frac{1}{2}$ ar (parallelogram $ABCD$) ...(i)

Similarly, ΔAPB and parallelogram $ABCD$ stand on the same base AB and lie between the same parallel lines AB and CD.

$\therefore \quad$ ar (ΔAPB) = $\frac{1}{2}$ ar (parallelogram $ABCD$) ...(ii)

From Eqs. (i) and (ii), we get

ar (ΔAPB) = ar(ΔBQC) **Hence proved.**

Example 6. Show that the area of a rhombus is half of product of its diagonals.

Sol. **Given** $ABCD$ is a rhombus.

To prove ar (rhombus $ABCD$) = $\frac{1}{2} \times AC \times BD$

Proof Since, the diagonals of a rhombus bisect at right angles.

$\therefore \quad OD \perp AC$ and $OB \perp AC$

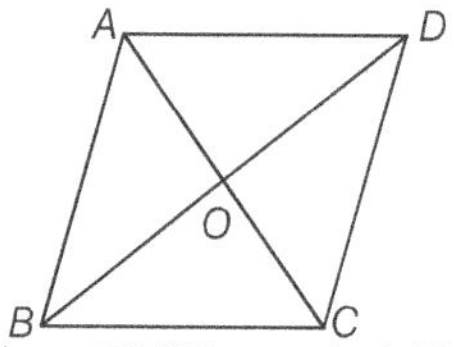

Now, ar (rhombus $ABCD$) = ar (ΔACD) + ar (ΔABC)

$= \frac{1}{2} \times AC \times OD + \frac{1}{2} \times AC \times OB$

$= \frac{1}{2} \times AC \times (OD + OB)$

$= \frac{1}{2} \times AC \times BD \quad [\because BD = OB + OD]$

$= \frac{1}{2} \times$ Product of diagonals **Hence proved.**

Example 7. Find the area of a trapezium, whose parallel sides are 9 cm and 6 cm and the distance between these sides is 8 cm.

Sol. We know that

$\therefore$ Area of trapezium = $\frac{1}{2} \times$ (Sum of parallel sides) $\times$ Height

Area of trapezium = $\frac{1}{2} \times (9 + 6) \times 8 = \frac{1}{2} \times 15 \times 8 = 60 \text{ cm}^2$

Hence, the area of a trapezium is 60 cm^2.

Example 8. The perimeter of an isosceles triangle is 32 cm and its base is 12 cm. One of its equal side forms the diagonal of a parallelogram. Find the area of parallelogram.

Sol. Let ABC be an isosceles triangle with base BC = 12 cm, perimeter = 32 cm and AC is a diagonal of a parallelogram $ABCD$.

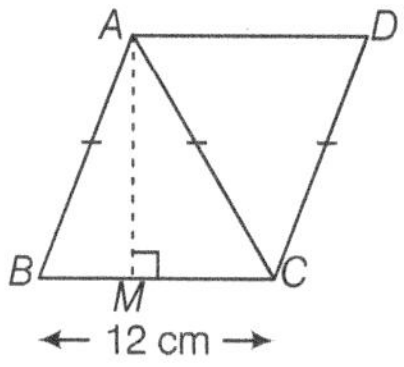

Draw $AM \perp BC$.

So, $\quad BM = CM = \frac{12}{2} = 6 \text{ cm}$

[$\because \Delta AMB \cong \Delta AMC$ by RHS congruence rule]

Also, $\quad AB = AC = \frac{32 - 12}{2} = 10 \text{ cm}$

In ΔAMC, $AM = \sqrt{AC^2 - CM^2} = \sqrt{10^2 - 6^2}$

$= \sqrt{100 - 36} = \sqrt{64} = 8 \text{ cm}$

$\therefore$ Area of parallelogram $ABCD = BC \times AM = 12 \times 8 = 96 \text{ cm}^2$

Example 9. Show that a median of a triangle divides it into two triangles of equal areas.

Sol. **Given** Let AD be a median of ΔABC.

To prove ar (ΔABD) = ar (ΔACD)

Construction Draw $AN \perp BC$.

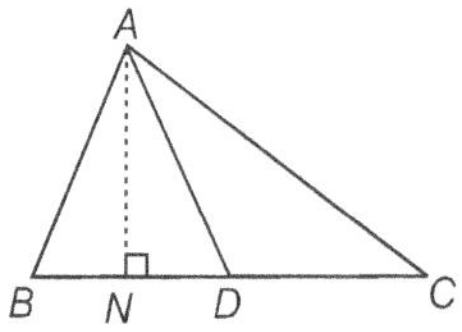

Proof Since, AD is a median of ΔABC. So, D is the mid-point of BC.

Then, $\quad BD = CD$ ...(i)

Now, $\quad$ ar (ΔABD) = $\frac{1}{2} \times BD \times AN$

$\left[\because \text{area of triangle} = \frac{1}{2} \times \text{base} \times \text{height}\right]$

$= \frac{1}{2} \times CD \times AN$ [from Eq. (i)]

$\Rightarrow \quad$ ar(ΔABD) = ar (ΔACD)

Hence, median of a triangle divides it into two triangles of equal areas. **Hence proved.**

Example 10. In the given figure, E is any point on median AD of a ΔABC. Show that ar (ΔABE) = ar (ΔACE).

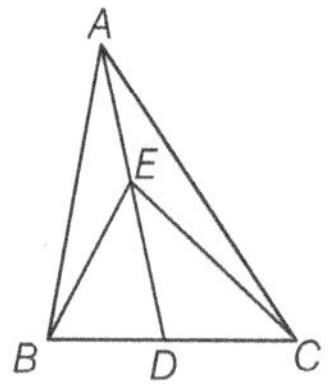

Sol. **Given** AD is a median of ΔABC and E is any point on AD.

To prove ar (ΔABE) = ar (ΔACE)

Proof Since, AD is the median of ΔABC.

$\therefore$ ar (ΔABD) = ar(ΔACD) ...(i)

[$\because$, a median of a triangle divides it into two triangles of equal areas]

Also, ED is the median of ΔEBC.

$\therefore$ ar (ΔBED) = ar (ΔCED) ...(ii)

On subtracting Eq. (ii) from Eq. (i), we get

ar (ΔABD) − ar (ΔBED) = ar (ΔACD) − ar (ΔCED)

$\Rightarrow$ ar (ΔABE) = ar (ΔACE) **Hence proved.**

Example 11. If E, F, G and H are respectively, the mid-points of the sides of a parallelogram $ABCD$, show that ar($EFGH$) = $\frac{1}{2}$ ar (parallelogram $ABCD$).

Sol. **Given** Points E, F, G and H are respectively, the mid-points of the sides AB, BC, CD and AD.

To prove ar ($EFGH$) = $\frac{1}{2}$ ar (parallelogram $ABCD$)

Construction Join HF.

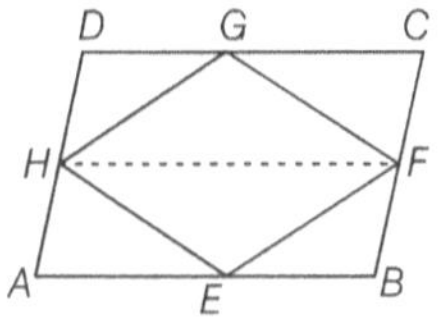

Proof Clearly, $ABFH$ and $HFCD$ both are parallelogram.

$\because$ A quadrilateral is a parallelogram, if a pair of opposite sides are equal and parallel and here $AH \parallel BF$, $AH = BF$ and $DH \parallel CF$ and $DH = CF$.

Now, as parallelogram $HDCF$ and ΔHGF stand on the same base HF and lie between the same parallel lines DC and HF.

$\therefore$ ar (ΔHGF) = $\frac{1}{2}$ ar (parallelogram $HDCF$) ...(i)

Similarly, parallelogram $ABFH$ and ΔHEF stand on the same base HF and lie between the same parallel lines HF and AB.

$\therefore$ ar (ΔHEF) = $\frac{1}{2}$ ar (parallelogram $ABFH$) ...(ii)

On adding Eqs. (i) and (ii), we get

ar (ΔHGF) + ar (ΔHEF) = $\frac{1}{2}$[ar (parallelogram $HDCF$) + ar (parallelogram $ABFH$)]

$\Rightarrow$ ar ($EFGH$) = $\frac{1}{2}$ ar (parallelogram $ABCD$)

Hence proved.

Example 12. Show that the area of the quadrilateral made by connecting the mid-points of the adjacent sides of a quadrilateral is half the area of the given quadrilateral.

Sol. **Given** A quadrilateral $WXYZ$ and $ABCD$ is the quadrilateral made by joining mid-points of the sides WX, XY, YZ and ZW, respectively.

To prove ar ($ABCD$) = $\frac{1}{2}$ ar ($WXYZ$)

Construction Join WY and WC.

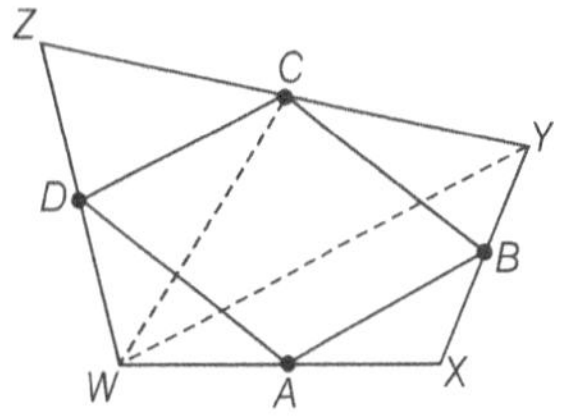

Proof We know that, a triangle is divided by its median in two triangles of equal area.

$\therefore$ ar (ΔWCZ) = $\frac{1}{2}$ ar (ΔWYZ) ...(i)

ar (ΔDCZ) = $\frac{1}{2}$ ar (ΔWCZ) ...(ii)

From Eqs. (i) and (ii), we get

ar (ΔDCZ) = $\frac{1}{4}$ ar (ΔWYZ) ...(iii)

Similarly, ar (ΔAXB) = $\frac{1}{4}$ ar (ΔWXY) ...(iv)

On adding Eqs. (iii) and (iv), we get

ar (ΔDCZ) + ar (ΔAXB) = $\frac{1}{4}$[ar (ΔWYZ) + ar (ΔWXY)] ...(v)

$\therefore$ ar (ΔDCZ) + ar (ΔAXB) = $\frac{1}{4}$ ar ($WXYZ$) ...(vi)

Similarly, ar (ΔWAD) + ar (ΔBYC) = $\frac{1}{4}$ ar ($WXYZ$) ...(vii)

On adding Eqs. (vi) and (vii), we get

ar (ΔWAD) + ar (ΔAXB) + ar (ΔBYC) + ar (ΔDCZ) = $\frac{1}{2}$ ar ($WXYZ$) ...(viii)

$\therefore$ ar (ΔWAD) + ar (ΔAXB) + ar (ΔBYC) + ar (ΔDCZ) + ar ($ABCD$) = ar ($WXYZ$) ...(ix)

On subtracting Eq. (viii) from Eq. (ix), we get

ar ($ABCD$) = $\frac{1}{2}$ ar ($WXYZ$) **Hence proved.**

Example 13. The medians BE and CF of a ΔABC intersect at G. Prove that ar (ΔGBC) = ar (quadrilateral $AFGE$).

Sol. **Given** BE and CF are medians of a ΔABC and they intersect at G.

To prove ar (ΔGBC) = ar (quadrilateral $AFGE$)

Proof We know that median of a triangle divide it into two parts of equal areas.

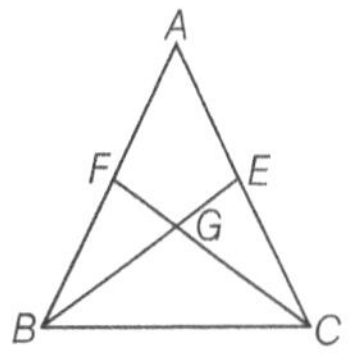

$\therefore$ ar (ΔFBC) = ar (ΔAFC)

$\Rightarrow$ ar (ΔFBC) = $\frac{1}{2}$ ar (ΔABC) ...(i)

Similarly, ar (ΔAEB) = $\frac{1}{2}$ ar (ΔABC) ...(ii)

From Eqs. (i) and (ii), we get ar (ΔFBC) = ar (ΔAEB)

On subtracting ar (ΔGBF) from both sides, we get

$$\text{ar}(\Delta FBC) - \text{ar}(\Delta GBF) = \text{ar}(\Delta AEB) - \text{ar}(\Delta GBF)$$

$\Rightarrow$ ar (ΔGBC) = ar (quadrilateral $AFGE$)

Hence proved.

Example 14. Let O be any point on the diagonal PR of a parallelogram $PQRS$ (see the figure). Prove that ar (ΔPSO) = ar (ΔPQO).

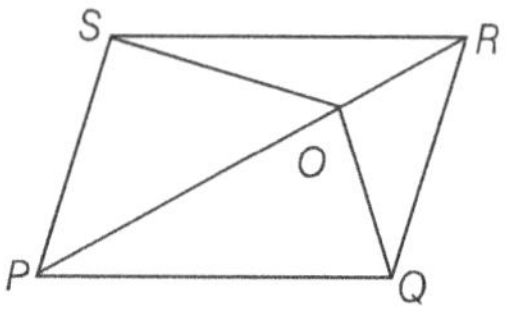

Sol. **Given** $PQRS$ is a parallelogram and O is any point on the diagonal PR.

To prove ar(ΔPSO) = ar(ΔPQO)

Construction Join SQ to intersect PR at B.

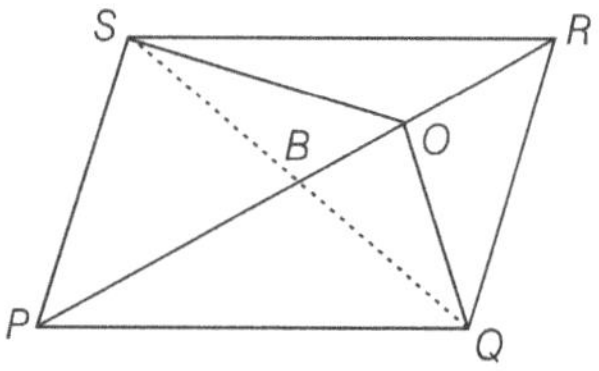

Proof We know that the diagonals of a parallelogram bisect each other, so B is the mid-point of SQ.

Thus, PB is a median of ΔQPS and median of a triangle divides it into two triangles of equal areas.

$\therefore$ ar (ΔBPQ) = ar (ΔBPS) ...(i)

Also, OB is a median of ΔOSQ.

ar (ΔOBQ) = ar (ΔOBS) ...(ii)

On adding Eqs. (i) and (ii), we get

$$\text{ar}(\Delta BPQ) + \text{ar}(\Delta OBQ) = \text{ar}(\Delta BPS) + \text{ar}(\Delta OSB)$$

$\Rightarrow$ ar (ΔPQO) = ar (ΔPSO) **Hence proved.**

Example 15. In the given figure, P is a point in the interior of a parallelogram $ABCD$. Show that

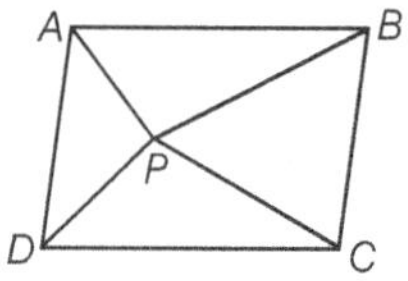

(i) ar (ΔAPB) + ar(ΔPCD) = $\frac{1}{2}$ ar (parallelogram $ABCD$)

(ii) ar(ΔAPD) + ar(ΔPBC) = ar(ΔAPB) + ar(ΔPCD).

Sol. **Given** $ABCD$ is a parallelogram.

So, $AB \parallel CD$ and $AD \parallel BC$.

To prove

(i) ar (ΔAPB) + ar (ΔPCD) = $\frac{1}{2}$ ar (parallelogram $ABCD$)

(ii) ar (ΔAPD) + ar (ΔPBC) = ar (ΔAPB) + ar (ΔPCD)

Proof

(i) Through the point P, draw MR parallel to AB.

$\because$ $MR \parallel AB$ and $AM \parallel BR$

So, $ABRM$ is a parallelogram.

Now, as ΔAPB and parallelogram $ABRM$ are on the same base AB and between the same parallel lines AB and MR.

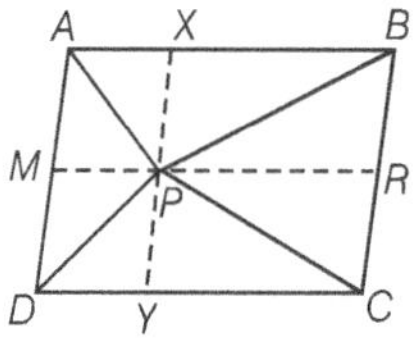

$\therefore$ ar (ΔAPB) = $\frac{1}{2}$ ar (parallelogram $ABRM$)

Similarly, ar (ΔPCD) = $\frac{1}{2}$ ar (parallelogram $MRCD$)

Now, ar (ΔAPB) + ar (ΔPCD)

= $\frac{1}{2}$ ar (parallelogram $ABRM$) + $\frac{1}{2}$ ar (parallelogram $MRCD$)

= $\frac{1}{2}$ ar (parallelogram $ABCD$) ...(i)

(ii) Draw a line XY through P parallel to AD.

$\because$ $XY \parallel AD$ and $AX \parallel DY$.

So, $AXYD$ is a parallelogram.

Now, ΔAPD and parallelogram $AXYD$ are on the same base AD and between the same parallels AD and XY.

$\therefore$ ar (ΔAPD) = $\frac{1}{2}$ ar (parallelogram $AXYD$)

Similarly, ar (ΔPBC) = $\frac{1}{2}$ ar (parallelogram $BXYC$)

Now, ar (ΔAPD) + ar (ΔPBC)

= $\frac{1}{2}$ ar (parallelogram $AXYD$) + $\frac{1}{2}$ ar (parallelogram $BXYC$)

$\Rightarrow$ ar (ΔAPD) + ar (ΔPBC)

= $\frac{1}{2}$ ar (parallelogram $ABCD$) ...(ii)

From Eqs. (i) and (ii), we get

ar (ΔAPD) + ar (ΔPBC) = ar (ΔAPB) + ar(ΔPCD)

Hence proved.

Exercise 12.1

1. In the given figure, if $l \parallel m$ and quadrilaterals *ABCD*, *CDEF* and *EFGH* are parallelograms, then prove that ar (parallelogram *ABCD*) = ar (parallelogram *EFGH*).

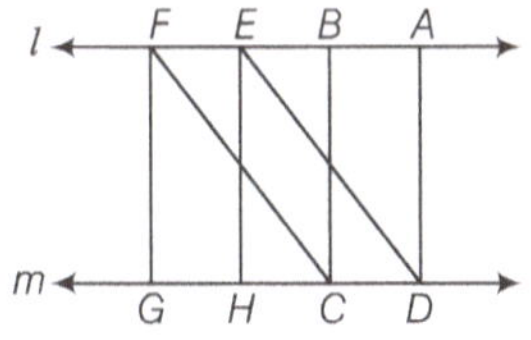

2. In the given figure, *ABCD* is a parallelogram, $DC = 5$ cm and $BD = 7$cm. Find the area of parallelogram *ABCD*.

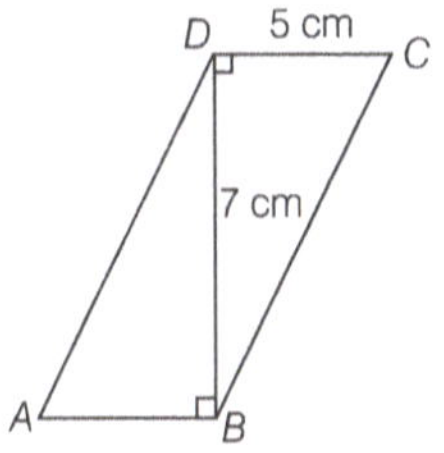

3. In the given figure, *ABCD* is a parallelogram. If $CD = 20$ cm, $AE = 12$ cm and $CF = 8$ cm, then find *AD*.

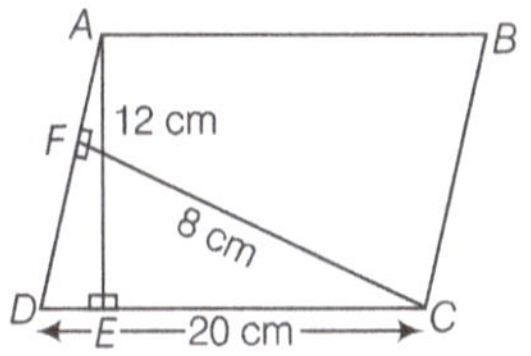

4. If the area, base and corresponding altitude of a parallelogram are x^2, $x - 3$, $x + 4$ respectively, then find the value of x.

5. If a triangle and a parallelogram are on the same base and between same parallels, then find the ratio of the area of the triangle to the area of the parallelogram.

6. In the given figure, the area of parallelogram *ABCD* is 140 cm^2.

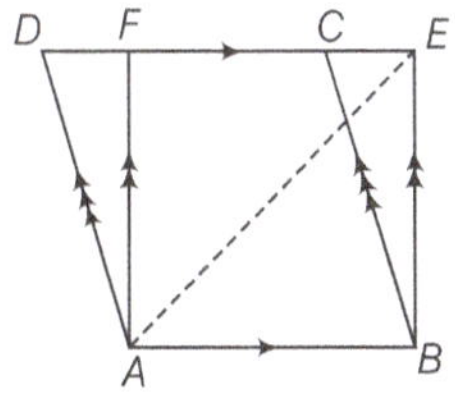

Find

(i) ar (parallelogram *ABEF*).

(ii) ar (ΔAEF).

7. ΔABC and ΔDBC are on the same base *BC* with *A*, *D* on opposite sides of *BC*. If area of ΔABC = area of ΔDBC, prove that *BC* bisects *AD*.

8. Find the area of a trapezium, whose parallel sides are 7 cm and 8 cm and the distance between these sides is 12 cm.

9. If *BD* is one of the diagonal of a quadrilateral *ABCD*. *AM* and *CN* are the perpendiculars from *A* and *C* respectively, on *BD*. Prove that ar (quadrilateral $ABCD) = \frac{1}{2} \cdot BD(AM + CN)$.

10. In ΔABC, if *D* is the mid-point of *BC* and *E* is the mid-point of median *AD*, then prove that ar $(\Delta ABE) = \frac{1}{4}$ ar (ΔABC).

11. Find the area of a rhombus, the lengths of whose diagonals are 16 cm and 24 cm, respectively.

12. The perimeter of an isosceles triangle is 16 cm and its base is 6 cm. One of its equal side forms the diagonal of a parallelogram. Find the area of parallelogram.

13. In trapezium *ABCD*, $AB \parallel DC$ and *L* is mid-point of *BC*. Through *L*, a line $PQ \parallel AD$ has been drawn which meets *AB* in *P* and *DC* produced in *Q*. Prove that ar (*ABCD*) = ar (*APQD*).

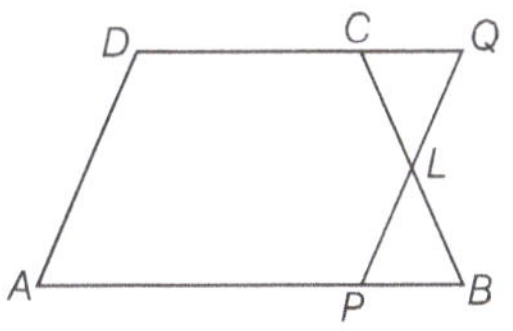

14. If *ABC* is a triangle, whose area is 50 cm^2. *E* and *F* are the mid-points of the sides *AB* and *AC*, respectively. Prove that *EBCF* is a trapezium. Also, find its area.

15. *XY* is a line parallel to side *BC* of a ΔABC. If $BE \parallel CA$ and $FC \parallel AB$ meet *XY* at *E* and *F* respectively, then show that ar(ΔABE) = ar(ΔACF).

Triangles on the Same Base and between the Same Parallels

Here, we will understand some important theorems, which are based on triangles having same base and between the same parallels.

Theorem 3

(i) Two triangles on the same base (or equal bases) and between the same parallels are equal in area.

Or

In other words, if ΔABC and ΔABD are on the same base AB and between the same parallel lines AB and CD, then

$$ar\ (\Delta ABC) = ar\ (\Delta ABD).$$

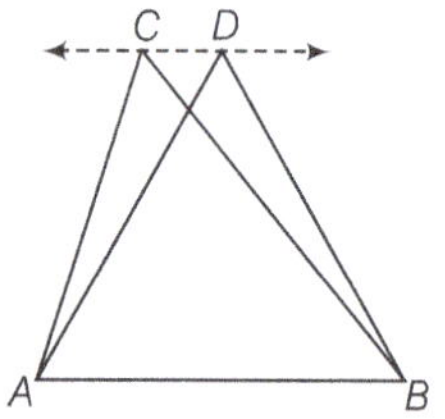

(ii) Also, if ΔABC and ΔPQR are two triangles with equal bases BC = QR and between the same parallel lines AP and BR, then $ar\ (\Delta ABC) = ar\ (\Delta PQR)$.

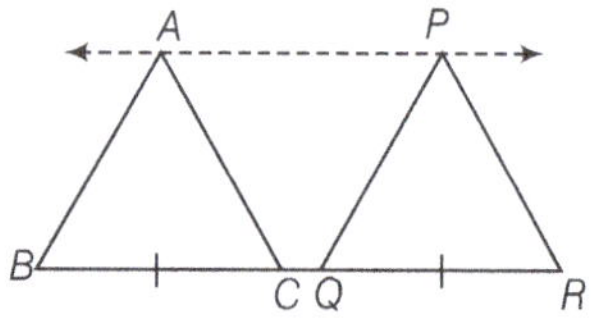

Example 16. Diagonals AC and BD of a trapezium $ABCD$ with $AB \parallel DC$ intersect each other at O. Prove that $ar(\Delta AOD) = ar(\Delta BOC)$.

Sol. **Given** Diagonals AC and BD of a trapezium $ABCD$ with $AB \parallel DC$ intersect each other at O.

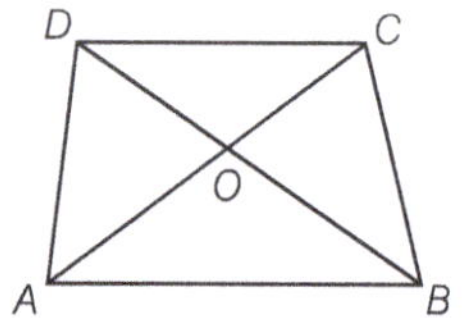

To prove $ar\ (\Delta AOD) = ar\ (\Delta BOC)$

Proof Here, ΔABC and ΔABD lie on the same base AB and between the same parallel lines AB and DC.

$\therefore \quad ar(\Delta ABD) = ar(\Delta ABC)$

On subtracting $ar(\Delta AOB)$ from both sides, we get

$ar(\Delta ABD) - ar(\Delta AOB) = ar(\Delta ABC) - ar(\Delta AOB)$

$\Rightarrow \quad ar(\Delta AOD) = ar(\Delta BOC)$ **Hence proved.**

Example 17. In ΔABC, if L and M are the mid-points on AB and AC respectively such that $LM \parallel BC$, then prove that $ar\ (\Delta LOB) = ar\ (\Delta MOC)$.

Sol. **Given** In ΔABC, L and M are mid-points on AB and AC, such that $LM \parallel BC$.

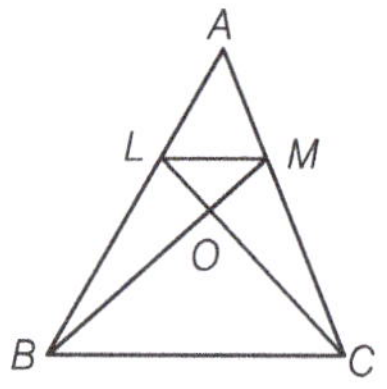

To prove $ar\ (\Delta LOB) = ar\ (\Delta MOC)$

Proof Since, ΔLBC and ΔMBC both lie on the same base BC and between the same parallel lines BC and LM.

$\therefore \quad ar\ (\Delta LBC) = ar\ (\Delta MBC)$

$\Rightarrow \quad ar\ (\Delta LOB) + ar\ (\Delta BOC) = ar\ (\Delta MOC) + ar\ (\Delta BOC)$

$\Rightarrow \quad ar\ (\Delta LOB) = ar\ (\Delta MOC)$

[eliminating $ar\ (\Delta BOC)$ from both sides]

Hence proved.

Example 18. In the given figure, $ABCD$ is a quadrilateral. BP is drawn parallel to AC and BP meets DC (produced) at P. Prove that $ar\ (\Delta ADP) = ar$ (quadrilateral $ABCD$).

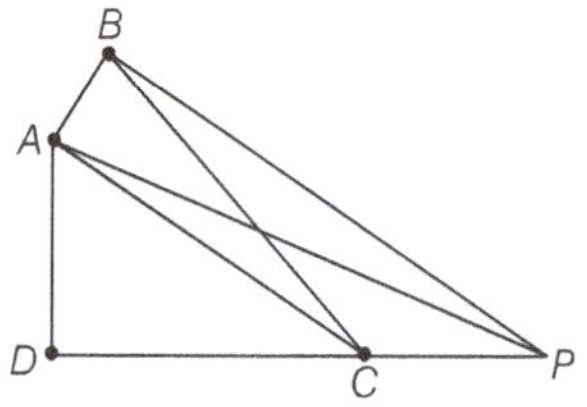

Sol. **Given** $ABCD$ is a quadrilateral and $BP \parallel AC$.

To prove $ar\ (\Delta ADP) = ar$(quadrilateral $ABCD$)

Proof Here, ΔACB and ΔACP lie on the same base AC and between the same parallel lines AC and BP.

So, $ar\ (\Delta ACB) = ar\ (\Delta ACP)$ [by theorem 3]

On adding $ar(\Delta ADC)$ both sides, we get

$ar\ (\Delta ACB) + ar\ (\Delta ADC) = ar\ (\Delta ACP) + ar\ (\Delta ADC)$

$\Rightarrow \quad ar\ (ABCD) = ar\ (\Delta ADP)$ **Hence proved.**

Example 19. In the given figure, $ABCDE$ is a pentagon. A line through B parallel to AC meets DC produced at F.

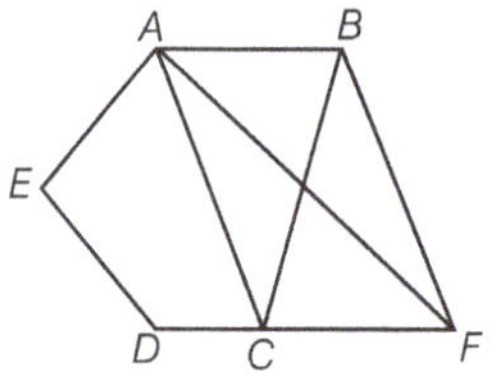

Show that

(i) $ar(\Delta ACB) = ar(\Delta ACF)$.

(ii) $ar\ (AEDF) = ar\ (ABCDE)$.

Sol. **Given** $ABCDE$ is a pentagon and $BF \parallel AC$.

To prove

(i) ar (ΔACB) = ar (ΔACF)

(ii) ar $(AEDF)$ = ar $(ABCDE)$

Proof

(i) ΔACB and ΔACF lie on the same base AC and between the same parallel lines AC and BF.

$\therefore \quad \text{ar}(\Delta ACB) = \text{ar}(\Delta ACF) \quad$ ...(i)

(ii) Now, $\text{ar}(AEDF) = \text{ar}(AEDC) + \text{ar}(\Delta ACF)$

$= \text{ar}(AEDC) + \text{ar}(\Delta ACB)$ [from Eq. (i)]

$= \text{ar}(ABCDE)$ **Hence proved.**

Example 20. A point E is taken on the side BC of a parallelogram $ABCD$. AE and DC are produced to meet at F. Prove that ar (ΔADF) = ar (quadrilateral $ABFC$).

Sol. **Given** $ABCD$ is a parallelogram.

To prove ar (ΔADF) = ar (quadrilateral $ABFC$)

Proof Here, ΔACB and ΔAFB are on the same base AB and between same parallel lines AB and DF.

[$\because AB \parallel DC \Rightarrow AB \parallel DF$]

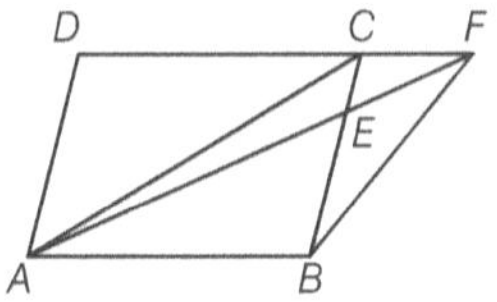

$\therefore \quad$ ar (ΔACB) = ar (ΔAFB) ...(i)

Now, ar (ΔACB) = ar (ΔADC) ...(ii)

[$\because$ diagonals of parallelogram divides it into two triangles of equal area]

From Eqs. (i) and (ii), we get

ar (ΔADC) = ar (ΔAFB)

On adding ar (ΔACF) both sides, we get

ar (ΔADC) + ar (ΔACF) = ar (ΔAFB) + ar (ΔACF)

$\Rightarrow$ ar (ΔADF) = ar $(ABFC)$ **Hence proved.**

Example 21. In the given figure, ABC is a triangle and D is the mid-point of AB. P is any point on BC. Line CQ is drawn parallel to PD to intersect AB at Q. PQ is joined. Show that ar $(\Delta BPQ) = \frac{1}{2}$ ar (ΔABC).

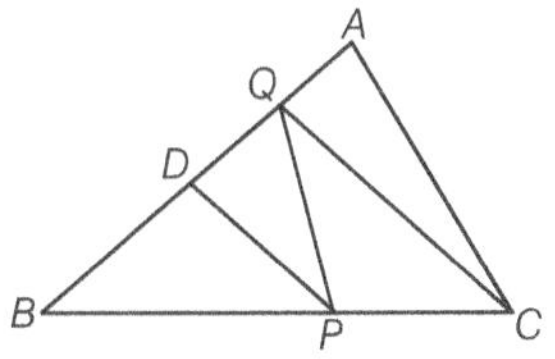

Sol. **Given** ΔABC in which D is the mid-point of AB and $CQ \parallel PD$.

To prove ar $(\Delta BPQ) = \frac{1}{2}$ ar (ΔABC)

Construction Join CD.

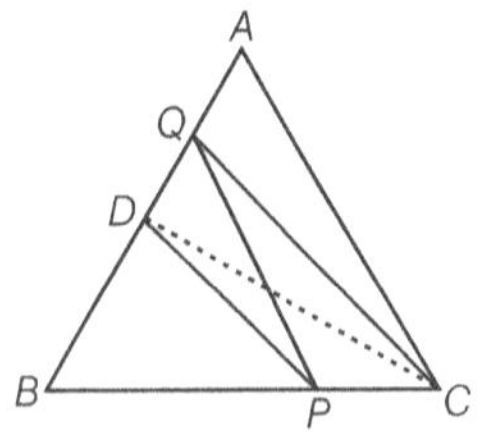

Proof Since, D is the mid-point of AB.

So, in ΔABC, CD is the median.

$\Rightarrow \quad$ ar $(\Delta BCD) = \frac{1}{2}$ ar (ΔABC) ...(i)

Since, ΔPDQ and ΔPDC are on the same base PD and between same parallels PD and CQ.

$\therefore \quad$ ar (ΔPDQ) = ar (ΔPDC) ...(ii)

Now, from Eq. (i), ar $(\Delta BCD) = \frac{1}{2}$ ar (ΔABC)

$\Rightarrow$ ar (ΔBDP) + ar $(\Delta PDC) = \frac{1}{2}$ ar (ΔABC)

$\Rightarrow$ ar (ΔBDP) + ar $(\Delta PDQ) = \frac{1}{2}$ ar (ΔABC) [from Eq. (ii)]

$\Rightarrow$ ar $(\Delta BPQ) = \frac{1}{2}$ ar (ΔABC) **Hence proved.**

Example 22. In the given figure, $ABCDE$ is any pentagon. BP drawn parallel to AC meets DC produced at P and EQ drawn parallel to AD meets CD produced at Q.

Prove that ar (Pentagon $ABCDE$) = ar (ΔAPQ).

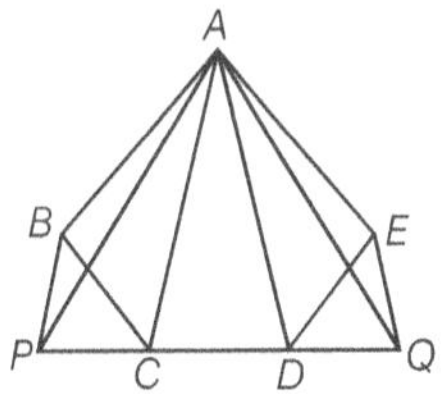

Sol. **Given** $ABCDE$ is a pentagon, $BP \parallel AC$ and $EQ \parallel AD$.

To prove ar (Pentagon $ABCDE$) = ar (ΔAPQ)

Proof We know that triangles on the same base and between the same parallels are equal in area.

$\therefore \quad$ ar (ΔADE) = ar (ΔADQ) ...(i)

Similarly, ar (ΔCAB) = ar (ΔCAP) ...(ii)

On adding Eqs. (i) and (ii), we get

ar (ΔADE) + ar (ΔCAB) = ar (ΔADQ) + ar (ΔCAP)

On adding ar (ΔCDA) both sides, we get

ar (ΔADE) + ar (ΔCAB) + ar (ΔCDA)

= ar (ΔADQ) + ar (ΔCAP) + ar (ΔCDA)

$\Rightarrow$ ar $(ABCDE)$ = ar (ΔAPQ) **Hence proved.**

Theorem 4 *Triangles with equal areas on the same base have equal corresponding altitudes.*

Given Two triangles, ΔABC and ΔABD are on the same base AB and ar (ΔABC) = ar (ΔABD). Further, $CM \perp AB$ and $DN \perp AB$.

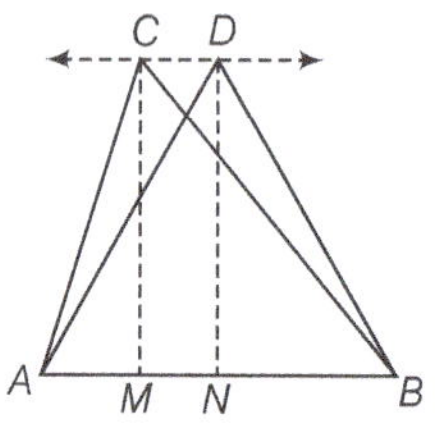

To prove $CM = DN$

Proof Clearly, ar $(\Delta ABC) = \frac{1}{2} \times AB \times CM$ ...(i)

and ar $(\Delta ABD) = \frac{1}{2} \times AB \times DN$ ...(ii)

$\because$ ar (ΔABC) = ar (ΔABD)

$\therefore$ $\frac{1}{2} \times AB \times CM = \frac{1}{2} \times AB \times DN$

[using Eqs. (i) and (ii)]

$\Rightarrow$ $CM = DN$ **Hence proved.**

Note

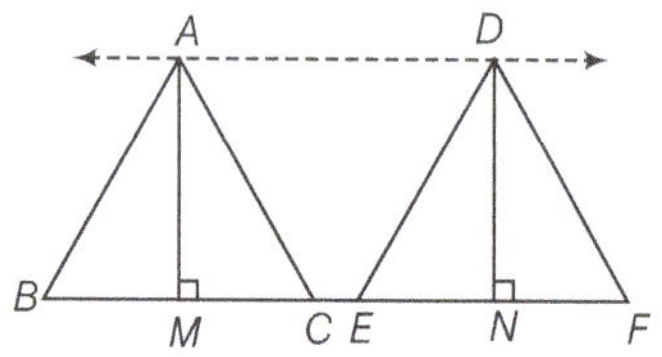

Corollary *Triangles on the same base and having equal areas lie between the same parallel lines.*

Given Two triangles, ΔABC and ΔABD are on the same base AB and ar (ΔABC) = ar (ΔABD).

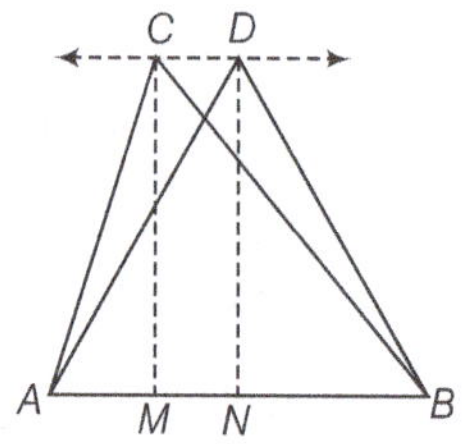

To prove $CD \parallel AB$

Construction From C and D, draw perpendiculars CM and DN on AB, respectively.

Proof $CM = DN$ [by the theorem]

$\Rightarrow$ $CM \parallel DN$

[$\because$ CM and DN are both perpendicular to the same line AB]

$\Rightarrow$ $CMND$ is a parallelogram.

[$\because$ a quadrilateral is a parallelogram, if a pair of opposite side of a quadrilateral are equal and parallel]

$\Rightarrow$ $CD \parallel MN$

$\Rightarrow$ $CD \parallel AB$

Note

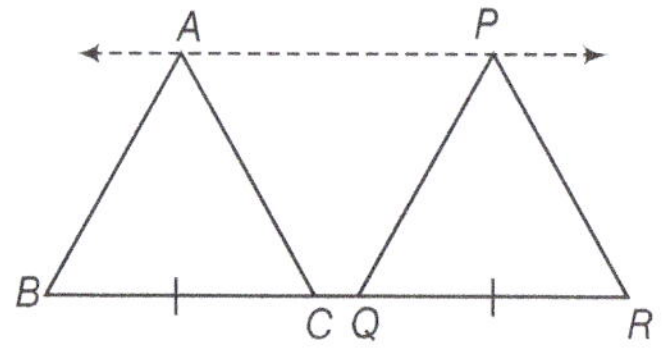

Example 23. D and E are mid-points on sides AB and AC respectively, of ΔABC such that ar(ΔDBC) = ar(ΔEBC). Prove that $DE \parallel BC$.

Sol. **Given** A ΔABC and D and E are mid-points on sides AB and AC, respectively.

Also, ar(ΔDBC) = ar(ΔEBC).

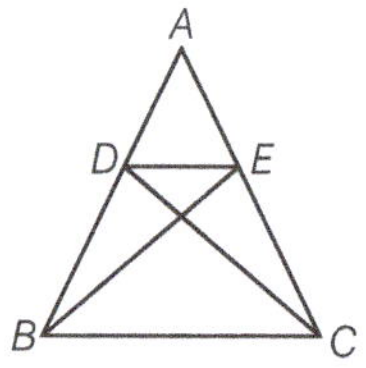

To prove $DE \parallel BC$

Proof Here, ΔDBC and ΔEBC are equal in area and have same base BC.

$\therefore$ Altitude from D of ΔDBC = Altitude from E of ΔEBC

Thus, ΔDBC and ΔEBC are between the same parallels.

$\Rightarrow$ $DE \parallel BC$ **Hence proved.**

Example 24. Diagonals AC and BD of a quadrilateral $ABCD$ intersect at O in such a way that ar (ΔAOD) = ar (ΔBOC). Prove that $ABCD$ is a trapezium.

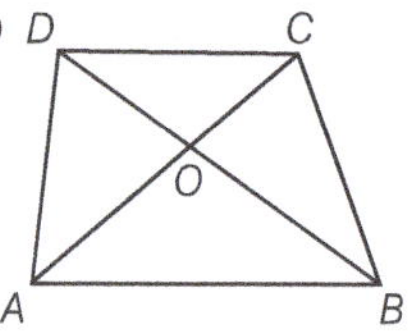

Sol. **Given** $ABCD$ is a quadrilateral and diagonals AC and BD intersect at O such that ar (ΔAOD) = ar (ΔBOC).

To prove $ABCD$ is a trapezium.

Proof Since, ar (ΔAOD) = ar (ΔBOC)

On adding ar (ΔAOB) both sides, we get

$$\text{ar}(\Delta AOD) + \text{ar}(\Delta AOB) = \text{ar}(\Delta BOC) + \text{ar}(\Delta AOB)$$

$$\Rightarrow \quad \text{ar}(\Delta ADB) = \text{ar}(\Delta ACB)$$

Now, ΔACB and ΔADB lie on same base AB.

and ar (ΔADB) = ar (ΔACB)

So, ΔACB and ΔADB will lie between same parallel lines.

$$\therefore \quad AB \parallel DC$$

Hence, $ABCD$ is a trapezium. **Hence proved.**

Some Important Results

1. If two triangles lie between the same parallels (i.e. have equal altitudes), then the ratio of their areas equals the ratio of their bases.

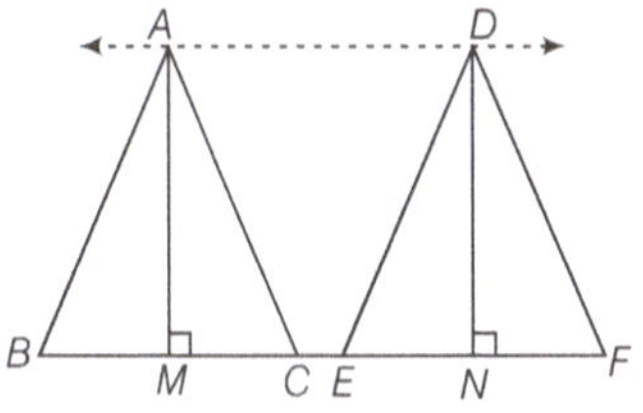

In the given figure, ΔABC and ΔDEF lie between the same parallel AD and BF.

$$\text{Then, } \frac{\text{ar}(\Delta ABC)}{\text{ar}(\Delta DEF)} = \frac{\frac{1}{2} \times BC \times AM}{\frac{1}{2} \times EF \times DN} = \frac{BC}{EF} \quad [\because AM = DN]$$

2. If two triangles have same base (or equal bases), then the ratio of their areas equals the ratio of their altitudes.

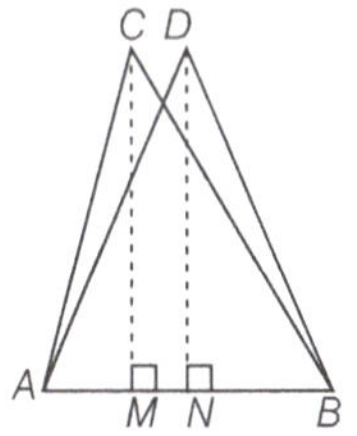

In the given figure, ΔABC and ΔABD are on the same base AB.

$$\text{Then, } \frac{\text{ar}(\Delta ABC)}{\text{ar}(\Delta ABD)} = \frac{\frac{1}{2} \times AB \times CM}{\frac{1}{2} \times AB \times DN} = \frac{CM}{DN}.$$

3. If the triangles have same vertex and the bases along the same line, then the areas of triangles are in the ratio of their bases.

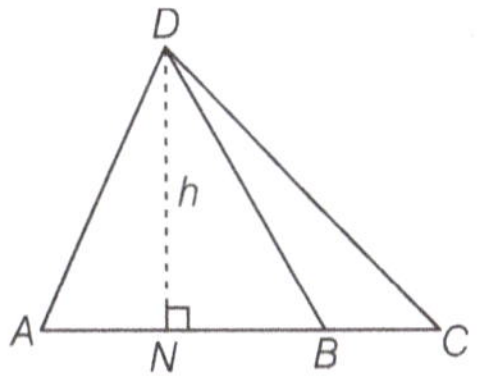

In the given figure, ΔABD, ΔBCD and ΔACD have the same vertex D and bases along the same straight line AC. So, they have the same height.

In such a case, we have the following ratios

(i) $$\frac{\text{ar}(\Delta ABD)}{\text{ar}(\Delta BCD)} = \frac{\frac{1}{2} \times AB \times DN}{\frac{1}{2} \times BC \times DN} = \frac{AB}{BC}$$

(ii) $$\frac{\text{ar}(\Delta ABD)}{\text{ar}(\Delta ACD)} = \frac{\frac{1}{2} \times AB \times DN}{\frac{1}{2} \times AC \times DN} = \frac{AB}{AC}$$

(iii) $$\frac{\text{ar}(\Delta BCD)}{\text{ar}(\Delta ACD)} = \frac{\frac{1}{2} \times BC \times DN}{\frac{1}{2} \times AC \times DN} = \frac{BC}{AC}$$

Example 25. In ΔABC, if D is a point on BC and divides it in the ratio 3 : 5, i.e. if $BD : DC = 3 : 5$, then find the ratio of ar (ΔADC) and ar (ΔABC).

Sol. Given, D is a point on BC such that

$$BD : DC = 3 : 5$$

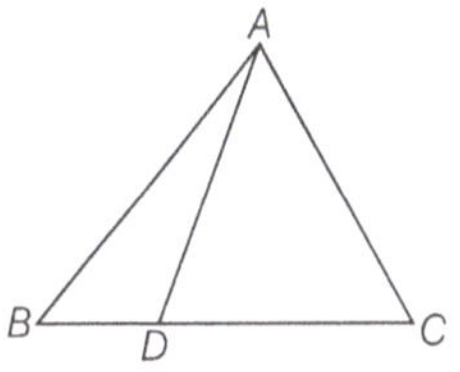

Since, ΔADC and ΔABC have same vertex A and bases (DC and BC) along the same line, therefore

$$\frac{\text{ar}(\Delta ADC)}{\text{ar}(\Delta ABC)} = \frac{DC}{BC} \quad \text{...(i)}$$

Now, consider $\frac{BD}{DC} = \frac{3}{5} \Rightarrow \frac{BD}{DC} + 1 = \frac{3}{5} + 1$

$$\Rightarrow \quad \frac{BD + DC}{DC} = \frac{3+5}{5}$$

$$\Rightarrow \quad \frac{BC}{DC} = \frac{8}{5} \Rightarrow \frac{DC}{BC} = \frac{5}{8} \quad \text{...(ii)}$$

From Eqs. (i) and (ii), we get

$$\frac{\text{ar}(\Delta ADC)}{\text{ar}(\Delta ABC)} = \frac{5}{8}$$

Example 26. The medians of a ΔABC intersect each other at point G. If one of its median is AD, then prove that

(i) $ar(\Delta ABD) = 3\,ar(\Delta BGD)$

(ii) $ar(\Delta ACD) = 3\,ar(\Delta CGD)$

(iii) $ar(\Delta BGC) = \frac{1}{3} ar(\Delta ABC)$

Sol. **Given** A ΔABC in which G is centroid of the triangle and AD is one of its median.

To prove (i) $ar(\Delta ABD) = 3 \times ar(\Delta BGD)$

(ii) $ar(\Delta ACD) = 3 \times ar(\Delta CGD)$

(iii) $ar(\Delta BGC) = \frac{1}{3} \times ar(\Delta ABC)$

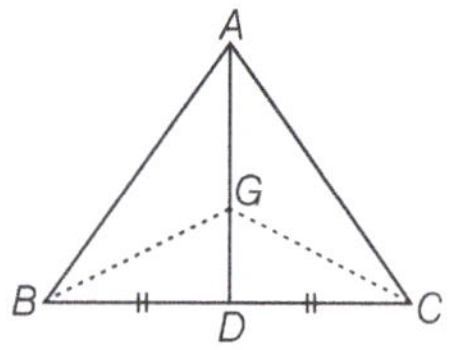

Proof We know that centroid divides each median in the ratio 2 : 1.

$\therefore \quad AG : GD = 2 : 1$

(i) Since, ΔABD and ΔBGD have the same vertex B and bases (AD and DG) along the same line,

$$\therefore \quad \frac{ar(\Delta ABD)}{ar(\Delta BGD)} = \frac{AD}{DG} \quad \text{...(i)}$$

We have, $\frac{AG}{GD} = \frac{2}{1} \Rightarrow \frac{AG}{GD} + 1 = \frac{2}{1} + 1$

$$\Rightarrow \frac{AG + GD}{GD} = \frac{3}{1} \Rightarrow \frac{AD}{GD} = 3 \quad \text{...(ii)}$$

From Eqs. (i) and (ii), we get

$$\frac{ar(\Delta ABD)}{ar(\Delta BGD)} = \frac{3}{1}$$

$$\Rightarrow \quad ar(\Delta ABD) = 3 \times ar(\Delta BGD) \quad \text{...(iii)}$$

(ii) Since, ΔACD and ΔCGD have the same vertex C and bases (AD and DG) along the same line,

$$\therefore \quad \frac{ar(\Delta ACD)}{ar(\Delta CGD)} = \frac{AD}{DG} = \frac{3}{1} \quad \text{[using Eq. (ii)]}$$

$$\Rightarrow \quad ar(\Delta ACD) = 3 \times ar(\Delta CGD) \quad \text{...(iv)}$$

(iii) On adding Eqs. (iii) and (iv), we get

$ar(\Delta ABD) + ar(\Delta ACD) = 3 \times ar(\Delta BGD) + 3 \times ar(\Delta CGD)$

$\Rightarrow ar(\Delta ABC) = 3\,[ar(\Delta BGD) + ar(\Delta CGD)] = 3\,[ar(\Delta BGC)]$

$\Rightarrow ar(\Delta BGC) = \frac{1}{3} ar(\Delta ABC)$ **Hence proved.**

Exercise 12.2

1. In the given figure, X and Y are points on the side LN of ΔLMN. Through X, a line is drawn parallel to LM to meet MN at Z. Prove that

   $ar(\Delta LZY) = ar(\text{quadrilateral } MZYX)$.

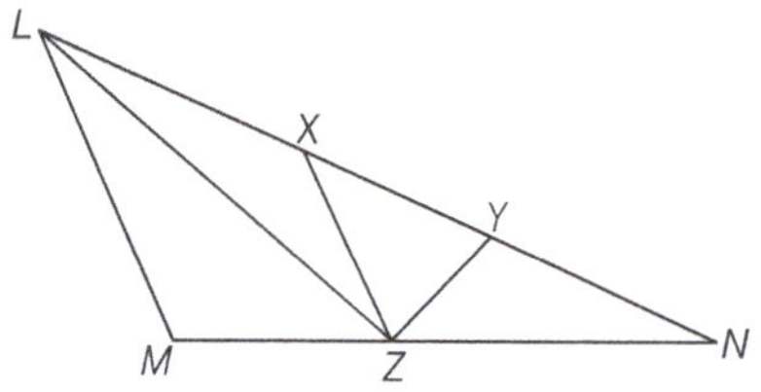

2. In the given figure, $AB \parallel CD$ and $ar(\Delta ABD) = 24$ sq units. If $AB = 8$ units, then find the height of ΔABC.

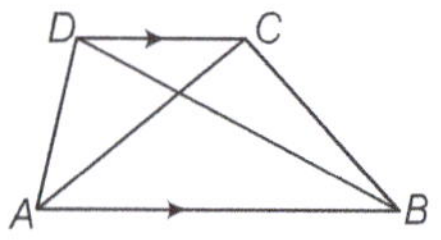

3. In the given figure, DE is parallel to BC. Show that $ar(\Delta ADC) = ar(\Delta AEB)$.

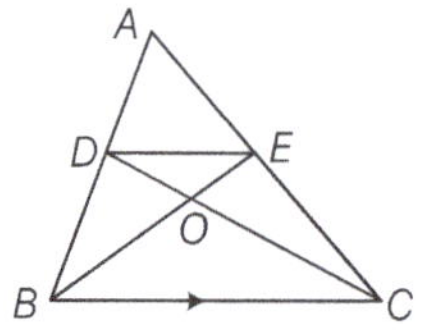

4. In the given figure, $ABCD$ is a parallelogram and BC is produced to a point Q such that $CQ = AD$. If AQ intersects DC at P, then show that $ar(\Delta BPC) = ar(\Delta DPQ)$.

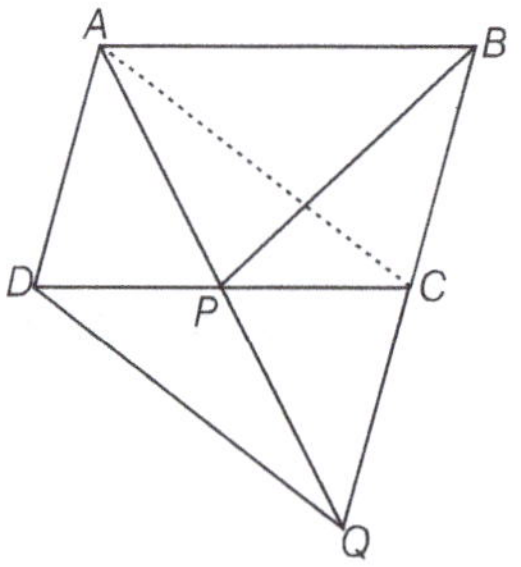

5. In the given figure, $PQRS$ and $PXYZ$ are two parallelograms of equal area. Prove that SX is parallel to YR.

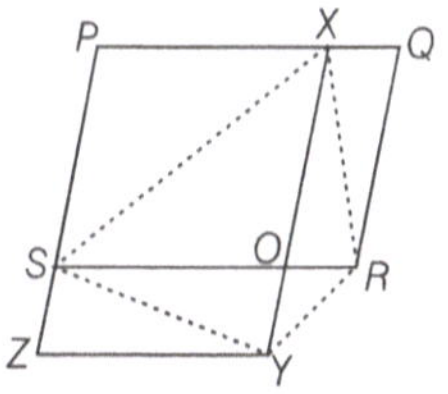

6. In the given figure, $AB \parallel DE$ and area of the parallelogram $ABFD$ is 24 cm². Find the areas of ΔAFB, ΔAGB and ΔAEB.

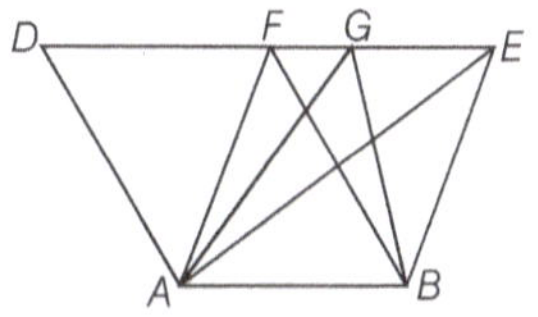

7. If $PQRS$ is a trapezium having PS and QR as parallel sides. A is any point on PQ and B is a point on SR such that $AB \parallel QR$. If area of ΔPBQ is $17\ \text{cm}^2$, then find the area of ΔASR.

8. The base BC of ΔABC is divided at D, so that

$BD = \frac{1}{2} DC$.

Prove that

$$\text{ar}(\Delta ABD) = \frac{1}{3} \times \text{ar}(\Delta ABC).$$

9. In the given figure, X and Y are the mid-points of AC and AB respectively, $QP \parallel BC$ and CYQ and BXP are straight lines. Prove that $\text{ar}(\Delta ABP) = \text{ar}(\Delta ACQ)$.

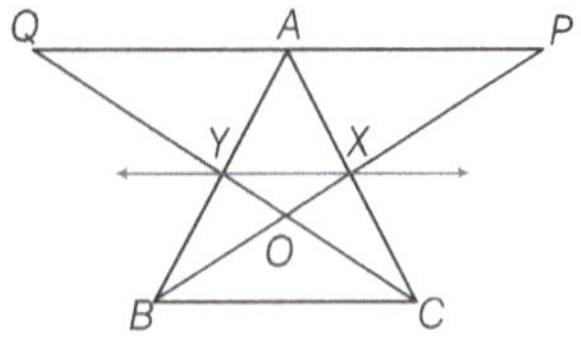

10. $ABCD$ is a trapezium with $AB \parallel DC$. A line parallel to AC intersects AB at X and BC at Y. Prove that $\text{ar}(\Delta ADX) = \text{ar}(\Delta ACY)$.

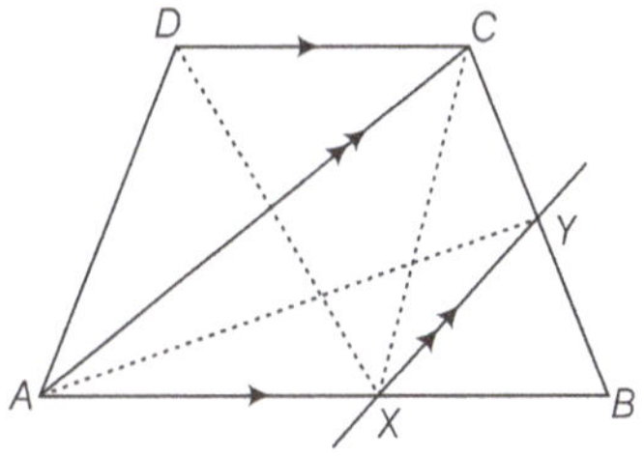

11. In the given figure, the side AB of a parallelogram $ABCD$ is produced to any point P. A line through A and parallel to CP meets CB produced at Q and then parallelogram $PBQR$ is completed. Show that area of parallelogram $ABCD$ = area of parallelogram $PBQR$.

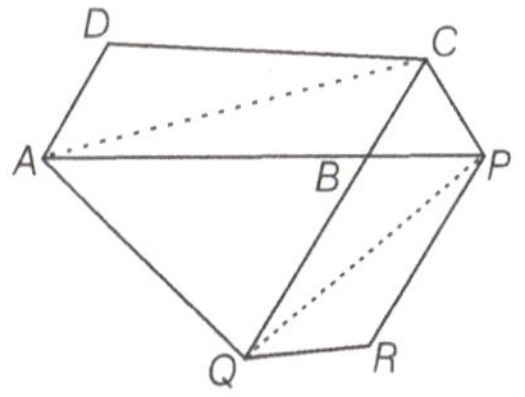

12. In a ΔABC, P is a point on the side BC such that $PC = 2BP$ and Q is a point on AP such that $QA = 5PQ$, determine

$$\text{ar}(\Delta AQC) : \text{ar}(\Delta ABC).$$

Chapter Practice

a. 1 Mark Questions

1. If two figures are equal in area, then they are
   (a) congruent (b) not congruent
   (c) both (a) or (b) (d) None of these

2. A diagonal of a parallelogram divides it into two
   (a) congruent triangles (b) isosceles triangles
   (c) equal trapezium (d) None of these

3. A median of a triangle divides it into two
   (a) right triangles
   (b) isosceles triangles
   (c) triangles of equal area
   (d) congruent triangles

4. If $BD = 2DC$ and ar $(\Delta ABC) = 60\text{ cm}^2$, then ar$(\Delta ADC)$

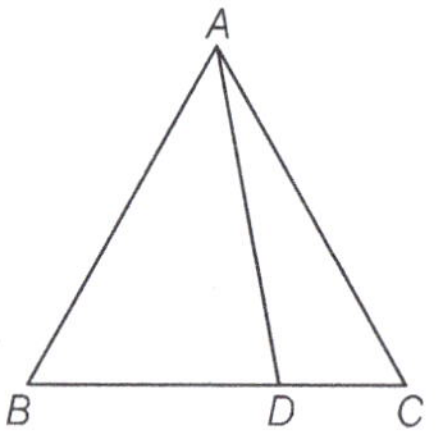

   (a) 180 cm^2 (b) 20 cm^2
   (c) 30 cm^2 (d) 10 cm^2

5. If $ABCD$ is a trapezium with $AB \parallel DC$, then ar(ΔDAO) is equal to

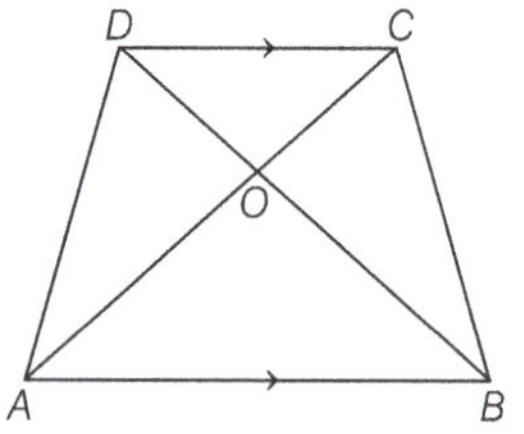

   (a) ar(ΔOAB) (b) ar(ΔOBC)
   (c) ar(ΔODC) (d) ar(ΔABC)

b. 3 Marks Questions

6. In the given figure below, $AB \parallel DC \parallel EF$, $AD \parallel BE$ and $DE \parallel AF$. Show that
   ar (parallelogram $ABCD$) = ar (parallelogram $DEFH$).

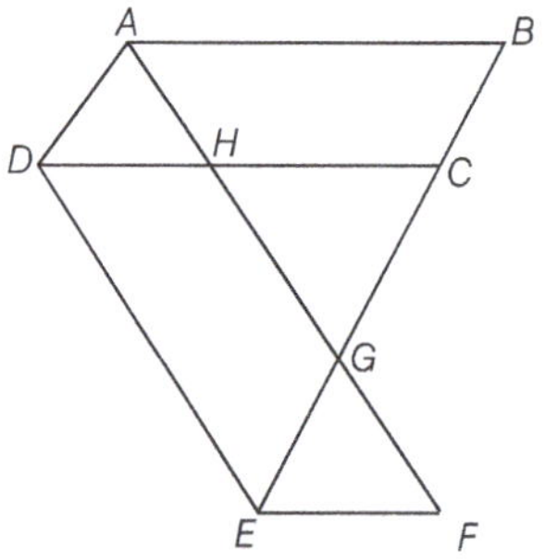

7. In a class, teacher gave two identical cardboard pieces which are in the shape of a parallelogram to two groups. First group was asked to find area of parallelogram using AB as base. Then, another group was asked to find height h of the parallelogram with AD as base. How will they find value of h?

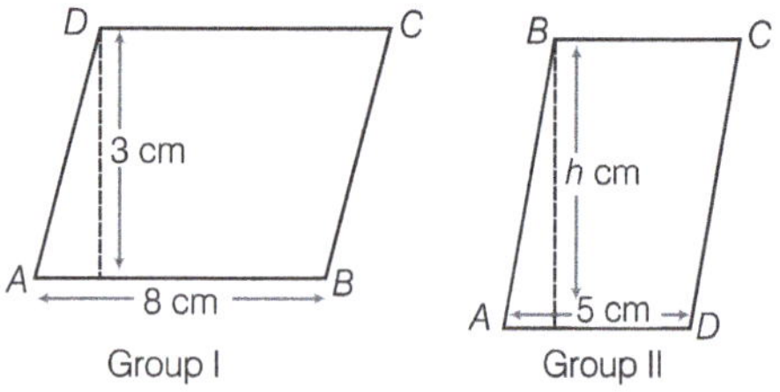

8. In the given figure, find the area of rhombus $ABCD$, if $AO = 4$ cm and $OD = 5$ cm.

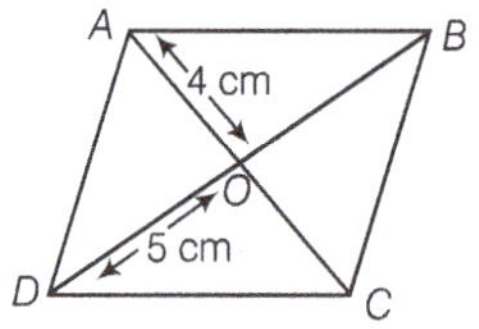

9. In a quadrilateral $ABCD$, it is being given that M is the mid-point of AC.

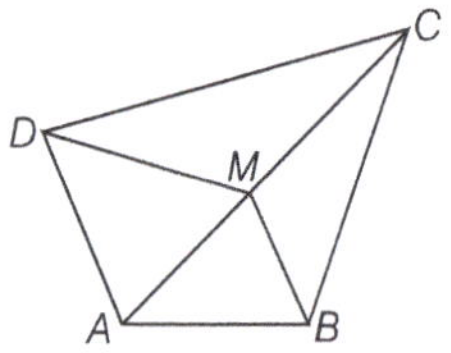

   Prove that ar (quadrilateral $ABMD$) = ar (quadrilateral $DMBC$).

10. In the given figure, ABC and ABD are two triangles on the same base AB. If line segment CD is bisected by AB at O, then show that ar (ΔABC) = ar (ΔABD).

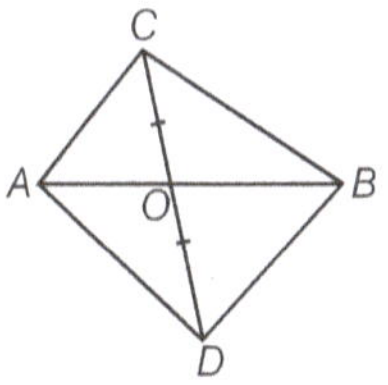

11. Suppose $ABCD$ is a parallelogram and O is the point of intersection of its diagonals (see the figure). If ar $(\Delta AOD) = 4\text{ cm}^2$, then find ar (ΔAOB).

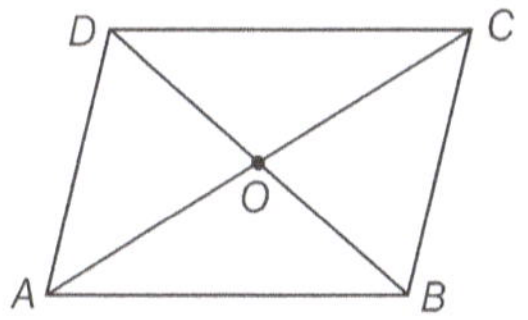

12. In ΔDEF, M and N are the mid-points of sides EF and DE, respectively. If ar $(\Delta ENM) = 4\text{ cm}^2$, then find ar (ΔDEF).

C. 4/5 Marks Questions

13. If $PQRS$ is a rectangle inscribed in a quadrant of a circle of radius 13 cm. A is any point on PQ (see the figure). If PS = 5 cm, then show that ar $(\Delta PAS) \leq 30\text{ cm}^2$.

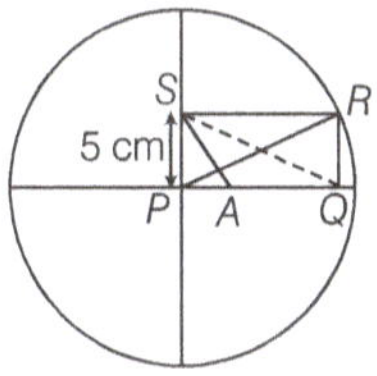

14. In the given figure, D is mid-point of side AB of ΔABC and $BDEC$ is a parallelogram. Prove that ar (ΔABC) = ar (parallelogram $BDEC$).

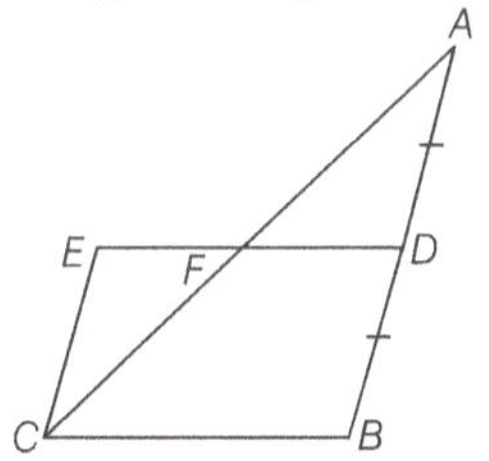

15. In the given figure, $AP \parallel BQ \parallel CR$. Prove that ar (ΔAQC) = ar (ΔPBR).

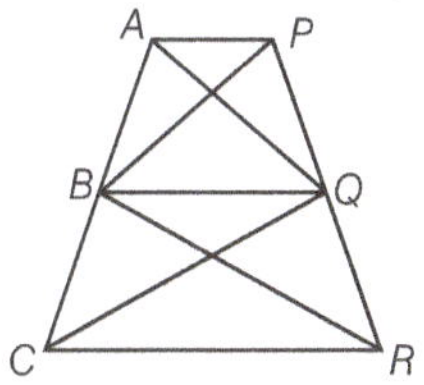

16. If ΔPQR is an equilateral triangle with $PM \perp QR$. Show that ar (ΔPQM) = ar (ΔPRM).

17. In the adjoining figure, D and E are two points on BC such that $BD = DE = EC$. Show that ar (ΔABD) = ar (ΔADE) = ar (ΔAEC).

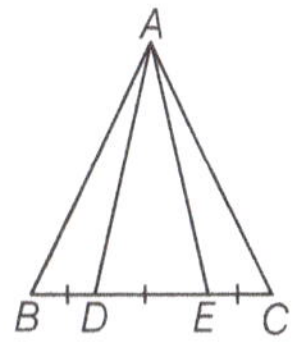

18. In the given figure, $BD \parallel CA$, E is mid-point of CA and $BD = \frac{1}{2} CA$. Prove that

ar $(\Delta ABC) = 2$ ar (ΔDBC).

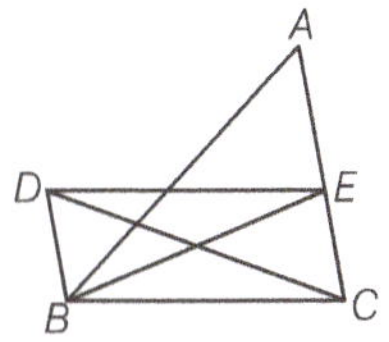

19. In the given figure $ABCD$ and $AEFG$ are two parallelograms. Prove that ar (parallelogram $ABCD$) = ar (parallelogram $AEFG$)

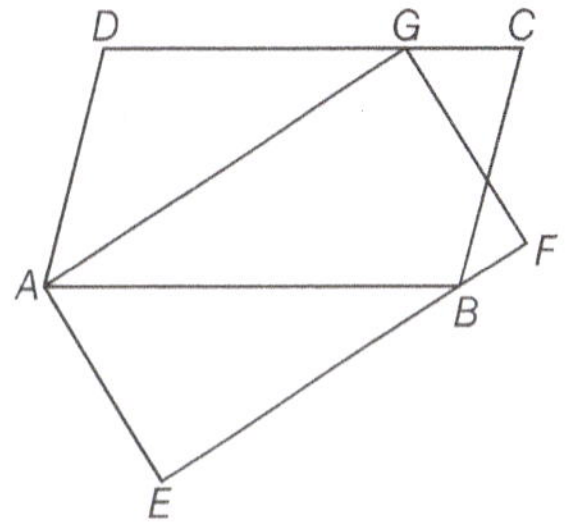

20. In the given figure, $ABCD$ is a parallelogram. Points P and Q on BC trisect BC in three equal parts. Prove that ar (ΔAPQ) = ar (ΔDPQ) $= \frac{1}{6}$ ar (parallelogram $ABCD$).

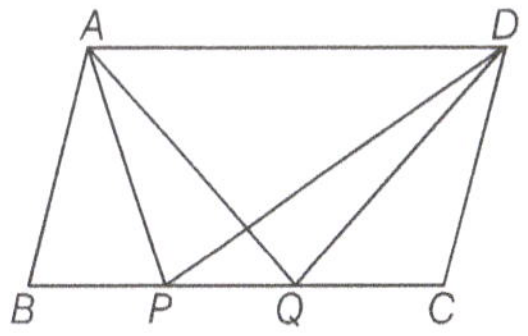

21. The diagonals of a parallelogram $ABCD$ intersect at O. A straight line through O meets AB at P and the opposite side CD at Q. Prove that ar (quadrilateral $APQD$)

$$= \frac{1}{2} \text{ ar (parallelogram } ABCD).$$

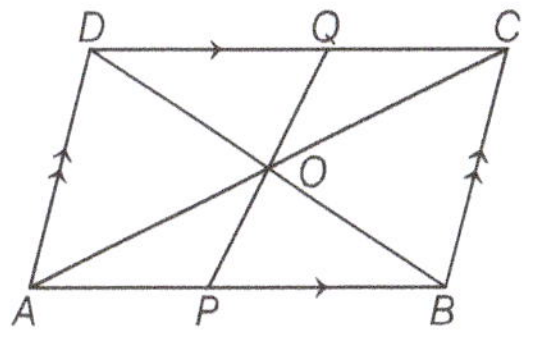

22. In the given figure, $ABCD$, $DCFE$ and $ABFE$ are parallelograms. Show that ar (ΔADE) = ar (ΔBCF).

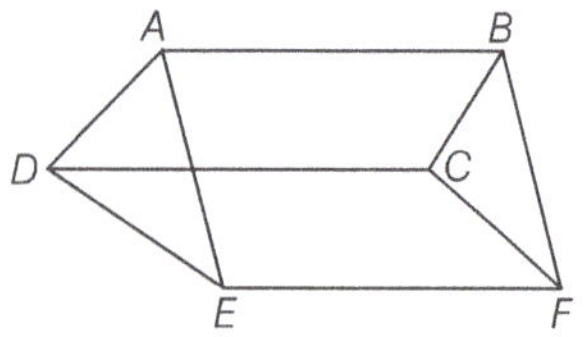

23. In the given figure, $BC \parallel XY$, $BX \parallel CA$ and $AB \parallel YC$. Prove that ar (ΔABX) = ar (ΔAYC).

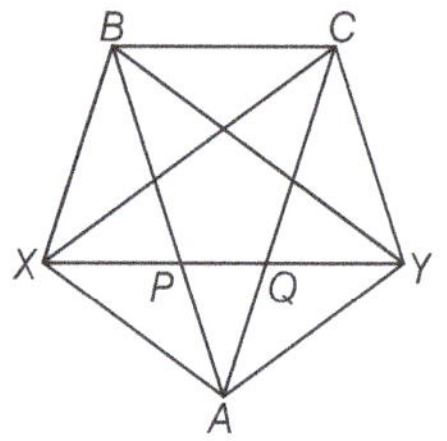

24. In the given figure, side AB of the parallelogram $ABCD$ is extended to E. A straight line through A is drawn parallel to CE to meet CB extended at F and parallelogram $BFGE$ is completed. Show that

ar (parallelogram $BFGE$)

= ar (parallelogram $ABCD$)

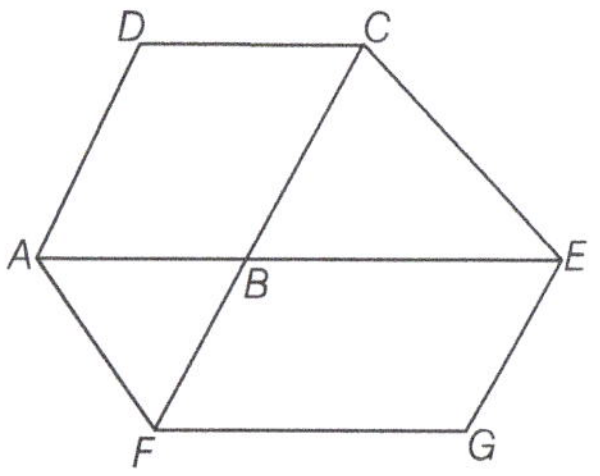

25. In the given figure, $ABCD$ is a rectangle with side $AB = 5$ cm and $AD = 8$ cm. Determine

(a) ar (parallelogram $DEFC$)

(b) ar (ΔEFG)

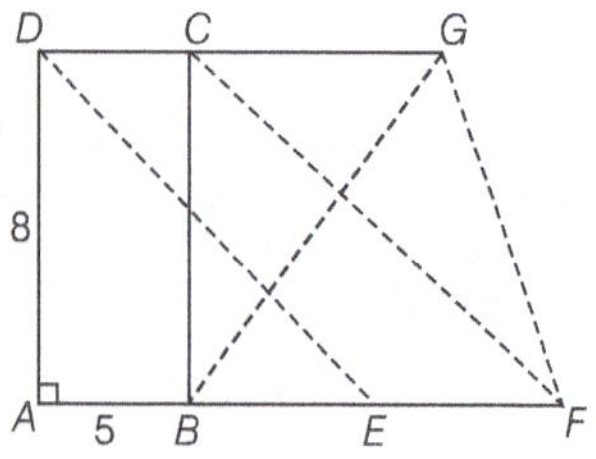

d. 6 Marks Questions

26. In the given figure, ABC is a right angled triangle, right angled at A, $BCED$, $ACFG$ and $ABMN$ are squares on the sides BC, CA and AB respectively. Line segment $AX \perp DE$ meets BC at Y.

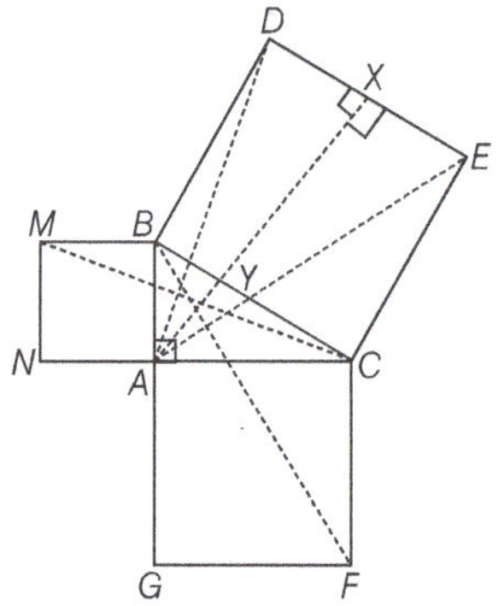

Show that

(i) $\Delta MBC \cong \Delta ABD$

(ii) ar $(BYXD)$ = 2 ar (ΔMBC)

(iii) ar $(BYXD)$ = ar $(ABMN)$

(iv) $\Delta FCB \cong \Delta ACE$

(v) ar $(CYXE) \cong$ 2 ar (ΔFCB)

(vi) ar $(CYXE)$ = ar $(ACFG)$

(vii) ar $(BCED)$ = ar $(ABMN)$ + ar $(ACFG)$

27. Show that the diagonals of a parallelogram divide it into four triangles of equal areas.

28. $ABCD$ is a parallelogram and X is the mid-point of AB. If ar $(\Delta ADC) = 24\text{ cm}^2$, then find ar $(AXCD)$.

29. If $ABCD$ is a parallelogram. X and Y are the mid-points of BC and CD, respectively. Prove that ar $(\Delta AXY) = \frac{3}{8}$ ar (parallelogram $ABCD$).

30. In the adjoining figure, D is the mid-point of side AB of the ΔABC. E is the mid-point of CD and F is the mid-point of AE. Prove that

8ar (ΔAFD) = ar (ΔABC).

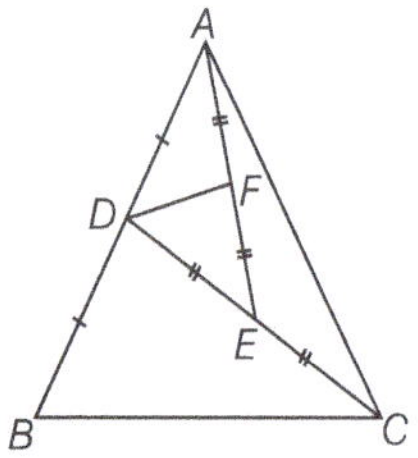

31. ABC is a triangle whose area is 56 cm^2. E and F are the mid-points of the sides AB and AC, respectively. Prove that $EBCF$ is a trapezium. Also, find its area.

32. In the given figure, $ABCD$ is a parallelogram, P is a point on DC such that ar $(\Delta APD) = 25\text{ cm}^2$ and ar $(\Delta BPC) = 15\text{ cm}^2$. Calculate

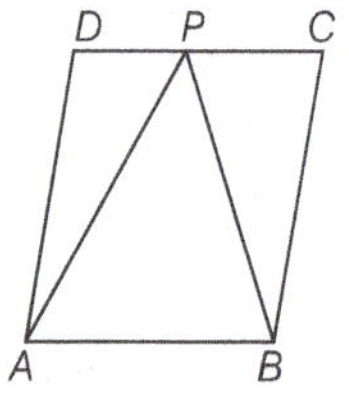

(i) ar (parallelogram $ABCD$).

(ii) $DP : PC$.

Hints and Answers

Exercise 12.1

1. **Hint** Use Theorem 1.
2. **Hint** Area of parallelogram = Base × Height
   Ans. 35 cm^2
3. **Hint** Do same as Example 2. **Ans.** 30 cm
4. **Hint** Area of parallelogram = Base × Height
   $\Rightarrow \quad x^2 = (x-3)(x+4)$ **Ans.** 12
5. **Hint** Use Theorem 2. **Ans.** 1 : 2
6. (i) **Hint** ar (parallelogram $ABEF$) = ar (parallelogram $ABCD$)
   Ans. 140 cm^2
   (ii) **Hint** ar (ΔAEF) $= \frac{1}{2}$ ar (parallelogram $ABCD$)
   Ans. 70 cm^2
7. **Hint** $\because$ ar (ΔABC) = ar (ΔDBC)
   $\Rightarrow \quad \frac{1}{2} BC \times AM = \frac{1}{2} BC \times DN$

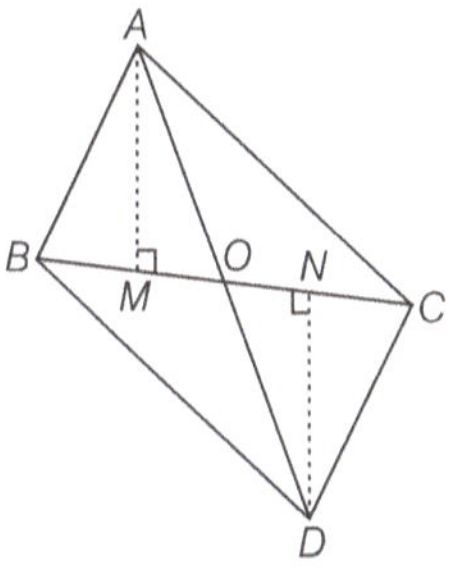

In ΔAMO and ΔDNO, $\angle AOM = \angle DON$
$\angle AMO = \angle DNO$ and $AM = DN$
$\therefore \Delta AMO \cong \Delta DNO$ [by AAS congruence rule]

8. **Hint** Do same as Example 7. **Ans.** 90 cm^2
9. **Hint** ar (ΔABD) $= \frac{1}{2} \times BD \times AM$ ...(i)

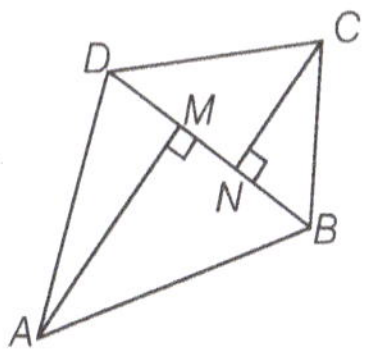

and ar (ΔBCD) $= \frac{1}{2} \times BD \times CN$ ...(ii)

On adding Eqs. (i) and (ii), we get the result.

10. **Hint** Clearly, ar (ΔABD) $= \frac{1}{2}$ ar (ΔABC)
    and ar (ΔABE) $= \frac{1}{2}$ ar (ΔABD)
    $\Rightarrow$ ar (ΔABE) $= \frac{1}{2} \times \frac{1}{2}$ ar (ΔABC) $= \frac{1}{4}$ ar (ΔABC)
11. **Hint** ar (rhombus) $= \frac{1}{2} \times$ product of diagonals
    Ans. 192 cm^2
12. **Hint** Do same as Example 8. **Ans.** 24 cm^2
13. **Hint** In ΔCLQ and ΔBLP,
    $CL = BL$ [$\because L$ is the mid-point of BC]
    $\angle LCQ = \angle LBP$ [alternate interior angles]
    and $\angle CQL = \angle LPB$ [alternate interior angles]
    $\therefore \Delta CLQ \cong \Delta BLP$ [by AAS congruence rule]
    $\Rightarrow$ ar (ΔCLQ) = ar (ΔBLP) ...(i)
    [since, congruent triangles have equal area]
    Now, ar ($ABCD$) = ar ($APQD$) − ar (ΔCQL) + ar (ΔBLP)
    $\Rightarrow$ ar ($ABCD$) = ar ($APQD$) [using Eq. (i)]
14. **Hint** Since, E and F are the mid-points of the sides AB and AC, respectively
    Also, $EF \parallel BC$ and $EF = \frac{1}{2} BC$
    As $EF \parallel BC$, therefore $EBCF$ is a trapezium.

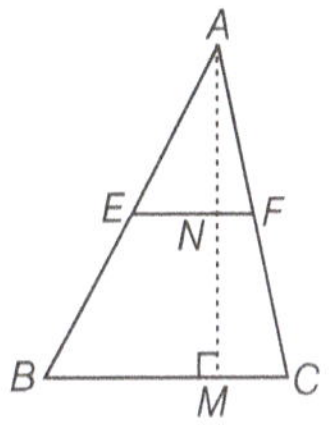

Now, ar (ΔAEF) $= \frac{1}{2} EF \times AN$
$= \frac{1}{2}\left(\frac{1}{2} BC \times \frac{1}{2} AM\right)$
$= \frac{1}{4}\left(\frac{1}{2} BC \times AM\right) = \frac{1}{4}$ ar (ΔABC)
$\therefore$ ar (trapezium $EBCF$) = ar (ΔABC) − ar (ΔAEF)
Ans. 37.5 cm^2

15. **Hint**

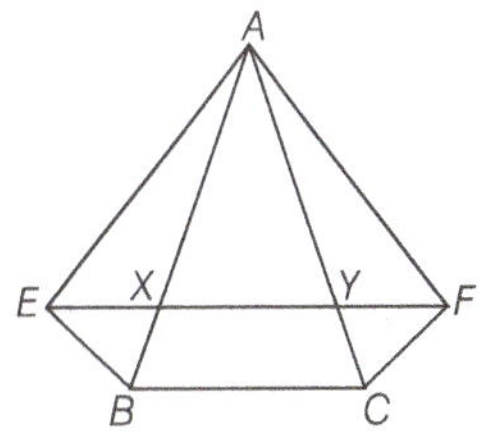

Here, ar (ΔABE) $= \frac{1}{2}$ ar (parallelogram $EBCY$)
and ar (ΔACF) $= \frac{1}{2}$ ar (parallelogram $XBCF$)
$\therefore$ ar (parallelogram $EBCY$) = ar (parallelogram $XBCF$).

Exercise 12.2

1. **Hint** Since, ΔLZX and ΔMZX are on the same base ZX and between same parallels XZ and LM,
ar (ΔLZX) = ar (ΔMZX).
Add ar (ΔXZY) on both sides.

2. **Hint** ar (ΔABC) = ar $(\Delta ABD) = 24$
[$\because$ triangles with same base and between same parallel lines]
$\Rightarrow \frac{1}{2} \times 8 \times$ Height $= 24$ **Ans.** 6 units

3. **Hint** Do same as Example 16.

4. **Hint** Here, ar (ΔBPC) = ar (ΔAPC)
In quadrilateral $ADQC$, $AD \parallel CQ$
and $AD = CQ$ [given]
In ΔAPC and ΔQPD,
$PC = DP$, $AP = PQ$ and $\angle APC = \angle QPD$
$\Delta APC \cong \Delta QPD$ [by SAS congruence rule]
$\therefore$ ar (ΔAPC) = ar (ΔDPQ)

5. **Hint** Here, ar (parallelogram $XORQ$)
= ar (parallelogram $SZYO$)
$\Rightarrow$ ar (ΔXOR) = ar (ΔSYO)
ar (ΔXYR) = ar (ΔSYR)
Also, ΔXYR and ΔSYR have the same base YR.
Therefore, these lie between the same parallel lines.
$\Rightarrow SX$ is parallel to YR.

6. **Hint** If a triangle and parallelogram are on the same base and between the same parallels, then the area of the triangle is equal to half the area of the parallelogram.
Also, two triangles on the same base and between the same parallels are equal in area.
Ans. Each 12 cm^2

7. **Hint** ar (ΔABQ) = ar (ΔABR) ...(i)
and ar (ΔPBA) = ar (ΔSAB) ...(ii)

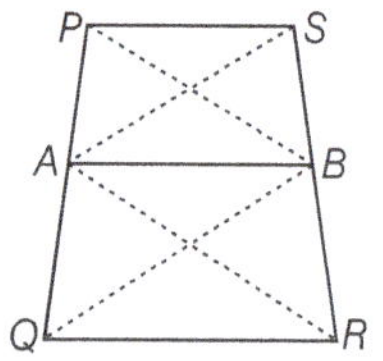

On adding Eqs. (i) and (ii), we get
ar (ΔABQ) + ar (ΔPBA)
= ar (ΔABR) + ar (ΔSAB)
$\therefore$ ar (ΔPBQ) = ar (ΔSAR)
or ar (ΔSAR) = ar (ΔPBQ) = 17 cm^2

8. **Hint** Do same as Example 24.

9. **Hint** In ΔAXP and ΔCXB,
$AX = CX$ [given]
$\angle AXP = \angle CXB$ [vertically opposite angles]
and $\angle PAX = \angle XCB$ [alternate interior angles]
$\therefore \Delta AXP \cong \Delta CXB$ [by ASA congruence rule]
$\Rightarrow AP = BC$ ...(i)
Similarly, $AQ = BC$ ...(ii)
From Eqs. (i) and (ii), we get
$AP = AQ$
Now, $AP \parallel BC$ and $AP = AQ$ [equal bases]
$\therefore$ ar (ΔABP) = ar (ΔACQ)

10. **Hint** Here, ar (ΔADX) = ar (ΔACX)
and ar (ΔACY) = ar (ΔACX)

11. **Hint** Here, ar (parallelogram $ABCD$)
= 2 ar (ΔABC) ...(i)
Also, PQ is a diagonal of parallelogram $PBQR$.
Here, area of parallelogram $PBQR$
= 2 ar (ΔPBQ) ...(ii)
Also, ar (ΔCAQ) = ar (ΔPAQ)
$\Rightarrow$ ar (ΔCAQ) − ar (ΔBAQ) = ar (ΔPAQ) − ar (ΔBAQ)
$\Rightarrow$ ar (ΔABC) = ar (ΔPBQ)

12. **Hint** $PC = \frac{2}{3} BC$ [$\because PC = 2\,BP$ (given)]
$\Rightarrow$ ar $(\Delta APC) = \frac{2}{3}$ ar (ΔABC) ...(i)

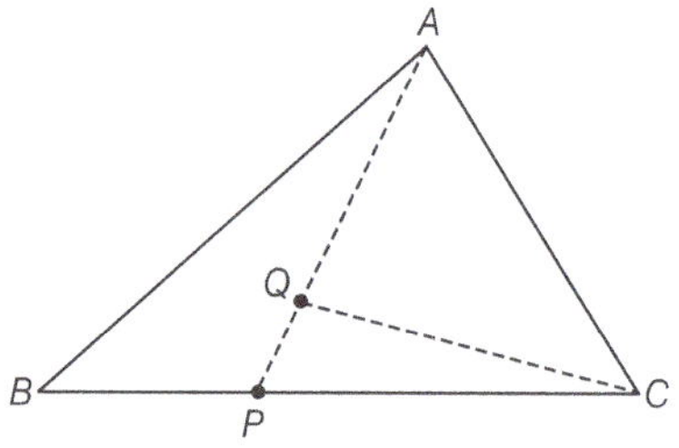

$AQ = \frac{5}{6} AP$ [$\because QA = 5PQ$(given)]
$\Rightarrow$ ar $(\Delta AQC) = \frac{5}{6}$ ar (ΔAPC)
$= \frac{5}{6} \cdot \frac{2}{3}$ ar (ΔABC) [from Eq. (i)]
$= \frac{5}{9}$ ar (ΔABC)
Ans. ar (ΔAQC) : ar (ΔABC) = 5 : 9

Chapter Exercise

1. (c) 2. (a)
3. (c) 4. (b)
5. (b)
6. **Hint** ar (parallelogram $DEFH$)
= ar (parallelogram $DEGA$)
[parallelograms on the same base and between same parallels]
Similarly, ar (parallelogram $ABCD$)
= ar (parallelogram $DEGA$)
7. **Hint For group I**
Base of cardboard = 8 cm
and height of cardboard = 3 cm
$\therefore$ Area of cardboard $= 8 \times 3 = 24$ cm^2
[$\because$ area of a parallelogram = base × height]

For group II

Base of cardboard = 5 cm

and height of cardboard = h cm

Then, $5 \times h = 24$ [$\because$ both boards are identical]

Ans. 4.8 cm

8. Hint Diagonals of rhombus bisect each other.

$\therefore BD = 2\,OD = 2 \times 5 = 10$ cm and $AC = 2OA = 8$ cm

Ans. 40 cm^2

9. Hint We know that median of a triangle divides it into two triangles of equal areas.

$\therefore$ ar (ΔABM) = ar (ΔBMC) ...(i)

and ar (ΔAMD) = ar (ΔDMC) ...(ii)

On adding Eqs. (i) and (ii), we get the result.

10. Hint Do same as Q. 8.

11. Hint ar (ΔAOD) = ar (ΔAOB) [$\because$ median divides the triangle into two triangles of equal area]

Ans. 4 cm^2

12. Hint Join D and M.

Then, ar (ΔDEF) = 2 ar (ΔDEM) = 2 × 2 ar (ΔENM)

Ans. 16 cm^2

13. Hint In ΔPQR, $PQ^2 = PR^2 - RQ^2 = (13)^2 - (5)^2$

[given, $PS = 5$ cm, $PR = 13$ cm]

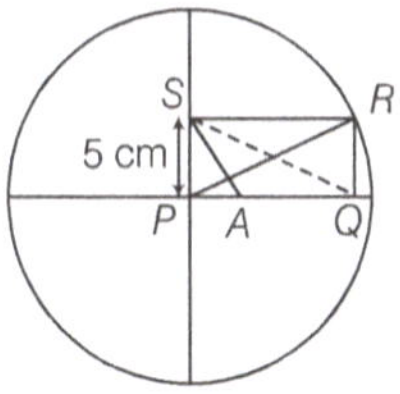

$\therefore \quad PQ = \sqrt{169 - 25} = \sqrt{144} = 12$ cm

Now, ar (rectangle $PQRS$) = $12 \times 5 = 60$ cm^2

$\Rightarrow$ ar (ΔPSQ) = $\frac{1}{2} \times 60 = 30$ cm^2

[$\because$ diagonal of a rectangle bisect it into two triangles of equal area]

Now, A is any point on PQ. So, the area of ΔAPS depends on the position of A.

If A is at point Q, then area will be 30 cm^2, otherwise.

ar (ΔPAS) $\le$ 30 cm^2

14. Hint $\therefore \Delta AFD \cong \Delta CFE$ [by AAS congruence rule]

$\Rightarrow$ ar (ΔAFD) = ar (ΔCFE)

Now, adding area of quadrilateral $CBDF$ on both sides, we get the result.

15. Hint We know that triangles on the same base and between the same parallels are equal in area.

$\therefore$ ar (ΔABQ) = ar (ΔPBQ) ...(i)

and ar (ΔBCQ) = ar (ΔBQR) ...(ii)

On adding Eqs. (i) and (ii), we get the result.

16. Hint Here, $\Delta PMQ \cong \Delta PMR$ [by AAS congruence rule]

$\Rightarrow$ $MQ = MR$ [by CPCT] ...(i)

Now, as ΔPQM and ΔPRM have the same vertex P and bases along the same line QR, therefore

$$\frac{\text{ar}(\Delta PQM)}{\text{ar}(\Delta PRM)} = \frac{QM}{MR} = 1 \quad \text{[using Eq. (i)]}$$

$\Rightarrow$ ar (ΔPQM) = ar (ΔPRM) **Hence proved.**

17. Hint Since, ΔABD and ΔADE have the same vertex A and bases along the same line BE, therefore

$$\frac{\text{ar}(\Delta ABD)}{\text{ar}(\Delta ADE)} = \frac{BD}{DE} = 1$$

$\Rightarrow$ ar (ΔABD) = ar (ΔADE) ...(i)

Similarly, ar (ΔADE) = ar (ΔAEC) ...(ii)

Now, from Eqs. (i) and (ii), we get the result.

18. Hint ar (ΔABC) = 2 ar (ΔBEC) = 2 ar (ΔBDC)

[$\because BD = CE$ and $BD \parallel CE$, therefore $BCED$ is parallelogram]

19. Hint Join BG

ar (ΔABG) = $\frac{1}{2}$ ar (parallelogram $ABCD$) ...(i)

and ar (ΔABG) = $\frac{1}{2}$ ar (parallelogram $AEFG$) ...(ii)

From Eqs. (i) and (ii), we get the result.

20. Hint

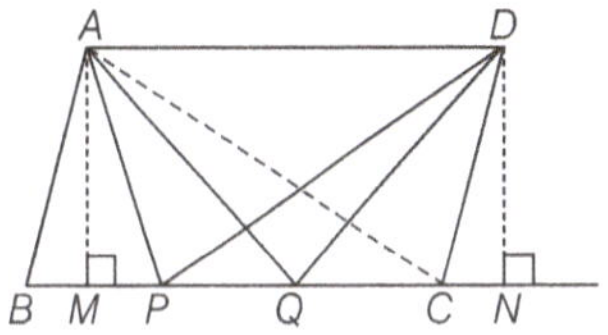

ar (ΔABP) = $\frac{1}{3} \times$ ar (ΔABC) ...(i)

ar (ΔABC) = $\frac{1}{2} \times$ ar (Parallelogram $ABCD$) ...(ii)

ar (ΔABP) = $\frac{1}{6} \times$ ar (Parallelogram $ABCD$) ...(iii)

ar (ΔABP) = ar (ΔAPQ) = ar (ΔDPQ)

ar (ΔAPQ) = ar (ΔDPQ) = $\frac{1}{6} \times$ ar (Parallelogram $ABCD$)

21. Hint ar (ΔOAP) = ar (ΔOCQ)

or adding ar (quadrilateral $AOQD$) both sides, we get

ar (quadrilateral $APQD$) = ar (ΔACD)

22. Hint $\Delta ADE \cong \Delta BCF$ (by SSS congruency rule)

23. Hint Triangles on the same base and between the same parallels are equal in area.

24. Hint Construction : Join AC and EF.

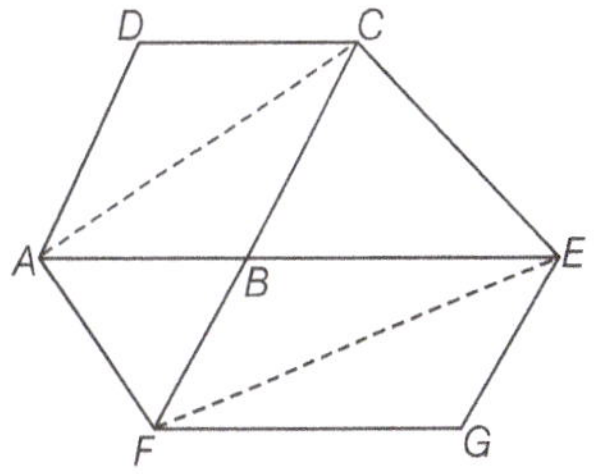

ar (ΔAFC) = ar (ΔAFE) ...(i)

[triangles on same base and between same parallels]

$\therefore \quad ar(\Delta ABC) = ar(\Delta BEF)$

[$\because$ subtract ar (ΔABF) from both sides of Eq. (i)]

Now, multiply by 2 on both sides and use theorem "a diagonal of a parallelogram divide it into two triangles of equal areas".

25. Hint A parallelogram, a rectangle and a triangle between the same parallels have equal height.

Also, opposite sides of a parallelogram are equal.

Ans. (a) 40 cm^2 (b) 20 cm^2

26. Hint

(i)

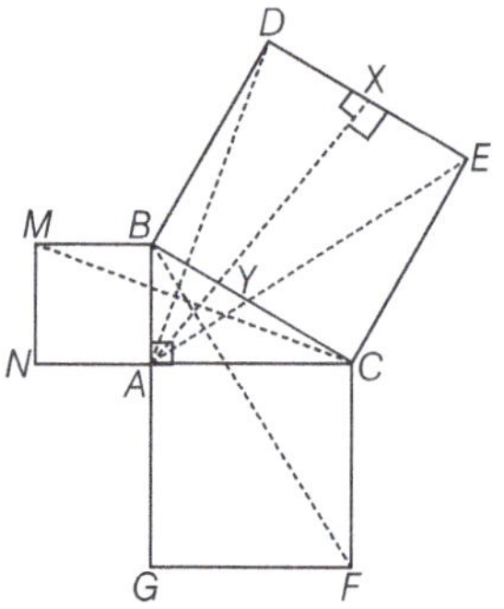

$$\angle MBA + \angle ABC = \angle ABC + \angle CBD$$

$$\Rightarrow \quad \Delta MBC \cong \Delta ABD$$

[by SAS congruency rule (axiom)]

(ii) $ar(\Delta ABD) = \frac{1}{2} ar(BYXD) \Rightarrow ar(BYXD) = 2\, ar(\Delta MBC)$

(iii) $ar(\Delta MBC) = \frac{1}{2} ar(ABMN)$

$\Rightarrow ar(BYXD) = ar(ABMN)$ [using part (ii)]

(iv) $\angle FCA + \angle ACB = \angle ACB + \angle BCE$ [adding $\angle ACB$]

$\Rightarrow \quad \Delta FCB \cong \Delta ACE$

[by SAS congruency rule (axiom)]

(v) $ar(\Delta ACE) = \frac{1}{2} ar(CYXE)$

$\Rightarrow 2\, ar(\Delta FCB) = ar(CYXE)$ [using part (iv)]

(vi) $ar(\Delta FCB) = \frac{1}{2} ar(ACFG)$

$2 ar(\Delta FCB) = ar(ACFG)$

Using part (v), we can get the result.

(vii) $\therefore$ By using Pythagoras Theorem,

$$BC^2 = AB^2 + AC^2$$

$$\Rightarrow \quad BC \times BD = AB \times MB + AC \times CF$$

$$\Rightarrow \quad ar(BCED) = ar(ABMN) + ar(ACFG)$$

27. Hint A median of a triangle divides it into two triangles of equal areas.

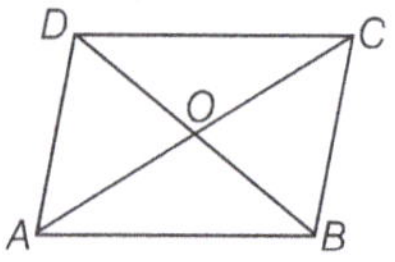

$\therefore \quad ar(\Delta OAB) = ar(\Delta OBC)$ ...(i)

$ar(\Delta OAB) = ar(\Delta OAD)$ ...(ii)

and $ar(\Delta AOD) = ar(\Delta OCD)$ ...(iii)

From Eqs. (i), (ii) and (iii), we get

$ar(\Delta OAB) = ar(\Delta OBC) = ar(\Delta OCD) = ar(\Delta OAD)$

28. Hint We know that diagonal of a parallelogram divides it into two triangles of equal areas.

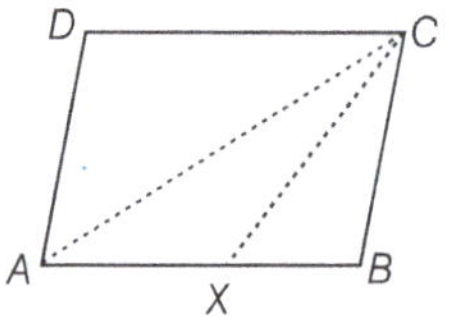

$\therefore \quad ar(\Delta ABC) = ar(\Delta ADC) = 24\ cm^2$

We know that median divides the triangle into two triangles of equal areas.

$\therefore \quad ar(\Delta ACX) = \frac{1}{2} ar(\Delta ABC) = \frac{1}{2} \times 24 = 12\ cm^2$

Ans. 36 cm^2

29. Hint Clearly, $ar(\Delta CYX) = \frac{1}{4} ar(\Delta DBC)$

and $ar(\Delta DBC) = \frac{1}{2}$ ar (parallelogram $ABCD$)

$\therefore \quad ar(\Delta CYX) = \frac{1}{8}$ ar (parallelogram $ABCD$)

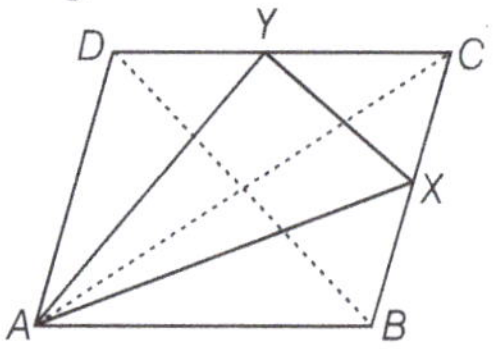

Also, $ar(\Delta AYD) = \frac{1}{2} ar(\Delta ADC)$

$= \frac{1}{2} \times \frac{1}{2}$ (parallelogram $ABCD$)

$= \frac{1}{4}$ ar (parallelogram $ABCD$)

Similarly, $ar(\Delta ABX) = \frac{1}{4}$ ar (parallelogram $ABCD$)

Now, $ar(\Delta AYX)$ = ar (parallelogram $ABCD$) $- [ar(\Delta ABX) + ar(\Delta AYD) + ar(\Delta CYX)]$

30. Hint Since, DF is median of a ΔADE.

Therefore, $ar(\Delta AFD) = \frac{1}{2} ar(\Delta ADE)$

$= \frac{1}{2} \times \frac{1}{2} ar(\Delta ADC) = \frac{1}{4} \times \frac{1}{2} ar(\Delta ABC)$

$\Rightarrow \quad 8\, ar(\Delta AFD) = ar(\Delta ABC)$

31. Hint Do same as Q. 14 of Exercise 12.1. **Ans.** 42 cm^2

32. (i) **Hint** $ar(\Delta APD) + ar(\Delta BPC) = ar(\Delta APB)$

$\Rightarrow ar(\Delta APB) = 25 + 15 = 40\ cm^2$

Also, $ar(\Delta APB) = \frac{1}{2}$ ar (parallelogram $ABCD$)

$\Rightarrow$ ar (parallelogram $ABCD$) $= 2\, ar(\Delta APB)$

Ans. 80 cm^2

(ii) **Hint** Clearly, $\frac{ar(\Delta APD)}{ar(\Delta BPC)} = \frac{DP}{PC}$

[$\because$ triangles lie between the same parallels and have bases along the line CD]

$\Rightarrow \quad \frac{25}{15} = \frac{DP}{PC}$ **Ans.** $DP : PC = 5 : 3$

Olympiad Section

Brain Teasing Questions of Olympiad Pattern

1 In the given figure, areas of parallelograms $ABCD$ and $FECG$ are equal. If ar $(\Delta AQE) = 12\text{ cm}^2$, then ar (parallelogram $FGBQ$ is equal to

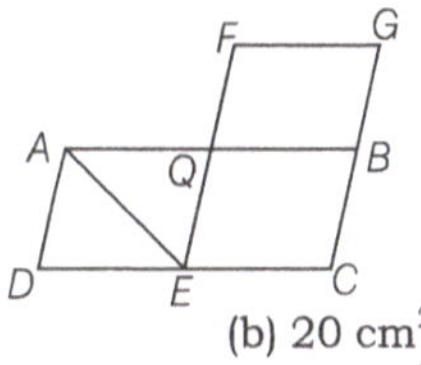

(a) 12 cm^2 (b) 20 cm^2
(c) 24 cm^2 (d) 36 cm^2

2 In the given figure, the angles $\angle BAD$ and $\angle ADC$ are right angles and $AX \parallel BC$. If $AB = BC = 5$ cm and $DC = 8$ cm, then the area of quadrilateral $ABCX$ is

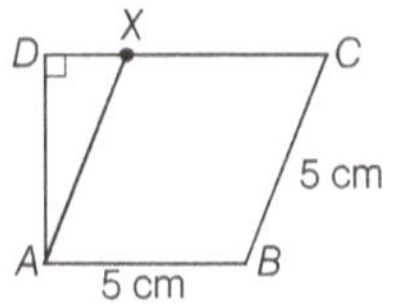

(a) 20 cm^2 (b) 64 cm^2
(c) 24 cm^2 (d) 42 cm^2

3 In the adjoining figure, P is a point in the interior of parallelogram $ABCD$. If the area of parallelogram $ABCD$ is 60 cm^2, then $[\text{ar}(\Delta ADP) + \text{ar}(\Delta BPC)]$ is equal to

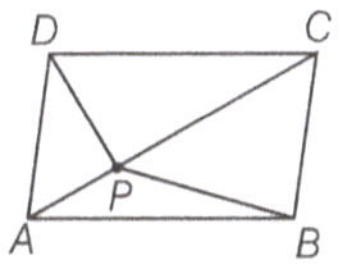

(a) 15 cm^2 (b) 30 cm^2
(c) 45 cm^2 (d) 20 cm^2

4 $ABCD$ is a trapezium with parallel sides $AB = a$ cm and $DC = b$ cm. E and F are the mid-points of the non-parallel sides. The ratio of ar $(ABFE)$ and ar $(EFCD)$ is

(a) $a : b$ (b) $(3a + b) : (a + 3b)$
(c) $(a + 3b) : (3a + b)$ (d) $(2a + b) : (3a + b)$

5 In the given figure,
ar (parallelogram $AFPE$) = ar (parallelogram $FBGM$) = ar (parallelogram $NGCH$) = ar (parallelogram $EOHD$)
The area of square $ABCD$ is 20 cm^2 more than that of square $EFGH$.
The area of square $EFGH$ is 6 times that of square $MNOP$, then the area of $MNOP$ is

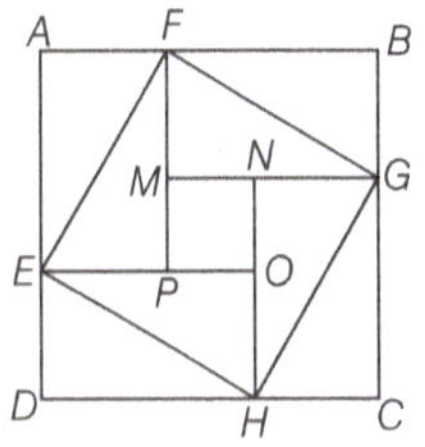

(a) 6 cm^2 (b) 4 cm^2
(c) 3 cm^2 (d) 2 cm^2

6 Let $ABCD$ be a parallelogram P, Q, R and S are points on sides AB, BC, CD and DA respectively, such that $AP = DR$. If the area of parallelogram $ABCD$ is 16 cm^2, then the area of the quadrilateral $PQRS$ is

(a) 8 cm^2 (b) 6 cm^2
(c) 10 cm^2 (d) 5 cm^2

7 Let $WXYZ$ be a square. Let P, Q and R be the mid-points of WX, XY and ZW, respectively and K and L be the mid-points of PQ and PR, respectively. Then, the value of

$$\frac{\text{area of } \Delta PKL}{\text{area of square } WXYZ} \text{ is}$$

(a) $\frac{1}{12}$ (b) $\frac{1}{15}$
(c) $\frac{1}{20}$ (d) $\frac{1}{16}$

8 In the given figure, two isosceles right angled triangles ΔDEF and ΔHGI are on the equal bases DE and GH, which are parallel to FI. If $DE = GH = 9$ cm and $DH = 20$ cm, then the area of the quadrilateral $FEGI$ is equal to

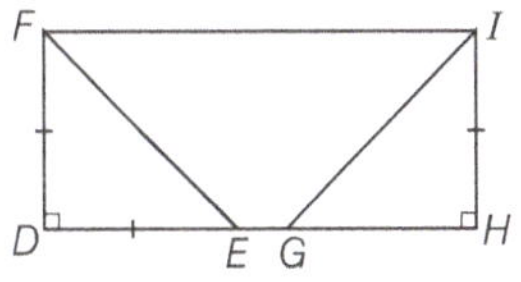

(a) 95 cm^2 (b) 99 cm^2
(c) 92 cm^2 (d) 90 cm^2

Answers

1. (c) **2.** (a) **3.** (b) **4.** (b) **5.** (b) **6.** (a) **7.** (d) **8.** (b)

** These questions may or may not be asked in the examination, have been given just for additional practice required for olympiads Scholarship Exams etc. For detailed explanations refer Page No. 346.*

CHAPTER
13

Circles

SYLLABUS

- (a) Chord Properties : (I) A straight line drawn from the centre of a circle to bisect a chord, which is not a diameter is at right angles to the chord. (ii) The perpendicular to a chord from the centre bisects the chord (without proof). (iii) Equal chords are equidistant from the centre. (iv) Chords equidistant from the centre are equal (without proof). (v) There is one and only one circle that passes through three given points not in a straight line.
- (b) Arc and Chord Properties : (I) If two arcs subtend equal angles at the centre, they are equal and its converse. (ii) If two chords are equal, they cut-off equal arcs and its converse (without proof).

The collection of all the points in a plane, which are at a fixed distance from a fixed point in the plane, is called a **circle**. The fixed point is called the **centre** of the circle and the fixed distance is called the **radius** of the circle.

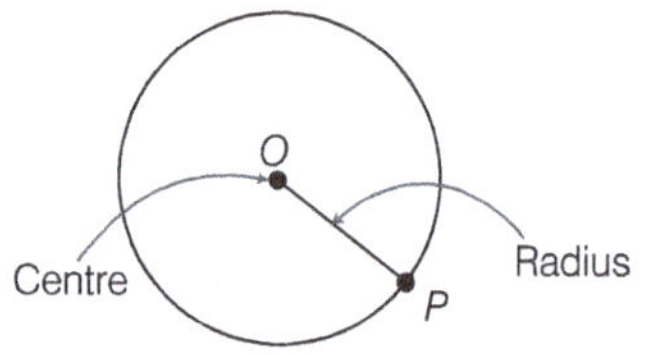

Parts of Plane Divided by a Circle

A circle divides the plane into three parts. These parts are

(i) inside the circle, called interior of the circle.
(ii) boundary of the circle.
(iii) outside the circle, called exterior of the circle.

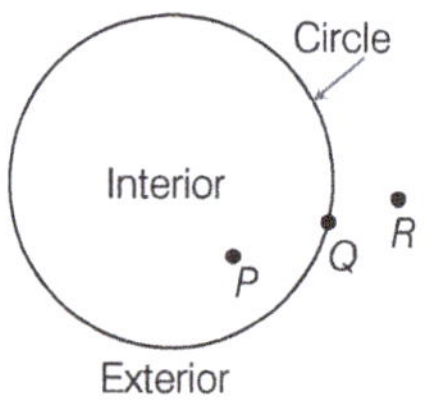

e.g. Point P, R and Q are inside, outside and on the circle, respectively

The length of the point P, R and Q from the centre is less than, greater than and equal to the radius, respectively.

The circle and its interior make up the **circular region**.

Semi-circle

Diameter of a circle divides the circle into two equal parts i.e. into two equal arcs. Each of these two arcs is called a semi-circle.

Semi-circular Region

When two arcs are semi-circles, then both segments and both sectors become same and each is known as semi-circular region.

Important Terms Related to a Circle

Chord

A line segment joining two points on the circle is called a chord of the circle. In figure, PQ is a chord of the circle.

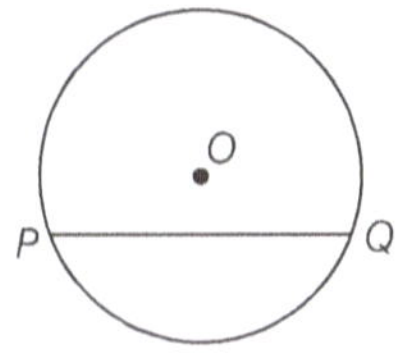

Diameter

A chord, which passes through the centre of the circle, is called a diameter of the circle. In figure, AB is the diameter of the circle. Diameter is the longest chord and all diameters have the same length, which is equal to two times the radius i.e. diameter = 2 × radius.

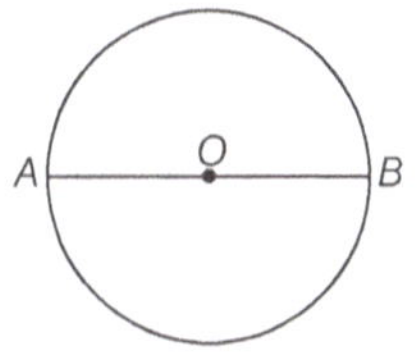

Circumference

The length of the complete circle is called its circumference.

Circumference = $\pi \times$ diameter

or $2\pi r$, r is the radius of the circle

Secant of a Circle

A line, which meets a circle in two points, is called a secant of the circle.

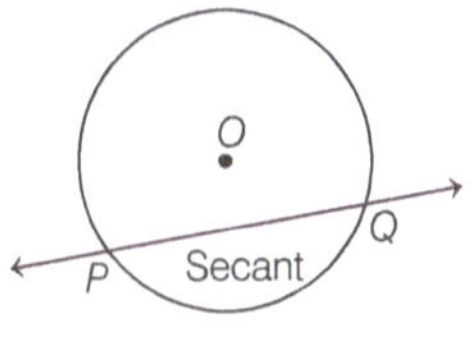

In figure, line PQ is a secant of the circle with centre O.

Arc

Any part of the circumference of a circle is called an arc of that circle. In the adjoining figure, there are two pieces, one longer and the other smaller. The longer one is called the **major arc** PRQ and the smaller one is called the **minor arc** PQ.

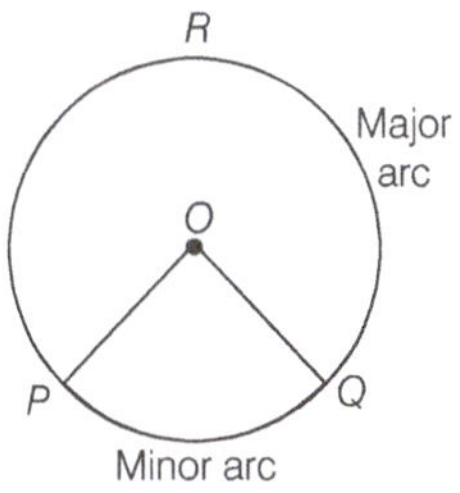

The minor arc PQ is denoted by $\overset{\frown}{PQ}$ and the major arc PRQ is denoted by $\overset{\frown}{PRQ}$.

Segment

The region between a chord and an arc is called a segment of the circle. This chord is called the **base** of the segment. The segment formed by minor arc along with chord, is called **minor segment** and the segment formed by major arc alongwith chord, is called the **major segment**.

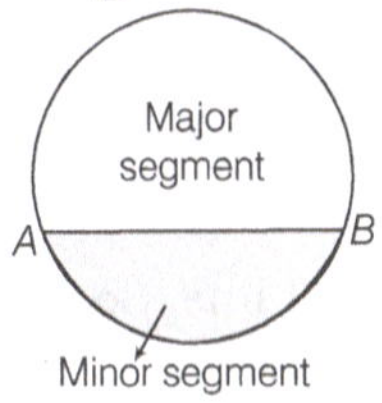

Sector

The region between an arc and two radii joining the centre to the end points of the arc is called a sector. The sector corresponding to minor and major arc is called **minor sector** and **major sector**, respectively.

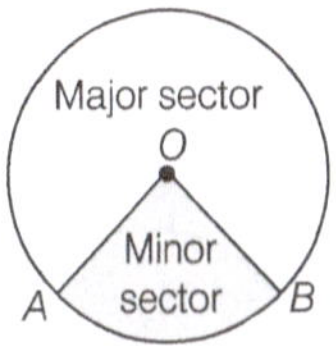

Concentric Circles

Two or more circles having common centre are called concentric circles.

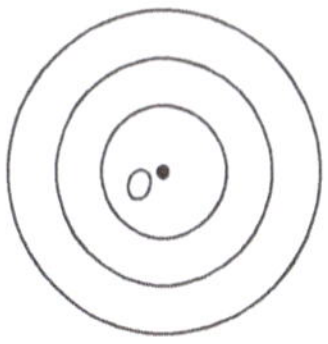

Congruent Circles

Two circles are said to be congruent, iff either they can superimposed or their radii are equals.

Chord Properties

Theorem 1 *The line drawn through the centre of a circle to bisect a chord, which is not a diameter, is perpendicular to the chord.*

Given AB is a chord of a circle with centre O. A line OM is drawn through the centre O to the chord AB such that M is the mid-point of AB i.e. $AM = MB$.

To prove $OM \perp AB$

Construction Join OA and OB.

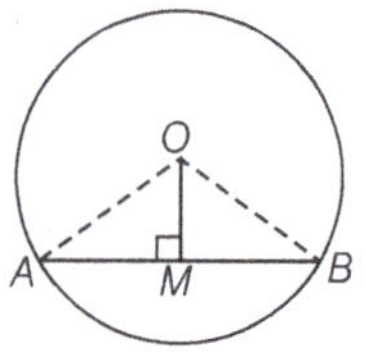

Proof In ΔOAM and ΔOBM, we have

$AM = MB$ [$\because M$ is the mid-point of AB]

$OA = OB$ [radii of same circle]

$OM = OM$ [common side]

$\therefore \quad \Delta OAM \cong \Delta OBM$ [by SSS congruence rule]

Then, $\angle OMA = \angle OMB$ [by CPCT] ...(i)

Now, AB is a straight line. So, by linear pair axiom,

$$\angle OMA + \angle OMB = 180^\circ$$

$\Rightarrow \quad 2\angle OMA = 180^\circ$ [using Eq. (i)]

$$\Rightarrow \quad \angle OMA = \frac{180^\circ}{2} = 90^\circ$$

Thus, $\angle OMA = \angle OMB = 90^\circ$

$\therefore \quad OM \perp AB$ **Hence proved.**

Theorem 2 **(Converse of Theorem 1)** *The perpendicular from the centre of a circle to a chord, bisects the chord i.e. if AB is a chord of a circle with centre O and $OM \perp AB$, then $AM = MB$.*

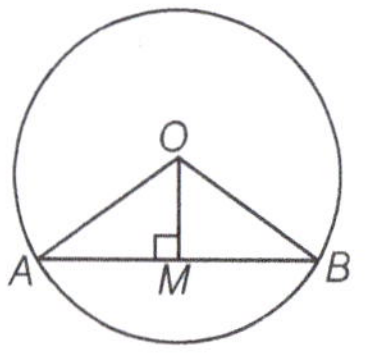

Example 1. Find the length of a chord of a circle, which is at a distance of 6 cm from the centre of the circle, whose radius is 10 cm.

Sol. Given, radius of circle = 10 cm and distance of chord AB from centre = 6 cm.

Draw $OM \perp AB$.

We know that the perpendicular drawn from the centre of a circle to a chord, bisects the chord.

i.e. OM bisects the chord AB.

$\therefore \quad AM = MB$

In right angled ΔOMA,

$OA = 10\text{ cm}$

and $OM = 6\text{ cm}$

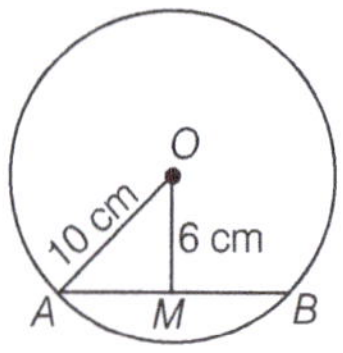

By Pythagoras theorem,

$$OA^2 = OM^2 + AM^2$$

$\Rightarrow \quad 10^2 = 6^2 + AM^2$

$\Rightarrow \quad AM^2 = 100 - 36 = 64$

$\Rightarrow \quad AM = 8\text{ cm}$ [taking positive square root]

$\therefore$ Length of the chord $AB = 2 \times AM$

$= 2 \times 8 = 16\text{ cm}.$

Example 2. The radius of a circle is 13 cm and the length of one of its chords is 10 cm. Find the distance of the chord from the centre.

Sol. Let AB be a chord of the given circle with centre O.

Given, radius $OA = 13\text{ cm}$ and $AB = 10\text{ cm}$.

From O, draw $OL \perp AB$.

We know that the perpendicular drawn from the centre of a circle to a chord, bisects the chord.

$$\therefore \quad AL = \frac{1}{2}AB = \frac{1}{2} \times 10 = 5\text{ cm}$$

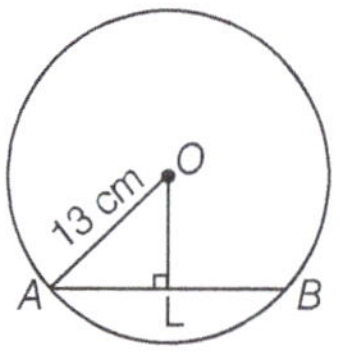

Now, in right angled ΔOLA,

$OA^2 = OL^2 + AL^2$ [by Pythagoras theorem]

$\Rightarrow \quad 13^2 = OL^2 + 5^2$

$\Rightarrow \quad OL^2 = 13^2 - 5^2$

$= 169 - 25$

$= 144$

$\Rightarrow \quad OL = 12\text{ cm}$ [taking positive square root]

Hence, the distance of the chord from the centre is 12 cm.

Example 3. A chord of a circle is 10 cm long and 20 cm away from the centre. Find the length of another chord of the circle, which is 5 cm from the centre.

Sol. Let CD and AB are the chords of the circle.

Draw $OM \perp AB$ and $ON \perp CD$

$\Rightarrow AM = MB$ and $CN = ND$ ...(i)

We know that perpendicular from the centre to a chord, bisects the chord.

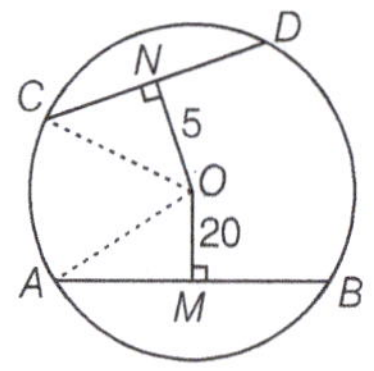

Since, $ON = 5\text{ cm}$

$\because \quad AM = \frac{1}{2}AB$

$\therefore \quad AM = \frac{10}{2}\text{ cm} = 5\text{ cm} = ON$

In right angled ΔAOM and ΔCON,

$AO = CO$ [radii]

$AM = ON$ [prove above]

$\angle OMA = \angle ONC$ [by (i)]

$\therefore \quad \Delta AMO \cong \Delta CNO$ [by RHS congruence Rule]

$\Rightarrow \quad CN = OM = 20$

$CD = 2 \times CN$

$= 2 \times 20 = 40\text{ cm}$

Example 4. In the given figure, if $OA = 5$ cm, $AB = 8$ cm and OD is perpendicular to AB, then find the length of CD.

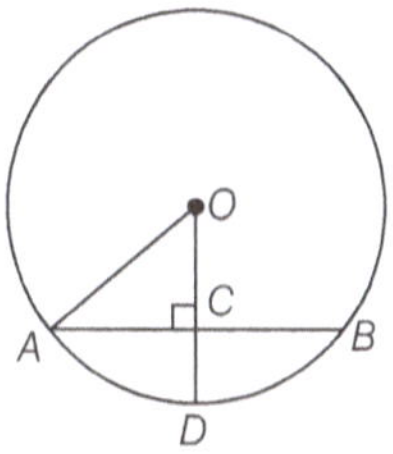

Sol. We know that the perpendicular from the centre of a circle to a chord, bisects the chord.

$\therefore \quad AC = CB = \frac{1}{2}AB = \frac{1}{2} \times 8 = 4\text{ cm}$ [$\because AB = 8\text{ cm}$]

$\because \quad OA = 5\text{ cm}$ [given]

In right angled ΔOCA, we have

$AO^2 = AC^2 + OC^2$ [by Pythagoras theorem]

$\Rightarrow \quad 5^2 = 4^2 + OC^2$

$\Rightarrow \quad 25 = 16 + OC^2$

$\Rightarrow \quad OC^2 = 25 - 16 = 9$

$\Rightarrow \quad OC = 3\text{ cm}$ [taking positive square root]

Now, $OA = OD$ [radii of same circle]

$\Rightarrow \quad OD = 5\text{ cm}$

$\therefore \quad CD = OD - OC$

$= 5 - 3 = 2\text{ cm}$

Example 5. Two circles of radii 10 cm and 8 cm are intersect and the length of the common chord is 12 cm. Find the distance between their centres.

Sol. Let O and O' be the centres of the circles of radii 10 cm and 8 cm, respectively and PQ be their common chord of length 12 cm.

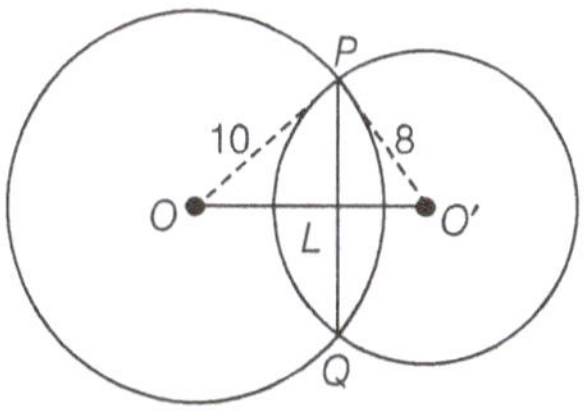

We have, $OP = 10$ cm, $O'P = 8$ cm and $PQ = 12$ cm

$\therefore \quad PL = \frac{1}{2}PQ = 6\text{ cm}$

[when two circles intersect at two points, then their centres lie on the perpendicular bisector of the common chord]

In right angled ΔOLP,

$OP^2 = OL^2 + LP^2$ [by Pythagoras theorem]

$\Rightarrow \quad OL = \sqrt{OP^2 - LP^2}$ [taking positive square root]

$= \sqrt{10^2 - 6^2} = \sqrt{100 - 36} = \sqrt{64} = 8\text{ cm}$

Similarly, in right angled $\Delta O'LP$,

$O'P^2 = O'L^2 + LP^2$ [by Pythagoras theorem]

$\Rightarrow \quad O'L = \sqrt{O'P^2 - LP^2}$

$= \sqrt{8^2 - 6^2} = \sqrt{64 - 36}$

$= \sqrt{28} = 5.29\text{ cm}$ [taking positive square root]

$\therefore$ Distance between their centres, $OO' = OL + LO'$

$= (8 + 5.29) = 13.29\text{ cm}$

Example 6. AB and CD are two chords of a circle such that $AB = 6$ cm, $CD = 12$ cm and $AB \parallel CD$. OM is perpendicular to AB. If the distance between AB and CD is 3 cm, then find the radius of the circle.

Sol. Given, $AB = 6$ cm, $CD = 12$ cm and $PM = 3$ cm

Clearly, $AM = MB = \frac{1}{2}AB = \frac{1}{2} \times 6\text{ cm} = 3\text{ cm}$

and $CP = PD = \frac{1}{2}CD = \frac{1}{2} \times 12\text{ cm} = 6\text{ cm}$ [$\because OM \perp AB$]

Let radius $= r = OC = OD$ and $OP = y$ cm. Then,

$OM = OP + PM = (y + 3)$ cm

In right angled ΔOPC and ΔAOM,

$CP^2 + OP^2 = r^2$ and $AM^2 + OM^2 = r^2$

[by Pythagoras theorem]

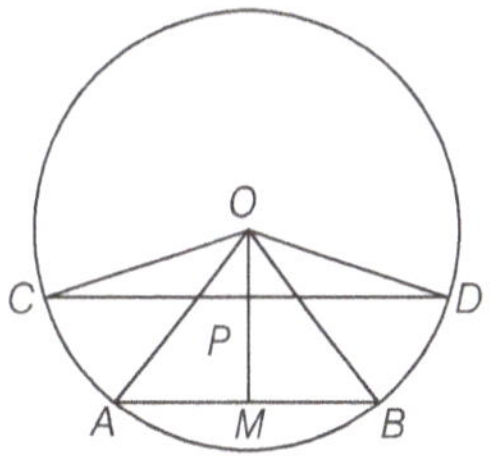

$\therefore \quad CP^2 + OP^2 = AM^2 + OM^2 = r^2$

$\Rightarrow \quad 6^2 + y^2 = 3^2 + (3 + y)^2 = r^2$ ...(i)

$\Rightarrow \quad 36 + y^2 = 9 + 9 + y^2 + 6y$ [$\because (a+b)^2 = a^2 + b^2 + 2ab$]

$\Rightarrow \quad 6y = 18 \Rightarrow y = 3\text{ cm}$

$\therefore \quad r^2 = 6^2 + y^2 = 36 + 9 = 45$ [from Eq. (i)]

$\Rightarrow \quad r = 3\sqrt{5}\text{ cm} = 6.708 \approx 6.71\text{ cm}$

Theorem 3 *Equal chords of a circle are equidistant from the centre.*

Given A circle with centre O and two equal chords AB and PQ.

To prove AB and PQ are equidistant from the centre O.

Construction Draw $OM \perp AB$ and $ON \perp PQ$.

Join OA, OB, OP and OQ.

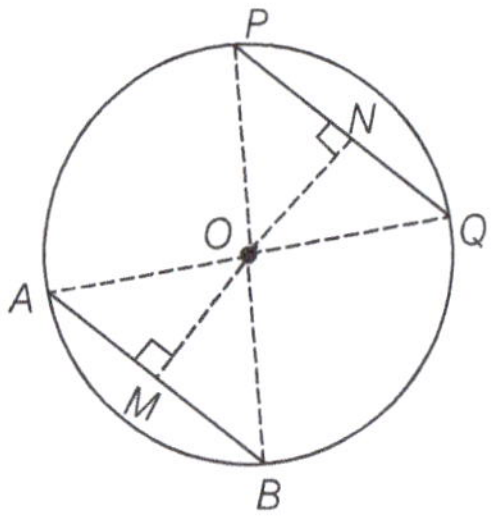

Proof We know that a perpendicular from the centre to a chord, bisects the chord.

$\therefore \quad AM = MB = \frac{1}{2} AB$ $\quad [\because OM \perp AB]$

and $\quad PN = NQ = \frac{1}{2} PQ$ $\quad [\because ON \perp PQ]$

Since, chord $AB =$ Chord PQ [given]

$\Rightarrow \quad \frac{1}{2} AB = \frac{1}{2} PQ$

Then, $\quad AM = MB = PN = NQ$

In right angled ΔOMA and ΔONQ,

$OA = OQ$ [radii of same circle]

$AM = NQ$ [proved above]

$\angle OMA = \angle ONQ$ [each 90°]

$\therefore \quad \Delta OMA \cong \Delta ONQ$ [by RHS congruence rule]

$\Rightarrow \quad OM = ON$ [by CPCT]

Hence, PQ and AB are equidistant from the centre O.

Hence proved.

Theorem 4 **(Converse of Theorem 3)** *Chords equidistant from the centre of a circle are equal in length.*

i.e. if OM and ON are equal in the figure with centre O of the circle, then $AB = CD$.

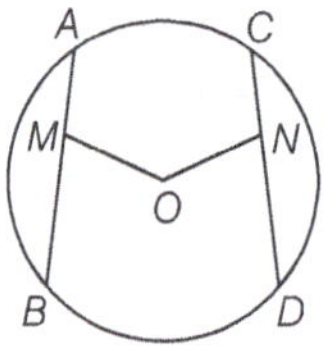

Example 7. If two chords intersect inside the circle, make equal angles with the line passing through the centre and their point of intersection (see the figure), then prove that the chords are equal.

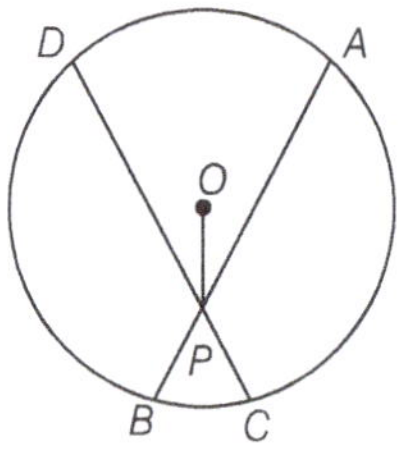

Or

In the given figure, O is the centre of a circle and PO bisects $\angle APD$. Prove that $AB = CD$.

Sol. Let AB and CD be two chords of a circle with centre O, intersecting at a point P. MN is a line passing through the centre O and point P such that MN bisects $\angle APD$ i.e. $\angle APO = \angle DPO$.

To prove $AB = CD$

Construction Draw $OE \perp AB$ and $OF \perp CD$

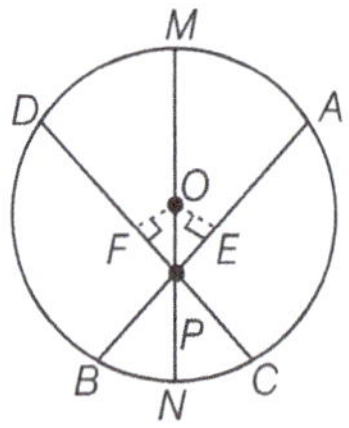

Proof In ΔOEP and ΔOFP,

$\angle OEP = \angle OFP$ [each 90°]

$OP = OP$ [common side]

and $\quad \angle OPE = \angle OPF$ $\quad [\because OP$ bisects $\angle APD]$

$\therefore \quad \Delta OEP \cong \Delta OFP$ [by AAS congruence rule]

Then, $\quad OE = OF$ [by CPCT]

Thus, chords AB and CD are equidistant from the centre O of the circle, then we know that chords of a circle, which are equidistant from the centre, are equal.

$\therefore \quad AB = CD$ **Hence proved.**

Example 8. In the given figure, equal chords AB and CD of a circle with centre O, cut at right angle at E. If M and N are the mid-points of AB and CD respectively, then prove that $OMEN$ is a square.

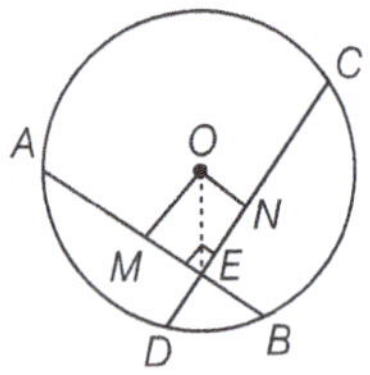

Sol. Since, M and N are the mid-points of AB and CD, respectively.

$\therefore \quad \angle OMB = \angle OND = 90°$

$\Rightarrow \quad \angle OME = \angle ONE = 90°$

[$\because$ we know that a line drawn from the centre to bisect a chord is perpendicular to chord

Since, equal chords of a circle are equidistant from the centre.

$\therefore \quad OM = ON$

Thus, in ΔOME and ΔONE, we have

$OM = ON$ [proved above]

$\angle OME = \angle ONE$ [each 90°]

and $OE = OE$ [common side]

$\therefore \quad \Delta OME \cong \Delta ONE$ [by RHS congruence rule]

$\angle MEO = \angle NEO$ [by CPCT]

$\Rightarrow \quad \angle MEO = \angle NEO = 45^\circ$

So, $\angle MOE = \angle NOE = 45^\circ$

[by using angle sum property of triangle]

Thus, each angle of quadrilateral $OMEN$ is 90°.

Hence, $OMEN$ is a square.

Example 9. In the given figure, O is the centre of a circle. If AB and AC are chords of the circle such that $AB = AC$, $OP \perp AB$ and $OQ \perp AC$, then prove that $PB = QC$.

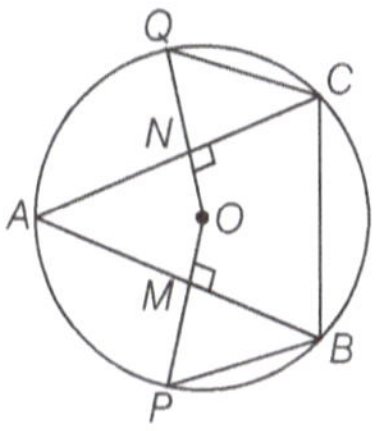

Sol. Given AB and AC are two equal chords of circle with centre O. Also, $OP \perp AB$ at M and $OQ \perp AC$ at N.

To prove $PB = QC$

Proof We know that the perpendicular from the centre of a circle to a chord, bisects the chord.

$\therefore \quad AM = MB = \frac{1}{2}AB$ [$\because OP \perp AB$]

and $AN = NC = \frac{1}{2}AC$ [$\because OQ \perp AC$]

Since, $AB = AC$

$\therefore \quad \frac{1}{2}AB = \frac{1}{2}AC$

$\Rightarrow \quad AM = MB = AN = NC$ ...(i)

$OM = ON$ ...(ii)

[$\because$ equal chords are equidistant from the centre]

$OP = OQ$ [radii of same circle] ...(iii)

$\Rightarrow \quad OP - OM = OQ - ON$ [subtracting Eq. (ii) from Eq. (iii)]

$\Rightarrow \quad PM = QN$ ...(iv)

Now, in ΔPMB and ΔQNC, we have

$MB = NC$ [from Eq. (i)]

$\angle PMB = \angle QNC$ [each 90°]

$\Rightarrow \quad PM = QN$ [from Eq. (iv)]

$\therefore \quad \Delta PMB \cong \Delta QNC$ [by SAS congruence rule]

$\Rightarrow \quad PB = QC$ [by CPCT] **Hence proved.**

Theorem 5 *There is one and only one circle, passing through three given non-collinear points.*

Given Three non-collinear points A, B and C.

To prove There is one and only one circle, passing through the points A, B and C.

Construction Draw line segments AB and BC and then draw perpendicular bisectors DP and EQ of AB and BC, respectively, which intersect at point O. Join OA, OB and OC.

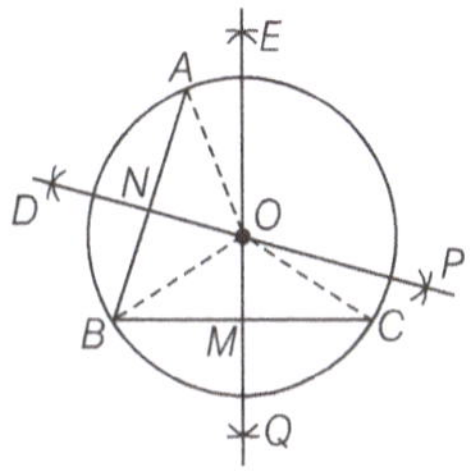

Proof Let perpendicular bisectors EQ and DP intersect BC and AB at M and N, respectively.

In ΔOMB and ΔOMC,

$BM = MC$

[$\because EQ$ is perpendicular bisector of BC]

$\angle OMB = \angle OMC$ [each 90°]

$OM = OM$ [common side]

$\therefore \quad \Delta OMB \cong \Delta OMC$ [by SAS congruence rule]

Then, $OB = OC$ [by CPCT] ...(i)

Similarly, $\Delta ONA \cong \Delta ONB$

Then, $OA = OB$ ...(ii)

From Eqs. (i) and (ii), we get

$OA = OB = OC = \text{Radius}$

Thus, circle of radius $OA = r$ with centre O passes through three non-collinear points A, B and C.

Uniqueness Since, the perpendicular bisectors of AB and BC intersect each other at only one point 'O'. So, O is the only point equidistant from A, B and C.

Hence, there is one and only one circle, passing through three non-collinear points A, B and C.

Hence proved.

Example 10. Given, an arc say PQ of a circle. Then, complete the circle.

Sol. Given, an arc PQ of a circle and we have to complete the circle i.e. we have to find its centre and radius.

Now, take a point R on the arc PQ. Join PR and RQ and then draw perpendicular bisectors of PR and RQ, which intersects at point O.

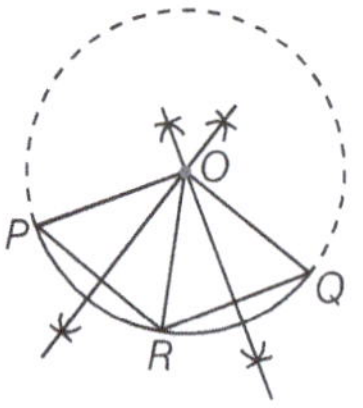

This point O is the required centre of circle and radius of circle is $PO = RO = OQ$. Now, take O as centre and PO as radius and then complete the circle.

Example 11. In isosceles triangle PQR inscribed in a circle $PQ = PR = 7$ cm and $QR = 6$ cm. Find the radius of the circle.

Sol. Let isosceles ΔPQR be inscribed in a circle with centre O and $PQ = PR = 7\text{cm}$, $QR = 6\text{cm}$.

Draw $OM \perp QR$

$$QM = \frac{1}{2}QR$$
$$= \frac{1}{2} \times 6 = 3\text{cm}$$

From right angled ΔPQM,

$$PM^2 = PQ^2 - QM^2$$
$$= 7^2 - 3^2 = 49 - 9$$

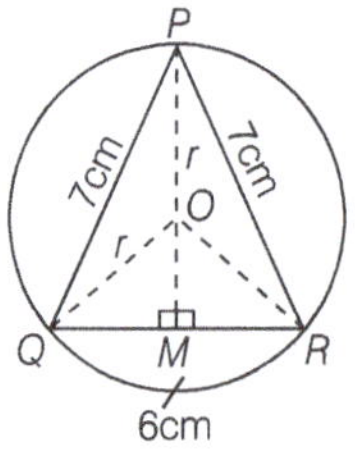

$$PM^2 = 40$$

$\therefore$ $$PM = 2\sqrt{10}\text{ cm}$$

$\therefore$ $$OM = PM - OP = 2\sqrt{10} - r$$

From right angled ΔOMQ

$$OQ^2 = QM^2 + OM^2$$

$\Rightarrow$ $$r^2 = 3^2 + (2\sqrt{10} - r)^2$$

$\Rightarrow$ $$r^2 = 9 + 40 + r^2 - 4\sqrt{10}r$$

$\Rightarrow$ $$4\sqrt{10}r = 49$$

$\Rightarrow$ $$r = \frac{49}{4\sqrt{10}}$$

$\Rightarrow$ $$r = \frac{49}{4\sqrt{10}} \times \frac{\sqrt{10}}{\sqrt{10}}$$

$$r = \frac{49\sqrt{10}}{40}\text{ cm}$$

Exercise 13.1

1. In the given figure, if $MP = PN$, then find the values of $\angle OPN$ and $\angle OPM$.

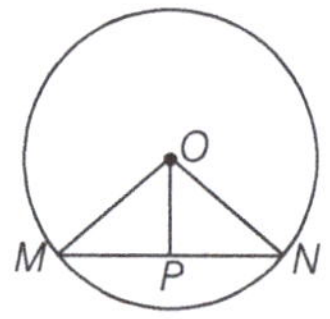

2. In the given figure, perpendicular is drawn from centre O to the chord AB. If $AB = 8$ cm, then find AP and PB.

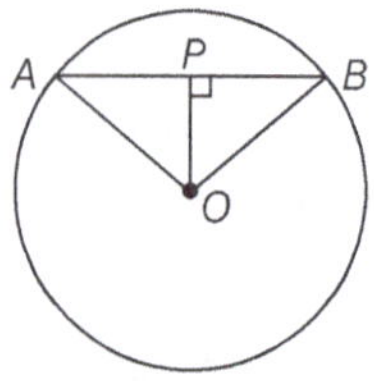

3. Two concentric circles with centre O have A, B, C and D as points of intersection with a line l as shown in the figure. If $AD = 12\text{cm}$ and $BC = 8\text{cm}$, then find the length of AB and CD.

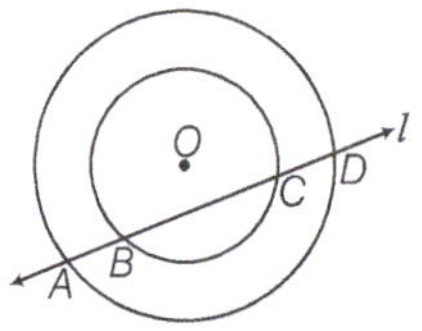

4. A chord is at a distance of 5 cm from the centre of a circle of radius 13 cm. Find the length of the chord.

5. A chord of length 6 cm is drawn in a circle of radius 5 cm. Calculate its distance from the centre of the circle.

6. A chord of length 8 cm is drawn at a distance of 3 cm from the centre of a circle. Calculate the radius of the circle.

7. Prove that the line joining the mid-points of two parallel chords of a circle passes through the centre.

8. Two circles of radii 4 cm and 3 cm intersect at two points and the distance between their centres is 5 cm. Find the length of the common chord.

9. In the given figure, PQ and RS are two chords of a circle having its centre O. If $PQ = RS$ and $ON = 3$ cm, then find OM.

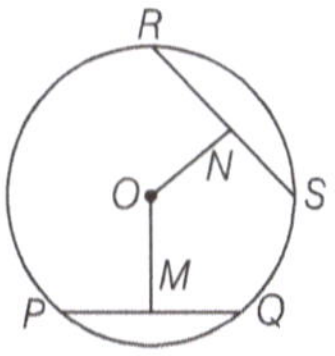

10. Two parallel chords are drawn in a circle of diameter 30 cm. If the length of one chord is 24 cm and the distance between the two chords is 21 cm, then find the length of the other chord.

11. AB and CD are equal chords of a circle with centre O. If $OM \perp AB$ and $ON \perp CD$, then prove that $\angle OMN = \angle ONM$.

12. AB and AC are two equal chords of a circle. Prove that the bisector of $\angle BAC$ passes through the centre of the circle.

13. AB and AC are two chords of a circle of radius r such that $AB = 2AC$. If p and q are the distances of AB and AC from the centre, prove that $4q^2 = p^2 + 3r^2$.

14. The centre of a circle of radius 13 units is the point (3, 6). $P(7, 9)$ is a point inside the circle. APB is a chord of the circle such that $AP = PB$. Calculate the length of AB.

15. Two circles with centres O and O' intersect each other at points P and Q. The straight line APB is parallel to centre-line OO'. Prove that $OO' = \frac{1}{2} AB$.

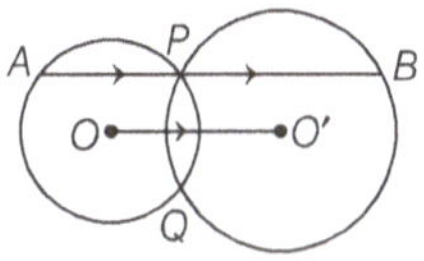

16. AB and CD are two equal chords of a circle with centre O. If AB and CD, on being produced, meet at a point P outside the circle, prove that

(i) $PA = PC$

(ii) $PB = PD$.

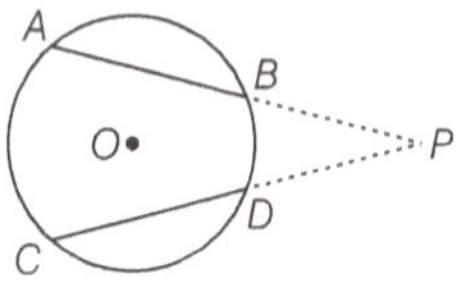

Arc and Chord Properties

Angle Subtended by a Chord

Let AB be a chord and points P and Q on the circle and join PA, PB, QA and QB. Then, $\angle APB$ and $\angle AQB$ are called the angles subtended by the chord AB.

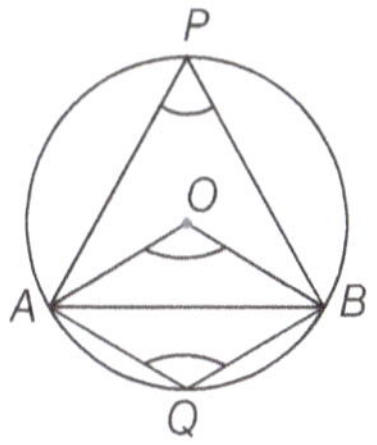

Angle Subtended by an Arc

Let PQ be the minor arc and the point R on the major arc. Join PR and RQ. Then, $\angle PRQ$ is called the angle subtended by an arc PQ.

Theorem 6 *If two chords are equal, they cut-off equal arcs.*

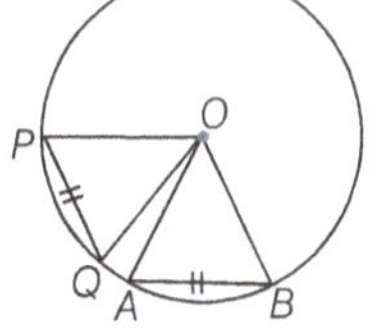

i.e. if $PQ = AB$, then $\overset{\frown}{PQ} = \overset{\frown}{AB}$.

Theorem 7 (Converse of Theorem 6) *If two arcs are equal, then their chords are equal i.e. if* $\overparen{PQ} = \overparen{AB}$, *then* $PQ = AB$.

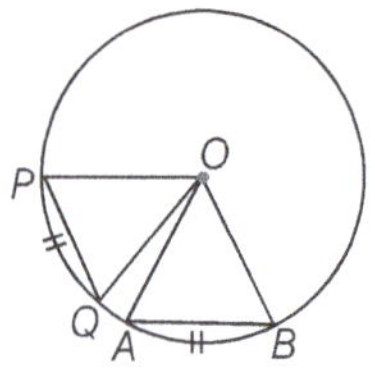

Theorem 8 *If two arcs subtend equal angles at the centre, then the arcs are equal.*

Given A circle with centre O. Let AB and CD be two arcs of a circle such that angles subtended by these arcs at the centre O of a circle are equal i.e. $\angle AOB = \angle COD$.

To prove $\overparen{AB} = \overparen{CD}$

Construction Join AB and CD.

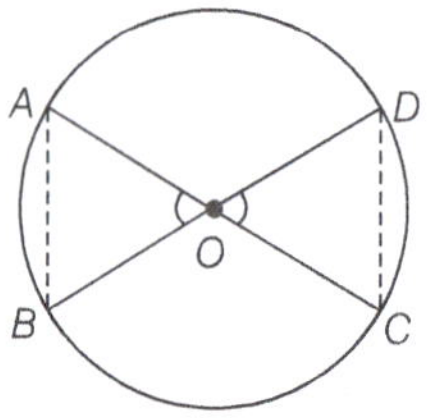

Proof In ΔAOB and ΔCOD, we have

$AO = CO$ [radii of same circle]

$\angle AOB = \angle COD$ [given]

and $OB = OD$ [radii of same circle]

$\therefore$ $\Delta AOB \cong \Delta COD$ [by SAS congruence rule]

So, $AB = CD$ [by CPCT]

$\Rightarrow$ $\overparen{AB} = \overparen{CD}$ [by Theorem 6]

Hence proved.

Theorem 9 (Converse of Theorem 8) *Equal arcs of a circle subtend equal angles at the centre.*

Given A circle with centre O. AB and CD are two equal arcs of the circle, which subtend $\angle AOB$ and $\angle COD$ at the centre O.

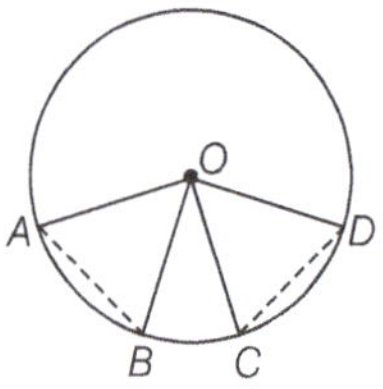

To prove $\angle AOB = \angle COD$

Construction Join AB and CD.

Proof In ΔAOB and ΔCOD,

$OA = OC$ [radii of same circle]

$OB = OD$ [radii of same circle]

$AB = CD$ [by using Theorem 7]

$\therefore$ $\Delta AOB \cong \Delta COD$ [by SSS congruence rule]

Then, $\angle AOB = \angle COD$ [by CPCT]

Hence proved.

Example 12. AB is an arc of a circle having centre O. If $\angle AOB = 60°$, then prove that the chord AB is of radius length.

Sol. Let O be the centre and r be the radius of the circle.

Arc AB subtends $\angle AOB = 60°$ at the centre of the circle.

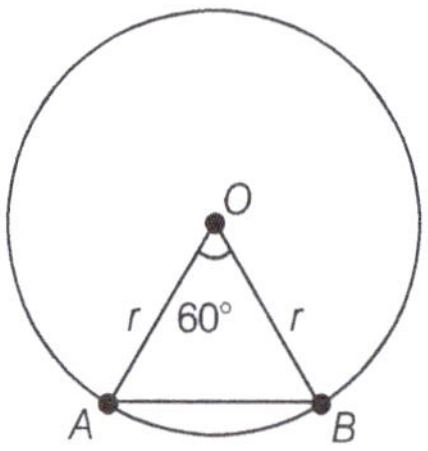

Here, $OB = OA = r$ [radii of same circle]

$\Rightarrow$ $\angle OAB = \angle OBA$ [$\because$ angles opposite to equal sides of a triangle are also equal]

i.e. $\angle A = \angle B$ ...(i)

In ΔOAB, $\angle O + \angle A + \angle B = 180°$ [angle sum property of a triangle]

$\Rightarrow$ $60° + \angle A + \angle B = 180°$

$\Rightarrow$ $\angle A + \angle B = 120°$ ...(ii)

From Eqs. (i) and (ii), we get

$2\angle A = 120°$

$\Rightarrow$ $\angle A = \frac{1}{2} \times 120° = 60°$

and $\angle B = 60°$

Thus, $\angle O = \angle A = \angle B = 60°$

$\Rightarrow$ ΔOAB is an equilateral triangle.

$\therefore$ $AB = OA = OB = r$, i.e. $AB = r$. **Hence proved.**

Example 13. If A, B and C are three points on a circle such that $AB = BC = CA$ and O is the centre of the circle, then find the angle subtended by the chords AB, BC and CA at the centre O.

Sol. Given, three points A, B and C are on a circle such that $AB = BC = CA$.

We know that equal chords of a circle subtend equal angles at the centre of circle.

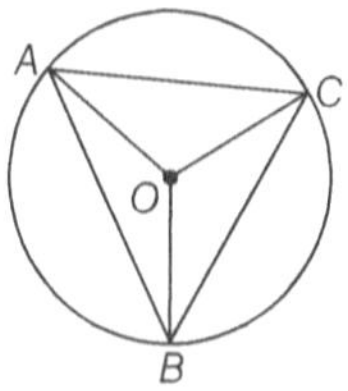

So, $\angle AOB = \angle BOC = \angle AOC$ ...(i)

Now, $\angle AOB + \angle BOC + \angle AOC = 360°$

[$\because$ sum of angles at a point is 360°]

$\Rightarrow$ $3\angle AOB = 360°$ [from Eq. (i)]

$\Rightarrow$ $\angle AOB = \dfrac{360°}{3} = 120°$

Hence, the angle subtended by the chords *AB*, *BC* and *CA* at the centre *O* is 120°.

Example 14. *AC* and *BD* are chords of a circle, which bisect each other. Prove that

(i) *AC* and *BD* are diameters.

(ii) *ABCD* is a rectangle.

Sol.

(i) Let *BD* and *AC* be two chords of a circle, bisect at *P*.

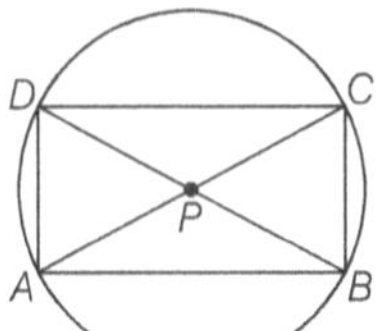

In ΔAPB and ΔCPD, we have

$PA = PC$ [$\because$ *P* is the mid-point of *AC*]

$\angle APB = \angle CPD$ [vertically opposite angles]

and $PB = PD$ [$\because$ *P* is the mid-point of *BD*]

$\therefore$ $\Delta CPD \cong \Delta APB$ [by SAS congruence rule]

Then, $CD = AB$ [by CPCT]

$\Rightarrow$ $\overset{\frown}{CD} = \overset{\frown}{AB}$ ...(i)

Similarly, in ΔCPB and ΔAPD,

$\overset{\frown}{CB} = \overset{\frown}{AD}$ ...(ii)

On adding Eqs. (i) and (ii), we get

$\Rightarrow$ $\overset{\frown}{CD} + \overset{\frown}{CB} = \overset{\frown}{AB} + \overset{\frown}{AD} \Rightarrow \overset{\frown}{BCD} = \overset{\frown}{BAD}$

Thus, *BD* divides the circle into two equal parts.

So, *BD* is a diameter.

Similarly, *AC* is a diameter.

(ii) Now, *BD* and *AC* bisect each other. So, *ABCD* is a parallelogram.

Also, $AC = BD$

Hence, *ABCD* is a rectangle. **Hence proved.**

Example 15. Prove that the right bisector of a chord of a circle bisects the corresponding arc of the circle.

Sol. Let *AB* be a chord of a circle having its centre *O*. Let *PQ* be the right bisector of the chord *AB*, intersecting *AB* at *L* and the arc *AB* at *Q*.

Since, the right bisector of a chord always passes through the centre.

So, *PQ* must pass through the centre *O*.

Join *OA* and *OB*.

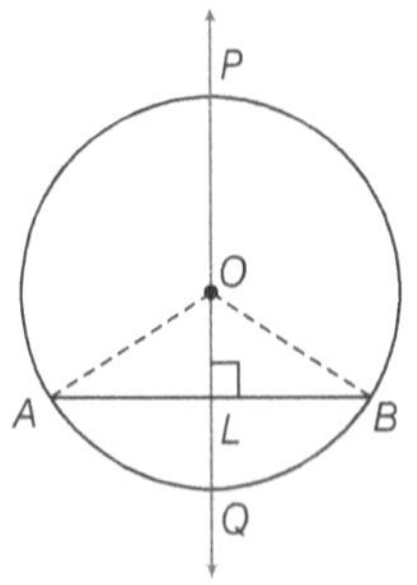

In ΔOLA and ΔOLB, we have

$OA = OB$ [radii of same circle]

$\angle ALO = \angle BLO = 90°$ [given]

$OL = OL$ [common side]

$\therefore$ $\Delta OLA \cong \Delta OLB$ [by RHS congruence rule]

Then, $\angle AOL = \angle BOL$ [by CPCT]

$\therefore$ $\overset{\frown}{AQ} = \overset{\frown}{BQ}$ [by Theorem 8] **Hence proved.**

Example 16. Prove that the line of centres of two intersecting circles subtends equal angles at the two points of intersection.

Sol. **Given** Two circles with centres *O* and *O'*, which intersect each other at *C* and *D*.

To prove $\angle OCO' = \angle ODO'$

Construction Join *OC*, *OD*, *O'C* and *O'D*.

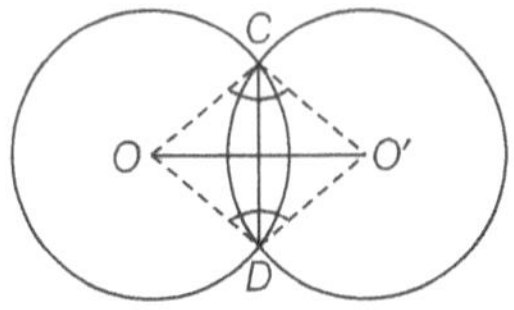

Proof In $\Delta OCO'$ and $\Delta ODO'$, we have

$OC = OD$ [radii of the same circle]

$O'C = O'D$ [radii of the same circle]

$OO' = OO'$ [common side]

$\therefore$ $\Delta OCO' \cong \Delta ODO'$ [by SSS congruence rule]

Then, $\angle OCO' = \angle ODO'$ [by CPCT]

Hence proved.

Exercise 13.2

1. In the given figure, chords AB and CD of a circle are equal. Prove that $AD = CB$.

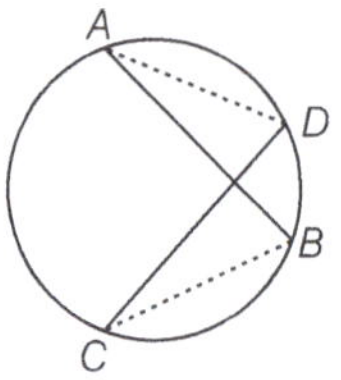

2. In the adjoining figure, AB is a diameter of a circle with centre O. If chord AC = chord AD, prove that arc BC = arc DB.

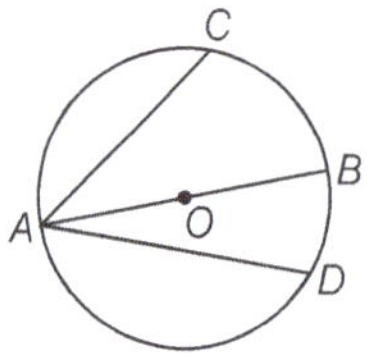

3. In the given figure, the length of arcs AB and BC are in the ratio 3 : 2. If $\angle AOB = 96°$, then find

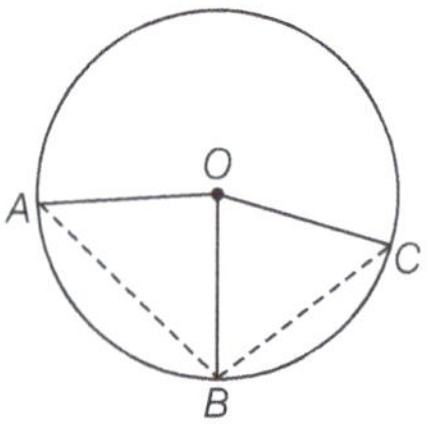

(i) $\angle BOC$ (ii) $\angle ABC$.

4. In the given figure, chords AB and CD are equal. If $\angle OBA = 55°$, then find the measure of $\angle COD$.

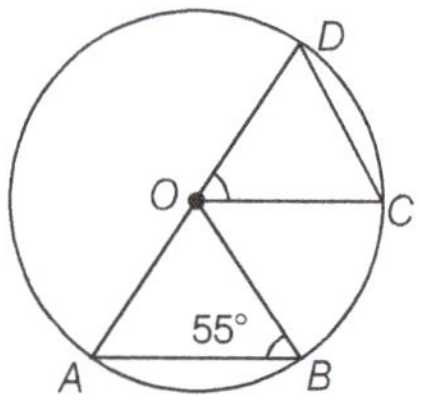

5. Write true or false. Give reason for your answer.
   (i) If two chords AB and AC of a circle with centre O are on the opposite sides of OA, then $\angle OAB = \angle OAC$.
   (ii) Congruent arcs of a circle subtend equal angles at the centre.

6. In the given figure, O is the centre of the circle and $CD = DE = EF = GF$. If $\angle COD = 40°$, then find the reflex $\angle COG$.

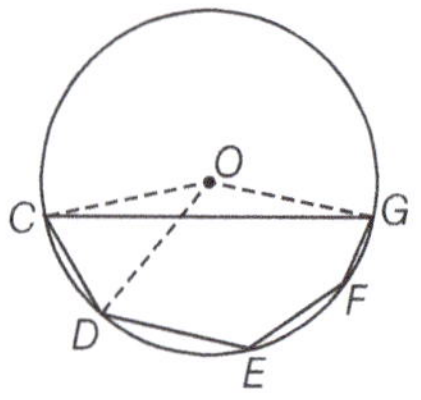

7. In the adjoining figure, the two chords AC and BC are equal and the radius OC intersects AB at M. Then, find the ratio $AM : BM$.

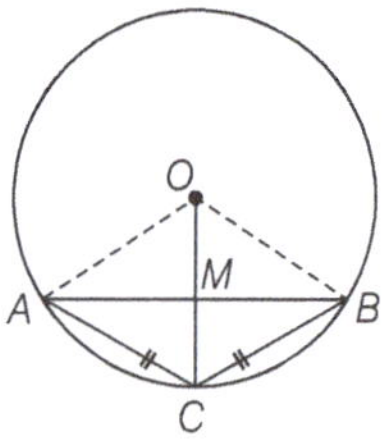

8. If O is the centre of a circle and points A, B, C, D, E, F, G and H are on the circle such that $AB = BC = CD = DE = EF = FG = GH = HA$. Find $\angle AOB$, $\angle AOC$, $\angle DOF$ and $\angle EOH$.

9. In the given figure, $\angle OAB = 30°$ and $\angle OCB = 57°$. Find $\angle BOC$ and $\angle AOC$.

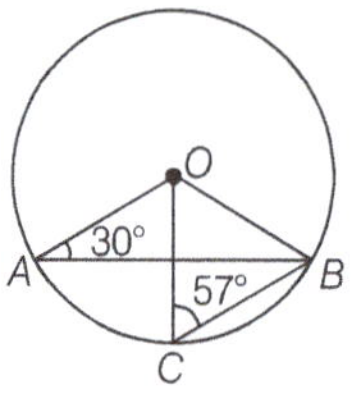

10. In the given figure, if the arc AXB and arc CYD of a circle are congruent, then find the ratio of AB and CD.

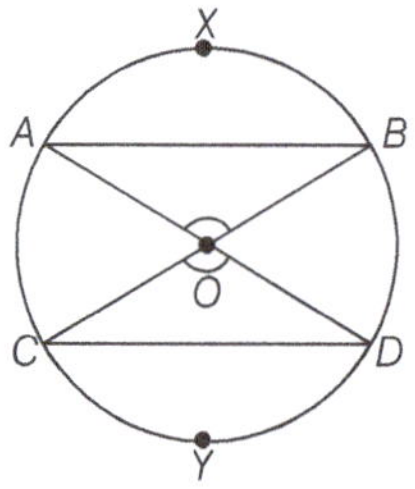

11. In the given figure, AOC is a diameter of the circle and arc $AXB = \frac{1}{2}$ arc BYC. Find $\angle BOC$.

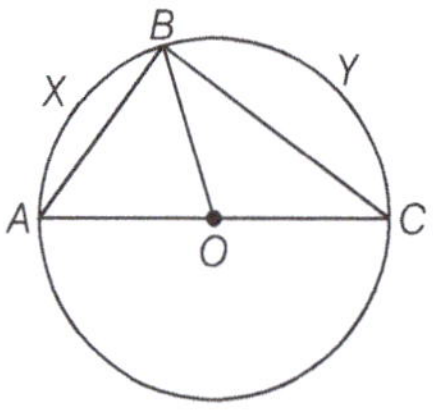

12. In the given figure, arc AB = arc CD. Prove that $\angle A = \angle B$.

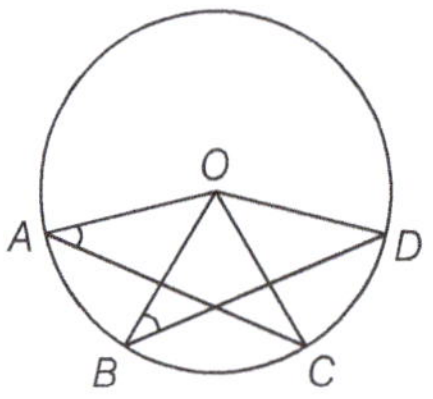

Chapter Practice

a. 1 Mark Questions

1. In given figure, if $AB = 8$ cm, then AC

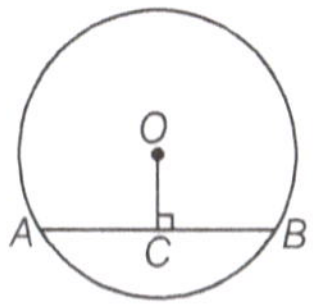

(a) 6 cm (b) 4 cm (c) 2 cm (d) 16 cm

2. In given figure, M is the mid-point of PQ, $OP = 13$ cm and $PQ = 24$ cm. Find the length of OM.

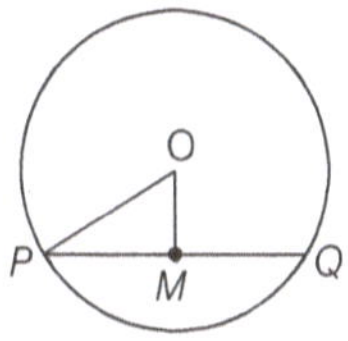

(a) 8 cm (b) 10 cm (c) 5.6 cm (d) 5 cm

3. In given figure, $MN = 8$ cm and $AB = 6$ cm, then find the length of CD.

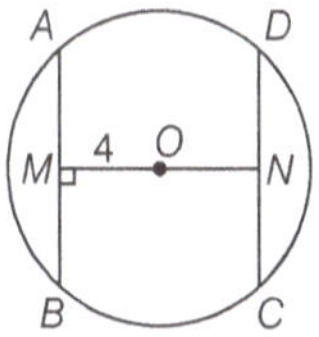

(a) 4 cm (b) 6 cm (c) 10 cm (d) 8 cm

4. In given figure, $OD = 9$ units and $PQ = 80$ units. Then, length of OQ is

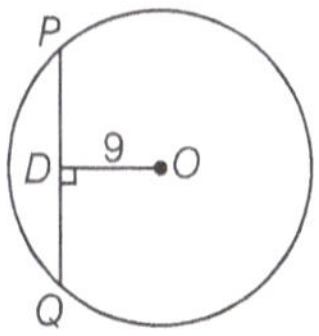

(a) 41 units (b) 48 units
(c) 45 units (d) 42 units

5. In two congruent circles having centres O and O', arc ABC and Arc PQR subtend equal angles at the centres O and O'. Then the ratio of AC and PR.

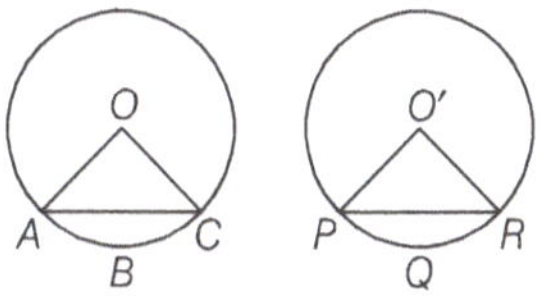

(a) 7 : 5
(b) 1 : 2
(c) 5 : 5
(d) 1 : 1

6. Perpendicular bisector of every chord of a circle always passes through its ....

7. Perpendicular bisectors of any two chords of a circle always intersect at the .... of the circle.

8. A point, whose distance from the centre of a circle is less than its radius, lies .... of the circle.

9. The region between a chord and either of the arc is called a ....

10. The region between an arc and the two radii, joining the centre to the ends of the arc, is called ....

b. 3 Marks Questions

11. Find the length of a chord, which is at a distance of 5 cm from the centre of a circle of radius 10 cm.

12. The radius of a circle is 5 cm and the length of a chord in the circle is 8 cm. Find the distance of the chord from the centre of the circle.

13. In the given figure, the diameter CD of a circle with centre O is perpendicular to the chord AB. If $AB = 8$ cm and $CM = 2$ cm, then find the radius of the circle.

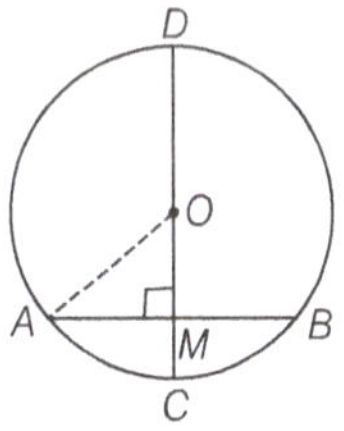

14. Prove that the diameter of a circle, which bisects a chord of the circle, also bisects the angle subtended by the chord at the centre of the circle.

15. If two equal chords of a circle intersect within the circle, then prove that the line joining the point of intersection to the centre makes equal angles with the chords.

16. OD is perpendicular on chord AB of the circle with centre O. If BC is a diameter, then prove that $CA = 2OD$.

17. In the given figure, O and O' are the centres of circles of radii 20 cm and 37 cm. If $AB = 24$ cm, then find the distance OO'.

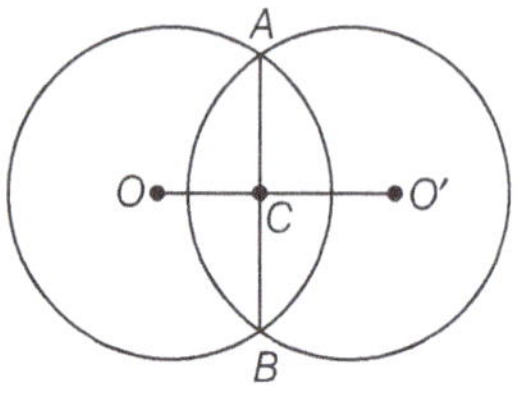

18. In the given figure, lengths of two parallel chords of a circle are 6 cm and 8 cm. If the smaller chord is at a distance of 4 cm from the centre, then what is the distance of the other chord from the centre?

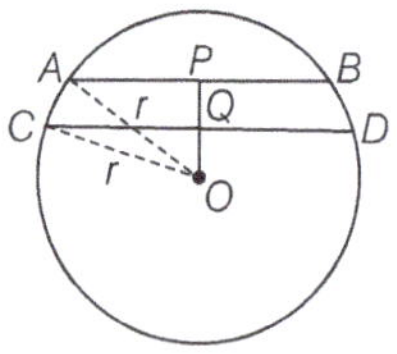

19. If two chords of a circle with a common end point are inclined equally to the diameter through this common end point, then prove that the chords are equal.

C. 4/5 Marks Questions

20. Prove that the circle drawn with any side of a rhombus as diameter, passes through the point of intersection of its diagonals.

21. Two parallel chords of a circle, whose diameter is 13 cm, are 5 cm and 12 cm, respectively. Find the distance between them, if they lie on opposite sides of the centre.

22. Prove that there is one and only one circle that passes through three given points not in a straight line.

23. If two equal chords of a circle intersect within the circle, then prove that the segments of one chord are equal to the corresponding segments of the other chord.

24. Two chords AB and AC of a circle with centre O are equal. Prove that centre of the circle lies on the bisector of $\angle BAC$.

25. In the given figure, O is the centre of a circle, AB is a side of regular octagon and AC is a side of regular hexagon.

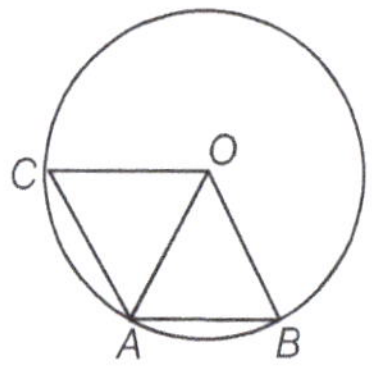

Find

(i) $\angle AOB$

(ii) $\angle AOC$

(iii) $\angle BOC$

Hints and Answers

Exercise 13.1

1. **Hint** Use Theorem 1.

Ans. $\angle OPM = \angle OPN = 90°$

2. **Hint** Use Theorem 2 [converse of theorem 1]

Ans. $AP = PB = 4$ cm

3. **Hint** Draw $OP \perp BC$. Then, $BP = PC$ and $AP = PD$

$\Rightarrow AP - BP = PD - PC \Rightarrow AB = CD$

Ans. $AB = CD = 2$ cm

4. Do same as Example 1.

Ans. 24 cm

5. Do same as Example 2. **Ans.** 4 cm

6. Use Theorem 2 [converse of theorem 1]

Ans. 5 cm

7. **Hint** Let AB and CD be two parallel chords having P and Q as their mid-points, respectively. Let O be the centre of the circle.

Then, $OP \perp AB$

But $OX \parallel AB$

$\therefore$ $\angle POX = \angle APO$ [alternate interior angles]

$\Rightarrow$ $\angle POX = 90°$

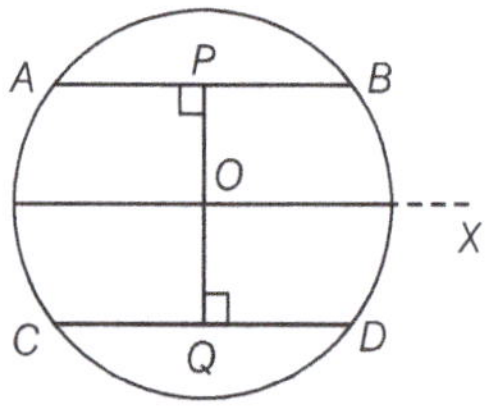

Similarly, Q is the mid-point of CD.

$\therefore$ $OQ \perp CD$

But $OX \parallel CD$

$\therefore$ $\angle XOQ = \angle CQO = 90°$ [alternate interior angles]

Now, $\angle POX + \angle XOQ = 90° + 90° = 180°$

8. **Hint** Since, $AO'^2 + AO^2 = 3^2 + 4^2$

$= 9 + 16 = 25 = OO'^2$

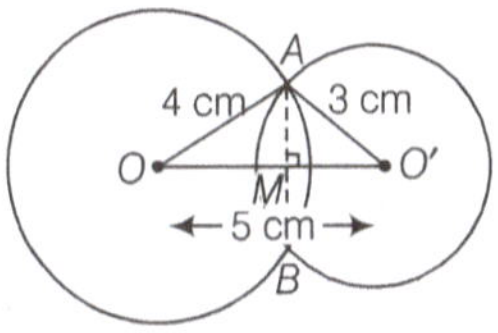

$\Rightarrow OO'A$ is a right angled triangle, right angled at A.

$\therefore \quad ar(\Delta OO'A) = \frac{1}{2} \times O'A \times OA$

$= \frac{1}{2} \times 3 \times 4 = 6\ cm^2 \quad \ldots(i)$

Now, $ar(\Delta OO'A) = \frac{1}{2} \times OO' \times AM$

$= \frac{1}{2} \times 5 \times AM = \frac{5}{2} AM \quad \ldots(ii)$

From Eqs. (i) and (ii), we get $AM = 2.4$ cm

Ans. 4.8 cm

9. **Hint** Since, equal chords of a circle are at equidistant from the centre.

Ans. 3 cm

10. Do same as Example 6. **Ans.** 18 cm

11. **Hint** Since, two chords are equal, so it is equidistant from the centre.

$\therefore \Delta OMN$ is isosceles.

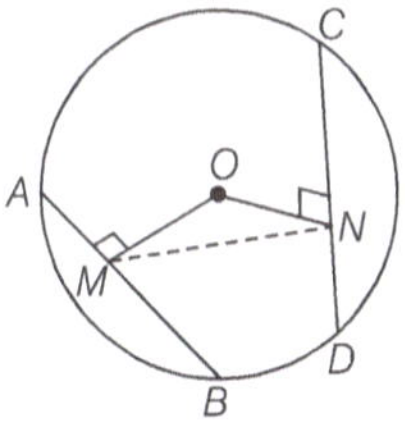

$\therefore \quad OM = ON \Rightarrow \angle ONM = \angle OMN$

12. **Hint** Given, AB and AC are two equal chords, whose centre is O.

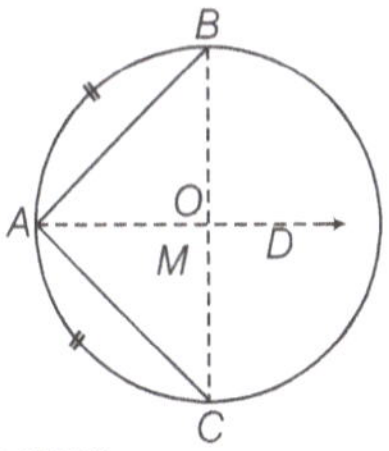

In ΔBAM and ΔCAM,

$AB = AC$ [given]

$\angle BAM = \angle CAM$ [given]

and $AM = AM$ [common side]

$\therefore \Delta BAM \cong \Delta CAM$ [by SAS congruence rule]

$\Rightarrow BM = CM$

and $\angle BMA = \angle CMA$ [by CPCT]

$\angle BMA = \angle CMA = 90°$ [$\because CB$ is a straight line]

Thus, AM is the perpendicular bisector of BC.

13. **Hint** Use Theorem 2.

Let $AC = 2x \Rightarrow AB = 4x$

$AM = \frac{1}{2} AB = \frac{1}{2} \times 4x = 2x$

$AN = \frac{1}{2} AC = \frac{1}{2} \times 2x = x$

14. **Hint** Use Theorem 1. and distance formula to find length CP.

$CP = 5$ units and $AP = 12$ units

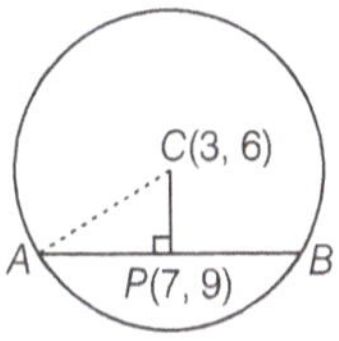

$\therefore$ The length of chord $AB = 24$ units

Ans. 24 units

15. **Hint** Use Theorem 2.

Draw $OM \perp AP$ and $ON' \perp PB$.

$OM \perp AP \Rightarrow PM = \frac{1}{2} AP$

and $O'N \perp PB \Rightarrow PN = \frac{1}{2} BP$

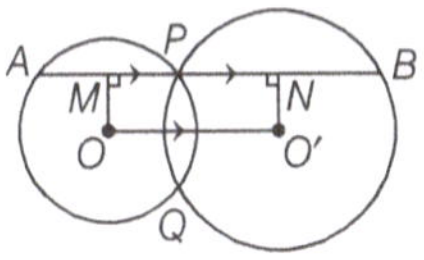

16. **Hint** Use Theorem 2.

Draw $OM \perp AB$, $ON \perp CD$ and join OP.

$AM = BM = \frac{1}{2} AB$

and $CN = DN = \frac{1}{2} CD$

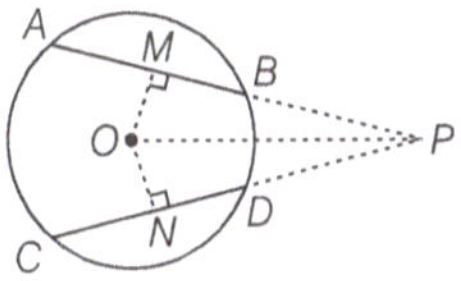

Exercise 13.2

1. Use Theorem 6.
2. Use Theorem 6.
3. (i) **Hint** $\widehat{AB} : \widehat{BC} = 3 : 2$

$\Rightarrow \quad AB = 3x$ and $BC = 2x$

Since, length $3x$ makes an angle 96°.

$\therefore$ Length x makes an angle 32°.

Hence, length $2x$ makes an angle 64°.

Ans. 64°

(ii) **Hint** Use the properties, angles opposite to equal sides of a triangle are equal and the sum of angles of a triangle is 180°.

Ans. 100°

4. **Hint** Since, $OA = OB \Rightarrow \angle OBA = \angle OAB = 55°$

$\therefore \angle AOB = 180° - (55° + 55°) = 70°$

Now, use Theorem 9. **Ans.** 70°

5. (i) **Hint** It is clear that from the figure

$\angle OAB \neq \angle OAC$

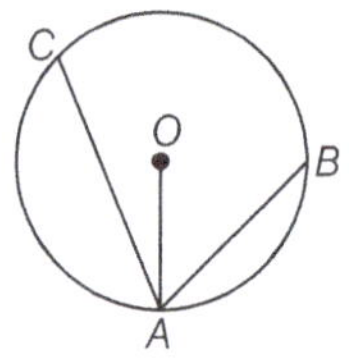

Ans. False

(ii) **Hint** Use Theorem 9.

Ans. True

6. **Hint** Since, equal chords subtends equal angles.

$\therefore \quad \angle COD = \angle DOE = \angle EOF = \angle FOG = 40°$

Ans. Reflex $\angle COG = 360° - (4 \times 40°) = 200°$

7. **Hint** Clearly, $\angle AOC = \angle BOC$ [$\because AC = BC$]

Now, in ΔOMA and ΔOMB, we have

$OA = OB$ [radii of circle]

$\angle AOC = \angle BOC$ [proved above]

and $OM = OM$ [common side]

$\Rightarrow \Delta OMA \cong \Delta OMB$ [by SAS congruence rule]

$\Rightarrow AM = BM$ [by CPCT]

Ans. 1 : 1

8. **Hint** We know that equal chords subtends equal angles.

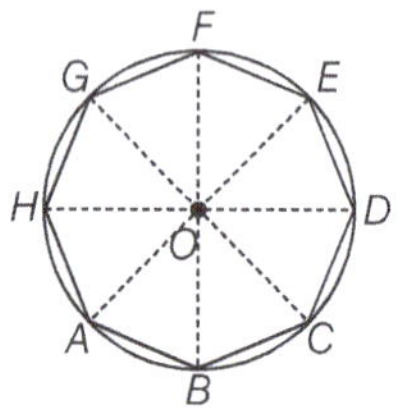

$\because \quad AB = BC = CD = DE = EF$

$= FG = GH = HA$

$\Rightarrow \angle AOB = \angle BOC = \angle COD$

$= \angle DOE = \angle EOF$

$= \angle FOG = \angle GOH = \angle HOA$

[$\because$ equal chords of a circle subtend equal angles at the centre of circle]

$\therefore \quad 8 \times \angle AOB = 360°$

$\Rightarrow \angle AOB = 45°$

Ans. $\angle AOB = 45°$, $\angle AOC = 90°$, $\angle DOF = 90°$ and $\angle EOH = 135°$

9. **Hint** Here, $OA = OB$ [radii of same circle]

$\Rightarrow \quad \angle OBA = \angle OAB = 30°$

[$\because$ angles opposite to equal sides are equal]

Similarly, $\angle OBC = 57°$

Now, in ΔBOC, $\angle BOC + \angle OCB + \angle OBC = 180°$

[by angle sum property of a triangle]

$\Rightarrow \quad \angle BOC = 66°$

In ΔAOB, $\angle AOB + \angle OAB + \angle OBA = 180°$

$\Rightarrow \quad \angle AOB = 120°$

Now, $\angle AOC = \angle AOB - \angle BOC$

Ans. 66°, 54°

10. **Hint** Let AXB and CYD be arcs of circle, whose centre and radius are O and r units, respectively.

So, $\quad OA = OB = OC = OD = r$ ...(i)

$\because$ arc $AXB \cong$ arc CYD

$\therefore \quad \angle AOB = \angle COD$ ...(ii)

[$\because$ equal arcs of a circle subtends equal angles at the centre]

In ΔAOB and ΔCOD,

$AO = CO$ [from Eq. (i)]

$BO = DO$ [from Eq. (i)]

and $\angle AOB = \angle COD$ [from Eq. (ii)]

$\therefore \quad \Delta AOB \cong \Delta COD$ [by SAS congruence rule]

$\Rightarrow \quad AB = CD$ [by CPCT]

Ans. 1 : 1

11. **Hint** arc $AXB = \frac{1}{2}$ arc BYC

$\Rightarrow \quad \angle AOB = \frac{1}{2} \angle BOC$

Ans. 120°

12. **Hint** $\angle AOB = \angle COD$,

$\Delta AOC \cong \Delta BOD$

Use Theorem 9.

Chapter Test

1. (b)
2. (d)
3. (b)
4. (a)
5. (d)
6. Centre
7. Centre
8. Inside or interior
9. Segment
10. Sector
11. Do same as Example 1.

    Ans. 17.32 cm or $10\sqrt{3}$ cm
12. Do same as Example 2.

    Ans. 3 cm
13. **Hint** $\because CD \perp AB \Rightarrow OM \perp AB$

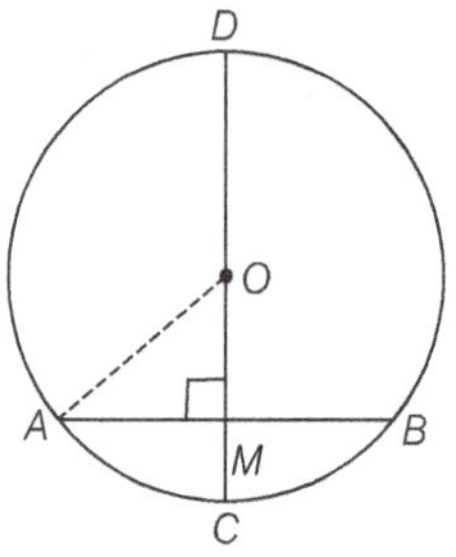

$\therefore\ AM = \frac{1}{2} AB = \frac{1}{2} \times 8 = 4$ cm

In ΔOAM, $OA^2 = AM^2 + OM^2$ [by Pythagoras Theorem]

$\Rightarrow\ r^2 = 4^2 + (r-2)^2$

Ans. $r = 5$ cm

14. Do same as Theorem 1.

15. Do same as Theorem 3.

Hint

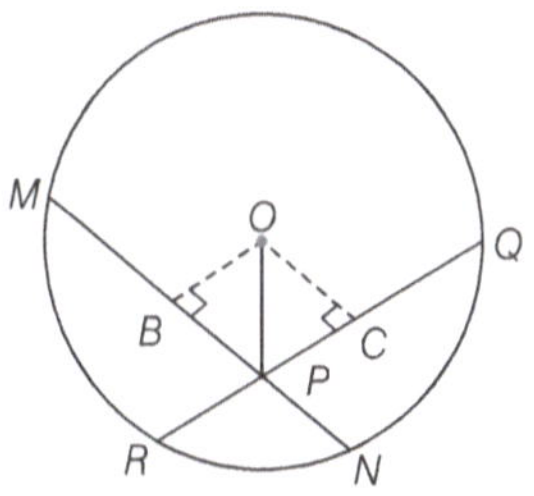

$\angle OPC = \angle OPB$

16. **Hint** $AD = BD$

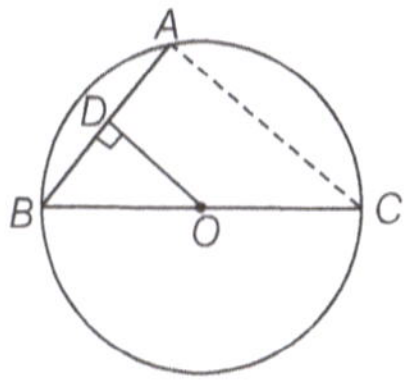

In ΔBAC, O and D are the mid-points of BC and BA.

$\therefore\ OD = \frac{1}{2} AC$

17. Do same as Example 5. **Ans.** 51 cm

18. Do same as Example 6.
Ans. 3 cm

19. Do same as Example 7..

20. **Hint Let** N, M be mid-points of PQ and SR, respectively.
Also, let E and F be mid-points of PS and QR, respectively.

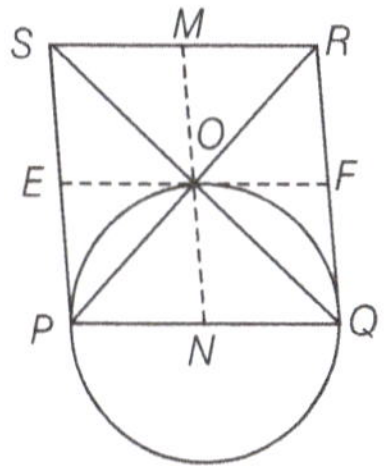

Here, $PQ = SR$

$\Rightarrow\ \frac{1}{2} PQ = \frac{1}{2} SR$

$\Rightarrow\ PN = NQ = SM = MR$

Similarly, $PE = SE = ON$

So, $PN = ON = NQ$

Therefore, a circle drawn with N as centre and radius PN passes through P, O and Q.

21. **Hint** In ΔOBC, $OB = \sqrt{(6.5)^2 - (2.5)^2} = \sqrt{36} = 6$ cm

In ΔOEF, $OE = \sqrt{(6.5)^2 - (6)^2} = \sqrt{6.25} = 2.5$ cm

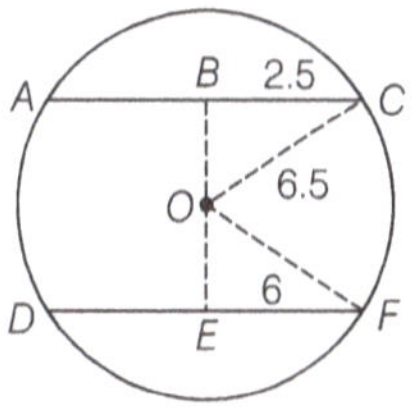

Ans. 8.5 cm

22. **Hint** Use Theorem 5.

23. **Hint**

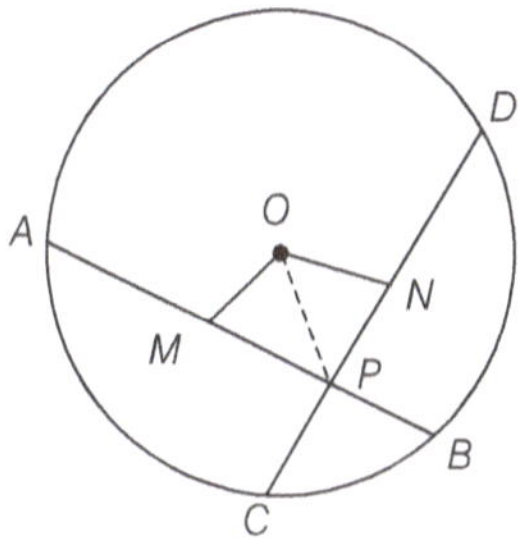

In ΔOMP and ΔONP,

$OM = ON$ [equal chords of a circle are equidistant from the centre]

$\angle OMP = \angle ONP = 90°$

$OP = OP$

$\therefore\ \Delta OMP \cong \Delta ONP$ [by RHS congruency rule]

$\Rightarrow\ MP = PN$ [by CPCT]

Also, $AM = ND = \frac{1}{2} CD$

$\Rightarrow\ AM + MP = PN + ND$

$\Rightarrow\ AP = PD$

Also, $MB - MP = CN - PN$

$\Rightarrow\ PB = CP$

Then, prove $PB = CP$

24. **Hint** Use Theorem 1.

25. **Hint**

(i) Since, AB is a side of a regular octagon

$\angle AOB = \frac{360°}{8} = 45°$

(ii) Since, AC is a side of regular hexagon

$\angle AOC = \frac{360°}{6} = 60°$

(iii) $\angle BOC = \angle AOB + \angle AOC$
$= 45° + 60°$
$= 105°$

Ans. (i) 45° (ii) 60° (iii) 105°

Olympiad Section

Brain Teasing Questions of Olympiad Pattern

1 In the adjoining figure, AB is a chord of a circle with centre O and BOC is a diameter. If $OD \perp AB$ such that $OD = 11$ cm, then AC is equal to

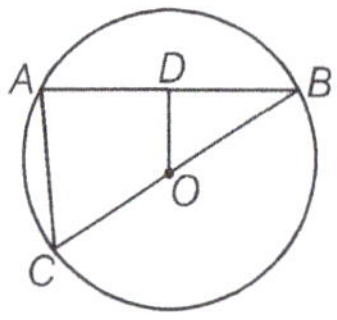

(a) 22 cm (b) 20 cm
(c) 15 cm (d) 18 cm

2 An equilateral triangle of side 12 cm is inscribed in a circle, then the radius of the circle is

(a) $5\sqrt{3}$ cm (b) $3\sqrt{3}$ cm (c) $2\sqrt{3}$ cm (d) $4\sqrt{3}$ cm

3 If AOB is a diameter of a circle with centre O such that $AB = 50$ cm and CD is a chord of length 48 cm, then distance of CD from AB is

(a) 7 cm (b) 8 cm (c) 5 cm (d) 9 cm

4 In a circle of radius 5 cm, AB and AC are two chords such that $AB = AC = 6$ cm. Find the length of the chord BC.

(a) 9.6 cm (b) 9.5 cm
(c) 9.4 cm (d) None of these

5 If two circles intersect in two points, then the line through their centres to the bisector of common chord is

(a) parallel
(b) perpendicular
(c) Neither parallel nor perpendicular
(d) None of the above

6 ABC is an equilateral triangle. A circle is drawn with centre A, so that it cuts AB and AC at points M and N respectively. Which of the option is correct?

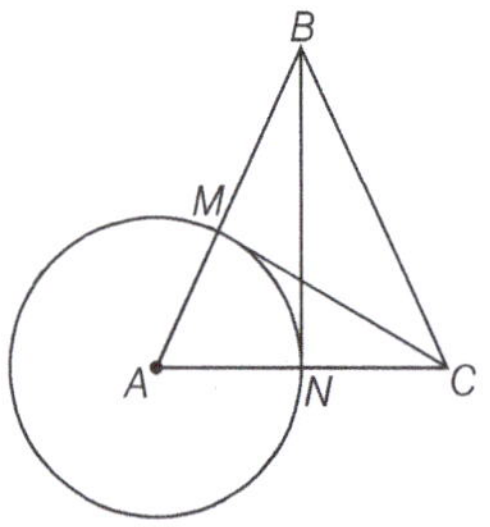

(a) $BN = CM$ (b) $BN = BM$
(c) $BC = CN$ (d) None of these

7 In the given figure, $OPQR$ is a square. A circle drawn with centre O and cut the square at X and Y. Then, what will be the relation between QX and QY?

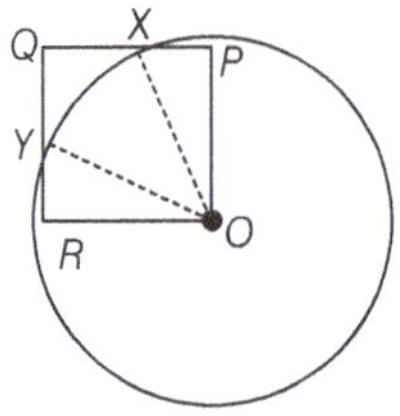

(a) $QX = 2QY$ (b) $QX = QY$
(c) $QX = 3QY$ (d) $QY = \frac{1}{3}QY$

8 A crescent is formed by two circular arcs ACB and ADB of equal radius with centres E and F in the given figure. The perpendicular bisector of AB cuts the crescent at C and D, where $CD = 12$ cm and $AB = 16$ cm. Then, what will be the value of the radius of the arcs?

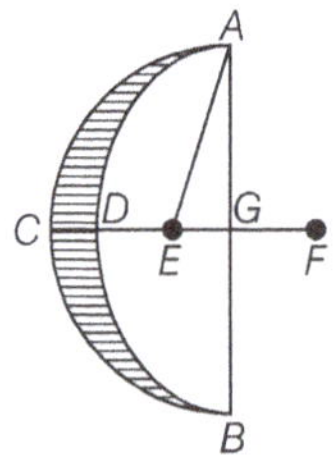

(a) 8 cm (b) 12 cm (c) 10 cm (d) 14 cm

9 Two congruent circles intersect each other at points A and B. Through A, any line segment PAQ is drawn, so that P and Q lie on the two circles. Then,

(a) $BP = BQ$ (b) $BP \neq BQ$
(c) $BP = AB$ (d) None of these

10 Two chords AB and CD of lengths 5 cm and 11 cm, respectively of a circle are parallel to each other and are on opposite sides of its centre. If the distance between AB and CD is 6 cm, then find the radius of the circle.

(a) 6.4 cm (b) 5.6 cm
(c) 5.9 cm (d) None of these

Answers

1. (a) **2.** (d) **3.** (a) **4.** (a) **5.** (b) **6.** (a) **7.** (b) **8.** (c) **9.** (a) **10.** (b)

* *These questions may or may not be asked in the examination, have been given just for additional practice required for olympiads Scholarship Exams etc. For detailed explanations refer Page No. 347.*

CHAPTER

14

Statistics

SYLLABUS

• Introduction, collection of data, presentation of data, Graphical representation of data, Mean, Median of ungrouped data. (i) Understanding and recognition of raw, arrayed and grouped data. (ii) Tabulation of raw data using tally-marks. (iii) Understanding and recognition of discrete and continuous variables. (iv) Mean, median of ungrouped data. (v) Class intervals, class boundaries and limits, frequency, frequency table, class size for grouped data. (vi) Grouped frequency distributions : the need to and how to convert discontinuous intervals to continuous intervals. (vii) Drawing a frequency polygon.

Statistics is a Science which deals with the collection, presentation, analysis and interpretation of numerical data. The word 'Statistics' is derived from the Latin word '*Status*' which means a political state.

Collection and Presentation of Data

Data

The word 'data' means the information, which are collected for a definite purpose.

Primary Data The data collected by the investigator himself for a definite plan or purpose.

Secondary Data The data which are not collected directly but obtained from some other sources (published or unpublished).

Raw (or Ungrouped) **Data** The data obtained in original form.

Grouped Data We may condense data into classes or groups.

Important Terms Related to Statistics

Variable A quantity which is being measured in collection of data.

(i) **Continuous Variable** A variable which can take any numerical values between two given values.

(ii) **Discontinuous** (or Discrete) **Variable** A variable which cannot take all possible numerical values between two given values.

Variate A particular value of a variable is called variate (observation).

Range The difference between the maximum and minimum values of a variable is called its range.

Tabulation Representation of data in the table form is called tabulation of the given data.

e.g.

Class IX	Boys	Girls	Total
Section A	3	2	5
Section B	1	3	4
Section C	4	2	6
Total	8	7	15

Frequency The frequency is the number which indicates how many times a variate appear in the given set of data.

Frequency Distribution A tabular arrangement of given numerical data showing the frequency of different variates and the table itself is called frequency distribution table.

Presentation of Data

Data Presented in Ascending or Descending Order

Consider the marks obtained by 10 students in a Mathematics test

55, 36, 95, 73, 60, 42, 25, 78, 75, 62

Now, arrange this raw data in ascending order as

25, 36, 42, 55, 60, 62, 73, 75, 78, 95

The raw data arranged in ascending or descending order is called the **arrayed data**.

Data Presented in the Form of Ungrouped Frequency Distribution

Example 1. Consider the marks obtained (out of 100 marks) by 30 students of Class IX of a school

10 20 36 92 95 40 50 56 60 70
92 88 80 70 72 70 36 40 36 40
92 40 50 50 56 60 70 60 60 88

Represent this data in the form of a frequency distribution table.

Sol. Required frequency distribution table is

Marks	Number of students (Frequency)
10	1
20	1
36	3
40	4
50	3
56	2
60	4
70	4
72	1
80	1
88	2
92	3
95	1
Total	30

Data Presented by using Tally Marks

To represent data using tally marks, we use following steps

Step I We take each observation from the data, one at a time and represent the frequency by small line or stroke called tally marks.

Step II We write tally marks in bunches of five lines, the fifth one crossing the four vertical lines diagonally.

e.g. 5 represented as 卌 and

7 represented as 卌 ||.

Step III In table, sum of all frequencies is equal to the total number of observations in the given data.

Example 2. Three coins tossed 30 times. Each time the number of heads occurring was noted down as follows

0, 1, 2, 2, 1, 2, 3, 1, 3, 0, 1, 3, 3, 0, 1
0, 1, 1, 2, 1, 2, 2, 0, 3, 1, 2, 2, 2, 1, 0

Construct a frequency distribution table by using tally marks.

Sol. The frequency distribution table, by using tally marks, is

Number of heads	Tally marks	Frequency
0	卌 I	6
1	卌 卌	10
2	卌 IIII	9
3	卌	5
Total		30

Data Presented in the Form of Grouped Frequency Distribution

When a data has a large number of values (entries) as $x_1, x_2, \ldots, x_n$ and most of them are distinct, it becomes inconvenient to present this data in the form of ungrouped frequency distribution. These groupings are called **classes** or **class intervals**. In each classes, the least number is called the **lower class limit**, the greatest number is called the **upper class limit** class width/class size = upper limit – lower limit, the number mid-way between the lower and upper limit is called **class mark**.

$$\text{Class mark} = \frac{\text{Lower limit} + \text{Upper limit}}{2}$$

e.g. Class mark of 10–20 is $\frac{10+20}{2} = 15$

The number of entries of the data having their values lying in a class is defined as the **frequency** of the class. The table in which the corresponding frequencies are written against each class, is called grouped frequency distribution of given data.

1. **Exclusive form** (Continuous form) A frequency distribution in which upper limit of each class is excluded and lower limit is included, the class units are called true or actual class limits or class boundaries.
2. **Inclusive form** (Discontinuous form or discrete form) A frequency distribution in which upper limit as well as lower limit are included.

Example 3. Consider the marks obtained by 20 students out of 50 marks of Class IX of a school in a test

42, 40, 41, 6, 8, 30, 34, 37, 14, 12,
47, 43, 49, 21, 23, 4, 10, 17, 35, 36

Present this data as a grouped data

(i) in exclusive form (ii) in inclusive form

Sol. We can classify the given data into group as given below

(i) **In exclusive form**

Marks (Class interval)	Tally marks	Number of students (Frequency)
0-10	|||	3
10-20	||||	4
20-30	||	2
30-40	卌	5
40-50	卌 |	6

(ii) **In inclusive form**

Marks (Class interval)	Number of students (Frequency)
0-10	4
11-20	3
21-30	3
31-40	5
41-50	5

Converting Discrete Distribution to Continuous Distribution

To convert discrete classes into continuous classes, we required some adjustment, which is called adjustment factor.

Adjustment factor

$$=\frac{\text{Lower limit of one class} - \text{Upper limit of previous class}}{2}$$

Subtract the adjustment factor from all the lower limits and add the adjustment factor to all the upper limits.

Example 4. Make following the continuous frequency distribution table.

Class interval	Frequency
25-34	2
35-44	7
45-54	8
55-64	6
65-74	2
75-84	5

Sol. We know that, Adjustment factor

$$=\frac{\text{Lower limit of one class} - \text{Upper limit of previous class}}{2}$$

$$=\frac{35-34}{2}=0.5$$

So, continuous frequency distribution table is as follows

Classes before adjustment	Classes after adjustment	Frequency
25-34	24.5-34.5	2
35-44	34.5-44.5	7
45-54	44.5-54.5	8
55-64	54.5-64.5	6
65-74	64.5-74.5	2
75-84	74.5-84.5	5

Example 5. The heights of 50 students, measured to the nearest centimetres have been found to be as follows

161, 150, 154, 165, 168, 161, 154, 162, 150, 151,
162, 164, 171, 165, 158, 154, 156, 172, 160, 170,
153, 159, 161, 170, 162, 165, 166, 168, 165, 164,
154, 152, 153, 156, 158, 162, 160, 161, 173, 166,
161, 159, 162, 167, 168, 159, 158, 153, 154, 159

(i) Represent the data given above by a grouped frequency distribution table, taking class intervals as 160-165, 165-170 etc., using tally marks.

(ii) What can you conclude about their heights from the table?

Sol.

(i) We condense the given data into groups, like 150-155, 155-160, ..., 170-175. The class width in this case is 5.

Heights (in cm)	Tally marks	Frequency
150-155	卌 卌 ||	12
155-160	卌 ||||	9
160-165	卌 卌 ||||	14
165-170	卌 卌	10
170-175	卌	5
Total		50

(ii) From the table, our conclusion is that more than 50% of students (i.e. $12+9+14=35$) are shorter than 165 cm height.

Cumulative Frequency

The sum of frequency of all the previous classes and that particular class is called the cumulative frequency of the class.

Example 6. The marks of 200 students in a test were recorded as follows :

Marks %	10-19	20-29	30-39	40-49	50-59
Number of Students	7	11	20	46	57

Draw the cumulative frequency table.

Sol.

Marks %	Tally	Number of Students Frequency	Cumulative Frequency
10-19	卌 II	7	7
20-29	卌 卌 I	11	18 (7 + 11)
30-39	卌 卌 卌 卌	20	38 (18 + 20)
40-49	卌 卌 卌 卌 卌 卌 卌 卌 卌 I	46	84 (38 + 46)
50-59	卌 卌 卌 卌 卌 卌 卌 卌 卌 卌 卌 II	57	141 (84 + 57)

Exercise 14.1

1. Find the lower limit, upper limit, class size and class mark of the class 70-80.

2. Solve the following.
   (i) In a grouped frequency distribution, the class intervals are 1-10, 11-20, 21-30,… . Find the class width.
   (ii) A data is such that, its minimum value is 86 and range is 32. What is its maximum value?
   (iii) In a grouped frequency distribution, the class intervals are 0-10, 10-20 and 20-30. In which class 20 is considered?

3. The weights (in kg) of 25 students are given as follows
   35, 38, 36, 37, 38, 35, 37, 36, 35, 38, 36, 36, 37, 37, 35, 38, 36, 35, 36, 37, 37, 38, 36, 38, 37.
   Complete the following frequency table.

Weight	35	36	37	38
Frequency	–	–	–	–

4. The sale of shirt of various size at a shop, on a particular day is given below
   30, 32, 34, 30, 32, 34, 28, 30, 32, 34,
   34, 32, 30, 28, 28, 30, 32, 30, 32, 32
   Make a frequency table for the given data.

5. The blood groups of 30 students of class VIII are recorded as follows
   A, B, O, O, AB, O, A, O, B, A, O, B, A, O, O
   A, AB, O, A, A, O, O, AB, B, A, O, B, A, B, O
   Represent this data in the form of a frequency distribution table. Find out which is the most common and which is the rarest blood group among these students?

6. Thirty girls, each of them 16 yr old, were tested to find their pulse rate. The following data is collected
   55, 72, 70, 66, 74, 70, 74, 53, 57, 62, 68, 75, 79, 68, 63, 59, 54, 51, 61, 58, 71, 66, 78, 73, 59, 52, 66, 60, 72, 56
   Using class intervals 51-55, 56-60 of equal width, prepare the frequency table. Here, the upper and lower limit of the classes are both inclusive.

7. Given below are the marks obtained by 30 students in Mathematics exam
   2, 7, 11, 13, 10, 18, 20, 23, 17, 18, 16,
   11, 13, 18, 24, 25, 27, 30, 31, 36, 37,
   8, 11, 13, 16, 15, 18, 27, 20, 3
   Arrange the data in increasing order and present the same as a grouped data in
   (i) discontinuous interval form, taking class intervals as 1-5, 6-10, 11-15, etc.
   (ii) continuous interval form, taking class interval as 1-5, 5-9, 9-13, etc.

8. Make a distribution with class width 5 in discrete form from the following data
   30, 25, 27, 28, 20, 22, 18, 19, 14, 10, 32, 34, 36, 37, 38, 39, 40, 35, 36, 37, 16, 17, 18, 24, 23, 26, 12, 13, 37, 18, 11, 21, 33, 20, 16

9. The weight in grams of 50 oranges picked at random from a consignment are as follows

131, 113, 82, 75, 204, 81, 84, 118, 104, 110, 80, 107, 111, 141, 136, 123, 90, 78, 90, 115, 110, 98, 106, 99, 107, 84, 76, 186, 82, 100, 109, 128, 115, 107, 115, 119, 93, 187, 139, 129, 130, 68, 195, 123, 125, 111, 92, 86, 70, 126

Form the grouped frequency table by dividing the variable range into intervals of equal width, each corresponding to 20 gm in such a way that the mid-value of the first class corresponds to 70 gm.

10. Convert the following frequency distribution from discontinuous to continuous form.

Marks (Class interval)	**Frequency**
1-10	11
11-20	8
21-30	7
31-40	8
41-50	9
51-60	12

11. Find the value of x, y, z, P, Q and R.

Class internal	Frequency	Cumulative frequency
25-34	x	15
35-44	y	28
45-54	21	z
55-64	16	P
65-74	Q	73
75-84	12	R

Mean and Median of Ungrouped Data

Mean or Arithmetic Mean

The average of a given set of numbers, is called the arithmetic mean or the mean and denoted by $\bar{x}$.

$\therefore$ Mean, $\bar{x} = \dfrac{\text{Sum of all observations}}{\text{Number of observations}}$

Thus, the mean of n observations $x_1, x_2, x_3, \ldots, x_n$ is given by

$$\bar{x} = \frac{(x_1 + x_2 + \ldots + x_n)}{n} = \frac{\sum_{i=1}^{n} x_i}{n} = \frac{\sum x}{n}$$

Property 1 If $\bar{x}$ is the mean of n number of observations $x_1, x_2, x_3 \ldots x_n$, then the sum of deviations of $\bar{x}$ from the observation $x_1, x_2, x_3 \ldots x_n$ is zero i.e. $\Sigma(x - \bar{x}) = 0$.

Property 2 If $\bar{x}$ is the mean of n number of observations $x_1, x_2, x_3 \ldots x_n$, then the mean of observations $x_1 + a, x_2 + a, x_3 + a \ldots x_n + a$ is $\bar{x} + a$ i.e. If each observation under consideration is increased by quantity a, then their mean is also increased by the same quantity a.

Property 3 If $\bar{x}$ is the mean of n number of observations $x_1, x_2, x_3 \ldots x_n$, then the mean of observations $x_1 - a, x_2 - a, x_3 - a \ldots x_n - a$ is $\bar{x} - a$. i.e. If each observation under consideration is decreased by quanitity a, then their mean is also decreased by the same quantity a.

Property 4 If $\bar{x}$ is the mean of n number of observations $x_1, x_2, x_3 \ldots x_n$, then mean of $ax_1, ax_2, ax_3 \ldots ax_n$ is $a\bar{x}$. i.e. If each observation under consideration is multiplied by quantity a, then mean is also multiplied by the same quantity a.

Property 5 If $\bar{x}$ is the mean of n number of observations $x_1, x_2, x_3 \ldots x_n$, then mean of $\frac{x_1}{a}, \frac{x_2}{a}, \frac{x_3}{a} \ldots \frac{x_n}{a}$ is $\frac{\bar{x}}{a}$.

i.e. If each observation under consideration is divided by quantity a, the mean is also divided by the same quantity a.

Example 7. If following are the marks obtained by 5 students of a class, then find their mean.

10, 5, 20, 25, 15

Sol. Mean, $\bar{x} = \dfrac{\Sigma x}{n} = \dfrac{10 + 5 + 20 + 25 + 15}{5} = \dfrac{75}{5} = 15$

Example 8. The mean of 18, 24, 15, $2x + 1$ and 12 is 25. Find the value of x.

Sol. We have, number of observations, $n = 5$ and mean $= 25$

$\therefore$ Mean $= \frac{1}{5}(18 + 24 + 15 + 2x + 1 + 12)$

$\left[\because \text{mean} = \dfrac{\text{sum of observations}}{\text{number of observations}}\right]$

$\Rightarrow$ $25 = \frac{1}{5}(70 + 2x)$

$\Rightarrow$ $125 = 70 + 2x$

$\Rightarrow$ $2x = 55$

$\Rightarrow$ $x = \frac{55}{2} = 27.5$

Example 9. The mean of 24 numbers is 12. If 2 is added to every number, what will be the new mean?

Sol. Let the given numbers be $x_1, x_2, \dots, x_{24}$.

$\therefore$ Mean $= \dfrac{x_1 + x_2 + \dots + x_{24}}{24}$

According to the question,

$$\frac{x_1 + x_2 + \dots + x_{24}}{24} = 12$$

$\Rightarrow \quad x_1 + x_2 + \dots + x_{24} = 288 \quad \dots(i)$

$\because$ 2 is added to every number.

$\therefore$ New numbers are $(x_1 + 2), (x_2 + 2), \dots, (x_{24} + 2)$.

Mean of the new numbers

$$= \frac{(x_1 + 2) + (x_2 + 2) + \dots + (x_{24} + 2)}{24}$$

$$= \frac{(x_1 + x_2 + \dots + x_{24}) + 48}{24}$$

$$= \frac{288 + 48}{24} \quad \text{[from Eq. (i)]}$$

$$= \frac{336}{24} = 14$$

Hence, the new mean is 14.

Example 10. The mean of 16 numbers is 50. If 5 is subtracted from each number, what will be the new mean?

Sol. Let the given numbers be $x_1, x_2, \dots, x_{16}$.

$\therefore$ Mean $= \dfrac{x_1 + x_2 + \dots + x_{16}}{16}$

According to the question,

$$\frac{x_1 + x_2 + \dots + x_{16}}{16} = 50$$

$\Rightarrow \quad x_1 + x_2 + \dots + x_{16} = 50 \times 16 = 800$

5 is subtracted from each number. Then, the new numbers are $(x_1 - 5), (x_2 - 5), \dots, (x_{16} - 5)$.

Mean of the new numbers

$$= \frac{(x_1 - 5) + (x_2 - 5) + \dots + (x_{16} - 5)}{16}$$

$$= \frac{(x_1 + x_2 + \dots + x_{16}) - 80}{16} = \frac{800 - 80}{16} = \frac{720}{16} = 45$$

Hence, the new mean is 45.

Mean of Ungrouped Frequency Distribution

If $x_1, x_2, \dots, x_n$ are n observations whose corresponding frequencies are $f_1, f_2, \dots, f_n$, then mean is given by

$$\bar{x} = \frac{x_1 f_1 + x_2 f_2 + \dots + x_n f_n}{f_1 + f_2 + \dots + f_n}$$

$$= \frac{\sum_{i=1}^{n} f_i x_i}{\sum_{i=1}^{n} f_i}$$

Example 11. Find the mean of the following distribution.

Variable	5	6	7	8	9
Frequency	4	8	14	11	3

Sol. Mean $= \dfrac{\Sigma f_i x_i}{\Sigma f_i} = \dfrac{5 \times 4 + 6 \times 8 + 7 \times 14 + 8 \times 11 + 9 \times 3}{4 + 8 + 14 + 11 + 3}$

$$= \frac{20 + 48 + 98 + 88 + 27}{40} = \frac{281}{40} = 7.025$$

Example 12. If the mean of the following data is 18.75, then find the value of p.

x_i	10	15	p	25	30
f_i	5	10	7	8	2

Sol. The product of observation and frequency is given in the table below

x_i	f_i	$f_i \times x_i$
10	5	50
15	10	150
p	7	$7p$
25	8	200
30	2	60
Total	$\Sigma f_i = 32$	$\Sigma f_i x_i = (460 + 7p)$

Now, mean $= \dfrac{\Sigma f_i x_i}{\Sigma f_i} = \dfrac{460 + 7p}{32}$

Also, mean = 18.75 [given]

$\Rightarrow \quad \dfrac{460 + 7p}{32} = 18.75$

$\Rightarrow \quad 460 + 7p = 18.75 \times 32$

$\Rightarrow \quad 460 + 7p = 600$

$\Rightarrow \quad 7p = 140$

$\therefore \quad p = 20$

Median

The value of the middle most observation, is called the median of the data.

Median of Ungrouped Data

Suppose there are n observations, first arrange the given observations in ascending or descending order.

(i) If n is odd, then

Median = Value of $\left(\dfrac{n+1}{2}\right)$th observation

(ii) If n is even, then

Median

$$= \frac{1}{2}\left[\text{Value of } \left(\frac{n}{2}\right)\text{th and } \left(\frac{n}{2} + 1\right)\text{th observations}\right]$$

Example 13. Find the median of the following observations.

15, 40, 25, 16, 28, 32, 36, 42, 16, 19, 28

Sol. On arranging the given data in ascending order, we get

15, 16, 16, 19, 25, 28, 28, 32, 36, 40, 42

Hence, the number of observations, $n = 11$, which is odd.

$\therefore$ Median = Value of $\left(\frac{n+1}{2}\right)$th term

= Value of $\left(\frac{11+1}{2}\right)$th term

= Value of $\left(\frac{12}{2}\right)$th term

= Value of 6th term = 28

Example 14. The percentage of marks obtained by students of a class in Mathematics are 65, 35, 37, 23, 0, 18, 82, 92, 72, 32, 10, 5. Find the median.

Sol. First, we write the given data in ascending order.

0, 5, 10, 18, 23, 32, 35, 37, 65, 72, 82, 92

Here, the number of observations is even, i.e. $n = 12$

$\therefore$ There are two middle terms $\frac{12}{2}$th and $\left(\frac{12}{2}+1\right)$th,

i.e. 6th and 7th terms.

So, the median is the mean of the values of the 6th and 7th terms.

$\therefore$ Median = $\frac{1}{2}$ [value of 6th observation + value of 7th observation]

$\therefore$ Median = $\frac{32+35}{2}$ [$\because$ 6th term = 32, 7th term = 35]

$= \frac{67}{2} = 33.5$

Example 15. The following observations have been arranged in ascending order. If the median of the data is 63, find the value of x.

29, 32, 48, 50, x, $x+2$, 72, 78, 84, 95

Sol. Given, number of observations $(n) = 10$, which is an even number.

$$\therefore \text{Median} = \frac{\left(\frac{n}{2}\right)\text{th observation} + \left(\frac{n}{2}+1\right)\text{th observation}}{2}$$

$$= \frac{\left(\frac{10}{2}\right)\text{th observation} + \left(\frac{10}{2}+1\right)\text{th observation}}{2}$$

$$= \frac{\text{5th observation} + \text{6th observation}}{2} = \frac{x+(x+2)}{2}$$

$= x + 1$

According to the question, Median = 63

$\therefore \quad x + 1 = 63 \Rightarrow x = 63 - 1 = 62$

Hence, the required value of x is 62.

Exercise 14.2

1. What is the mean of the data 48, 42, 39, 46, 51, 57, 59, 42, 43, 47?
2. If the weight of 10 students (in kg) are 15, 17, 18, 20, 19, 17, 22, 24, 18, 20, then find the average weight of 10 students?
3. If the mean of observations p, $p+2$, $p+4$, $p+6$ and $p+8$ is 11, then find
   (i) the value of p.
   (ii) the mean of first three observation.
4. Suppose the mean of 20 observations is 11. If 3 is added to every number, then find the new mean of 20 observations.
5. If 12 is the mean of 10 observations and 10 is added to each observation, then what is the new mean?
6. Obtain the mean of the following distribution.

Frequency (f_i)	4	8	14	11	3
Variable (x_i)	4	6	8	10	12

7. The traffic police recorded the speed (in km/h) of 10 motorists as 47, 53, 49, 60, 39, 42, 55, 57, 52, 48. Later on an error in recording instrument was found. Find the correct average speed of the motorists, if the instrument recorded 5 km/h less in each case.
8. The mean of 12 observations is 24. If each observation is divided by 3, then find the new mean.
9. The mean of a set of observations is a. If each observation is multiplied by b and each product is decreased by c, then find the mean of new set of observations.
10. The mean of five items of 15. If the mean of first three items is 14 and that of the last three is 17, then find the third item.
11. Let $\bar{x}$ is the mean of $x_1, x_2, x_3, \ldots, x_n$ and $\bar{y}$ the mean of $y_1, y_2, y_3, \ldots, y_n$. If $\bar{z}$ is the mean of $x_1, x_2, x_3, \ldots, x_n, y_1, y_2, y_3, \ldots y_n$, then find the value of $\bar{z}$.
12. Find the sum of the deviations of the data 5, 7, 9, 15 and 21 from their mean.
13. Find the mean of 8, 12, 16, 22, 10 and 4. Find the resulting mean, if each of the observations, given above be
   (i) increased by 25%
   (ii) decreased by 40%

14. The pass percentage in different subjects and the number of students who appeared in the subjects are given below.

Subjects	Number of Students	Pass Percentage
English	45	66
Hindi	40	95
Sanskrit	20	80
Mathematics	60	55
Science and Technology	55	70
Social Science	60	60

Find the arithmetic mean of pass percentage and the weighted arithmetic mean.

15. The sum of the deviations of a set of n values $x_1, x_2, x_3, \ldots, x_n$, measured from 50 is – 10 and the sum of deviations of the values from 46 is 70. Find the values of n and the mean.

16. The weight (in kg) of 7 students are given below

32.5, 36.4, 39.2, 41.3, 42.9, 37.2, 41.2

Then, find its median.

17. Find the median of the following data.

2.0025, 2.0205, – 2.206, –2.006

18. The data 32, 35, 54, 56, x, $x+2$, 78, 84, 90 and 100 are arranged in ascending order, if their median is 63, find the value of x.

19. Find the median of the following data.

19, 25, 59, 48, 35, 31, 30, 32, 51

If 25 is replaced by 52, then what will be the new median?

20. The median of following observations arranged in ascending order is 25. If observation is 11, 13, 15, 19, $x+4$, $x+2$, 30, 35, 39, 46, then find the value of x.

Graphical Representation of Data

Bar Graph

Bars of uniform width are drawn with equal spacing between them on one axis with various heights. The height of a bar represents the frequency of the corresponding observation on the other axis.

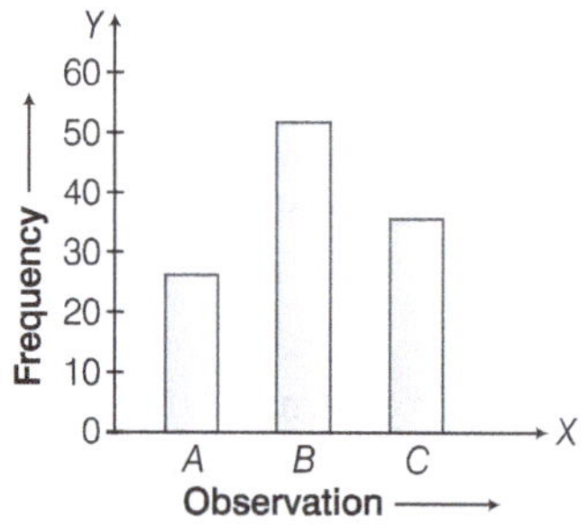

Example 16. 70 students from a locality, use different modes of transport to go to school as given below

Mode of transport	Car	Bus	Moped	Bicycle	Rickshaw
Number of students	4	27	12	19	8

Draw a bar graph representing the above data.

Sol. Take the mode of transport along the X-axis choosing any scale and the number of students along the Y-axis.

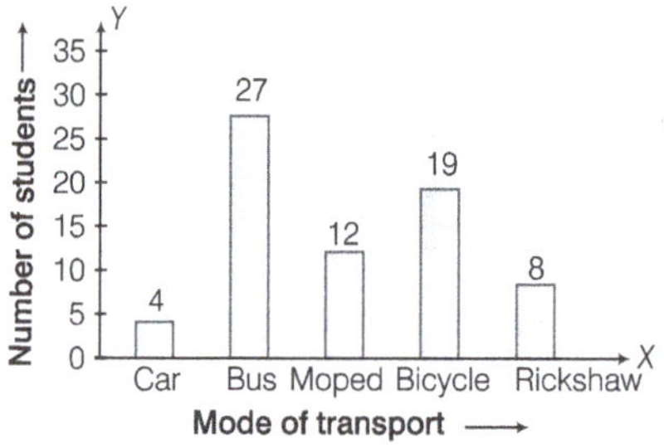

Histogram

A histogram is the graphical representation of a grouped frequency distribution with continuous classes in the form of rectangles. There is no gap between any two consecutive rectangles.

Example 17. Represent the following frequency distribution by means of a histogram.

Marks	Number of students
10-20	7
20-30	11
30-40	9
40-50	13
50-60	16
60-70	4
70-80	2

Sol. X-axis, 1 cm = 10 units

Y-axis, 1 cm = 1 student

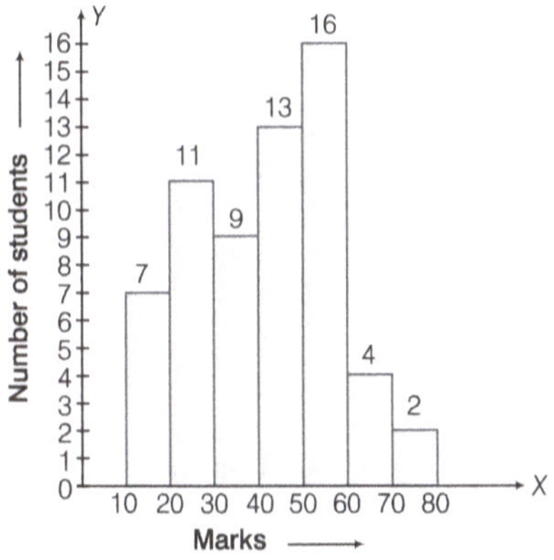

Histogram, when Class Intervals are of Unequal Size

We know that in a histogram, the areas of the rectangles are proportional to the frequencies but in this case, the widths of the rectangles are varying. So, we need to make certain modifications in the lengths of the rectangles (i.e. frequencies), so that the areas are again proportional to the frequencies.

$$\text{Adjusted frequency} = \frac{\text{Minimum class size}}{\text{Class size of the class}} \times \text{Frequency of the class}$$

Example 18. A random survey of the number of children of various age groups playing football match in a park was found as follows

Age (in years)	Number of children
1-2	5
2-3	4
3-5	10
5-7	12
7-10	9
10-15	10
15-17	8

Draw a histogram to represent the above data.

Sol. Here, minimum class size = $2 - 1 = 1$

Adjusted frequency of a class

$$= \frac{\text{Minimum class size}}{\text{Class size of the class}} \times \text{Frequency of the class}$$

Frequency distribution after adjusting frequency

Age (in years)	Number of children (Frequency)	Width of the class	Adjusted frequency
1-2	5	1	$\frac{1}{1} \times 5 = 5$
2-3	4	1	$\frac{1}{1} \times 4 = 4$
3-5	10	2	$\frac{1}{2} \times 10 = 5$
5-7	12	2	$\frac{1}{2} \times 12 = 6$
7-10	9	3	$\frac{1}{3} \times 9 = 3$
10-15	10	5	$\frac{1}{5} \times 10 = 2$
15-17	8	2	$\frac{1}{2} \times 8 = 4$

The required histogram is as follows

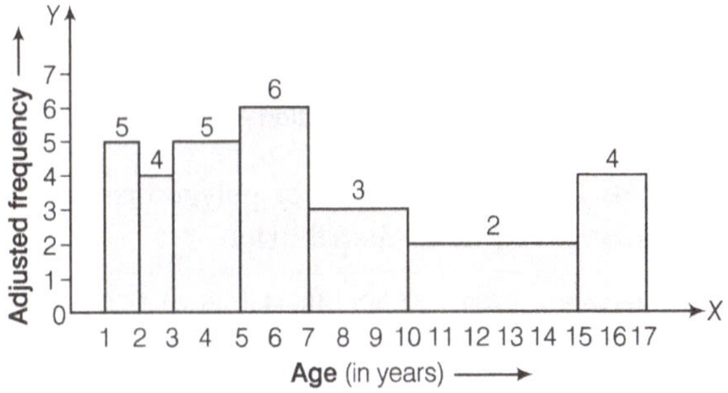

Frequency Polygon

A frequency polygon is the polygon obtained by joining the mid-points of upper horizontal sides of all the rectangles in the histogram. Frequency polygons can also be drawn independently without drawing histograms.

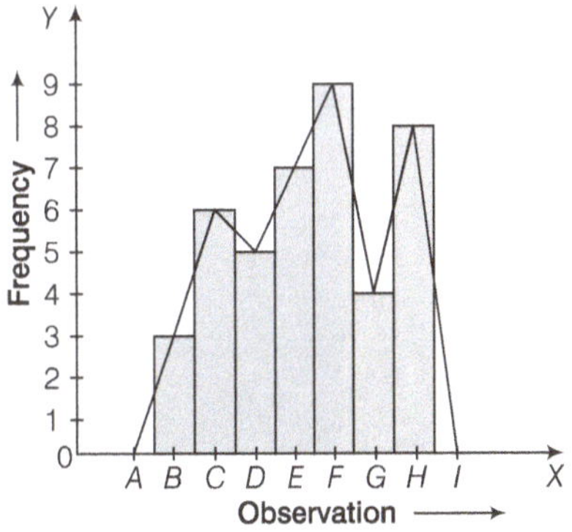

Now, take the class marks along the horizontal axis (i.e. X-axis) and frequencies along the vertical axis (i.e. Y-axis). After that, plot the points (x_i, f_i) and join these points by line segments join all the class marks to get required frequency polygon.

To complete frequency polygon, a class interval with frequency zero before first interval and one after last interval. Such class intervals are called **imagined class intervals.**

A break near origin is shown by a zig-zag curve to indicate that the graph does not begin from origin. This break is known as Kink.

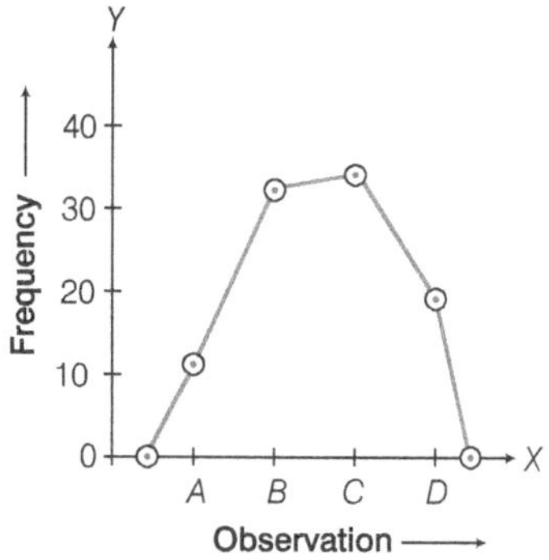

Example 19. Draw a frequency polygon representing the following frequency distribution.

Class intervals	30-34	35-39	40-44	45-49	50-54	55-59
Frequency	12	16	20	8	10	4

Sol. Given, class intervals are discontinuous, so we make them continuous by subtracting and adding 0.5 in lower and upper limits of each class interval.

We take the imagined class 24.5-29.5 and 59.5-64.5.

Class intervals	Class marks	Frequency
24.5-29.5	$\frac{24.5+29.5}{2}=27$	0
29.5-34.5	32	12
34.5-39.5	37	16
39.5-44.5	42	20
44.5-49.5	47	8
49.5-54.5	52	10
54.5-59.5	57	4
59.5-64.5	62	0

Along the X-axis, we take class marks 27, 32, 37, 42, 47, 52, 57 and 62 with a suitable scale.

Along the Y-axis, we take corresponding frequencies 0, 12, 16, 20, 8, 10, 4 and 0 with a suitable scale.

Now, plot the points $A(27, 0)$, $B(32, 12)$, $C(37, 16)$, $D(42, 20)$, $E(47, 8)$, $F(52, 10)$, $G(57, 4)$ and $H(62, 0)$.

We join line segments AB, BC, CD, DE, EF, FG and GH to obtain the required frequency polygon as shown below

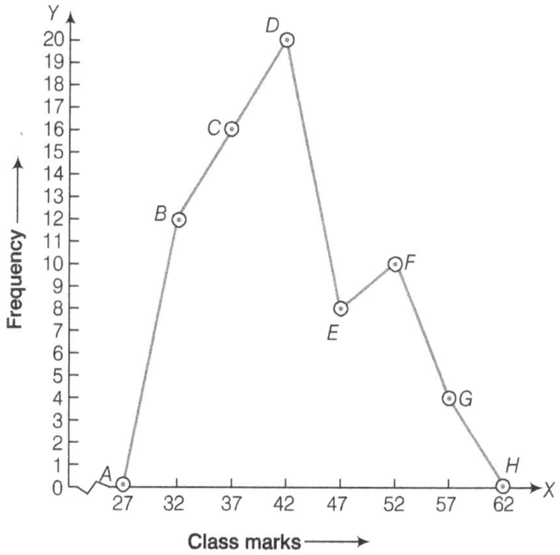

Exercise 14.3

1. Given below are the seats won by different political parties in the polling outcome of a State Assembly Election.

Political parties	Seats won
A	75
B	55
C	37
D	29
E	10
F	37

(i) Draw a bar graph to represent the polling results.

(ii) Which political party won the maximum number of seats?

2. The following figure represents the amount of money spent in various years.

Years	Amount (in crore)
1996-97	45
1997-98	70
1998-99	95
1999-2000	90

Represent this with bar graph.

3. The following data gives the demand estimates of the Government of India, Department of Electronics for the personnel in the Computer sector during the Eighth Plan period (1990-95)

Qualifications	Personnel required
MCA (Master in Computer applications)	40600
DCA (Diploma in Computer Applications)	181600
DCE (Diploma in Computer Engineering)	18600
CL (Certificate Level Course)	67060
ST (Short-term Course)	180290

(i) Represent the data with the help of a bar graph.

(ii) Indicate with the help of the bar graph the course where estimated requirement is least.

4. Draw a histogram for the daily earnings of 30 drug stores in the following table.

Daily earning (in ₹)	Number of stores
450-500	16
500-550	10
550-600	7
600-650	3
650-700	1

5. The following table gives the life-times of 400 neon lamps.

Life-times (in hours)	Number of lamps
300-400	14
400-500	56
500-600	60
600-700	86
700-800	74
800-900	62
900-1000	48

(i) Represent the given information with the help of a histogram.

(ii) How many lamps have a life-time of more than 700 h?

6. The following table shows the number of literate females in the age group (10-57) yr in a village

Age group (in years)	Number of females (Frequency)
10-17	300
18-25	980
26-33	740
34-41	580
42-49	260
50-57	140
Total	3000

Draw a histogram to represent the above data.

7. The frequency distribution has been represented graphically as follows

Marks	0-20	20-40	40-60	60-100
Number of students	10	15	20	25

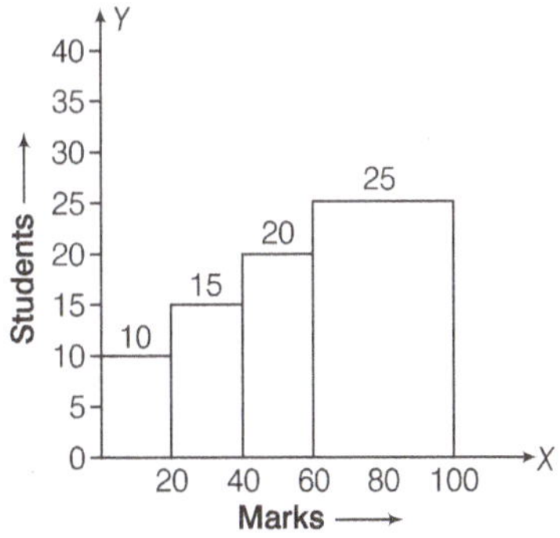

Do you think this representation is correct and why?

8. The length of 40 leaves of a plant measured correct to one millimetre and the obtained data is represented in the following table.

Length (in mm)	Number of leaves
118-126	3
127-135	5
136-144	9
145-153	12
154-162	5
163-171	4
172-180	2

(i) Draw a histogram to represent the given data.
(ii) Is there any other suitable graphical representation for the same data?
(iii) Is it correct to conclude that the maximum number of leaves are 153 mm long and why?

9. Construct a combined histogram and frequency polygon for the following frequency distribution.

Class interval	Frequency
0-20	3
20-40	5
40-60	6
60-80	4
80-100	2

10. The monthly profits (in ₹) of 100 shops are distributed as follows

Profits per shop	Number of shops
0-50	12
50-100	18
100-150	27
150-200	20
200-250	17
250-300	6

Draw a histogram for the data and show the frequency polygon for it.

11. Draw a frequency polygon for each of the following frequency distribution.
(a) Using histogram
(b) Without using histogram

Class interval	10-30	30-50	50-70	70-90	90-110	110-130	130-150
Frequency	4	7	5	9	5	6	4

Chapter Practice

a. 1 Mark Questions

1. Fill in the blanks
   (i) The number of observations in a particular class is called .... of the class.
   (ii) The difference between the class marks of two consecutive classes in the .... of the class.
   (iii) The range of the data 16, 19, 23, 13, 11, 25, 18 is ....
   (iv) The mid-point of the class interval is called its ....
   (v) The class mark of the class 4-9 is ....

2. If m is the mid-point and l is the upper limit of a class in a continuous frequency distribution, then what is the lower limit of the class?
   (a) $m - 2l$ (b) $2m - l$ (c) $m + 2l$ (d) $2m + l$

3. In discrete distribution, the given class limits are called
   (a) stated class limits (b) unstated class limits
   (c) actual class limits (d) class boundaries

4. If the mean of the data 6, 8, 10, 3, 7 and m is 7, then the value of m is
   (a) 6 (b) 7 (c) 8 (d) 9

5. The mean of the first five prime numbers is
   (a) 5.6 (b) 6.5 (c) 4.5 (d) 5.2

6. The mean of the (positive) factors of 24 is
   (a) 7.6 (b) 7.5 (c) 5.7 (d) 5.6

7. Find the mean of first six natural numbers.
   (a) 3.5 (b) 5.3 (c) 3.2 (d) 4.3

8. Find the class mark of class-interval 15-25.
   (a) 20 (b) 22 (c) 25 (d) 40

9. Find the mean of prime numbers between 20 and 30.
   (a) 26 (b) 27 (c) 28 (d) 25

10. Find the mean of first 10 whole numbers.
    (a) 4.5 (b) 4.6 (c) 5.5 (d) 5.6

11. If the mean of the data $x_1, x_2, x_3 \ldots, x_n$ is 'α', then find the mean of the data $x_1 + a, x_2 + a, x_3 + a, \ldots, x_n + a$.
    (a) $\alpha - a$ (b) $\alpha + a$ (c) $\alpha - a$ (d) $2\alpha + a$

12. Range of the points scored by a basketball team in a series of matches are follows

    17, 7, 10, 25, 5, 10, 18, 10 and 24 is

    (a) 24 (b) 25 (c) 21 (d) 20

b. 3 Mark Questions

13. Given below are the marks obtained by 27 students in a test

    21, 3, 28, 38, 6, 40, 20, 26, 9, 8, 14, 18, 20, 16, 17, 10, 8, 5, 22, 27, 34, 2, 35, 31, 16, 28, 37

    (i) Using the class intervals 1-10, 11-20 etc. Construct a frequency table.
    (ii) State the class mark of 3rd class of your frequency table.

14. Use the following table to find

Class	Frequency
18-22	5
23-27	8
28-32	13
33-37	9
38-42	7
43-47	5
48-52	2

    (i) upper and lower limits of 5th class.
    (ii) true class limits of the 5th class.
    (iii) class boundaries of 3rd class.
    (iv) class mark of 4th class.
    (v) width of 6th class.

15. The water tax bill of 30 houses in a locality are given below

    144, 184, 130, 195, 132, 134, 196, 114, 212, 174, 188, 210, 202, 145, 175, 154, 174, 178, 166, 146, 135, 115, 120, 114, 140, 188, 176, 166, 210, 208

    Construct a frequency distribution table with class size 10.

16. The heights of 72 plants in a garden are given below

Height (in cm)	58	60	62	64	66	68
Number of plants	12	14	20	13	8	5

    Find the mean height per plant.

17. Find the arithmetic mean from the following data.

x	18	19	20	21	22	23	24
f	170	320	530	700	230	140	110

18. If the mean of the following data is 20.2, then find the value of p.

x	10	15	20	25	30
f	6	8	p	10	6

19. The mean of six number is 23. If one of the numbers is excluded, the mean of the remaining numbers is 20. Find the excluded number.

20. If the mean of the marks of five students is 33 and that of the marks of four of them is 32.5 m, then find the marks obtained by fifth student.

21. The mean of 25 observations was found to be 78.4. But later on, it was discovered that 96 was misread as 69. Find the correct mean.

22. A batsman in his 12th inning makes a score of 63 runs and thereby increases his average score by 2. What is his average after the 12th inning?

23. Mean of n observations $x_1, x_2, x_3 \ldots, x_n$ is $\bar{x}$ and if each observation is multiplied by 3, then find the new mean.

c. 4/5 Marks Questions

24. Find the median of the first ten prime numbers.

25. The following data on the number of girls (to the nearest ten) per thousand boys in different sections of Indian society is given below

Section	Number of girls per thousand boys
Scheduled Caste (SC)	940
Scheduled Tribe (ST)	970
Non-SC/ST	920
Backward Districts (BD)	950
Non-backward Districts	920
Rural	930
Urban	910

(i) Represent the information above by a bar graph.

(ii) In the classroom, discuss what conclusions can be arrived from the graph?

26. The following table presents the number of illiterate females in the age group (10-34) in a town.

Age group	10-14	15-19	20-24	25-29	30-34
Number of females	300	980	800	580	290

Draw a histogram to represent the above data.

27. Draw a frequency polygon for the following.

Class interval	Frequency
40-50	15
50-60	28
60-70	45
70-80	32
80-90	41
90-100	18

28. Draw a frequency polygon for the following frequency distribution.

Class interval	Frequency
1-10	8
11-20	3
21-30	6
31-40	12
41-50	2
51-60	7

d. 6 Marks Questions

29. The relative humidity (in %) of a certain city for a month of 30 days was as follows

98.1, 98.6, 99.2, 90.3, 86.5, 95.3, 92.9, 96.3, 94.2, 95.1, 89.2, 92.3, 97.1, 93.5, 92.7, 95.1, 97.2, 93.3, 95.2, 97.3, 96.2, 92.1, 84.9, 90.2, 95.7, 98.3, 97.3, 96.1, 92.1, 89.0

(i) Construct a grouped frequency distribution table with classes 84-86, 86-88 etc.

(ii) Which month or season do you think this data is about?

30. The distance (in km) of 40 engineers from their residence to their place of work were found as follows

5, 3, 10, 20, 25, 11, 13, 7, 12, 31, 19, 10, 12, 17, 18, 11, 32, 17, 16, 2, 7, 9, 7, 8, 3, 5, 12, 15, 18, 3, 12, 14, 2, 9, 6, 15, 15, 7, 6, 12

Construct a grouped frequency distribution table with class size 5 for the data given above taking the first interval as 0-5 (5 is not included). What main features do you observe from this tabular representation?

31. There are 50 numbers. Each number is subtracted from 53 and the mean number so obtained is found to be – 3.5. Find the mean of the given numbers.

32. The following observations have been arranged in ascending order. If the median of these observations is 58, then find the value of x.

24, 27, 43, 48, $x-1$, $x+3$, 68, 73, 80, 90

33. 100 boys and 100 girls of a locality, use different modes of transport to go to school as given below

Mode	Number of boys	Number of girls
Walk	16	4
Bicycle	24	36
Bus	12	28
Car	30	26
Others	18	6

Draw a bar graph representing the above data.

34. A survey conducted by an organisation for the cause of illness and death among the women between the ages 15-44 (in years) worldwide, found the following figures (in %)

S.No.	Causes	Female fatality rate (in %)
1.	Reproductive health conditions	31.8
2.	Neuropsychiatric conditions	25.4
3.	Injuries	12.4
4.	Cardiovascular conditions	4.3
5.	Respiratory conditions	4.1
6.	Other causes	22.0

(i) Represent the information given above graphically.

(ii) Which condition is the major cause of women's ill health and death worldwide?

(iii) Try to find out, with the help of your teacher, any two factors which play a major role in the above being the major causes.

35. The mean height of 10 students is 151.8 cm. Two more student of heights 157.6 cm and 154.4 cm join the group. What is the new mean height?

36. Mean temperature of a city of a certain week was 25°C. If the mean temperature of Monday, Tuesday, Wednesday and Thursday was 23°C and that of Thursday, Friday, Saturday and Sunday was 28°, find the temperature of Thursday.

37. The mean marks (out of 100) of boys and girls in an examination are 70 and 73, respectively. If the mean marks of all the students in that examination is 71, find the ratio of the number of boys to the number of girls.

38. In a class average score of girls in an examination is 80 and that of boys is 70. The average score of the whole class is 74. Find the percentage of girls and boys in the class.

39. The mean of the following distribution is 50.

x	10	30	50	70	90
f	17	$5a+3$	32	$7a-11$	19

Find the value of a.

40. (i) Find the mean $(\bar{x})$ of first 5 even natural numbers.

(ii) If x denotes the different even natural numbers, taken in part (i) above, show that $\Sigma(x-\bar{x})=0$

41. The water bills (in rupees) of 32 houses in a locality are given below : 30, 48, 52, 78, 103, 85, 37, 94, 72, 73, 66, 52, 92, 65, 78, 81, 64, 60, 75, 78, 108, 63, 71, 54, 59, 75, 100, 103, 35, 89, 95, 73 taking class intervals 30-40, 40-50, 50-60, ... form frequency distribution table construct a combined histogram and frequency polygon.

42. The following table gives the distribution of students of two sections according to the marks obtained by them

Section A		Section B	
Marks	Frequency	Marks	Frequency
0-10	3	0-10	5
10-20	9	10-20	19
20-30	17	20-30	15
30-40	12	30-40	10
40-50	9	40-50	1

Represent the marks of the students of both on the same graph by two frequency polygons. From the two polygons compare the performance of the two sections.

Hints and Answers

Exercise 14.1

1. **Hint** Class mark = $\frac{\text{Upper limit} + \text{Lower limit}}{2}$

   Ans. 70, 80, 10 and 75

2. (i) **Hint** The given interval is a discontinuous class interval, so both 1 and 10 are included in the interval. **Ans.** 10

   (ii) **Hint** Range = Maximum value – Minimum value

   Ans. 118

   (iii) **Hint** Given data is an exclusive form.

   Ans. 20-30

3. **Hint** Do same as Example 1.

   Ans.

Weight	35	36	37	38
Frequency	5	7	7	6

4. **Hint** Do same as Example 1.

   Ans.

Size of shirts	28	30	32	34
Frequency	3	6	7	4

5. **Hint** Do same as Example 1.

   Ans.

Blood group	Number of students
A	9
B	6
O	12
AB	3

Blood group *O* is the most common and blood group *AB* is the rarest among the students.

6. **Hint** Do same as Example 3(ii).

   Ans.

Class interval	51-55	56-60	61-65	66-70	71-75	76-80
Frequency	5	6	3	7	7	2

7. **Hint** Do same as Example 3.

   Ans. (i)

Class Interval	Frequency
1-5	2
6-10	3
11-15	7
16-20	9
21-25	3
26-30	3
31-35	1
36-40	2

Ans. (ii)

Class Interval	Frequency
1-5	2
5-9	2
9-13	4
13-17	6
17-21	7
21-25	2
25-29	3
29-33	2
33-37	1
37-41	1

8. **Hint** Do same as Example 3(ii).

   Ans.

Class interval	10-14	15-19	20-24	25-29	30-34	35-39	40-44
Frequency	5	7	6	4	4	8	1

9. **Hint** Size of each class = 20, mid-value of first class = 70

   So, the lower limit of the first class interval

   $$= 70 - 10 = 60$$

   and the upper limit of the first class interval

   $$= 70 + 10 = 80$$

   ∴ First class interval is 60-80.

   Ans.

Weight (in gm)	Tally marks	Frequency
60-80	𝍸	5
80-100	𝍸 𝍸 |||	13
100-120	𝍸 𝍸 𝍸 ||	17
120-140	𝍸 𝍸	10
140-160	|	1
160-180		0
180-200	|||	3
200-220	|	1
Total		50

10. **Hint** Do same as Example 4.

    Ans.

Class interval	Frequency
0.5-10.5	11
10.5-20.5	8
20.5-30.5	7
30.5-40.5	8
40.5-50.5	9
50.5-60.5	12

11. We know that cumulative frequency of a class interval is the sum of the frequencies of all class upto that classes.

Ans. $x = 15$, $y = 13$, $z = 49$

and $P = 65$, $Q = 8$, $R = 85$

Exercise 14.2

1. **Hint** Do same as Example 7.
Ans. 47.4

2. **Hint** Do same as Example 7.
Ans. 19 kg

3. **Hint** Do same as Example 8.
Ans. (i) 7 (ii) 9

4. **Hint** Do same as Example 9.
Ans. 14

5. **Hint** Do same as Example 9.
Ans. 22

6. **Hint** Do same as Example 11.
Ans. 8.05

7. **Hint** First, find the mean of given observations, then do same as Example 10.
Ans. 55.2 km/h

8. **Hint** New mean $= \dfrac{\left(\dfrac{x_1}{3} + \dfrac{x_2}{3} + \ldots + \dfrac{x_{12}}{3}\right)}{12}$

$$= \frac{\frac{1}{3} \cdot (x_1 + x_2 + \ldots + x_{12})}{12}$$

Ans. 8

9. **Hint** New mean $= \dfrac{(bx_1 - c) + (bx_2 - c) + \ldots + (bx_n - c)}{n}$

$$= \frac{b(x_1 + x_2 + \ldots + x_n) - nc}{n}$$

Ans. $ab - c$

10. **Hint** Clearly, sum of five items $= 15 \times 5 = 75$,

sum of first three items $= 14 \times 3 = 42$

and sum of last three items $= 17 \times 3 = 51$

$\therefore$ Third item = (Sum of first three items + Sum of last three items) − Sum of five items

$= (42 + 51) - 75$ **Ans.** 18

11. **Hint** Here, $\bar{x}$ is the mean of $x_1, x_2, \ldots, x_n$ and $\bar{y}$ is the mean of $y_1, y_2, \ldots, y_n$.

$$\bar{z} = \frac{\bar{x} + \bar{y}}{2}$$

Ans. $\dfrac{\bar{x} + \bar{y}}{2}$

12. **Hint** Mean of given data $= \dfrac{\quad + \quad + \quad + \quad}{\quad} =$

$\therefore$ Sum of deviations of the given data from their mean $= 1(5 - 12) + (7 - 12) + (9 - 12) + (15 - 12) + (24 - 12)$

$= -7 - 5 - 3 + 3 + 12 = 0$

13. **Hint** Mean of the given data

$$= \frac{8 + 12 + 16 + 22 + 10 + 4}{6} = \frac{72}{6} = 12$$

(i) Increased by 25%

New mean = Original mean + 25% original mean

Ans. 15

(ii) Decreased by 40%

New mean = Original mean − 40% of original mean

$= 12 - \dfrac{40}{100} \times 12$ **Ans.** 7.2

14. **Hint** Do same as Example 11.

Ans. 68.28 $\left[\text{Arithmetic mean} = \dfrac{\text{Sum of pass\%}}{\text{Number of pass\%}}\right]$

15. **Hint** $\because$ $x_1 - 50 + x_2 - 50 + \ldots + x_n - 50 = -10$

$\Rightarrow \quad (x_1 + x_2 + \ldots + x_n) = -10 + 50n \quad \ldots \text{(i)}$

Also given that

$x_1 - 46 + x_2 - 46 + \ldots + x_n - 46 = 70$

$\Rightarrow \quad (x_1 + x_2 + \ldots + x_n) = 70 + 64n \quad \ldots \text{(ii)}$

From Eqs. (i) and (ii), we get

$n = 20$

$\Rightarrow \quad \text{Mean} = \dfrac{x_1 + x_2 + \ldots + x_n}{n}$ **Ans.** 49.5

16. **Hint** Do same as Example 13. **Ans.** 39.2

17. **Hint** Do same as Example 14. **Ans.** −0.00175

18. **Hint** Do same as Example 15. **Ans.** 62

19. **Hint** First, do same as Example 13.

Now, if 25 is replaced by 52, then the new observations in ascending order are 19, 30, 31, 32, 35, 48, 51, 52, 59

$\therefore$ New median = Value of 5th observation

Ans. 32, New median = 35

20. **Hint** =

$\therefore$ Median = Average of 5th and 6th observations.

Ans. $x = 22$

Exercise 14.3

1. (i) **Hint** Do same as Example 16. **Ans.**

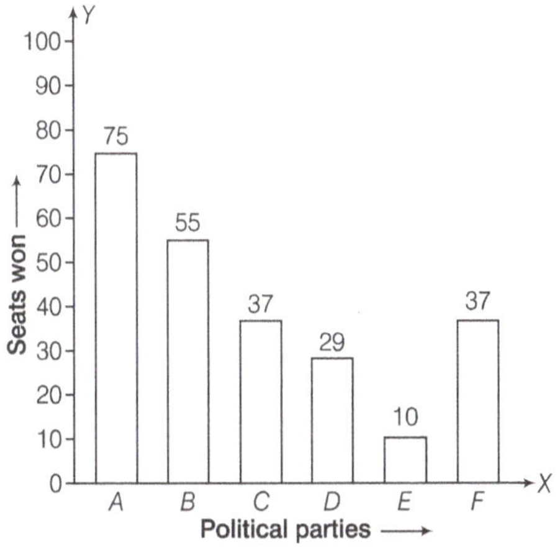

(ii) **Hint** From the bar graph, it is clear that party *A* won the maximum number of seats, i.e. 75.

Ans. *A*

2. **Hint** Do same as Example 16.

Ans.

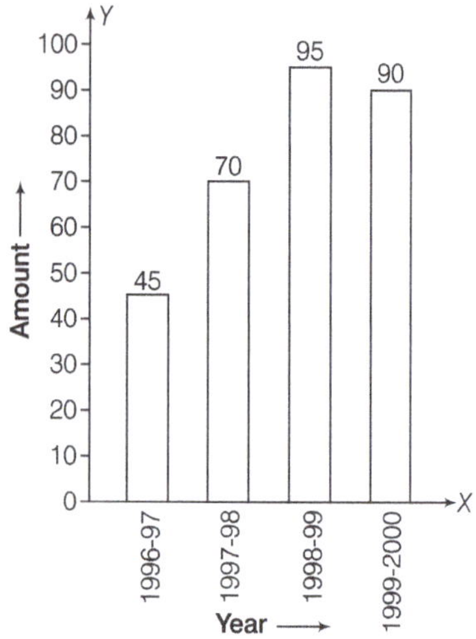

3. **Hint** Do same as Example 16.

Ans. (i)

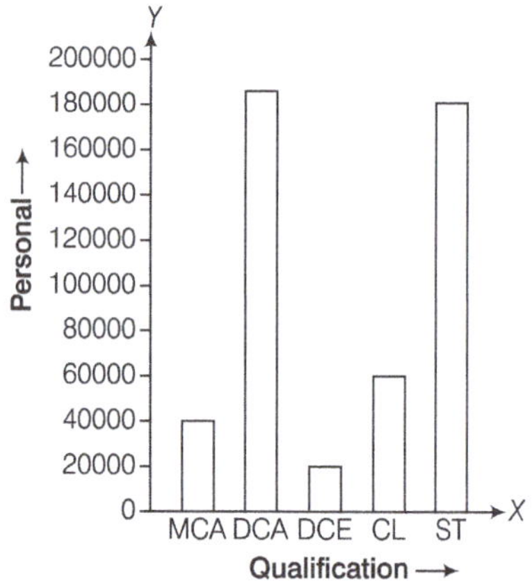

(ii) DCE

4. Do same as Example 17.

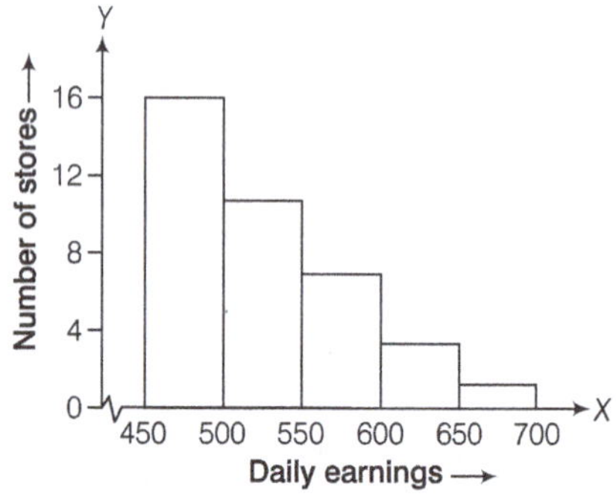

5. (i) **Hint** Do same as Example 17.

Ans.

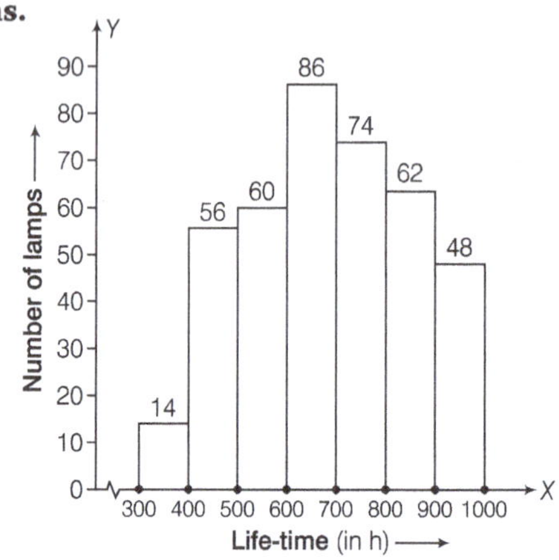

(ii) **Hint** Number of lamps have a life-time of more than 700 h = 74 + 62 + 48 **Ans.** 184

6. **Hint** First, convert it into a continuous frequency distribution. Then, do same as Example 17.

Ans.

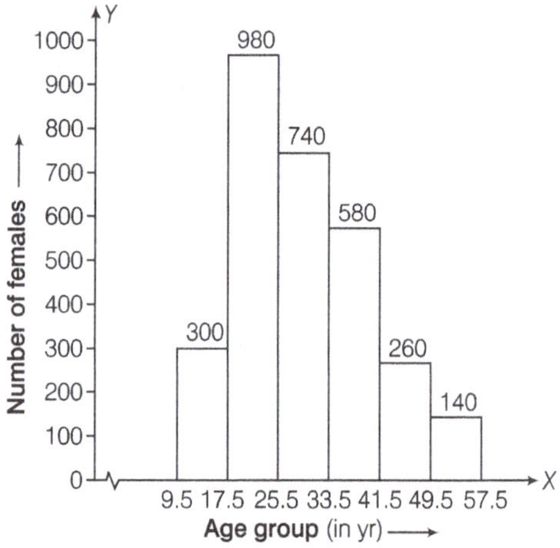

7. **Hint** Do same as Example 18.

Ans. No, here the widths of the rectangle are varying. So, we need to make certain modification in the lengths of the rectangles, so that the areas are proportional to the frequencies.

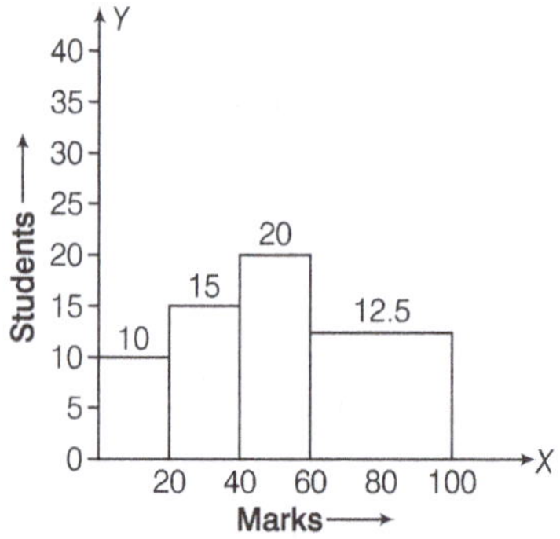

8. (i) **Ans.**

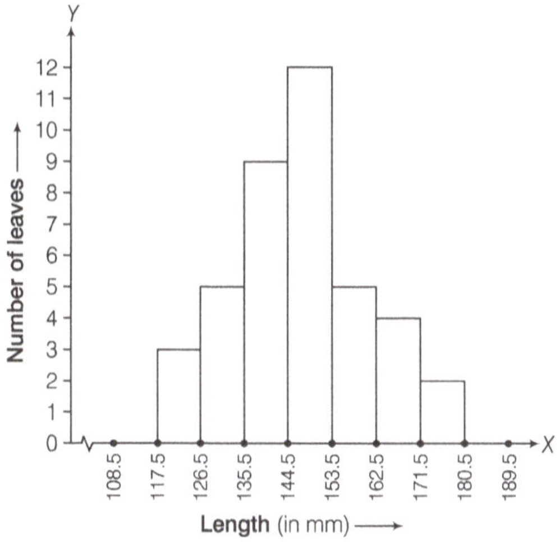

(ii) Frequency polygon

(iii) No, because the maximum number of leaves have their lengths lying in the interval 145-153.

9. Hint First, do same as Example 17, then join the mid-points of upper horizontal sides of all the rectangles in the histogram.

Ans.

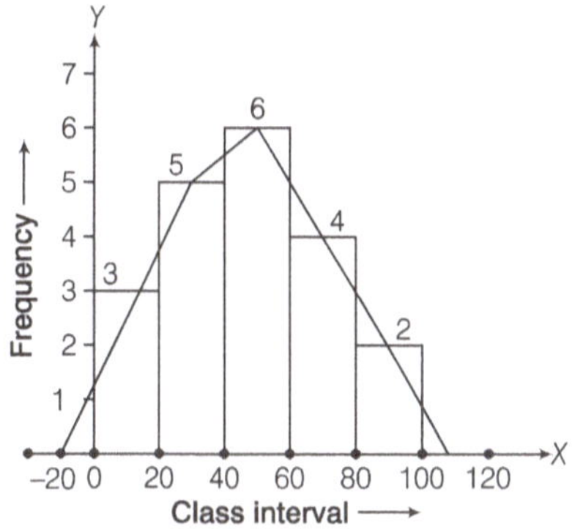

10. Hint Do same as Q. 9.

Ans.

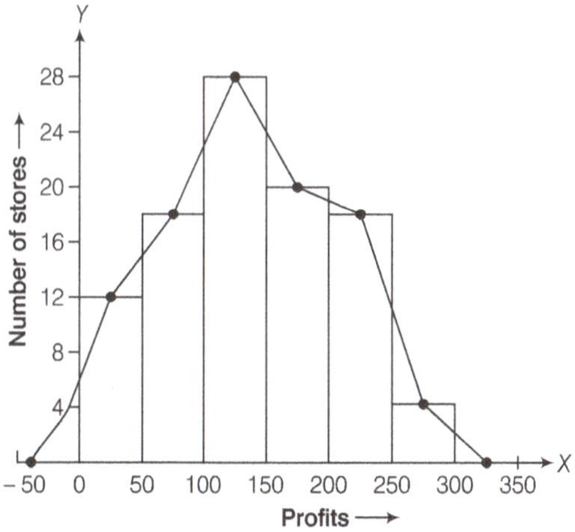

11. Ans. (a) Do same as Q. 9.

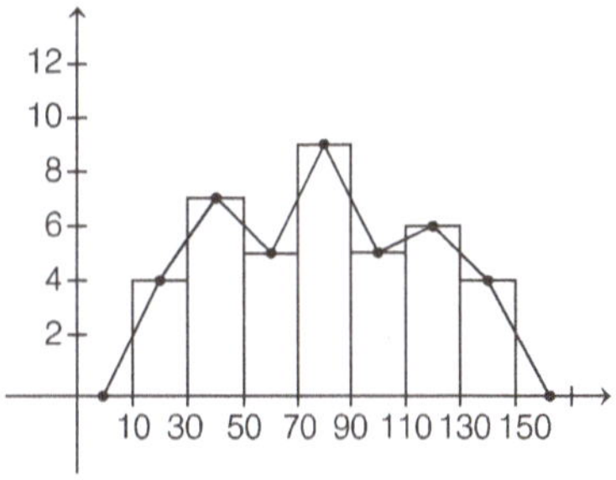

(b)

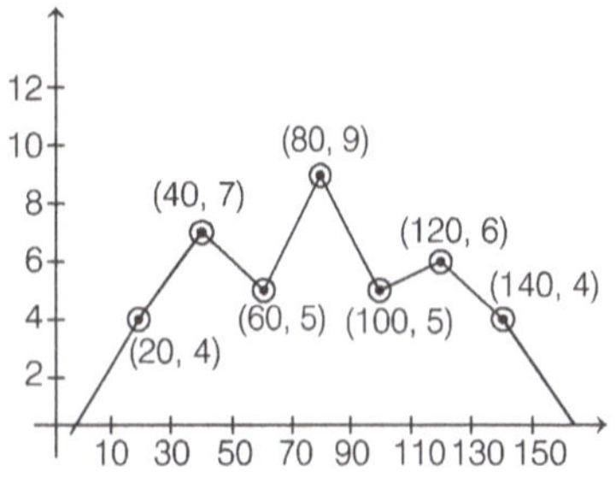

Chapter Exercise

1. (i) Frequency (ii) Size (iii) 14 (iv) Class mark (v) 6.5

2. (b) **3.** (a) **4.** (c)

5. (a) **6.** (b) **7.** (a)

8. (a) **9.** (a) **10.** (a)

11. (b) **12.** (d)

13. Hint Do same as Example 3 (ii).

Ans. (i)

Class	1-10	11-20	21-30	31-40
Frequency	8	7	6	6

(ii) 25.5

14. (i) 42 and 38 (ii) 42.5 and 37.5 (iii) 27.5 and 32.5 (iv) 35 (v) 4

15. The frequency distribution table may be presented as shown below

Bill (in ₹)	Tally marks	Frequency
114-124	||||	4
124-134	||	2
134-144	|||	3
144-154	|||	3
154-164	|	1
164-174	||	2
174-184	~~||||~~	5
184-194	|||	3
194-204	|||	3
204-214	||||	4
Total		30

16. **Hint** Do same as Example 11.

Ans. 62.17 cm

17. **Hint** Do same as Example 11.

Ans. 20.62

18. **Hint** Do same as Example 12.

Ans. $p = 20$

19. **Hint** Sum of six numbers $= 23 \times 6 = 138$

Sum of five numbers $= 138 -$ Excluded number

Now, as mean of five numbers $= 20$

$$\therefore \quad \frac{138 - \text{Excluded number}}{5} = 20$$

Ans. 38

20. **Hint** Sum of marks of five students $= 33 \times 5$

Sum of marks of four students $= 32.5 \times 4$

Required marks $= (33 \times 5) - (32.5 \times 4)$

Ans. 35

21. **Hint** Correct sum $= (78.4 \times 25) - 69 + 96 = 1987$

Ans. 79.48

22. **Hint** Let upto 11th innings his average score be x.

Then, total number of runs would be $11x$.

Now, after 12 innings, total number of runs

$= 11x + 63$

and average after 12 innings $= \dfrac{11x + 63}{12}$

$$\Rightarrow \quad x + 2 = \frac{11x + 63}{12}$$

Ans. 41

23. **Hint** $x_1 + x_2 + x_3 + \ldots + x_n = n\bar{x}$

New mean $= \dfrac{3x_1 + 3x_2 + 3x_3 + \ldots + 3x_n}{n}$

$= \dfrac{3(x_1 + x_2 + x_3 + \ldots + x_n)}{n}$

Ans. $3\bar{x}$

24. **Hint** Do same as Example 14.

Ans. 12

25. **Hint** Choose the scale on Y-axis as 1 unit = 10 girls.

Ans. (i)

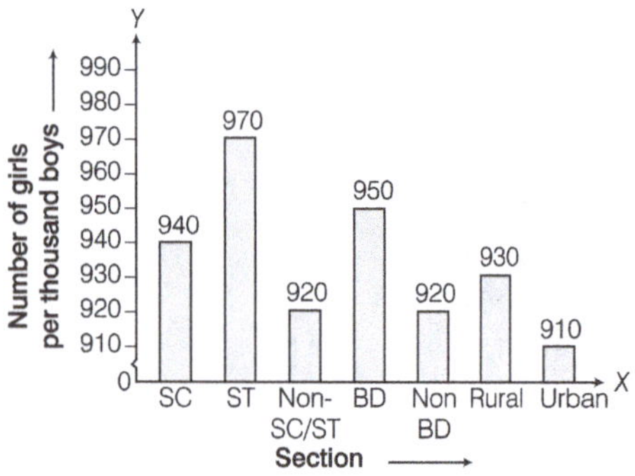

(ii) From the graph, we observe that in Scheduled Tribe (ST), there is maximum number of girls per thousand boys among different sections of Indian society.

26. **Hint** The given frequency distribution is not continuous. So, we will first convert it into a continuous frequency distribution.

The distribution so obtained is as given below

Age group	Number of females
9.5-14.5	300
14.5-19.5	980
19.5-24.5	800
24.5-29.5	580
29.5-34.5	290

Ans.

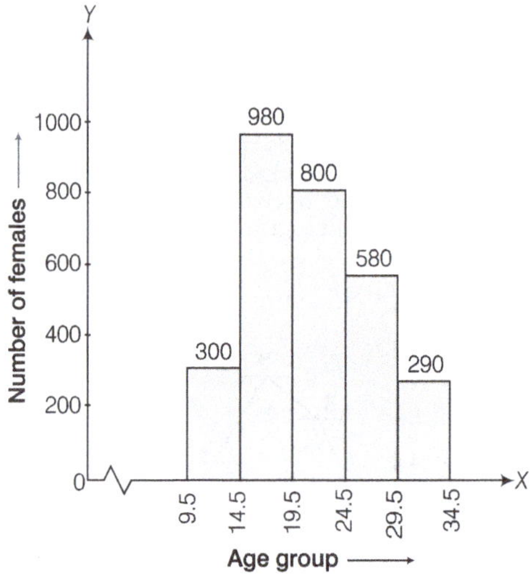

27. **Hint** Do same as Example 19.

Ans.

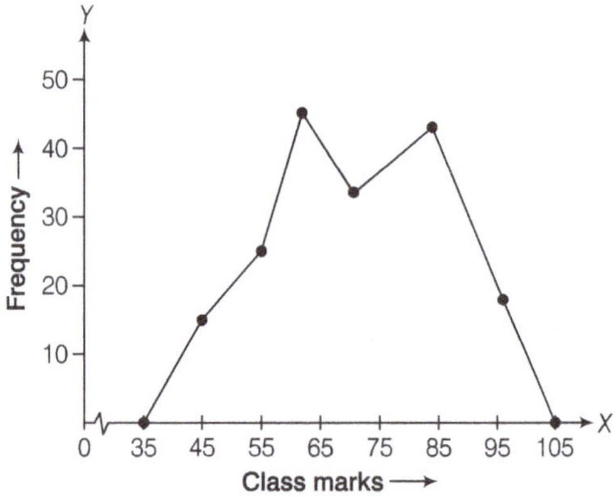

28. Hint Do same as Example 19.

Ans.

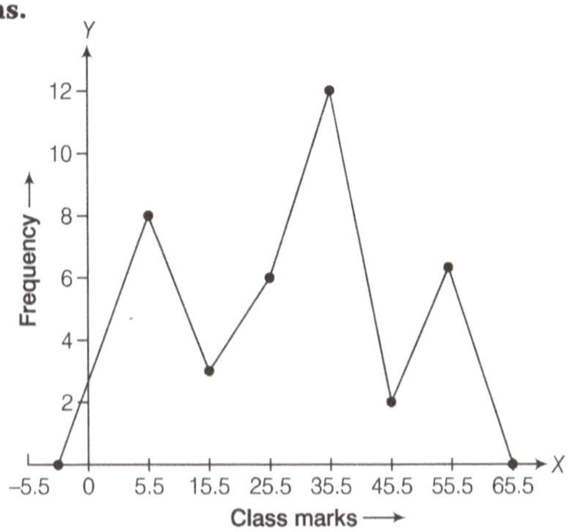

29. (i) **Hint** Do same as Example 5.

Ans.

Relative humidity (in %)	Tally marks	Frequency
84-86	|	1
86-88	|	1
88-90	||	2
90-92	||	2
92-94	卌||	7
94-96	卌|	6
96-98	卌||	7
98-100	||||	4
Total		30

(ii) **Ans.** From the table, we observe that the data appears to be taken in the rainy season as the relative humidity is high.

30. Hint Do same as Example 5.

Ans.

Distance (in km)	Tally marks	Frequency
0-5	卌	5
5-10	卌 卌 |	11
10-15	卌 卌 |	11
15-20	卌 ||||	9
20-25	|	1
25-30	|	1
30-35	||	2
Total		40

(i) Frequencies of class intervals 5-10 and 10-15 are equal, i.e. 11 each. It shows that maximum number of engineers have their residence within the distance of 5 km to 15 km from their workplace.

(ii) Frequencies of class intervals 20-25 and 25-30 are also equal, i.e. 1 each. It shows that minimum number of engineers have their residences within 20 km to 30 km from their workplace.

31. Hint Let the number are $x_1, x_2, \dots, x_{50}$

Then, $\frac{(53 - x_1) + (53 - x_2) + \dots + (53 - x_n)}{50} = -3.5$

$\Rightarrow \quad \frac{x_1 + x_2 + \dots + x_n}{50}$

Ans. 56.5

32. Hint Do same as Example 15. **Ans.** 57

33. Ans.

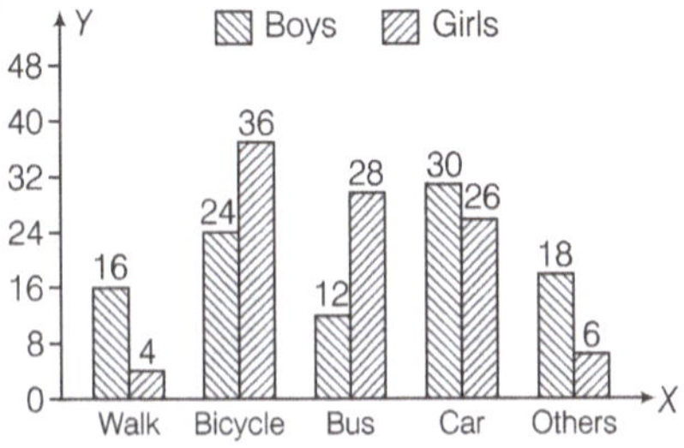

34. Ans. (i)

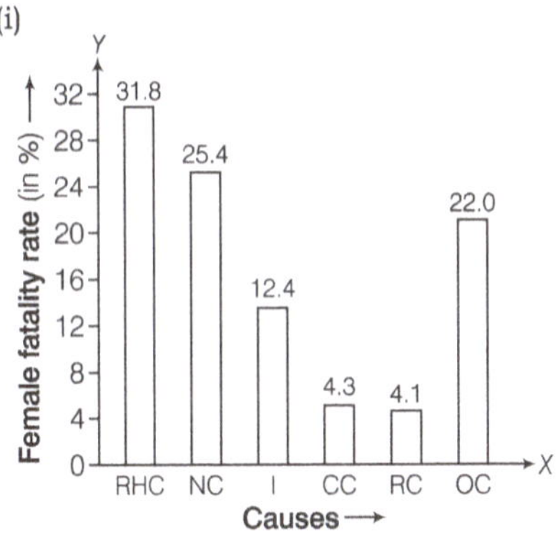

(ii) From the graph, we observe that 'reproductive health conditions' is the major cause of women's ill health and death worldwide because it has maximum percentage among the causes, i.e. 31.8%.

(iii) The factors are as follows

(a) Lack of medical facilities.

(b) Lack of and infrastructure good doctors.

35. Hint Mean height of 10 students

$= \frac{\text{sum of heights of 10 students}}{10}$

$\therefore$ Sum of heights of 12 students

$= (1518 + 157.6 + 154.4)$ cm

$= 1830$ cm

$\therefore$ New mean height

$= \frac{\text{sum of heights of 12 students}}{12}$

Ans. 152.5 cm

36. Hint Mean temperature of the week = 25° C

Temperature of 7 days of the week

$= 7 \times 25° \text{C} = 175° \text{C}$ ...(i)

Temperature of Monday, Tuesday, Wednesday and Thursday

$= 4 \times 23° \text{C} = 92° \text{C}$ ... (ii)

Temperature of Thursday, Friday, Saturday and Sunday

$= 4 \times 28° C = 112° C$ ...(iii)

Temperature of Monday to Sunday and Thursday
$= 92° C + 112° C$

[using Eqs. (ii) and (iii)]

$= 204° C$ ...(iv)

$\therefore$ Temperature of Thursday $= 204° C - 175° C$

[using Eqs. (iv) and (i)]

Ans. 29° C

37. Hint Number of boys and girls be n_1 and n_2 respectively.

$$\therefore \quad \frac{n_1(70) + n_2(73)}{n_1 + n_2} = 71$$

$$\Rightarrow \quad 70n_1 + 73n_2 = 71n_1 + 71n_2$$

$$\Rightarrow \quad 73n_2 - 71n_2 = 71n_1 - 70n_1$$

$$\Rightarrow \quad 2n_2 = n_1 \Rightarrow \frac{n_1}{n_2} = \frac{2}{1}$$

Hence the required ratio is 2 : 1.

38. Hint The number of girls be x and boys be y.

Average of the whole class = 74

$$\therefore \quad \frac{80x + 70y}{x + y} = 74$$

Percentage of girls in the class

$$= \frac{x}{x + y} \times 100 = 40\%$$

Percentage of boys in the class = (100 – 40) = 60%

Ans. 40% and 60%

39. Hint

x	f	fx
10	17	170
30	$5a + 3$	$150a + 90$
50	32	1600
70	$7a - 11$	$490a - 770$
90	19	1710
Total	$12a + 60$	$640a + 2800$

Mean = 50

$$\therefore \quad \frac{640a + 2800}{12a + 60} = 50$$

Ans. 5

40. (i) **Ans.** 6

(ii) **Hint**

x	$x - \bar{x}$
2	$2 - 6 = -4$
4	$4 - 6 = -2$
6	$6 - 6 = 0$
8	$8 - 6 = 2$
10	$10 - 6 = 4$

$\therefore \Sigma(x - \bar{x}) = -4 - 2 + 0 + 2 + 4 = 0$

41. Hint

Class Intervals	Tally marks	Frequency
30-40	|||	3
40-50	|	1
50-60	||||	4
60-70	~~||||~~	5
70-80	~~||||~~ ||||	9
80-90	|||	3
90-100	|||	3
100-110	||||	4

Ans.

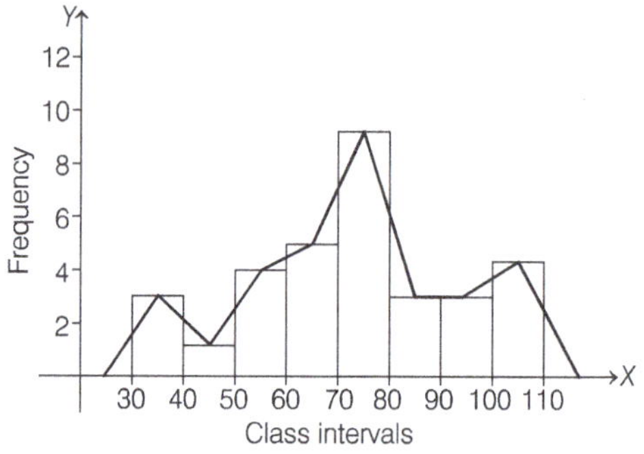

42. Hint

Class	Class Marks	Section A (Number of students)	Section B (Number of students)
0-10	5	3	5
10-20	15	9	19
20-30	25	17	15
30-40	35	12	10
40-50	45	9	1

For section (5, 3), (15, 9), (25, 17) (35, 12) and (45, 9)

For section B (5, 5), (15, 19), (25, 15) (35, 10) and (45, 1)

Ans.

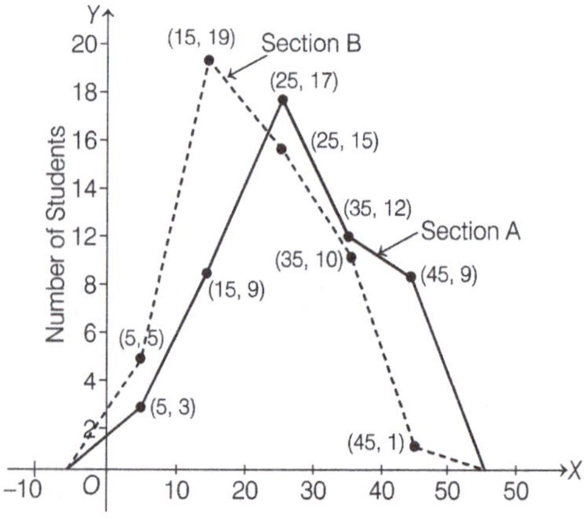

Olympiad Section

Brain Teasing Questions of Olympiad Pattern

1 If the arithmetic mean of 6, 8, 5, 7, x and 4 is 7, then x is equal to

(a) 12 (b) 6
(c) 8 (d) 4

2 The median of the data 46, 64, 87, 41, 58, 77, 35, 90, 55, 33 and 92 is

(a) 87 (b) 77
(c) 58 (d) 60.2

3 The mean of all factors of 24 is

(a) 7 (b) 7.75
(c) 7.25 (d) 7.5

4 If each entry of a data is increased by 5, then the arithmetic mean

(a) remains the same (b) increases by 5
(c) decreases by 5 (d) None of these

5 The following observations have been arranged in ascending order. If the median of the data is 48.5, then the value of x is

16, 21, 23, 29, 30, 40, x, 50, 60, 73, 80, 93

(a) 57 (b) 60
(c) 55 (d) 50

6 The mean of 100 observations was found to be 30. If two observations were wrongly taken as 32 and 12 instead of 23 and 11, then the correct mean is

(a) 29 (b) 30
(c) 29.90 (d) 28

Answers

1. (a) **2.** (c) **3.** (d) **4.** (b) **5.** (a) **6.** (c)

* *These questions may or may not be asked in the examination, have been given just for additional practice required for olympiads Scholarship Exams etc. For detailed explanations refer Page No. 349.*

CHAPTER

15

Perimeter and Area

SYLLABUS

- Area and perimeter of a triangle and a quadrilateral. Area and circumference of circle Surface area and volume of Cube and Cuboids. (a) Area and perimeter of triangle (including Heron's formula), all types of Quadrilaterals. (b) Circle : Area and Circumference. Direct application problems including Inner and Outer area. Areas of sectors of circles other than quarter-circle and semicircle are not included.

Perimeter and Area of Triangle and Quadrilateral

Perimeter The total length of boundary of a plane figure is called its perimeter. The unit of perimeter is cm, m etc.

Area The measurement of the region enclosed by a plane figure is called its area. The unit of area is cm^2, m^2 etc.

Perimeter and Area of a Triangle

(i) Perimeter of ΔABC = Sum of all sides of a triangle $= a + b + c$.

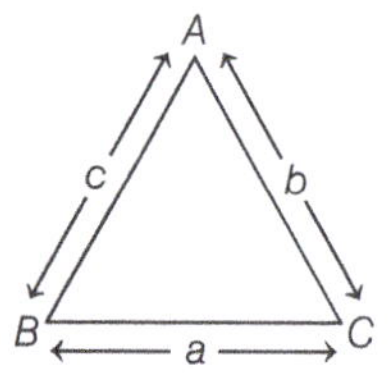

(ii) Area of $\Delta ABC = \frac{1}{2} \times \text{Base} \times \text{Height} = \frac{1}{2} \times BC \times AD$

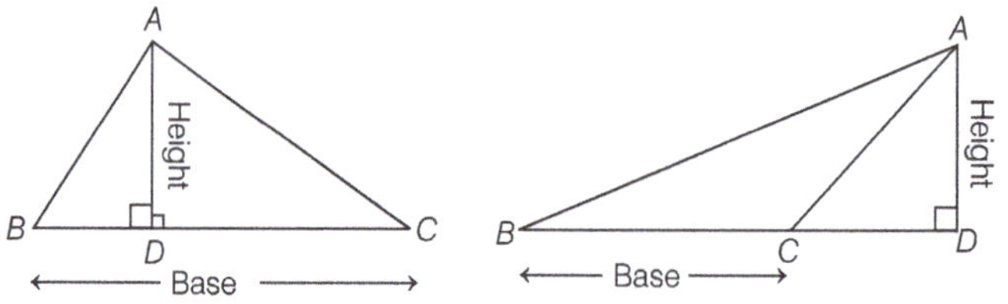

(iii) When all three sides are given, Heron's formula is

$$\text{Area of } \Delta ABC = \sqrt{s(s-a)(s-b)(s-c)}$$

where a, b and c are the sides of triangle,

$$s = \text{semi-perimeter} = \frac{a+b+c}{2}$$

Example 1. If the sides of a triangle are 15 cm, 5 cm and 12 cm and its area equal to 30 cm^2, then find the altitude using the longest side as base.

Sol. Let h be the length of altitude corresponding to the longest side.

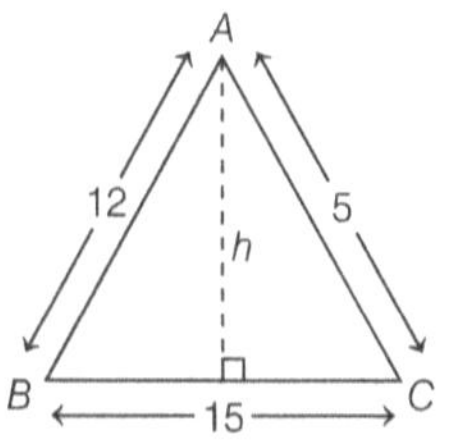

$$\text{Area of } \Delta ABC = 30 = \frac{1}{2} \times 15 \times h$$

$\Rightarrow$ $60 = 15 \times h$ $\left[\because \text{area of triangle} = \frac{1}{2} \times \text{base} \times \text{height}\right]$

$\Rightarrow$ $h = \frac{60}{15} = 4\,\text{cm}$

Hence, the altitude corresponding to longest side is 4 cm.

Example 2. Find the area of a triangle whose sides are 12 cm, 16 cm and 20 cm, respectively.

Sol. Let the sides of triangle be $a = 12\,\text{cm}$, $b = 16\,\text{cm}$ and $c = 20\,\text{cm}$.

We know that, semi-perimeter, $s = \frac{a+b+c}{2}$

$= \frac{12+16+20}{2} = \frac{48}{2} = 24\,\text{cm}$

By Heron's formula,

Area of triangle $= \sqrt{s(s-a)(s-b)(s-c)}$

$= \sqrt{24\,(24-12)\,(24-16)\,(24-20)}$

$= \sqrt{24 \times 12 \times 8 \times 4} = \sqrt{9216} = 96\,\text{cm}^2$

Hence, the area of the given triangle is 96 cm^2.

Example 3. Calculate the area of triangle, whose sides are in the ratio 7 : 5 : 4 and perimeter equal to 32 cm.

Sol. Let ABC be the given triangle with sides $a = 7x$, $b = 5x$ and $c = 4x$.

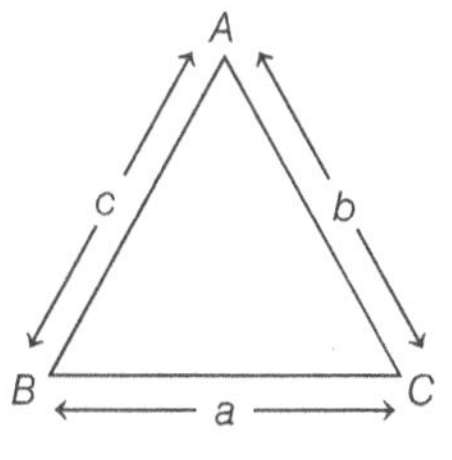

Since, perimeter, $p = 32\,\text{cm}$

$\therefore$ $7x + 5x + 4x = 32$

$\Rightarrow$ $16x = 32$

$\Rightarrow$ $x = \frac{32}{16}$

$\Rightarrow$ $x = 2\,\text{cm}$

Thus, the sides of a triangle are $7x = 7 \times 2 = 14\,\text{cm}$, $5x = 5 \times 2 = 10\,\text{cm}$ and $4x = 4 \times 2 = 8\,\text{cm}$.

Now, semi-perimeter, $s = \frac{p}{2} = \frac{32}{2} = 16\,\text{cm}$

and area of triangle $= \sqrt{s(s-a)(s-b)(s-c)}$ [by Heron's formula]

$= \sqrt{16(16-14)(16-10)(16-8)}$

$= \sqrt{16 \times 2 \times 6 \times 8} = 4 \times 4 \times \sqrt{6}$

$= 16\sqrt{6}\,\text{cm}^2$

Example 4. A conical tent is made by stitching 12 triangular pieces of cloth of two different colours, red and white alternately, each piece measuring 10 cm, 20 cm and 20 cm.

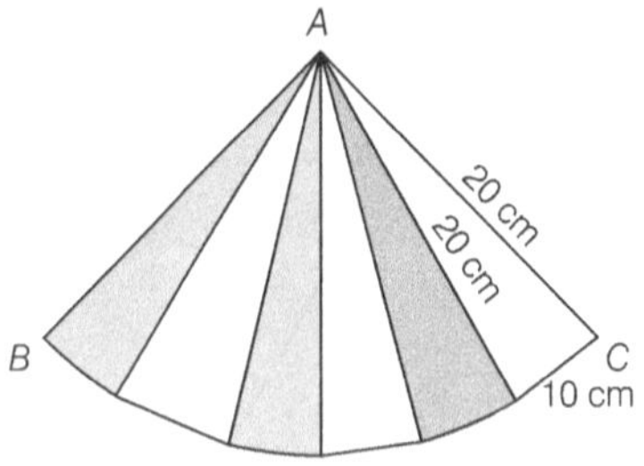

(i) How much cloth of red colour is required to make a conical tent?

(ii) Find the total length of triangular pieces of white colour.

Sol.

(i) In a conical tent, let sides are $a = 10$ cm, $b = 20$ cm and $c = 20\,\text{cm}$.

Semi-perimeter of triangle,

$$s = \frac{a+b+c}{2} = \frac{10+20+20}{2} = \frac{50}{2} = 25\,\text{cm}$$

and area of triangle

$= \sqrt{s(s-a)(s-b)(s-c)}$ [by Heron's formula]

$= \sqrt{25(25-10)(25-20)(25-20)}$

$= \sqrt{25 \times 15 \times 5 \times 5} = \sqrt{5 \times 5 \times 3 \times 5 \times 5 \times 5}$

$= 5 \times 5\sqrt{15} = 25\sqrt{15}\,\text{cm}^2$

Thus, area of one red colour triangular piece is $25\sqrt{15}\,\text{cm}^2$.

Since, tent is made of 12 pieces of two colours.

So, number of triangular pieces of red colour is 6.

Hence, cloth of red colour required to make a conical tent is $6 \times 25\sqrt{15} = 150\sqrt{15}\,\text{cm}^2$.

(ii) Perimeter of one triangular piece, $= 10 + 20 + 20 = 50\,\text{cm}$

$\therefore$ Total perimeter of 6 white colour pieces

$= 6 \times$ Perimeter of one triangular piece

$= 6 \times 50 = 300\,\text{cm}$

Area and Perimeter of different types of Triangles

1. **Right angled triangle** The triangle whose one angle is right angle is called right angled triangle.

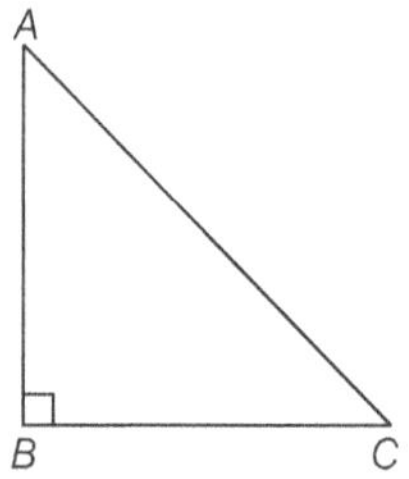

Area of $\Delta ABC = \frac{1}{2} \times BC \times AB$

and perimeter of $\Delta ABC = AB + BC + CA$.

2. **Equilateral triangle** The triangle whose all the three sides are equal, is called an equilateral triangle.

Area of $\Delta ABC = \frac{\sqrt{3}}{4}a^2$ sq units

and perimeter of $\Delta ABC = 3a$ units.

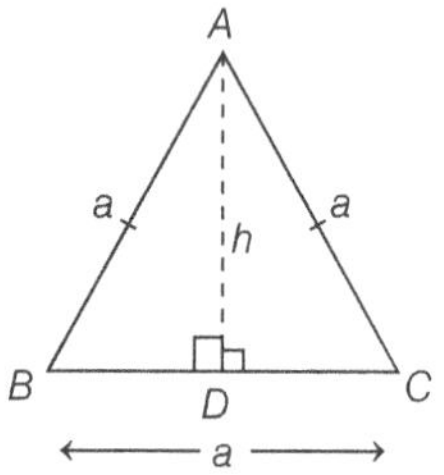

3. **Isosceles triangle** The triangle whose two sides are equal, is called an isosceles triangle.

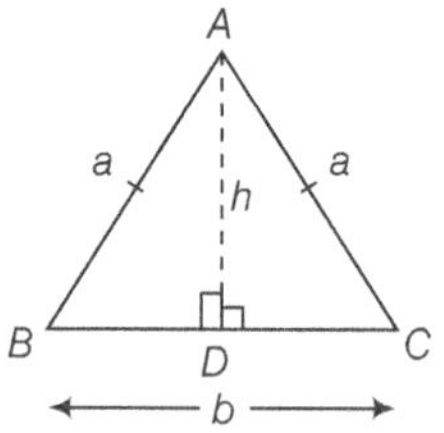

Perimeter of $\Delta ABC = a + a + b = (2a + b)$ units

and area of an isosceles ΔABC

$$= \frac{1}{4}b\sqrt{4a^2 - b^2} \text{ sq units}$$

Example 5. The base and hypotenuse of a right angled triangle are, respectively 5 cm and 13 cm long. Find its area.

Sol. Given, base (B) and hypotenuse (H) are 5 cm and 13 cm, respectively.

Now, let the length of perpendicular be x cm. Then, by using Pythagoras theorem,

$$H^2 = P^2 + B^2$$

$\Rightarrow$ $(13)^2 = (x)^2 + (5)^2$

$\Rightarrow$ $169 - 25 = x^2 \Rightarrow 144 = x^2$

$\Rightarrow$ $x = \sqrt{144} \Rightarrow x = 12$ cm

[taking positive square root as side cannot be negative]

$\therefore$ Area of right angled triangle

$$= \frac{1}{2} \times \text{Base} \times \text{Height}$$

$$= \frac{1}{2} \times 5 \times 12 = 30 \text{ cm}^2$$

Hence, the required area of the right angled triangle is 30 cm^2.

Example 6. Find the area of an equilateral triangle whose each side, is 12 cm.

Sol. Given, each side is 12 cm.

We know that

Area of an equilateral triangle $= \frac{\sqrt{3}}{4}(\text{side})^2$

$$= \frac{\sqrt{3}}{4} \times 12 \times 12$$

$$= \sqrt{3} \times 3 \times 12$$

$$= 36\sqrt{3} \text{ cm}^2$$

Example 7. Find the area of an equilateral triangle, whose height is 5 cm. [Take, $\sqrt{3} = 1.73$]

Sol. Given, $AD = 5$ cm

Let each side $= a$

$BD = DC = \frac{a}{2}$ [$\because D$ is the mid-point of BC]

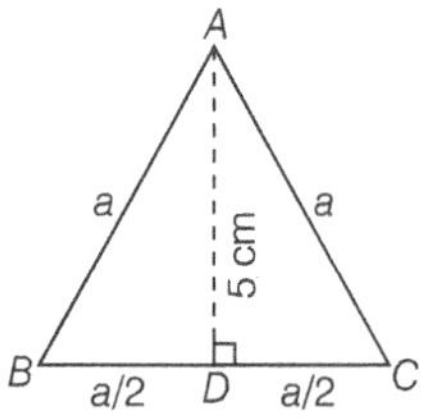

Now, applying Pythagoras theorem in ΔADB, we get

$$AB^2 = AD^2 + BD^2$$

$$a^2 = (5)^2 + \left(\frac{a}{2}\right)^2$$

$\Rightarrow$ $25 = a^2 - \frac{a^2}{4}$

$\Rightarrow$ $25 = \frac{3a^2}{4}$

$\Rightarrow$ $a^2 = \frac{25 \times 4}{3} = \frac{100}{3}$

$\therefore$ Area of an equilateral ΔABC

$$= \frac{\sqrt{3}}{4}a^2 = \frac{\sqrt{3}}{4} \times \frac{100}{3} = \frac{25}{\sqrt{3}}$$

$$= \frac{25}{1.73} = 14.45 \text{ cm}^2$$

Example 8. Find the area of an isosceles triangle whose equal sides are 5 cm each and base is 6 cm.

Sol. Let each of equal side, $a = 5\text{cm}$ and base, $b = 6\text{cm}$.

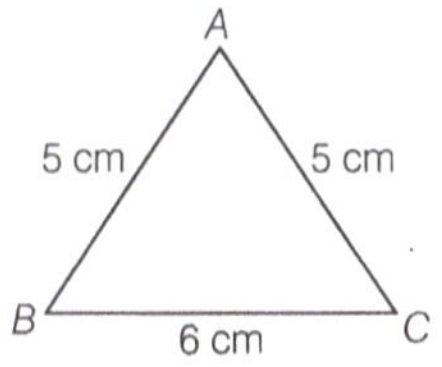

We know that

Area of an isosceles triangle $= \frac{1}{4} b\sqrt{4a^2 - b^2}$

$\therefore$ Area of $\Delta ABC = \frac{1}{4} \times 6\sqrt{4 \times (5)^2 - (6)^2} = \frac{1}{4} \times 6\sqrt{100 - 36}$

$= \frac{1}{4} \times 6\sqrt{64} = \frac{1}{4} \times 6 \times 8 = 12\,\text{cm}^2$

Alternate Method 1

Draw $AD \perp BC \Rightarrow BD = DC = 3\,\text{cm}$

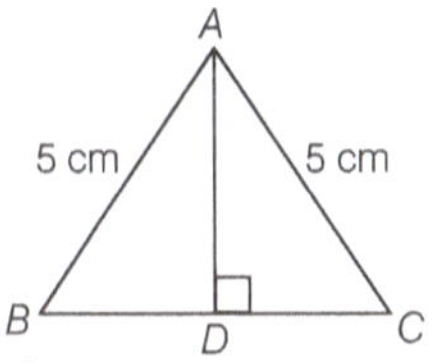

By Pythagoras theorem,

$AD = \sqrt{AC^2 - DC^2}$

$AD = 4\,\text{cm}$

Area of $\Delta ABC = 2 \times$ Area of ΔADC

$= 2 \times \frac{1}{2} \times 3 \times 4$

$\left[\because \text{area of } \Delta = \frac{1}{2} \times \text{base} \times \text{height}\right]$

$= 12\,\text{cm}^2$

Alternate Method 2

Semi-perimeter$(s) = \frac{5+5+6}{2} = \frac{16}{2} = 8\,\text{cm}$

By using Heron's formula,

Area of $\Delta = \sqrt{s(s-a)(s-b)(s-c)}$, where $a = b = 5, c = 6$

$= \sqrt{8(8-5)(8-5)(8-6)}$

$= \sqrt{8 \times 3 \times 3 \times 2}$

$= 4 \times 3 = 12\,\text{cm}^2$

Perimeter and Area of a Quadrilateral

Consider a quadrilateral *ABCD*.

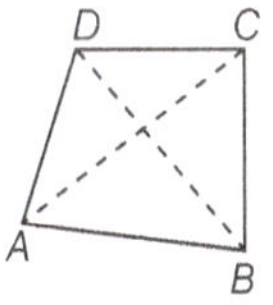

Perimeter of quadrilateral *ABCD*

= Sum of all four sides of a quadrilateral

$= AB + BC + CD + DA$

Area of quadrilateral *ABCD*

= Area of ΔABD + Area of ΔBDC

Or

= Area of ΔADC + Area of ΔABC

Area of Quadrilateral under Certain Conditions

(i) **When one diagonal and the perpendicular drawn from the remaining vertices to this diagonal are given**

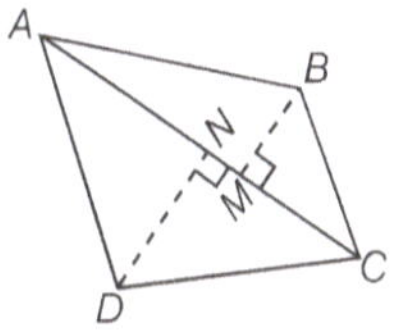

Area of quadrilateral *ABCD*

$= \text{ar}(\Delta ADC) + \text{ar}(\Delta ABC) = \frac{1}{2} \times AC \times (DN + BM)$

(ii) **When diagonals of a quadrilateral intersect each other at right angles**

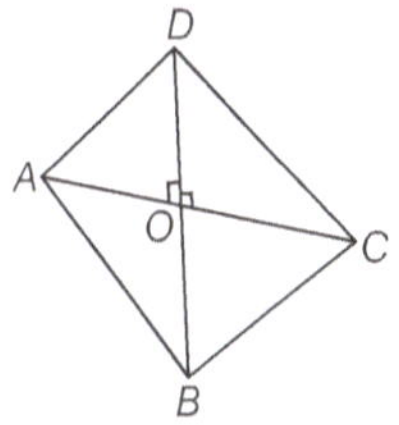

Area of quadrilateral *ABCD*

$= \frac{1}{2} \times AC \times BD = \frac{1}{2} \times$ (Product of diagonals)

Example 9. Find the area of a quadrilateral *ABCD*, in which $AB = 5$ cm, $BC = 4$ cm, $CD = 4$ cm, $DA = 5$ cm and $AC = 7$ cm.

Sol. Given, $AB = 5\text{cm}$, $BC = 4\text{cm}$, $CD = 4\text{cm}$, $DA = 5\text{cm}$ and $AC = 7\text{cm}$.

Clearly, length of sides of ΔABC are equal to length of corresponding sides of ΔADC.

$\therefore$ Area of ΔABC = Area of ΔADC

Now, area of quadrilateral $ABCD = 2$ (area of ΔADC) ...(i)

For ΔABC, let $a = 4$ cm, $b = 7$ cm and $c = 5$ cm.

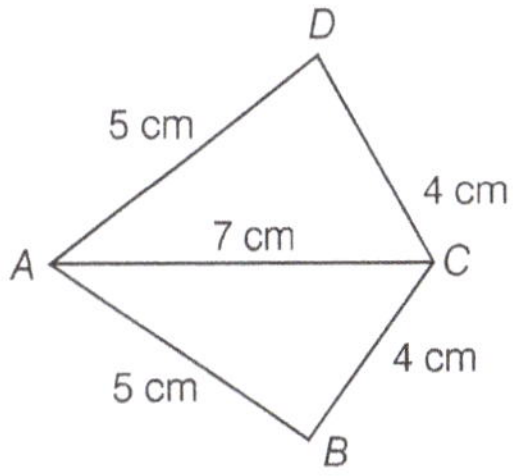

Then, semi-perimeter of ΔABC,

$$s = \frac{a+b+c}{2} = \frac{4+7+5}{2} = \frac{16}{2} = 8 \text{ cm}$$

$\therefore$ Area of $\Delta ABC = \sqrt{s(s-a)(s-b)(s-c)}$ [by Heron's formula]

$$= \sqrt{8(8-4)(8-7)(8-5)}$$
$$= \sqrt{8 \times 4 \times 1 \times 3}$$
$$= \sqrt{96} = 9.80 \text{ cm}^2$$

From Eq. (i), we get

Area of quadrilateral $ABCD = 2 \times 9.80 = 19.6 \text{ cm}^2$

Hence, required area of quadrilateral $ABCD$ is 19.6 cm^2.

Example 10. Calculate the area of quadrilateral $ABCD$, in which ΔBCD is equilateral with each side equal to 10 cm, $\angle A = 90°$ and $AD = 8$ cm.

Sol. Given, a quadrilateral $ABCD$, equal side is 10 cm, $\angle A = 90°$ and $AD = 8$ cm.

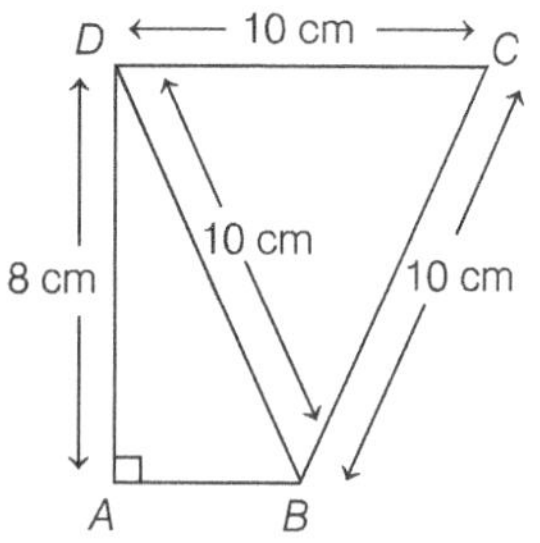

In ΔDAB, $BD^2 = AD^2 + AB^2$ [by Pythagoras theorem]

$\Rightarrow \quad AB^2 = BD^2 - AD^2$

$\Rightarrow \quad AB^2 = (10)^2 - (8)^2 = 100 - 64$

$\Rightarrow \quad AB^2 = 36$

$\Rightarrow \quad AB = 6 \text{ cm}$

[taking positive square root as side cannot be negative]

ar (quadrilateral $ABCD$) = ar (ΔBCD) + ar (ΔDAB)

$$= \frac{\sqrt{3}}{4}(10)^2 + \frac{1}{2} \times AB \times AD$$

$\left[\because \text{area of } \Delta = \frac{1}{2} \times \text{base} \times \text{height and area of an equilateral triangle} = \frac{\sqrt{3}}{4} \times (\text{side})^2\right]$

$$= \frac{\sqrt{3}}{4} \times (10)^2 + \frac{1}{2} \times 6 \times 8$$

$\therefore 25\sqrt{3} + 4 \times 6$

$$= 25\sqrt{3} + 24$$
$$= 25 \times 1.732 + 24$$
$$= 43.3 + 24$$
$$= 67.3 \text{ cm}^2$$

Example 11. Find the area of a quadrilateral whose one diagonal is 20 cm long and lengths of perpendicular from the other two vertices on it are 16.4 cm and 11.6 cm, respectively.

Sol. Let $AC = 20$ cm, $BM = 16.4$ cm and $DN = 11.6$ cm.

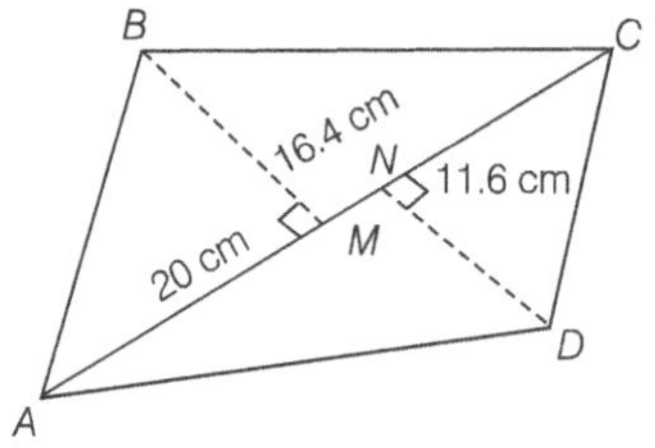

$\therefore$ Area of quadrilateral $ABCD$

$$= \frac{1}{2} \times AC \times (BM + DN)$$
$$= \frac{1}{2} \times 20 \times (16.4 + 11.6) = \frac{1}{2} \times 20 \times 28 = 280 \text{ cm}^2$$

Example 12. The diagonals of a quadrilateral intersect each other at right angles. If the length of these diagonals be 16 cm and 18 cm respectively, then find the area of the quadrilateral.

Sol. Let $AC = 16$ cm, $BD = 18$ cm and $AC \perp BD$.

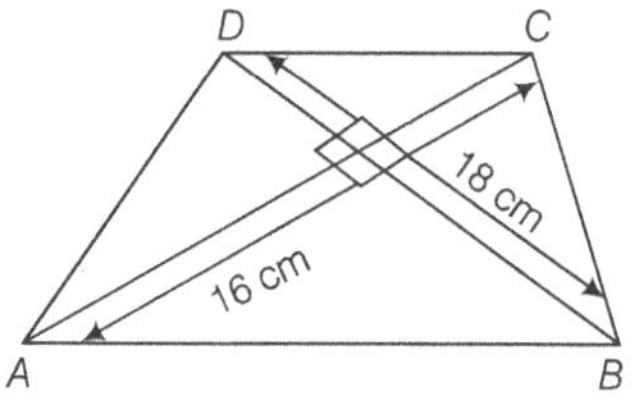

$\therefore$ Area of quadrilateral $ABCD = \frac{1}{2} \times AC \times BD$

$$= \frac{1}{2} \times 16 \times 18 = 144 \text{ cm}^2$$

Area and Perimeter of Different types of Quadrilaterals

1. **Trapezium**

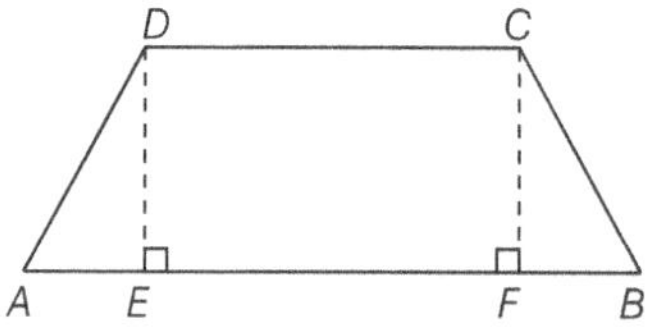

Perimeter of trapezium

= Sum of all sides of trapezium

$= AB + BC + CD + DA$

Area of trapezium

$= \frac{1}{2} \times$ (Sum of parallel sides) $\times$ (Distance between them)

$= \frac{1}{2} \times (AB + DC) \times DE$

Or

$= \frac{1}{2} \times (AB + DC) \times CF$

2. **Parallelogram**

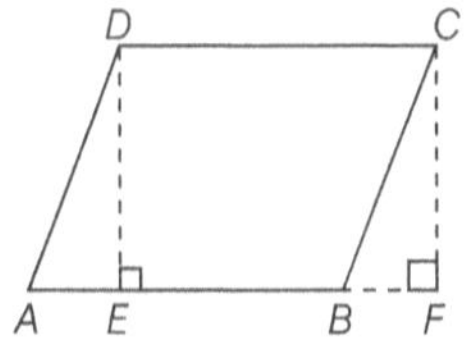

Perimeter of parallelogram

= Sum of all sides of parallelogram

$= AB + BC + CD + DA$

Area of parallelogram = Base × Height

$= AB \times DE$ (or $AB \times CF$)

3. **Rectangle**

Perimeter of rectangle $= 2(l + b)$

Area of rectangle $= l \times b$.

4. **Square**

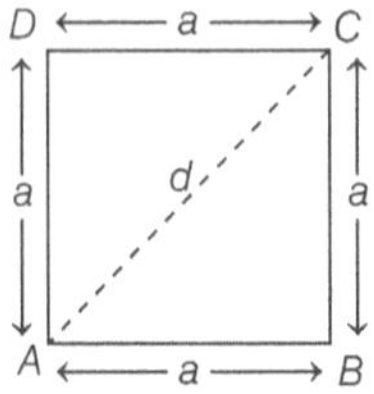

Perimeter of square $= 4a$

$= 4 \times$ (Side)

Area of square $= a^2 =$ (Side)^2.

5. **Rhombus**

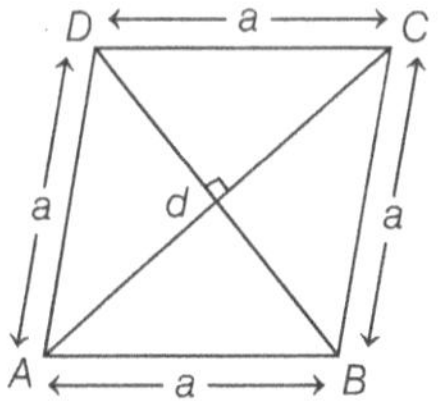

Perimeter of rhombus $= 4a = 4 \times$ (side)

Area of rhombus $= \frac{1}{2} \times$ Product of diagonals

[∵ diagonals of rhombus bisect each other at 90°]

Example 13. In the trapezium $ABCD$, $AB \parallel DC$ and $\angle ADC = 90°$, $AB = 10$ cm, $DC = 40$ cm and the diagonal $AC = 41$ cm. Then, find the area of trapezium.

Sol. Given, $\angle ADC = 90°$, $AB = 10$ cm, $DC = 40$ cm.

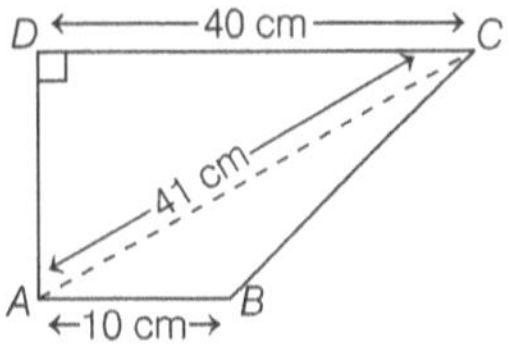

In ΔADC, $AC^2 = AD^2 + DC^2$ [using Pythagoras theorem]

$\Rightarrow \quad 41^2 = AD^2 + 40^2$

$\Rightarrow \quad AD^2 = 41^2 - 40^2 = (41 + 40)(41 - 40)$

$= 81 \times 1 = 81 \quad [\because a^2 - b^2 = (a+b)(a-b)]$

$\Rightarrow \quad AD = 9$ cm [taking positive square root as side cannot be negative]

$\therefore$ Area of trapezium $= \frac{1}{2} \times (AB + CD) \times AD$

[∵ area of trapezium $= \frac{1}{2} \times$ sum of parallel sides × distance between them]

$= \frac{1}{2} \times (10 + 40) \times 9 = \frac{1}{2} \times 50 \times 9 = 25 \times 9$

$= 225 \text{ cm}^2$

Example 14. The area of a parallelogram is 392 m^2. If its altitude is twice the corresponding base, then find its base and altitude.

Sol. Let DE is altitude.

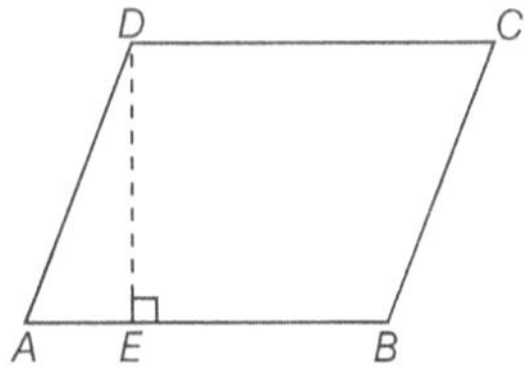

According to the question,

$DE = 2AB$

$\because$ Area of parallelogram $ABCD = 392 \text{ m}^2$

$\therefore \quad AB \times DE = 392$

[∵ area of parallelogram = base × height]

$\Rightarrow \quad AB \times 2AB = 392 \Rightarrow 2(AB)^2 = 392$

$\Rightarrow \quad (AB)^2 = \frac{392}{2} = 196 \Rightarrow AB = 14$ m

[taking positive square root as side cannot be negative]

Hence, the required base is 14 m and altitude is 28 m.

Example 15. Find the area of a parallelogram given in the following figure. Also, find the length of the altitude from vertex A on the side DC.

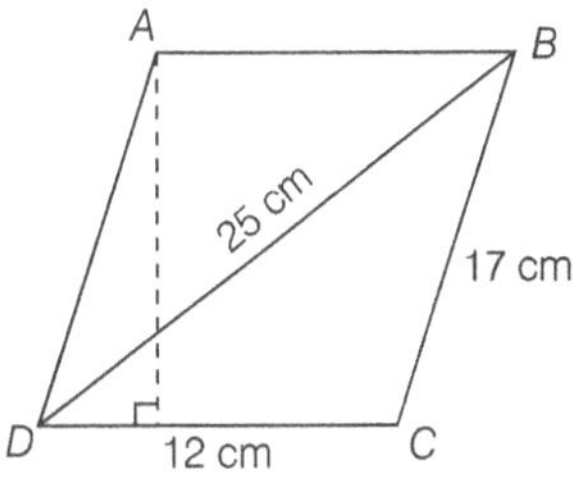

Sol. Clearly, ar (parallelogram $ABCD$) = 2× ar (ΔBCD) ...(i)

Let the sides of ΔBCD be $a = 12$ cm, $b = 17$ cm and $c = 25$ cm.

Semi-perimeter of ΔBCD,

$$s = \frac{a+b+c}{2} = \frac{12+17+25}{2} = \frac{54}{2} = 27 \text{ cm}$$

and ar (ΔBCD) = $\sqrt{s(s-a)(s-b)(s-c)}$ [by Heron's formula]

$$= \sqrt{27(27-12)(27-17)(27-25)}$$
$$= \sqrt{27 \times 15 \times 10 \times 2}$$
$$= \sqrt{3 \times 3 \times 3 \times 3 \times 5 \times 5 \times 2 \times 2}$$
$$= 3 \times 3 \times 5 \times 2$$
$$= 90 \text{ cm}^2$$

On substituting the value of area of ΔBCD in Eq. (i), we get

Area of parallelogram $ABCD$ = 2 × 90 = 180 cm^2 ...(ii)

Let altitude of the parallelogram corresponding to base DC be h cm.

Area of parallelogram $ABCD$ = Base × Altitude

$\Rightarrow$ $180 = DC \times h$ [from Eq. (ii)]

$\Rightarrow$ $180 = 12 \times h$

$\therefore$ $h = \frac{180}{12} = 15$ cm

Hence, the required area of parallelogram is 180 cm^2 and the length of altitude is 15 cm.

Example 16. The area of a square field is 576 m^2. Find the length of its one side and one diagonal.

Sol. Let each side of square is a metres.

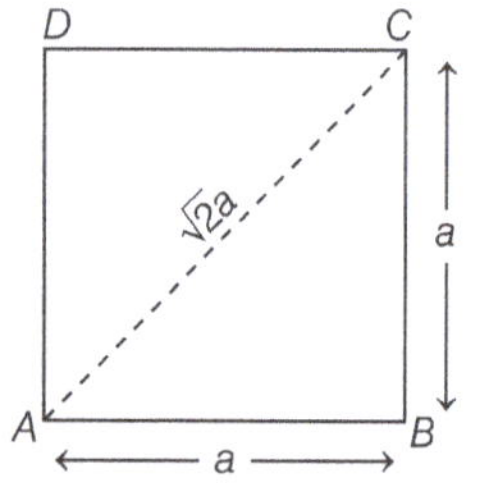

$\therefore$ Area of square $ABCD = a^2$

$\Rightarrow$ $576 = a^2$ [$\because$ area of square = 576 m^2]

$\Rightarrow$ $a = \sqrt{576} = 24$ m

[taking positive square root as side cannot be negative]

and length of diagonal = $\sqrt{2}a = 24\sqrt{2}$ m.

Example 17. In the given figure, triangle is drawn inside the rectangle. Find the area and perimeter of the shaded region.

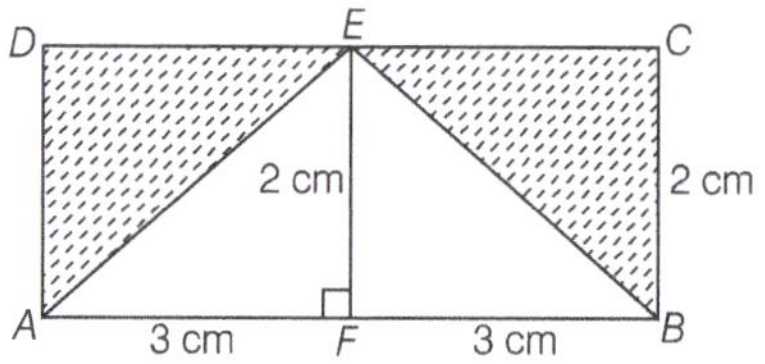

Sol. Now, area of $\Delta ABE = \frac{1}{2} \times AB \times EF$

$\left[\because \text{area of triangle} = \frac{1}{2} \times \text{base} \times \text{height}\right]$

$= \frac{1}{2} \times 6 \times 2 = 6 \text{ cm}^2$

and area of the rectangle $ABCD$

$= AB \times BC$

$= 6 \times 2 = 12 \text{ cm}^2$

[$\because$ area of rectangle = length × breadth]

$\therefore$ Area of the shaded region = Area of rectangle $ABCD$ − Area of a ΔABE

$= 12 - 6 = 6 \text{ cm}^2$

Now, in right angled ΔAFE,

$AE = \sqrt{AF^2 + FE^2}$ [using Pythagoras theorem]

$= \sqrt{(3)^2 + (2)^2} = \sqrt{9+4}$

$= \sqrt{13} = 3.6$ cm

$\therefore$ Perimeter of the shaded region

$= (AD + DE + EA) + (BC + CE + EB)$

$= 2(AD + DE + EA)$

[$\because AD = BC, AE = EB$ and $DE = CE$]

$= 2(2 + 3 + 3.6)$

$= 2(8.6) = 17.2$ cm

Exercise 15.1

1. The sides of a right angled triangle containing the right angle are $5x$ cm and $(3x - 1)$ cm. If its area is 60 cm^2, then find its perimeter.
2. ABC is a triangle, in which $AB = AC = 4$ cm and $\angle A = 90°$. Find
   (i) the area of ΔABC.
   (ii) the length of perpendicular from A to BC.
3. Find the area of an isosceles triangle, by using Heron's formula having base 4 cm and length of one of equal side as 6 cm.
4. Find the area of this triangle.
   (i) If the sides of a triangle are 8 m, 9 m and 13 m.
   (ii) If the sides of a triangle are 7 cm, 9 cm and 14 cm.
5. The perimeter of a triangular field is 420 m and its sides are in the ratio 6 : 7 : 8. Find the area of the triangular field.
6. If the sides of a triangle are 20 cm, 24 cm and 28 cm, find the length of longest altitude.
7. The base of an isosceles triangle is 18 cm and its area is 108 cm^2. Find its perimeter.

8. Calculate the area of the shaded region in the following figure.

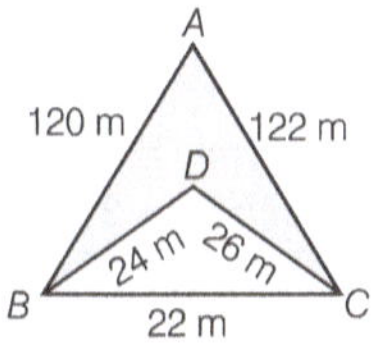

9. The sides of a quadrilateral $ABCD$ are 6 cm, 8 cm, 12 cm and 14 cm (taken in order) respectively and the angle between the first two sides is a right angle. Find its area.

10. Find the area of the trapezium $PQRS$, with height PQ, which is in the figure given below.

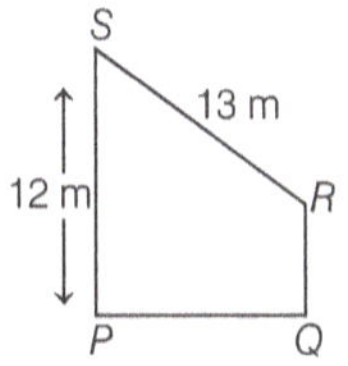

11. Find the area of a field which is in the shape of trapezium having parallel sides are 20 m and 42 m and non-parallel sides are 21 m and 23 m.

12. Two adjacent sides of a parallelogram are 28 cm and 21 cm. If the distance between the longer sides is 12 cm, then find the distance between shorter sides.

13. The area of a parallelogram is 338 m^2. If its altitude is twice the corresponding base, determine the base and the altitude.

14. In the given figure, $ABCD$ is a rectangle of dimensions 4 cm and 6 cm. E and F are the mid-points of AB and BC, respectively. Find the area of the shaded portion.

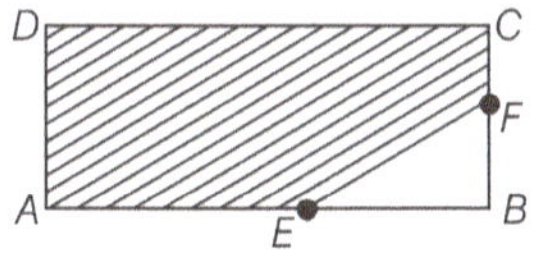

15. The side of a square exceeds the side of another square by 4 cm and the sum of the areas of the two squares is 656 cm^2. Find the perimeters of the squares.

16. The area of a rhombus is 72 cm^2. If one of the diagonal is 18 cm long, find the length of the other diagonal.

17. Find the area of a rhombus, one side of which is 20 cm and one of whose diagonal is 32 cm.

18. A kite is in the shape of a square with diagonal 40 cm and an isosceles triangle of base 6 cm and side 4 cm. Find the area of the given figure.

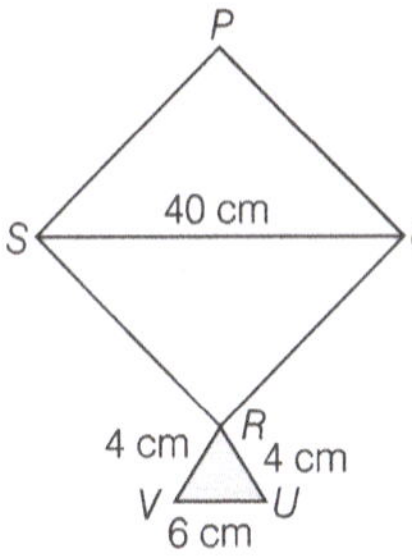

19. Calculate the area of pentagon $ABCDE$ show in figure below, given that $AX = BX = 6$ cm, $EY = CY = 4$ cm, $DE = DC = 5$ cm, $DX = 9$ cm and DX is perpendicular to EC and AB.

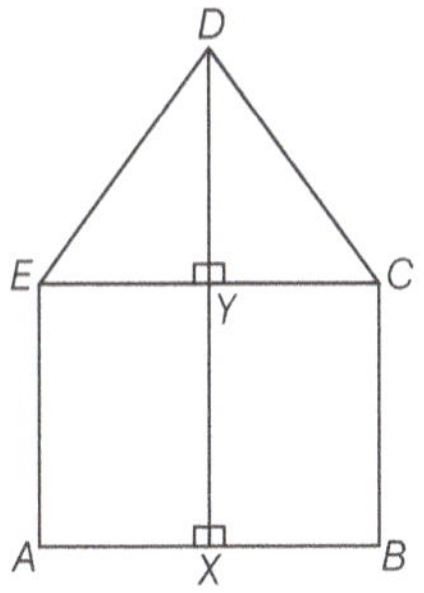

20. In the given figure, $ABCD$ is a rectangle with sides $AB = 10$ cm and $BC = 8$ cm, SAD and BQC are equilateral triangles; APB and DRC are right angled isosceles triangles. Find the area of the shaded region and the perimeter of the figure.

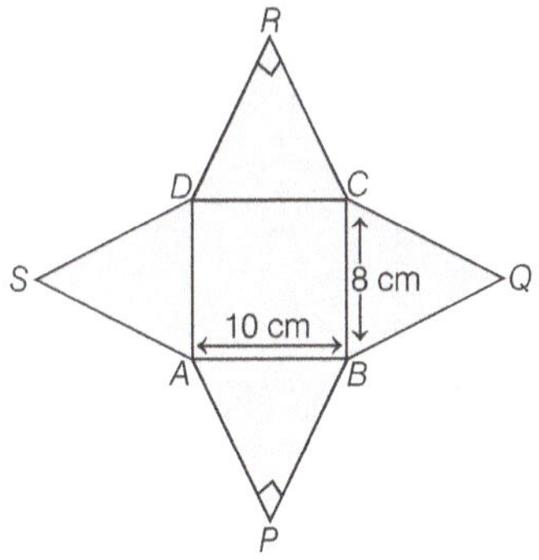

Circle

A circle is the locus of a point that moves in a plane in such a way that its distance from a fixed point remains same. This fixed point is called the **centre** and the constant distance is called the **radius** of the circle.

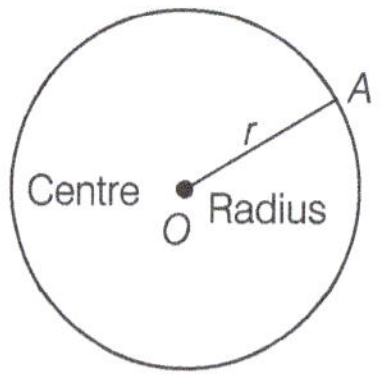

Diameter of a Circle

A line-segment joining any two points on a circle and passing through its centre is called a **diameter** of the circle.

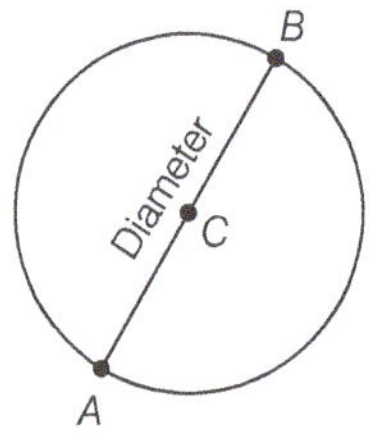

∴ Diameter = 2 × Radius

Circumference of a Circle

The length of the boundary of a circle is known as **circumference** (or perimeter) of a circle.

Circumference = $\pi \times$ Diameter = $\pi \times 2r = 2\pi r$

Area of a Circle

The surface enclosed by the circumference of the circle is called **area** of a circle.

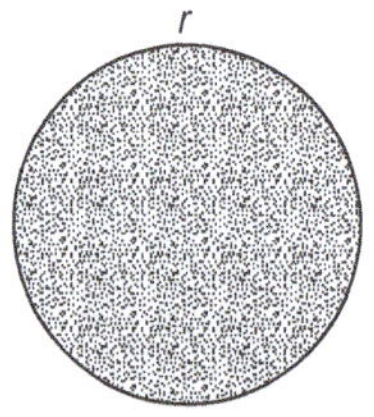

Area of circle = πr^2 where, r is radius of a circle.

Some Important Facts Related to Circle

(i) Distance covered by a wheel in 1 rotation
= Circumference of the wheel

(ii) Number of rotations taken by wheel (n)
$= \dfrac{\text{Total distance covered by the wheel}}{\text{Circumference of the wheel}}$

Example 18. Find the circumference of a circle of radius 8 cm. Give your answer correct to one decimal place. [take $\pi = 3.14$]

Sol. Given, radius of a circle, $r = 8$ cm

∵ Circumference of a circle = $2\pi r$

∴ Circumference of a circle = $2 \times 3.14 \times 8 = 50.2$ cm

Example 19. Find the area of a circle, whose

(i) radius is 5 cm.

(ii) diameter is 16 cm. [take $\pi = 3.14$]

Sol.

(i) Given, radius of a circle, $r = 5$ cm

∴ Area of a circle = $\pi r^2 = (3.14)\,(5)^2 = 25 \times 3.14 = 78.5\text{ cm}^2$

(ii) Given, diameter of a circle, $d = 16$ cm

∴ Radius of the circle, $r = \dfrac{d}{2} = \dfrac{16}{2} = 8$ cm

∴ Area of a circle = $\pi r^2 = (3.14)\,(8)^2$
$= 64 \times 3.14 = 200.96\text{ cm}^2$

Example 20. How many times, will the wheel of a car rotate in a journey of 44 km, if it is known that the diameter of the wheel is 28 cm? [take $\pi = 22/7$]

Sol. Given, diameter of the wheel, $d = 28$ cm

∴ Radius of the wheel, $r = \dfrac{d}{2} = \dfrac{28}{2} = 14$ cm

Now, distance covered by wheel in one rotation
= Circumference of a circle = $2\pi r$
$= 2 \times \dfrac{22}{7} \times 14 = 2 \times 22 \times 2 = 88$ cm

Clearly, total distance covered by the wheel in the journey
= 44 km = $44 \times 1000 \times 100$ cm
[∵ 1 km = $1 \times 1000 \times 100$ cm]
= 4400000 cm

Number of rotations
$= \dfrac{\text{Total distance covered by the wheel}}{\text{Distance covered by the wheel in one rotation}}$
$= \dfrac{4400000}{88} = 50000$

Hence, wheel of the car will, take 50000 rotations to cover a distance of 44 km.

Example 21. The radius of the wheel of a bus is 25 cm. If the speed of the bus is 33 km/h, then how many revolutions will the wheel make in 1 min?

Sol. In 1 h, distance covered by wheel = 33 km.

In 1 min, distance covered by wheel = $\dfrac{33 \times 1000}{60} = 550$ m

Now, Number of revolutions made in 1 min
$= \dfrac{\text{Distance covered by wheel}}{\text{Circumference of the wheel}}$
$= \dfrac{550}{2 \times \dfrac{22}{7} \times \dfrac{25}{100}}$ $\left[\because 25 \text{ cm} = \dfrac{25}{100}\text{ m}\right]$
$= \dfrac{550 \times 7 \times 100}{2 \times 22 \times 25} = 350$

Example 22. The short and long hands of a clock are 6 cm and 8 cm long, respectively. Find the sum of the distance travelled by their tips in 1 day. [take, $\pi = 22/7$]

Sol. In 1 day, i.e. 24 h, short (hour) hand of the clock make 2 revolutions and long (minute) hand make 24 revolutions.

In 1 revolution, distance travelled by tip of hour hand

= Circumference of circle of radius 6 cm

$= 2\times\frac{22}{7}\times 6$

In 1 revolution, distance travelled by tip of minute hand

= Circumference of circle of radius 8 cm

$= 2\times\frac{22}{7}\times 8$

$\therefore$ Sum of distances travelled by tips of both hand in 1 day

$$= 2\times 2\times\frac{22}{7}\times 6 + 24\times 2\times\frac{22}{7}\times 8$$

$$= 2\times\frac{22}{7}\times(12+192)$$

$$= 2\times\frac{22}{7}\times 204 = 1282.29\text{ cm (approx.)}$$

Example 23. The radii of two circles are 13 cm and 6 cm, respectively. Find the radius of the circle which has circumference equal to sum of the circumferences of the two circles.

Sol. Circumference of the circle having radius 13 cm

$= 2\pi\times 13 = 26\pi$ cm [$\because$ radius = 13 cm]

and circumference of the circle having radius 6 cm

$= 2\pi\times 6 = 12\pi$ cm [$\because$ radius = 6 cm]

$\therefore$ Sum of the circumferences of the two circles

$= 26\pi + 12\pi = 38\pi$ cm

Let r be the radius of the required circle whose circumference is 38π cm.

Then, $2\pi r = 38\pi \Rightarrow r = 19$ cm

Hence, the radius of the new circle is 19 cm.

Example 24. The cost of fencing a circular field at the rate of ₹ 24 per m is ₹ 5280. The field is to be ploughed at the rate of ₹ 0.50 per m^2. Find the cost of ploughing the field. [take $\pi = 22/7$]

Sol. Length of fence of a circular field

$$= \frac{\text{Total cost}}{\text{Rate}} = \frac{5280}{24} = 220\text{ m}$$

So, the circumference of the field is 220 m.

Let r be the radius of the field, then

$$2\pi r = 220$$

$$\Rightarrow \quad 2\times\frac{22}{7}\times r = 220 \Rightarrow r = \frac{220\times 7}{2\times 22} = 35\text{ m}$$

So, the radius of the field is 35 m.

Now, area of the field $= \pi r^2$

$$= \frac{22}{7}\times 35\times 35 = 22\times 5\times 35\text{ m}^2$$

Given, cost of ploughing 1 m^2 of the field = ₹ 0.50

$\therefore$ Total cost of ploughing the field $= 0.5\times 22\times 5\times 35$

= ₹ 1925

Area of a Circular Ring

The region bounded by the circumferences of two concentric circles is called an area of a circular ring.

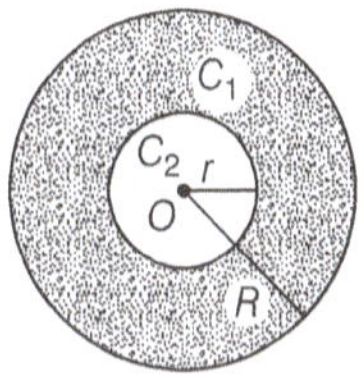

Area of circular ring = Area of shaded region

= Area of outer circle – Area of inner circle

$= \pi R^2 - \pi r^2 = \pi(R^2 - r^2)$

Example 25. In the given figure, find the area of the shaded portion.

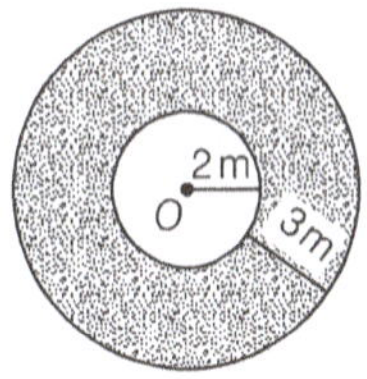

Sol. Let r and R be the radii of inner and outer circle, respectively. Then, we have

$r = 2$ m and $R = (2+3)$ m $= 5$ m

Now, area of shaded portion $= \pi(R^2 - r^2)$

$= \pi(5^2 - 2^2) = 3.14(25-4)$

$= 21\times 3.14 = 65.94\text{ cm}^2$

Semi-circle

A semi-circle is a half circle, formed by dividing the whole circle along its diameter.

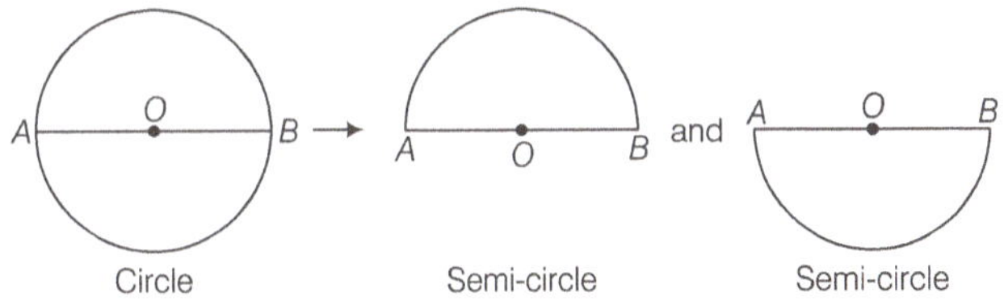

Perimeter of a Semi-circle

The perimeter of a semi-circle is equal to the sum of half circumference of a circle and length of the diameter.

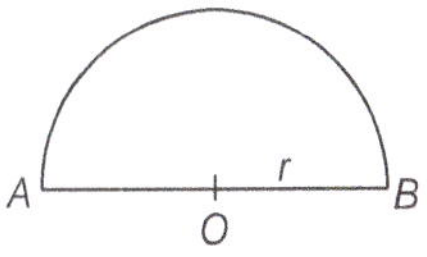

i.e. Perimeter of semi-circle $= \frac{1}{2}$ (Circumference of circle) + Length of the diameter

$$= \frac{1}{2}(2\pi r) + 2r = \pi r + 2r = r(\pi + 2)\text{ units}$$

Area of a Semi-circle

The area of semi-circle is equal to the half of area of circle,

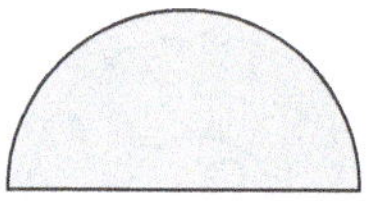

i.e. area of semi-circle $= \frac{1}{2}$ (area of a circle)

$$= \frac{1}{2}(\pi r^2) = \frac{\pi r^2}{2} \text{ sq units}$$

Example 26. Find the area and perimeter of the given figure. [take $\pi = 3.14$]

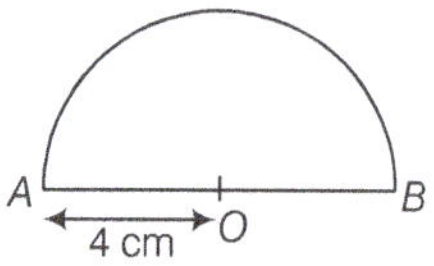

Sol. Given, radius of circle, $r = 4$ cm

Now, area of a semi-circle $= \frac{\pi r^2}{2} = \frac{3.14 \times (4)^2}{2}$

$= 3.14 \times 8 = 25.12 \text{ cm}^2$

$\because$ Perimeter of a semi-circle $= \pi r + 2r = (\pi + 2)r$

$= (3.14 + 2) \times 4$

$= 5.14 \times 4 = 20.56$ cm

Example 27. Find the area of the shaded region in figure as shown below, where *ABCD* is a square of side 12 cm.

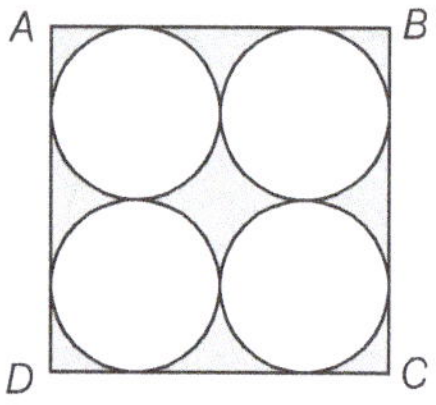

Sol. $\because$ Area of square $= (\text{Side})^2$

$\therefore$ Area of square $ABCD = 12 \times 12 = 144 \text{ cm}^2$

$\because$ Diameter of each circle $= \frac{12}{2} = 6$ cm

[here, length of square $= 2 \times$ diameter of circle]

$\therefore$ Radius of each circle $(r) = \frac{6}{2} = 3$ cm

Area of one circle $= \pi r^2 = \frac{22}{7} \times 3 \times 3 = \frac{198}{7} \text{ cm}^2$

Therefore, area of four circles $= 4 \times \frac{198}{7} = \frac{792}{7} \text{ cm}^2$

Hence, area of the shaded region

= Area of square – Area of four circles

$= 144 - \frac{792}{7}$

$= \frac{1008 - 792}{7} = \frac{216}{7} = 30.86 \text{ cm}^2$

Example 28. Find the area of shaded design in the given figure, where *ABCD* is a square of side 10 cm and semi-circles are drawn with each of the side as diameter. [take, $\pi = 3.14$]

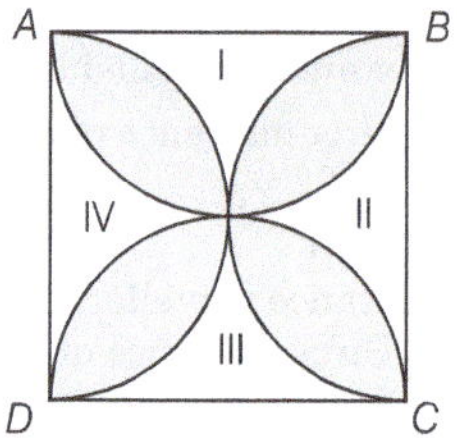

Sol. Let the four unshaded regions be denoted by I, II, III and IV as shown in the figure.

Given, side of square = 10 cm

Diameter of each semi-circle = 10 cm

$\therefore$ Radius of each semi-circle $= \frac{10}{2} = 5$ cm

Now, area of I region + area of III region

= Area of *ABCD* – Area of two semi-circles each of radius 5 cm

$= \left(10 \times 10 - 2 \times \frac{1}{2} \times \pi \times 5^2\right)$

$= (100 - 3.14 \times 25) = (100 - 78.5) = 21.5 \text{ cm}^2$

Similarly, area of II region + area of IV region $= 21.5 \text{ cm}^2$

$\therefore$ Area of the shaded design

= Area of *ABCD* – Area of (I + II + III + IV) region

$= (100 - 2 \times 21.5) = (100 - 43) = 57 \text{ cm}^2$

Problems Based on Inner and Outer Circles

1. Circumscribed Circle

The circle passing through vertices of a square *ABCD* is called circumscribed circle its radius '*R*' is called the **circumradius** and its centre is known as **circumcentre** of a circle.

2. Inscribed Circle

The circle touching all sides of square *ABCD* internally is known as an inscribed circle. Its radius '*r*' is called the **inradius** and its centre is called **incentre** of a circle.

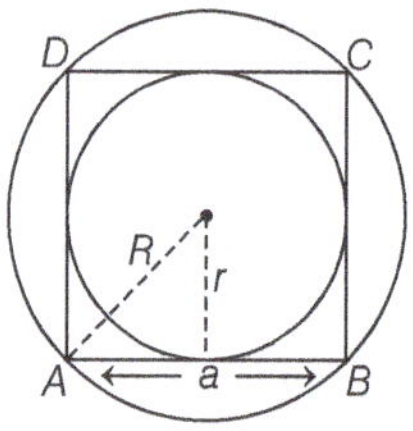

Let *ABCD* be a square of side *a* unit.

Let R and r be the radii of circumscribed and inscribed circle, respectively.

Then, $2r = a$

$\Rightarrow \quad r = \frac{a}{2}$

and $\quad 2R = \sqrt{a^2 + a^2}$

$\Rightarrow \quad R = \frac{a}{2}\sqrt{2} = \frac{a}{\sqrt{2}}$

(i) Area of inscribed circle $= \pi r^2$

$$= \pi\left(\frac{a}{2}\right)^2 = \frac{\pi a^2}{4}$$

(ii) Area of circumscribed circle $= \pi R^2$

$$= \pi\left(\frac{a}{\sqrt{2}}\right)^2 = \frac{\pi a^2}{2}$$

Example 29. In the given figure, a circle is inscribed and circumscribed in a square of side 14 cm.

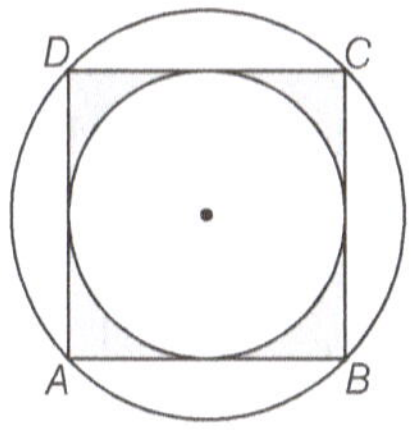

(i) Determine the inradius and circumradius of a circle.
(ii) Find the area of inscribed and circumscribed of circle.
(iii) Find the area of the shaded region.

Sol.

(i) Given, side of a square, $a = 14$ cm

Let r and R be the radii of inscribed and circumscribed circle, respectively.

Then, inradius, $r = \frac{a}{2} = \frac{14}{2} = 7$ cm

and circumradius, $R = \frac{a}{2}\sqrt{2} = \frac{14}{2}\sqrt{2}$

$= 7\sqrt{2}$ cm

(ii) $\therefore$ Area of inscribed circle $= \frac{\pi a^2}{4}$

$$= \frac{22}{7} \times \frac{(14)^2}{4} = 22 \times 7$$

$$= 154 \text{ cm}^2$$

$\therefore$ Area of circumscribed circle $= \frac{\pi a^2}{2} = \frac{22}{7} \times \frac{(14)^2}{2}$

$$= 22 \times 14 = 308 \text{ cm}^2$$

(iii) Area of shaded region

= Area of a square – Area of inscribed circle

$= (14)^2 - 154 = 196 - 154 = 42 \text{ cm}^2$

Example 30. A square $OABC$ is inscribed in a quadrant $OPBQ$ of a circle as shown in figure.
If $OA = 14$ cm, then find the area of shaded region. [take, $\pi = 22/7$]

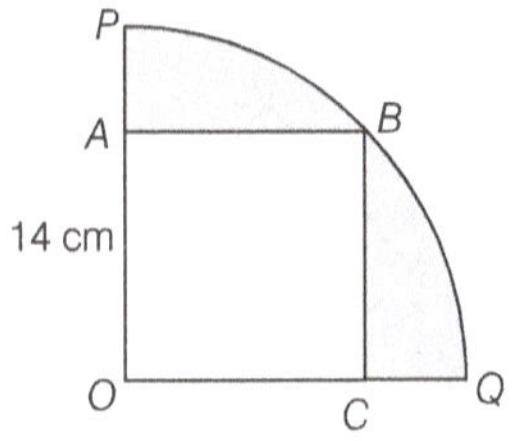

Sol. $\because$ Diagonal of a square $= OB =$ Radius $(r) =$ Side $\sqrt{2}$

$= 14\sqrt{2}$ cm [$\because$ diagonal of square = side $\sqrt{2}$]

$\therefore$ Area of shaded region

= Area of quadrant $OPBQ$ – Area of square $OABC$

$$= \frac{1}{4}\pi r^2 - (\text{Side})^2 = \frac{1}{4} \times \frac{22}{7} \times (14\sqrt{2})^2 - (14)^2$$

$$= \frac{11}{14} \times 14 \times 14 \times 2 - 196 = 308 - 196 = 112 \text{ cm}^2$$

Sector of a Circle

The region enclosed by two radii and the corresponding arc of a circle is called the **sector** of circle.

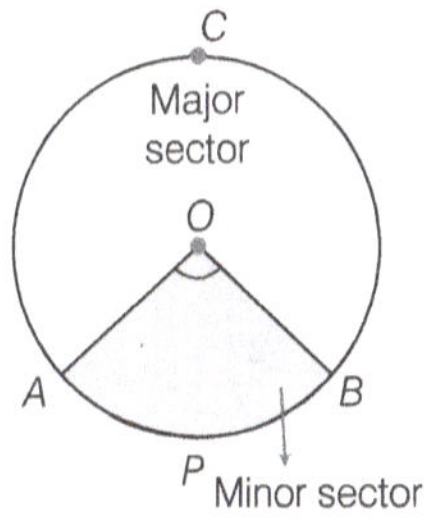

Here, $\angle AOB$ is called the **angle of sector**. The sector containing minor arc is called **minor sector** and the sector containing major arc is called **major sector.**

Area of Sector of a Circle

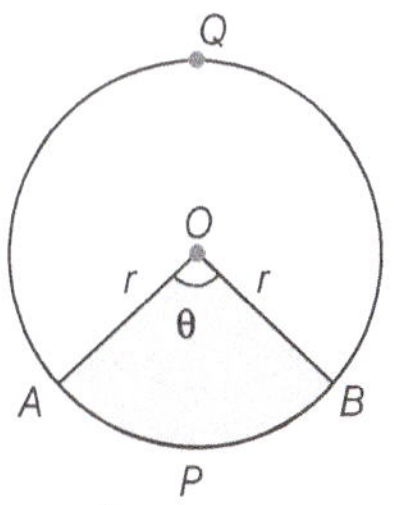

Area of the sector $= \frac{\theta}{360^\circ} \times \pi r^2$

Also, Area of the major sector

$= \pi r^2 -$ Area of minor sector

Area of minor sector $= \pi r^2 -$ Area of major sector

Length of an Arc of a Sector

The arc corresponding to a sector is called an arc of the sector.

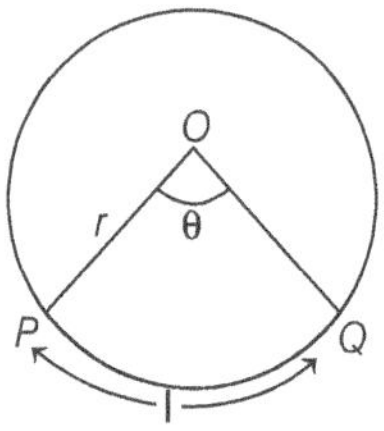

Length of an arc of a sector, $l = \frac{\theta}{360°} \times 2\pi r$

Also, area of sector in terms of length of arc $= \frac{1}{2} lr$

Example 31. The length of minute hand of a clock is 14 cm. Find the area swept by the minute hand in one minute. [take $\pi = 22/7$]

Sol. The minute hand of a clock describes a circle of radius equal to its length, i.e. 14 cm in 1 hour.

So, the angle described by minute hand in 60 min = 360°.

$\therefore$ Angle described by minute hand in 1 min $= \frac{360°}{60} = 6°$

So, the area swept by the minute hand in 1 min is the area of a sector of angle 6° in a circle of radius 14 cm.

$$\therefore \text{Required area} = \frac{\theta}{360°} \times \pi r^2$$
$$= \frac{6°}{360°} \times \frac{22}{7} \times (14)^2$$
$$= \frac{1}{60} \times \frac{22}{7} \times 14 \times 14$$
$$= 10.27 \text{ cm}^2$$

Example 32. In a circle of radius 28 cm, an arc subtends an angle of 45° at the centre. Find the length of the arc and using it, find the area of the sector.

Sol. Given, $r = 28$ cm and $\theta = 45°$.

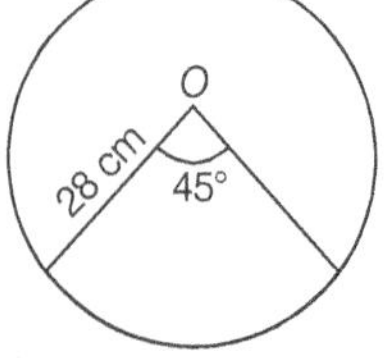

$$\therefore \text{Arc length} = \frac{\theta}{360°} \times 2\pi r$$
$$= \frac{45°}{360°} \times 2 \times \frac{22}{7} \times 28 = \frac{1}{8} \times 2 \times 22 \times 4 = 22 \text{ cm}$$

Now, area of sector $= \frac{1}{2} \times l \times r$ [where, l = arc length]

$$= \frac{1}{2} \times 22 \times 28 = 22 \times 14 = 308 \text{ cm}^2$$

Example 33. The area of an equilateral triangle is $49\sqrt{3}$ cm^2. With each vertex of the triangle as centre, a circle is described with radius equal to half the length of the side of the triangle as shown in the adjoining figure. Find the area of the shaded region.

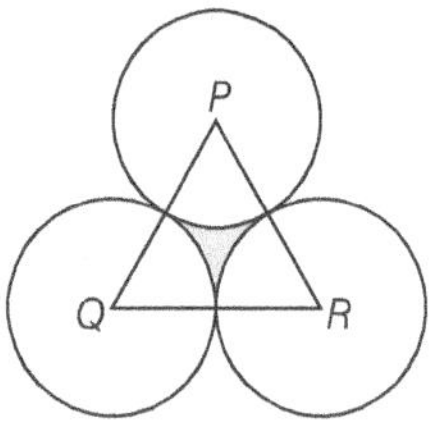

Sol. Let a cm be the side of equilateral triangle.

Then area of $\Delta PQR = \frac{\sqrt{3}}{4} a^2 = 49\sqrt{3}$ [given]

$\Rightarrow$ $a^2 = 196 \Rightarrow a = 14$ cm

$\therefore$ Each side of triangle = 14 cm

So, radius of the each circle $= \frac{1}{2} \times 14 = 7$ cm

$\therefore$ Required area = Area of ΔPQR – Sum of area of three sectors of central angle 60°.

$$= 49\sqrt{3} - 3 \times \left[\frac{60°}{360°} \times \frac{22}{7} \times 7^2\right] \text{cm}^2$$
$$= 49\sqrt{3} - 3 \times \left[\frac{1}{6} \times \frac{22}{7} \times 49\right] \text{cm}^2$$
$$= (49\sqrt{3} - 77) \text{ cm}^2$$

Example 34. A memento is made as shown in the figure. Its base *PBCR* is silver plated from the front side at the rate of ₹ 20 per cm^2. Find the total cost of the silver plating. $\left[\text{take } \pi = \frac{22}{7}\right]$

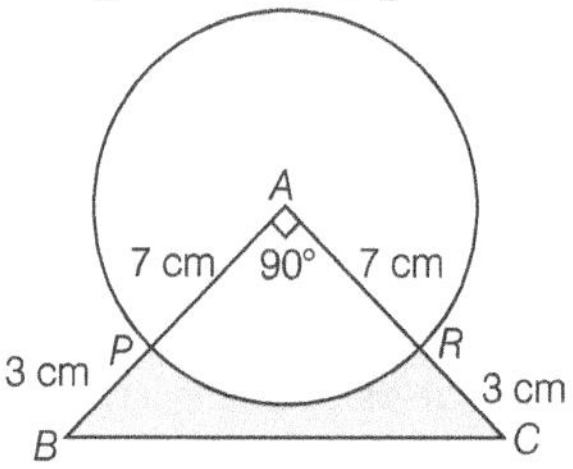

Sol. From the figure, we have

$AB = 7 + 3 = 10$ cm, $AC = 7 + 3 = 10$ cm and $\angle BAC = 90°$

Also, radius of circle $= AP = AR = 7$ cm

$\therefore$ Area of right angled $\Delta BAC = \frac{1}{2} \times AB \times AC$

$$= \frac{1}{2} \times 10 \times 10 = 50 \text{ cm}^2$$

Area of the sector $APR = \frac{90°}{360°} \times \pi r^2 = \frac{1}{4} \times \pi \times (7)^2$

$\left[\because \text{area of sector} = \frac{\theta}{360°} \times \pi r^2\right]$

$$= \frac{1}{4} \times \frac{22}{7} \times 49 = \frac{11 \times 7}{2} = 38.5 \text{ cm}^2$$

Then, area of base *PBCR* (shaded), which is to be silver plated

= Area of the right angled ΔBAC – Area of the sector APR

$= 50 - 38.5 = 11.5 \text{cm}^2$

$\therefore$ Total cost of silver plating at the rate of ₹ 20 per cm^2

= ₹20 × 11.5 = ₹ 230

Exercise 15.2

1. The diameter of a circle is 28 cm. Find its circumference and area.
2. A wheel has a diameter of 42 cm. How many times would the wheel rotate to cover a distance of 6.6 km?
3. The perimeter of a circle exceeds its diameter by 300 cm. Find its diameter. [take $\pi = 22/7$]
4. The radii of two circles are in the ratio 3 : 8. If the difference between their areas is 385π cm^2, then find the area of bigger circle. [take $\pi = 22/7$]
5. The radii of two circles are 16 cm and 12 cm. Find the area of the circle which has its circumference equal to the difference of the circumferences of the given two circles. [take $\pi = 22/7$]
6. The diameters of three circles are 12 cm, 16 cm and 48 cm. Find the perimeter of the circle having its area equal to sum of the areas of three given circles.
7. The circumference of a circle is 123.2 cm. Calculate
   (i) the radius of the circle in cm.
   (ii) the area of the circle in cm^2, correct to the nearest cm^2.
   (iii) the effect on the area of the circle, if the radius is doubled.
8. Two circles touch internally. The sum of their areas is 116π cm^2 and distance between their centres is 6 cm. Find the radii of the circles.
9. The sum of the radii of two circles is 140 cm and the difference of their circumferences is 88 cm. Find the diameters of the circles.
10. The radii of two circles are 19 cm and 9 cm, respectively. Find the radius and area of the circle, which has its circumference equal to the sum of the circumferences of the two circles.
11. The cost of fencing a circular field at the rate of ₹ 400 per meter is ₹ 52800. The field is to be ploughed at the rate ₹ 10 per m^2. Find the cost of ploughing the field. [take $\pi = 22/7$]
12. A racing track is bounded by two concentric circles with circumference 396 cm and 352 cm. Find the area of the racing track.
13. The area of a circular ring enclosed between two concentric circles is 550 cm^2. Find the radii of two circles, given that their difference is 5 cm. [take $\pi = 22/7$]
14. A 7 m wide road surrounds a circular plot whose circumference is 88 m. Find the cost of paving the road at ₹ 100 per m^2. [take $\pi = 22/7$]
15. If the area of semi-circle is 693 cm^2, then find the perimeter of the semi-circle.
16. Calculate the length of the boundary and the area of the shaded region in the given diagrams.

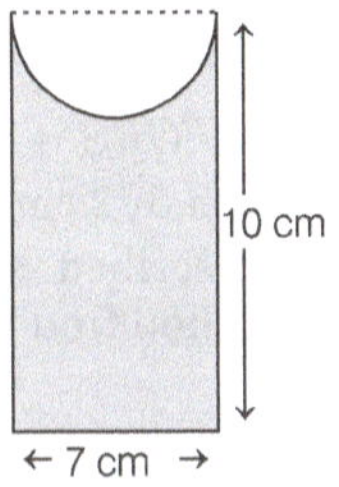

17. The length of hour hand of a clock is 7 cm. Find the area swept by the hour hand in one hour.
18. The minute hand of a clock is 12 cm long. Find the area of the face of the clock described by the minute hand between 9 : 00 am to 9 : 35 am.
19. A horse is placed for grazing inside a rectangular field 70 m by 52 m and is tethered to one corner by a rope 21 m long. On how much area can it graze?
20. A square park has each side of 100 m. At each corner of the park, there is a flower bed in the form of a quadrant of radius 14 m as shown in the figure below. Find the area of the remaining part of the park.

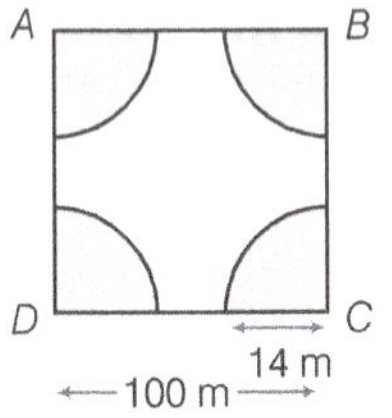

21. In the given figure, diameter AB is 12 cm long. AB is trisected at points P and Q. Find the area of the shaded region. [take $\pi = 3.14$]

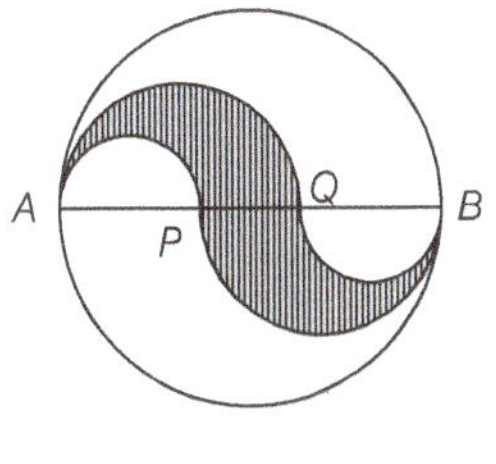

22. There are three semi-circles A, B and C having diameter 3 cm each and another semi-circle E having a circle D with diameter 4.5 cm as shown in the figure below. Find the area of the shaded region.

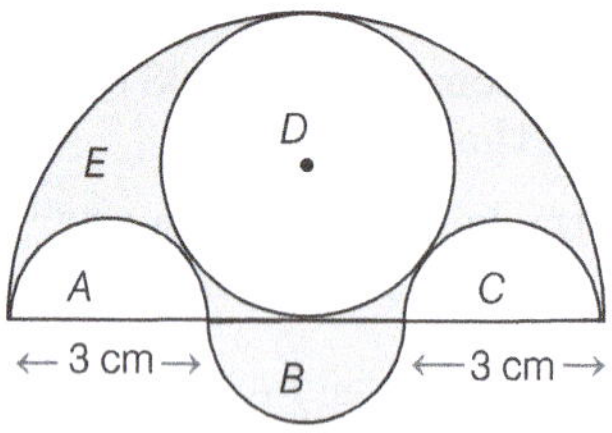

23. In the given figure, $PQRS$ is a rectangle of length $10\sqrt{2}$ cm and breadth $5\sqrt{2}$ cm. If PEQ is an isosceles triangle inscribed in the semi-circle with diameter PQ, then find the area of the shaded region.

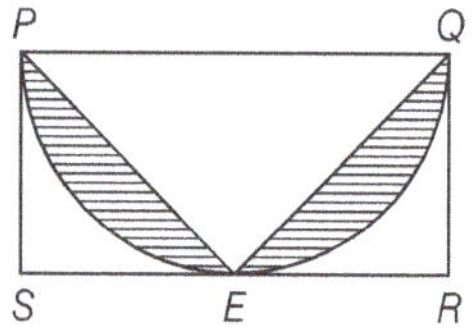

24. In the given figure, O is the centre and AOC is a diameter of the circle.

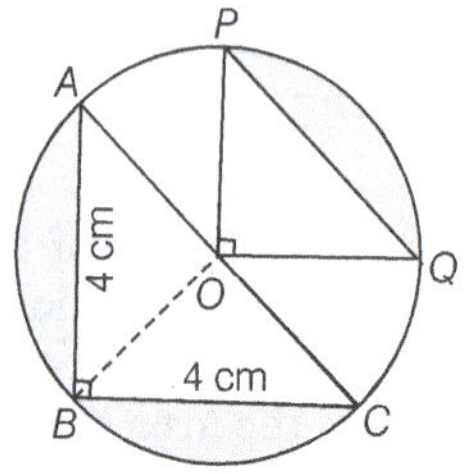

Find

(i) the sum of the areas of the two shaded segments made by the chords AB and BC.

(ii) the area of the shaded segment made by the chord PQ. $\left[\text{take } \pi = \frac{22}{7}\right]$

25. Find the area of the shaded region in the given figure, if $PQ = 24$ cm, $PR = 7$ cm and O is the centre of the circle.

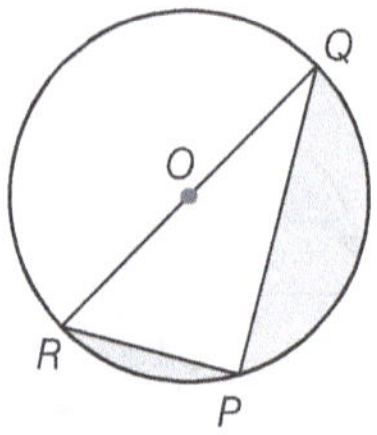

26. Find the area of the shaded region in figure, if radii of the two concentric circles with centre O are 7 cm and 14 cm respectively and $\angle AOC = 40°$.

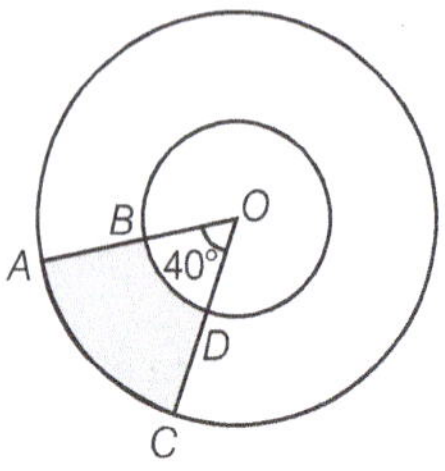

27. Find the area of the shaded region in figure, if $ABCD$ is a square of side 14 cm and APD and BPC are semi- circles.

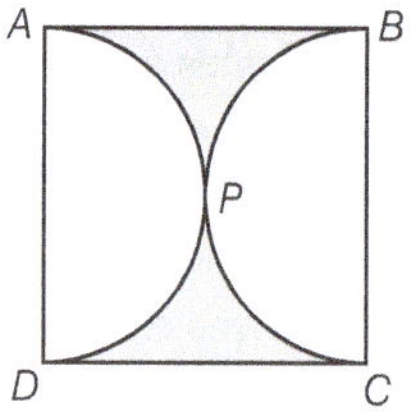

28. Find the area of the shaded region in figure, where a circular arc of radius 6 cm has been drawn with vertex O of an equilateral triangle OAB of side 12 cm as centre.

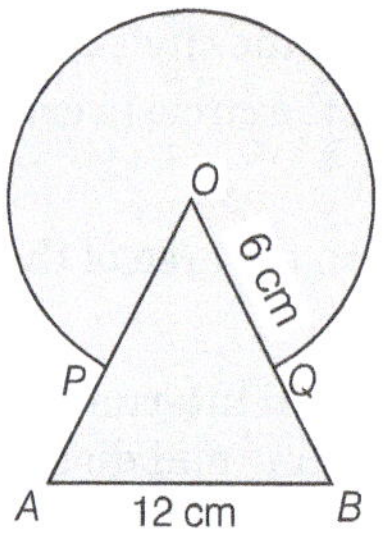

29. In the given figure, $ABCD$ is a square of side 14 cm. With centres A, B, C and D, four circles are drawn such that each circle touch externally two of the remaining three circles. Find the area of the shaded region.

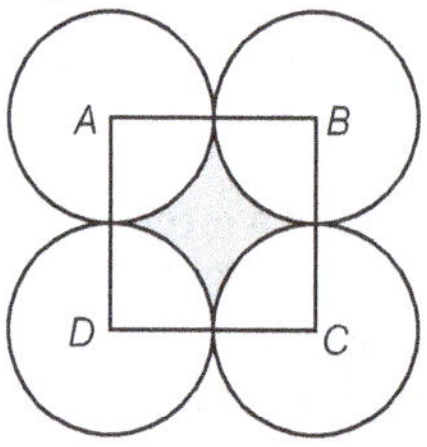

30. Following figure depicts a racing track whose left and right ends are semi-circular. The distance between two inner parallel line segments is 60 m and they are each 106 m long. If the track is 10 m wide, find

(i) the distance around the track along its inner edge.

(ii) the area of the track.

31. In the given figure, AB and CD are two diameters of a circle (with centre O) perpendicular to each other and OD is the diameter of the smaller circle. If $OA = 7$ cm, then find the area of the shaded region.

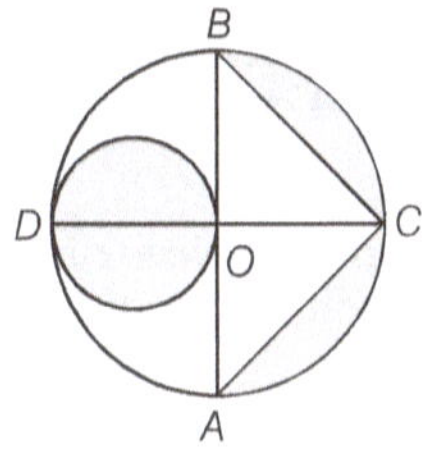

32. The area of an equilateral $\Delta\ ABC$ is 17320.5 cm^2. With each vertex of the triangle as centre, a circle is drawn with radius equal to half the length of the side of the triangle (see the figure). Find the area of the shaded region.

[take $\pi = 3.14$ and $\sqrt{3} = 1.73205$]

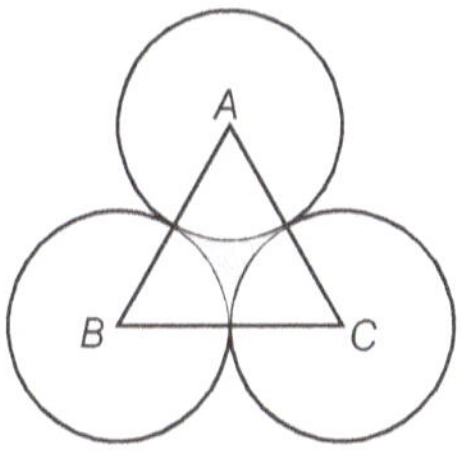

33. On a square handkerchief, nine circular designs each of radius 7 cm are made (see the figure). Find the area of the remaining portion of the handkerchief.

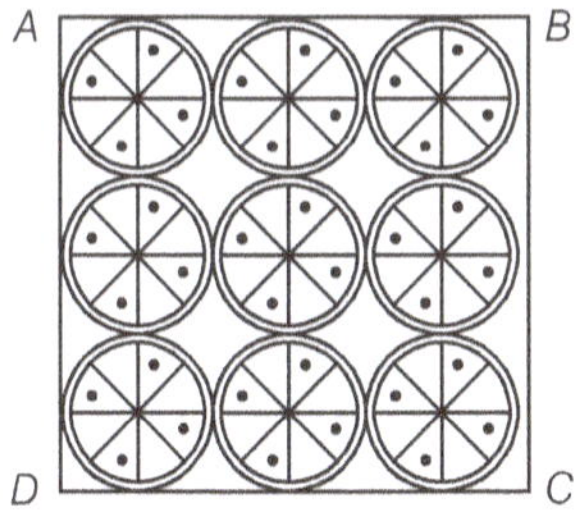

34. In the given figure, $OACB$ is a quadrant of a circle with centre O and radius 3.5 cm. If $OD = 2$ cm, then find the area of the

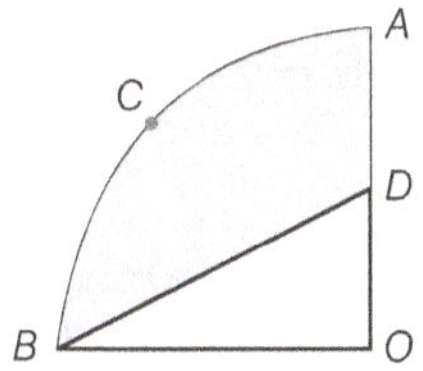

(i) quadrant $OACB$. (ii) shaded region.

35. In the given figure, a square $OABC$ is inscribed in a quadrant $OPBQ$. If $OA = 20$ cm, then find the area of the shaded region.

[take $\pi = 3.14$]

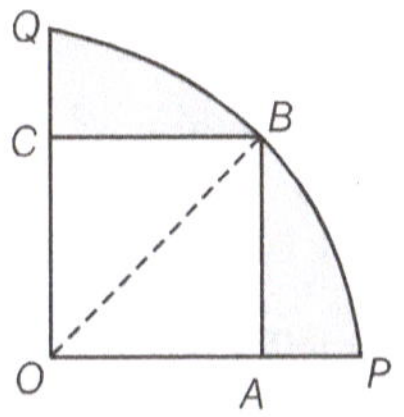

36. AB and CD are respectively arcs of two concentric circles of radii 21 cm and 7 cm, and centre O (see the figure).

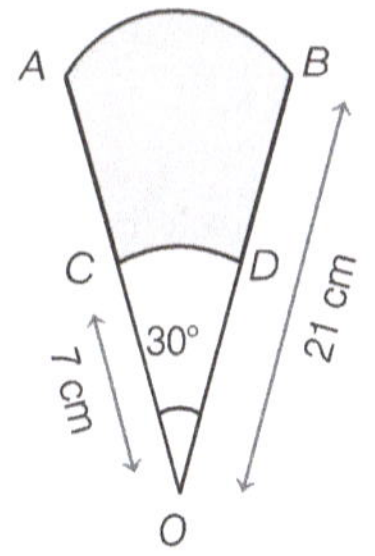

If $\angle AOB = 30°$, then find the area of the shaded region.

37. In the given figure, ABC is a quadrant of a circle of radius 14 cm and a semi-circle is drawn with BC as diameter. Find the area of the shaded region.

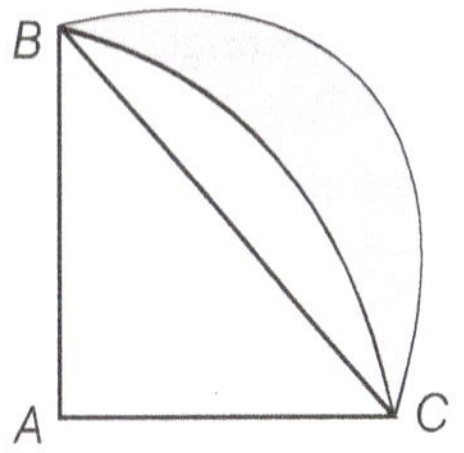

38. Calculate the area of the designed region in figure, common between the two quadrants of circles of radius 8 cm each.

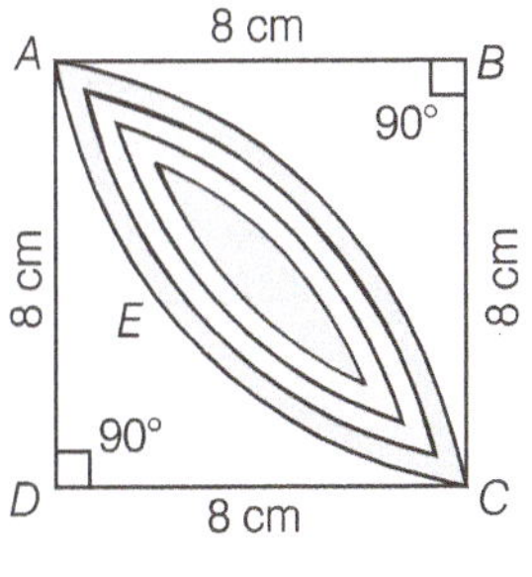

Chapter Practice

a. 1 Mark Questions

1. Area of a triangle is 30 cm^2 and base is 10 cm, then its height is
(a) 6 cm (b) 4 cm (c) 8 cm (d) 5 cm

2. The base of an isosceles triangle is 24 cm and its area is 192 sq cm. Its perimeter is
(a) 48 cm (b) 60 cm (c) 54 cm (d) 64 cm

3. The arc of a quadrilateral $ABCD$ in which $AB = 3$ cm, $BC = 4$ cm, $CD = 4$ cm, $DA = 5$ cm and $AC = 5$ cm, is
(a) 18 cm^2 (b) 27 cm^2
(c) $2(3+\sqrt{21})$ cm^2 (d) $3(2+\sqrt{21})$ cm^2

4. If perimeter of a circle is 96π cm. Then, find the perimeter of semi-circle.
(a) 26.472 cm (b) 24.672 cm
(c) 264.72 cm (d) 246.72 cm

5. If the area of the quadrant $= \frac{1}{4}\pi r^2$, then the perimeter of the quadrant?
(a) $\left(\frac{\pi}{2}+2\right)r$ (b) $(\pi+4)r$
(c) $\left(\frac{\pi}{2}+4\right)r$ (d) $\left(\frac{\pi}{4}+2\right)r$

b. 3 Marks Questions

6. Find the area of a triangle, whose height is 6 cm and base is 10 cm.

7. The area of a triangle is 216 cm^2 and its sides are in the ratio 3 : 4 : 5, find the perimeter of the triangle.

8. Find the area of a triangle whose sides are 42 cm, 34 cm and 20 cm. Hence, find the length of the altitude corresponding to the shortest side.

9. Find the semi-perimeter of an equilateral triangle of side $2a$.

10. If the altitude of an equilateral triangle is $12\sqrt{3}$ cm, then find its perimeter and area.

11. One side of an equilateral triangle is 8 cm. Find its area using Heron's formula. Also, find its altitude.

12. Find the perimeter of an equilateral triangle whose area is equal to that of a triangle with sides 21 cm, 16 cm and 13 cm.

13. Find the perimeter of an isosceles right angled triangle, whose area is 72 cm^2.

14. The area of an isosceles triangle is 12 cm^2 and then the base is 8 cm in length. Find the perimeter of the triangle.

15. If the area of an isosceles triangle is 120 cm^2 and the length of each of its equal sides is 17 cm, then find its base.

16. Each of equal sides of an isosceles triangle is 4 cm greater than its height. If the base of the triangle is 24 cm, calculate the perimeter and area of the triangle.

17. In the following figure, ABC and BDE are two equilateral triangles such that D is the mid-point of BC. If $BC = 20$ cm, then find the area of the shaded portion.

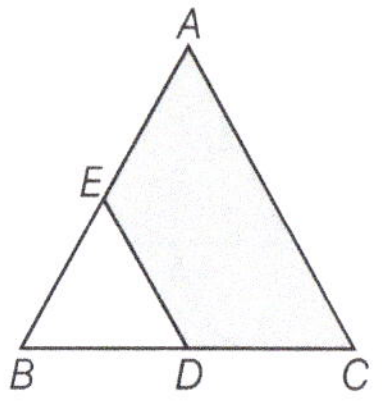

18. The given figure shows an equilateral ΔABC, whose each side is 10 cm and a right angled ΔBDC whose side $BD = 8$ cm and $\angle D = 90°$. Find the area of the shaded portion.

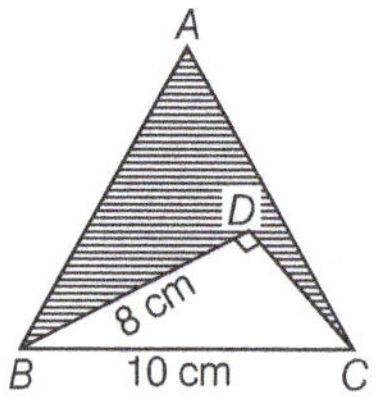

19. Find the area of a triangle whose perimeter is 22 cm, one side is 9 cm and the difference of the other two sides is 3 cm.

20. If the difference between the two sides of a right angled-triangle is 2 cm and the area of the triangle is 24 cm^2, find the perimeter of the triangle.

21. Find the area of a quadrilateral, one of whose diagonals is 30 cm long and the perpendiculars from the other two vertices are 19 cm and 11 cm, respectively.

22. In the given figure, $PQRS$ is a rhombus with $PQ = 3$ cm and height 2.5 cm. Find its area.

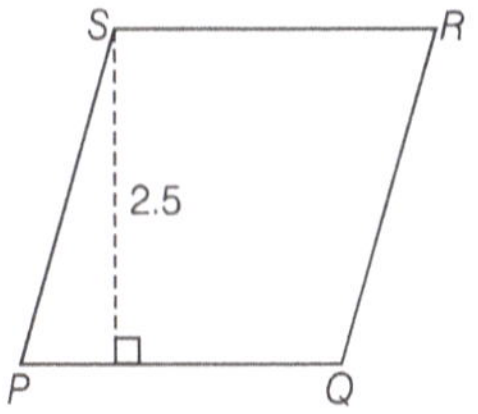

23. Find the area and the circumference of a circle, whose radius is 12.6 cm.

24. Find the area of a circle whose circumference is 22 cm.

25. The perimeter of a semi-circular protractor is 108 cm. Find the diameter of the protractor.

26. The outer and inner diameters of a circular ring are 34 cm and 32 cm, respectively. Then, find the area of ring.

27. The shaded area in the adjacent figure between the circumference of two concentric circles is 346.5 cm^2.

The circumference of the inner circle is 88 cm. Calculate the radius of the outer circle.

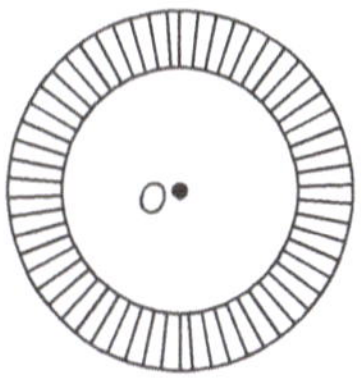

28. A footpath of uniform width runs all around the inside of a rectangular field 38 m long and 32 m wide. If the path occupies 600 m^2, find its width.

29. Area of a square is a same as that of rectangle. The length and the breadth of the rectangle are respectively 5 cm more and 4 cm less than the side of the square. Find the side of the square.

30. Two circles touch externally. The sum of their areas is 58 π cm^2 and the distance between their centre is 10 cm. Find the radii of the two circles.

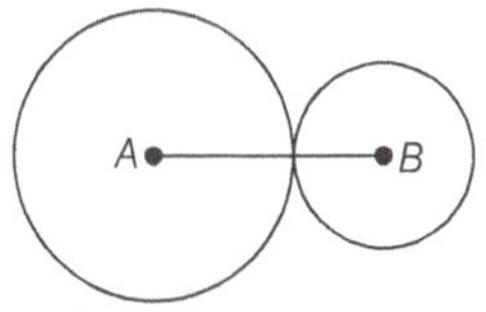

31. In a circle of radius 21 cm an arc subtends an angle of 60° at the centre. Find the length of the arc.

32. In the following figure, O is the centre of the circle with radius equal to 14 cm. The length of the arc $AB = 13.2$ cm. Find the area of the shaded sector of the circle.

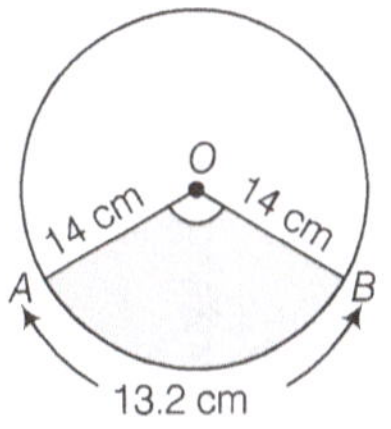

C. 4/5 Marks Questions

33. Find the area of a triangle two sides of which are 18 cm and 10 cm and the perimeter is 42 cm.

34. The sides of a triangle are in the ratio of 12 : 17 : 25 and its perimeter is 540 cm. Find its area.

35. Find the area of a quadrilateral $ABCD$, in which $AB = 3$ cm, $BC = 4$ cm, $CD = 4$ cm, $DA = 5$ cm and $AC = 5$ cm.

36. A kite is made as shown alongside in which ABC is an equilateral triangle with side 20 cm, BOC is an isosceles triangle with $OB = OC = 26$ cm and ODE is an isosceles triangle with base $DE = 8$ cm and height 6 cm. Find the whole area of the kite.

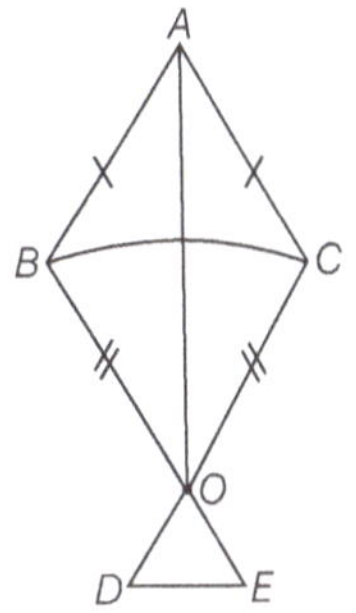

37. A park in the shape of a quadrilateral $ABCD$ has $\angle C = 90°$, $AB = 9$ m, $BC = 12$ m, $CD = 5$ m and $AD = 8$ m. How much area does it occupy?

38. From a point in the interior of an equilateral triangle, perpendicular are drawn on the three sides. If the lengths of the perpendiculars are 14 cm, 10 cm and 6 cm, find the area of the triangle.

39. A triangle and a parallelogram have the same base and the same area. If the sides of the triangle are 15 cm, 14 cm and 13 cm and the parallelogram stands on the base 15 cm, find the height of the parallelgoram.

40. $ABCD$ is a square with sides of length of 6 cm. Find point M on BC such that area of ΔABM : area of trap $ADCM = 1 : 3$.

41. Area of a sector of a circle of radius 36 cm is 54π cm^2. Find the length of the corresponding arc of sector.

42. The given figure shows a cross-section of a railway tunnel.

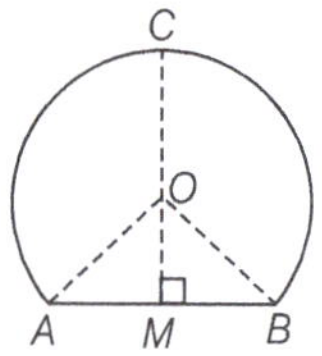

The radius OA of the circular part is 2 m. If $\angle AOB = 90°$, calculate

(i) the height of the tunnel.

(ii) the perimeter of the cross-section.

(iii) the area of the cross-section.

(Leave the answer in π and surds.)

43. In the given figure, ABC is right angled triangle at A.

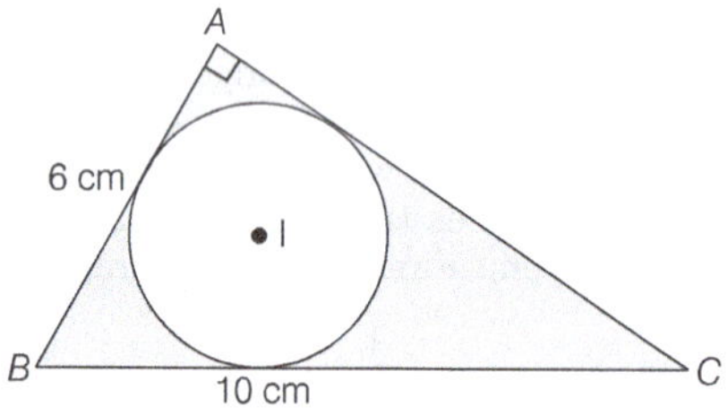

Find the area of the shaded region if $AB = 6$ cm, $BC = 10$ cm and I is the centre of incircle of ΔABC.

$\left(\text{take } \pi = \frac{22}{7}\right)$

44. The cost of cultivating a square field at the rate of ₹ 90 per hec is ₹ 1440. Find the cost of putting a fence around it, at the rate of 75 paise per metre.

45. In the given figure, $ABCD$ is a trapezium with $AB \parallel DC$, $AB = 18$ cm, $DC = 32$ cm and distance between AB and $DC = 14$ cm.

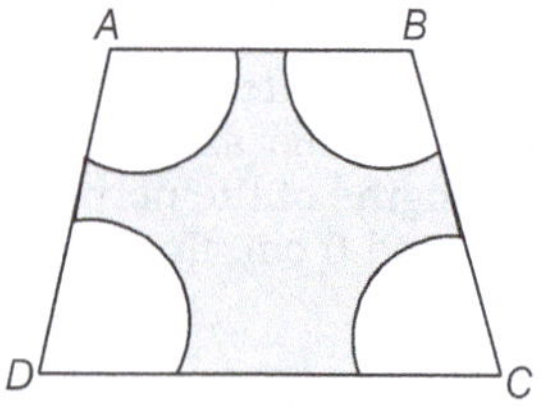

If the arcs of equal radii 7 cm with centre A, B, C and D have drawn, then find the area of the shaded region.

46. Kamla has a triangular field with sides 240 m, 200 and 300 m, where she grew wheat.

In another triangular field with sides 240 m, 320 m and 400 m adjacent to the previous field, she wanted to grow potatoes and onions. She divided the field into two parts by joining the mid-point of the longest side to the opposite vertex and grew potatoes in one part and onions in the other part. How much area (in hectares) has been used for wheat, potatoes and onions? (1 hec = 10000 m^2).

d. 6 Marks Questions

47. The triangular side walls of a flyover have been used for advertisements. The sides of the walls are 122 m, 22 m and 120 m (shown in the figure).

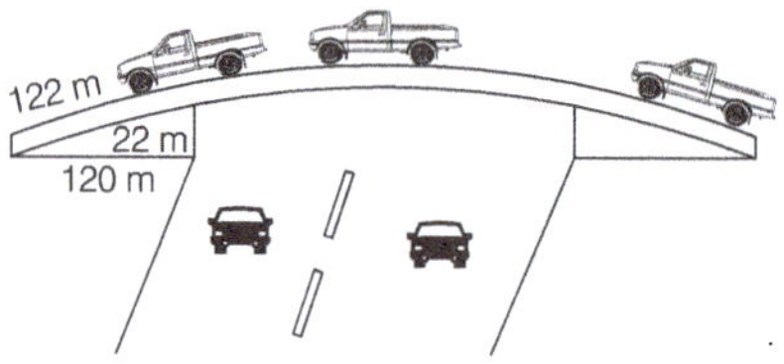

The advertisements yield an earning of ₹ 5000 per m^2 per year. A company hired one of its walls for 3 months. How much rent did it pay?

48. In the given figure, $ABCD$ is a rectangle and $PQRS$ is a rhombus whose vertices are mid-points of the sides of the rectangle.

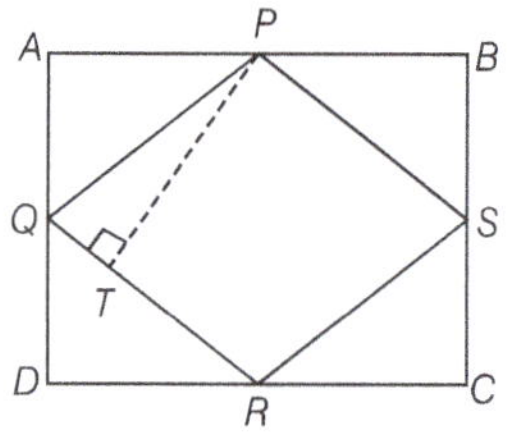

Given that $AB = 8$ cm and $AD = 6$ cm, find

(i) the area of the rhombus $PQRS$

(ii) the area of the ΔPBS

(iii) the length of PT, where PT is the perpendicular drawn from P to QR.

49. The shaded region of the given diagram represents the lawn in the form of a house. On the three sides of the lawn there are flower-beds having a uniform width of 2m.

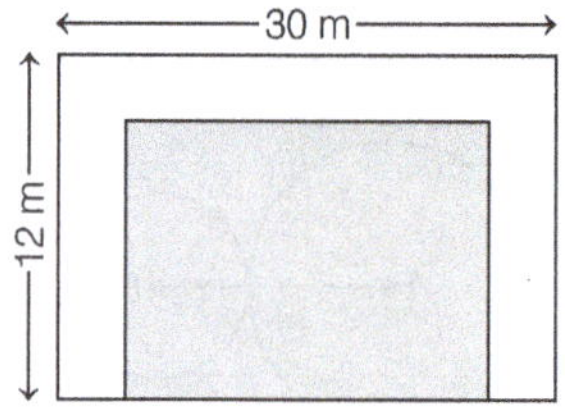

(i) Find the length and the breadth of the lawn.

(ii) Find the area of the flower-beds.

50. The diagram, given below, shows two paths drawn inside a rectangular field 80 m long and 45 m wide. The widths of the two paths are 8 m and 15 m as shown.

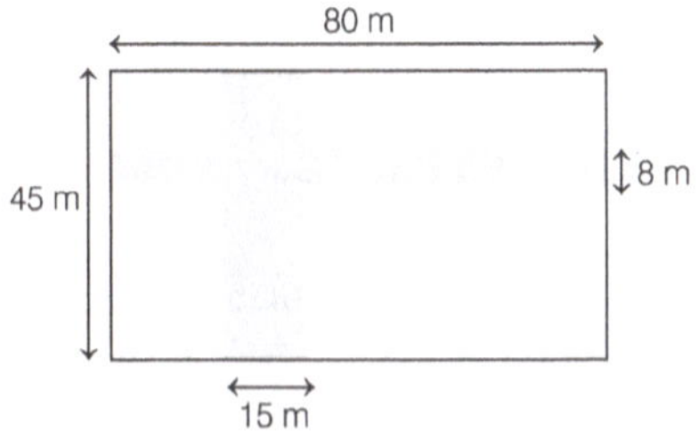

Find the area of the shaded portion.

51. In the centre of a room 10 m^2 there is a square of turkey carpet and the rest of the floor is covered with oil cloth. The carpet and the oil cloth cost respectively ₹ 15 and ₹ 6.50 per m^2 and the total cost of the carpet and the oil cloth is ₹ 1338.50. Find the width of the oil cloth border.

52. Radha made a picture of an aeroplane with coloured paper as shown in adjoining figure.

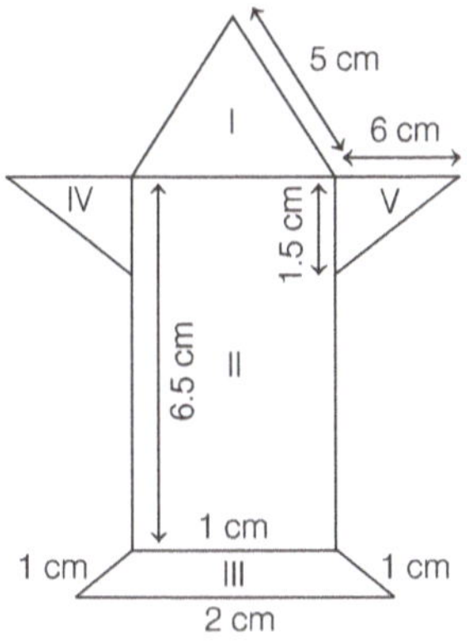

Find the total area of the paper used.

53. A cow is tied with a rope of length 14 m at the corner of a rectangular field of dimensions $20 \text{ m} \times 16 \text{ m}$. Find the area of the field in which the cow can graze.

54. In the given figure, AOB is a flower bed in the shape of a sector of a circle of radius 40 m and $\angle AOB = 60°$. Also, a 15 m wide concrete track is made as shown in the figure. Flower bed is made at the rate of ₹ 2.40 per m^2 and rate of making the concrete track is ₹ 20 per m^2. Find the total amount spent for the job. [take, $\pi = 3.14$]

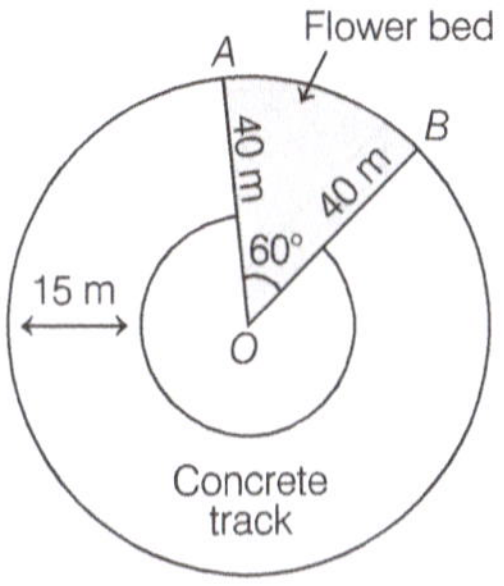

55. In the given figure, $ABCD$ is a square drawn inside a circle with centre O. The centre of the square coincides with O and the diagonal AC is horizontal.

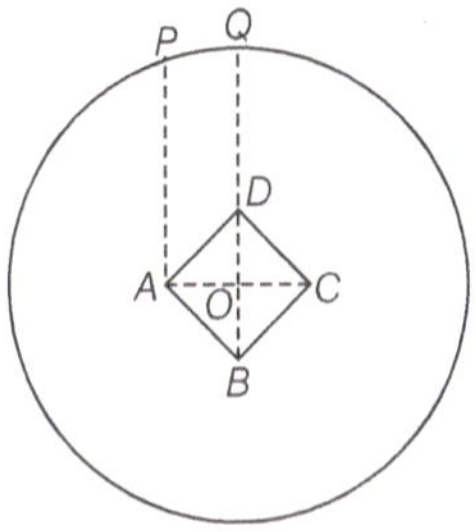

If AP, DQ are vertical and $AP = 45$ cm, $DQ = 25$ cm, find

(i) the radius of the circle.

(ii) the side of the square.

(iii) the area of the shaded region.

(take $\sqrt{2} = 1.41$ and $\pi = 3.14$)

Hints and Answers

Exercise 15.1

1. Hint Area of right angled $\Delta ABC = 60 \text{ cm}^2$

$$\Rightarrow \quad \frac{1}{2} \times BC \times AB = 60$$

$$\Rightarrow \quad 5x \times (3x - 1) = 120$$

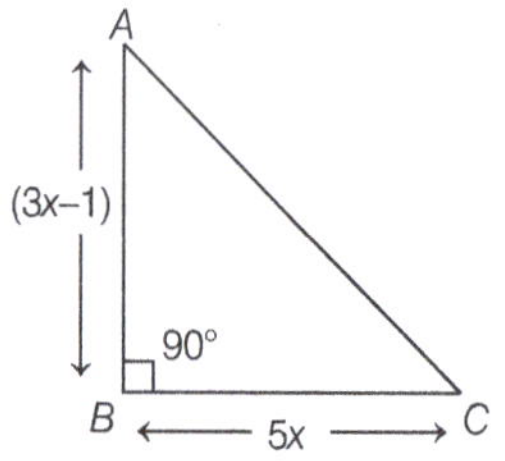

After solving, we get

$$x = 3 \text{ or } x = -\frac{8}{3}$$

[∵ length cannot be negative]

∴ $BC = 15$ cm, $AB = 8$ cm

In ΔABC, $AC^2 = AB^2 + BC^2 = (8)^2 + (15)^2 = 289$

$$\Rightarrow \quad AC = 17 \text{ cm}$$

∴ Perimeter of $\Delta ABC = BC + AB + AC$

$$= 15 + 8 + 17$$

Ans. 40 cm

2. (i) **Hint** Do same as Example 5. **Ans.** 8 cm^2

(ii) **Hint** Do same as Example 1. **Ans.** 2.82 cm

3. Hint Do same as Example 8 by Alternate Method-2. **Ans.** $8\sqrt{2} \text{ cm}^2$

4. (i) **Hint** Do same as Example 2. **Ans.** $6\sqrt{35} \text{ m}^2$

(ii) **Hint** Do same as Example 2. **Ans.** $12\sqrt{5} \text{ cm}^2$

5. Do same as Example 3. **Ans.** $2100\sqrt{15}$ m

6. Hint First, find the area of the given triangle by Heron's formula, then proceed same as Example 1.

Ans. $\frac{48\sqrt{6}}{5}$ cm

7. Hint ∵ Area of isosceles triangle $= \frac{1}{4} b\sqrt{4a^2 - b^2}$

where, a = length of each side and b = base.

$$\therefore \quad 108 = \frac{1}{4} \times 18\sqrt{4a^2 - (18)^2}$$

$$\Rightarrow \quad \frac{108 \times 4}{18} = \sqrt{4a^2 - 324}$$

$$\Rightarrow \quad (24)^2 = 4a^2 - 324$$

$$\Rightarrow \quad a^2 = \frac{576 + 324}{4} = 225$$

$$\Rightarrow \quad a = 15 \text{ cm}$$

We know that, perimeter of isosceles triangle $= 2a + b$.

Ans. 48 cm

8. Hint Here, $s_1 = \frac{120 + 122 + 22}{2} = 132$ m

$$\therefore \quad \Delta_1 = \sqrt{132(132 - 120)(132 - 122)(132 - 22)}$$

$$= \sqrt{132 \times 12 \times 10 \times 110} = 1320 \text{ m}^2$$

and $\quad s_2 = \frac{24 + 26 + 22}{2} = 36$

$$\therefore \quad \Delta_2 = \sqrt{36(36 - 24)(36 - 26)(36 - 22)}$$

$$= \sqrt{36 \times 12 \times 10 \times 14} = 245.93 \text{ m}^2$$

∴ Area of shaded region $= 1320 - 245.93$

Ans. 1074.07 m^2

9. Hint

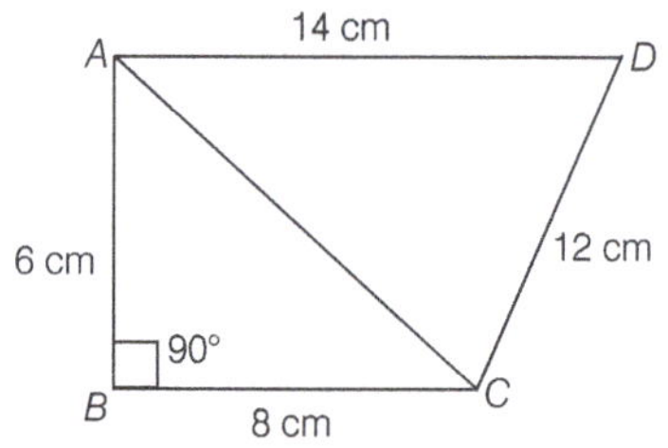

Now, do same as Example 9.

Ans. 82.79 cm^2

10. Hint In right angled ΔRMS,

$$MR = \sqrt{(13)^2 - (5)^2} = 12 \text{ m}$$

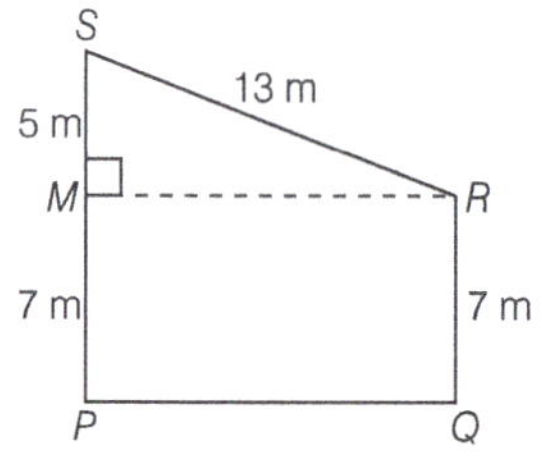

Now, area of trapezium $PQRS$

$$= \frac{1}{2} \times (\text{Sum of parallel sides}) \times \text{Height}$$

$$= \frac{1}{2} \times 19 \times 12 \quad \textbf{Ans. } 114 \text{ m}^2$$

11. Hint Let $ABCD$ be the trapezium with $AB \parallel DC$, then semi-perimeter of ΔEBC is

$$s = \frac{21 + 23 + 22}{2} = \frac{66}{2} = 33 \text{ m}$$

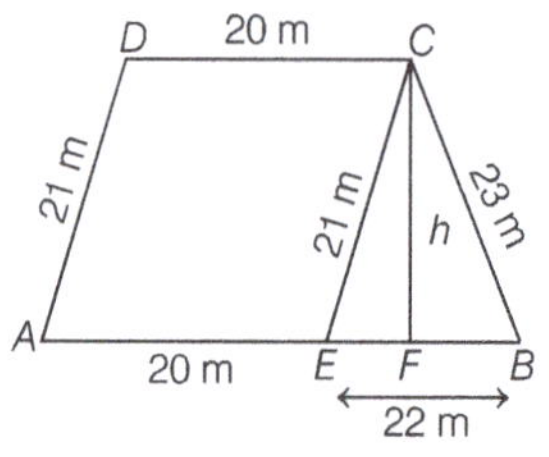

Area of $\Delta\ EBC = \sqrt{s(s-a)(s-b)(s-c)}$

$= \sqrt{33(33-21)(33-23)(33-22)}$

$= 66\sqrt{10}\ \text{m}^2$

Now, area of $\Delta\ EBC = \frac{1}{2} \times \text{Base} \times \text{Height}$

$= \frac{1}{2} \times BE \times CF$

$\Rightarrow \quad 66\sqrt{10} = \frac{1}{2} \times 22 \times h \Rightarrow h = 6\sqrt{10}$ m

$\therefore$ Area of trapezium $ABCD$

$= \frac{1}{2} \times$ (Sum of parallel sides) $\times$ Height

$= \frac{1}{2} \times (20 + 42) \times 6\sqrt{10}$

Ans. $186\sqrt{10}\ \text{m}^2$

12. Hint Given, distance between longer side,

$DE = 12$ cm.

Now, let distance between shorter side, $CF = x$ cm.

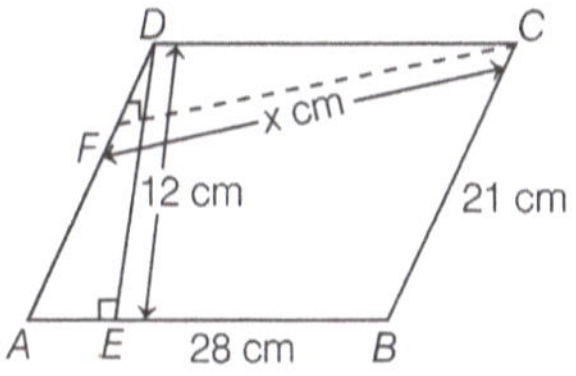

$\Rightarrow \quad AB \times DE = BC \times CF$

$\Rightarrow \quad 28 \times 12 = 21 \times x$

$\Rightarrow \quad x = \frac{28 \times 12}{21}$

Ans. 16 cm

13. Hint Let the base be x m long. Then, altitude $= 2x$.

$\therefore$ Area = Base $\times$ altitude $\Rightarrow 338 = x \times 2x$

Ans. 13 m, 26 cm

14. Hint Area of rectangle $ABCD = AB \times BC$

$= 6 \times 4 = 24\ \text{cm}^2$

and area of $\Delta BEF = \frac{1}{2} \times BE \times BF$

$= \frac{1}{2} \times 3 \times 2 = 3\ \text{cm}^2$

$\therefore$ Area of shaded region

= Area of rectangle $ABCD$ − Area of $\Delta\ BEF$

$= 24 - 3 = 21\ \text{cm}^2$

Ans. Area of shaded region is 21 cm^2

15. Hint Let the side of one square be x cm, then the side of other square be $(x + 4)$ cm.

According to the given condition, we have

$x^2 + (x+4)^2 = 656$

After solving above equation, we get

$x = -20$ or $x = 16$.

Since, length of side cannot be negative.

$\therefore$ Sides of two squares are 16 cm and 20 cm.

Ans. Perimeters of the two squares are 64 cm and 80 cm.

16. Hint Area $= \frac{1}{2} \times$ (Product of diagonals)

$\Rightarrow \quad 72 = \frac{1}{2}(18 \times d)$ **Ans.** 8 cm

17. Hint Area of rhombus $ABCD = \frac{1}{2} \times AC \times BD$

$= \frac{1}{2} \times 32 \times BD$

$= 16\ BD \quad [\because AC = 32\ \text{cm}]$

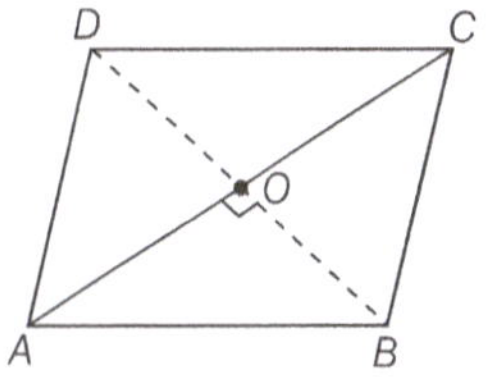

Since, the diagonals of a rhombus bisects each other 90°.

$\therefore \quad AB^2 = OA^2 + OB^2$

$\Rightarrow \quad OB = 12$ cm

Now, $\quad BD = 2 \times 12 = 24$ cm

Ans. Area of rhombus $= 16 \times 24 = 384\ \text{cm}^2$

18. Hint $\because$ Diagonal of a square,

$\sqrt{2}a = 40 \Rightarrow a = 20\sqrt{2}$ cm

$\therefore$ Area of square $= (20\sqrt{2})^2 = 800\ \text{cm}^2$

Ans. $(800 + 3\sqrt{7})\ \text{cm}^2$

19. Hint In right angled ΔEYD

$DY^2 = DE^2 - EY^2 = (5)^2 - (4)^2$

$\Rightarrow \quad DY = 3$ cm

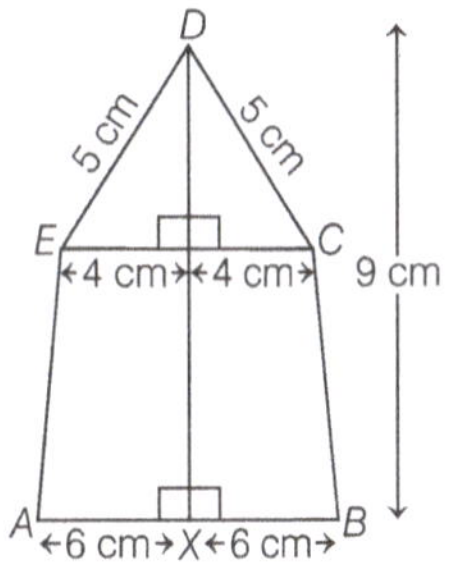

$\therefore$ Area of $\Delta ECD = \frac{1}{2} \times 8 \times 3\ \text{cm}^2$

$= 12\ \text{cm}^2$

$\Rightarrow \quad DX = 9$ cm (given)

$\therefore \quad XY = DX - DY$

$= 9 - 3 = 6$ cm

$\therefore \quad EC \parallel AB$

So, $ABCE$ is a trapezium.

$\therefore$ Area of trapezium

$ABCE = \frac{1}{2} \times (EC + AB) \times \text{height}$

$= \frac{1}{2}(8 + 12) \times 6$

$= 60\ \text{cm}^2$

$\therefore$ Area of pentagon $ABCDE$ = Area of ΔECD + Area of trapezium $ABCE$

Ans. 72 cm^2

20. Hint Area of the shaded region

$= 2$ (Area of ΔAPB) + 2 (Area of ΔBQC) + Area of rectangle $ABCD$

and perimeter of the figure

$= AP + PB + BQ + QC + CR + RD + DS + SA$

Ans. $(130 + 32\sqrt{3})$ cm^2, $4(5\sqrt{2} + 8)$ cm

Exercise 15.2

1. Hint Given, $2r = 28$ cm $\Rightarrow r = \frac{28}{2} = 14$ cm

Now, apply, circumference of a circle $= 2\pi r$ and area of a circle $= \pi r^2$

Ans. 88 cm, 616 cm^2

2. Hint Do same as Example 20.

Ans. 5000

3. Hint According to the question, we have

$$2\pi r - 2r = 300$$
$$\Rightarrow \quad r = 70 \text{ cm}$$

Ans. 140 cm

4. Hint Let the radii of the two circles be $3x$ cm and $8x$ cm.

According to the question, we get

$$\pi(8x)^2 - \pi(3x)^2 = 385\pi \Rightarrow x = \sqrt{7}$$

$\therefore$ Radius of bigger circle $= 8x = 8\sqrt{7}$

$\therefore$ Area of bigger circle $= \pi r^2 = \pi(8\sqrt{7})^2$

Ans. 1408 cm^2

5. Hint According to the question,

Circumference of required circle

$= 2\pi(16) - 2\pi(12) = 8\pi$

$\therefore \quad 2\pi r = 8\pi \Rightarrow r = 4$ cm

Ans. 50.28 cm^2

6. Hint Area of circle with radius (R)

= Area of circle with radius 6 cm + Area of circle with radius 8 cm + Area of circle with radius 24 cm

$$\therefore \quad \pi R^2 = \pi(6)^2 + \pi(8)^2 + \pi(24)^2$$
$$\Rightarrow \quad R^2 = 676$$
$$\Rightarrow \quad R = 26 \text{ cm}$$

Now, perimeter of a circle with radius $(R) = 2\pi R$

$$= 2 \times \frac{22}{7} \times 26$$

Ans. $163\frac{3}{7}$ cm

7. (i) **Hint** Given, $2\pi r = 123.2$

$$\Rightarrow \quad 2 \times \frac{22}{7} \times r = 123.2$$

Ans. 19.6 cm

(ii) **Hint** Area of the circle $= \pi r^2 = \frac{22}{7} \times (19.6)^2$

Ans. 1207.36 cm^2

(iii) **Hint** Let A be the area of the circle of radius r and A_1 be the area of the circle whose radius is $2r$.

Then, $A = \pi r^2$ and $A_1 = \pi(2r)^2 = 4\pi r^2$

Ans. 4 times

8. Let R and r be the radii of the circles having centres at O and O', respectively. Then,

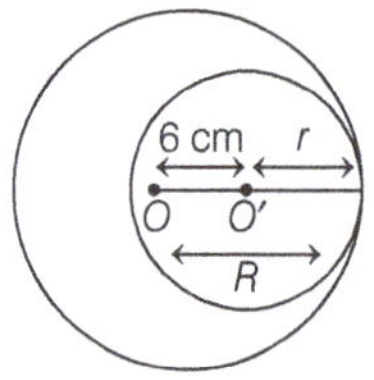

Sum of areas $= 116\pi$ cm^2

$$\Rightarrow \quad \pi R^2 + \pi r^2 = 116\pi$$
$$\Rightarrow \quad R^2 + r^2 = 116 \quad \ldots(i)$$

Distance between the centres = 6 cm

$$\Rightarrow \quad OO' = 6 \text{ cm} \Rightarrow R - r = 6 \quad \ldots(ii)$$

Now, $(R + r)^2 + (R - r)^2 = 2(R^2 + r^2)$

$$\Rightarrow \quad (R + r)^2 + 36 = 2 \times 116$$

[using Eqs. (i) and (ii)]

$$\Rightarrow \quad (R + r)^2 = (2 \times 116 - 36) = 196$$
$$\Rightarrow \quad R + r = 14 \quad \ldots(iii)$$

Now, solve Eqs. (ii) and (iii) to find r and R.

Ans. 10 cm, 4 cm

9. Hint Let r_1 and r_2 be the radii of two given circles.

Then, $\quad r_1 + r_2 = 140$

and $\quad 2\pi r_1 - 2\pi r_2 = 88$

$$\Rightarrow \quad 2\pi(r_1 - r_2) = 88$$
$$\Rightarrow \quad r_1 - r_2 = 14$$

Ans. 154 cm and 126 cm

10. Hint Let the radius of the circle be r cm.

Then, $\quad 2\pi r = 2\pi \times 19 + 2\pi \times 9 \Rightarrow r = 28$ cm

$\therefore$ Area of the circle $= \pi r^2 = \frac{22}{7} \times 28 \times 28$ cm^2

Ans. 28 cm, 2464 cm^2

11. Hint Do same as Example 24. **Ans.** ₹ 13860

12. Hint Let r cm and R cm be the radius of the concentric circles.

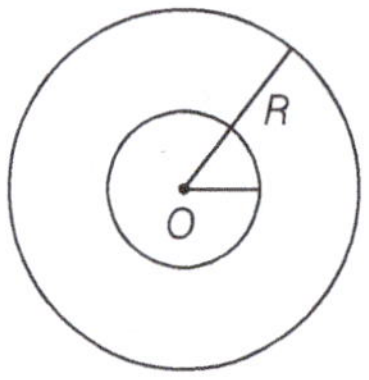

Then, $2\pi R = 396$ and $2\pi r = 352$

$$\Rightarrow \quad R = 63 \text{ cm and } r = 56 \text{ cm}$$

Now, do same as Example 25.

Ans. 2618 cm^2

13. Hint We have,

$$R - r = 5 \quad \ldots(i)$$

and $\pi(R^2 - r^2) = 550$

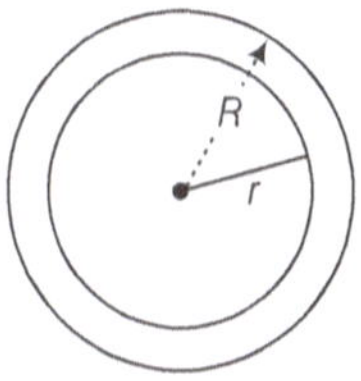

$\Rightarrow \quad R + r = 35 \quad \ldots(ii)$

Now, solve Eqs. (i) and (ii), to find r and R.

Ans. $R = 20$ cm and $r = 15$ cm

14. Hint We have, $R - r = 7 \quad \ldots(i)$

and $2\pi r = 88 \Rightarrow r = \frac{88 \times 7}{44} = 14$ m

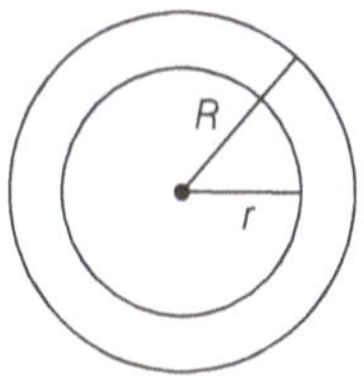

On putting $r = 14$ m in Eq. (i), we get $R = 21$ m

Now, area of paving the road $= \pi(R^2 - r^2)$

$= \pi(R - r)(R + r)$

$= \frac{22}{7} \times (21 - 14)(21 + 14) = 770 \text{ m}^2$

Cost of paving at ₹ 100 per sq m = ₹ 100×770

Ans. ₹ 77000

15. Hint We have, $\frac{1}{2}\pi r^2 = 693 \Rightarrow r = 21$ cm

$\therefore$ Perimeter of the semi-circle $= \pi r + 2r$

Ans. 108 cm

16. (i) **Hint** Length of boundary $= 2 \times 10 + 7 + \pi \times \left(\frac{7}{2}\right)$

Ans. 38 cm

(ii) **Hint** Area of the shaded region

= Area of rectangle

– Area of semi-circle with radius $\times \left(\frac{7}{2}\right)$

Ans. 50.75 cm^2

17. Hint Angle described by hour hand in 1 hour

$= \frac{360°}{12} = 30°$

$\therefore$ Area swept $= \frac{30°}{360°} \times \pi \times (7)^2 \text{ cm}^2$ **Ans.** 12.83 cm^2

18. Hint 1 h of minute hand = 360°

60 min = 360°

1 min = 6°

Angle described by minute hand between 9:00 am to 9:35 am $= 6° \times 35 = 210°$ **Ans.** 264 cm^2

19. Hint Here, required area $= \frac{90°}{360°} \times \pi r^2$.

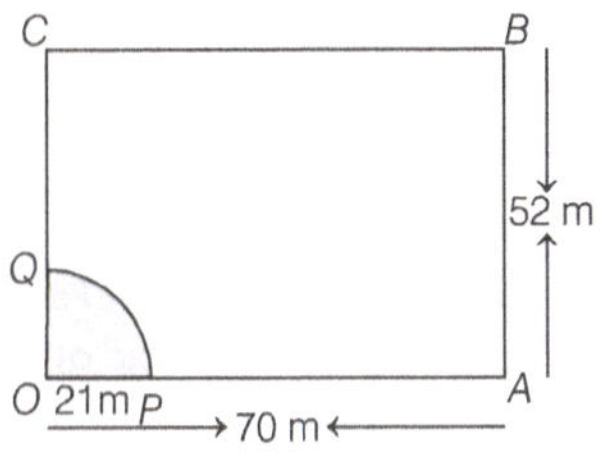

Ans. 346.5 m^2

20. Hint Area of remaining part

= Area of square – 4 × Area of quadrant

Ans. 9384 m^2

21. Hint Area of shaded region = 2 ×

[Area of semi-circle with diameter AQ

– Area of semi-circle with diameter AP].

Ans. 37.68 cm^2

22. Hint Area of shaded region = Area of semi-circle E + Area of semi-circle B – [Area of circle D + 2 × Area of semi-circle A].

Ans. $\frac{63}{16}\pi \text{ cm}^2$

23. Hint Area of shaded region = Area of semi-circle with diameter PQ – Area of ΔPEQ.

Ans. $\frac{200}{7} \text{ cm}^2$

24. (i) **Hint** Area of shaded region

= Area of semi-circle – Area of ΔABC

Ans. $\frac{32}{7} \text{ cm}^2$

(ii) **Hint** Area of shaded region

= Area of quadrant $OPQO$ – Area of ΔPOQ

Ans. $\frac{16}{7} \text{ cm}^2$

25. Hint Area of right angled $\Delta RPQ = \frac{1}{2} \times RP \times PQ$

$\therefore$ Area of semi-circle $= \frac{\pi r^2}{2}$ **Ans.** $\frac{4523}{28} \text{ cm}^2$

26. Hint Area of sector $OBD = \frac{\theta}{360°} \times \pi r^2$

and area of sector $OAC = \frac{\theta}{360°} \times \pi r^2$

$\therefore$ Area of shaded region

= Area of sector OAC – Area of sector OBD

$= \frac{616}{9} - \frac{154}{9} = \frac{462}{9}$ **Ans.** $\frac{154}{3} \text{ cm}^2$

27. Hint Area of semi-circle APD

= Area of semi-circle $BPC = \frac{\pi r^2}{2}$

and area of square $ABCD = (\text{Side})^2$

$\therefore$ Area of shaded region

= Area of square – (Area of semi-circle APD

+ Area of semi-circle BPC)

Ans. 42 cm^2

28. **Hint** Area of an equilateral $\Delta OAB = \frac{\sqrt{3}}{4}(\text{Side})^2$

$\therefore$ Area of circle outside the triangle

$= \text{Area of circle} - \text{Area of sector } OPQO$

$= \pi r^2 - \frac{60^\circ}{360^\circ} \times \pi r^2$

Total area of the shaded region

$= \text{Area of an equilateral } \Delta OAB$

$+ \text{Area of circle outside the triangle}$

Ans. $\left(36\sqrt{3} + \frac{660}{7}\right) \text{cm}^2$

29. **Hint** Radius of circle $= \frac{1}{2} \times$ (Side of a square)

$\therefore$ Area of quadrant of one circle $= \frac{\pi r^2}{4}$

$\therefore$ Area of shaded region

$= \text{Area of square} - \text{Area of four quadrants}$

Ans. 42 cm^2

30.

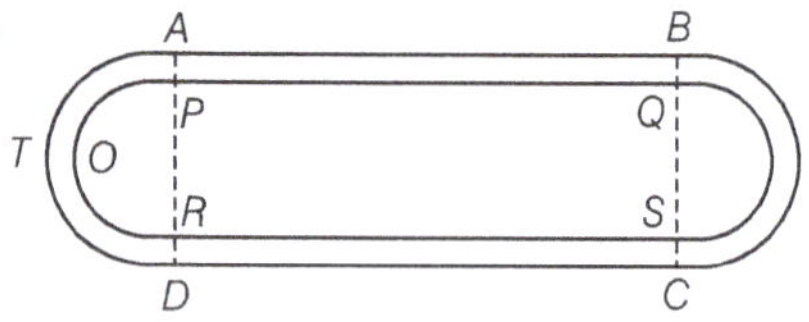

(i) **Hint** Distance around the track along its inner edge $= PQ + RS + 2 \times$ Circumference of semi-circle POR

Ans. $\frac{2804}{7}$ m

(ii) **Hint** Area of the track = Area of outer track − Area of inner track

= [Area of rectangle $ABCD$ + 2 × Area of semi-circle ATD] − [Area of rectangle $PQSR$ + 2 × Area of semi-circle POR]

Ans. 4320 m^2

31. **Hint** Area of smaller circle $= \pi r^2$

Area of $\Delta ABC = \frac{1}{2} \times AB \times OC$

and area of semi-circle $ABCA = \frac{\pi R^2}{2}$

$\therefore$ Area of total shaded region = Area of small circle + [Area of semi-circle $ABCA$ − Area of ΔABC]

Ans. 66.5 cm^2

32. **Hint** Let the side of an equilateral triangle be a.

$\therefore$ Area of an equilateral $\Delta ABC = \frac{\sqrt{3}}{4}(a)^2$

Since, ΔABC is an equilateral triangle.

$\therefore \quad \angle A = \angle B = \angle C = 60^\circ$

$\therefore$ Area of sector of a circle $= \frac{\theta}{360^\circ} \times \pi r^2$

$\therefore$ Area of required shaded region

= Area of ΔABC − Area of three sectors

Ans. 1620.5 cm^2

33. **Hint** Length of a side of square

$= 3 \times$ Diameter of one circle

Now, area of one circle $= \pi r^2$

$\therefore$ Area of the remaining portion of the handkerchief

= Area of square − Area of nine circles

Ans. 378 cm^2

34. (i) **Hint** Area of quadrant $OACB$

$= \frac{1}{4} \times$ Area of the circle

Ans. $\frac{77}{8}$ cm^2

(ii) **Hint** Area of $\Delta BOD = \frac{1}{2} \times OB \times OD$

$\therefore$ Area of shaded region

= Area of quadrant $OACB$ − Area of ΔOBD

Ans. $\frac{49}{8}$ cm^2

35. **Hint** Diagonal of a square $= \sqrt{2} \times$ Side

$\therefore$ Area of quadrant $OPBQO = \frac{\pi r^2}{4}$

$\therefore$ Area of shaded region

= Area of quadrant − Area of square

Ans. 228.57 cm^2

36. **Hint** $\therefore$ Area of sector $COD = \frac{\theta}{360^\circ} \times \pi r_1^2$

$\therefore$ Area of sector $AOB = \frac{\theta}{360^\circ} \times \pi r_2^2$

$\therefore$ Area of shaded region

= Area of sector AOB − Area of sector COD

Ans. $\frac{308}{3}$ cm^2

37. **Hint** Area of right angled $\Delta BAC = \frac{1}{2} \times AC \times AB$

and area of quadrant $ABDC = \frac{\pi r^2}{4}$

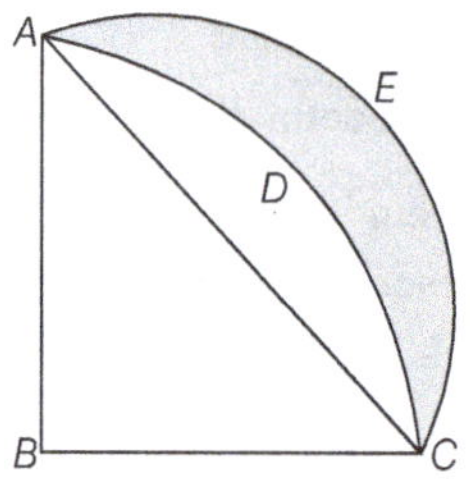

Now, area of semi-circle $BCE = \frac{\pi r^2}{2}$

$\therefore$ Area of shaded region = Area of semi-circle BCE − (Area of quadrant $ABDC$ − Area of right angled ΔBAC)

Ans. 98 cm^2

38. Hint Area of sector, $BAEC = \frac{\pi r^2}{4}$

Area of right angled, $\Delta ABC = \frac{1}{2} \times AB \times BC$

$\therefore$ Area of shaded region AEC

$= $ Area of sector $BAEC$ − Area of right angled ΔABC

Shaded region = 2 × Area of shaded region AEC

Ans. $\frac{256}{7}$ cm^2

Chapter Exercise

1. (a) 2. (d) 3. (c) 4. (d) 5. (a)

6. Hint Area of triangle $= \frac{1}{2} \times$ Base × Height.

Ans. 30 cm^2

7. Hint Do same as Example 3. **Ans.** 72 cm

8. Hint First, find the area of the given triangle by Heron's formula, then proceed same as Example 1. **Ans.** 336 cm^2, 33.6 cm

9. Hint Semi-perimeter of equilateral triangle

$$s = \frac{2a + 2a + 2a}{2}$$ **Ans.** $3a$

10. Hint Do same as Example 7.

Ans. 72 cm, $144\sqrt{3}$ cm^2.

11. Hint Perimeter of an equilateral triangle,

$$2s = 3 \text{ (side)}$$

$$\Rightarrow \quad 2s = 3 \times 8 \Rightarrow s = 12 \text{ cm}$$

$$\therefore \text{ Area of triangle} = \sqrt{s(s-a)(s-b)(s-c)}$$

$$= \sqrt{12(12-8)(12-8)(12-8)}$$

$$= \sqrt{12 \times 4 \times 4 \times 4} = 16\sqrt{3} \text{ cm}^2$$

$$\therefore \text{ Area of triangle} = \frac{1}{2} \times 8 \times h$$

$$\Rightarrow \quad 16\sqrt{3} = \frac{1}{2} \times 8 \times h$$

Ans. $h = 4\sqrt{3}$ cm

12. Hint First, find the area of triangle by Heron's formula, then apply.

Area of equilateral triangle = Area of triangle by Heron's formula.

Ans. 46.48 cm

13. Hint Area of isosceles right angled triangle

$$= \frac{1}{2} \times \text{Base} \times \text{Height}$$

$$\Rightarrow \quad 72 = \frac{1}{2} \times a \times a \quad \text{[let base = height = } a\text{]}$$

$$\Rightarrow \quad a^2 = 144 \Rightarrow a = 12 \text{ cm}$$

Applying Pythagoras theorem in an isosceles right angled triangle, we get

Hypotenuse $= \sqrt{(12)^2 + (12)^2} = 12\sqrt{2}$ cm

$\therefore$ Perimeter of an isosceles right angled triangle

$$= 2 \times 12 + 12\sqrt{2} = 24 + 12\sqrt{2}$$

Ans. 40.97 cm

14. Hint Do same as Example 8.

Using, Perimeter of isoceles triangle = $2a + b$

Ans. 18 cm

15. Hint Do same as Example 8.

Using, Perimeter of isoceles triangle = $2a + b$

Ans. 30 cm or 16 cm

16. Hint Given, $a = 4 + h$ ...(i)

$$\therefore \quad \frac{1}{2} \times 24 \times h = \frac{1}{4} \times 24\sqrt{4a^2 - (24)^2}$$

$$\Rightarrow \quad \frac{1}{2} \times 24(a-4) = \frac{1}{4} \times 24\sqrt{4a^2 - 576} \quad \text{[from Eq. (i)]}$$

Ans. 64 cm, 192 cm^2

17. Hint Area of shaded portion = Area of equilateral triangle ABC − Area of equilateral BDE

Ans. 129.9 cm^2

18. Hint Area of shaded region = Area of equilateral ΔABC − Area of right angled ΔBDC.

Ans. 19.3 cm^2

19. Hint Given,

$$9 + a + b = 22$$

$$\Rightarrow \quad a + b = 13 \quad \text{...(i)}$$

$$\text{and} \quad a - b = 3 \quad \text{...(ii)}$$

On solving Eqs. (i) and (ii), and using Heron's formula. **Ans.** $6\sqrt{11}$ cm^2

20. Hint Let ΔABC is right angled triangle.

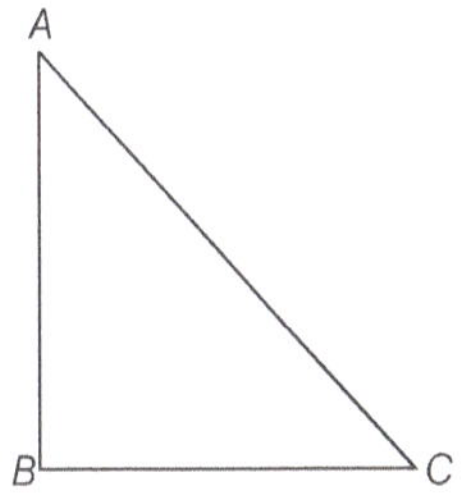

Then, according to question

$$AB - BC = 2 \text{ cm}$$

$$\Rightarrow \quad AB = 2 + BC \quad \text{... (i)}$$

Given, area of the triangle = 24 cm^2

$$\Rightarrow \quad \frac{1}{2} \times BC \times AB = 24$$

$$\Rightarrow \quad \frac{1}{2} \times BC(2 + BC) = 24 \quad \text{[From Eq. (i)]}$$

$$\Rightarrow \quad BC^2 + 2BC = 48$$

On solving, we get

$$BC = 6$$

[Side can not be negative]

From Eq. (i)

$$AB = 2 + 6 = 8$$

In right angled triangle ABC

$$AB^2 + BC^2 = AC^2$$
$$\Rightarrow \quad 8^2 + 6^2 = AC^2$$
$$\Rightarrow \quad AC = 10$$

$\therefore$ Perimeter of the triangle $= AB + BC + AC$

Ans. 24 cm

21. Hint Do same as Example 11. **Ans.** 450 cm^2

22. Hint Area of rhombus = Base × Height.

Ans. 7.5 cm^2

23. Hint Area of circle $= \pi r^2$

and circumference of circle $= 2\pi r$

Ans. 498.96 cm^2, 79.2 cm

24. Hint Given, $2\pi r = 22$ and area $= \pi r^2$ **Ans.** 38.5 cm^2

25. Hint Given, $\pi r = 108$ and use diameter $= 2r$

Ans. 42 cm

26. Hint Let $R = \frac{34}{2}$ and $r = \frac{32}{2}$.

Now, area of ring $= \pi(R^2 - r^2)$.

Ans. 103.71 cm^2

27. Hint Let r and R be inner and outer radii respectively, then

$$2\pi r = 88 \quad \ldots(i)$$

and $$\pi(R^2 - r^2) = 346.5 \quad \ldots(ii)$$

Solve Eqs. (i) and (ii) to find R. **Ans.** 17.5 cm

28. Hint

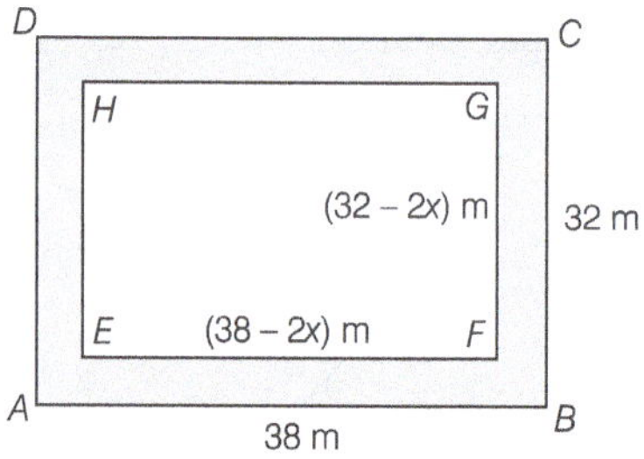

Let width of the uniform path = x m

Area of path = Area of rectangle $ABCD$

– Area of rectangle $EFGH$ **Ans.** 5 m

29. Hint

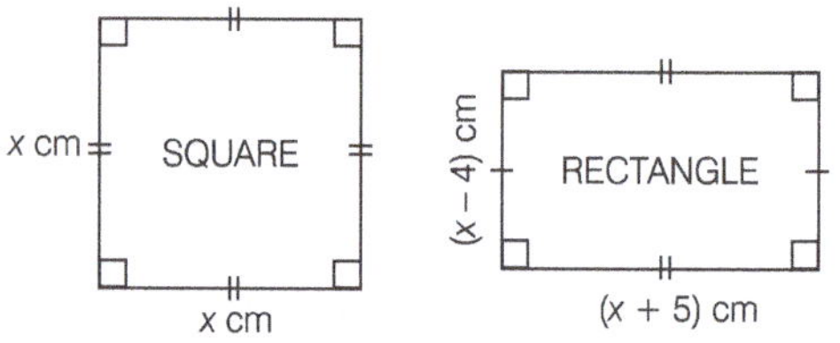

Ans. 20 cm

30. Hint Let R cm and r cm be the radii of two circles, then

$$R + r = 10 \Rightarrow r = 10 - R \quad \ldots(i)$$

Also, $\pi R^2 + \pi r^2 = 58\pi$

$\Rightarrow R = 7$ or $R = 3$, and $r = 3$ or 7

Ans. radii of the two circles are 7 cm and 3 cm.

31. Hint Length of the arc, $l = \frac{\theta}{360^\circ} \times 2\pi r$

$$= \frac{60^\circ}{360^\circ} \times 2 \times \frac{22}{7} \times 21$$

Ans. 22 cm

32. Hint Area of shaded region

$$= \frac{1}{2} \times \text{Length of arc} \times \text{Radius}$$

Ans. 92.4 cm^2

33. Hint $18 + 10 + c = 42 \Rightarrow c = 14$.

Here, $s = \frac{42}{2} = 21$ cm.

$\therefore$ Area of a triangle $= \sqrt{s(s-a)(s-b)(s-c)}$

$$= \sqrt{21(21-18)(21-10)(21-14)}$$

Ans. $21\sqrt{11}$ cm^2

34. Hint Do same as Example 3. **Ans.** 9000 cm^2

35. Hint Do same as Example 9. **Ans.** 15.1 cm^2

36. Hint Area of $\Delta ABC = \frac{\sqrt{3}}{4} \times (20)^2$ cm^2

Join BC and draw $OP \perp BC$

Since, BOC is an isosceles triangle, OP will bisect BC

$\Rightarrow \quad BP = CP = 10$ cm

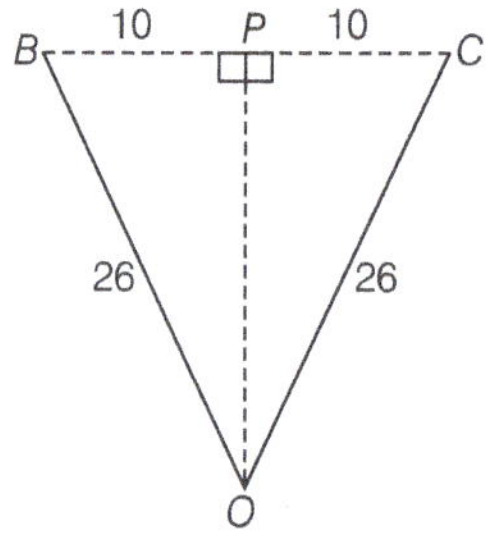

In right angled triangle OPB,

Using Pythagoras theorem and find OP

$\therefore$ Area of $\Delta BOC = \frac{1}{2} \times BC \times OP$

and area of $\Delta ODE = \frac{1}{2} \times 8 \times 6$ cm^2

Required area = [Area of ΔABC

+ Area of ΔBOC + Area of ΔODE]

Ans. 437.2 cm^2

37. Hint

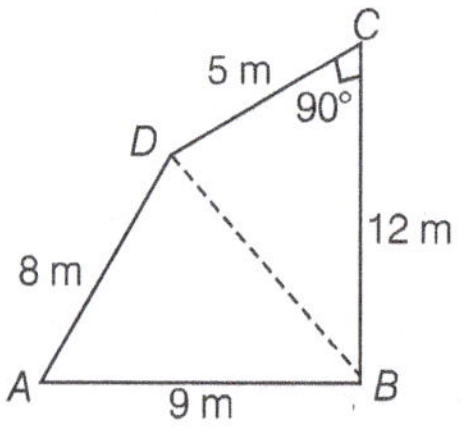

In right angled triangle BCD

$$BD^2 = BC^2 + CD^2$$
$$BD^2 = 12^2 + 5^2 \Rightarrow BD = 13 \text{ m}$$

$\therefore$ Area of $\Delta BCD = \frac{1}{2} \times BC \times CD$

$= \frac{1}{2} \times 12 \times 5 = 30 \text{ m}^2$

For ΔABD, $s = \frac{9 + 13 + 8}{2} = 15 \text{ m}$

$\therefore$ Area of $\Delta ABD = \sqrt{15(15-9)(15-13)(15-8)}$

$= \sqrt{15 \times 6 \times 2 \times 7} = 35.5 \text{ m}^2$

$\therefore$ Area of quadrilateral $ABCD$ = Area of ΔBCD + Area of ΔABD

Ans. 65.5 m^2

38. Hint Area of equilateral $\Delta ABC = \frac{\sqrt{3}}{4} a^2 \text{ cm}^2$

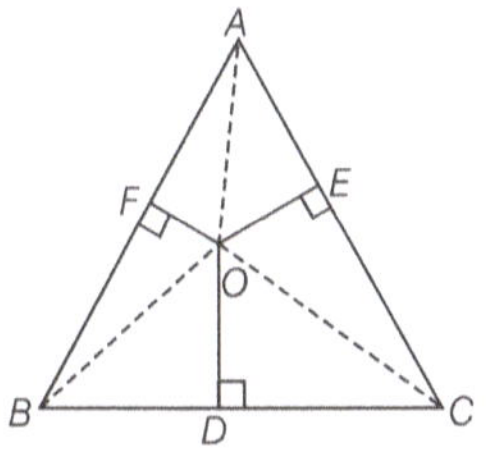

$\therefore$ Area of ΔABC = Area of ΔOBD + Area of ΔOCA + Area of ΔOAB

Ans. $300\sqrt{3}$ cm^2

39. Hint For ΔABC, $s = 21$ cm

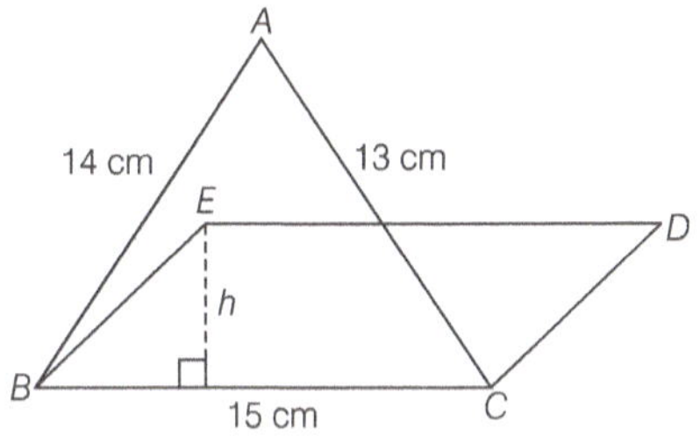

$\therefore$ Area of $\Delta ABC = 84 \text{ cm}^2$ (by Heron's formula)

$\therefore$ Area of parallelogram $BCDE$ = Base × Height

Ans. 5.6 cm

40. Hint Let $BM = x$ cm, then $MC = (6 - x)$ cm

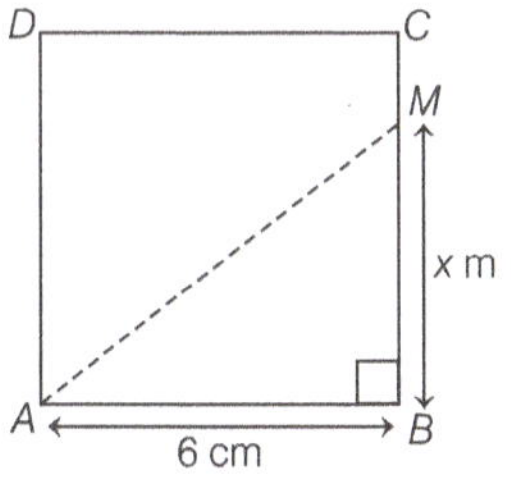

$\therefore$ Area of $\Delta ABM = \left(\frac{1}{2} \times 6 \times x\right) \text{cm}^2 = 3x \text{ cm}^2$,

$\therefore$ Area of trapezium $ADCM = \frac{1}{2}[6 + (6 - x)] \times 6 \text{ cm}^2$

$= 3(12 - x) \text{ cm}^2$

Ans. M is mid-point of BC.

41. Hint Length of arc $= \frac{2 \times \text{Area of sector}}{\text{Radius}}$.

Ans. 3π cm

42. Hint

(i) Draw $OM \perp AB$.

By Pythagoras theorem,

$OA^2 = AM^2 + OM^2$

$\Rightarrow \quad OM = \sqrt{2}$ m

The height of the tunnel $= OC + OM$

Ans. $(2 + \sqrt{2})$ m

(ii) Since, $OM \perp AB$, M is mid-point of AB.

$\therefore$ $AB = 2\sqrt{2}$ m.

$\therefore$ Length of the major arc ACB

$= \frac{3}{4}$ of circumference

Ans. The perimeter of the cross-section $= (3\pi + 2\sqrt{2})$ m

(iii) $\therefore$ Area of $\Delta OAB = \frac{1}{2} \times AB \times OM$

$\therefore$ Area of the sector $OACB$

$= \frac{3}{4}$ of area of circle of radius 2 m

Ans. The area of the cross-section $= (3\pi + 2)$ m^2

43. Hint

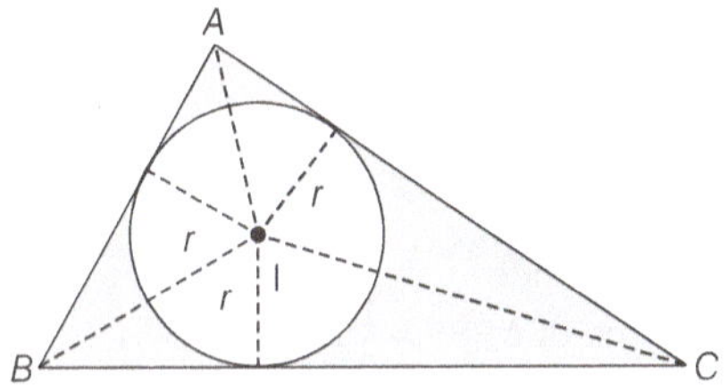

ar $(\Delta ABC) = 24$ cm^2

ar(ΔABC) = ar(ΔIBC) + ar (ΔICA) + ar (ΔIAB)

$24 = 12r$

$\Rightarrow \quad r = 2$

and area of shaded region

= ar (ΔABC) − Area of incircle

Ans. $11\frac{3}{7}$ cm^2

44. Hint Area of square, $a^2 = \frac{1440}{90}$

$\Rightarrow \quad a^2 = 16 \text{ hec} = (16 \times 10000) \text{ m}^2$

$\therefore$ Perimeter of square field $= 4a = 4 \times 400$

$= 1600$ m

Ans. Cost of putting a fence around the square field $= 1600 \times 0.75 = ₹\ 1200$

45. Hint Area of trapezium $ABCD$

$= \frac{1}{2}$ (sum of parallel sides) × height

$\therefore$ Required area = Area of trapezium $ABCD$ − area of four sectors

Ans. 196 cm^2

46. Hint By using Heron's formula,

Area for growing wheat = Area of ΔABC

$= 2.26$ hectares (approx.)

$ar(\Delta ACD) = 3.84$ hec

$\therefore$ Area for growing potatoes

= Area for growing onions

$= \frac{1}{2} \times ar(\Delta ACD)$

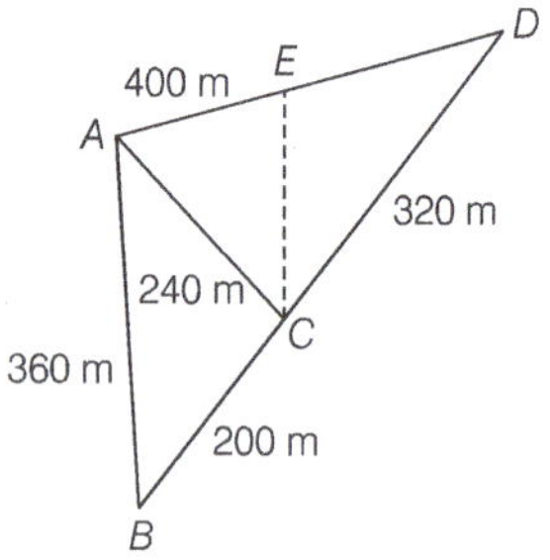

Ans. 2.26 hec, 1.92 hec and 1.92 hec.

47. Hint Using Heron's formula,

Area of one triangular wall $= 1320\ m^2$

Rent = ₹ 5000 per m^2 per year.

$\therefore$ Rent of one wall for 3 months

$= ₹\left(\frac{1320 \times 5000 \times 3}{12}\right)$

Ans. ₹ 1650000

48. Hint

(i) Area of rhombus $PQRS = \frac{1}{2} \times QS \times PR$

Ans. 24 cm^2

(ii) $\therefore$ Area of $\Delta PBS = \frac{1}{2} PB \times BS$

Ans. 6 cm^2.

(iii) $\because QR = PS$ side of rhombus

Area of rhombus $PQRS = 24\ cm^2$

[from part (i)]

$\Rightarrow \quad QR \times PT = 24$

$\Rightarrow \quad 5 \times PT = 24$

Ans. 4.8 cm

49. Hint

(i) Length of the lawn

= [30 – 2 times of flower-bids width]

$= 30 - 2 \times 2 = 26$ m

and Breadth of the Lawn

= [12 – width of flower-beds]

$= 12 - 2 = 10$ m

(ii) $\therefore$ Area of flower-beds $= (26 \times 10)\ m^2$

$= 260\ m^2$

Ans. (i) 26 m and 10 m

(ii) 260 m^2

50. Hint Area of shaded portion

$= [80 \times 8 + 15 \times 45 - 15 \times 8]\ m^2$

$= [640 + 675 - 120]\ m^2$

$= 1195\ m^2$

Ans. 1195 m^2

51. Hint Total cost = area of covered by carpet

× ₹ 15 + Area of remaining part × ₹ 6.50

$= x^2 \times 15 + (100 - x^2)\,6.50$

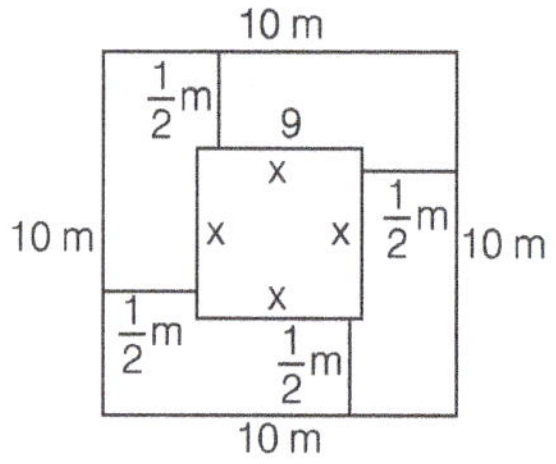

Ans. $\frac{1}{2}$ m

52. Hint By using Heron's formula,

Area of part I = 2.487 cm^2

For part II

Area of part II = 6.5 cm^2

For part III

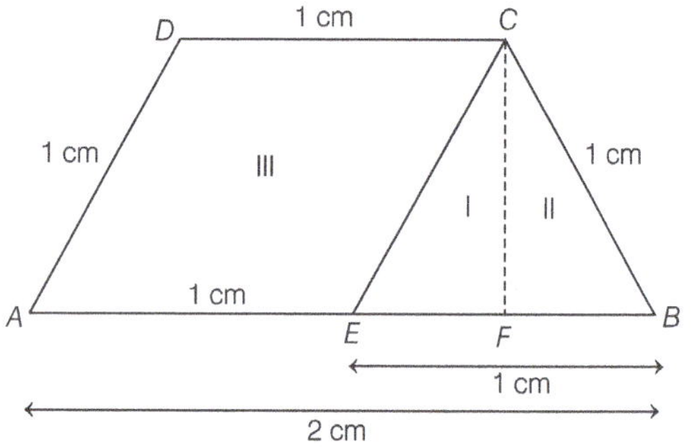

It is a trapezium $ABCD$.

$1\ cm = EB$

$\frac{1}{2} \times EB \times CF = \frac{\sqrt{3}}{4} \times (1)^2$

[$\because \Delta EBC$ is an equilateral triangle]

$\Rightarrow \quad CF = \frac{\sqrt{3}}{2}$ cm

Area of trapezium $= \frac{1}{2}$ (Sum of parallel sides × Height)

$= \frac{1}{2}(AB + CD) \times CF$

$= 1.299\ cm^2$

For part V

Area of part V = 4.5 cm^2

Similarly, area of part IV = 4.5 cm^2

Total area of paper used

= Area of part (I + II + III + IV + V)

Ans. 19.3 cm^3 (approx)

53. Hint Required area = Area of quadrant APQ of radius 14 m

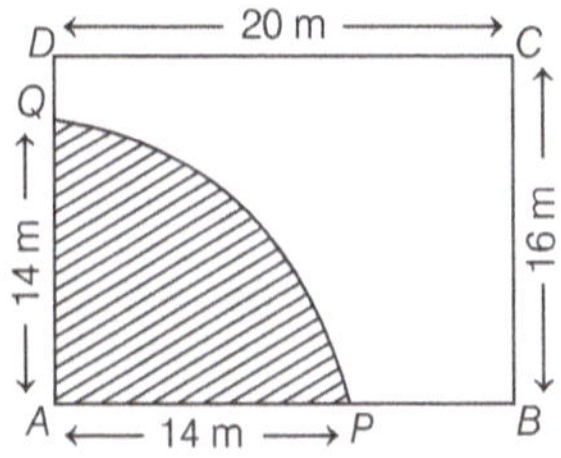

Ans. 154 m^2

54. Hint Area of the sector AOB

$$= \frac{60°}{360°} \times 3.14 \times (40)^2$$

$$= \frac{1}{6} \times 3.14 \times 1600 = \frac{2512}{3}\ m^2$$

Amount spent for making the flower bed at the rate of

₹ 2.40 per m^2 = ₹ $2.40 \times \frac{2512}{3}$ = ₹ 2009.60

Radius of inner circle = 40 − 15 = 25 m

∴ Area of concrete track

$$= \left\{\frac{300°}{360°} \times \pi \times (40)^2 - \frac{300°}{360°} \times \pi \times (25^2)\right\}$$

$$= \frac{5}{6} \times \pi \times (1600 - 625) = \frac{5}{6} \times 3.14 \times 975$$

$$= 2551.25\ m^2$$

Amount spent for making the concrete track at the rate of ₹ 20 per m^2 = 20×2551.25

= ₹ 51025

Ans. Total amount spent for both the jobs

= 2009.60 + 51025

= ₹ 53034.60

55. Hint

(i) Radius of the circle = $OP = OQ = OD + DQ$

$= (x + 25)$ cm

By Pythagoras theorem,

$$OP^2 = AP^2 + AO^2$$

Ans. The radius of the circle = OP

= (28 + 25) cm

= 53 cm

(ii) By Pythagoras theorem,

$$AD^2 = AO^2 + OD^2$$

Ans. AD = 39.48 cm

(iii) ∴ Area of of the shaded region

= Area of the circle − Area of the square

Ans. 7252.26 cm^2

Olympiad Section

Brain Teasing Questions of Olympiad Pattern

1 The perimeter of a right angled triangle is 12 cm and its area is 6 cm^2. Then, the sum of the lengths of its perpendicular sides is

(a) 6 cm (b) 7 cm (c) 8 cm (d) 5 cm

2 In a triangle, the average of any two sides is 6 cm more than half of the third side. Then, the area of the triangle is equal to

(a) $36\sqrt{3}$ cm^2 (b) $36\sqrt{2}$ cm^2

(c) $39\sqrt{2}$ cm^2 (d) $30\sqrt{5}$ cm^2

3 The lengths of the diagonals of a rhombus are 9 cm and 12 cm. Then, the distance between any two parallel sides of the rhombus is equal to

(a) 6.5 cm (b) 7.2 cm (c) 7.8 cm (d) 6.2 cm

4 The circumradius of a right triangle is 10 cm and one of the perpendicular side is 12 cm. Then, find the area of the triangle is

(a) 94 cm^2 (b) 96 cm^2 (c) 91 cm^2 (d) 92 cm^2

5 The given figure shows two cross paths drawn inside a rectangular field 45 m long and 38 m wide, one parallel to its length and the other parallel to the breadth. The width of each path is 4 m. The cost of gravelling the paths at ₹ 5.60 per m^2 is

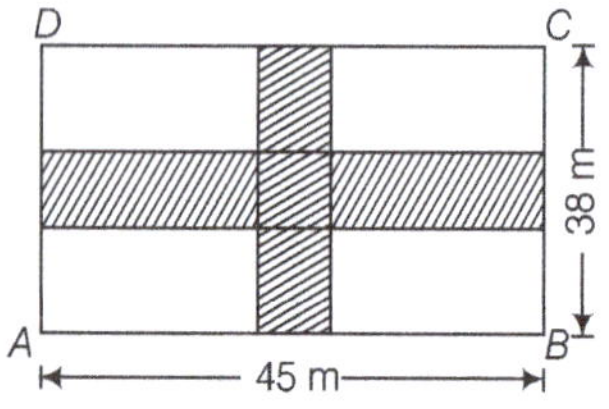

(a) ₹ 1769.60 (b) ₹ 1750 (c) ₹ 1870 (d) ₹ 1775.50

6 The given figure shows a field with the measurement given in metres, then the area of the field is

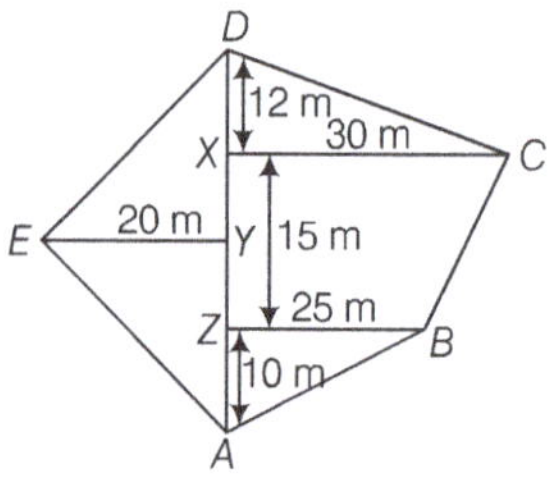

(a) 110.0 m^2 (b) 1087.5 m^2

(c) 1075.5 m^2 (d) 1090.5 m^2

7 In a pentagon *ABCDE*, *DP* is drawn perpendicular to *AB* and it is also perpendicular to *CE* at point *Q*. If $AP = BP = 12$ cm, $EQ = CQ = 8$ cm, $DE = DC = 10$ cm and $DP = 18$ cm, then the area of the pentagon *ABCDE* is

(a) 280 cm^2 (b) 290 cm^2

(c) 288 cm^2 (d) 290 cm^2

8 Two circles touch each other externally. The sum of their areas is 58π cm^2 and the distance between their centres is 10 cm, then the radii of the two circles are

(a) $r_1 = 6$ cm, $r_2 = 3$ cm

(b) $r_1 = 7$ cm, $r_2 = 3$ cm

(c) $r_1 = 5$ cm, $r_2 = 4$ cm

(d) $r_1 = 7$ cm, $r_2 = 5$ cm

9 In the following figure, rectangle *ABCD* inscribed in a circle. If $AB = 28$ cm and $BC = 21$ cm, then the area of the shaded portion of the given is equal to

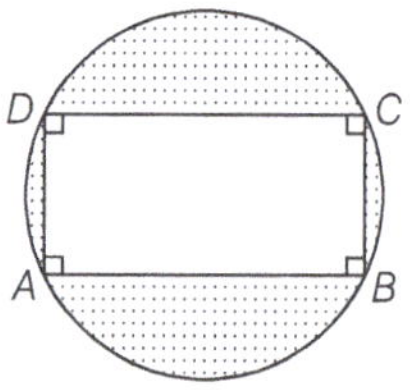

(a) 374.5 cm^2

(b) 370.6 cm^2

(c) 380.4 cm^2

(d) 378.5 cm^2

10 In the given figure, the area of the shaded portion with given measurements is

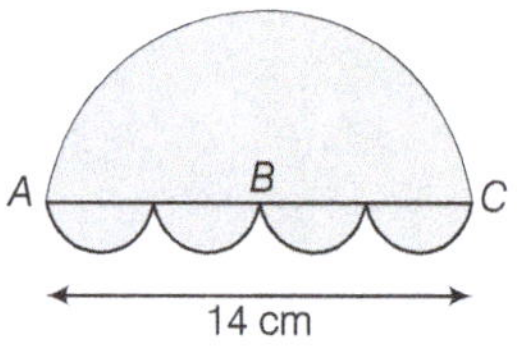

(a) 95.50 cm^2 (b) 96.25 cm^2

(c) 94.3 cm^2 (d) 97.5 cm^2

Answers

1. (b) **2.** (a) **3.** (b) **4.** (b) **5.** (a) **6.** (b) **7.** (c) **8.** (b) **9.** (a) **10.** (b)

* *These questions may or may not be asked in the examination, have been given just for additional practice required for olympiads Scholarship Exams etc. For detailed explanations refer Page No. 349.*

CHAPTER

16

Surface Area and Volume of 3-D Solids

SYLLABUS

- Surface area and volume of 3-D solids: cube and cuboid including problems of type involving (i) Different internal and external dimensions of the solid. (ii) Cost. (iii) Concept of volume being equal to area of cross-section x height. (iv) Open/closed cubes/cuboids.

Solid Figures

The objects having definite shape, size and occupy a fixed amount of space in three dimensions are called solids as cube, cuboid, cylinder, cone, sphere and hemisphere etc.

Cuboid

A cuboid is a solid bounded by six rectangular plane surfaces e.g. match box, brick, box, etc. Opposite faces of a cuboid are equal and parallel.

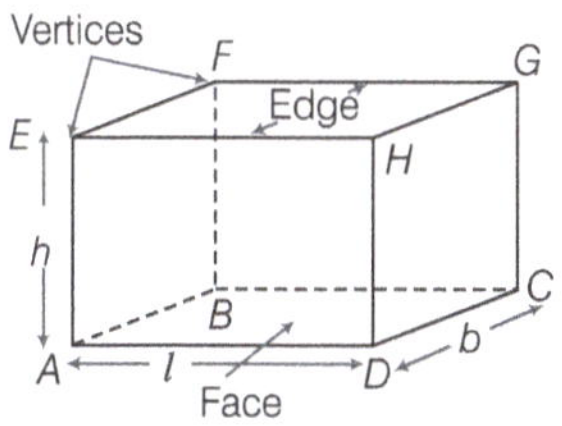

Let the length of the cuboid be l units, breadth b units and height h units. Then,

(i) **Surface Area** (SA) or **Total Surface Area** (TSA) **of the cuboid**

= Sum of areas of six rectangular faces

$= lb + lb + bh + bh + hl + hl$

$\therefore$ $\boxed{\text{SA or TSA} = 2(lb + bh + hl) \text{ sq units}}$

(ii) **Lateral Surface Area** If out of the six faces of a cuboid, we do not include the bottom and top faces, then the area of remaining four faces is called the lateral surface area of the cuboid. So, Lateral surface area = Sum of area of four rectangular faces (excluding top and bottom faces)

$= bh + bh + lh + lh = 2(l + b)h$

$\therefore$ Lateral surface area of a cuboid $= 2(l + b)h$ sq units

Or

Lateral surface area of a cuboid

= Perimeter of the base × Height

(iii) **Diagonal of a Cuboid** $= \sqrt{l^2 + b^2 + h^2}$ units

(iv) **Total Length of Cuboid** = Length of all 12 edges of the cuboid = Sum of semi-perimeter of all faces of the cuboid $= 4(l + b + h)$ units

Volume

The space occupied by an object/solid body is called the volume of that particular object/solid body.

Volume of a Cuboid

Let length of the cuboid is l units, breadth is b units and height is h units, then

Volume of the cuboid = Length × Breadth × Height

or Volume of the cuboid = lbh cu units

Also, Volume of the cuboid = Base area × Height

The unit of measurement of volume is cubic units.

Cube

A cuboid whose length, breadth and height all are equal, is called a cube. e.g. ice cubes, sugar cubes, dice etc.

Surface Area of a Cube

Let each edge of the cube be 'a' units. Then,

(i) Total surface area of the cube

$$= \text{Sum of areas of six faces}$$
$$= 2(aa + aa + aa)$$
$$= 2(a^2 + a^2 + a^2)$$

∴ **SA or TSA of cube = $6a^2$ sq units**

(ii) Lateral surface area of the cube = Sum of areas of four faces (excluding top and bottom)

$$= 2(aa + aa)$$

∴ **Lateral surface area = $4a^2$ sq units**

(iii) Diagonal of a cube $= \sqrt{a^2 + a^2 + a^2} = \sqrt{3a^2}$

∴ **Diagonal of a cube = $\sqrt{3}a$ units**

(iv) Total length of a cube = Length of all 12 edges of a cube = $12a$ units.

Volume of a Cube

We know that cube is a cuboid whose length, breadth and height are all equal. So, if one side of a cube be a units, then

Volume of cube $= l \times b \times h = a \times a \times a$

∴ **Volume of cube** $= a^3 = (\text{Side})^3$ cu units

Unit Conversions Related to Volume

$$1\text{ cm}^3 = 1\text{ cm} \times 1\text{ cm} \times 1\text{ cm}$$
$$= 10\text{ mm} \times 10\text{ mm} \times 10\text{ mm} = 1000\text{ mm}^3$$
$$1\text{ L} = 1000\text{ mL} = 1000\text{ cm}^3$$
$$1\text{ m}^3 = 1\text{ m} \times 1\text{ m} \times 1\text{ m} = 100\text{ cm} \times 100\text{ cm} \times 100\text{ cm}$$
$$= 10^6\text{ cm}^3 = 1000\text{ L} = 1\text{ kL}$$
$$1\text{ dm}^3 = 1000\text{ cm}^3$$
$$1\text{ m}^3 = 1000\text{ dm}^3$$
$$1\text{ km}^3 = 10^9\text{ m}^3$$

Example 1. The length, breadth and height of a cuboid are 8 m, 6 m and 4 m, respectively. Find its total surface area, diagonal and area of four walls.

Sol. Given, length of cuboid (l) = 8 m, breadth (b) = 6 m and height (h) = 4 m.

∴ Total surface area of cuboid $= 2(lb + bh + hl)$
$$= 2(8 \times 6 + 6 \times 4 + 4 \times 8)$$
$$= 2(48 + 24 + 32)$$
$$= 2 \times 104 = 208\text{ m}^2$$

∴ Diagonal of cuboid $= \sqrt{l^2 + b^2 + h^2}$
$$= \sqrt{(8)^2 + (6)^2 + (4)^2}$$
$$= \sqrt{64 + 36 + 16} = \sqrt{116} = 10.77\text{ m}$$

and area of the four walls = lateral surface area of cuboid
$$= 2(l + b)h = 2(8 + 6) \times 4 = 2 \times 14 \times 4 = 112\text{ m}^2$$

Example 2. The dimensions of a cuboid are in the ratio 1 : 2 : 3 and its total surface area is 88 m². Find the dimensions of the cuboid.

Sol. Given, dimensions of the cuboid are in the ratio 1 : 2 : 3.

So, let the dimensions of cuboid are x, $2x$ and $3x$.

Then, total surface area $= 2(lb + bh + hl)$
$$= 2(x \times 2x + 2x \times 3x + 3x \times x)$$

But surface area = 88 m²

∴ $2(x \times 2x + 2x \times 3x + 3x \times x) = 88$

⇒ $2(2x^2 + 6x^2 + 3x^2) = 88$

⇒ $2 \times 11x^2 = 88$

⇒ $22x^2 = 88 \Rightarrow x^2 = \dfrac{88}{22}$

⇒ $x^2 = 4$

⇒ $x = 2\text{ m}$ [taking positive square root]

∴ $2x = 2 \times 2 = 4\text{ m}$ and $3x = 3 \times 2 = 6\text{ m}$

Hence, the dimensions of cuboid are 2 m, 4 m and 6 m.

Example 3. A cuboidal oil tin is 30 cm × 40 cm × 50 cm. Find the cost of the tin required for making 20 such tins, if the cost of tin sheet is ₹ 20 per sq m.

Sol. Here, oil tin is in cuboidal form whose length (l) = 30 cm, breadth (b) = 40 cm and height (h) = 50 cm

∴ Surface area of one tin $= 2(lb + bh + hl)$
$$= 2(30 \times 40 + 40 \times 50 + 30 \times 50)$$
$$= 2(1200 + 2000 + 1500) = 2 \times 4700 = 9400\text{ cm}^2$$

Now, surface area of 20 such tins

$= 20 \times 9400 = 188000\,\text{cm}^2 = \frac{188000}{10000}\,\text{m}^2$

$\left[\because (100\text{ cm})^2 = (1\text{ m})^2 \Rightarrow 1\,\text{cm}^2 = \frac{1}{10000}\,\text{m}^2\right]$

$= 18.8\ \text{m}^2$

Given cost of 1 m^2 of tin sheet = ₹ 20

$\therefore$ Cost of $18.8\,\text{m}^2$ of tin sheet = ₹20×18.8 = ₹ 376

Hence, the cost of tin sheet for making 20 such tins is ₹ 376.

Example 4. Mary wants to decorate her Christmas tree. She wants to place the tree on a wooden box covered with coloured paper with picture of Santa Claus on it (see figure). She must know the exact quantity of paper to buy for this purpose. If the box has length, breadth and height as 80 cm, 40 cm and 20 cm, respectively, then how many square sheets of paper of side 40 cm would she require?

Sol. Here, Mary wants to cover a cuboidal box with square sheets of paper. So, the quantity of paper required to cover the box will be equal to the surface area of the box.

Given, dimensions of the box are length $(l) = 80\,\text{cm}$, breadth $(b) = 40\,\text{cm}$ and height $(h) = 20\,\text{cm}$.

$\therefore$ Surface area of the box $= 2(lb + bh + hl)$

$= 2[80 \times 40 + 40 \times 20 + 20 \times 80]$

$= 2[3200 + 800 + 1600] = 2 \times 5600 = 11200\,\text{cm}^2$

Dimension of square sheet of paper is 40 cm.

$\therefore$ Area of each square sheet of the paper

$= 40 \times 40 = 1600\,\text{cm}^2$ $\quad [\because \text{area of square} = (\text{side})^2]$

Now, surface area of the box = Number of sheets required × Area of each square sheet of paper

$\therefore$ Number of sheets required

$= \frac{\text{Surface area of the box}}{\text{Area of each square sheet of paper}} = \frac{11200}{1600} = 7$

Hence, 7 square sheets of paper, she would require.

Example 5. The dimension of a rectangular box are in the ratio 2 : 3 : 4 and the difference between the cost of covering it with sheet of paper at the rate of ₹ 4 and ₹ 4.50 per sq m is ₹ 416. Find the dimensions of the box.

Sol. Let the dimensions of the rectangular box be $2x$, $3x$ and $4x$.

$\therefore$ Surface area $= 2(2x \times 3x + 3x \times 4x + 4x \times 2x)$

$[\because \text{surface area} = 2(lb + bh + hl)]$

$= 2(6x^2 + 12x^2 + 8x^2)$

$= 2 \times 26x^2 = 52x^2$

Cost of covering the box with sheet of paper at the rate of ₹ 4 per m^2 = ₹ $52x^2 \times 4$ = ₹ $208\,x^2$.

and cost of covering the box with sheet of paper at the rate of ₹ 4.50 per m^2 = ₹ $4.50 \times 52x^2$

= ₹ $234x^2$.

According to the question,

Difference of the cost at different rate = 416

$\Rightarrow \quad 234x^2 - 208x^2 = 416$

$\Rightarrow \quad 26x^2 = 416$

$\Rightarrow \quad x^2 = 16 \quad \Rightarrow \quad x = 4$

[taking positive square root]

Hence, the dimension of the box are 8 m, 12 m and 16 m.

Example 6. Find the surface area and diagonal of a cube whose edge is 11 cm.

Sol. Given, edge of cube $(a) = 11\text{cm}$

$\therefore$ Surface area of cube $= 6a^2 = 6\,(11)^2$

$= 6 \times 121$

$= 726\,\text{cm}^2$

and diagonal of cube $= \sqrt{3}a = 11\sqrt{3}$ cm.

Example 7. The total surface area of a cube is 486cm^2. Find its lateral surface area.

Sol. Given, total surface area of the cube = 486 cm^2

But we know that, total surface area of cube $= 6a^2$

$[\because a = \text{edge of the cube}]$

$\therefore \quad 6a^2 = 486$

$\Rightarrow \quad a^2 = \frac{486}{6} = 81$

$\Rightarrow \quad a = \sqrt{81} = 9$ cm $\quad$ [taking positive square root]

Thus, lateral surface area of cube

$= 4a^2 = 4(9)^2$

$= 324\,\text{cm}^2$

Example 8. A cubical box has each edge 10 cm and another cuboidal box is 12.5 cm long, 10 cm wide and 8 cm high.

(i) Which box has the greater lateral surface area and by how much?

(ii) Which box has the smaller total surface area and by how much?

Sol. Given, length of the cubical box $(l) = 10$ cm

For cuboidal box, length $(l) = 12.5$ cm, breadth $(b) = 10$ cm and height $(h) = 8$ cm

(i) Lateral surface area of cubical box

$= 4l^2 = 4(10)^2 = 4 \times 100 = 400\text{cm}^2$

$\therefore$ Lateral surface area of cuboidal box

$= 2\,(l + b) \times h = 2\,(12.5 + 10) \times 8$

$= 2\,(22.5) \times 8 = 45 \times 8 = 360\,\text{cm}^2$

Lateral surface area of cubical box > Lateral surface area of cuboidal box

$[\because 400 > 360]$

$\therefore$ Required difference $= 400 - 360 = 40\,\text{cm}^2$

Hence, cubical box has 40 cm^2 more lateral surface area.

(ii) Total surface area of cubical box

$= 6l^2 = 6(10)^2$

$= 6 \times 100 = 600\,\text{cm}^2$

∴ Total surface area of cuboidal box

$= 2(l \times b + b \times h + h \times l)$

$= 2(12.5 \times 10 + 10 \times 8 + 8 \times 12.5)$

$= 2(125 + 80 + 100)$

$= 2 \times 305 = 610\ cm^2$

Area of cuboidal box > Area of cubical box [∵ 610 > 600]

∴ Required difference = 610 − 600 = 10 cm^2

Hence, cubical box has 10 cm^2 less total surface area.

Example 9. A cuboidal water tank is 4 m long, 5 m wide and 8 m deep. How many litres of water can it hold?

Sol. Given, the cuboidal water tank have length = 4 m, breadth = 5 m and height = 8 m.

Volume of the tank = Length × Breadth × Height

$= 4 \times 5 \times 8 = 160 m^3$

Quantity of water which the tank can hold

$= 160 \times 1000 = 160000\ L$ [∵ $1 m^3 = 1000 L$]

Example 10. The areas of three adjacent faces of a cuboid are x, y and z. If its volume is V, then find its volume.

Sol. Let the dimensions of cuboid be l, b and h.

Given, area of three adjacent faces of a cuboid are x, y and z.

∴ $x = lb,\ y = bh$ and $z = hl$ ...(i)

and volume of cuboid = V

∴ $V = lbh$

On squaring both sides, we get

$V^2 = l^2b^2h^2 = (lb)(bh)(hl)$

⇒ $V^2 = xyz$ [from Eq. (i)]

⇒ $V = \sqrt{xyz}$ [taking positive square root]

Example 11. If the total surface area of a cube is 96 cm^2, then what is the volume of cube?

Sol. Given, surface area of a cube = 96 cm^2.

∴ $6(\text{Side})^2 = 96$ [∵ surface area of a cube = $6(\text{side})^2$]

⇒ $(\text{Side})^2 = 16$ ⇒ Side = 4 cm

[taking positive square root as length cannot be negative]

∴ Volume of the cube = $(\text{Side})^3 = (4)^3 = 64\ cm^3$.

Example 12. Find the surface area and the length of the diagonal of a cube, if the volume of a cube is 2197 cu cm.

Sol. Given, volume of cube = 2197 cu cm

⇒ $(\text{Side})^3 = 2197$ [∵ volume of cube = $(\text{side})^3$]

⇒ Side of cube = $\sqrt[3]{2197} = 13$ cm

[taking cube root both sides]

Now, surface area of cube = $6(\text{Side})^2$

$= 6(13)^2$ sq cm

$= 1014$ sq cm

and length of the diagonal of cube = $\sqrt{3} \times$ Side

$= \sqrt{3} \times 13 = 22.517$ cm

Example 13. Three cubes are joined end-to-end forming a cuboid. If side of a cube is 2 cm, then find the dimensions of the cuboid. Also, find the volume of cuboid.

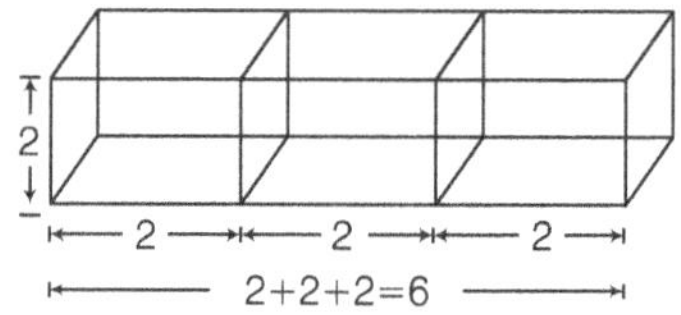

Sol. When we join three cubes with edge 2 cm, then we get a cuboid whose length is changed but breadth and height are not changed.

∴ Length = 2 + 2 + 2 = 6 cm

breadth = 2 cm and height = 2 cm

Now, volume of cuboid = $l \times b \times h$

$= 6 \times 2 \times 2$

$= 24\ cm^3$

Example 14. A hollow square-shaped tube open at both ends is made of iron. The internal square is of 8 cm side and the length of the table is 10 cm. There are 800 cm^3 of iron in this tube. Find its thickness.

Sol. Let thickness of the tube = x cm

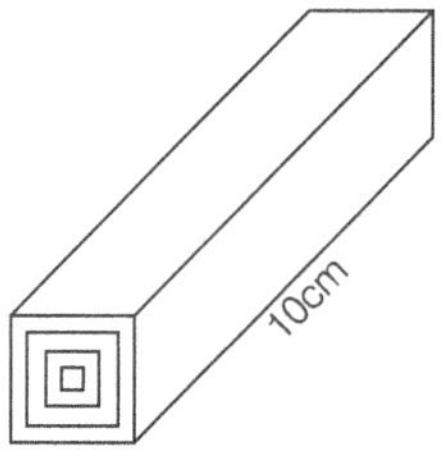

∴ Side of external square = $(8 + 2x)$ cm

∵ Volume of the tube − its internal volume

= Volume of iron in the tube.

$= (8 + 2x) \times (8 + 2x) \times 10 - 8 \times 8 \times 10 = 800$

⇒ $(8 + 2x) \times (8 + 2x) = \dfrac{800 - 640}{10} = \dfrac{160}{10}$

⇒ $(8 + 2x)^2 = 16$

Taking square root on both side,

$8 + 2x = 4$

$2x = -4$

⇒ $x = -2, 2$

[∵ thickness can not be negative]

⇒ Thickness of the tube = 2 cm

Example 15. A wall of length 10 m was to be built across an open ground. The height of the wall is 4 m and thickness of the wall is 24 cm. If this wall is to be built up with bricks whose dimensions are 24 cm × 12 cm × 8 cm, then how many bricks would be required?

Sol. Given, dimensions of wall are length = 10 m = 1000 cm, thickness = 24 cm and height = 4 m = 400 cm.

$\therefore$ Volume of the wall = Length × Thickness × Height

$= 1000 \times 24 \times 400 \text{ cm}^3$

Now, each brick is a cuboid with length = 24 cm, breadth = 12 cm and height = 8 cm.

$\therefore$ Volume of each brick

= Length × Breadth × Height

$= 24 \times 12 \times 8 \text{ cm}^3$

Since, the cuboidal wall is built up with cuboidal bricks. So, volume of the cuboidal wall = Volume of each brick × Number of bricks required

$\Rightarrow$ Number of bricks required

$$= \frac{\text{Volume of the wall}}{\text{Volume of each brick}} = \frac{1000 \times 24 \times 400}{24 \times 12 \times 8} = 4166.7$$

Hence, the wall requires 4167 bricks.

Example 16. A certain quantity of wood costs ₹ 180 per m^3. A solid cubical block of such wood is bought for ₹ 737.28. Calculate the volume of the block and find the length of one edge of the cube.

Sol. Volume of cubical block × Rate = Cost

$$\Rightarrow \text{Volume of cubical block} = \frac{737.28}{180} \text{ m}^3$$

$$= 4.096 \text{ m}^3 \quad \left[\because \text{Volume} = \frac{\text{Cost}}{\text{Rate}}\right]$$

Now, for edge of the cube

$$(\text{edge})^3 = 4.096 \quad [\because \text{Volume of cube} = (\text{edge})^3]$$

$$= \frac{4096}{1000}$$

$$= \frac{4 \times 4 \times 4 \times 4 \times 4 \times 4}{2 \times 2 \times 2 \times 5 \times 5 \times 5}$$

$$\Rightarrow \text{Edge of the cube} = \frac{4 \times 4}{2 \times 5} \text{ m} = 1.6 \text{ m}$$

Example 17. A field is 14 m long and 10 m broad. At one corner of this field a rectangular well of dimensions 8 m × 2.5 m × 2 m is dug and dug-out soil is spread evenly over the rest of the field. Find the rise in the level of the rest of the field.

Sol.

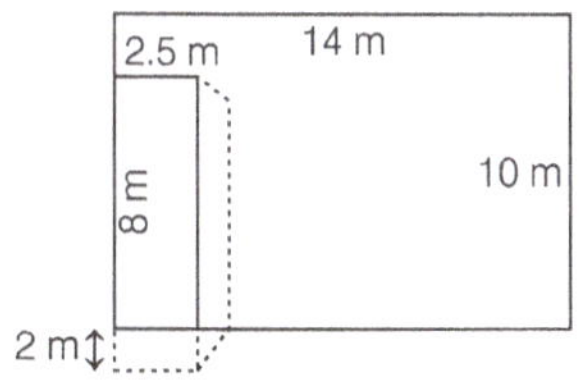

The volume of the solid removed

= Volume of the well dug

$= 8 \times 2.5 \times 2\text{m}^3 = 40 \text{ m}^3$

Let the level of the remaining field be raised by h m. Since, the area of remaining field

$= (14 \times 10 - 8 \times 2.5) \text{ m}^2$

$= 120 \text{ m}^2$

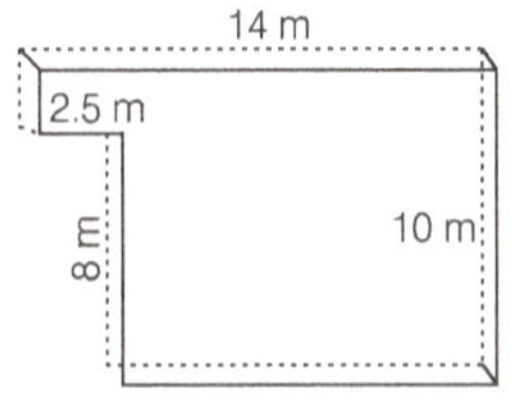

Volume of the solid spread

= Area of the remaining field × Rise in level

$\Rightarrow \quad 40 \text{ m}^3 = 120 \text{ m}^2 \times h$

$\Rightarrow \quad h = \frac{40}{120} \text{ m}$

$= \frac{1}{3} \text{ m}$

$= 33.33 \text{ cm}$

$\therefore$ The rise in level of rest of the field = 33.33 cm

Cross-section

The cross-section is a part or piece, which is cut from a given solid, perpendicular to its length (breadth or height).

A solid is said to have uniform cross-section, if this perpendicular cut is of the same shape and size at each point of its length (breadth or height).

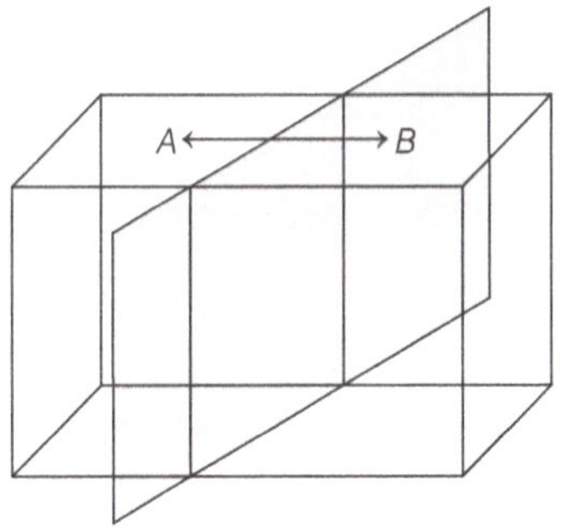

Cross-section Perpendicular to Length

When a solid has uniform cross-section, then

(i) Volume = Area of cross-section × length (breadth or height)

(ii) Surface area (excluding cross-section)

= Lateral surface area

= Perimeter of cross-section × Length (or Breadth or Height)

Example 18. The cross-section of a piece of metal 2 m in length is as shown in the figure below

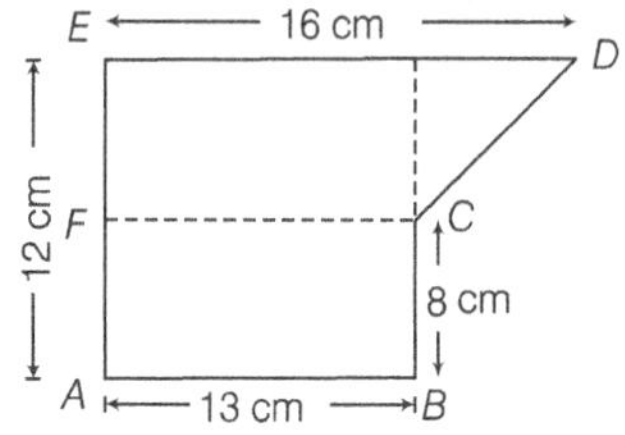

Calculate

(i) the area of cross-section.

(ii) the volume of piece of metal.

(iii) the weight of piece of metal to the nearest kg, if $1 cm^3$ of metal weight 6.5 gm.

Sol.

(i) Area of cross-section = Area of rectangle *ABCF* + Area of trapezium *CDEF*

$= (13 \times 8) + \frac{1}{2}(13 + 16) \times 4$

[∵ area of rectangle = length × breadth and area of trapezium = 1/2 (sum of parallel sides) × height]

$= 104 + \frac{1}{2} \times 29 \times 4$

$= 104 + 58$

$= 162 \text{ cm}^2$

(ii) Volume of metal piece

= Area of cross-section × Height

$= 162 \times 200$

$= 32400 \text{ cm}^3$ [∵ 1 m = 100 cm]

(iii) Weight of the metal piece

$= 32400 \times 6.5$ gm

= 210600 gm

= 210.6 kg

∴ Weight of the metal piece = 211 kg (approx).

Chapter Practice

a. 1 Mark Questions

1. A small indoor green house (herbarium) is made entirely of glass panes (including base) held together with tape. The dimensions of the green house are 40 cm × 30 cm × 25 cm. Find the length of the tape required.
   (a) 380 cm^2 (b) 382 cm^2 (c) 382 m^2 (d) 380 m^2

2. The length of the longest rod that can be placed in a rectangular box or in a room is called
   (a) diagonal (b) breadth
   (c) height (d) None of these

3. How many litres of water flows out of a pipe of cross-section area 5 cm^2 in 1 min, if the speed of the water in the pipe is 30 cm/s?
   [1 L = 1000 cm^3]
   (a) 10 L (b) 9.2 L (c) 9 L (d) 10.2 L

4. A solid piece of metal, cuboidal in shape, with dimensions 24 cm, 18 cm and 4 cm is recast into a cube. Calculate the lateral surface area of the cube.
   (a) 576 m^2 (b) 576 cm^2 (c) 567 cm^2 (d) 567 m^2

5. The length, breadth and height of a rectangular solid are in the ratio 5 : 4 : 2. If the total surface area is 1216 cm^2, find the length of the solid.
   (a) 10 cm (b) 16 cm (c) 8 cm (d) 20 cm

b. 3 Marks Questions

6. Find the surface area of a box whose length, breadth and height are 12 cm, 8 cm and 5 cm, respectively.

7. Find the surface area of a box whose length is 40 cm, breadth 27 cm and height 10 cm.

8. Find the length of the longest pole that can be put in a room of dimensions (10 m × 10 m × 5 m).

9. Find the length of the longest rod that can be placed in a room 12 m long, 9 m broad and 8 m high.

10. 75 persons can sleep in a room 25 m by 9.6 m. If each person requires 16 m^3 of air, find the height of the room.

11. The total surface area of a cube is 216 m^2. Find its diagonal.

12. A cuboidal water tank is 8 m long, 4 m wide and 3 m deep. How many litres of water can it hold?

13. A solid cube is cut into two cuboids of equal volumes. Find the ratio of the total surface area of the given cube and that of one of the cuboids.

14. A cuboidal oil tin is 3 m × 4 m × 5 m. Find the cost of the tin required for making 30 such tins, if the cost of tin sheet is ₹ 10 per sq m.

15. The sum of length, breadth and height of a cuboid is 38 cm and the length of its diagonal is 22 cm. Find the surface area of the cuboid.

16. The perimeter of one face of a cube is 20 cm. Find the lateral surface area of the cube.

17. The perimeter of one face of a cube is 40 cm. Find the volume of the cube (in cm^3).

18. Find the cost of digging a cuboidal pit 8 m long, 6 m broad and 3 m deep at the rate of ₹ 30 per m^3.

19. A plastic box 1.5 m long, 1.25 m wide and 65 cm deep is to be made. It is opened at the top. Ignoring the thickness of the plastic sheet, determine
   (i) the area of the sheet required for making the box.
   (ii) the cost of sheet for it, if a sheet measuring 1 m^2 costs ₹ 20.

20. The length, breadth and height of a room are 5 m, 4 m and 3 m, respectively. Find the cost of white-washing the walls of the room and the ceiling at the rate of ₹ 7.50 per m^2.

21. The whole surface area of rectangular block is 1300 cm^2. Find its volume, if their dimensions are in the ratio of 4 : 3 : 2.

22. A cube of 9 cm edge is immersed completely in a rectangular vessel containing water. If the dimensions of base are 15 cm and 12 cm. Then, find the rise in water level in the vessel.

23. How many litres of water flows out of a pipe of cross-section area 5 cm^2 in 1 min, if the speed of the water in the pipe is 30 cm/s?
   [1 L = 1000 cm^3]

24. A river 3 m deep and 40 m wide is flowing at the rate of 2 km/h. How much water will fall into the sea in a minute?

c. 4/5 Marks Questions

25. The length of a hall is 24 m and its width is 16 m. If the lateral surface area of the hall is $\frac{2}{3}$rd of the sum of the areas of the roof and the floor, find its height.

26. A hollow square shaped tube open at both ends, is made of iron. the internal square is of 5 cm side and the length of the tube is 8 cm. There are 192 cm^3 of iron in this tube. Find the thickness.

27. To construct a wall 25 m long, 0.3 m thick and 6 m high, bricks of dimensions 25 cm × 15 cm × 10 cm, each are used. If mortar occupies $\frac{1}{10}$ th of the volume of the wall, find the number of bricks used.

28. A rectangular tank is 25 m long and 9.5 m deep. If 600 cu m of water be drawn off the tank, the level of water in the tank goes down by 1.5 m.
Calculate
(i) the width of the tank.
(ii) the total volume of water which the tank can hold.

29. A rectangular water-tank measuring 80 cm × 60 cm × 60 cm is filled from a pipe of cross sectional area 1.5 cm^2. The water emerging at 3.2 m/s. How long does it take to fill the tank?

30. A classroom is 8 m long 6 m wide and 4.5 m high. The room has one door of size 2.5 m × 1 m and three windows of size 1 m × 80 cm. Find the area of the walls excluding doors and windows. Also, find the cost of polishing the walls at the rate of ₹ 10 per sq m.

31. A school auditorium is 40 m long, 30 m broad and 12 m height. If each student requires 1.2 m^2 of the floor area. Find the maximum number of students that can be accomodated in this auditorium. Also, find the volume of air available in the auditorium, for each student.

32. Three equal cubes are placed adjacently in a row. Find the ratio of the total surface area of the resulting cuboid to that of the sum of the total surface areas of the three cubes.

33. The following figure shows a solid of uniform cross-section.

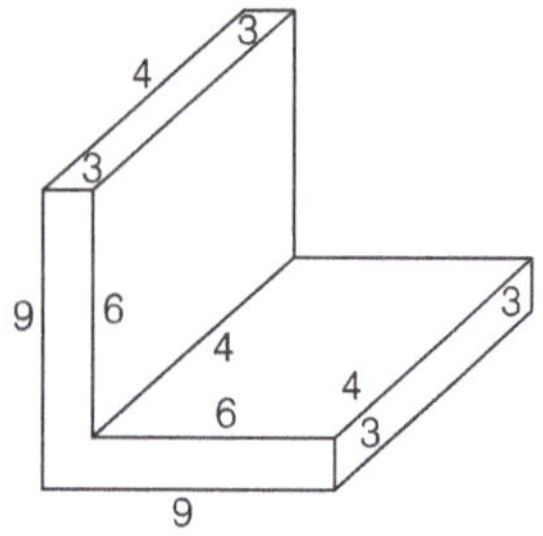

Find the volume of the solid all measurements are (in cm) and assuming that all angles in the figure are right angles.

34. A wall of length 20 m was to be built across an open ground. The height of the wall is 5 m and thickness of the wall is 20 cm. If this wall is to be built up with bricks whose dimensions are 15 cm × 10 cm × 5 cm, then how many bricks would be required?

35. A small village having the population of 5000, requires 75 L of water per head per day. The village has got an overhead tank of measurement 40 m × 25 m × 15 m. For how many days will the water of this tank last?

36. A woodcutter desires to make dusters for schools. He plans to make duster of dimensions 10 cm × 4 cm × 3 cm. How many dusters can be made from a wooden plank of dimensions 4 m × 3 m × 1 m?

37. A storage tank is in the form of a cube. When it is full of water, the volume of water is 15.625 m^3. If the present depth of water is 1.3 m, find the volume of water already used from the tank.

38. Three cubes of metal whose edges are in the ratio 3 : 4 : 5, are melted to form a cube whose diagonal is $12\sqrt{3}$ cm. Find the edges of the three cubes.

39. The dimensions of a rectangular box are in the ratio 2 : 3 : 4 and the difference between the cost of covering it with sheet of paper at the rate of ₹ 5 and ₹ 6.50 per m^2 is ₹ 1950. Then, find the length of box.

40. The length of a room is 50% more than its breadth. The cost of carpeting the room at the rate of ₹ 38.50 m^2 is ₹ 924 and the cost of perpering the walls at ₹ 3.30 m^2 is 214.50. If the room has one door of dimensions 1 m × 2 m and two windows each of dimensions 1 m × 1.5 m. Find the dimensions of the room.

41. A house-pipe of cross-section area 2 cm^2 deliver 1500 L of water in 5 min. What is the speed of water (in m/s) through the pipe?

42. The area of cross-section of a pipe is 5.4 cm^2 and water is pumped out of it at the rate of 27 km/h. Find in litres the volume of water which flows out of the pipe in one minute.

43. A rectangular field is 112 m long and 62 m broad. A cubical tank of edge 6 m is dug at each of four corners of the field and the earth so removed is evenly spread on the remaining field. Find the rise in level.

44. A field is 15 m long and 12 m broad. At one corner of this field a rectangular well of dimensions 8 m × 2.5 m × 2 m is dug and the

dug-out soil is spread evenly over the rest of the field. Find the rise in the level of the rest of the field.

d. 6 Marks Questions

45. The cross-section of a tunnel perpendicular to its length is *PQRS* as shown in figure. Also, given that $PM = QN$, $PQ = 7$ m, $RS = 5$ m and the height of the tunnel is 40 m long.

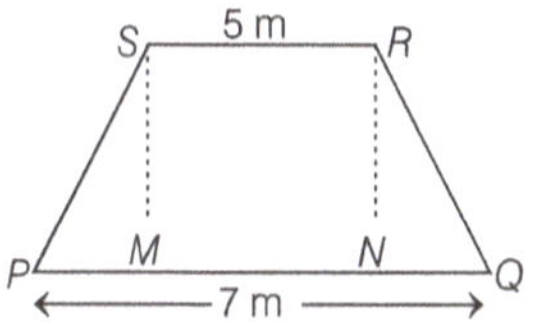

Calculate

(i) the cost of painting the internal surface of the tunnel (excluding the floor) at the rate of ₹ 5 per m^2.

(ii) the cost of painting the floor at the rate of 18 per m^2.

46. The cross-section of swimming pool 10 m broad, 2 m deep at one end and 3 m deep at the other end as shown in figure.

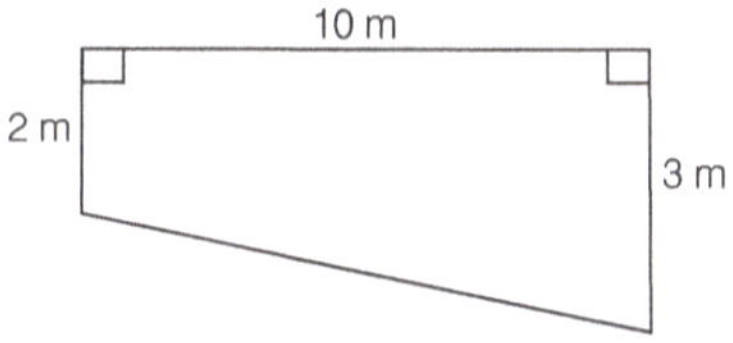

Calculate the volume of water it hold when full given that its length is 40 m.

47. A wooden bookshelf has external dimensions as follows

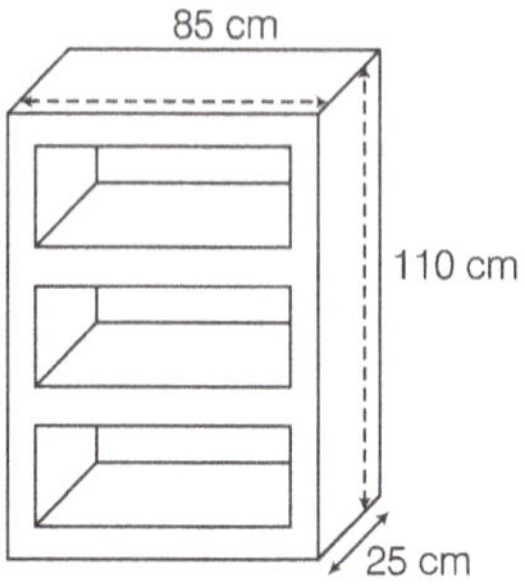

Height = 110 cm, depth = 25 cm,

and breadth = 85 cm (see the figure).

The thickness of the plank is 5 cm everywhere. The external faces are to be polished and the inner faces are to be painted. If the rate of polishing is 20 paise per cm^2 and the rate of painting is 10 paise per cm^2, find the total expenses required for polishing and painting the surface of the bookshelf.

48. The following figure shows a closed victory-stand whose dimensions (in cm).

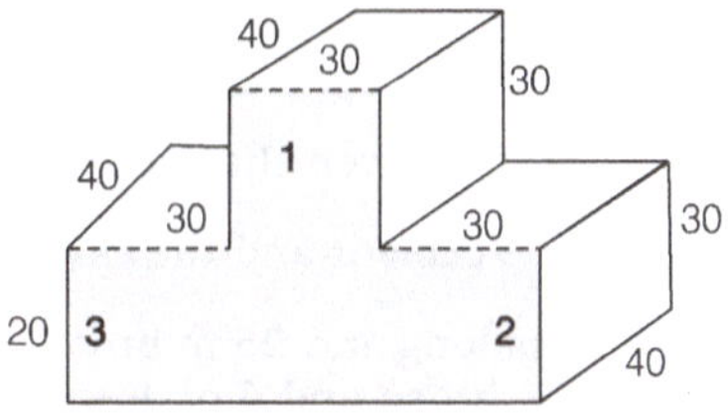

If the bottom of the stand is open, find the volume and total surface area.

49. In the given figure the cross-section of a concrete wall to be constructed. It is 2 m wide at the top, 3.5 m at the bottom and its height is 6 m and length is 400 m. Find

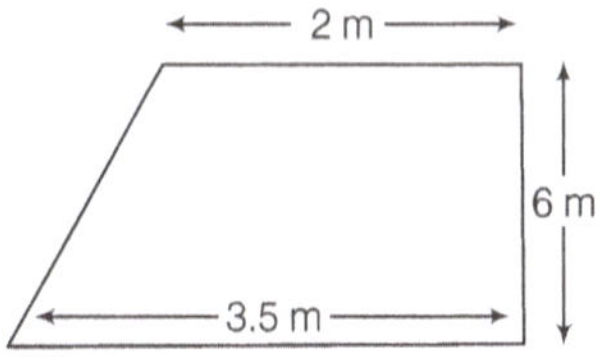

(i) the area of cross-section.

(ii) the volume of concrete in the wall.

50. When length of each side of a cube is increased by 3 cm its volume is increased by 2457 cm^3. Find its side how much will its volume decrease, if length of each side of it is reduced by 20%?

51. Hammed has built a cubical water tank with lid for his house, with each outer edge 1.5 m long. He gets the outer surface of the tank excluding the base, covered with square tiles of side 25 cm (shown in the adjoining figure). Find how much he would spend for the tiles, if the cost of the tiles is ₹ 360 per dozen.

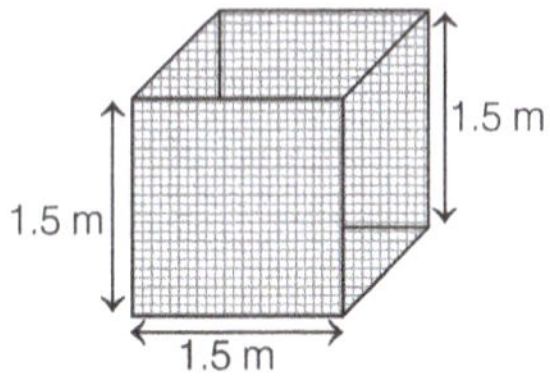

52. A rectangular container, whose base is a square of side 15 cm, stands on a horizontal table and holds water upto 3 cm from the top. When a cube is placed in the water and is completely submerged, the water rises to the top and 54 cm^3 of water overflows. Calculate the volume of the cube and its surface area.

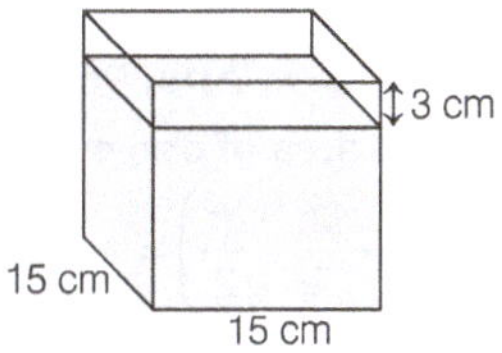

53. How many bricks, (each measuring 20 cm × 16 cm × 8 cm), will be required to build a wall 30 m long, 30 cm thick and 5 m high, with a provision of 2 doors, each measuring 2.5 m × 1.2 m. It is given that $\frac{1}{9}$th of the wall is occupied by the cement and the sand mixture.

54. A field is 102 m long and 25 m broad. A tank 10 m long, 5 m broad and 4 m deep is dug out from the middle of the field and the earth removed is evenly spread over the remaining part of the field.

Find the rise in the level of the remaining part of the field (in cm).

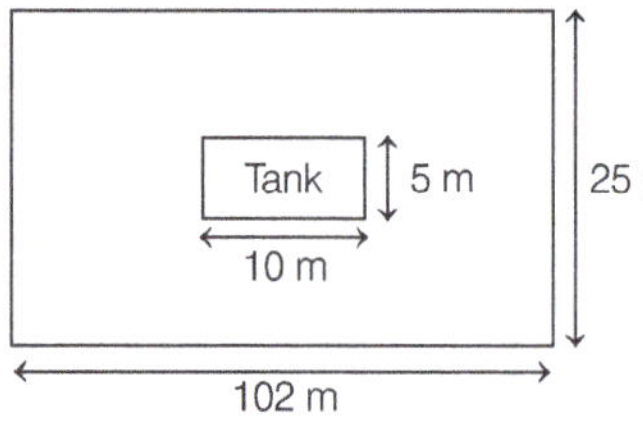

55. Shanti Sweets wants to place an order for cardboard boxes for packing sweets. They need two types of boxes, one with dimensions 25 cm × 20 cm × 5 cm and another with dimensions 15 cm × 12 cm × 5 cm.

For all the overlaps, 5% of the total surface is required extra. If the cost of the cardboard is ₹ 4 for 1000 cm^2, find the cost of cardboard required for supplying 250 boxes of each type.

56. *ABCDE* is the end view of a factory shed which is 50 m long. The roofing of the shed consists of asbestos sheets as shown in the figure. The two ends of the shed are completely closed by brick walls.

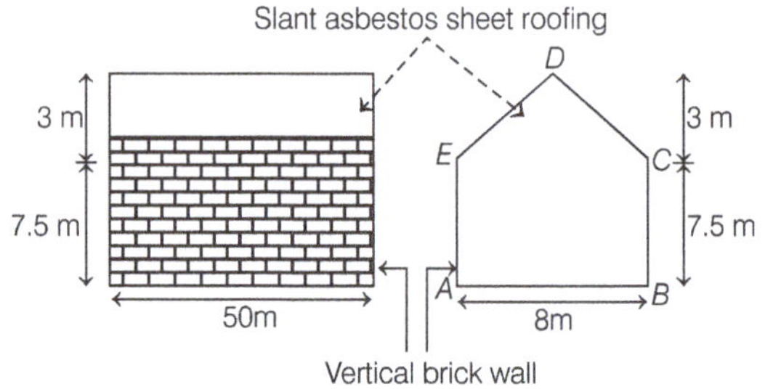

(i) Calculate the total volume content of the shed.

(ii) If the cost of asbestos sheet roofing is ₹ 25 per m^2 (sq metre), find the cost of roofing.

(iii) If the whole outside surface of the shed (including roofing) is to be painted, find the cost of painting it at ₹ 5 per m^2 (sq metre).

Hints and Answers

1. (a) **2.** (a)

3. (c) **4.** (b)

5. (d)

6. Do same as Example 1. **Ans.** 392 cm^2

7. Do same as Example 1. **Ans.** 3500 cm^2

8. **Hint** Length of the longest pole

$$= \text{Diagonal of a cuboid}$$
$$= \sqrt{(10)^2 + (10)^2 + (5)^2}$$

Ans. 15 m

9. Do same as Q. 8. **Ans.** 17 m

10. **Hint** 75 persons requires air = 75 × 16

$$= 1200 \text{ m}^3$$

$$\text{height } (h) = \frac{1200 \times 10}{25 \times 96} = 5 \text{ m}$$

11. **Hint** From the question, $6\,(\text{Side})^2 = 216 \text{ m}^2$

$\therefore$ Diagonal $= \sqrt{(6)^2 + (6)^2 + (6)^2}$ **Ans.** $6\sqrt{3}$ m

12. Do same as Example 9. **Ans.** 96000 L

13. **Hint** Total surface area of one cuboid

$$= 2\left(a^2 + \frac{a^2}{2} + \frac{a^2}{2}\right) = 4a^2 \text{ cm}^2$$

and total surface area of the cube

$$= 6\,(\text{Edge})^2 = 6a^2 \text{cm}^2$$

Ans. 3 : 2

14. **Hint** Surface area of one tin = $2(lb + bh + hl) = 94 \text{ m}^2$

Now, surface area of 30 such tins = $30 \times 94 \text{ m}^2$

$$= 2820 \text{ m}^2$$

$\therefore$ Cost of 2820 m^2 of tin sheet = ₹ (10 × 2820

Ans. ₹ 28200

15. **Hint** From the question,

$$x + y + z = 38 \text{ cm}$$

and $\sqrt{x^2 + y^2 + z^2} = 22$ cm

Now, $(x + y + z)^2 = x^2 + y^2 + z^2 + 2(xy + yz + zx)$

$\Rightarrow 2\,(xy + yz + zx) = 960 \text{ cm}^2$ **Ans.** 960 cm^2

16. **Hint** Edge of cube $= \frac{20}{4} = 5$ cm

$\therefore$ Lateral surface area of the cube = $4 \times (5)^2$

Ans. 100 cm^2

17. **Hint** Here, edge of cube $= \frac{40}{4} = 10$ cm

Now, volume of the cube = $(10)^3$

Ans. 1000 cm^3

18. **Hint** Volume of a cuboidal pit = $(8 \times 6 \times 3) = 144 \text{ m}^3$

Now, cost of digging 144 m^3 = ₹ 30×144

Ans. ₹ 4320

19. **Hint** Surface area of the box

$= 2(1.5 \times 1.25 + 1.25 \times 0.65 + 0.65 \times 1.5)$

(i) Area of the sheet required for making the box

$= 7.325 \; - l \times b$

Ans. 5.45 m^2

(ii) Cost of 5.45 m^2 sheet = ₹ 20×5.45 **Ans.** ₹109

20. **Hint** Required area for white-washing

$= 2(l + b) \times h + (l \times b)$

$= 2(5 + 4) \times 3 + (5 \times 4) = 74 \text{ m}^2$

Cost of white-washing 74 m^2 = ₹ 7.50×74

Ans. ₹ 555

21. **Hint** Let the dimensions of rectangular block are $4x$, $3x$ and $2x$, respectively.

According to the question,

$2[(4x \times 3x) + (3x \times 2x) + (2x \times 4x)] = 1300$

$\therefore \quad x = 5 \text{ cm}$ [taking positive square part]

Now, required volume = $[(4 \times 5) \times (3 \times 5) \times (2 \times 5)] \text{ cm}^3$

Ans. 3000 cm^3

22. **Hint** Let the rise in the water level be x cm.

Then, volume of vessel = $15 \times 12 \times x$

According to the question, $15 \times 12 \times x = 9 \times 9 \times 9$

Ans. 4.05 cm

23. **Hint** Volume of water flowing in 1 s = $5 \times 30 \text{ cm}^3$

$= 150 \text{ cm}^3$

$\Rightarrow$ Volume of water flowing in 1 min = $150 \times 60 \text{ cm}^3$

$= 9000 \text{ cm}^3$

Ans. 9 L

24. **Hint** Volume of water flowing in 1 h

= Area of cross-section × Speed of water flowing × Time

$= 40 \times 3 \times 2000 \times 1$

Hence, volume of water flowing into the sea in

$1 \text{ min} = \dfrac{240000}{60}$

Ans. 4000 m^3

25. Given, $l = 24$ m, $b = 16$ m and height = h m

Lateral surface Area = $2(l + b)h = 2(24 + 16)h = 80h \text{ m}^2$

Sum of area of the roof and floor = 768 m^2

$\Rightarrow \quad 80h = \dfrac{2}{3} \times 768$

$h = 6.4$ m

26. $\therefore$ Internal volume of a square = $(5 \times 5 \times 8) \text{ cm}^3$

$= 200 \text{ cm}^3$.

Let the thickness of a side be x cm.

Then, the external square is of $(5 + 2x)$ cm side.

As the tube is open at both ends, its length remains 8 cm.

$\therefore$ The external volume of the tube

$= [(5 + 2x)(5 + 2x) \times 8] \text{ cm}^3$.

Given, volume of iron = 192 cm^3

$(5 + 2x)^2 \times 8 - 200 = 192$

$\Rightarrow \quad x = 1$

27. $\therefore$ The volume of wall = $l \times b \times h$

$= (2500 \times 30 \times 600) \text{ cm}^3$.

$\therefore$ Volume of each brick = $(25 \times 15 \times 10) \text{ cm}^3$.

$\Rightarrow$ The volume of wall occupied by bricks

$= \left(1 - \dfrac{1}{10}\right)$th of volume of wall

$= \left(\dfrac{9}{10} \times 2500 \times 30 \times 600\right) \text{cm}^3$

$\therefore$ The number of bricks required to construct the wall

$= \dfrac{\text{Volume of wall occupied by bricks}}{\text{Volume of one brick}}$

$= \dfrac{2500 \times 27 \times 600}{25 \times 15 \times 10} = 10800.$

28. **Ans.** (i) 16 m

(ii) Volume = $l \times b \times h = 3800 \text{ m}^3$

29. **Hint** Volume of rectangular tank

$= (80 \times 60 \times 60) \text{ cm}^3 = 288000 \text{ cm}^3$

Water flow = $1.5 \times 320 = 480 \text{ cm}^3/\text{s}$

Time of fill tank = $\dfrac{288000}{480} = 600$ s

600 s = 10 min

30. **Hint** Area of four walls = $2h(l + b)$

$= 2 \times 4.5(8 + 6)$

$= 126 \text{ m}^2$

$\therefore$ Area of door + 3 windows = $2.5 + 2.4 = 4.9 \text{ m}^2$

Hence, remaining area = 121.1 m^2

$\therefore$ Cost of polishing the walls = ₹ 10×121.1 = ₹ 1211

31. **Hint** Flour area of auditorium = $l \times b$

$40 \times 30 = 1200 \text{ m}^2$

Maximum number of students = $\dfrac{1200}{1.2} = 1000$

Volume of air of the auditorium

$= 40 \times 30 \times 12 = 14400 \text{ m}^3$

Volume of air for each student = $\dfrac{14400}{1000} \text{ m}^3 = 14.4 \text{ m}^3$

32. Do same as Q. 13. **Ans.** 7 : 9

33. **Hint** Required volume of solid

= Volume of I cuboid + Volume of II cuboid

$= (6 \times 4 \times 3 + 4 \times 3 \times 9) \text{ cm}^3$

Ans. 180 cm^3

34. **Hint** Volume of the wall = $(2000 \times 20 \times 500) \text{ cm}^3$

$\therefore$ Volume of each brick = $(15 \times 10 \times 5) \text{ cm}^3$

$\therefore$ Number of bricks required = $\dfrac{2000 \times 20 \times 500}{15 \times 10 \times 5}$

Ans. 26667

35. **Hint** Volume of the overhead tank

$= 40\text{ m} \times 25\text{ m} \times 15\text{ m} = 15000\text{ m}^3$

Volume of water in the tank

$= 15000 \times 1000 = 15000000\text{ L}$

$\therefore$ Number of days $= \dfrac{15000000}{75 \times 5000}$

Ans. 40 days

36. **Hint** Number of dusters $= \dfrac{400\text{ cm} \times 300\text{ cm} \times 100\text{ cm}}{10\text{ cm} \times 4\text{ cm} \times 3\text{ cm}}$

Ans. 100000

37. **Hint** Let side of a cubical tank $= x$ m

$\Rightarrow \quad x^3 = 15.625 \Rightarrow x = 2.5$ m

$\therefore$ Height of water used $= (2.5 - 1.3)$ m $= 1.2$ m

Hence, volume of water used $= (1.2 \times 2.5 \times 2.5)\text{ m}^3$

Ans. 7500 L

38. **Hint** Total volume of the three cubes

$= (3x)^3 + (4x)^3 + (5x)^3$

[$\because$ volume of a cube = (edge)^3]

$= 216x^3$

Now, diagonal of new cube

$= \sqrt{3}a = 12\sqrt{3} \Rightarrow a = 12$

Volume of new cube $= (12)^3 = 1728\text{ cm}^3$

Now, $\quad 216x^3 = 1728 \quad$ [from the question]

$\Rightarrow \quad x = 2$

Ans. 6 cm, 8 cm, 10 cm

39. Total surface area of the box

$= 2(2x \times 3x + 3x \times 4x + 4x \times 2x) = 52x^2\text{ m}^2$

Cost of covering with sheet of paper at the rate of ₹ 5 per m^2 $= 52x^2 \times 5 =$ ₹ $260x^2$

Cost of covering with sheet of paper at the rate of ₹ 6.50 per m^2 $= 52x^2 \times 6.50 =$ ₹ $338x^2$

Difference between costs $= 338x^2 - 260x^2 = 78x^2$

According to the question,

$78x^2 = 1950 \Rightarrow x = 5$

Now, length of the box $= 2 \times x$

$= 2 \times 5 = 10$ m

40. Let the breadth of the room be x m.

$\Rightarrow$ Length of the room $= \left(1 + \dfrac{50}{100}\right)$ of x m $= \dfrac{3}{2}x$ m

$\therefore$ The area of the floor of the room

$= \dfrac{3}{2}x \times x\text{ m}^2 = \dfrac{3}{2}x^2\text{m}^2$

$\Rightarrow$ Cost of carpeting the room $\dfrac{3x^2}{2} \times 38.5 = 924$

$\Rightarrow \quad x^2 = 16 \Rightarrow x = 4$

Hence, the length of the room $= \dfrac{3}{2}x$ m $= \dfrac{3}{2} \times 4 = 6$ m

$\therefore$ Surface area of all the walls of the room

= 2 (length + breadth) × height

Surface area to be papered = Surface area of wall − Surface area of door and windows

According to question,

Surface area to be papered × 3.30 = 214.50

The dimensions of the room are 6 m × 4 m × 3.5 m.

41. **Hint** Speed of water through pipe

$= \dfrac{\text{Volume of water}}{\text{Area of cross - section} \times \text{Time}}$

$v = \dfrac{1500 \times 1000}{60000} = \dfrac{150}{6}$ **Ans.** 25 m/s

42. Area of cross-section of the pipe = 5.4 cm^2

Length of water which flows out of pipe in 1 min

$= \dfrac{27}{60}$ km

$\therefore$ Volume of water which flows out of pipe in 1 min

$= \left[\dfrac{5.4}{100 \times 100} \times \dfrac{27}{60} \times 1000\right]\text{m}^3$

$= 243$ L $\quad$ [$\because 1\text{ m}^3 = 1000$ L]

43. Area of the field $= 112 \times 62 = 6944\text{ m}^2$

Now, area of four tanks of upper face

$= 4 \times (6 \times 6) = 144\text{ m}^2$

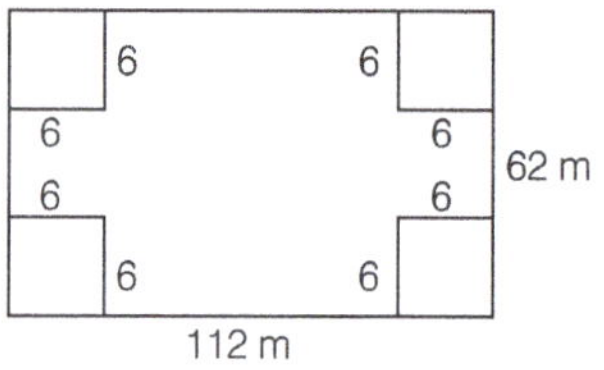

Volume of earth dug out from each tank

$= (6)^3 = 216\text{ m}^3$

$\therefore$ Total volume of earth dug out from 4 tanks

$= 216 \times 4 = 864\text{ m}^3$

$\therefore$ Height of the earth level spread over the remaining.

Total $= \dfrac{864}{6800} \times 100\text{ cm} = \dfrac{864}{68}$ cm

$= 12\dfrac{12}{17}$ cm

44. Do same as Example 17. **Ans.** 25 cm

45. Do same as Example 18.

Ans. (i) ₹ 2040 (ii) ₹ 5040

46. Do same as Example 18. **Ans.** 1000 m^3

47. Area to be polished = Area of four walls + Area of back + Area of front beading

$= (2 \times 85 \times 25 + 2 \times 25 \times 110) + (85 \times 110) + [(85 \times 110) - (3 \times 75 \times 30)]$

$= 21700\text{ cm}^2$

Cost of polishing 21700 cm^2 = ₹ 4340

$\therefore$ Internal surface area = Total surface area of 3 cuboids each of dimensions 75 cm × 30 cm × 20 cm − Area of front face of 3 cuboids of same dimensions

$= 3\{2(75 \times 30 + 30 \times 20 + 20 \times 75)\} - 3 \times (75 \times 30)$

$= 19350\text{ cm}^2$

Cost of painting 19350 cm^2 $= 19350 \times \dfrac{10}{100} =$ ₹ 1935

Hence, total expenses = ₹(4340 + 1935) = ₹ 6275

48. **Hint** We can divide the victory stand into 3 blocks.

So, the volume of block 1 = $30 \times 40 \times 60 = 72000 \text{ cm}^3$

Volume of block 2 = $30 \times 30 \times 40 = 36000 \text{ cm}^3$

Volume of block 3 = $30 \times 40 \times 20 = 24000 \text{ cm}^3$

$\therefore$ Total volume = $(72000 + 36000 + 24000) \text{ cm}^3$

Total surface area of the victory-stand

= Area of front portion

+ Area of back + Area of sides + Area of top

Ans. 132000 cm^3, 14600 cm^2

49. (i) **Hint** Area of cross-section = $\frac{1}{2}(2 + 3.5) \times 6$

Ans. 16.5 m^2

(ii) **Hint** Volume = Area of cross-section × length

$= 16.5 \times 400$ **Ans.** 6600 m^3

50. Let each side of a cube = x cm.

then volume = x^3

by increasing each side of 3 cm, then side of cube

$= (x + 3)$ cm

Volume = $(x + 3)^3 \text{ cm}^3 \Rightarrow (x + 3)^3 = 2457$

$x^2 + 3x - 270 = 0 \Rightarrow (x + 18)(x - 15) = 0$

Either $x + 18 = 0$, then $x = -18$ which is not possible

as $x - 15 = 0$, $x = 15$ side of the cube = 15 cm

Volume of the cube = $(15)^3 = 3375$

Decrease in side = $20\% = 15 \times \frac{80}{100} = 12$ cm

Volume of decreased cube = $(12)^3 \text{ cm}^3 = 1728 \text{ cm}^3$

Required decrease in volume = $3375 - 1728 = 1647 \text{ cm}^3$

51. Each side (edge) of the tank = 1.5m = 150 cm.

$\therefore$ Outer surface area of the tank (excluding base)

$= (5 \times 150 \times 150) \text{ cm}^2$.

$\therefore$ Area of each square tile = $(25 \times 25) \text{ cm}^2$.

$\therefore$ Number of tiles required = $\frac{5 \times 150 \times 150}{25 \times 25} = 180.$

Cost of one dozen i.e. 12 tiles = ₹ 360

$\therefore$ Cost of one tile = ₹ $\frac{360}{12}$ = ₹ 30

$\therefore$ The cost of 180 tiles = ₹ (30 × 180) = ₹ 5400

52. The volume of the cube submerged

= volume of water that fills 3 cm height of the container + volume of the water that overflows

$= [(15 \times 15 \times 3) \text{ cm}^3 + 54 \text{ cm}^3] = 729 \text{ cm}^3$

If side of the cube submerged = x cm

Its volume = $x^3 \text{cm}^3$

$\therefore$ $x^3 = 729$

$\Rightarrow$ The side of the cube = 9 cm

Surface area = $6 \times (\text{side})^2 = 486 \text{ cm}^2$

53. Do same as Example 15. **Ans.** 15000.

54. Do same as Example 17. **Ans.** 8 cm.

55. Surface area of a big box

$= 2(25 \times 20 + 20 \times 5 + 25 \times 5) \text{ cm}^2$

$= 1450 \text{ cm}^2$.

Given 5% of total surface is required extra for overlaps,

Then, area of cardboard required for making one big box

$= \left[\left(1 + \frac{5}{100}\right) \times 1450\right] \text{cm}^2$

$= 1522.5 \text{ cm}^2$.

$\therefore$ Required area of cardboard for making 250 big boxes

$= (1522.5 \times 250) \text{ cm}^2 = 380625 \text{ cm}^2$.

$\therefore$ Surface area of 1 small box

$= 2(15 \times 12 + 12 \times 5 + 15 \times 5) \text{ cm}^2 = 630 \text{ cm}^2$.

$\therefore$ Required area of cardboard for making one small box

$= \left[\left(1 + \frac{5}{100}\right) \times 630\right] \text{cm}^2 = 661.5 \text{ cm}^2$.

Area of cardboard for making 250 small boxes

$= 661.5 \times 250 \text{ cm}^2 = 165375 \text{ cm}^2$

$\therefore$ Total area cardboard required for supplying 250 big boxes and 250 small boxes = $(380625 + 165375) \text{ cm}^2$

As cost of 1000 cm^2 cardboard is ₹ 4

Cost of 546000 cm^2 of cardboard

$= \frac{₹\, 546000 \times 4}{1000}$ = ₹ 2184

56. (i) Area of cross-section = Area of $ABCDE$

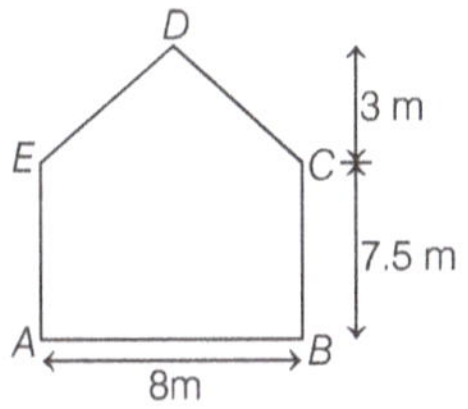

$\therefore$ Total volume contents of the shed

= Area of cross-section × length

$= 3600 \text{ m}^3$

(ii) Using Pythagoras theorem,

$DE = DC = 5$ m

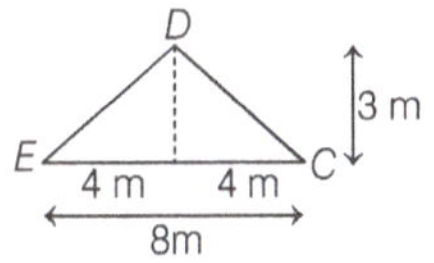

$\therefore$ Area of asbestos sheet roofing

$= [DE \times 50 \text{ m}^2 + CD \times 50 \text{ m}^2]$

$\therefore$ The cost of asbestos roofing

= Area of the sheet × Rate

= 500 × ₹ 25 = ₹ 12500

(iii) The whole outside surface area of the shed

= 2 × Area of cross-section

+ 2 × Area of each side wall + Area of roofing

$= 2 \times 72 \text{ m}^2 + 2(50 \text{ m} \times 7.5 \text{ m}) + 500 \text{ m}^2$

$\therefore$ The cost of painting = 1394 × ₹ 5 = ₹ 6970.

Olympiad Section

Brain Teasing Questions of Olympiad Pattern

1 In a shower, 5 cm of rain falls. Find the volume of water that falls on 2 hectare of ground.

(a) 1000 m^3 (b) 100 m^3
(c) 10000 m^3 (d) None of these

2 A field is 70 m long and 40 m broad. In one corner of the field, a pit which is 10 m long, 8 m broad and 5 m deep, has been dug out. The earth taken out of it is evenly spread over the remaining part of the field. Find the rise in the level of the field.

(a) 14.70 cm (b) 15.70 cm
(c) 10.70 cm (d) None of these

3 If volume of a cuboidal metal of dimensions 44 cm $\times$ 30 cm $\times$ 15 cm is two more than the four times of volume of cube, then each side of cube is

(a) 16.12 cm (b) 17.04 cm
(c) 15.13 cm (d) None of these

4 If each side of a cube is increased by 50%, then the surface area of the cube is increased by

(a) 50% (b) 100%
(c) 125% (d) 150%

5 The paint in a certain container is sufficient to paint an area equal to 9.375 m^2. How many bricks of dimensions 22.5 cm $\times$ 10 cm $\times$ 7.5 cm be painted out of this container?

(a) 100 (b) 110
(c) 200 (d) 120

6 The volume of a cuboid whose sides are in the ratio of 1 : 2 : 4, is same as that of a cube. Then, what is the ratio of lengths of diagonals of cuboid to that of the cube?

(a) 2 : 1 (b) 1 : 1
(c) $2 : \sqrt{7}$ (d) $\sqrt{7} : 2$

7 The length and width of a swimming pool are 50 m and 15 m, respectively. If the depth of the swimming pool at one end is 10 m and at the other end is 20 m, then what will be the volume of water in the swimming pool?

(a) 12150 m^3 (b) 11250 m^3
(c) 11520 m^3 (d) 10052 m^3

8 The diagonals of the three faces of a cuboid are x, y and z, respectively then what will be the volume of the cuboid if $x = 5$ m, $y = 7$ m and $z = 8$ m.

(a) $20\sqrt{11}\ m^3$ (b) $40\sqrt{11}\ m^3$
(c) $20\sqrt{22}\ m^3$ (d) $40\sqrt{22}\ m^3$

Answers

1. (a) **2.** (a) **3.** (b) **4.** (c) **5.** (a) **6.** (d) **7.** (b) **8.** (a)

** These questions may or may not be asked in the examination, have been given just for additional practice required for olympiads Scholarship Exams etc. For detailed explanations refer Page No. 351.*

CHAPTER

17

Trigonometry

SYLLABUS

- (a) Trigonometric Ratios : sine, cosine, tangent of an angle and their reciprocals. (b) Trigonometric ratios of standard angle 0, 30, 45, 60, 90 degrees. Evaluation of an expression involving these ratios. (c) Simple 2-D problems involving are right-angled triangle. (d) Concept of trigonometric ratios of complementary angles and their direct application:
$\sin A = \cos (90° - A)$, $\cos A = \sin (90° - A)$; $\tan A = \cot (90° - A)$, $\cot A = \tan (90° - A)$;
$\sec A = \text{cosec} (90° - A)$, $\text{cosec} A = \sec (90° - A)$

The word trigonometry is derived from the Greek words '*tri*' (meaning three), '*gon*' (meaning sides) and '*metron*' (meaning measure). Trigonometry is the branch of mathematics, which studies of the relationships between the sides and angles of a right angled triangle.

In this chapter, we will study ratios of the sides of a right angled triangle with respect to its acute angles. Here, ratios are called trigonometric ratios. Here, we will define the values of trigonometric ratio for angles between 0° and 90° and will learn to solve different problems related to right angled triangle.

Trigonometric Ratios

The ratios of the sides of a right angled triangle with respect to its acute angles are called **trigonometric ratios**. Trigonometric ratios are also called **T-ratios.** To understand the trigonometric ratios, first of all we will understand the concept of perpendicular, base and hypotenuse in a right angled triangle.

For any acute angle (which is also known as the **angle of reference**) in a right angled triangle, the side opposite to the acute angle is called the **perpendicular** (P), the side adjacent to this acute angle is called the **base** (B) and side opposite to the right angle is called the **hypotenuse** (H).

(i)

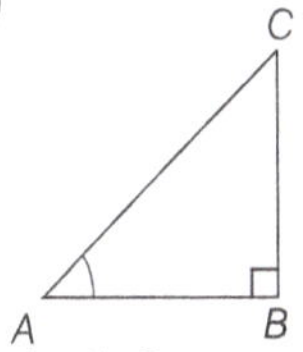

Angle of reference = $\angle A$
Perpendicular = BC
Base = AB
Hypotenuse = AC

(ii)

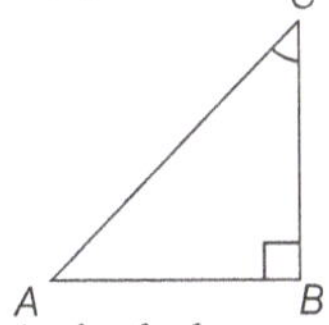

Angle of reference = $\angle C$
Perpendicular = AB
Base = BC
Hypotenuse = AC

(iii)

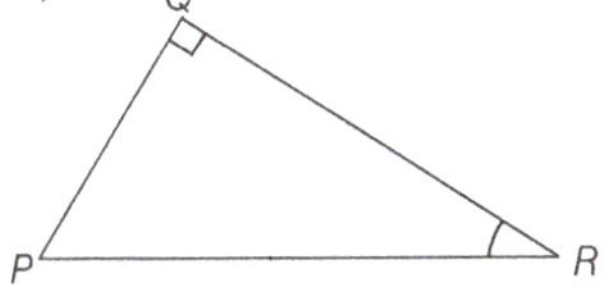

Angle of reference = $\angle R$
Perpendicular = PQ
Base = QR
Hypotenuse = PR

Trigonometric ratios of $\angle A$ in right angled ΔABC are defined as follow:

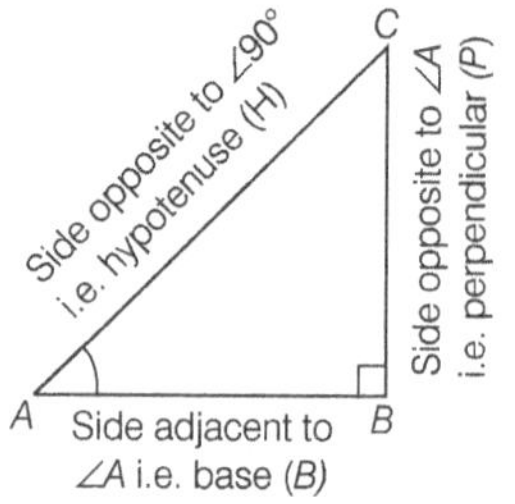

(i) sine of $\angle A$ or $\sin A = \dfrac{\text{Perpendicular}}{\text{Hypotenuse}} = \dfrac{P}{H} = \dfrac{BC}{AC}$

(ii) cosine of $\angle A$ or $\cos A = \dfrac{\text{Base}}{\text{Hypotenuse}} = \dfrac{B}{H} = \dfrac{AB}{AC}$

(iii) tangent of $\angle A$ or $\tan A = \dfrac{\text{Perpendicular}}{\text{Base}} = \dfrac{P}{B} = \dfrac{BC}{AB}$

(iv) cosecant of $\angle A$ or $\text{cosec } A = \dfrac{\text{Hypotenuse}}{\text{Perpendicular}}$

$$= \frac{H}{P} = \frac{AC}{BC}$$

(v) secant of $\angle A$ or $\sec A = \dfrac{\text{Hypotenuse}}{\text{Base}} = \dfrac{H}{B} = \dfrac{AC}{AB}$

(vi) cotangent of $\angle A$ or $\cot A = \dfrac{\text{Base}}{\text{Perpendicular}}$

$$= \frac{B}{P} = \frac{AB}{BC}$$

Similarly, trigonometric ratios of $\angle C$ in right angled ΔABC are as follow:

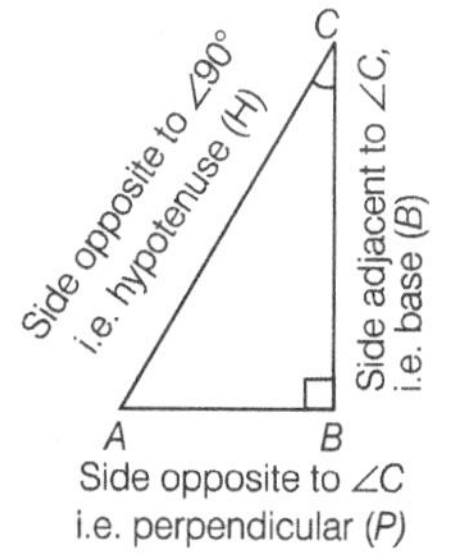

(i) $\sin C = \dfrac{AB}{AC}$ (ii) $\cos C = \dfrac{BC}{AC}$

(iii) $\tan C = \dfrac{AB}{BC}$ (iv) $\text{cosec } C = \dfrac{AC}{AB}$

(v) $\sec C = \dfrac{AC}{BC}$ (vi) $\cot C = \dfrac{BC}{AB}$

Note The symbol $\sin A$ used as an abbreviation for 'the sine of the $\angle A$'. $\sin A$ is not the product of 'sin' and 'A'. 'sin' separated from A has no meaning. This interpretation follows for other trigonometric ratios also.

Some important points about trigonometric ratios are given below

(i) Each trigonometric ratio is a real number and has no unit.

(ii) The value of each of the trigonometric ratios of an angle does not depend on the size of the triangle. It only depends on the angle.

(iii) The values of the trigonometric ratios of an angle do not vary with the lengths of the sides of the triangle, if the angle remains the same.

(iv) If one of the trigonometric ratios of an acute angle is known, then the remaining trigonometric ratios of that angle can be easily determined.

(v) In an isosceles right angled ΔABC, right angled at B, the trigonometric ratios obtained by taking either $\angle A$ or $\angle C$, both give the same value.

(vi) As we know that the hypotenuse is the longest side in a right angled triangle, so the value of $\sin A$ or $\cos A$ is always less than 1 (or in particular equal to 1), whereas the value of $\sec A$ or $\text{cosec } A$ is always greater than or equal to 1.

Example 1. Indicate the perpendicular, the hypotenuse and the base (in that order), with respect to the angle marked x.

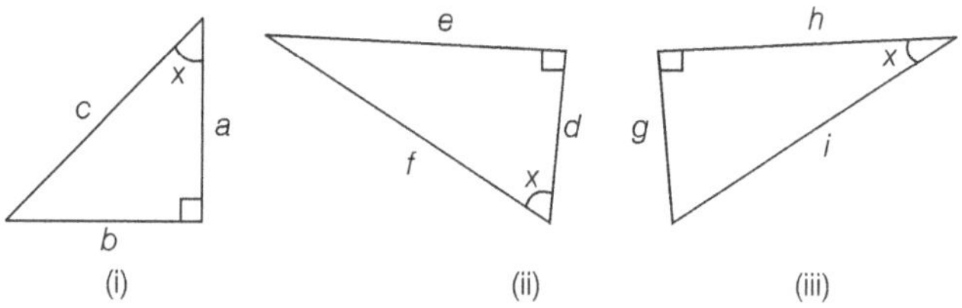

Sol. With reference to angle x,

(i) Perpendicular = b, hypotenuse = c and base = a.

(ii) Perpendicular = e, hypotenuse = f and base = d.

(iii) Perpendicular = g, hypotenuse = i and base = h.

Example 2. From the following figure, find

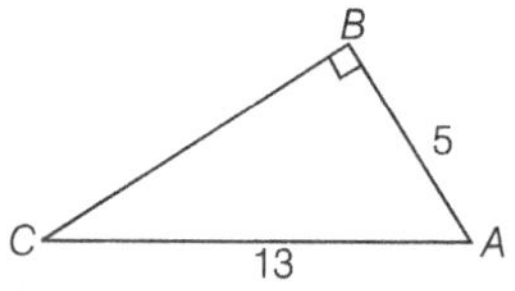

(i) $\sin A$ (ii) $\cos C$

(iii) $\tan A$ (iv) $\text{cosec}\, C$

Sol. Given, $\angle ABC = 90°$, $AC = 13$ and $AB = 5$

Now, $AC^2 = AB^2 + BC^2$ [using Pythagoras theorem]

$\Rightarrow$ $13^2 = 5^2 + BC^2$

$\Rightarrow$ $BC^2 = 169 - 25 = 144$

$\Rightarrow$ $BC = \sqrt{144} = 12$

[taking positive square root as side cannot be negative]

(i) $\sin A = \dfrac{\text{Perpendicular}}{\text{Hypotenuse}} = \dfrac{BC}{AC} = \dfrac{12}{13}$

(ii) $C = \dfrac{\text{Base}}{\text{Hypotenuse}} = \dfrac{BC}{AC} = \dfrac{12}{13}$

(iii) $\tan A = \dfrac{\text{Perpendicular}}{\text{Base}} = \dfrac{BC}{AB} = \dfrac{12}{5}$

(iv) $\text{cosec } C = \dfrac{\text{Hypotenuse}}{\text{Perpendicular}} = \dfrac{AC}{AB} = \dfrac{13}{5}$

Example 3. If $\tan A = \dfrac{4}{3}$, then find the other trigonometric ratios of $\angle A$.

Sol. First, draw a ΔABC, right angled at B.

Given, $\tan A = \dfrac{4}{3} \Rightarrow \dfrac{\text{Perpendicular}}{\text{Base}} = \dfrac{4}{3}$

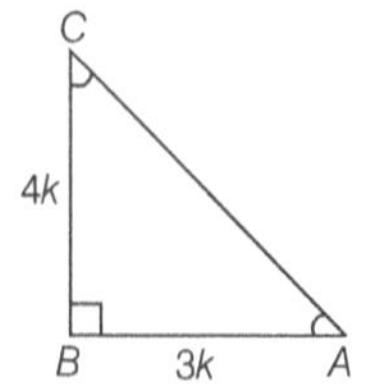

$\Rightarrow \quad \dfrac{BC}{AB} = \dfrac{4}{3} = k \text{ (say)}$ [where, k is any positive integer]

$\therefore \quad BC = 4k$ and $AB = 3k$

Using Pythagoras theorem in ΔABC, we have

$AC^2 = BC^2 + AB^2$

$\Rightarrow \quad AC^2 = (4k)^2 + (3k)^2 = 16k^2 + 9k^2$

$\Rightarrow \quad AC^2 = 25k^2 \Rightarrow AC = \sqrt{25k^2} = 5k$

[taking positive square root as side cannot be negative]

Now, $\sin A = \dfrac{BC}{AC} = \dfrac{4k}{5k} = \dfrac{4}{5}$, $\cos A = \dfrac{AB}{AC} = \dfrac{3k}{5k} = \dfrac{3}{5}$

$\cot A = \dfrac{AB}{BC} = \dfrac{3k}{4k} = \dfrac{3}{4}$, $\text{cosec} A = \dfrac{AC}{BC} = \dfrac{5k}{4k} = \dfrac{5}{4}$

and $\sec A = \dfrac{AC}{AB} = \dfrac{5k}{3k} = \dfrac{5}{3}$

Example 4. In the following figure, find $\tan P - \cot R$.

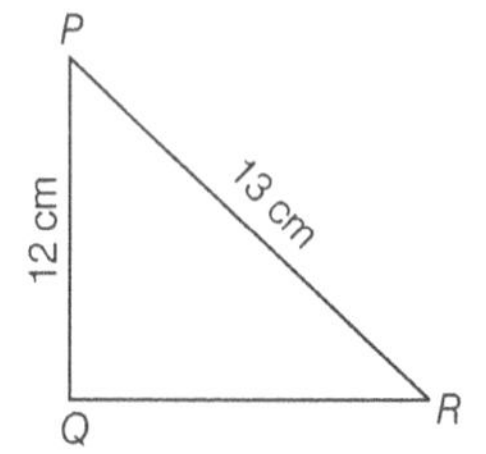

Sol. In right angled ΔPQR, we have

$PQ = 12\text{ cm}$ and $PR = 13\text{ cm}$

Using Pythagoras theorem in ΔPQR, we have

$PQ^2 + QR^2 = PR^2$

$\Rightarrow \quad (12)^2 + QR^2 = (13)^2$

$\Rightarrow \quad 144 + QR^2 = 169$

$\Rightarrow \quad QR^2 = 169 - 144 = 25$

$\therefore \quad QR = 5$

[taking positive square root as side cannot be negative]

Now, $\tan P = \dfrac{\text{Perpendicular}}{\text{Base}} = \dfrac{QR}{PQ} = \dfrac{5}{12}$

and $\cot R = \dfrac{\text{Base}}{\text{Perpendicular}} = \dfrac{QR}{PQ} = \dfrac{5}{12}$

$\therefore \tan P - \cot R = \dfrac{5}{12} - \dfrac{5}{12} = 0$

Example 5. In a ΔPQR, right angled at Q, $PR + QR = 25\text{ cm}$ and $PQ = 5\text{ cm}$. Determine the values of $\sin P$, $\cos P$ and $\tan P$.

Sol. Let $QR = x$ and $PR = y$.

Then, $PR + QR = 25$ [given]

$\Rightarrow \quad y + x = 25 \Rightarrow y = 25 - x$ ...(i)

In right angled ΔPQR, we have

$QR^2 + PQ^2 = PR^2$ [using Pythagoras theorem]

$\Rightarrow \quad x^2 + (5)^2 = y^2$

$\Rightarrow \quad x^2 + 25 = (25 - x)^2$ [from Eq. (i)]

$\Rightarrow \quad x^2 + 25 = 625 + x^2 - 50x$

[$\because (a - b)^2 = a^2 + b^2 - 2ab$]

$\Rightarrow \quad x^2 - x^2 + 50x = 625 - 25$

$\Rightarrow \quad 50x = 600$

$\therefore \quad x = \dfrac{600}{50} = 12 = QR$

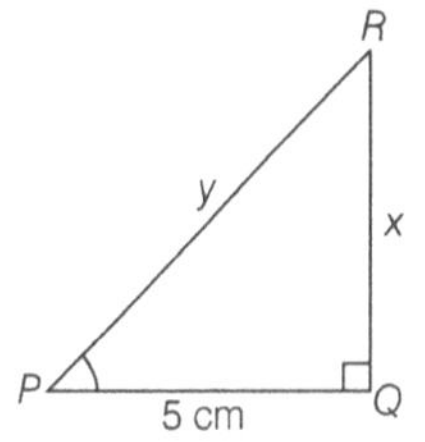

From Eq. (i), we get $y = 25 - x = 25 - 12 = 13 = PR$

Now, $\sin P = \dfrac{QR}{PR} = \dfrac{12}{13}$, $\cos P = \dfrac{PQ}{PR} = \dfrac{5}{13}$

and $\tan P = \dfrac{QR}{PQ} = \dfrac{12}{5}$

Example 6. In a ΔABC, right angled at B, if $\tan A = 1$, then verify that $2 \sin A \cos A = 1$.

Sol. Given, a ΔABC in which $\angle B = 90°$.

In ΔABC, we have

$\tan A = \dfrac{\text{Perpendicular}}{\text{Base}}$

$\Rightarrow \quad 1 = \dfrac{BC}{AB}$

$\Rightarrow \quad BC = AB$

Let $AB = BC = k$, where k is any positive number.

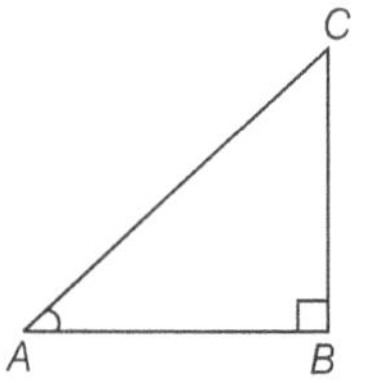

Then, $AC = \sqrt{AB^2 + BC^2}$ [using Pythagoras theorem]

$= \sqrt{(k)^2 + (k)^2} = k\sqrt{2}$

Now, $\sin A = \dfrac{\text{Perpendicular}}{\text{Hypotenuse}} = \dfrac{BC}{AC} = \dfrac{k}{\sqrt{2}k} = \dfrac{1}{\sqrt{2}}$

and $\cos A = \dfrac{\text{Base}}{\text{Hypotenuse}} = \dfrac{AB}{AC} = \dfrac{k}{\sqrt{2}k} = \dfrac{1}{\sqrt{2}}$

$\therefore\ 2\sin A \cos A = 2\left(\dfrac{1}{\sqrt{2}}\right)\left(\dfrac{1}{\sqrt{2}}\right) = 1$ **Hence verified.**

Example 7. From the given figure, evaluate

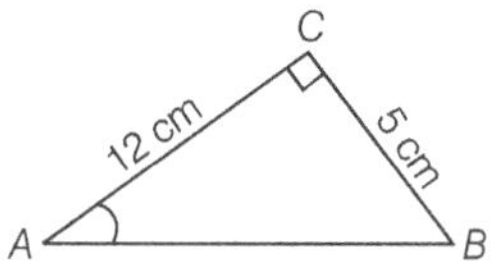

(i) $\cos^2 A - \sin^2 A$ (ii) $\text{cosec}^2 A - \cot^2 A$

Sol. We have, ΔABC, right angled at C, $AC = 12$ cm and $BC = 5$ cm.

On applying Pythagoras theorem in ΔABC, we get

$AB^2 = AC^2 + BC^2$

$\Rightarrow AB^2 = 12^2 + 5^2 = 144 + 25 = 169$

$\therefore\ AB = 13$ cm [taking positive square root as side cannot be negative]

Now, $\sin A = \dfrac{P}{H} = \dfrac{BC}{AB} = \dfrac{5}{13}$, $\text{cosec}\, A = \dfrac{H}{P} = \dfrac{AB}{BC} = \dfrac{13}{5}$,

$\cos A = \dfrac{B}{H} = \dfrac{AC}{AB} = \dfrac{12}{13}$ and $\cot A = \dfrac{B}{P} = \dfrac{AC}{BC} = \dfrac{12}{5}$

(i) Now, $\cos^2 A - \sin^2 A$

$= \left(\dfrac{12}{13}\right)^2 - \left(\dfrac{5}{13}\right)^2 = \dfrac{144}{169} - \dfrac{25}{169} = \dfrac{119}{169}$

(ii) Now, $\text{cosec}^2 A - \cot^2 A$

$= \left(\dfrac{13}{5}\right)^2 - \left(\dfrac{12}{5}\right)^2$

$= \dfrac{169}{25} - \dfrac{144}{25} = \dfrac{25}{25} = 1$

Note $\sin^2 A = (\sin A)^2$ but $\sin\theta^2 \neq (\sin\theta)^2$, true for all t-ratios.

Example 8. In ΔABC, right angled at B, $AB = 24$ cm and $BC = 7$ cm. Determine

(i) $\sin A$ and $\cos A$ (ii) $\sin C$ and $\cos C$

Sol. In right angled ΔABC, we have

$AC^2 = AB^2 + BC^2$ [using Pythagoras theorem]

$= (24)^2 + (7)^2 = 576 + 49 = 625$

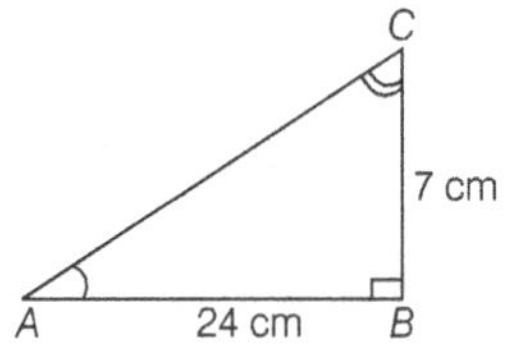

$\therefore\ AC = 25$ cm

[taking positive square root as side cannot be negative]

(i) With reference to $\angle A$, we have

Base $= AB = 24$ cm, perpendicular $= BC = 7$ cm and hypotenuse $= AC = 25$ cm

Now, $\sin A = \dfrac{P}{H} = \dfrac{BC}{AC} = \dfrac{7}{25}$ and $\cos A = \dfrac{B}{H} = \dfrac{AB}{AC} = \dfrac{24}{25}$

(ii) With reference to $\angle C$, we have

Perpendicular $= AB = 24$ cm, base $= BC = 7$ cm and hypotenuse $= AC = 25$ cm

Now, $\sin C = \dfrac{P}{H} = \dfrac{AB}{AC} = \dfrac{24}{25}$ and $\cos C = \dfrac{B}{H} = \dfrac{BC}{AC} = \dfrac{7}{25}$

Example 9. From the given figure, find the value of

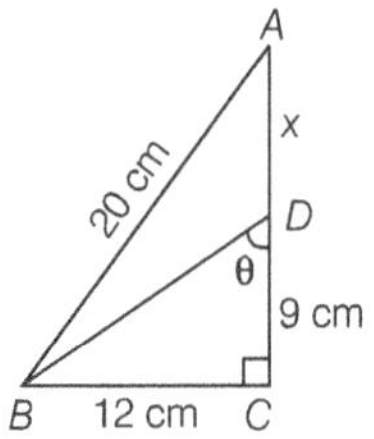

(i) $\sin \angle ABC$ (ii) $\tan\theta + \cos\theta - 2\sin\theta$

Sol. Let $AD = x$. Then, $AC = AD + CD = (x + 9)$ cm

In ΔACB, right angled at C, we have

$AB^2 = BC^2 + AC^2$ [using Pythagoras theorem]

$\Rightarrow (20)^2 = (12)^2 + (x + 9)^2$

$\Rightarrow (x + 9)^2 = 400 - 144 = 256 = (16)^2$

$\Rightarrow x + 9 = 16$ [taking positive square root as side cannot be negative]

$\Rightarrow x = 16 - 9 = 7$ ...(i)

(i) $\sin \angle ABC = \dfrac{P}{H} = \dfrac{AC}{AB} = \dfrac{x + 9}{20} = \dfrac{7 + 9}{20} = \dfrac{16}{20} = \dfrac{4}{5}$

(ii) In right angled ΔBCD, we have

$BD^2 = BC^2 + CD^2$

$\Rightarrow BD^2 = 12^2 + 9^2 = 144 + 81 = 225 = (15)^2$

$\therefore\ BD = 15$ cm [taking positive square root]

Now, $\sin\theta = \dfrac{P}{H} = \dfrac{BC}{BD} = \dfrac{12}{15} = \dfrac{4}{5}$

$\cos\theta = \dfrac{B}{H} = \dfrac{CD}{BD} = \dfrac{9}{15} = \dfrac{3}{5}$

and $\tan\theta = \dfrac{P}{B} = \dfrac{BC}{CD} = \dfrac{12}{9} = \dfrac{4}{3}$

$\therefore\ \tan\theta + \cos\theta - 2\sin\theta = \dfrac{4}{3} + \dfrac{3}{5} - 2 \times \dfrac{4}{5} = \dfrac{4}{3} + \dfrac{3}{5} - \dfrac{8}{5}$

$= \dfrac{20 + 9 - 24}{15} = \dfrac{29 - 24}{15} = \dfrac{5}{15} = \dfrac{1}{3}$

Relations between Trigonometric Ratios

1. Reciprocal Relations

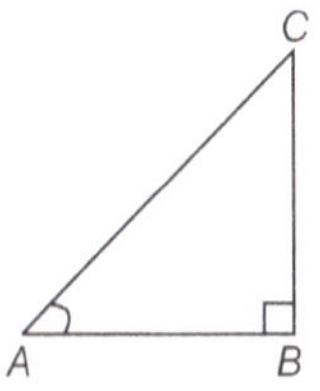

(i) $\sin A = \dfrac{1}{\text{cosec } A}$ or $\text{cosec } A = \dfrac{1}{\sin A}$,

i.e. $\sin A \cdot \text{cosec } A = 1$

(ii) $\cos A = \dfrac{1}{\sec A}$ or $\sec A = \dfrac{1}{\cos A}$, i.e. $\cos A \cdot \sec A = 1$

(iii) $\tan A = \dfrac{1}{\cot A}$ or $\cot A = \dfrac{1}{\tan A}$, i.e. $\tan A \cdot \cot A = 1$

2. Quotient Relations

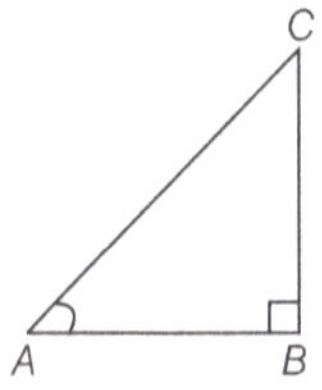

(i) $\tan A = \dfrac{\sin A}{\cos A}$ $\left[\because \tan A = \dfrac{\text{perpendicular}}{\text{base}} = \dfrac{BC}{AB} = \dfrac{BC/AC}{AB/AC} = \dfrac{\sin A}{\cos A}\right]$

(ii) $\cot A = \dfrac{\cos A}{\sin A}$ $\left[\because \cot A = \dfrac{\text{base}}{\text{perpendicular}} = \dfrac{AB}{BC} = \dfrac{AB/AC}{BC/AC} = \dfrac{\cos A}{\sin A}\right]$

Example 10. If $m \cot A = n$, then find the value of $\dfrac{m \sin A - n \cos A}{n \cos A + m \sin A}$.

Sol. Given, $m \cot A = n \Rightarrow m \cdot \dfrac{1}{\tan A} = n$ $\left[\because \cot \theta = \dfrac{1}{\tan \theta}\right]$

$$\Rightarrow \quad \tan A = \frac{m}{n} \qquad \text{...(i)}$$

Now, $\dfrac{m \sin A - n \cos A}{n \cos A + m \sin A} = \dfrac{m \cdot \dfrac{\sin A}{\cos A} - n}{n + m \cdot \dfrac{\sin A}{\cos A}}$

[dividing numerator and denominator by $\cos A$]

$$= \frac{m \tan A - n}{n + m \tan A} = \frac{m \cdot \dfrac{m}{n} - n}{n + m \cdot \dfrac{m}{n}} \quad \text{[from Eq. (i)]}$$

$$= \frac{\dfrac{m^2 - n^2}{n}}{\dfrac{n^2 + m^2}{n}} = \frac{m^2 - n^2}{m^2 + n^2}$$

Example 11. If θ is an acute angle and $3 \sin \theta = 4 \cos \theta$, then find the value of $4 \sin^2 \theta - 3 \cos^2 \theta + 2$.

Sol. Given, equation is $3 \sin \theta = 4 \cos \theta$

$$\Rightarrow \quad \frac{\sin \theta}{\cos \theta} = \frac{4}{3} \Rightarrow \tan \theta = \frac{4}{3} \qquad \text{...(i)}$$

Now, draw a right angled ΔABC, such that $\angle B = 90°$ and let $\angle A = \theta$.

From Eq. (i), we get

$$\tan \theta = \frac{4}{3} = \frac{\text{Perpendicular}}{\text{Base}} = \frac{BC}{AB}$$

$\therefore$ $BC = 4k$ and $AB = 3k$.

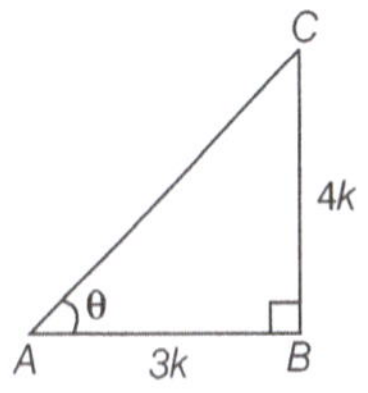

Using Pythagoras theorem, we have

$$CA^2 = AB^2 + BC^2$$

$$\Rightarrow \quad CA^2 = (3k)^2 + (4k)^2 = 9k^2 + 16k^2$$

$$\Rightarrow \quad CA^2 = 25k^2$$

$$\therefore \quad CA = 5k \qquad \text{[taking positive square root]}$$

Now, $\sin \theta = \dfrac{\text{Perpendicular}}{\text{Hypotenuse}} = \dfrac{BC}{CA} = \dfrac{4k}{5k} = \dfrac{4}{5}$

and $\cos \theta = \dfrac{\text{Base}}{\text{Hypotenuse}} = \dfrac{AB}{CA} = \dfrac{3k}{5k} = \dfrac{3}{5}$

$$\therefore \quad 4 \sin^2 \theta - 3 \cos^2 \theta + 2 = 4\left(\frac{4}{5}\right)^2 - 3\left(\frac{3}{5}\right)^2 + 2$$

$$= 4\left(\frac{16}{25}\right) - 3\left(\frac{9}{25}\right) + 2$$

$$= \frac{64}{25} - \frac{27}{25} + 2 = \frac{64 - 27 + 50}{25} = \frac{87}{25} = 3\frac{12}{25}$$

Example 12. Evaluate $\dfrac{5 \sin A - 3 \cos A}{2 \cos A + \sin A}$, if $5 \cos A - 12 \sin A = 0$.

Sol. We have, $5 \cos A - 12 \sin A = 0$

$$\Rightarrow \quad 5 \cos A = 12 \sin A$$

$$\Rightarrow \quad \frac{\sin A}{\cos A} = \frac{5}{12}$$

$$\therefore \quad \tan A = \frac{5}{12}$$

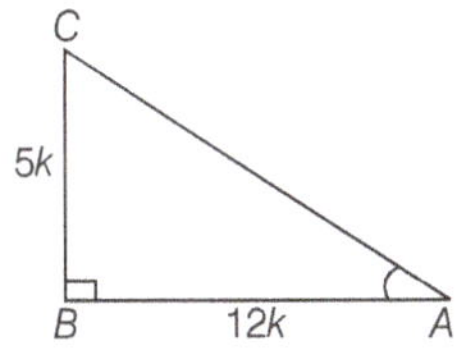

Since, $\tan A = \dfrac{P}{B} = \dfrac{BC}{AB} = \dfrac{5}{12}$

Let $BC = 5k$, $AB = 12k$, where k be any positive number.

Using Pythagoras theorem in ΔABC, we have

$AC^2 = AB^2 + BC^2 = (12k)^2 + (5k)^2 = 144k^2 + 25k^2 = 169k^2$

$\therefore\ AC = 13k$

[taking positive square root as side cannot be negative]

Hence, $\sin A = \dfrac{5}{13}$ and $\cos A = \dfrac{12}{13}$.

Now, $\dfrac{5\sin A - 3\cos A}{2\cos A + \sin A}$

$$= \frac{5\times\frac{5}{13} - 3\times\frac{12}{13}}{2\times\frac{12}{13}+\frac{5}{13}} = \frac{\frac{25}{13}-\frac{36}{13}}{\frac{24}{13}+\frac{5}{13}} = \frac{-\frac{11}{13}}{\frac{29}{13}} = -\frac{11}{29}$$

Example 13. If $\tan x + \cot x = 2$, then find the value of $\tan^2 x + \cot^2 x$.

Sol. We have, $\tan x + \cot x = 2$

On squaring both sides, we get $(\tan x + \cot x)^2 = 2^2$

$\Rightarrow\quad \tan^2 x + \cot^2 x + 2\tan x \cdot \cot x = 4$

$[\because (a+b)^2 = a^2 + b^2 + 2ab]$

$\Rightarrow\quad \tan^2 x + \cot^2 x + 2 = 4 \qquad [\because \tan\theta \cdot \cot\theta = 1]$

$\Rightarrow\quad \tan^2 x + \cot^2 x = 4 - 2 \Rightarrow \tan^2 x + \cot^2 x = 2$

Example 14. Prove that

$$\frac{\text{cosec}^2\theta - \cos^2\theta}{\cot^2\theta} = \sec^2\theta - \sin^2\theta.$$

Sol. LHS $= \dfrac{\text{cosec}^2\theta - \cos^2\theta}{\cot^2\theta} = \dfrac{\frac{1}{\sin^2\theta} - \cos^2\theta}{\frac{\cos^2\theta}{\sin^2\theta}}$

$\left[\because \text{cosec}\, A = \dfrac{1}{\sin A} \text{ and } \cot A = \dfrac{\cos A}{\sin A}\right]$

$$= \frac{\frac{1-\cos^2\theta\sin^2\theta}{\sin^2\theta}}{\frac{\cos^2\theta}{\sin^2\theta}} = \frac{1-\cos^2\theta\sin^2\theta}{\sin^2\theta} \times \frac{\sin^2\theta}{\cos^2\theta}$$

$$= \frac{1-\cos^2\theta\sin^2\theta}{\cos^2\theta} = \frac{1}{\cos^2\theta} - \frac{\cos^2\theta\sin^2\theta}{\cos^2\theta}$$

$= \sec^2\theta - \sin^2\theta \qquad \left[\because \dfrac{1}{\cos A} = \sec A\right]$

= RHS **Hence proved**

Exercise 17.1

1. From the given figure, the values of

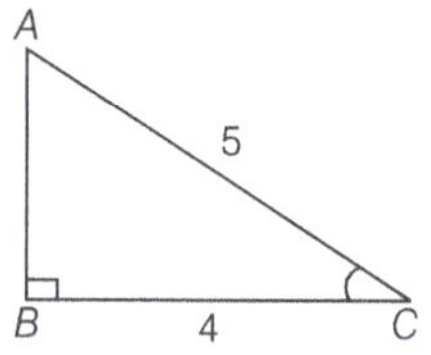

(i) $\sin A$ (ii) $\sin C$
(iii) $\tan A$ (iv) $\sec C$

2. If $\cos\theta = \dfrac{12}{13}$ and θ is acute angle, then find
(i) $\text{cosec}\,\theta$ (ii) $\sec\theta$
(iii) $\tan\theta$.

3. If $\tan\theta = \dfrac{a}{b}$, then find the value of $\sec\theta$.

4. If $\cot A = \dfrac{5}{12}$, then find $\dfrac{\cot A - \sec A}{\text{cosec}\, A}$.

5. If $\text{cosec}\, A = \dfrac{29}{21}$, then evaluate
(i) $\sin A - \dfrac{1}{\tan A}$ (ii) $\cos A - \dfrac{1}{\cot A}$.

6. If $\sec\theta = \dfrac{4}{\sqrt{7}}$, prove that $\sqrt{\dfrac{2\tan^2\theta - \text{cosec}^2\theta}{2\cos^2\theta - \cot^2\theta}} = \dfrac{20}{7}$.

7. If $\sin A = \dfrac{1}{2}$ and $\cos B = \dfrac{1}{\sqrt{2}}$, then find the value of $\dfrac{\tan A - \tan B}{\tan A \tan B + 1}$.

8. In ΔABC, right angled at B, $AC + BC = 49$ cm, $AB = 7$ cm. Determine the values of $\sin A$, $\cos A$, $\tan C$ and $\sec C$.

9. From the given figure, find

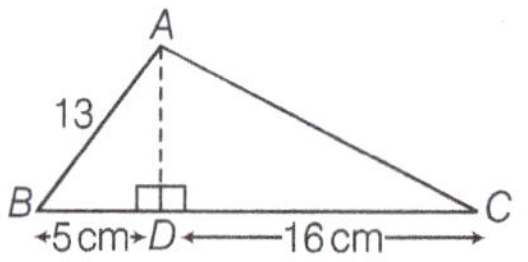

(i) $\sec^2 B - \tan^2 B$ (ii) $\sin^2 C + \cos^2 C$.

10. If $\tan\theta = p/q$, then find the value of $\tan\theta + \cot\theta$ in terms of p and q.

11. If $12\cos x - 5\sin x = 0$, then find the value of $\dfrac{2\cos x - \sin x}{\sin x + \cos x}$.

12. If $\tan\theta = \dfrac{4}{3}$, then find $\dfrac{\sin\theta + \cos\theta}{\sin\theta - \cos\theta}$.

13. If $5\tan\alpha = 4$, prove that $\dfrac{5\sin\alpha - 3\cos\alpha}{5\sin\alpha + 2\cos\alpha} = \dfrac{1}{6}$.

14. If $13\sin\theta = 5$, then find the value of $\dfrac{\text{cosec}\,\theta - \cot\theta}{\text{cosec}\,\theta + \cot\theta}$.

15. If $3\tan A = 4$, then prove that
(i) $\sqrt{\dfrac{\sec A - \text{cosec}\, A}{\sec A + \text{cosec}\, A}} = \dfrac{1}{\sqrt{7}}$. (ii) $\sqrt{\dfrac{1-\sin A}{1+\cos A}} = \dfrac{1}{2\sqrt{2}}$.

16. If $\sqrt{3}\sin\theta = \cos\theta$, then find the value of $\dfrac{\sin\theta\tan\theta(1+\cot\theta)}{\sin\theta+\cos\theta}$.

17. If $\tan x + \cot x = 6$, then find the value of $\tan^2 x + \cot^2 x$.

18. If $\sin A + \operatorname{cosec} A = 4\frac{1}{4}$, then find the value of $\sin^2 A + \operatorname{cosec}^2 A$.

19. Prove that $\dfrac{\sec^2\theta - \sin^2\theta}{\tan^2\theta} = \operatorname{cosec}^2\theta - \cos^2\theta$.

20. Prove that $(1+\tan A+\cos A)(\sin A-\cos A)$
$= \sin A\tan A - \cot A\cos A$.

21. Prove that $\dfrac{\sec A - 1}{\sec A + 1} = \dfrac{1-\cos A}{1+\cos A}$.

22. Prove that $(1+\tan A)^2 - (1-\tan A)^2 = 4\sin A\sec A$.

23. Prove that $\dfrac{\sin\theta\cot\theta}{1-\cos\theta} = \dfrac{1}{\sec\theta - 1}$.

24. Prove that $\dfrac{\cos A}{1-\tan A} + \dfrac{\sin A}{1-\cot A} = \cos A + \sin A$.

Trigonometric Ratios of Standard Angles

Trigonometric Ratios for Angles of 30° and 60°

Let ΔABC be an equilateral triangle with each side equal to $2a$ units and $\angle A = \angle B = \angle C = 60°$

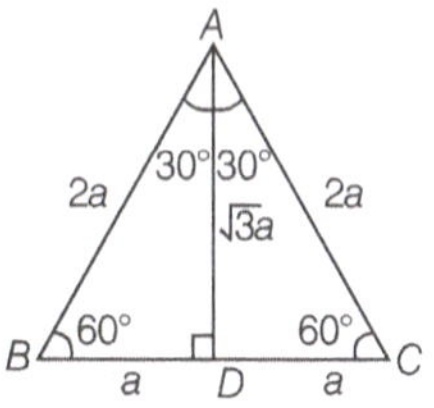

Now, draw perpendicular AD from A to the side BC.

Here, $\Delta ADB \cong \Delta ADC$ [by RHS congruence rule]

Thus, $BD = DC = a$ units and $\angle BAD = \angle CAD = 30°$.

On applying Pythagoras theorem, we get

$$AD = \sqrt{(AB)^2 - (BD)^2} = \sqrt{4a^2 - a^2} = \sqrt{3}a \text{ units}$$

For Angle 30°

In right angled ΔADB, we have

$$\sin 30° = \frac{\text{Perpendicular}}{\text{Hypotenuse}} = \frac{BD}{AB} = \frac{a}{2a} = \frac{1}{2}$$

$$\sin 30° = \frac{1}{2}$$

Similarly, we can find other trigonometric ratios.

$$\cos 30° = \frac{\text{Base}}{\text{Hypotenuse}} = \frac{AD}{AB} = \frac{\sqrt{3}a}{2a} = \frac{\sqrt{3}}{2}$$

$$\tan 30° = \frac{\text{Perpendicular}}{\text{Base}} = \frac{BD}{AD} = \frac{a}{\sqrt{3}a} = \frac{1}{\sqrt{3}}$$

$$\operatorname{cosec} 30° = \frac{1}{\sin 30°} \quad \text{[from reciprocal relation]}$$

$$= \frac{1}{1/2} = 2$$

$$\sec 30° = \frac{1}{\cos 30°} = \frac{1}{\sqrt{3}/2} = \frac{2}{\sqrt{3}}$$

[from reciprocal relation]

$$\cot 30° = \frac{1}{\tan 30°} = \frac{1}{1/\sqrt{3}} = \sqrt{3}$$

[from reciprocal relation]

For Angle 60°

In right angled ΔADB, we have

$$\sin 60° = \frac{\text{Perpendicular}}{\text{Hypotenuse}} = \frac{AD}{AB} = \frac{\sqrt{3}a}{2a} = \frac{\sqrt{3}}{2}$$

$$\sin 60° = \frac{\sqrt{3}}{2}$$

Similarly, we can find other trigonometric ratios.

$$\cos 60° = \frac{1}{2}, \ \tan 60° = \sqrt{3}, \ \operatorname{cosec} 60° = \frac{2}{\sqrt{3}}$$

$$\sec 60° = 2, \quad \cot 60° = \frac{1}{\sqrt{3}}$$

Trigonometric Ratios for Angle of 45°

Let ΔABC be a right angled triangle, in which $\angle B = 90°$ and $\angle A = 45°$, i.e. $\angle C = 45°$.

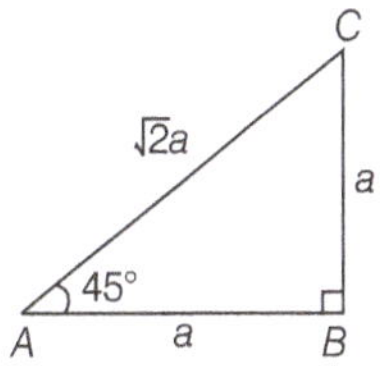

Here, $\angle A = \angle C \Rightarrow BC = AB = a$ units (say)

[$\because$ sides opposite to equal angles of a triangle are also equal]

Then, $AC = \sqrt{2}a$ units [using Pythagoras theorem]

Now, $\sin 45° = \dfrac{\text{Perpendicular}}{\text{Hypotenuse}} = \dfrac{BC}{AC} = \dfrac{a}{\sqrt{2}a} = \dfrac{1}{\sqrt{2}}$

$$\sin 45° = \frac{1}{\sqrt{2}}$$

Similarly, we can find other trigonometric ratios.

$$\cos 45° = \frac{1}{\sqrt{2}}, \tan 45° = 1, \text{cosec } 45° = \sqrt{2},$$

$$\sec 45° = \sqrt{2}, \cot 45° = 1$$

Trigonometric Ratios for Angles of 0° and 90°

For Angle 0°

In ΔABC, as $\angle A$ gets smaller and smaller, the length of the side BC decreases and the point C gets closer to point B.

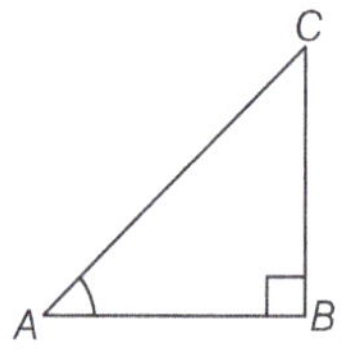

Finally, when $\angle A$ becomes very close to 0°, AC becomes almost the same as AB and BC gets very close to 0, so the value of $\sin A = \dfrac{BC}{AC}$ is very close to 0. Also, when $\angle A$ is very close to 0°, AC is nearly the same as AB and so the value of $\cos A = \dfrac{AB}{AC}$ is very close to 1.

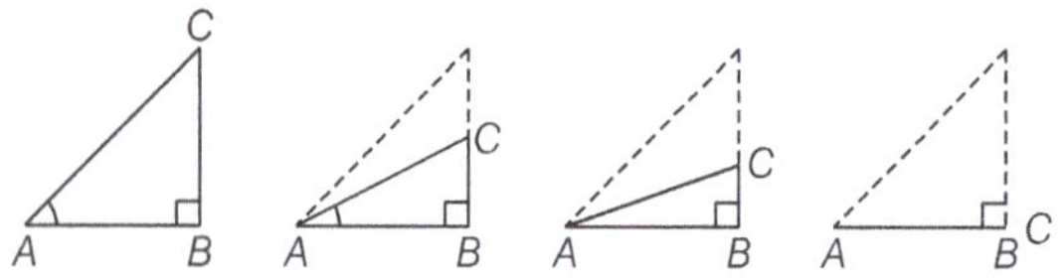

Thus, when $\angle A = 0°$, $\sin 0° = 0$ and $\cos 0° = 1$.

Similarity, we can find values of other trigonometric ratios $\tan 0° = 0$, $\text{cosec } 0° = \infty$, $\sec 0° = 1$, $\cot 0° = \infty$

For Angle 90°

In ΔABC, as $\angle A$ gets larger and larger, $\angle C$ gets smaller and smaller and the length of the side AB goes on decreasing, i.e. point A gets closer to point B.

Finally, when $\angle A$ is very close to 90°, $\angle C$ becomes very close to 0° and the side AC almost coincides with side BC.

So, $\sin A = \dfrac{BC}{AC}$ is very close to 1.

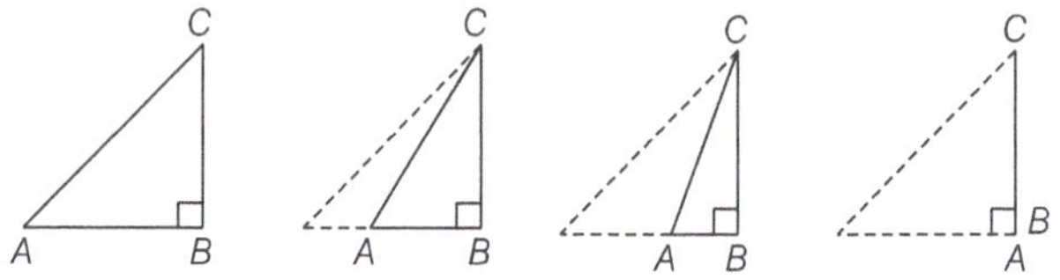

Also, when side AC is nearly the same as side BC, $\angle A$ is very close to 90° and the side AB is nearly zero, so $\cos A$ is very close to 0.

Thus, when $\angle A = 90°$, then

$$\sin 90° = \frac{BC}{AC} = \frac{BC}{BC} = 1, \cos 90° = \frac{AB}{AC} = \frac{0}{AC} = 0.$$

$\sin 90° = 1$ and $\cos 90° = 0$

Using these, we can find other trigonometric ratios.

$\tan 90° = \infty$, $\text{cosec } 90° = 1$, $\sec 90° = \infty$, $\cot 90° = 0$

Values of Trigonometric Ratios for Some Specific Angles

Angles	0° or 0	30° or $\frac{\pi}{6}$	45° or $\frac{\pi}{4}$	60° or $\frac{\pi}{3}$	90° or $\frac{\pi}{2}$
$\sin\theta$	0	$\frac{1}{2}$	$\frac{1}{\sqrt{2}}$	$\frac{\sqrt{3}}{2}$	1
$\cos\theta$	1	$\frac{\sqrt{3}}{2}$	$\frac{1}{\sqrt{2}}$	$\frac{1}{2}$	0
$\tan\theta$	0	$\frac{1}{\sqrt{3}}$	1	$\sqrt{3}$	∞ (undefined)
$\text{cosec }\theta$	∞	2	$\sqrt{2}$	$\frac{2}{\sqrt{3}}$	1
$\sec\theta$	1	$\frac{2}{\sqrt{3}}$	$\sqrt{2}$	2	∞
$\cot\theta$	∞	$\sqrt{3}$	1	$\frac{1}{\sqrt{3}}$	0

Example 15. Evaluate

$$\cos^2 30° + \sin^2 45° - \frac{1}{3}\tan^2 60°.$$

Sol. We have, $\cos^2 30° + \sin^2 45° - \frac{1}{3}\tan^2 60°$

$$= (\cos 30°)^2 + (\sin 45°)^2 - \frac{1}{3}(\tan 60°)^2$$

$$= \left(\frac{\sqrt{3}}{2}\right)^2 + \left(\frac{1}{\sqrt{2}}\right)^2 - \frac{1}{3}(\sqrt{3})^2$$

$$\left[\because \cos 30° = \frac{\sqrt{3}}{2}, \sin 45° = \frac{1}{\sqrt{2}} \text{ and } \tan 60° = \sqrt{3}\right]$$

$$= \frac{3}{4} + \frac{1}{2} - \frac{3}{3} = \frac{3+2}{4} - 1 = \frac{5}{4} - 1 = \frac{5-4}{4} = \frac{1}{4}$$

Example 16. Find the value of

$$\frac{\cos 60° + \sin 45° - \cot 30°}{\tan 60° + \sec 45° - \text{cosec}\, 30°}.$$

Sol. We have, $\dfrac{\cos 60° + \sin 45° - \cot 30°}{\tan 60° + \sec 45° - \text{cosec}\, 30°}$

$$= \frac{\frac{1}{2} + \frac{1}{\sqrt{2}} - \sqrt{3}}{\sqrt{3} + \sqrt{2} - 2} = \frac{\frac{\sqrt{2} + 2 - 2\sqrt{2} \times \sqrt{3}}{2\sqrt{2}}}{\sqrt{3} + \sqrt{2} - 2}$$

$\left[\because \cos 60° = 1/2, \sin 45° = 1/\sqrt{2}, \cot 30° = \sqrt{3}, \tan 60° = \sqrt{3}, \sec 45° = \sqrt{2} \text{ and cosec } 30° = 2\right]$

$$= \frac{\sqrt{2} + 2 - 2\sqrt{6}}{2\sqrt{2}\,(\sqrt{3} + \sqrt{2} - 2)} = \frac{\sqrt{2} + 2 - 2\sqrt{6}}{2\sqrt{6} + 2\sqrt{2} \times \sqrt{2} - 2\sqrt{2} \times 2}$$

$$= \frac{\sqrt{2} + 2 - 2\sqrt{6}}{2\sqrt{6} + 4 - 4\sqrt{2}}$$

Example 17. Find the value of

$$\frac{\sin 30° + \tan 45° - \text{cosec}\, 60°}{\sec 30° + \cos 60° + \cot 45°}.$$

Sol. We have, $\dfrac{\sin 30° + \tan 45° - \text{cosec}\, 60°}{\sec 30° + \cos 60° + \cot 45°}$

$$= \frac{\frac{1}{2} + 1 - \frac{2}{\sqrt{3}}}{\frac{2}{\sqrt{3}} + \frac{1}{2} + 1} = \frac{\frac{\sqrt{3} + 2\sqrt{3} - 4}{2\sqrt{3}}}{\frac{4 + \sqrt{3} + 2\sqrt{3}}{2\sqrt{3}}}$$

$\left[\because \sin 30° = \frac{1}{2}, \tan 45° = 1, \text{cosec } 60° = \frac{2}{\sqrt{3}}, \sec 30° = \frac{2}{\sqrt{3}}, \cos 60° = \frac{1}{2} \text{ and } \cot 45° = 1\right]$

$$= \frac{3\sqrt{3} - 4}{4 + 3\sqrt{3}} = \frac{3\sqrt{3} - 4}{4 + 3\sqrt{3}} \times \frac{4 - 3\sqrt{3}}{4 - 3\sqrt{3}}$$

[by rationalising the denominator]

$$= \frac{12\sqrt{3} - 27 - 16 + 12\sqrt{3}}{(4)^2 - (3\sqrt{3})^2} \quad [\because (a+b)(a-b) = a^2 - b^2]$$

$$= \frac{24\sqrt{3} - 43}{16 - 27} = \frac{-(43 - 24\sqrt{3})}{-11}$$

$$= \frac{43 - 24\sqrt{3}}{11}$$

Example 18. If $\angle A = \angle B = 45°$, then verify that $\sin(A + B) = \sin A \cos B + \cos A \sin B$.

Sol. Given, $\angle A = \angle B = 45°$.

Now, LHS $= \sin(A + B)$

$= \sin(45° + 45°)$

$= \sin 90° = 1$

and RHS $= \sin A \cos B + \cos A \sin B$

$= \sin 45° \cos 45° + \cos 45° \sin 45°$

$$= \frac{1}{\sqrt{2}} \cdot \frac{1}{\sqrt{2}} + \frac{1}{\sqrt{2}} \cdot \frac{1}{\sqrt{2}} = \frac{1}{2} + \frac{1}{2} = 1$$

$\left[\because \sin 45° = \cos 45° = \frac{1}{\sqrt{2}}\right]$

$\therefore$ LHS = RHS **Hence verified**

Example 19. Find the value of

$$\frac{5\cos^2 60° + 4\sec^2 30° - \tan^2 45°}{\sin^2 30° + \cos^2 30°}.$$

Sol. We have, $\dfrac{5\cos^2 60° + 4\sec^2 30° - \tan^2 45°}{\sin^2 30° + \cos^2 30°}$

$$= \frac{5\left(\frac{1}{2}\right)^2 + 4\left(\frac{2}{\sqrt{3}}\right)^2 - (1)^2}{\left(\frac{1}{2}\right)^2 + \left(\frac{\sqrt{3}}{2}\right)^2} = \frac{5\left(\frac{1}{4}\right) + 4\left(\frac{4}{3}\right) - 1}{\frac{1}{4} + \frac{3}{4}}$$

$\left[\because \cos 60° = \frac{1}{2}, \sec 30° = \frac{2}{\sqrt{3}}, \tan 45° = 1, \sin 30° = \frac{1}{2} \text{ and } \cos 30° = \frac{\sqrt{3}}{2}\right]$

$$= \frac{\frac{5}{4} + \frac{16}{3} - 1}{\frac{1}{4} + \frac{3}{4}} = \frac{\frac{15 + 64 - 12}{12}}{\frac{1 + 3}{4}} = \frac{67}{12} \times \frac{4}{4} = \frac{67}{12}$$

Example 20. If $A = 15°$, then find the value of

$$\frac{\sin 3A - 2\cos 4A}{\cos 3A + 2\sin 4A}.$$

Sol. Given, $A = 15°$.

On substituting the value of A in given expression, we get

$$\frac{\sin 3A - 2\cos 4A}{\cos 3A + 2\sin 4A} = \frac{\sin 3 \times 15° - 2\cos 4 \times 15°}{\cos 3 \times 15° + 2\sin 4 \times 15°}$$

$$= \frac{\sin 45° - 2\cos 60°}{\cos 45° + 2\sin 60°} = \frac{\frac{1}{\sqrt{2}} - 2 \times \frac{1}{2}}{\frac{1}{\sqrt{2}} + 2 \times \frac{\sqrt{3}}{2}} = \frac{\frac{1}{\sqrt{2}} - 1}{\frac{1}{\sqrt{2}} + \sqrt{3}}$$

$\left[\because \sin 45° = \cos 45° = \frac{1}{\sqrt{2}}, \cos 60° = \frac{1}{2} \text{ and } \sin 60° = \frac{\sqrt{3}}{2}\right]$

$$= \frac{\frac{1 - \sqrt{2}}{\sqrt{2}}}{\frac{1 + \sqrt{2} \times \sqrt{3}}{\sqrt{2}}} = \frac{1 - \sqrt{2}}{1 + \sqrt{6}}$$

Example 21. If $2\cos 3\theta = \sqrt{3}$, then find the value of θ.

Sol. We have, $2\cos 3\theta = \sqrt{3}$

$\Rightarrow \quad \cos 3\theta = \frac{\sqrt{3}}{2} \Rightarrow \cos 3\theta = \cos 30° \quad \left[\because \cos 30° = \frac{\sqrt{3}}{2}\right]$

$\Rightarrow \quad 3\theta = 30°$

$\therefore \quad \theta = 10°$

Example 22. If $\tan(3x + 30°) = 1$, then find the value of x.

Sol. We have, $\tan(3x + 30°) = 1$

$\Rightarrow \quad \tan(3x + 30°) = \tan 45° \quad [\because \tan 45° = 1]$

$\Rightarrow \quad 3x + 30° = 45°$

$\Rightarrow \quad 3x = 45° - 30° = 15° \Rightarrow x = 5°$

Note $\tan(A + B) \neq \tan A + \tan B$, true for all t-ratios

Example 23. Find the magnitude of $\angle A$, if $4\sin A \sin 2A + 1 - 2\sin 2A = 2\sin A$.

Sol. Given, $4\sin A \sin 2A + 1 - 2\sin 2A = 2\sin A$

$\Rightarrow \quad 4\sin A \sin 2A - 2\sin 2A - 2\sin A + 1 = 0$

$\Rightarrow \quad 2\sin 2A\ (2\sin A - 1) - 1\ (2\sin A - 1) = 0$

$\Rightarrow \quad (2\sin A - 1)\ (2\sin 2A - 1) = 0$

$\Rightarrow \quad 2\sin A - 1 = 0 \text{ or } 2\sin 2A - 1 = 0$

$\Rightarrow \quad \sin A = \frac{1}{2} \text{ or } \sin 2A = \frac{1}{2}$

$\Rightarrow \quad \sin A = \sin 30^\circ \text{ or } \sin 2A = \sin 30^\circ \quad \left[\because \sin 30^\circ = \frac{1}{2}\right]$

$\Rightarrow \quad \angle A = 30^\circ \text{ or } \angle 2A = 30^\circ \Rightarrow \angle A = 30^\circ \text{ or } \angle A = 15^\circ$

Hence, the required values of A are 15° and 30°, respectively.

Example 24. If $\sin(A - B) = \frac{1}{2}$, $\cos(A + B) = \frac{1}{2}$, $0^\circ < A + B \le 90^\circ$, $A > B$, find the values of A and B.

Sol. Given, $\sin(A - B) = \frac{1}{2}$

$\Rightarrow \quad \sin(A - B) = \sin 30^\circ \quad [\because \sin 30^\circ = 1/2]$

On equating both sides, we get

$$A - B = 30^\circ \quad \text{...(i)}$$

Also, $\cos(A + B) = \frac{1}{2}$

$\Rightarrow \quad \cos(A + B) = \cos 60^\circ \quad [\because \cos 60^\circ = 1/2]$

On equating both sides, we get

$$A + B = 60^\circ \quad \text{...(ii)}$$

On adding Eqs. (i) and (ii), we get

$$2A = 90^\circ \Rightarrow A = 45^\circ$$

From Eq. (i), we get $45^\circ - B = 30^\circ$

$\Rightarrow \quad B = 45^\circ - 30^\circ \quad [\because A = 45^\circ]$

$\therefore \quad B = 15^\circ$

Hence, $A = 45^\circ$ and $B = 15^\circ$.

Example 25. In ΔABC right angled at B, $AB = 5$ cm and $\angle ACB = 30^\circ$. Determine the lengths of the sides BC and AC.

Sol. Given, $\angle C = \angle ACB = 30^\circ$ and $AB = 5$ cm.

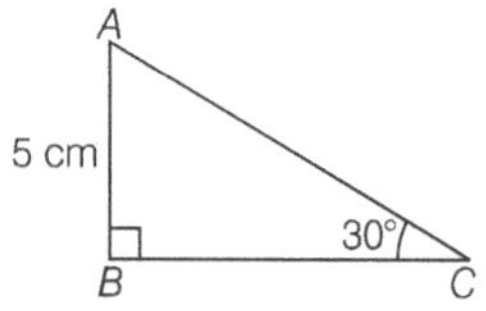

For side BC, $\tan 30^\circ = \frac{5}{BC} \quad \left[\because \tan C = \frac{\text{perpendicular}}{\text{base}} = \frac{AB}{BC}\right]$

$\Rightarrow \quad \frac{1}{\sqrt{3}} = \frac{5}{BC} \quad \left[\because \tan 30^\circ = \frac{1}{\sqrt{3}}\right]$

$\Rightarrow \quad BC = 5\sqrt{3}$ cm

and for side AC, $\sin 30^\circ = \frac{AB}{AC} \quad \left[\because \sin C = \frac{\text{perpendicular}}{\text{hypotenuse}}\right]$

$\Rightarrow \quad \frac{1}{2} = \frac{5}{AC} \quad \left[\because \sin 30^\circ = \frac{1}{2}\right]$

$\Rightarrow \quad AC = 10$ cm

Hence, the lengths of sides $BC = 5\sqrt{3}$ cm and $AC = 10$ cm.

Example 26. In a ΔABC, right angled at B, side $AB = 40$ cm and acute $\angle A = 60^\circ$. Find BC and AC. [take $\sqrt{3} = 1.732$]

Sol. In ΔABC, AB is base and BC is perpendicular.

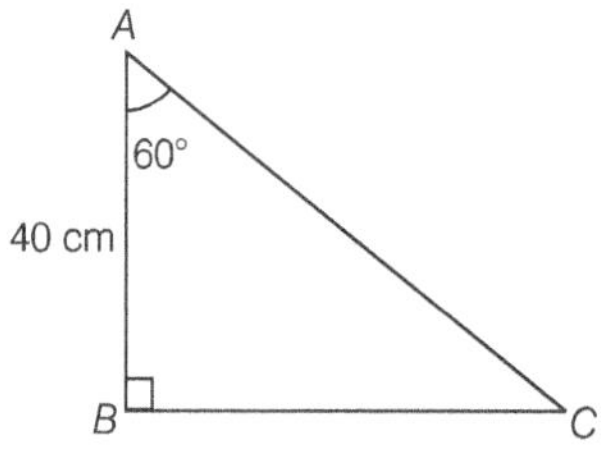

Now, $\tan 60^\circ = \frac{\text{Perpendicular}}{\text{Base}}$

$\Rightarrow \quad \sqrt{3} = \frac{BC}{AB} = \frac{BC}{40}$

[given, $AB = 40$ cm, $\because \tan 60^\circ = \sqrt{3}$]

$\Rightarrow \quad \sqrt{3} = \frac{BC}{40}$

$\Rightarrow \quad BC = 40 \times \sqrt{3} = 40 \times 1.732 = 69.28 \text{ cm} \quad \text{...(i)}$

and $\cos 60^\circ = \frac{\text{Base}}{\text{Hypotenuse}} = \frac{AB}{AC}$

$\Rightarrow \quad \frac{1}{2} = \frac{40}{AC} \quad \left[\because \cos 60^\circ = \frac{1}{2}\right]$

$\therefore \quad AC = 2 \times 40 = 80$ cm

Example 27. In the given figure, PQR is a right angled triangle, where $\angle Q = 90^\circ$, $PQ = 3$ cm and $PR = 6$ cm. Determine $\angle QPR$ and $\angle PRQ$.

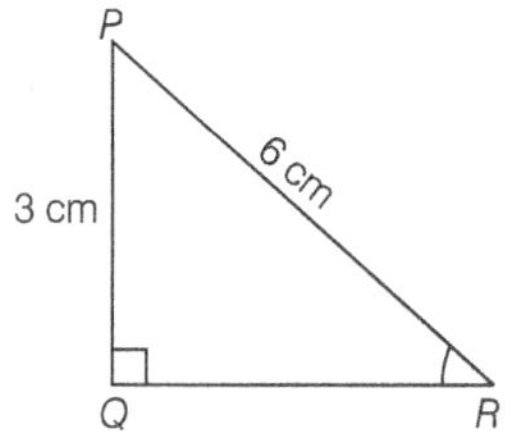

Sol. Given, $PQ = 3$ cm and $PR = 6$ cm.

In ΔPQR, $\sin R = \frac{PQ}{PR}$

$\Rightarrow \quad \sin R = \frac{3}{6} = \frac{1}{2}$

$\Rightarrow \quad \sin R = \sin 30^\circ \quad \left[\because \sin 30^\circ = \frac{1}{2}\right]$

$\therefore \quad \angle R = 30^\circ \text{ or } \angle PRQ = 30^\circ$

On applying angle sum property of ΔPQR, we get

$$\angle P + \angle Q + \angle R = 180^\circ$$

$\Rightarrow \quad \angle P + 90^\circ + 30^\circ = 180^\circ$

$\Rightarrow \quad \angle P = 180^\circ - 120^\circ = 60^\circ$

Hence, $\angle P = 60^\circ$ or $\angle QPR = 60^\circ$.

Exercise 17.2

1. Find the value of $\sin^2 30° + \cos^2 45° + \cos^2 30°$.

2. Show that
$2(\cos^2 45° + \tan^2 60°) - 6(\sin^2 45° - \tan^2 30°) = 6$.

3. Evaluate
$$\frac{\tan^2 60° + 4\sin^2 45° + 3\sec^2 30° + 5\cos^2 90°}{\operatorname{cosec} 30° + \sec 60° - \cot^2 30°}.$$

4. Show that
$$2(\cos^4 60° + \sin^4 30°) - (\tan^2 60° - \cot^2 45°) + 3\sec^2 30° = \frac{9}{4}.$$

5. Show that
$(\sqrt{3}+1)(3 - \cot 30°) = \tan^3 60° - 2\sin 60°$.

6. Prove that $\sqrt{\dfrac{1+\sin 30°}{1-\sin 30°}} = \cot 30°$.

7. If $\theta = 30°$, then verify that
(i) $4\cos^3\theta = 3\cos\theta + \cos 3\theta$.
(ii) $\tan 2\theta = \dfrac{2\tan\theta}{1-\tan^2\theta}$.

8. If $A = 60°$ and $B = 30°$, then verify that
(i) $\cos(A - B) = \cos A \cdot \cos B + \sin A \cdot \sin B$.
(ii) $\cot(A+B) = \dfrac{\cot A \cdot \cot B - 1}{\cot B + \cot A}$.

9. Solve the following equations for θ, if
(i) $2\sin\theta = 1$
(ii) $\sqrt{2}\cos 3\theta = 1$
(iii) $\sqrt{3}\cot 2\theta = 1$
(iv) $\tan 3\theta = 1$

10. If $\cos\left(\dfrac{\theta}{2} + 10°\right) = \dfrac{\sqrt{3}}{2}$, then find the value of θ.

11. Find the magnitude of angle α, if
$$4\cos\alpha\cos 2\alpha + 1 - 2\cos 2\alpha = 2\cos\alpha.$$

12. If $\sin(A+B) = 1$ and $\cos(A-B) = \dfrac{\sqrt{3}}{2}$, find the values of A and B.

13. In a ΔABC, right angled at B, $AB = 7$ cm and $\angle ACB = 30°$. Determine the lengths of the sides BC and AC.

14. In the following figure, ABC is a right angled triangle at B, $AB = 3$ cm and $AC = \sqrt{12}$ cm. Determine $\angle BAC$ and $\angle ACB$.

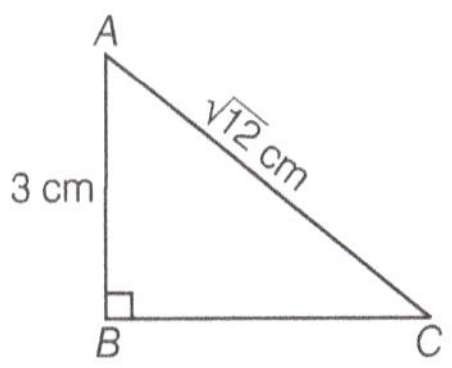

Trigonometric Ratios of Complementary Angles

Two angles are said to be complementary, if their sum is equal to 90°.

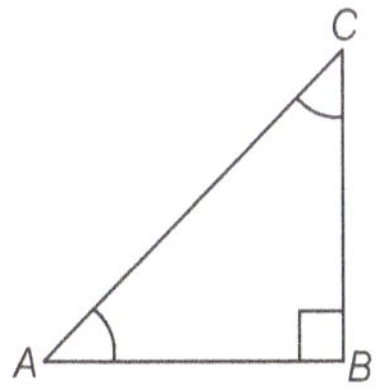

In right angled ΔABC,
if $\angle B = 90°$, then $\angle A + \angle C = 90°$
[$\because$ in a ΔABC, $\angle A + \angle B + \angle C = 180°$]

$\sin(90° - A) = \cos A$, $\cos(90° - A) = \sin A$
$\tan(90° - A) = \cot A$, $\cot(90° - A) = \tan A$
$\sec(90° - A) = \operatorname{cosec} A$, $\operatorname{cosec}(90° - A) = \sec A$

Example 28. Evaluate
(i) $\dfrac{\sin 41°}{\cos 49°}$ (ii) $\dfrac{\tan 29°}{\cot 61°}$ (iii) $\dfrac{\operatorname{cosec} 70°}{\sec 20°}$.

Sol. (i) $\dfrac{\sin 41°}{\cos 49°} = \dfrac{\sin(90° - 49°)}{\cos 49°} = \dfrac{\cos 49°}{\cos 49°} = 1$
[$\because \sin(90° - \theta) = \cos\theta$]

(ii) $\dfrac{\tan 29°}{\cot 61°} = \dfrac{\tan(90° - 61°)}{\cot 61°} = \dfrac{\cot 61°}{\cot 61°} = 1$
[$\because \tan(90° - \theta) = \cot\theta$]

(iii) $\dfrac{\operatorname{cosec} 70°}{\sec 20°} = \dfrac{\operatorname{cosec}(90° - 20°)}{\sec 20°} = \dfrac{\sec 20°}{\sec 20°} = 1$
[$\because \operatorname{cosec}(90° - \theta) = \sec\theta$]

Example 29. Evaluate
(i) $\cos 53° - \sin 37°$ (ii) $\tan 42° - \cot 48°$.

Sol. (i) $\cos 53° - \sin 37° = \cos(90° - 37°) - \sin 37°$
$= \sin 37° - \sin 37° = 0$ [$\because \cos(90° - \theta) = \sin\theta$]

(ii) $\tan 42° - \cot 48° = \tan(90° - 48°) - \cot 48°$
$= \cot 48° - \cot 48° = 0$ [$\because \tan(90° - \theta) = \cot\theta$]

Example 30. Express cosec 48° + tan 88° in terms of T-ratios of angles between 0° and 45°.

Sol. We have, cosec 48° + tan 88°

$= \text{cosec}\,(90° - 42°) + \tan\,(90° - 2°) = \sec 42° + \cot 2°$

$[\because \text{cosec}\,(90° - \theta) = \sec\theta \text{ and } \tan\,(90° - \theta) = \cot\theta]$

Example 31. Evaluate $\frac{\tan 15°}{\cot 75°} + \frac{\sin 25°}{\cos 65°}$.

Sol. $\frac{\tan 15°}{\cot 75°} + \frac{\sin 25°}{\cos 65°} = \frac{\tan\,(90° - 75°)}{\cot 75°} + \frac{\sin\,(90° - 65)}{\cos 65°}$

$= \frac{\cot 75°}{\cot 75°} + \frac{\cos 65°}{\cos 65°}$ $\left[\because \tan\,(90° - \theta) = \cot\theta \text{ and } \sin\,(90° - \theta) = \cos\theta\right]$

$= 1 + 1 = 2$

Example 32. Find the value of (tan 1° tan 2° tan 3° ...tan 89°).

Sol. tan 1° tan 2° tan 3° ...tan 89°

$= \tan\,(90° - 89°)\tan\,(90° - 88°)\tan\,(90° - 87°) \ldots \tan 45° \ldots \tan 87° \tan 88° \tan 89°$

$= \cot 89° \cot 88° \cot 87° \ldots \tan 45° \ldots \tan 87° \tan 88° \tan 89°$

$[\because \tan\,(90° - \theta) = \cot\theta]$

$= (\cot 89° \tan 89°) \cdot (\cot 88° \tan 88°) \ldots \tan 45°$

$= 1 \times 1 \times 1 \times \ldots \times 1 = 1$ $[\because \tan\theta \cdot \cot\theta = 1 \text{ and } \tan 45° = 1]$

Example 33. Evaluate $\frac{\tan 50° + \sec 50°}{\cot 40° + \text{cosec } 40°} + \cos 40° \text{ cosec } 50°$.

Sol. Given, expression $= \frac{\tan 50° + \sec 50°}{\cot 40° + \text{cosec } 40°} + \cos 40° \text{ cosec } 50°$

$= \frac{\tan 50° + \sec 50°}{\cot\,(90° - 50°) + \text{cosec}\,(90° - 50°)} + \cos 40° \text{ cosec}\,(90° - 40°)$

$= \frac{\tan 50° + \sec 50°}{\tan 50° + \sec 50°} + \cos 40° \sec 40°$

$[\because \cot\,(90° - \theta) = \tan\theta, \text{cosec}\,(90° - \theta) = \sec\theta]$

$= 1 + 1 = 2$

Example 34. Evaluate $\frac{\sin 70°}{\cos 20°} + \frac{\text{cosec } 36°}{\sec 54°} - \frac{2\cos 43° \text{ cosec } 47°}{\tan 10° \tan 40° \tan 50° \tan 80°}$.

Sol. $\frac{\sin 70°}{\cos 20°} + \frac{\text{cosec } 36°}{\sec 54°} - \frac{2\cos 43° \text{ cosec } 47°}{\tan 10° \tan 40° \tan 50° \tan 80°}$

$= \frac{\sin\,(90° - 20°)}{\cos 20°} + \frac{\text{cosec}\,(90° - 54°)}{\sec 54°} - \frac{2\cos 43° \text{ cosec}\,(90° - 43°)}{\tan\,(90° - 80°)\tan\,(90° - 50°)\tan 50° \tan 80°}$

$= \frac{\cos 20°}{\cos 20°} + \frac{\sec 54°}{\sec 54°} - \frac{2\cos 43° \sec 43°}{\cot 80° \cot 50° \tan 50° \tan 80°}$

$\left[\because \sin\,(90° - \theta) = \cos\theta, \text{cosec}\,(90° - \theta) = \sec\theta, \tan\,(90° - \theta) = \cot\theta\right]$

$= 1 + 1 - \frac{2\cos 43° \cdot \frac{1}{\cos 43°}}{\frac{1}{\tan 80°} \cdot \tan 80° \cdot \frac{1}{\tan 50°} \cdot \tan 50°}$

$\left[\because \tan\theta = \frac{1}{\cot\theta} \text{ and } \sec\theta = \frac{1}{\cos\theta}\right]$

$= 2 - \frac{2 \cdot 1}{1 \cdot 1} = 2 - 2 = 0$

Example 35. If A and B are acute angles such that $\sin A = \cos B$, prove that $(A + B) = 90°$.

Sol. $\sin A = \cos B \Rightarrow \sin A = \sin\,(90° - B)$

$\Rightarrow \quad A = 90° - B$ [$\because A$ and $(90° - B)$ are acute angles]

$\therefore \quad A + B = 90°$ **Hence proved**

Example 36. If $\sin 3A = \cos\,(A - 26°)$, where $3A$ is an acute angle, then find the value of A.

Sol. Given, $\sin 3A = \cos\,(A - 26°)$ ...(i)

where, $3A$ is an acute angle.

We know that, $\sin\theta = \cos\,(90° - \theta)$

From Eq. (i), $\cos\,(90° - 3A) = \cos\,(A - 26°)$

Since, $(90° - 3A)$ and $(A - 26°)$ both are acute angles.

$\therefore \quad 90° - 3A = A - 26°$

$\Rightarrow \quad 4A = 116°$

$\Rightarrow \quad A = \frac{116°}{4} = 29°$

Example 37. If $\sec 5A = \text{cosec}(A + 30°)$, then find A.

Sol. We have, $\sec 5A = \text{cosec}\,(A + 30°)$

$\Rightarrow \sec 5A = \sec\,[90° - (A + 30°)]$ $[\because \sec\,(90° - \theta) = \text{cosec}\,\theta]$

$\Rightarrow \sec 5A = \sec\,(60° - A)$

$\Rightarrow \quad 5A = 60° - A$ [$\because 5A$ and $(60° - A)$ are acute angles]

$\Rightarrow \quad 6A = 60°$

$\therefore \quad A = 10°$

Example 38. If $\cos\,(A - B) = \cos A \cos B + \sin A \sin B$, then find the value of (i) cos 15° (ii) sin 75°.

Sol. Given, $\cos\,(A - B) = \cos A \cos B + \sin A \sin B$ ...(i)

Let $A = 45°$ and $B = 30°$.

Then, we have

(i) $\cos 15° = \cos\,(45° - 30°)$

$= \cos 45° \cos 30° + \sin 45° \sin 30°$ [using Eq. (i)]

$= \frac{1}{\sqrt{2}} \cdot \frac{\sqrt{3}}{2} + \frac{1}{\sqrt{2}} \cdot \frac{1}{2}$

$= \frac{\sqrt{3}}{2\sqrt{2}} + \frac{1}{2\sqrt{2}} = \frac{\sqrt{3} + 1}{2\sqrt{2}}$

$\Rightarrow \cos 15° = \frac{\sqrt{3} + 1}{2\sqrt{2}}$ ...(ii)

(ii) $\sin 75° = \sin\,(90° - 15°) = \cos 15°$ $[\because \sin\,(90° - \theta) = \cos\theta]$

$= \frac{\sqrt{3} + 1}{2\sqrt{2}}$ [from Eq. (ii)]

Exercise 17.3

1. Evaluate

   (i) $\dfrac{\sin 36^\circ}{\cos 54^\circ}$ (ii) $\dfrac{\cot 18^\circ}{\tan 72^\circ}$

   (iii) $\dfrac{\sec 81^\circ}{\operatorname{cosec} 9^\circ}$

2. Evaluate

   (i) $\cos 15^\circ - \sin 75^\circ$ (ii) $\sec 49^\circ - \operatorname{cosec} 41^\circ$

3. Express each of the following in terms of trigonometric ratio of angles lying between 0° and 45°.

   (i) $\sin 64^\circ + \cos 54^\circ$

   (ii) $\tan 80^\circ + \cot 70^\circ$

4. Find the value of $\dfrac{\cot 40^\circ}{\tan 50^\circ} - \dfrac{\cos 35^\circ}{2 \sin 55^\circ}$.

5. Evaluate $\left(\dfrac{\sin 25^\circ}{\cos 65^\circ}\right)^2 + \left(\dfrac{\tan 65^\circ}{\cot 25^\circ}\right)^2 - 2\cos^2 45^\circ$.

6. Prove that

   (i) $\dfrac{\sin\theta}{\cos(90^\circ - \theta)} + \dfrac{\sec(90^\circ - \theta)}{\operatorname{cosec}\theta} = 2$

   (ii) $\sin(70^\circ + \theta) - \cos(20^\circ - \theta) = 0$

7. Evaluate

   (i) $\cot 12^\circ \cot 38^\circ \cot 52^\circ \cot 60^\circ \cot 78^\circ$.

   (ii) $\tan 5^\circ \tan 25^\circ \tan 30^\circ \tan 65^\circ \tan 85^\circ$.

8. If $\sec 5A = \operatorname{cosec}(A + 60^\circ)$, then find A.

9. If $\sin\left(50^\circ - \dfrac{3}{2}\theta\right) = \cos(3\theta - 50^\circ)$, then find the value of θ and hence evaluate

   $\tan\theta \sec\theta \sin\theta - \cot\theta \sin\theta \cos\theta$.

10. If A, B and C are the angles of a ΔABC, then prove that $\tan\left(\dfrac{B+C}{2}\right) = \cot\dfrac{A}{2}$.

Chapter Practice

a. 1 Mark Questions

1. From the given figure, find the value of $\cos y$

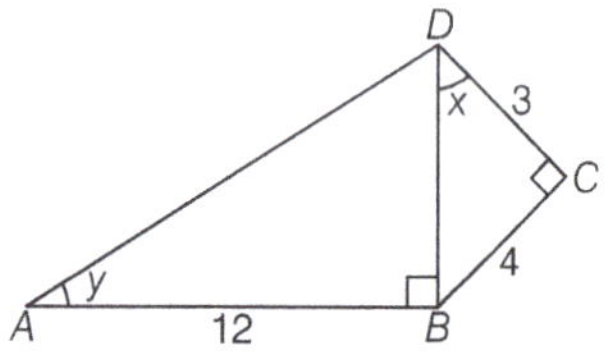

(a) $\frac{12}{13}$ (b) $\frac{5}{13}$ (c) $\frac{13}{12}$ (d) $\frac{13}{5}$

2. Find the value of $\sin y$

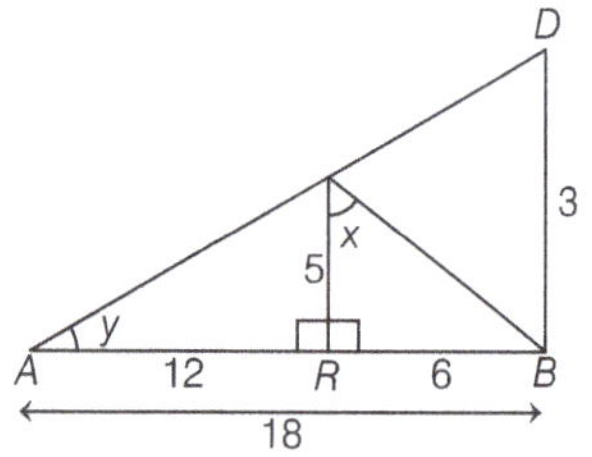

(a) $\frac{6}{13}$ (b) $\frac{12}{13}$ (c) $\frac{5}{12}$ (d) $\frac{5}{13}$

3. The value of $(\sin 45^\circ + \cos 45^\circ)$ is

(a) $\frac{1}{\sqrt{2}}$ (b) $\sqrt{2}$ (c) 1 (d) $\frac{\sqrt{3}}{2}$

4. If $\tan A = \frac{3}{4}$, then $\sin A \cos A$ is

(a) $\frac{24}{25}$ (b) $\frac{12}{25}$ (c) $\frac{5}{6}$ (d) $\frac{6}{5}$

5. Find the value of x, if $\tan(2x + 34^\circ) = 1$

(a) $6\frac{1}{2}$ (b) $5\frac{1}{2}$ (c) $7\frac{1}{3}$ (d) $6\frac{1}{3}$

b. 3 Mark Questions

6. If $\sec\theta = 13/12$, then calculate all other trigonometric ratios.

7. In ΔABC, right angled at B, if $\tan A = 1/\sqrt{3}$, then find the value of
   (i) $\sin A \cos C + \cos A \sin C$
   (ii) $\cos A \cos C - \sin A \sin C$

8. If $\cos\theta = 2/3$, then find the value of $2\sec^2\theta + 2\tan^2\theta - 7$.

9. If $\sin\alpha = \frac{1}{2}$ and α is an acute angle, then find the value of $(3\cos\alpha - 4\cos^3\alpha)$.

10. In a ΔABC, $\angle B = 90^\circ$. If $AB = 2$ cm and $AC = 3$ cm, then find the value of $\sin A$.

11. Prove that $\left(\frac{1 - \tan A}{1 - \cot A}\right)^2 = \tan^2 A$.

12. If $\cot\theta = \frac{7}{8}$, then evaluate
    (i) $\frac{(1 + \sin\theta)(1 - \sin\theta)}{(1 + \cos\theta)(1 - \cos\theta)}$ (ii) $\cot^2\theta$

13. If $4\tan\theta = 3$, then find the value of $\left(\frac{4\sin\theta - \cos\theta}{4\sin\theta + \cos\theta}\right)$.

14. If $\tan\theta = \frac{20}{21}$, then show that $\frac{1 - \sin\theta + \cos\theta}{1 + \sin\theta + \cos\theta} = \frac{3}{7}$.

15. If $\angle A = 45^\circ$, then verify that $\frac{\cos A}{1 + \sin A} = \frac{1 - \sin A}{\cos A}$.

16. Prove that $\frac{2\tan 30^\circ}{1 + \tan^2 30^\circ} = \frac{\sqrt{3}}{2}$.

17. Find the value of $\sin^2 60^\circ + \cos^2 45^\circ + \cos^2 60^\circ$.

18. Find the value of $(\sin 30^\circ + \cos 30^\circ) - (\sin 60^\circ + \cos 60^\circ)$.

19. Evaluate $\frac{\cos 45^\circ}{\sec 30^\circ + \operatorname{cosec} 30^\circ}$.

20. Find the value of $3\sin 30^\circ - 4\sin^3 60^\circ$.

21. If $\tan(6x + 15^\circ) = 1$, then find the value of x.

22. If $x \tan 45^\circ \cos 60^\circ = \sin 60^\circ \cot 60^\circ$, find the value of x.

23. Without using trigonometric tables, prove the following.
    (i) $\sin^2 28^\circ - \cos^2 62^\circ = 0$
    (ii) $\frac{\cot 54^\circ}{\tan 36^\circ} + \frac{\tan 20^\circ}{\cot 70^\circ} = 2$
    (iii) $\frac{\cos 80^\circ}{\sin 10^\circ} + \cos 59^\circ \cdot \operatorname{cosec} 31^\circ = 2$

24. Evaluate
    $\frac{\sin 65^\circ}{\cos 25^\circ} + \frac{\cos 32^\circ}{\sin 58^\circ} - \sin 28^\circ \cdot \sec 62^\circ + \operatorname{cosec}^2 30^\circ$.

25. Prove that $\frac{2\sin 43^\circ}{\cos 47^\circ} - \frac{\cot 30^\circ}{\tan 60^\circ} - \sqrt{2}\sin 45^\circ = 0$.

26. Prove that $\dfrac{\sin(90^\circ-\theta)+5\cos\theta}{\tan\theta}=6\cot\theta\cdot\cos\theta.$

27. For the given figure, if $\cos\alpha=\dfrac{5}{13}$ and $\sin\beta=\dfrac{8}{10}$, find the length of BD.

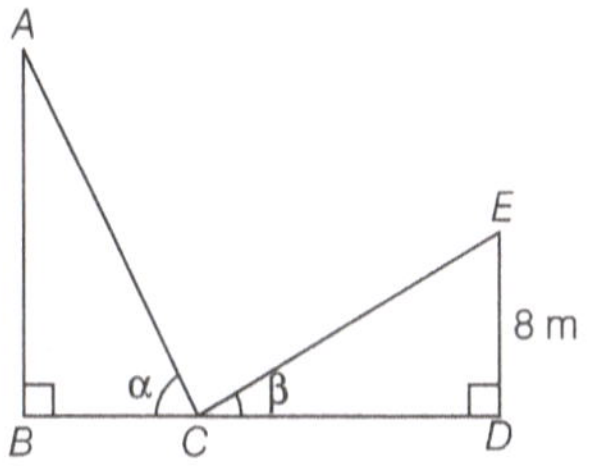

28. Find the length of PD, if $\angle PQR=60^\circ$, $\angle DQR=45^\circ$ and $QR=30$ cm and D is any point on PR.

29. In the given figure; $\angle C=90^\circ$ and $BD=DC$. Find

(i) $\dfrac{\cot\angle ABC}{\cot\angle ADC}$ (ii) $\dfrac{\tan\angle DAC}{\tan\angle BAC}$

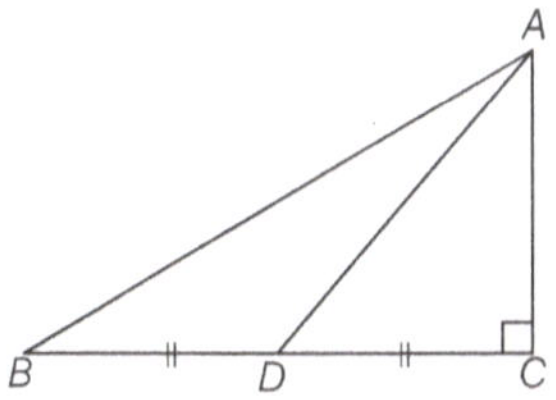

30. Without using trigonometric tables, evaluate the following.

(i) $\dfrac{\tan 38^\circ}{\cot 52^\circ}$ (ii) $\dfrac{\sec 62^\circ}{\text{cosec } 28^\circ}$

(iii) $\dfrac{\cos 25^\circ}{\sin 65^\circ}$ (iv) $\dfrac{\cos 37^\circ}{\sin 53^\circ}$

(v) $\dfrac{\text{cosec } 32^\circ}{\sec 58^\circ}$ (vi) $\dfrac{\tan 15^\circ}{\cot 75^\circ}$

31. Without using trigonometric table, evaluate the following.

(i) $\tan^2 42^\circ-\cot^2 48^\circ$

(ii) $\sec^2 18^\circ-\text{cosec } 72^\circ$

(iii) $\dfrac{\sin 72^\circ}{\cos 18^\circ}-\dfrac{\sec 32^\circ}{\text{cosec } 58^\circ}.$

(iv) $\dfrac{\cos 75^\circ}{\sin 15^\circ}+\dfrac{\sin 12^\circ}{\cos 78^\circ}-\dfrac{\cos 18^\circ}{\sin 72^\circ}.$

(v) $3\cos 80^\circ\cdot\text{cosec } 10^\circ+2\cos 59^\circ\cdot\text{cosec } 31^\circ.$

(vi) $2\left(\dfrac{\tan 35^\circ}{\cot 55^\circ}\right)^2+\left(\dfrac{\cot 55^\circ}{\tan 35^\circ}\right)^2-3\left(\dfrac{\sec 40^\circ}{\text{cosec } 50^\circ}\right).$

(vii) $\dfrac{\sin 80^\circ}{\cos 10^\circ}+\sin 59^\circ\cdot\sec 31^\circ.$

C. 6 Mark Questions

32. Express the following in terms of trigonometric ratios of angles lying between 0° and 45°.

(i) $\tan 68^\circ+\sec 68^\circ$

(ii) $\text{cosec } 85^\circ+\sin 85^\circ$

(iii) $\text{cosec } 75^\circ+\cot 75^\circ$

(iv) $\sin 85^\circ+\tan 82^\circ$

33. $ABCD$ is a rhombus whose diagonal AC makes an angle α with AB. If $\cos\alpha=\dfrac{2}{3}$ and $OB=3$ cm, then find the side and the diagonals of the rhombus.

34. In a rhombus $ABCD$, length of each side is 10 cm and $\angle A=60^\circ$. Find the lengths of its diagonals AC and BD.

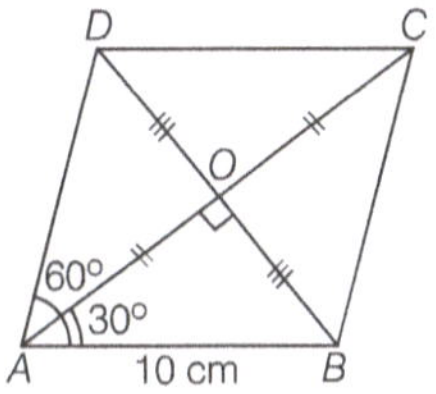

35. In the given figure, a rocket is fired vertically upwards from its launching pad A. It first rises 40 km vertically upwards and then 40 km at 60° to the vertical. AL represents the first stage of the journey and LM the second stage. N is a point vertically below M on the horizontal level as A. Calculate

(i) the height of the rocket when it is at point M.

(ii) the horizontal distance of point N from A.

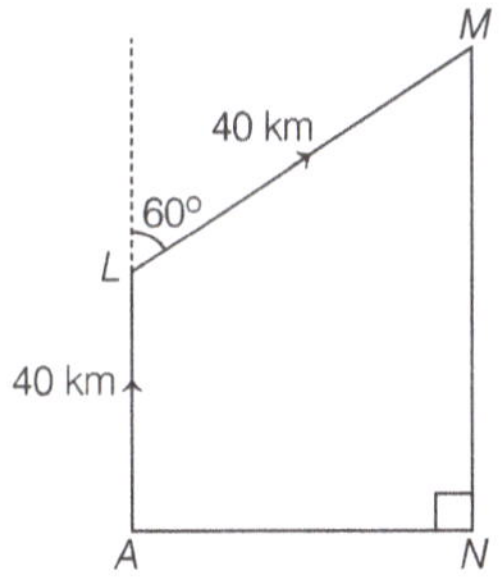

36. In the given figure $PQ\perp QR$, $SR\perp QR$, $QS\perp PR$, $\angle S=30^\circ$ and $SR=60\sqrt{3}$ m. Find the length of PQ

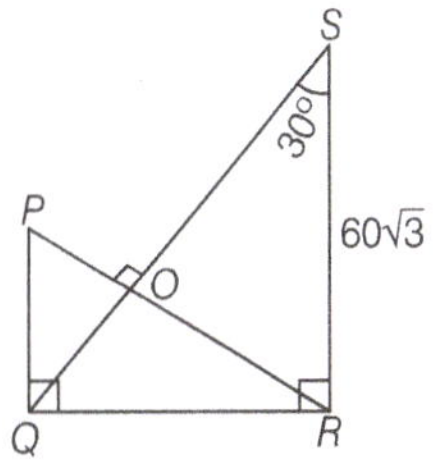

37. In the given figure, $PD \perp QR$, $PR = 17$, $RD = 15$, $QR = 36$. $\angle DPR = x$ and $\angle PQD = y$, find value of

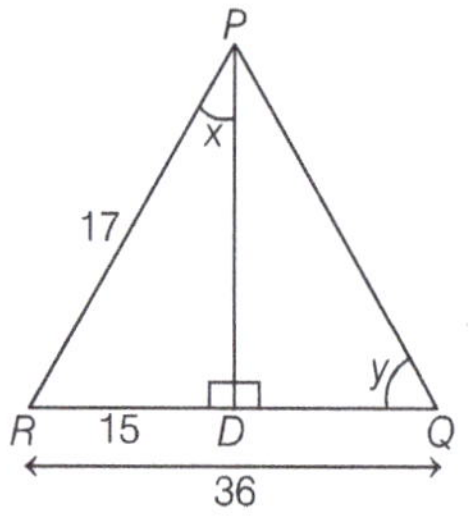

(i) $\tan x$

(ii) $\frac{1}{\cos^2 y} - \frac{1}{\cot^2 y}$

(iii) $\frac{6}{\cos x} - \frac{7}{\cos y} + 8\tan y$

38. In the given figure, $PQRS$ is a rectangle. Its diagonal $PR = 15$ cm and $\angle PRS = \theta$. If $\cot\theta = \frac{3}{2}$, find the perimeter and area of the rectangle.

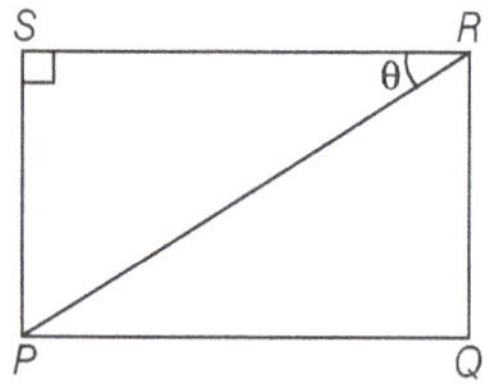

39. In the given figure, $ABCD$ is a trapezium with $\angle C = 120°$, $DC = 28$ cm and $BC = 40$ cm. Find

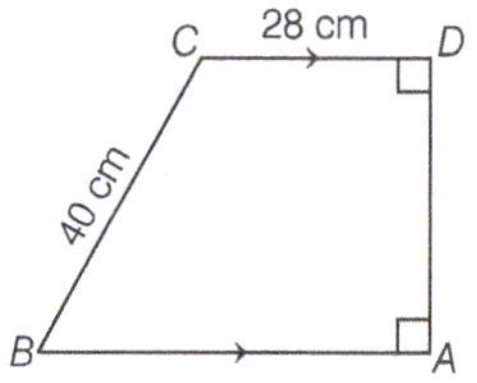

(i) Length of AB
(ii) Length of AD
(iii) The area of trapezium

40. Prove that

(i) $2(\cos^2 45° + \tan^2 60°) - 6(\sin^2 45° - \tan^2 30°) = 6$

(ii) $\frac{\tan 45°}{\text{cosec}\,30°} + \frac{\sec 60°}{\cot 45°} - \frac{5\sin 90°}{2\cos 0°} = 0$

41. Evaluate $\frac{\sin 70°}{\cos 20°} + \frac{\text{cosec}\,36°}{\sec 54°} - \frac{2\cos 43° \text{cosec}\,47°}{\tan 10° \tan 40° \tan 50° \tan 80°}$.

42. Evaluate

$\frac{\cos 28°}{\sin 62°} + \frac{\sin 36°}{\cos 54°} - \cos 22° \cdot \text{cosec}\,68° + 2\cot^2 45°$.

43. If $2\tan 3A \cos 3A - \tan 3A + 1 = 2\cos 3A$, then find the value of A.

44. If $\sin(A+B) = 1$ and $\sin(A-B) = \frac{1}{2}$; $0 \le A+B \le 90°$ and $A > B$, find the values of A and B.

Hints and Answers

Exercise 17.1

1. **Hint** Do same as Example 2.

Ans. (i) $\frac{4}{5}$ (ii) $\frac{3}{5}$ (iii) $\frac{4}{3}$ (iv) $\frac{5}{4}$

2. **Hint** Do same as Example 3.

Ans. (i) $\frac{13}{5}$ (ii) $\frac{13}{12}$ (iii) $\frac{5}{12}$

3. **Hint** Do same as Example 3.

Ans. $\frac{\sqrt{a^2+b^2}}{b}$

4. **Hint** First, do same as Example 3. Then, put the values of $\cot A$, $\sec A$ and $\text{cosec}\,A$ in given expression.

Ans. $\frac{-131}{65}$

5. **Hint** First, do same as Example 3. Then, put the values of $\sin A$, $\cos A$, $\tan A$ and $\cot A$ in the given expression.

Ans. (i) $\frac{-139}{609}$ (ii) $-\frac{209}{580}$

6. **Hint** $\sec\theta = \frac{4}{\sqrt{7}} = \frac{H}{B}$

Using Pythagoras theorem,

$$P^2 = H^2 - B^2 = 16 - 7 = 9$$

$$\Rightarrow \quad P = 3$$

Now, $\tan\theta = \frac{P}{B} = \frac{3}{\sqrt{7}}$, $\text{cosec}\,\theta = \frac{H}{P} = \frac{4}{3}$,

$\cos\theta = \frac{B}{H} = \frac{\sqrt{7}}{4}$, $\cot\theta = \frac{\sqrt{7}}{3}$

Now, put these values in LHS of given expression.

7. **Hint** Given, $\sin A = \frac{1}{2} = \frac{P_1}{H_1}$ and $\cos B = \frac{1}{\sqrt{2}} = \frac{B_2}{H_2}$.

Let $P_1 = k_1$, $H_1 = 2k_1$ and $B_2 = k_2$, $H_2 = \sqrt{2}k_2$, where k_1 and k_2 be any positive numbers.

By Pythagoras theorem, we get

$$B_1 = \sqrt{H_1^2 - P_1^2} \text{ and } P_2 = \sqrt{H_2^2 - B_2^2}$$

$$\Rightarrow B_1 = \sqrt{(2k_1)^2 - (k_1)^2} \text{ and } P_2 = \sqrt{(\sqrt{2}k_2)^2 - (k_2)^2}$$

$$\Rightarrow B_1 = \sqrt{4k_1^2 - k_1^2} \text{ and } P_2 = \sqrt{2k_2^2 - k_2^2}$$

$$\Rightarrow B_1 = \sqrt{3}\,k_1 \text{ and } P_2 = k_2$$

Now, $\tan A = \dfrac{P_1}{B_1} = \dfrac{k_1}{\sqrt{3}\,k_1} = \dfrac{1}{\sqrt{3}}$

and $\tan B = \dfrac{P_2}{B_2} = \dfrac{k_2}{k_2} = 1$

On putting the values of tan A and tan B in the given expression, we get the required result.

Ans. $\dfrac{1-\sqrt{3}}{1+\sqrt{3}}$

8. **Hint** Do same as Example 5.

Ans. $\sin A = \dfrac{24}{25}, \tan C = \dfrac{7}{24}, \cos A = \dfrac{7}{25}$

and $\sec C = \dfrac{25}{24}$

9. **Hint** $AD = \sqrt{(13)^2 - (5)^2} = 12$

and $AC = \sqrt{(16)^2 + (12)^2} = 20$

Ans. (i) 1 (ii) 1

10. **Hint** Use $\cot\theta = \dfrac{1}{\tan\theta}$ **Ans.** $\dfrac{p^2+q^2}{pq}$

11. **Hint** Do same as Example 12. **Ans.** $\dfrac{-2}{17}$

12. **Hint** Do same as Example 12. **Ans.** 7

13. **Hint** Do same as Example 12.

14. **Hint** $13\sin\theta = 5 \Rightarrow \sin\theta = \dfrac{5}{13} = \dfrac{P}{H}$

Using Pythagoras theorem

$$(13)^2 = (5)^2 + B^2 \Rightarrow B = 12$$

$$\text{cosec}\,\theta = \frac{H}{P} = \frac{13}{5}, \cot\theta = \frac{B}{P} = \frac{12}{5}$$ **Ans.** $\dfrac{1}{25}$

15. **Hint** $3\tan A = 4 \Rightarrow \tan A = \dfrac{4}{3} = \dfrac{P}{B}$

Using Pythagoras theorem,

$$H^2 = 4^2 + 3^2 \Rightarrow H = 5$$

$$\sec A = \frac{H}{B} = \frac{5}{3}, \quad \text{cosec}\,A = \frac{H}{P} = \frac{5}{4},$$

$$\cos A = \frac{B}{H} = \frac{3}{5} \text{ and } \sin A = \frac{P}{H} = \frac{4}{5}$$

16. **Hint** $\sqrt{3}\sin\theta = \cos\theta \Rightarrow \tan\theta = \dfrac{1}{\sqrt{3}}$

Now, $\dfrac{\sin\theta\tan\theta(1+\cot\theta)}{\sin\theta+\cos\theta} = \dfrac{\tan\theta\tan\theta(1+\cot\theta)}{\tan\theta+1}$

[dividing numerator and denominator by cos θ]

Ans. $\dfrac{1}{\sqrt{3}}$

17. **Hint** Do same as Example 13. **Ans.** 34

18. **Hint** Do same as Example 13. **Ans.** $\dfrac{257}{16}$

19. **Hint** LHS $= \dfrac{\sec^2\theta - \sin^2\theta}{\tan^2\theta}$

$$= \frac{\dfrac{1}{\cos^2\theta} - \sin^2\theta}{\dfrac{\sin^2\theta}{\cos^2\theta}} \quad \left[\because \sec A = \frac{1}{\cos A}\right]$$

$$= \frac{1-\sin^2\theta\cos^2\theta}{\cos^2\theta} \times \frac{\cos^2\theta}{\sin^2\theta} \quad \left[\because \frac{a/b}{c/d} = \frac{a\times d}{b\times c}\right]$$

$$= \frac{1-\sin^2\theta\cos^2\theta}{\sin^2\theta} = \text{cosec}^2\theta - \cos^2\theta$$

20. **Hint** LHS $= (1+\tan A + \cot A)(\sin A - \cos A)$

$$= \left(1 + \frac{\sin A}{\cos A} + \frac{\cos A}{\sin A}\right)(\sin A - \cos A)$$

$$= \left(\frac{\sin A\cos A + \sin^2 A + \cos^2 A}{\sin A\cos A}\right)(\sin A - \cos A)$$

$$= \frac{\sin^3 A - \cos^3 A}{\sin A\cos A} = \frac{\sin^2 A}{\cos A} - \frac{\cos^2 A}{\sin A}$$

$$= \sin A\tan A - \cos A\cot A$$

21. **Hint** Use $\sec A = \dfrac{1}{\cos A}$

22. **Hint** LHS

$$= 1 + \tan^2 A + 2\tan A - 1 - \tan^2 A + 2\tan A \quad [\because (a \pm b)^2 = a^2 + b^2 \pm 2ab]$$

$$= 4\tan A = 4\frac{\sin A}{\cos A}$$

$$= 4\sin A\cdot\sec A \quad \left[\because \frac{1}{\cos\theta} = \sec\theta\right]$$

23. **Hint** LHS $= \dfrac{\sin\theta\cot\theta}{1-\cos\theta} = \dfrac{\sin\theta\cdot\dfrac{\cos\theta}{\sin\theta}}{1-\cos\theta}$

$$= \frac{\cos\theta}{\cos\theta\left(\dfrac{1}{\cos\theta} - 1\right)} = \frac{1}{\sec\theta - 1}$$

24. **Hint** LHS $= \dfrac{\cos A \times \cos A}{\cos A - \sin A} + \dfrac{\sin A\cdot\sin A}{\sin A - \cos A}$

$$\left[\because \tan\theta = \frac{\sin\theta}{\cos\theta} \text{ and } \cot\theta = \frac{\cos\theta}{\sin\theta}\right]$$

$$= \frac{\cos^2 A - \sin^2 A}{\cos A - \sin A} = \cos A + \sin A$$

Exercise 17.2

1. **Hint** $\left(\dfrac{1}{2}\right)^2 + \left(\dfrac{1}{\sqrt{2}}\right)^2 + \left(\dfrac{\sqrt{3}}{2}\right)^2$ **Ans.** $\dfrac{3}{2}$

2. **Hint** LHS $= 2\left[\left(\dfrac{1}{\sqrt{2}}\right)^2 + (\sqrt{3})^2\right] - 6\left[\left(\dfrac{1}{\sqrt{2}}\right)^2 - \left(\dfrac{1}{\sqrt{3}}\right)^2\right]$

3. Hint $\dfrac{(\sqrt{3})^2 + 4\left(\frac{1}{\sqrt{2}}\right)^2 + 3\left(\frac{2}{\sqrt{3}}\right)^2 + 5(0)^2}{2 + 2 - (\sqrt{3})^2}$

Ans. 9

4. Hint LHS $= 2\left[\left(\frac{1}{2}\right)^4 + \left(\frac{1}{2}\right)^4\right] - [(\sqrt{3})^2 - (1)^2] + 3\left(\frac{2}{\sqrt{3}}\right)^2$

5. Hint LHS $= (\sqrt{3}+1)(3-\sqrt{3})$

and RHS $= (\sqrt{3})^3 - 2\left(\frac{\sqrt{3}}{2}\right)$

6. Hint LHS $= \sqrt{\dfrac{1+1/2}{1-1/2}}$ and RHS $= \cot 30°$

7. (i) **Hint** LHS $= 4\cos^3 30° = 4\left(\frac{\sqrt{3}}{2}\right)^3$

and RHS $= 3\cos 30° + \cos 90°$

(ii) **Hint** LHS $= \tan 2\theta = \tan(2 \times 30°) = \sqrt{3}$

and RHS $= \dfrac{2\tan\theta}{1-\tan^2\theta} = \dfrac{2\tan 30°}{1-\tan^2 30°} = \dfrac{2\left(\frac{1}{\sqrt{3}}\right)}{1-\left(\frac{1}{\sqrt{3}}\right)^2}$

8. (i) **Hint** LHS $= \cos(60° - 30°)$

and RHS $= \cos 60° \cdot \cos 30° + \sin 60° \cdot \sin 30°$

(ii) **Hint** Let, LHS $= \cot(60° + 30°)$

and RHS $= \dfrac{\cot 60° \cot 30° - 1}{\cot 30° + \cot 60°}$

9. (i) **Hint** $\sin\theta = \frac{1}{2} \Rightarrow \sin\theta = \sin 30°$ **Ans.** 30°

(ii) **Hint** $\cos 3\theta = \frac{1}{\sqrt{2}} \Rightarrow \cos 3\theta = \cos 45°$ **Ans.** 15°

(iii) **Hint** $\cot 2\theta = \frac{1}{\sqrt{3}} \Rightarrow \cot 2\theta = \cot 60°$ **Ans.** 30°

(iv) **Hint** $\tan 3\theta = \tan 45°$ **Ans.** 15°

10. Hint Do same as Example 22.

$$\cos\left(\frac{\theta}{2} + 10\right) = \cos 30°$$

Ans. $\theta = 40°$

11. Hint Do same as Example 23.

Ans. 60° and 30°

12. Hint Do same as Example 24.

Ans. $A = 60°$ and $B = 30°$

13. Hint

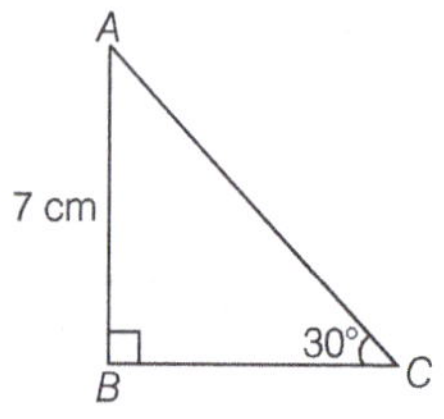

$\tan 30° = \dfrac{7}{BC}$ $\left[\because \tan C = \dfrac{\text{Perpendicular}}{\text{Base}} = \dfrac{AB}{BC}\right]$

$\sin 30° = \dfrac{AB}{AC}$ $\left[\because \sin C = \dfrac{\text{Perpendicular}}{\text{Hypotenuse}} = \dfrac{AB}{AC}\right]$

Ans. $BC = 7\sqrt{3}$ cm, $AC = 14$ cm

14. Hint Do same as Example 27.

Ans. $\angle BAC = 30°$ and $\angle ACB = 60°$

Exercise 17.3

1. Hint Do same as Example 28.

Ans. (i) 1 (ii) 1 (iii) 1

2. Hint Do same as Example 29.

Ans. (i) 0 (ii) 0

3. Hint Do same as Example 30.

Ans. (i) $\cos 26° + \sin 36°$ (ii) $\cot 10° + \tan 20°$

4. Hint Do same as Example 31. **Ans.** $\frac{1}{2}$

5. Hint $\cos 65° = \cos(90° - 25°) = \sin 25°$

$\cot 25° = \cot(90° - 65°) = \tan 65°$

and $\cos 45° = \frac{1}{\sqrt{2}}$

Ans. 1

6. Hint (i) $\cos(90° - \theta) = \sin\theta$, $\sec(90° - \theta) = \text{cosec}\,\theta$

(ii) $\sin(70° + \theta) = \sin[90° - (20° - \theta)]$

$= \cos(20° - \theta)$

7. Hint Do same as Example 32.

Ans. (i) $\frac{1}{\sqrt{3}}$ (ii) $\frac{1}{\sqrt{3}}$

8. Hint Do same as Example 37. **Ans.** $A = 5°$

9. Hint $\sin\left(50° - \frac{3}{2}\theta\right) = \cos(3\theta - 50°)$

$\Rightarrow \quad 50° - \frac{3}{2}\theta + 3\theta - 50° = 90°$

$[\because \sin A = \cos B \Rightarrow A + B = 90°]$

$\therefore \quad \theta = 60°$

Ans. $\theta = 60°, \frac{11}{4}$

10. Hint $A + B + C = 180°$

$\Rightarrow \quad \dfrac{B+C}{2} = 90° - \dfrac{A}{2}$

$\Rightarrow \quad \tan\left(\dfrac{B+C}{2}\right) = \tan\left(90° - \dfrac{A}{2}\right)$

$\Rightarrow \quad \tan\dfrac{B+C}{2} = \cot\dfrac{A}{2}$

Chapter Exercise

1. (a) **2.** (d)

3. (b) **4.** (b)

5. (b)

6. Hint Do same as Example 3.

Ans. $\sin\theta = \frac{5}{13}$, $\cos\theta = \frac{12}{13}$, $\tan\theta = \frac{5}{12}$,

$\text{cosec}\,\theta = \frac{13}{5}$, $\cot\theta = \frac{12}{5}$

7. Hint $\because \tan A = \frac{1}{\sqrt{3}}$

$\therefore \quad \frac{BC}{AB} = \frac{1}{\sqrt{3}} = k$ (say)

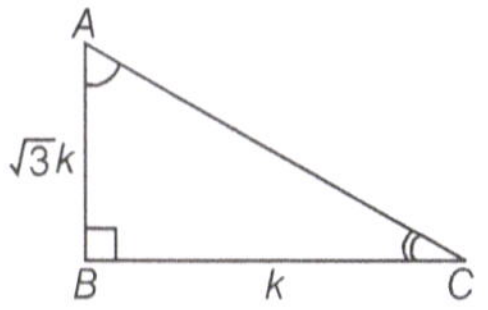

By Pythagoras theorem, we get

$$AC = \sqrt{(k)^2 + (\sqrt{3}k)^2} = \sqrt{k^2 + 3k^2} = 2k$$

$$\therefore \sin A = \frac{k}{2k} = \frac{1}{2}, \cos A = \frac{\sqrt{3}k}{2k} = \frac{\sqrt{3}}{2},$$

$$\sin C = \frac{\sqrt{3}k}{2k} = \frac{\sqrt{3}}{2} \text{ and } \cos C = \frac{k}{2k} = \frac{1}{2}$$

Ans. (i) 1 (ii) 0

8. Hint $\because \cos\theta = \frac{2}{3}$

$\Rightarrow \quad \frac{BC}{AC} = \frac{2}{3} = k$ (say)

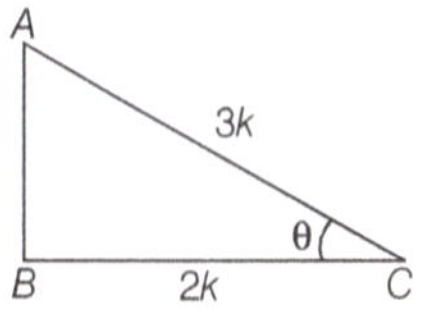

By Pythagoras theorem, we get

$$AB = \sqrt{(3k)^2 - (2k)^2} = \sqrt{5}\,k$$

$$\therefore \quad \sec\theta = \frac{3k}{2k} = \frac{3}{2}$$

and $\quad \tan\theta = \frac{\sqrt{5}k}{2k} = \frac{\sqrt{5}}{2}$ **Ans.** 0

9. Hint Do same as Q.8. **Ans.** 0

10. Hint $BC = \sqrt{(3)^2 - (2)^2} = \sqrt{5}$ [using Pythagoras theorem]

Angle of reference = $\angle A$

$\Rightarrow$ Base = AB

and perpendicular = BC

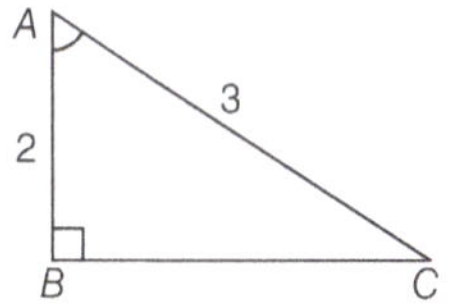

Ans. $\frac{\sqrt{5}}{3}$

11. Hint $\left(\frac{1 - \tan A}{1 - \cot A}\right)^2 = \left(\frac{1 - \frac{\sin A}{\cos A}}{1 - \frac{\cos A}{\sin A}}\right)^2$

$$= \left(\frac{\cos A - \sin A}{\sin A - \cos A} \times \frac{\sin A}{\cos A}\right)^2$$

12. Hint $\because \cot\theta = \frac{7}{8}$

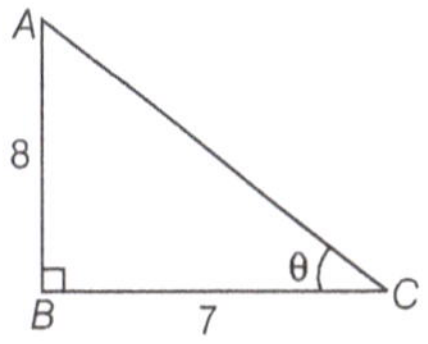

Now, $\quad \frac{BC}{AB} = \frac{7}{8} = k$ (say)

$\therefore \quad AC = \sqrt{(8k)^2 + (7k)^2} = \sqrt{113}\,k$

(i) **Hint** $\sin\theta = \frac{AB}{AC} = \frac{8}{\sqrt{113}}$ and $\cos\theta = \frac{BC}{AC} = \frac{7}{\sqrt{113}}$

Ans. $\frac{49}{64}$

(ii) **Hint** $\cot^2\theta = \left(\frac{7}{8}\right)^2$ **Ans.** $\frac{49}{64}$

13. Hint $\tan\theta = \frac{3}{4}$

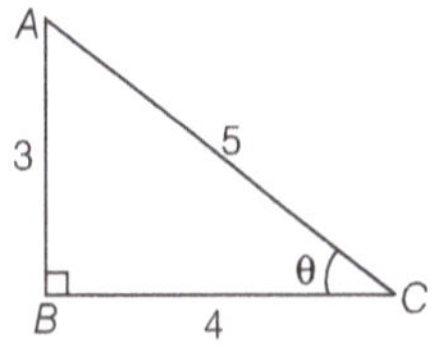

$$\left(\frac{4\sin\theta - \cos\theta}{4\sin\theta + \cos\theta}\right) = \left(\frac{\frac{4\sin\theta}{\cos\theta} - 1}{\frac{4\sin\theta}{\cos\theta} + 1}\right)$$

$$\frac{4\tan\theta - 1}{4\tan\theta + 1} = \left(\frac{4 \times \frac{3}{4} - 1}{4 \times \frac{3}{4} + 1}\right) = \frac{1}{2}$$

Ans. $\frac{1}{2}$

14. Hint $\sin\theta = \frac{20}{29}$ and $\cos\theta = \frac{21}{29}$

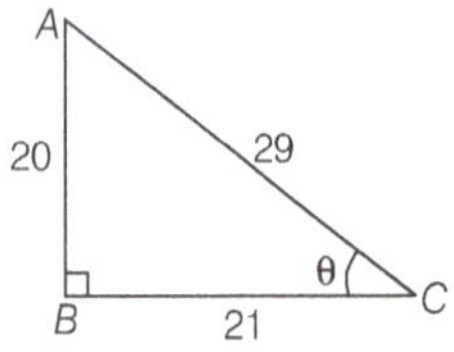

$$\frac{1 - \frac{20}{29} + \frac{21}{29}}{1 + \frac{20}{29} + \frac{21}{29}} = \frac{30}{70} = \frac{3}{7} \quad \textbf{Ans. } \frac{3}{7}$$

15. Hint LHS $= \frac{\cos 45^\circ}{1 + \sin 45^\circ} = \frac{1/\sqrt{2}}{1 + \frac{1}{\sqrt{2}}} = \frac{1}{1 + \sqrt{2}}$

and RHS $= \frac{1 - \sin 45^\circ}{\cos 45^\circ} = \frac{1 - \frac{1}{\sqrt{2}}}{1/\sqrt{2}} = \sqrt{2} - 1 \times \frac{\sqrt{2} + 1}{\sqrt{2} + 1}$

16. **Hint** LHS $= \dfrac{2\tan 30^\circ}{1+\tan^2 30^\circ} = \dfrac{2\times \frac{1}{\sqrt{3}}}{1+\left(\frac{1}{\sqrt{3}}\right)^2}$

17. **Hint** Do same as Example 15. **Ans.** $\dfrac{3}{2}$

18. **Hint** $\sin 30^\circ = \cos 60^\circ = \dfrac{1}{2}$ and $\cos 30^\circ = \sin 60^\circ = \dfrac{\sqrt{3}}{2}$

Ans. 0

19. **Hint** $\dfrac{1/\sqrt{2}}{\frac{2}{\sqrt{3}}+2}$ **Ans.** $\dfrac{3\sqrt{2}-\sqrt{6}}{8}$

20. **Hint** Do same as Example 15. **Ans.** $\dfrac{3(1-\sqrt{3})}{2}$

22. **Hint** $x\times 1\times \dfrac{1}{2} = \dfrac{\sqrt{3}}{2}\times\dfrac{1}{\sqrt{3}}$ **Ans.** $x=1$

21. **Hint** Do same as Example 22. **Ans.** $x = 5$

23. (i) **Hint** LHS $= \sin^2(90^\circ - 62^\circ) - \cos^2 62^\circ$

$= \cos^2 62^\circ - \cos^2 62^\circ = 0$

(ii) **Hint** LHS $= \dfrac{\cot(90^\circ-36^\circ)}{\tan 36^\circ} + \dfrac{\tan(90^\circ-70^\circ)}{\cot 70^\circ}$

$= \dfrac{\tan 36^\circ}{\tan 36^\circ} + \dfrac{\cot 70^\circ}{\cot 70^\circ}$

(iii) **Hint** LHS

$= \dfrac{\cos(90^\circ-10^\circ)}{\sin 10^\circ} + \cos(90^\circ-31^\circ)\cdot \text{cosec}\, 31^\circ$

$= \dfrac{\sin 10^\circ}{\sin 10^\circ} + \sin 31^\circ \cdot \text{cosec}\, 31^\circ = 1 + 1$

24. **Hint** $\dfrac{\sin(90^\circ-25^\circ)}{\cos 25^\circ} + \dfrac{\cos(90^\circ-58^\circ)}{\sin 58^\circ}$

$- \sin(90^\circ - 62^\circ)\cdot \sec 62^\circ + (2)^2$

$= \dfrac{\cos 25^\circ}{\cos 25^\circ} + \dfrac{\sin 58^\circ}{\sin 58^\circ} - \cos 62^\circ \cdot \sec 62^\circ + 4$

Ans. 5

25. **Hint** LHS $= \dfrac{2\sin(90^\circ-47^\circ)}{\cos 47^\circ} - \dfrac{\cot(90^\circ-60^\circ)}{\tan 60^\circ} - \sqrt{2}\times\dfrac{1}{\sqrt{2}}$

$= \dfrac{2\cos 47^\circ}{\cos 47^\circ} - \dfrac{\tan 60^\circ}{\tan 60^\circ} - 1$

26. **Hint** LHS $= \dfrac{\cos\theta + 5\cos\theta}{\tan\theta}$ $\left[\because \dfrac{1}{\tan A} = \cot A\right]$

27. **Hint** $\cos\alpha = \dfrac{5}{13} = \dfrac{\text{Base}}{\text{Hypotenuse}}$

$BC = 5$ [using pythagoras theorem in ΔABC]

$\sin\beta = \dfrac{8}{10} = \dfrac{\text{Perpendicular}}{\text{Hypotenuse}}$

$CD = 6$ [using pythagoras theorem in ΔCDE]

$\therefore$ $BD = BC + CD$

Ans. $BD = 11$ m

28. **Hint** $\tan 45^\circ = \dfrac{DR}{QR} = \dfrac{DR}{30}$

$DR = 30$

$\tan 60^\circ \Rightarrow \dfrac{PD+30}{30} = \dfrac{\sqrt{3}}{1}$

$PD = 30\sqrt{3} - 30$

$PD = 30(\sqrt{3}-1)$

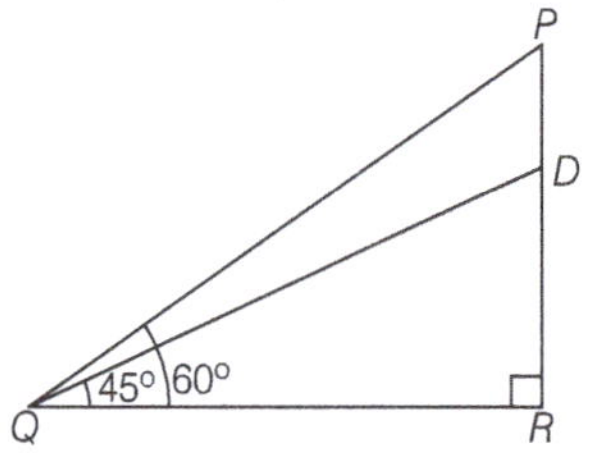

Ans. $30(\sqrt{3}-1)$

29. **Hint** Let $BD = DC = x$

Ans. (i) 2 (ii) $\dfrac{1}{2}$

30. (i) **Hint** $\dfrac{\tan(90^\circ-52^\circ)}{\cot 52^\circ}$ **Ans.** 1

(ii) **Hint** $= \dfrac{\sec(90^\circ-28^\circ)}{\text{cosec}\, 28^\circ}$ **Ans.** 1

(iii) **Hint** $\dfrac{\cos(90^\circ-65^\circ)}{\sin 65^\circ}$ **Ans.** 1

(iv) **Hint** $\dfrac{\cos(90^\circ-53^\circ)}{\sin 53^\circ}$ **Ans.** 1

(v) **Hint** $\dfrac{\text{cosec}\ 90^\circ-58^\circ}{\sec 58^\circ}$ **Ans.** 1

(vi) **Hint** $\dfrac{\tan(90^\circ-75^\circ)}{\cot 75^\circ}$ **Ans.** 1

31. (i) **Hint** $\tan^2(90^\circ-48^\circ) - \cot^2 48^\circ$

$= \cot^2 48^\circ - \cot^2 48^\circ$ **Ans.** 0

(ii) **Hint** $\sec^2(90^\circ-72^\circ) - \text{cosec}^2 72^\circ$

$= \text{cosec}^2 72^\circ - \text{cosec}^2 72^\circ$ **Ans.** 0

(iii) **Hint** $\dfrac{\sin(90^\circ-18^\circ)}{\cos 18^\circ} - \dfrac{\sec(90^\circ-58^\circ)}{\text{cosec}\, 58^\circ}$

$= \dfrac{\cos 18^\circ}{\cos 18^\circ} - \dfrac{\text{cosec}\, 58^\circ}{\text{cosec}\, 58^\circ}$ **Ans.** 0

(iv) **Hint** $\dfrac{\cos(90^\circ-15^\circ)}{\sin 15^\circ} + \dfrac{\sin(90^\circ-78^\circ)}{\cos 78^\circ} - \dfrac{\cos(90^\circ-72^\circ)}{\sin 72^\circ}$

$= \dfrac{\sin 15^\circ}{\sin 15^\circ} + \dfrac{\cos 78^\circ}{\cos 78^\circ} - \dfrac{\sin 72^\circ}{\sin 72^\circ}$ **Ans.** 1

(v) **Hint** $3\cos(90^\circ-10^\circ)\cdot \text{cosec}\, 10^\circ$

$+ 2\cos(90^\circ-31^\circ)\cdot \text{cosec}\, 31^\circ$

$= 3\sin 10^\circ \cdot \text{cosec}\, 10^\circ + 2\sin 31^\circ \cdot \text{cosec}\, 31^\circ$

Ans. 5

(vi) **Hint** $2\left[\dfrac{\tan(90^\circ-55^\circ)}{\cot 55^\circ}\right]^2 + \left[\dfrac{\cot(90^\circ-35^\circ)}{\tan 35^\circ}\right]^2$

$-3\left[\dfrac{\sec(90^\circ-50^\circ)}{\text{cosec}\, 50^\circ}\right]$

$= 2\left(\dfrac{\cot 55^\circ}{\cot 55^\circ}\right)^2 + \left(\dfrac{\tan 35^\circ}{\tan 35^\circ}\right)^2 - 3\left(\dfrac{\text{cosec}\, 50^\circ}{\text{cosec}\, 50^\circ}\right)$

Ans. 0

(vii) **Hint** $\frac{\sin(90° - 10°)}{\cos 10°} + \sin(90° - 31°) \cdot \sec 31°$

$= \frac{\cos 10°}{\cos 10°} + \cos 31° \cdot \sec 31°$

Ans. 2

32. (i) **Hint** $\tan(90° - 22°) + \sec(90° - 22°)$

Ans. $\cot 22° + \text{cosec}\, 22°$

(ii) **Hint** $\text{cosec}(90° - 5°) + \sin(90° - 5°)$

Ans. $\sec 5° + \cos 5°$

(iii) **Hint** $\text{cosec}(90° - 15°) + \cot(90° - 15°)$

Ans. $\sec 15° + \tan 15°$

(iv) **Hint** $\sin(90° - 5°) + \tan(90° - 8°)$

Ans. $\cos 5° + \cot 8°$

33. Hint

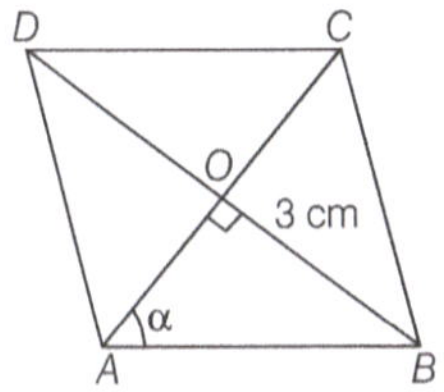

By Pythagoras theorem,

$AB = \frac{9}{\sqrt{5}}$

$\Rightarrow \quad OA = \frac{6}{\sqrt{5}}$

Ans. Side $= \frac{9}{\sqrt{5}}$ cm

Diagonal $BD = 6$ cm and $AC = \frac{12}{\sqrt{5}}$ cm

34. Hint Diagonals of a rhombus bisects each other at 90 ° and also bisects the angle of the vertex.

In right angled ΔAOB,

$\sin 30° = \frac{OB}{AB}$

$\Rightarrow \quad \frac{1}{2} = \frac{OB}{10} \Rightarrow OB = 5$

$BD = OB + OD \quad [\because OB = OD]$

$BD = 5 + 5 = 10$

In right angled ΔAOD,

$\cos 30° = \frac{AO}{AD} \Rightarrow \frac{\sqrt{3}}{2} = \frac{AO}{10} \quad \left[\because \angle DAO = \frac{60}{2} = 30°\right]$

$\Rightarrow \quad AO = 5\sqrt{3}$

$AC = 2 \times AO = 10\sqrt{3} = 17.32$

Ans. Length of diagonal $AC = 17.32$ cm and $BD = 10$ cm.

35. Hint Draw $LO \perp MN$

$LO = AN$

$NM = NO + OM$

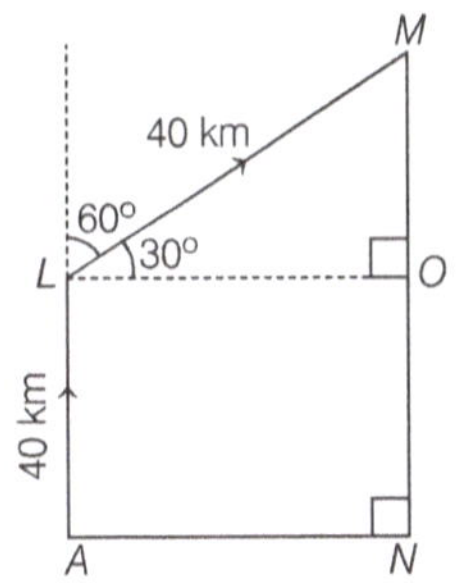

Ans. (i) 60 km

(ii) 34.64 km

36. Hint $\tan 30° = \frac{QR}{60\sqrt{3}}$

$QR = 60$

$\Delta PQR, \quad \tan 30° = \frac{PQ}{60}$

$PQ = 20\sqrt{3}$

37. Hint

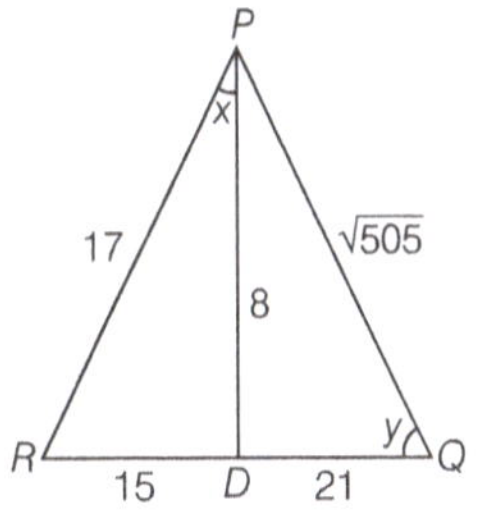

(i) In right angled ΔPDR

$PR^2 = PD^2 + RD^2$

[by Phythagoras theorem]

$\Rightarrow \quad 17^2 = PD^2 + 15^2$

$\Rightarrow \quad PD = \sqrt{64} = 8$

Now, $\tan x = \frac{\text{Perpendicular}}{\text{Base}}$

$= \frac{RD}{PD} = \frac{15}{8}$

Ans. 1.875

(ii) **Hint** $DQ = 36 - 15 = 21$

$PD = 8$

$PQ = \sqrt{441 + 64}$

[by Pythagoras theorem in right angled ΔPDQ]

In right angled ΔPDQ

$\cos y = \frac{21}{\sqrt{505}}, \cot y = \frac{21}{8}$

Putting the value of $\cos y$ and $\cot y$ in $\frac{1}{\cos^2 y} - \frac{1}{\cot^2 y}$, we get

$\Rightarrow \left(\frac{\sqrt{505}}{21}\right)^2 - \left(\frac{8}{21}\right)^2$ **Ans.** 1

(iii) **Hint** In right angled ΔPDR

$$\cos x = \frac{RD}{PR} = \frac{8}{17}$$

In right angled ΔPDQ

$$\cos y = \frac{21}{\sqrt{505}}$$

and $$\tan y = \frac{PD}{PQ} = \frac{8}{21}$$

Put the value of $\cos x$, $\cos y$ and $\tan y$ in given terms and find.

Ans. 8.29

38. Hint

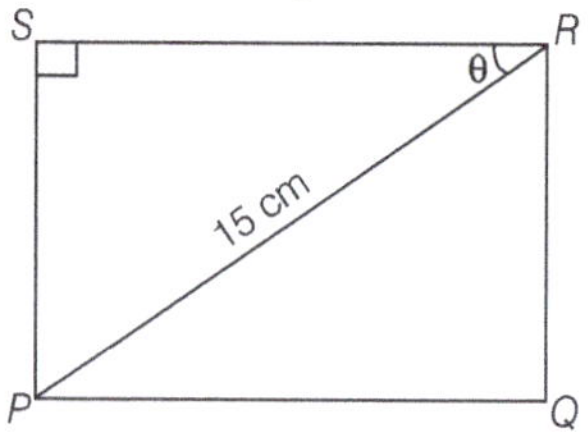

$$\cot\theta = \frac{3}{2} = \frac{\text{Base}}{\text{Perpendicular}}$$

[apply in right angled ΔPSR]

$PQ = RS = 3K$ (say)

$QR = PS = 2K$

In right angled ΔPSR

$$\cos\theta = \frac{\text{Base}}{\text{Hypotenuse}} = \frac{RS}{15}$$

$\left[\because \cot\theta = \frac{3}{2}, \text{ then } \cos\theta = \frac{3}{\sqrt{3}}\right]$

$$\Rightarrow \frac{3}{\sqrt{3}} = \frac{3K}{15}$$

$$\Rightarrow K = \frac{15}{\sqrt{3}}$$

$$PQ = RS = \frac{45}{\sqrt{3}}$$

$$QR = PS = \frac{30}{\sqrt{3}}$$

Perimeter of rectangle $PQRS = 2(PQ + QR)$

Area $= PQ \times RS$

Perimeter $= \frac{150}{\sqrt{3}}$ cm

and area $= 103\frac{11}{13}$ cm^2

39. Hint $\angle ABC + \angle BCD = 180°$

$\angle ABC = 180° - 120°$ $[\because \angle C = 120°$ (given)$]$

$= 60°$

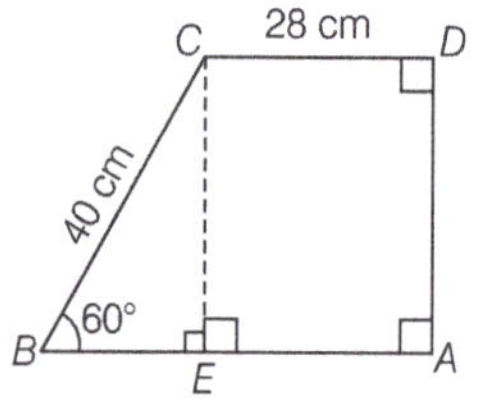

Draw $CE \perp BA$

In right angled ΔCBE

$$\sin 60° = \frac{CE}{BC} = \frac{CE}{40}$$

$$\Rightarrow CE = 40 \times \frac{\sqrt{3}}{2} \quad \left[\therefore \sin 60° = \frac{\sqrt{3}}{2}\right]$$

And $$\cos 60° = \frac{BE}{BC} = \frac{BE}{40}$$

$$BE = 40 \times \frac{1}{2} = 20 \quad \left[\therefore \cos 60° = \frac{1}{2}\right]$$

(i) $AB = BE + AE$

$= BE + CD$ $[\therefore AE = CD]$

(ii) $AD = CE$

(iii) Area of trapezium $= \frac{1}{2}(AB + CD) \times AD$

Ans.

(i) 48 cm

(ii) $20\sqrt{3}$ cm

(iii) Area of trapezium $= 760\sqrt{3}$ cm^2

40. (i) **Hint** On putting the values of

$\cos 45° = \sin 45° = \frac{1}{\sqrt{2}}$, $\tan 60° = \sqrt{3}$ and $\tan 30° = \frac{1}{\sqrt{3}}$

in the given expression.

(ii) **Hint** On putting the values of $\tan 45° = 1$, $\sec 60° = 2$, $\sin 90° = 1$, $\text{cosec} 30° = 2$, $\cot 45° = 1$ and $\cos 0° = 1$ in the given expression.

41. Hint We have,

$$\frac{\sin(90°-20°)}{\cos 20°} + \frac{\text{cosec}(90°-54°)}{\sec 54°} - \frac{2\cos(90°-47°) = \frac{RD}{PD} = \frac{15}{8} 47°}{\tan(90°-80°)\tan(90°-50°)\tan 50°\tan 80°}$$

$$= \frac{\cos 20°}{\cos 20°} + \frac{\sec 54°}{\sec 54°} - \frac{2\sin 47°\,\text{cosec}\,47°}{\cot 80° \cdot \cot 50° \tan 50° \tan 80°}$$

Ans. 0

42. Hint $\frac{\cos(90°-62°)}{\sin 62°} + \frac{\sin(90°-54°)}{\cos 54°}$

$- \cos(90° - 68°) \cdot \text{cosec} 68° + 2 \times 1$

$$= \frac{\sin 62°}{\sin 62°} + \frac{\cos 54°}{\cos 54°} - \sin 68° \cdot \text{cosec } 68° + 2$$

Ans. 3

43. Hint $2\tan 3A \cos 3A - \tan 3A - 2\cos 3A + 1 = 0$

$(\tan 3A - 1)(2\cos 3A - 1) = 0$

Either $\tan 3A - 1 = 0$ or $2\cos 3A - 1 = 0$

$\tan 3A = \tan 45°$ or $\cos 3A = \cos 60°$z **Ans.** 15° and 20°

44. Hint $\sin(A + B) = 1 = \sin 90°$

$$A + B = 90°$$

$$\sin(A - B) = \frac{1}{2} = \sin 30°$$

$$A = 60°$$

$$B = 30°$$

Ans. $A = 60°$ and $B = 30°$

Olympiad Section

Brain Teasing Questions of Olympiad Pattern

1 If $f(x) = \cos^2 x + \sec^2 x$, then $f(x)$ is

(a) ≥ 1 (b) ≤ 1
(c) ≥ 2 (d) ≤ 2

2 If $A = 30°$, then the value of $\frac{1 + \sin 2A + \cos 2A}{(\sin A + \cos A)}$ is

(a) $\sqrt{2}$ (b) $\sqrt{5}$
(c) $\sqrt{3}$ (d) $\sqrt{3-1}$

3 If ABC is a right angled triangle, then

$$\tan\left(\frac{A-B-C}{2}\right) \text{ and } -\tan\left(\frac{A+B-C}{2}\right)$$

(a) are equal
(b) are unequal
(c) sum of these equal to 1
(d) None of the above

4 If $m = a\cos^3\theta + 3a\cos\theta\sin^2\theta$ and $n = a\sin^3\theta + 3a\cos^2\theta\sin\theta$, then $(m+n)^{2/3} + (m-n)^{2/3}$ is equal to

(a) $4a^{2/3}\sin\theta\cos\theta$
(b) $a^{2/3}\sin\theta\cos\theta$
(c) $4a^{3/2}\sin\theta$
(d) $a^{3/2}\sin\theta\cos\theta$

5 If $a\sec\theta + b\tan\theta + c = 0$, $p\sec\theta + q\tan\theta + r = 0$ and $\sec^2\theta - \tan^2\theta = 1$, then $(br - qc)^2 - (pc - ar)^2$ is equal to

(a) $(ap - bq)^2$ (b) $(aq - bp)^2$
(c) $(ap - bq)$ (d) $(aq - bp)$

6 The acute angles A and B, if $\sin(A + 2B) = \frac{\sqrt{3}}{2}$ and $\cos(A + 4B) = 0$, where $A > B$, are respectively

(a) 15°, 25°
(b) 30°, 15°
(c) 25°, 45°
(d) 45°, 90°

7 In a ΔABC, right angled at B, $BC = 5$ cm and $AC - AB = 1$ cm, then the value of $\frac{\cos^2 C}{1 - \sin C}$ is

(a) $\frac{25}{13}$ (b) $\frac{25}{9}$
(c) $\frac{9}{13}$ (d) $\frac{13}{25}$

8 Find the lengths of diagonals AC and BD of rhombus $ABCD$, given that $AB = 60$ cm and $\angle BAD = 60°$ are respectively [take $\sqrt{3} = 1.732$]

(a) 100.85 cm, 55 cm (b) 101.90 cm, 55.2 cm
(c) 103.92 cm, 60 cm (d) None of these

Directions (Q. Nos. 9-11) In trapezium $ABCD$, as shown in the figure below, $AB \parallel DC$, $AD = DC = 20$ cm and $\angle A = 60°$.

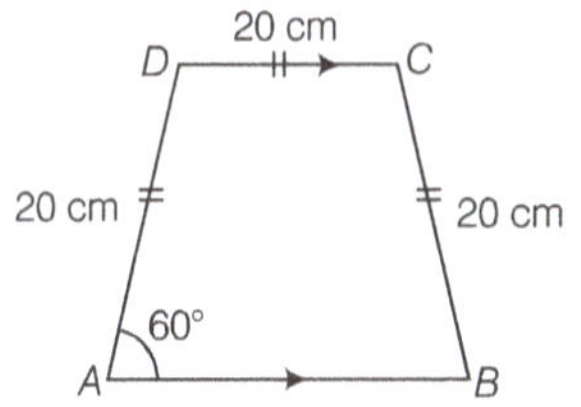

9 The distance between AB and DC is

(a) 17.32 cm (b) 18.02 cm
(c) 19.50 cm (d) 25.02 cm

10 The length of AB is

(a) 10 cm
(b) 15 cm
(c) 25 cm
(d) 40 cm

11 The value of $\sin(50° + \theta) - \cos(40° - \theta) + \tan 1° \cdot \tan 10° \cdot \tan 20° \cdot \tan 70° \cdot \tan 80° \cdot \tan 89°$ is

(a) 0 (b) 1
(c) 2 (d) 4

Answers

1. (c) **2.** (c) **3.** (b) **4.** (a) **5.** (b) **6.** (b) **7.** (a) **8.** (c) **9.** (a) **10.** (d) **11.** (b)

* *These questions may or may not be asked in the examination, have been given just for additional practice required for olympiads Scholarship Exams etc. For detailed explanations refer Page No. 353.*

CHAPTER 18

Coordinate Geometry and Distance Formula

SYLLABUS

- (i) Dependent and independent variables. (ii) Ordered pairs, coordinates of points and plotting them in the Cartesian plane. (iii) Solution of Simultaneous Linear Equations graphically. (iv) Distance formula.

Cartesian System

The system used to described the position of a point in a plane, is called the **cartesian system**. In cartesian system, there are two mutual perpendicular straight lines XX' (horizontal line) and YY' (vertical line) which intersect at point O, is called the **origin** and it is denoted by O. The horizontal line XOX' is called **X-axis** and the vertical line YOY' is called **Y-axis**. Directions OX, OY and OX', OY' are called the **positive directions** and **negative directions** of X-axis and Y-axis, respectively.

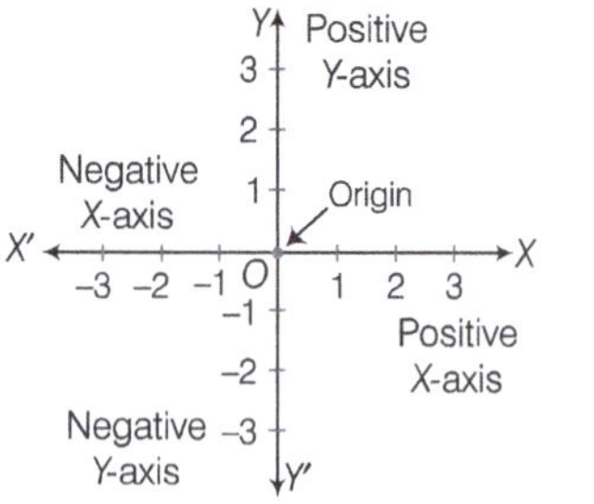

Directions OX, OY and OX' and OY' are called the **positive directions** and **negative directions** of X-axis and Y-axis, respectively.

Ordered Pair

It is a pair of two objects taken in a specific order. e.g. (a, b) is called ordered pair, in which a is called first element and b is called second element.

Two ordered pair are equal, if their corresponding components are equal,
i.e. $(a, b) = (c, d) \Rightarrow a = c$ and $b = d$.

Example 1. Find x and y, if

(i) $(x, 4) = (-8, y)$ (ii) $(x-3, 6) = (5, x+2y)$

Sol. We know that $(a, b) = (c, d)$, if $a = c$ and $b = d$

(i) $(x, 4) = (-8, y)$

$\therefore x = -8$ and $4 = y \Rightarrow x = -8$ and $y = 4$

(ii) $(x-3, 6) = (5, x+2y)$

$\therefore x - 3 = 5 \Rightarrow x = 5 + 3 = 8$ and $x + 2y = 6$

Put $x = 8$ in the equation $x + 2y = 6$, we get

$8 + 2y = 6 \Rightarrow 2y = 6 - 8 = -2 \Rightarrow 2y = -2 \Rightarrow y = -1$

Hence, $x = 8$ and $y = -1$.

Quadrants and Sign Convention

The axes divide the plane into four parts. These four parts are called **quadrant** (i.e. 1/4th part), numbered I, II, III and IV anti-clockwise from OX.

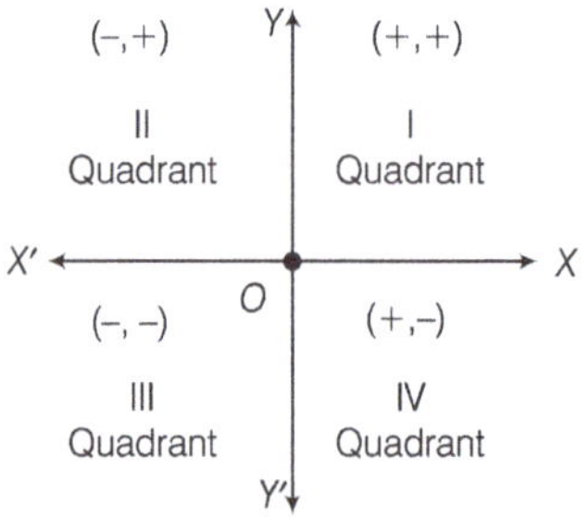

(i) XOY is called I quadrant, where both x and y-coordinates are positive.
(ii) $X'OY$ is called II quadrant, where x-coordinate is negative and y-coordinate is positive.
(iii) $X'OY'$ is called III quadrant, where both x and y-coordinates are negative.
(iv) XOY' is called IV quadrant, where x-coordinate is positive and y-coordinate is negative.

In tabular form, we can define the signs of coordinates in the following way

Region	Quadrant	Nature of x and y-coordinates	Sign of x-coord inate	Sign of y-coordinate	Sign of coordinates of a point
XOY	I	$x > 0, y > 0$	+	+	(+, +)
$X'OY$	II	$x < 0, y > 0$	−	+	(−, +)
$X'OY'$	III	$x < 0, y < 0$	−	−	(−, −)
XOY'	IV	$x > 0, y < 0$	+	−	(+, −)

Thus, the plane consists of two axes and four quadrants is known as **XY-plane** or **cartesian plane** or **coordinate plane** and the axes are known as the **coordinate axes.**

Coordinates of a Point in Cartesian Plane

To locate a point in the cartesian plane, its perpendicular distances from X-axis and Y-axis are required, these distances are called **coordinates** of the point. Each point in cartesian plane has two coordinates; x-coordinate and y-coordinate.

(i) The **x-coordinate** of a point is the perpendicular distance from the Y-axis. The x-coordinate is also called the **abscissa.**

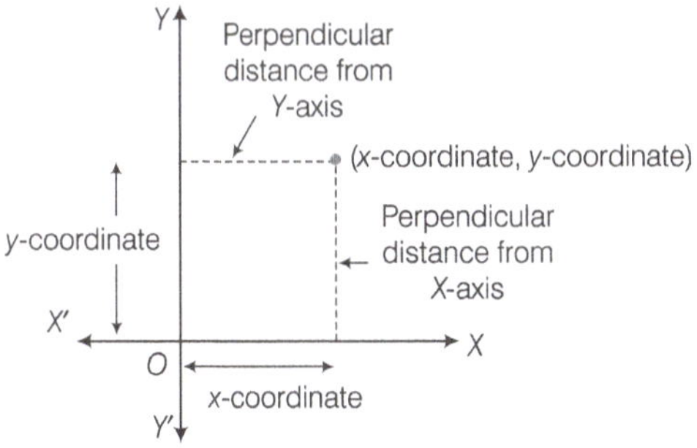

(ii) The **y-coordinate** of a point is the perpendicular distance from the X-axis. The y-coordinate is also called the **ordinate**.
(iii) The x-coordinate and y-coordinate taken together are called **cartesian coordinates** or **coordinates** of a point and it is denoted by (x, y). Here, the x-coordinate comes first and y-coordinate comes second.

Some Important Points

(i) If x-coordinate of two or more points are same, then the line joining these points is parallel to Y-axis.
(ii) If y-coordinate of two or more points are same, then the line joining these points is parallel to X-axis.
(iii) Suppose coordinates of a point (x, y) are not equal (i.e. $x \neq y$). If we interchange the coordinates x and y, then the position of (y, x) will be different from the position of (x, y).
Here, ordered pair $(x, y) \neq$ ordered pair (y, x).
(iv) If coordinates of a point are equal (i.e. $x = y$), then interchanging the coordinates x and y does not change the position of that point.

Example 2. Write the coordinates of the point which lies at a distance of x units from X-axis and y units from Y-axis.

Sol. The coordinates of the point which lies at a distance of x units from X-axis and y units from Y-axis is $P(y, x)$.

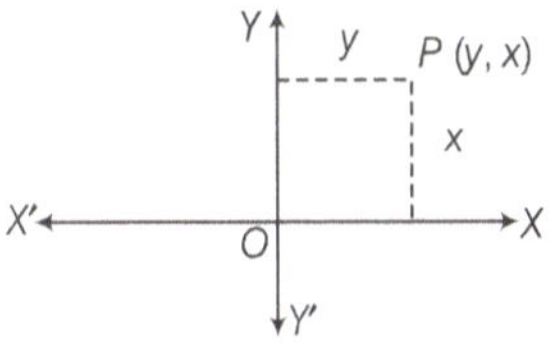

Example 3. If the coordinates of two points are $A(3, 4)$ and $B(-2, 5)$, then find

(Abscissa of A) – (Abscissa of B).

Sol. Given, point A (3, 4), i.e. abscissa of $A = 3$
and point B (– 2, 5), i.e. abscissa of $B = -2$
$\therefore$ Abscissa of A – Abscissa of $B = 3 - (-2) = 3 + 2 = 5$

Example 4. In the given figure, LM is a line parallel to the Y-axis at a distance of 3 units from origin.

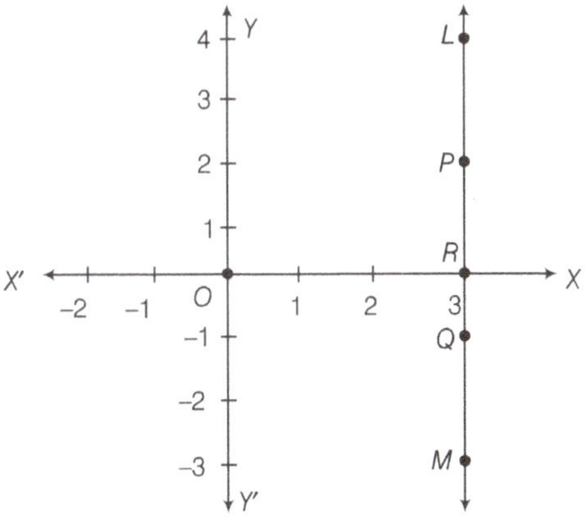

(i) What are the coordinates of the points P, R and Q?
(ii) What is the difference between the abscissae of the points L and M?

Sol. Given, LM is a line parallel to the Y-axis and its perpendicular distance from Y-axis is 3 units.

(i) Coordinates of point P are (3, 2).

[∵ its perpendicular distance from X-axis is 2 units in positive direction of Y-axis]

Coordinates of point R are (3, 0).

[∵ it lies on X-axis, so its y-coordinate is zero]

Coordinates of point Q are (3, – 1).

[∵ its perpendicular distance from X-axis is 1 in negative direction of Y-axis]

(ii) Abscissa of point $L = 3$, abscissa of point $M = 3$

∴ Difference between the abscissa of points L and M $= 3 - 3 = 0$

Example 5. Write the coordinates of the points given in the following graph.

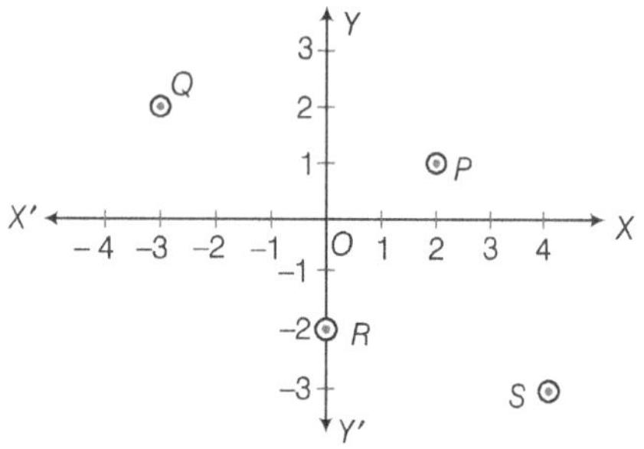

Sol. Here, the given points on the graph are P, Q, R and S.

Now, draw the perpendicular lines from points P, Q, R and S on X and Y-axes.

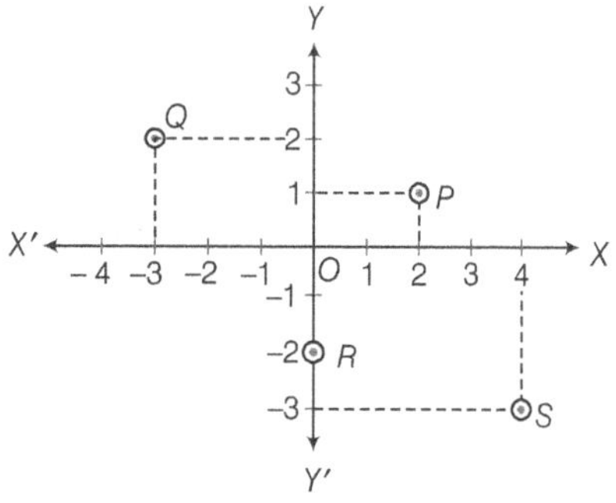

Coordinates of Point P

The point P is at a distance of 2 units from the Y-axis and 1 unit from the X-axis.

Point P lies in I quadrant.

∴ Coordinates of point P are (2, 1).

Coordinates of Point Q

The point Q is at a distance of 3 units from the Y-axis and 2 units from the X-axis.

Point Q lies in II quadrant.

∴ Coordinates of point Q are (–3, 2).

Coordinates of Point R

The point R is at a distance of 0 unit from the Y-axis and 2 units from the X-axis.

Point R is in negative direction of Y-axis.

∴ Coordinates of point R are (0, – 2).

Coordinates of Point S

The point S is at a distance of 4 units from the Y-axis and 3 units from the X-axis.

Point S lies in IV quadrant.

∴ Coordinates of point S are (4, – 3).

Example 6. In the following figure, O is the intersecting points of OA and OC and $OABC$ is a square of side 2 units. Find the positions of A, B and C.

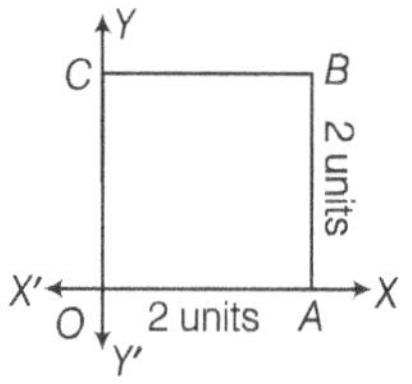

Sol. Here, position means coordinates of the point.

As the point A, lies on side OA, is at a distance of 2 units from the intersection point O, so its position will be (2, 0).

Point B lies 2 units away from both the sides, so its position will be (2, 2) and point C lies on the side OC, at a distance of 2 units from the intersection of point O, so its position will be (0, 2).

Example 7. Write down the

(i) abscissa (ii) ordinate

(iii) coordinates (iv) quadrant

in which points P, Q, R and S lie.

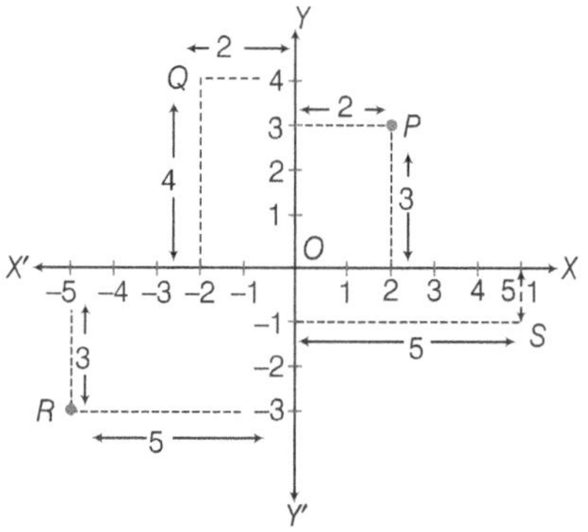

Sol. **For point P**

(i) Abscissa of the point = 2

(ii) Ordinate of the point = 3

(iii) Coordinates of the point = (2, 3)

(iv) Point of the type (+, +) lies in the I quadrant, hence the point (2, 3) lies in the I quadrant.

For point Q

(i) Abscissa of the point = – 2

(ii) Ordinate of the point = 4

(iii) Coordinates of the point = (– 2, 4)

(iv) Point of the type (–, +) lies in the II quadrant, hence the point (–2, 4) lies in the II quadrant.

For point *R*

(i) Abscissa of the point = – 5

(ii) Ordinate of the point = – 3

(iii) Coordinates of the point = (– 5, – 3)

(iv) Point of the type (–, –) lies in the III quadrant, hence the point (– 5, – 3) lies in the III quadrant.

For point *S*

(i) Abscissa of the point = 5

(ii) Ordinate of the point = – 1

(iii) Coordinates of the point = (5, – 1)

(iv) Point of the type (+, –) lies in the IV quadrant, hence the point (5, – 1) lies in the IV quadrant.

Example 8. If the coordinates of a point M are $(-2, 9)$ which can also be expressed as $(1 + x, y^2)$ and $y > 0$, then find in which quadrant do the following points lie : $A(y, x)$, $B(2, x)$, $C(x^2, y - 1)$, $D(2x, -3y)$.

Sol. Given, $(-2, 9) = (1 + x, y^2)$, $y > 0$

$\Rightarrow \quad 1 + x = -2$ and $y^2 = 9$, $y > 0$

$\Rightarrow \quad x = -3$ and $y = 3$

$\therefore$ The point $A(y, x)$ is $(3, -3)$, which lie in the IVth quadrant.

The point $B(2, x)$ is $(2, -3)$, lie in IVth quadrant.

The point $C(x^2, y - 1)$ is $(9, 2)$, lie in Ist quadrant.

The point $D(2x, -3y)$ is $(-6, -9)$, lie in IIIrd quadrant.

Plotting of Point in Cartesian Plane

Here, we will learn how to plot a point in cartesian plane, if its coordinates are given. This can be explained with the help of following example.

Example 9. Plot the points (4, 5) and (–4, 5) on a graph paper.

Sol. First, draw the coordinate axes and mark the units on both the axes such that 1 cm represents one unit.

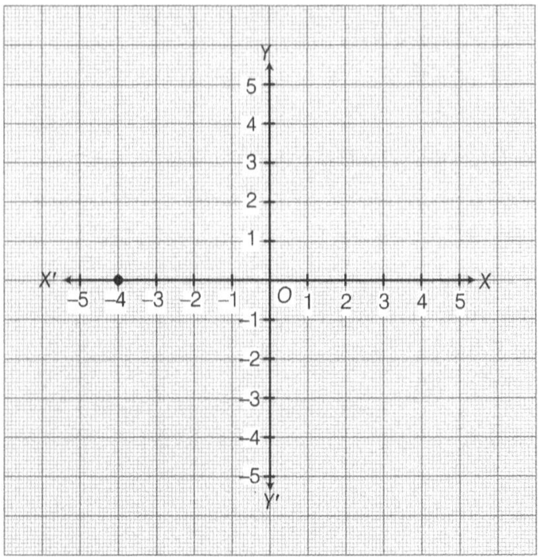

Then, the coordinates of point (4, 5) shows that the distance of this point from the Y-axis along the positive X-axis is 4 units and its distance from X-axis along the positive Y-axis is 5 units.

Similarly, (–4, 5) shows that the distance from the Y-axis along the negative X-axis is 4 units and its distance from X-axis along the positive Y-axis is 5 units.

Plotting of given points

Now, count 4 units, starting from origin on the positive X-axis and mark the point as A. Also, count the 4 units starting from origin on the negative X-axis and mark the point as P.

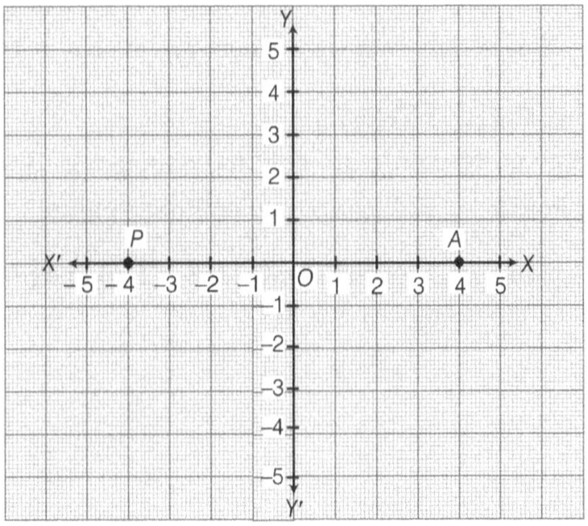

Now, start from the point A, count 5 units along the positive direction of the Y-axis and mark that point as B.

Similarly, start from the point P, count 5 units along the positive direction of the Y-axis and mark that point as Q.

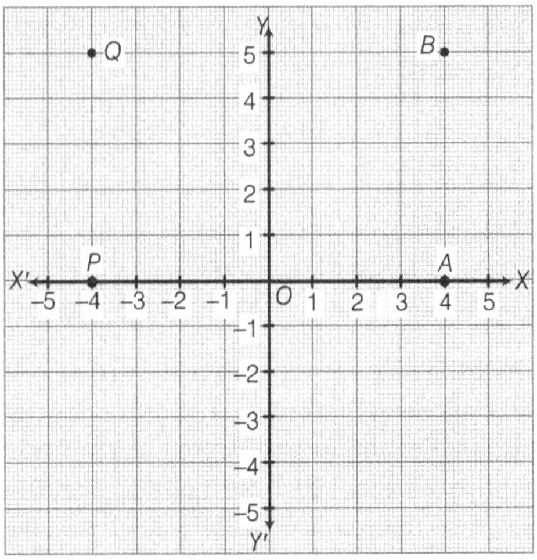

Finally, the position of the given points are

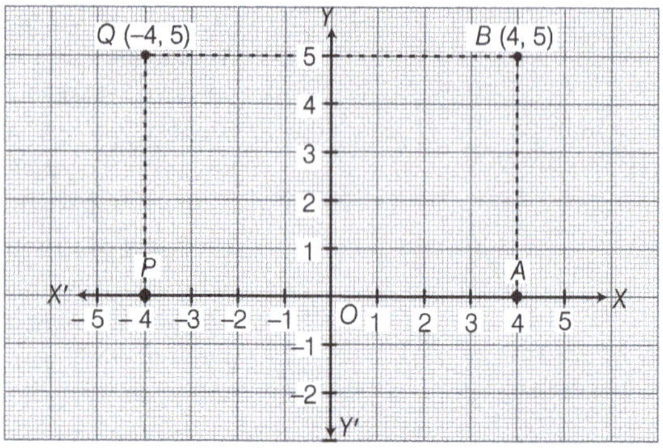

Here, B represents the position of point (4, 5) and Q represents the position of point (–4, 5) on the graph paper.

Collinear Points

Two or more points are said to collinear, if they lie on a straight line.
e.g. Points A, B, C and D are collinear points.

Example 10. Plot the points (1, 3), (2, 6) and $(-3,0)$ on a graph paper and check whether they are collinear or not.

Sol. Let the points be $A\,(1,3), B\,(2,6)$ and $C\,(-3,0)$. Now, plot these points on the graph paper.

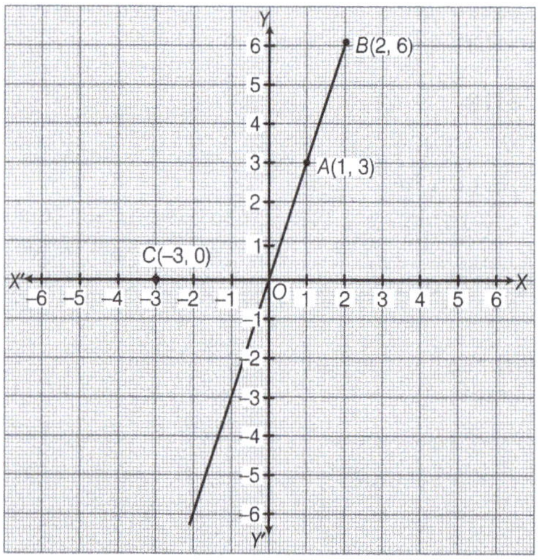

Then, join these points A and B by a straight line and extend it, we find that the point $C\,(-3,0)$ does not lie on this line. Hence, the given points (1, 3), (2, 6) and (–3, 0) are not collinear.

Example 11. Three vertices of a square are $A(2,3)$, $B(-3,3)$ and $C(-3,-2)$. Plot these points on a graph paper and hence, use it to find the coordinates of the fourth vertex. Also, find the area of the square.

Sol. Plot the points $A\ (2,3)$, $B\ (-3,3)$ and $C(-3,-2)$. Draw a parallel line to X and Y-axes from the points C and A respectively. Join the points to complete the square $ABCD$.

Now, we read the coordinates of the point D from the graph paper is $D\,(2,-2)$.

Side of square $ABCD\ = 3+2 = 5$ units

$\therefore$ Area of square $ABCD = (\text{Side})^2$

$= (5)^2$

$= 25$ sq units

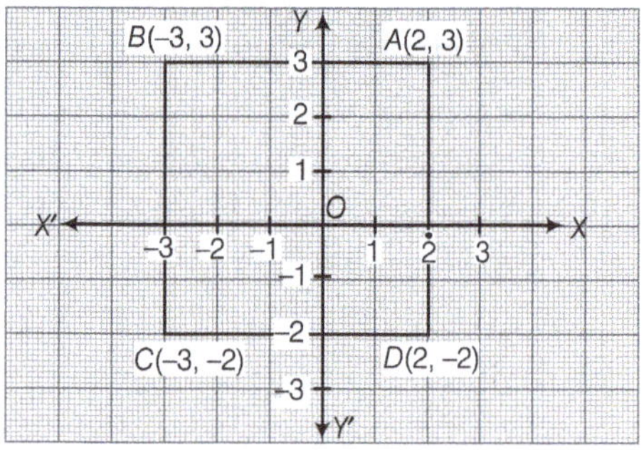

Exercise 18.1

1. Find the values of x and y, if
   (i) $(5x+1, 2y-7) = (11, -5)$.
   (ii) $(2x-3y, y-3x) = (4, -3)$.
2. Find the coordinates of points whose
   (i) abscissa is -4 and ordinate is 3.
   (ii) abscissa is -3 and lies on X-axis.
   (iii) ordinate is $\frac{5}{3}$ and lies on Y-axis.
3. In which quadrant or on which axis each of the following points lie?
   (i) $(-3, 5)$ (ii) $(4, -1)$
   (iii) $(2, 0)$ (iv) $(2, 2)$
   (v) $(-3, -6)$ (vi) $(0, -3)$
4. Consider the figure and then write the following.

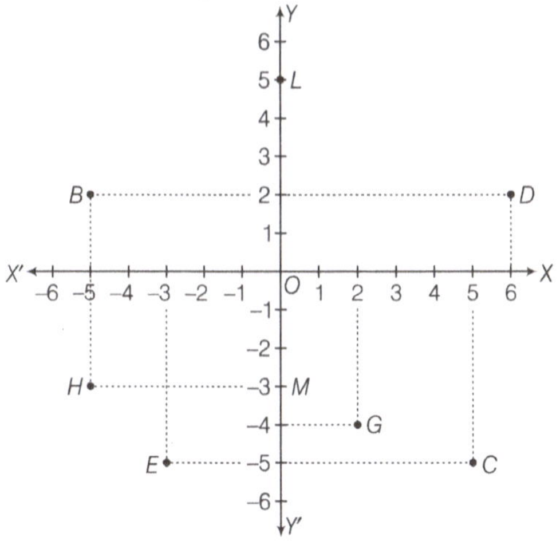

   (i) The coordinates of the point B.
   (ii) The coordinates of the point C.
   (iii) The point identified by the coordinates $(-3, -5)$.
   (iv) The point identified by the coordinates $(2, -4)$.
   (v) The abscissa of the point D.
   (vi) The ordinate of the point H.
   (vii) The coordinates of the point L.
   (viii) The coordinates of the point M.
5. Plot the points $P(2, 5)$, $Q(3, 7)$ and $R(-4, -3)$ on a graph paper and check whether they are collinear or not.
6. Plot the points $A(0, 3)$, $B(1, 5)$ and $C(-2, -1)$ on a graph paper and check whether they are collinear or not.
7. If the coordinates of a point M are $(-4, 16)$ which expressed as $(1-x, y^2)$ and $y > 0$, then find in which quadrant do the following points lie :
   (i) $P(x^2, y-1)$ (ii) $Q(2x, -3y)$
8. If $P(-2, 2)$, $Q(3, -5)$, $R(2, -2)$, $S(-3, -4)$ and $T(-6, 3)$ are plotted on the graph paper, then find the points lie in the IV quadrant.
9. On plotting the points $O(0, 0)$, $A(3, 0)$, $B(3, 4)$, $C(0, 4)$ and joining OA, AB, BC and CO. Which shape is obtained?
10. Plot the following points and write the name of the figure obtained by joining them in order.
    $P(-3, 2)$, $Q(-7, -3)$, $R(6, -3)$ and $S(2, 2)$
11. Draw the quadrilateral with vertices $(-4, 4)$, $(-6, 0)$, $(-4, -4)$ and $(-2, 0)$.
    (i) Name the type of quadrilateral.
    (ii) Find the area of the formed figure.
12. Plot the points $A(1, 2)$, $B(-4, 2)$, $C(-4, -1)$ and $D(1, -1)$.
    (i) What kind of quadrilateral is $ABCD$?
    (ii) Find the area of the quadrilateral $ABCD$.
13. Plot the points $(0, 2)$, $(3, 0)$, $(0, -2)$ and $(-3, 0)$ on a graph paper. Join these points (in order).
    (i) Name the figure so obtained.
    (ii) Find the area of the figure obtained.
14. In the adjoining figure, ΔABC and ΔADB are equilateral triangles. Find the coordinates of the point C and D.

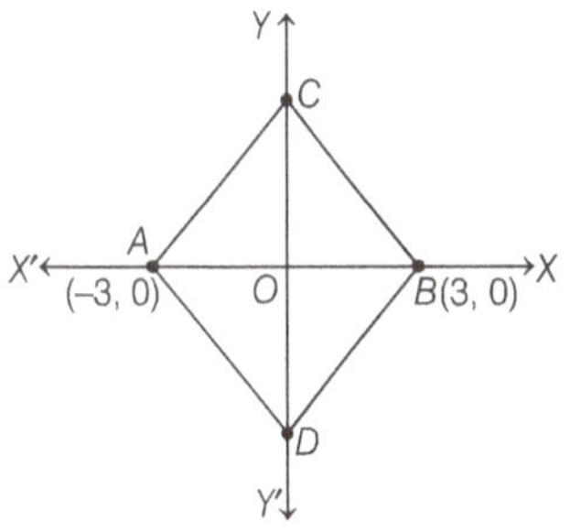

15. Three vertices of a square are $A(1, 3)$, $B(-4, 3)$ and $C(-4, -2)$. Plot these points on a graph paper.
    (i) Find the coordinates of the fourth vertex.
    (ii) Find the area of the square.
16. Three vertices of a parallelogram are $A(-2, 2)$, $B(6, 2)$ and $C(4, -3)$. Plot these points on a graph paper.
    (i) Find the coordinates of the fourth vertex D.
    (ii) Find the coordinates of the mid-point of the side CD.
    (iii) What is the area of the parallelogram?

Dependent and Independent Variables and Graphs of Linear Equations in Two Variables

Variable

Variables mean the terms which varies in their values,
e.g. the linear equation of the form $4x - 5y = 6$, $y = mx + c$ etc. the letters x and y are called variables.

Variables are of two types which are discussed below

Independent and Dependent Variables

If a linear equation in x and y is expressed as y in terms of x, then x is called **independent variable** and y is called **dependent variable**.

e.g. (i) $y = 2x + 3$ (ii) $y = 5 - \frac{x}{3}$

Here, x is independent variable and y is dependent variable. Similarly, if a linear equation in x and y is expressed as x in terms of y, then y is called independent variable and x is dependent variable.

e.g. (i) $x = 3y + 7$ (ii) $x = 3 - \frac{4y}{7}$

Example 12. Express the equation $3x - 4y + 12 = 0$ in the form, so that

(i) x is independent variable and y is dependent variable.
(ii) y is independent variable and x is dependent variable.

Sol.

(i) We have, $3x - 4y + 12 = 0 \Rightarrow -4y = -12 - 3x$

$\Rightarrow \quad 4y = 12 + 3x \Rightarrow y = \frac{12 + 3x}{4} = 3 + \frac{3x}{4}$

(ii) We have, $3x - 4y + 12 = 0$

$\Rightarrow \quad 3x = 4y - 12 \Rightarrow x = \frac{4y}{3} - \frac{12}{3} \Rightarrow x = \frac{4y}{3} - 4$

Graph of Linear Equations

The graph of linear equations of the form $ax + by + c = 0$, where a, b and c are real numbers and $a \neq 0$, $b \neq 0$ will always, be a straight line.

To draw its graph, we use the following steps

***Step* I** Write the given linear equation and express y in terms of x

$$\Rightarrow \quad y = -\frac{a}{b}x - \frac{c}{b} \quad \ldots(i)$$

***Step* II** Put the different arbitrary values of x in Eq. (i) and find the corresponding values of y.

***Step* III** A table as follow by writing the values of y below the corresponding value of x as

x	x_1	x_2	x_3	x_4
y	y_1	y_2	y_3	y_4

***Step* IV** Draw the coordinate axes on graph paper and take a suitable scale to plot points $(x_1, y_1), (x_2, y_2), \ldots$ on graph paper.

***Step* V** Join the points $(x_1, y_1), (x_2, y_2), \ldots$ we get a straight line. The line so obtained is the required graph of the given linear equation.

Example 13. Draw the graph of the equation $3 = 2x + y$.

Sol. Given equation is $3 = 2x + y$ and it can be written as

$$y = 3 - 2x \quad \ldots(i)$$

When $x = 0$, then $y = 3 - 2(0) = 3$

When $x = 1$, then $y = 3 - 2(1) = 1$

When $x = -1$, then $y = 3 - 2(-1) = 5$

Thus, we have the following table

x	0	1	–1
y	3	1	5
(x, y)	A(0, 3)	B(1, 1)	C(–1, 5)

Now, draw the coordinate axes XOX' and YOY' and then plot the points $A(0, 3)$, $B(1, 1)$ and $C(-1, 5)$ on the graph. and join these points, we get a line BC.

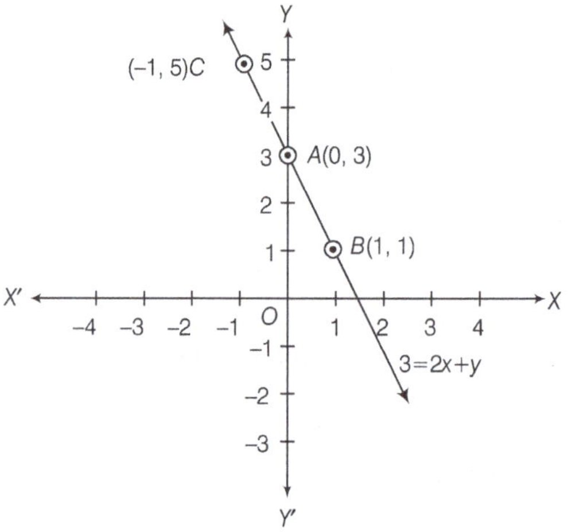

Hence, the line BC represents the required graph of given linear equation.

Solutions of Pair of Linear Equations

Any pair of values of x and y which satisfies both the equations $a_1x + b_1y + c_1 = 0$ and $a_2x + b_2y + c_2 = 0$, is called a solution of a given pair of linear equations.

A pair of linear equations in two variables can be solved by two methods namely graphical method and algebraic method. But here we will discuss only graphical method.

Graphical Method for Solution of a Pair of Linear Equations

Let us consider a pair of linear equations in two variables as $a_1x + b_1y + c_1 = 0$ and $a_2x + b_2y + c_2 = 0$. These linear equations will represent pair of straight lines, both to be considered together, with only one of the following three possibilities

***Case* I** When the graph of system of linear equations will represent two intersecting lines, the coordinates of point of intersection, say (a, b), is the solution of the pair of linear equations. In this case, there is only one point of intersection which is unique, so the system has unique solution and such pair of linear equations is called **consistent**.

***Case* II** When the graph of system of linear equations will represent two parallel lines, there is no point of intersection and lines are parallel consequently there is no pair of values of x and y which satisfy the given linear equations. Thus, system has no solution and such pair of linear equations is called **inconsistent.**

***Case* III** When the graph of system of linear equations will represent coincident or overlapping lines, there are infinitely many common points.

Thus, system has infinitely many solutions and such pair of linear equations is called **dependent/consistent**.

Example 14. Solve graphically the pair of equations $2x + y = 6$ and $2x - y + 2 = 0$.

Sol. Given, equations are $2x + y = 6$ and $2x - y + 2 = 0$.

Table for equation $2x + y = 6$ or $y = 6 - 2x$ is

x	0	1	3
$y = 6 - 2x$	6	4	0
Points	$B(0, 6)$	$E(1, 4)$	$A(3, 0)$

Now, plot all these points on a graph paper and join them to get a line AB.

Table for equation $2x - y + 2 = 0$ or $y = 2x + 2$

x	0	−1	1
$y = 2x + 2$	2	0	4
Points	$D(0, 2)$	$C(-1, 0)$	$E(1, 4)$

Now, plot all these points on a graph paper and join them to get a line CE.

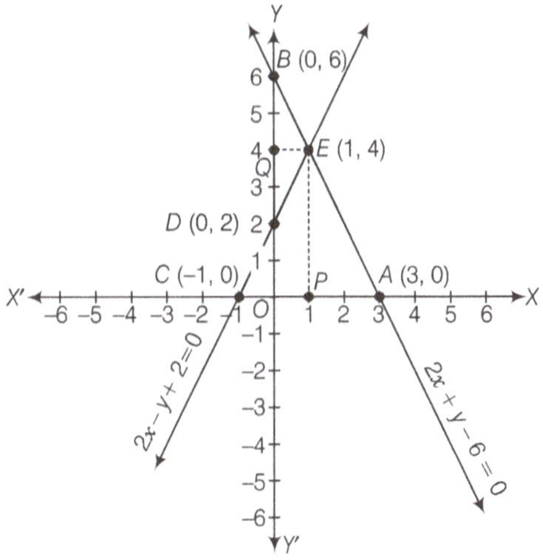

It is clear from the graph that pair of equations intersects graphically at point $E(1, 4)$, i.e. $x = 1$ and $y = 4$.

Hence, $x = 1$ and $y = 4$ is the solution of the given pair of linear equations.

Example 15. Solve graphically the pair of linear equations $3x - 4y + 3 = 0$ and $3x + 4y - 21 = 0$. Find the coordinate of the vertices of triangular region formed by these lines and X-axis. Also, calculate the area of this triangle.

Sol. Given, pair of linear equations is $3x - 4y + 3 = 0$ ...(i)

and $3x + 4y - 21 = 0$ ...(ii)

Table for $3x - 4y + 3 = 0$ or $y = \dfrac{3x + 3}{4}$ is

x	3	−1
$y = \dfrac{3x+3}{4}$	3	0
Points	$A(3, 3)$	$B(-1, 0)$

Plot the points $A(3, 3)$ and $B(-1, 0)$ on the graph paper and join them to get the straight line AB.

Now, table for $3x + 4y - 21 = 0$

or $y = \dfrac{21 - 3x}{4}$ is

x	3	7
$y=\dfrac{21-3x}{4}$	3	0
Points	$A(3, 3)$	$C(7, 0)$

Plot the points A (3, 3) and C (7, 0) on same graph paper and join them to get the straight line AC.

The graph of given equations is

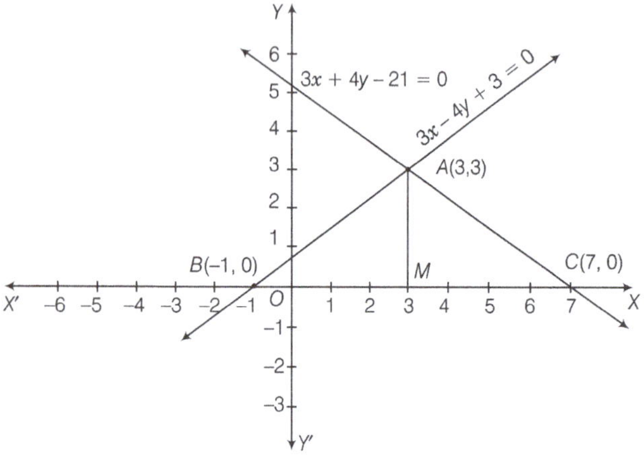

The coordinates of the vertices of ΔABC are $A(3, 3)$, $B(-1, 0)$ and $C(7, 0)$.

$\therefore$ Area of $\Delta ABC = \frac{1}{2} \times BC \times AM$

$= \frac{1}{2} \times 8 \times 3 = 12$ sq units

[Here, $BC = 1 + 7 = 8$ units and $AM = 3$ units]

Example 16. Write an equation of a line passing through the point representing solution of the pair of linear equations $x + y = 2$ and $2x - y = 1$. How many such lines can we find?

Sol. Given, pair of linear equations is

$x + y - 2 = 0$ ...(i)

and $2x - y - 1 = 0$ ...(ii)

Now, table for $x + y = 2$ or $y = 2 - x$ is

x	0	2
$y = 2 - x$	2	0
Points	$A(0, 2)$	$B(2, 0)$

Plot the points A (0, 2) and B (2, 0) and join them to get the straight line AB.

Table for $2x - y - 1 = 0$ or $y = 2x - 1$ is

x	0	2
$y = 2x - 1$	−1	3
Points	$C(0, -1)$	$D(2, 3)$

Now, plot the points C (0, −1) and D (2, 3) and join them to get the straight line CD. The lines AB and CD intersect at E (1, 1). So, the solution of the given pair of linear equations is (1, 1).

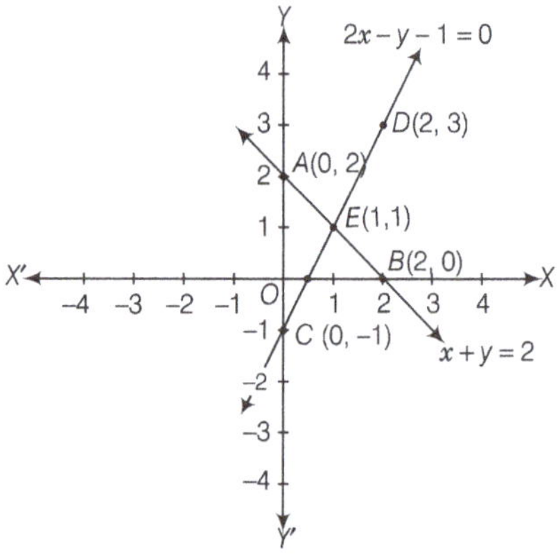

It is clear from the graph that infinite lines can pass through the intersection point of linear equations $x + y = 2$ and $2x - y = 1$.

Exercise 18.2

1. Find the independent and dependent variables of the following.
   (i) $y = \dfrac{3x+5}{8}$ (ii) $x = \dfrac{4y-3}{2}$ (iii) $x = 3y - 2$.
2. Draw the graph of the following equations.
   (i) $2x + y = 6$ (ii) $y = 3x - 4$ (iii) $y = -2x + \dfrac{3}{2}$
3. Draw the graph of $7 - 3(1 - y) = -5 + 2x$ and find the area of triangle enclosed by the graph and the coordinate axes.
4. For each of the following linear equation, sketch the graph and state whether the lines drawn are parallel or perpendicular to each other.
   (i) $y = 3x - 1$ and $y = 3x + 2$
   (ii) $2x - 3y = 6$ and $\dfrac{x}{2} + \dfrac{y}{3} = 1$
5. Solve graphically the following pair of equations.
   $2x - y + 3 = 0$ and $3x - 5y + 1 = 0$
6. Solve graphically the pair of linear equations $x - y = -1$ and $2x + y - 1 = 0$. Also, find the vertices of the triangle formed by these lines and X-axis.
7. Solve graphically the pair of linear equations $3x + y - 11 = 0$, $x - y - 1 = 0$. Also, find the vertices of the triangle formed by these lines and Y-axis.
8. Solve the following pairs of linear equations graphically and find the vertices of the triangle formed by these lines and Y-axis.
   $x - y + 1 = 0$, $3x + 2y - 12 = 0$
9. Sketch the graph of following linear equation, $2x + 3y = 10$ and $4x + 6y = 20$.
   (i) State the lines are parallel, intersect or coincide.
   (ii) State equations are consistent or inconsistent.

Distance Formula

Distance between Two Points in a Cartesian Plane

The distance between any two points $P(x_1, y_1)$ and $Q(x_2, y_2)$ is given by $PQ = \sqrt{(x_2 - x_1)^2 + (y_2 - y_1)^2}$

or $\quad PQ = \sqrt{(x_1 - x_2)^2 + (y_1 - y_2)^2}$

i.e. $\quad PQ = \sqrt{(\text{Difference of abscissae})^2 + (\text{Difference of ordinates})^2}$

Proof Let $X'OX$ and $Y'OY$ be the coordinate axes. Let $P(x_1, y_1)$ and $Q(x_2, y_2)$ be the given points in XY-plane.

Draw perpendicular lines PR and QS to the X-axis. Again, draw a perpendicular line from the point P on QS to meet it at the point T.

Now, $\quad OR = x_1$ and $OS = x_2$

$\therefore \quad RS = OS - OR = x_2 - x_1 = PT$

Also, $\quad SQ = y_2$ and $ST = PR = y_1$

$\therefore \quad QT = QS - ST = y_2 - y_1$

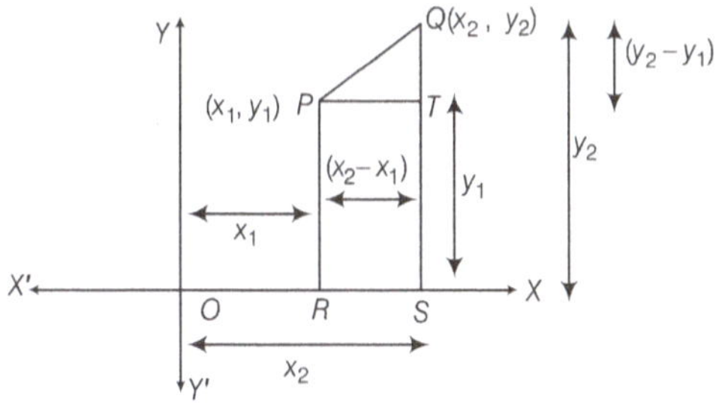

In right angled ΔPTQ,

$$PQ^2 = PT^2 + QT^2 \quad \text{[by Pythagoras theorem]}$$
$$= (x_2 - x_1)^2 + (y_2 - y_1)^2$$

$\Rightarrow \quad PQ = \sqrt{(x_2 - x_1)^2 + (y_2 - y_1)^2}$

or $\quad PQ = \sqrt{(x_1 - x_2)^2 + (y_1 - y_2)^2}$

Here, we will take only positive square root, because distance is always non-negative.

Note Let $P(x, y)$ be a point and $O(0, 0)$ be the origin. Then, by distance formula, distance of P from O is $OP = \sqrt{x^2 + y^2}$

Example 17. Find the distance between the points $P(-6, 7)$ and $Q(-1, -5)$.

Sol. Here, $x_1 = -6, y_1 = 7, x_2 = -1$ and $y_2 = -5$

$\therefore$ Distance between two points,

$$PQ = \sqrt{(x_2 - x_1)^2 + (y_2 - y_1)^2} \quad \text{[by distance formula]}$$
$$= \sqrt{(-1 + 6)^2 + (-5 - 7)^2}$$
$$= \sqrt{(5)^2 + (-12)^2}$$
$$= \sqrt{25 + 144} = \sqrt{169} = 13 \text{ units}$$

Example 18. Find the distance of the point (20, 15) from origin.

Sol. Given, points are P (20, 15) and origin O (0, 0).

Here, $(x_1, y_1) = (20, 15)$ and $(x_2, y_2) = (0, 0)$

$\therefore$ Distance between two points,

$$OP = \sqrt{(x_2 - x_1)^2 + (y_2 - y_1)^2} \quad \text{[by distance formula]}$$
$$= \sqrt{(0 - 20)^2 + (0 - 15)^2} = \sqrt{(20)^2 + (15)^2}$$
$$= \sqrt{400 + 225} = \sqrt{625} = 25 \text{ units}$$

Example 19. Find the value of y, if the distance between the points $(2, y)$ and $(-4, 3)$ is 10 units.

Sol. Let the points $A(2, y)$ and $B(-4, 3)$.

Here, $(x_1, y_1) = (2, y)$ and $(x_2, y_2) = (-4, 3)$

$\therefore$ Distance between two points,

$$AB = \sqrt{(x_1 - x_2)^2 + (y_1 - y_2)^2} \quad \text{[by distance formula]}$$

$\Rightarrow \quad AB = \sqrt{(2 + 4)^2 + (y - 3)^2} \Rightarrow 10 = \sqrt{(6)^2 + y^2 + 9 - 6y}$

$[\because AB = 10 \text{ and } (a - b)^2 = a^2 + b^2 - 2ab]$

On squaring both sides, we get

$$100 = 36 + y^2 + 9 - 6y \Rightarrow 100 = 45 + y^2 - 6y$$

$\Rightarrow \quad y^2 - 6y - 55 = 0$

$\Rightarrow \quad y^2 - 11y + 5y - 55 = 0 \quad$ [by factorisation]

$\Rightarrow \quad y(y - 11) + 5(y - 11) = 0$

$\Rightarrow \quad (y - 11)(y + 5) = 0$

$\Rightarrow \quad y - 11 = 0$ or $y + 5 = 0 \Rightarrow y = 11$ or $y = -5$

Hence, the required values of y are 11 and -5.

Different Types of Problems Based on Distance Formula

There are so many problems which can be solved by using distance formula. Some of them are discussed below

Type I Problems Based on Collinearity of Points

If collinearity of three points, say A, B and C, then show that sum of two shorter lengths is equal to the largest length.

Example 20. Check the points $(1, -1)$, $(5, 2)$ and $(9, 5)$ are collinear.

Sol. Let the given points be $A = (1, -1)$, $B = (5, 2)$ and $C = (9, 5)$.

Then, distance between the point A and B

$$AB = \sqrt{(5 - 1)^2 + (2 + 1)^2}$$

$\left[\because \text{distance} = \sqrt{(x_2 - x_1)^2 + (y_2 - y_1)^2}\right]$

$$= \sqrt{(4)^2 + (3)^2} = \sqrt{16 + 9} = \sqrt{25} = 5 \text{ units}$$

$BC = \sqrt{(9-5)^2 + (5-2)^2}$

$= \sqrt{(4)^2 + (3)^2} = \sqrt{25} = 5$ units

$AC = \sqrt{(9-1)^2 + (5+1)^2} = \sqrt{(8)^2 + (6)^2} = \sqrt{100} = 10$ units

Clearly, $AC = AB + BC$

Hence, A, B and C are collinear points.

Type II Problems Based on Equidistant Points

To find a point, say P, which is equidistant from two points, say A and B, we take $AP = BP$.

Example 21. If the point $P(x, y)$ is equidistant from the points $A(5, 1)$ and $B(1, 5)$, then prove that $x = y$.

Sol. Given, point $P(x, y)$ is equidistant from the points A (5,1) and B(1,5).

$\therefore \quad AP = BP$

$\Rightarrow \quad (AP^2 = BP^2$ [squaring both sides]

$\Rightarrow \quad (x-5)^2 + (y-1)^2 = (x-1)^2 + (y-5)^2$

[$\because$ distance $= \sqrt{(x_2 - x_1)^2 + (y_2 - y_1)^2}$]

$\Rightarrow x^2 + 25 - 10x + y^2 + 1 - 2y = x^2 + 1 - 2x + y^2 + 25 - 10y$

$\Rightarrow \quad -10x + 2x = -10y + 2y$

$\Rightarrow \quad -8x = -8y$

$\Rightarrow \quad x = y$ **Hence proved**

Example 22. Find a point on X-axis, which is equidistant from the points (7, 6) and (−3, 4).

Sol. Let $A(x, 0)$ be any point on the X-axis, which is equidistant from B (7, 6) and C(−3, 4).

$\therefore \quad AB = AC$

$\Rightarrow \quad AB^2 = AC^2$ [squaring both sides]

$\Rightarrow \quad (7-x)^2 + (6-0)^2 = (-3-x)^2 + (4-0)^2$

[$\because$ distance $= \sqrt{(x_2 - x_1)^2 + (y_2 - y_1)^2}$]

$\Rightarrow \quad 49 + x^2 - 14x + 36 = 9 + x^2 + 6x + 16$

$\Rightarrow \quad 20x = 60$

$\Rightarrow \quad x = 3$

Hence, the required point is (3, 0).

Example 23. Find the coordinates of the circumcentre of the ΔABC; whose vertices A, B and C are (4, 6), (0, 4) and (6, 2) respectively.

Sol. Let the circumcentre of the triangle be $P(x, y)$.

Then, $PA = PB$ [$\because A \equiv (4, 6), B \equiv (0, 4)$]

$PA^2 = PB^2$ [$\because$ squaring both sides]

$\Rightarrow \quad (x-4)^2 + (y-6)^2 = (x-0)^2 + (y-4)^2$

$\Rightarrow x^2 - 8x + 16 + y^2 - 12y + 36 = x^2 + y^2 - 8y + 16$

$\Rightarrow \quad -8x - 4y = -36$

$\Rightarrow \quad 2x + y = 9$ ...(i)

and $PA = PC$ [$\because A \equiv (4, 6), C \equiv (6, 2)$]

$PA^2 = PC^2$ [$\because$ squaring both sides]

$\Rightarrow \quad (x-4)^2 + (y-6)^2 = (x-6)^2 + (y-2)^2$

$\Rightarrow x^2 - 8x + 16 + y^2 - 12y + 36$

$= x^2 - 12x + 36 + y^2 - 4y + 4$

$\Rightarrow \quad 4x - 8y = -12$

$\Rightarrow \quad x - 2y = -3$ ...(ii)

On solving Eqs. (i) and (ii), we get $x = 3$ and $y = 3$

$\therefore$ The circumcentre of the given triangle = (3, 3)

Note Circumcentre is the point which is equidistant from the vertices of the triangle if P is the circumcentre, then $PA = PB = PC =$ Circumradius.

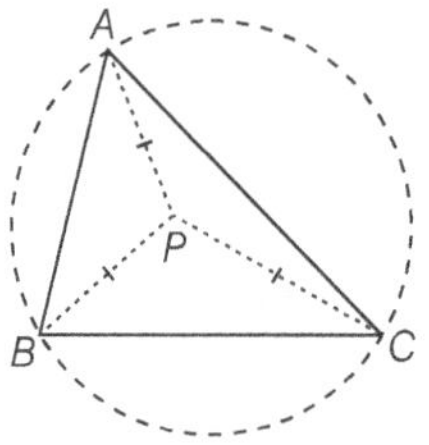

Type III Problems Based on Geometrical Figure

Sometimes, three or four points are given and we have to show that the given points form given geometrical figure or not.

(i) **triangle**, prove that sum of lengths of any two sides is greater than the length of third side.

(ii) **isosceles triangle**, prove that two sides are equal.

(iii) **right angled triangle**, prove that sides of triangle satisfy Pythagoras theorem.

(iv) **equilateral triangle**, prove that all three sides are equal and parallel.

(v) **parallelogram**, prove that the opposite sides are equal and parallel.

(vi) **rectangle**, prove that opposite sides are equal and the diagonals are also equal.

(vii) **square**, prove that the four sides are equal and the diagonals are also equal.

(viii) **rhombus**, prove that the four sides are equal.

Example 24. Do the points (3, 2), (−2, −3) and (2, 3) form a triangle? If so, name the type of triangle formed.

Sol. Let the given points be A (3, 2), B (−2, −3) and C (2,3).

Here, $AB = \sqrt{(-2-3)^2 + (-3-2)^2}$

[$\because$ distance $= \sqrt{(x_2 - x_1)^2 + (y_2 - y_1)^2}$]

$= \sqrt{(-5)^2 + (-5)^2} = \sqrt{25 + 25} = \sqrt{50}$

$= 7.07$ units (approx.)

$BC = \sqrt{(2+2)^2 + (3+3)^2} = \sqrt{(4)^2 + (6)^2}$

$= \sqrt{16 + 36} = \sqrt{52} = 7.21$ units (approx.)

and $CA = \sqrt{(3-2)^2 + (2-3)^2} = \sqrt{(1)^2 + (-1)^2} = \sqrt{1+1}$

$= \sqrt{2} = 1.41$ units (approx.)

Given points A, B and C will form a triangle, if sum of

any two sides is greater than third side.
Here, $CA + AB > BC$.
So, the given points forms a triangle.
Also, $(\sqrt{52})^2 = (\sqrt{50})^2 + (\sqrt{2})^2 \Rightarrow BC^2 = AB^2 + CA^2$
So, by converse of Pythagoras theorem, $\angle A = 90°$.
Hence, ΔBAC is a right angled triangle.

Example 25. Show that the points (2, 3), (3, 4), (5, 6) and (4, 5) are the vertices of a parallelogram.

Sol. Let $A(2, 3)$, $B(3, 4)$, $C(5, 6)$ and $D(4, 5)$ be the given points.
Then, by distance formula,

$$AB = \sqrt{(3-2)^2 + (4-3)^2} = \sqrt{(1)^2 + (1)^2} = \sqrt{2} \text{ units}$$

$$BC = \sqrt{(5-3)^2 + (6-4)^2} = \sqrt{(2)^2 + (2)^2} = \sqrt{4+4} = \sqrt{8} = 2\sqrt{2} \text{ units}$$

$$CD = \sqrt{(4-5)^2 + (5-6)^2} = \sqrt{(-1)^2 + (-1)^2} = \sqrt{2} \text{ units}$$

and $AD = \sqrt{(4-2)^2 + (5-3)^2} = \sqrt{(2)^2 + (2)^2} = \sqrt{4+4} = \sqrt{8} = 2\sqrt{2}$ units

Thus, $AB = CD$ and $AD = BC$
Hence, the opposite sides are equal.
So, it is a parallelogram.

Also, $AC = \sqrt{(5-2)^2 + (6-3)^2} = \sqrt{3^2 + 3^2} = \sqrt{9+9} = 3\sqrt{2}$ units

and $BD = \sqrt{(4-3)^2 + (5-4)^2} = \sqrt{(1)^2 + (1)^2} = \sqrt{1+1} = \sqrt{2}$ units

$\because$ $AC \neq BD$
So, the diagonals are not equal.
Hence, the given vertices represent a parallelogram.

Exercise 18.3

1. Find the distance between the following points, using distance formula.
   (i) $(-7, -3)$ and $(-5, 11)$ (ii) (3, 1) and (5, 3)
   (iii) (0, 8) and (6, 0) (iv) $(-1, 1)$ and $(3, -5)$
   (v) $(2a, a)$ and $(-a, 3a)$
2. Find the distance of the following points from the origin.
   (i) $(3, -4)$
   (ii) (7, 0)
   (iii) $(0, -10)$
   (iv) (a, a)
   (v) $(\sqrt{2}, 1)$
3. (i) Find the perpendicular distance of $A(5, 12)$ from the Y-axis.
   (ii) Find the perpendicular distance of the point $P(2, 3)$ from the X-axis.
4. Find the points on the X-axis which are at a distance of $2\sqrt{5}$ units from the point $(7, -4)$. How many such points are there?
5. (i) Show that $A(2, 3)$, $B(1, 4)$ and $C(-2, 7)$ are collinear points.
   (ii) Show that the points (3, 2), $\left(4, \frac{5}{2}\right)$ and (5, 3) are collinear.
6. Find the relation between x and y such that the point (x, y) is equidistant from (7, 1) and (3, 5).
7. Find the point on Y-axis, equidistant from two points $A(-3, 4)$ and $B(3, 6)$ on the same plane.
8. Do the points (4, 2), (7, 5) and (9, 7) form a triangle?
9. If the point $A(2, -4)$ is equidistant from $P(3, 8)$ and $Q(-10, y)$, then find the value of y. Also, find distance PQ.
10. Find the points which are at a distance of $\sqrt{10}$ units from the point (4, 3) given that the ordinate of the points is twice the abscissa.
11. Find the coordinates of the circumcentre of the ΔABC, whose vertices A, B and C are (4, 6), (0, 4) and (6, 12), respectively.
12. $AOBC$ is a rectangle whose three vertices are $A(0, 3)$, $O(0, 0)$ and $B(5, 0)$. What are the length of its diagonals?
13. (i) Prove that the points $A(0, 1)$, $B(1, 4)$, $C(4, 3)$ and $D(3, 0)$ are the vertices of a square.
    (ii) Show that the points $A(2, -2)$, $B(14, 10)$, $C(11, 13)$ and $D(-1, 1)$ are the vertices of a rectangle.
    (iii) Show that quadrilateral $PQRS$ formed by vertices $P(22, 5)$, $Q(7, 10)$, $R(12, 11)$ and $S(3, 24)$ is not a parallelogram.
    (iv) Show that the points $A(5, -1)$, $B(8, 3)$, $C(4, 0)$ and $D(1, -4)$ are the vertices of a rhombus.

Chapter Practice

a. 1 Mark Questions

1. Which quadrant the point (– 2, 5) lies?

(a) I quadrant (b) II quadrant
(c) III quadrant (d) IV quadrant

2. Abscissa of the coordinate (5.7, – 2) is

(a) 3.7 (b) 5.7
(c) – 2 (d) None of these

3. The area of a square whose vertices are $A(0, -2)$, $B(3, 1)$, $C(0, 4)$ and $D(-3, 1)$ is

(a) 18 sq units (b) 15 sq units
(c) $\sqrt{18}$ sq units (d) $\sqrt{15}$ sq units

4. The point which lies on Y-axis at a distance of 5 units in the negative direction of Y-axis is

(a) (0, 5) (b) (5, 0) (c) (0, –5) (d) (– 5, 0)

5. The pair of equation $x = a$ and $y = b$ graphically represents lines which are

(a) parallel (b) intersecting at (b, a)
(c) coincident (d) intersecting at (a, b)

6. If the point $P(a, b)$ lies in the fourth quadrant, then

(a) $a > b$ (b) $a < b$
(c) $a = b$ (d) None of these

b. 3 Marks Questions

7. In the given figure, O is the intersecting points of OA and OC and $OABC$ is a square of side 4 units. Find the positions of A, B and C.

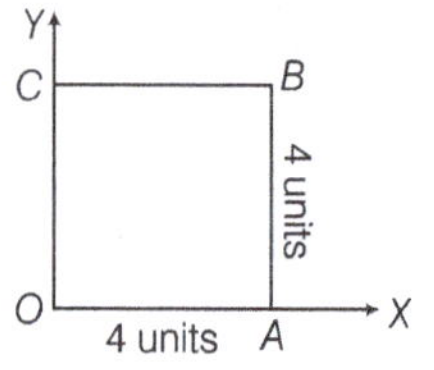

8. Draw the graph of the equation $y = 3x$.

9. Plot the points (x, y) given in the following table on the plane, choosing suitable units of distance on the axes.

x	– 2	– 1	0	1	3
y	8	7	–1.25	3	– 1

10. Draw the graph of the equation $6 - 1.5x = 0$.

11. (i) Plot the points $M(5, -3)$ and $N(-3, -3)$.

(ii) What is the length of MN?

(iii) Find the coordinates of points A, B and C lying on MN such that $MA = AB = BC = CN$.

12. Find the distance between the following points.

(i) $\left(-\frac{6}{3}, -3\right)$ and $\left(-4, \frac{-7}{5}\right)$

(ii) (a, b) and $(-a, -b)$

(iii) (– 5, 7) and (–1, 3)

13. Find the distance of the following points from the origin.

(i) (– 5, 3)

(ii) (3, – 6)

(iii) (0, 3)

14. Find the perimeter of a triangle with vertices (0, 4), (0, 0) and (3, 0).

15. If the distance between the points $(4, p)$ and $(1, 0)$ is 5, then find the value(s) of p.

c. 4/5 Marks Questions

16. From the given graph, write

(i) the coordinates of the points B and F.

(ii) the abscissa of points D and H.

(iii) the ordinate of the points A and C.

(iv) the perpendicular distance of the point G from the X-axis.

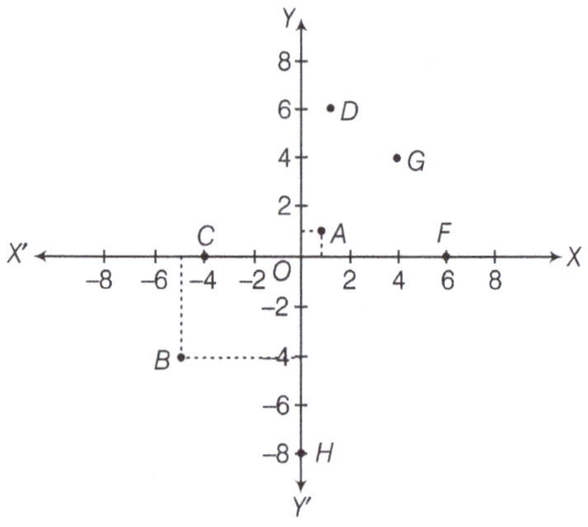

17. In which quadrant or on which axes do these points (–2, 4), (3, – 1), (–1, 0), (1, 2) and (–3, – 5) lie? Verify your answer by locating them on the cartesian plane.

18. Write down the
(i) abscissa for the points A, B, C and D.
(ii) ordinate for the points A, B, C and D.
(iii) coordinates for the points A, B, C and D.
(iv) quadrant in which these points lie.

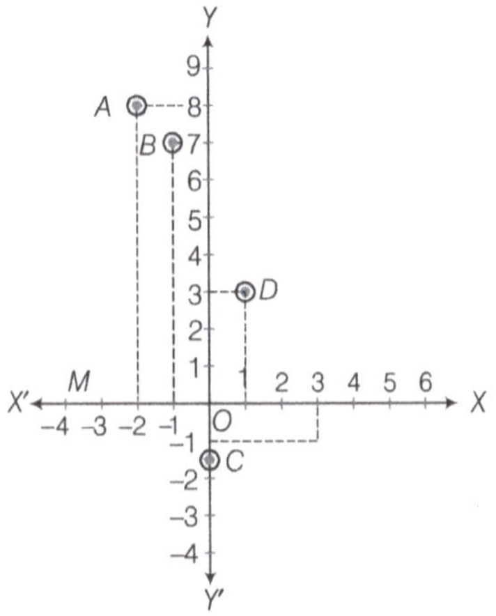

19. Plot the points (1, 1), (2, – 3) and (–1, – 2) and check whether they are collinear or not.

20. Plot the points (1, 1), (2, – 2) and (–1, – 2) and check whether they are collinear or not. If not collinear, then determine the area of the figure.

21. Draw the graph of following linear equations.
(i) $4y - 9 = 0$ (ii) $x - 2y = 3$ (iii) $x - 3y = -7$

22. Draw the graphs of the lines represent by the equations $y = 2x + 1$ and $x + 2y + 3 = 0$. Are these lines perpendicular to each other? Also, find the coordinates of their point of intersection.

23. Draw the graphs of the equations $x - y + 1 = 0$ and $3x + 2y - 12 = 0$. Determine the coordinates of the vertices of the triangle formed by these lines and the X-axis and shade the triangular region.

24. A triangle is formed by the lines $x + 2y - 3 = 0$, $3x - 2y + 7 = 0$ and $y + 1 = 0$. Find graphically
(i) the coordinates of the vertices of the triangle.
(ii) the area of the triangle.

25. Solve graphically the equations $4x - 3y = 0$ and $2x + 3y - 18 = 0$. Also, find the ratio of the areas of the triangles formed by these lines and the coordinates axes.

d. 6 Marks Questions

26. Draw the graph of a linear equation in x and y passing through $A(-1, -1)$ and $B(2, 5)$. Find the values of h and k, if the graph of linear equation passes through $(h, 4)$ and $\left(\frac{1}{2}, k\right)$.

27. Draw the graph (straight line) given by equation $x - 3y = 18$. If the straight line drawn passes through the point $(P, -5)$ and $(6, q)$, find the values of p and q.

28. If the distance between the points $A(1, 1)$ and $B(x, 1)$ is 5 units, then find the value(s) of x.

29. Find the point on Y-axis, which is equidistant from two points $A(-3, 4)$ and $B(3, 6)$ on the same plane.

30. If $A(x, y)$ is a point on the line joining the points $B(2, -3)$ and $C(-4, 5)$ and A is equidistant from B and C, then prove that $3x - 4y + 7 = 0$.

31. Name the types of quadrilateral formed, if any, by the following points and give reason for your answer.
(i) $A(-1, -2)$, $B(1, 0)$, $C(-1, 2)$, $D(-3, 0)$
(ii) $A(-3, 5)$, $B(3, 1)$, $C(0, 3)$, $D(-1, -4)$
(iii) $A(4, 5)$, $B(7, 6)$, $C(4, 3)$, $D(1, 2)$

32. Points $A(-1, y)$ and $B(5, 7)$ lie on a circle with centre $O(2, -3y)$. Find the value of y. Hence, find the radius of the circle.

33. Find the points on the X-axis whose distance from the points (2, 3) and $\left(\frac{3}{2}, -1\right)$ are in ratio 2 : 1.

34. The centre of a circle is $(2a, a - 7)$. Find the values of a if the circle passes through the point $(11, -9)$ and has diameter $10\sqrt{2}$ units.

35. If the point $P(x, y)$ is equidistant from the points $A(a + b, b - a)$ and $B(a - b, a + b)$, prove that $bx = ay$.

Hints and Answers

Exercise 18.1

1. **Hint** Do same as Example 1.

   Ans. (i) $x = 2$ and $y = 1$ (ii) $x = \frac{5}{7}$ and $y = -\frac{6}{7}$

2. (i) **Hint** Here, $x = -4$ and $y = 3$.

   The coordinate of points are (x, y). **Ans.** $(-4, 3)$

   (ii) **Hint** Point lies on X-axis have ordinate 0.

   Ans. $(-3, 0)$

   (iii) **Hint** Point lies on Y-axis have abscissa 0.

   Ans. $\left(0, \frac{5}{3}\right)$

3. **Hint** Do same as Example 7 (iv).

   Ans. (i) II quadrant (ii) IV quadrant
   (iii) X-axis (iv) I quadrant
   (v) III quadrant (vi) Y-axis

4. **Ans.** (i) $(-5, 2)$ (ii) $(5, -5)$ (iii) E (iv) G (v) 6
   (vi) -3 (vii) $(0, 5)$ (viii) $(-3, 0)$

5. **Hint** Do same as Example 10.

   Ans. Not collinear

6. **Hint** Do same as Example 10.

   Ans. Collinear

7. **Hint** Given $(-4, 16) = (1 - x, y^2)$, $y > 0$

   $\Rightarrow 1 - x = -4$ and $y^2 = 16$, $y > 0$

   $\Rightarrow x = 5$ and $y = 4$

   The point $P(x^2, y - 1) = (25, 3)$

   The point $Q(2x, -3y) = (10, -12)$

   Ans. (i) Ist quadrant (ii) IVth quadrant

8. **Hint** In IV quadrant, $x > 0$ and $y < 0$, i.e. $(+, -)$.

   Ans. Points $R(2, -2)$ and $Q(3, -5)$ lie in the IV quadrant.

9. **Hint**

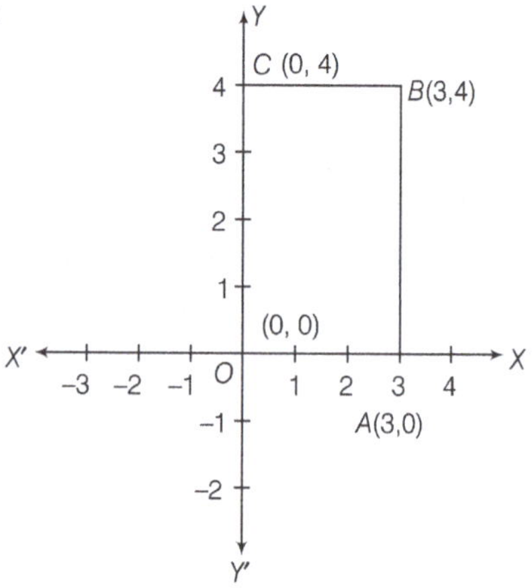

Ans. Rectangle

10. **Hint**

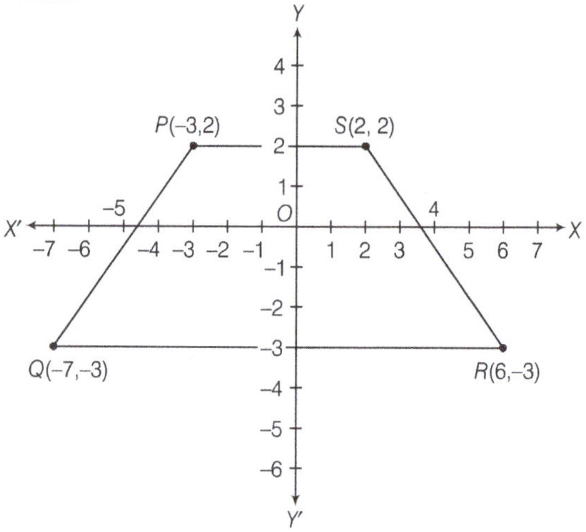

Ans. Trapezium

11. (i) **Hint**

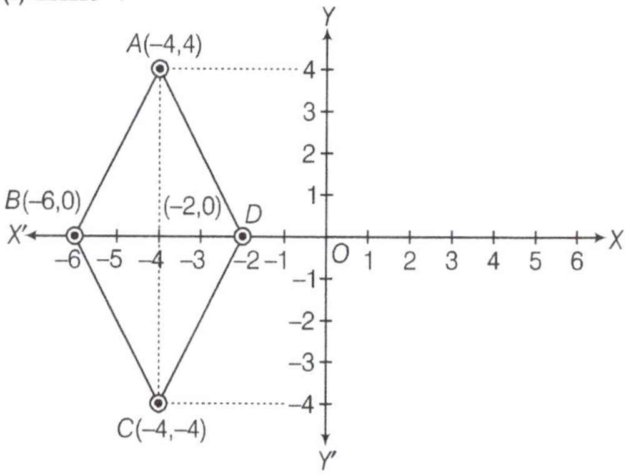

Ans. Rhombus

(ii) **Hint** Area of rhombus $= \frac{1}{2} \times d_1 \times d_2 = \frac{1}{2} \times 8 \times 4$

$[\because d_1 = AC = 4 + 4 = 8$ and $d_2 = BD = 4]$

Ans. 16 sq units

12. **Hint** Do same as Q. 11.

    Ans. (i) Rectangle (ii) 15 sq units

13. **Hint** Do same as Q. 11.

    Ans. (i) Rhombus (ii) 12 sq units

14. **Hint** From figure,

    Distance $AO = 3$ units

    Distance $OB = 3$ units

    $\Rightarrow \quad AB = 6$ units

    and $\quad BC = 6$ units

    In ΔOBC, $\angle COB = 90°$

    $\Rightarrow \quad BC^2 = OB^2 + OC^2$

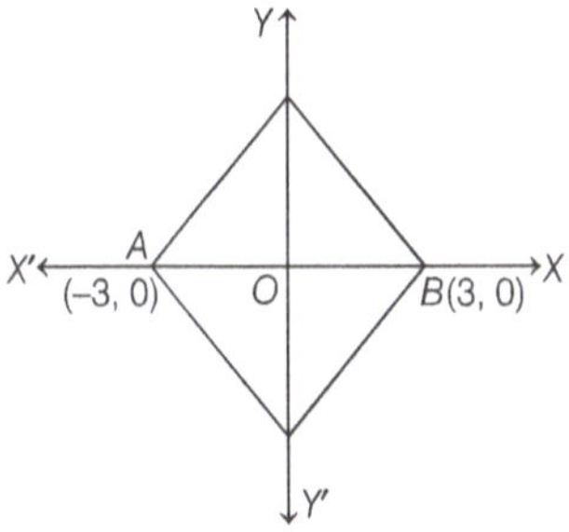

$\Rightarrow \quad 6^2 = 3^2 + (OC)^2$

$\Rightarrow \quad OC = \sqrt{27}$ units

$= 3\sqrt{3}$ units

Also, $OD = OC$

Ans. The coordinates of point C are $(0, 3\sqrt{3})$.

The coordinates of point D are $(0, -3\sqrt{3})$.

15. Hint Do same as Example 11.

Ans. (i) (1, – 2) (ii) 25 sq units

16. Hint Do same as Example 11.

Ans. (i) (–4, –3)

(ii) **Hint** The coordinates of point C is (4, – 3) and the coordinates of point D is (– 4, – 3).

Let mid-point of CD is M whose coordinates are (p, k).

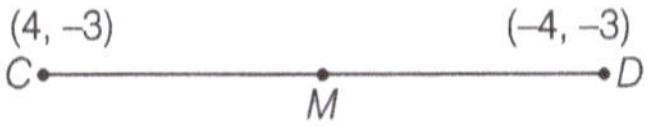

$\therefore \quad (p, k) = \left(\frac{4 + (-4)}{2}, \frac{(-3) + (-3)}{2}\right)$

$= (0, -3)$

Ans. (0, – 3)

(iii) 40 sq units

Exercise 18.2

1. Hint Do same as Example 12.

Ans.

(i) Independent variable = x, Dependent variable = y

(ii) Independent variable = y, Dependent variable = x

(iii) Independent variable = y, Dependent variable = x

2. Hint Do same as Example 13.

Ans. (i) Given, equation is $2x + y = 6$ and it can be written as $y = 6 - 2x$

When $x = 0$, then $y = 6 - 2(0) = 6$

When $x = 1$, then $y = 6 - 2(1) = 4$

When $x = 2$, then $y = 6 - 2(2) = 2$

Thus, we have the following table

x	0	1	2
y	6	4	2
(x, y)	A(0,6)	B (1, 4)	C (2, 2)

Now, plot the point A (0, 6), B (1, 4), C (2, 2) on the graph and join these points, we get a line AC.

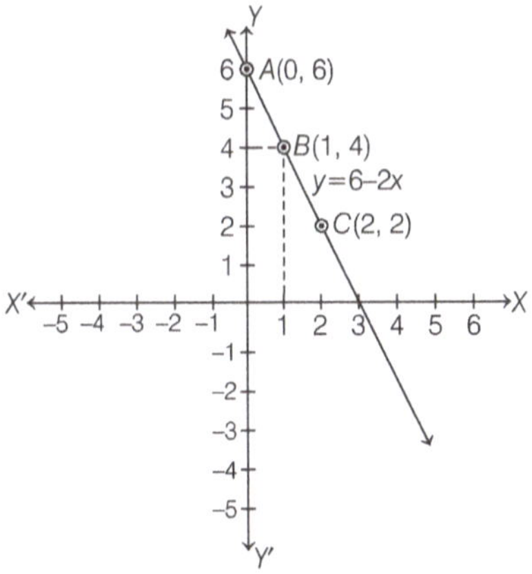

(ii)

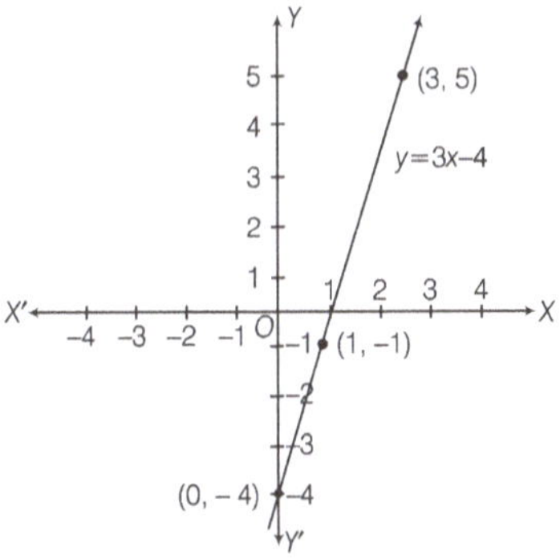

(iii)

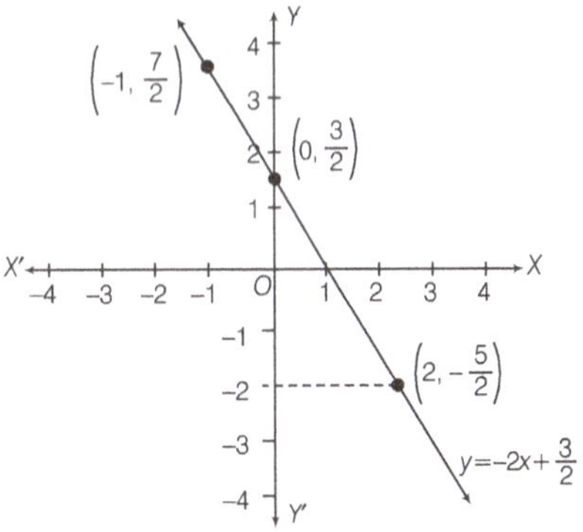

3. Hint Table for $2x - 3y = 9$ is

x	0	– 3	– 6
y	– 3	– 5	– 7

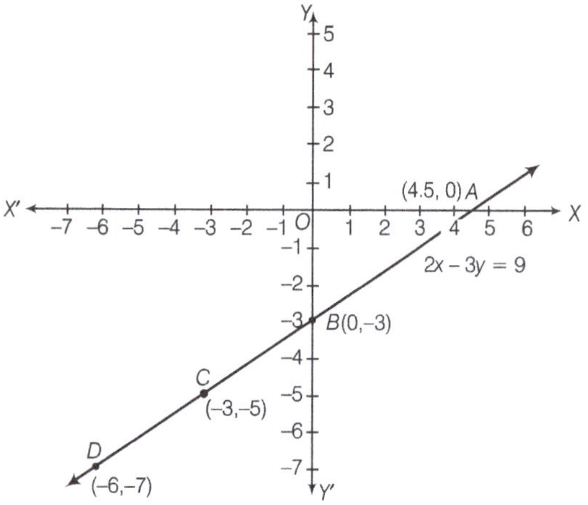

$\therefore$ Area of $\Delta OAB = \frac{1}{2} \times OA \times OB$

Ans. 6.75 sq units

4. (i) **Hint** Table for $y = 3x - 1$ is

x	1	2	− 1
y	2	5	− 4

and table for $y = 3x + 2$ is

x	1	− 2	0
y	5	− 4	2

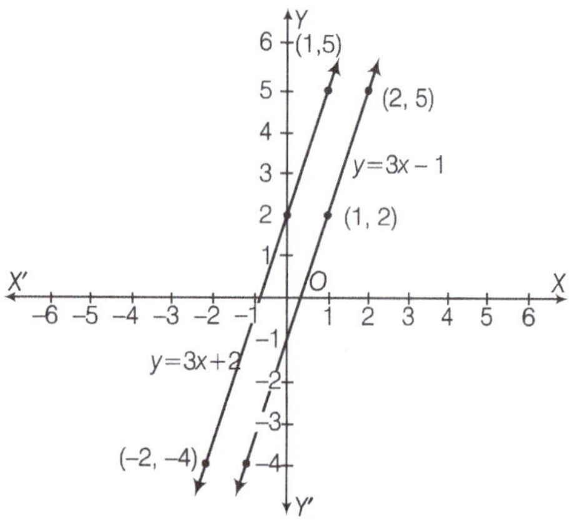

Ans. Parallel

(ii) **Hint** Table for $2x - 3y = 6$ is

x	0	3	− 3
y	− 2	0	− 4

and table for $\frac{x}{2} + \frac{y}{3} = 1$ is

x	0	2	− 2
y	3	0	6

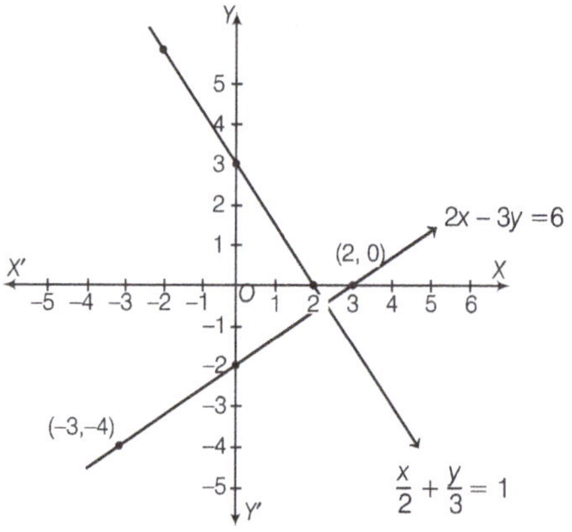

Ans. Perpendicular

5. **Hint** Table for $2x - y + 3 = 0$ is

x	0	− 1
y	3	1

and table for $3x - 5y + 1 = 0$ is

x	−2	3
y	−1	2

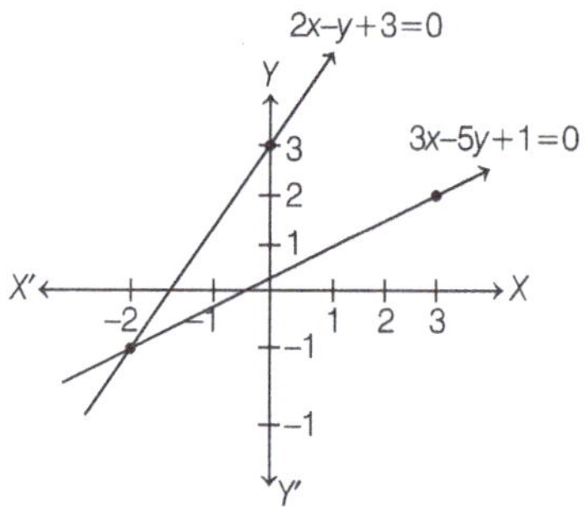

Point of intersect is (−2, − 1).

Ans. $x = -2$, $y = -1$

6. **Hint** First draw graph of the equations. Then, find the intersecting point between the lines and then intersection point of lines with X-axis.

Ans. $x = 0$, $y = 1$; (0, 1), (− 1, 0) and (1/2, 0)

7. **Hint** Do same as Q. 6.

Ans. $x = 3$, $y = 2$; (3, 2), (0, − 1) and (0, 11)

8. **Hint** Do same as Q. 6.

Ans. $x = 2$, $y = 3$; (0, 6), (0, 1) and (2, 3)

9. **Hint** Table for $2x + 3y = 10$ is

x	2	−1	5
y	2	4	0
(x, y)	A(2, 2)	B (−1, 4)	C (5, 0)

Table for $4x + 6y = 20$

x	2	−1	5
y	2	4	0
(x, y)	(2, 2)	(−1, 4)	(5, 0)

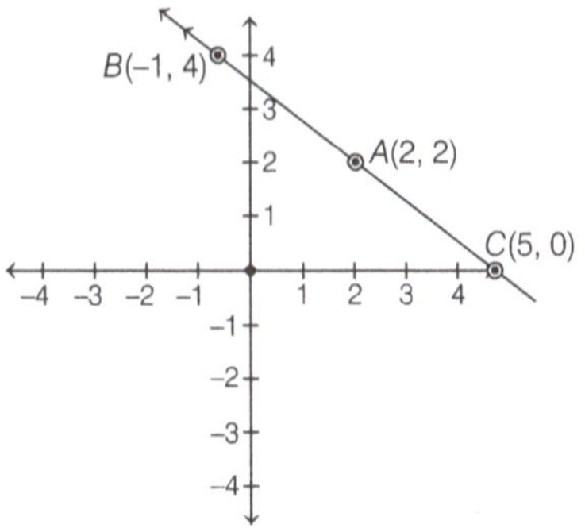

Ans.

(i) Many points are common for both table, line lie on top of each other

So lines coincide here.

(ii) These lines coincide with each other and exist many solutions.

$\therefore$ Equations are consistent.

Exercise 18.3

1. Hint Do same as Example 17.

Ans. (i) $10\sqrt{2}$ units (ii) $2\sqrt{2}$ units (iii) 10 units (iv) $2\sqrt{13}$ units (v) $a\sqrt{13}$ units

2. Hint Do same as Example 18.

Ans. (i) 5 units (ii) 7 units (iii) 10 units (iv) $a\sqrt{2}$ units (v) $\sqrt{3}$ units

3. (i) **Hint**

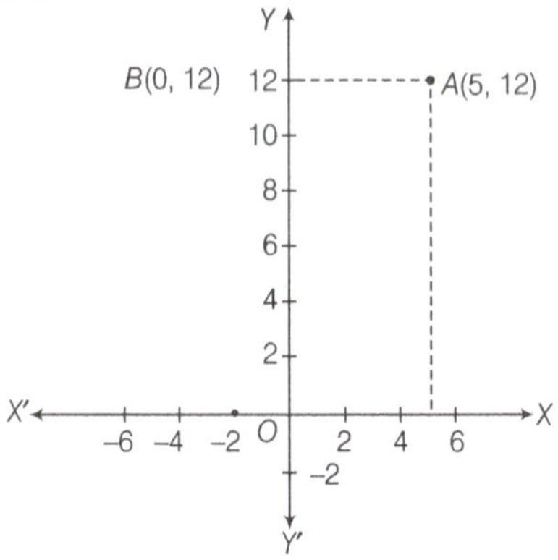

$\therefore$ Distance $(AB) = \sqrt{(5-0)^2 + (12-12)^2}$

Ans. 5 units

(ii) **Hint** Do same as part (i). **Ans.** 3 units

4. Hint Let the point on X-axis be $(x, 0)$. Now, use the distance formula.

Ans. (9, 0) and (5, 0); Required number of points = 2

5. (i) **Hint** Do same as Example 20.

(ii) **Hint** Do same as Example 20.

6. Do same as Example 21.

Ans. $x - y = 2$

7. Do same as Example 22.

Ans. (0, 5)

8. Hint Let $A(4, 2)$, $B(7, 5)$, $C(9, 7)$ be the given points.

Then, by distance formula,

$$AB = \sqrt{(7-4)^2 + (5-2)^2} = \sqrt{(3)^2 + (3)^2} = 3\sqrt{2} \text{ units}$$

$$BC = \sqrt{(9-7)^2 + (7-5)^2} = \sqrt{(2)^2 + (2)^2} = 2\sqrt{2} \text{ units}$$

$$AC = \sqrt{(9-4)^2 + (7-2)^2} = \sqrt{(5)^2 + (5)^2} = 5\sqrt{2} \text{ units}$$

For form of a triangle-

Sum of two sides must be greater than the third side.

But here,

$$(AB + BC) \not> AC$$

Ans. No

9. Hint $\because \; AP = AQ$ [given]

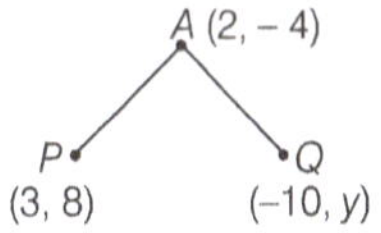

$\Rightarrow \quad AP^2 = AQ^2$ [squaring both sides]

Now, use the distance formula.

Ans. $y = -5, -3$, $PQ = \sqrt{338}$ units and $\sqrt{290}$ units

10. Hint The points are of the form $(x, 2x)$ and given point is (4, 3).

$$d = \sqrt{(x_2 - x_1)^2 + (y_2 - y_1)^2}$$

$\Rightarrow \quad d = \sqrt{(x-4)^2 + (3-2x)^2}$ [by distance formula]

$\Rightarrow \quad \sqrt{10} = \sqrt{(x-4)^2 + (3-2x)^2}$

[given, distance, $d = \sqrt{10}$ units]

$\Rightarrow \quad x = 3$ or $x = 1$

$\therefore \quad y = 2x = 6$ or $y = 2$

So, points are (3, 6) and (1, 2).

Ans. (3, 6), (1, 2)

11. Hint Let the circumcentre be $P(x, y)$.

$$PA = PB$$

$\Rightarrow \sqrt{(x-4)^2 + (y-6)^2} = \sqrt{(x-0)^2 + (y-4)^2}$ ...(i)

and $\quad PA = PC$

$\sqrt{(x-4)^2 + (y-6)^2} = \sqrt{(x-6)^2 + (y-2)^2}$ ...(ii)

On solving Eqs. (i) and (ii), we get

$$x = 3 \text{ and } y = 3$$

Ans. (3, 3)

12. **Hint** Given, $AOBC$ is a rectangle.

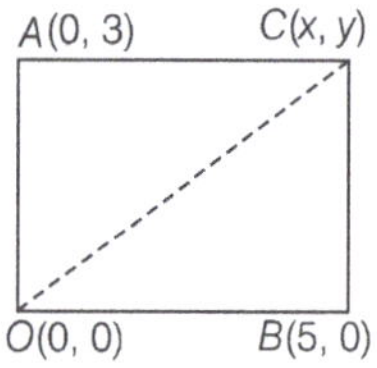

Vertices are $A(0, 3)$, $O(0, 0)$, $B(5, 0)$ [Given]

Point O is origin, given coordinates $(0, 0)$ in rectangle $AOBC$, $AC = OB$

[opposite sides of a rectangle are equal]

Let the coordinate of C is (x, y).

Then, by distance formula

$\Rightarrow \quad \sqrt{(x-0)^2 + (y-3)^2} = \sqrt{(5-0)^2 + (0-0)^2}$

$\Rightarrow \quad (x-0)^2 + (y-3)^2 = (5-0)^2 + (0-0)^2$ [$\because$ Squaring both sides]

$\Rightarrow \quad (x, y) = (5, 3)$ [on solving]

Now, diagonal of rectangle $AOBC$ is

$OC = \sqrt{(5-0)^2 + (3-0)^2}$ [by distance formula]

$= \sqrt{34}$

Length of diagonals of a rectangle are same.

Ans. $\sqrt{34}$ units

13. (i) **Hint** See the properties of square and use distance formula.

(ii) **Hint** See the properties of rectangle and use distance formula.

(iii) **Hint** See the properties of parallelogram and use distance formula.

(iv) **Hint** See the properties of rhombus and use the distance formula.

Chapter Exercise

1. (b) **2.** (b) **3.** (a)

4. (c) **5.** (d) **6.** (a)

7. **Hint** Do same as Example 6.

Ans. Coordinates of $A \equiv (4, 0)$, Coordinates of $B \equiv (4, 4)$

Coordinates of $C \equiv (0, 4)$

8. **Hint**

x	1	-1
y	3	-3
(x, y)	$A(1, 3)$	$B(-1, -3)$

Ans.

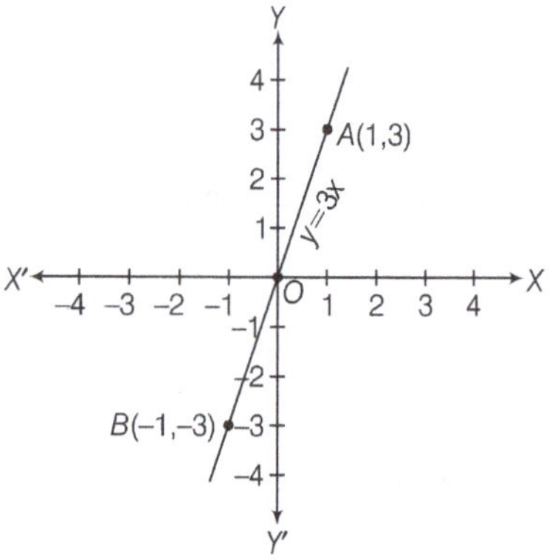

9. **Hint** Do same as Q. 8.

Ans.

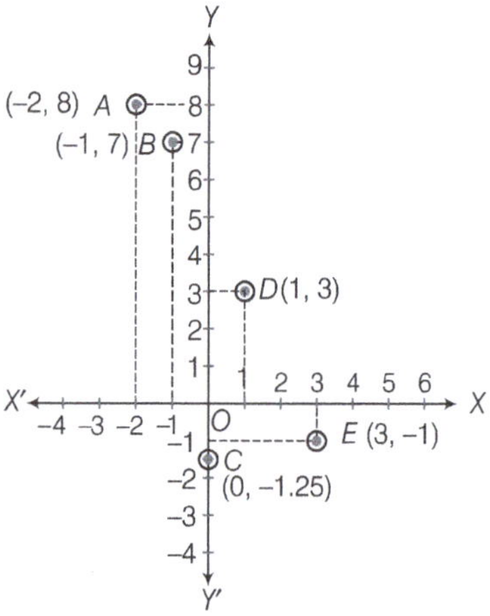

10. **Hint** $6 - \frac{3}{2}x = 0$

$\Rightarrow \quad x = 6 \times \frac{2}{3} = 4$

$\Rightarrow \quad x = 4$

Ans.

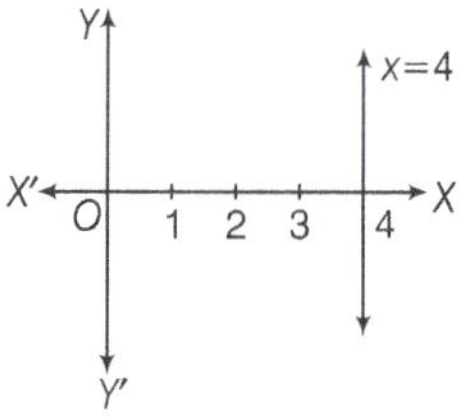

11. (i) **Hint** Do same as Example 9.

Ans.

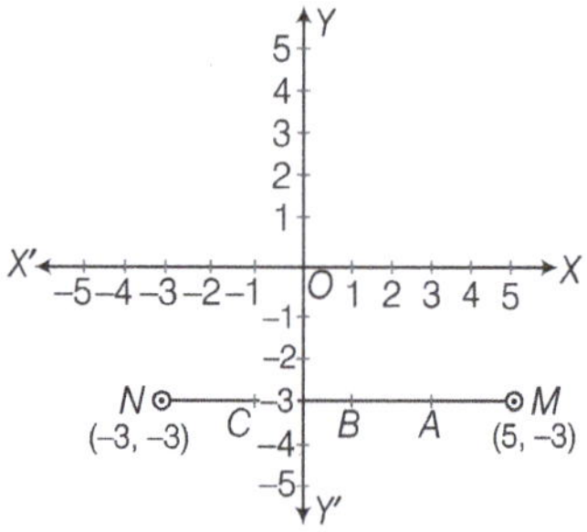

(ii) **Hint** Length of $MN = 5 + 3$. **Ans.** 8 units

(iii) **Ans.** Coordinates of $A = (3, -3)$, coordinates of $B = (1, -3)$ and coordinates of $C = (-1, -3)$.

12. **Hint** Do same as Example 17.

Ans. (i) $\frac{2\sqrt{41}}{5}$ units (ii) $2\sqrt{a^2 + b^2}$ units

(iii) $4\sqrt{2}$ units

13. **Hint** Do same as Example 18.

Ans. (i) $\sqrt{34}$ units (ii) $3\sqrt{5}$ units (iii) 3 units

14. **Hint** First find the length of three sides and then add them. **Ans.** 12 units

15. Hint $\sqrt{(4-1)^2 + p^2} = 5$ **Ans.** $p = \pm 4$

16. Hint Do same as Example 5.

Ans.
(i) Coordinates of $B = (-5, -4)$
Coordinates of $F = (6, 0)$
(ii) The abscissa of point $D = 1$
The abscissa of point $H = 0$
(iii) The ordinate of point $A = 1$
The ordinate of point $C = 0$
(iv) The perpendicular distance of the point G from X-axis = y-coordinate of $G = 4$

17. Hint Do same as Example 7
and plot these point on the cartesian plane.
Ans. $(-2, 4)$: II quadrant, $(3, -1)$: IV quadrant
$(-1, 0)$: negative direction of X-axis, $(1, 2)$: I quadrant, and $(-3, -5)$: III quadrant

18. Hint Do same as Example 7.

Ans. For point A,
(i) Abscissa = -2 (ii) Ordinate = 8
(iii) Coordinates = $(-2, 8)$ (iv) II quadrant

For point B,
(i) Abscissa = -1 (ii) Ordinate = 7
(iii) Coordinates = $(-1, 7)$ (iv) II quadrant

For point C,
(i) Abscissa = 0 (ii) Ordinate = -1.50
(iii) Coordinates = $(0, -1.50)$ (iv) Y-axis

For point D,
(i) Abscissa = 1 (ii) Ordinate = 3
(iii) Coordinates = $(1, 3)$ (iv) I quadrant

19. Hint Do same as Example 10.

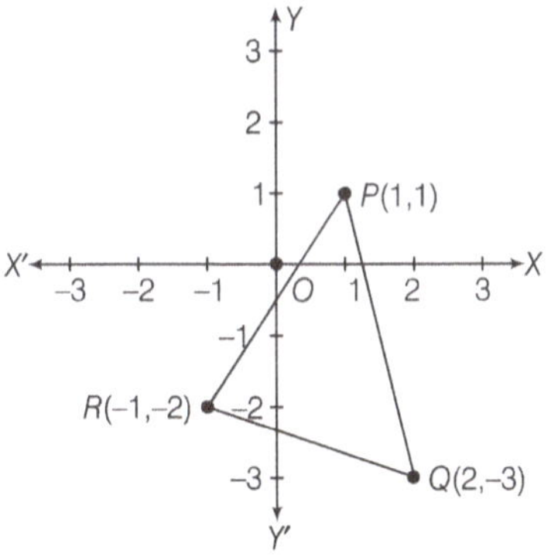

Ans. Points are not collinear.

20. Hint Draw the graph same as Example 10.
$\therefore$ Area of $\Delta PQR = (1/2) \times$ Base $\times$ Height

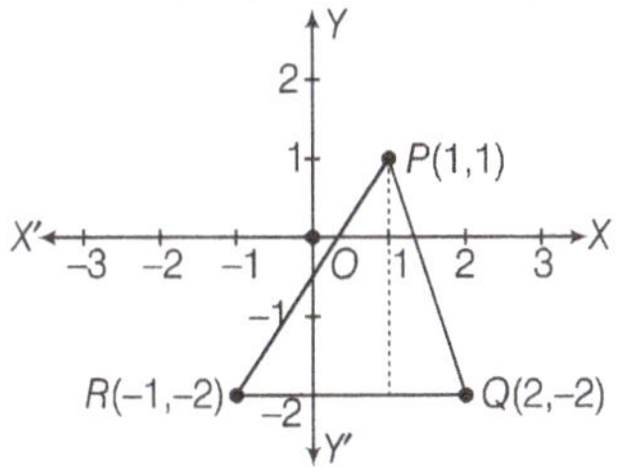

Ans. Not collinear, 9/2 sq units

21. Hint Do same as Example 13.

Ans. (i)

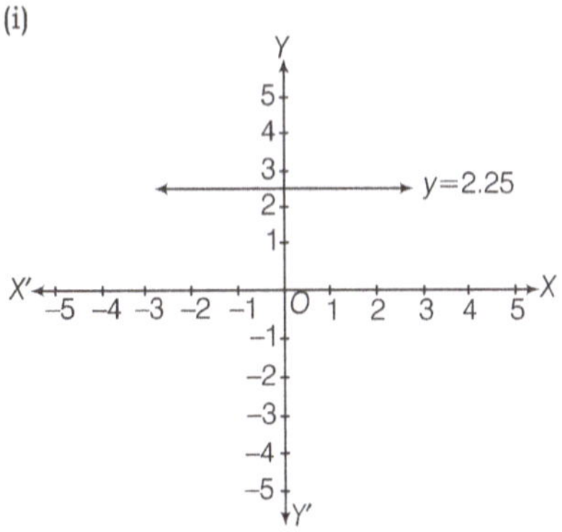

(ii)

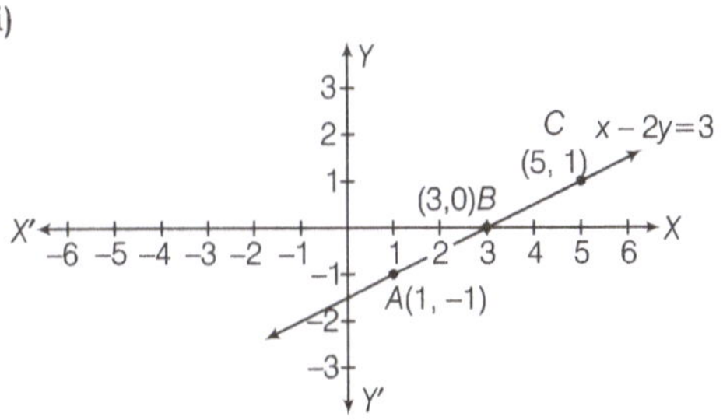

(iii)

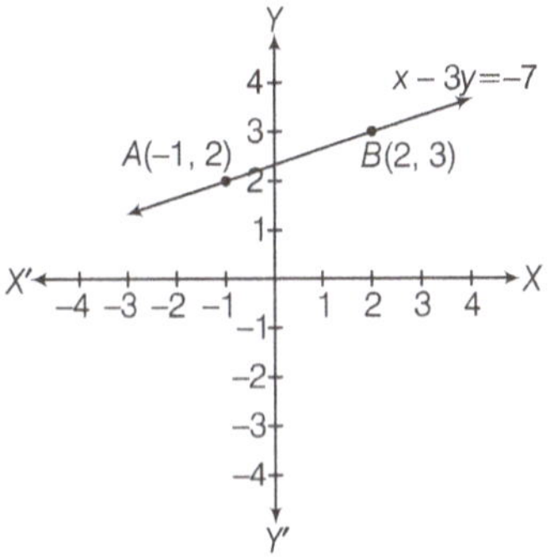

22. Hint Table for $y = 2x + 1$ is

x	0	1	–1
y	1	3	–1

Table for $y = -(x/2) - (3/2)$ is

x	3	–3	–1
y	–3	0	–1

Draw the graph of both equations same as Example 12.

Ans. Yes, intersection point = $(-1, -1)$

23. **Hint** Do same as Example 15.

Ans.

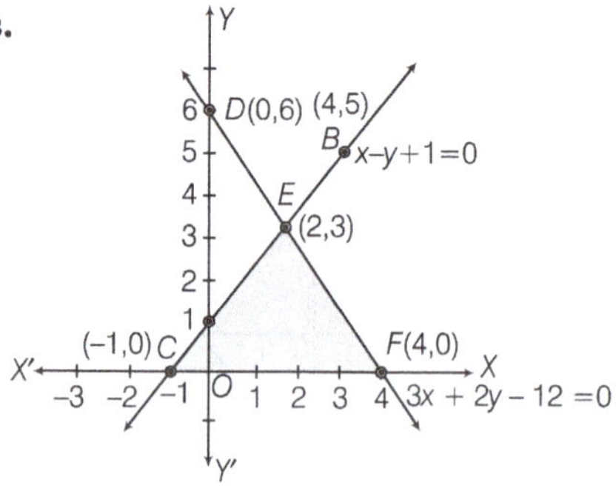

Also, coordinates are (– 1, 0), (4, 0) and (2, 3).

24. **Hint** Do same as Example 15.

Ans. (i) (– 1, 2), (– 3, – 1) and (5, – 1)

(ii) 12 sq units

25. **Hint** Do same as Example 15.

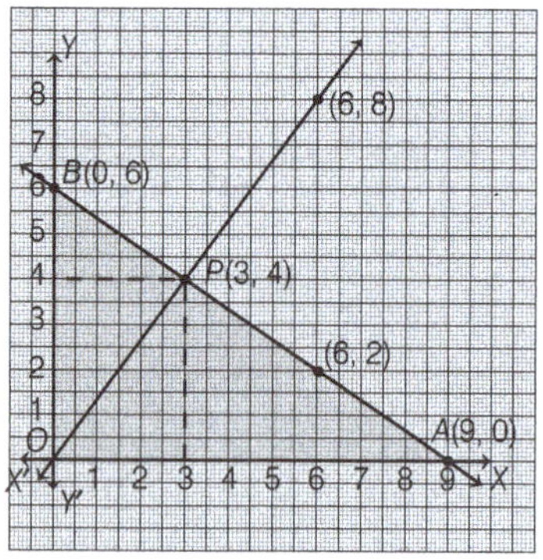

Ans. ar (ΔPOA) : ar $(\Delta OPB) = 2:1$

26. **Hint** Draw horizontal and vertical line on X and Y-axes.

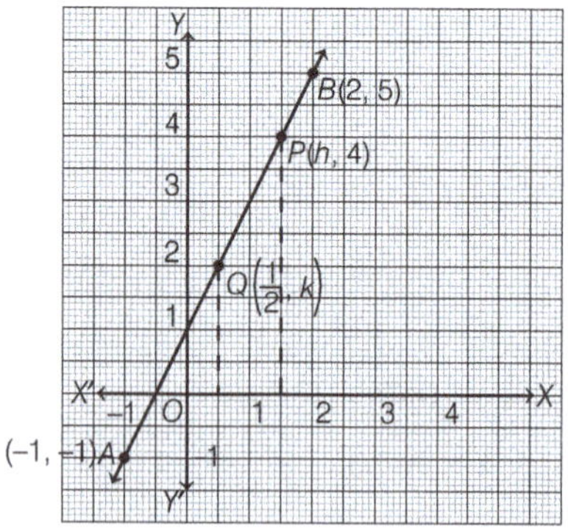

Ans. $h = \frac{3}{2}$ and $k = 2$

27. **Hint** Do same as Q. 26. **Ans.** $p = 3, q = -4$

28. **Hint** Do same as Example 19. **Ans.** $x = -4, 6$

29. **Hint** Do same as Example 22. **Ans.** (0, 5)

30. **Hint** Do same as Example 21.

Distance AB = Distance AC

31. (i) **Hint** Here, $AB = BC = CD = DA$ and $AC = BD$

Ans. Square

(ii) **Hint** Here, $AC + BC = AB$

Ans. Not a quadrilateral

(iii) **Hint** Here, $AB = CD$ and $BC = DA$

Also, $AC \neq BD$

Ans. Parallelogram

32. **Hint** $OA = OB \Rightarrow y = 7, -1$

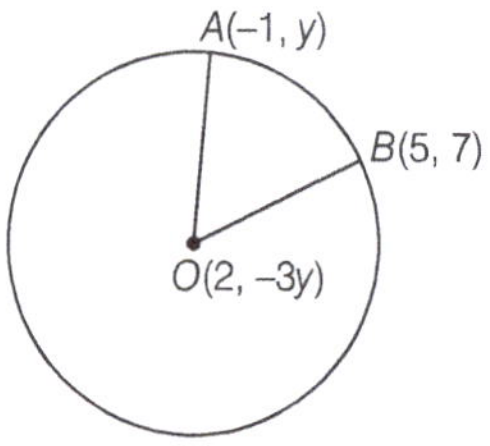

Ans. $y = 7, -1$

Radius = $\sqrt{793}$ units, 5 units

33. **Hint** Let $P(x, 0)$ on X-axis and $A(2, 3)$, $B\left(\frac{3}{2}, -1\right)$. Then,

$$\frac{AP}{BP} = \frac{2}{1}$$

Ans. (0, 0) or $\left(\frac{8}{3}, 0\right)$

34. **Hint** Radius = $5\sqrt{2}$ units

Let $C = (2a, a - 7)$ and $P \equiv (11, -9)$,

CP = radius of circle.

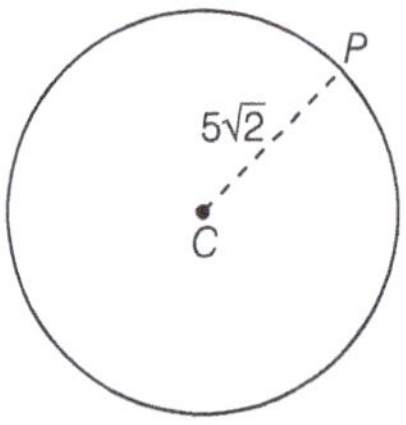

Ans. 3, 5

35. **Hint** $AP = BP$ and use distance formula.

Olympiad Section

Brain Teasing Questions of Olympiad Pattern

1 The line $x = my$, where $m < 0$, lies in the quadrants

(a) I, II (b) II, IV (c) III, IV (d) III, I

2 In a parallelogram $PQRS$, if $P(15, 9)$, $Q(7, 10)$ and $R(-5, -4)$, then the fourth vertex S is

(a) $(3, -2)$ (b) $(3, -4)$
(c) $(9, -5)$ (d) $(3, -5)$

3 A figure is shown below

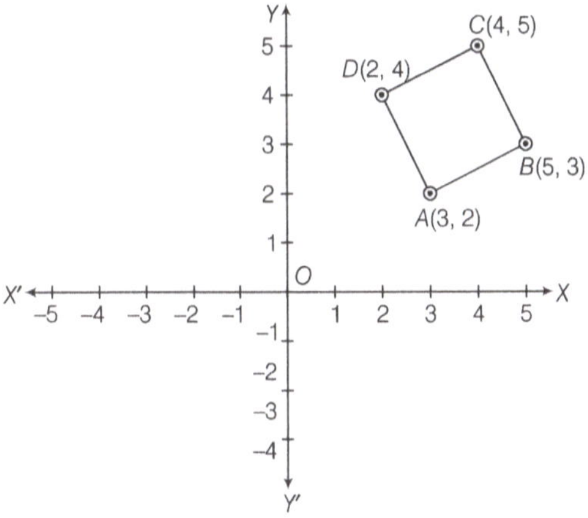

If we shift the coordinate axes from (0, 0) to (1, 1), then the new coordinates of the above figure is

(a) $A(2, 1)$, $B(4, 2)$, $C(3, 4)$, $D(1, 3)$
(b) $A(2, 2)$, $B(4, 4)$, $C(3, 3)$, $D(3, 1)$
(c) $A(1, 2)$, $B(2, 4)$, $C(4, 3)$, $D(3, 1)$
(d) None of the above

Directions (Q.Nos. 4-6) A graph is given below

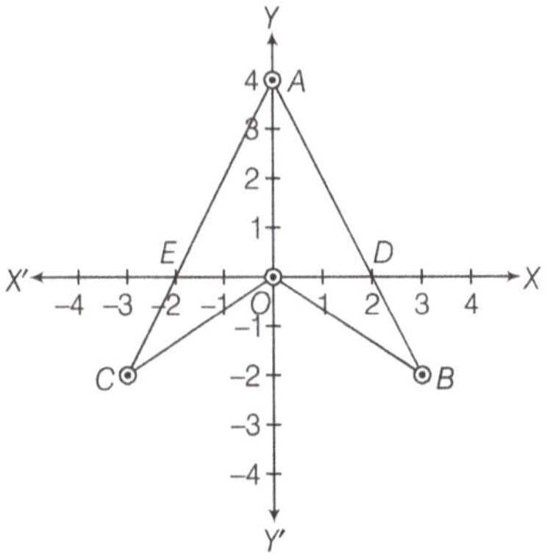

4 The coordinates of the points A, B and C are

(a) (4, 0), (−2, 3), (2, 3) (b) (0, 4), (3, −2), (−3, −2)
(c) (0, 2), (0, 3), (4, 3) (d) None of these

5 Find the area of the given figure.

(a) 10 sq units (b) 12 sq units
(c) 14 sq units (d) None of these

6 If we rotate the given figure at an angle of 270° clockwise, then draw the graph and find their coordinates.

(a) (−4, 0), (2, 3), (2, −3) (b) (4, 4), (2, 2), (2, 3)
(c) (4, 3), (2, 3), (3, 3) (d) None of these

7 Find the length of the longest side of the triangle formed by the line $3x + 4y = 12$ with the coordinate axes

(a) 9 units (b) 16 units (c) 5 units (d) 7 units

8 Plot the following points, join them in order and identify the figure, thus formed.

$A(1, 3)$, $B(1, -1)$, $C(7, -1)$, $D(7, 3)$

Also, write the coordinates of the point of intersection of the diagonals.

(a) Square, (4, 1) (b) Rectangle, (4, 1)
(c) Rectangle, (1, 4) (d) None of these

9 If the point $A(5, 1)$ is centre of the circle with radius 13 units, $AB \perp$ chord PQ and the coordinates of B are $(2, -3)$. Then, the length of chord PQ is

(a) 2 units (b) 26 units
(c) 24 units (d) 27 units

10 Join two points $P(2, 2)$ and $Q(4, 2)$ in a plane. Fixed the point P and rotate the line PQ in anti-clockwise direction at an angle of 270°. The area formed by this figure is

(a) 9 sq units (b) 9.5 sq units
(c) 9.42 sq units (d) 9.45 sq units

Answers

1. (b)	**2.** (d)	**3.** (a)	**4.** (b)	**5.** (b)
6. (a)	**7.** (c)	**8.** (b)	**9.** (c)	**10.** (c)

* *These questions may or may not be asked in the examination, have been given just for additional practice required for olympiads Scholarship Exams etc. For detailed explanations refer Page No. 354.*

Solutions to Olympiad Section

Chapter 1 Rational and Irrational Numbers

1. (a) We have, $\sqrt[3]{4}, \sqrt[4]{5}$ and $\sqrt[4]{3}$

i.e $\quad 4^{\frac{1}{3}}, 5^{\frac{1}{4}}$ and $3^{\frac{1}{4}}$

Here, LCM of 3 and 4 = 12

or $\quad 4^{\frac{1}{3}\times\frac{12}{12}}, 5^{\frac{1}{4}\times\frac{12}{12}}, 3^{\frac{1}{4}\times\frac{12}{12}}$

or $\quad 4^{\frac{4}{12}}, 5^{\frac{3}{12}}, 3^{\frac{3}{12}}$

or $\quad (256)^{\frac{1}{12}}, (125)^{\frac{1}{12}}, (27)^{\frac{1}{12}}$

Clearly, $(256)^{1/12}$ is the greatest number.

2. (d) We have, $\sqrt{\frac{1}{2}}, \sqrt[3]{\frac{2}{3}}, \sqrt{\frac{1}{3}}, \sqrt{\frac{1}{4}}$

i.e. $\left(\frac{1}{2}\right)^{\frac{1}{2}}, \left(\frac{2}{3}\right)^{\frac{1}{3}}, \left(\frac{1}{3}\right)^{\frac{1}{2}}, \left(\frac{1}{4}\right)^{\frac{1}{2}}$

$\because$ LCM of 2 and 3 = 6

$\therefore \quad \left(\frac{1}{2}\right)^{\frac{1}{2}\times\frac{6}{6}}, \left(\frac{2}{3}\right)^{\frac{1}{3}\times\frac{6}{6}}, \left(\frac{1}{3}\right)^{\frac{1}{2}\times\frac{6}{6}}, \left(\frac{1}{4}\right)^{\frac{1}{2}\times\frac{6}{6}}$

or $\quad \left(\frac{1}{2}\right)^{\frac{3}{6}}, \left(\frac{2}{3}\right)^{\frac{2}{6}}, \left(\frac{1}{3}\right)^{\frac{3}{6}}, \left(\frac{1}{4}\right)^{\frac{3}{6}}$

or $\quad \left[\left(\frac{1}{2}\right)^3\right]^{\frac{1}{6}}, \left[\left(\frac{2}{3}\right)^2\right]^{\frac{1}{6}}, \left[\left(\frac{1}{3}\right)^3\right]^{\frac{1}{6}}, \left[\left(\frac{1}{4}\right)^3\right]^{\frac{1}{6}}$

or $\quad \left(\frac{1}{8}\right)^{\frac{1}{6}}, \left(\frac{4}{9}\right)^{\frac{1}{6}}, \left(\frac{1}{27}\right)^{\frac{1}{6}}, \left(\frac{1}{64}\right)^{\frac{1}{6}}$

or $\quad (0.125)^{\frac{1}{6}}, (0.4)^{\frac{1}{6}}, (0.037)^{\frac{1}{6}}, (0.015625)^{\frac{1}{6}}$

Clearly, $\left(\frac{1}{64}\right)^{\frac{1}{6}}$ is the smallest number.

3. (a) We have, $x = \frac{\sqrt{3}+1}{2}$

On putting x in $4x^3 + 2x^2 - 8x + 7$, we get

$$4\left(\frac{\sqrt{3}+1}{2}\right)^3 + 2\left(\frac{\sqrt{3}+1}{2}\right)^2 - 8\left(\frac{\sqrt{3}+1}{2}\right) + 7$$

$$= \frac{4}{8}[(\sqrt{3})^3 + 1 + 3\sqrt{3}(\sqrt{3}+1)] + \frac{2}{4}(3 + 1 + 2\sqrt{3}) - 4(\sqrt{3}+1) + 7$$

[using the identities, $(a+b)^3 = a^3 + b^3 + 3ab(a+b)$ and $(a+b)^2 = a^2 + b^2 + 2ab$]

$$= \frac{1}{2}(3\sqrt{3} + 1 + 9 + 3\sqrt{3}) + \frac{1}{2}(4 + 2\sqrt{3}) - 4\sqrt{3} - 4 + 7$$

$$= \frac{1}{2}(10 + 6\sqrt{3}) + \frac{2}{2}(2 + \sqrt{3}) - 4\sqrt{3} + 3$$

$$= 5 + 3\sqrt{3} + 2 + \sqrt{3} - 4\sqrt{3} + 3 = 10$$

4. (b) We have, $\frac{4+\sqrt{3}}{4-\sqrt{3}} = a + b\sqrt{3}$

Now, rationalising the denominator, we get

$$\frac{4+\sqrt{3}}{4-\sqrt{3}} \times \frac{4+\sqrt{3}}{4+\sqrt{3}} = a + b\sqrt{3}$$

$$\Rightarrow \frac{(4+\sqrt{3})^2}{(4)^2 - (\sqrt{3})^2} = a + b\sqrt{3} \Rightarrow \frac{16 + 3 + 8\sqrt{3}}{16 - 3} = a + b\sqrt{3}$$

$$\Rightarrow \frac{19 + 8\sqrt{3}}{13} = a + b\sqrt{3} \Rightarrow \frac{19}{13} + \frac{8}{13}\sqrt{3} = a + b\sqrt{3}$$

On comparing both sides, we get $a = \frac{19}{13}$ and $b = \frac{8}{13}$

5. (a) We have to find $\frac{\sqrt{3}+1}{\sqrt{3}-1} + \frac{\sqrt{3}-1}{\sqrt{3}+1} + \frac{4+\sqrt{3}}{4-\sqrt{3}}$

Rationalising the denominator of each term, we get

$$\frac{\sqrt{3}+1}{\sqrt{3}-1} \times \frac{\sqrt{3}+1}{\sqrt{3}+1} + \frac{\sqrt{3}-1}{\sqrt{3}+1} \times \frac{\sqrt{3}-1}{\sqrt{3}-1} + \frac{4+\sqrt{3}}{4-\sqrt{3}} \times \frac{4+\sqrt{3}}{4+\sqrt{3}}$$

$$= \frac{(\sqrt{3}+1)^2}{3-1} + \frac{(\sqrt{3}-1)^2}{3-1} + \frac{(4+\sqrt{3})^2}{16-3}$$

[$(a+b)(a-b) = a^2 - b^2$]

$$= \frac{3 + 1 + 2\sqrt{3}}{2} + \frac{3 + 1 - 2\sqrt{3}}{2} + \frac{16 + 3 + 8\sqrt{3}}{13}$$

$$= \frac{4 + 2\sqrt{3} + 4 - 2\sqrt{3}}{2} + \frac{19 + 8\sqrt{3}}{13}$$

$$= \frac{8}{2} + \frac{19 + 8\sqrt{3}}{13} = 4 + \frac{19 + 8\sqrt{3}}{13} = \frac{52 + 19 + 8\sqrt{3}}{13}$$

$$= \frac{71 + 8\sqrt{3}}{13} = \frac{71 + 8 \times 1.7321}{13} = \frac{71 + 13.8568}{13}$$

$$= \frac{84.868}{13} = 6.5274$$

6. (d) We have, $\sqrt{\sqrt{63} + \sqrt{56}}$

$$= \sqrt{\sqrt{3 \times 3 \times 7} + \sqrt{2 \times 2 \times 14}}$$

$$= \sqrt{3\sqrt{7} + 2\sqrt{7 \times 2}} = \sqrt{\sqrt{7}(3 + 2\sqrt{2})}$$

$$= \sqrt{\sqrt{7}}\sqrt{3 + 2\sqrt{2}} = (7^{\frac{1}{2}})^{\frac{1}{2}}\sqrt{2 + 1 + 2\sqrt{2}}$$

$$= 7^{\frac{1}{4}}\sqrt{(\sqrt{2})^2 + 1^2 + 2\sqrt{2}}$$

$$= 7^{\frac{1}{4}}\sqrt{(\sqrt{2}+1)^2} = 7^{\frac{1}{4}}(\sqrt{2}+1)$$

7. (a) We have, $\sqrt[3]{9}, \sqrt[9]{5}, \sqrt[3]{7}$, i.e. $9^{\frac{1}{3}}, 5^{\frac{1}{9}}, 7^{\frac{1}{3}}$

$\because$ LCM of 3 and 9 = 9

$$9^{\frac{1}{3}\times\frac{9}{9}}, 5^{\frac{1}{9}}, 7^{\frac{1}{3}\times\frac{9}{9}}$$

$\because \quad 9^{\frac{3}{9}}, 5^{\frac{1}{9}}, 7^{\frac{3}{9}}$

or $\quad (9^3)^{\frac{1}{9}}, (5)^{\frac{1}{9}}, (7^3)^{\frac{1}{9}}$ or $(729)^{\frac{1}{9}}, (5)^{\frac{1}{9}}, (343)^{\frac{1}{9}}$

Clearly, $5 < 343 < 729$

or $5^{\frac{1}{9}} < (343)^{\frac{1}{9}} < (729)^{\frac{1}{9}}$ or $\sqrt[9]{5} < \sqrt[3]{7} < \sqrt[3]{9}$

8. (b) We have, $x = \dfrac{1}{7 + 4\sqrt{3}}$, $y = \dfrac{1}{7 - 4\sqrt{3}}$

$\because \quad xy = \dfrac{1}{7 + 4\sqrt{3}} \times \dfrac{1}{7 - 4\sqrt{3}} = \dfrac{1}{49 - (4\sqrt{3})^2}$

$\Rightarrow \quad xy = \dfrac{1}{49 - 48} = 1$ $[\because (a + b)(a - b) = a^2 - b^2]$ ...(i)

Now, $5x^2 - 7xy - 5y^2 = 5x^2 - 5y^2 - 7$

$= 5\left(x^2 - \dfrac{1}{x^2}\right) - 7$ [from Eq. (i)]

$= 5\left[\dfrac{1}{(7 + 4\sqrt{3})^2} - (7 + 4\sqrt{3})^2\right] - 7$

$= 5[(7 - 4\sqrt{3})^2 - (7 + 4\sqrt{3})^2] - 7$

$= 5[(49 + 48 - 56\sqrt{3}) - (49 + 48 + 56\sqrt{3})] - 7$

$= 5(-112\sqrt{3}) - 7 = -7(1 + 80\sqrt{3})$

9. (a) Given, $x = (4 + \sqrt{15})^{1/3} + (4 - \sqrt{15})^{1/3}$

On cubing both sides, we get

$$x^3 = (4 + \sqrt{15})^{\frac{1}{3} \times 3} + (4 - \sqrt{15})^{\frac{1}{3} \times 3} + 3\{(4 + \sqrt{15})^{1/3}(4 - \sqrt{15})^{1/3}\}[(4 + \sqrt{15})^{1/3} + (4 - \sqrt{15})^{1/3}]$$

$[\because (a + b)^3 = a^3 + b^3 + 3ab(a + b)]$

$$= (4 + \sqrt{15}) + (4 - \sqrt{15}) + 3(4 + \sqrt{15})^{1/3}(4 - \sqrt{15})^{1/3}[(4 + \sqrt{15})^{1/3} + (4 - \sqrt{15})^{1/3}]$$

$\Rightarrow \quad x^3 = 8 + 3(16 - 15)^{\frac{1}{3}}x$ $[\because x = (4 + \sqrt{15})^{1/3} + (4 - \sqrt{15})^{1/3}]$

$\Rightarrow \quad x^3 = 8 + 3x \Rightarrow x^3 - 3x = 8$

10. (a) Given, $x = \dfrac{1}{2}\left(\sqrt{a} + \dfrac{1}{\sqrt{a}}\right)$

Now, $\quad x = \dfrac{1}{2}\left(\dfrac{\sqrt{a} \times \sqrt{a} + 1}{\sqrt{a}}\right) \Rightarrow x = \dfrac{1}{2}\left(\dfrac{a + 1}{\sqrt{a}}\right)$ ...(i)

On squaring both sides of Eq. (i), we get

$$x^2 = \frac{1}{(2)^2} \times \frac{(a + 1)^2}{(\sqrt{a})^2} = \frac{(a + 1)^2}{4a}$$

On subtracting both sides by 1, we get

$$x^2 - 1 = \frac{(a + 1)^2}{4a} - 1$$

$\Rightarrow \quad x^2 - 1 = \dfrac{(a + 1)^2 - 4a}{4a} = \dfrac{(a - 1)^2}{4a}$

$\Rightarrow \quad \sqrt{x^2 - 1} = \dfrac{a - 1}{2\sqrt{a}}$ [taking square roots both sides]

$\therefore \quad x - \sqrt{x^2 - 1} = \dfrac{a + 1}{2\sqrt{a}} - \dfrac{(a - 1)}{2\sqrt{a}}$ $\left[\because x = \dfrac{(a + 1)}{2\sqrt{a}}\right]$

$= \dfrac{2}{2\sqrt{a}} = \dfrac{1}{\sqrt{a}}$

So, $\quad \dfrac{\sqrt{x^2 - 1}}{x - \sqrt{x^2 - 1}} = \dfrac{(a - 1)/2\sqrt{a}}{1/\sqrt{a}} = \dfrac{a - 1}{2}$

Chapter 2 Compound Interest

1. (c) Here, $A = ₹\,2560$, $R = 2\dfrac{1}{2} = \dfrac{5}{2}\%$ and $T = 2$ yr

Let the amount borrowed by Ramu be ₹ P.

Then, $\quad A = P\left(1 + \dfrac{R}{100}\right)^T$

$\therefore \quad 2560 = P\left(1 + \dfrac{5}{200}\right)^2 \Rightarrow 2560 = P\left(\dfrac{41}{40}\right)^2$

$\therefore \quad P = \dfrac{2560 \times 40 \times 40}{41 \times 41} = ₹\,2436.64$

2. (b) Let A be the amount, P be the principal and R be the rate of interest per annum.

Here, $A = 2P$ when, $T = 4$ yr

$\because \quad A = P\left(1 + \dfrac{R}{100}\right)^T$

$\therefore \quad 2P = P\left(1 + \dfrac{R}{100}\right)^4$

$\Rightarrow \quad 2 = \left(1 + \dfrac{R}{100}\right)^4$

On squaring both sides, we get

$$2^2 = \left[\left(1 + \frac{R}{100}\right)^4\right]^2 \Rightarrow 4 = \left(1 + \frac{R}{100}\right)^8$$

On multiplying both sides by P, we get

$$4P = P\left(1 + \frac{R}{100}\right)^8$$

Thus, the amount becomes 4 times the principal in 8 yr.

Hence, 4 more years are required.

3. (a) In first case, $P = ₹4000$, $R = 10\%$ and $T = 2$ yr

$\therefore \quad SI = \dfrac{P \times R \times T}{100} = \dfrac{4000 \times 10 \times 2}{100} = ₹\,800$

In second case, $P = ₹4000$, $R = 10\%$ and $T = 2$ yr

$\therefore \quad CI = P\left[\left(1 + \dfrac{R}{100}\right)^T - 1\right] = 4000\left[\left(1 + \dfrac{10}{100}\right)^2 - 1\right]$

$= 4000\left[\left(\dfrac{11}{10}\right)^2 - 1\right] = ₹\,840$

Thus, total interest for 4 yr = 800 + 840 = ₹1640

If simple interest is used for entire period, then total interest

$= 4 \times \dfrac{4000 \times 10 \times 1}{100} = ₹1600$

[$\because$ simple interest is same for every year]

Hence, Ajay have to pay ₹ (1640 – 1600) = ₹ 40 more.

4. (b) Here, $P = ₹\,25600$, $R = 25\%$ and $A = ₹28900$

Now, let the number of conversion periods is n.

Then, $\quad A = P\left(1 + \dfrac{R}{400}\right)^n$

$\Rightarrow \quad 28900 = 25600\left(1 + \dfrac{25}{400}\right)^n$

$\Rightarrow \quad \frac{289}{256} = \left(1+\frac{25}{400}\right)^n$

$\Rightarrow \quad \frac{289}{256} = \left(\frac{17}{16}\right)^n$

$\Rightarrow \quad \left(\frac{17}{16}\right)^2 = \left(\frac{17}{16}\right)^n$

$\therefore \quad n = 2$

i.e. $\frac{n}{4} = \frac{2}{4} = \frac{1}{2}$ yr sum of ₹ 25600 amount to ₹ 28900.

5. (b) Let I_1, I_2 and I_3 be the interest of first, second and third year, respectively. Let the principal be ₹ P.

Clearly, $I_1 = \frac{P \times 8 \times 1}{100} = ₹\ \frac{2P}{25}$

Now, for second year, $R = 10\%$

and principal $= P + \frac{2P}{25} = ₹\ \frac{27P}{25}$

$\therefore \quad I_2 = \frac{\frac{27P}{25} \times 10 \times 1}{100} = ₹\ \frac{27P}{250}$

Now, for third year, $R = 12\%$

and principal $= \frac{27P}{25} + \frac{27P}{250} = ₹\ \frac{297P}{250}$

$\therefore \quad I_3 = \frac{\frac{297P}{250} \times 12 \times 1}{100} = ₹\ \frac{891P}{6250}$

$\because$ It is given that the interest earned in the third year = ₹ 891

$\therefore \quad \frac{891P}{6250} = 891 \Rightarrow P = ₹\ 6250$

6. (c) Let the rate of interest be $R\%$.

According to the question,

$$4000\left[\left(1+\frac{R}{100}\right)^2 - 1\right] - \frac{4000 \times R \times 2}{100} = 250$$

$$\left[\because \text{CI} = P\left[\left(1+\frac{R}{100}\right)^n - 1\right] \text{ and SI} = \frac{P \times R \times T}{100}\right]$$

$\Rightarrow \quad \left[\left(\frac{100+R}{100}\right)^2 - 1\right] - \frac{R \times 2}{100} = \frac{250}{4000}$

$\Rightarrow \quad \frac{[(100+R)^2 - (100)^2] - 200R}{(100)^2} = \frac{250}{4000}$

$\Rightarrow \quad [(100+R+100)(100+R-100)] - 200R = \frac{250 \times 10000}{4000} \quad [\because a^2 - b^2 = (a+b)(a-b)]$

$\Rightarrow \quad (200+R)R - 200R = 625$

$\Rightarrow \quad R^2 = 625 \Rightarrow R = 25$

[taking positive square root]

Hence, the rate of interest per annum is 25%.

7. (b) Let the sum of money invested be ₹ P and rate of interest be $R\%$.

Given, the amount doubles itself in 6 yr.

$\therefore \quad 2P = P\left(1+\frac{R}{100}\right)^6 \quad \left[\because \text{CI} = P\left\{\left(1+\frac{R}{100}\right)^n - 1\right\}\right]$

$\Rightarrow \quad \left(1+\frac{R}{100}\right)^6 = 2 \quad \ldots \text{(i)}$

Now, according to the question, we get

$$64P = P\left(1+\frac{R}{100}\right)^n$$

$\Rightarrow \quad 64 = \left[\left(1+\frac{R}{100}\right)^6\right]^{n/6}$

$\Rightarrow \quad 64 = 2^{n/6}$ [from Eq. (i)]

$\Rightarrow \quad 2^6 = 2^{n/6}$

On comparing both sides, we get

$$\frac{n}{6} = 6 \Rightarrow n = 36$$

Hence, the amount becomes 64 times itself in 36 yr.

8. (b) Let the money lent at simple interest be ₹ x. Then, the money lent at compound interest will be ₹ $(4000 - x)$.

Given, rate of interest is 20% per annum and time is 2 yr.

$\therefore \quad \frac{x \times 20 \times 2}{100} + (4000 - x)\left[\left(1+\frac{20}{100}\right)^2 - 1\right] = 1720$

$$\left[\because \text{SI} = \frac{P \times R \times T}{100} \text{ and CI} = P\left\{\left(1+\frac{R}{100}\right)^n - 1\right\}\right]$$

$\Rightarrow \quad \frac{x \times 2}{5} + (4000 - x)\left[\left(\frac{6}{5}\right)^2 - 1\right] = 1720$

$\Rightarrow \quad \frac{2x}{5} + (4000 - x)\left(\frac{11}{25}\right) = 1720$

$\Rightarrow \quad \frac{10x + 44000 - 11x}{25} = 1720$

$\Rightarrow \quad 44000 - x = 25 \times 1720$

$\Rightarrow \quad x = 44000 - 25 \times 1720$

$\Rightarrow \quad x = 44000 - 43000$

$\Rightarrow \quad x = 1000$

Hence, the sum of money lent at simple interest is ₹ 1000.

9. (c) Given, present cost = ₹ 32490, rate of depreciation = 5% per annum and $n = 2$ yr.

Let the cost before 2 yr be ₹ P.

$\therefore \quad 32490 = P\left[1 - \frac{5}{100}\right]^2 \quad \left[\because V = V_0\left(1 - \frac{r}{100}\right)^n\right]$

$\Rightarrow \quad 32490 = P\left[1 - \frac{1}{20}\right]^2$

$\Rightarrow \quad 32490 = P\left[\frac{20-1}{20}\right]^2$

$\Rightarrow \quad 32490 = P \times \frac{19}{20} \times \frac{19}{20}$

$\Rightarrow \quad P = \frac{32490 \times 20 \times 20}{19 \times 19} = 36000$

Hence, the cost of electronic device is ₹ 36000 two years ago.

10. (a) Let the amount lent by two persons P and Q be ₹ P_1 and ₹ P_2, respectively. The rate of interest be $R\%$.

Now, according to the question, we get

$$\frac{P_1\left(1+\frac{R}{100}\right)^2}{P_2\left(1+\frac{R}{100}\right)^3} = \frac{3}{5} \quad \left[\because A = P\left(1+\frac{R}{100}\right)^n\right]$$

$\Rightarrow \quad \dfrac{P_1}{P_2\left(1+\dfrac{R}{100}\right)} = \dfrac{3}{5} \Rightarrow \dfrac{P_1}{8500} = \dfrac{3}{5}$

$\Rightarrow \quad P_1 = \dfrac{8500 \times 3}{5} = 5100$

Given, interest earned by P at the end of first year is ₹ 510.

$\therefore \quad \dfrac{P_1 \times 1 \times R}{100} = 510 \quad \left[\because \text{SI} = \dfrac{P \times R \times T}{100}\right]$

$\Rightarrow \quad \dfrac{5100 \times R}{100} = 510$

$\Rightarrow \quad R = \dfrac{510 \times 100}{5100} = 10\%$

$\Rightarrow \quad R = 10\%$

Also, $P_2\left(1+\dfrac{R}{100}\right) = 8500$

$\Rightarrow \quad P_2\left(1+\dfrac{10}{100}\right) = 8500 \Rightarrow P_2 \times \dfrac{11}{10} = 8500$

$\Rightarrow \quad P_2 = 8500 \times \dfrac{10}{11}$

$\therefore \quad P_1 : P_2 = 5100 : 8500 \times \dfrac{10}{11}$

$= 3 : \dfrac{50}{11} = 33 : 50$

Hence, the ratio of their principals, i.e. $P_1 : P_2$ is 33 : 50.

Chapter 3 Expansions

1. (a) We know that, $a^3 + b^3 + c^3 - 3abc = (a + b + c)(a^2 + b^2 + c^2 - ab - bc - ca)$

$\therefore x^3 + y^3 + z^3 - 3xyz$

$= (x + y + z)(x^2 + y^2 + z^2 - xy - yz - zx)$

$\Rightarrow (x + y + z)(x^2 + y^2 + z^2 - xy - yz - zx) = 0$

$[\because x^3 + y^3 + z^3 = 3xyz]$

$\Rightarrow$ Either $x + y + z = 0$

or $x^2 + y^2 + z^2 - xy - yz - zx = 0$ ...(i)

Now, consider $x^2 + y^2 + z^2 - xy - yz - zx = 0$

$\Rightarrow \quad 2x^2 + 2y^2 + 2z^2 - 2xy - 2yz - 2zx = 0$

[multiplying both sides by 2]

$\Rightarrow (x^2 + y^2 - 2xy) + (y^2 + z^2 - 2yz) + (x^2 + z^2 - 2zx) = 0$

$\Rightarrow \quad (x - y)^2 + (y - z)^2 + (z - x)^2 = 0$

$\Rightarrow \quad x - y = 0,\ y - z = 0,\ z - x = 0$

$\Rightarrow \quad x = y, \quad y = z, \quad z = x \Rightarrow x = y = z$ ...(ii)

Thus, from Eqs. (i) and (ii), we get either

$x + y + z = 0$ or $x = y = z$

2. (c) $\because x^{1/3} + y^{1/3} + z^{1/3} = 0$

$\therefore \quad (x^{1/3})^3 + (y^{1/3})^3 + (z^{1/3})^3 - 3x^{1/3}y^{1/3}z^{1/3} = 0$

[$\because$ if $a + b + c = 0$, then $a^3 + b^3 + c^3 = 3abc$]

$\Rightarrow \quad x + y + z = 3(xyz)^{1/3}$

On cubing both sides, we get

$(x + y + z)^3 = 27xyz$

3. (b) We have, $a^{1/2} + b^{1/2} - c^{1/2} = 0$

$\Rightarrow \quad a^{1/2} + b^{1/2} = c^{1/2}$

On squaring both sides, we get

$(a^{1/2} + b^{1/2})^2 = (c^{1/2})^2$

$\Rightarrow \quad (a^{1/2})^2 + (b^{1/2})^2 + 2(a^{1/2})(b^{1/2}) = (c^{1/2})^2$

$[\because (A + B)^2 = A^2 + B^2 + 2AB]$

$\Rightarrow \quad a + b + 2\sqrt{ab} = c$

$\Rightarrow \quad a + b - c = -2\sqrt{ab}$

Again, on squaring both sides, we get

$(a + b - c)^2 = (-2\sqrt{ab})^2 = 4ab$

4. (d) We have, $p = 2 - a$

$\Rightarrow \quad a + p + (-2) = 0$

$\Rightarrow \quad a^3 + p^3 + (-2)^3 = 3 \times a \times p \times (-2)$

[$\because$ if $a + b + c = 0$, then $a^3 + b^3 + c^3 = 3abc$]

$\Rightarrow \quad a^3 + p^3 - 8 = -6ap$

$\Rightarrow \quad a^3 + 6ap + p^3 - 8 = 0$

5. (a) Now, $(3a + 2b - c + d)^2 - 12a(2b - c + d)$

$= [3a + (2b - c + d)]^2 - 4(3a)(2b - c + d)$

$= (3a)^2 + (2b - c + d)^2 + 2(3a)(2b - c + d) - 4(3a)(2b - c + d)$

$= (3a)^2 + (2b - c + d)^2 - 2(3a)(2b - c + d)$

$= [3a - (2b - c + d)]^2 = (3a - 2b + c - d)^2$

which is a perfect square.

6. (a) We know that, $a^3 + b^3 + c^3 - 3abc$

$= (a + b + c)(a^2 + b^2 + c^2 - ab - bc - ca)$

$= (a + b + c)\{(a^2 + b^2 + c^2) - (ab + bc + ca)\}$

$= 15\{83 - (ab + bc + ca)\}$ ...(i)

[$\because a + b + c = 15$ and $a^2 + b^2 + c^2 = 83$, given]

Now, consider $(a + b + c)^2 = a^2 + b^2 + c^2 + 2(ab + bc + ca)$

$\Rightarrow \quad (ab + bc + ca) = \dfrac{(a + b + c)^2 - (a^2 + b^2 + c^2)}{2}$

$= \dfrac{(15)^2 - 83}{2} = \dfrac{225 - 83}{2} = \dfrac{142}{2} = 71$

Now, putting $ab + bc + ca = 71$ in Eq. (i), we get

$a^3 + b^3 + c^3 - 3abc = 15(83 - 71) = 15 \times 12 = 180$

7. (a) $\left(x - \dfrac{1}{x}\right)^3 = x^3 - \dfrac{1}{x^3} - 3 \cdot x \cdot \dfrac{1}{x}\left(x - \dfrac{1}{x}\right) = x^3 - \dfrac{1}{x^3} - 3\left(x - \dfrac{1}{x}\right)$

$\Rightarrow \quad x^3 - \dfrac{1}{x^3} = \left(x - \dfrac{1}{x}\right)^3 + 3\left(x - \dfrac{1}{x}\right)$ ...(i)

$\because \quad x + \dfrac{1}{x} = \dfrac{5}{2}$

and as $\left(x - \dfrac{1}{x}\right)^2 = \left(x + \dfrac{1}{x}\right)^2 - 4$

$\therefore \quad \left(x - \dfrac{1}{x}\right)^2 = \dfrac{25}{4} - 4 \quad \left[\because \dfrac{x^2 + 1}{x} = x + \dfrac{1}{x} = \dfrac{5}{2}, \text{ given}\right]$

$\Rightarrow \quad \left(x - \dfrac{1}{x}\right)^2 = \dfrac{9}{4} \Rightarrow x - \dfrac{1}{x} = \pm\dfrac{3}{2}$ ...(ii)

When we take $x - \dfrac{1}{x} = \dfrac{3}{2}$, then from Eqs. (i) and (ii), we get

$x^3 - \dfrac{1}{x^3} = \left(\dfrac{3}{2}\right)^3 + 3 \cdot \dfrac{3}{2} = \dfrac{27}{8} + \dfrac{9}{2} = \dfrac{63}{8} = 7\dfrac{7}{8}$

When we take $x - \frac{1}{x} = -\frac{3}{2}$, then from Eqs. (i) and (ii), we get

$$x^3 - \frac{1}{x^3} = \left(-\frac{3}{2}\right)^3 + 3 \times \left(-\frac{3}{2}\right) = -\frac{27}{8} - \frac{9}{2} = -7\frac{7}{8}$$

8. (a) We know that,

$$(a + b + c)^2 = a^2 + b^2 + c^2 + 2(ab + bc + ca)$$

$\therefore \quad (x - y + z)^2 = x^2 + (-y)^2 + z^2 + 2[x(-y) + (-y)(z) + xz]$

$\Rightarrow \quad (4)^2 = x^2 + y^2 + z^2 + 2(-xy - yz + xz)$

$\Rightarrow \quad 16 = 38 + 2(xz - yz - xy)$

$\Rightarrow \quad 2(xz - yz - xy) = 16 - 38 = 22 \Rightarrow xy + yz - xz = 11$

9. (c) We know that,

$a^3 + b^3 + c^3 - 3abc = (a + b + c)(a^2 + b^2 + c^2 - ab - bc - ca)$

$= (a + b + c)(a^2 + b^2 + c^2 + 2ab + 2bc + 2ca - 3ab - 3bc - 3ca)$

$= (a + b + c)[(a + b + c)^2 - 3(ab + bc + ca)]$

$= 2[(2)^2 - 3(-1)] = 2(4 + 3) = 14$

$\Rightarrow \quad a^3 + b^3 + c^3 - 3(-2) = 14$

$\Rightarrow \quad a^3 + b^3 + c^3 + 6 = 14$

$\Rightarrow \quad a^3 + b^3 + c^3 = 8$

10. (a) Now, $a^2 + 4b^2 + 25c^2 - 2ab - 10bc - 5ca = 0$

$\Rightarrow \quad a^2 + (2b)^2 + (5c)^2 - (a)(2b) - (2b)(5c) - (a)(5c) = 0$

$\Rightarrow \quad [2a^2 + 2(2b)^2 + 2(5c)^2 - 2(a)(2b) - 2(2b)(5c) - 2(a)(5c)] = 0$

[multiply both sides by 2]

$\Rightarrow \quad \{a^2 + (2b)^2 - 2(a)(2b)\} + \{(2b)^2 + (5c)^2 - 2(2b)(5c)\} + \{a^2 + (5c)^2 - 2(a)(5c)\} = 0$

$\Rightarrow \quad (a - 2b)^2 + (2b - 5c)^2 + (a - 5c)^2 = 0$

$\Rightarrow \quad a - 2b = 0, 2b - 5c = 0, a - 5c = 0$

$\Rightarrow \quad a = 2b = 5c$

Chapter 4 Factorisation

1. (a) We have, $(3 - 4y - 7y^2)^2 - (4y + 1)^2$

$= (3 - 4y - 7y^2 + 4y + 1)(3 - 4y - 7y^2 - 4y - 1)$

$[\because a^2 - b^2 = (a + b)(a - b)]$

$= (4 - 7y^2)(2 - 8y - 7y^2)$

2. (b) We have, $px^2 + (4p^2 - 3q)x - 12pq$

$= px^2 + 4p^2x - 3qx - 12pq$

$= (px^2 + 4p^2x) - 3q(x + 4p)$

$= px(x + 4p) - 3q(x + 4p)$

$= (x + 4p)(px - 3q)$

[taking $(x + 4p)$ common]

3. (a) We have, $y^3 - 2y^2 - y + 2$

$= (y^3 - 2y^2) - (y - 2)$

$= y^2(y - 2) - 1(y - 2)$

$= (y - 2)(y^2 - 1)$ [taking $(y - 2)$ common]

$= (y - 2)(y + 1)(y - 1)$

$[\because a^2 - b^2 = (a + b)(a - b)]$

4. (a) We have, $\left(3x - \frac{1}{y}\right)^2 + 8\left(3x - \frac{1}{y}\right) + 16 + \left(z + \frac{1}{y} - 2x\right)\left(3x - \frac{1}{y} + 4\right)$

$= \left(3x - \frac{1}{y}\right)^2 + 2 \cdot 4 \cdot \left(3x - \frac{1}{y}\right) + 4^2 + (z + \frac{1}{y} - 2x)(3x - \frac{1}{y} + 4)$

$= \left(3x - \frac{1}{y} + 4\right)^2 + \left(z + \frac{1}{y} - 2x\right)\left(3x - \frac{1}{y} + 4\right)$

$[\because a^2 + 2ab + b^2 = (a + b)^2]$

$= \left(3x - \frac{1}{y} + 4\right)\left(3x - \frac{1}{y} + 4 + z + \frac{1}{y} - 2x\right)$

$\left[\text{taking}\left(3x - \frac{1}{y} + 4\right)\text{common}\right]$

$= \left(3x - \frac{1}{y} + 4\right)(x + z + 4)$

5. (b) We have, $xya^2 = (x - y)^2(a + 1)$

$\Rightarrow \quad \frac{a^2}{a + 1} = \frac{(x - y)^2}{xy}$ ...(i)

On adding 4 both sides, we get

$$\frac{a^2}{a + 1} + 4 = \frac{(x - y)^2}{xy} + 4$$

$\Rightarrow \quad \frac{a^2 + 4a + 4}{a + 1} = \frac{(x - y)^2 + 4xy}{xy}$

$\Rightarrow \quad \frac{(a + 2)^2}{a + 1} = \frac{(x + y)^2}{xy}$ $[\because A^2 + 2AB + B^2 = (A + B)^2$ and $(A - B)^2 + 4AB = (A + B)^2]$

On dividing both sides by a^2, we get

$$\frac{(a + 2)^2}{a^2} = \frac{(x + y)^2}{xy} \times \frac{a + 1}{a^2}$$

Now, on putting the value of $\frac{a + 1}{a^2}$ from Eq. (i), we get

$$\frac{(a + 2)^2}{a^2} = \frac{(x + y)^2}{xy} \times \frac{xy}{(x - y)^2}$$

$\Rightarrow \quad \frac{a^2 + 4 + 4a}{a^2} = \left(\frac{x + y}{x - y}\right)^2$

$\Rightarrow \quad 1 + \frac{4}{a} + \frac{4}{a^2} = \left(\frac{x + y}{x - y}\right)^2$

6. (c) We have, $5x^2 - y^2 - 4xy + 7x - 7y$

$= (x^2 - y^2) + (4x^2 - 4xy) + (7x - 7y)$

$= (x + y)(x - y) + 4x(x - y) + 7(x - y)$

$[\because a^2 - b^2 = (a + b)(a - b)]$

$= (x - y)(x + y + 4x + 7)$ [taking $(x - y)$ common]

$= (x - y)(5x + y + 7)$

7. (d) We have, $12(3x - 4y)^2 - 3x + 4y - 1$

$= 12(3x - 4y)^2 - (3x - 4y) - 1$

Put $3x - 4y = t$, then the given expression reduces,

$12t^2 - t - 1 = 12t^2 + (-4 + 3)t - 1$

$= 12t^2 - 4t + 3t - 1$

$= (12t^2 - 4t) + (3t - 1)$

$= 4t(3t - 1) + 1(3t - 1)$
$= (3t - 1)(4t + 1)$

Now, on substituting $t = 3x - 4y$, we get
$= [3(3x - 4y) - 1][4(3x - 4y) + 1]$
$= (9x - 12y - 1)(12x - 16y + 1)$

8. (b) We have, $(x^2 + 4y^2 - 9z^2)^2 - 16x^2y^2$
$= (x^2 + 4y^2 - 9z^2)^2 - (4xy)^2$
$= (x^2 + 4y^2 - 9z^2 + 4xy)(x^2 + 4y^2 - 9z^2 - 4xy)$ $[\because a^2 - b^2 = (a + b)(a - b)]$
$= [(x^2 + 4xy + 4y^2) - 9z^2][(x^2 - 4xy + 4y^2) - 9z^2]$
$= [(x + 2y)^2 - (3z)^2][(x - 2y)^2 - (3z)^2]$ $[\because a^2 \pm 2ab + b^2 = (a \pm b)^2]$
$= (x + 2y + 3z)(x + 2y - 3z)(x - 2y + 3z)(x - 2y - 3z)$ $[\because a^2 - b^2 = (a + b)(a - b)]$

9. (a) We have, $x^4 - 625 = (x^2)^2 - (25)^2$
$= (x^2 + 25)(x^2 - 25)$ $[\because a^2 - b^2 = (a + b)(a - b)]$
$= (x^2 + 25)[x^2 - (5)^2] = (x^2 + 25)(x + 5)(x - 5)$ $[\because a^2 - b^2 = (a + b)(a - b)]$

10. (a) We have, $4x^2 - 12ax - y^2 - z^2 - 2yz + 9a^2$
$= 4x^2 - 12ax - (y^2 + z^2 + 2yz) + 9a^2$
$= 4x^2 - 12ax - (y + z)^2 + 9a^2$ $[\because A^2 + B^2 + 2AB = (A + B)^2]$
$= 4x^2 - 12ax + 9a^2 - (y + z)^2$
$= (2x)^2 - 2 \cdot 2x \cdot 3a + (3a)^2 - (y + z)^2$
$= (2x - 3a)^2 - (y + z)^2$ $[\because A^2 - 2AB + B^2 = (A - B)^2]$
$= (2x - 3a + y + z)(2x - 3a - y - z)$ $[\because A^2 - B^2 = (A + B)(A - B)]$
$= (2x + y + z - 3a)(2x - y - z - 3a)$

Chapter 5 Simultaneous Linear Equations

1. (d) Given, $(a + b, a - b)$ is the solution of the following equations

$3x + 2y = 20$ ...(i)
and $4x - 5y = 42$ ...(ii)

$\therefore$ $(a + b, a - b)$ satisfies both the equations.
Now, Eq. (i) can be written as
$3(a + b) + 2(a - b) = 20$
$\Rightarrow$ $3a + 3b + 2a - 2b = 20 \Rightarrow 5a + b = 20$ ...(iii)
and Eq. (ii) can be written as
$4(a + b) - 5(a - b) = 42$
$\Rightarrow$ $4a + 4b - 5a + 5b = 42 \Rightarrow -a + 9b = 42$ ...(iv)
On multiplying Eq. (iv) by 5 and then adding with Eq. (iii), we get
$46b = 210 + 20$
$\therefore$ $b = \frac{230}{46} = 5$

2. (b) Let the larger number be x and the smaller number be y.
According to the question, $x + y = 32$ ...(i)
and $(x - 1) - (y + 1) = 6$
$\Rightarrow$ $x - 1 - y - 1 = 6 \Rightarrow x - y = 8$ ...(ii)
On adding Eqs. (i) and (ii), we get $2x = 40 \Rightarrow x = 20$
On substituting $x = 20$ in Eq. (i), we get
$20 + y = 32 \Rightarrow y = 32 - 20 = 12$
Thus, the difference of numbers $= 20 - 12 = 8$

3. (a) Let X be abc. Then, the number formed by reversing the digits $= cba$. Now, according to the question,
$cba = abc - 891 \Rightarrow 891 = abc - cba$
$\Rightarrow$ $891 = 100a + 10b + c - (100c + 10b + a)$
$\Rightarrow$ $891 = 99a - 99c \Rightarrow 891 = 99(a - c)$
$\Rightarrow$ $a - c = \frac{891}{99} = 9 \Rightarrow a - c = 9 \Rightarrow a = c + 9$ ...(i)
Since, $c \geq 0$, therefore $a \geq 9$. But $a \leq 9$, therefore $a = 9$
$\Rightarrow$ $c = 0$ [from Eq. (i)]
Hence, the unit's digit is 0.

4. (a) Let us first convert them into linear equations by putting $7^x = p$ and $5^y = q$. Then, the given equations become
$p + q = 74$ ...(i)
and $7p - 5q = 218$ ...(ii)
On substituting $p = 74 - q$ from Eq. (i) in Eq. (ii), we get
$7(74 - q) - 5q = 218 \Rightarrow -12q = 218 - 518 = -300$
$\therefore$ $q = 25$
On substituting the value of q in Eq. (i), we get
$p + 25 = 74 \Rightarrow p = 49$
Thus, $7^x = 49$ and $5^y = 25 \Rightarrow 7^x = 7^2$ and $5^y = 5^2$
Hence, $x = 2$ and $y = 2$.

5. (d) Let the speed of Shashi on first day be x km/h and let the time taken on first day be y h. Thus, distance walked everyday by Shashi is xy.
Now, when she increases her speed by 1 km/h, then according to given condition,
$(x + 1)(y - 0.1) = xy$ $\left[\because 6 \text{ min} = \frac{6}{60} \text{ h} = 0.1 \text{ h}\right]$
$\Rightarrow$ $-0.1x + y = 0.1$ ...(i)
and when she decides to decrease her speed by 1 km/h, then according to given condition,
$(x - 1)(y + 0.15) = xy$ $\left[\because 9 \text{ min} = \frac{9}{60} \text{ h} = 0.15 \text{ h}\right]$
$\Rightarrow$ $0.15x - y = 0.15$ ...(ii)
On adding Eqs. (i) and (ii), we get
$0.05x = 0.25 \Rightarrow x = 5$
On substituting the value of x in Eq. (i), we get
$y = 0.1 + 0.5 = 0.6$
Hence, the distance that Shashi decided to walk everyday is $xy = 5 \times 0.6 = 3$ km.

6. (c) Let x L of mixture be taken from 1st vessel and y L of the mixture be taken from 2nd vessel and kept in 3rd vessel, such that $(x + y)$ L of the mixture in 3rd vessel may contain 25 L of milk and 10 L of water.
A mixture of x L from 1st vessel contains $\frac{24}{30}x = \frac{4}{5}x$ L of milk and $\frac{x}{5}$ L of water and a mixture of y L from 2nd vessel contains $\frac{3y}{5}$ L of milk and $\frac{2y}{5}$ L of water.

According to the question,

$$\frac{4}{5}x + \frac{3}{5}y = 25 \Rightarrow 4x + 3y = 125 \quad \ldots(i)$$

and $$\frac{x}{5} + \frac{2}{5}y = 10 \Rightarrow x + 2y = 50 \quad \ldots(ii)$$

On multiplying Eq. (ii) by 4 and then subtracting Eq. (i) from it, we get

$$5y = 200 - 125 \Rightarrow 5y = 75 \Rightarrow y = 15$$

On substituting $y = 15$ in Eq. (ii), we get

$$x + 2 \times 15 = 50 \Rightarrow x = 20$$

Hence, 20 L of mixture be taken from first vessel and 15 L of mixture be taken from second vessel.

7. (c) In the first half life, let every year, the number of mangoes that cannot become fruits is y.

According to the question,

The number of fruits produced in the first half life

$$= 11\,n - y$$

$\therefore$ Number of fruits produced in 4th year = 36

$\Rightarrow \quad 11(4) - y = 36 \Rightarrow y = 8$

Number of fruits produced in the second half life $= 11n - \frac{y}{2}$

$\therefore$ Number of fruits produced in the 9th year

$$= 11(9) - \frac{8}{2} = 99 - 4 = 95$$

Chapter 6 Indices/Exponents

1. (b) We have, $\left(\sqrt[6]{27} - \sqrt{6\frac{3}{4}}\right)^2$

$$= \left(\sqrt[6]{27} - \sqrt{\frac{24+3}{4}}\right)^2 = \left(\sqrt[6]{27} - \sqrt{\frac{27}{4}}\right)^2$$

$$= \left[(27)^{1/6} - \left(\frac{27}{4}\right)^{1/2}\right]^2 \quad [\because \sqrt[m]{a} = a^{1/m}]$$

$$= \left[(3 \times 3 \times 3)^{1/6} - \left(\frac{3 \times 3 \times 3}{2 \times 2}\right)^{1/2}\right]^2$$

$$= \left[(3^3)^{1/6} - \left(\frac{3^3}{2^2}\right)^{1/2}\right]^2 = \left(3^{3 \times \frac{1}{6}} - \frac{3^{3 \times \frac{1}{2}}}{2^{2 \times \frac{1}{2}}}\right)^2 \quad [\because (a^m)^n = a^{mn}]$$

$$= \left(3^{1/2} - \frac{3^{3/2}}{2}\right)^2 = \left[3^{1/2}\left(1 - \frac{3^{3/2}}{2 \times 3^{1/2}}\right)\right]^2$$

[taking $3^{1/2}$ common]

$$= \left[3^{1/2}\left(1 - \frac{3}{2}\right)\right]^2 = (3^{1/2})^2\left(\frac{2-3}{2}\right)^2$$

$$= 3^{2 \times \frac{1}{2}}\left(-\frac{1}{2}\right)^2 = 3 \times \frac{1}{4} = \frac{3}{4}$$

2. (a) We have, $x = \sqrt{3} + \sqrt{2}$

Then, $$\frac{1}{x} = \frac{1}{\sqrt{3} + \sqrt{2}}$$

On multiplying numerator and denominator by $\sqrt{3} - \sqrt{2}$, we get

$$\frac{1}{x} = \frac{\sqrt{3} - \sqrt{2}}{(\sqrt{3} + \sqrt{2}) \times (\sqrt{3} - \sqrt{2})}$$

$$\Rightarrow \quad \frac{1}{x} = \frac{\sqrt{3} - \sqrt{2}}{3 - 2} \quad [\because (a+b)(a-b) = a^2 - b^2]$$

$$\Rightarrow \quad \frac{1}{x} = \sqrt{3} - \sqrt{2}$$

Now, $x + \frac{1}{x} = \sqrt{3} + \sqrt{2} + \sqrt{3} - \sqrt{2} \Rightarrow x + \frac{1}{x} = 2\sqrt{3}$

On squaring both sides, we get

$$\left(x + \frac{1}{x}\right)^2 = (2\sqrt{3})^2$$

$$\Rightarrow \quad x^2 + \frac{1}{x^2} + 2x \times \frac{1}{x} = 2 \times \sqrt{3} \times 2 \times \sqrt{3}$$

$[\because (a+b)^2 = a^2 + b^2 + 2ab]$

$$\Rightarrow \quad x^2 + \frac{1}{x^2} + 2 = 12$$

$$\Rightarrow \quad x^2 + \frac{1}{x^2} = 10$$

3. (c) We have, $x = 7 - 4\sqrt{3}$

Then, $$\frac{1}{x} = \frac{1}{7 - 4\sqrt{3}}$$

On multiplying numerator and denominator by $7 + 4\sqrt{3}$, we get

$$\frac{1}{x} = \frac{1}{7 - 4\sqrt{3}} \times \frac{7 + 4\sqrt{3}}{7 + 4\sqrt{3}} = \frac{7 + 4\sqrt{3}}{(7)^2 - (4\sqrt{3})^2}$$

$[\because (a+b)(a-b) = a^2 - b^2]$

$$\Rightarrow \quad \frac{1}{x} = \frac{7 + 4\sqrt{3}}{49 - 48} = 7 + 4\sqrt{3}$$

Now, $x + \frac{1}{x} = 7 - 4\sqrt{3} + 7 + 4\sqrt{3}$

$$\Rightarrow \quad x + \frac{1}{x} = 14 \Rightarrow \frac{x^2 + 1}{x} = 14$$

$$\therefore \quad \frac{x^2 + 1}{7x} = \frac{14}{7} = 2 \quad [\because \text{dividing both sides by 7}]$$

4. (a) We have, $x^3 = \sqrt[3]{8} + \sqrt[3]{27} + \sqrt[3]{64} + \sqrt[3]{125} + \sqrt[3]{216} + \sqrt[3]{343}$

$$= (8)^{1/3} + (27)^{1/3} + (64)^{1/3} + (125)^{1/3} + (216)^{1/3} + (343)^{1/3}$$

$[\because \sqrt[m]{a} = a^{1/m}]$

$$= (2^3)^{1/3} + (3^3)^{1/3} + (4^3)^{1/3} + (5^3)^{1/3} + (6^3)^{1/3} + (7^3)^{1/3}$$

$$= 2^{3 \times \frac{1}{3}} + 3^{3 \times \frac{1}{3}} + 4^{3 \times \frac{1}{3}} + 5^{3 \times \frac{1}{3}} + 6^{3 \times \frac{1}{3}} + 7^{3 \times \frac{1}{3}}$$

$$= 2 + 3 + 4 + 5 + 6 + 7$$

$\Rightarrow x^3 = 27 = 3 \times 3 \times 3 = (3)^3$

$\Rightarrow x = 3$ [taking cube root on both sides]

$\therefore x^2 = 9$ [squaring both sides]

5. (c) We have, $\frac{3^{30} + 3^{29} + 3^{28}}{3^{31} + 3^{30} - 3^{29}} + \frac{2^{30} + 2^{29} + 2^{28}}{2^{31} + 2^{30} - 2^{29}}$

On taking minimum exponent of 3 and 2 common from each term in both numerator and denominator, we get

$$= \frac{3^{28}\left(\frac{3^{30}}{3^{28}} + \frac{3^{29}}{3^{28}} + \frac{3^{28}}{3^{28}}\right)}{3^{29}\left(\frac{3^{31}}{3^{29}} + \frac{3^{30}}{3^{29}} - \frac{3^{29}}{3^{29}}\right)} + \frac{2^{28}\left(\frac{2^{30}}{2^{28}} + \frac{2^{29}}{2^{28}} + \frac{2^{28}}{2^{28}}\right)}{2^{29}\left(\frac{2^{31}}{2^{29}} + \frac{2^{30}}{2^{29}} - \frac{2^{29}}{2^{29}}\right)}$$

$$= \frac{3^{28}(3^2+3+1)}{3^{29}(3^2+3-1)} + \frac{2^{28}(2^2+2+1)}{2^{29}(2^2+2-1)}$$

$$= \frac{3^{28}\times 13}{3^{29}\times 11} + \frac{2^{28}\times 7}{2^{29}\times 5} = \frac{13}{3\times 11} + \frac{7}{2\times 5} = \frac{13}{33} + \frac{7}{10}$$

$$= \frac{130+231}{33\times 10} = \frac{361}{330}$$

6. (d) We have, $\sqrt{3^2\sqrt{9^2\sqrt{81^2\sqrt{16^{16}}}}}$

$$= 3^{2\times\frac{1}{2}} \times 9^{2\times\frac{1}{4}} \times 81^{2\times\frac{1}{8}} \times 16^{16\times\frac{1}{16}} \quad [\because \sqrt[n]{\sqrt[m]{a}} = a^{1/(m\times n)}]$$

$$= 3 \times 9^{1/2} \times 81^{1/4} \times 16 = 3 \times 3^{2\times\frac{1}{2}} \times 3^{4\times\frac{1}{4}} \times 16$$

$$= 3 \times 3 \times 3 \times 16 = 27 \times 16 = 432$$

7. (b) We have, $x = \frac{1}{2-\sqrt{3}}$

On multiplying numerator and denominator by $2+\sqrt{3}$, we get

$$x = \frac{1}{2-\sqrt{3}} \times \frac{2+\sqrt{3}}{2+\sqrt{3}} = \frac{2+\sqrt{3}}{4-3}$$

$[\because (a-b)(a+b) = a^2 - b^2]$

$\Rightarrow \quad x = 2+\sqrt{3} \Rightarrow x - 2 = \sqrt{3}$

On squaring both sides, we get

$$(x-2)^2 = (\sqrt{3})^2$$

$\Rightarrow \quad x^2 + 4 - 4x = 3 \quad [\because (a-b)^2 = a^2 + b^2 - 2ab]$

$\Rightarrow \quad x^2 - 4x + 1 = 0 \quad \ldots(\text{i})$

Now, divide $x^3 - 2x^2 - 7x + 10$ by $x^2 - 4x + 1$.

$$\begin{array}{r|l} & x + 2 \\ x^2-4x+1 & x^3 - 2x^2 - 7x + 10 \\ & x^3 - 4x^2 + x \\ & - \quad + \quad - \\ \hline & 2x^2 - 8x + 10 \\ & 2x^2 - 8x + 2 \\ & - \quad + \quad - \\ \hline & 8 \end{array}$$

$\therefore \quad x^3 - 2x^2 - 7x + 10 = (x+2)(x^2-4x+1) + 8$

$= (x+2)\times 0 + 8 \quad [\because \text{from Eq. (i)}]$

$= 0 + 8 = 8$

8. (a) We have, $x = 1 + 5^{1/3} + 5^{2/3}$

$\Rightarrow \quad x - 1 = 5^{1/3} + 5^{2/3} \quad \ldots(\text{i})$

On cubing both sides, we get

$$(x-1)^3 = (5^{1/3} + 5^{2/3})^3$$

$\Rightarrow \quad x^3 - 1 - 3x(x-1) = 5 + 5^2 + 3\cdot 5(5^{1/3} + 5^{2/3})$

$[\because (a \pm b)^3 = a^3 \pm b^3 \pm 3ab(a \pm b)]$

$\Rightarrow x^3 - 1 - 3x^2 + 3x = 5 + 25 + 15(x-1) \quad$ [from Eq. (i)]

$\Rightarrow x^3 - 1 - 3x^2 + 3x = 30 + 15(x-1)$

$\Rightarrow x^3 - 3x^2 + 3x - 1 = 15x + 15$

$\Rightarrow \quad x^3 - 3x^2 - 12x = 16$

$\Rightarrow x^3 - 3x^2 - 12x + 6 = 16 + 6 \quad$ [adding 6 on both sides]

$\therefore \quad x^3 - 3x^2 - 12x + 6 = 22$

Chapter 7 Logarithms

1. (d) We have, $x = \log_3 27 = \log_3 3^3$

$= 3\log_3 3 \quad [\because \log m^n = n\log m]$

$= 3 \times 1 = 3 \quad [\because \log_m m = 1]$

and $\quad y = \log_9 27 = \log_{3^2} 3^3$

$= \frac{3}{2}\log_3 3 \quad \left[\because \log_{b^n} a^m = \frac{m}{n}\log_b a\right]$

$= \frac{3}{2} \times 1 = \frac{3}{2} \quad [\because \log_m m = 1]$

Now, $\quad \frac{x+y}{xy} = \frac{3+\frac{3}{2}}{3\times\frac{3}{2}} = \frac{9/2}{9/2} = 1$

2. (b) We have, $\log_{(a-b)}(a^3 - b^3) - \log_{(a-b)}(a^2 + ab + b^2)$

$= \log_{(a-b)}\frac{a^3-b^3}{a^2+ab+b^2} \quad \left[\because \log m - \log n = \log\frac{m}{n}\right]$

$= \log_{(a-b)}\frac{(a-b)(a^2+ab+b^2)}{a^2+ab+b^2}$

$[\because A^3 - B^3 = (A-B)(A^2+AB+B^2)]$

$= \log_{(a-b)}(a-b) = 1 \quad [\because \log_m m = 1]$

3. (b) We have, $\log_2 1 \times \log_3 2 \times \log_4 3 \times \ldots \times \log_{99} 100$

We know that, $\log_2 1 = 0$

Hence, $0 \times \log_3 2 \times \log_4 3 \ldots \times \log_{99} 100 = 0$

4. (a) We have, $\log_a \frac{13^2}{\sqrt{2^3}\times 5} = 2\log_a 13 - \log_a 5 - x$

$\Rightarrow \log_a 13^2 - \log_a[(2^3)^{1/2}\times 5)]$

$= 2\log_a 13 - \log_a 5 - x \quad \left[\because \log\frac{m}{n} = \log m - \log n\right]$

$\Rightarrow \quad \log_a 13^2 - \log_a 2^{3/2} - \log_a 5$

$= 2\log_a 13 - \log_a 5 - x \quad [\because \log mn = \log m + \log n]$

$\Rightarrow \quad 2\log_a 13 - \frac{3}{2}\log_a 2 - \log_a 5 = 2\log_a 13 - \log_a 5 - x$

$[\because \log m^n = n\log m]$

$\Rightarrow \quad -\frac{3}{2}\log_a 2 = -x \Rightarrow x = \frac{3}{2}\log_a 2$

$\Rightarrow \quad x = \log_a(2)^{3/2} \quad [\because n\log m = \log m^n]$

$\Rightarrow \quad (2)^{3/2} = a^x \quad [\because \log_a n = m \Rightarrow a^m = n]$

Hence, $\quad a^x = (2)^{3/2}$

5. (d) We have, $\log[4 - 5\log_{32}(x+3)] = 0$

$\Rightarrow \quad 4 - 5\log_{32}(x+3) = (10)^0 = 1$

$[\because \log_a n = m \Rightarrow a^m = n \text{ and } a^0 = 1]$

$\Rightarrow \quad -5\log_{32}(x+3) = 1 - 4 = -3$

$\Rightarrow \quad \log_{32}(x+3) = \frac{3}{5}$

$\Rightarrow \quad (x+3) = (32)^{3/5} \quad [\because \log_a n = m \Rightarrow a^m = n]$

$\Rightarrow \quad (x+3) = (2^5)^{3/5}$

$\Rightarrow \quad x + 3 = 2^{5\times\frac{3}{5}} \quad [\because (a^m)^n = a^{m\times n}]$

$\Rightarrow \quad x + 3 = 2^3 = 8$

$\Rightarrow \quad x = 8 - 3 = 5$

6. (d) Given, $x^6 - y^6 = k^6$

Now, $\log_k(x^2 - y^2) + \log_k(x^2 + y^2 + xy) + \log_k(x^2 + y^2 - xy)$

$= \log_k (x^2 - y^2) \times (x^2 + y^2 + xy) \times (x^2 + y^2 - xy)$

$[\because \log m + \log n + \log p = \log mnp]$

$= \log_k(x + y)(x - y)(x^2 + y^2 - xy)(x^2 + y^2 + xy)$

$[\because a^2 - b^2 = (a + b)(a - b)]$

$= \log_k (x + y)(x^2 - xy + y^2)(x - y)(x^2 + xy + y^2)$

$= \log_k(x^3 + y^3)(x^3 - y^3)$

$\left[\begin{array}{l}\because a^3 + b^3 = (a + b)(a^2 - ab + b^2) \\ \text{and } a^3 - b^3 = (a - b)(a^2 + ab + b^2)\end{array}\right]$

$= \log_k (x^6 - y^6) = \log_k k^6$

$= 6 \log_k k = 6 \times 1 = 6$

7. (a) We have, $\log_2 [\log_4 \{\log_5 (625)^4\}]$

$= \log_2[\log_4 \{\log_5(5^4)^4\}]$

$= \log_2 [\log_4 \{\log_5 5^{16}\}]$ $[\because (a^m)^n = a^{m \times n}]$

$= \log_2 [\log_4 \{16 \log_5 5\}]$

$= \log_2[\log_4 16]$ $[\because \log_m m = 1]$

$= \log_2 [\log_4 4^2] = \log_2[2 \log_4 4]$ $[\because \log m^n = n \log m]$

$= \log_2 2 = 1$ $[\because \log_m m = 1]$

8. (a) We have, $x^4 + y^4 = 83x^2y^2$

On subtracting $2x^2y^2$ from both sides, we get

$x^4 + y^4 - 2x^2y^2 = 81x^2y^2$

$\Rightarrow (x^2 - y^2)^2 = (9xy)^2 \Rightarrow x^2 - y^2 = 9xy$

$\Rightarrow \dfrac{x^2 - y^2}{9} = xy$

Taking log on both sides, we get

$\log\left(\dfrac{x^2 - y^2}{9}\right) = \log xy$

$\therefore \log\left(\dfrac{x^2 - y^2}{9}\right) = \log x + \log y$

$[\because \log mn = \log m + \log n]$

9. (b) We have, $\log x + \log 5 = 2 + \log 64$

$\Rightarrow \log x + \log 5 = 2 + \log 2^6$

$\Rightarrow \log x + \log\dfrac{10}{2} = 2 + 6 \log 2$

$\Rightarrow \log x + \log 10 - \log 2 = 2 + 6 \log 2$

$\Rightarrow \log x + 1 - \log 2 = 2 + 6 \log 2$

$\Rightarrow \log x = 1 + 7 \log 2$

$\Rightarrow \log x = \log 10 + \log 2^7$

$\Rightarrow \log x = \log 10 + \log 128$

$\Rightarrow \log x = \log 128 \times 10$

$[\because \log m + \log n = \log mn]$

$\Rightarrow \log x = \log 1280$

$\therefore x = 1280$

10. (c) We have, $\log_{11} 3 \times \log_3 1331 = \log_{11} 3 \times \log_3 11^3$

$= \log_{11} 3 \times 3 \log_3 11$

$= \dfrac{\log 3}{\log 11} \times 3 \times \dfrac{\log 11}{\log 3}$ $\left[\because \log_n m = \dfrac{\log m}{\log n}\right]$

$= 3$

Chapter 8 Triangles

1. (a) We have, $A - B = 15° \Rightarrow A = B + 15°$ ...(i)

and $B - C = 30° \Rightarrow C = B - 30°$ ...(ii)

As we know that the sum of interior angles of triangle is 180°, therefore we have

$A + B + C = 180°$

$\Rightarrow B + 15° + B + B - 30° = 180°$ [using Eqs.(i) and (ii)]

$\Rightarrow 3B - 15° = 180°$

$\Rightarrow 3B = 195°$

$\Rightarrow B = 65°$

Now, from Eqs. (i) and (ii), we get

$A = 65° + 15° = 80°$

and $C = 65° - 30° = 35°$

2. (d) In ΔABP, we have

$\angle ABP > \angle BAP \Rightarrow AP > BP$ ... (i)

Also, in ΔACP, we have

$\angle ACP > \angle CAP \Rightarrow AP > CP$ ... (ii)

[∵ side opposite to greater angle is greater]

Now, from the given options, we can see that only option (d) is correct, i.e. $CP < BP < AP$.

3. (d) From the inequality of triangle, we have

$6002 + 2006 > m$ and $6002 - 2006 < m$

$\Rightarrow 8008 > m$ and $3996 < m \Rightarrow 3996 < m < 8008$

Since, m is an integer, therefore it can take

$8008 - 3996 - 1 = 4011$

Hence, 4011 triangles are possible.

4. (a) We know that if in a triangle median is same as altitude, then the triangle is isosceles.

In ΔABD, we have AC is the median as well as altitude to BD.

$\therefore AB = AD$ ...(i)

In ΔACE, AD is median to CE, therefore

$CD = DE$ ...(ii)

Now, in ΔADE, we have

$AD + DE > AE$

$\Rightarrow AB + CD > AE$ [using Eqs. (i) and (ii)]

5. (a) Given, $AY = ZY$ and $BY = XY$

$\because BY \perp XY$ and $AY \perp ZY$.

$\therefore \angle BYX = 90°$ and $\angle AYZ = 90°$

$\Rightarrow \angle BYX = \angle AYZ$

On adding $\angle AYX$ both sides, we get

$\angle BYX + \angle AYX = \angle AYZ + \angle AYX$

$\Rightarrow \angle AYB = \angle ZYX$

Now, in ΔAYB and ΔZYX, we have

$AY = ZY$ [given]

$BY = XY$ [given]

and $\angle AYB = \angle ZYX$ [proved above]

$\therefore \Delta AYB \cong \Delta ZYX$ [by SAS congruence rule]

Hence, $AB = ZX$ [by CPCT]

6. (c) Given, $AB = AC$ and $AD = DC = BC$.

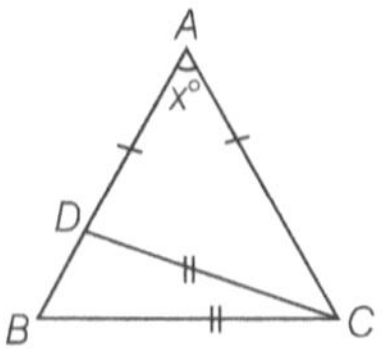

Let $\angle BAC = x$

Now in ΔADC, we have $AD = DC$

$\Rightarrow \quad \angle DAC = \angle ACD = x$

[$\because$ angles opposite to equal sides are equal]

$\Rightarrow \quad \angle BDC = x + x = 2x$

[$\because \angle BDC$ is an exterior angle of ΔADC]

Now, in ΔBDC, we have

$DC = BC$

$\Rightarrow \quad \angle DBC = \angle BDC = 2x$

$\Rightarrow \quad \angle ABC = 2x \quad [\because \angle ABC = \angle DBC]$ ...(i)

$\therefore$ In ΔABC, we have

$\angle ACB = 2x \quad [\because AB = AC \Rightarrow \angle ABC = \angle ACB]$ ...(ii)

Now, consider ΔABC, then

$\angle A + \angle B + \angle C = 180°$

$\Rightarrow \quad x + 2x + 2x = 180°$ [from Eqs. (i) and (ii)]

$\Rightarrow \quad 5x = 180° \Rightarrow x = 36°$

Hence, $\angle BAC$ is 36°.

7. (c) Given, $AC = CD$

$\therefore \quad \angle CAD = \angle CDA$ ...(i)

$CDEF$ is a parallelogram.

$\therefore \quad DE \parallel CF$ or $DE \parallel AF$ and $CD \parallel FE$.

Since in parallelogram $CDEF$,

$CD \parallel FE$ and EC is a transversal.

$\therefore \quad \angle DCE = \angle FEC = 10°$ [alternate interior angle]

[$\because \angle FEC = 10°$ (given)]

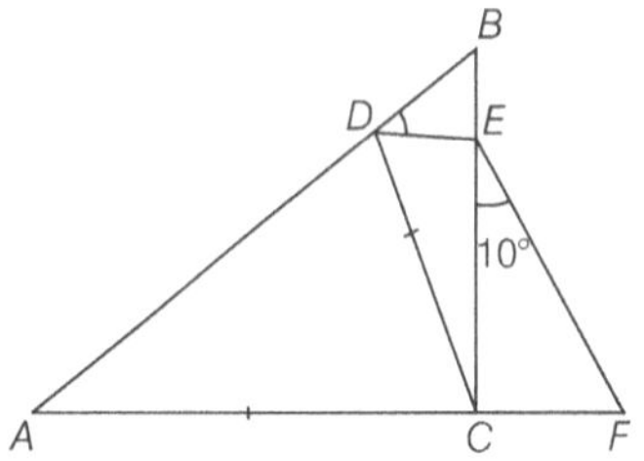

Now, $\quad \angle ACB = 90°$

$\Rightarrow \quad \angle ACD = 90° - 10° = 80°$

In ΔACD,

$\angle CAD + \angle CDA + \angle ACD = 180°$

[by angle sum property of a triangle]

$\Rightarrow \angle CAD + \angle CAD + 80° = 180°$

$\Rightarrow \quad \angle CAD = 50°$

Again, in parallelogram $CDEF$, $DE \parallel AF$ and DA is the transversal.

$\because \quad \angle BDE = \angle CAD = 50°$ [corresponding angles]

$\therefore \quad \angle BDE = 50°$

8. (d) Extend AF and AG, such that they touch CD at M and N respectively.

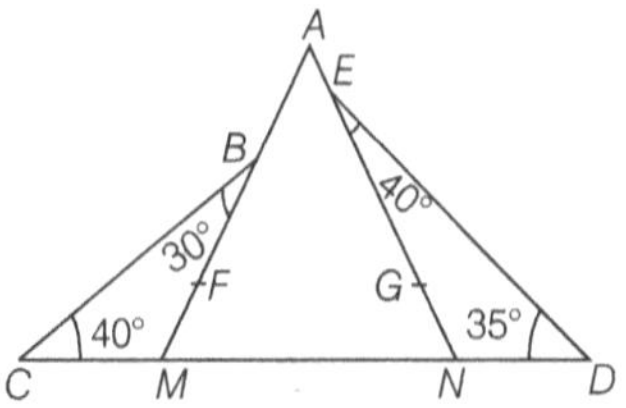

Now, $\angle MCB + \angle MBC = \angle AMN$

[as, exterior angle of a triangle equals to the sum of interior opposite angles]

$\angle AMN = 40° + 30° = 70° \Rightarrow \angle AMN = 70°$ ...(i)

Similarly,

$\angle ANM = \angle NED + \angle NDE$

and $\quad \angle ANM = 40° + 35° = 75°$ ...(ii)

In ΔAMN,

$\angle AMN + \angle ANM + \angle MAN = 180°$

[angle sum property of a triangle]

$\Rightarrow \quad 70° + 75° + \angle MAN = 180°$

$\Rightarrow \quad \angle MAN = 180° - 145° = 35°$

$\Rightarrow \quad \angle MAN = 35° \quad [\because \angle BAE = \angle MAN]$

9. (b) Given $PQRS$ is a quadrilateral. PQ is the longest side and RS is the shortest side.

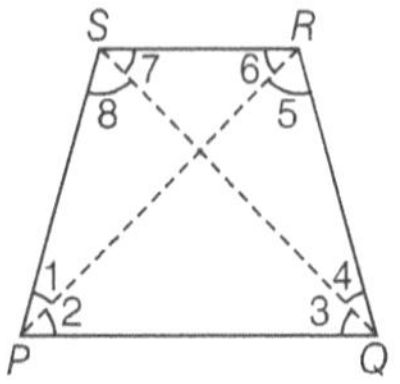

Since, PQ is the longest side of quadrilateral $PQRS$.

Therefore, in ΔPQR, we have

$PQ > QR$

$\Rightarrow \quad \angle 5 > \angle 2$ ...(i)

[as, angle opposite to longer side of a triangle is greater]

Since, RS is the smallest side of quadrilateral $PQRS$.

Therefore, in ΔPSR, we have

$PS > RS$

$\Rightarrow \quad \angle 6 > \angle 1$ ...(ii)

On adding Eqs. (i) and (ii), we get

$\angle 5 + \angle 6 > \angle 2 + \angle 1$

$\Rightarrow \quad \angle R > \angle P$

In ΔPQS, $\quad PQ > PS$ [as, PQ is the longest side]

$\Rightarrow \quad \angle 8 > \angle 3$ ...(iii)

[as, angle opposite to longer side of a triangle is greater]

In ΔSRQ,

$RQ > RS$ [as, RS is the shortest side]

$\Rightarrow \quad \angle 7 > \angle 4$ ...(iv)

[as, angle opposite to longer side of a triangle is greater]

On adding Eqs. (iii) and (iv), we get

$\angle 8 + \angle 7 > \angle 3 + \angle 4 \Rightarrow \angle S > \angle Q$

Hence, $\angle R > \angle P$ and $\angle S > \angle Q$.

10. (a) Given M and N are the mid-points of parallel sides AB and DC, respectively of a trapezium $ABCD$ and MN is perpendicular to both sides AB and DC, i.e. $MN \perp AB$ and $MN \perp CD$. Join AN and BM

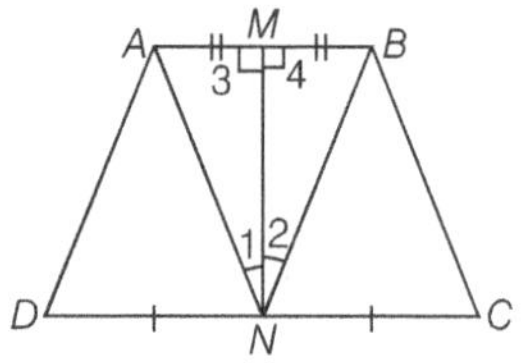

Since, M is the mid-point of AB.

$\therefore \quad AM = MB$

Now, in ΔAMN and ΔBMN, we have

$AM = MB$ [proved above]

$\angle 3 = \angle 4$ [each 90°]

and $MN = MN$ [common side]

$\therefore \quad \Delta AMN \cong \Delta BMN$ [by SAS congruence rule]

Then, $\angle 1 = \angle 2$ [by CPCT]

$\Rightarrow \quad 90° - \angle 1 = 90° - \angle 2$

$\Rightarrow \quad \angle AND = \angle BNC$ ...(i)

Now, in ΔADN and ΔBCN, we have

$\angle AND = \angle BNC$ [from Eq. (i)]

$AN = BN$ [proved above]

and $DN = NC$ [as, N is the mid-point of CD]

$\therefore \quad \Delta ADN \cong \Delta BCN$ [by SAS congruence rule]

$AD = BC$ [by CPCT]

Chapter 9 Mid-Point and Pythagoras Theorems

1. (d) We know that, if M is the mid-point of hypotenuse AB, then

$AM = MB = MC$

$\Rightarrow \quad MC = MB = \frac{1}{2} AB$

$\Rightarrow \quad MC = \frac{1}{2} AB$ ...(i)

Now, applying Pythagoras theorem in ΔABC, we get

$AB^2 = BC^2 + AC^2 = (60)^2 + (32)^2$

$\Rightarrow \quad AB^2 = 3600 + 1024 = 4624$

$\Rightarrow \quad AB = 68$

$\therefore$ From Eq. (i), we get $MC = \frac{1}{2} \times 68 = 34$ cm

2. (b) In ΔABC, as D is mid-point of BC and $DQ \parallel BA$, therefore Q is mid-point of AC, i.e. $AQ = QC$

[by converse of mid-point theorem]

Now, as $FA \parallel DQ \parallel CP$ and AC makes equal intercepts AQ and QC on the parallel lines. Therefore, by equal intercept theorem, we can say that the transversal FP also makes equal intercepts.

$\therefore \quad FD = DP$ ...(i)

$\because \quad EC = \frac{1}{2} AC$

$\therefore \quad EC = QC$ ...(ii)

Now, in ΔEQD, C is mid-point of EQ and $CP \parallel DQ$.

$\therefore$ P must be the mid-point of DE.

[by converse of mid-point theorem]

$\Rightarrow \quad DP = PE$ ...(iii)

Now, from Eqs. (i), (ii) and (iii), we get

$FD = DP = PE$

$\Rightarrow \quad FD = \frac{1}{3} FE$

3. (d) Since, D and E are the mid-points of sides BC and AC, therefore $DE \parallel AB$ and $DE = \frac{1}{2} AB$

[by mid-point theorem]

Similarly, $DF \parallel AC$ and $DF = \frac{1}{2} AC$

$\because \quad AB = AC \Rightarrow \frac{1}{2} AB = \frac{1}{2} AC$

$\Rightarrow \quad DE = DF$ ...(i)

Since, $DE \parallel AB$ and $DE = \frac{1}{2} AB$

$\Rightarrow \quad DE \parallel AF$ and $DE = AF$ [$\because$ F is mid-point of AB]

$\Rightarrow$ $DEAF$ is a parallelogram.

[$\because$ a pair of opposite side are equal and parallel]

$\therefore \quad DE = AF$ and $DF = AE$ ...(ii)

[$\because$ opposite sides of parallelogram are equal]

From Eqs. (i) and (ii), we get

$DE = DF = AF = AE$

$\Rightarrow$ $DEAF$ is a rhombus.

$\Rightarrow \quad AD \perp FE$ and $AM = MD$

[$\because$ diagonals of a rhombus bisect each other at right angles]

Hence, $AD \perp FE$ and AD is bisected by FE.

4. (b) **Given** A ΔABC, in which D, E and F are the mid-points of AB, BC and CA, respectively. Further P and Q are the mid-point of OB and OC, where O is the point of intersection of AE and DF.

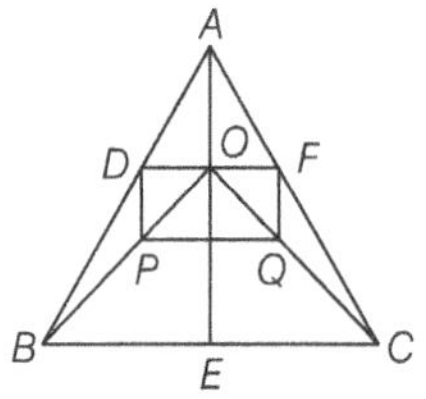

Since, D and F are the mid-points of AB and AC, therefore

$DF \parallel BC$ and $DF = \frac{1}{2} BC$ ...(i)

[by mid-point theorem]

Also, in ΔOBC, P and Q are the mid-points of OB and OC.

Therefore, $PQ \parallel BC$ and $PQ = \frac{1}{2} BC$ ...(ii)

[by mid-point theorem]

From Eqs. (i) and (ii), we get

$DF \parallel PQ$ and $DF = PQ$

$\therefore$ $DPQF$ is a parallelogram.

[$\because$ a pair of opposite sides are equal and parallel]

5. (a) **Given**, A ΔABC and through A, B and C lines are drawn parallel to BC, CA and AB respectively intersecting at P, Q and R.

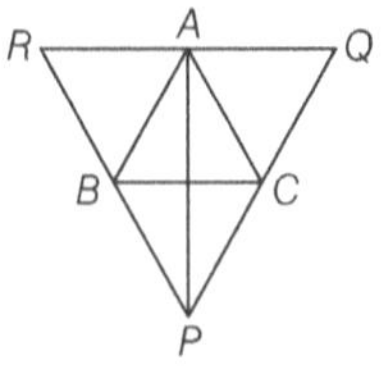

$PQ + QR + RP = 2(AB + BC + CA)$

Since, $BC \parallel RQ$ and $AB \parallel PQ$,

$\therefore$ $BC \parallel AQ$ and $AB \parallel CQ$

$\Rightarrow$ $ABCQ$ is a parallelogram.

Similarly, $ARBC$ is a parallelogram.

$\therefore$ $BC = AQ$ and $BC = AR$

[$\because$ opposite sides of parallelogram are equal]

$\Rightarrow$ A is mid-point of RQ.

Similarly, B and C are the mid-points of PR and PQ, respectively.

$\therefore$ $AB = \frac{1}{2}PQ$, $BC = \frac{1}{2}QR$

and $CA = \frac{1}{2}PR$ [by mid-point theorem]

$\Rightarrow$ $PQ = 2AB$, $QR = 2BC$, $PR = 2CA$

$\Rightarrow$ $PQ + QR + PR = 2AB + 2BC + 2CA$

$= 2(AB + BC + CA)$

$\Rightarrow$ Perimeter of ΔPQR = 2 (Perimeter of ΔABC)

6. (c) Let P, Q and R be the mid-points of AB, BC and AC, respectively.

$\therefore$ $PQ \parallel AC$, $PR \parallel BC$, $QR \parallel AB$

[by mid-point theorem]

$\Rightarrow$ $PQ \parallel RC$ and $PR \parallel QC$

$\Rightarrow$ $PQCR$ is a parallelogram.

$\Rightarrow$ $\angle QPR = \angle QCR = 80°$

[opposite angle of parallelogram are equal]

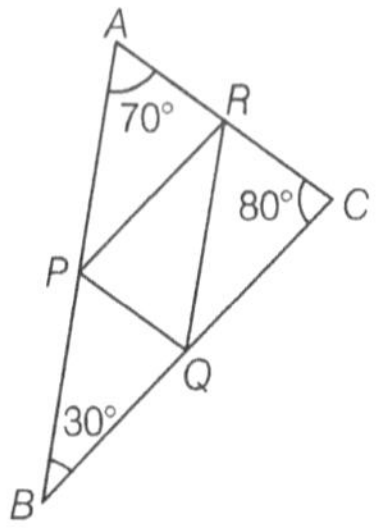

Similarly, $PBQR$ is a parallelogram.

$\Rightarrow$ $\angle PBQ = \angle PRQ = 30°$

and $APQR$ is a parallelogram.

$\Rightarrow$ $\angle PAR = \angle PQR = 70°$

Hence, in ΔPQR, $\angle P = 80°$, $\angle Q = 70°$ and $\angle R = 30°$.

7. (b) Let AC be the ladder of length 5 m and BC = 4 m be the height of the wall, which ladder is placed.

If the foot of the ladder is moved 1.6 m towards the wall, i.e. AD = 1.6 m, then the ladder is slide upward, i.e. $CE = x$ m.

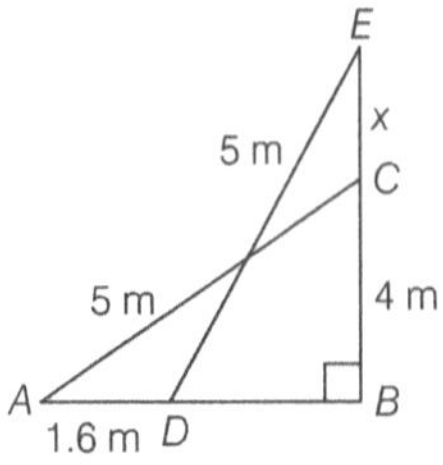

In right angled ΔEBD,

$ED^2 = EB^2 + BD^2$ [by Pythagoras theorem]

$\Rightarrow$ $(5)^2 = (AB)^2 + (4)^2$

$\Rightarrow$ $AB^2 = 25 - 16 = 9$

$\Rightarrow$ $AB = 3$ m

$\therefore$ $DB = AB - AD = 3 - 1.6 = 1.4$ m

In right angled ΔEBD,

$ED^2 = EB^2 + BD^2$ [by Pythagoras theorem]

$\Rightarrow$ $(5)^2 = (EB)^2 + (1.4)^2$ [$\because BD = 1.4$ m]

$\Rightarrow$ $25 = (EB)^2 + 1.96$

$\Rightarrow$ $(EB)^2 = 25 - 1.96$

$\Rightarrow$ $EB = \sqrt{23.04} = 4.8$

Now, $EC = EB - BC = 4.8 - 4 = 0.8$

Hence, the top of the ladder would slide upwards on the wall at distance 0.8 m.

8. (a) By using Pythagoras theorem,

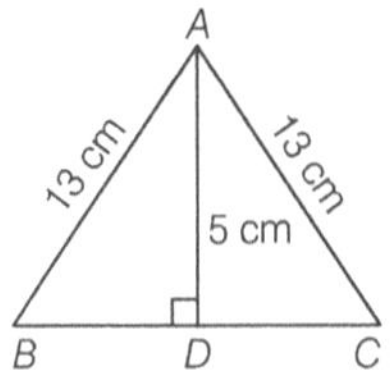

$BD^2 = (AB)^2 - (AD)^2$

$BD^2 = (13)^2 - (5)^2 = 169 - 25 = 144$

$\Rightarrow$ $BD = 12$ cm

$\therefore$ $BC = 2 \times BD = 2 \times 12 = 24$ cm

9. (b) In right angled ΔAOC,

$AC^2 = AO^2 + OC^2 = 6^2 + 8^2$

$\Rightarrow$ $AC^2 = 36 + 64 = 100$

$\Rightarrow$ $AC = 10$ cm

Now, in right angled ΔBAC,

$BC^2 = AB^2 + AC^2$

$= (24)^2 + (10)^2$

$= 576 + 100 = 676$

$\therefore$ $BC = \sqrt{676} = 26$ cm

10. (c) According to the given statement, we draw the following figure.

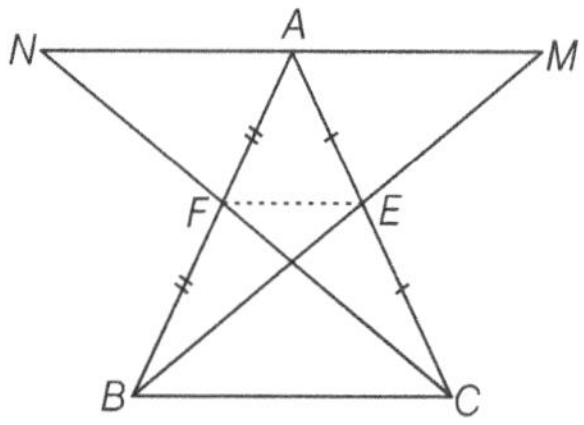

It is clear from the given statement that E is the mid-point of AC and BM whereas F is the mid-point of AB and CN.

Since, the line joining the mid-points of any two sides of a triangle is parallel and half of the third side.

$\therefore$ In ΔACN, $EF \parallel AN$ and $EF = \frac{1}{2} AN$ ...(i)

and in ΔABM, $EF \parallel AM$ and $EF = \frac{1}{2} AM$ ...(ii)

(i) From Eqs. (i) and (ii), we get

$AN \parallel AM$ [both are parallel to EF]

As, AN and AM are parallel and have a common point (say A), this is possible only if NAM is a straight line.

Hence, Statement I is true.

(ii) From Eqs. (i) and (ii), we have

$EF = \frac{1}{2} AN$ and $EF = \frac{1}{2} AM$

$\Rightarrow AN = AM \Rightarrow A$ is mid-point of MN.

Hence, Statement II is true.

Chapter 10 Rectilinear Figures

1. (b) Using angle sum property of quadrilateral, we have

$p + q + r + s = 360°$ ...(i)

and $w + x + y + z = 360°$ ...(ii)

From Eqs. (i) and (ii), we get

$p + q + r + s = w + x + y + z$

2. (d) We know that oposite sides of the parallelogram are equal.

Therefore, we have

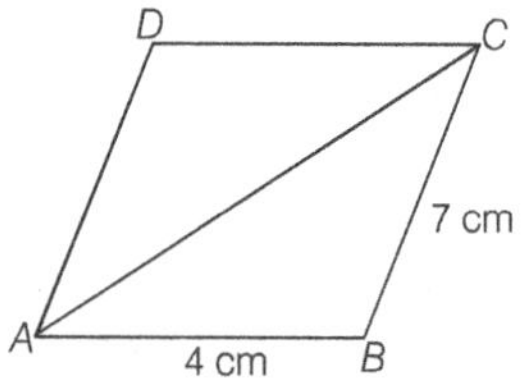

$DC = AB = 4$ cm and $AD = BC = 7$ cm

Also, we know that sum of any two sides must be greater than the third side.

In ΔABC, we have

$AB + BC > AC \Rightarrow AC < AB + BC$

$\Rightarrow AC < 4 + 7$

$\Rightarrow AC < 11$ cm

Similarly, $BD < 11$ cm

Hence, the length of the diagonals must be less than 11 cm.

3. (b) Given, $AB = AC$, $AEDC$ is a parallelogram, $\angle CDF = 70°$ and $\angle BFE = 100°$.

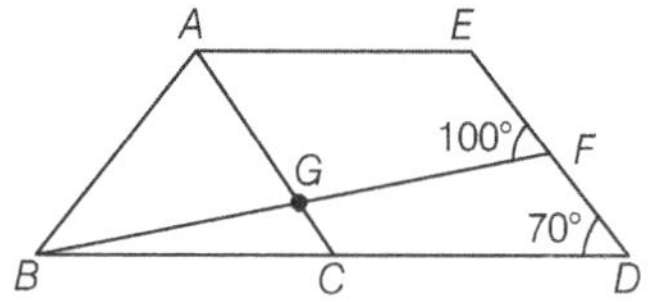

Since, $AB = AC$, therefore we have

$\angle ACB = \angle ABC$ ...(i)

[$\because$ angles opposite to equal sides are equal]

Also, $\angle ACB = \angle EDC = 70°$ ...(ii)

[$\because AC \parallel ED$ and BD is a transversal]

$\therefore$ From Eqs. (i) and (ii), we get

$\angle ABC = \angle ACB = 70°$

Now, in ΔABC, we have

$\angle BAC + \angle ABC + \angle ACB = 180°$

$\Rightarrow \angle BAC = 180° - 140° = 40°$ ...(iii)

Since, $AC \parallel ED$ and FG is a transversal. Therefore, we have

$\angle CGF = \angle EFG = 100°$

[alternate interior angles and $\angle BFE = \angle GFE$]

$\Rightarrow \angle AGB = 100°$ ...(iv)

[vertically opposite angles]

Now, in ΔAGB, we have

$\angle BAG + \angle ABG + \angle AGB = 180°$

$\Rightarrow 40° + \angle ABG + 100° = 180°$ [$\because \angle BAG = \angle BAC$]

$\Rightarrow \angle ABG = 40°$

$\Rightarrow \angle FBA = 40°$ [$\because \angle ABG = \angle FBA$]

4. (d) Let $\angle XOB = x$

In ΔOXB, $\angle XOB + \angle OXB + \angle XBO = 180°$

[by angle sum property of a triangle]

$\Rightarrow x + \angle OXB + 45° = 180°$

$\Rightarrow \angle OXB = 135° - x$

Now, $\angle OXB + \angle OXA = 180°$ [linear pair]

$\Rightarrow \angle OXA = 180° - (135° - x) = 45° + x$

Also, given $AX = OA$

$\Rightarrow \angle XOA = \angle OXA = 45° + x$

[$\because$ angles opposite to corresponding sides of a triangle are equal]

But $\angle AOX + \angle XOB = 90°$

[$\because$ diagonals of a square intersect at right angles]

$\Rightarrow 45° + x + x = 90°$

$\Rightarrow 2x = 45°$

$\therefore x = \frac{45°}{2} = 22.5°$

5. (a) Let $\angle BAX = \theta$.

Then, $\angle XAD = 90° - \theta$

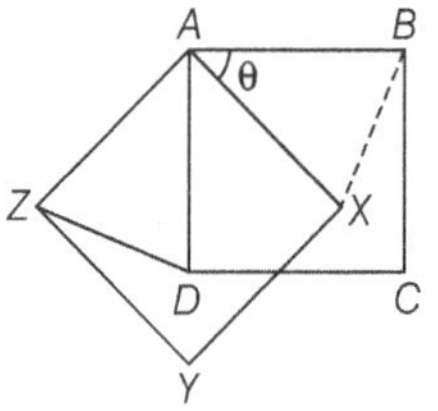

Also, $AXYZ$ is a square.

$\therefore \quad \angle ZAX = 90°$

$\Rightarrow \quad \angle ZAD + \angle XAD = 90°$

$\Rightarrow \quad \angle ZAD = 90° - \angle XAD$

$= 90° - (90° - \theta) = \theta$

$\Rightarrow \quad \angle BAX = \angle ZAD \quad$ ...(i)

Now, in ΔABX and ΔADZ,

$AB = AD \quad$ [sides of square $ABCD$]

$AX = AZ \quad$ [sides of square $AXYZ$]

and $\angle BAX = \angle ZAD \quad$ [from Eq. (i)]

$\therefore \quad \Delta ABX \cong \Delta ADZ \quad$ [by SAS congruence rule]

Hence, $BX = DZ$. $\quad$ [by CPCT]

6. (a) Given, $ABCD$ is a square. P, Q, R and S are points on the sides AB, BC, CD and DA respectively, such that $AP = BQ = CR = DS$.

Now, join SP and QP.

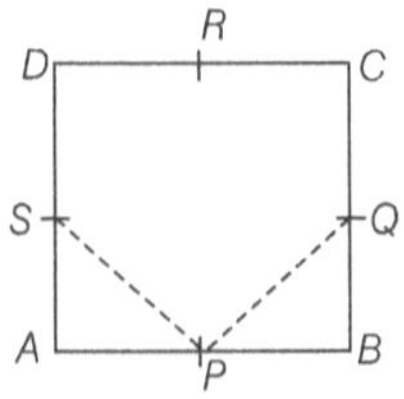

In ΔAPS and ΔPBQ,

$AS = PB \quad [\because AB = AD \Rightarrow AP = DS]$

$AP = BQ \quad$ [given]

and $\angle A = \angle B = 90° \quad$ [angles of square]

$\therefore \quad \angle APS \cong \Delta BQP \quad$ [SAS congruence rule]

$\Rightarrow \quad \angle ASP = \angle BPQ \quad$ [by CPCT] ...(i)

Now, in ΔASP,

$\angle SPB = \angle ASP + \angle PAS$

[by exterior angle property of a triangle]

$\Rightarrow \angle SPQ + \angle BPQ = \angle ASP + 90°$

$\Rightarrow \quad \angle SPQ = 90° \quad$ [using Eq. (i)]

7. (b) In quadrilateral $ABCD$, join AC

In ΔABC

$AB = BC \quad$ [given]

$\therefore \quad \angle BAC = \angle BCA \quad$ ...(i)

[angles opposite to equal sides are also equal]

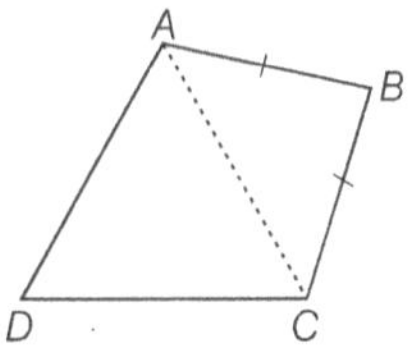

In ΔADC,

$CD > AD \quad$ [given]

$\therefore \quad \angle DAC > \angle DCA \quad$ ...(ii)

[in a triangle, angle opposite to greater side is bigger than the angle opposite to smaller side]

On adding Eqs. (i) and (ii), we get

$\angle BAC + \angle DAC > \angle BCA + \angle DCA$

$\angle BAD > \angle BCD$

8. (b) Produce AP and BQ to meet at R.

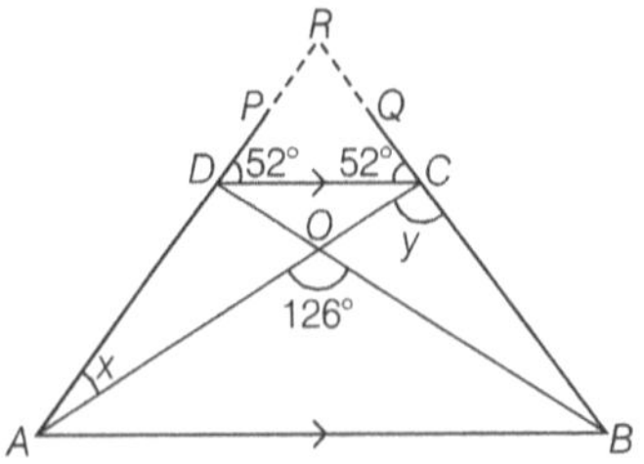

In ΔRDC, $\angle RDC = \angle RCD \quad$ [each angle = 52°]

$\therefore \quad DR = CR \quad$ ...(i)

[sides opposite to equal angles are equal]

$\Rightarrow \quad \angle RAB = \angle RDC$

[corresponding angles are equal as $AB \parallel DC$]

Similarly, $\angle RBA = \angle RCD$

$\therefore \quad \angle RAB = \angle RBA$

$\Rightarrow \quad RB = AR \quad$ ...(ii)

[sides opposite to equal angles are equal]

$\therefore \quad AD = AR - DR = RB - CR = BC$

[from Eqs. (i) and (ii)]

$\Rightarrow$ $ABCD$ is an isosceles trapezium.

$\therefore \quad OA = OB \quad$ [properties of an isosceles trapezium]

$\Rightarrow \quad \angle OBA = \angle OAB$

$\therefore \quad \angle OAB = \dfrac{180° - 126°}{2} = 27°$

Now, $\angle DAC = \angle DAB - \angle OAB = 52° - 27° = 25°$

$\therefore \quad x = 25°$

In ΔABC, $\angle ACB + \angle CAB + \angle ABC = 180°$

[use angle sum property of a triangle]

$\Rightarrow \quad y + 27° + 52° = 180°$

$\Rightarrow \quad y = 180° - 27° - 52° \Rightarrow y = 101°$

9. (a) Given, $ABCD$ is a parallelogram, AP bisects $\angle A$ and CQ bisects $\angle C$.

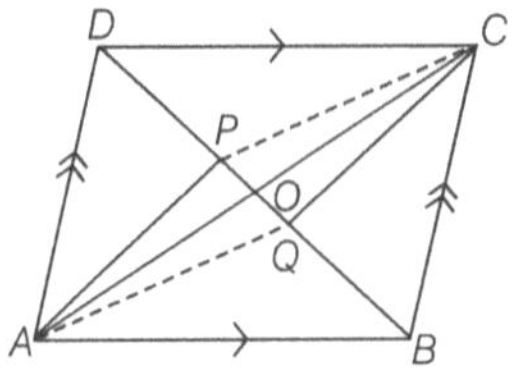

From figure,

$\angle BAP = \dfrac{1}{2} \angle A \quad [\because AP$ is bisector of $\angle A]$

$\angle DCQ = \dfrac{1}{2} \angle C \quad [\because CQ$ is bisector of $\angle C]$

$\angle BAP = \angle DCQ \quad$ ...(i)

[$\because$ opposite angles in a parallelogram are equals]

$\angle BAC = \angle DCA \quad$ ...(ii)

[$\because AB \parallel DC$ and AC is transversal]

On subtracting Eq. (i) from Eq. (ii), we get

$\angle BAP - \angle BAC = \angle DCQ - \angle DCA \Rightarrow \angle CAP = \angle ACQ$

$\Rightarrow \quad AP \parallel QC$

[$\because$ if alternate angles are equal, then lines $AP \parallel QC$]

Similarly, $PC \parallel AQ$.

Hence, $PCQA$ is a parallelogram.

Chapter 12 Areas Theorems on Parallelograms and Triangles

1. (c) We have,

ar (parallelogram $ABCD$) = ar (parallelogram $FECG$)

$\Rightarrow$ ar (parallelogram $ABCD$) – ar (parallelogram $BQEC$)

= ar (parallelogram $FECG$) – ar (parallelogram $BQEC$)

[subtracting ar (parallelogram $BQEC$) on both sides]

$\Rightarrow$ ar $(ADEQ)$ = ar $(FGBQ)$

Now, ar (parallelogram $AQED$) = ar (ΔADE) + ar (ΔAQE)

$= 12 + 12 = 24 \text{ cm}^2$

$\Rightarrow$ ar (parallelogram $FGBQ$) = 24 cm^2

2. (a) Since, $\angle ADC + \angle DAB = 180°$.

Therefore, $AB \parallel CD \Rightarrow AB \parallel XC$

Also, $AX \parallel BC$ [$\because$ sum of interior angles on the same side of transversal is 180°]

$\therefore$ $ABCX$ is a parallelogram.

$\Rightarrow$ $AB = CX = 5$ cm

Now, in ΔAXD, $AD^2 = AX^2 - XD^2$ [by Pythagoras theorem]

$= 5^2 - 3^2 = 25 - 9 = 16 \Rightarrow AD = 4$ cm

$\therefore$ Area of parallelogram $ABCX = AB \times AD = 5 \times 4 = 20 \text{ cm}^2$

3. (b) Clearly,

$$\text{ar}(\Delta ADP) + \text{ar}(\Delta BPC) = \frac{1}{2} \text{ ar (parallelogram } ABCD)$$

$$= \frac{1}{2} \times 60 = 30 \text{ cm}^2$$

4. (b) Given, $AB = a$ cm, $DC = b$ cm and $AB \parallel DC$.

Also, E and F are the mid-points of AD and BC, respectively. So, distance between CD, EF and AB, EF will be same (say h).

Join BD, which intersects EF at M.

Now, in ΔABD, E is the mid-point of AD and $EM \parallel AB$.

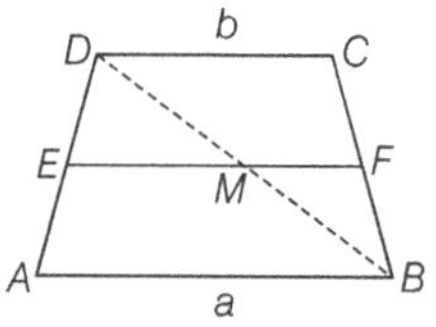

So, M is the mid-point of BD [by mid-point theorem]

and $EM = \frac{1}{2} AB$ ...(i)

Similarly, in ΔCBD, $MF = \frac{1}{2} CD$ ...(ii)

On adding Eqs. (i) and (ii), we get

$$EM + MF = \frac{1}{2} AB + \frac{1}{2} CD$$

$$\Rightarrow \quad EF = \frac{1}{2}(AB + CD) = \frac{1}{2}(a + b)$$

Now, area of trapezium $ABFE$

$= \frac{1}{2} \times$ (Sum of parallel sides) $\times$ (Distance between parallel sides)

$$= \frac{1}{2}\left(a + \frac{1}{2}(a + b)\right) \times h = \frac{1}{4}(3a + b)h$$

Now, area of trapezium $EFCD$

$$= \frac{1}{2}\left[b + \frac{1}{2}(a + b)\right] \times h = \frac{1}{4}(3b + a)h$$

$$\therefore \text{ Required ratio} = \frac{\text{Area of trapezium } ABFE}{\text{Area of trapezium } EFCD}$$

$$= \frac{\frac{1}{4}(3a + b)h}{\frac{1}{4}(3b + a)h} = \frac{(3a + b)}{(a + 3b)}$$

$$= (3a + b) : (a + 3b)$$

5. (b) Given

(i) ar (parallelogram $AFPE$) = ar (parallelogram $FBGM$) = ar (parallelogram $NGCH$) = ar (parallelogram $EOHD$)

(ii) ar $(ABCD) = 20 +$ ar $(EFGH)$

(iii) ar $(EFGH) = 6$ ar $(MNOP)$

As we know that diagonal of a parallelogram divides it into two triangles of equal areas. Therefore, we have

(A) ar (ΔAEF) = ar (ΔEPF)
(B) ar (ΔFBG) = ar (ΔFMG)
(C) ar (ΔGCH) = ar (ΔGNH)
(D) ar (ΔEOH) = ar (ΔEDH)

Clearly, (A) = (B) = (C) = (D) [using given condition (i)] ...(i)

Now , since ar $(ABCD)$ – ar $(EFGH) = 20$

$\Rightarrow$ ar (ΔAEF) + ar (ΔFBG) + ar (ΔGCH) + ar $(\Delta EDH) = 20$

$\Rightarrow$ 4 ar $(\Delta AEF) = 20$ [using Eq. (i)]

$\Rightarrow$ ar (ΔAEF) = ar (ΔFBG) = ar (ΔGCH)

= ar (ΔEDH)

$= 5 \text{ cm}^2$

Now, we have the following figure

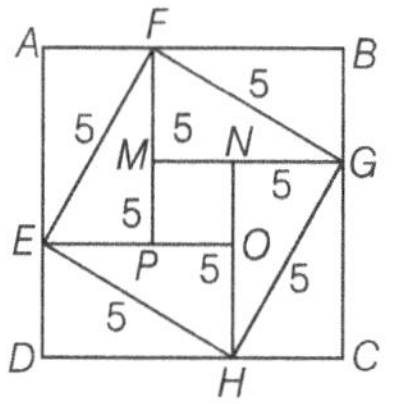

Let the area of $MNOP$ be $x \text{ cm}^2$.

Then, ar $(EFGH) = 6$ ar $(MNOP)$

$$\Rightarrow \quad x = \frac{1}{6} \text{ ar }(EFGH)$$

$$\Rightarrow \quad x = \frac{1}{6}[\text{ar}(\Delta EPF) + \text{ar}(\Delta FMG) + \text{ar}(\Delta EOH) + \text{ar}(\Delta GNH) + \text{ar}(MNOP)]$$

$$\Rightarrow \quad x = \frac{1}{6}(5 \times 4 + x)$$

$\Rightarrow$ $6x = 20 + x$

$\Rightarrow$ $5x = 20$

$\therefore$ $x = 4 \text{ cm}^2$

Hence, the area of $MNOP$ is 4 cm^2.

6. (a) Given, $ABCD$ is a parallelogram and P, Q, R and S are the points on the parallelogram such that $AP = DR$.

Clearly, $AP \parallel DR$. [$\because AB \parallel CD$]

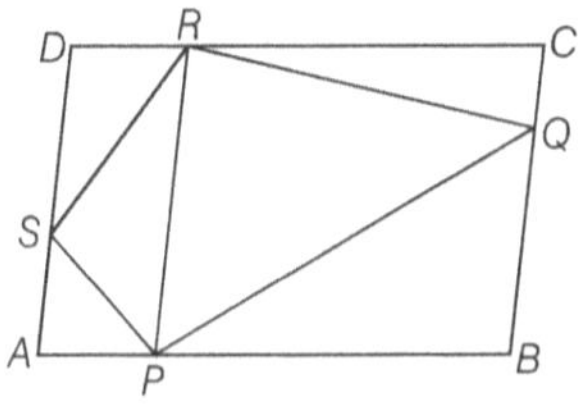

$\therefore$ *APRD* is a parallelogram.

Consequently, $PR \parallel AD$.

Now, as ΔPRS and parallelogram *PRDA* are on the same base *PR* and between the same parallel lines *AD* and *PR*.

$\therefore$ ar $(\Delta PSR) = \frac{1}{2} \times$ ar (parallelogram *PRDA*)

Similarly, ar $(\Delta PQR) = \frac{1}{2} \times$ ar (parallelogram *PBCR*)

$\therefore$ ar (quadrilateral *PSRQ*) = ar (ΔPSR) + ar (ΔPQR)

$= \frac{1}{2} \times$ ar (parallelogram *PRDA*) + $\frac{1}{2} \times$ ar (parallelogram *PRCB*)

$= \frac{1}{2}$[ar (parallelogram *PRDA*) + ar (parallelogram *PRCB*)]

$= \frac{1}{2} \times$ ar (parallelogram *ABCD*) $= \frac{1}{2} \times 16 = 8 \text{ cm}^2$

7. (d) Clearly, ar $(\Delta PRQ) = \frac{1}{2}$ ar $(WXQR)$

$$= \frac{1}{2}\left\{\frac{1}{2} \text{ ar } (WXYZ)\right\} = \frac{1}{4} \text{ ar } (WXYZ) \quad \text{...(i)}$$

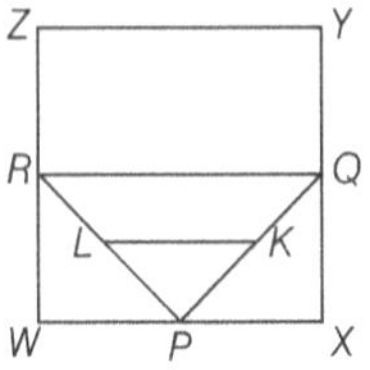

Also, ar $(\Delta PRQ) = 4$ ar (ΔPKL) ...(ii)

Now, from Eqs. (i) and (ii), we get

$$4 \text{ ar } (\Delta PKL) = \frac{1}{4} \text{ ar } (WXYZ)$$

$$\therefore \quad \frac{\text{ar } (\Delta PKL)}{\text{ar } (WXYZ)} = \frac{1}{16}$$

8. (b) Given, ΔDEF and ΔHGI are isosceles triangle on the equal bases *DE* and *GH*, which are parallel to *FI* with $DE = GH = 9$ cm and $DH = 20$ cm.

Clearly, *FEGI* is a trapezium, $[\because DH \parallel FI]$

and ar (trapezium *FEGI*) $= \frac{1}{2}(EG + FI) \times DF$ ...(i)

Since, ΔDEF is an isosceles right angled triangle.

Therefore, $DE = FD = 9$ cm

Now, from Eq. (i), we have

$$\text{ar (trapezium } FEGI) = \frac{1}{2}[(20 - 9 - 9) + 20] \times 9$$

$$= \frac{1}{2}(2 + 20) \times 9$$

$$= 11 \times 9 = 99 \text{ cm}^2$$

Chapter 13 Circles

1. (a) $OD \perp AB \Rightarrow D$ is the mid-point of *AB* and also, *O* is the mid-point of *BC*.

Now, in ΔBAC, *D* is the mid-point of *AB* and *O* is the mid-point of *BC*.

$$\therefore \quad OD = \frac{1}{2}AC \Rightarrow 11 = \frac{1}{2}AC \Rightarrow AC = 2 \times 11 = 22 \text{ cm}$$

2. (d) Let ΔABC be an equilateral triangle of side 12 cm.

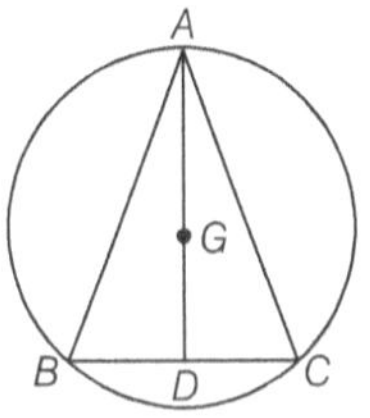

Let *AD* be one of its median, then

$$AD \perp BC \text{ and } BD = \frac{12}{2} = 6 \text{ cm}$$

$$\therefore \quad AD = \sqrt{AB^2 - BD^2} = \sqrt{(12)^2 - (6)^2}$$

[using Pythagoras theorem in right angled ΔADB]

$$= \sqrt{144 - 36} = \sqrt{108} = 6\sqrt{3}$$

Let *G* be the centroid of ΔABC, then $AG : GD = 2:1$

$\therefore$ Radius $= AG = \frac{2}{3}AD = \frac{2}{3} \times 6\sqrt{3} = 4\sqrt{3}$ cm

3. (a) Here, $OP \perp CD$

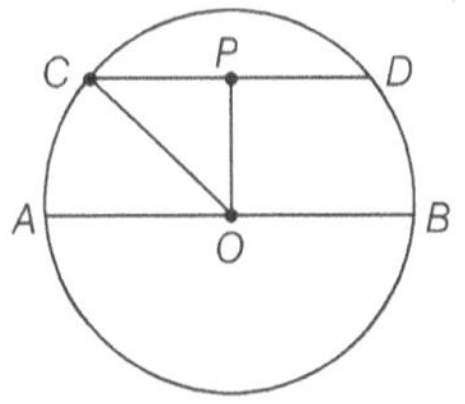

$\therefore CP = \frac{1}{2}CD = \frac{1}{2} \times 48 = 24$ cm

Radius of circle, $OC = \frac{AB}{2} = \frac{50}{2} = 25$ cm

Now, $OP = \sqrt{OC^2 - CP^2} = \sqrt{(25)^2 - (24)^2}$

[using Pythagoras theorem in right angled ΔOPC]

$$= \sqrt{625 - 576}$$

$$= \sqrt{49} = 7$$

4. (a) Let *O* be the centre of the circle.

Let the bisector of $\angle BAC$ meet the chord *BC* at *M*.

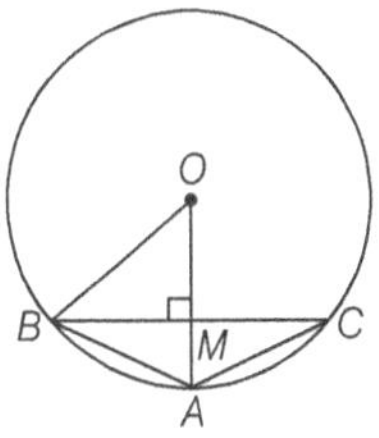

In ΔBAM and ΔCAM,

$\angle BAM = \angle MAC$ [by construction]

$AB = AC$ [given]

$AM = AM$ [common side]

$\therefore \Delta BAM \cong \Delta CAM$ [by SAS congruence rule]

$\therefore BM = MC$ and $\angle BMA = \angle AMC$ [by CPCT]

But $\angle BMA + \angle AMC = 180°$ [$\because$ BMC is a straight line]

$\Rightarrow \angle BMA = 90°$

Therefore, AM is perpendicular bisector of BC and hence it passes through the centre O of the circle.

Let $BM = y$ cm and $OM = x$ cm, then

$MA = OA - OM = (5 - x)$ cm [$\because$ radius = 5 cm]

In right angled ΔOMB, $y^2 + x^2 = 5^2$ ...(i)

In right angled ΔBMA, $y^2 + (5 - x)^2 = 6^2$

i.e. $y^2 + x^2 - 10x = 11$ ...(ii)

[by Pythagoras theorem]

On subtracting Eq. (ii) from Eq. (i), we get

$$10x = 25 - 11 \Rightarrow 10x = 14 \Rightarrow x = \frac{7}{5}$$

On substituting the value of x in Eq. (i), we get

$$y^2 + \frac{19}{25} = 25 \Rightarrow y^2 = 25 - \frac{49}{25} = \frac{625 - 49}{25}$$

$$\Rightarrow y^2 = \frac{576}{25} \Rightarrow y = \frac{24}{5}$$

$\therefore$ Length of chord $BC = 2BM = 2 \cdot \frac{24}{5}$ cm $= \frac{48}{5}$ cm $= 9.6$ cm

5. (b) Given that the two circles with centres C, D and intersecting at points A, B so that AB is their common chord.

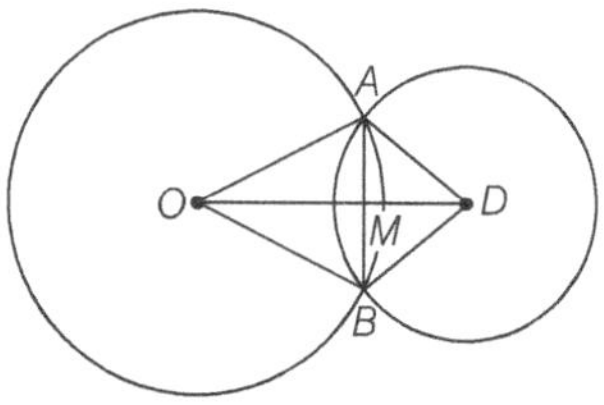

In ΔACD and ΔBCD,

$CA = CB$ [radii of same circle]

$AD = BD$ [radii of same circle]

$CD = CD$ [common side]

$\therefore \Delta ACD \cong \Delta BCD$ [by SSS congruence rule]

$\Rightarrow \angle ACM = \angle MCB$ [by CPCT]

In ΔACM and ΔBCM,

$\angle ACM = \angle MCB$

$CA = CB$ [radii of same circle]

$CM = CM$ [common side]

$\therefore \Delta ACM \cong \Delta BCM$ [by SAS congruence rule]

$\Rightarrow AM = MB$

and $\angle CMA = \angle CMB$ [by CPCT]

$\therefore \angle CMA + \angle CMB = 180°$

[$\because$ AMB is a straight line]

$\Rightarrow \angle CMA = 90°$ [$\because \angle CMA = \angle CMB$]

Hence, CD is perpendicular bisector of AB.

6. (a) $AB = AC$ [sides of an equilateral ΔABC]

$AM = AN$ [radii of the same circle]

$\therefore AB - AM = AC - AN$

$\Rightarrow BM = CN$ ...(i)

Now, in ΔBMC and ΔCNB,

$BM = CN$ [from Eq. (i)]

$BC = BC$ [common side]

and $\angle MBC = \angle BCN = 60°$

[each angle of an equilateral triangle is 60°]

$\therefore \Delta BMC \cong \Delta CNB$ [by SAS congruence rule]

$\Rightarrow BN = CM$ [by CPCT]

7. (b) Given a circle with centre O and $OPQR$ is a square.

In ΔOXP and ΔOYR, we have

$OP = OR$ [sides of square]

$OX = OY$ [radii of circle]

and $\angle OPX = \angle ORY = 90°$ [angles of a square]

$\therefore \Delta OXP \cong \Delta OYR$ [by RHS congruence rule]

$\Rightarrow PX = RY$ [by CPCT]

$\Rightarrow PQ - QX = QR - QY$

$\Rightarrow PQ - QX = PQ - QY$ [$\because PQ = QR$]

$\Rightarrow -QX = -QY$

$\therefore QX = QY$

8. (c) Let radius of two crescents be r.

We have, $EC = FD$ [radii of arcs]

On subtracting DE from both sides, we get

$EC - DE = FD - DE$

$\Rightarrow CD = EF = 12$ cm [given]

$\Rightarrow EG = GF = 6$ cm

[$\because$ AG is perpendicular bisector of EF]

Now, in ΔAEG,

$AG = \frac{1}{2} AB = \frac{1}{2} \times 16 = 8$ cm [$\because AB = 16$ cm]

In right angled ΔAGE,

$AE^2 = AG^2 + EG^2$ [by Pythagoras theorem]

$\Rightarrow r^2 = 8^2 + 6^2 = 64 + 36 = 100$

$\therefore r = 10$ cm

9. (a) Let O' and O be the centres of two congruent circles.

Since, AB is a common chord of these circles.

$\therefore \angle BPA = \angle BQA$

[since, angles subtended by equal chords are equal]

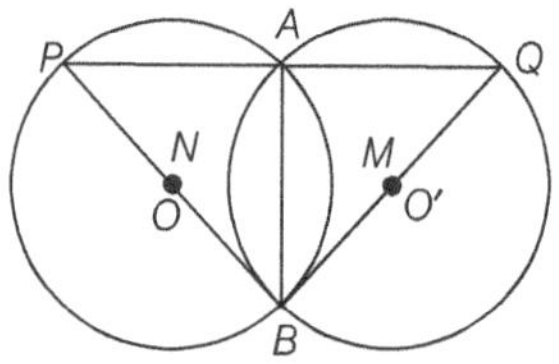

Hence, $BP = BQ$

[$\because$ sides opposite to equal angles of a triangle are also equal]

10. (b) Let O be the centre of the given circle and its radius be b cm. Given, $AB = 5$ cm and $CD = 11$ cm are two chords on opposite sides of its centre. Draw $ON \perp AB$ and $OM \perp CD$.

Since, $ON \perp AB$, $OM \perp CD$ and $AB \parallel CD$, therefore the points N, O and M are collinear.

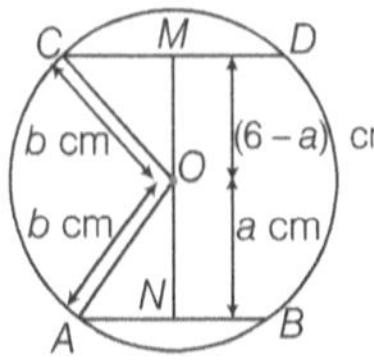

Given, distance between AB and $CD = MN = 6$ cm

Let $ON = a$ cm

$\therefore$ $OM = (6 - a)$ cm

Join OA and OC.

Then, $OA = OC = b$ cm

We know that the perpendicular from the centre to a chord of the circle bisects the chord.

Then, $AN = NB = \frac{5}{2} = 2.5$ cm

and $CM = MD = \frac{11}{2} = 5.5$ cm

In right angled ΔONA and ΔOMC,

$OA^2 = ON^2 + AN^2$

and $OC^2 = OM^2 + CM^2$ [by Pythagoras theorem]

$\Rightarrow$ $b^2 = a^2 + (2.5)^2$ ...(i)

and $b^2 = (6 - a)^2 + (5.5)^2$ ...(ii)

So, $a^2 + (2.5)^2 = (6 - a)^2 + (5.5)^2$ [from Eqs. (i) and (ii)]

$\Rightarrow$ $a^2 + 6.25 = 36 - 12a + a^2 + 30.25$

$\Rightarrow$ $12a = 60 \Rightarrow a = 5$

On putting $a = 5$ in Eq. (i), we get

$b^2 = (5)^2 + (2.5)^2 = 25 + 6.25 = 31.25$

$\therefore$ Radius $= b = \sqrt{31.25} = 5.6$ cm (approx.)

Chapter 14 Statistics

1. (a) We know that, AM $= \frac{\text{Sum of all observations}}{\text{Number of observations}}$

$\therefore$ Mean $= \frac{6 + 8 + 5 + 7 + x + 4}{6} = 7$

$\Rightarrow$ $\frac{30 + x}{6} = 7 \Rightarrow 30 + x = 42$

$\Rightarrow$ $x = 42 - 30 = 12$

2. (c) Firstly, we arrange the given data in ascending order. We have, 33, 35, 41, 46, 55, 58, 64, 77, 87, 90 and 92.

Here, number of terms = 11 which is an odd number.

Hence, median $= \left(\frac{11+1}{2}\right)$th observation = 6th observation

$\therefore$ Median = 58

3. (d) The factors of 24 are 1, 2, 3, 4, 6, 8, 12 and 24.

Here, $n = 8$

$\therefore$ Mean $= \frac{1 + 2 + 3 + 4 + 6 + 8 + 12 + 24}{8} = 7.5$

$\left[\because \text{mean} = \frac{\Sigma x_i}{n}\right]$

4. (b) Let the observations be $x_1, x_2, \ldots, x_n$. After the increase they become $x_1 + 5, x_2 + 5, x_3 + 5, \ldots, x_n + 5$.

$\therefore$ Mean $= \frac{x_1 + 5 + x_2 + 5 + \ldots + x_n + 5}{n}$

$= \frac{x_1 + x_2 + \ldots + x_n + 5n}{n}$

$= \frac{x_1 + x_2 + \ldots + x_n}{n} + \frac{5n}{n}$

$= \frac{x_1 + x_2 + \ldots + x_n}{n} + 5$

$\therefore$ New mean = Old mean + 5

5. (a) Here, number of observations, $n = 12$ and median = 48.5

$\therefore$ Median $= \frac{\text{6th observation} + \text{7th observation}}{2}$

$\Rightarrow$ $48.5 = \frac{40 + x}{2} \Rightarrow 40 + x = 97$

$\Rightarrow$ $x = 97 - 40 = 57$

6. (c) Here, mean = 30 and $n = 100$

$\because$ Mean $= \frac{\Sigma x_i}{n} \Rightarrow 30 = \frac{\Sigma x_i}{100}$

$\therefore$ $\Sigma x_i = 3000$, which is incorrect as per the question.

Now, correct value of Σx_i

$= 3000 - (32 + 12) + (23 + 11) = 2990$

$\therefore$ Correct mean $= \frac{2990}{100} = 29.90$

Hence, the correct mean is 29.90.

Chapter 15 Perimeter and Area of Plane Figures

1. (b) Let ABC be the right angled triangle with sides a, b and c, where $a < b < c$, i.e. c is the hypotenuse and a and b are the perpendicular sides.

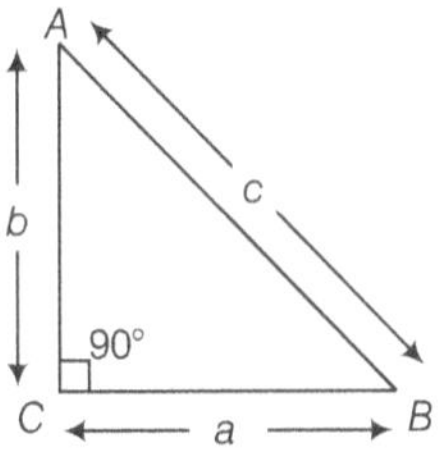

$\because$ Perimeter of $\Delta ABC = 12$ cm

$\therefore$ $a + b + c = 12$ ...(i)

and area of $\Delta ABC = 6$ cm^2

$\therefore$ $\frac{1}{2} \times a \times b = 6 \Rightarrow ab = 12$ ...(ii)

Now, from Eq. (i), we have $a + b = 12 - c$ ...(iii)

On squaring both sides, we get $(a + b)^2 = (12 - c)^2$

$\Rightarrow$ $a^2 + b^2 + 2ab = 144 + c^2 - 24c$

$\Rightarrow$ $a^2 + b^2 + 2 \times 12 = 144 + c^2 - 24c$ [using Eq. (ii)]

$\Rightarrow$ $c^2 + 24 = 144 + c^2 - 24c$

[$\because a^2 + b^2 = c^2$, using Pythagoras theorem in ΔABC]

$\Rightarrow$ $24c = 144 - 24$

$\Rightarrow$ $24c = 120 \Rightarrow c = 5$

$\therefore$ $a + b = 12 - c = 12 - 5 = 7$ cm

2. (a) Let ABC be the given triangle with sides a, b and c.

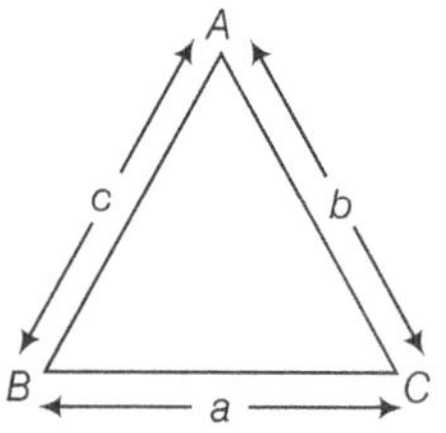

Now, according to given condition, we get

$$\frac{a+b}{2} = 6 + \frac{c}{2}, \frac{a+c}{2} = 6 + \frac{b}{2} \text{ and } \frac{b+c}{2} = 6 + \frac{a}{2}$$

$\Rightarrow \quad a + b = 12 + c \quad$ ...(i)

$a + c = 12 + b \quad$ ...(ii)

and $\quad b + c = 12 + a \quad$ ...(iii)

Now, on adding Eqs. (i), (ii) and (iii), we get

$2(a + b + c) = 36 + (a + b + c)$

$\Rightarrow \quad 2(a + b + c) - (a + b + c) = 36$

$\Rightarrow \quad a + b + c = 36 \quad$ ...(iv)

$\Rightarrow \quad 12 + c + c = 36 \quad$ [using Eq. (i)]

$\Rightarrow \quad 2c = 24 \Rightarrow c = 12$

Similarly, using Eqs. (ii) and (iii) in Eq. (iv), we get

$b = 12$ and $a = 12$

Hence, $a = b = c = 12$.

Now, ar $(\Delta ABC) = \frac{\sqrt{3}}{4} \times (12)^2 = \frac{\sqrt{3}}{4} \times 144 = 36\sqrt{3}$ cm^2

3. (b) Let $ABCD$ be the given rhombus, with $AC = 12$ cm and $BD = 9$ cm.

Now, draw $BE \perp CD$.

As, we know that diagonals of a rhombus bisect each other at 90°.

$\therefore$ $OB = 4.5$ cm, $OC = 6$ cm and $\angle BOC = 90°$.

Thus, in ΔBOC, we have

$BC^2 = OB^2 + OC^2 \Rightarrow BC^2 = (4.5)^2 + 6^2$

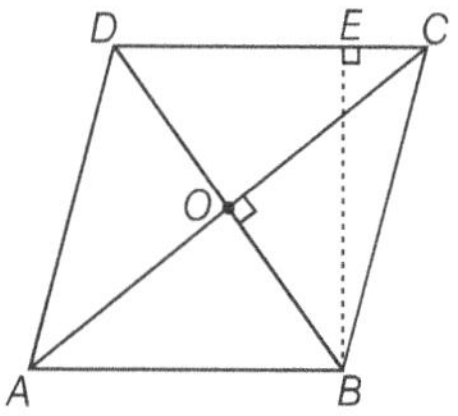

$\Rightarrow \quad BC^2 = 20.25 + 36 = 56.25 = (7.5)^2$

$\Rightarrow \quad BC = 7.5$ cm

$\Rightarrow \quad AB = BC = CD = DA = 7.5$ cm

Now, as $AC = 12$ cm and $BD = 9$ cm, therefore

ar (rhombus $ABCD$)

$= \frac{1}{2} \times AC \times BD$

$= \frac{1}{2} \times 12 \times 9 = 54$ cm$^2 \quad$ ...(i)

Also, area of rhombus $ABCD$ = base × height

$= DC \times BE$

[$\because$ rhombus is also a parallelogram] ...(ii)

From Eqs. (i) and (ii), we get

$7.5 \times BE = 54 \quad$ [$\because DC = 7.5$ cm]

$\Rightarrow \quad BE = \frac{54}{7.5} = 7.2$ cm

4. (b) Let ABC be the right angled triangle, right angled at B, with circumradius $r = 10$ cm and $BC = 12$ cm.

We know that, circumradius is half of the hypotenuse, therefore

$AC = 2(10) = 20$ cm

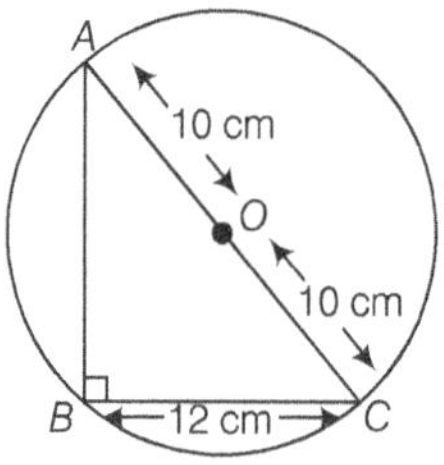

Now, in ΔABC, we have

$AC^2 + AB^2 + BC^2 \quad$ [by using Pythagoras theorem]

$\Rightarrow \quad (20)^2 = (12)^2 + AB^2$

$\Rightarrow \quad AB^2 = 400 - 144 = 256$

$\Rightarrow \quad AB = 16$ cm $\quad$ [taking positive sign]

Area of $\Delta ABC = \frac{1}{2} \times BC \times AB = \frac{1}{2} \times 12 \times 16 = 96$ cm^2

5. (a) Let $ABCD$ be the given rectangular field with $AB = 45$ m and $BC = 38$ m.

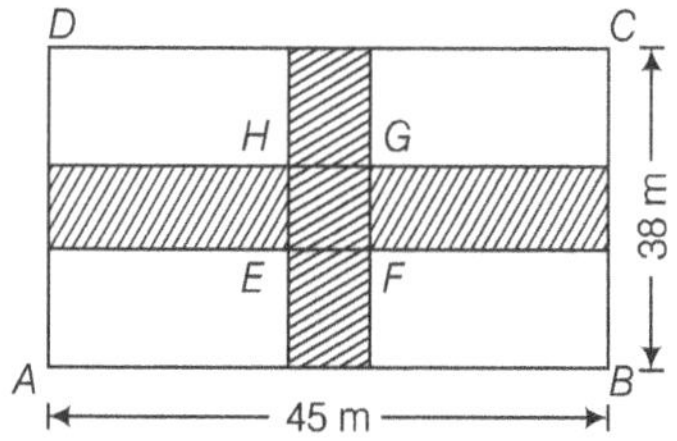

Now, as width of path is 4 m, therefore

area of path parallel to length = 45 × 4 = 180 m^2

and area of path parallel to breadth = 38 × 4 = 152 m^2.

$\therefore$ Area of two paths = 180 + 152

− Area of the common part $EFGH$

= 332 − 4 × 4 = 332 − 16 = 316 m^2

Since, the cost of gravelling 1 m^2 path is ₹ 5.60.

$\therefore$ Total cost of gravelling the path = ₹ (316 × 5.60)

= ₹ 1769.60

6. (b) Area of the given field = ar (ΔAZB) + ar (trapezium $ZBCX$) + ar (ΔDXC) + ar (ΔDAE)

$= \frac{1}{2} \times 25 \times 10 + \frac{1}{2} \times (25 + 30) \times 15 + \frac{1}{2} \times 30 \times 12 + \frac{1}{2} \times (12 + 15 + 10) \times 20$

$= 125 + 412.5 + 180 + 370 = 1087.5$ m^2

Hence, the required area is 1087.5 m^2.

7. (c) According to the given information, we have the following figure.

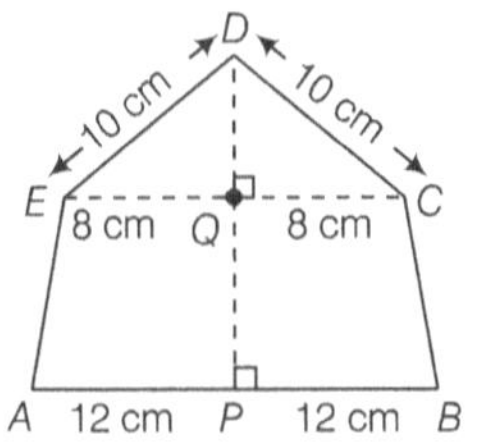

Clearly, area of pentagon $ABCDE$

$= \text{ar}(\Delta\, DQE) + \text{ar}(\Delta\, DQC) + \text{ar}(\text{trapezium}\ \Delta\, EABC)$

$= \frac{1}{2} \times EQ \times DQ + \frac{1}{2} \times QC \times DQ + \frac{1}{2}(EC + AB) \times PQ$ ...(i)

Now, in $\Delta\, DEQ$, we have

$DE^2 = DQ^2 + EQ^2$

$\Rightarrow \quad 10^2 = DQ^2 + 8^2 \Rightarrow DQ^2 = 100 - 64 = 36$

$\Rightarrow \quad DQ = 6$ cm [taking positive sign]

$\Rightarrow \quad PQ = DP - DQ = 18 - 6 = 12$ cm [$\because DP = 18$ cm]

From Eq. (i), we get

$\text{ar}(\text{pentagon}\ ABCDE) = \frac{1}{2} \times 8 \times 6 + \frac{1}{2} \times 8 \times 6 + \frac{1}{2} \times (16 + 24) \times 12$

$= 24 + 24 + 240 = 288\ \text{cm}^2$

8. (b) Let r_1 and r_2 (assume $r_1 > r_2$) be the radii of two circles, which touch externally at A and their centres are O and O', respectively.

Now, according to given conditions, we have

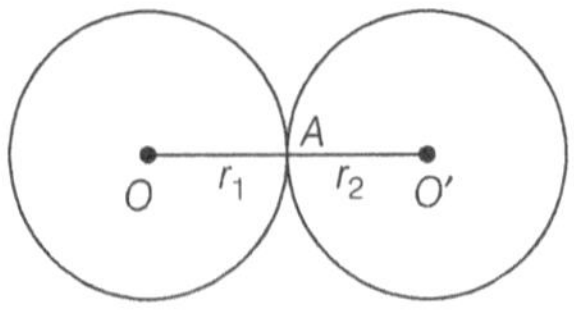

$r_1 + r_2 = 10$ ...(i)

and $\pi r_1^2 + \pi r_2^2 = 58\pi \Rightarrow r_1^2 + r_2^2 = 58$ ...(ii)

Now, $(r_1 + r_2)^2 = r_1^2 + r_2^2 + 2r_1 r_2$

$\Rightarrow \quad (10)^2 + 58 = 2 r_1 r_2$ [from Eqs. (i) and (ii)]

$\Rightarrow \quad 100 - 58 = 2r_1 r_2 \Rightarrow 2r_1 r_2 = 42$ ...(iii)

Now, $(r_1 - r_2)^2 = r_1^2 + r_2^2 - 2r_1 r_2 \Rightarrow (r_1 - r_2)^2 = 58 - 42 = 16$

$\Rightarrow \quad r_1 - r_2 = 4$ [$\because r_1 > r_2$] ...(iv)

Now, on solving Eqs. (i) and (iv), we get

$r_1 = 7$ cm and $r_2 = 3$ cm

9. (a) Given a rectangle $ABCD$ inscribed in a circle, with $AB = 28$ cm and $BC = 21$ cm.

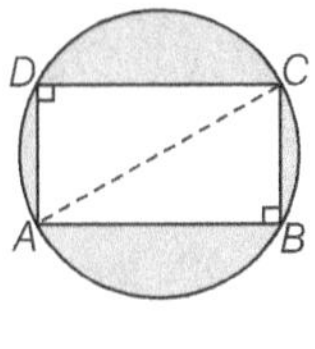

Now, join A and C, then in $\Delta\, ABC$, we have

$AC^2 = AB^2 + BC^2 = (28)^2 + (21)^2$

$= 784 + 441 = 1225$

$\Rightarrow \quad AC = 35$ cm [taking positive square root]

$\therefore$ Diameter of the circle = 35 cm

$\Rightarrow \quad$ Radius of circle $= \frac{35}{2}$ cm

$\therefore$ Area of circle $= \pi r^2 = \frac{22}{7} \times \frac{35}{2} \times \frac{35}{2} = \frac{1925}{2} = 962.5\ \text{cm}^2$

Also, area of rectangle $ABCD = 28 \times 21 = 588\ \text{cm}^2$

Hence, required area = Area of circle − Area of rectangle

$= 962.5 - 588 = 374.5\ \text{cm}^2$

10. (b) Radius of the semi-circle with AC as diameter,

$r_1 = \frac{14}{2} = 7$ cm

and radius of the semi-circle with AD as diameter,

$r_2 = \frac{7}{4}$ cm

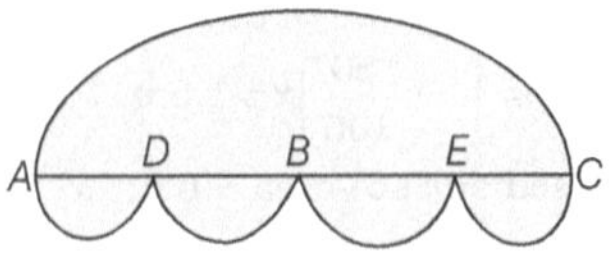

Now, area of shaded portion

= Area of radius of semi-circle with AC as diameter + 4 × Area of semi-circle with AD as diameter

$= \frac{1}{2} \times \pi r_1^2 + 4 \times \frac{\pi r_2^2}{2}$

$= \frac{1}{2} \times \frac{22}{7} \times 7 \times 7 + 4 \times \frac{1}{2} \times \frac{22}{7} \times \frac{7}{4} \times \frac{7}{4}$

$= 77 + 19.25 = 96.25\ \text{cm}^2$

Hence, the required area of the shaded portion is $96.25\ \text{cm}^2$.

Chapter 16 Surface Area and Volume of 3-D Solids

1. (a) Given, area = 2 hect $= 2 \times 10000\ \text{m}^2$

and depth = 5 cm $= \frac{5}{100}$ m

Now, volume of water = area × depth

$= 2 \times 10000 \times \frac{5}{100} = 1000\ \text{m}^3$

2. (a) Area of the field $= (70 \times 40)\ \text{m}^2 = 2800\ \text{m}^2$

Area of pit $= (10 \times 8)\ \text{m}^2 = 80\ \text{m}^2$

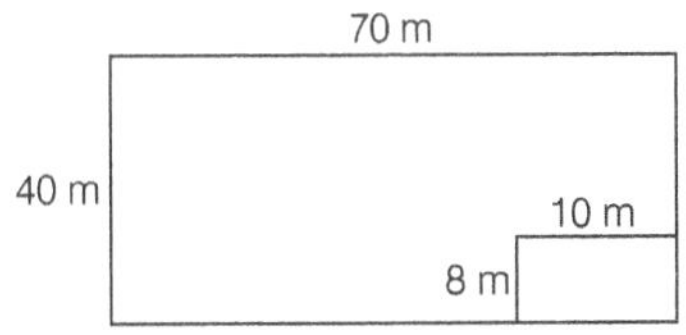

Area over which the earth is spread over

$= (2800 - 80)\ \text{m}^2 = 2720\ \text{m}^2$

Volume of the earth dug out $= (10 \times 8 \times 5)\ \text{m}^3$

$= 400\ \text{m}^3$

$\therefore$ Rise in level of the field

$$= \frac{\text{Volume of the earth dug out}}{\text{Area on which the earth is spread}}$$

$$= \left(\frac{400}{2720}\right) \text{m} = \left(\frac{400 \times 100}{2720}\right) \text{cm} = \frac{250}{17} \text{cm} = 14.70 \text{ cm}$$

3. (b) Given, volume of cuboid is two more than four times the volume of cube.

Let each side of cube be a cm.

According to the question,

$$44 \times 30 \times 15 = 4a^3 + 2$$

$\Rightarrow \quad 4a^3 = 19800 - 2$

$\Rightarrow \quad 4a^3 = 19798$

$\Rightarrow \quad a^3 = 4949.5$

$\Rightarrow \quad a = 17.04$ cm [taking cube root both sides]

Hence, the side of cube is 17.04 cm.

4. (c) Let each side of cube be x.

Then, surface area of cube = $6x^2$

If side is increased by 50%, then increased length

$$= \left(1 + \frac{50}{100}\right)x = 1.5\,x$$

Then, increased surface area = $6\,(1.5\,x)^2$

$$= 6 \times 1.5 \times 1.5 \times x^2$$

$\therefore$ Percentage increase in surface area

$$= \frac{\text{Increase in surface area}}{\text{Total surface area}} \times 100\%$$

$$= \frac{6 \times 1.5 \times 1.5 \times x^2 - 6x^2}{6x^2} \times 100$$

$$= \frac{6x^2(2.25 - 1)}{6x^2} \times 100$$

$$= 1.25 \times 100\% = 125\%$$

5. (a) Given, dimensions of a brick are

$$l = 22.5 \text{ cm},\ b = 10 \text{ cm and } h = 7.5 \text{ cm}$$

and total surface area of container = 9.375 m^2

Now, total surface area of a brick

$$= 2\,(l \times b + b \times h + h \times l)$$

$$= 2(22.5 \times 10 + 10 \times 7.5 + 7.5 \times 22.5)$$

$$= 2(225 + 75 + 168.75) = 2 \times 468.75 = 937.5 \text{ cm}^2$$

$$= \frac{937.5}{100 \times 100} \text{m}^2 \quad [\because 1 \text{ m} = 100 \text{ cm}]$$

$\therefore$ Number of bricks that painted out of this container

$$= \frac{\text{Total surface area of container}}{\text{Total surface area of bricks}}$$

$$= \frac{9.375}{\frac{937.5}{100 \times 100}} = \frac{9.375 \times 100 \times 100}{937.5} = \frac{937500}{9375} = 100$$

Hence, 100 bricks can be painted out.

6. (d) Let the sides of the cuboid are x, $2x$ and $4x$ and the side of the cube is y.

$\therefore$ Volume of the cuboid = $x \times 2x \times 4x = 8x^3$

and volume of the cube = y^3

According to the given condition,

Volume of the cuboid = Volume of the cube

$\therefore \quad 8x^3 = y^3$

$\Rightarrow \quad \left(\frac{x}{y}\right)^3 = \left(\frac{1}{2}\right)^3$

$\Rightarrow \quad \frac{x}{y} = \frac{1}{2}$ [taking cube root on both sides]

$\therefore$ Diagonal of the cuboid $= \sqrt{x^2 + (2x)^2 + (4x)^2}$

$$= \sqrt{x^2 + 4x^2 + 16x^2}$$

$$= \sqrt{21}\,x$$

and diagonal of the cube = $\sqrt{3}y = 2\sqrt{3}x$

Hence, required ratio $= \frac{\sqrt{21}x}{2\sqrt{3}x} = \frac{1}{2} \cdot \sqrt{\frac{21}{3}} = \frac{\sqrt{7}}{2} = \sqrt{7} : 2$

7. (b) If we take the vertical cross-section of the face of the swimming pool, then it is a trapezium *ABCD* with parallel sides *AD* and *BC* respectively of lengths 10 m and 20 m and distance between parallel sides is 50 m. The width of the swimming pool is 15 m.

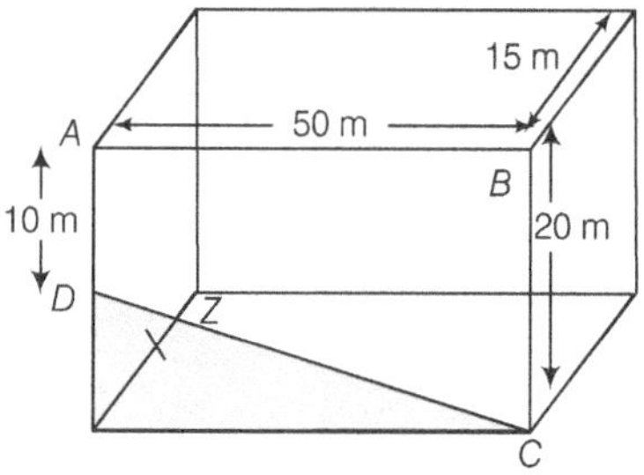

$\therefore$ Volume of water in the swimming pool

= Area of vertical cross-section (*ABCD*) × Width of swimming pool

$$= \left[\frac{1}{2}(10 + 20) \times 50\right] \times 15$$

$$= 15 \times 50 \times 15 = 11250 \text{ m}^3$$

8. (a) Let l, b and h be the sides of cuboid.

Then, $\quad l^2 + b^2 = x^2, \quad \ldots\text{(i)}$

$\quad b^2 + h^2 = y^2 \quad \ldots\text{(ii)}$

and $\quad h^2 + l^2 = z^2 \quad \ldots\text{(iii)}$

On adding Eqs. (i), (ii) and (iii), we get

$$2(l^2 + b^2 + h^2) = x^2 + y^2 + z^2$$

$\Rightarrow \quad l^2 + b^2 + h^2 = \frac{1}{2}(x^2 + y^2 + z^2) \quad \ldots\text{(iv)}$

From Eqs. (i), (ii), (iii) and (iv), we get

$$x^2 + h^2 = \frac{1}{2}(x^2 + y^2 + z^2)$$

$\Rightarrow \quad h^2 = \frac{(x^2 + y^2 + z^2)}{2} - x^2$

$\Rightarrow \quad h^2 = \frac{y^2 + z^2 - x^2}{2}$

$\Rightarrow \quad h = \sqrt{\frac{y^2 + z^2 - x^2}{2}}$

Similarly, $\quad l = \sqrt{\frac{z^2 + x^2 - y^2}{2}}$

and $\quad b = \sqrt{\frac{x^2 + y^2 - z^2}{2}}$

Hence, volume of cuboid = lbh

$$= \sqrt{\frac{(y^2 + z^2 - x^2)(z^2 + x^2 - y^2)(x^2 + y^2 - z^2)}{2 \times 2 \times 2}}$$

$$= \frac{1}{2\sqrt{2}} \sqrt{(y^2 + z^2 - x^2)(z^2 + x^2 - y^2)(x^2 + y^2 - z^2)}$$

Now, we have $x = 5$ m, $y = 7$ m and $z = 8$ m.

Volume of cuboid

$$= \frac{1}{2\sqrt{2}} \sqrt{\{(7^2 + 8^2 - 5^2)(8^2 + 5^2 - 7^2)(5^2 + 7^2 - 8^2)\}}$$

$$= \frac{1}{2\sqrt{2}} \sqrt{(49 + 64 - 25)(64 + 25 - 49)(25 + 49 - 64)}$$

$$= \frac{1}{2\sqrt{2}} \sqrt{(88)(40)(10)} = \frac{1}{2\sqrt{2}} \times 2 \times 2 \times 10\sqrt{2 \times 11}$$

$$= 20\sqrt{11} \text{ m}^3$$

Chapter 17 Trigonometry

1. (c) Given, $f(x) = \cos^2 x + \sec^2 x = \cos^2 x + \sec^2 x - 2 + 2$ [adding and subtracting 2]

$$= \cos^2 x + \sec^2 x - 2\cos x \cdot \sec x + 2 \quad [\because \cos x \cdot \sec x = 1]$$

$$= (\cos x - \sec x)^2 + 2 \quad [\because a^2 + b^2 - 2ab = (a-b)^2]$$

We know that square of any expression is always greater than equal to zero.

$\therefore \quad f(x) \geq 2$

2. (c) We have, $A = 30°$

$$\therefore \frac{1 + \sin 2A + \cos 2A}{\sin A + \cos A}$$

$$= \frac{1 + \sin 2 \times 30° + \cos 2 \times 30°}{\sin 30° + \cos 30°} \quad \text{[putting } A = 30°]$$

$$= \frac{1 + \sin 60° + \cos 60°}{\sin 30° + \cos 30°}$$

$$= \frac{1 + \frac{\sqrt{3}}{2} + \frac{1}{2}}{\frac{1}{2} + \frac{\sqrt{3}}{2}} \quad \left[\begin{array}{l}\because \sin 30° = \frac{1}{2}, \cos 30° = \frac{\sqrt{3}}{2} \\ \text{and } \sin 60° = \frac{\sqrt{3}}{2}, \cos 60° = \frac{1}{2}\end{array}\right]$$

$$= \frac{\frac{2 + \sqrt{3} + 1}{2}}{\frac{1 + \sqrt{3}}{2}} = \frac{3 + \sqrt{3}}{1 + \sqrt{3}} = \frac{\sqrt{3}(\sqrt{3} + 1)}{\sqrt{3} + 1} = \sqrt{3}$$

3. (b) Given, ABC is a right angled triangle.

Since, the sum of the angles of a triangle is 180°.

$\therefore \quad A + B + C = 180° \quad$ ...(i)

Now, $\tan\left(\frac{A - B - C}{2}\right) = \tan\left[\frac{A - (180° - A)}{2}\right]$ [from Eq. (i)]

$$= \tan\left(\frac{2A - 180°}{2}\right) = \tan(A - 90°)$$

$$= \tan[-(90° - A)]$$

$$= -\tan(90° - A) \quad [\because \tan(-\theta) = -\tan\theta]$$

$$= -\cot A \quad [\because \tan(90° - A) = \cot A] \quad \text{...(ii)}$$

and $-\tan\left(\frac{A + B - C}{2}\right) = -\tan\left[\frac{(180° - C) - C}{2}\right]$ [from Eq. (i)]

$$= -\tan(90° - C) = \cot C \quad \text{...(iii)}$$

From Eqs. (ii) and (iii), we get

$$\tan\left(\frac{A - B - C}{2}\right) \neq -\tan\left(\frac{A + B - C}{2}\right)$$

4. (a) Given, $\quad m = a\cos^3\theta + 3a\cos\theta\sin^2\theta \quad$ ...(i)

and $\quad n = a\sin^3\theta + 3a\cos^2\theta\sin\theta \quad$ ...(ii)

On adding Eqs. (i) and (ii), we get

$$m + n = a\cos^3\theta + 3a\cos\theta\sin^2\theta + a\sin^3\theta + 3a\cos^2\theta\sin\theta$$

$$= a[\cos^3\theta + \sin^3\theta + 3\cos\theta\sin\theta(\sin\theta + \cos\theta)]$$

$$= a(\cos\theta + \sin\theta)^3$$

$$[\because (a+b)^3 = a^3 + b^3 + 3ab(a+b)] \quad \text{...(iii)}$$

On subtracting Eq. (ii) from Eq. (i), we get

$$m - n = a\cos^3\theta + 3a\cos\theta\sin^2\theta - a\sin^3\theta - 3a\cos^2\theta\sin\theta$$

$$= a[\cos^3\theta - \sin^3\theta - 3\cos\theta\sin\theta(\cos\theta - \sin\theta)]$$

$$= a[\cos\theta - \sin\theta]^3 \quad \text{...(iv)}$$

$$[\because (a-b)^3 = a^3 - b^3 - 3ab(a-b)]$$

Now, $(m+n)^{2/3} - (m-n)^{2/3}$

$$= [a(\cos\theta + \sin\theta)^3]^{2/3} - [a(\cos\theta - \sin\theta)^3]^{2/3}$$

[from Eqs. (iii) and (iv)]

$$= a^{2/3}(\cos\theta + \sin\theta)^2 - a^{2/3}(\cos\theta - \sin\theta)^2$$

$$= a^{2/3}[(\cos\theta + \sin\theta)^2 - (\cos\theta - \sin\theta)^2]$$

$$= a^{2/3}[\cos^2\theta + \sin^2\theta + 2\cos\theta\sin\theta - \cos^2\theta - \sin^2\theta + 2\sin\theta\cos\theta]$$

$$[\because (a+b)^2 = a^2 + b^2 + 2ab, (a-b)^2 = a^2 + b^2 - 2ab]$$

$$= a^{2/3}\, 4\sin\theta\cos\theta \quad [\because \cos^2\theta + \sin^2\theta = 1]$$

$$= 4a^{2/3}\sin\theta\cos\theta$$

5. (b) We have, $a\sec\theta + b\tan\theta + c = 0$

and $\quad p\sec\theta + q\tan\theta + r = 0$

On solving these two equations for $\sec\theta$ and $\tan\theta$ by the cross-multiplication method, we get

$$\frac{\sec\theta}{br - qc} = \frac{\tan\theta}{cp - ar} = \frac{1}{aq - bp}$$

$$\Rightarrow \quad \sec\theta = \frac{br - cq}{aq - bp} \text{ and } \tan\theta = \frac{cp - ar}{aq - bp}$$

Now, $\sec^2\theta - \tan^2\theta = 1$

$$\Rightarrow \quad \left(\frac{br - cq}{aq - bp}\right)^2 - \left(\frac{cp - ar}{aq - bp}\right)^2 = 1$$

$$\Rightarrow \quad (br - cq)^2 - (cp - ar)^2 = (aq - bp)^2$$

6. (b) We have, $\sin(A + 2B) = \frac{\sqrt{3}}{2}$

$$\Rightarrow \quad \sin(A + 2B) = \sin 60° \quad \left[\because \sin 60° = \frac{\sqrt{3}}{2}\right]$$

$$\Rightarrow \quad A + 2B = 60° \quad \text{...(i)}$$

and $\cos(A + 4B) = 0° \Rightarrow \cos(A + 4B) = \cos 90°$

$$\Rightarrow \quad A + 4B = 90° \quad \text{...(ii)}$$

On subtracting Eq. (i) from Eq. (ii), we get

$$A + 4B - A - 2B = 90° - 60°$$

$$\Rightarrow \quad 2B = 30° \Rightarrow B = \frac{30°}{2} = 15°$$

On putting the value of $B = 15°$ in Eq. (i), we get

$A + 2 \times 15° = 60° \Rightarrow A + 30° = 30°$

$\Rightarrow \quad A = 60° - 30° = 30°$

Hence, $A = 30°$, $B = 15°$

7. (a) In ΔABC, right angled at B,

$$AC^2 = BC^2 + AB^2 \quad \text{[by using Pythagoras theorem]}$$

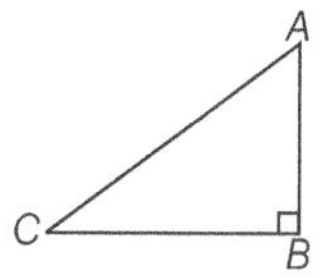

$\Rightarrow \quad AC^2 - AB^2 = BC^2$

$\Rightarrow \quad (AC + AB)(AC - AB) = (5)^2 \; [\because a^2 - b^2 = (a-b)(a+b)]$

$\Rightarrow \quad (AC + AB)(1) = 25 \; [\because AC - AB = 1 \text{ cm, given}]$

$\Rightarrow AC + AB = 25$ and $AC - AB = 1$

On solving above equations, we get

$$AC = 13 \text{ and } AB = 12$$

Now, in ΔABC, $\sin C = \dfrac{AB}{AC} = \dfrac{12}{13}$ and $\cos C = \dfrac{BC}{AC} = \dfrac{5}{13}$

$$\therefore \quad \frac{\cos^2 C}{1 - \sin C} = \frac{\left(\frac{5}{13}\right)^2}{1 - \frac{12}{13}} = \frac{\frac{25}{169}}{\frac{13-12}{13}} = \frac{25 \times 13}{169} = \frac{25}{13}$$

8. (c) We know that diagonals of a rhombus bisect each other at right angle and also bisect the angle of sector.

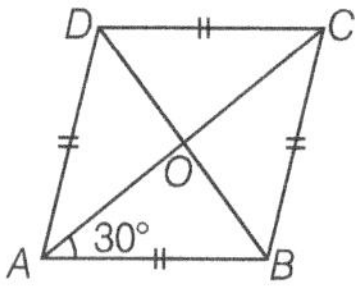

$\therefore \quad OA = OC = \dfrac{1}{2} AC$

$\Rightarrow \quad OB = OD = \dfrac{1}{2} BD$

$\Rightarrow \quad \angle AOB = 90°$

and $\quad \angle OAB = \dfrac{60°}{2} = 30° \quad [\because \angle BAD = 60, \text{ given}]$

Also, we have

$$AB = 60 \text{ cm}$$

In right angled ΔAOB, we have

$$\sin 30° = \frac{OB}{AB}$$

$\Rightarrow \quad \dfrac{1}{2} = \dfrac{OB}{60}$

$\Rightarrow \quad OB = \dfrac{60}{2} = 30 \text{ cm}$

and $\quad \cos 30° = \dfrac{OA}{AB}$

$\Rightarrow \quad \dfrac{\sqrt{3}}{2} = \dfrac{OA}{60}$

$\Rightarrow \quad OA = \dfrac{60 \times \sqrt{3}}{2} = 30 \times \sqrt{3}$

Hence, length of diagonal $AC = 2 \times OA$

$$= 2 \times 30 = 60\sqrt{3}$$
$$= 60 \times 1.732$$
$$= 103.92 \text{ cm}$$

and length of diagonal $BD = 2 \times OB$

$$= 2 \times 30 = 60 \text{ cm}$$

Solutions (Q. Nos. 9-11) Draw DL perpendicular to AB and CM perpendicular to AB.

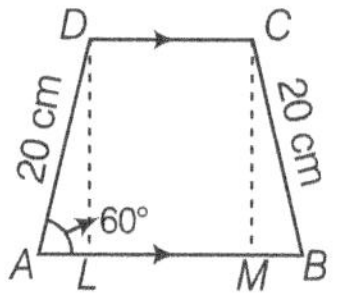

9. (a) In right angled ΔALD,

$$\sin 60° = \frac{DL}{AD} = \frac{DL}{20}$$

$\Rightarrow \quad \dfrac{\sqrt{3}}{2} = \dfrac{DL}{20} \quad \left[\because \sin 60° = \dfrac{\sqrt{3}}{2}\right]$

$\therefore \quad DL = \dfrac{20 \times \sqrt{3}}{2} = 10 \times \sqrt{3} \text{ cm}$

Hence, distance between AB and DC

$$= 10\sqrt{3} = 10 \times 1.732 = 17.32 \text{ cm}$$

10. (d) Now, in ΔALD,

$$\cos 60° = \frac{AL}{AD} = \frac{AL}{20}$$

$\Rightarrow \quad \dfrac{1}{2} = \dfrac{AL}{20} \quad \left[\because \cos 60° = \dfrac{1}{2}\right]$

$\therefore \quad AL = \dfrac{20}{2} = 10 \text{ cm}$

Similarly, $MB = 10$ cm, because ΔALD and ΔCMB are congruent.

Now, $\quad AB = AL + LM + MB = 10 + 20 + 10 = 40$ cm

$[\because LM = CD = 20 \text{ cm, given}]$

11. (b) We have, $\sin(50° + \theta) - \cos(40° - \theta)$

$+ \tan 1° \tan 10° \tan 20° \tan 70° \tan 80° \tan 89°$

$= \cos[90° - (50° + \theta)] - \cos(40° - \theta)$

$+ \tan 1° \tan 10° \tan 20° \cot(90° - 70°)$

$\cot(90° - 80°) \cot(90° - 89°)$

$[\because \sin\theta = \cos(90° - \theta) \text{ and } \tan\theta = \cot(90° - \theta)]$

$= \cos(90° - 50° - \theta) - \cos(40° - \theta)$

$+ \tan 1° \tan 10° \tan 20° \cot 20° \cot 10° \cot 1°$

$= \cos(40° - \theta) - \cos(40° - \theta)$

$+ \tan 1° \cot 1° \tan 10° \cot 10° \tan 20° \cot 20°$

$= 1 \times 1 \times 1 = 1 \quad [\because \tan\theta \cot\theta = 1]$

Chapter 18 Coordinate Geometry and Distance Formula

1. (b) Let us identify the sign of y for each sign of x.

We have, $x = my \Rightarrow y = \dfrac{x}{m}$, where $m < 0$

When x is (+ve), then y is (–ve) and when x is (–ve), then y is (+ve).

Thus, the coordinate of points lying on the line are of the form $(+x, -y)$ and $(-x, +y)$, which implies that points lying in second and fourth quadrants.

Hence, the line $x = my$, where $m < 0$, lies in II and IV quadrants.

2. (d) Let us plot the points $P(15, 9)$, $Q(7, 10)$ and $R(-5, -4)$ on the graph paper and join PQ and QR.

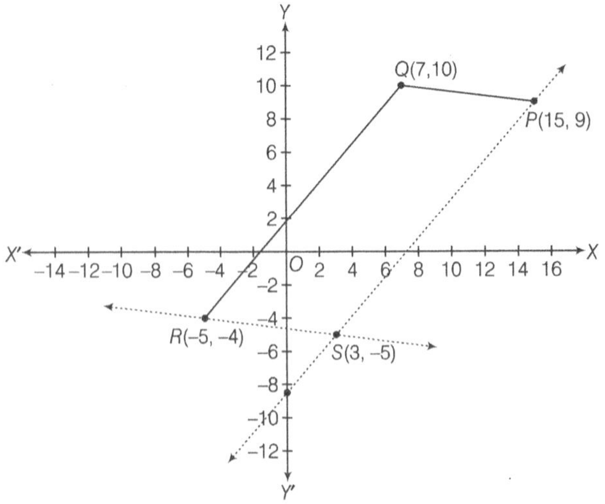

Now, through P, draw a line parallel to QR and through R, draw a line parallel to PQ. It can be seen that these lines cut each other at $(3, -5)$.

Hence, the fourth vertex is $S(3, -5)$.

3. (a) If we shift the coordinate axes from (0, 0) to (1, 1), then for finding the new coordinates, we will subtract 1 from both coordinates of each point. The new coordinates with respect to new axes are $A(3-1, 2-1)$, $B(5-1, 3-1)$, $C(4-1, 5-1)$ and $D(2-1, 4-1)$, i.e. $A(2, 1)$, $B(4, 2)$, $C(3, 4)$ and $D(1, 3)$.

4. (b) The coordinates of points A, B and C are $(0, 4)$, $(3, -2)$ and $(-3, -2)$, respectively.

5. (b) Area of figure = Area of ΔAED + Area of ΔOCE + Area of ΔOBD

$$= \frac{1}{2} \times 4 \times 4 + \frac{1}{2} \times 2 \times 2 + \frac{1}{2} \times 2 \times 2$$

$$= 8 + 2 + 2 = 12 \text{ sq units}$$

Alternate-Method

Area of the figure = ar(ΔAOC) + ar (ΔAOB)

$$= \frac{1}{2} \times 4 \times 3 + \frac{1}{2} \times 4 \times 3 = 6 + 6 = 12 \text{ sq units}$$

6. (a) On rotating the given figure at an angle of 270° clockwise, we get the following graph

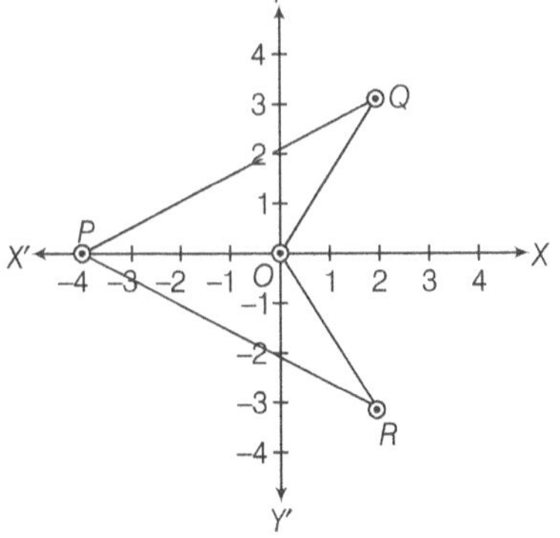

Hence, the coordinates are $P(-4, 0)$, $Q(2, 3)$ and $R(2, -3)$.

7. (c) The graph of given linear equation is shown below

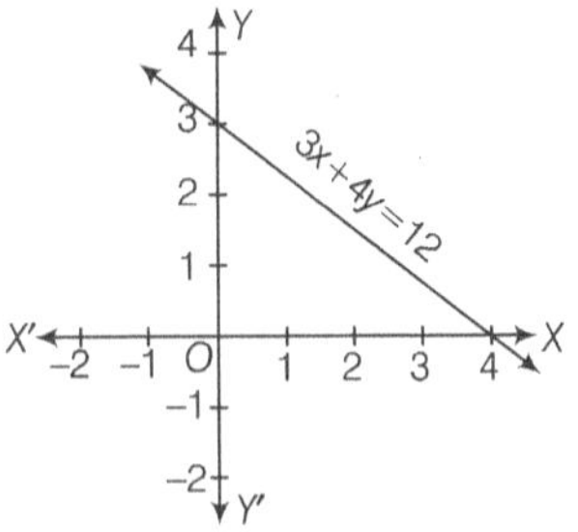

Here, vertices of the triangle formed are (4, 0), (0, 3) and (0, 0). Clearly, the longest side is the hypotenuse joining (4, 0) and (0, 3).

$\therefore$ Its length $= \sqrt{4^2 + 3^2} = \sqrt{16+9} = \sqrt{25} = 5$ units

8. (b) Given points can be plotted as shown below

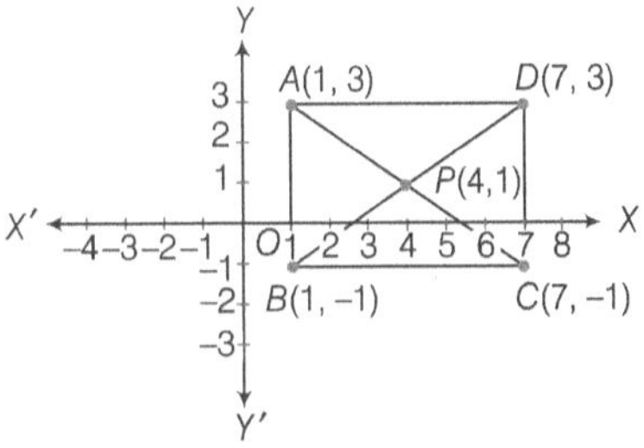

The figure so obtained is a rectangle. The coordinates of the point of intersection of the diagonals are $P(4, 1)$.

9. (c) $\because$ $AB \perp$ chord PQ

$\therefore$ AB bisects chord PQ.

Here, $PQ = 2PB$

Now, $AB = \sqrt{(2-5)^2 + (-3-1)^2}$ units

$= \sqrt{9+16} = \sqrt{25} = 5$ units

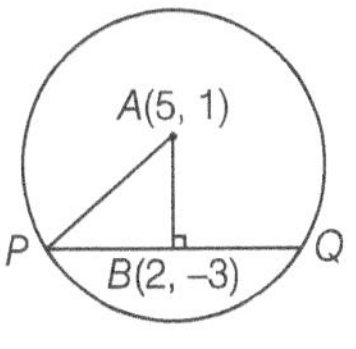

$\therefore$ AP = Radius of circle = 13 units

By using Pythagoras theorem, we get

$PB = \sqrt{AP^2 - AB^2} = \sqrt{169-25} = \sqrt{144} = 12$ units

$\therefore$ $PQ = 2 \times PB = 24$ units

10. (c) When we rotate the line PQ in anti-clockwise direction at an angle of 270°, then the new coordinates of point Q will be at R, which touches the X-axis at (2, 0).

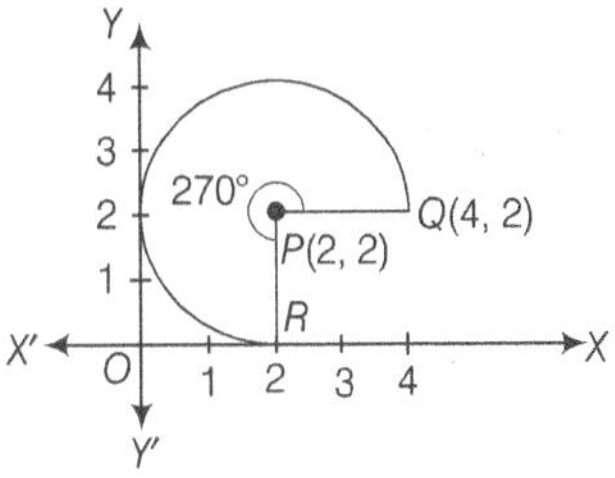

Hence, the coordinates of R are (2, 0).

Now, $PQ = \sqrt{(4-2)^2 + (2-2)^2}$

$[\because \text{distance} = \sqrt{(x_2 - x_1)^2 + (y_2 - y_1)^2}]$

$= \sqrt{2^2 + 0} = 2$ units

$\therefore$ Area of the figure $= \frac{3}{4}\pi r^2$

$= \frac{3}{4} \times 3.14 \times 4 = 9.42$ sq units

Internal Assessment of Practical Work

Project 1

Topic

Conduct a survey of a group of students and represent it graphically regarding their height, weight, number of family members, pocket money etc.

Table of Contents

1. Introduction

In the present time, statistics is applied to almost everything. It is a tool for science and technology, banking, etc. The study of statistics involves collection, organisation, analysis, interpretation and presentation of data.

For above surveys, I will use the concept of statistics, collect the data through a questionnaire and then organise into a table using tally marks.

After that I will present the data pictorially by means of bar graphs, histograms, frequency polygons, etc.

I will also process the data by calculating parameters such as mean, median and mode, so that these parameters and pictorial representations can be used to draw analysis about the data. These analysis may again be used to present a report.

2. Data Collection

In order to collect my data. I surveyed 7 boys and 8 girls from my school of my grade. I asked about their height, weight, number of family members, weekly pocket money and monthly family income, using a questionnaire form, which is given below

Class IX/Maths Project

Please provide the following information

- Name ....
- Height (in cm) ....
- Weight (in kg) ....
- Number of family members ....
- Weekly pocket money (in ₹) ....
- Monthly family income (in ₹) ....

3. Tabulation of Data

Here, I will represent the collected data in the tabular form, as shown below

I. Height

S.No.	Girls	Height (in cm)	S.No.	Boys	Height (in cm)
1.	Megha	146	9.	Naveen	145
2.	Kriti	163	10.	Arjun	165
3.	Neha	142	11.	Tarun	149
4.	Manisha	160	12.	Varun	162
5.	Charu	175	13.	Rahul	179
6.	Divya	152	14.	Saurabh	163
7.	Kanchan	171	15.	Karan	153
8.	Anju	140			

II. Weight

S.No.	Girls	Weight (in kg)	S.No.	Boys	Weight (in kg)
1.	Megha	70	9.	Naveen	45
2.	Kriti	60	10.	Arjun	62
3.	Neha	65	11.	Tarun	65
4.	Manisha	55	12.	Varun	50
5.	Charu	54	13.	Rahul	70
6.	Divya	50	14.	Saurabh	62
7.	Kanchan	52	15.	Karan	58
8.	Anju	62			

III. Number of Family Members

S.No.	Girls	Number of family members	S.No.	Boys	Number of family members
1.	Megha	3	9.	Naveen	3
2.	Kriti	2	10.	Arjun	4
3.	Neha	8	11.	Tarun	5
4.	Manisha	5	12.	Varun	6
5.	Charu	6	13.	Rahul	4
6.	Divya	3	14.	Saurabh	4
7.	Kanchan	4	15.	Karan	7
8.	Anju	5			

IV. Weekly Pocket Money

S.No.	Girls	Weekly pocket money (in ₹)	S.No.	Boys	Weekly pocket money (in ₹)
1.	Megha	200	9.	Naveen	100
2.	Kriti	500	10.	Arjun	200
3.	Neha	300	11.	Tarun	200
4.	Manisha	400	12.	Varun	350
5.	Charu	150	13.	Rahul	150
6.	Divya	200	14.	Saurabh	50
7.	Kanchan	250	15.	Karan	100
8.	Anju	350			

V. Monthly Family Income

S.No.	Girls	Monthly family income (in ₹)	S.No.	Boys	Monthly family income (in ₹)
1.	Megha	25000	9.	Naveen	20000
2.	Kriti	40000	10.	Arjun	25000
3.	Neha	45000	11.	Tarun	35000
4.	Manisha	30000	12.	Varun	40000
5.	Charu	25000	13.	Rahul	22000
6.	Divya	20000	14.	Saurabh	15000
7.	Kanchan	22000	15.	Karan	23000
8.	Anju	23000			

Now, let us summarise the above data in the frequency distribution tables, by taking 5 classes in each frequency table. For this, let us first find the class size and classes.

I. Height

Minimum 140 cm, Maximum 179 cm.

$$\therefore \text{Estimated class size} = \frac{179-140}{5} = \frac{39}{5} = 7.8 \approx 8$$

Hence, classes are 140-148, 148-156, 156-164, 164-172, 172-180.

II. Weight

Minimum 45 kg, Maximum 70 kg.

$$\therefore \text{Estimated class size} = \frac{70-45}{5} = \frac{25}{5} = 5 \approx 6$$

Hence, classes are 45-51, 51-57, 57-63, 63-69, 69-75.

III. Number of Family Members

Minimum 2, Maximum 8.

$$\therefore \text{Estimated class size} = \frac{8-2}{5} = \frac{6}{5} = 1.2 \approx 2$$

Hence, classes are 2-4, 4-6, 6-8, 8-10, 10-12.

IV. Weekly Pocket Money

Minimum ₹ 50, Maximum ₹ 500.

$$\therefore \text{Estimated class size} = \frac{500-50}{5} = \frac{450}{5} = 90 \approx 91$$

Hence, classes are

50-141, 141-232, 232-323, 323-414, 414-505.

V. Monthly Family Income

Minimum ₹ 15000, Maximum ₹ 45000

$$\therefore \text{Estimated class size} = \frac{45000-15000}{5} = \frac{30000}{5}$$

$$= 6000 \approx 7000$$

Hence, classes are 15000-22000, 22000-29000, 29000-36000, 36000-43000, 43000-50000.

Now, let us tabulate the data in the following frequency distribution by using tally marks.

I. Frequency Table for Height

Height (cm)	Tally marks	Number of students
140-148	||||	4
148-156	|||	3
156-164	||||	4
164-172	||	2
172-180	||	2

II. Frequency Table for Weight

Weight (in kg)	Tally marks	Number of students
45-51	III	3
51-57	III	3
57-63	~~IIII~~	5
63-69	II	2
69-75	II	2

III. Frequency Table for Family Member

Number of family members	Tally marks	Number of students
2-4	IIII	4
4-6	~~IIII~~ II	7
6-8	III	3
8-10	I	1
10-12		0

IV. Frequency Table for Weekly Pocket Money

Weekly pocket money (in ₹)	Tally marks	Number of students
50-141	III	3
141-232	~~IIII~~ I	6
232-323	II	2
323-414	III	3
414-505	I	1

V. Frequency Table for Monthly Family Income

Monthly family income (in ₹)	Tally marks	Number of students
15000-22000	III	3
22000-29000	~~IIII~~ II	7
29000-36000	II	2
36000-43000	II	2
43000-50000	I	1

4. Graphical Representation of Data

Here, we represent the above data with the help of bar graphs, histogram and frequency polygon.

Graphical Representation of Height

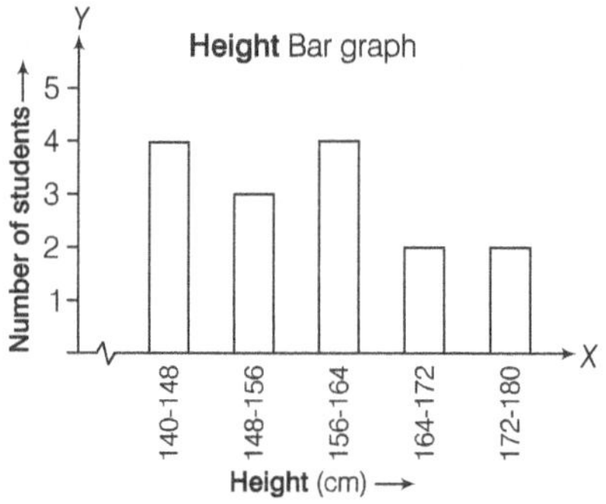

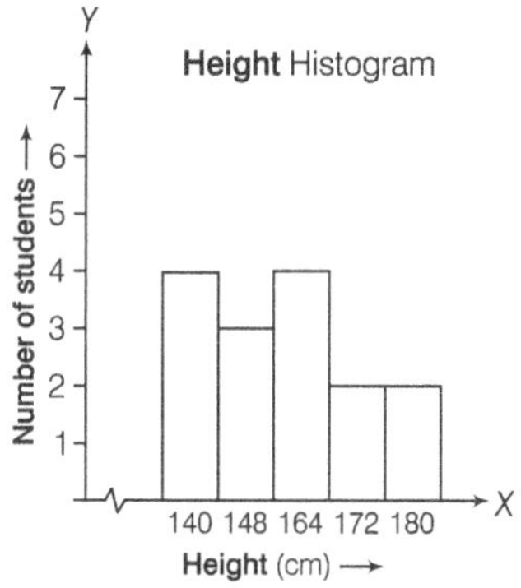

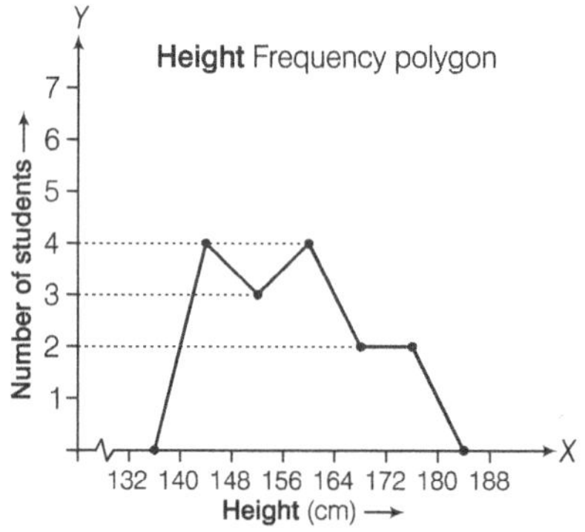

Graphical Representation of Weight

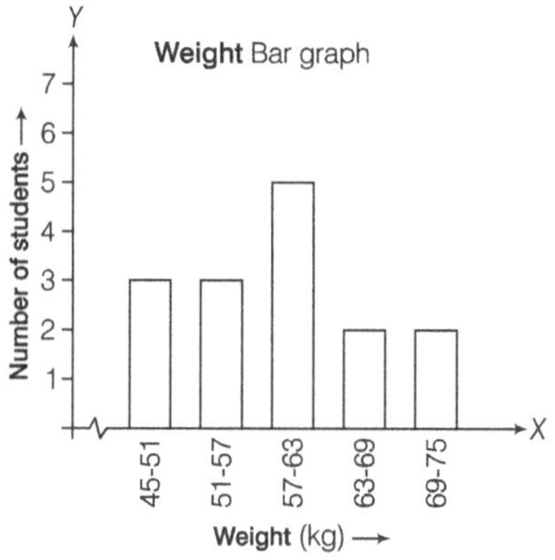

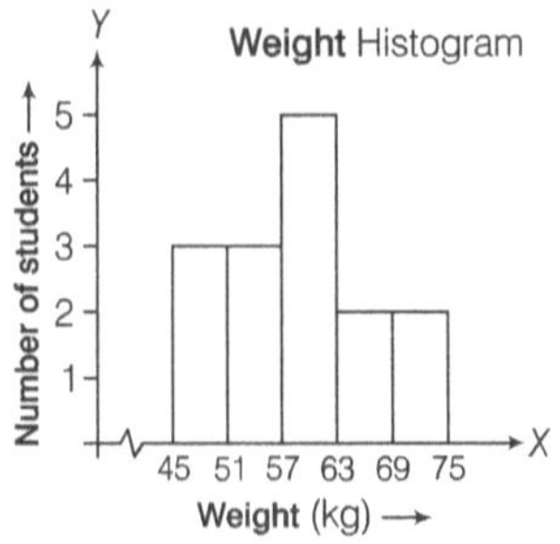

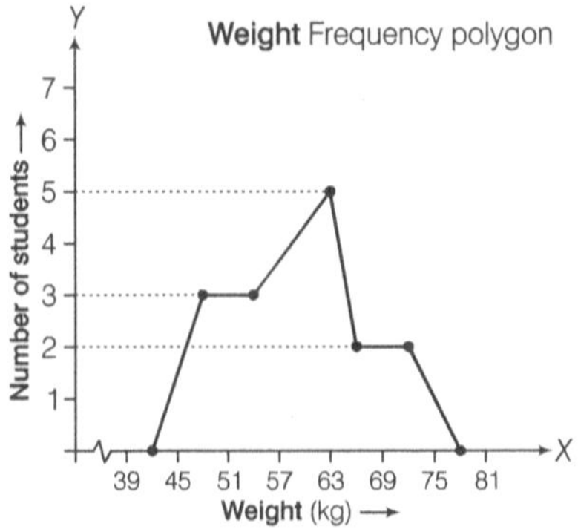

Graphical Representation of Number of Family Members

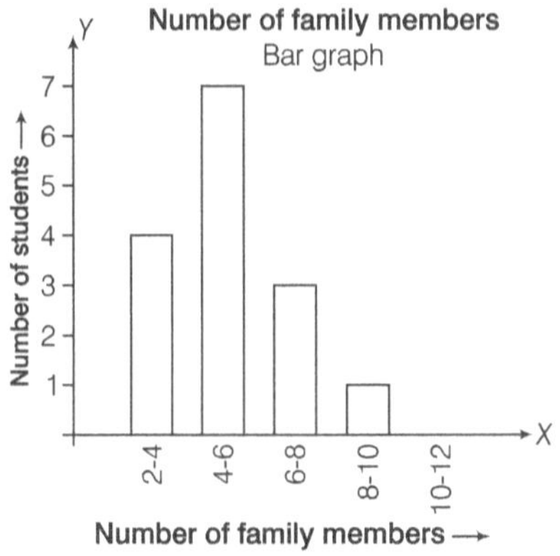

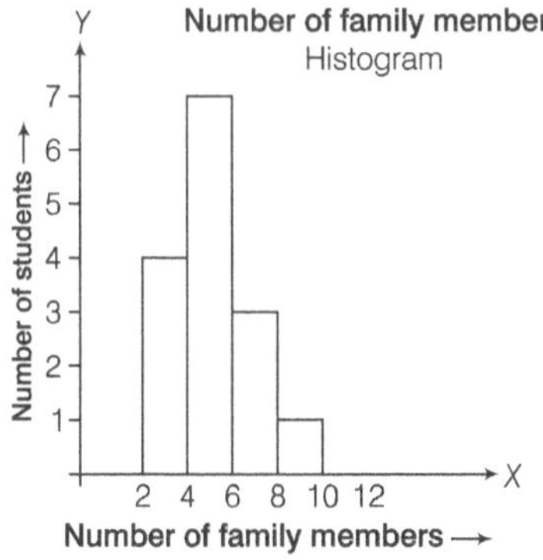

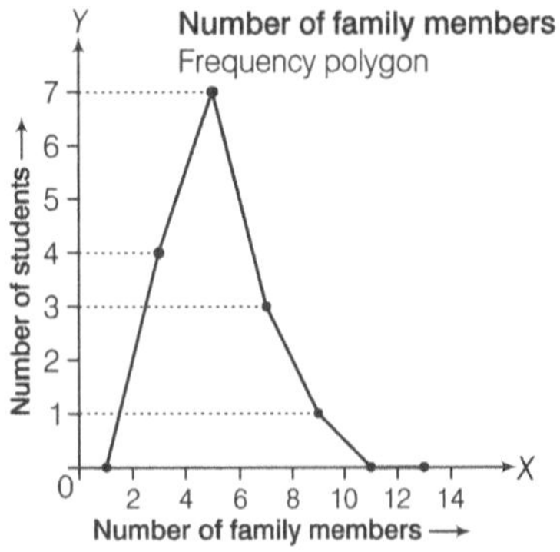

Graphical Representation of Weekly Pocket Money

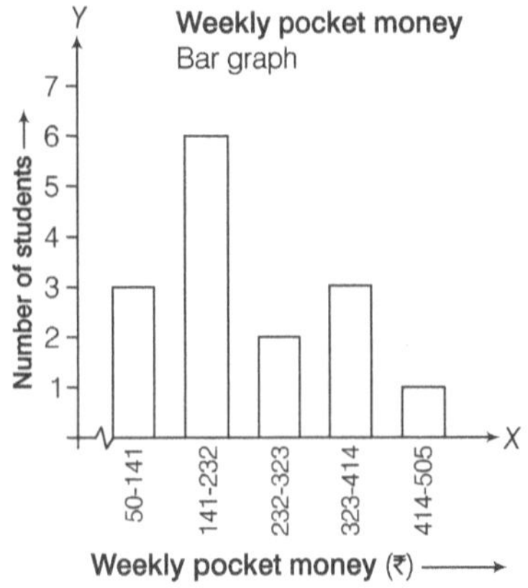

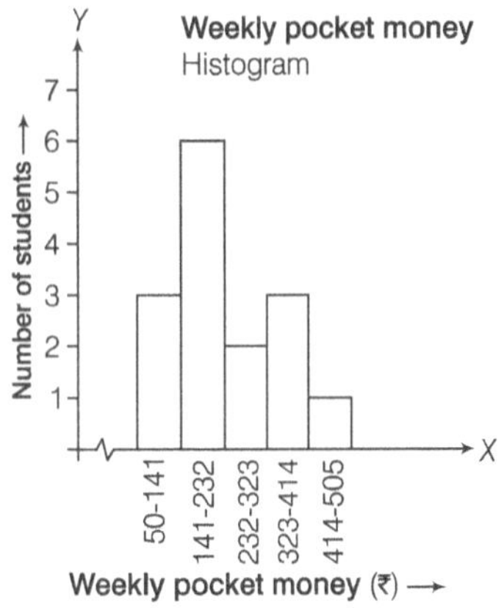

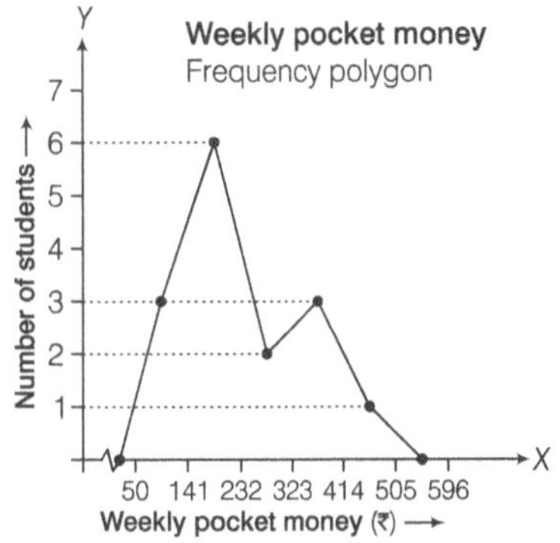

Graphical Representation of Families Monthly Income

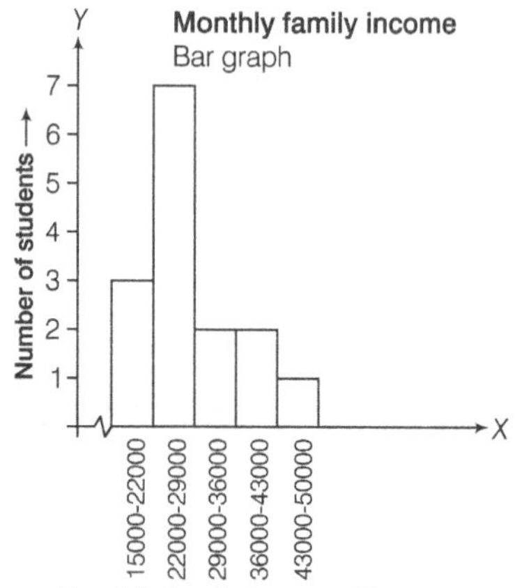

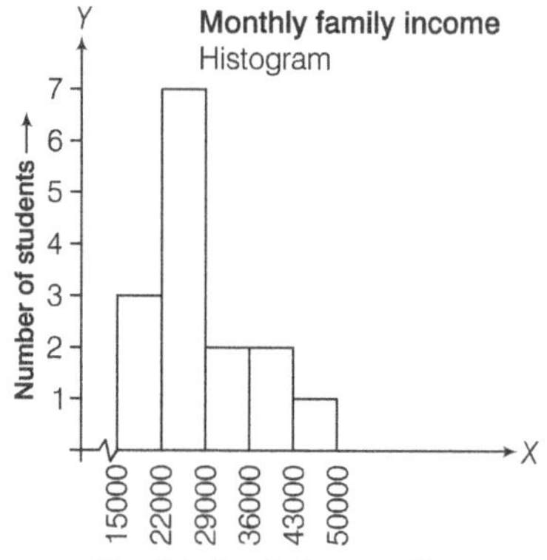

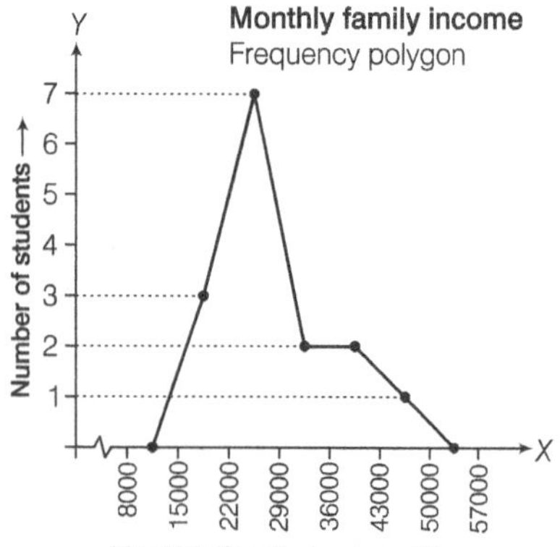

5. Data Processing

Here, we will find the mean, median and mode for each of the parameters (height, weight, number of family members etc.)

I. Height

$$\text{Mean (Average)} = \frac{\text{Sum of all observations}}{\text{Total number of observations}}$$

$$\therefore \text{ Mean height} = \frac{2365}{15} = 157.67 \text{ cm}$$

$$\text{Median} = \left(\frac{n+1}{2}\right)\text{th observation, as } n \text{ is odd.}$$

To find median, let us arrange the observations in ascending order, i.e. 140, 142, 145, 146, 149, 152, 153, 160, 162, 163, 163, 165, 171, 175, 179.

$$\therefore \text{Median} = \left(\frac{15+1}{2}\right)\text{th observation}$$

$$= \textbf{8th observation} = \textbf{160 cm}$$

Mode = Most frequently occurring observation.

$\therefore$ **Mode = 163 cm**

II. Weight

$$\text{Mean (Average)} = \frac{\text{Sum of all observations}}{\text{Total number of observations}}$$

$$\therefore \text{Mean weight} = \frac{880}{15} = 58.67 \text{ kg}$$

$$\text{Median} = \left(\frac{n+1}{2}\right)\text{th observation, as } n \text{ is odd.}$$

To find median, let us arrange the observations in ascending order.

45, 50, 50, 52, 54, 55, 58, 60, 62, 62, 62, 65, 65, 70, 70.

$$\therefore \text{Median} = \left(\frac{15+1}{2}\right)\text{th observation} = \text{8th observation}$$

$= 60$kg

Mode = Most frequently occurring observation

$\therefore$ Mode = 62 kg

III. Number of Family Members

$$\text{Mean (Average)} = \frac{\text{Sum of all observations}}{\text{Total number of observations}}$$

$$\therefore \text{Mean, number of family members} = \frac{69}{15} = 4.6$$

$$\text{Median} = \left(\frac{n+1}{2}\right)\text{th observation, as } n \text{ is odd.}$$

To find median, let us arrange the observations in ascending order.

2, 3, 3, 3, 4, 4, 4, 4, 5, 5, 5, 6, 6, 7, 8

$\therefore$ Median = 8th observation = 4

Mode = Most frequently occurring observation

$\therefore$ Mode = 4

IV. Weekly Pocket Money

$$\text{Mean (Average)} = \frac{\text{Sum of all observations}}{\text{Total number of observations}}$$

$$\therefore \text{Mean, pocket money} = \frac{3500}{15}$$

$$= ₹\ 233.33$$

$$\text{Median} = \left(\frac{n+1}{2}\right)\text{th observation, as } n \text{ is odd.}$$

To find median, let us arrange the observations in descending order.

500, 400, 350, 350, 300, 250, 200, 200, 200, 200, 150, 150, 100, 100, 50

$\therefore$ Median 8th observation = ₹ 200

Mode = Most frequently occurring observation.

$\therefore$ Mode = ₹ 200

V. Monthly Family Income

$$\text{Mean} = \frac{\text{Sum of all observations}}{\text{Total number of observations}}$$

$$\therefore \text{Mean, family income} = \frac{410000}{15}$$

$$= ₹\ 27333.33$$

$$\text{Median} = \left(\frac{n+1}{2}\right)\text{th observation, as } n \text{ is odd.}$$

To find median, let us arrange the observations in ascending order.

15000, 20000, 20000, 22000, 22000, 23000, 23000, 25000, 25000, 25000, 30000, 35000, 40000, 40000, 45000.

$\therefore$ Median = 8th observation = ₹ 25000

Mode = Most frequently occurring observation

= ₹ 25000

6. Observations

From the above information, we observe the following

Central values/ Parameters	Height (in cm)	Weight (in kg)	Family size	Pocket money (in ₹)	Family income (in ₹)
Average	157.67	58.67	4.6	233.33	27333.33
Median	160	60	4	200	25000
Modal	163	62	4	200	25000

7. Conclusions

1. In case of height and weight, as mode is greater than the mean and the median lies in between mean and mode, therefore we can say that there are few students which have small height and less weight than the majority of students.
2. In case of family size, pocket money and family income, as mode and median are alike, and mean is far away, therefore we can say there are few students which have higher family size, pocket money and family income than the majority of students.
3. On comparing the average height and average weight, we can say that students are surveyed in good health.
4. On the basis of pocket money and family income, we can conclude that most of the students surveyed have a modest family background whereas few are perhaps in higher income group.

(i) If mean is greater than the mode and median lies in between mean and mode, then the data contains some values that are much larger than the majority of other observations.

(ii) If mode is greater than the mean and median lies some where in between mean and mode, then the data contains some values that are much smaller than the majority of other observations.

8. Further Study

1. We may conduct survey on the number of cars in the family, number of siblings etc.
2. For more accurate values of parameter, we may increase the size of data.
3. We may find out statistical parameters for girls and boys separately and compare them.

Project 2

Topic

Planning delivery routes for a milkman/postman.

Table of contents

1. Introduction

A milkman is a person who delivers milk in milk cartons or bottles. Generally, milkman delivers milk on the cycle and they deliver from milk dairy to various houses, daily. To save time and energy a milkman plans his route.

Let us help Raju, a milkman to plan his route. Suppose, Raju delivers milk to three localities X, Y and Z. These localities are situated on a straight road as shown in the figure below.

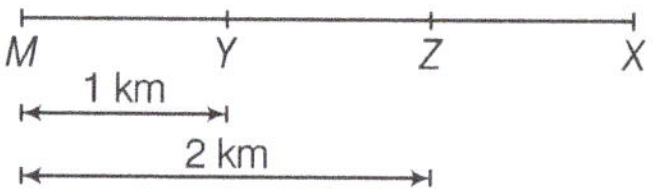

Here, M is 'milk dairy' and localities X, Y and Z are 3 km, 1 km and 2 km away from milk dairy, respectively.

Let, locality X has 60 houses and their total demand is 100 L, Y has 40 houses and their total demand is 60 L, whereas Z has 50 houses and their total demand is 40 L. Suppose, milkman has a sufficient amount of milk to meet their demands and has a capacity to carry 100 L at a time.

2. Planning the Routes

Route 1

(i) Taking 100 L milk, first goes towards locality Y.

(ii) After delivering milk of locality Y, he moves forward to deliver milk to locality Z.

(iii) Cycle back to the milk dairy.

(iv) Takes 100 L milk and goes towards locality X.

(v) After delivering milk to locality X, again cycle back to the milk dairy.

Total Distance Covered by Him

(i) Travelling from M to Y, he cover 1 km with a load of 100 L.

(ii) Travelling from Y to Z, he cover 1 km with a load of 40 L.

(iii) Travelling from Z to M, he cover 2 km with no load.

(iv) Travelling from M to X, he cover 3 km with a load of 100 L.

(v) Travelling from X to M, he cover 3 km with no load.

So, he need to cycle 10 km.

Route 2

(i) Taking 100 L milk, first goes towards locality Z.

(ii) After delivering milk of locality Z, cycle back to the locality Y.

(iii) After delivering milk of locality Y, cycle back to the milk dairy.

(iv) Takes 100 L milk and goes towards locality X.

(v) After delivering milk to locality X, again cycle back to the milk dairy.

Total Distance Covered by Him

(i) Travelling from M to Z, he cover 2 km with a load of 100 L.

(ii) Travelling from Z to Y, he cover 1 km with a load of 60 L.

(iii) Travelling from Y to M, he cover 1km with no load.

(iv) Travelling from M to X, he cover 3 km with a load of 100 L.

(v) Travelling from X to M, he cover 3 km with no load.

So, he need to cycle 10 km.

3. Comparison of Routes

In routes 1 and 2, he travels same distance but in route 2 he has to carry an extra load of 40 L, while travelling from M to Z and Z to Y, i.e. he carries extra load of 40 L for 4 km, where as in route 1, he need not to carry any extra load.

4. Conclusion

Route 1 is better, as it requires lesser energy.

5. Further Study

1. We can assume that a milkman delivers milk on motorcycle and then apply transportation cost.
2. In the same way, we can plan a route for a postman.

   Remember that your postman neither have cycle nor carry too much load.

Project 3

Topic

Running a tuck shop/canteen.

Table of Contents

1. Introduction

The term "tuck shop" is interchangeable with the word "canteen". Usually, the term "tuck shop" is used in boarding schools. A tuck shop is a small, food-selling retailer. It typically sells confectionery items, such as sweets, potato chips, soft drinks and so on. When the tuck shop is in a school, it is frequently the one place where monetary transactions can be made. In some schools, they often sell items of stationary too, although food is still their primary source of income. Suppose Ram Lal has got a contract to run a "tuck shop" in a school for two years. According, to the contract he has to set up a healthy tuck shop, so that it encourages children to make healthy choices in what they eat. He is also responsible to keep the tuck shop clean. Besides, he has to deposit ₹ 100000 as security. To run a successful healthy tuck shop, some past sale records has been made available to him, so that he can plan this tuck shop accordingly.

2. Items on Sale

According to past sales records, he decided to sell the following items

(i) **Healthy Snacks** Sandwich and fruit salad.

(ii) **Confectionary items** Healthy biscuits and potato chips.

(iii) **Beverages** Tea, coffee, fruit juice and milk bottles.

3. Tables Showing their Cost Price, Selling Price and Expected Sale.

Based on the previous data, the following table shows the cost price, selling price and expected sale of each item

S. No.	Items	Cost price/ item (CP)	Selling price (SP)	Daily expected sale
	Healthy Snacks			
1.	Sandwich	₹ 12	₹ 15	300
2.	Fruit salad	₹ 20	₹ 25	200
	Confectionary Items			
3.	Healthy biscuits	₹ 8	₹ 10	50
4.	Potato chips	₹ 10	₹ 13	150
	Beverages			
5.	Tea	₹ 6	₹ 8	50
6.	Coffee	₹ 10	₹ 12	100
7.	Milk bottle	₹ 18	₹ 20	150
8.	Fruit juice	₹ 20	₹ 25	400

4. Total Profit on Each Item

The following table shows the total profit on each item.

S. No.	Items	Daily expected sale	Profit = SP – CP	Total profit on an item
1.	Sandwich	300	₹ (15 – 12) = ₹ 3	₹ (300 × 3) = ₹ 900
2.	Fruit salad	200	₹ (25 – 20) = ₹ 5	₹ (200 × 5) = ₹ 1000
3.	Healthy biscuits	50	₹ (10 – 8) = ₹ 2	₹ (50 × 2) = ₹ 100
4.	Potato chips	150	₹ (13 – 10) = ₹ 3	₹ (150 × 3) = ₹ 450
5.	Tea	50	₹ (8 – 6) = ₹ 2	₹ (50 × 2) = ₹ 100
6.	Coffee	100	₹ (12 – 10) = ₹ 2	₹ (100 × 2) = ₹ 200
7.	Milk bottle	150	₹ (20 – 18) = ₹ 2	₹ (150 × 2) = ₹ 300
8.	Fruit juice	400	₹ (25 – 20) = ₹ 5	₹ (400 × 5) = ₹ 2000
			Total profit	₹ 5050

5. Miscellaneous Expenses and Expected Monthly Profit

Based on previous records the following table shows the other expenses.

Monthly expenses	Amount (in ₹)
Rent	₹ 25000
Electricity and water bill	₹ 5000
Salary of 4 sales men	₹ 25000
Wastage	₹ 20000
Total	₹ 75000

Now, expected monthly profit is given by

$= \text{Total monthly profit on each item} - \text{Monthly expenses}$

$= \text{Number of days school open} \times \text{Total profit} - \text{Monthly expenses}$

$= ₹\,(26 \times 5050) - ₹\,75000$

$= ₹\,131300 - ₹\,75000$

$= ₹\,56300$

6. Observations

In order to start a 'tuck shop', Ram Lal needs,

Security deposit = ₹ 100000

One month rent = ₹ 25000

Amount needed to purchase items

$= ₹\,(12 \times 300 + 20 \times 200 + 8 \times 50 + 10 \times 150 + 6 \times 50 + 10 \times 100 + 18 \times 150 + 20 \times 400)$

$= ₹\,(3600 + 4000 + 400 + 1500 + 300 + 1000 + 2700 + 8000)$

$= ₹\,21500$

Total = ₹ 146500 (₹ 150000 approx).

7. Conclusion

As, Ram Lal will not earn any interest on his security deposit, i.e. he will lose ₹ 1000 per month on it. (12% per annum simple interest).

∴ Gross monthly profit of Ram Lal

$= ₹\,(56300 - 1000) = ₹\,55300$

which is sufficient as compared to investment.

8. Further Study

(i) We may add some more items to the items available in the tuck shop.

(ii) If Ram Lal borrowed ₹ 150000 @ 36% per annum simple interest from a money lender, then plan how will he repay, if he require ₹ 40000 per month to run his home.

Project 4

Topic

Study ways of raising a loan to buy a car or house, e.g. Bank loan or purchase a refrigerator or a television set through hire purchase.

Purchasing a Refrigerator on Hire Purchase

Table of Contents

1. Introduction
2. Hire purchase
3. Purchasing a refrigerator
4. Observations
5. Conclusion
6. Further study

1. Introduction

A loan refers to the money borrowed from financial institutions like banks or other lenders. People take out loans for several different reasons like to purchase some heavy cost items. With the current economic condition, taking out loan is something that has become a norm for a lot of people. We know, income has not been increasing for years, while prices kept soaring high. For this reason, people are usually cash strapped and are forced to borrow money in order to fulfill their needs.

2. Hire Purchase

Hire purchase is a form of instalment credit. In this a financial institution provides loan to a customer for buying a product on instalment. Under hire purchase, we only need to pay a part of purchase price (called **down payment**) at the time of purchase and rest amount in instalment. The size of down payment depends on the finance company's policy and its assessment about the customer. Here, the customer does not actually own the product until the last instalment is paid, although he or she has full control on use of product throughout the repayment period.

3. Purchasing a Refrigerator

Suppose Ravi, a sales executive, wishes to buy a refrigerator for his family. It costs ₹ 50000. Which is difficult for him to arrange amount, so he asks the shopkeeper for finance options. Then, shopkeeper offers him the following finance options

1. **Finance by a bank** According to bank policy, Ravi has to pay ₹ 10000 as cash down payment and 5 monthly instalments of ₹ 9000 each. Also, he has to pay a processing fee of ₹ 500. Under this finance option, Ravi has to wait for 7-10 days, because bank will take 7-10 days to process his application.

2. **Finance by a private finance company** According to finance company's policy, Ravi has to pay ₹ 10000 as cash down payment and 5 monthly instalment of ₹ 9600 each. Under this finance option, there is no waiting period and no processing fee.

4. Observations

Option 1

Total cost $= ₹\ 10000 + 5 \times ₹\ 9000 + ₹\ 500$

$= ₹\ (10000 + 45000 + 500)$

$= ₹\ 55500$

Extra amount paid $= ₹\ (55500 - 50000)$

$= ₹\ 5500$

Waiting period $= (7 - 10)$ days

Option 2

Total cost $= ₹\ 10000 + 5 \times ₹\ 9600$

$= ₹\ (10000 + 48000)$

$= ₹\ 58000$

Extra amount paid $= ₹\ (58000 - 50000) = ₹\ 8000$

Waiting period = 0 days

5. Conclusion

Ravi, should go for option 1. Although option 2 requires no waiting period but it cost ₹ 2500 more than option 1.

6. Further Study

In the same way, we can study the ways of financing a car or house, etc. We may compare the instalments and interest charged if an item is financed for 2 yr, 3 yr etc.

Project 5

Topic

Cutting a circle into equal sections of a small central angle to find the area of a circle by using the formula $A = \pi r^2$.

Pre-requisite Knowledge

(i) Formula of the circumference of a circle

(ii) Formula of the area of a rectangle

Requirement

Pencil, pair of compasses, scale, drawing sheet, white paper colour box, a pair of scissors and fevistik.

Procedure

1. Draw a circle with centre O and radius (say) r [let, $r = 9$ cm] on a drawing sheet.
2. Draw the diameter of a circle with the help of scale and pencil.
3. Paint the halves of the circle with two different colours. Let us paint red colour on the upper half and green colour on the lower half.

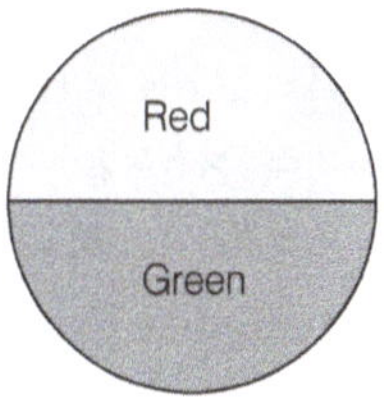

4. Divide the circle into 16 equal parts by paper folding, i.e. first fold the circle to get two equal semi-circles and then continue folding till you have folded the circle four times and you will get a circle divided into 16 equal parts.
5. Now, cut all 16 equal parts of the circle as shown in the following figure.

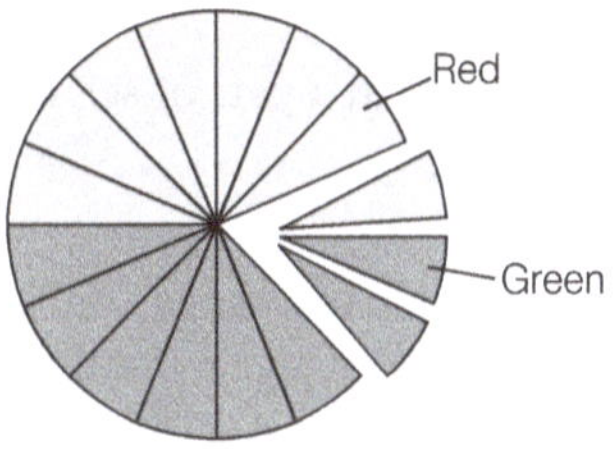

6. Take any one part and cut this part into two equal halves as shown in the given figure. Let us take green part of a circle and cut this part into two equal halves.

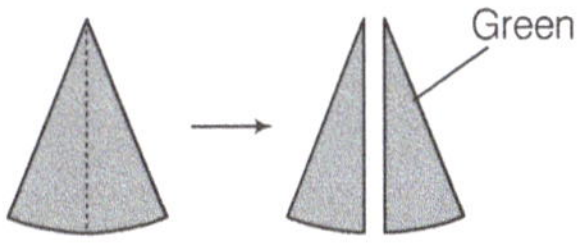

7. Paste all the parts of the circle on a white sheet exactly as shown in the following figure and paste two equal halves at the ends which were cut in the step 6th.

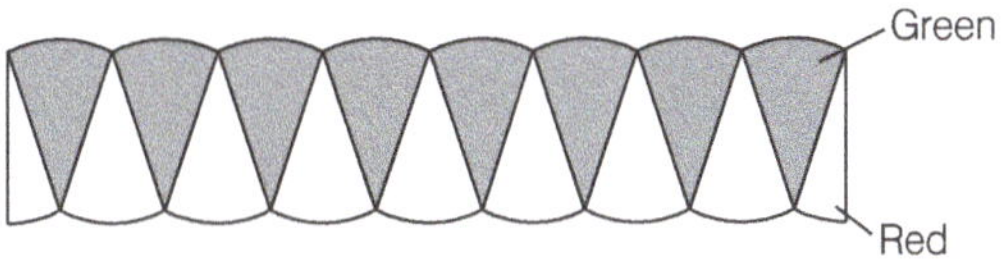

Observations

From the last figure obtained in step 7, we get a rectangle

Length of this rectangle $= \frac{1}{2} \times 2\pi r = \pi r$

and breadth of this rectangle

$= \text{radius of a circle} = r.$

Calculation

Area of circle = Area of rectangle obtained in step 7

$= \text{length} \times \text{breadth}$

$= \pi r \times r = \pi r^2$

Result

Area of a circle of radius r units $= \pi r^2$

Project Report

1. Students learn the elementary concept of changing one geometrical shape into another. In this project, we transform a circle into an approximate shape of rectangle.
2. If the circle is further divided into 32, 64, ... equal parts, then the figure obtained in step 7 appears more and more like a rectangle.
3. Area of a circle πr^2 is the geometrical observation of the students.

Project 6

Topic

To use flat cutouts to form cube, cuboids and pyramids to obtain the formulae for volume and total surface area.

Pre-requisite Knowledge

Concept of perimeter and area of a square, a rectangle, a triangle, an equilateral triangle, etc., and the concept of surface area and volume of a cube, a cuboid, a pyramid and a cone.

Requirement

Geometry box, chart paper, a pair of scissors/paper cutter, adhesive transparent tape.

Procedure

1. On a coloured chart paper draw the nets of a cube, a cuboid and a right triangular pyramid as shown below.
2. Fold the nets to make cube, cuboid and the right triangular pyramid. Use adhesive tape to make them rigid.
3. Find the surface areas and volumes of the following as shown.

(i) **Net of a cube**

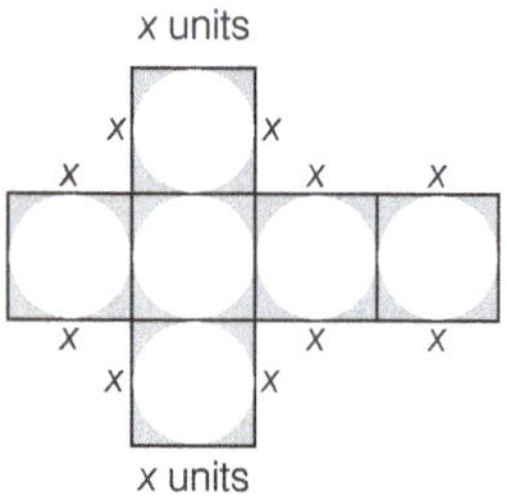

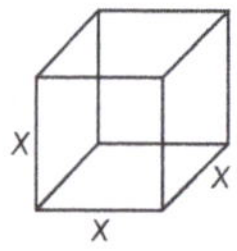

Observations Area of each face of the cube equals to

$= x \times x = x^2$ sq units

Total faces in a cube are 6.

$\therefore$ Total surface area of the cube $= 6x^2$

Volume of cube = (Area of base) $\times$ Height

$= x^2 \times x = x^3$ cubic units.

(ii) **Net of a cuboid**

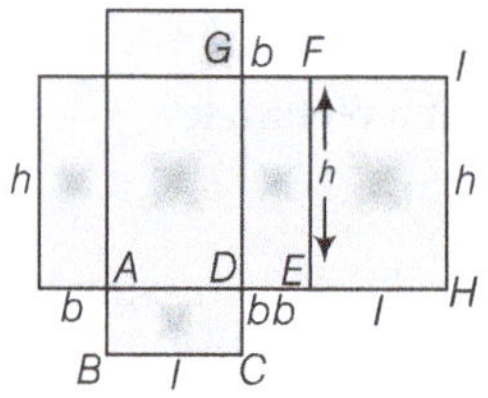

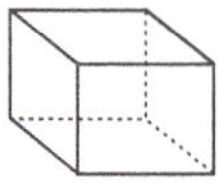

Observation

Area of face $ABCD = l \times b = lb$

Area of face $DEFG = b \times h = bh$

Area of face $EHIF = l \times h = lh$

$\therefore$ Total surface area of a cuboid

$= 2$ (Area of face $ABCD$)

$+ 2$ (Area of face $DEFG$) $+ 2$ (Area of face $EHIF$)

$= 2(lb) + 2(bh) + 2(hl) = 2(lb + bh + hl)$ sq units

Volume of cuboid = (Area of the base) $\times$ Height

$= l \times b \times h$

$= lbh$ cubic units

(iii) **Net of a Right Triangular Pyramid**

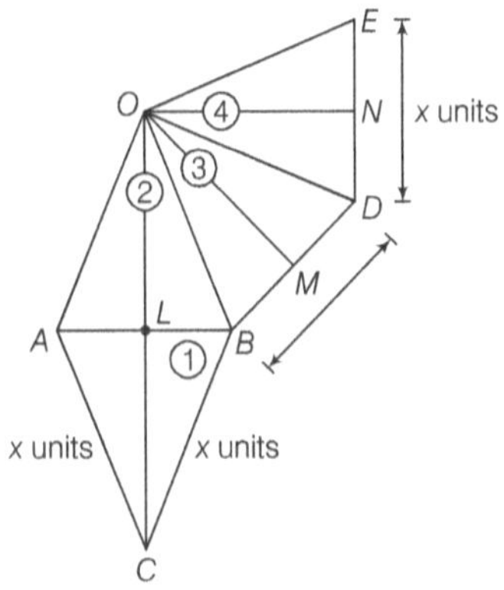

Observations

Triangle 1 is an equilateral triangle of side of length x units.

Triangles 2, 3 and 4 are three congruent triangles.

In ΔAOB, ΔBOD and ΔDOE, OL, OM and ON are perpendicular bisectors of AB, BD and DE respectively, and $OL = OM = ON = l$ (say)

$\therefore$ Lateral surface area of the right pyramid = Sum of areas of three faces AOB, BOD and DOE

$$= \text{ar}(\Delta AOB) + \text{ar}(\Delta BOD) + \text{ar}(\Delta DOE)$$

$$= \frac{1}{2} x \times l + \frac{1}{2} x \times l + \frac{1}{2} x \times l = \frac{3}{2} xl$$

Volume of the right pyramid

$$= \frac{1}{3}(\text{Area of base}) \times \text{Height}$$

$$= \frac{1}{3} \times \frac{\sqrt{3}}{4} x^2 \times h$$

$$= \frac{\sqrt{3}}{12} x^2 \times h$$

[where, h is vertical height of the pyramid]

(iv) **Net of a Right Square Pyramid**

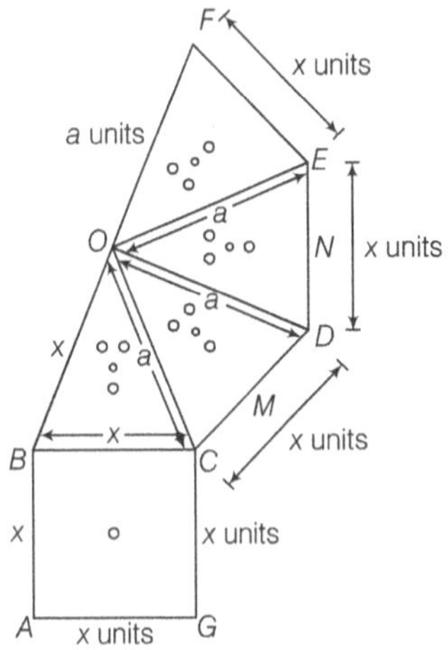

Observations $ABCG$ is a square and ΔBOC, ΔCOD, ΔDOE and ΔEOF are isosceles triangles with base x units and equal sides a units.

To find the lateral surface area and volume, students can proceed as explained in the right triangular pyramid.

Project Report

Solid figures	Surface area	Volume
Cuboid	$2(lb + bh + hl)$	lbh
Cube	$6a^2$	a^3
Pyramid	Base area + $\frac{1}{2}$ × Perimeter of base × Height	$\frac{1}{3}$ × (Base area) × Height

Further Study

Take different dimensions of cuboid, cube and pyramid, put in the formulae and find the surface area and volume.

Project 7

Topic

Draw a circle of radius r on a 1/2 cm graph paper and then on a 2 mm graph paper. Estimate the area enclosed in each case by actually counting the squares. Now, try out with circles of different radii. Establish the pattern if any, between the two observed values and the theoretical value (area $= \pi r^2$). Any modifications?

Requirement

Pencil, 2 graph papers, scale, a pair of compasses.

1. **Definition of circle** A circle is the locus of all points equidistant from a central point.
2. **Construct the circle on a graph paper**

   (i) Take $r = 6$ cm, draw a circle on $\frac{1}{2}$ cm graph paper.

   (ii) Draw a circle of radius, $r = 6$ cm on 2 mm graph paper.

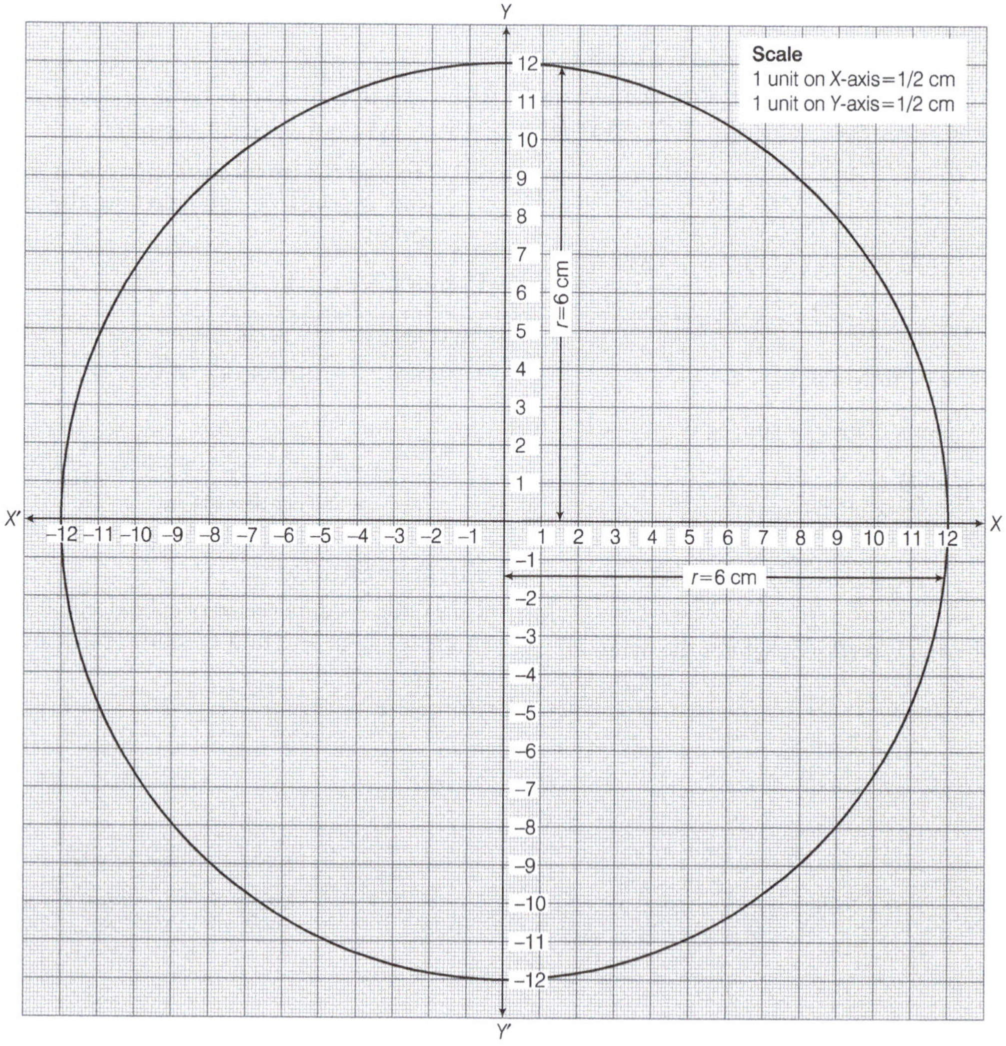

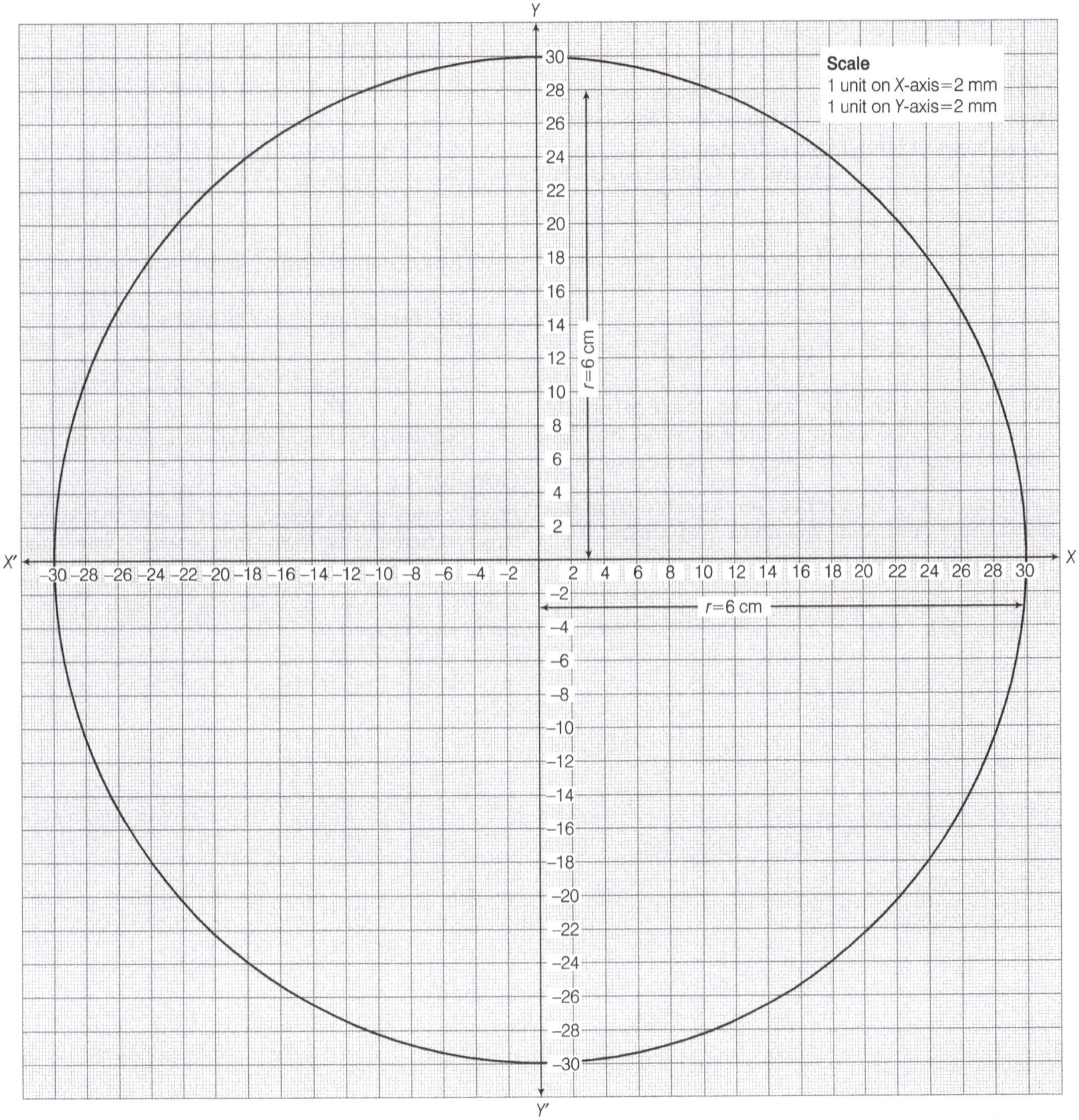

3. Counting of squares enclosed by circle on each graph paper.

(i) On $\frac{1}{2}$ cm graph paper,

Let x_1 = Number of full squares and x_2 = Number of half squares

(ii) On 2 mm graph paper,

Let y_1 = Number of full squares and y_2 = Number of half squares

4. **Observations** From both graphs, we observe that $y_1 > x_1$ and $y_2 > x_2$.

5. **Calculation**

(i) On $\frac{1}{2}$ cm graph paper,

Area of circle = (Area of each full square × Numbers of full squares) + (Area of each half square × Number of half squares)

$$= \left(\frac{1}{2}\right)^2 \times x_1 + \frac{1}{2} \times \left(\frac{1}{2}\right)^2 \times x_2$$

$$= \frac{1}{4}x_1 + \frac{1}{2} \times \frac{1}{4}x_2 = \frac{1}{4}\left[x_1 + \frac{1}{2}x_2\right]\text{cm}^2$$

(ii) On 2 mm graph paper,

Area of circle = (Area of each full square × Number of full squares) + (Area of each half square × Number of half squares)

$$= (2)^2 \times y_1 + \frac{1}{2}(2)^2 \times y_2$$

$$= 4y_1 + \frac{1}{2} \times 4y_2$$

$$= 4\left(y_1 + \frac{1}{2}y_2\right)\text{mm}^2$$

But the area of circle on both the graph papers is same because the radius of circle is same. So, by calculation, using $A = \pi r^2$, we get the same result.

6. Draw circles of different radii on these two types of graph papers and count the number of squares and find the area for each of them.

We see the pattern on $\frac{1}{2}$ cm graph paper

Radii → r_1, r_2, r_3 [let]

Number of full and half squares →

$$x_1 + x_2,\ x_1' + x_2',\ x_1'' + x_2''.$$

and let $a\left(= x_1 + \frac{1}{2}x_2\right)$, $b\left(= x_1' + \frac{1}{2}x_2'\right)$,

$c\left(= x_1'' + \frac{1}{2}x_2''\right)$

By calculation area of circles → $\pi r_1^2, \pi r_2^2, \pi r_3^2$

By observation area of circles → $\frac{1}{4}a, \frac{1}{4}b, \frac{1}{4}c$

$\therefore \quad \frac{1}{4}a \approx \pi r_1^2, \frac{1}{4}b \approx \pi r_2^2, \frac{1}{4}c \approx \pi r_3^2$

Similarly result is observed on 2 mm graph paper.

Conclusion

From the above discussion, we conclude that there is no larger difference between the observed value and the theoretical value of the area of circle by using $\frac{1}{2}$ cm and 2 mm graph papers.

3 Sample Question Papers

SAMPLE QUESTION PAPER 1

A HIGHLY SIMULATED Sample Question Paper for ICSE Class IX

Mathematics (Unsolved)

GENERAL INSTRUCTIONS

1. Answers to this paper must be written on the paper provided saperately.
2. You will not be allowed to write during the first 15 minutes. This time is to be spent in reading the question paper.
3. The time given at the head of this paper is the time allowed for writing the answers.
4. Attempt all **questions** from **Section A** and **any 4 questions** from **Section B.**
5. All working, including rough work, must be clearly shown and must be done on the same sheet as the rest of the answer.
6. Omission of essential working will result in loss of marks.
7. The intended marks for questions or parts of questions are given in bracket [ ].
8. Mathematical tables are provided.

Time : 2.5 Hrs **Max. Marks : 80**

Section A [40 *Marks*]

(Attempt all questions from this section)

1. Choose the correct answers to the questions from the given options. [15]

(i) In how many years will a sum of ₹ 25600, interest compounded quarterly, at the rate of 25% per annum amount to ₹ 28900?

(a) 1 yr (b) $\frac{1}{2}$ yr

(c) 2 yr (d) 4 yr • ***Evaluation***

(ii) In the given figure, AC is the median as well as altitude to BD. In ΔACE, AD is the median to CE.

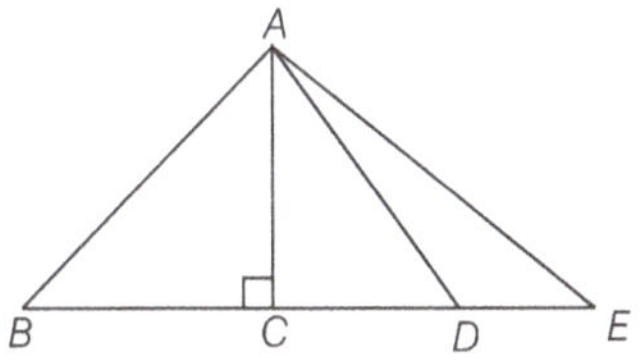

Which one of the following is true?

(a) $AB + CD > AE$

(b) $AB + BC = AE$

(c) $AB + DE < AE$

(d) None of the above • ***Analysis***

(iii) **Assertion** (A) The distance of $P(a,b)$ from origin is $a^2 + b^2$.

Reason (R) The distance between two points $A(x_1, y_1)$ and $B(x_2, y_2)$ is $\sqrt{(x_2 - x_1)^2 + (y_2 - y_1)^2}$.

(a) A is true, R is false.

(b) A is false, R is true.

(c) Both A and R are true, and R is the correct Reason for A.

(d) Both A and R are true, and R is the incorrect Reason for A. • ***Application***

(iv) If $\log[4 - 5\log_{32}(x + 3)] = 0$ then the value of x is

(a) 32 (b) 8

(c) 2 (d) 5 • ***Evaluation***

(v) Shashi has decided fixed distance to walk on a tread-mill. First day, she walks at a certain speed. Next day, she increases the speed of the tread-mill by 1 km/h, she takes 6 min less and if she reduces the speed by 1 km/h then she takes 9 min more. What is the distance that she has decided to walk everyday?

(a) 4 km (b) 6 km

(c) 5 km (d) 3 km • ***Application***

(vi) In the given figure, O is a point inside a $\triangle ABC$ such that $\angle AOC = 90°$, $OA = 6$ cm and $OR = 8$ cm. If $AB = 24$ cm and $\angle BAC = 90°$ then BC is equal to

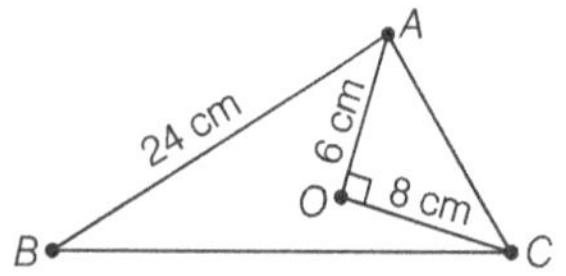

(a) 25 cm (b) 26 cm
(c) 30 cm (d) 32 cm • *Evaluation*

(vii) $\log_2 [\log_4 \{\log_5 (625)^4\}]$ is equal to
(a) 1 (b) 0
(c) 3 (d) None of these
• *Evaluation*

(viii) The greatest among $\sqrt[3]{4}$, $\sqrt[4]{5}$ and $\sqrt[4]{3}$ is
(a) $\sqrt[3]{4}$ (b) $\sqrt[4]{5}$
(c) $\sqrt[4]{3}$ (d) None of these
• *Evaluation*

(ix) If $m = a\cos^3\theta + 3a\cos\theta\sin^2\theta$ and $n = a\sin^3\theta + 3a\cos^2\theta\sin\theta$ then $(m+n)^{2/3} + (m-n)^{2/3}$ is equal to
(a) $4a^{2/3}\sin\theta\cos\theta$ (b) $a^{2/3}\sin\theta\cos\theta$
(c) $4a^{3/2}\sin\theta$ (d) $a^{3/2}\sin\theta\cos\theta$
• *Evaluation*

(x) Find the length of the longest side of the triangle formed by the line $3x + 4y = 12$ with the coordinate axes
(a) 9 units (b) 16 units
(c) 5 units (d) 7 units
• *Application*

(xi) **Statement I** If the mean of 18, 24, 15, $(2x+1)$ and 12 is 25 then the value of x is 17.5.

Statement II The mean of 24 numbers is 12.
• *Analysis*

If 2 is added to every number then new mean will be 14.
(a) Both the statements are true.
(b) Both the statements are false.
(c) Statement I is true and Statement II is false.
(d) Statement I is false and Statement II is true.

(xii) $(\sin\theta + \cos\theta)^2 + (\sin\theta - \cos\theta)^2$ is equal to
(a) $\sin^2\theta$ (b) $\cos^2\theta$
(c) 1 (d) 2 • *Understanding*

(xiii) **Assertion** (A) The length of a chord which is at a distance of 5 cm from the centre of a circle of radius 10 cm is 17.32 cm.

Reason (R) The perpendicular from the centre of a circle to a chord bisects the chord.
(a) A is true, R is false.
(b) A is false, R is true.
(c) Both A and R are true, and R is the correct Reason for A.
(d) Both A and R are true, and R is the incorrect Reason for A.
• *Analysis*

(xiv) If $\frac{343}{49} = 7^{2x}$ then x is equal to
(a) 1 (b) 2
(c) $\frac{1}{2}$ (d) 3
• *Evaluation*

(xv) The value of $\left(\sqrt[6]{27} - \sqrt{6\frac{3}{4}}\right)^2$ is
(a) $\frac{1}{4}$ (b) $\frac{3}{4}$
(c) $\frac{1}{3}$ (d) $\frac{5}{4}$ • *Evaluation*

2. (i) Simplify $\frac{5 \times (25)^{x+1} - 25 \times 5^{2x}}{5 \times 5^{2x+3} - (25)^{x+1}}$. • *Evaluation* [4]

(ii) Line segment AB is parallel to another line segment CD. O is the mid-point of AD. Show that
(a) $\triangle AOB \cong \triangle DOC$
(b) O is also the mid-point of BC.
• *Application* [4]

(iii) In the given figure, LM is a line parallel to the Y-axis at a distance of 3 units from origin.
• *Analysis* [4]

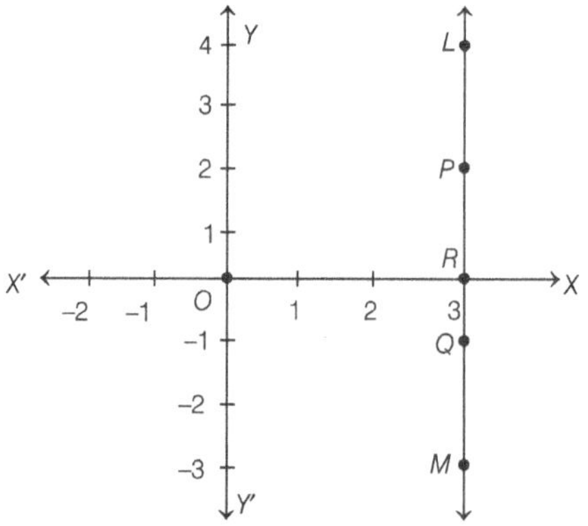

(a) What are the coordinates of the point Q?
(b) What is the sum of abscissa and ordinate of the point P?
(c) What is the difference between the abscissae of the points L and M? • *Analysis*

3. (i) Factorise $p^2x + pqy + qy + px - (px + qy)^2$.
• *Evaluation* [4]

(ii) Solve the pair of linear equation by cross-multiplication method $x + 9y = 10$ and $9x + 16y = 25$. • *Understanding* [4]

(iii) If $a^2 - 4a - 1 = 0$ and $a \neq 0$ then find the values of [5]
(a) $\frac{a^2 - 1}{a}$ (b) $a - \frac{1}{a}$
(c) $a + \frac{1}{a}$ (d) $a^2 - \frac{1}{a^2}$ • *Evaluation*

Section B [40 Marks]

(Attempt any four questions from this section)

4. (i) If one side of a parallelogram is 15 cm, and its diagonals are 18 cm and 24 cm then find the area of the parallelogram and also prove that the diagonals are perpendicular to each other. • ***Analysis*** [3]

(ii) Using class interval 0-5, 6-11, 12-17, 18-23, 24-29, construct a frequency distribution table for the following raw data.

17, 28, 26, 14, 13, 4, 9, 21, 26, 27, 28, 18, 17, 13, 12, 5, 6, 11, 12, 4 • ***Analysis*** [3]

(iii) If $\log_{10} 2 = a$ and $\log_{10} 3 = b$ then find

$\log_{10}\left(3\frac{1}{8}\right) + \log_{10} 18.$ • ***Evaluation*** [4]

5. (i) If $\sin A = \frac{6}{7}$ and $A + B = 90°$, then find the value of $\cos B$. • ***Evaluation*** [3]

(ii) In the given figure, perpendicular is drawn from centre O to the chord AB. If $AB = 8$ cm then find • ***Evaluation*** [3]

(a) PB (b) OP

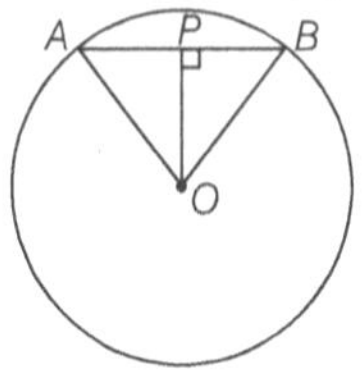

• ***Understanding***

(iii) If $y = 2x + \sqrt{x^2 + t}$, express t in terms of x and y. • ***Understanding*** [4]

6. (i) Without using trigonometric tables, evaluate the following.

(a) $\frac{\tan 38°}{\cot 52°}$ (b) $\frac{\sec 62°}{\operatorname{cosec} 28°}$ (c) $\frac{\cos 25°}{\sin 65°}$

(d) $\frac{\cos 37°}{\sin 53°}$ (e) $\frac{\operatorname{cosec} 32°}{\sec 58°}$ • ***Evaluation*** [5]

(ii) (a) A match box measure $4 \text{ cm} \times 2.5 \text{ cm} \times 1.5$ cm. What will be the volume of a packet containing 12 such boxes? • ***Analysis***

(b) Find the total surface area of the match box. • ***Analysis*** [5]

7. (i) In the given figure, ABC and DBC are two isosceles triangles on the same base BC such that $AB = AC$ and $DB = DC$. Prove that $\angle ABD = \angle ACD$. [3] • ***Applicationns***

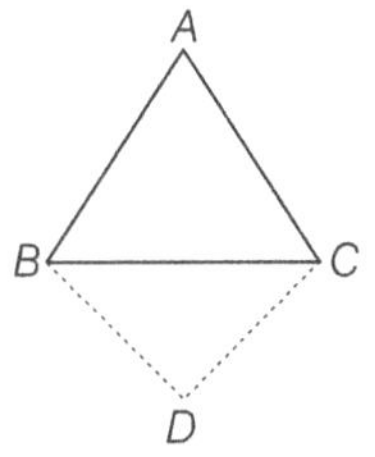

(ii) Ram deposited in a bank ₹ 7500 for 6 months at the rate of 8% interest compounded quarterly.

(a) Find the amount he received after 6 months.

(b) Find the compound interest after 6 months. • ***Application*** [3]

(iii) Solve the following system of linear equations.

$2x - y - 4 = 0, x + y + 1 = 0$ • ***Application*** [4]

8. (i) In the given figure, diagonal is AC and BD of quadrilateral $ABCD$ intersect at O, such that $OB = OD$. If $AD = BC$, show that

(a) ar (ΔAOD) = ar (ΔBOC)

(b) ar (ΔABD) = ar (ΔABC)

(c) $AB \parallel DC$ • ***Analys*** [3]

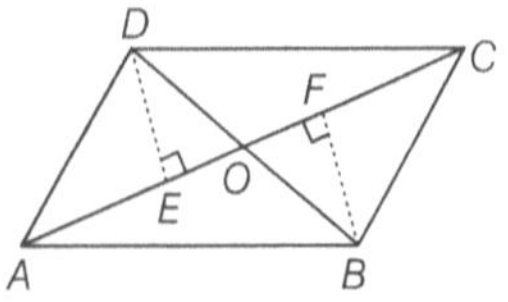

(ii) Factorise

(a) $2x^5 - 2x$ • ***Analysis*** [3]

(b) $4x^2 - 169y^2$

(iii) Show that the following repeating decimals are rational number. • ***Understanding*** [4]

(a) $1.\bar{9}$ (b) $0.\overline{325}$

9. (i) A rhombus shaped field has green grass for 18 cows to graze. If each side of the rhombus is 30 m and its longer diagonal is 48 m. How much area of grass field will each cow be grazing? • ***Application*** [3]

(ii) In a ΔABC, $AC > AB$, D is the mid-point of BC and $AE \perp BC$.

Prove that

(a) $AC^2 = AD^2 + BC \cdot DE + \frac{1}{4}BC^2$

(b) $AB^2 = AD^2 - BC \cdot DE + \frac{1}{4}BC^2$ • ***Application*** [3]

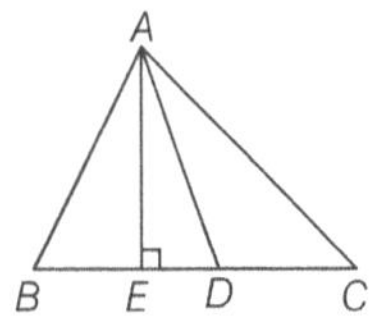

(iii) Write the lowest rationalising factor of the following.

(a) $\sqrt{32}$ (b) $(\sqrt{2} - 2)$

(c) $\sqrt{40} - \sqrt{360}$ (d) $15 - 3\sqrt{2}$

• ***Evaluation*** [4]

10. (i) The perimeter of rectangular field is 80 m. If the length of field is decreased by 2 m and its breadth is increased by 2 m then the area is increased by 36 m^2.
(a) Find the length of the rectangular field.
(b) Find the breadth of the rectangular field. • *Analysis* [4]
(ii) Construct a rectangle with side 4.5 cm and diagonal 6 cm. • *Analysis* [3]
(iii) Find the area of quadrilateral $ABCD$, in which $AB = 7$ cm, $BC = 6$ cm, $CD = 12$ cm, $DA = 15$ cm and $AC = 9$ cm. • *Application* [3]

ANSWERS

1. (i) (b) (ii) (a) (iii) (c) (iv) (d) (v) (d)
(vi) (b) (vii) (a) (viii) (a) (ix) (a) (x) (c)
(xi) (d) (xii) (d) (xiii) (c) (xiv) (c) (xv) (b)

2. (i) $\frac{1}{6}$ (iii) (a) $(3, -1)$ (b) 5 (c) 0

3. (i) $(px + qy)(p + 1 - px - qy)$
(ii) 1, 1
(iii) (a) 4 (b) 4 (c) $\pm 2\sqrt{5}$ (d) $\pm 8\sqrt{5}$

4. (i) 216 cm^2 (iii) $2b - 4a + 2$

5. (i) $\frac{6}{7}$ (ii) (a) $PB = 4$ cm (b) $OP = 3$ cm
(iii) $t = 3x^2 + y^2 - 4xy$

6. (i) (a) 1 (b) 1 (c) 1 (d) 1 (e) 1
(ii) (a) 180 cm (b) 39.5 cm^2

7. (ii) (a) ₹ 7803 (b) ₹ 303 (iii) 1, – 2

8. (ii) (a) $2x(x^2 + 1)(x + 1)(x - 1)$
(b) $(2x + 13y)(2x - 13y)$

9. (i) 48 m^2
(iii) (a) $\sqrt{2}$ (b) $\sqrt{2} + 2$ (c) $\sqrt{10}$ (d) $5 + \sqrt{2}$

10. (i) (a) 30 m (b) 10 m
(iii) 74.98 cm^2

SAMPLE QUESTION PAPER 2

A HIGHLY SIMULATED Sample Question Paper for ICSE Class IX

Mathematics (Unsolved)

GENERAL INSTRUCTIONS

1. Answers to this paper must be written on the paper provided saperately.
2. You will not be allowed to write during the first 15 minutes. This time is to be spent in reading the question paper.
3. The time given at the head of this paper is the time allowed for writing the answers.
4. Attempt all **questions** from **Section A** and **any 4 questions** from **Section B.**
5. All working, including rough work, must be clearly shown and must be done on the same sheet as the rest of the answer.
6. Omission of essential working will result in loss of marks.
7. The intended marks for questions or parts of questions are given in bracket [ ].
8. Mathematical tables are provided.

Time : 2.5 Hrs **Max. Marks : 80**

Section A [40 *Marks*]

(Attempt all questions from this section)

1. Choose the correct answers to the questions from the given options. [15]

(i) In ΔABC, if $\angle A - \angle B = 15°$ and $\angle B - \angle C = 30°$ then $\angle A$, $\angle B$ and $\angle C$ are respectively

(a) 80°, 65°, 35°
(b) 65°, 80°, 35°
(c) 35°, 80°, 65°
(d) 80°, 35°, 65°

• ***Application***

(ii) Ajay borrowed a sum of ₹ 4000 at 10% per annum for 4 yr under simple interest. But after 2 yr he was asked to pay compound interest for the remaining 2 yr on the sum borrowed initially. How much more did Ajay have to pay, if interest was compounded annually?

(a) ₹ 40 (b) ₹ 20
(c) ₹ 80 (d) ₹ 160 • ***Application***

(iii) A 5 m long ladder is placed leaning towards a vertical wall such that it reaches the wall at a point 4 m high. If the foot of the ladder is moved 1.6 m towards the wall, then find the distance by which the top of the ladder would slide upwards on the wall.

(a) 0.5 m (b) 0.8 m
(c) 0.4 m (d) 0.6 m • ***Analysis***

(iv) If $x = \log_3 27$ and $y = \log_9 27$ then the value of $\frac{x+y}{xy}$ is

(a) $\frac{1}{3}$ (b) $\frac{1}{9}$
(c) 3 (d) 1 • ***Evaluation***

(v) X is a three-digit number. The number formed by reversing the digits of X is 891 less than X. Find its unit's digit.

(a) 0
(b) 1
(c) 2
(d) Cannot be determined • ***Application***

(vi) If $\log x + \log 5 = 2 + \log 64$ then the value of x is

(a) 1240 (b) 1280
(c) 1310 (d) 1100 • ***Analysis***

(vii) In the given figure, ΔABC is an isosceles triangle, in which $AB = AC$ and D, E and F are the mid-points of BC, CA and AB, respectively. Then,

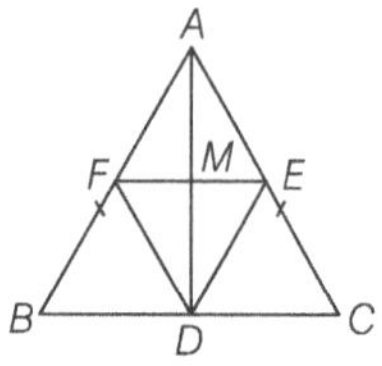

(a) $AD \perp FE$
(b) $AD \parallel FE$
(c) AD is bisected by FE.
(d) Both (a) and (c) • *Analysis*

(viii) The smallest of the surds $\sqrt{\frac{1}{2}}, \sqrt[3]{\frac{2}{3}}, \sqrt{\frac{1}{3}}, \sqrt{\frac{1}{4}}$ is
(a) $\frac{1}{2}$ (b) $\sqrt[3]{\frac{2}{3}}$
(c) $\sqrt{\frac{1}{3}}$ (d) $\sqrt{\frac{1}{4}}$
• *Understanding*

(ix) **Assertion** (A) If $\tan x + \cot x = 2$ then the value of $\tan^2 x + \cot^2 x$ is equal to 2.

Reason (R) $\tan x \cdot \cot x = 1$
(a) A is true, R is false.
(b) A is false, R is true.
(c) Both A and R are true, and R is the correct Reason for A.
(d) Both A and R are true, and R is the incorrect Reason for A. • *Analysis*

(x) Plot the following points, join them in order and identify the figure, thus formed.

$A(1, 3), B(1, -1), C(7, -1), D(7, 3)$

Also, write the coordinates of the point of intersection of the diagonals.
(a) Square, (4, 1)
(b) Rectangle, (4, 1)
(c) Rectangle, (1, 4)
(d) None of these
• *Application*

(xi) **Statement I**
$\text{cosec } 48° + \tan 88° = \sec 42° + \cot 2°$
Statement II The value of $\frac{\tan 15°}{\cot 75°} + \frac{\sin 25°}{\cos 65°}$ is equal to 3.
(a) Both the statements are true.
(b) Both the statements are false.
(c) Statement I is true and Statement II is false.
(d) Statement I is false and Statement II is true.
• *Analysis*

(xii) If the point $A(5, 1)$ is centre of the circle with radius 13 units, $AB \perp$ chord PQ and the coordinates of B are $(2, -3)$. Then, the length of chord PQ is
(a) 2 units (b) 26 units
(c) 24 units (d) 27 units
• *Application*

(xiii) $(1+\tan\theta)(1-\tan\theta)$ is equal to
(a) $\sec^2\theta$ (b) $\sec^2\theta - 1$
(c) $1-\sec^2\theta$ (d) $2-\sec^2\theta$ • *Analysis*

(xiv) In ΔABC, $AB = BC = 6$ cm and $\angle B = 90°$ then area of ΔABC is
(a) 24 cm^2 (b) 36 cm^2
(c) 18 cm^2 (d) 32 cm^2 • *Evaluation*

(xv) **Assertion** (A) If the coordinate of two points are $A(3, 4)$ and $B(-2, 5)$ then the value of (Abscissa of A) - (Abscissa of B) is 1.

Reason (R) The y-coordinate of a point is the perpendicular distance from the X-axis. The y-coordinate is also called the ordinate.
(a) A is true, R is false.
(b) A is false, R is true.
(c) Both A and R are true, and R is the correct Reason for A.
(d) Both A and R are true, and R is the incorrect Reason for A. • *Analysis*

2. (i) If $x = 5$ then find the value of
$$(x^{1/3} + x^{-1/3})(x^{2/3} + x^{-2/3} - 1).$$
• *Evaluation* [4]

(ii) Find the sum of 0.0333 ... and 0.444... . [4]

(iii) If $A = 30°$, verify
(a) $\cot 2A = \frac{\cot^2 A - 1}{2\cot A}$.
(b) $4\sin A \sin 2A + 1 - 2\sin 2A = 2\sin A$
• *Application* [4]

3. (i) If $x^2 + \frac{1}{x^2} = 23$ and $x \neq 0$ then find the value of $x^3 + \frac{1}{x^3}$.
• *Evaluation* [4]

(ii) If $5^{3x} = 125$ and $10^y = 0.001$ then find
(a) $5x + y$
(b) $x + 2y^2 - 8$
(c) $2x^2 - y$
(d) $3x + 2y^2 + 6xy$ • *Evaluation* [4]

(iii) If the numerator and denominator of a fraction are increased by 1 and 2 respectively, it becomes 3/5. If this numerator and denominator are decreased by 2 and 1 respectively, it becomes 1/2. Find the fraction. • *Application* [5]

Section B [40 Marks]

(Attempt any four questions from this section)

4. (i) In the given figure, O is the mid-point of AB and CD. Prove that

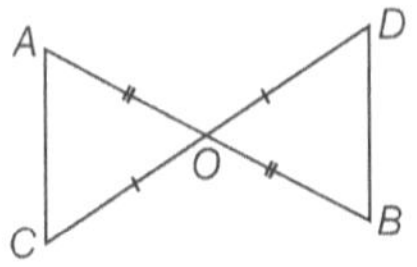

(a) $\triangle AOC \cong \triangle BOD$
(b) $AC = BD$
(c) $AC \parallel BD$ • *Analysis* [3]

(ii) Given below are the marks obtained by 40 students in an examination.

29, 45, 23, 30, 40, 48, 11, 01, 35, 15
07, 43, 09, 49, 19, 13, 32, 39, 25, 03
31, 32, 25, 22, 27, 41, 12, 13, 02, 44
40, 03, 12, 48, 49, 18, 30, 24, 25, 29

Taking the class interval 1-10, 11-20, ..., 41-50 make a frequency table for the above distribution. • *Analysis* [4]

(iii) A rectangular sheet of paper is 35 cm long and 28 cm wide. Find the area of the largest circle that can be cut from this sheet. • *Analysis* [3]

5. (i) Construct a parallelogram in which $AC = 6$ cm, $BD = 4.6$ cm and $\angle CAD = 60°$. • *Analysis* [3]

(ii) Solve the following system of equation by using the method of elimination.
$2x + 3y = 7$ and $3x - y = 5$ • *Application* [4]

(iii) If $a^2 = \log x$, $b^3 = \log y$ and $3a^2 - 2b^3 = 6\log z$, express y in terms of x and z. • *Analysis* [3]

6. (i) Solve the following equation for θ, if
(a) $2\sin\theta = 1$ (b) $\sqrt{2}\cos 3\theta = 1$
(c) $\sqrt{3}\cot 2\theta = 1$ (d) $\tan 3\theta = 1$
(e) $2\sin^2\theta = \sqrt{2}$ • *Understanding* [5]

(ii) Find the distance between the following points.
(a) $\left(-\frac{6}{3}, -3\right)$ and $\left(-4, \frac{-7}{5}\right)$
(b) (a, b) and $(-a, -b)$
(c) $(-5, 7)$ and $(-1, 3)$
(d) $(-5, 3)$
(e) $(3, -6)$ • *Evaluation* [5]

7. (i) (a) Factorise : $27x^3 - 54x^2y + 36xy^2 - 7y^3$. • *Evaluation*

(b) $\left(x - \frac{1}{x}\right)^2 + 6x - \frac{6}{x} + 9$ • *Evaluation* [3]

(ii) Divide ₹ 39030 between A and B so that when their shares are lent out, the amount that A receives in 2 yr is the same as what B receives in 4 yr. The interest is compounded annually at the rate of 4% per annum. • *Analysis* [4]

(iii) Construct a rhombus $ABCD$ of side 45 cm and $\angle BCD = 135°$. • *Analysis* [3]

8. (i) A field is 15 m long and 12 m broad. At one corner of this field a rectangular well of dimensions 8 m × 25 m × 2 m is dug and the dug-out soil is spread evenly over the rest of the field. Find the rise in the level of the rest of the field. • *Analysis* [4]

(ii) Show that $\frac{1}{3-\sqrt{8}} - \frac{1}{\sqrt{8}-\sqrt{7}} + \frac{1}{\sqrt{7}-\sqrt{6}} - \frac{1}{\sqrt{6}-\sqrt{5}} + \frac{1}{\sqrt{5}-2} - 1 = 4$ • *Evaluation* [3]

(iii) The present population of a village is 10816. If it has increased at the rate of 4% every year, then what was the population 2 yr ago? • *Analysis* [3]

9. (i) In the given figure, $ABCD$ is a rectangle with sides $AB = 10$ cm and $BC = 8$ cm, SAD and BQC are equilateral triangles. APB and DRC are right angled isosceles triangles, find the area of the shaded region. • *Analysis* [3]

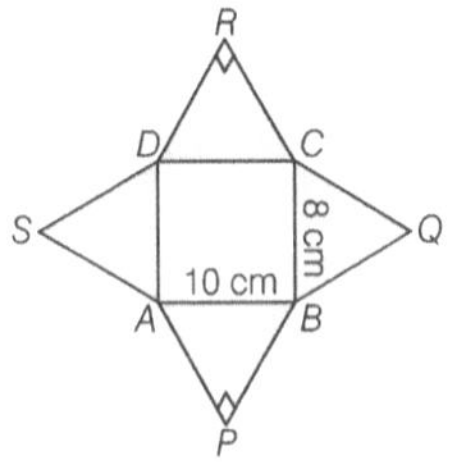

(ii) If $\sin A = \frac{\sqrt{3}}{2}$ and $\cos B = \frac{1}{\sqrt{2}}$ then find the value of $\frac{\tan A - \tan B}{1 + \tan A \tan B}$, where A and B are acute angles. • *Evaluation* [3]

(iii) In $\triangle ABC$, AD is perpendicular to BC and $AD^2 = BD \times DC$. Prove that $\angle BAC = 90°$. • *Evaluation* [4]

10. (i) If $ABCD$ is rhombus then prove that $AC^2 + BD^2 = 4\,AB^2$. • *Understanding* [3]

(ii) Find the median of the following data 19, 25, 59, 48, 35, 31, 30, 32 and 51. If 25 is replaced by 52, what will be the new median? • *Understanding* [4]

(iii) How many 3 m cubes can be cut from a cuboid measuring 18 m × 12 m × 9 m. • *Analysis* [3]

ANSWERS

1. (i) (a) (ii) (a) (iii) (b) (iv) (d) (v) (a)
(vi) (b) (vii) (d) (viii) (d) (ix) (c) (x) (c)
(xi) (c) (xii) (c) (xiii) (d) (xiv) (c) (xv) (b)

2. (i) $\frac{26}{5}$ (ii) $\frac{43}{90}$

3. (i) ± 110 (ii) (a) 2 (b) 11 (c) 5 (d) 3
(iii) $\frac{8}{13}$

4. (iii) 616 cm^2

5. (ii) $x = 2$ and $y = 1$ (iii) $y = (x^3 z^{-6})^{\frac{1}{2}}$

6. (i) (a) 30° (b) 15° (c) 30° (d) 15° (e) 90°
(ii) (a) $\frac{2\sqrt{41}}{5}$ units (b) $2\sqrt{a^2 + b^2}$ units
(c) $4\sqrt{2}$ units (d) $\sqrt{34}$ units
(d) $3\sqrt{5}$ units

7. (i) (a) $(3x - y)(9x^2 + 7y^2 - 15xy)$
(b) $\left(x - \frac{1}{x} + 3\right)^2$
(ii) A's amount = ₹ 20280 and B's amount = ₹ 18750

8. (i) 25 cm (iii) 10000

9. (i) $(32\sqrt{3} + 50)$ cm^2
(ii) $2 - \sqrt{3}$

10. (ii) 32; 35 (iii) 72 cubes

SAMPLE QUESTION PAPER 3

A HIGHLY SIMULATED Sample Question Paper for ICSE Class IX

Mathematics (Unsolved)

GENERAL INSTRUCTIONS

1. Answers to this paper must be written on the paper provided saperately.
2. You will not be allowed to write during the first 15 minutes. This time is to be spent in reading the question paper.
3. The time given at the head of this paper is the time allowed for writing the answers.
4. Attempt all **questions** from **Section A** and **any 4 questions** from **Section B.**
5. All working, including rough work, must be clearly shown and must be done on the same sheet as the rest of the answer.
6. Omission of essential working will result in loss of marks.
7. The intended marks for questions or parts of questions are given in bracket [ ].
8. Mathematical tables are provided.

Time : 2.5 Hrs **Max. Marks : 80**

Section A [40 *Marks*]

(Attempt all questions from this section)

1. Choose the correct answers to the questions from the given options. [15]

(i) The sides of a triangle are 2006 cm, 6002 cm and m cm, where m is a positive integer. The number of such possible triangles is

(a) 1 (b) 2006
(c) 3996 (d) 4011 • ***Analysis***

(ii) The difference between the compound interest on a sum of ₹ 4000, interest being compounded annually and the simple interest on it for 2 yr is ₹ 250. Find the rate of interest (p.a.).

(a) 15% (b) 10%
(c) 25% (d) 20% • ***Analysis***

(iii) **Assertion** (A) The decimal value of $\frac{437}{999}$ is 0.437437 ..., which is rational.

Reason (R) A non-terminating repeating decimal number is a rational number.

(a) A is true, R is false.
(b) A is false, R is true.
(c) Both A and R are true, and R is the correct Reason for A.
(d) Both A and R are true, and R is the incorrect Reason for A. • ***Understanding***

(iv) The value of $\log_{(a-b)}(a^3 - b^3) - \log_{(a-b)}(a^2 + ab + b^2), (a > b)$ is

(a) 0 (b) 1
(c) 3 (d) Not defined • ***Analysis***

(v) There are two numbers. The predecessor of the larger number exceeds the successor of the smaller number by 6. The sum of the numbers is 32. Then, the difference of numbers is

(a) 0 (b) 8
(c) 10 (d) 12 • ***Application***

(vi) If $x^6 - y^6 = k^6$ then $\log_k(x^2 - y^2) + \log_k(x^2 + y^2 - xy) + \log_k(x^2 + y^2 + xy)$ is equal to

(a) 3 (b) 4
(c) 5 (d) 6 • ***Evaluation***

(vii) A vessel contains a mixture of 24 L milk and 6 L water and second vessel contains a mixture of 15 L milk and 10 L water then how much mixture of milk and water should be taken from the first and the second vessel separately and kept in a third vessel, so that the third vessel may contain a mixture of 25 L milk and 10 L water?

(a) 15 L and 15 L (b) 20 L and 10 L
(c) 20 L and 15 L (d) None of these

• *Analysis*

(viii) The value of $\sqrt{\sqrt{63}+\sqrt{56}}$ is

(a) $7^{1/6}(\sqrt{3}+1)$ (b) $7^{1/4}(\sqrt{3}+1)$
(c) $7^{1/5}(\sqrt{5}+1)$ (d) $7^{1/4}(\sqrt{2}+1)$

• *Evaluation*

(ix) **Statement I** If $a+b=6$ and $ab=8$ then the value of $(a-b)$ is $\pm$ 2.

Statement II If $x^2+\frac{1}{x^2}=20$ then the value of $x+\frac{1}{x}$ is 22.

(a) Both the statements are true.
(b) Both the statements are false.
(c) Statement I is true and Statement II is false.
(d) Statement I is false and Statement II is true.

• *Analysis*

(x) Join two points $P(2, 2)$ and $Q(4, 2)$ in a plane. Fixed the point P and rotate the line PQ in anti-clockwise direction at an angle of 270°. The area formed by this figure is

(a) 9 sq units (b) 9.5 sq units
(c) 9.42 sq units (d) 9.45 sq units

• *Application*

(xi) The acute angles A and B, if $\sin(A+2B)=\frac{\sqrt{3}}{2}$ and $\cos(A+4B)=0$, where $A>B$, are respectively

(a) 15°, 25° (b) 30°, 15°
(c) 25°, 45° (d) 45°, 90° • *Analysis*

(xii) A figure is shown below

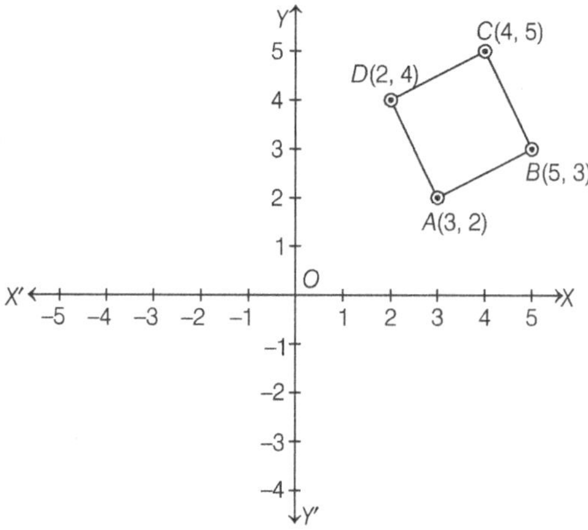

If we shift the coordinate axes from (0, 0) to (1, 1) then the new coordinates of the above figure is

(a) $A(2, 1), B(4, 2), C(3, 4), D(1, 3)$
(b) $A(2, 2), B(4, 4), C(3, 3), D(3, 1)$
(c) $A(1, 2), B(2, 4), C(4, 3), D(3, 1)$
(d) None of the above • *Application*

(xiii) $(\sec\theta+1)(\sec\theta-1)$ is equal to

(a) $-\tan^2\theta$ (b) $\tan^2\theta$
(c) $\cos^2\theta$ (d) $-\cos^2\theta$

• *Understanding*

(xiv) **Assertion** (A) If we draw triangles with angles 30°, 70° and 80° and the length of the sides of one triangle be different than that of the corresponding sides of the other triangles, then they are not congruent.

Reason (R) If two triangles are constructed, which have all corresponding angles equal but have a pair of unequal corresponding sides, then two triangles cannot be congruent to each other.

(a) A is true, R is false.
(b) A is false, R is true.
(c) Both A and R are true, and R is the correct Reason for A.
(d) Both A and R are true, and R is the incorrect Reason for A. • *Analysis*

(xv) The distance between (3, 1) and (–7, 2) is

(a) 10 (b) 12
(c) $\sqrt{101}$ (d) $\sqrt{120}$ • *Application*

2. (i) Prove that $\sqrt{7}-\sqrt{5}$ is an irrational number.

• *Analysis* [4]

(ii) The triangular side walls of a flyover have been used for advertisements. The sides of the walls are 122 m, 22 m and 120 m (see figure). The advertisements yield an earning of ₹ 5000 per m² per year. A company hired one of its walls for 3 months.

(a) How much rent did it pay?
(b) What is the value of the advertisements for the people in daily life? • *Evaluation* [4]

(iii) In the given figure, $ABCD$ is a square, $EF \parallel BD$ and R is the mid-point of EF.

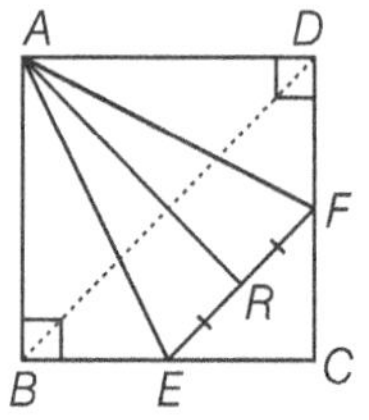

Prove that

(a) $BE = DF$. (b) AR bisects $\angle BAD$.
(c) If AR is produced, then it will pass through C. • *Analysis* [4]

3. (i) Show that
$\frac{1}{2}\log 9 + 2\log 6 + \frac{1}{4}\log 81 - \log 12 = 3\log 3$
• ***Understanding*** [4]

(ii) Simplify the following expressions
(a) $(x+y+z)^2 + (x+y-z)^2$.
(b) $(2x+p-c)^2 - (2x-p+c)^2$.
(c) $(x-4)(x+6)$
(d) $(x-2)(x-5)$ • ***Analysis*** [5]

(iii) Rationalise the denominator of the following. [4]

(a) $\frac{4}{3\sqrt{5}}$ (b) $\frac{3}{4-\sqrt{7}}$
(c) $\frac{1}{\sqrt{6}-\sqrt{5}}$ (d) $\frac{6}{3\sqrt{2}-2\sqrt{3}}$ • ***Application***

Section B [40 Marks]

(Attempt any four questions from this section)

4. (i) In the following figure, $AB = AC$ and $BE = CF$ are bisectors of $\angle B$ and $\angle C$, respectively. Prove that $\Delta EBC \cong \Delta FCB$.

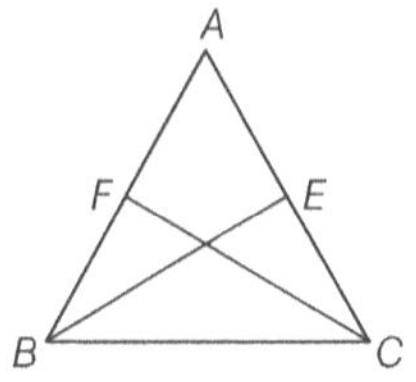

• ***Understanding*** [3]

(ii) Factorise $8x^3 - 2x^2y - 15xy^2$. • ***Evaluation*** [3]

(iii) The base of a triangular field is three times its altitude. If the cost of cultivating the field at ₹ 24.60 per hectare is ₹ 332.10 then find its base and height. • ***Analysis*** [4]

5. (i) A steel wire when bent in the form of a square, encloses an area of 121 cm^2. If the same wire is bent in the form of a circle, then find the area of the circle. • ***Analysis*** [3]

(ii) If $x+y+z=15$ and $x^2+y^2+z^2=83$ then find the value of
(a) $x^3+y^3+z^3-3xyz$.
(b) $(xy+yz+zx)$ • ***Application*** [3]

(iii) P and Q are the points on the sides CA and CB, respectively of ΔABC, right angled at C as shown in figure. Prove that
$AQ^2 + BP^2 = AB^2 + PQ^2$.
• ***Analysis*** [4]

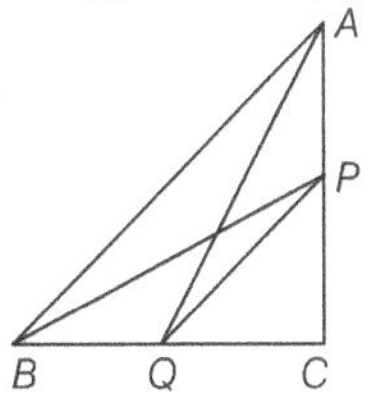

6. (i) Find the values of x in each of the following.
(a) $\log_3 x = 3$ (b) $\log_4 x = \frac{3}{2}$
(c) $\log_{10} x = -3$ (d) $\log_x 16 = 2$
(e) $\log_9 27 = 2x + 3$ • ***Evaluation*** [5]

(ii) AB is a line segment and P is its mid-point. D and E are points on the same side of AB, such that $\angle BAD = \angle ABE$ and $\angle EPA = \angle DPB$ (see the figure). Show that
(a) $\Delta DAP \cong \Delta EBP$
(b) $AD = BE$

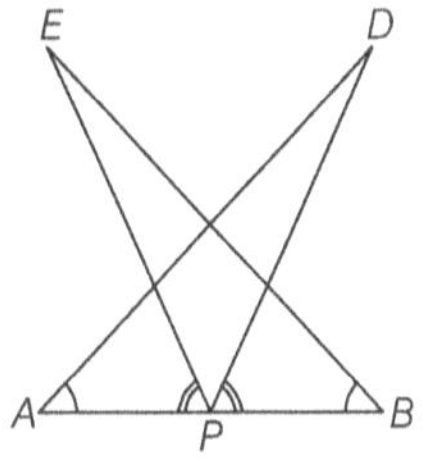

• ***Analysis*** [5]

7. (i) In the given figure, BM and DN are both perpendiculars to the segment AC and $BM = DN$. Prove that AC bisects BD. [3]

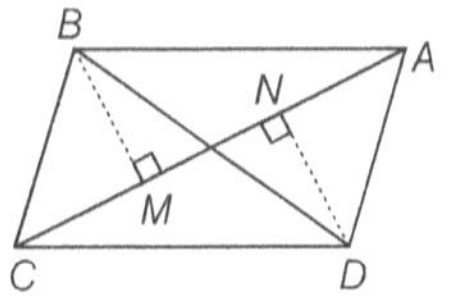

• ***Analysis***

(ii) 4 yr ago, a mother was four times as old as her daughter. 6 yr later, the mother will be two and a half times as old as her daughter at that time. Find the present ages of
(a) mother (b) her daughter
• ***Analysis*** [4]

(iii) The following table gives the marks scored by 100 students in an entrance examination.

Marks	Number of Students
0-10	4
10-20	9
20-30	17
30-40	21
40-50	20
50-60	19
60-70	8
70-80	2

Represent this data in the form of a histogram.
• ***Analysis*** [3]

8. (i) Using a ruler and a compass only, construct a parallelogram $ABCD$, in which $AB = 4$ cm, $AC = 10$ cm and $BD = 5$ cm. • *Analysis* [3]

(ii) A figure is shown below.

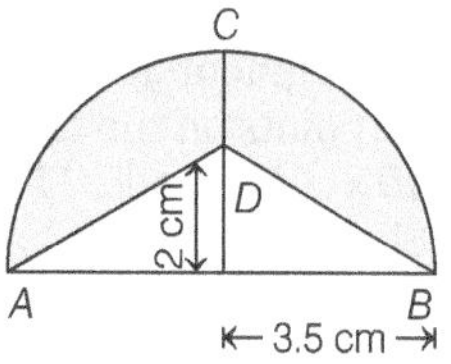

$ABCA$ represents a semi-circle of radius 3.5 cm with centre O. Calculate the area of shaded portion. $\left[\text{Take, } \pi = \frac{22}{7}\right]$ • *Understanding* [4]

(iii) The numbers 51, 42, 35, 32, $2x + 10$, $2x$, 12, 11, 9 and 5 are written in descending order and their median is 25. Find x. • *Analysis* [3]

9. (i) The dimensions of a rectangular box are in the ratio of 2 : 3 : 4 and the difference between the costs of covering it with sheet of paper at the rates of ₹ 8 and ₹ 9.50 per m^2 is ₹ 1248. Find the volume of the box. • *Evaluation* [3]

(ii) The cost of cultivating a square field at the rate of ₹ 90 per hectare is ₹ 1440. Find the cost of putting a fence around it, at rate of 75 paise per metre. • *Evaluation* [3]

(iii) Draw the graph of the line $3x - 7y + 21 = 0$. Find the points where it cuts X-axis and Y-axis. • *Application* [4]

10. (i) A triangle and a parallelogram have the same base and same area. If the sides of the triangle are 26 cm, 28 cm and 30 cm, and the parallelogram stands on the base 28 cm then find the height of the parallelogram. • *Application* [3]

(ii) Factorise $(a^2 - 4a)(a^2 - 4a - 1) - 20$. • *Evaluation* [3]

(iii) Two parallel chords of a circle whose diameter is 13 cm are 5 cm and 12 cm, respectively. Find the distance between them, if they lie on opposite sides of the centre. • *Understanding* [4]

ANSWERS

1. (i) (d) (ii) (c) (iii) (c) (iv) (b) (v) (b)
(vi) (d) (vii) (c) (viii) (d) (ix) (a) (x) (c)
(xi) (b) (xii) (a) (xiii) (b) (xiv) (c) (xv) (c)

2. (ii) (a) ₹ 1650000
(b) Advertisements play major role in people life. By the advertisement, people can aware about social activities, government schemes and laws, new products launching by the company, etc.
(iii) $x = 15$ and $y = 5$

3. (ii) (a) $2x^2 + 2y^2 + 2z^2 + 4xy$ (b) $8x(p - c)$
(c) $x^2 + 2x - 24$ (d) $x^2 - 7x + 10$
(iii) (a) $\frac{4\sqrt{5}}{15}$ (b) $\frac{4 + \sqrt{7}}{3}$ (c) $\sqrt{6} + \sqrt{5}$
(d) $3\sqrt{2} + 2\sqrt{3}$

4. (ii) $x(2x - 3y)(4x + 5y)$
(iii) Base = 900 m, height = 300 m

5. (i) 154 cm^2 (ii) (a) 71 (b) 180

6. (i) (a) 27 (b) 8 (c) $\frac{1}{1000}$ (d) 4 (e) $\frac{-3}{4}$

7. (ii) (a) 44 yr (b) 14 yr

8. (ii) 12.25 cm^2 (iii) 10

9. (i) 1536 m^3 (ii) ₹ 1200
(iii) (0, 3), (−7, 0)

10. (i) 12 cm (ii) $(a - 5)(a + 1)(a - 2)^2$
(iii) 8.5 cm